MW00788900

INTERACTIVE CASEBOOK SERIES[SM]

# LEGISLATION AND REGULATION

*A Contemporary Approach*

SECOND EDITION

**Peter J. Smith**
ARTHUR SELWYN MILLER RESEARCH PROFESSOR OF LAW
THE GEORGE WASHINGTON UNIVERSITY LAW SCHOOL

860 Blue Gentian Road, Suite 350
Eagan, MN 55121
1-877-888-1330



Printed in the United States of America

ISBN: 978-1-68561-470-6

*To my family and my students.*

# *Preface*

Legislation and Regulation was not a regular part of the typical law school curriculum for almost two centuries. Most schools required first-year students to take Torts, Contracts, and Property—the classic common-law subjects—as well as Civil Procedure and Criminal Law, but there was no first-year course that focused on statutory interpretation or regulation in the administrative state. For the last half-century or so, many schools offered upper-level courses in Administrative Law or Legislation, but not all students took those courses before graduating.

Things are different at many law schools today. If you are using this book, you likely are a student at a law school that now requires a course in Legislation and Regulation in the first year. There are a few things that you should know about this course at the outset. First, even though it was not traditionally part of the required first-year curriculum, changes in the practice and nature of law have made the course an essential part of a legal education. If you have friends attending other schools that do not require this course, they will be at a disadvantage when they begin their legal careers. The practice of law today is much more likely to require you to be able to interpret a statute or a regulation issued by an agency than it is to require you to rely on common-law doctrines developed by judges long ago.

Second, this course will be different from your other first-year courses in at least two important ways. Although you will read many judicial opinions in this course, the opinions in this course will usually be about the meaning of some text—a statute enacted by a legislature or a rule issued by some administrative agency. In most of your other classes, the judicial opinions are more likely to be about things that other courts have previously said.

More important, this course will be principally methodological. In your other courses, you will spend a good deal of time trying to learn the substantive law—of Torts, or of Property, or of Contracts. In Legislation and Regulation, in contrast, you will learn to use a set of lawyerly tools—arguments about how to determine the meaning of text. In your other courses, each case will be about some doctrine relevant to the subject—such as a Contracts case about consideration, or a Torts case about negligence. In this class, in contrast, the cases will involve statutes that address a wide range of topics—securities regulation, environmental protection, criminal law—but we won't be reading those cases to master the law in those disparate areas. Instead, we will be reading them to see what tools judges use when they address a dispute about the meaning of a statute. As you read the materials, pay attention to the types of arguments that the parties and judges make about the meaning of the statutes or rules at issue.

There are a few things about this book that I think make it distinctive and especially effective in teaching the subject. First, the book comes with a digital version that students can access on their computers. The digital version contains live hyperlinks to cases, statutes, law review articles, and other materials available on Westlaw and other websites. Accordingly, students who wish to explore the material in greater depth have the tools at their fingertips to do so. In addition, students who use laptop computers in the classroom will be able to view the course materials on their computers in class.

Second, I have tried to avoid the problem created by the aggressive editing in many books, which present excerpts so brief that the students in effect read only *about* what the court has decided. In my view, judicial opinions should be presented as more than a series of conclusory assertions that have been stitched together by a space-sensitive editor. I have tried to edit the principal cases to ensure that they are short enough to read, but rich enough to give the students a clear sense of the court's reasoning. I have also chosen not to create the illusion of breadth that characterizes many books in the field. Rather than provide summaries of dozens of decisions in each area that I address, I focus on fuller excerpts of the principal cases, which are designed to be illustrative. This book is self-consciously a casebook, and does not aspire to be a treatise.

Third, rather than follow the principal cases with pages and pages of notes and questions—an ineffective approach that students universally resent—I include multiple sidebars in the excerpts of each principal case to focus the students' attention on important questions at the very moment when they are reading the relevant portions of the opinion. Among other things, the sidebars focus attention on particularly salient passages of the opinions; draw connections between the discussion in the case and other topics that the students have explored (or will explore) in the book; supply food for thought; and direct the students to secondary materials to enrich their studies. After each case, I provide brief points for discussion, to focus the students' attention on the central themes in the case. The book also contains hypothetical problems—often drawn from real cases—to encourage the students to apply the material that they have learned.

Although I have attempted to provide fuller excerpts of the principal cases than is perhaps common in casebooks in the field, I of course nevertheless have had to do substantial editing. I have used three asterisks ("* * *") to indicate that text has been omitted within a paragraph, although I have often omitted entire paragraphs without providing a similar indication. (Because the cases are hyperlinked, students can easily read the full opinions, if they so choose.) I have omitted most footnotes from the cases; when I have included them, I have used the original numbering from the cases. Footnotes that I have inserted in the cases, on the other hand, are indicated by an asterisk and conclude with the notation "—*Ed.*" I have also omitted many of the citations, but I have attempted to preserve the most important ones.

I hope that reading this book is as enjoyable for you as writing it was for me.

Peter J. Smith
January 2023
Washington, D.C.

# *Table of Contents*

# *Table of Cases*

***The principal cases are in bold type.***

# LEGISLATION AND REGULATION

*A Contemporary Approach*

SECOND EDITION

# Chapter One

# *Legislation and Regulation*

## A. Introduction

### Problem

1. The Town Council in Ardsmore, West Carolina, recently enacted the Parks Safety Act of 2019. It provides:

> "No vehicles shall be permitted in any municipal park. Violation of this section shall constitute a misdemeanor, which may be punished by a fine not exceeding $500 or by a two-day incarceration in the municipal jail, or both."

Diego Ramirez, a sixteen-year-old student at Ardsmore High School, was recently cited under the Act for riding his bicycle in Sunshine Park as he was on the way home from his volunteer job helping elderly people at a local nursing home. He has challenged the fine in a local court. How should the court rule?

2. Now imagine that the minutes of the session at which the Town Council enacted the Parks Safety Act reveal that the Council enacted the ordinance after two incidents in which people who were trying to avoid traffic jams rode motorcycles through a downtown park, resulting in serious injuries to park-goers. At the session, Council Member Jones proposed a bill that would have stated, "No motorcycles shall be permitted in any municipal park." Council Member Robinson responded by noting that by singling out motorcycles, the language might imply that other, more dangerous vehicles, such as cars, *are* permitted in the park. Council Member Jones then changed his proposal to read, "No vehicles shall be permitted in any municipal park."

But then Council Member Chen argued that this broad language might be read to include bicycles and other non-motorized (and largely non-threatening) vehicles. She moved to amend the language to read, "No cars, trucks, or motorcycles shall be permitted in the park." Council Member Robinson responded by arguing that bicycles can be dangerous to park goers, too;

Council Member Jones, conversely, said that he didn't "think that the word 'vehicle' includes bikes." The Council then voted 3–2 against the amendment, and then voted 4–1 to adopt the bill above, simply stating (in relevant part), "No vehicles shall be permitted in any municipal park."

Does this change your view about how a court should resolve Ramirez's challenge?

3. Now imagine that the ordinance includes a second section, which provides:

> "Section 2. A 'vehicle' is any mechanism for conveying a person from one place to another, including motorcycles, automobiles, trucks, and motor scooters."

Does this change your view about how a court should resolve Ramirez's challenge?

---

## Points for Discussion

***a. Statutes as a Source of Law***

What is the first thing that you considered in trying to determine whether Ramirez violated the ordinance by riding his bicycle through the park? Was it the words used in the ordinance? If so, how do you know what they mean? Did you consider anything else in trying to determine the meaning of the ordinance? How, if at all, did your inquiry differ from what you would have done in your Torts or Contracts class to determine if a person had run afoul of some legal requirement?

***b. Understanding Written Instructions***

In order to resolve the issue presented by Ramirez's challenge, we have to determine the meaning of the Parks Safety Act. All of us have experience, from our everyday lives, interpreting written directives. For example, imagine that your friend is having several people over for dinner. She sends you a text that says, "Remember to bring refreshments." Should you bring something to drink or instead something to eat? If the former, should it be something alcoholic? Soda? Bottled water? Something else? If the latter, what counts? You would have figure out what she meant by "refreshments." In answering that question, would you rely on the dictionary definition of "refreshments"? On something else? Would it matter if your friend doesn't drink alcohol? Or is diabetic?

In what way is interpreting an ordinance such as the Parks Safety Act different?

---

In the late-nineteenth century, Christopher Columbus Langdell, the Dean of Harvard Law School, radically restructured the school's curriculum. He replaced a lecture system with an interactive approach known as the "case method." Rather than using lectures to summarize legal rules, the case method requires students to read judicial opinions, to answer questions that force them to articulate the governing legal principles, and to apply those principles in different circumstances. Virtually every law school in the United States continues to use the Langdellian case method today.

The case method works particularly well in the standard first-year curriculum at most American law schools, which require students to take (among other things) Torts, Contracts, Property, and Criminal Law. Until not very long ago, those subjects were governed almost entirely by the common law. Common law is the body of law created and applied by judges in the course of deciding cases. (It was called "common" law because it was applied uniformly in the King's Courts throughout England.) In a system of common law, judges not only decide cases, but also generate new legal rules. Common-law systems depend heavily on the doctrine of *stare decisis*, which requires courts to follow precedent, and in particular to follow the reasoning used in prior decisions. It is not difficult to see why the case method is well suited for training students to practice in a system in which binding legal rules are formulated and applied by judges in written opinions.

The common-law subjects still dominate the first-year curriculum at most American law schools, mostly because they are good vehicles for the case method, which many professors believe is a useful way to teach legal reasoning. But law in the United States today is much more likely to be enacted by a legislature or promulgated by an administrative agency than it is to be announced by a court. As a consequence, the actual practice of law in the United States today requires an understanding of those sources of law.

This is likely why your law school now offers a course in Legislation and Regulation. Although the coverage in the course varies from school to school, most Legislation and Regulation courses focus on statutory interpretation and basic elements of administrative law. Statutory interpretation is the process of determining the meaning of written enactments, usually those passed by a legislature or similar body. Administrative law is the body of law that applies to the actions of administrative agencies, such as the Environmental Protection Agency or the Federal Communications Commission. Most law schools have courses that address specific substantive areas of regulation—such as Environmental Law or Communications Law—but the course in Administrative Law is different. Administrative law is concerned with the general legal framework in which administrative agencies operate.

To practice law today, a competent lawyer must understand how to interpret statutes. For example, imagine that you are an Assistant United States Attorney and you must decide whether to seek indictments under 18 U.S.C. § 924(c)(1). The statute provides that a person who commits a drug crime faces a longer sentence if

**Make the Connection**

We will consider cases that present these facts in Chapter 3, when we consider *Smith v. United States*, 508 U.S. 223 (1993), and *Muscarello v. United States*, 524 U.S. 125 (1998).

he "uses or carries a firearm" "during and in relation to" a drug trafficking crime. In the first case, a man traded a gun for cocaine; in the second, a man drove his car, which had a gun in the glove compartment, to a drug transaction. Did the first man "use" a gun during and in relation to a drug crime? Did the second man "carry" one? To answer those questions, you will need to know how to interpret the statute.

A competent lawyer also needs to understand the rules that govern administrative decision-making. If the Securities and Exchange Commission issues a rule that imposes substantial costs on your client, you will want to know if the rule is subject to challenge under the Administrative Procedure Act—perhaps for failure to comply with the procedural requirements for rule-making—or if there are limits on your client's ability to challenge the rule in court.

In the modern regulatory state, the topics of statutory interpretation and administrative law also frequently intersect. Imagine, for example, that a federal statute prohibits the use in the workplace of toxins that cause "material health impairments" after "consistent exposure." The Occupational Safety and Health Administration has issued a rule defining "material health impairment" as "any affliction requiring medical treatment, including over-the-counter medication," and defining "consistent exposure" as "exposure for at least ten minutes one or more times per week." If you represent a company that uses harsh chemicals in its manufacturing process, you will need to figure out not only what the statute means, but also whether the agency's interpretation of the statute is entitled to any special status.

Questions of this sort arise at least as frequently today as do questions about the scope of the common-law duty of reasonable care or the common-law definition of breach of contract. But none of this is to suggest that the common-law method, and the skills that you can develop from studying it, are irrelevant to the practice of law today. Even in the context of statutory interpretation and administrative law, courts follow precedent. When a court interprets a statute or concludes that the Due Process Clause of the Constitution requires an agency to grant a hearing to a regulated party, the court's decision becomes binding precedent in cases implicating the statute or administrative practice. The ability to interpret statutes and understand the rules governing administrative regulation complements, rather than replaces, the skills that you are developing in your other classes.

In the rest of this Chapter, we will address theories of regulation and when regulation might be warranted. We'll also think about the relative virtues of legislation, the common law, and agency action as ways to regulate private behavior. Then we will turn to the federal legislative process and the many obstacles to enacting legislation at the federal level.

In Chapters 2–5, we will consider the process of statutory interpretation and its associated doctrines. Then, in Chapters 6 and 7, we will introduce the core elements of administrative law. In Chapter 8, we will consider the intersection between statutory interpretation and administrative law—and specifically what to do when an administrative agency has, in the process of regulating, offered an interpretation of the statute that it is responsible for implementing.

---

## B. Regulation and Legislation

### Problem

To: Legislative Aide

From: Representative Smith*

Re: Rainmaking

---

I need your advice about rainmaking—not about rainmaking in any metaphorical sense, but about rainmaking in the literal sense. It seems that there are now businesses that will come to an agricultural area, set up what they call a "silver-iodide generator," and make rain. Although they make no general promises, the advertisements that I have seen claim an average 20% increase in precipitation over the course of a growing season.

In one sense, of course, this seems great. A 20% increase in rain in a drought year is the difference between profit and loss in many of the agricultural parts of the state; and if we look beyond farming, it could really help our municipal water supplies in lean years, too.

But I've already heard some constituent complaints. One was from a farmer who had a bad year and griped that a farmer in a neighboring county hired a rainmaker and stole his rain. Another was from a resort owner in the lake district, who said that she had a terrible summer season because there were so

---

* This problem is based on teaching materials from Professor Todd Rakoff's Administrative Law course at Harvard Law School and is reprinted here with Professor Rakoff's gracious permission.

many rainy days—brought on, she claimed, by a nearby rainmaking operation. And a third was from a farmer who paid a rainmaker and got no results.

I'd like to do something before the next election. Over the summer break, I had an intern look into what other states have been doing. She reported that in some states there are statutes regarding rainmaking; in some there appears to be no law except the occasional private lawsuit; and in some there are "Rainmaking Bureaus," which are administrative agencies that have authority over the matter.

I meant to ask her whether she thought we should set up such a Bureau, but by the time I got around to it she had left for school. What do you think? Should we establish a Rainmaking Bureau? If so, what tasks should it be given? Or are we better off doing something else?

---

## Points for Discussion

### *a. Whether to Regulate*

What factors should the legislator consider in determining whether to regulate rainmaking—or, for that matter, any new technology? Is it a question of economics? Of social justice? A combination of the two? Or is it, in practice, a question of which interest group has the most influence over the legislator? If the question is ultimately one of costs and benefits, how can a legislator determine what those costs and benefits are—and assign values to them?

### *b. How to Regulate*

If the legislature decides that rainmaking warrants regulation, what form should the regulation take? Answering this question requires resolving several questions of institutional competence and design. Should the legislature simply enact a statute that bans rainmaking—or, conversely, immunizes from liability those who engage in it? How would such a statute be enforced? Or should the legislature give regulatory power to an administrative agency? If so, what sorts of power and guidance should it give to the agency?

Suppose for a moment that the legislature does not take any action at all to address rainmaking. Would the consequence be that the aggrieved hotel owner or the farmer who believes that his neighbor stole his rain has no remedy? In the absence of legislation about rainmaking, what would you advise the hotel owner or farmer to do? Are existing remedies an adequate substitute for legislation specifically about rainmaking?

---

As the rainmaking example suggests, the questions whether and how to regulate do not have straightforward answers. Many law school courses address these questions in specific substantive contexts. For example, a course in Environmental Law might consider how the legal regime ought to balance the interest in economic development with the interest in ensuring clean air and water; a course in Securities Law might address the best way to reconcile the desire to use the power of the market efficiently to allocate capital with the need to prevent exploitative behavior. The course in Legislation and Regulation, in contrast, is not about Environmental Law or Securities Law (or any other substantive area of the law). Instead, the course is about the legal framework in which the government regulates and about how the relevant actors—legislators, judges, and regulated parties—should approach and make sense of that legal framework.

Most of the course—and, consequently, most of this book—is about the rules that constrain the government's regulatory decisions and about how we should understand and interpret those decisions. But it is important not to lose sight of the threshold question that government actors must answer before making those decisions. Before we can have a statute (or a rule issued by an administrative agency) regulating private conduct, the legislature (or agency) must decide that some regulatory response is warranted.

As you can see from the rainmaking example, this is often a complicated decision. Given our tradition of individual liberty and private choice, should there be a presumption against government regulation? If so, what sorts of justifications are sufficient to overcome the presumption against regulation? Entire disciplines are dedicated to providing a framework for answering these kinds of questions. For present purposes, it suffices to note that most justifications for government regulation fall into one of two categories: economic rationales and non-economic rationales.

Most economic justifications start from the premise that well-functioning markets are likely to produce an efficient allocation of resources that maximizes total social welfare. On this view, because resources will tend to be deployed where they produce the most value, any government intervention that disrupts the market is likely to result in a less efficient allocation of resources. As a consequence, economic justifications for regulation generally require some reason to suspect that there has been a market failure—that is, that a market is not operating efficiently. See generally Stephen G. Breyer, Regulation and Its Reform 15–34 (1982). To take an obvious example, if one firm has a monopoly on a particular good or service, then the firm can charge unreasonably high prices or rates without having to worry about the disciplining effects of competition. Such market failures might justify government regulation—in this case, antitrust rules that prohibit monopoly pricing or the acquisition of monopoly power in the first place.

Market failures can take other forms, as well. Sometimes the information necessary for businesses or consumers to make rational decisions is not widely available or is too complex for the ordinary consumer to understand. In other cases, rational behavior might lead to externalities, which are costs that one party's conduct imposes on another party. For example, if a factory emits large quantities of a pollutant, people who live downwind of the factory will be forced to breathe dirty air. Absent regulation limiting the permissible emissions of pollutants, the factory will reap the benefits of its industrial process—by getting to sell products made through its polluting process—and the factory's neighbors will bear the costs.

Conversely, some goods or services provide great value to the public without fully compensating the parties who provide them. For example, a lighthouse is a valuable service that ensures that ships do not run aground; but no private actor would bear the cost of constructing a lighthouse, because she will not be able to recoup those costs from passing ships, which benefit from the lighthouse without having to pay any fee. The same is true of roads and flood-control systems. These are all examples of "public goods," which private actors typically will not produce absent government intervention.

---

## Perspective and Analysis

In 2003, the Office of Management and Budget (OMB), an office within the Executive Office of the President, issued guidance to federal agencies about when regulation might be warranted. Here is an excerpt of that guidance:

> Before recommending Federal regulatory action, an agency must demonstrate that the proposed action is necessary. * * * If the regulation is designed to correct a significant market failure, you should describe the failure both qualitatively and (where feasible) quantitatively. * * *
>
> The major types of market failure include: externality, market power, and inadequate or asymmetric information. * * * An externality occurs when one party's actions impose uncompensated benefits or costs on another party. Environmental problems are a classic case of externality. * * * Resources that may become congested or overused, such as fisheries or the broadcast spectrum, represent common property resources. "Public goods," such as defense or basic scientific research, are goods where provision of the good to some individuals cannot occur without providing the same level of benefits free of charge to other individuals.
>
> Firms exercise market power when they reduce output below what would be offered in a competitive industry in order to obtain higher prices. * * * Generally, regulations that increase market power for selected entities should

> be avoided. * * * Nevertheless, you should keep in mind that technological advances often affect economies of scale. This can, in turn, transform what was once considered a natural monopoly into a market where competition can flourish.
>
> Market failures may also result from inadequate or asymmetric information. * * * Even when adequate information is available, people can make mistakes by processing it poorly. * * * When it is time-consuming or costly for consumers to evaluate complex information about products or services (e.g., medical therapies), they may expect government to ensure that minimum quality standards are met. However, the mere possibility of poor information processing is not enough to justify regulation. If you think there is a problem of information processing that needs to be addressed, it should be carefully documented. * * *
>
> Even where a market failure clearly exists, you should consider other means of dealing with the failure before turning to Federal regulation. Alternatives to Federal regulation include antitrust enforcement, consumer-initiated litigation in the product liability system, or administrative compensation systems.

**OMB Circular A-4 (September 17, 2003).**

---

The OMB approach focuses on economic justifications for regulation. But regulation sometimes seeks to advance values other than wealth maximization. Consider three examples. First, a legislature might decide that the society's values are offended by a lopsided distribution of wealth and, in response, pursue policies that redistribute wealth from the rich to the poor. A legislature might do so by imposing higher tax rates on the wealthy and using the revenue to provide food stamps or health insurance to those who cannot afford it. Second, a legislature might take steps to alleviate burdens on marginalized groups. For example, the legislature might prohibit private businesses from discriminating on the basis of race in hiring or providing services, or it might require private businesses to install ramps to provide access for people who use wheelchairs. Third, a legislature might decide that we have an ethical obligation to preserve the Earth's rich diversity and prohibit private actions that impair the habitats of endangered species.

These policies are justified largely by moral considerations—respectively, that we have a moral obligation to ensure that all persons are entitled to food, shelter, and decent medical care; that "differences that are irrelevant from the moral point of view ought not to be turned into social disadvantages," CASS SUNSTEIN, AFTER THE RIGHTS REVOLUTION: RECONCEIVING THE REGULATORY STATE 57 (1990); and that all species have intrinsic value. An economist might resist regulation in these circumstances if the costs of the regulation—increasing total health care costs or installing ramps, for example—exceed the quantifiable benefits. But it should come as no surprise that many regulatory decisions are designed to advance moral and ethical values, rather than merely to maximize total welfare.

---

## Points for Discussion

### *a. Whether to Regulate*

Deciding whether to regulate is often a difficult and contested question. For example, imagine that the legislature or an administrative agency is trying to decide whether to limit the permissible level of emissions from coal-burning factories. Does the economic approach to regulation provide a clear answer to whether the government should do so? What about the non-economic approach? Ultimately, either approach requires the government to make judgments about the respective costs and benefits of regulation. What sorts of questions would the government need to answer in order to decide whether emissions limits are warranted?

### *b. How to Regulate*

Once the government decides that regulation is warranted, what form should the regulation take? Does economic theory (or social justice theory or any other approach) answer that question? There are countless regulatory responses that the government could plausibly adopt for any given problem. To stick with the example of emissions from coal-burning factories, the government could ban the use of coal in factories; permit it but only up to a particular limit; authorize liability for health problems that develop as a result of inhaling polluted air; permit the trading of the right to emit pollutants; and so on. Is one approach likely to be more effective than the others?

---

As the rainmaking problem suggested, regulation can come in many forms. We will spend most of our time in this course on legislative initiatives—either statutes directly regulating some matter or statutes delegating power to administrative agencies to formulate regulatory policy. But the common law, which likely is the focus of most of your other first-year courses, is another source of regulation. For example, products liability doctrine, which is largely the result of judicial innovation, regulates the manufacture and sale of all sorts of items. If your client invented a useful but potentially dangerous product and asks for your advice about whether she should sell it in its current form, you would need to advise her about the likelihood that she would face liability for injuries sustained by users of the product. Your advice might lead her to change the product's design. In this way, products-liability doctrine governs private decision-making.

Is the common law likely to be an effective source of regulation? Does it depend on the issue that the legislature is confronting? Consider the Problems that follow.

For each, ask yourself: (1) whether there is a problem that warrants some regulatory response; and (2) if so, what the form and content of that response should be.

---

## Problem

In 1971, Ford began to sell the Pinto, a light, fuel-efficient, and low-priced subcompact car. Ford designed the Pinto and brought it to market in just 25 months, considerably faster than the typical new car model, because the company was worried about losing market share to low-cost options manufactured by companies in Germany and Japan.

In 1972, Lilly Gray's Pinto stalled as she tried to change lanes on a California freeway. Another car traveling about thirty miles per hour rear-ended her. The Pinto's gas tank ruptured, releasing vapors that spread through the car. A spark ignited the mixture, and the Pinto exploded in a ball of fire. Gray died a few days later. Her passenger, a thirteen-year-old boy named Richard Grimshaw, suffered disfiguring burns and had to undergo facial reconstruction surgery. Gray's estate and Grimshaw filed suit against Ford, claiming that the Pinto's gas tank was defectively designed and that the car was unreasonably dangerous.

Internal company documents showed that Ford had performed more than forty crash tests with the Pinto before it became available on the market, and that the Pinto's fuel tank had ruptured in every single test conducted at speeds over twenty miles per hour. Ford engineers were aware that such a rupture created a risk of fire; in response, they considered several low-cost design fixes. Lining the fuel tank with a nylon bladder would have cost somewhere between $5 and $8 per vehicle; adding structural protection to the rear of the car would have cost $4.20 per vehicle; and putting a plastic baffle between the fuel tank and the differential housing would have cost about $1 per vehicle.

Documents disclosed during discovery revealed that executives at Ford had conducted an analysis to determine whether it was cost-effective to install the extra protective devices on the car. Ford was planning to manufacture about 11 million Pintos, and it assumed that adding the extra parts would cost an additional $11 per vehicle. By not installing the extra parts, in other words, Ford would save over $120 million.

Ford also considered the likely consequences of declining to install the extra parts. Executives estimated that, without the new parts, roughly 180 Pinto drivers or passengers would be killed by explosions caused by a ruptured gas tank; another 180 Pinto drivers or passengers would suffer severe burns as a result of such accidents; and about 2,000 Pintos would be damaged or destroyed by fire. The executives then estimated that, if Ford were sued by all of those accident victims, it would have to pay out about $200,000 to the family of each person killed in an accident involving an exploding gas tank; $67,000 to each person injured in such an accident; and $700 for each car damaged in such an accident. By Ford's calculation, in other words, it would have to pay out about $50 million in tort judgments as a result of the dangerous fuel tank. Because this cost was substantially lower than the amount Ford would save by declining to install the extra parts, executives at Ford decided not to install the extra parts. (In addition, the Executive Vice President of Ford had also insisted that the car weigh no more than 2,000 pounds and cost no more than $2,000, goals that would be difficult to achieve with the extra parts.)

After hearing this evidence, the jury awarded $2.5 million to Grimshaw and around $500,000 to Gray's estate to compensate them for their injuries. In addition, the jury awarded punitive damages of $125 million. An appellate court later reduced the punitive damages award to $3.5 million.

Did the common-law tort system function as an adequate regulatory regime for automobile safety? If not, what alternatives are available to ensure safe cars while promoting innovation and reducing prices for consumers?

---

## Problem

In the nineteenth century, industry discovered the insulating and fire-proofing properties of asbestos. In World War II, asbestos was used in large quantities to insulate the effects of heat on Navy ships; by the middle of the twentieth century, the product was widely used in manufacturing and building construction, not only as insulation, but also to make cement stronger without adding much weight. By the 1970s, however, it had become clear that exposure to asbestos fibers causes lung cancer and other fatal diseases.

Under modern product liability rules, the manufacturer of an unreasonably dangerous product is liable to persons injured by the product, even if the manufacturer exercised all due care in the preparation and sale of the product. Asbestos indisputably is an unreasonably dangerous—indeed, deadly—product.

But there were several serious obstacles to providing a remedy through the tort system to people who were injured by exposure to asbestos. First, in most states, the statute of limitations for a tort claim is three years. But asbestos exposure is not like a car accident; there is not one definable moment when the exposure has caused an injury, and many people who were exposed were not even aware of their exposure. In addition, there often was a long time between exposure and the manifestation of the injury.

Second, it is more difficult to prove causation for diseases than it is for injuries sustained in other types of incidents, such as a car accident. Some conditions caused by asbestos exposure, such as lung cancer, can also be caused by other products, such as cigarettes. Of course, this was not a problem when the plaintiff had developed asbestosis, which is caused only by exposure to asbestos. But even those plaintiffs faced serious obstacles to recovery: there were over a dozen large manufacturers of asbestos, and it usually was very difficult to identify which company had manufactured the asbestos to which the plaintiff had been exposed. If a plaintiff has to prove that it's more likely than not that the defendant caused her injuries, and it's equally plausible that any one of 15 manufacturers was responsible, then the plaintiff won't be able to satisfy the burden of proof against any of them, even though we know for sure that at least one of them must have been responsible.

Third, the sheer number of potential plaintiffs threatened to overwhelm the court system. Millions of people were exposed to asbestos; not just people who worked at the factories that manufactured it, but also people who worked in construction and countless people who lived and worked in buildings constructed with asbestos.

Fourth, it wasn't clear that all of the hundreds of thousands of potential claimants could receive compensation, even if they could overcome these other problems. Given the severity of the diseases caused by asbestos exposure, successful plaintiffs likely would recover substantial amounts of money. But there was a risk that the first wave of plaintiffs who recovered damages from asbestos manufacturers would bankrupt those companies, leaving nothing for the thousands of others who developed asbestos-related diseases.

What options are available to overcome the tort system's limitations in providing compensation to victims of asbestos exposure?

---

The examples that we have considered so far suggest that there are at least three possible responses to some problem that warrants regulation: leave the problem to the common-law system; enact legislation that directly regulates the problem (such as by banning a particular practice that causes the problem); or create an administrative agency and give it power to address the problem. Why might a legislature choose the last option?

There are three main justifications for relying on administrative agencies. First, agencies develop expertise in their fields of regulation. Imagine, for example, that Congress is concerned about increasing levels of air pollution and what it means for public health. Congress could try to impose emissions limits for various pollutants, but deciding the appropriate limits requires considerable scientific and economic expertise. Members of Congress are likely to be generalists, not experts in these areas. In addition, the appropriate limits might change over time, in light of population changes, technological changes, or other developments. Congress might not have the time regularly to revisit its prior decisions about appropriate emissions limits. An agency charged with monitoring air pollution levels, staffed with scientists and economists, and focused only on questions of environmental protection, in contrast, can be expected to have considerable expertise in answering these types of questions.

Second and relatedly, agency decision-making is less likely to be driven by crass political calculations, and more likely to be based on neutral scientific or technical principles, than legislative decision-making. Members of Congress are primarily concerned with ensuring their re-election and might be tempted to choose regulatory policies based on short-term political expedience rather than on sound policy judgment. Agency officials are not subject to election—they are appointed, and therefore one step removed from politics—and thus are more likely to base their decisions on the best evidence.

Third, agency decision-making might be more efficient than legislative decision-making. Legislative decision-making is often slow and cumbersome, in practice requiring something approximating super-majoritarian consensus. Administrative decision-making often uses less burdensome procedures. In addition, legislative regulation requires enforcement by another branch, which might not share the legislature's priorities. Agencies, in contrast, can both issue rules and implement those rules, eliminating the potential for inter-branch conflict.

There are also drawbacks to relying on administrative agencies to regulate. First, because the officials who run agencies are not directly accountable to the voters, agency decision-making lacks the democratic legitimacy that characterizes legislative decision-making. Second, conferring powers on one entity to formulate rules and to implement them—and, in at least some cases, to adjudicate disputes that arise under those rules—might be inconsistent with a commitment to the separation of powers. Third, because each agency has responsibility for regulating one particular subject—such as environmental protection or consumer product safety—there is the risk that its decisions will suffer from a "silo effect," walled off from (and possibly even inconsistent with) the policy decisions of other agencies or parts of the government. See, e.g., Richard E. Levy & Robert L. Glicksman, *Agency-Specific Precedents*, 89 TEX. L. REV. 499 (2011).

We will consider the virtues and drawbacks of administrative agencies, as well as the rules governing administrative decision-making, in Chapters 6–8. For now, it is enough to note that regulation by administrative agencies is a common, even if controversial, feature of our system.

---

## C. The Legislative Process

As we have seen, the decision whether to regulate by legislation is a complicated question of policy. But put that threshold question to one side. What happens once the legislature decides to address a problem by enacting regulatory legislation?

In the middle-school-civics version of our system of government, the members of the legislature, all of whom are motivated by the desire to serve the general welfare, find common ground and enact a law. In the real world, matters are a bit more complicated. First, interest groups with a stake in the dispute might mobilize to oppose action. (In the rainmaking problem, for example, the industry group representing the manufacturer of the rainmaking technology might lobby members of the legislature to oppose any action.) Leaders of one of the political parties might see electoral advantage in resisting action, perhaps because private groups will use their financial muscle to run television advertisements against candidates who support such action. To be sure, there might be well-financed and influential interest groups on the other side of the issue, as well—say, the travel industry or farmers—but there is no guarantee that the voting public's preferences will align perfectly with the relative influence of these competing groups. See generally MANCUR OLSON, THE LOGIC OF COLLECTIVE ACTION (1965).

Second, the legislative process is filled with opportunities for opponents of the legislation to obstruct its passage. At the federal level and in most states, two houses of the legislature must agree. (Nebraska, on the other hand, has a unicameral, or one-house, legislature.) As a consequence, opponents of legislative action usually need to frustrate progress only in one house to defeat regulation.

At the federal level, which we will focus on here, the Constitution provides that both the House of Representatives and the Senate must pass a bill, and that the president must sign it (or that the two houses must override a veto by super-majority votes), in order to make binding law. But this sketch leaves open many questions about how exactly a bill works its way through each house of Congress. In practice, the quirky rules of the legislative process in each house create multiple choke points at which legislative proposals can wither and die. Even assuming a strong case for regulation by legislation, the actual likelihood that Congress will successfully enact a law turns on just how difficult it is to navigate this legislative process.

The Constitution provides that "[e]ach House may determine the Rules of its proceedings." U.S. CONST., art. I, § 5, cl. 2. Each house has adopted complicated rules to govern how a bill makes its way through the chamber. What follows below is a brief overview of the legislative process created by those rules.

Knowledge of how a bill can become law is useful for any lawyer, and particularly for one who decides to work on Capitol Hill. But more important for our purposes, it might also be relevant to how we think about the meaning of laws that Congress succeeds in passing. If there are many choke points in the process—points at which opponents of pending legislation can obstruct or prevent its enactment—then the compromises that the legislature reaches in order successfully to navigate those choke points might tell us a good deal about the legislative bargain, and thus what the legislation ultimately means. We will return to this point in Chapter 4, when we consider the role of legislative history in statutory interpretation. For now, keep in mind that, to the extent that statutory interpretation requires us to identify the manner in which the legislature resolved competing interests, a bill's evolution as it makes its way through the legislative process might be highly relevant to the task of statutory interpretation.

## 1. The House of Representatives

**FYI**

The Rules of the House of Representatives are available on the website of the House Committee on Rules, which you can access at https://rules.house.gov/rules-and-resources.

Most bills can originate in either house of Congress. (The Constitution, however, provides that bills for raising revenue must originate in the House. See U.S. CONST., art. I, § 7, cl. 1.) The process in the House of Representatives begins with the **introduction of a bill** by a member of the House. Any member may introduce a bill, and only members may introduce a bill.

The President will often announce that he is proposing legislation to advance his agenda, but the President has no formal power to introduce a bill; he must find a member to introduce it in the chamber. To introduce a bill, a member—even today, in the digital era—drops a paper copy of the bill in a wooden box, known as the "hopper," next to the Clerk's desk.

111TH CONGRESS
1ST SESSION

# H. R. 3962

To provide affordable, quality health care for all Americans and reduce the growth in health care spending, and for other purposes.

---

IN THE HOUSE OF REPRESENTATIVES

OCTOBER 29, 2009

Mr. DINGELL (for himself, Mr. RANGEL, Mr. WAXMAN, Mr. GEORGE MILLER of California, Mr. STARK, Mr. PALLONE, and Mr. ANDREWS) introduced the following bill; which was referred to the Committee on Energy and Commerce, and in addition to the Committees on Education and Labor, Ways and Means, Oversight and Government Reform, the Budget, Rules, Natural Resources, and the Judiciary, for a period to be subsequently determined by the Speaker, in each case for consideration of such provisions as fall within the jurisdiction of the committee concerned

---

# A BILL

To provide affordable, quality health care for all Americans and reduce the growth in health care spending, and for other purposes.

Once a bill is introduced, the Speaker of the House generally directs that it be **referred to one or more of the House's standing committees**. Today, there are 20 standing committees in the House, including the Ways and Means Committee, the Judiciary Committee, and the Oversight and Reform Committee. Sometimes the Speaker will instruct that a bill be referred to more than one committee for consideration. The bill (shown above) that ultimately became the Affordable Care Act, for example, was referred to seven committees. Other times the Speaker will direct that a bill be referred to only one committee. Politics plays some role in these decisions: sending a bill to more than one committee might make it less likely that it will

**FYI**

Standing committees are permanent committees whose jurisdiction is identified and defined in the House Rules. "Select Committees," in contrast, are created by a resolution, usually to conduct an investigation or to consider a particular measure, and do not usually continue to serve after they complete their assigned task. Joint committees, such as the Joint Committee on Taxation, have members from both the House and the Senate and usually conduct studies rather than consider legislation.

ultimately advance; in contrast, sending a bill to a committee with a sympathetic chair might make it more likely to advance. The House's Rules also do not require that a bill be referred to any committee, and occasionally a bill will advance without committee consideration.

If the bill is referred to a committee, it often will be further **referred to a subcommittee**. Most committees (though not all) have multiple subcommittees, each of which is responsible for a particular subject matter. For example, the House Committee on the Judiciary has five subcommittees: the Antitrust, Commercial, and Administrative Law Subcommittee; the Courts, Intellectual Property, and Internet Subcommittee; the Crime, Terrorism, and Homeland Security Subcommittee; the Immigration and Citizenship Subcommittee; and the Constitution, Civil Rights, and Civil Liberties Subcommittee.

A subcommittee to which a bill has been referred will usually hold **hearings** on the bill. At the hearings, witnesses (called by members of the subcommittee) often testify about the problem to be addressed by the bill and about the bill itself. Sometimes this process is a genuine effort to gather information to help craft a sensible legislative solution; other times, it results in a kind of theater designed to win political points. The subcommittee process also entails the process of "**mark-up**," which involves the crafting of statutory language to respond to objections or to improve the bill. During this process, the subcommittee members vote on each proposed amendment to the language of the bill.

When a subcommittee completes this process, it **reports the bill to the full committee**. The committee to which a bill has been referred will also often hold hearings and, if the bill advances far enough, engage in the process of mark-up. Once the committee has completed its consideration of a bill, it will sometimes **issue a report** describing the bill, usually section by section, and any changes made to the bill in committee.

| 116TH CONGRESS<br>*1st Session* | HOUSE OF REPRESENTATIVES | REPORT<br>116–317 |
|---|---|---|

VOTING RIGHTS ADVANCEMENT ACT OF 2019

NOVEMBER 29, 2019.—Committed to the Committee of the Whole House on the State of the Union and ordered to be printed

Mr. NADLER, from the Committee on the Judiciary, submitted the following

R E P O R T

together with

DISSENTING VIEWS

[To accompany H.R. 4]

The Committee on the Judiciary, to whom was referred the bill (H.R. 4) to amend the Voting Rights Act of 1965 to revise the criteria for determining which States and political subdivisions are subject to section 4 of the Act, and for other purposes, having considered the same, report favorably thereon with an amendment and recommend that the bill as amended do pass.

CONTENTS



A bill that survives the committee process then **proceeds to the House Rules Committee**, which is responsible for setting the terms of the House debate over the bill. This process dates to the late nineteenth century, when the House decided to systematize the consideration of proposed legislation on the floor of the House. Before the full House can consider a bill, the Rule Committee issues a "rule," which specifies how much time will be available for debate and whether amendments can be offered (and, if so, what kind). For some bills, usually uncontroversial ones, the members might vote to suspend the requirement of a rule for debate. For other bills, the rule might provide that there will be one or two hours of floor debate and a limit to the number of amendments that may be proposed.

Once the Rules Committee issues a rule, **the rule itself is subject to a brief debate by the full House**. Assuming the rule—which, again, only governs the terms of debate—is approved, **debate begins on the bill itself**, as amended during the committee process. This process takes place in the "Committee of the Whole," which for all intents and purposes is the entire membership of the House. (The quorum rules are slightly different for the Committee of the Whole, but at this point all of the members are entitled to participate.) Members might speak for or against the proposed bill, and some might offer amendments (subject, of course, to the limits identified in the rule approved for the bill).

**Food for Thought**

The Constitution requires each house to keep a "Journal of its Proceedings," and it provides that "the Yeas and Nays of the Members of either House on any questions shall, at the Desire of one fifth of those present, be entered on the Journal." U.S. CONST., art. I, § 5, cl. 3. As a practical matter, this means that how a Member votes is always a matter of public record. Why do you think the framers of the Constitution wanted such information to be publicly available?

At the end of the floor debate, the **House votes on the bill**. A tiny percentage of bills that are introduced in the House ultimately are passed by the full House. And even those that are cannot become law unless they also make it through the Senate.

## 2. The Senate

In some ways, the process for passing a bill in the Senate parallels the process in the House. But there are important differences, and those differences make passage in the Senate even more challenging than it is in the House.

**FYI**

The Standing Rules of the Senate are available on the website of the United States Senate at https://www.senate.gov/reference/reference_index_subjects/Rules_and_Procedure_vrd.htm.

As in the House, any Senator may **introduce a bill**. The bill will then be **referred to committee**, usually the committee with responsibility for the primary subject matter addressed by the bill. The Senate's rules, however, do not require that a bill go through a committee before it can be considered by the full Senate on the floor. Sometimes, the majority and minority leaders agree to move a bill directly to the floor. Other times, a Senator offers a bill as an amendment to another pending bill, even if the bill he seeks to advance has nothing to do with the bill pending before the Senate. (The Senate's rules do not require that amendments to proposed legislation be germane to the bill already under consideration.)

If a bill goes through the committee process, then the process looks very much like the process in the House: a subcommittee might hold **hearings** and **mark-up** the proposed bill, and then the committee might do the same. Senate committees often issue reports about the bill, the committee's consideration of the bill, and the substantive changes that the committee made to the text of the bill.

| 115TH CONGRESS 2d Session | SENATE | REPORT 115–432 |
|---|---|---|

VICTIMS OF CHILD ABUSE ACT REAUTHORIZATION ACT OF 2018

DECEMBER 12, 2018.—Ordered to be printed

Mr. GRASSLEY, from the Committee on Judiciary, submitted the following

REPORT

[To accompany S. 2961]

[Including cost estimate of the Congressional Budget Office]

The Committee on the Judiciary, to which was referred the bill (S. 2961) to reauthorize subtitle A of the Victims of Child Abuse Act of 1990, having considered the same, reports favorably thereon with an amendment in the nature of a substitute and recommends that the bill, as amended, do pass.

CONTENTS



I. BACKGROUND AND PURPOSE OF THE VICTIMS OF CHILD ABUSE ACT REAUTHORIZATION ACT OF 2018

A. BACKGROUND

"[T]he interest [of] safeguarding the physical and psychological well-being of a minor . . . is a compelling one." *Packingham v. North Carolina*, 137 S. Ct. 1730, 1739 (2017) (quoting *Globe Newspaper Co. v. Superior Court, County of Norfolk*, 457 U.S. 596, 607 (1982) (alterations in original)). Prior to 1990, child victims of sexual abuse, physical abuse, or neglect were required to undergo a difficult disclosure and investigation process. The discovery of an

The next step in the process in the Senate reflects an important difference between the rules of the House and the Senate. Rather than using a committee to determine the rules of debate—which culminates in a vote by the full membership, permitting the majority to pass its preferred bills—the Senate's default mode of proceeding requires "**unanimous consent.**" In other words, all Senators must agree to advance a bill for consideration by the full body. As a consequence, an objection from any one of the 100 Senators can delay (and sometimes defeat) successful passage of a bill.

Uncontroversial bills usually proceed because of unanimous consent, which the majority leader can seek to facilitate passage of the bill. Sometimes a request for unanimous consent will specify the time for the debate and the procedure for offering amendments. But if any one Senator objects, then the bill cannot proceed until either the objecting Senator consents or the objection is overcome by a super-majority of Senators. **Objections to proceeding** are very common in the Senate, which has long been referred to (almost certainly hyperbolically and often ironically) as the "world's greatest deliberative body."

Objections to proceeding come in different forms. Traditionally, a Senator would object to unanimous consent and follow the objection with a **filibuster**. The classic filibuster involved a long speech to delay consideration of a bill. For example, Strom Thurmond, a pro-segregation Senator from South Carolina, spoke for over 24 hours straight on the Senate floor to obstruct passage of the Civil Rights Act of 1957. Most objections to proceeding today, however, do not involve such drama; instead, a single Senator can merely state an objection and, because the Senate rules require a super-majority vote to end debate, prevent a vote on the bill in question.

To overcome an objection—whether a stated objection to proceeding, a speaking filibuster, or a "hold"—Senators who wish to proceed to a vote must invoke **cloture**, the mechanism for ending debate. For a long time, successfully invoking cloture required a vote of two-thirds of the Senators. As a consequence, in 1964, when the Senate was debating the Civil Rights Act, supporters of the measure needed the support of 67 Senators to end the filibuster of a bloc of Senators from the South. Today, cloture requires the support of three-fifths of the Senators, which means that, as a practical matter, at least 60 Senators must support a proposed piece of legislation for it to achieve passage in the Senate.

In practice, cloture might be achieved by negotiations between proponents of the bill and Senators who have objected to proceeding, who might insist on changes to the bill as the price for their support. In such cases, the Senate usually takes up a "**substitute bill**," which replaces the previous version of the bill (and the one that went through the committee process). If cloture is successfully invoked, the Senate will **debate** the bill—either the one that emerged from the committee process or the substitute bill—and then **vote**.

### 3. Resolving Differences

Under Article I of the Constitution, only a "Bill which shall have passed the House of Representatives and the Senate" can become "a Law." U.S. Const., art. I, § 7, cl. 2. This means that both chambers must pass the *same* bill before it can become law. This is easier said than done. Often only one of the houses is interested in taking action to address a particular issue. (This might happen, among other reasons, if the chambers are controlled by different political parties, or if the leaders of one of the chambers see electoral risk for the most vulnerable members of their party.) Even if both the House and the Senate decide to take up a bill to consider a problem, the bill might make it successfully through only one of the chambers. And in those rare cases in which both chambers succeed in passing a bill, the bills that they ultimately approve might not be identical. Indeed, even if a member in the House and a Senator introduced identical bills in their respective chambers—which is actually somewhat unusual—the bills likely will diverge at some point during the process.

When the two houses pass bills that differ, there is no "Bill," within the meaning of the Constitution, that has been passed by both chambers. In those cases, the two chambers need to take further action to ensure enactment of a law. Sometimes, one of the houses will simply take up the bill passed by the other chamber and successfully pass it without amendments. (This is what happened in 1964, after the Civil Rights Act finally made it through the Senate in a way that differed from the version that the House had previously passed.) But in other cases, the two houses will need to confer to agree on a compromise measure that can get sufficient support in both houses. They do so by constituting a committee—known as a **conference committee**—composed of members from both chambers. The leaders in the House and Senate appoint members of the committee—known as "conferees"—to craft a bill that is likely to attract support in both chambers.

The conference committee then must determine the text of the bill. As a general matter, the rules of the two chambers prevent the committee from adding provisions to the bill that did not appear in the versions approved by either house. Once the conference committee agrees on the text of a bill, it drafts and issues a report explaining the differences between the prior bills and the new one. This is known as the "**conference report and joint explanation**," and it includes the actual text of the new bill.

| 106th Congress<br>*2d Session* | HOUSE OF REPRESENTATIVES | Report<br>106–606 |
|---|---|---|

# TRADE AND DEVELOPMENT ACT OF 2000

May 4, 2000.—Ordered to be printed

**Mr. Archer, from the committee of conference, submitted the following**

## CONFERENCE REPORT

[To accompany H.R. 434]

**The committee of conference on the disagreeing votes of the two Houses on the amendments of the Senate to the bill (H.R. 434), to authorize a new trade and investment policy for sub-Sahara Africa, having met, after full and free conference, have agreed to recommend and do recommend to their respective Houses as follows:**

**That the House recede from its disagreement to the amendment of the Senate to the text of the bill and agree to the same with an amendment as follows:**

**In lieu of the matter proposed to be inserted by the Senate amendment, insert the following:**

***SECTION 1. SHORT TITLE; TABLE OF CONTENTS.***

***(a) Short Title.—This Act may be cited as the "Trade and Development Act of 2000".***

***(b) Table of Contents.—***

*TITLE I—EXTENSION OF CERTAIN TRADE BENEFITS TO SUB-SAHARAN AFRICA*

*Subtitle A—Trade Policy for Sub-Saharan Africa*



The conference report then proceeds to consideration in each house. Ordinarily, amendments are out of order at this point, as they would defeat the purpose of the conference process. Both houses must approve the conference report before it can become law.

## 4. The President's Role

Even a bill that successfully makes it through both houses does not automatically become law. The Constitution provides that "[e]very Bill which shall have passed the House of Representatives and the Senate, shall, before it become a Law, be presented to the President of the United States." U.S. Const., art. I, § 7, cl. 2. If the President signs the bill, it becomes law. But the President can veto (or "return") it; in that case, it can become law only if a two-thirds majority in each house votes to approve the bill notwithstanding the President's objections. Even when the President signs a bill, he sometimes issues a "signing statement" to announce his understanding of the law or a reservation that he has about some applications of the law. Such statements typically do not carry the binding force of law, but they might instruct other Executive Branch officials about how to enforce the law, and they might inform subsequent interpreters about the intended meaning of the law.

---

## Points for Discussion

### *a. Efficiency and the Lawmaking Process*

The process for enacting legislation at the federal level is filled with pitfalls and obstacles. Each point during the legislative process described above is a potential choke point for proposed legislation: a committee chair in the House who is hostile to proposed legislation can bottle the bill up in committee and delay its consideration indefinitely; a Senator who opposes action can withhold consent to proceed or offer a poison-pill amendment designed to unravel a delicate compromise; the President might threaten to veto the bill without substantial changes; and so forth. This is a highly inefficient process, if the goal is to enact legislation to address pressing public problems. (Indeed, a tiny percentage of bills introduced in one or the other house of Congress ultimately become law.) Why would we adopt such a process for lawmaking? What is the virtue of a system that erects multiple obstacles to successful legislation?

### *b. Majority Rule and Minority Concerns*

One of the consequences of this process for enacting law is that proposals favored by the majority might not successfully become law. The Senate's rules, for example, allow a small but dedicated minority to obstruct the progress of a bill. Who benefits from this system? What is the justification for giving something approximating a veto power to the political minority?

Whatever one can say about the virtue of this system, historically one of its consequences has been that, when bills do successfully make it through the process, they have passed by large margins. Laws that pass by large margins, in turn, tend to reflect broad societal consensus. Does this consequence justify the significant barriers to successful policy-making imposed by the rules of the legislative process?

---

So far, we have been thinking about when regulation is warranted, when regulation by legislation is a sensible response, and how Congress actually goes about adopting such legislation. As we will see soon, the enactment of legislation is just the first step in determining the scope of the government's regulatory response. Questions about the meaning of enacted law inevitably arise, and someone—a prosecutor, a judge, an official at an administrative agency, or some other actor—will have to figure out what duties the law actually imposes or what entitlements the law actually confers.

We will spend a substantial amount of time thinking about those questions in Chapters 2 through 5. For now, it is worth starting to consider what the complicated process for enacting legislation suggests about how we might engage in that process of statutory interpretation. Should a bill's progress through the House and Senate—and the bargains and compromises reached in order to advance the bill through the various choke points—influence how we think about the meaning of the statute that Congress ultimately adopted?

Consider the example of the Civil Rights Act of 1964. After the Supreme Court's decision in *Brown v. Board of Education*, 347 U.S. 483 (1954), the Court directed lower courts to order school authorities to take steps towards integration "with all deliberate speed." *Brown v. Board of Education*, 349 U.S. 294 (1955). The most charitable thing that can be said about officials in many parts of the country, and particularly in the South, is that they focused on the "deliberate" rather than on the "speed." A decade after the Court's decision, many schools remained segregated, and the promise of a country untainted by discrimination remained unfilled.

In 1963, after the March on Washington, at which the Reverend Martin Luther King, Jr., gave his famous "I Have a Dream" speech, President Kennedy urged the enactment of legislation to prohibit segregation in public schools and discrimination in public accommodations, employment, and housing. At first blush, the stars seemed aligned for passage of a federal law addressing these matters: Kennedy's Democratic Party had solid majorities in both houses of Congress. But the party was divided between northern liberals, who favored aggressive steps to end discrimination, and southern conservatives, who opposed measures to end racial discrimination. At the time, however, the parties were separated by fewer ideological differences than they are today. Many Republican members of Congress supported the cause of civil rights, but they were more likely to oppose regulations that limited the autonomy of businesses and employers.

Proponents of the bill in the House had to invoke some of the more obscure rules of House procedure to get the bill through the Rules Committee, whose Southern chair, Howard "Judge" Smith, was an ardent opponent of federal protections for civil rights. The bill faced further challenges on the House floor, where Representative Smith offered an amendment to extend the bill's workplace protections (contained in Title VII of the bill) to prohibit discrimination on the basis of sex. (Smith supported equal rights for women, but there is evidence to suggest that he offered the amendment as a "poison pill," to make the bill unpalatable to some of its less dedicated supporters.) Although Congressman Smith's amendment was successful, the full House eventually approved the bill anyway 290–130.

Not surprisingly, the Senate's unique rules posed a greater threat to passage of the bill. The Democrats held 66 seats in the Senate in 1964, but because of the ideological split between northern and southern Democrats, proponents of the bill needed Republican support to break the southerners' filibuster. Republicans eventually supported a motion for cloture, but not before extracting concessions that would limit the effects of the bill on businesses. As the price for their support of cloture, Republicans obtained provisions limiting the power of the Equal Employment Opportunity Commissions to issue rules governing the workplace; expanding the defenses available to employers facing claims of discrimination; and making clear that the law does not require affirmative action in the workplace. Although Republicans held only 34 seats in the Senate, they got most of the protections that they wanted for employers.

In the end, the Senate held more than 500 hours of continuous debate over almost two months, the longest filibuster in the history of the Senate. But with Republican support, the motion for cloture passed 71–29. After further attempts at delay in the debate before the full Senate, the Senators approved a substitute bill 73–27, with the support of 46 Democrats and 27 Republicans.

Given the struggle to pass the bill in the Senate, the House decided to take up the Senate's bill rather than risk further gamesmanship at a conference between the two houses. After limited debate, the House approved the Senate's version of the bill, and President Johnson signed it on July 2, 1964.

What is the significance of this story for the meaning of the Civil Rights Act of 1964? We will return in Chapter 4 to the role of legislative history in determining statutory meaning. For now, think about the ways in which a bill's progress through the complicated legislative process in the two houses might be relevant to the law's ultimate meaning. Consider the three cases that follow, all of which involved the meaning of Title VII of the Act.

The core protection of Title VII is stated in section 703(a), which provides:

"It shall be an unlawful employment practice for an employer—

(1) to fail or refuse to hire or to discharge any individual, or otherwise to discriminate against any individual with respect to his compensation, terms, conditions, or privileges of employment, because of such individual's race, color, religion, sex, or national origin; or

(2) to limit, segregate, or classify his employees or applicants for employment in any way which would deprive or tend to deprive any individual of employment opportunities or otherwise adversely affect his status as an employee, because of such individual's race, color, religion, sex, or national origin."

---

## *Griggs v. Duke Power Co.*

420 F.2d 1225 (4th Cir. 1970)

BOREMAN, CIRCUIT JUDGE:

[Duke Power Company ran an electrical generating plant at Dan River Stream Station in Draper, North Carolina. Employees were divided into five departments: Operations, Maintenance, Laboratory and Testing, Coal Handling, and Labor. Employees who worked in the Labor Department, which was responsible for janitorial services, received by far the lowest hourly wages.

Before 1955, Duke Power permitted black employees to work only in the Labor Department. In 1955, the company eliminated that restriction. The company also began to require that every new employee, except those in the Labor Department, have a high school diploma. In addition, the new policy required an incumbent employee to have a high school education or its equivalent before he could be considered for promotion from the Labor Department to another department. Between 1955 and 1965, none of the black employees in the Labor Department were promoted to a different department.

In 1965, after the enactment of the Civil Rights Act of 1964, Duke Power instituted a new policy that permitted employees in the Labor Department to be promoted to another department if they either had a high school diploma or passed two general intelligence tests with scores equivalent to those achieved by an average high school graduate. Between 1965 and 1968, three black employees with high school diplomas were promoted to another department.

Black employees in the Labor Department sued Duke Power, asserting claims for discrimination in violation of Title VII. Ten of the plaintiffs lacked high school diplomas; of those, six had been hired before 1955. The court held that those six employees were the victims of a discriminatory policy that limited black employees to the Labor Department, and thus that they were entitled to relief.

The other four employees who lacked high school diplomas had been hired after 1955, when Duke Power instituted the diploma requirement. They admitted that the defendant had abandoned its policy of restricting all black employees to the Labor Department, but they claimed that the 1965 policy—and specifically its diploma and testing requirements—violated Title VII.]

Pointing out that it uses an intra-company promotion system to train its own employees for supervisory positions inside the company rather than hire supervisory personnel from outside, Duke claims that it initiated the high school education requirement, at least partially, so that it would have some reasonable assurance that its employees could advance into supervisory positions; further, that its educational and testing requirements are valid because they have a legitimate business purpose, and because the tests are professionally developed ability tests, as sanctioned under § 703(h) of the Act, 42 U.S.C. § 2000e–2(h).

**Food for Thought**

The 1955 policy did not by its terms discriminate on the basis of race; it simply required existing employees to have a high school diploma or its equivalent as a requirement for promotion. If the Civil Rights Act had been in effect in 1955, would the policy have violated Title VII? In thinking about that question, consider whether a white employee hired in a department other than Labor before 1955 could be promoted without a high school diploma.

[I]t seems reasonably clear that [the high school diploma] requirement did have a genuine business purpose and that the company initiated the policy with no intention to discriminate against Negro employees who might be hired after the adoption of the educational requirement. This conclusion would appear to be not merely supported, but actually compelled by the following facts:

(1) Duke had long ago established the practice of training its own employees for supervisory positions rather than bring in supervisory personnel from outside.

(2) Duke instituted its educational requirement in 1955, nine years prior to the passage of the Civil Rights Act of 1964 and well before the civil rights movement had gathered enough momentum to indicate the inevitability of the passage of such an act.

(3) Duke has, by plaintiffs' own admission, discontinued the use of discriminatory tactics in employment, promotions and transfers.

(4) The company's expert witness, Dr. Moffie, testified that he had observed the Dan River operation; had observed personnel in the performance of jobs; had studied the written summary of job duties; had spent several days with company representatives discussing job content; and he concluded that a high school education would provide the training, ability and judgment to perform tasks in the higher skilled classifications. This testimony is uncontroverted in the record.

(5) When the educational requirement was adopted it adversely affected the advancement and transfer of white employees who

were Watchmen or were in the Coal Handling Department as well as Negro employees in the Labor Department.

(6) Duke has a policy of paying the major portion of the expenses incurred by an employee who secures a high school education or its equivalent. In fact, one of the plaintiffs recently obtained such equivalent, the company paying seventy-five percent of the cost.

Next, we consider the testing requirements to determine their validity and we conclude that they, too, are valid under § 703(h) of the Civil Rights Act of 1964, 42 U.S.C. § 2000e–2(h). In pertinent part, § 703(h) reads: ". . . nor shall it be an unlawful employment practice for an employer to give and to act upon the results of any professionally developed ability test provided that such test, its administration or action upon the results is not designed, intended or used to discriminate because of race, color, religion, sex, or national origin."

There is no evidence in the record that there is any discrimination in the administration and scoring of the tests. Nor is there any evidence that the tests are not professionally developed. * * * The plaintiffs claim that tests must be job-related in order to be valid under § 703(h). The Equal Employment Opportunity Commission which is charged with administering and implementing the Act supports plaintiffs' view. The EEOC has ruled that tests are unlawful ". . . in the absence of evidence that the tests are properly related to specific jobs and have been properly validated . . . ." Decision of EEOC, December 2, 1966, reprinted in CCH, Employment Practices Guide, P17,304.53. * * *

**Food for Thought**

The plaintiffs argued that the intelligence test requirement violated §§ 703(a). In what sense did the challenged policy, which required a high school diploma or a particular score on general intelligence tests, "discriminate * * * because of * * * race"?

We cannot agree with plaintiffs' contention that such an interpretation by EEOC should be upheld where, as here, it is clearly contrary to compelling legislative history and, as will be shown, the legislative history of § 703(h) will not support the view that a "professionally developed ability test" must be job-related.

The amendment which incorporated the testing provision of § 703(h) was proposed in a modified form by Senator Tower, who was concerned about a then-recent finding by a hearing examiner for the Illinois Fair Employment Practices Commission in a case involving Motorola, Inc. The examiner had found that a pre-employment general intelligence test which Motorola had given to a Negro applicant for a job had denied the applicant an equal employment opportunity because Negroes were a culturally deprived or disadvantaged group. In proposing his original amendment, essentially the same as the version later unanimously accepted by the Senate, Senator Tower stated:

> "[The amendment] is an effort to protect the system whereby employers give general ability and intelligence tests to determine the trainability of prospective employees. The amendment arises from my concern about what happened in the Motorola FEPC case . . . .
>
> "If we should fail to adopt language of this kind, there could be an Equal Employment Opportunity Commission ruling which would in effect invalidate tests of various kinds of employees by both private business and Government to determine the professional competence or ability or trainability or suitability of a person to do a job." 110 Cong. Rec. 13492, June 11, 1964.

The discussion which ensued among members of the Senate reveals that proponents and opponents of the Act agreed that general intelligence and ability tests, if fairly administered and acted upon, were not invalidated by the Civil Rights Act of 1964. See 110 Cong. Rec. 13503–13505, June 11, 1964.

[The interpretative memorandum prepared by Senators Clark and Case, co-managers of the bill,] pertaining to Title VII fortifies the conclusion that Congress did not intend to invalidate an employer's use of bona fide general intelligence and ability tests. It was stated in said memorandum:

> "There is no requirement in Title VII that employers abandon bona fide qualification tests where, because of differences in background and education, members of some groups are able to perform better on these tests than members of other groups. An employer may set his qualifications as high as he likes, he may test to determine which applicants have these qualifications, and he may hire, assign, and promote on the basis of test performance." 110 Cong. Rec. 7213, April 8, 1964.

When Senator Tower called up his modified amendment, which became the ability testing provision of § 703(h), Senator Humphrey—one of the leading proponents and the principal floor leader of the fight for passage of the entire Act—[urged its adoption].

Having determined that Duke's educational and testing requirements were valid under Title VII, we reach the conclusion that those four Negro employees without a high school education who were hired after the adoption of the educational requirement are not entitled to relief.

Sobeloff, Circuit Judge [concurring in part and dissenting from the court's refusal to grant relief to the four employees hired after 1955]:

The case presents the broad question of the use of allegedly objective employment criteria resulting in the denial to Negroes of jobs for which they are potentially qualified. * * * The pattern of racial discrimination in employment parallels that which we have witnessed in other areas. Overt bias, when prohibited, has ofttimes been supplanted by more cunning devices designed to impart the appearance of neutrality, but to operate with the same invidious effect as before. * * * It is long recognized constitutional doctrine that "sophisticated as well as simple-minded modes of discrimination" are prohibited. *Lane v. Wilson*, 307 U.S. 268, 275 (1938) (Frankfurter, J.). We should approach enforcement of the Civil Rights Act in the same spirit.

The statute is unambiguous. Overt racial discrimination in hiring and promotion is banned [by § 703(a)(1)]. So too, the statute interdicts practices that are fair in form but discriminatory in substance. Thus it has become well settled that "objective" or "neutral" standards that favor whites but do not serve business needs are indubitably unlawful employment practices. * * * For example, a requirement that all applicants for employment shall have attended a particular type of school would seem racially neutral. But what if it develops that the specified schools were open only to whites, and if, moreover, they taught nothing of particular significance to the employer's needs? No one can doubt that the requirement would be invalid. It is the position of the Equal Employment Opportunities Commission (EEOC) that educational or test requirements which are irrelevant to job qualifications and which put blacks at a disadvantage are similarly forbidden.

Whites fare overwhelmingly better than blacks on all the criteria [considered by Duke Power for promotion],[6] as evidenced by the relatively small promotion rate from the Labor Department since 1965. Therefore, the EEOC contends that use of the standards as conditions for transfer, unless they have significant relation to performance on the job, is improper. The requirements, to withstand attack, must be shown to appraise accurately those characteristics (and only those) necessary for the job or jobs an employee will be expected to perform. In other words, the standards must be "job-related."

**Make the Connection**

We will consider agency interpretations of statutes, and the role that those interpretations should play in the process of statutory interpretation, in Chapter 8.

Under settled doctrine the Commission's interpretation should be accepted. The Supreme Court has held that "when faced with a problem of statutory construction, this Court shows great deference to the interpretation given the statute by the officers or agency charged with its administration."

---

6 In North Carolina, census statistics show, as of 1960, while 34% of white males had completed high school, only 12% of Negro males had done so. On a gross level, then, use of the high school diploma requirement would favor whites by a ratio of approximately 3 to 1. * * * Since for generations blacks have been afforded inadequate educational opportunities and have been culturally segregated from white society, it is no more surprising that their performance on "intelligence" tests is significantly different than whites' than it is that fewer blacks have high school diplomas. In one instance, for example, it was found that 58% of whites could pass a battery of standardized tests, as compared with only 6% of blacks. Included among those tests were the [tests used by Duke Power].

Not only is the Commission's interpretation of § 703(h) not unreasonable, but it makes eminent common sense. The Company would have us hold that any test authored by a professional test designer is "professionally developed" and automatically merits the court's blessing. But, what is professionally developed for one purpose is not necessarily so far another. [A] test that is adequately designed to determine academic ability, such as a college entrance examination, may be grossly wide of the mark when used in hiring a machine operator. Moreover, the Commission's is the only construction compatible with the purpose to end discrimination and to give effect to § 703(a). Although certainly not so intended, my brethren's resolution of the issue contains a built-in invitation to evade the mandate of the statute. To continue his discriminatory practices an employer need only choose any test that favors whites and is irrelevant to actual job qualifications.

Congressional discussion of employment testing came in the swath of the famous decision of an Illinois Fair Employment Practices Commission hearing examiner, *Myart v. Motorola*. That case went to the extreme of suggesting that standardized tests on which whites performed better than Negroes could never be used. The decision was generally taken to mean that such tests could never be justified even if the needs of the business required them.

Understandably, there was an outcry in Congress that Title VII might produce a *Motorola* decision. * * * Read against the context of the *Motorola* controversy, the import of the [legislative history] plainly appears: employers were not to be prohibited from using tests that determine qualifications. "Qualification" implies qualification for something. A reasonable interpretation of what the Senators meant, in light of the events, was that nothing in the Act prevents employers from requiring that applicants be fit for the job. Tests for that purpose may be as difficult as an employer may desire. * * * It is highly noteworthy that Senator Tower's exertions were not on behalf of tests unrelated to job qualifications, but his aim was to make sure that job-related tests would be permitted. He squarely disavowed any broader aim.

There can be no serious question that Duke Power's criteria are not job-related. * * * [T]he Company's criteria unfairly apply only to outsiders seeking entrance to the inside departments. This policy disadvantages those who were not favored with the lax criteria used for whites before 1955. [T]his when juxtaposed with the history and racial composition of the Dan River plant, is itself sufficient to constitute a violation of Title VII.

It is true * * * that the uneven-handed administration of transfer procedures works against some whites as well as blacks. * * * On the other hand, it cannot be ignored that while this practice does not constitute forthright racial discrimination, the policy disfavoring the outside employees has primary impact on blacks. This effect is possible only because a history of overt bias caused the departments to become so imbalanced in the first place. The result is that in 1969, four years after the passage of

Title VII, Dan River looks substantially like it did before 1965. The Labor Department is all black; the rest is virtually lily-white.

There no longer is room for doubt that a neutral superstructure built upon racial patterns that were discriminatorily erected in the past comes within the Title VII ban. * * * [T]he judgment of the District Court should be reversed with directions to grant relief to all of the plaintiffs.

---

## *Griggs v. Duke Power Co.*

401 U.S. 424 (1971)

MR. CHIEF JUSTICE BURGER delivered the opinion of the Court.

We granted the writ in this case to resolve the question whether an employer is prohibited by the Civil Rights Act of 1964, Title VII, from requiring a high school education or passing of a standardized general intelligence test as a condition of employment in or transfer to jobs when (a) neither standard is shown to be significantly related to successful job performance, (b) both requirements operate to disqualify Negroes at a substantially higher rate than white applicants, and (c) the jobs in question formerly had been filled only by white employees as part of a longstanding practice of giving preference to whites.

The Court of Appeals [concluded that] there was no showing of a racial purpose or invidious intent in the adoption of the high school diploma requirement or general intelligence test and that these standards had been applied fairly to whites and Negroes alike. It held that, in the absence of a discriminatory purpose, use of such requirements was permitted by the Act. In so doing, the Court of Appeals rejected the claim that because these two requirements operated to render ineligible a markedly disproportionate number of Negroes, they were unlawful under Title VII unless shown to be job related.

The objective of Congress in the enactment of Title VII is plain from the language of the statute. It was to achieve equality of employment opportunities and remove barriers that have operated in the past to favor an identifiable group of white employees over other employees. Under the Act, practices, procedures, or tests neutral on their face, and even neutral in terms of intent, cannot be maintained if they operate to 'freeze' the status quo of prior discriminatory employment practices.

The Court of Appeals' opinion, and the partial dissent, agreed that, on the record in the present case, "whites register far better on the Company's alternative requirements" than Negroes. This consequence would appear to be directly traceable to race. Basic intelligence must have the means of articulation to manifest itself fairly in a testing process. Because they are Negroes, petitioners have long received inferior education in segregated schools and this Court expressly recognized these differences in *Gaston County v. United States*, 395 U.S. 285 (1969). There, because of the inferior education received by Negroes in North Carolina, this Court barred the institution of a literacy test for voter registration on the ground that the test would abridge the right to vote indirectly on account of race. Congress did not intend by Title VII, however, to guarantee a job to every person regardless of qualifications. In short, the Act does not command that any person be hired simply because he was formerly the subject of discrimination, or because he is a member of a minority group. Discriminatory preference for any group, minority or majority, is precisely and only what Congress has proscribed. What is required by Congress is the removal of artificial, arbitrary, and unnecessary barriers to employment when the barriers operate invidiously to discriminate on the basis of racial or other impermissible classification.

Congress has now provided that tests or criteria for employment or promotion may not provide equality of opportunity merely in the sense of the fabled offer of milk to the stork and the fox. On the contrary, Congress has now required that the posture and condition of the job-seeker be taken into account. It has—to resort again to the fable—provided that the vessel in which the milk is proffered be one all seekers can use. The Act proscribes not only overt discrimination but also practices that are fair in form, but discriminatory in operation. The touchstone is business necessity. If an employment practice which operates to exclude Negroes cannot be shown to be related to job performance, the practice is prohibited.

**FYI**

In "The Fox and the Stork," one of Aesop's Fables, a fox invites a stork to dine and serves milk (or, in some versions, soup) in a bowl. The fox can eat it with no problem, but the stork cannot drink it with its beak. The stork then invites the fox to share milk, which he serves in a narrow-necked vessel. The stork can drink it with his beak, but the fox cannot. The moral of the fable is that one should do for others what one would wish for oneself.

On the record before us, neither the high school completion requirement nor the general intelligence test is shown to bear a demonstrable relationship to successful performance of the jobs for which it was used. Both were adopted, as the Court of Appeals noted, without meaningful study of their relationship to job-performance ability. Rather, a vice president of the Company testified, the requirements were instituted on the Company's judgment that they generally would improve the overall quality of the work force.

The evidence, however, shows that employees who have not completed high school or taken the tests have continued to perform satisfactorily and make progress in departments for which the high school and test criteria are now used.[7] The promotion record of present employees who would not be able to meet the new criteria thus suggests the possibility that the requirements may not be needed even for the limited purpose of preserving the avowed policy of advancement within the Company. In the context of this case, it is unnecessary to reach the question whether testing requirements that take into account capability for the next succeeding position or related future promotion might be utilized upon a showing that such long-range requirements fulfill a genuine business need. In the present case the Company has made no such showing.

The Court of Appeals held that the Company had adopted the diploma and test requirements without any "intention to discriminate against Negro employees." We do not suggest that either the District Court or the Court of Appeals erred in examining the employer's intent; but good intent or absence of discriminatory intent does not redeem employment procedures or testing mechanisms that operate as "built-in headwinds" for minority groups and are unrelated to measuring job capability. * * * Congress directed the thrust of the Act to the consequences of employment practices, not simply the motivation. More than that, Congress has placed on the employer the burden of showing that any given requirement must have a manifest relationship to the employment in question.

The Company contends that its general intelligence tests are specifically permitted by § 703(h) of the Act.[8] That section authorizes the use of "any professionally developed ability test" that is not "designed, intended or used to discriminate because of race . . . ."

The Equal Employment Opportunity Commission, having enforcement responsibility, has issued guidelines interpreting § 703(h) to permit only the use of job-related tests. The administrative interpretation of the Act by the enforcing agency is entitled to great deference. Since the Act and its legislative history support the Commission's construction, this affords good reason to treat the guidelines as expressing the will of Congress.

Section 703(h) was not contained in the House version of the Civil Rights Act but was added in the Senate during extended debate. For a period, debate revolved around claims that the bill as proposed would prohibit all testing and force employers to hire unqualified persons simply because they were part of a group formerly subject to job discrimination.[10] Proponents of Title VII sought throughout the debate to assure

---

7 For example, between July 2, 1965, and November 14, 1966, the percentage of white employees who were promoted but who were not high school graduates was nearly identical to the percentage of nongraduates in the entire white work force.

8 Section 703(h) applies only to tests. It has no applicability to the high school diploma requirement.

10 The congressional discussion was prompted by the decision of a hearing examiner for the Illinois Fair Employment Commission in *Myart v. Motorola Co.* (The decision is reprinted at 110 Cong. Rec.

the critics that the Act would have no effect on job-related tests. Senators Case of New Jersey and Clark of Pennsylvania, comanagers of the bill on the Senate floor, issued a memorandum explaining that the proposed Title VII "expressly protects the employer's right to insist that any prospective applicant, Negro or white, must meet the applicable job qualifications. Indeed, the very purpose of title VII is to promote hiring on the basis of job qualifications, rather than on the basis of race or color." 110 Cong. Rec. 7247.[11] Despite these assurances, Senator Tower of Texas introduced an amendment authorizing "professionally developed ability tests." Proponents of Title VII opposed the amendment because, as written, it would permit an employer to give any test, "whether it was a good test or not, so long as it was professionally designed. Discrimination could actually exist under the guise of compliance with the statute." 110 Cong. Rec. 13504 (remarks of Sen. Case).

The amendment was defeated and two days later Senator Tower offered a substitute amendment which was adopted verbatim and is now the testing provision of § 703(h). Speaking for the supporters of Title VII, Senator Humphrey, who had vigorously opposed the first amendment, endorsed the substitute amendment, [finding it] "in accord with the intent and purpose of that title." 110 Cong. Rec. 13724. The amendment was then adopted. From the sum of the legislative history relevant in this case, the conclusion is inescapable that the EEOC's construction of § 703(h) to require that employment tests be job related comports with congressional intent.

Nothing in the Act precludes the use of testing or measuring procedures; obviously they are useful. What Congress has forbidden is giving these devices and mechanisms controlling force unless they are demonstrably a reasonable measure of job performance. Congress has not commanded that the less qualified be preferred over the better qualified simply because of minority origins. Far from disparaging job qualifications as such, Congress has made such qualifications the controlling factor, so that race, religion, nationality, and sex become irrelevant. What Congress

---

5662.) That case suggested that standardized tests on which whites performed better than Negroes could never be used. The decision was taken to mean that such tests could never be justified even if the needs of the business required them. A number of Senators feared that Title VII might produce a similar result. See remarks of Senators Ervin, 110 Cong. Rec. 5614–5616; Smathers, *id.*, at 5999–6000; Holland, *id.*, at 7012–7013; Hill, *id.*, at 8447; Tower, *id.*, at 9024; Talmadge, *id.*, at 9025–9026; Fulbright, *id.*, at 9599–9600; and Ellender, *id.*, at 9600.

11 The Court of Appeals majority, in finding no requirement in Title VII that employment tests be job related, relied in part on a quotation from an earlier Clark-Case interpretative memorandum addressed to the question of the constitutionality of Title VII. * * * However, nothing there stated conflicts with the later memorandum dealing specifically with the debate over employer testing, 110 Cong. Rec. 7247 (quoted from in the text above), in which Senators Clark and Case explained that tests which measure "applicable job qualifications" are permissible under Title VII. In the earlier memorandum Clark and Case assured the Senate that employers were not to be prohibited from using tests that determine qualifications. Certainly a reasonable interpretation of what the Senators meant, in light of the subsequent memorandum directed specifically at employer testing, was that nothing in the Act prevents employers from requiring that applicants be fit for the job.

has commanded is that any tests used must measure the person for the job and not the person in the abstract.

The judgment of the Court of Appeals is, as to that portion of the judgment appealed from, reversed.

---

## Points for Discussion

***a. Disparate Treatment and Disparate Impact***

Both the Court of Appeals and the Supreme Court concluded that the employer had not adopted the testing requirement in order to exclude black employees from eligibility for promotion. Accordingly, the case did not present a claim of "disparate treatment." The Supreme Court concluded, however, that Title VII also prohibits some employment practices that have a "disparate impact" on the basis of race. The Court further held that employment tests that have a racially disparate impact must measure some skill that is related to the job in question. Do you agree that a prohibition on practices that "discriminate" on the basis of race is properly interpreted to extend to policies that are not motivated by a discriminatory purpose but that have a discriminatory effect?

***b. The Legislative Process***

One of the provisions at issue in *Griggs*—section 703(h) in Title VII—became part of the bill in the Senate after Republican Senators expressed concern about the burdens that the ban on discrimination might impose on employers. Given the need for Republican support to advance the bill through the Senate, are the views of those Senators entitled to significant weight in determining the legislative bargain ultimately adopted by Congress? If so, did the Court accurately discern their views? How do you know?

---

## *United Steelworkers of America, AFL-CIO-CLC v. Weber*

443 U.S. 193 (1979)

MR. JUSTICE BRENNAN delivered the opinion of the Court.

In 1974, petitioner United Steelworkers of America (USWA) and petitioner Kaiser Aluminum & Chemical Corp. (Kaiser) entered into a master collective-bargaining agreement covering terms and conditions of employment at 15 Kaiser plants. The agreement contained * * * an affirmative action plan designed to eliminate conspicuous racial imbalances in Kaiser's then almost exclusively white craft-work forces. Black craft-hiring goals were set for each Kaiser plant equal to the percentage of blacks in the respective local labor forces. To enable plants to meet these goals, on-the-job training programs were established to teach unskilled production workers—black and white—the skills necessary to become craftworkers. The plan reserved for black employees 50% of the openings in these newly created in-plant training programs.

This case arose from the operation of the plan at Kaiser's plant in Gramercy, La. Until 1974, Kaiser hired as craftworkers for that plant only persons who had had prior craft experience. Because blacks had long been excluded from craft unions, few were able to present such credentials. As a consequence, prior to 1974 only 1.83% (5 out of 273) of the skilled craftworkers at the Gramercy plant were black, even though the work force in the Gramercy area was approximately 39% black.

Pursuant to the national agreement Kaiser altered its craft-hiring practice in the Gramercy plant. Rather than hiring already trained outsiders, Kaiser established a training program to train its production workers to fill craft openings. Selection of craft trainees was made on the basis of seniority, with the proviso that at least 50% of the new trainees were to be black until the percentage of black skilled craftworkers in the Gramercy plant approximated the percentage of blacks in the local labor force.

During 1974, the first year of the operation of the Kaiser-USWA affirmative action plan, 13 craft trainees were selected from Gramercy's production work force. Of these, seven were black and six white. The most senior black selected into the program had less seniority than several white production workers whose bids for admission were rejected. Thereafter one of those white production workers, respondent Brian Weber (hereafter respondent), instituted this class action in the United States District Court for the Eastern District of Louisiana.

The complaint alleged that the filling of craft trainee positions at the Gramercy plant pursuant to the affirmative action program had resulted in junior black employees' receiving training in preference to senior white employees, thus discriminating against respondent and other similarly situated white employees in violation of

§§ 703(a)[2] and (d)[3] of Title VII [of the Civil Rights Act of 1964]. The District Court held that the plan violated Title VII * * *. A divided panel of the Court of Appeals for the Fifth Circuit affirmed, holding that all employment preferences based upon race, including those preferences incidental to bona fide affirmative action plans, violated Title VII's prohibition against racial discrimination in employment. * * * We reverse.

We emphasize at the outset the narrowness of our inquiry. Since [the] Kaiser-USWA plan was adopted voluntarily, we are not concerned with what Title VII requires or with what a court might order to remedy a past proved violation of the Act. The only question before us is the narrow statutory issue of whether Title VII *forbids* private employers and unions from voluntarily agreeing upon bona fide affirmative action plans that accord racial preferences in the manner and for the purpose provided in the Kaiser-USWA plan. That question was expressly left open in *McDonald v. Santa Fe Trail Transp. Co.*, 427 U.S. 273, 281 n. 8 (1976), which held, in a case not involving affirmative action, that Title VII protects whites as well as blacks from certain forms of racial discrimination.

Respondent argues that Congress intended in Title VII to prohibit all race-conscious affirmative action plans. Respondent's argument rests upon a literal interpretation of §§ 703(a) and (d) of the Act. Those sections make it unlawful to "discriminate . . . because of . . . race" in hiring and in the selection of apprentices for training programs. Since, the argument runs, *McDonald* settled that Title VII forbids discrimination against whites as well as blacks, and since the Kaiser-USWA affirmative action plan operates to discriminate against white employees solely because they are white, it follows that the Kaiser-USWA plan violates Title VII.

Respondent's argument is not without force. But it overlooks the significance of the fact that the Kaiser-USWA plan is an affirmative action plan voluntarily adopted by private parties to eliminate traditional patterns of racial segregation. In this context respondent's reliance upon a literal construction of §§ 703(a) and (d) and

---

2 Section 703(a) [42 U.S.C. § 2000e–2(a)] provides:

"(a) . . . It shall be an unlawful employment practice for an employer—

"(1) to fail or refuse to hire or to discharge any individual, or otherwise to discriminate against any individual with respect to his compensation, terms, conditions, or privileges of employment, because of such individual's race, color, religion, sex, or national origin; or

"(2) to limit, segregate, or classify his employees or applicants for employment in any way which would deprive or tend to deprive any individual of employment opportunities or otherwise adversely affect his status as an employee, because of such individual's race, color, religion, sex, or national origin."

3 Section 703(d) [42 U.S.C. § 2000e–2(d)] provides:

"It shall be an unlawful employment practice for any employer, labor organization, or joint labor-management committee controlling apprenticeship or other training or retraining, including on-the-job training programs to discriminate against any individual because of his race, color, religion, sex, or national origin in admission to, or employment in, any program established to provide apprenticeship or other training."

upon *McDonald* is misplaced. It is a "familiar rule that a thing may be within the letter of the statute and yet not within the statute, because not within its spirit nor within the intention of its makers." *Holy Trinity Church v. United States*, 143 U.S. 457, 459 (1892).

**Make the Connection**

We will consider the Court's decision in *Holy Trinity Church*, and the tension between the "letter" and the "spirit" of a law, in Chapter 2.

The prohibition against racial discrimination in §§ 703(a) and (d) of Title VII must therefore be read against the background of the legislative history of Title VII and the historical context from which the Act arose. Examination of those sources makes clear that an interpretation of the sections that forbade all race-conscious affirmative action would "bring about an end completely at variance with the purpose of the statute" and must be rejected. *United States v. Public Utilities Comm'n*, 345 U.S. 295, 315 (1953).

Congress' primary concern in enacting the prohibition against racial discrimination in Title VII of the Civil Rights Act of 1964 was with "the plight of the Negro in our economy." 110 Cong. Rec. 6548 (1964) (remarks of Sen. Humphrey). Before 1964, blacks were largely relegated to "unskilled and semi-skilled jobs." *Ibid.* (remarks of Sen. Humphrey); *id.*, at 7204 (remarks of Sen. Clark); *id.*, at 7379–7380 (remarks of Sen. Kennedy). Because of automation the number of such jobs was rapidly decreasing. See *id.*, at 6548 (remarks of Sen. Humphrey); *id.*, at 7204 (remarks of Sen. Clark). As a consequence, "the relative position of the Negro worker [was] steadily worsening. In 1947 the nonwhite unemployment rate was only 64 percent higher than the white rate; in 1962 it was 124 percent higher." *Id.*, at 6547 (remarks of Sen. Humphrey). See also *id.*, at 7204 (remarks of Sen. Clark). Congress considered this a serious social problem. * * *

Congress feared that the goals of the Civil Rights Act—the integration of blacks into the mainstream of American society—could not be achieved unless this trend were reversed. And Congress recognized that that would not be possible unless blacks were able to secure jobs "which have a future." *Id.*, at 7204 (remarks of Sen. Clark). See also *id.*, at 7379–7380 (remarks of Sen. Kennedy). * * * Accordingly, it was clear to Congress that "[t]he crux of the problem [was] to open employment opportunities for Negroes in occupations which have been traditionally closed to them," 10 Cong. Rec. 6548 (1964) (remarks of Sen. Humphrey), and it was to this problem that Title VII's prohibition against racial discrimination in employment was primarily addressed.

It plainly appears from the House Report accompanying the Civil Rights Act that Congress did not intend wholly to prohibit private and voluntary affirmative action efforts as one method of solving this problem. The Report provides:

> "No bill can or should lay claim to eliminating all of the causes and consequences of racial and other types of discrimination against minorities. There is reason to believe, however, that national leadership provided by the enactment of Federal legislation

> dealing with the most troublesome problems *will create an atmosphere conducive to voluntary or local resolution of other forms of discrimination.*" H.R. Rep. No. 914, 88th Cong., 1st Sess., pt. 1, p. 18 (1963). (Emphasis supplied.)

Given this legislative history, we cannot agree with respondent that Congress intended to prohibit the private sector from taking effective steps to accomplish the goal that Congress designed Title VII to achieve. The very statutory words intended as a spur or catalyst to cause "employers and unions to self-examine and to self-evaluate their employment practices and to endeavor to eliminate, so far as possible, the last vestiges of an unfortunate and ignominious page in this country's history," *Albemarle Paper Co. v. Moody*, 422 U.S. 405, 418 (1975), cannot be interpreted as an absolute prohibition against all private, voluntary, race-conscious affirmative action efforts to hasten the elimination of such vestiges. It would be ironic indeed if a law triggered by a Nation's concern over centuries of racial injustice and intended to improve the lot of those who had "been excluded from the American dream for so long," 110 Cong. Rec. 6552 (1964) (remarks of Sen. Humphrey), constituted the first legislative prohibition of all voluntary, private, race-conscious efforts to abolish traditional patterns of racial segregation and hierarchy.

Our conclusion is further reinforced by examination of the language and legislative history of § 703(j) of Title VII.[5] Opponents of Title VII raised two related arguments against the bill. First, they argued that the Act would be interpreted to *require* employers with racially imbalanced work forces to grant preferential treatment to racial minorities in order to integrate. Second, they argued that employers with racially imbalanced work forces would grant preferential treatment to racial minorities, even if not required to do so by the Act. See 110 Cong. Rec. 8618–8619 (1964) (remarks of Sen. Sparkman). Had Congress meant to prohibit all race-conscious affirmative action, as respondent urges, it easily could have answered both objections by providing that Title VII would not require or *permit* racially preferential integration efforts. But Congress did not choose such a course. Rather, Congress added § 703(j) which addresses only the first objection. The section provides that nothing contained in Title VII "shall be interpreted to *require* any employer . . . to grant

---

5 Section 703(j) [42 U.S.C. § 2000e–2(j)] provides:

"Nothing contained in this title shall be interpreted to require any employer, employment agency, labor organization, or joint labor-management committee subject to this title to grant preferential treatment to any individual or to any group because of the race, color, religion, sex, or national origin of such individual or group on account of an imbalance which may exist with respect to the total number or percentage of persons of any race, color, religion, sex, or national origin employed by any employer, referred or classified for employment by any employment agency or labor organization, admitted to membership or classified by any labor organization, admitted to membership or classified by any labor organization, or admitted to, or employed in, any apprenticeship or other training program, in comparison with the total number or percentage of persons of such race, color, religion, sex, or national origin in any community, State, section, or other area, or in the available work force in any community, State, section, or other area." * * *

preferential treatment . . . to any group because of the race . . . of such . . . group on account of" a *de facto* racial imbalance in the employer's work force. The section does *not* state that "nothing in Title VII shall be interpreted to *permit*" voluntary affirmative efforts to correct racial imbalances. The natural inference is that Congress chose not to forbid all voluntary race-conscious affirmative action.

The reasons for this choice are evident from the legislative record. Title VII could not have been enacted into law without substantial support from legislators in both Houses who traditionally resisted federal regulation of private business. Those legislators demanded as a price for their support that "management prerogatives, and union freedoms . . . be left undisturbed to the greatest extent possible." H.R. Rep. No. 914, 88th Cong., 1st Sess., pt. 2, p. 29 (1963).

**Take Note**

The Court here describes the need for the bill's proponents to accommodate Republicans' concerns in order to secure passage. How did the bill's progress through the legislative process influence the Court's interpretation of the Act?

Section 703(j) was proposed by Senator Dirksen to allay any fears that the Act might be interpreted in such a way as to upset this compromise. The section was designed to prevent § 703 of Title VII from being interpreted in such a way as to lead to undue "Federal Government interference with private businesses because of some Federal employee's ideas about racial balance or racial imbalance." 110 Cong. Rec. 14314 (1964) (remarks of Sen. Miller). See also *id.*, at 9881 (remarks of Sen. Allott); *id.*, at 10520 (remarks of Sen. Carlson); *id.*, at 11471 (remarks of Sen. Javits); *id.*, at 12817 (remarks of Sen. Dirksen). Clearly, a prohibition against all voluntary, race-conscious, affirmative action efforts would disserve these ends. Such a prohibition would augment the powers of the Federal Government and diminish traditional management prerogatives while at the same time impeding attainment of the ultimate statutory goals. In view of this legislative history and in view of Congress' desire to avoid undue federal regulation of private businesses, use of the word "require" rather than the phrase "require or permit" in § 703(j) fortifies the conclusion that Congress did not intend to limit traditional business freedom to such a degree as to prohibit all voluntary, race-conscious affirmative action.[7]

---

7 Respondent argues that our construction of § 703 conflicts with various remarks in the legislative record. See, *e.g.*, 110 Cong. Rec. 7213 (1964) (Sens. Clark and Case); *id.*, at 7218 (Sens. Clark and Case); *id.*, at 6549 (Sen. Humphrey); *id.*, at 8921 (Sen. Williams). We do not agree. In Senator Humphrey's words, these comments were intended as assurances that Title VII would not allow establishment of systems "to *maintain* racial balance in employment." *Id.*, at 11848 (emphasis added). They were not addressed to temporary, voluntary, affirmative action measures undertaken to eliminate manifest racial imbalance in traditionally segregated job categories. Moreover, the comments referred to by respondent all preceded the adoption of § 703(j). After § 703(j) was adopted, congressional comments were all to the effect that employers would not be *required* to institute preferential quotas to avoid Title VII lia-

We therefore hold that Title VII's prohibition in §§ 703(a) and (d) against racial discrimination does not condemn all private, voluntary, race-conscious affirmative action plans.

We need not today define in detail the line of demarcation between permissible and impermissible affirmative action plans. It suffices to hold that the challenged Kaiser-USWA affirmative action plan falls on the permissible side of the line. * * * Accordingly, the judgment of the Court of Appeals for the Fifth Circuit is [reversed].

MR. JUSTICE POWELL and MR. JUSTICE STEVENS took no part in the consideration or decision of these cases.

[JUSTICE BLACKMUN's concurring opinion and CHIEF JUSTICE BURGER's dissenting opinion have been omitted.]

MR. JUSTICE REHNQUIST, with whom THE CHIEF JUSTICE joins, dissenting.

The operative sections of Title VII prohibit racial discrimination in employment *simpliciter*. Taken in its normal meaning and as understood by all Members of Congress who spoke to the issue during the legislative debates, this language prohibits a covered employer from considering race when making an employment decision, whether the race be black or white. * * *

Were Congress to act today specifically to prohibit the type of racial discrimination suffered by Weber, it would be hard pressed to draft language better tailored to the task than that found in § 703(d) [and § 703(a)(2)] of Title VII * * *. Entirely consistent with these two express prohibitions is the language of § 703(j) of Title VII, which provides that the Act is not to be interpreted "to require any employer . . . to grant preferential treatment to any individual or to any group because of the race . . . of such individual or group" to correct a racial imbalance in the employer's work force. Seizing on the word "require," the Court infers that Congress must have intended to "permit" this type of racial discrimination. Not only is this reading of

---

bility, see, *e.g.*, 110 Cong. Rec. 12819 (1964) (remarks of Sen. Dirksen); *id.*, at 13079–13080 (remarks of Sen. Clark); *id.*, at 15876 (remarks of Rep. Lindsay). There was no suggestion after the adoption of § 703(j) that wholly voluntary, race-conscious, affirmative action efforts would in themselves constitute a violation of Title VII. On the contrary, as Representative MacGregor told the House shortly before the final vote on Title VII:

> "Important as the scope and extent of this bill is, it is also vitally important that all Americans understand what this bill does not cover. Your mail and mine, your contacts and mine with our constituents, indicates a great degree of misunderstanding about this bill. People complain about . . . preferential treatment or quotas in employment. There is a mistaken belief that Congress is legislating in these areas in this bill. When we drafted this bill we excluded these issues largely because the problems raised by these controversial questions are more properly handled at a governmental level closer to the American people and by communities and individuals themselves." 110 Cong. Rec. 15893 (1964).

§ 703(j) outlandish in the light of the flat prohibitions of §§ 703(a) and (d), but also [is] totally belied by the Act's legislative history.

Quite simply, Kaiser's racially discriminatory admission quota is flatly prohibited by the plain language of Title VII. This normally dispositive fact, however, gives the Court only momentary pause. An "interpretation" of the statute upholding Weber's claim would, according to the Court, "bring about an end completely at variance with the purpose of the statute." To support this conclusion, the Court calls upon the "spirit" of the Act, which it divines from passages in Title VII's legislative history indicating that enactment of the statute was prompted by Congress' desire "to open employment opportunities for Negroes in occupations which [had] been traditionally closed to them."[10] But the legislative history invoked by the Court to avoid the plain language of §§ 703(a) and (d) simply misses the point. To be sure, the reality of employment discrimination against Negroes provided the primary impetus for passage of Title VII. But this fact by no means supports the proposition that Congress intended to leave employers free to discriminate against white persons. In most cases, "[l]egislative history . . . is more vague than the statute we are called upon to interpret." *United States v. Public Utilities Comm'n*, 345 U.S. 295, 320 (1953) (Jackson, J., concurring). Here, however, the legislative history of Title VII is as clear as the language of §§ 703(a) and (d), and it irrefutably demonstrates that Congress meant precisely what it said in §§ 703(a) and (d)—that *no* racial discrimination in employment is permissible under Title VII, not even preferential treatment of minorities to correct racial imbalance.

Introduced on the floor of the House of Representatives on June 20, 1963, the bill—H.R. 7152—that ultimately became the Civil Rights Act of 1964 contained no compulsory provisions directed at private discrimination in employment. The bill was promptly referred to the Committee on the Judiciary, where it was amended to include Title VII. With two exceptions, the bill

**Take Note**

Justice Rehnquist gives a play-by-play account of the bill's progress through the two houses of Congress. In his view, what is the significance of this history? What role does it play in his effort to interpret the meaning of the statute's provisions?

10 In holding that Title VII cannot be interpreted to prohibit use of Kaiser's racially discriminatory admission quota, the Court reasons that it would be "ironic" if a law inspired by the history of racial discrimination in employment against blacks forbade employers from voluntarily discriminating against whites in favor of blacks. I see no irony in a law that prohibits *all* voluntary racial discrimination, even discrimination directed at whites in favor of blacks. The evil inherent in discrimination against Negroes is that it is based on an immutable characteristic, utterly irrelevant to employment decisions. The characteristic becomes no less immutable and irrelevant, and discrimination based thereon becomes no less evil, simply because the person excluded is a member of one race rather than another. Far from ironic, I find a prohibition on all preferential treatment based on race as elementary and fundamental as the principle that "two wrongs do not make a right."

reported by the House Judiciary Committee contained §§ 703(a) and (d) as they were ultimately enacted. Amendments subsequently adopted on the House floor added § 703's prohibition against sex discrimination and § 703(d)'s coverage of "on-the-job training."

After noting that "[t]he purpose of [Title VII] is to eliminate . . . discrimination in employment based on race, color, religion, or national origin," the Judiciary Committee's Report simply paraphrased the provisions of Title VII without elaboration. H.R. Rep., pt. 1, p. 26. In a separate Minority Report, however, opponents of the measure on the Committee advanced a line of attack which was reiterated throughout the debates in both the House and Senate and which ultimately led to passage of § 703(j). Noting that the word "discrimination" was nowhere defined in H.R. 7152, the Minority Report charged that the absence from Title VII of any reference to "racial imbalance" was a "public relations" ruse and that "the administration intends to rely upon its own construction of 'discrimination' as including the lack of racial balance . . . ." H.R. Rep., pt. 1, pp. 67–68. To demonstrate how the bill would operate in practice, the Minority Report posited a number of hypothetical employment situations, concluding in each example that the employer "*may be forced to hire according to race*, to 'racially balance' those who work for him *in every job classification* or be in violation of Federal law." *Id.*, at 69.

When H.R. 7152 reached the House floor, the opening speech in support of its passage was delivered by Representative Celler, Chairman of the House Judiciary Committee and the Congressman responsible for introducing the legislation. A portion of that speech responded to criticism "seriously misrepresent[ing] what the bill would do and grossly distort[ing] its effects":

> "[T]he charge has been made that the Equal Employment Opportunity Commission to be established by title VII of the bill would have the power to prevent a business from employing and promoting the people it wished, and that a 'Federal inspector' could then order the hiring and promotion only of employees of certain races or religious groups. This description of the bill is entirely wrong. . . . The Bill would do no more than prevent . . . employers from discriminating against *or in favor* of workers because of their race, religion, or national origin.
>
> "It is likewise not true that the Equal Employment Opportunity Commission would have power to rectify existing 'racial or religious imbalance' in employment by requiring the hiring of certain people without regard to their qualifications simply because they are of a given race or religion. Only actual discrimination could be stopped." 110 Cong. Rec. 1518 (1964) (emphasis added).

Representative Celler's construction of Title VII was repeated by several other supporters during the House debate.

Thus, the battle lines were drawn early in the legislative struggle over Title VII, with opponents of the measure charging that agencies of the Federal Government such as the Equal Employment Opportunity Commission (EEOC), by interpreting the word "discrimination" to mean the existence of "racial imbalance," would "require" employers to grant preferential treatment to minorities, and supporters responding that the EEOC would be granted no such power and that, indeed, Title VII prohibits discrimination "in favor of workers because of their race." Supporters of H.R. 7152 in the House ultimately prevailed by a vote of 290 to 130, and the measure was sent to the Senate to begin what became the longest debate in that body's history.

Formal debate on the merits of H.R. 7152 began on March 30, 1964. * * * Senator Humphrey, the majority whip, and Senator Kuchel, the minority whip, were selected as the bipartisan floor managers on the entire civil rights bill. Responsibility for explaining and defending each important title of the bill was placed on bipartisan "captains." Senators Clark and Case were selected as the bipartisan captains responsible for Title VII.

In the opening speech of the formal Senate debate on the bill, Senator Humphrey addressed the main concern of Title VII's opponents, advising that not only does Title VII not require use of racial quotas, *it does not permit* their use. "The truth," stated the floor leader of the bill, "is that this title forbids discriminating against anyone on account of race. This is the simple and complete truth about title VII." 110 Cong. Rec. 6549 (1964). Senator Humphrey continued:

> "Contrary to the allegations of some opponents of this title, there is nothing in it that will give any power to the Commission or to any court to require hiring, firing, or promotion of employees in order to meet a racial 'quota' or to achieve a certain racial balance.
>
> "That bugaboo has been brought up a dozen times; but it is nonexistent. In fact, *the very opposite is true. Title VII prohibits discrimination.* In effect, it says that race, religion and national origin are not to be used as the basis for hiring and firing. Title VII is designed to encourage hiring on the basis of ability and qualifications, not race or religion." *Ibid.* (emphasis added).

At the close of his speech, Senator Humphrey returned briefly to the subject of employment quotas: "It is claimed that the bill would require racial quotas for all hiring, when in fact it provides that race shall not be a basis for making personnel decisions." *Id.*, at 6553.

A few days later the Senate's attention focused exclusively on Title VII, as Senators Clark and Case rose to discuss the title of H.R. 7152 on which they shared floor "captain" responsibilities. In an interpretative memorandum submitted jointly to the Senate, Senators Clark and Case took pains to refute the opposition's charge that Title VII would result in preferential treatment of minorities. Their words were clear and unequivocal:

> "There is no requirement in title VII that an employer maintain a racial balance in his work force. On the contrary, any deliberate attempt to maintain a racial balance, whatever such a balance may be, would involve a violation of title VII because maintaining such a balance would require an employer to hire or to refuse to hire on

> the basis of race. It must be emphasized that discrimination is prohibited as to any individual." *Id.*, at 7213.

Of particular relevance to the instant litigation were their observations regarding seniority rights. As if directing their comments at Brian Weber, the Senators said:

> "Title VII would have no effect on established seniority rights. Its effect is prospective and not retrospective. Thus, for example, if a business has been discriminating in the past and as a result has an all-white working force, when the title comes into effect the employer's obligation would be simply to fill future vacancies on a nondiscriminatory basis. He would not be obliged—*or indeed permitted*—to fire whites in order to hire Negroes, *or to prefer Negroes for future vacancies, or, once Negroes are hired, to give them special seniority rights at the expense of the white workers hired earlier.*" *Ibid.* (emphasis added).

Despite these clear statements from the bill's leading and most knowledgeable proponents, the fears of the opponents were not put to rest. * * * While the debate in the Senate raged, a bipartisan coalition under the leadership of Senators Dirksen, Mansfield, Humphrey, and Kuchel was working with House leaders and representatives of the Johnson administration on a number of amendments to H.R. 7152 designed to enhance its prospects of passage. The so-called "Dirksen-Mansfield" amendment was introduced on May 26 by Senator Dirksen as a substitute for the entire House-passed bill. The substitute bill, which ultimately became law, left unchanged the basic prohibitory language of §§ 703(a) and (d), as well as the remedial provisions in § 706(g). It added, however, several provisions defining and clarifying the scope of Title VII's substantive prohibitions. One of those clarifying amendments, § 703(j), was specifically directed at the opposition's concerns regarding racial balancing and preferential treatment of minorities, providing in pertinent part: "Nothing contained in [Title VII] shall be interpreted to require any employer . . . to grant preferential treatment to any individual or to any group because of the race . . . of such individual or group on account of" a racial imbalance in the employer's work force. 42 U.S.C. § 2000e–2(j).

Contrary to the Court's analysis, the language of § 703(j) is precisely tailored to the objection voiced time and again by Title VII's opponents. Not once during the 83 days of debate in the Senate did a speaker, proponent or opponent, suggest that the bill would allow employers *voluntarily* to prefer racial minorities over white persons. In light of Title VII's flat prohibition on discrimination "against any individual . . . because of such individual's race," § 703(a), such a contention would have been, in any event, too preposterous to warrant response. Indeed, speakers on both sides of the issue, as the legislative history makes clear, recognized that Title VII would tolerate no *voluntary* racial preference, whether in favor of blacks or whites. The complaint consistently voiced by the opponents was that Title VII, particularly the word "discrimination," would be *interpreted* by federal agencies such as the EEOC to *require* the correction of racial imbalance through the granting of preferential treatment to minorities. Verbal assurances that Title VII would not require—indeed, would not permit—preferential treatment of blacks having failed, supporters of H.R. 7152 responded by proposing an amendment carefully worded to meet, and put to rest, the opposition's charge. Indeed, unlike §§ 703(a) and (d), which are by their terms directed at entities—*e.g.*, employers, labor unions—whose actions are restricted by Title VII's prohibitions, the language of § 703(j) is specifically directed at entities—federal agencies and courts—charged with the responsibility of interpreting Title VII's provisions.

Section 703(j) apparently calmed the fears of most of the opponents; after its introduction, complaints concerning racial balance and preferential treatment died down considerably. * * * On June 10, the Senate, for the second time in its history, imposed cloture on its Members. [On June 19,] the Dirksen-Mansfield substitute bill was passed. [Less than two weeks later, the House adopted the Senate version without amendments. On July 2, the President signed the bill and the Civil Rights Act of 1964 became law.]

Reading the language of Title VII, as the Court purports to do, "against the background of [its] legislative history . . . and the historical context from which the Act arose," one is led inescapably to the conclusion that Congress fully understood what it was saying and meant precisely what it said. * * * In passing Title VII, Congress outlawed *all* racial discrimination, recognizing that no discrimination based on race is benign, that no action disadvantaging a person because of his color is affirmative. * * * By going not merely *beyond*, but directly *against* Title VII's language and legislative history, the Court has sown the wind. Later courts will face the impossible task of reaping the whirlwind.

---

## *Johnson v. Transportation Agency, Santa Clara County*

480 U.S. 616 (1987)

Justice Brennan delivered the opinion of the Court.

In December 1978, the Santa Clara County Transit District Board of Supervisors adopted an Affirmative Action Plan (Plan) for the County Transportation Agency. The Plan implemented a County Affirmative Action Plan, which had been adopted, declared the County, because "mere prohibition of discriminatory practices is not enough to remedy the effects of past practices and to permit attainment of an equitable representation of minorities, women and handicapped persons." Relevant to this case, the Agency Plan provides that, in making promotions to positions within a traditionally segregated job classification in which women have been significantly underrepresented, the Agency is authorized to consider as one factor the sex of a qualified applicant.

In reviewing the composition of its work force, the Agency noted in its Plan that women were represented in numbers far less than their proportion of the County labor force in both the Agency as a whole and in five of seven job categories. Specifically, while women constituted 36.4% of the area labor market, they composed only 22.4% of Agency employees. Furthermore, women working at the Agency were concentrated largely in EEOC job categories traditionally held by women: women made up 76% of Office and Clerical Workers, but only 7.1% of Agency Officials and Administrators, 8.6% of Professionals, 9.7% of Technicians, and 22% of Service and Maintenance Workers. As for the job classification relevant to this case, none of the 238 Skilled Craft Worker positions was held by a woman. * * *

The Agency's Plan [set] aside no specific number of positions for minorities or women, but authorized the consideration of ethnicity or sex as a factor when evaluating qualified candidates for jobs in which members of such groups were poorly represented. One such job was the road dispatcher position that is the subject of the dispute in this case.

[Pursuant to the Plan, the Agency promoted Diane Joyce, the first woman in the County to fill a position as a road maintenance worker, to the position of road dispatcher. Nine of the applicants for the position, including Joyce and Paul Johnson,] were deemed qualified for the job, and were interviewed by a two-person board. Seven of the applicants scored above 70 on this interview, which meant that they were certified as eligible for selection by the appointing authority. The scores awarded ranged from 70 to 80. Johnson was tied for second with a score of 75, while Joyce ranked next with a score of 73. [The official responsible for making the promotion decision stated that he "looked at the whole picture" and took many factors into account, including the affirmative action plan and Joyce's sex.]

[Johnson filed suit and asserted that the County's failure to promote him constituted unlawful sex discrimination under Title VII of the Civil Rights Act of 1964. The district court granted relief, but the court of appeals reversed.]

The assessment of the legality of the Agency Plan must be guided by our decision in *Steelworkers v. Weber*, 443 U.S. 193 (1979). In that case, [w]e upheld the employer's decision to select less senior black applicants over the white respondent, for we found that taking race into account was consistent with Title VII's objective of "break[ing] down old patterns of racial segregation and hierarchy." *Id.*, at 208. As we stated:

> "It would be ironic indeed if a law triggered by a Nation's concern over centuries of racial injustice and intended to improve the lot of those who had 'been excluded from the American dream for so long' constituted the first legislative prohibition of all voluntary, private, race-conscious efforts to abolish traditional patterns of racial segregation and hierarchy." *Id.*, at 204 (quoting remarks of Sen. Humphrey, 110 Cong. Rec. 6552 (1964)).[7]

---

7 Justice SCALIA's dissent maintains that *Weber*'s conclusion that Title VII does not prohibit voluntary affirmative action programs "rewrote the statute it purported to construe." *Weber*'s decisive

* * * Our decision was grounded in the recognition that voluntary employer action can play a crucial role in furthering Title VII's purpose of eliminating the effects of discrimination in the workplace, and that Title VII should not be read to thwart such efforts.

[The Court considered in detail the elements of the Agency's affirmative action plan.]

We [hold] that the Agency appropriately took into account as one factor the sex of Diane Joyce in determining that she should be promoted to the road dispatcher position. The decision to do so was made pursuant to an affirmative action plan that represents a moderate, flexible, case-by-case approach to effecting a gradual improvement in the representation of minorities and women in the Agency's work force. Such a plan is fully consistent with Title VII, for it embodies the contribution that voluntary employer action can make in eliminating the vestiges of discrimination in the workplace. * * *

JUSTICE STEVENS, concurring.

Prior to 1978 the Court construed the Civil Rights Act of 1964 as an absolute blanket prohibition against discrimination which neither required nor permitted

---

rejection of the argument that the "plain language" of the statute prohibits affirmative action rested on (1) legislative history indicating Congress' clear intention that employers play a major role in eliminating the vestiges of discrimination, and (2) the language and legislative history of § 703(j) of the statute, which reflect a strong desire to preserve managerial prerogatives so that they might be utilized for this purpose. As Justice BLACKMUN said in his concurrence in *Weber*, "[I]f the Court has misperceived the political will, it has the assurance that because the question is statutory Congress may set a different course if it so chooses." *Id.*, at 216. Congress has not amended the statute to reject our construction, nor have any such amendments even been proposed, and we therefore may assume that our interpretation was correct.

Justice SCALIA's dissent faults the fact that we take note of the absence of congressional efforts to amend the statute to nullify *Weber*. It suggests that congressional inaction cannot be regarded as acquiescence under all circumstances, but then draws from that unexceptional point the conclusion that *any* reliance on congressional failure to act is necessarily a "canard." The fact that inaction may not always provide crystalline revelation, however, should not obscure the fact that it may be probative to varying degrees. *Weber*, for instance, was a widely publicized decision that addressed a prominent issue of public debate. Legislative inattention thus is not a plausible explanation for congressional inaction. Furthermore, Congress not only passed no contrary legislation in the wake of *Weber*, but not one legislator even proposed a bill to do so. The barriers of the legislative process therefore also seem a poor explanation for failure to act. By contrast, when Congress has been displeased with our interpretation of Title VII, it has not hesitated to amend the statute to tell us so. For instance, when Congress passed the Pregnancy Discrimination Act of 1978, 42 U.S.C. § 2000e(k), "it unambiguously expressed its disapproval of both the holding and the reasoning of the Court in [*General Electric Co. v. Gilbert*, 429 U.S. 125 (1976)]." *Newport News Shipbuilding & Dry Dock Co. v. EEOC*, 462 U.S. 669, 678 (1983). Surely, it is appropriate to find some probative value in such radically different congressional reactions to this Court's interpretations of the same statute.

As one scholar has put it, "When a court says to a legislature: 'You (or your predecessor) meant X,' it almost invites the legislature to answer: 'We did not.' " G. Calabresi, A Common Law for the Age of Statutes 31–32 (1982). Any belief in the notion of a dialogue between the judiciary and the legislature must acknowledge that on occasion an invitation declined is as significant as one accepted.

discriminatory preferences for any group, minority or majority. * * * If the Court had adhered to that construction of the Act, petitioner would unquestionably prevail in this case. But it has not done so.

In [*Regents of University of California v. Bakke,* 438 U.S. 265 (1978), which addressed affirmative action plans at public universities,] and again in *Steelworkers v. Weber,* 443 U.S. 193 (1979), a majority of the Court interpreted the antidiscriminatory strategy of the statute in a fundamentally different way. [T]he only problem for me is whether to adhere to an authoritative construction of the Act that is at odds with my understanding of the actual intent of the authors of the legislation. I conclude without hesitation that I must answer that question in the affirmative * * *.

*Bakke* and *Weber* have been decided and are now an important part of the fabric of our law. This consideration is sufficiently compelling for me to adhere to the basic construction of this legislation that the Court adopted in *Bakke* and in *Weber.* There is an undoubted public interest in "stability and orderly development of the law." * * * Respondent's voluntary decision [to adopt and apply an affirmative action plan] is surely not prohibited by Title VII as construed in *Weber.*

[Justice O'Connor's opinion concurring in the judgment and Justice White's dissenting opinion have been omitted.]

Justice Scalia, with whom The Chief Justice joins, and with whom Justice White joins in Parts I and II, dissenting.

The Court today completes the process of converting [Title VII] from a guarantee that race or sex will *not* be the basis for employment determinations, to a guarantee that it often *will.* Ever so subtly, without even alluding to the last obstacles preserved by earlier opinions that we now push out of our path, we effectively replace the goal of a discrimination-free society with the quite incompatible goal of proportionate representation by race and by sex in the workplace. * * *

[In Part I of his dissent, Justice Scalia contended that the County had not previously discriminated in hiring on the basis of sex, and that accordingly the Plan was not designed to remedy past discrimination. In Part II, Justice Scalia criticized the Court's opinion for permitting affirmative action plans that seek to remedy past societal, rather than past employer-specific, discrimination.]

[III] * * * It is well to keep in mind just how thoroughly *Weber* rewrote the statute it purported to construe. The language of that statute * * * is unambiguous: it is an unlawful employment practice "to fail or refuse to hire or to discharge any individual, or otherwise to discriminate against any individual with respect to his compensation, terms, conditions, or privileges of employment, because of such individual's race, color, religion, sex, or national origin." 42 U.S.C. § 2000e–2(a). *Weber* disregarded the text of the statute, invoking instead its "spirit," and "practical and equitable [considerations] only partially perceived, if perceived at all, by the 88th Congress," 443 U.S., at 209 (BLACKMUN, J., concurring). It concluded, on the basis of these intangible guides, that Title VII's prohibition of intentional discrimination on the basis of race and sex does not prohibit intentional discrimination on the basis of race and sex, so long as it is "designed to break down old patterns of racial [or sexual] segregation and hierarchy," "does not unnecessarily trammel the interests of the white [or male] employees," "does not require the discharge of white [or male] workers and their replacement with new black [or female] hirees," "does [not] create an absolute bar to the advancement of white [or male] employees," and "is a temporary measure . . . not intended to maintain racial [or sexual] balance, but simply to eliminate a manifest racial [or sexual] imbalance." *Id.,* at 208. In effect, *Weber* held that the legality of intentional discrimination by private employers against certain disfavored groups or individuals is to be judged not by Title VII but by a judicially crafted code of conduct, the contours of which are determined by no discernible standard, aside from (as the dissent convincingly demonstrated) the divination of congressional "purposes" belied by the face of the statute and by its legislative history. We have been recasting that self-promulgated code of conduct ever since—and what it has led us to today adds to the reasons for abandoning it.

The majority's response to this criticism of *Weber* asserts that, since "Congress has not amended the statute to reject our construction, . . . we . . . may assume that our interpretation was correct." This assumption, which frequently haunts our opinions, should be put to rest. It is based, to begin with, on the patently false premise that the correctness of statutory construction is to be measured by what the current Congress desires, rather than by what the law as enacted meant. To make matters worse, it assays the current Congress' desires *with respect to the particular provision in isolation,* rather than (the way the provision was originally enacted) as part of a total legislative package containing many *quids pro quo.* * * * But even accepting the flawed premise that the intent of the current Congress, with respect to the provision in isolation, is determinative, one must ignore rudimentary principles of political science to draw any conclusions regarding that intent from the *failure* to enact legislation. The "complicated check on legislation," The Federalist No. 62, p. 378 (C. Rossiter ed. 1961), erected by our Constitution creates an inertia that makes it impossible to assert with any degree of assurance that congressional failure to act represents (1) approval of the status quo, as opposed to (2) inability to agree upon how to alter the status quo, (3) unawareness of the status quo, (4) indifference to the status quo, or even

**Food for Thought**

What is the significance, if any, of Congress's response (or lack thereof) to a judicial decision interpreting a statute that a previous Congress enacted? Do you agree with Justice Scalia that congressional silence in response to such a judicial decision should be irrelevant in assessing the meaning of the statute?

(5) political cowardice. * * * I think we should admit that vindication by congressional inaction is a canard.

Justice STEVENS' concurring opinion emphasizes the "undoubted public interest in 'stability and orderly development of the law' " that often requires adherence to an erroneous decision. [But] today's decision is a demonstration not of stability and order but of the instability and unpredictable expansion which the substitution of judicial improvisation for statutory text has produced. For a number of reasons, *stare decisis* ought not to save *Weber.* First, this Court has applied the doctrine of *stare decisis* to civil rights statutes less rigorously than to other laws. See *Maine v. Thiboutot,* 448 U.S. 1, 33 (1980) (POWELL, J., dissenting). Second, as Justice STEVENS acknowledges in his concurrence, *Weber* was itself a dramatic departure from the Court's prior Title VII precedents * * *. Third, *Weber* was decided a mere seven years ago, and has provided little guidance to persons seeking to conform their conduct to the law, beyond the proposition that Title VII does not mean what it says. Finally, "even under the most stringent test for the propriety of overruling a statutory decision . . .—'that it appear beyond doubt . . . that [the decision] misapprehended the meaning of the controlling provision,' " *Monell v. New York City Dept. of Social Services,* 436 U.S. 658, 700 (1978) (quoting *Monroe v. Pape,* 365 U.S. 167, 192 (1961) (HARLAN, J., concurring)), *Weber* should be overruled.

In addition to complying with the commands of the statute, abandoning *Weber* would have the desirable side effect of eliminating the requirement of willing suspension of disbelief that is currently a credential for reading our opinions in the affirmative-action field—from *Weber* itself, which demanded belief that the corporate employer adopted the affirmative-action program "voluntarily," rather than under practical compulsion from government contracting agencies, see 443 U.S., at 204; to *Bakke,* a Title VI case cited as authority by the majority here, which demanded belief that the University of California took race into account as merely one of the many diversities to which it felt it was educationally important to expose its medical students, see 438 U.S., at 311–315, to today's opinion, which—in the face of a plan obviously designed to force promoting officials to prefer candidates from the favored racial and sexual classes * * *—[demands] belief that we are dealing here with no more than a program that "merely authorizes that consideration be given to affirmative action concerns when evaluating qualified applicants." Any line of decisions rooted so firmly in naiveté must be wrong.

The majority emphasizes, as though it is meaningful, that "*No* persons are automatically excluded from consideration; *all* are able to have their qualifications weighed against those of other applicants." * * * Johnson was indeed entitled to have his qualifications weighed against those of other applicants—but more to the point, he was virtually assured that, after the weighing, if there was any minimally qualified applicant from one of the favored groups, he would be rejected.

Today's decision does more, however, than merely reaffirm *Weber*, and more than merely extend it to public actors. It is impossible not to be aware that the practical effect of our holding is to accomplish *de facto* what the law—in language even plainer than that ignored in *Weber*, see 42 U.S.C. § 2000e–2(j)—forbids anyone from accomplishing *de jure*: in many contexts it effectively *requires* employers, public as well as private, to engage in intentional discrimination on the basis of race or sex.

**Definition**

*De jure* is Latin for "of law," and it refers to some fact that exists because of the operation of the law. *De facto* is Latin for "of fact," and it refers to something that exists as a matter of fact (but not because of a legal requirement).

This Court's prior interpretations of Title VII, especially the decision in *Griggs v. Duke Power Co.*, 401 U.S. 424 (1971), subject employers to a potential Title VII suit whenever there is a noticeable imbalance in the representation of minorities or women in the employer's work force. Even the employer who is confident of ultimately prevailing in such a suit must contemplate the expense and adverse publicity of a trial, because the extent of the imbalance, and the "job relatedness" of his selection criteria, are questions of fact to be explored through rebuttal and counterrebuttal of a "prima facie case" consisting of no more than the showing that the employer's selection process "selects those from the protected class at a 'significantly' lesser rate than their counterparts." B. Schlei & P. Grossman, Employment Discrimination Law 91 (2d ed. 1983). If, however, employers are free to discriminate through affirmative action, without fear of "reverse discrimination" suits by their nonminority or male victims, they are offered a threshold defense against Title VII liability premised on numerical disparities. Thus, after today's decision the *failure* to engage in reverse discrimination is economic folly, and arguably a breach of duty to shareholders or taxpayers, wherever the cost of anticipated Title VII litigation exceeds the cost of hiring less capable (though still minimally capable) workers. (This situation is more likely to obtain, of course, with respect to the least skilled jobs—perversely creating an incentive to discriminate against precisely those members of the nonfavored groups *least* likely to have profited from societal discrimination in the past.) It is predictable, moreover, that this incentive will be greatly magnified by economic pressures brought to bear by government contracting agencies upon employers who refuse to discriminate in the fashion we have now approved. A statute designed to establish a color-blind and gender-blind workplace has thus been converted into a powerful engine of racism and sexism, not merely *permitting* intentional race- and sex-based discrimination, but often making it, through operation of the legal system, practically compelled.

It is unlikely that today's result will be displeasing to politically elected officials, to whom it provides the means of quickly accommodating the demands of organized groups to achieve concrete, numerical improvement in the economic status of particular constituencies. Nor will it displease the world of corporate and governmental employers (many of whom have filed briefs as *amici* in the present case, all on the side of Santa Clara) for whom the cost of hiring less qualified workers is often substantially less—and infinitely more predictable—than the cost of litigating Title VII cases and of seeking to convince federal agencies by nonnumerical means that no discrimination exists. In fact, the only losers in the process are the Johnsons of the country, for whom Title VII has been not merely repealed but actually inverted. The irony is that these individuals—predominantly unknown, unaffluent, unorganized—suffer this injustice at the hands of a Court fond of thinking itself the champion of the politically impotent. I dissent.

---

## Points for Discussion

***a. Title VII and Affirmative Action***

At least two of Title VII's provisions are relevant to determining whether voluntary affirmative action policies are lawful. First, section 703(a) prohibits employment practices that "discriminate" on the basis of race or sex. Does a policy that gives a preference based on race or sex as a means to remedy past societal discrimination "discriminate" within the meaning of section 703(a)? In your view, what is the most sensible interpretation of the word "discriminate"?

Second, section 703(j) provides that "nothing contained in this title shall be interpreted to require any employer * * * to grant preferential treatment to any individual or to any group because of the race, color, religion, sex, or national origin of such individual or group on account of an imbalance" in the make-up of the workforce. Do you agree with Justice Brennan that, because the provision does not say "require *or permit*," it does not prohibit voluntary affirmative action plans? Does the legislative history recounted by Justices Brennan and Rehnquist convince you one way or the other?

***b. The Legislative Process***

Both Justice Brennan and Justice Rehnquist sought to determine the nature of the legislative bargain extracted by those whose votes were needed for the passage of the Civil Rights Act, a compromise necessitated by the multiple opportunities for obstruction in our legislative process. Is the text of the statute a good indicator of the nature of that bargain, as Justice Scalia contended? Does the legislative history shed light on the question? If so, what should an interpreting judge do about the fact that there are hundreds of members of Congress, and that they likely held widely divergent views about how the law ought to apply? We will take up those questions in the Chapters that follow.

**Test Your Knowledge**

To assess your understanding of the material in this Chapter, click here to take a quiz.

# Chapter Two

# *Statutory Interpretation: The Letter and the Spirit*

## Introduction

Chapter 1 considered why, when, and how we might choose legislative action to regulate private conduct. Let's assume that the legislature has done so, enacting a statute that provides, "The use of a mechanical device to produce rain shall be permitted only by first obtaining a license from the Rainmaking Bureau, but under no circumstances may such a device be used to produce a quantity of rain that constitutes a nuisance to businesses or residents in the area affected." It is not difficult to imagine conflicts that might arise about the meaning of the statute. For example, what counts as a "mechanical device"? What quantity of rain "constitutes a nuisance"? Is the term "nuisance" defined according to its meaning in the common law of torts, or does it have a distinctive statutory meaning? To apply the statute, these questions (and presumably many others) require authoritative answers. In other words, to apply the statute, we will need to *interpret* it.

As we saw in Chapter 1, it is not immediately clear who should have responsibility for announcing the authoritative meaning of the statute. For example, perhaps the Rainmaking Bureau, with its expertise in the subject, should have power to define the contested terms in the statute. Or perhaps a court should have the last word on the meaning of the statute. In Chapter 8, we will squarely address this institutional question. For present purposes, however, we can assume that a court will answer questions about statutory meaning, and we can return to the complicating presence of an administrative agency later in the course.

How should a court go about answering questions of statutory meaning? Statutory interpretation is, at its core, about understanding a directive expressed in writing. You almost certainly have experience in that task, even if you haven't ever stopped to think systematically about the techniques that you use to understand such directives. For example, if your roommate leaves you a note asking you pick up some "healthy food" when you go to the grocery store, you have to interpret the directive (even if you don't do so consciously) to decide what counts as "healthy." (Does yogurt with added fruit and sugars count? What about pasta?)

Before we proceed to examples of courts engaging in statutory interpretation, therefore, it might help to identify the basic tools of interpretation with which we are all familiar from daily experience.

---

## *The Food Stays in the Kitchen: Everything I Needed to Know About Statutory Interpretation I Learned by the Time I Was Nine*

**Hillel Y. Levin**

12 Green Bag 2d 337 (2009)*

On March 23, 1986, the following proclamation, henceforth known as Ordinance 7.3, was made by the Supreme Lawmaker, Mother:

> I am tired of finding popcorn kernels, pretzel crumbs, and pieces of cereal all over the family room. From now on, no food may be eaten outside the kitchen.

Thereupon, litigation arose.

FATHER, C.J., issued the following ruling on March 30, 1986:

Defendant Anne, age 14, was seen carrying a glass of water into the family room. She was charged with violating Ordinance 7.3 ("the Rule"). We hold that drinking water outside of the kitchen does not violate the Rule.

The Rule prohibits "food" from being eaten outside of the kitchen. This prohibition does not extend to water, which is a beverage rather than food. Our interpretation is confirmed by Webster's Dictionary, which defines food to mean, in relevant part, a "material consisting essentially of protein, carbohydrate, and fat used in the body of an organism to sustain growth, repair, and vital processes and to furnish energy" and "nutriment in solid form." Plainly, water, which contains no protein, carbohydrate, or fat, and which is not in solid form, is not a food.

Customary usage further substantiates our distinction between "food" and water. Ordinance 6.2, authored by the very same Supreme Lawmaker, declares: "[a]fter you get home from school, have some food and something to drink, and then do your homework." This demonstrates that the Supreme Lawmaker speaks of food and drink separately and is fully capable of identifying one or both as appropriate. After all, if "food," as used in the Family Code, included beverages, then the word

---

* Reprinted with the generous permission of the author.

"drink" in Ordinance 6.2 would be redundant and mere surplusage. Thus, had the Supreme Lawmaker wished to prohibit beverages from being taken out of the kitchen, she could easily have done so by declaring that "no food or drink is permitted outside the kitchen."

Our understanding of the word "food" to exclude water is further buttressed by the evident purpose of the Rule. The Supreme Lawmaker enacted the Rule as a response to the mess produced by solid foods. Water, even when spilled, does not produce a similar kind of mess. Some may argue that the cup from which the Defendant was drinking water may, if left in the family room, itself be a mess. But we are not persuaded. The language of the Rule speaks to the Supreme Lawmaker's concern with small particles of food rather than to a more generalized concern with the containers in which food is held. A cup or other container bears a greater resemblance to other bric-a-brac, such as toys and backpacks, to which the Rule does not speak, than it does to the food spoken of in the Rule. * * *

BABYSITTER SUE, J., issued the following ruling on April 12, 1986:

Defendant Beatrice, age 12, is charged with violating Ordinance 7.3 by drinking a beverage, to wit: orange juice, in the family room. The Defendant relies on our ruling of March 30, 1986, which "h[e]ld that drinking water outside of the kitchen does not violate the [Ordinance]," and urges us to conclude that all beverages are permitted in the family room under Ordinance 7.3. While we believe this is a difficult case, we agree. As we have previously explained, the term "food" does not extend to beverages.

Our hesitation stems not from the literal meaning of the Ordinance, which strongly supports the Defendant's claim, but rather from an understanding of its purpose. As we have previously stated, and as evidenced by the language of the Ordinance itself, the Ordinance was enacted as a result of the Supreme Lawmaker's concern with mess. Unlike the case with water, if the Defendant were to spill orange juice on the couch or rug in the family room, the mess would be problematic—perhaps even more so than the mess produced by crumbs of food. It is thus difficult to infer why the Supreme Lawmaker would choose to prohibit solid foods outside of the kitchen but to permit orange juice.

Nevertheless, we are bound the plain language of the Ordinance and by precedent. We are confident that if the Supreme Lawmaker disagrees with the outcome in this case, she can change or clarify the law accordingly.

GRANDMA, SENIOR J., issued the following ruling on May 3, 1986:

Defendant Charlie, age 10, is charged with violating Ordinance 7.3 by eating popcorn in the family room. The Defendant contends, and we agree, that the Ordinance does not apply in this case.

Ordinance 7.3 was enacted to prevent messes outside of the kitchen. This purpose is demonstrated by the language of the Ordinance itself, which refers to food being left "all over the family room" as the immediate cause of its adoption. Such messes are produced only when one transfers food from a container to his or her mouth outside of the kitchen. During that process—what the Ordinance refers to as "eat[ing]"—crumbs and other food particles often fall out of the eater's hand and onto the floor or sofa. As the record shows, the Defendant placed all of the popcorn into his mouth prior to leaving the kitchen. He merely masticated and swallowed while in the family room. At no time was there any danger that a mess would be produced.

We are certain that there was no intent to prohibit merely the chewing or swallowing of food outside of the kitchen. After all, the Supreme Lawmaker has expressly permitted the chewing of gum in the family room. It would be senseless and absurd to treat gum differently from popcorn that has been ingested prior to leaving the kitchen.

If textual support is necessary to support this obvious and commonsensical interpretation, abundant support is available. First, the Ordinance prohibits food from being "eaten" outside of the kitchen. The term "eat" is defined to mean "to take in through the mouth as food: ingest, chew, and swallow in turn." The Defendant, having only chewed and swallowed, did not "eat." Further, the Ordinance prohibits the "eat[ing]" rather than the "bringing" of food outside of the kitchen; and indeed, food is often brought out of the kitchen and through the family room, as when school lunches are delivered to the front door for carpool pickup. There is no reason to treat food enclosed in a brown bag any differently from food enclosed within the Defendant's mouth. * * *

UNCLE RICK, J., issued the following ruling on May 20, 1986:

Defendant Charlie, age 10, is charged with violating Ordinance 7.3 ("the Rule") by bringing a double thick mint chocolate chip milkshake into the family room. Were I writing on a clean slate, I would surely conclude that the Defendant has violated the Rule. A double thick milkshake is "food" because it contains protein, carbohydrate, and/or fat. Further, the purpose of the Rule—to prevent messes—would be undermined by permitting a double thick milkshake to be brought into the family room. Indeed, it makes little sense to treat a milkshake differently from a pretzel or a scoop of ice cream.

However, I am not writing on a clean slate. Our precedents have now established that all beverages are permitted outside of the kitchen under the Rule. The Defendant relied on those precedents in good faith. Further, the Supreme Lawmaker has had ample opportunity to clarify or change the law to prohibit any or all beverages from being brought out of the kitchen, and she has elected not to exercise that authority. I can only conclude that she is satisfied with the status quo.

GRANDMA, SENIOR J., issued the following ruling on July 2, 1986:

Defendant Anne, age 14, is charged with violating Ordinance 7.3 by eating apple slices in the family room. As we have repeatedly held, the Ordinance pertains only to messy foods. Moreover, the Ordinance explicitly refers to "popcorn kernels, pretzel crumbs, and pieces of cereal." Sliced apples, not being messy (and certainly being no worse than orange juice and milkshakes, which have been permitted by our prior decisions), and being wholly dissimilar from the crumbly foods listed in the Ordinance, do not come within the meaning of the Ordinance.

We also find it significant that the consumption of healthy foods such as sliced apples is a behavior that this jurisdiction supports and encourages. It would be odd to read the Ordinance in a way that would discourage such healthy behaviors by limiting them to the kitchen.

AUNT SARAH, J., issued the following ruling on August 12, 1986:

Defendant Beatrice, age 13, is charged with violating Ordinance 7.3 by eating pretzels, popcorn, cereal, and birthday cake in the family room. Under ordinary circumstances, the Defendant would clearly be subject to the Ordinance. However, the circumstances giving rise to the Defendant's action in this case are far from ordinary.

The Defendant celebrated her thirteenth birthday on August 10, 1986. For the celebration, she invited four of her closest friends to sleep over. During the evening, and as part of the festivities, the celebrants watched a movie in the family room. Chief Justice Father provided those present with drinks and snacks, including the aforesaid pretzels, popcorn, and cereal, for consumption during the movie-watching. Father admonished the Defendant to clean up after the movie, and there is no evidence in the record suggesting that the Defendant failed to do so.

We frankly concede that the Defendant's action were violative of the plain meaning of the Ordinance. However, given the special and unique nature of the occasion, the fact that Father, a representative of the Supreme Lawmaker—as well as of this Court—implicitly approved of the Defendant's actions, and the apparent efforts of the Defendant in upholding the spirit of the Ordinance by cleaning up after her friends, we believe that the best course of action is to release the Defendant.

In light of the growing confusion in the interpretation of this ambiguous Ordinance, we urge the Supreme Lawmaker to exercise her authority to clarify and/or change the law if and as she deems it appropriate.

FATHER, C.J., issued the following ruling on September 17, 1986:

Defendant Derek, age 9, was charged with violating Ordinance 7.3 ("the Rule") by eating pretzels, potato chips, popcorn, a bagel with cream cheese, cottage cheese, and a chocolate bar in the family room.

The Defendant argues that our precedents have clearly established a pattern permitting food to be eaten in the family room so long as the eater cleans up any mess. He further maintains that it would be unjust for this Court to punish him after having permitted past actions such as drinking water, orange juice, and a milkshake, as well as swallowing popcorn, eating apple slices, and eating pretzels, popcorn, and cereal on a special occasion. The Defendant avers that there is no rational distinction between his sister's eating foods in the family room during a movie on a special occasion and his eating foods in the family room during a weekly television show.

We agree. The citizens of this jurisdiction look to the rulings of this Court, as well as to general practice, to understand their rights and obligations as citizens. In the many months since the Rule was originally announced, the cumulative rulings of this Court on the subject would signify to any citizen that, whatever the technical language of the Rule, the real Rule is that they must clean up after eating any food outside of the kitchen. To draw and enforce any other line now would be arbitrary and, as such, unjust.

* * * *

On November 4, 1986, the following proclamation, henceforth known as The New Ordinance 7.3, was made by the Supreme Lawmaker, Mother:

> Over the past few months, I have found empty cups, orange juice stains, milkshake spills, slimy spots of unknown origin, all manner of crumbs, melted chocolate, and icing from cake in the family room. I thought I was clear the first time! And you've all had a chance to show me that you could use your common sense and clean up after yourselves. So now let me be clearer: No food, gum, or drink of any kind, on any occasion or in any form, is permitted in the family room. Ever, Seriously. I mean it.

---

## Points for Discussion

### *a. The Object of Interpretation*

The "judicial opinions" in Professor Levin's light-hearted piece are of course tongue in cheek, but they reveal how our ordinary, every-day interactions often require us to engage in the process of interpretation. Do the "judges" who wrote the various opinions all follow the same approach to interpreting the directive at issue? If not, in what ways are they different?

More specifically, what is the "object" of interpretation in each of the opinions? Do the judges seek the ordinary meaning of the words of the proclamation? Some more technical meaning, or instead a colloquial meaning? Or do they seek to implement the lawgiver's intent? Or to resolve the disputed issues in light of her broader set of purposes? What else do the opinions rely on in "interpreting" the proclamation?

Do you find one or some of these inquiries more convincing or legitimate than others? If so, why?

#### *b. Interpretation and Context*

As we will see shortly, when judges interpret statutes, they use many of the techniques of interpretation that we use in our daily lives when we try to decipher instructions or directives from others. This makes sense because, as noted above, interpretation is first and foremost a process of making sense of written directives. But there are also important differences between our interpretation of our mother's household rules (or our roommate's grocery list), on the one hand, and judicial interpretation of statutes enacted by a legislature, on the other.

Legislative enactments (at least in theory) reflect the will of the people, and thus come with democratic legitimacy. The same is not true of our roommate's grocery list. In addition, failure to comply with a statute could lead to damages or, worse, jail. It's fair to say that the stakes are usually considerably lower when we try to make sense of our parents' household rules. Should these differences in context affect the way that we think about interpretation? For example, should judicial interpretation of duly enacted statutes be more constrained than the type of interpretation in which we engage in our daily lives? Do judges have a duty of fidelity to legislative will that simply isn't present when we go shopping for our roommate? If so, what does that tell us, if anything, about what a judge's object should be when she interprets a statute?

---

## A. The Touchstones of Interpretation

For an introduction to how courts approach the task of statutory interpretation, consider the case that follows. The case involved this statute:

The Alien Contract Labor Act of 1885, 23 Stat. 332

> Chap. 164—An act to prohibit the importation and migration of foreigners and aliens under contract or agreement to perform labor in the United States, its Territories, and the District of Columbia.
>
> [Section 1.] *Be it enacted by the Senate and House of Representatives of the United States of America in Congress assembled*, That from and after the passage of this act it shall be unlawful for any person, company, partnership, or corporation, in any manner whatsoever, to prepay the transportation, or in any way assist or encourage the importation or migration of any alien or aliens, any foreigner or foreigners, into the United States, its Territories, or the District of Columbia, under contract or agreement, parol or special, express or implied, made previous to the importation or migration of such alien or aliens, foreigner or foreigners,

to perform labor or service of any kind in the United States, its Territories, or the District of Columbia.

Section 2. That all contracts or agreements, express or implied, parol or special, which may hereafter be made by and between any person, company, partnership, or corporation, and any foreigner or foreigners, alien or aliens, to perform labor or service or having reference to the performance of labor or service by any person in the United States, its Territories, or the District of Columbia previous to the migration or importation of the person or persons whose labor or service is contracted for into the United States, shall be utterly void and of no effect.

Section 3. That for every violation of any of the provisions of section one of this act the person, partnership, company or corporation violating the same * * * shall forfeit and pay for every such offence the sum of one thousand dollars, which may be sued for and recovered by the United States * * *.

Section 4. That the master of any vessel who shall knowingly bring within the United States any such vessel, and land, or permit to be landed, from any foreign port of place, any alien laborer, mechanic, or artisan who, previous to embarkation on such vessel, had entered into contract or agreement * * * to perform labor or service in the United States, shall be deemed guilty of a misdemeanor * * *.

Section 5. That nothing in this act shall be so construed * * * as to prevent any person, persons, partnership, or corporation from engaging, under contract or agreement, skilled workman [sic] in foreign countries to perform labor in the United States in or upon any new industry not at present established in the United States; *Provided*, That skilled labor for that purpose cannot be otherwise obtained; nor shall the provisions of this act apply to professional actors, artists, lecturers, or singers, nor to persons employed strictly as personal or domestic servants * * *.

---

## *Church of the Holy Trinity v. United States*

143 U.S. 457 (1892)

MR. JUSTICE BREWER delivered the opinion of the court.

Plaintiff in error is a corporation duly organized and incorporated as a religious society under the laws of the state of New York. E. Walpole Warren was, prior to September, 1887, an alien residing in England. In that month the plaintiff in error made a contract with him, by which he was to remove to the city of New York, and enter into its service as rector and pastor; and, in pursuance of such contract, Warren

**Take Note**

Stop for a moment and consider how the statute applies to the facts of this case. On which provisions of the statute do you think the government relied?

did so remove and enter upon such service. It is claimed by the United States that this contract on the part of the plaintiff in error was forbidden by chapter 164, 23 St. 332; and an action was commenced to recover the penalty prescribed by that act. The circuit court held that the contract was within the prohibition of the statute, and rendered judgment accordingly, and the single question presented for our determination is whether it erred in that conclusion.

It must be conceded that the act of the corporation is within the letter of [section 1], for the relation of rector to his church is one of service, and implies labor on the one side with compensation on the other. Not only are the general words "labor" and "service" both used, but also, as it were to guard against any narrow interpretation and emphasize a breadth of meaning, to them is added "of any kind;" and, further, * * * the fifth section, which makes specific exceptions, among them professional actors, artists, lecturers, singers, and domestic servants, strengthens the idea that every other kind of labor and service was intended to be reached by the first section. While there is great force to this reasoning, we cannot think congress intended to denounce with penalties a transaction like that in the present case. It is a familiar rule that a thing may be within the letter of the statute and yet not within the statute, because not within its spirit nor within the intention of its makers. This has been often asserted, and the Reports are full of cases illustrating its application.

**Take Note**

This statement—that it "is a familiar rule that a thing may be within the letter of the statute and yet not within the statute, because not within its spirit nor within the intention of its makers"—is one of the most famous, and controversial, assertions about statutory interpretation in Supreme Court history. What did the Court mean by it? Does it strike you as a common-sense statement about interpretation, or as a declaration of an intention to ignore Congress?

This is not the substitution of the will of the judge for that of the legislator; for frequently words of general meaning are used in a statute, words broad enough to include an act in question, and yet a consideration of the whole legislation, or of the circumstances surrounding its enactment, or of the absurd results which follow from giving such broad meaning to the words, makes it unreasonable to believe that the legislator intended to include the particular act. As said in *Stradling v. Morgan*, Plow. 205: "[It] appears that the sages of the law heretofore have construed statutes quite contrary to the letter in some appearance, and those statutes which comprehend all things in the letter they have expounded to extend to but some things, and those which generally prohibit all people from doing such an act they have interpreted to permit some people to do it, and those which include every person in the letter they have adjudged to reach to some persons only, which expositions have always been founded upon the intent of the legislature, which they have collected sometimes by considering the cause and necessity of making the act, sometimes by comparing one part of the act with another, and sometimes by foreign circumstances."

Among other things which may be considered in determining the intent of the legislature is the title of the act. We do not mean that it may be used to add to or take from the body of the statute, *Hadden v. Collector*, 72 U.S. 107 (1866), but it may help to interpret its meaning. * * * It will be seen that words as general as those used in the first section of this act were by that decision limited, and the intent of congress with respect to the act was gathered partially, at least, from its title. Now, the title of this act is, "An act to prohibit the importation and migration of foreigners and aliens under contract or agreement to perform labor in the United States, its territories, and the District of Columbia." Obviously the thought expressed in this reaches only to the work of the manual laborer, as distinguished from that of the professional man. No one reading such a title would suppose that congress had in its mind any purpose of staying the coming into this country of ministers of the gospel, or, indeed, of any class whose toil is that of the brain. The common understanding of the terms "labor" and "laborers" does not include preaching and preachers, and it is to be assumed that words and phrases are used in their ordinary meaning. So whatever of light is thrown upon the statute by the language of the title indicates an exclusion from its penal provisions of all contracts for the employment of ministers, rectors, and pastors.

Again, another guide to the meaning of a statute is found in the evil which it is designed to remedy; and for this the court properly looks at contemporaneous events, the situation as it existed, and as it was pressed upon the attention of the legislative body. The situation which called for this statute was briefly but fully stated by Mr. Justice BROWN when, as district judge, he decided the case of *U.S. v. Craig*, 28 Fed. Rep. 795, 798 (E.D. Mich. 1886): "The motives and history of the act are matters of common knowledge. It had become the practice for large capitalists in this country to contract with their agents abroad for the shipment of great numbers of an ignorant and servile class of foreign laborers, under contracts by which the employer agreed, upon the one hand, to

**Food for Thought**

The Court here seeks to determine the statute's application to Pastor Walpole by considering the "evil" that the statute "was designed to remedy." On this approach, it might not matter that members of Congress never paused to consider how the statute would apply to members of the clergy; instead, the Court can seek to determine whether application of the statute in such circumstances would be consistent with Congress's broader objectives. How does the Court know what evil Congress was seeking to address?

prepay their passage, while, upon the other hand, the laborers agreed to work after their arrival for a certain time at a low rate of wages. The effect of this was to break down the labor market, and to reduce other laborers engaged in like occupations to the level of the assisted immigrant. The evil finally became so flagrant that an appeal was made to congress for relief by the passage of the act in question, the design of which was to raise the standard of foreign immigrants, and to discountenance the migration of those who had not sufficient means in their own hands, or those of their friends, to pay their passage."

It appears, also, from the petitions, and in the testimony presented before the committees of congress, that it was this cheap, unskilled labor which was making the trouble, and the influx of which congress sought to prevent. It was never suggested that we had in this country a surplus of brain toilers, and, least of all, that the market for the services of Christian ministers was depressed by foreign competition. Those were matters to which the attention of congress, or of the people, was not directed. So far, then, as the evil which was sought to be remedied interprets the statute, it also guides to an exclusion of this contract from the penalties of the act.

A singular circumstance, throwing light upon the intent of congress, is found in this extract from the report of the senate committee on education and labor, recommending the passage of the bill: "The general facts and considerations which induce the committee to recommend the passage of this bill are set forth in the report of the committee of the house. The committee report the bill back without amendment, although there are certain features thereof which might well be changed or modified, in the hope that the bill may not fail of passage during the present session. Especially would the committee have otherwise recommended amendments, substituting for the expression, 'labor and service,' whenever it occurs in the body of the bill, the words 'manual labor' or 'manual service,' as sufficiently broad to accomplish the purposes of the bill, and that such amendments would remove objections which a sharp and perhaps unfriendly criticism may urge to the proposed legislation. The committee, however, believing that the bill in its present form will be construed as including only those whose labor or service is manual in character, and being very desirous that the bill become a law before the adjournment, have reported the bill without change." Page 6059, Congressional Record, 48th Cong. And, referring back to the report of the committee of the house, there appears this language: "It seeks to restrain and prohibit the immigration or importation of laborers who would have never seen our shores but for the inducements and allurements of men whose only object is to obtain labor at the lowest possible rate, regardless of the social and material well-being of our own citizens, and regardless of the evil consequences which result to American laborers from

**Take Note**

This was the first time in its history that the Supreme Court relied on legislative history to interpret a statute in a way ostensibly in conflict with the plain meaning of the statute's text.

such immigration. This class of immigrants care nothing about our institutions, and in many instances never even heard of them. They are men whose passage is paid by the importers. They come here under contract to labor for a certain number of years. They are ignorant of our social condition, and, that they may remain so, they are isolated and prevented from coming into contact with Americans. They are generally from the lowest social stratum, and live upon the coarsest food, and in hovels of a character before unknown to American workmen. They, as a rule, do not become citizens, and are certainly not a desirable acquisition to the body politic. The inevitable tendency of their presence among us is to degrade American labor, and to reduce it to the level of the imported pauper labor." Page 5359, Congressional Record, 48th Cong.

We find, therefore, that the title of the act, the evil which was intended to be remedied, the circumstances surrounding the appeal to congress, the reports of the committee of each house, all concur in affirming that the intent of congress was simply to stay the influx of this cheap, unskilled labor.

But, beyond all these matters, no purpose of action against religion can be imputed to any legislation, state or national, because this is a religious people. * * * From the discovery of this continent to the present hour, there is a single voice making this affirmation. The commission to Christopher Columbus, prior to his sail westward, is from "Ferdinand and Isabella, by the grace of God, king and queen of Castile," etc., and recites that "it is hoped that by God's assistance some of the continents and islands in the ocean will be discovered," etc. * * * The first charter of Virginia, granted by King James I in 1606 [stated]: "We, greatly commending, and graciously accepting of, their Desires for the Furtherance of so noble a Work, which may, by the Providence of Almighty God, hereafter tend to the Glory of his Divine Majesty, in propagating of Christian Religion to such People, as yet live in Darkness and miserable Ignorance of the true Knowledge and Worship of God, and may in time bring the Infidels and Savages, living in those parts, to human Civility, and to a settled and quiet Government; DO, by these our Letters-Patents, graciously accept of, and agree to, their humble and well-intended Desires."* * * Coming nearer to the present time, the declaration of independence recognizes the presence of the Divine in human affairs in these words: "We hold these truths to be self-evident, that all men are created equal, that they are endowed by their Creator with certain unalienable Rights, that among these are Life, Liberty, and the pursuit of Happiness." * * *

* * * Every constitution of every one of the 44 states contains language which, either directly or by clear implication, recognizes a profound reverence for religion, and an assumption that its influence in all human affairs is essential to the well-being of the community. [The Illinois Constitution begins:] "We, the people of the state of Illinois, grateful to Almighty God for the civil, political, and religious liberty which He hath so long permitted us to enjoy, and looking to Him for a blessing upon our endeavors to secure and transmit the same unimpaired to succeeding generations," etc. Even the constitution of the United States, which is supposed to have little touch

upon the private life of the individual, contains in the first amendment a declaration common to the constitutions of all the states, as follows: "Congress shall make no law respecting an establishment of religion, or prohibiting the free exercise thereof," etc.,—and also provides in article 1, § 7, (a provision common to many constitutions,) that the executive shall have 10 days (Sundays excepted) within which to determine whether he will approve or veto a bill.

There is no dissonance in these declarations. There is a universal language pervading them all, having one meaning. They affirm and reaffirm that this is a religious nation. These are not individual sayings, declarations of private persons. They are organic utterances. They speak the voice of the entire people. * * *

If we pass beyond these matters to a view of American life, as expressed by its laws, its business, its customs, and its society, we find everywhere a clear recognition of the same truth. Among other matters note the following: The form of oath universally prevailing, concluding with an appeal to the Almighty; the custom of opening sessions of all deliberative bodies and most conventions with prayer; the prefatory words of all wills, "In the name of God, amen;" the laws respecting the observance of the Sabbath, with the general cessation of all secular business, and the closing of courts, legislatures, and other similar public assemblies on that day * * *. These, and many other matters which might be noticed, add a volume of unofficial declarations to the mass of organic utterances that this is a Christian nation. In the face of all these, shall it be believed that a congress of the United States intended to make it a misdemeanor for a church of this country to contract for the services of a Christian minister residing in another nation?

**Food for Thought**

The Establishment Clause of the First Amendment is the textual basis for the familiar concept of the separation of church and state. In light of that concept, are you surprised by the Court's declaration that "this is a religious nation"—and that "this is a Christian nation"? Either way, why does the Court make these assertions? What role do they play in the Court's conclusion?

Suppose, in the congress that passed this act, some member had offered a bill which in terms declared that, if any Roman Catholic church in this country should contract with Cardinal Manning to come to this country, and enter into its service as pastor and priest, or any Episcopal church should enter into a like contract with Canon Farrar, or any Baptist church should make similar arrangements with Rev. Mr. Spurgeon, or any Jewish synagogue with some eminent rabbi, such contract should be adjudged unlawful and void, and the church making it be subject to prosecution and punishment. Can it be believed that it would have received a minute of approving thought or a single vote? Yet it is contended that such was, in effect, the meaning of this statute. The construction invoked cannot be accepted as correct. It is a case where there was presented a definite evil, in view of which the legislature used general terms with the purpose of reaching all phases of that evil; and thereafter, unexpectedly, it is developed that the general language thus employed is broad enough to reach cases and acts which the whole history and life of the country affirm could not have been intentionally legislated against. It is the duty of the courts, under those circumstances, to say that, however broad the language of the statute may be, the act, although within the letter, is not within the intention of the legislature, and therefore cannot be within the statute. [Reversed.]

---

## Points for Discussion

### *a. Statutory Text*

The Court began by "conced[ing]" that the church's contract with Pastor Walpole was "within the letter" of the statute. What was the basis for that concession? Is it clear to you that the ordinary meaning of the phrase "perform labor or service" embraces the work of a pastor ministering to a congregation? What else might those terms mean—and where might we look to determine their meaning?

The Court also noted that section 5 creates an exception for "professional actors, artists, lecturers, * * * singers, [and] persons employed strictly as personal or domestic servants." Does this strengthen the conclusion that contracts to hire members of the clergy fall within the "letter" of section 1 of the statute, or does it undermine it? What about section 4 of the statute, which the Court did not cite?

### *b. The Evil to Be Remedied*

The Court declared that "another guide to the meaning of a statute is found in the evil which it is designed to remedy." On the one hand, this assertion seems utterly conventional. For example, in seeking to determine whether a bicycle counts as a "vehicle" within the meaning of an ordinance prohibiting "vehicles" in the park, most people would find it highly relevant that the town council enacted the law after two highly publicized incidents in which bicycle couriers injured visitors to the park—or after motorcycles disrupted the tranquility of an outdoor yoga class in the park. Consistent with this intuition, the Court in *Church of the Holy Trinity* looked to the impetus for the law in seeking to determine the meaning of the terms in the statute.

On the other hand, just because Congress might have been *inspired to act* because of a specific problem doesn't mean that the *solution* that it crafted addresses only that particular problem. Isn't it possible that Congress decided to paint with a broader brush, and to prohibit a broader class of activities than the ones that first came to its attention? And even if the Court is right that the terms of the statute should be confined by the evil that motivated Congress, how does the Court know which exact problem Congress was trying to remedy? What evidence does the Court cite for its conclusion? Are you confident that the Court accurately described Congress's motivation in enacting the law?

### *c. Intent*

The Court also focused on the "intent of Congress." Usually, when courts refer to legislative "intent," they have in mind the actual, specific intent of the legislature with respect to the particular question at issue. How did the Court in *Church of the Holy Trinity* use the term? One clue is the evidence on which the Court relied to demonstrate Congress's intent: a report of the Senate committee responsible for drafting the bill. Although the report does not speak specifically of the status of contracts with foreign clergy, it did (in the Court's view) provide insight into Congress's specific understanding of the relevant terms in the statute. Is a report of a committee in one house of Congress convincing evidence of Congress's intentions in enacting the law?

Assume for the sake of argument that it is appropriate for courts to seek to determine legislative intent from sources beyond the statutory text, and that a committee report is proper evidence of Congress's intent. Did the committee's report in *Church of the Holy Trinity* strengthen the Court's argument or undermine it? As it turns out, Congress did not actually enact the statute during the legislative session in 1884 (when the committee produced its report), but instead took up the bill the following year. When Congress finally did so in 1885, it made changes to the version of the bill that the committee report addressed, but it did not amend the language about labor and service. Now do you think that the Court properly relied on the committee report as evidence of Congress's intent?

### *d. Background Norms*

The Court also declared that "no purpose of action against religion can be imputed to any legislation, state or national, because this is a religious people." What role did this assertion play in the Court's analysis? Was the Court's point that, because there is a background norm of respect for religion in our society, we should not be quick to presume that Congress sought to regulate the relationship between a church and its pastor? If this was the Court's point, then wouldn't the statute have to be ambiguous for the presumption to apply? After all, if the statute clearly applies to clergy—as the Court seemed to concede, in noting that the pastor's contract fell within the letter of the law—then the presumption would be overcome. Or is the Court's point that Congress lacks power to regulate the relationship between a church and its pastor? If so, then the rest of the Court's discussion would have been entirely beside the point.

Yet surely there are background norms against which we usually understand statutory enactments. (We will consider a particular type of such norms in Chapter 3, when we consider the so-called substantive canons of construction.) For example, federalism norms might lead us to read narrowly statutes that interfere with state sovereignty. But where did the Court find the norm on which it relied in *Church of the Holy Trinity*? In thinking about that question, consider whether the Court's assertion that "this is a Christian nation" seemed uncontroversial to you or instead quite shocking. Are there background norms about which there is broad consensus, and thus that we can assume Congress has in mind when it legislates?

#### e. Congressional Action

After the federal trial court held that the Alien Contract Labor Act applied to the contract with Pastor Warren, but before the Supreme Court's decision, Congress passed a new statute that amended the 1885 Act. The new statute added the following to the list of exceptions in section 5 of the original statute: "ministers of any religious denomination, [and] persons belonging to any recognized profession, [and] professors for colleges and seminaries." 26 Stat. 1084, 1086 (1891). By its terms, however, the amendment did not apply to any proceeding, "civil or criminal, begun under any existing act or any acts hereby amended," but instead provided that such proceedings "shall proceed as if this act had not been passed." Perhaps as a consequence, the Supreme Court did not mention this statute in its opinion. But was the statute relevant to determining Congress's intent with respect to contracts to hire ministers from abroad? If so, which way did it cut?

#### f. Criticism

As we will see shortly, the Court's decision in *Church of the Holy Trinity* is very controversial. Justice Scalia, who often criticized judicial attempts to discern legislative intent (which he described as a "handy cover for judicial intent"), wrote that "*Church of the Holy Trinity* is cited to us whenever counsel wants us to ignore the narrow, deadening text of the statute, and pay attention to the life-giving legislative intent. It is nothing but an invitation to judicial lawmaking." In his view, Pastor Warren's contract "was within the letter of the statute, and was therefore within the statute: end of case." Antonin Scalia, *Common-Law Courts in a Civil-Law System: The Role of United States Federal Courts in Interpreting the Constitution and Laws*, in A Matter of Interpretation 20–21 (Amy Gutmann ed., 1998).

Do you agree that judicial efforts to determine the legislature's "intent" inevitably will lead to judges imposing their personal views about good policy under the guise of interpretation?

---

As you can tell from the Court's opinion in *Church of the Holy Trinity*, there are several possible "touchstones" of interpretation. A "touchstone" is a criterion by which something is judged. In the context of statutory interpretation, the term refers to the court's focus or object in determining statutory meaning. For example, a court might focus on the plain or ordinary meaning of the text of the statute; or the legislature's specific intent with respect to the question presented; or the legislature's more general purpose, which might shed light on the answer even if the members of the legislature never actually thought about the specific question at issue.

The Court in *Church of the Holy Trinity* went beyond the mere text of the statute, considering the implications of other parts of the statute (such as the title), the purpose of the law, and Congress's specific intent. As we will see shortly, the Court's approach has been subject to considerable criticism in recent decades. Indeed, not even the Court in the late-nineteenth and early-twentieth centuries consistently adhered to the *Church of the Holy Trinity* approach. Consider the case that follows.

---

## *Caminetti v. United States*

242 U.S. 470 (1917)

MR. JUSTICE DAY delivered the opinion of the court:

These three cases were argued together, and may be disposed of in a single opinion. In each of the cases there was a conviction and sentence for violation of the so-called White Slave Traffic Act of June 25, 1910 (36 Stat. at L. 825, chap. 395, Comp. Stat. 1913, § 8813),* the judgments were affirmed by the circuit courts of appeals, and writs of certiorari bring the cases here.

In the Caminetti Case, the petitioner was indicted in the United States district court for the northern district of California * * * for alleged violations of the act. The [first count of the indictment] charged him with transporting and causing to be transported, and aiding and assisting in obtaining transportation for a certain woman from Sacramento, California, to Reno, Nevada, in interstate commerce, for the purpose of debauchery, and for an immoral purpose, to wit, that the aforesaid woman should be and become his mistress and concubine. [D]efendant was found

---

* The Act provided, in relevant part:

"Chap. 395—An Act to further regulate interstate commerce and foreign commerce by prohibiting the transportation therein for immoral purposes of women and girls, and for other purposes.

Be it enacted by the Senate and House of Representatives of the United States of America in Congress assembled, * * *

Sec. 2. That any person who shall knowingly transport or cause to be transported, or aid or assist in obtaining transportation for, or in transporting, in interstate or foreign commerce * * * any woman or girl for the purpose of prostitution or debauchery, or for any other immoral purpose, or with the intent and purpose to induce, entice, or compel such woman or girl to become a prostitute or to give herself up to debauchery, or to engage in any other immoral practice * * * shall be punished by a fine not exceeding five thousand dollars, or by imprisonment of not more than five years, or by both such fine and imprisonment, in the discretion of the court. * * *

Sec. 8. That this Act shall be known and referred to as the 'White-slave traffic Act.' "
—*Ed.*

guilty and sentenced to imprisonment for eighteen months and to pay a fine of $1,500. [The facts of the two other cases before the Court were similar.]

It is contended that the act of Congress is intended to reach only "commercialized vice," or the traffic in women for gain, and that the conduct for which the several petitioners were indicted and convicted, however reprehensible in morals, is not within the purview of the statute when properly construed in the light of its history and the purposes intended to be accomplished by its enactment. In none of the cases was it charged or proved that the transportation was for gain or for the purpose of furnishing women for prostitution for hire, and it is insisted that, such being the case, the acts charged and proved, upon which conviction was had, do not come within the statute.

It is elementary that the meaning of a statute must, in the first instance, be sought in the language in which the act is framed, and if that is plain, and if the law is within the constitutional authority of the lawmaking body which passed it, the sole function of the courts is to enforce it according to its terms. Where the language is plain and admits of no more than one meaning, the duty of interpretation does not arise, and the rules which are to aid doubtful meanings need no discussion. There is no ambiguity in the terms of this act. It is specifically made an offense to knowingly transport or cause to be transported, etc., in interstate commerce, any woman or girl for the purpose of prostitution or debauchery, or for "any other immoral purpose," or with the intent and purpose to induce any such woman or girl to become a prostitute or to give herself up to debauchery, or to engage in any other immoral practice.

**Take Note**

How does the Court's description of the judicial role in interpretation here differ from the Court's approach in *Church of the Holy Trinity*? Taking the Court on its own terms, is it clear to you that there is no ambiguity in the language of the statute?

Statutory words are uniformly presumed, unless the contrary appears, to be used in their ordinary and usual sense, and with the meaning commonly attributed to them. To cause a woman or girl to be transported for the purposes of debauchery, and for an immoral purpose, to wit, becoming a concubine or mistress, for which Caminetti [was] convicted * * *, would seem by the very statement of the facts to embrace transportation for purposes denounced by the act, and therefore fairly within its meaning.

While such immoral purpose would be more culpable in morals and attributed to baser motives if accompanied with the expectation of pecuniary gain, such considerations do not prevent the lesser offense against morals of furnishing transportation in order that a woman may be debauched, or become a mistress or a concubine, from being the execution of purposes within the meaning of this law. To say the contrary would shock the common understanding of what constitutes an immoral purpose when those terms are applied, as here, to sexual relations.

But it is contended that though the words are so plain that they cannot be misapprehended when given their usual and ordinary interpretation, and although the sections in which they appear do not in terms limit the offense defined and punished to acts of "commercialized vice," * * * such limited purpose is to be attributed to Congress and engrafted upon the act in view of the language of § 8 and the report which accompanied the law upon its introduction into and subsequent passage by the House of Representatives.

In this connection, it may be observed that while the title of an act cannot overcome the meaning of plain and unambiguous words used in its body, the title of this act embraces the regulation of interstate commerce "by prohibiting the transportation therein for immoral purposes of women and girls, and for other purposes." It is true that § 8 of the act provides that it shall be known and referred to as the "White Slave Traffic Act," and the report accompanying the introduction of the same into the House of Representatives set forth the fact that a material portion of the legislation suggested was to meet conditions which had arisen in the past few years, and that the legislation was needed to put a stop to a villainous interstate and international traffic in women and girls. Still, the name given to an act by way of designation or description, or the report which accompanies it, cannot change the plain import of its words. If the words are plain, they give meaning to the act, and it is neither the duty nor the privilege of the courts to enter speculative fields in search of a different meaning. [Affirmed.]

MR. JUSTICE MCREYNOLDS took no part in the consideration or decision of these cases.

MR. JUSTICE MCKENNA, [joined by CHIEF JUSTICE WHITE and JUSTICE CLARKE,] dissenting:

Undoubtedly, in the investigation of the meaning of a statute we resort first to its words, and, when clear, they are decisive. The principle has attractive and seemingly disposing simplicity, but that it is not easy of application, or, at least, encounters other principles, many cases demonstrate. The words of a statute may be uncertain in their signification or in their application. If the words be ambiguous, the problem they present is to be resolved by their definition; the subject matter and the lexicons become our guides. * * * [And if] the words be clear in meaning, but the objects to which they are addressed be uncertain, the problem then is to determine the uncertainty. And for this a realization of conditions that provoked the statute must inform our judgment. * * *

* * * Our present concern is with the words "any other immoral practice" * * *. "Immoral" is a very comprehensive word. It means a dereliction of morals. In such

sense it covers every form of vice, every form of conduct that is contrary to good order. It will hardly be contended that in this sweeping sense it is used in the statute. But, if not used in such sense, to what is it limited and by what limited? * * * By its context, necessarily, and the purpose of the statute.

For the context I must refer to the statute; of the purpose of the statute Congress itself has given us illumination. It devotes a section to the declaration that the "act shall be known and referred to as the 'White Slave Traffic Act.' " And its prominence gives it prevalence in the construction of the statute. It cannot be pushed aside or subordinated by indefinite words in other sentences, limited even there by the context. It is a peremptory rule of construction that all parts of a statute must be taken into account in ascertaining its meaning, and it cannot be said that § 8 has no object. Even if it gives only a title to the act, it has especial weight. But it gives more than a title; it makes distinctive the purpose of the statute. The designation "white slave traffic" has the sufficiency of an axiom. If apprehended, there is no uncertainty as to the conduct it describes. It is commercialized vice, immoralities having a mercenary purpose, and this is confirmed by other circumstances.

The author of the bill was Mr. Mann, and in reporting it from the House committee on interstate and foreign commerce he declared for the committee that it was not the purpose of the bill to interfere with or usurp in any way the police power of the states * * *. And further explaining the bill, it was said that the sections of the act had been "so drawn that they are limited to the cases in which there is an act of transportation in interstate commerce of women for the purposes of prostitution." And again:

> "The White Slave Trade—A material portion of the legislation suggested and proposed is necessary to meet conditions which have arisen within the past few years. The legislation is needed to put a stop to a villainous interstate and international traffic in women and girls. The legislation is not needed or intended as an aid to the states in the exercise of their police powers in the suppression or regulation of immorality in general. It does not attempt to regulate the practice of voluntary prostitution, but aims solely to prevent panderers and procurers from compelling thousands of women and girls against their will and desire to enter and continue in a life of prostitution." Cong. Rec. vol. 50, pp. 3368, 3370.

In other words, it is vice as a business at which the law is directed, using interstate commerce as a facility to procure or distribute its victims.

* * * The report [excerpted above] was by the committee charged with the duty of investigating the necessity for the act, and to inform the House of the results of that investigation, both of evil and remedy. * * * There is a presumption [that] the measure it recommends has the purpose it declares and will accomplish it as declared.

This being the purpose, the words of the statute should be construed to execute it, and they may be so construed even if their literal meaning be otherwise. In *Church of the Holy Trinity v. United States*, 143 U.S. 457 (1892), [the Court] declared that "it is a familiar rule that a thing may be within the letter of the statute and yet not within the statute, because not within its spirit, nor within the intention of its makers." It is hardly necessary to say that the application of the rule does not depend upon the objects of the legislation, to be applied or not applied as it may exclude or include good things or bad things. Its principle is the simple one that the words of a statute will be extended or restricted to execute its purpose.

The rule that [this case] illustrate[s] is a valuable one and in varying degrees has daily practice. * * * Language, even when most masterfully used, may miss sufficiency and give room for dispute. Is it a wonder, therefore, that when used in the haste of legislation, in view of conditions perhaps only partly seen or not seen at all, the consequences, it may be, beyond present foresight, it often becomes necessary to apply the rule? And it is a rule of prudence and highest sense. It rescues from crudities, excesses, and deficiencies, making legislation adequate to its special purpose, rendering unnecessary repeated qualifications, and leaving the simple and best exposition of a law the mischief it was intended to redress. Nor is this judicial legislation. It is seeking and enforcing the true sense of a law notwithstanding its imperfection or generality of expression.

There is much in the present case to tempt to a violation of the rule. Any measure that protects the purity of women from assault or enticement to degradation finds an instant advocate in our best emotions; but the judicial function cannot yield to emotion—it must, with poise of mind, consider and decide. It should not shut its eyes to the facts of the world and assume not to know what everybody else knows. And everybody knows that there is a difference between the occasional immoralities of men and women and that systematized and mercenary immorality epitomized in the statute's graphic phrase "white slave traffic." And it was such immorality that was in the legislative mind, and not the other. * * *

---

## Points for Discussion

### *a. Touchstone of Interpretation*

How would you describe the Court's approach to statutory interpretation in *Caminetti*? Notice that the Court focused on the "plain" meaning of the words in the statute's text. The Court mentioned the statute's title provision and some legislative history, but it also said that, because the words were plain, the Court should not "enter speculative fields in search of a different meaning." Yet the statutory phrase at issue was "immoral purpose," which seems like a phrase whose meaning varies in the eyes of the beholder. How did the Court know what those words meant in the statute without consulting any other sources? How can a court rely on the touchstone of ordinary textual meaning given such difficulties?

### *b. Results*

Why didn't the Court in *Caminetti* follow an approach similar to the one that the Court used in *Church of the Holy Trinity*? The dissent would have relied on evidence of Congress's intent in enacting the provision in concluding that the term "immoral purpose" had a much more narrow meaning than the one that the Court found. Is it possible that the Court's approach was designed to produce a particular outcome? Consider the substantive outcomes in *Church of the Holy Trinity* and *Caminetti*. In the former, the Court construed the statute narrowly to exempt ministers from a statute that applied to many other employees, and in the latter the Court construed the statute expansively to prohibit a sexual relationship outside of marriage. Do you think that the subject matters regulated, or the outcomes that would have been produced by the competing approaches to interpretation, influenced the Justices in their views of the two statutes? Is it possible for statutory interpretation to be "neutral," in the sense that the judges are not influenced by the policy questions at issue?

---

## B. The Letter and the Spirit

The most famous line in the Court's opinion in *Church of the Holy Trinity* is the Court's invocation of the "familiar rule" that "a thing may be within the letter of the statute and yet not within the statute, because not within its spirit nor within the intention of its makers." The Court thus suggested that the plain language of a statute—the "letter"—might not define the true scope of the statute's reach; instead, some act that falls within the literal reach of the terms in the statute might actually be excluded if there is reason to believe that the legislature thought that it should be excluded, or if the "spirit" of the law so requires.

In many cases, this seems like a common-sense, and perhaps even uncontroversial, idea. Imagine that your roommate leaves you a note asking you to "get some green vegetables" when you go to the grocery store. Kale pretty clearly counts as a green vegetable, but would you buy it if you knew that your roommate despises kale? In that case, you likely would interpret the directive on the grocery list in light of your roommate's ascertainable, specific intent—which is for you to get some green vegetable other than kale, even though the actual directive didn't mention kale one way or the other.

The same is true about the Court's focus on the "spirit" of the law. Recall the ordinance prohibiting vehicles in the park. Imagine that an elderly visitor to the park experiences symptoms of a heart attack and calls her doctor, who dispatches a private ambulance to pick her up and transport her to the hospital. Because the symptoms prevent her from walking, the ambulance enters the park to pick her up. Has the ambulance violated the ordinance? Most people would find it problematic to say that the ambulance has violated the law, even though it plainly is a vehicle and was in the park. This intuition is based on the idea that the ambulance's presence in the park is consistent with the spirit of the law, which presumably is to protect park visitors from the risk of injury.

Yet the Court's approach in *Church of the Holy Trinity* is controversial, in part because it is often difficult to identify the intent of the legislature or the "spirit" of a law. For example, how can we be confident that legislative history properly reflects the will of a majority of legislators? Similarly, how do we know that the spirit of the ban on vehicles in the park is to prevent injury, rather than, say, to ensure quiet and tranquility in the park? As a consequence, judges have long debated whether and when courts should depart from the plain or literal meaning of statutory text. To frame our thinking about that debate, consider the case that follows.

---

## *Riggs v. Palmer*

22 N.E. 188 (N.Y. 1889)

EARL, J.

On the 13th day of August, 1880, Francis B. Palmer made his last will and testament, in which he gave small legacies to his two daughters, Mrs. Riggs and Mrs. Preston, the plaintiffs in this action, and the remainder of his estate to his grandson, the defendant Elmer E. Palmer * * *. At the date of the will, and subsequently to the death of the testator, Elmer lived with him as a member of his family, and at his death was 16 years old. He knew of the provisions made in his favor in the will, and, that he might prevent his grandfather from revoking such provisions, which he had manifested some intention to do, and to obtain the speedy enjoyment and immediate possession of his property, he willfully murdered him by poisoning him. He now claims the property, and the sole question for our determination is, can he have it?

The defendants say that the testator is dead; that his will was made in due form, and has been admitted to probate; and that therefore it must have effect according to the letter of the law. It is quite true that statutes regulating the making, proof, and effect of wills and the devolution of property, if literally construed, and if their force and effect can in no way and under no circumstances be controlled or modified, give this property to the murderer.

[The New York statute of wills provided: "All persons, except idiots, persons of unsound mind and infants, may devise their real estate, by a last will and testament, duly executed according to the provisions of this title." 3 N.Y. Rev. Stat. 2283 (7th ed. 1882). After specifying how wills were to be executed and attested, the law stated: "No will in writing . . . shall be revoked, or altered, otherwise than by some other will in writing, or some other writing of the testator, declaring such revocation or alteration and executed with the same formalities with which the will itself was required by law to be executed; or unless such be burnt, torn, cancelled, obliterated or destroyed, with the intent and for the purpose of revoking the same, by the testator himself, or by another person in his presence, by his direction and consent; and when so done by another person, the direction and consent of the testator, and the fact of such injury or destruction, shall be proved by at least two witnesses." *Id.* At 1186.]

The purpose of those statutes was to enable testators to dispose of their estates to the objects of their bounty at death, and to carry into effect their final wishes legally expressed; and in considering and giving effect to them this purpose must be kept in view. It was the intention of the law-makers that the donees in a will should have the property given to them. But it never could have been their intention that a donee who murdered the testator to make the will operative should have any benefit under it. If such a case had been present to their minds, and it had been supposed necessary to make some provision of law to meet it, it cannot be doubted that they would have provided for it. It is a familiar canon of construction that a thing which is within the intention of the makers of a statute is as much within the statute as if it were within the letter; and a thing which is within the letter of the statute is not within the statute unless it be within the intention of the makers. The writers of laws do not always express their intention perfectly, but either exceed it or fall short of it, so that judges are to collect it from probable or rational conjectures only, and this is called "rational interpretation;" and Rutherford, in his *Institutes*, says: "Where we make use of rational interpretation, sometimes we restrain the meaning of the writer so as to take in less, and sometimes we extend or enlarge his meaning so as to take in more, than his words express."

Such a construction ought to be put upon a statute as will best answer the intention which the makers had in view * * *. In Bac. Abr. "Statutes," 1, 5; Puff. Law Nat. bk. 5, c. 12; Ruth. Inst. 422, 427, and in Smith's Commentaries, 814, many cases are mentioned where it was held that matters embraced in the general words of statutes nevertheless were not within the statutes, because it could not have been the intention of the law-makers that they should be included. They were taken out of the statutes by an equitable construction; and it is said in Bacon:

> "By an equitable construction a case not within the letter of a statute is sometimes [held] to be within the meaning, because it is within the mischief for which a remedy is provided. The reason for such construction is that the law-makers could not set down every case in express terms. In order to form a right judgment whether a case [be] within the equity of a statute, it is a good way to suppose the law-maker present, and that you have asked him this question: Did you intend to comprehend this case? Then you must give yourself such answer as you imagine he, being an upright and reasonable man, would have given. If this be that he did mean to comprehend it, you may safely

> hold the case to be within the equity of the statute; for while you do no more than he would have done, you do not act contrary to the statute, but in conformity thereto."

9 Bac. Abr. 248. In some cases the letter of a legislative act is restrained by an equitable construction; in others, it is enlarged; in others, the construction is contrary to the letter. * * * If the law-makers could, as to this case, be consulted, would they say that they intended by their general language that the property of a testator or of an ancestor should pass to one who had taken his life for the express purpose of getting his property? In 1 Blackstone's Commentaries 91, the learned author, speaking of the construction of statutes, says:

> "If there arise out of them collaterally any absurd consequences manifestly contradictory to common reason, they are with regard to those collateral consequences void. . . . Where some collateral matter arises out of the general words, and happens to be unreasonable, there the judges are in decency to conclude that this consequence was not foreseen by the parliament, and therefore they are at liberty to expound the statute by equity, and only [with respect to this] disregard it;"

and he gives as an illustration, if an act of parliament gives a man power to try all causes that arise within his manor of Dale, yet, if a cause should arise in which he himself is party, the act is construed not to extend to that, because it is unreasonable that any man should determine his own quarrel.

There was a statute in Bologna that whoever drew blood in the streets should be severely punished, and yet it was held not to apply to the case of a barber who opened a vein in the street. It is commanded in the decalogue that no work shall be done upon the Sabbath, and yet giving the command a rational interpretation founded upon its design the Infallible Judge held that it did not prohibit works of necessity, charity, or benevolence on that day.

What could be more unreasonable than to suppose that it was the legislative intention in the general laws passed for the orderly, peaceable, and just devolution of property that they should have operation in favor of one who murdered his ancestor that he might speedily come into the possession of his estate? Such an intention is inconceivable. We need not, therefore, be much troubled by the general language contained in the laws.

**Take Note**

The court declares that it is "inconceivable" that the legislature would have wanted Elmer to inherit the estate under these circumstances. Is the court making an assertion about the actual intentions of the members of the legislature, or is it instead "imagining" what a rational legislature would have concluded? If the latter, how does the court know?

Besides, all laws * * * may be controlled in their operation and effect by general, fundamental maxims of the common law. No one shall be permitted to profit by his own fraud, or to take advantage of his own wrong, or to found any claim upon his own iniquity, or to acquire property by his own crime. These maxims are dictated by public policy, have their foundation in universal law administered in all civilized countries, and have nowhere been superseded by statutes. * * *

Here there was no certainty that this murderer would survive the testator, or that the testator would not change his will, and there was no certainty that he would get this property if nature was allowed to take its course. He therefore murdered the testator expressly to vest himself with an estate. Under such circumstances, what law, human or divine, will allow him to take the estate and enjoy the fruits of his crime? The will spoke and became operative at the death of the testator. He caused that death, and thus by his crime made it speak and have operation. Shall it speak and operate in his favor? If he had met the testator, and taken his property by force, he would have had no title to it. Shall he acquire title by murdering him? If he had gone to the testator's house, and by force compelled him, or by fraud or undue influence had induced him, to will him his property, the law would not allow him to hold it. But can he give effect and operation to a will by murder, and yet take the property? To answer these questions in the affirmative it seems to me would be a reproach to the jurisprudence of our state, and an offense against public policy.

My view of this case does not inflict upon Elmer any greater or other punishment for his crime than the law specifies. It takes from him no property, but simply holds that he shall not acquire property by his crime, and thus be rewarded for its commission.

The judgment of the [trial court] should therefore be reversed, and judgment should be entered as follows: That Elmer E. Palmer and the administrator be enjoined from using any of the personalty or real estate left by the testator for Elmer's benefit; that the devise and bequest in the will to Elmer be declared ineffective to pass the title to him; that by reason of the crime of murder committed upon the grandfather he is deprived of any interest in the estate left by him; [and] that the plaintiffs are the true owners of the real and personal estate left by the testator * * *.

GRAY, J., joined by DANFORTH, J., *dissenting.*

This appeal presents an extraordinary state of facts, and the case, in respect of them, I believe, is without precedent in this state. The respondent, a lad of 16 years of age, being aware of the provisions in his grandfather's will, which constituted him the residuary legatee of the testator's estate, caused his death by poison, in 1882. For this crime he was tried, and was convicted of murder in the second degree, and at the time of the commencement of this action he was serving out his sentence in the state reformatory. This action was brought by two of the children of the testator for the purpose of having those provisions of the will in the respondent's favor canceled and annulled. The appellants' argument for a reversal of the judgment, which dismissed their complaint, is that the respondent unlawfully prevented a revocation of the existing will, or a new will from being made, by his crime; and that he terminated the enjoyment by the testator of his property, and effected his own succession to it, by the same crime. They say that to permit the respondent to take the property willed to him would be to permit him to take advantage of his own wrong.

To sustain their position the appellants' counsel has submitted an able and elaborate brief, and, if I believed that the decision of the question could be effected by considerations of an equitable nature, I should not hesitate to assent to views which commend themselves to the conscience. But the matter does not lie within the domain of conscience. We are bound by the rigid rules of law, which have been established by the legislature, and within the limits of which the determination of this question is confined.

The question we are dealing with is whether a testamentary disposition can be altered, or a will revoked, after the testator's death, through an appeal to the courts, when the legislature has by its enactments prescribed exactly when and how wills may be made, altered, and revoked, and apparently, as it seems to me, when they have been fully complied with, has left no room for the exercise of an equitable jurisdiction by courts over such matters. Modern jurisprudence, in recognizing the right of the individual, under more or less restrictions, to dispose of his property after his death, subjects it to legislative control, both as to extent and as to mode of exercise. * * * To the statutory restraints which are imposed upon the disposition of one's property by will are added strict and systematic statutory rules for the execution, alteration, and revocation of the will, which must be, at least substantially, if not exactly, followed to insure validity and performance.

The reason for the establishment of such rules, we may naturally assume, consists in the purpose to create those safeguards about these grave and important acts which experience has demonstrated to be the wisest and surest. That freedom which is permitted to be exercised in the testamentary disposition of one's estate by the laws of the state is subject to its being exercised in conformity with the regulations of the statutes. The capacity and the power of the individual to dispose of his property after death, and the mode by which that power can be exercised, are matters of which the legislature has assumed the entire control, and has undertaken to regulate with comprehensive particularity.

The appellants' argument is not helped by reference to * * * those laws of other governments, by which the heir, or legatee, is excluded from benefit under the testament if he has been convicted of killing, or attempting to kill, the testator. In the absence of such legislation here, the courts are not empowered to institute such a system of remedial justice. * * * I concede that rules of law which annul testamentary provisions made for the benefit of those who have become unworthy of them may be based on principles of equity and of natural justice. It is quite reasonable to suppose that a testator would revoke or alter his will, where his mind has been so angered and changed as to make him unwilling to have his will executed as it stood. But these principles only suggest sufficient reasons for the enactment of laws to meet such cases.

**Food for Thought**

Judge Gray relies on the language of the statute in asserting that Elmer is entitled to inherit his grandfather's estate. Do you agree that the text of the New York Statute of Wills requires this conclusion? Judge Gray reaches this conclusion by noting that the statute's rules about altering or revoking a will "impl[y]" that a will that hasn't been altered or revoked pursuant to those rules must be followed. Would it be possible to reach a different conclusion about the meaning of the language in the statute?

The statutes of this state have prescribed various ways in which a will may be altered or revoked; but the very provision defining the modes of alteration and revocation implies a prohibition of alteration or revocation in any other way. The words of the section of the statute are: "No will in writing, except in the cases hereinafter mentioned, nor any part thereof, shall be revoked or altered otherwise," etc. Where, therefore, none of the cases mentioned are met by the facts, and the revocation is not in the way described in the section, the will of the testator is unalterable. I think that a valid will must continue as a will always, unless revoked in the manner provided by the statutes. * * * The finding of fact of the referee that presumably the testator would have altered his will had he known of his grantor's murderous intent cannot affect the question. We may concede it to the fullest extent; but still the cardinal objection is undisposed of—that the making and the revocation of a will are purely matters of statutory regulation, by which the court is bound in the determination of questions relating to these acts.

I cannot find any support for the argument that the respondent's succession to the property should be avoided because of his criminal act, when the laws are silent. Public policy does not demand it; for the demands of public policy are satisfied by the proper execution of the laws and the punishment of the crime. There has been no convention between the testator and his legatee nor is there any such contractual element, in such a disposition of property by a testator, as to impose or imply conditions in the legatee. The appellants' argument practically amounts to this: that, as the legatee has been guilty of a crime, by the commission of which he is placed in a position to sooner receive the benefits of the testamentary provision, his rights to the property should be forfeited, and he should be divested of his estate. To allow their argument to prevail, would involve the diversion by the court of the testator's estate into the hands of persons whom, possibly enough, for all we know, the testator might not have chosen or desired as its recipients. Practically the court is asked to make another will for the testator. The laws do not warrant this judicial action, and mere presumption would not be strong enough to sustain it.

But, more than this, to concede the appellants' views would involve the imposition of an additional punishment or penalty upon the respondent. What power or warrant have the courts to add to the respondent's penalties by depriving him of property? The law has punished him for his crime, and we may not say that it was an insufficient punishment. In the trial and punishment of the respondent the law has vindicated itself for the outrage which he committed, and further judicial utterance upon the subject of punishment or deprivation of rights is barred. We may not, in the language of the court in *People v. Thornton*, 25 Hun 456, "enhance the pains, penalties, and forfeitures provided by law for the punishment of crime." The judgment should be affirmed * * *.

---

## Points for Discussion

### *a. Legislative Intent and Rational Interpretation*

The court in *Riggs* stated, as did the Court later in *Church of the Holy Trinity*, that "a thing which is within the letter of the statute is not within the statute unless it be within the intention of the makers." In *Church of the Holy Trinity*, the Court sought to demonstrate that the statute did not prohibit the contract in question in part by relying on the statute's legislative history. In other words, the Court in that case set out to determine Congress's actual understanding of the meaning of the terms in the statute, and thus of the statute's application to a contract with a member of the clergy. The court in *Riggs*, in contrast, did not cite any evidence about what the members of the New York legislature actually thought about whether a person who murdered the testator should be permitted to inherit. Indeed, it is not clear that the possibility ever occurred to the members of the legislature. Instead, the court said that its task was to engage in "rational interpretation," under which the interpreter "suppose[s] the law-maker present, and that you have asked him this question: Did you intend to comprehend this case? Then you must give yourself such answer as you imagine he, being an upright and reasonable man, would have given." How does a court know what a legislator would have thought about an issue about which he apparently never thought?

The process that the court describes is known as "imaginative reconstruction," Roscoe Pound, *Spurious Interpretation*, 7 COLUM. L. REV. 379, 381–82 (1907), because it requires the court to imagine what the legislature would have said had it been presented with the legal question at issue. Is this approach meaningfully different from an approach that focuses on the legislature's broad purpose or the spirit of the law? At bottom, all of these approaches require the court to ascertain the principal objectives of the law, and then to answer the question presented in a manner consistent with those objectives. How does a court know what the principal objective—or purpose or spirit—of a law is?

### *b. Plain Language and the Letter of the Law*

Judge Gray would have relied on the plain language of the New York statute of wills, which did not create any explicit exception from the ordinary enforceability of wills for cases involving the murder of the testator. Judge Gray conceded that his approach would lead to potentially inequitable consequences in this case, but he asserted that he was "bound by the rigid rules of law, which have been established by the legislature." What is the justification for this view of the judicial role? Do democratic norms or the separation of powers help to explain Judge Gray's approach? If the judge's role is faithfully to implement the legislature's directives, is it obvious to you that the court's approach conflicted with that obligation?

### *c. Wills and Intentions*

The dueling opinions focused primarily on the legislature's wishes, and whether it had (or would have) created an exception in cases in which the heir murders the testator in order to inherit. Could the court have avoided the conflict over the *legislature's* intentions by focusing instead on *Francis's* intentions? After all, Judge Earl and Judge Gray agreed that the point of inheritance law is to effectuate the wishes of the testator. Can't we understand the court's decision ultimately to be based on the assumption that, if Francis had known that Elmer would murder him in order to ensure his inheritance, Francis would have changed his will? If so, is there any problem with this assumption? Even if not, how would the court know who Francis would have wanted to inherit instead? Judge Gray noted that the court's resolution of the case involved "the diversion * * * of the testator's estate into the hands of persons whom, possibly enough, for all we know, the testator might not have chosen or desired as its recipients." He thought that, in effect, the court had "ma[d]e another will for the testator." Was Judge Gray's approach likely to be more faithful to Francis's wishes?

---

The dueling approaches in *Riggs* represent the two sides in an age-old debate about the proper inquiry and judicial role in statutory interpretation. In the late-nineteenth century, the dominant approach was to seek the legislature's intent. Although most judges viewed the statutory text as the best evidence of legislative intent, they were often willing to go beyond the text, as did the Court in *Church of the Holy Trinity*, in interpreting statutes. Indeed, judges were willing to reach conclusions arguably in conflict with the statutory text—as in *Church of the Holy Trinity* and *Riggs*—in order to effectuate the legislature's apparent intent.

To be sure, the notion of legislative "intent" did not have one clear, agreed-upon meaning. Sometimes courts used the term to refer to the actual, specific intent of particular members of the legislature; other times courts used the term to refer to the actual, collective intent of the legislature as a whole; and still other times, as in *Riggs*, courts used the term to refer to a hypothesized intent about matters that the legislature had not considered at all. (In addition, courts sometimes used the term "intent" to refer to the legislature's broader purposes or the spirit of the law. We will return to this concept, and the ways that it might differ from "intent," shortly.)

In the early-twentieth century, some judges and scholars began to criticize judicial reliance on legislative intent. These critics raised several objections to the practice. First, some critics charged that judges used the concept of legislative intent as a cover to smuggle their personal policy preferences—in that era, usually conservative or libertarian views—into the law. For example, Roscoe Pound, who became the Dean of Harvard Law School, noted that judges read the antitrust laws to limit the power of labor unions, and that they read statutes such as the one at issue in *Caminetti* to advance a puritanical moral vision. See Roscoe Pound, *Mechanical Jurisprudence*, 8 Colum. L. Rev. 605 (1908); Roscoe Pound, *Common Law and Legislation*, 21 Harv. L. Rev. 383 (1908).

Second, some critics, such as Justice Oliver Wendell Holmes, Jr., contended that departures from the plain meaning of statutory text frustrated the will of the people. Holmes noted that such departures inevitably relied on the judges' sensibilities and policy preferences, rather than the choices of the legislature; but legislators, not judges, are elected to make policy. In addition, if judges can read statutes to reach results that an ordinary person reading the statute would not contemplate, then the law ceases to be predictable. As such, Justice Holmes asserted that a quest for legislative intent, to the extent that it departed from the ordinary meaning of statutory text, was both anti-democratic and contrary to the rule of law. See Oliver Wendell Holmes, Jr., *The Theory of Legal Interpretation*, 12 Harv. L. Rev. 417 (1899); Oliver Wendell Holmes, Jr., The Common Law (1881).

Third, legal realists, writing in the 1920s and 1930s, attacked the concept of legislative intent by noting that it is impossible to uncover one single, collective intent when a legislature enacts a statute. They pointed out that each member of the legislature might have a distinctive motivation, or multiple motivations, and a distinctive understanding of the meaning of the terms in the statute and how they might apply. As a consequence, legal realists argued that the concept of legislative intent was a fiction. See Max Radin, *Statutory Interpretation*, 43 Harv. L. Rev. 863 (1930).

In the 1940s, some judges and scholars began to urge a new way of thinking about the task of statutory interpretation. Consider this famous hypothetical case that Professor Fuller used to illustrate the range of approaches in statutory interpretation.

---

## *The Case of the Speluncean Explorers*

**Lon L. Fuller**

62 Harv. L. Rev. 616 (1949)*

In the Supreme Court of Newgarth, 4300

Truepenny, C.J. The four defendants are members of the Speluncean Society, an organization of amateurs interested in the exploration of caves. Early in May of

---

* Reprinted with permission.

4299 they, in the company of Roger Whetmore, then also a member of the Society, penetrated into the interior of a limestone cavern of the type found in the Central Plateau of this Commonwealth. While they were in a position remote from the entrance to the cave, a landslide occurred. Heavy boulders fell in such a manner as to block completely the only known opening to the cave. * * * On the failure of Whetmore and the defendants to return to their homes, the Secretary of the Society was notified by their families, [and a] rescue party was promptly dispatched to the spot.

The task of rescue proved one of overwhelming difficulty. * * * The work of removing the obstruction was several times frustrated by fresh landslides, [one of which killed ten men working on the rescue]. * * * Success was finally achieved on the thirty-second day after the men entered the cave.

Since it was known that the explorers had carried with them only scant provisions, and since it was also known that there was no animal or vegetable matter within the cave on which they might subsist, anxiety was early felt that they might meet death by starvation before access to them could be obtained. On the twentieth day of their imprisonment it was learned for the first time that they had taken with them into the cave a portable wireless machine capable of both sending and receiving messages. [Upon establishing communication, they] asked to be informed how long a time would be required to release them. The engineers in charge of the project answered that at least ten days would be required even if no new landslides occurred. The explorers then [were] placed in communication with a committee of medical experts. The imprisoned men * * * asked for a medical opinion whether they would be likely to live without food for ten days longer. The chairman of the committee of physicians told them that there was little possibility of this. * * * Whetmore, speaking on behalf of himself and the defendants, asked whether they would be able to survive for ten days longer if they consumed the flesh of one of their number. The physicians' chairman reluctantly answered this question in the affirmative. * * * When the imprisoned men were finally released it was learned that on the twenty-third day after their entrance into the cave Whetmore had been killed and eaten by his companions.

From the testimony of the defendants, which was accepted by the jury, it appears that it was Whetmore who first proposed that they might find the nutriment without which survival was impossible in the flesh of one of their own number. It was also Whetmore who first proposed the use of some method of casting lots, calling the attention of the defendants to a pair of dice he happened to have with him. The defendants were at first reluctant to adopt so desperate a procedure, but after the conversations by wireless related above, they finally agreed on the plan proposed by Whetmore. After much discussion of the mathematical problems involved, agreement was finally reached on a method of determining the issue by the use of the dice.

Before the dice were cast, however, Whetmore declared that he withdrew from the arrangement, as he had decided on reflection to wait for another week before embracing an expedient so frightful and odious. The others charged him with a breach of faith and proceeded to cast the dice. When it came Whetmore's turn, the dice were cast for him by one of the defendants, and he was asked to declare any objections he might have to the fairness of the throw. He stated that he had no such objections. The throw went against him, and he was then put to death and eaten by his companions.

After the rescue of the defendants, and after they had completed a stay in a hospital where they underwent a course of treatment for malnutrition and shock, they were indicted for the murder of Roger Whetmore. At the trial, after the testimony had been concluded, the foreman of the jury (a lawyer by profession) inquired of the court whether the jury might not find a special verdict, leaving it to the court to say whether on the facts as found the defendants were guilty. After some discussion, both the Prosecutor and counsel for the defendants indicated their acceptance of this procedure, and it was adopted by the court. In a lengthy special verdict the jury found the facts as I have related them above, and found further that if on these facts the defendants were guilty of the crime charged against them, then they found the defendants guilty. On the basis of this verdict, the trial judge ruled that the defendants were guilty of murdering Roger Whetmore. The judge then sentenced them to be hanged, the law of our Commonwealth permitting him no discretion with respect to the penalty to be imposed. After the release of the jury, its members joined in a communication to the Chief Executive asking that the sentence be commuted to an imprisonment of six months. The trial judge addressed a similar communication to the Chief Executive. As yet no action with respect to these pleas has been taken, as the Chief Executive is apparently awaiting our disposition of this petition of error.

* * * The language of our statute is well known: "Whoever shall willfully take the life of another shall be punished by death." N.C.S.A. § 12–A. This statute permits of no exception applicable to this case, however our sympathies may incline us to make allowance for the tragic situation in which these men found themselves.

In a case like this the principle of executive clemency seems admirably suited to mitigate the rigors of the law, and I propose to my colleagues that we follow the example of the jury and the trial judge by joining in the communications they have addressed to the Chief Executive. There is every reason to believe that these requests for clemency will be heeded, coming as they do from those who have studied the case and had an opportunity to become thoroughly acquainted with all its circumstances. * * * I think we may [assume] that some form of clemency will be extended to these defendants. If this is done, then justice will be accomplished without impairing either the letter or spirit of our statutes and without offering any encouragement for the disregard of law.

FOSTER, J. I am shocked that the Chief Justice, in an effort to escape the embarrassments of this tragic case, should have adopted, and should have proposed to his colleagues, an expedient at once so sordid and so obvious. I believe something more is on trial in this case than the fate of these unfortunate explorers; that is the law of our Commonwealth. If this Court declares that under our law these men have committed a crime, then our law is itself convicted in the tribunal of common sense, no matter what happens to the individuals involved in this petition of error. For us to assert that the law we uphold and expound compels us to a conclusion we are ashamed of, and from which we can only escape by appealing to a dispensation resting within the personal whim of the Executive, seems to me to amount to an admission that the law of this Commonwealth no longer pretends to incorporate justice.

For myself, I do not believe that our law compels the monstrous conclusion that these men are murderers. I believe, on the contrary, that it declares them to be innocent of any crime. I rest this conclusion on two independent grounds, either of which is of itself sufficient to justify the acquittal of these defendants.

The first of these grounds rests on [the] premise that * * * the enacted or positive law of this Commonwealth, including all of its statutes and precedents, is inapplicable to this case, and that the case is governed instead by what ancient writers in Europe and America called "the law of nature." This conclusion rests on the proposition that our positive law is predicated on the possibility of men's coexistence in society. When a situation arises in which the coexistence of men becomes impossible, then a condition that underlies all of our precedents and statutes has ceased to exist. When that condition disappears, then it is my opinion that the force of our positive law disappears with it. * * * [A]t the time Roger Whetmore's life was ended by these defendants, they were, to use the quaint language of nineteenth-century writers, not in a "state of civil society" but in a "state of nature." This has the consequence that the law applicable to them is not the enacted and established law of this Commonwealth, but the law derived from those principles that were appropriate to their condition. I have no hesitancy in saying that under those principles they were guiltless of any crime. What these men did was done in pursuance of an agreement accepted by all of them and first proposed by Whetmore himself. Since it was apparent that their extraordinary predicament made inapplicable the usual principles that regulate men's relations with one another, it was necessary for them to draw, as it were, a new charter of government appropriate to the situation in which they found themselves.

* * * My second ground [for decision] proceeds by [conceding for] purposes of argument that * * * the Consolidated Statutes have the power to penetrate five hundred feet of rock and to impose themselves upon these starving men huddled in their underground prison. Now it is, of course, perfectly clear that these men did an act that violates the literal wording of the statute which declares that he who "shall willfully take the life of another" is a murderer. But one of the most ancient bits of legal wisdom is the saying that a man may break the letter of the law without breaking the law itself. Every proposition of positive law, whether contained in a statute or a judicial precedent, is to be interpreted reasonably, in the light of its evident purpose. This is a truth so elementary that it is hardly necessary to expatiate on it. * * *

The statute before us for interpretation has never been applied literally. Centuries ago it was established that a killing in self-defense is excused. There is nothing in the wording of the statute that suggests this exception. Various attempts have been made to reconcile the legal treatment of self-defense with the words of the statute, but in my opinion these are all merely ingenious sophistries. The truth is that the exception in favor of self-defense cannot be reconciled with the *words* of the statute, but only with its *purpose*.

The true reconciliation of the excuse of self-defense with the statute making it a crime to kill another is to be found in the following line of reasoning. One of the principal objects underlying any criminal legislation is that of deterring men from crime. Now it is apparent that if it were declared to be the law that a killing in self-defense is murder such a rule could not operate in a deterrent manner. A man whose life is threatened will repel his aggressor, whatever the law may say. Looking therefore to the broad purposes of criminal legislation, we may safely declare that this statute was not intended to apply to cases of self-defense.

When the rationale of the excuse of self-defense is thus explained, it becomes apparent that precisely the same reasoning is applicable to the case at bar. If in the future any group of men ever find themselves in the tragic predicament of these defendants, we may be sure that their decision whether to live or die will not be controlled by the contents of our criminal code. Accordingly, if we read this statute intelligently it is apparent that it does not apply to this case. The withdrawal of this situation from the effect of the statute is justified by precisely the same considerations that were applied by our predecessors in office centuries ago to the case of self-defense.

There are those who raise the cry of judicial usurpation whenever a court, after analyzing the purpose of a statute, gives to its words a meaning that is not at once apparent to the casual reader who has not studied the statute closely or examined the objectives it seeks to attain. Let me say emphatically that I accept without reservation the proposition that this Court is bound by the statutes of our Commonwealth and that it exercises its powers in subservience to the duly expressed will of the Chamber of Representatives. The line of reasoning I have applied above raises no question of fidelity to enacted law, though it may possibly raise a question of the distinction between intelligent and unintelligent fidelity. No superior wants a servant who lacks the capacity to read between the lines. The stupidest housemaid knows that when she is told "to peel the soup and skim the potatoes" her mistress does not mean what she says. She also knows that when her master tells her to "drop everything and come running" he has overlooked the possibility that she is at the moment in the act of rescuing the baby from the rain barrel. Surely we have a right to expect the same modicum of intelligence from the judiciary. The correction of obvious legislative errors or oversights is not to supplant the legislative will, but to make that will effective.

I therefore conclude that on any aspect under which this case may be viewed these defendants are innocent of the crime of murdering Roger Whetmore, and that the conviction should be set aside.

Tatting, J. As I analyze the opinion just rendered by my brother Foster, I find that it is shot through with contradictions and fallacies. Let us begin with his first proposition: these men were not subject to our law because they were not in a "state of civil society" but in a "state of nature." I am not clear why this is so, whether it is because of the thickness of the rock that imprisoned them, or because they were hungry, or because they had set up a "new charter of government" by which the usual rules of law were to be supplanted by a throw of the dice. Other difficulties intrude themselves. If these men passed from the jurisdiction of our law to that of "the law of nature," at what moment did this occur? Was it when the entrance to the cave was blocked, or when the threat of starvation reached a certain undefined degree of intensity, or when the agreement for the throwing of the dice was made? * * *

Let us look at the contents of this code of nature that my brother proposes we adopt as our own and apply to this case. What a topsy-turvy and odious code it is! It is a code in which the law of contracts is more fundamental than the law of murder. It is a code under which a man may make a valid agreement empowering his fellows to eat his own body. Under the provisions of this code, furthermore, such an agreement once made is irrevocable, and if one of the parties attempts to withdraw, the others may take the law into their own hands and enforce the contract by violence—for though my brother passes over in convenient silence the effect of Whetmore's withdrawal, this is the necessary implication of his argument.

* * * I come now to the second part of my brother's opinion, in which he seeks to show that the defendants did not violate the provisions of N.C.S.A. § 12–A. * * * It is true that a statute should be applied in the light of its purpose, and that *one* of the purposes of criminal legislation is recognized to be deterrence. The difficulty is that other purposes are also ascribed to the law of crimes. It has been said that one of its objects is to provide an orderly outlet for the instinctive human demand for retribution. It has also been said that its object is the rehabilitation of the wrongdoer. Other theories have been propounded. Assuming that we must interpret a statute in the light of its purpose, what are we to do when it has many purposes or when its purposes are disputed?

A similar difficulty is presented by the fact that although there is authority for my brother's interpretation of the excuse of self-defense, there is other authority which assigns to that excuse a different rationale. * * * The taught doctrine of our law schools, memorized by generations of law students, runs in the following terms: The statute concerning murder requires a "willful" act. The man who acts to repel an aggressive threat to his own life does not act "willfully," but in response to an impulse deeply ingrained in human nature. * * *

Now the familiar explanation for the excuse of self-defense just expounded obviously cannot be applied by analogy to the facts of this case. These men acted not only "willfully" but with great deliberation and after hours of discussing what they should do. Again we encounter a forked path, with one line of reasoning leading us in one direction and another in a direction that is exactly the opposite. * * *

[W]hat are we to do with one of the landmarks of our jurisprudence, which again my brother passes over in silence? [In] *Commonwealth v. Valjean*, [the] defendant was indicted for the larceny of a loaf of bread, and offered as a defense that he was in a condition approaching starvation. The court refused to accept this defense. If hunger cannot justify the theft of wholesome and natural food, how can it justify the killing and eating of a man? Again, if we look at the thing in terms of deterrence, is it likely that a man will starve to death to avoid a jail sentence for the theft of a loaf of bread? My brother's demonstrations would compel us to overrule *Valjean*, and many other precedents that have been built on that case.

**FYI**

The "precedent" that Justice Tatting cites here is based on Victor Hugo's famous novel *Les Misérables*, which begins with the protagonist, Jean Valjean, serving a nineteen-year prison term for stealing a loaf of bread.

There is still a further difficulty in my brother Foster's proposal to read an exception into the statute to favor this case, though again a difficulty not even intimated in his opinion. What shall be the scope of this exception? Here the men cast lots and the victim was himself originally a party to the agreement. What would we have to decide if Whetmore had refused from the beginning to participate in the plan? Would a majority be permitted to overrule him? Or, suppose that no plan were adopted at all and the others simply conspired to bring about Whetmore's death, justifying their act by saying that he was in the weakest condition. Or again, that a plan of selection was followed but one based on a different justification than the one adopted here, as if the others were atheists and insisted that Whetmore should die because he was the only one who believed in an afterlife. These illustrations could be multiplied, but enough have been suggested to reveal what a quagmire of hidden difficulties my brother's reasoning contains.

I have given this case the best thought of which I am capable. I have scarcely slept since it was argued before us. When I feel myself inclined to accept the view of my brother Foster, I am repelled by a feeling that his arguments are intellectually unsound and approach mere rationalization. On the other hand, when I incline toward upholding the conviction, I am struck by the absurdity of directing that these men be put to death when their lives have been saved at the cost of the lives of ten heroic workmen. It is to me a matter of regret that the Prosecutor saw fit to ask for an indictment for murder. * * * Since I have been wholly unable to resolve the doubts that beset me about the law of this case, I am with regret announcing a step that is, I believe, unprecedented in the history of this tribunal. I declare my withdrawal from the decision of this case.

Keen, J. I should like to begin by setting to one side two questions which are not before this Court. The first of these is whether executive clemency should be extended to these defendants if the conviction is affirmed. Under our system of government, that is a question for the Chief Executive, not for us. I therefore disapprove of that passage in the opinion of the Chief Justice in which he in effect gives instructions to the Chief Executive as to what he should do in this case * * *. [I]f I were the Chief Executive, * * * I would pardon these men altogether, since I believe that they have already suffered enough to pay for any offense they may have committed. [But in] the discharge of my duties as judge, it is neither my function to address directions to the Chief Executive, nor to take into account what he may or may not do, in reaching my own decision, which must be controlled entirely by the law of this Commonwealth.

The second question that I wish to put to one side is that of deciding whether what these men did was "right" or "wrong," "wicked" or "good." That is also a question that is irrelevant to the discharge of my office as a judge sworn to apply, not my conceptions of morality, but the law of the land. In putting this question to one side I think I can also safely dismiss without comment the first and more poetic portion of my brother Foster's opinion. * * *

The sole question before us for decision is whether these defendants did, within the meaning of N.C.S.A. § 12–A, willfully take the life of Roger Whetmore. * * * Now I should suppose that any candid observer, content to extract from these words their natural meaning, would concede at once that these defendants did "willfully take the life" of Roger Whetmore.

Whence arise all the difficulties of the case, then, and the necessity for so many pages of discussion about what ought to be so obvious? The difficulties, in whatever tortured form they may present themselves, all trace back to a single source, and that is a failure to distinguish the legal from the moral aspects of this case. To put it bluntly, my brothers do not like the fact that the written law requires the conviction of these defendants. Neither do I, but unlike my brothers I respect the obligations of an office that requires me to put my personal predilections out of my mind when I come to interpret and apply the law of this Commonwealth.

Now, of course, my brother Foster does not admit that he is actuated by a personal dislike of the written law. Instead he develops a familiar line of argument according to which the court may disregard the express language of a statute when something not contained in the statute itself, called its "purpose," can be employed to justify the result the court considers proper. * * * We are all familiar with the process by which the judicial reform of disfavored legislative enactments is accomplished. [It] requires three steps. The first of these is to divine some single "purpose" which the statute serves. This is done although not one statute in a hundred has any such single purpose, and although the objectives of nearly every statute are differently interpreted by the different classes of its sponsors. The second step is to discover that a mythical being called "the legislator," in the pursuit of this imagined "purpose," overlooked something or left some gap or imperfection in his work. Then comes the final and most refreshing part of the task, which is, of course, to fill in the blank thus created. * * *

My brother Foster's penchant for finding holes in statutes reminds one of the story told by an ancient author about the man who ate a pair of shoes. Asked how he liked them, he replied that the part he liked best was the holes. That is the way my brother feels about statutes; the more holes they have in them the better he likes them. In short, he doesn't like statutes.

One could not wish for a better case to illustrate the specious nature of this gap-filling process than the one before us. My brother thinks he knows exactly what was sought when men made murder a crime, and that was something he calls "deterrence." My brother Tatting has already shown how much is passed over in that interpretation. But I think the trouble goes deeper. I doubt very much whether our statute making murder a crime really has a "purpose" in any ordinary sense of the term. Primarily, such a statute reflects a deeply-felt human conviction that murder is wrong and that something should be done to the man who commits it. If we were forced to be more articulate about the matter, we would probably take refuge in the more sophisticated theories of the criminologists, which, of course, were certainly not in the minds of those who drafted our statute. We might also observe that men will do their own work more effectively and live happier lives if they are protected against the threat of violent assault. Bearing in mind that the victims of murders are often unpleasant people, we might add some suggestion that the matter of disposing of undesirables is not a function suited to private enterprise, but should be a state monopoly. * * * If we do not know the purpose of § 12–A, how can we possibly say there is a "gap" in it? * * *

Now I know that the line of reasoning I have developed in this opinion will not be acceptable to those who look only to the immediate effects of a decision and ignore the long-run implications of an assumption by the judiciary of a power of dispensation. A hard decision is never a popular decision. * * * Hard cases may even have a certain moral value by bringing home to the people their own responsibilities toward the law that is ultimately their creation, and by reminding them that there is no principle of personal grace that can relieve the mistakes of their representatives.

Indeed, I will go farther and say that not only are the principles I have been expounding those which are soundest for our present conditions, but that we would have inherited a better legal system from our forefathers if those principles had been observed from the beginning. For example, with respect to the excuse of self-defense, if our courts had stood steadfast on the language of the statute the result would undoubtedly have been a legislative revision of it. Such a revision would have drawn on the assistance of natural philosophers and psychologists, and the resulting regulation of the matter would have had an understandable and rational basis, instead of the hodgepodge of verbalisms and metaphysical distinctions that have emerged from the judicial and professorial treatment. * * * I conclude that the conviction should be affirmed.

HANDY, J. I have listened with amazement to the tortured ratiocinations to which this simple case has given rise. I never cease to wonder at my colleagues' ability to throw an obscuring curtain of legalisms about every issue presented to them for decision. We have heard this afternoon learned disquisitions on the distinction between positive law and the law of nature, the language of the statute and the purpose of the statute, judicial functions and executive functions, judicial legislation and legislative legislation. * * *

What have all these things to do with the case? The problem before us is what we, as officers of the government, ought to do with these defendants. That is a question of practical wisdom, to be exercised in a context, not of abstract theory, but of human realities. When the case is approached in this light, it becomes, I think, one of the easiest to decide that has ever been argued before this Court.

I have never been able to make my brothers see that government is a human affair, and that men are ruled, not by words on paper or by abstract theories, but by other men. They are ruled well when their rulers understand the feelings and conceptions of the masses. They are ruled badly when that understanding is lacking.

* * * [W]herever you have rules and abstract principles lawyers are going to be able to make distinctions. To some extent [this] is a necessary evil attaching to any formal regulation of human affairs. But I think that the area which really stands in need of such regulation is greatly overestimated. * * * I believe that all government officials, including judges, will do their jobs best if they treat forms and abstract concepts as instruments. We should take as our model, I think, the good administrator, who accommodates procedures and principles to the case at hand, selecting from among the available forms those most suited to reach the proper result.

The most obvious advantage of this method of government is that it permits us to go about our daily tasks with efficiency and common sense. My adherence to this philosophy has, however, deeper roots. I believe that it is only with the insight this philosophy gives that we can preserve the flexibility essential if we are to keep our actions in reasonable accord with the sentiments of those subject to our rule. More governments have been wrecked, and more human misery caused, by the lack of this accord between ruler and ruled than by any other factor that can be discerned in history. Once drive a sufficient wedge between the mass of people and those who direct their legal, political, and economic life, and our society is ruined. Then neither Foster's law of nature nor Keen's fidelity to written law will avail us anything.

Now when these conceptions are applied to the case before us, its decision becomes, as I have said, perfectly easy. In order to demonstrate this I shall have to introduce certain realities that my brothers in their coy decorum have seen fit to pass over in silence, although they are just as acutely aware of them as I am.

The first of these is that this case has aroused an enormous public interest, both here and abroad. * * * One of the great newspaper chains made a poll of public opinion on the question, "What do you think the Supreme Court should do with the Speluncean explorers?" About ninety per cent expressed a belief that the defendants should be pardoned or let off with a kind of token punishment. It is perfectly clear, then, how the public feels about the case. We could have known this without the poll, of course, on the basis of common sense, or even by observing that on this Court there are apparently four-and-a-half men, or ninety per cent, who share the common opinion.

This makes it obvious, not only what we should do, but what we must do if we are to preserve between ourselves and public opinion a reasonable and decent accord. Declaring these men innocent need not involve us in any undignified quibble or trick. No principle of statutory construction is required that is not consistent with the past practices of this Court. Certainly no layman would think that in letting these men off we had stretched the statute any more than our ancestors did when they created the excuse of self-defense. If a more detailed demonstration of the method of reconciling our decision with the statute is required, I should be content to rest on the arguments developed in the second and less visionary part of my brother Foster's opinion. * * *

* * * *

The Supreme Court being evenly divided, the conviction and sentence of the Court of General Instances is *affirmed*. It is ordered that the execution of the sentence shall occur at 6 A.M., Friday, April 2, 4300, at which time the Public Executioner is directed to proceed with all convenient dispatch to hang each of the defendants by the neck until he is dead.

---

## Points for Discussion

### *a. Identifying the Competing Approaches*

Professor Fuller's fictional judges advanced a wide range of views about the proper judicial role in interpreting statutes, some of which we've already seen and others of which are new. Justice Keen echoed Judge Gray in *Riggs* (and Justice Holmes in his academic writing), asserting that the way for judges to be faithful to legislative will, and to avoid substituting their own views about good policy, is to rely solely on the statutory text. Justice Handy rejected this approach, and its "legalisms" and "abstract theory," instead urging reliance on "efficiency and common sense." Justice Handy embodied the legal realist, who presumes that the entire enterprise of interpretation and decision ultimately is an exercise in moral and political reasoning. And Justice Foster urged interpretation in light of the statute's purposes.

In the real judicial opinions that we've seen so far in this Chapter, some judges have sought to determine the legislature's "intent." No member of Professor Fuller's fictional court engaged in that inquiry. Notice again that the touchstone of legislative intent is distinct from the concept of legislative "purpose," on which Justice Foster relied. Although courts (including, perhaps, the Court in *Church of the Holy Trinity*) sometimes use these terms interchangeably, they have slightly different connotations. When courts speak of the legislature's purpose—or, sometimes, the statute's "spirit"—they are usually referring to the broad motivating objectives of the statute. For example, the purpose (or spirit) of the law prohibiting vehicles in the park might be the desire to protect park visitors from injury. When courts seek to implement the legislature's purpose, they usually try to interpret the statute in a way that advances the general goals that motivated the enacting the legislature. In order for a court to read a statute in light of its purpose, it is not necessary that the members of the legislature have actually thought about the particular matter in question. It's possible, for example, that the members of the town council in our hypothetical town hadn't thought about how the ordinance banning vehicles in parks would apply to bicycles. But this wouldn't be an obstacle to a court seeking to implement the spirit or purpose of the ban on vehicles in the park, as long as the court could confidently identify that purpose.

The concept of legislative intent is different. Usually, when courts refer to the legislature's "intent," they have in mind the specific intent of the legislature with respect to the particular question at issue. For example, a court trying to determine the town council's intent in a case involving a citation for a person who rode a bicycle in the park would look for evidence of what the members of the council thought about the application of the statute to bicycles. If there is clear evidence—such as a speech during the debate over the ordinance or a report issued by a committee advising the members—that the council thought that the ordinance does not ban bicycles, then a court might choose to give effect to that intent even though the literal terms of the text that the council chose might fairly be read to embrace bicycles.

#### *b. The Turn to Statutory Purpose*

As we've seen, the tendency of courts in the late-nineteenth and early-twentieth century to seek legislative intent had been the subject of considerable criticism. Critics charged that the concept of legislative intent was a fiction, and that a focus on legislative intent inevitably led to unelected judges substituting their own policy views for those of the legislature.

Professor Fuller and other scholars, however, were uncomfortable with the alternative approaches that some critics proposed. Justice Holmes (like the fictional Justice Keen) urged reliance on statutory text. But the realists had also made a convincing case that statutory text, which is often vague and open-ended, was as subject to manipulation and results-oriented decision-making as reliance on legislative intent. (As an example, recall the *Caminetti* case, which we considered earlier in this Chapter.)

The realists endeavored to show that both "imaginative reconstruction," which Judge Earl used in *Riggs*, and interpretation based on "plain meaning," which Justice Holmes had proposed, gave judges tremendous discretion to decide legal questions. Because the realists thought that legal decision-making inevitably was unconstrained by text or legal principle, they encouraged judges to engage in instrumental, policy-driven decision-making to produce sensible, rational rules. But that solution—unabashed policy-making by judges, based on moral and political considerations, of the form urged by the fictional Justice Handy—arguably was inconsistent with democracy, the separation of powers, and the rule of law.

In the 1930s and 1940s, Professor Fuller and other legal scholars sought to resolve this dilemma by urging judges to focus on legislative purpose when they interpreted statutes. Proponents of this view acknowledged that judges, as the realists had suggested, will inevitably engage in some policy-making. The indeterminacy of language and impossibility of anticipating every circumstance that might arise makes this unavoidable. But they argued that this policy-making was legitimate when it derived from legislative choices. See Felix Frankfurter, *Some Reflections on the Reading of Statutes*, 47 COLUM. L. REV. 527, 538–39 (1947). The idea was that judges could decide cases based on the objectives that the legislature had sought to achieve in enacting the statute, which could be identified by considering the statute's context and legislative history. On this view, judges would fill in the gaps in statutes in a way that was faithful to the legislature's purposes—and thus with democratic principles.

The fictional Justice Foster advanced this view in the second part of his opinion in *The Case of the Speluncean Explorers*. (The first part of his opinion might sound jarring to modern ears, but makes more sense when understood in light of then-recent events. Justice Foster's reliance on natural law was likely a response to World War II, advancing the idea that, under certain circumstances, we have reason to doubt the binding quality of enacted law and must resort to another set of principles, much like the concept of international human rights law that arose in the wake of the world's experience with Nazism. See LON L. FULLER, THE LAW IN QUEST OF ITSELF 122–25 (1940).) Professor Fuller was well aware of the potential criticisms of a focus on statutory purpose. His fictional Justice Keen worried that departing from the text enacted by the legislature threatened the separation of powers and democracy. Justice Tatting suggested that a focus on purpose is just as indeterminate and subject to judicial willfulness as any other approach, with Justices Tatting and Keen both pointing out that most statutes have multiple, or even countless, purposes, and that those purposes don't always point in the same direction. See generally William N. Eskridge, Jr., The Case of the Speluncean Explorers: *Twentieth Century Statutory Interpretation in a Nutshell*, 61 GEO. WASH. L. REV. 1731 (1993). But the focus on statutory purpose was attractive to many scholars and judges.

---

After Professor Fuller published *The Case of the Speluncean Explorers*, two of his colleagues at Harvard Law School created a set of teaching materials that sought to implement Fuller's insights. (The materials were eventually published as a casebook in the 1990s. See HENRY M. HART, JR. & ALBERT M. SACKS, THE LEGAL PROCESS: BASIC PROBLEMS IN THE MAKING AND APPLICATION OF LAW (W. Eskridge & P. Frickey, eds. 1994)). They argued that the creation of law did not end with the enactment of a statute; instead, they asserted that the creation of law is a process that merely begins with enactment, but that ends with judges (and administrative agencies) engaging in reasoned elaboration based on statutory purpose. They called their approach the "Legal Process."

Proponents of the legal process school generally rejected the pure plain meaning approach of Justice Keen, Justice Holmes, and Judge Gray. But they were also skeptical of imaginative reconstruction—urged by Professor Roscoe Pound, and by Judge Earl in *Riggs*—at least to the extent that it purported to rely on the legislature's specific intentions. Instead, they urged judges (and agency administrators) to focus explicitly on the legislature's broader objectives, interpreting statutes to reach results consistent with those broader purposes.

Hart and Sacks explained that, in interpreting a statute, a court should "[d]ecide what purpose ought to be attributed to the statute and to any subordinate provision of it which may be involved," and then "[i]nterpret the words of the statute immediately in question so as to carry out the purpose as best it can." They cautioned that a court should not give the words of a statute "a meaning they will not bear," and that courts should enforce the plain meaning of statutory text when "the words fit with all the relevant elements of their context to convey a single meaning, as applied to the matter at hand." But they urged courts, in seeking to determine statutory purposes, to "try to put" themselves in "the position of the legislature which enacted the measure" and to assume that "the legislature was made up of reasonable persons pursuing reasonable purposes reasonably."

The legal process approach dominated in the legal academy and on the Supreme Court for several decades. For example, in *United States v. American Trucking Associations, Inc.*, 310 U.S. 534, 543–44 (1940), the Court explained its role in interpreting statutes:

> "There is, of course, no more persuasive evidence of the purpose of a statute than the words by which the legislature undertook to give expression to its wishes. Often these words are sufficient in and of themselves to determine the purpose of the legislation. In such cases we have followed their plain meaning. When that meaning has led to absurd or futile results, however, this Court has looked beyond the words to the purpose of the act. Frequently, however, even when the plain meaning did not produce absurd results but merely an unreasonable one 'plainly at variance with the policy of the legislation as a whole' this Court has followed that purpose, rather than the literal words. When aid to construction of the meaning of words, as used in the statute, is available, there certainly can be no 'rule of law' which forbids its use, however clear

> the words may appear on 'superficial examination.' * * * Obviously there is danger that the courts' conclusion as to legislative purpose will be unconsciously influenced by the judges' own views or by factors not considered by the enacting body. A lively appreciation of the danger is the best assurance of escape from its threat but hardly justifies an acceptance of a literal interpretation dogma which withholds from the courts available information for reaching a correct conclusion."

Because of its focus on statutory purpose, the legal process school is perhaps the best-known variant of an approach to interpretation known as "purposivism."

---

### Problem

The defendant was convicted under a statute that provides: "It shall be a misdemeanor punishable by a fine not exceeding $500 to leave one's car parked on Pennsylvania Avenue for a period longer than two hours." It was undisputed that the defendant had attempted to remove his car from its parking spot on Pennsylvania Avenue before he had reached the two-hour limit, but that he was unable to do so because the streets were obstructed by a political demonstration in which he took no part and that he had no reason to anticipate. The defendant has appealed his conviction. How should the court rule? In thinking about this question, consider how a judge who focuses on the statutory text would resolve the case, and how a judge who focuses on statutory purpose would do so. Which approach seems more sensible to you?

---

### Problem

In 2005, a few high schools in Connecticut became notorious for running up the score in football games against over-matched opponents. In one game, the New London High School Whalers beat the Griswold High School Wolverines 90–0. Later that year, the coach of another team playing New London High School was arrested after a fight with Jack Cochran, New London's coach; to preserve a scoring opportunity, Cochran had called a timeout near the end of the first half of a game that his team was dominating (and ultimately won 60–0).

Because it was considered unsporting to beat the opposing team by such wide margins, in 2006 the Connecticut Interscholastic Athletic Conference adopted the following rule:

> "At the conclusion of any regular season game, if a team wins by a differential of more than 50 points, the head coach of the winning team shall be ineligible to participate in the next contest at the same level of play."

The rule was colloquially known as the "Jack Cochran rule," after the coach whose unyielding approach prompted the adoption of the rule.

Not long after the rule was adopted, New Canaan High School's football team took a big lead in the first quarter of a football game against Westport High School's team, which had not won a game in two years. In response, the New Canaan coach pulled all of his starters from the field and put only second-string players in the game. But New Canaan kept scoring and led 49–0 at halftime. In the second half, New Canaan's coach instructed his quarterback not to pass the ball. But Westport's defense nevertheless continued to struggle, and New Canaan scored again. In the end, New Canaan won the game 56–0.

Does the rule require the coach of the winning team to be suspended for one game? Does the answer depend on whether we focus on the text of the rule or instead the rule's purpose? Which approach seems more sensible to you?

---

These two problems, like *The Case of the Speluncean Explorers* and *Riggs v. Palmer*, suggest that strict adherence to statutory text sometimes produces results that seem contrary to what we assume to be the spirit or purpose of the law. This problem becomes even more complex when the statutory text has remained static, but the world has changed in ways that the enacting legislature did not anticipate. What should courts do when confronted with such situations? Is reliance on statutory text particularly problematic in such cases? Does a focus on statutory purpose—or the legal process approach, which encourages judges to fill gaps in order to advance statutory objectives—help to resolve any such problems? Or should courts instead resolve such disputes based on the actual intent or understanding of the enacting legislature? Consider the cases that follow.

---

## *Commonwealth v. Maxwell*

114 A. 825 (Pa. 1921)

Schaffer, J.

In this case, the court below quashed an indictment, charging the defendants with murder, because one of the grand jury which found it was a woman. The commonwealth has appealed; and this brings before us the important question whether women are eligible to serve as jurors in Pennsylvania.

[When the Pennsylvania] Constitution was adopted the uniform method of selecting jurors and determining their qualifications was by legislation, both here and in England. This was known to the framers of the first and all succeeding Constitutions, in the first being specifically recognized; and it and all the others, in guaranteeing the right to trial by jury, did not in any way limit the Legislature from determining from time to time how juries should be composed.

**FYI**

Pennsylvania adopted its first constitution in 1776. It adopted new constitutions in 1790, 1838, 1873, and 1968. When the court decided this case, the 1873 version was in effect, but all versions of the state's constitution have protected a right to a jury trial in criminal cases.

[The Pennsylvania legislature enacted a series of statutes to govern eligibility for jury service. Most of the older statutes provided that jurors should be drawn from among the pool of "taxable citizens" or "white male taxable citizens." In 1867, the legislature enacted a statute] providing that the jury commissioners are required to select "from the whole qualified electors of the respective county . . . persons, to serve as jurors in the several courts of such county" * * *. [In 1920, the requisite number of states ratified the Nineteenth Amendment] to the federal Constitution, putting women in the body of electors.

**FYI**

The Nineteenth Amendment provides: "The right of citizens of the United States to vote shall not be denied or abridged by the United States or by any State on account of sex."

"The term 'elector' is a technical, generic term, descriptive of a citizen having constitutional and statutory qualifications that enable him to vote, and including not only those who vote, but also those who are qualified, yet fail to exercise the right of franchise." 20 Corpus Juris, 58.

If the act of 1867 is prospective in operation, and takes in new classes of electors as they come to the voting privilege from time to time, then, necessarily, women, being electors, are eligible to jury service. That the act of 1867 does cover those who at any time shall come within the designation of electors there can be no question. "Statutes framed in general terms apply to new cases that arise, and to new subjects that are created from time to time, and which come within their general scope and policy. It is a rule of statutory construction that legislative enactments in general and comprehensive terms, prospective in operation, apply alike to all persons, subjects, and business within their general purview and scope coming into existence subsequent to their passage." 25 Ruling Case Law, 778.

Summing up, we conclude [that] the designation "qualified elector" embraces all electors at the time jurors are selected from the body of electors; [and that] the term "electors" embraces those who may be added to the electorate from time to time. [As a consequence,] women are eligible to serve as jurors in all the commonwealth's courts. The order quashing the indictment is reversed, and the indictment is reinstated, with direction to the court below to proceed with the trial of the defendants in due course.

---

## *People ex rel. Fyfe v. Barnett*

150 N.E. 290 (Ill. 1925)

HEARD, J.

Mrs. Hannay Beye Fyfe * * * filed in the circuit court of Cook County her petition for a writ of mandamus against the appellants, who are the jury commissioners for Cook county, to compel them to replace her name upon the jury lists of Cook county. [Fyfe was a 46-year-old woman who had lived in Oak Park, Illinois, for more than 15 years. Although she had previously been briefly included on the list of eligible jurors, in 1925 the jury commissioners removed her name from the list because she did not "possess the necessary legal qualifications for jury duty, in that she was a woman." The trial court ruled in favor of Fyfe and issued a writ of mandamus to compel the jury commissioners to place Fyfe on the list of eligible jurors.]

Appellants contend that such order must be reversed for the reason that the existing statutes of the state of Illinois cannot be construed so as to impose upon women electors the obligation to serve on juries, and because by the issuance of the writ in question the court has obligated appellants to perform a duty in conflict with the Constitution of this state.

The Jury Commissioners' Act in force July 1, 1887, as amended July 1, 1897, and April 24, 1899 (Cahill's Stat. 1923, c. 78, par. 26), for the appointment of jury commissioners in counties having more than 250,000 inhabitants, provides, in part, as follows:

> "The said commissioners upon entering upon the duties of their office, and every four years thereafter, shall prepare a list of all electors between the ages of twenty-one and sixty years, possessing the necessary legal qualifications for jury duty, to be known as the jury list. The list may be revised and amended annually in the discretion of the commissioners. * * *"

* * * On August 26, 1920, the Secretary of State of the United States in an official proclamation declared the [Nineteenth Amendment] ratified by three-fourths of the states, and it became a part of the Constitution of the United States. That amendment [provides]: "The right of citizens of the United States to vote shall not be denied or abridged by the United States or by any state on account of sex. * * *"

The Nineteenth Amendment to the Constitution of the United States makes no provision whatever with reference to the qualifications of jurors. Since the adoption of the amendment to the Constitution, the Legislature of the state of Illinois has not enacted any legislation on the subject of the eligibility or liability of women for jury service. While this amendment had the effect of nullifying every expression in the Constitution and laws of the state denying or abridging the right of suffrage to women on account of their sex, it did not purport to have any effect whatever on the subject of liability or eligibility of citizens for jury service. Since the adoption of the amendment, the Legislature of Illinois in 1921 granted to women the full right of suffrage, and they became, equally with men, electors and legal voters.

It is a primary rule in the interpretation and construction to be placed upon a statute that the intention of the Legislature should be ascertained and given effect. *People v. Price*, 101 N.E. 196 (Ill. 1913). * * * What the framers of the statute would have done had it been in their minds that a case like the one here under consideration would arise is not the point in dispute. The inquiry is what, in fact, they did enact, possibly without anticipating the existence of such facts. This should be determined, not by conjecture as to their meaning, but by the construction of the language used. The only legitimate function of the court is to declare and enforce the law as enacted by the Legislature. The office of the court is to interpret the language used by the Legislature where it requires interpretation, but not to annex new provisions or substitute different ones. The endeavor should be made always, in construing one or more statutes, to ascertain, by the history of the legislation on the subject, the purpose and intent of the Legislature * * *. The true rule is that statutes are to be construed as they were intended to be understood when they were passed. Statutes are to be read in the light of attendant conditions and that state of the law existent at the time of their enactment. The words of a statute must be taken in the sense in which they were understood at the time the statute was enacted. * * *

At the time of the passage by the Legislature of the act above mentioned, providing for the appointment of a jury commission and the making of jury lists, the words "voters" and "electors" were not ambiguous terms. They had a well-defined and settled meaning. [Article VII, section 1 of the state Constitution of 1870 and the Act on elections in force at the time in question] provided:

> "Every person having resided in this state one year, in the county ninety days, and in the election district thirty days next preceding any election therein who was an elector in this state on the first day of April, in the year of our Lord 1848, or obtained a certificate of naturalization before any court of record in this state prior to the first day of January, in the year of our Lord, 1870, or who shall be a male citizen of the United States, above the age of twenty-one years, shall be entitled to vote at such election."

The legislative intent that controls in the construction of a statute has reference to the Legislature which passed the given act. Applying the rules of construction herein mentioned, it is evident that when the Legislature enacted the law in question, which provided for the appointment of jury commissioners in counties having more than 250,000 inhabitants and imposing upon them the duty of making a jury list, using the words "shall prepare a list of all electors between the ages of twenty-one and sixty years, possessing the necessary legal qualifications for jury duty, to be known as the jury list," it was intended to use the words "electors" and "elector" as the same were then defined by the Constitution and laws of the state of Illinois. At that time the Legislature did not intend that the name of any women should be placed on the jury list, and must be held to have intended that the list should be composed of the names of male persons, only. In interpreting a statute, the question is what the words used therein meant to those using them. The word "electors," in the statute here in question, meant male persons, only, to the legislators who used it. We must therefore hold that the word "electors," as used in the statute, means male persons, only, and that the petitioner was not entitled to have her name replaced upon the jury list of Cook county. The judgment of the circuit court is therefore reversed.

---

## Points for Discussion

### *a. Touchstones of Interpretation*

On which touchstone of interpretation did the Pennsylvania court rely in concluding that women could serve as jurors? On which touchstone did the Illinois court rely in concluding that they could not? In one sense, both courts focused on the meaning of the word "elector" in the jury-eligibility statute. But the Pennsylvania court defined that term at a high level of generality—that is, as a word describing all persons currently eligible to vote, even those persons who were not eligible when the legislature enacted the statute—whereas the Illinois court defined the term in light of the specific connotation of the term at the time that the legislature enacted the jury-eligibility statute.

Or perhaps it is more accurate to say that the Pennsylvania court focused on the *plain meaning* of the word elector, whereas the Illinois court focused on the *intent of the legislature* when it enacted the jury-eligibility statute. But is it possible to determine the meaning of the words in a statute without considering the context in which they were adopted? If not, was there really a methodological difference between the two courts' approaches?

Either way, how would a court following the legal process approach have addressed the question of interpretation presented in the two cases? Would a focus on statutory purposes help to resolve these cases? What was the purpose (or purposes) of the jury-eligibility statutes?

### *b. Static Text in a Dynamic World*

The central question in the jury-eligibility cases was how to interpret a statute that has not changed when the world, and the circumstances to which the statute applies, has changed dramatically. Even if you are sympathetic to the approach of the Illinois Supreme Court in *People ex rel. Fyfe*, is it obvious to you that only persons who were eligible to vote at the time the legislature enacted the jury-eligibility statute should be eligible to serve on juries today?

In thinking about this question, consider that, in most states, suffrage was originally limited not only to males, and not even only to white males, but to white males who owned property. Over time, the states expanded the pool of eligible voters to include white males who did not own property (and, at least formally even if not in practice after the adoption of the Fifteenth Amendment, all males). Imagine that a state had a statute governing jury eligibility similar to the statutes in *Maxwell* and *People ex rel. Fyfe*, and that the legislature did not amend the jury-eligibility statute after males who did not own property gained the right to vote. Under the court's approach in *People ex rel. Fyfe*, would males who did not own property have become eligible to serve as jurors in that state after they gained the right to vote? If so, why wouldn't women similarly have gained the right to serve as jurors once the Nineteenth Amendment guaranteed them the right to vote?

Consider the reasoning of the Massachusetts Supreme Judicial Court, in *Commonwealth v. Welosky*, 177 N.E. 656 (Mass. 1931), which presented the same question that was at issue in *Maxwell* and *People ex rel. Fyfe*:

> Possession of property of specified value and payment of taxes as qualifications for voters were required in earlier days and from time to time, but these were gradually eliminated by Amendments to the [state] Constitution until the last of such limitations disappeared with the approval of Amendment 32 in 1891. When the suffrage has been thus widened among male citizens, there has followed, without further legislation and without change in the phrase of the statute, a like extension of citizens liable to service as jurors. These concurring enlargements of those liable to jury service were simply an extension to larger numbers of the same classification of persons. Since the word 'person' in the statutes respecting jurors meant men, when there was an

> extension of the right to vote to other men previously disqualified, the jury statutes by specific definition included them. No amendment to the statute can be conceived which could have made that meaning more clear. * * *
>
> Changes in suffrage and in liability for jury service in the past differ in kind from the change here urged. The Nineteenth Amendment to the federal Constitution conferred the suffrage upon an entirely new class of human beings. It did not extend the right to vote to members of an existing classification theretofore disqualified, but created a new class. It added to qualified voters those who did not fall within the meaning of the word 'person' in the jury statutes. No member of the class thus added to the body of voters had ever theretofore in this commonwealth had the right to vote for candidates for offices created by the Constitution. The change in the legal status of women wrought by the Nineteenth Amendment was radical, drastic and unprecedented. While it is to be given full effect in its field, it is not to be extended by implication. It is unthinkable that those who first framed and selected the words for the [jury-eligibility] statute [had] any design that it should ever include women within its scope. * * * When they used the word 'person' in connection with those qualified to vote for members of the more numerous branch of the general court, to describe those liable to jury service, no one contemplated the possibility of women becoming so qualified.

Do you find this distinction convincing? Exactly what sorts of social change can fixed text accommodate?

The question about how to interpret static statutory text in a changing world has arisen in the context of adoption, as well. Consider the case that follows.

**Make the Connection**

We will return to the jurisprudential challenge presented in these cases—what to do when the world changes but statutory text remains static—in Chapter 5, when we consider *Bostock v. Clayton County* and the application of Title VII of the Civil Rights Act of 1964 to discrimination on the basis of sexual orientation and gender identity.

---

## *In the Interest of Angel Lace M.*

516 N.W.2d 678 (Wis. 1994)

STEINMETZ, JUSTICE.

Angel [Lace M.] was born on March 10, 1986. On September 20, 1988, Georgina and Terry M. adopted Angel. Georgina and Terry were married at the time of the adoption. They separated in February, 1990, and divorced in June of that same year. Aside from paying court-ordered child support, Terry has played no part in Angel's life since late 1990.

In June, 1990, Georgina and Angel began living with Annette. The two women have shared equally in raising Angel since that time. Georgina and Annette symbolically solemnized their commitment to each other by partaking in a marriage-like ceremony in Milwaukee on August 11, 1991.[1] On February 17, 1992, Annette filed a petition in the Brown county circuit court to adopt Angel. Simultaneously, Georgina filed a petition to terminate Terry's parental rights and a petition for the adoptive placement of Angel with Annette. No party filed a petition to terminate Georgina's parental rights.

Judge Dietz held a hearing on the various petitions on March 25, 1992. At the hearing, Terry signed a statement consenting to the termination of his parental rights and testified that his consent was both voluntary and knowing. The Community Adoption Center filed a report with the court recommending the adoption. In addition, a social worker from the center testified at the hearing that the termination of Terry's parental rights and the adoption of Angel by Annette would be in Angel's best interests.

Based on the testimony and other evidence presented at the hearing, the circuit court determined that the proposed adoption would be in Angel's best interests. However, the court also determined that pursuant to ch. 48, Stats., Annette is not competent to adopt Angel and Angel is not competent to be adopted by Annette. Hence, the court denied each of the petitions * * *. Annette and Georgina appealed the circuit court's order. The court of appeals certified the appeal for review by this court. We accepted the certification and now affirm the order of the circuit court.

The petitioners argue that the circuit court should have granted Annette's petition for adoption because the court found that the adoption is in Angel's best interests. *See* sec. 48.01(2), Stats.[3] There is no doubt that a court must find that an adoption is in the best interests of the child before the court may grant the petition for adoption. However, the fact that an adoption—or any other action affecting a child—is in the child's best interests, by itself, does not authorize a court to grant the adoption. * * * [B]efore we apply the best interests standard in this case, we must determine whether Annette's proposed adoption of Angel satisfies the statutory requirements for adoption.

1 [At the time of the court's decision, Wisconsin did not recognize same-sex marriages.] *See* sec. 765.001(2), Stats., *Phillips v. Wisconsin Personnel Commission*, 482 N.W.2d 121 (Wis. Ct. App. 1992). Hence, under the laws of Wisconsin, Georgina and Annette are not married. As a result, Annette is not Angel's stepparent.

3 Section 48.01(2), Stats., provides as follows: "This chapter shall be liberally construed to effect the objectives contained in this section. The best interests of the child shall always be of paramount consideration, but the court shall also consider the interest of the parents or guardian of the child, the interest of the person or persons with whom the child has been placed for adoption and the interests of the public."

In Wisconsin, the requirements for adoption are found in ch. 48, Stats. Our purpose in interpreting a statute is to give effect to the intent of the legislature, with the plain language of the statute acting as our primary guide.

Section 48.82, Stats.,[4] controls who may adopt a minor. A party petitioning to adopt a minor must satisfy two requirements. First, the party must be a resident of Wisconsin. Annette satisfies this first requirement. Second, the party must fit the description from either sec. 48.82(1)(a) or sec. 48.82(1)(b). Annette does not qualify under sec. 48.82(1)(a) because she is not legally "the husband or wife" of Georgina who is the "parent of the minor." However, Annette does fit the description in sec. 48.82(1)(b) because she is "[a]n unmarried adult."

For the adoption to be valid, not only must Annette qualify as a party who may adopt Angel, but Angel must also be eligible for adoption. Section 48.81, Stats.,[5] controls who may be adopted. A minor must also satisfy two requirements to be eligible for adoption. Angel satisfies the first requirement of the statute because she was present in the state of Wisconsin at the time Annette filed the petition for adoption. *See* sec. 48.81(2). It is less clear whether Angel satisfies the second requirement. Pursuant to sec. 48.81(1), a minor may only be adopted if her "parental rights have been terminated. . . ."[6] Angel's adoptive father, Terry, has consented to the termination of his parental rights. Georgina's parental rights, on the other hand, remain intact.

The petitioners claim that sec. 48.81(1), Stats., is ambiguous. According to the petitioners, the statute could mean that Angel is eligible for adoption * * * as long as the rights of *at least one* of her parents have been terminated. The petitioners ask this court to construe the statute liberally to further the best interests of Angel, pursuant to sec. 48.01(2), and accept [this] interpretation of the statute.

Under [this] interpretation of the statute [a] minor would be eligible to be adopted even if the remaining parent is legally fit to raise the child alone and prefers to raise the child alone. Ostensibly, a complete stranger could petition to adopt a minor who is a member of this stable family; and, at least pursuant to sec. 48.81, Stats., the proposed adoption would be permissible. The legislature could not have

---

4 Section 48.82, Stats., provides as follows:

48.82 Who may adopt. (1) The following persons are eligible to adopt a minor if they are residents of this state: (a) A husband and wife jointly, or either the husband or wife if the other spouse is a parent of the minor; (b) An unmarried adult. * * *

5 Section 48.81, Stats., provides as follows:

48.81 Who may be adopted. Any minor who meets all of the following criteria may be adopted:

(1) * * * [A] minor whose parental rights have been terminated under subch. VIII or in another state or a foreign jurisdiction; (2) A minor who is present within this state at the time the petition for adoption is filed.

6 We first note that this statute is poorly worded. A minor does not have parental rights that may be terminated. Rather, her parents possess these rights. The legislature must have intended to state that a minor may be adopted if her "parents' rights have been terminated. . . ."

intended to declare a minor eligible for adoption under those circumstances. This would be an absurd result. This court will not construe a statute so as to work absurd or unreasonable results. *Estate of Evans,* 135 N.W.2d 832 (Wis. 1965). Hence, we hold that pursuant to sec. 48.81(1), a minor is not eligible for adoption unless the rights of both of her parents have been terminated.[8] Because Georgina's parental rights remain intact, Angel is not eligible to be adopted by Annette.

Section 48.92, Stats.,[9] also stands in the way of Annette's proposed adoption of Angel. This statute severs the ties between the birth parent[10] and the adopted minor after a court enters the order of adoption.[11] Pursuant to sec. 48.92(2), if the circuit court grants Annette's petition to adopt Angel, "all the rights, duties and other legal consequences of [Georgina's relationship with Angel] *shall* cease to exist." (Emphasis added.) If the legislature had intended to sanction adoptions by nonmarital partners, it would not have mandated this "cut-off" of the "rights, duties and other legal consequences" of the birth parents in these adoptions. [Because the term] " 'shall' is presumed to be mandatory when it appears in a statute," *State v. Speer,* 501 N.W.2d 429 (Wis. 1993), * * * we hold that the "cut-off" provision of sec. 48.92(2), Stats., is mandatory. Hence, Georgina would lose the "rights, duties and other legal consequences of" her relationship with Angel if the circuit court granted Annette's petition to adopt Angel. This result would frustrate rather than further the petitioners' intentions. We also hold that, pursuant to sec. 48.81(1), Angel is not eligible for adoption. Therefore, we conclude that the proposed adoption does not satisfy the essential requirements of the adoption statutes and is, in fact, prohibited by these statutes. The circuit court properly denied the petitions before it despite its finding that the adoption would be in Angel's best interests.

---

8 This holding obviously does not apply to stepparent adoptions. In a stepparent adoption, the minor is eligible to be adopted if the rights of one of her parents are terminated. Section 48.81, Stats., does not clearly provide for this exception in the case of stepparent adoptions. However, it is clear from surrounding statutes that the legislature intended to sanction stepparent adoptions. *See* sec. 48.92(2) ("unless the birth parent is the spouse of the adoptive parent") and sec. 48.835(3)(b) ("[i]f the person filing the adoption petition is a stepparent"). The same cannot be said for the proposed adoption in this case. No neighboring statutes indicate that the legislature intended to allow any adoptions, other than stepparent adoptions, unless the rights of both of the child's parents have been terminated.

9 Section 48.92, Stats., provides as follows:

> 48.92 Effect of adoption. (1) After the order of adoption is entered the relation of parent and child and all the rights, duties and other legal consequences of the natural relation of child and parent thereafter exists between the adopted person and the adoptive parents.
>
> (2) After the order of adoption is entered the relationship of parent and child between the adopted person and the adoptive person's birth parents, unless the birth parent is the spouse of the adoptive parent, shall be completely altered and all the rights, duties and other legal consequences of the relationship shall cease to exist. Notwithstanding the extinction of all parental rights under this subsection, a court may order reasonable visitation under § 48.925. * * *

10 This case involves "[t]he adoption of an adopted person . . . [and thus] the references to parent and birth parent [in the statutes] are to adoptive parent." *See* sec. 48.96, Stats.

11 The statute does exempt the birth parent from this "cut-off" provision in stepparent adoptions. However, because Georgina and Annette are not married, this exception does not apply.

[The court also held that the statute, in prohibiting the adoption in question, did not violate Angel's or Annette's rights under the Due Process or Equal Protection Clauses of the Fourteenth Amendment to the United States Constitution.]

GESKE, JUSTICE (*concurring*).

I join in the majority opinion because I believe that it correctly analyzes current Wisconsin law. * * * I write separately only to encourage the Wisconsin legislature to revisit ch. 48 in light of all that is occurring with children in our society. The legislators, as representatives of the people of this state, have both the right and the responsibility to establish the requirements for a legal adoption, for custody, and for visitation. This court cannot play that role. We can only interpret the law, not rewrite it.

HEFFERNAN, CHIEF JUSTICE (*dissenting*).

The issue addressed in this case is whether the Wisconsin statutes governing adoption allow Annette G. to adopt Angel, a child with whom she already has a functional parent-child relationship. The adoption statutes on their face do not address this issue. * * * In the present case, however, this court is provided with helpful guidance from the legislature on the appropriate canon of construction to apply to the adoption statutes. Section 48.01(2), Stats., states that the children's code, of which the adoption statutes are a part, "shall be liberally construed to effect the objectives contained in this section." * * * Section 48.01(2) adds: "The best interests of the child shall always be of paramount consideration, but the court shall also consider the interest of the parents or guardian of the child, the interest of the person or persons with whom the child has been placed for adoption and the interests of the public." Because the best interests of the child is "paramount," it appears that the legislature deems liberal construction of the statutes particularly appropriate when such construction effectuates the best interests of the child unless the other concerns listed outweigh the child's best interests. This court should interpret the adoption statutes following the approach mandated by the legislature.

In the present case everyone involved agrees that the adoption is in Angel's best interests. * * * [N]one of the other interests listed in sec. 48.01(2) preclude liberal construction of the statute with the paramount consideration being the child's best interests. The interests of Angel's current parents would be furthered by allowing this adoption. * * * The circuit court found that Terry, Angel's legal father, strongly supports the adoption and has consented to termination of his parental rights. * * * Georgina, Angel's legal mother, is one of the petitioners requesting that Annette be allowed to adopt Angel and clearly believes that the adoption is consistent with her own interests.

The second interest, that of the person or persons with whom the child has been placed for adoption, is not at issue in this case. Angel is not being placed outside her present family for adoption—if the adoption is allowed she will remain with Georgina and have a legally-recognized relationship with Annette as well. The third interest, that of the public, is also consistent with Angel's best interests. Given the shrinking percentage of children that are raised in two-parent families, and the shrinking percentage of children who receive even minimally adequate care regardless of family structure, the public interest is enhanced by granting legal recognition to two-parent families that do further the express objective in sec. 48.01(1)(g) of "provid[ing] children in the state with permanent and stable family relationships." Because the adoption in this case would further Angel's best interests while either having no effect on or enhancing the additional legislatively-recognized interests, this court should proceed to employ the legislatively-prescribed approach of interpreting the adoption statutes liberally in light of the "paramount consideration" of the best interests of the child.

The first relevant section in the adoption statutes is sec. 48.82(1), Stats., which governs who may adopt. The statute provides: "The following persons are eligible to adopt a minor if they are residents of this state: (a) A husband and wife jointly, or either the husband or wife if the other spouse is a parent of the minor[;] (b) An unmarried adult." Annette meets the sec. 48.82(1)(b) requirement—she is an unmarried adult. The second relevant statute is sec. 48.81, Stats., which sets forth the criteria governing who may be adopted: "Any minor who meets all of the following criteria may be adopted: (1) * * * a minor whose parental rights have been terminated * * *[;] (2) A minor who is present within this state at the time the petition for adoption is filed."

* * * The question in the present case is whether sec. 48.81 requires that parental rights of both parents be terminated before a minor is eligible for adoption. Looking solely at sec. 48.81, this court need not employ the legislatively-mandated canon of liberal construction in order to conclude that this statute requires that the parental rights of only one parent be terminated in order for a child to be eligible for adoption in those situations in which the remaining parent supports the adoption. Stepparent adoption is a common form of adoption but would be prohibited if sec. 48.81 is read to require that both parents' parental rights must be terminated before an adoption can take place.

In a footnote, the majority states that sec. 48.835(3)(b),[7] which expressly refers to stepparent adoption, and sec. 48.81(1), read *in pari materia,* clearly allow a minor to be adopted by a steppar-

**Definition**

*In pari materia* means "on the same matter" and refers to a maxim of statutory interpretation that statutes on the same subject should be read together. We will consider this and other maxims in Chapter 3.

---

7 Section 48.835(3)(b) provides: "If the person filing the adoption petition is a stepparent with whom the child and the child's parent reside, the stepparent shall file only a petition to terminate the parental rights of the parent who does not have custody of the child."

ent. I agree. However, this conclusion does not preclude further interpretation of sec. 48.81 to determine whether a child may be eligible for adoption in other circumstances in which the rights of only one parent have been terminated. If sec. 48.81 is construed utilizing the canon of liberal construction mandated by the legislature, a child may be eligible for adoption after the rights of only one parent have been terminated as long as the remaining legal parent supports the adoption. Such an adoption will still be subject to all of the additional statutory criteria. * * *

The third relevant statute is sec. 48.92, Stats., which provides in relevant part: "Effect of adoption. . . . (2) After the order of adoption is entered the relationship of parent and child between the adopted person and the adoptive person's birth parents, unless the birth parent is the spouse of the adoptive parent, shall be completely altered and all the rights, duties and other legal consequences of the relationship shall cease to exist." * * * Section 48.92 does not establish requirements that must be met in order for an adoption to occur; rather, it defines the legal status of the parties after the adoption has been approved. A court granting an adoption is not required to take any action to effectuate sec. 48.92. This court need not determine whether the statute is mandatory or directory because it is not a command but rather a definition of post-adoption status of the family that results from the adoption.

The majority construes the adoption statutes strictly, ignoring the legislatively-mandated canon of liberal construction and applying canons of its own choosing without providing any reasons for doing so. * * * Although strict construction of a statute is often seen as an exercise of judicial restraint, in the present case such construction is precisely the opposite and flouts the legislative will.

When interpreting sec. 48.81, governing who may be adopted, the majority employs the canon that a statute is not to be construed so as to work absurd or unreasonable results. [T]he majority concludes that if sec. 48.81 is interpreted to mean that a minor is eligible for adoption after the parental rights of only one parent have been terminated, then a child could be adopted by a second person even against the wishes of the child's present legal parent. * * * It seems highly unlikely that a court would find such an adoption to be in the best interests of the child. Moreover, such an adoption would undoubtedly be prohibited as a violation of the constitutionally protected liberty interest of the legal parent to control the upbringing of that parent's child.

The concurring opinion asks the legislature to act to protect the best interests of Wisconsin children. The concurrence rests on the faulty premise that the legislature has not spoken. As I have discussed at length, the legislature has provided guidance—each statutory provision is to be liberally construed to further the best interests of the child. The concurring opinion provides no explanation for the majority's decision to ignore the legislature's expressed direction in respect to construction of the adoption statutes.

I am authorized to state that Justices Shirley S. Abrahamson and Bablitch, join this dissenting opinion.

Bablitch, Justice (*dissenting*).

I join the dissenting opinion filed by Chief Justice Heffernan. Respectfully, I write only to address the concurring opinion which strongly urges the legislature to address this issue. My experience as a former member of the legislature tells me this: that will not happen.

In some legislation the legislature, recognizing that the future will bring issues to the fore that it cannot anticipate at the time of passage of the bill, meets its obligation to the future by placing the burden on the courts to deal with those issues consistent with its expressed intent. This is just such an issue. That is why the dissent by the Chief Justice is so very correct.

The Legislative Council highlighted the adoption statutes as just such legislation. The Council, in its notes to the bill, took great care to point out to the legislature that the proposed adoption legislation effected a major change in the area of future interpretation: that not only would the principle of best interest of the child remain but also that the principle of strict construction of the adoption statutes would be rejected in favor of liberal construction. * * * This was the "red flag" that told the legislature that if it adopted this legislation, future interpretation of even the thorniest of issues would be left to the courts, with the only canon being liberal construction in the best interests of the child.

**FYI**

The Legislative Council is a non-partisan legislative service agency of the Wisconsin Legislature. The Council provides legal advice and guidance to the legislature's standing committees and prepares legal and informational publications for members of the legislature and the public.

The legislature at times, as here, deliberately paints with a very broad and ambiguous brush. By design, it left the details to us, even the most controversial ones. We abdicate our responsibility by passing this back to the legislature, particularly when we know the likelihood of the legislature ever acting is minimal at best. The legislature, by being deliberately ambiguous, is telling the courts, "We will not because we cannot spell out in detail every conceivable situation that might arise in the future, particularly the very sensitive ones. Look to the best interests of the child when these situations arise." As the dissent eloquently points out, everybody agrees what the best interests are here.

---

## Points for Discussion

### *a. Statutory Language and Social Context*

When the Wisconsin legislature enacted the adoption standards at issue in *In the Interest of Angel Lace M.*, the state did not recognize same-sex marriages, and social norms strongly disapproved of same-sex relationships (and co-habitation between opposite-sex but unmarried partners). Over a period of decades, these social norms shifted. By the time that the court decided the case, cohabitation between unmarried partners was commonplace, and same-sex relationships were increasingly accepted. But the operative provisions of the state's adoption law remained largely static. To be sure, there were some changes, such as the recognition of step-parent adoptions (which became more common as the divorce rate increased) and the addition of provisions instructing courts to construe the statute liberally and to advance the best interests of the child. But the legislature had not amended the statute specifically to authorize adoption by a same-sex, unmarried partner of the biological parent. What should a court do when confronted with such a case?

### *b. Touchstones of Interpretation*

In addressing the petitioners' claims, on which touchstone of interpretation did the court rely? Did the court rely solely on the plain meaning of the terms in the statute? If so, did the court seek to understand the meaning of those terms from the perspective of the legislators who enacted them years earlier? And if so, is there a meaningful difference between seeking the "plain" or "ordinary" meaning of statutory text, on the one hand, and seeking the legislature's "intent," on the other? In thinking about this question, consider whether the dissent conceded that the text of the statute did *not* authorize the adoption at issue. Is it clear to you that a focus on the plain meaning of the statutory text requires the result that the majority reached?

How might a legal process approach have looked different from the court's (and the dissent's) approach? In most cases, the legal process approach requires the judge to discern the statute's broad purposes from the text and the context in which the legislature enacted the statute. But in this case, the Wisconsin statute included some explicit instructions about the legislature's goals. The statute provided that it should "be liberally construed to effect the objectives contained" in the statute, and it further instructed that the "best interests of the child shall always be of paramount consideration." Section 48.01(2), Stats. Must one adhere to the legal process school of interpretation in order to interpret such a statute to permit an adoption by a same-sex couple in a committed relationship?

Assume for a moment that the statute did not include section 48.01(2). Do you think that the statute's purposes are difficult to identify? What would an opinion interpreting the statute in light of its purposes have said?

In some cases, a focus on statutory purpose will result in the extension of a statutory right to persons that the enacting legislature did not think would benefit. This was (more or less) what happened in the Pennsylvania jury-eligibility case and what would have happened had the dissenters in the Wisconsin adoption case convinced one more Justice of their view of the statute. But sometimes a judicial focus on the purpose or spirit of a law will result in the *withholding* of a statutory benefit from persons or entities that the legislature probably assumed would benefit. Consider the case that follows.

---

## *Bob Jones University v. United States*

461 U.S. 574 (1983)

CHIEF JUSTICE BURGER delivered the opinion of the Court.

We granted certiorari to decide whether petitioners, nonprofit private schools that prescribe and enforce racially discriminatory admissions standards on the basis of religious doctrine, qualify as tax-exempt organizations under § 501(c)(3) of the Internal Revenue Code of 1954.

Until 1970, the Internal Revenue Service granted tax-exempt status to private schools, without regard to their racial admissions policies, under § 501(c)(3) of the Internal Revenue Code, 26 U.S.C. § 501(c)(3),[1] and granted charitable deductions for contributions to such schools under § 170 of the Code, 26 U.S.C. § 170.[2]

On January 12, 1970, a three-judge District Court for the District of Columbia [enjoined] the IRS from according tax-exempt status to private schools in Mississippi that discriminated as to admissions on the basis of race. *Green v. Kennedy*, 309 F. Supp. 1127 (D.D.C.), *app. dismissed sub nom. Cannon v. Green*, 398 U.S. 956 (1970). [In response, the IRS changed its policy to make clear that racially discriminatory private schools were not entitled to exemption under § 501(c)(3) and that donors were not entitled to deductions for contributions to such schools under § 170.]

The revised policy on discrimination was formalized in Revenue Ruling 71–447, 1971–2 Cum. Bull. 230:

---

1 Section 501(c)(3) lists the following organizations, which, pursuant to § 501(a), are exempt from taxation unless denied tax exemptions under other specified sections of the Code: "Corporations, and any community chest, fund, or foundation, *organized and operated exclusively for religious, charitable,* scientific, testing for public safety, literary, *or educational purposes* * * *." (Emphasis added).

2 Section 170(a) allows deductions for certain "charitable contributions." Section 170(c)(2)(B) includes within the definition of "charitable contribution" a contribution or gift to or for the use of a corporation "organized and operated exclusively for religious, charitable, scientific, literary, or educational purposes. . . ."

> "Both the courts and the Internal Revenue Service have long recognized that the statutory requirement of being 'organized and operated exclusively for religious, charitable, . . . or educational purposes' was intended to express the basic common law concept [of 'charity']. . . . All charitable trusts, educational or otherwise, are subject to the requirement that the purpose of the trust may not be illegal or contrary to public policy." *Id.,* at 230.

Based on the "national policy to discourage racial discrimination in education," the IRS ruled that "a private school not having a racially nondiscriminatory policy as to students is not 'charitable' within the common law concepts reflected in sections 170 and 501(c)(3) of the Code." *Id.,* at 231. The application of the IRS construction of these provisions to petitioners, two private schools with racially discriminatory admissions policies, is now before us.

Bob Jones University is a nonprofit corporation located in Greenville, South Carolina. Its purpose is "to conduct an institution of learning . . ., giving special emphasis to the Christian religion and the ethics revealed in the Holy Scriptures." [The University's] teachers are required to be devout Christians, and all courses at the University are taught according to the Bible. Entering students are screened as to their religious beliefs, and their public and private conduct is strictly regulated by standards promulgated by University authorities.

The sponsors of the University genuinely believe that the Bible forbids interracial dating and marriage. To effectuate these views, Negroes were completely excluded until 1971. From 1971 to May 1975, the University accepted no applications from unmarried Negroes, but did accept applications from Negroes married within their race. Following the decision of the United States Court of Appeals for the Fourth Circuit in *McCrary v. Runyon,* 515 F.2d 1082 (4th Cir. 1975), *aff'd* 427 U.S. 160 (1976), prohibiting racial exclusion from private schools, the University revised its policy. Since May 29, 1975, the University has permitted unmarried Negroes to enroll; but a disciplinary rule prohibits interracial dating and marriage. * * * The University continues to deny admission to applicants engaged in an interracial marriage or known to advocate interracial marriage or dating.

Until 1970, the IRS extended tax-exempt status to Bob Jones University under § 501(c)(3). [In 1976,] the IRS officially revoked the University's tax-exempt status, effective as of December 1, 1970, the day after the University was formally notified of the change in IRS policy. [The University challenged the IRS's determination that it was not entitled to tax-exempt status. The District Court held that the revocation of the University's tax-exempt status was unlawful, but the Court of Appeals reversed.]

In Revenue Ruling 71–447, the IRS formalized the policy first announced in 1970, that § 170 and § 501(c)(3) embrace the common law "charity" concept. Under that view, to qualify for a tax exemption pursuant to § 501(c)(3), an institution must show, first, that it falls within one of the eight categories expressly set forth in that section, and second, that its activity is not contrary to settled public policy.

Section 501(c)(3) provides that "[c]orporations . . . organized and operated exclusively for religious, charitable . . . or educational purposes" are entitled to tax exemption. Petitioners argue that the plain language of the statute guarantees them tax-exempt status. They emphasize the absence of any language in the statute expressly requiring all exempt organizations to be "charitable" in the common law sense, and they contend that the disjunctive "or" separating the categories in § 501(c)(3) precludes such a reading. Instead, they argue that if an institution falls within one or more of the specified categories it is automatically entitled to exemption, without regard to whether it also qualifies as "charitable." * * *

It is a well-established canon of statutory construction that a court should go beyond the literal language of a statute if reliance on that language would defeat the plain purpose of the statute * * *. Section 501(c)(3) therefore must be analyzed and construed within the framework of the Internal Revenue Code and against the background of the Congressional purposes. Such an examination reveals unmistakable evidence that, underlying all relevant parts of the Code, is the intent that entitlement to tax exemption depends on meeting certain common law standards of charity—namely, that an institution seeking tax-exempt status must serve a public purpose and not be contrary to established public policy.

This "charitable" concept appears explicitly in § 170 of the Code. That section contains a list of organizations virtually identical to that contained in § 501(c)(3). It is apparent that Congress intended that list to have the same meaning in both sections. In § 170, Congress used the list of organizations in defining the term "charitable contributions." On its face, therefore, § 170 reveals that Congress' intention was to provide tax benefits to organizations serving charitable purposes. The form of § 170 simply makes plain what common sense and history tell us: in enacting both § 170 and § 501(c)(3), Congress sought to provide tax benefits to charitable organizations, to encourage the development of private institutions that serve a useful public purpose or supplement or take the place of public institutions of the same kind.

Tax exemptions for certain institutions thought beneficial to the social order of the country as a whole, or to a particular community, are deeply rooted in our history, as in that of England. The origins of such exemptions lie in the special privileges that have long been extended to charitable trusts.[12]

---

12 The form and history of the charitable exemption and deduction sections of the various income tax acts reveal that Congress was guided by the common law of charitable trusts. See Simon, The Tax-Exempt Status of Racially Discriminatory Religious Schools, 36 Tax L. Rev. 477, 485–489 (1981). Congress acknowledged as much in 1969. The House Report on the Tax Reform Act of 1969, Pub. L. 91–172, 83 Stat. 487, stated that the § 501(c)(3) exemption was available only to institutions that served "the specified charitable purposes," H.R. Rep. No. 413 (Part 1), 91st Cong., 1st Sess. 35 (1969), and described "charitable" as "a term that has been used in the law of trusts for hundreds of years." *Id.*, at 43. * * *

More than a century ago, this Court [declared]: "[I]t has now become an established principle of American law, that courts of chancery will sustain and protect . . . a gift . . . to public charitable uses, *provided the same is consistent with local laws and public policy. . . .*" *Perin v. Carey*, 24 How. 465, 501 (1861) (emphasis added). Soon after that, in 1878, the Court commented: "A charitable use, *where neither law nor public policy forbids,* may be applied to almost any thing *that tends to promote the well-doing and well-being of social man.*" *Ould v. Washington Hospital for Foundlings*, 95 U.S. 303, 311 (1878) (emphasis added). * * * These statements clearly reveal the legal background against which Congress enacted the first charitable exemption statute in 1894: charities were to be given preferential treatment because they provide a benefit to society.

A corollary to the public benefit principle is the requirement, long recognized in the law of trusts, that the purpose of a charitable trust may not be illegal or violate established public policy. * * * When the Government grants exemptions or allows deductions all taxpayers are affected; the very fact of the exemption or deduction for the donor means that other taxpayers can be said to be indirect and vicarious "donors." Charitable exemptions are justified on the basis that the exempt entity confers a public benefit—a benefit which the society or the community may not itself choose or be able to provide, or which supplements and advances the work of public institutions already supported by tax revenues. History buttresses logic to make clear that, to warrant exemption under § 501(c)(3), an institution must fall within a category specified in that section and must demonstrably serve and be in harmony with the public interest. The institution's purpose must not be so at odds with the common community conscience as to undermine any public benefit that might otherwise be conferred.

We are bound to approach these questions with full awareness that determinations of public benefit and public policy are sensitive matters with serious implications for the institutions affected; a declaration that a given institution is not "charitable" should be made only where there can be no doubt that the activity involved is contrary to a fundamental public policy. But there can no longer be any doubt that racial discrimination in education violates deeply and widely accepted views of elementary justice. Prior to 1954, public education in many places still was conducted under the pall of *Plessy v. Ferguson*, 163 U.S. 537 (1896); racial segregation in primary and secondary education prevailed in many parts of the country.[20] This Court's decision

---

20 In 1894, when the first charitable exemption provision was enacted, racially segregated educational institutions would not have been regarded as against public policy. Yet contemporary standards must be considered in determining whether given activities provide a public benefit and are entitled to the charitable tax exemption. In *Walz v. Tax Comm'n*, 397 U.S. 664, 672–673 (1970), we observed: "Qualification for tax exemption is not perpetual or immutable; some tax-exempt groups lose that status when their activities take them outside the classification and new entities can come into being and qualify for the exemption." Charitable trust law also makes clear that the definition of "charity" depends upon contemporary standards. See, *e.g.*, Restatement (Second) of Trusts, § 374, comment a (1959).

in *Brown v. Board of Education*, 347 U.S. 483 (1954), signalled an end to that era. Over the past quarter of a century, every pronouncement of this Court and myriad Acts of Congress and Executive Orders attest a firm national policy to prohibit racial segregation and discrimination in public education.

An unbroken line of cases following *Brown v. Board of Education* establishes beyond doubt this Court's view that racial discrimination in education violates a most fundamental national public policy, as well as rights of individuals. "The right of a student not to be segregated on racial grounds in schools . . . is indeed so fundamental and pervasive that it is embraced in the concept of due process of law." *Cooper v. Aaron*, 358 U.S. 1, 19 (1958). In *Norwood v. Harrison*, 413 U.S. 455, 468–469 (1973), we dealt with a non-public institution: "[A] private school—even one that discriminates—fulfills an important educational function; *however, . . . [that] legitimate educational function cannot be isolated from discriminatory practices . . . [D]iscriminatory treatment exerts a pervasive influence on the entire educational process.*" (Emphasis added).

Congress, in Titles IV and VI of the Civil Rights Act of 1964, clearly expressed its agreement that racial discrimination in education violates a fundamental public policy. Other sections of that Act, and numerous enactments since then, testify to the public policy against racial discrimination. See, *e.g.*, the Voting Rights Act of 1965; Title VIII of the Civil Rights Act of 1968; the Emergency School Aid Act of 1972 [and 1978].

The Executive Branch has consistently placed its support behind eradication of racial discrimination. Several years before this Court's decision in *Brown v. Board of Education*, President Truman issued Executive Orders prohibiting racial discrimination in federal employment decisions, Exec. Order No. 9980, 3 CFR 720 (1943–1948 Comp.), and in classifications for the Selective Service, Exec. Order No. 9988, *id.* 726, 729. In 1957, President Eisenhower employed military forces to ensure compliance with federal standards in school desegregation programs. Exec. Order No. 10730, 3 CFR 389 (1954–1958 Comp.). And in 1962, President Kennedy announced: "[T]he granting of federal assistance for . . . housing and related facilities from which Americans are excluded because of their race, color, creed, or national origin is unfair, unjust, and inconsistent with the public policy of the United States as manifested in its Constitution and laws." Exec. Order No. 11063, 3 CFR 652 (1959–1963 Comp.). These are but a few of numerous Executive Orders over the past three decades demonstrating the commitment of the Executive Branch to the fundamental policy of eliminating racial discrimination.

Few social or political issues in our history have been more vigorously debated and more extensively ventilated than the issue of racial discrimination, particularly in education. * * * It would be wholly incompatible with the concepts underlying tax exemption to grant the benefit of tax-exempt status to racially discriminatory educational entities * * *. Whatever may be the rationale for such private schools' policies, and however sincere the rationale may be, racial discrimination in education is contrary to public policy. Racially discriminatory educational institutions cannot be viewed as conferring a public benefit within the "charitable" concept discussed earlier, or within the Congressional intent underlying § 170 and § 501(c)(3).

Petitioners contend that, regardless of whether the IRS properly concluded that racially discriminatory private schools violate public policy, only Congress can alter the scope of § 170 and § 501(c)(3). * * * Yet ever since the inception of the tax code, Congress has seen fit to vest in those administering the tax laws very broad authority to interpret those laws. * * * [T]his Court has long recognized the primary authority of the IRS and its predecessors in construing the Internal Revenue Code * * *. Congress, the source of IRS authority, can modify IRS rulings it considers improper * * *. In the first instance, however, the responsibility for construing the Code falls to the IRS.

The actions of Congress since 1970 leave no doubt that the IRS reached the correct conclusion in exercising its authority. * * * Ordinarily, and quite appropriately, courts are slow to attribute significance to the failure of Congress to act on particular legislation. * * * Here, however, we do not have an ordinary claim of legislative acquiescence. Only one month after the IRS announced its position in 1970, Congress held its first hearings on this precise issue. *Equal Educational Opportunity: Hearings Before the Senate Select Comm. on Equal Educational Opportunity*, 91st Cong., 2d Sess. 1991 (1970). Exhaustive hearings have been held on the issue at various times since then. These include hearings in February 1982, after we granted review in this case. *Administration's Change in Federal Policy Regarding the Tax Status of Racially Discriminatory Private Schools: Hearing Before the House Comm. on Ways and Means*, 97th Cong., 2d Sess. (1982).

Non-action by Congress is not often a useful guide, but the non-action here is significant. During the past 12 years there have been no fewer than 13 bills introduced to overturn the IRS interpretation of § 501(c)(3). Not one of these bills has emerged from any committee, although Congress has enacted numerous other amendments to § 501 during this same period, including an amendment to § 501(c)(3) itself. Tax Reform Act of 1976, Pub. L. 94–455, § 1313(a), 90 Stat. 1520, 1730 (1976). It is hardly conceivable that Congress—and in this setting, any Member of Congress—was not abundantly aware of what was going on. In view of its prolonged and acute awareness of so important an issue, Congress' failure to act on the bills proposed on this subject provides added support for concluding that Congress acquiesced in the IRS rulings of 1970 and 1971.

The evidence of Congressional approval of the policy embodied in Revenue Ruling 71–447 goes well beyond the failure of Congress to act on legislative proposals. Congress affirmatively manifested its acquiescence in the IRS policy when it enacted the present § 501(i) of the Code, Act of October 20, 1976, Pub. L. 94–568, 90 Stat. 2697 (1976). That provision denies tax-exempt status to social clubs whose charters or policy statements provide for "discrimination against any person on the basis of race, color, or religion." Both the House and Senate committee reports on that bill articulated the national policy against granting tax exemptions to racially discriminatory private clubs. S. Rep. No. 1318, 94th Cong., 2d Sess., 8 (1976); H.R. Rep. No. 1353, 94th Cong., 2d Sess., 8 (1976).

Even more significant is the fact that both reports focus on this Court's affirmance of *Green v. Connally* as having established that "discrimination on account of race is inconsistent with an *educational institution's* tax exempt status." S. Rep. No. 1318, *supra,* at 7–8 and n. 5; H.R. Rep. No. 1353, *supra,* at 8 and n. 5 (emphasis added). These references in Congressional committee reports on an enactment denying tax exemptions to racially discriminatory private social clubs cannot be read other than as indicating approval of the standards applied to racially discriminatory private schools by the IRS subsequent to 1970, and specifically of Revenue Ruling 71–447.

Petitioners contend that, even if the Commissioner's policy is valid as to nonreligious private schools, that policy cannot constitutionally be applied to schools that engage in racial discrimination on the basis of sincerely held religious beliefs. As to such schools, it is argued that the IRS construction of § 170 and § 501(c)(3) violates their free exercise rights under the Religion Clauses of the First Amendment. * * * [The Court concluded that the IRS's policy did not violate the Constitution.] *Affirmed.*

[Justice Powell's opinion concurring in part and concurring in the judgment has been omitted.]

Justice Rehnquist, dissenting.

The Court points out that there is a strong national policy in this country against racial discrimination. To the extent that the Court states that Congress in furtherance of this policy could deny tax-exempt status to educational institutions that promote racial discrimination, I readily agree. But, unlike the Court, I am convinced that Congress simply has failed to take this action and, as this Court has said over and over again, regardless of our view on the propriety of Congress' failure to legislate we are not constitutionally empowered to act for them.

In approaching this statutory construction question the Court quite adeptly avoids the statute it is construing. This I am sure is no accident, for there is nothing in the language of § 501(c)(3) that supports the result obtained by the Court. * * * With undeniable clarity, Congress has explicitly defined the requirements for § 501(c)(3) status. An entity must be (1) a corporation, or community chest, fund, or foundation, (2) organized for one of the eight enumerated purposes, (3) operated on a nonprofit basis, and (4) free from involvement in lobbying activities and political campaigns. Nowhere is there to be found some additional, undefined public policy requirement.

The Court first seeks refuge from the obvious reading of § 501(c)(3) by turning to § 170 * * * which provides a tax deduction for contributions made to § 501(c)(3) organizations. In setting forth the general rule, § 170 states: "There shall be allowed as a deduction any charitable contribution * * * payment of which is made within the taxable year. * * *" 26 U.S.C. § 170(a)(1). The Court seizes the words "charitable contribution" and with little discussion concludes that "[o]n its face, therefore, § 170 reveals that Congress' intention was to provide tax benefits to organizations serving charitable purposes," intimating that this implies some unspecified common law charitable trust requirement.

The Court would have been well advised to look to subsection (c) where, as § 170(a)(1) indicates, Congress has defined a "charitable contribution" * * *. Plainly, § 170(c) simply tracks the requirements set forth in § 501(c)(3). Since § 170 is no more than a mirror of § 501(c)(3) and § 170 followed § 501(c)(3) by more than two decades, it is at best of little usefulness in finding the meaning of § 501(c)(3).

[The Court concludes that] Congress intended that an organization seeking § 501(c)(3) status "must fall within a category specified in that section *and must demonstrably serve and be in harmony with the public interest.*" To the contrary, I think that the legislative history of § 501(c)(3) unmistakably makes clear that *Congress has decided* what organizations are serving a public purpose and providing a public benefit within the meaning of § 501(c)(3) and has clearly set forth in § 501(c)(3) the characteristics of such organizations. In fact, there are few examples which better illustrate Congress' effort to define and redefine the requirements of a legislative act.

**FYI**

Congress first conferred tax-exempt status on charitable organizations in 1894 and first permitted the deduction of contributions to charitable organizations in 1917.

The first general income tax law was passed by Congress in the form of the Tariff Act of 1894. A provision of that Act provided an exemption for "corporations, companies, or associations organized and conducted solely for charitable, religious, or educational purposes." Ch. 349, § 32, 28 Stat. 509, 556 (1894). The income tax portion of the 1894 Act was held unconstitutional by this Court, see *Pollock v. Farmers' Loan & Trust Co.*, 158 U.S. 601 (1895), but a similar exemption appeared in the Tariff Act of 1909 which imposed a tax on corporate income. The 1909 Act provided an exemption for "any corporation or association organized and operated exclusively for religious, charitable, or educational purposes, no part of the net income of which inures to the benefit of any private stockholder or individual." Ch. 6, § 38, 36 Stat. 11, 113 (1909).

With the ratification of the Sixteenth Amendment, Congress again turned its attention to an individual income tax with the Tariff Act of 1913. And again, in the direct predecessor of § 501(c)(3), a tax exemption was provided for "any corporation or association organized and operated exclusively for religious, charitable, scientific, or educational purposes, no part of the net income of which inures to the benefit of any private stockholder or individual." Ch. 16, § II(G)(a), 38 Stat. 114, 172 (1913).

In subsequent acts Congress continued to broaden the list of exempt purposes. The Revenue Act of 1918 added an exemption for corporations or associations organized "for the prevention of cruelty to children or animals." Ch. 18, § 231(6), 40 Stat. 1057, 1076 (1918). The Revenue Act of 1921 expanded the groups to which the exemption applied to include "any community chest, fund, or foundation" and added "literary" endeavors to the list of exempt purposes. Ch. 136, § 231(6), 42 Stat. 227, 253 (1921). * * * In the Revenue Act of 1934 Congress added the requirement that no substantial part of the activities of any exempt organization can involve the carrying on of "propaganda" or "attempting to influence legislation." Ch. 277, § 101(6), 48 Stat. 680, 700 (1934). * * *

The tax laws were overhauled by the Internal Revenue Code of 1939, but this exemption was left unchanged. Ch. 1, § 101(6), 53 Stat. 1, 33 (1939). When the 1939 Code was replaced with the Internal Revenue Code of 1954, the exemption was adopted in full in the present § 501(c)(3) with the addition of "testing for public safety" as an exempt purpose and an additional restriction that tax-exempt organizations could not "participate in, or intervene in (including the publishing or distributing of statements), any political campaign on behalf of any candidate for public office." Ch. 1, § 501(c)(3), 68A Stat. 1, 163 (1954). Then in 1976 the statute was again amended adding to the purposes for which an exemption would be authorized, "to foster national or international amateur sports competition," provided the activities did not involve the provision of athletic facilities or equipment. Tax Reform Act of 1976, Pub. L. No. 94–455, § 1313(a), 90 Stat. 1520, 1730 (1976).

One way to read the opinion handed down by the Court today leads to the conclusion that this long and arduous refining process of § 501(c)(3) was certainly a waste of time, for when enacting the original 1894 statute Congress intended to adopt a common law term of art, and intended that this term of art carry with it all of the common law baggage which defines it. Such a view, however, leads also to the unsupportable idea that Congress has spent almost a century adding illustrations simply to clarify an already defined common law term.

Another way to read the Court's opinion leads to the conclusion that even though Congress has set forth *some* of the requirements of a § 501(c)(3) organization, it intended that the IRS additionally require that organizations meet a higher standard of public interest, not stated by Congress, but to be determined and defined by the IRS and the courts. This view I find equally unsupportable. Almost a century of statutory history proves that Congress itself intended to decide what § 501(c)(3) requires. * * *

Perhaps recognizing the lack of support in the statute itself, or in its history, for the 1970 IRS change in interpretation, the Court finds that "[t]he actions of Congress since 1970 leave no doubt that the IRS reached the correct conclusion in exercising its authority," concluding that there is "an unusually strong case of legislative acquiescence in and ratification by implication of the 1970 and 1971 rulings." The Court relies first on several bills introduced to overturn the IRS interpretation of

§ 501(c)(3). But we have said before, and it is equally applicable here, that this type of congressional inaction is of virtually no weight in determining legislative intent. See *United States v. Wise*, 370 U.S. 405, 411 (1962); *Waterman Steamship Corp. v. United States*, 381 U.S. 252, 269 (1965). These bills and related hearings indicate little more than that a vigorous debate has existed in Congress concerning the new IRS position.

The Court next asserts that "Congress affirmatively manifested its acquiescence in the IRS policy when it enacted the present § 501(i) of the Code," a provision that "denies tax exempt status to social clubs whose charters or policy statements provide for" racial discrimination. Quite to the contrary, it seems to me that in § 501(i) Congress showed that when it wants to add a requirement prohibiting racial discrimination to one of the tax-benefit provisions, it is fully aware of how to do it.

This Court continuously has been hesitant to find ratification through inaction. This is especially true where such a finding "would result in a construction of the statute which not only is at odds with the language of the section in question and the pattern of the statute taken as a whole, but also is extremely far reaching in terms of the virtually untrammeled and unreviewable power it would vest in a regulatory agency." *SEC v. Sloan*, 436 U.S. 103, 121 (1978). Few cases would call for more caution in finding ratification by acquiescence than the present one. The new IRS interpretation is not only far less than a long standing administrative policy, it is at odds with a position maintained by the IRS, and unquestioned by Congress, for several decades prior to 1970. The interpretation is unsupported by the statutory language, it is unsupported by legislative history, the interpretation has lead to considerable controversy in and out of Congress, and the interpretation gives to the IRS a broad power which until now Congress had kept for itself. Where in addition to these circumstances Congress has shown time and time again that it is ready to enact positive legislation to change the tax code when it desires, this Court has no business finding that Congress has adopted the new IRS position by failing to enact legislation to reverse it.

I have no disagreement with the Court's finding that there is a strong national policy in this country opposed to racial discrimination. I agree with the Court that Congress has the power to further this policy by denying § 501(c)(3) status to organizations that practice racial discrimination. But as of yet Congress has failed to do so. Whatever the reasons for the failure, this Court should not legislate for Congress.

---

## Points for Discussion

### *a. The Spirit of the Law*

The Court declared that "a court should go beyond the literal language of a statute if reliance on that language would defeat the plain purpose of the statute," and reasoned that Section 501(c)(3) "therefore must be analyzed and construed within the framework of the Internal Revenue Code and against the background of the Congressional purposes." How did the Court determine what those purposes were? Is it a problem for the Court's approach that most members of the Congress that enacted the provision at issue probably didn't think that it would exclude educational institutions with discriminatory policies?

***b. The Letter of the Law***

Justice Rehnquist asserted in dissent that, with "undeniable clarity, Congress has explicitly defined the requirements for § 501(c)(3) status." Do you agree with him that the terms in section 501(c)(3), read in context, plainly exclude a "public policy" requirement for tax-exempt status? If so, is there nevertheless a justification for reading the statute to impose such a requirement?

---

## C. Plain Meaning and the Rise of Textualism

We have now seen many examples of cases where there were strong arguments for why courts should depart from the plain meaning of the statutory text. In some cases, there was evidence that the legislature did not intend the particular result that strict adherence to statutory text would produce; in others, fidelity to the text would have produced results in tension with the statute's apparent purposes.

But in each of those cases, the court seemed to proceed from the premise that *ordinarily* the plain meaning of the statutory text governs. In *Bob Jones University*, for example, Chief Justice Burger stated that "a court should go beyond the literal language of a statute *if* reliance on that language would defeat the plain purpose of the statute" (emphasis added), implying that, absent such circumstances, the literal language controls.

This premise likely seems uncontroversial to you. When you first read the "no vehicles in the park" ordinance, you probably began by thinking about what the word "vehicle" means. Similarly, if you are looking for a place to park your car, you would likely not park it right next to a "No Parking" sign, because you would assume that the plain language of the sign governs. Statutes are expressed in words; if we could ignore the plain meaning of those words, then statutes would not be binding or authoritative. When judges confront statutes written in clear, plain terms, it seems uncontroversial to say that they should be bound by the plain meaning of the words, too. In most cases, we assume that the letter of the law controls.

To be sure, we have seen cases in which the letter and the spirit of the law appear to be in conflict. For example, perhaps you would park next to a "No Parking" sign if it were in front of a hospital, and your pregnant friend in the back seat was in labor—and perhaps there is a plausible argument that, under those circumstances, you have not violated the law. We have already explored the reasons why a court might choose to depart from the letter of the law in such cases.

Such conflicts between the letter and the spirit of the law, however, are relatively rare. In most cases, the letter of the law governs. For example, even though there is some ambiguity about its reach, the "no vehicles in the park" law presumably would prohibit you from driving your car through the park because you did not feel like walking from the entrance to the basketball courts. But courts are rarely called upon to construe statutes in such cases; parties are not likely to bear the cost of litigating questions that have obvious answers. Instead, courts tend to decide cases in which there are plausible arguments on both sides about the meaning of the statute.

As long we have lawyers (especially lawyers who have studied legislation and regulation), courts will be asked to decide when the letter of the law should yield to the spirit of the law. The question that we turn to now is just how frequently courts should accept such invitations. Are there reasons to enforce the plain meaning of a law *even when* it would produce surprising or seemingly unjust results—and even when it is difficult to believe that the legislature could have intended such a result?

Although approaches based on legislative intent were prominent in the late-nineteenth and early-twentieth century, and approaches based on statutory purpose were dominant in the middle of the twentieth century, a focus on the plain meaning of statutory text also has deep roots in our legal system. We have already seen judges who have expressed that view; recall the Court's opinion in *Caminetti*, Judge Gray's dissent in *Riggs*, Justice Rehnquist's dissent in *Bob Jones University*, and the fictional Justice Keen's opinion in the *Case of the Speluncean Explorers*.

In the 1970s and 1980s, a growing number of judges indicated discomfort with approaches based on legislative intent or purpose. They urged instead an approach that focuses on the plain meaning of statutory text. Consider the cases that follow.

---

## *Tennessee Valley Authority v. Hill*

437 U.S. 153 (1978)

MR. CHIEF JUSTICE BURGER delivered the opinion of the Court.

[In 1967, the Tennessee Valley Authority, a wholly owned public corporation of the United States, began constructing the Tellico Dam and Reservoir Project using funds that Congress appropriated for that purpose. The project was designed to generate electricity for local residents, provide flood control, and improve economic conditions in a poor area. Six years later, Congress enacted the Endangered Species

Act of 1973. Section 7 of the Act, 16 U.S.C. § 1536, provides that all federal agencies shall "insure that actions authorized, funded, or carried out by them do not jeopardize the continued existence of . . . endangered species" or "result in the destruction or modification of habitat of such species."

The construction of the dam would result in the flooding of a portion of the Little Tennessee River. But that portion of the river was believed to be the only remaining habitat of the snail darter, a small fish. Nevertheless, the TVA continued work on the project, and Congress continued to appropriate funds for its construction. In 1975, as the TVA was nearing completion of the project, the Secretary of the Interior acted pursuant to Section 4 of the Endangered Species Act, 16 U.S.C. § 1533, to designate the snail darter as an endangered species. The Secretary determined that the snail darter lived only in the portion of the Little Tennessee River that would be completely flooded by the Tellico Dam and Reservoir Project, and that the flooding would result in the total destruction of the snail darter's habitat. In a lawsuit asserting that the project would violate the Endangered Species Act, the District Court concluded that the completion of the project wouldn't violate the Act, but the Court of Appeals enjoined continued work on the project. The Supreme Court began "with the premise that operation of the Tellico Dam will either eradicate the known population of snail darters or destroy their critical habitat."]

It may seem curious to some that the survival of a relatively small number of three-inch fish among all the countless millions of species extant would require the permanent halting of a virtually completed dam for which Congress has expended more than $100 million. The paradox is not minimized by the fact that Congress continued to appropriate large sums of public money for the project, even after congressional Appropriations Committees were apprised of its apparent impact upon the survival of the snail darter. We conclude, however, that the explicit provisions of the Endangered Species Act require precisely that result.

One would be hard pressed to find a statutory provision whose terms were any plainer than those in § 7 of the Endangered Species Act. Its very words affirmatively command all federal agencies "to *insure* that actions *authorized, funded,* or *carried out* by them do not *jeopardize* the continued existence" of an endangered species or "*result* in the destruction or modification of habitat of such species . . . ." 16 U.S.C. § 1536 (1976 ed.). (Emphasis added.) This language admits of no exception. Nonetheless, petitioner urges, as do the dissenters, that the Act cannot reasonably be interpreted as applying to a federal project which was well under way when Congress passed the Endangered Species Act of 1973. To sustain that position, however, we would be forced to ignore the ordinary meaning of plain language. It has not been shown, for example, how TVA can close the gates of the Tellico Dam without "carrying out" an action that has been "authorized" and "funded" by a federal agency. Nor can we understand how such action will "*insure*" that the snail darter's habitat is not disrupted.[18] Accepting the Secretary's determinations, as we must, it is clear that TVA's proposed operation of the dam will have precisely the opposite effect, namely the *eradication* of an endangered species.

Concededly, this view of the Act will produce results requiring the sacrifice of the anticipated benefits of the project and of many millions of dollars in public funds. But examination of the language, history, and structure of the legislation under review here indicates beyond doubt that Congress intended endangered species to be afforded the highest of priorities.

When Congress passed the Act in 1973, it was not legislating on a clean slate. The first major congressional concern for the preservation of the endangered species had come with passage of the Endangered Species Act of 1966, 80 Stat. 926, repealed, 87 Stat. 903. In that legislation Congress gave the Secretary power to identify "the names of the species of native fish and wildlife found to be threatened with extinction," § 1(c), 80 Stat. 926, as well as authorization to purchase land for the conservation, protection, restoration, and propagation of "selected species" of "native fish and wildlife" threatened with extinction. §§ 2(a)–(c), 80 Stat. 926–927. Declaring the preservation of endangered species a national policy, the 1966 Act directed all federal agencies both to protect these species and *"insofar as is practicable and consistent with the[ir] primary purposes,"* § 1(b), 80 Stat. 926, "preserve the habitats of such threatened species on lands under their jurisdiction." *Ibid.* (Emphasis added.) The 1966 statute was not a sweeping prohibition on the taking of endangered species, however, except on federal lands, § 4(c), 80 Stat. 928, and even in those federal areas the Secretary was authorized to allow the hunting and fishing of endangered species. § 4(d)(1), 80 Stat. 928.

In 1969 Congress enacted the Endangered Species Conservation Act, 83 Stat. 275, repealed, 87 Stat. 903, which continued the provisions of the 1966 Act while at the same time broadening federal involvement in the preservation of endangered species. Under the 1969 legislation, the Secretary was empowered to list species "threatened with worldwide extinction," § 3(a), 83 Stat. 275; in addition, the impor-

---

18 In dissent, Mr. Justice POWELL argues that the meaning of "actions" in § 7 is "far from 'plain,' " and that "it seems evident that the 'actions' referred to are not all actions that an agency can ever take, but rather actions that the agency is *deciding whether* to authorize, to fund, or to carry out." Aside from this bare assertion, however, no explanation is given to support the proffered interpretation. This recalls Lewis Carroll's [classic] advice on the construction of language: " 'When *I* use a word,' Humpty Dumpty said, in rather a scornful tone, 'it means just what *I* choose it to mean—neither more nor less.' " Through the Looking Glass, in The Complete Works of Lewis Carroll 196 (1939). Aside from being unexplicated, the dissent's reading of § 7 is flawed on several counts. First, under its view, the words "or carry out" in § 7 would be superfluous since all prospective actions of an agency remain to be "authorized" or "funded." Second, the dissent's position logically means that an agency would be obligated to comply with § 7 only when a project is in the planning stage. But if Congress had meant to so limit the Act, it surely would have used words to that effect, as it did in the National Environmental Policy Act, 42 U.S.C. §§ 4332(2)(A), (C).

tation of any species so recognized into the United States was prohibited. § 2, 83 Stat. 275. * * *

Despite the fact that the 1966 and 1969 legislation represented "the most comprehensive of its type to be enacted by any nation" up to that time, Congress was soon persuaded that a more expansive approach was needed if the newly declared national policy of preserving endangered species was to be realized. By 1973, when Congress held hearings on what would later become the Endangered Species Act of 1973, it was informed that species were still being lost at the rate of about one per year, 1973 House Hearings 306 (statement of Stephen R. Seater, for Defenders of Wildlife), and "the pace of disappearance of species" appeared to be "accelerating." H.R. Rep. No. 93–412, p. 4 (1973). Moreover, Congress was also told that the primary cause of this trend was something other than the normal process of natural selection: "[M]an and his technology [have] continued at any ever-increasing rate to disrupt the natural ecosystem. * * *" 1973 House Hearings 202 (statement of Assistant Secretary of the Interior).

The legislative proceedings in 1973 are * * * replete with expressions of concern over the risk that might lie in the loss of *any* endangered species. Typifying these sentiments is the Report of the House Committee on Merchant Marine and Fisheries on H.R. 37, a bill which contained the essential features of the subsequently enacted Act of 1973; in explaining the need for the legislation, the Report stated:

> "As we homogenize the habitats in which these plants and animals evolved, and as we increase the pressure for products that they are in a position to supply (usually unwillingly) we threaten their—and our own—genetic heritage. The value of this genetic heritage is, quite literally, incalculable. From the most narrow possible point of view, *it is in the best interests of mankind to minimize the losses of genetic variations.* The reason is simple: they are potential resources. * * * Who knows, or can say, what potential cures for cancer or other scourges, present or future, may lie locked up in the structures of plants which may yet be undiscovered, much less analyzed? . . . Sheer self-interest impels us to be cautious. *The institutionalization of that caution* lies at the heart of H.R. 37 . . . ." H.R. Rep. No. 93–412, pp. 4–5 (1973). (Emphasis added.)

As the examples cited here demonstrate, Congress was concerned about the *unknown* uses that endangered species might have and about the *unforeseeable* place such creatures may have in the chain of life on this planet.

In shaping legislation to deal with the problem thus presented, Congress started from the finding that "[t]he two major causes of extinction are hunting and destruction of natural habitat." S. Rep. No. 93–307, p. 2 (1973). Of these twin threats, Congress was informed that the greatest was destruction of natural habitats; see 1973 House Hearings 236 (statement of Associate Deputy Chief for National Forest System, Dept. of Agriculture) * * *. Virtually every bill introduced in Congress during the 1973 session responded to this concern by incorporating language similar, if not identical, to that found in the present § 7 of the Act. These provisions were designed, in the words of an administration witness, "for the first time [to] *prohibit* [a] federal agency from taking action which does jeopardize the status of endangered species," Hearings on S. 1592 and S. 1983 before the Subcommittee on Environment of the Senate Committee on Commerce, 93d Cong., 1st Sess., 68 (1973) (statement of Deputy Assistant Secretary of the Interior) (emphasis added); furthermore, the proposed bills would "*direc[t]* all . . . Federal agencies to utilize their authorities for carrying out programs *for the protection* of endangered animals." 1973 House Hearings 205 (statement of Assistant Secretary of the Interior). (Emphasis added.)

As it was finally passed, the Endangered Species Act of 1973 represented the most comprehensive legislation for the preservation of endangered species ever enacted by any nation. Its stated purposes were "to provide a means whereby the ecosystems upon which endangered species and threatened species depend may be conserved," and "to provide a program for the conservation of such . . . species . . . ." 16 U.S.C. § 1531(b) (1976 ed.). In furtherance of these goals, Congress expressly stated in § 2(c) that "all Federal departments and agencies *shall* seek *to conserve endangered species* and threatened species . . . ." 16 U.S.C. § 1531(c) (1976 ed.). (Emphasis added.) Lest there be any ambiguity as to the meaning of this statutory directive, the Act specifically defined "conserve" as meaning "to use and the use of *all methods and procedures which are necessary* to bring *any endangered species or threatened species* to the point at which the measures provided pursuant to this chapter are no longer necessary." § 1532(2). (Emphasis added.) Aside from § 7, other provisions indicated the seriousness with which Congress viewed this issue: Virtually all dealings with endangered species, including taking, possession, transportation, and sale, were prohibited, 16 U.S.C. § 1538 (1976 ed.), except in extremely narrow circumstances, see § 1539(b). The Secretary was also given extensive power to develop regulations and programs for the preservation of endangered and threatened species. § 1533(d). Citizen involvement was encouraged by the Act, with provisions allowing interested persons to petition the Secretary to list a species as endangered or threatened, § 1533(c)(2), and bring civil suits in United States district courts to force compliance with any provision of the Act, §§ 1540(c) and (g).

Section 7 of the Act * * * provides a particularly good gauge of congressional intent. As we have seen, this provision had its genesis in the Endangered Species Act of 1966, but that legislation qualified the obligation of federal agencies by stating that they should seek to preserve endangered species only "*insofar as is practicable and consistent with the[ir] primary purposes* . . . ." Likewise, every bill introduced in 1973 contained a qualification similar to that found in the earlier statutes. * * * This type of language did not go unnoticed by those advocating strong endangered species legislation. A representative of the Sierra Club, for example, attacked the use of the phrase "consistent with the primary purpose" in proposed H.R. 4758, cautioning that the qualification "could be construed to be a declaration of congressional policy that other agency purposes are necessarily more important than protection of endangered species and would always prevail if conflict were to occur." 1973 House Hearings 335 (statement of the chairman of the Sierra Club's National Wildlife Committee); see *id.*, at 251 (statement for the National Audubon Society).

What is very significant in this sequence is that the final version of the 1973 Act carefully omitted all of the reservations described above. In the bill which the Senate initially approved (S. 1983), however, the version of the current § 7 merely required federal agencies to "carry out such programs *as are practicable* for the protection of species listed . . . ." S. 1983, § 7(a). (Emphasis added.) By way of contrast, the bill that originally passed the House, H.R. 37, contained a provision which was essentially a mirror image of the subsequently passed § 7—indeed all phrases which might have qualified an agency's responsibilities had been omitted from the bill. In explaining the expected impact of this provision in H.R. 37 on federal agencies, the House Committee's Report states:

> "This subsection *requires* the Secretary and the heads of all other Federal departments and agencies to use their authorities in order to carry out programs for the protection of endangered species, and it further *requires* that those agencies take *the necessary action* that will *not jeopardize* the continuing existence of endangered species or result in the destruction of critical habitat of those species." H.R. Rep. No. 93–412, p. 14 (1973). (Emphasis added.)

Resolution of this difference in statutory language, as well as other variations between the House and Senate bills, was the task of a Conference Committee. See 119 Cong. Rec. 30174–30175, 31183 (1973). The * * * conferees rejected the Senate version of § 7 and adopted the stringent, mandatory language in H.R. 37. While the Conference Report made no specific reference to this choice of provisions, the House manager of the bill, Representative Dingell, provided an interpretation of what the Conference bill would require, making it clear that the mandatory provisions of § 7 were not casually or inadvertently included:

> "[Section 7] substantially amplifie[s] the obligation of [federal agencies] to take steps within their power to carry out the purposes of this act. A recent article . . . illustrates the problem which might occur absent this new language in the bill. It appears that the whooping cranes of this country, perhaps the best known of our endangered species, are being threatened by Air Force bombing activities along the gulf coast of Texas. Under existing law, the Secretary of Defense has some discretion as to whether or not he will take the necessary action to see that this threat disappears . . . . [O]nce the bill is enacted, [the Secretary of Defense] *would be required to take the proper steps.* * * * The purposes of the bill included the conservation of the species and of the ecosystems upon which they depend, and *every agency of government is committed* to see that those purposes are carried out. . . . [T]he agencies of Government can no longer plead that they can do nothing about it. *They can, and they must. The law is clear.*" 119 Cong. Rec. 42913 (1973). (Emphasis added.)

It is against this legislative background[29] that we must measure TVA's claim that the Act was not intended to stop operation of a project which, like Tellico Dam, was near completion when an endangered species was discovered in its path. While there is no discussion in the legislative history of precisely this problem, the totality of congressional action makes it abundantly clear that the result we reach today is wholly in accord with both the words of the statute and the intent of Congress. The plain intent of Congress in enacting this statute was to halt and reverse the trend toward species extinction, whatever the cost. * * *

It is not for us to speculate, much less act, on whether Congress would have altered its stance had the specific events of this case been anticipated. In any event, we discern no hint in the deliberations of Congress relating to the 1973 Act that would compel a different result than we reach here. Indeed, the repeated expressions of congressional concern over what it saw as the potentially enormous danger presented by the eradication of *any* endangered species suggest how the balance would have been struck had the issue been presented to Congress in 1973.

Furthermore, it is clear Congress foresaw that § 7 would, on occasion, require agencies to alter ongoing projects in order to fulfill the goals of the Act. Congressman Dingell's discussion of Air Force practice bombing, for instance, obviously pinpoints a particular activity—intimately related to the national defense—which a major federal department would be obliged to alter in deference to the strictures of § 7. A similar example is provided by the House Committee Report:

> "Under the authority of [§ 7], the Director of the Park Service would be required *to conform the practices of his agency* to the need for protecting the rapidly dwindling stock of grizzly bears within Yellowstone Park * * *, *by curtailing the destruction of habitat by clearcutting National Forests surrounding the Park*, and by preventing hunting until their numbers have recovered sufficiently to withstand these pressures." H.R. Rep. No. 93–412, p. 14 (1973). (Emphasis added.)

Notwithstanding Congress' expression of intent in 1973, we are urged to find that the continuing appropriations for Tellico Dam constitute an implied repeal of the 1973 Act, at least insofar as it applies to the Tellico Project. In support of this view, TVA points to the statements found in various House and Senate Appropriations Committees' Reports [that] generally reflected the attitude of the *Committees* either that the Act did not apply to Tellico or that the dam should be completed regardless of the provisions of the Act. Since we are unwilling to assume that these latter Committee statements constituted advice to ignore the provisions of a duly enacted law, we assume that these Committees believed that the Act simply was not applicable

29 When confronted with a statute which is plain and unambiguous on its face, we ordinarily do not look to legislative history as a guide to its meaning. *Ex parte Collett*, 337 U.S. 55, 61 (1949). Here it is not *necessary* to look beyond the words of the statute. We have undertaken such an analysis only to meet Mr. Justice POWELL's suggestion that the "absurd" result reached in this case is not in accord with congressional intent.

in this situation. But even under this interpretation of the Committees' actions, we are unable to conclude that the Act has been in any respect amended or repealed.

There is nothing in the appropriations measures, as passed, which states that the Tellico Project was to be completed irrespective of the requirements of the Endangered Species Act. These appropriations, in fact, represented relatively minor components of the lump-sum amounts for the *entire* TVA budget. To find a repeal of the Endangered Species Act under these circumstances would surely do violence to the "cardinal rule . . . that repeals by implication are not favored." *Morton v. Mancari*, 417 U.S. 535, 549 (1974). * * *

The doctrine disfavoring repeals by implication "applies with full vigor when . . . the subsequent legislation is an *appropriations* measure." *Committee for Nuclear Responsibility v. Seaborg*, 463 F.2d 783, 785 (1971) (emphasis added). This is perhaps an understatement since it would be more accurate to say that the policy applies with even *greater* force when the claimed repeal rests solely on an Appropriations Act. We recognize that both substantive enactments and appropriations measures are "Acts of Congress," but the latter have the limited and specific purpose of providing funds for authorized programs. When voting on appropriations measures, legislators are entitled to operate under the assumption that the funds will be devoted to purposes which are lawful and not for any purpose forbidden. Without such an assurance, every appropriations measure would be pregnant with prospects of altering substantive legislation, repealing by implication any prior statute which might prohibit the expenditure. Not only would this lead to the absurd result of requiring Members to review exhaustively the background of every authorization before voting on an appropriation, but it would flout the very rules the Congress carefully adopted to avoid this need. House Rule XXI(2), for instance, specifically provides: "No [provision in any general appropriation bill] or amendment thereto changing existing law [shall] be in order." See also Standing Rules of the Senate, Rule 16.4. Thus, to sustain petitioner's position, we would be obliged to assume that Congress meant to repeal *pro tanto* § 7 of the Act by means of a procedure expressly prohibited under the rules of Congress.

**Definition**

*Pro tanto* is a Latin phrase that means "to such an extent."

[W]e are urged to view the Endangered Species Act "reasonably," and hence shape a remedy "that accords with some modicum of common sense and the public weal." But is that our function? We have no expert knowledge on the subject of endangered species, much less do we have a mandate from the people to strike a balance of equities on the side of the Tellico Dam. Congress has spoken in the plainest of words, making it abundantly clear that the balance has been struck in favor of affording endangered species the highest of priorities, thereby adopting a policy which it described as "institutionalized caution." * * * [I]n our constitutional system the commitment to the separation of powers is too fundamental for us to pre-empt congressional action by judicially decreeing what accords with "common sense and the public weal." Our Constitution vests such responsibilities in the political branches. *Affirmed.*

MR. JUSTICE POWELL, with whom MR. JUSTICE BLACKMUN joins, dissenting.

In my view § 7 cannot reasonably be interpreted as applying to a project that is completed or substantially completed when its threat to an endangered species is discovered. Nor can I believe that Congress could have intended this Act to produce the "absurd result"—in the words of the District Court—of this case. If it were clear from the language of the Act and its legislative history that Congress intended to authorize this result, this Court would be compelled to enforce it. It is not our province to rectify policy or political judgments by the Legislative Branch, however egregiously they may disserve the public interest. But where the statutory language and legislative history, as in this case, need not be construed to reach such a result, I view it as the duty of this Court to adopt a permissible construction that accords with some modicum of common sense and the public weal.

In 1966, Congress authorized and appropriated initial funds for the construction by the Tennessee Valley Authority (TVA) of the Tellico Dam and Reservoir Project on the Little Tennessee River in eastern Tennessee. * * * Construction began in 1967, and Congress has voted funds for the project in every year since. In August 1973, when the Tellico Project was half completed, a new species of fish known as the snail darter was discovered in the portion of the Little Tennessee River that would be impounded behind Tellico Dam. The Endangered Species Act was passed the following December. 87 Stat. 884, 16 U.S.C. § 1531 *et seq.* (1976 ed.). More than a year later, in January 1975, respondents joined others in petitioning the Secretary of the Interior to list the snail darter as an endangered species. On November 10, 1975, when the Tellico Project was 75% completed, the Secretary placed the snail darter on the endangered list and concluded that the "proposed impoundment of water behind the proposed Tellico Dam would result in total destruction of the snail darter's habitat." 40 Fed. Reg. 47506 (1975). In respondents' view, the Secretary's action meant that completion of the Tellico Project would violate § 7 of the Act. TVA nevertheless determined to continue with the Tellico Project in accordance with the prior authorization by Congress. In February 1976, respondents filed the instant suit to enjoin its completion. By that time the Project was 80% completed.

In March 1976, TVA informed the House and Senate Appropriations Committees about the Project's threat to the snail darter and about respondents' lawsuit. Both Committees were advised that TVA was attempting to preserve the fish by relocating them in the Hiwassee River, which closely resembles the Little Tennessee. It stated explicitly, however, that the success of those efforts could not be guaranteed.

In a decision of May 25, 1976, the District Court for the Eastern District of Tennessee held that "the Act should not be construed as preventing completion of the project." * * * In 1975, 1976, and 1977, Congress, with full knowledge of the Tellico Project's effect on the snail darter and the alleged violation of the Endangered Species Act, continued to appropriate money for the completion of the Project. In doing so, the Appropriations Committees expressly stated that the Act did not prohibit the Project's completion, a view that Congress presumably accepted in approving the appropriations each year. For example, in June 1976, the Senate Committee on Appropriations released a report noting the District Court decision and recommending approval of TVA's full budget request for the Tellico Project. The Committee observed further that it did "not view the Endangered Species Act as prohibiting the completion of the Tellico project at its advanced stage," and it directed "that this project be completed as promptly as possible in the public interest." The appropriations bill was passed by Congress and approved by the President.

The Court of Appeals for the Sixth Circuit nevertheless reversed the District Court in January 1977. * * * In June 1977, and after being informed of the decision of the Court of Appeals, the Appropriations Committees in both Houses of Congress again recommended approval of TVA's full budget request for the Tellico Project. Both Committees again stated unequivocally that the Endangered Species Act was not intended to halt projects at an advanced stage of completion:

> "[The Senate] Committee has not viewed the Endangered Species Act as preventing the completion and use of these projects which were well under way at the time the affected species were listed as endangered. If the act has such an effect, which is contrary to the Committee's understanding of the intent of Congress in enacting the Endangered Species Act, funds should be appropriated to allow these projects to be completed and their benefits realized in the public interest, the Endangered Species Act notwithstanding." S. Rep. No. 95–301, p. 99 (1977).
>
> "It is the [House] Committee's view that the Endangered Species Act was not intended to halt projects such as these in their advanced stage of completion, and [the Committee] strongly recommends that these projects not be stopped because of misuse of the Act." H.R. Rep. No. 95–379, p. 104 (1977).

Once again, the appropriations bill was passed by both Houses and signed into law.

Today the Court, like the Court of Appeals below, adopts a reading of § 7 of the Act that gives it a retroactive effect and disregards 12 years of consistently expressed congressional intent to complete the Tellico Project. With all due respect, I view this result as an extreme example of a literalist construction, not required by the language of the Act and adopted without regard to its manifest purpose. Moreover, it ignores established canons of statutory construction.

The starting point in statutory construction is, of course, the language of § 7 itself. [It] can be viewed as a textbook example of fuzzy language, which can be read according to the "eye of the beholder." [But under] the Court's reasoning, the Act covers every existing federal installation, including great hydroelectric projects and reservoirs, every river and harbor project, and every national defense installation—however essential to the Nation's economic health and safety. The "actions" that an agency would be prohibited from "carrying out" would include the continued operation of such projects or any change necessary to preserve their continued usefulness. The only precondition, according to respondents, to thus destroying the usefulness of even the most important federal project in our country would be a finding by the Secretary of the Interior that a continuation of the project would threaten the survival or critical habitat of a newly discovered species of water spider or amoeba.

"[F]requently words of general meaning are used in a statute, words broad enough to include an act in question, and yet a consideration of the whole legislation, or of the circumstances surrounding its enactment, or of the absurd results which follow from giving such broad meaning to the words, makes it unreasonable to believe that the legislator intended to include the particular act." *Church of the Holy Trinity v. United States*, 143 U.S. 457, 459 (1892). The result that will follow in this case by virtue of the Court's reading of § 7 makes it unreasonable to believe that Congress intended that reading. Moreover, § 7 may be construed in a way that avoids an "absurd result" without doing violence to its language.

The critical word in § 7 is "actions" and its meaning is far from "plain." [I]t seems evident that the "actions" referred to are not all actions that an agency can ever take, but rather actions that the agency is *deciding whether* to authorize, to fund, or to carry out. In short, these words reasonably may be read as applying only to *prospective actions, i.e.*, actions with respect to which the agency has reasonable decisionmaking alternatives still available, actions *not yet* carried out. At the time respondents brought this lawsuit, the Tellico Project was 80% complete at a cost of more than $78 million. [U]nder a prospective reading of § 7, the action already had been "carried out" in terms of any remaining reasonable decisionmaking power. This is a reasonable construction of the language and also is supported by the presumption against construing statutes to give them a retroactive effect. * * *

The Court recognizes that the first purpose of statutory construction is to ascertain the intent of the legislature. * * * If the relevant Committees that considered the Act, and the Members of Congress who voted on it, had been aware that the Act could be used to terminate major federal projects authorized years earlier and nearly completed, or to require the abandonment of essential and long-completed federal installations and edifices, we can be certain that there would have been hearings, testimony, and debate concerning consequences so wasteful, so

**Food for Thought**

Is Justice Powell here urging the Court to engage in "imaginative reconstruction"? If so, is that a sensible way to interpret the statutes in question? We saw this approach to interpretation earlier in this Chapter when we considered *Riggs v. Palmer*.

inimical to purposes previously deemed important, and so likely to arouse public outrage. The absence of any such consideration by the Committees or in the floor debates indicates quite clearly that no one participating in the legislative process considered these consequences as within the intendment of the Act.

[T]his view of legislative intent at the time of enactment is abundantly confirmed by the subsequent congressional actions and expressions. We have held, properly, that post-enactment statements by individual Members of Congress as to the meaning of a statute are entitled to little or no weight. The Court also has recognized that subsequent Appropriations Acts themselves are not necessarily entitled to significant weight in determining whether a prior statute has been superseded. But these precedents are inapposite. There was no effort here to "bootstrap" a post-enactment view of prior legislation by isolated statements of individual Congressmen. Nor is this a case where Congress, without explanation or comment upon the statute in question, merely has voted apparently inconsistent financial support in subsequent Appropriations Acts. Testimony on this precise issue was presented before congressional committees, and the Committee Reports for three consecutive years addressed the problem and affirmed their understanding of the original congressional intent. We cannot assume—as the Court suggests—that Congress, when it continued each year to approve the recommended appropriations, was unaware of the contents of the supporting Committee Reports. All this amounts to strong corroborative evidence that the interpretation of § 7 as not applying to completed or substantially completed projects reflects the initial legislative intent.

I have little doubt that Congress will amend the Endangered Species Act to prevent the grave consequences made possible by today's decision. Few, if any, Members of that body will wish to defend an interpretation of the Act that requires the waste of at least $53 million, and denies the people of the Tennessee Valley area the benefits of the reservoir that Congress intended to confer. There will be little sentiment to leave this dam standing before an empty reservoir, serving no purpose other than a conversation piece for incredulous tourists.

But more far reaching than the adverse effect on the people of this economically depressed area is the continuing threat to the operation of every federal project, no matter how important to the Nation. If Congress acts expeditiously, as may be anticipated, the Court's decision probably will have no lasting adverse consequences. But I had not thought it to be the province of this Court to force Congress into otherwise unnecessary action by interpreting a statute to produce a result no one intended.

[JUSTICE REHNQUIST's dissenting opinion has been omitted.]

---

## Points for Discussion

### *a. Touchstones of Interpretation*

The Court began its consideration of the statute by focusing on the "plain[ ]" terms of the Act, and asserted that to accept the government's view would force the Court "to ignore the ordinary meaning of plain language." In other words, the Court's principal touchstone of interpretation was the ordinary meaning of the statutory text. Do you agree that the language of the statute plainly required the agency to cease work on the dam project?

Even if it did, wasn't there a strong argument that Congress did not intend such an outcome? Justice Powell focused on Congress's repeated decisions to continue funding the project after the enactment of the Endangered Species Act. He also urged the Court to interpret the statute in a way that would accord "with some modicum of common sense and the public weal." In other words, Justice Powell sought to determine the legislature's intent and, more obliquely, the statute's spirit or purpose. Do you agree with Justice Powell's account of Congress's intent and more general objectives?

Notice that the Court did not focus solely on the statutory text; after seeking to determine the meaning of the words in the statute, the Court turned to the Act's legislative history to confirm its understanding of the statutory text. But the Court advanced a theory for why courts should focus first and foremost on plain language of the statute, explaining that "[o]ur Constitution vests" the responsibility to determine public policy "in the political branches." In other words, for the Court to interpret the statute in tension with its plain language would amount to judicial policy-making in conflict with our "commitment to the separation of powers."

There is considerable appeal to this view. After all, we elect members of Congress to make policy for the nation. Federal judges, in contrast, are not elected, and we have little recourse if they make policy decisions with which we disagree. But the Court's approach is based on the premise that any departure from statutory text amounts to a departure from the policy that Congress enacted. Isn't it possible that the Court's conclusion in *Hill*—which enjoined a project that Congress had repeatedly funded—itself represented a departure from the policy that Congress sought to pursue? If so, is it obvious that Justice Powell's approach is in conflict with the separation of powers?

### *b. Congress's Response*

In thinking about whether the Court or instead Justice Powell acted consistent with Congress's policy preferences, consider Congress's response to the Court's decision. After the Court's decision, Congress enacted the Endangered Species Act Amendments of 1978, Pub. L. No. 95–632, 92 Stat. 3751 (1978), which established an inter-agency committee that had power to grant exemptions from the requirements of the Endangered Species Act. After the committee declined to grant a request to exempt the Tellico Dam Project, Congress passed a statute specifically granting an exemption for the project. Pub. L. No. 96–69, 93 Stat. 437, 449 (1979) ("[N]otwithstanding the provisions of 16 U.S.C., chapter 35 or any other law, the [TVA] is authorized and directed to complete construction, operate and maintain the Tellico Dam and Reservoir project for navigation, flood control, electric power generation and other purposes * * *.") What does this subsequent history suggest about whose view of the Endangered Species Act was correct?

---

Part of the reason why the courts in cases such as *Church of the Holy Trinity* and *Riggs v. Palmer* departed from the text of the statutes at issue was that strict adherence to the statutes' plain language would have produced what the judges apparently thought would be unfair, and thus likely unintended, results. Justice Powell thought that *Hill* was such a case, as well, but the outcome of the case—the cessation of a project that likely would cause environmental harm—was not obviously unjust, or implausibly within Congress's contemplation, even if it probably surprised many members of Congress. Can a commitment to enforcing the plain meaning of text survive in cases in which strict adherence to the text produces unfair results that Congress likely did not intend? Consider the case that follows.

---

## *United States v. Locke*

471 U.S. 84 (1985)

JUSTICE MARSHALL delivered the opinion of the Court.

From the enactment of the general mining laws in the 19th century until 1976, those who sought to make their living by locating and developing minerals on federal lands were virtually unconstrained by the fetters of federal control. The general mining laws, 30 U.S.C. § 22 *et seq.*, still in effect today, allow United States citizens to go onto unappropriated, unreserved public land to prospect for and develop certain minerals. "Discovery" of a mineral deposit, followed by the minimal procedures required to formally "locate" the deposit, gives an individual the right of exclusive possession of the land for mining purposes, 30 U.S.C. § 26; as long as $100 of assessment work is performed annually, the individual may continue to extract and sell minerals from the claim without paying any royalty to the United States, 30 U.S.C. § 28. For a nominal sum, and after certain statutory conditions are fulfilled, an individual may patent the claim, thereby purchasing from the Federal Government the land and minerals and obtaining ultimate title to them. Patenting, however, is not required, and an unpatented mining claim remains a fully recognized possessory interest. *Best v. Humboldt Placer Mining Co.*, 371 U.S. 334, 335 (1963).

By the 1960's, it had become clear that this 19th-century laissez-faire regime had created virtual chaos with respect to the public lands. In 1975, it was estimated that more than 6 million unpatented mining claims existed on public lands other than the national forests; in addition, more than half the land in the National Forest System was thought to be covered by such claims. S. Rep. No. 94–583, p. 65 (1975). * * * As a result, federal land managers had to proceed slowly and cautiously in taking any action affecting federal land lest the federal property rights of claimants be unlawfully disturbed. * * *

After more than a decade of studying this problem in the context of a broader inquiry into the proper management of the public lands in the modern era, Congress in 1976 enacted the [Federal Land Policy and Management Act of 1976 (FLPMA)], Pub. L. 94–579, 90 Stat. 2743 (codified at 43 U.S.C. § 1701 *et seq.*). Section 314 of the Act establishes a federal recording system that is designed both to rid federal lands of stale mining claims and to provide federal land managers with up-to-date information that allows them to make informed land management decisions. For claims located before FLPMA's enactment, the federal recording system imposes two general requirements. First, the claims must initially be registered with the [Bureau of Land Management (BLM)] by filing, within three years of FLPMA's enactment, a copy of the official record of the notice or certificate of location. 43 U.S.C. § 1744(b). Second, in the year of the initial recording, and "prior to December 31" of every year after that, the claimant must file with state officials and with BLM a notice of intention to hold the claim, an affidavit of assessment work performed on the claim, or a detailed reporting form. 43 U.S.C. § 1744(a). Section 314(c) of the Act provides that failure to comply with either of these requirements "shall be deemed conclusively to constitute an abandonment of the mining claim . . . by the owner." 43 U.S.C. § 1744(c).

The second of these requirements—the annual filing obligation—has created the dispute underlying this appeal. Appellees, four individuals engaged "in the business of operating mining properties in Nevada," purchased in 1960 and 1966 10 unpatented mining claims on public lands near Ely, Nevada. These claims were major sources of gravel and building material: the claims are valued at several million dollars, and, in the 1979–1980 assessment year alone, appellees' gross income totaled more than $1 million. [A]ppellees satisfied FLPMA's initial recording requirement by properly filing with BLM a notice of location, thereby putting their claims on record for purposes of FLPMA.

At the end of 1980, however, appellees failed to meet on time their first annual obligation to file with the Federal Government. After allegedly receiving misleading information from a BLM employee,[7] appellees waited until December 31 to submit to BLM the annual notice of intent to hold or proof of assessment work performed required under 43 U.S.C. § 1744(a). As noted above, that section requires these documents to be filed annually "prior to December 31." * * * Thus, appellees' filing was one day too late.

This fact was brought painfully home to appellees when they received a letter from the BLM Nevada State Office informing them that their claims had been declared abandoned and void due to their tardy filing. In many cases, loss of a claim in this way would have minimal practical effect; the claimant could simply locate the same claim again and then rerecord it with BLM. In this case, however, relocation of appellees' claims, which were initially located by appellees' predecessors in 1952 and 1954, was prohibited by the Common Varieties Act of 1955, 30 U.S.C. § 611; that Act prospectively barred location of the sort of minerals yielded by appellees' claims. Appellees' mineral deposits thus escheated to the Government. [Appellees filed suit to recover their mining rights. The District Court ruled in their favor.]

[Appellees asserted that the § 314(a) requirement of a filing "prior to December 31 of each year" should be construed to require a filing "on or before December 31."] It is clear to us that the plain language of the statute simply cannot sustain the gloss appellees would put on it. * * * While we will not allow a literal reading of a statute to produce a result "demonstrably at odds with the intentions of its drafters," *Griffin v. Oceanic Contractors, Inc.*, 458 U.S. 564, 5713 (1982), with respect to filing deadlines a literal reading of Congress' words is generally the only proper reading of those words. To attempt to decide whether some date other than the one set out in the statute is the date actually "intended" by Congress is to set sail on an aimless journey, for the purpose of a filing deadline would be just as well served by nearly any date a court might choose as by the date Congress has in fact set out in the statute. "Actual purpose is sometimes unknown," *United States Railroad Retirement Board v. Fritz*, 449 U.S. 166, 180 (1980) (Stevens, J., concurring), and such is the case with filing deadlines;

---

7 An affidavit submitted to the District Court by one of appellees' employees stated that BLM officials in Ely had told the employee that the filing could be made at the BLM Reno office "on or before December 31, 1980." Affidavit of Laura C. Locke ¶ 3. The 1978 version of a BLM question and answer pamphlet erroneously stated that the annual filings had to be made "on or before December 31" of each year. Staking a Mining Claim on Federal Lands 9–10 (1978). Later versions have corrected this error to bring the pamphlet into accord with the BLM regulations that require the filings to be made "on or before December 30." * * * Justice Stevens and Justice Powell seek to make much of this pamphlet and of the uncontroverted evidence that appellees were told a December 31 filing would comply with the statute. However, at the time appellees filed in 1980, BLM regulations and the then-current pamphlets made clear that the filing was required "on or before December 30." Thus, the dissenters' reliance on this pamphlet would seem better directed to the claim that the United States was equitably estopped from forfeiting appellees' claims, given the advice of the BLM agent and the objective basis the 1978 pamphlet provides for crediting the claim that such advice was given. The District Court did not consider this estoppel claim. Without expressing any view as to whether, as a matter of law, appellees could prevail on such a theory, we leave any further treatment of this issue, including fuller development of the record, to the District Court on remand.

as might be expected, nothing in the legislative history suggests why Congress chose December 30 over December 31, or over September 1 (the end of the assessment year for mining claims, 30 U.S.C. § 28), as the last day on which the required filings could be made. But "[d]eadlines are inherently arbitrary," while fixed dates "are often essential to accomplish necessary results." *United States v. Boyle*, 469 U.S. 241, 249 (1984). Faced with the inherent arbitrariness of filing deadlines, we must, at least in a civil case, apply by its terms the date fixed by the statute.

Moreover, BLM regulations have made absolutely clear since the enactment of FLPMA that "prior to December 31" means what it says. As the current version of the filing regulations states: "The owner of an unpatented mining claim located on Federal lands . . . shall have filed or caused to have been filed *on or before December 30* of each calendar year . . . evidence of annual assessment work performed during the previous assessment year or a notice of intention to hold the mining claim." 43 CFR § 3833.2–1(b)(1) (1984) (emphasis added). Leading mining treatises similarly inform claimants that "[i]t is important to note that the filing of a notice of intention or evidence of assessment work must be done *prior* to December 31 of each year, *i.e.*, on or before December 30." 2 American Law of Mining § 7.23D, p. 150.2 (Supp.1983) (emphasis in original). If appellees, who were businessmen involved in the running of a major mining operation for more than 20 years, had any questions about whether a December 31 filing complied with the statute, it was incumbent upon them, as it is upon other businessmen, to have checked the regulations or to have consulted an attorney for legal advice. Pursuit of either of these courses, rather than the submission of a last-minute filing, would surely have led appellees to the conclusion that December 30 was the last day on which they could file safely.

In so saying, we are not insensitive to the problems posed by congressional reliance on the words "prior to December 31." But the fact that Congress might have acted with greater clarity or foresight does not give courts a *carte blanche* to redraft statutes in an effort to achieve that which Congress is perceived to have failed to do. "There is a basic difference between filling a gap left by Congress' silence and rewriting rules that Congress has affirmatively and specifically enacted." *Mobil Oil Corp. v. Higginbotham*, 436 U.S. 618, 625 (1978). Nor is the Judiciary licensed to attempt to soften the clear import of Congress' chosen words whenever a court believes those words lead to a harsh result. On the contrary, deference to the supremacy of the Legislature, as well as recognition that Congressmen typically vote on the language of a bill, generally requires us to assume that "the legislative purpose is expressed by the ordinary meaning of the words used." *Richards v. United States*, 369 U.S. 1, 9 (1962). * * * The phrase "prior to" may be clumsy, but its meaning is clear. Under these circumstances, we are obligated to apply the "prior to December 31" language by its terms. * * * We therefore hold that BLM did not act ultra vires in concluding that appellees' filing was untimely. [The Court also concluded that the statute did not violate the Takings or Due Process Clauses of the Fifth Amendment, and it remanded for "further proceedings consistent with this opinion."]

Justice O'Connor, concurring.

I agree that the judgment below must be reversed. Nonetheless, I share many of the concerns expressed in the dissenting opinions * * *. If the facts are as alleged by appellees, allowing the Bureau of Land Management (BLM) to extinguish active mining claims that appellees have owned and worked for more than 20 years would seem both unfair and inconsistent with the purposes underlying FLPMA.

The Government has not disputed that appellees sought in good faith to comply with the statutory deadline. Appellees contend that in order to meet the requirements of § 314, they contacted the BLM and were informed by agency personnel that they could file the required materials on December 31, 1980. Appellees apparently relied on this advice and hand-delivered the appropriate documents to the local BLM office on that date. The BLM accepted the documents for filing, but some three months later sent appellees a notice stating that their mining claims were "abandoned and void" because the filing was made on, rather than prior to, December 31, 1980. * * * The unusual facts alleged by appellees suggest that the BLM's actions might estop the Government from relying on § 314(c) to obliterate a property interest that has provided a family's livelihood for decades.

[Justice Powell's dissenting opinion has been omitted.]

Justice Stevens, with whom Justice Brennan joins, dissenting.

Congress enacted § 314 of the Federal Land Policy and Management Act to establish for federal land planners and managers a federal recording system designed to cope with the problem of stale claims, and to provide "an easy way of discovering which Federal lands are subject to either valid or invalid mining claim locations." [S. Rep. No. 94–583, p. 65 (1975).] I submit that the appellees' actions in this case did not diminish the importance of these congressional purposes; to the contrary, their actions were entirely consistent with the statutory purposes, despite the confusion created by the "inartful draftsmanship" of the statutory language.

A careful reading of § 314 discloses at least [two] respects in which its text cannot possibly reflect the actual intent of Congress. First, the description of what must be filed in the initial filing and subsequent annual filings is quite obviously garbled. Read literally, § 314(a)(2) seems to require that a notice of intent to hold the claim and an affidavit of assessment work performed on the claim must be filed "*on* a detailed report provided by § 28–1 of Title 30."* One must substitute the word "or" for the word "on" to make any sense at all out of this provision. This error should

* The statute provides that the person asserting the claim must "[f]ile for record [with BLM] an affidavit of assessment work performed thereon, on a detailed report provided by section 28–1 of title 30, relating thereto." —*Ed.*

cause us to pause before concluding that Congress commanded blind allegiance to the remainder of the literal text of § 314.

Second, [BLM's] regulations do not use the language "prior to December 31;" instead, they use "on or before December 30 of each year." The Bureau's drafting of the regulations using this latter phrase indicates that the meaning of the statute itself is not quite as "plain" as the Court assumes; if the language were plain, it is doubtful that the Bureau would have found it necessary to change the language at all. Moreover, the Bureau, under the aegis of the Department of the Interior, once issued a pamphlet entitled "Staking a Mining Claim on Federal Lands" that contained the following information: * * * "Once the claim or site is recorded with BLM, *these documents must be filed on or before December 31 of each subsequent year*" (emphasis added). "Plain language," indeed.

In light of the foregoing, I cannot believe that Congress intended the words "prior to December 31 of each year" to be given the literal reading the Court adopts today. The statutory scheme requires periodic filings on a calendar-year basis. The end of the calendar year is, of course, correctly described either as "prior to the close of business on December 31," or "on or before December 31," but it is surely understandable that the author of § 314 might inadvertently use the words "prior to December 31" when he meant to refer to the end of the calendar year. As the facts of this case demonstrate, the scrivener's error is one that can be made in good faith.

The risk of such an error is, of course, the greatest when the reference is to the end of the calendar year. That it was in fact an error seems rather clear to me because no one has suggested any rational basis for omitting just one day from the period in which an annual filing may be made, and I would not presume that Congress deliberately created a trap for the unwary by such an omission. * * * I have no doubt that Congress would have chosen to adopt a construction of the statute that filing take place by the end of the calendar year if its attention had been focused on this precise issue.

**Make the Connection**

We will consider the "scrivener's error doctrine" in Chapter 3.

---

## Points for Discussion

### *a. Touchstone of Interpretation*

The Court in *Locke* relied on the "plain language" of the statute even though, as the Court acknowledged, the statute's wording produced a "harsh result." Was the

Court's approach motivated by a particular understanding of the judicial role—which would argue in favor of fidelity to statutory text in *all* cases—or instead by the fact that this case involved a deadline? On the one hand, the Court said that judges are not "licensed to attempt to soften the clear import of Congress' chosen words" simply because they believe that "those words lead to a harsh result." Indeed, the Court suggested that reliance on statutory text is required by the need for "deference to the supremacy of the Legislature." On the other hand, the Court stated that "with respect to filing deadlines a literal reading of Congress' words is generally the only proper reading of those words," because such deadlines are "inherently arbitrary." Either way, do you agree that the separation of powers—and the "supremacy of the Legislature"—requires courts to adhere to the plain meaning of statutory text even when it produces harsh results?

***b. Aftermath of the Decision***

In a footnote, the Court noted that the Lockes, who claimed that they had relied on the advice of a BLM employee who told them that they could file on or before December 31, could argue on remand that the government was estopped from relying on the statutory deadline to forfeit their claims. After the Court's decision, the government reached a settlement with the Lockes that enabled them to keep their mining claims. What does this suggest, if anything, about the legitimacy of the Court's adherence to the plain meaning of the statutory text?

---

Not long after the Court's decision in *Locke*, President Reagan appointed Antonin Scalia as an Associate Justice on the Supreme Court. Justice Scalia became the most prominent advocate of "textualism," a theory of statutory interpretation that holds that "the text is the law, and it is the text that must be observed." Antonin Scalia, *Common-Law Courts in a Civil-Law System: The Role of United States Federal Courts in Interpreting the Constitution and Laws*, in A MATTER OF INTERPRETATION 22 (Amy Gutmann ed., 1998). In his opinions in the cases that follow, he explained his approach to statutory interpretation.

---

## *Chisom v. Roemer*

501 U.S. 380 (1991)

JUSTICE STEVENS delivered the opinion of the Court.

Petitioners * * * represent a class of approximately 135,000 black registered voters in Orleans Parish, Louisiana. They brought this action against the Governor and other state officials [to] challenge the method of electing justices of the Louisiana Supreme Court from the New Orleans area. * * *

The Louisiana Supreme Court consists of seven justices, five of whom are elected from five single-member [districts], and two of whom are elected from one multi-member [district]. * * * The one multimember district, the First Supreme Court District, consists of the parishes of Orleans, St. Bernard, Plaquemines, and Jefferson. Orleans Parish contains about half of the population of the First Supreme Court District and about half of the registered voters in that district. More than one-half of the registered voters of Orleans Parish are black, whereas more than three-fourths of the registered voters in the other three parishes are white.

**Food for Thought**

Orleans Parish, which was majority black, was roughly the same size as all of the other single-member districts in the state, but voters from the Parish were part of a larger Supreme Court District that elected two members of the court. In a multi-member district, voters in a particular area elect more than one candidate to office. Can you see why the voting system diluted minority voting strength?

Petitioners allege that "the present method of electing two Justices to the Louisiana Supreme Court at-large from the New Orleans area impermissibly dilutes minority voting strength" in violation of § 2 of the Voting Rights Act. [At the time of the Court's decision, no black person had ever been elected to the Louisiana Supreme Court.] * * * Petitioners seek a remedy that would divide the First District into two districts, one for Orleans Parish and the second for the other three parishes. If this remedy were adopted, the seven members of the Louisiana Supreme Court would each represent a separate single-member judicial district, and each of the two new districts would have approximately the same population. According to petitioners, the new Orleans Parish district would also have a majority black population and majority black voter registration. [The district court dismissed the complaint, relying on *League of United Latin American Citizens Council No. 4434 v. Clements*, 914 F.2d 620 (5th Cir. 1990) ("LULAC"), which held that judicial elections are not covered under § 2 of the Act as amended in 1982.]

It is * * * undisputed that § 2 [of the Voting Rights Act] applied to judicial elections prior to the 1982 amendment [to the Act] * * *. Moreover, there is no question that the terms "standard, practice, or procedure" [used in § 2] are broad enough to encompass the use of multimember districts to minimize a racial minority's ability to influence the outcome of an election covered by § 2. The only matter in dispute is whether the test for determining the legality of such a practice, which was added to the statute in 1982, applies in judicial elections as well as in other elections.

The text of § 2 of the Voting Rights Act as originally enacted read as follows:

> "No voting qualification or prerequisite to voting, or standard, practice, or procedure shall be imposed or applied by any State or political subdivision to deny or abridge the right of any citizen of the United States to vote on account of race or color." 79 Stat. 437.

The terms "vote" and "voting" were defined elsewhere in the Act to include "all action necessary to make a vote effective *in any primary, special, or general election.*" § 14(c)(1) of the Act, 79 Stat. 445 (emphasis added). The statute further defined vote and voting as "votes cast with respect to candidates for public or party office and propositions for which votes are received in an election." *Ibid.*

At the time of the passage of the Voting Rights Act of 1965, § 2, unlike other provisions of the Act, did not provoke significant debate in Congress because it was viewed largely as a restatement of the Fifteenth Amendment. This Court took a similar view of § 2 in *Mobile v. Bolden*, 446 U.S. 55, 60–61 (1980). * * * Section 2 protected the right to vote, and it did so without making any distinctions or imposing any limitations as to which elections would fall within its purview. As Attorney General Katzenbach made clear during his testimony before the House, "[e]very election in which registered electors are permitted to vote would be covered" under § 2.

Justice Stewart's opinion for the plurality in *Mobile v. Bolden,* which held that there was no violation of either the Fifteenth Amendment or § 2 of the Voting Rights Act absent proof of intentional discrimination, served as the impetus for the 1982 amendment. One year after the decision in *Mobile,* Chairman Rodino of the House Judiciary Committee introduced a bill to extend the Voting Rights Act and its bilingual requirements, and to amend § 2 by striking out "to deny or abridge" and substituting "in a manner which *results* in a denial or abridgment of." The "results" test proposed by Chairman Rodino was incorporated into S.1992, and ultimately into the 1982 amendment to § 2, and is now the focal point of this litigation.

Under the amended statute, proof of intent is no longer required to prove a § 2 violation. Now plaintiffs can prevail under § 2 by demonstrating that a challenged election practice has resulted in the denial or abridgment of the right to vote based on color or race. * * * The full text of § 2 as amended in 1982 reads as follows:

> "SEC. 2. (a) No voting qualification or prerequisite to voting or standard, practice, or procedure shall be imposed or applied by any State or political subdivision in a manner which results in a denial or abridgement of the right of any citizen of the United States to vote on account of race or color, or in contravention of the guarantees set forth in section 4(f)(2), as provided in subsection (b).
>
> "(b) A violation of subsection (a) is established if, based on the totality of circumstances, it is shown that the political processes leading to nomination or election in the State or political subdivision are not equally open to participation by members of a class of citizens protected by subsection (a) in that its members have less opportunity than other members of the electorate to participate in the political process and to elect representatives of their choice. The extent to which members of a protected

class have been elected to office in the State or political subdivision is one circumstance which may be considered: *Provided,* That nothing in this section establishes a right to have members of a protected class elected in numbers equal to their proportion in the population." 96 Stat. 134.

**Take Note**

Before you read on, can you anticipate what the state argued in defending its system for electing members of the Supreme Court? Specifically, on which word in the amended statute do you think the state relied?

The two purposes of the amendment are apparent from its text. Section (a) adopts a results test, thus providing that proof of discriminatory intent is no longer necessary to establish *any* violation of the section. Section (b) provides guidance about how the results test is to be applied.

Respondents contend, and the [Fifth Circuit] agreed, that Congress' choice of the word "representatives" in the phrase "have less opportunity than other members of the electorate to participate in the political process and to elect representatives of their choice"[22] in section (b) is evidence of congressional intent to exclude vote dilution claims involving judicial elections from the coverage of § 2. We reject that construction because we are convinced that if Congress had such an intent, Congress would have made it explicit in the statute, or at least some of the Members would have identified or mentioned it at some point in the unusually extensive legislative history of the 1982 amendment.[23] * * *

The statutory language is patterned after the language used by Justice WHITE in his opinions for the Court in *White v. Regester,* 412 U.S. 755 (1973), and *Whitcomb v. Chavis,* 403 U.S. 124 (1971). In both opinions, the Court identified the opportunity to participate and the opportunity to elect as inextricably linked. In *White v. Regester,* the Court described the connection as follows: "The plaintiffs' burden is to produce evidence . . . that its members had less opportunity than did other residents

22 The phrase is borrowed from Justice White's opinion for the Court in *White v. Regester,* 412 U.S. 755 (1973), which predates *Mobile v. Bolden.* Congress explained that its purpose in adding section 2(b) was to "embod[y] the test laid down by the Supreme Court in *White.*" S. Rep. No. 97–417, at 27. In *White,* the Court said that the "plaintiffs' burden is to produce evidence . . . that [the minority group's] members had less opportunity than did other residents in the district to participate in the political processes and to elect legislators of their choice." 412 U.S., at 766.

23 Congress' silence in this regard can be likened to the dog that did not bark. See A. Doyle, Silver Blaze, in The Complete Sherlock Holmes 335 (1927). Cf. *Harrison v. PPG Industries, Inc.,* 446 U.S. 578, 602 (1980) (Rehnquist, J., dissenting) ("In a case where the construction of legislative language such as this makes so sweeping and so relatively unorthodox a change as that made here, I think judges as well as detectives may take into consideration the fact that a watchdog did not bark in the night"). See also *American Hospital Assn. v. NLRB,* 499 U.S. 606 (1991).

in the district to participate in the political processes *and* to elect legislators of their choice." 412 U.S., at 766 (emphasis added). And earlier, in *Whitcomb v. Chavis,* the Court described the plaintiffs' burden as entailing a showing that they "had less opportunity than did other . . . residents to participate in the political processes *and* to elect legislators of their choice." 403 U.S., at 149 (emphasis added).

The results test mandated by the 1982 amendment is applicable to all claims arising under § 2. If the word "representatives" did place a limit on the coverage of the Act for judicial elections, it would exclude all claims involving such elections from the protection of § 2. For all such claims must allege an abridgment of the opportunity to participate in the political process *and* to elect representatives of one's choice. Even if the wisdom of Solomon would support the [Fifth Circuit's] proposal to preserve claims based on an interference with the right to vote in judicial elections while eschewing [vote dilution] claims based on the opportunity to elect judges, we have no authority to divide a unitary claim created by Congress.

**Take Note**

The court of appeals read § 2(b) to draw a distinction between claims involving tests or other devices that interfere with individual participation in an election, on the one hand, and claims of vote dilution that challenge impairment of a group's opportunity to elect representatives of their choice, on the other hand. The court reasoned that the amended § 2 would continue to apply to judicial elections with respect to claims in the first category, but that the word "representatives" excludes judicial elections from claims in the second category. The Court here responds to that argument. Whose reading of the provision makes more sense?

Both respondents and the [Fifth Circuit] place their principal reliance on Congress' use of the word "representatives" instead of "legislators" in the phrase "to participate in the political process and to elect representatives of their choice." 42 U.S.C. § 1973. When Congress borrowed the phrase from *White v. Regester,* it replaced "legislators" with "representatives."[26] This substitution indicates, at the very least, that Congress intended the amendment to cover more than legislative elections. Respondents argue, and the [Fifth Circuit] agreed, that the term "representatives" was used to extend § 2 coverage to executive officials, but not to judges. We think,

---

26 The word "representatives" rather than "legislators" was included in Senator Robert Dole's compromise, which was designed to assuage the fears of those Senators who viewed the House's version, H.R. 3112, as an invitation for proportional representation and electoral quotas. Senator Dole explained that the compromise was intended both to embody the belief "that a voting practice or procedure which is discriminatory in result should not be allowed to stand, regardless of whether there exists a discriminatory purpose or intent" and to "delineat[e] what legal standard should apply under the results test and clarif[y] that it is not a mandate for proportional representation." Hearings on S. 53 et al. before the Subcommittee on the Constitution of the Senate Committee on the Judiciary, 97th Cong., 2d Sess., 60 (1982). Thus, the compromise was not intended to exclude any elections from the coverage of subsection (a), but simply to make clear that the results test does not require the proportional election of minority candidates in *any* election.

however, that the better reading of the word "representatives" describes the winners of representative, popular elections. If executive officers, such as prosecutors, sheriffs, state attorneys general, and state treasurers, can be considered "representatives" simply because they are chosen by popular election, then the same reasoning should apply to elected judges.

Respondents suggest that if Congress had intended to have the statute's prohibition against vote dilution apply to the election of judges, it would have used the word "candidates" instead of "representatives." But that confuses the ordinary meaning of the words. The word "representative" refers to someone who has prevailed in a popular election, whereas the word "candidate" refers to someone who is seeking an office. Thus, a candidate is nominated, not elected. When Congress used "candidate" in other parts of the statute, it did so precisely because it was referring to people who were aspirants for an office. See, *e.g.*, 42 U.S.C. § 1971(b) ("any candidate for the office of President").

The [Fifth Circuit] was, of course, entirely correct in observing that "judges need not be elected at all," 914 F.2d, at 622, and that ideally public opinion should be irrelevant to the judge's role because the judge is often called upon to disregard, or even to defy, popular sentiment. The Framers of the Constitution had a similar understanding of the judicial role, and as a consequence, they established that Article III judges would be appointed, rather than elected, and would be sheltered from public opinion by receiving life tenure and salary protection. * * * Louisiana, however, has chosen a different course. It has decided to elect its judges and to compel judicial candidates to vie for popular support just as other political candidates do.

The fundamental tension between the ideal character of the judicial office and the real world of electoral politics cannot be resolved by crediting judges with total indifference to the popular will while simultaneously requiring them to run for elected office. When each of several members of a court must be a resident of a separate district, and must be elected by the voters of that district, it seems both reasonable and realistic to characterize the winners as representatives of that district. * * * Louisiana could, of course, exclude its judiciary from the coverage of the Voting Rights Act by changing to a system in which judges are appointed, and, in that way, it could enable its judges to be indifferent to popular opinion. The reasons why Louisiana has chosen otherwise are precisely the reasons why it is appropriate for § 2 * * * of the Voting Rights Act to continue to apply to its judicial elections.

Congress enacted the Voting Rights Act of 1965 for the broad remedial purpose of "rid[ding] the country of racial discrimination in voting." *South Carolina v. Katzenbach*, 383 U.S. 301, 315 (1966). In *Allen v. State Board of Elections*, 393 U.S. 544, 567 (1969), we said that the Act should be interpreted in a manner that provides "the broadest possible scope" in combating racial discrimination. Congress amended the Act in 1982 in order to relieve plaintiffs of the burden of proving discriminatory intent, after a plurality of this Court had concluded that the original Act, like the Fifteenth

Amendment, contained such a requirement. See *Mobile v. Bolden*. Thus, Congress made clear that a violation of § 2 could be established by proof of discriminatory results alone. It is difficult to believe that Congress, in an express effort to broaden the protection afforded by the Voting Rights Act, withdrew, without comment, an important category of elections from that protection. Today we reject such an anomalous view and hold that state judicial elections are included within the ambit of § 2 as amended. [Reversed.]

JUSTICE SCALIA, with whom THE CHIEF JUSTICE and JUSTICE KENNEDY join, dissenting.

Section 2 of the Voting Rights Act of 1965 is not some all-purpose weapon for well-intentioned judges to wield as they please in the battle against discrimination. It is a statute. I thought we had adopted a regular method for interpreting the meaning of language in a statute: first, find the ordinary meaning of the language in its textual context; and second, using established canons of construction, ask whether there is any clear indication that some permissible meaning other than the ordinary one applies. If not—and especially if a good reason for the ordinary meaning appears plain—we apply that ordinary meaning.

Today, however, the Court adopts a method quite out of accord with that usual practice. It begins not with what the statute says, but with an expectation about what the statute must mean absent particular phenomena ("[*W*]*e are convinced* that if Congress had . . . an intent [to exclude judges] Congress would have made it explicit in the statute, or at least some of the Members would have identified or mentioned it at some point in the unusually extensive legislative history" (emphasis added)); and the Court then interprets the words of the statute to fulfill its expectation. Finding nothing in the legislative history affirming that judges were excluded from the coverage of § 2, the Court gives the phrase "to elect representatives" the quite extraordinary meaning that covers the election of judges.

As method, this is just backwards, and however much we may be attracted by the result it produces in a particular case, we should in every case resist it. Our job begins with a text that Congress has passed and the President has signed. We are to read the words of that text as any ordinary Member of Congress would have read them, see Holmes, *The Theory of Legal Interpretation*, 12 Harv. L. Rev. 417 (1899), and apply the meaning so determined. In my view, that reading reveals that § 2 extends to vote dilution claims for the elections of representatives only, and judges are not representatives.

As the Court suggests, the 1982 amendments to the Voting Rights Act were adopted in response to our decision in *Mobile v. Bolden*, 446 U.S. 55 (1980), which had held that the scope of the original Voting Rights Act was coextensive with the Fifteenth Amendment, and thus proscribed intentional discrimination only. I agree with the Court that that original legislation, directed toward intentional discrimination, applied to all elections, for it clearly said so:

> "No voting qualification or prerequisite to voting, or standard, practice, or procedure shall be imposed or applied by any State or political subdivision to deny or abridge the right of any citizen of the United States to vote on account of race or color." 79 Stat. 437.

The 1982 amendments, however, radically transformed the Act. As currently written, the statute proscribes intentional discrimination only if it has a discriminatory effect, but proscribes practices with discriminatory effect whether or not intentional. This new "results" criterion provides a powerful, albeit sometimes blunt, weapon with which to attack even the most subtle forms of discrimination. The question we confront here is how broadly the new remedy applies. The foundation of the Court's analysis, the itinerary for its journey in the wrong direction, is the following statement: "It is difficult to believe that Congress, in an express effort to broaden the protection afforded by the Voting Rights Act, withdrew, without comment, an important category of elections from that protection." There are two things wrong with this. First is the notion that Congress cannot be credited with having achieved anything of major importance by simply saying it, in ordinary language, in the text of a statute, "without comment" in the legislative history. As the Court colorfully puts it, if the dog of legislative history has not barked nothing of great significance can have transpired. Apart from the questionable wisdom of assuming that dogs will bark when something important is happening, see 1 T. Livius, The History of Rome 411–413 (1892) (D. Spillan transl.), we have forcefully and explicitly rejected the Conan Doyle approach to statutory construction in the past. See *Harrison v. PPG Industries, Inc.*, 446 U.S. 578, 592 (1980) ("In ascertaining the meaning of a statute, a court cannot, in the manner of Sherlock Holmes, pursue the theory of the dog that did not bark"). We are here to apply the statute, not legislative history, and certainly not the absence of legislative history. Statutes are the law though sleeping dogs lie.

The more important error in the Court's starting point, however, is the assumption that the effect of excluding judges from the revised § 2 would be to "withdr[aw] . . . an important category of elections from [the] protection [of the Voting Rights Act]." There is absolutely no question here of *withdrawing* protection. Since the pre-1982 content of § 2 was coextensive with the Fifteenth Amendment, the entirety of that protection subsisted in the Constitution, and could be enforced through the other provisions of the Voting Rights Act. Nothing was lost from the prior coverage; *all* of the new "results" protection was an add-on. The issue is not, therefore, as the Court would have it, whether Congress has cut back on the coverage of the Voting Rights Act; the issue is how far it has extended it. Thus, even if a court's expectations were a proper basis for interpreting the text of a statute, while there would be reason to expect that Congress was not "withdrawing" protection, there is no particular reason to expect that the supplemental protection it provided was any more extensive than the text of the statute said.

* * * The Court, petitioners, and petitioners' *amici* have labored mightily to establish that there is *a* meaning of "representatives" that would include judges, and no doubt there is. But our job is not to scavenge the world of English usage to discover whether there is any possible meaning of "representatives" which suits our preconception that the statute includes judges; our job is to determine whether the *ordinary* meaning includes them, and if it does not, to ask whether there is any solid indication in the text or structure of the statute that something other than ordinary meaning was intended.

**Food for Thought**

Do you agree with Justice Scalia that the ordinary meaning of the word "representative" does not include judges who are elected from separate districts? If so, how could Congress have drafted the statute if it had wanted to include all state officials who are subject to election?

There is little doubt that the ordinary meaning of "representatives" does not include judges, see Webster's Second New International Dictionary 2114 (1950). The Court's feeble argument to the contrary is that "representatives" means those who "are chosen by popular election." On that hypothesis, the fan-elected members of the baseball all-star teams are "representatives"—hardly a common, if even a permissible, usage. Surely the word "representative" connotes one who is not only *elected by* the people, but who also, at a minimum, *acts on behalf of* the people. Judges do that in a sense—but not in the ordinary sense. As the captions of the pleadings in some States still display, it is the prosecutor who represents "the People"; the judge represents the Law—which often requires him to rule against the People. It is precisely because we do not *ordinarily* conceive of judges as representatives that we held judges not within the Fourteenth Amendment's requirement of "one person, one vote." *Wells v. Edwards*, 347 F. Supp. 453 (MD La.1972), aff'd, 409 U.S. 1095 (1973). The point is not that a State could not make judges in some senses representative, or that all judges must be conceived of in the Article III mold, but rather, that giving "representatives" its ordinary meaning, the ordinary speaker in 1982 would not have applied the word to judges. It remains only to ask whether there is good indication that ordinary meaning does not apply.

[T]here is assuredly nothing whatever that points in the opposite direction, indicating that the ordinary meaning here should *not* be applied. Far from that, in my view the ordinary meaning of "representatives" gives clear purpose to congressional action that otherwise would seem pointless. As an initial matter, it is evident that Congress paid particular attention to the scope of elections covered by the "to elect" language. As the Court suggests, that language for the most part tracked this Court's opinions in *White v. Regester*, 412 U.S. 755, 766 (1973), and *Whitcomb v. Chavis*, 403 U.S. 124, 149 (1971), but the word "legislators" was not copied. Significantly, it was replaced not with the more general term "candidates" used repeatedly elsewhere in the Act, but with the term "representatives," which appears nowhere else in the Act (except as a proper noun referring to Members of the federal lower House, or designees of the Attorney General). The normal meaning of this term is broader than "legislators" (it includes, for example, school boards and city councils as well as senators and representatives) but narrower than "candidates."

The Court says that the seemingly significant refusal to use the term "candidate" and selection of the distinctive term "representative" are really inconsequential, because "candidate" could not have been used. According to the Court, since "candidate" refers to one who has been nominated but *not yet* elected, the phrase "to elect candidates" would be a contradiction in terms. The only flaw in this argument is that it is not true, as repeated usage of the formulation "to elect candidates" by this Court itself amply demonstrates. See, *e.g., Davis v. Bandemer*, 478 U.S. 109, 131 (1986). * * * In other words, far from being an impermissible choice, "candidates" would have been the natural choice, even if it had not been used repeatedly elsewhere in the statute. It is quite absurd to think that Congress went out of its way to replace that term with "representatives," in order to convey what "candidates" naturally suggests (viz., coverage of *all* elections) and what "representatives" naturally does not.

A second consideration confirms that "representatives" in § 2 was meant in its ordinary sense. When given its ordinary meaning, it causes the statute to reproduce an established, eminently logical, and perhaps practically indispensable limitation upon the availability of vote dilution claims. Whatever other requirements may be applicable to elections for "representatives" (in the sense of those who are not only elected by but act on behalf of the electorate), those elections, unlike elections for *all* officeholders, must be conducted in accordance with the equal protection principle of "one person, one vote." And it so happens—more than coincidentally, I think—that in every case in which, prior to the amendment of § 2, we recognized the possibility of a vote dilution claim, the principle of "one person, one vote" was applicable. Indeed, it is the principle of "one person, one vote" that gives meaning to the concept of "dilution." One's vote is diluted if it is not, *as it should be*, of the same practical effect as everyone else's. * * * Well before Congress amended § 2, we had held that the principle of "one person, one vote" does not apply to the election of judges, *Wells v. Edwards*. If Congress was (through use of the extremely inapt word "representatives") making vote dilution claims available with respect to the election of judges, it was, for the first time, extending that remedy to a context in which "one person, one vote" did not apply. *That* would have been a significant change in the law, and given the need to identify some other baseline for computing "dilution," *that* is a matter which those who believe in barking dogs should be astounded to find unmentioned in the legislative history. If "representatives" is given its normal meaning, on the other hand, there is no change in the law (except elimination of the intent requirement) and the silence is entirely understandable.

All this is enough to convince me that there is sense to the ordinary meaning of "representative" in § 2(b)—that there is reason to Congress' choice—and since there is, then, under our normal presumption, that ordinary meaning prevails. * * *

As I said at the outset, these cases are about method. The Court transforms the meaning of § 2, not because the ordinary meaning is irrational, or inconsistent with other parts of the statute, see, *e.g.*, *Green v. Bock Laundry Machine Co.*, 490 U.S. 504, 510–511 (1989), but because it does not fit the Court's conception of what Congress must have had in mind. When we adopt a method that psychoanalyzes Congress rather than reads its laws, when we employ a tinkerer's toolbox, we do great harm. Not only do we reach the wrong result with respect to the statute at hand, but we poison the well of future legislation, depriving legislators of the assurance that ordinary terms, used in an ordinary context, will be given a predictable meaning. Our highest responsibility in the field of statutory construction is to read the laws in a consistent way, giving Congress a sure means by which it may work the people's will. We have ignored that responsibility today. I respectfully dissent.

**Make the Connection**

We will consider the Court's decision in *Bock Laundry*, and the so-called "absurdity doctrine," in Chapter 3.

[JUSTICE KENNEDY's dissenting opinion has been omitted.]

---

## Points for Discussion

### *a. Touchstone of Interpretation*

Justice Scalia insisted in his dissent that the only appropriate touchstone for interpreting statutes is the ordinary meaning of the text. What is the theoretical justification for this view? Taking Justice Scalia on his own terms, is it clear to you that the ordinary meaning of the word "representatives" excludes judges who are subject to election?

On which touchstones of interpretation did Justice Stevens rely in his opinion for the Court? Did he ignore the ordinary meaning of the text? Or did he read the word "representatives" in light of the context in which Congress enacted the statute? To the extent that Justice Stevens focused on congressional intent or purpose, what evidence did he advance to demonstrate that intent or purpose?

### *b. Consequences of the Decision*

Before the Court's decision in *Chisom*, Louisiana voters had never elected a black person to serve on the state Supreme Court. After the decision, the Louisiana legislature enacted legislation that permitted the Justices then serving from the multi-member district to serve out their terms, temporarily added an eighth Justice, and redrew the district lines to create the majority-black single-member Seventh District. The temporary eighth Justice, Revius Ortique, Jr., from Orleans Parish, became the first black Justice elected to the Louisiana Supreme Court. In 2013, Bernette Joshua Johnson, elected from the Seventh District, became the first black Chief Justice of the Louisiana Supreme Court.

---

## *West Virginia University Hospitals, Inc. v. Casey*

499 U.S. 83 (1991)

Justice Scalia delivered the opinion of the Court.

This case presents the question whether fees for services rendered by experts in civil rights litigation may be shifted to the losing party pursuant to 42 U.S.C. § 1988, which permits the award of "a reasonable attorney's fee."

Petitioner West Virginia University Hospitals, Inc. (WVUH), operates a hospital in Morgantown, W.Va., near the Pennsylvania border. The hospital is often used by Medicaid recipients living in southwestern Pennsylvania. In January 1986, Pennsylvania's Department of Public Welfare notified WVUH of new Medicaid reimbursement schedules for services provided to Pennsylvania residents by the Morgantown hospital. [WVUH objected to the new reimbursement rates on both federal statutory and federal constitutional grounds.] After exhausting administrative remedies, WVUH filed suit in Federal District Court under 42 U.S.C. § 1983. Named as defendants (respondents here) were Pennsylvania Governor Robert Casey and various other Pennsylvania officials.

Counsel for WVUH employed Coopers & Lybrand, a national accounting firm, and three doctors specializing in hospital finance to assist in the preparation of the lawsuit and to testify at trial. WVUH prevailed at trial in May 1988. The District Court subsequently awarded fees pursuant to 42 U.S.C. § 1988,[1] including over $100,000 in fees attributable to expert services. The District Court found these services to have been "essential" to presentation of the case—a finding not disputed by respondents. Respondents appealed both the judgment on the merits and the fee award. The Court of Appeals for the Third Circuit affirmed as to the former, but

---

1 42 U.S.C. § 1988 provides in relevant part: "In any action or proceeding to enforce a provision of sections 1981, 1982, 1983, 1985, and 1986 of this title, title IX of Public Law 92–318 . . ., or title VI of the Civil Rights Act of 1964 . . ., the court, in its discretion, may allow the prevailing party, other than the United States, a reasonable attorney's fee as part of the costs."

reversed as to the expert fees, disallowing them except to the extent that they fell within the $30-per-day fees for witnesses prescribed by 28 U.S.C. § 1821(b).

[28 U.S.C. § 1920 authorizes federal judges to impose costs on the party that loses a lawsuit. Among the permissible costs are "[f]ees and disbursements for printing and witnesses." At the time of this suit, 28 U.S.C. § 1821(b) limited the witness fees authorized by § 1920 to an attendance fee of $30 per day for each day's attendance and for "the time necessarily occupied in going to and returning from the place of attendance."] In *Crawford Fitting Co. v. J.T. Gibbons, Inc.*, 482 U.S. 437 (1987), we held that these provisions define the full extent of a federal court's power to shift litigation costs absent express statutory authority to go further. * * * The question before us [is] whether the term "attorney's fee" in § 1988 provides the "explicit statutory authority" required by *Crawford Fitting.*

**FYI**

The default approach to litigation financing in the United States—the so-called "American Rule"—is that each side pays its own lawyers. Accordingly, in the ordinary suit, the winning party still has to pay its attorney's fees. This is in contrast to the typical approach in Great Britain, where the losing party usually pays the fees of the winning party's attorney.

The record of statutory usage demonstrates convincingly that attorney's fees and expert fees are regarded as separate elements of litigation cost. While some fee-shifting provisions, like § 1988, refer only to "attorney's fees," see, *e.g.*, Civil Rights Act of 1964, 42 U.S.C. § 2000e–5(k), many others explicitly shift expert witness fees *as well as* attorney's fees. In 1976, just over a week prior to the enactment of § 1988, Congress passed those provisions of the Toxic Substances Control Act, 15 U.S.C. §§ 2618(d), 2619(c)(2), which provide that a prevailing party may recover "the costs of suit and reasonable fees for attorneys *and expert witnesses.*" (Emphasis added.) Also in 1976, Congress amended the Consumer Product Safety Act, 15 U.S.C. §§ 2060(c), 2072(a), 2073, which as originally enacted in 1972 shifted to the losing party "cost[s] of suit, including a reasonable attorney's fee," see 86 Stat. 1226. In the 1976 amendment, Congress altered the fee-shifting provisions to their present form by adding a phrase shifting expert witness fees *in addition to* attorney's fees. See Pub. L. 94–284, § 10, 90 Stat. 506, 507. Two other significant Acts passed in 1976 contain similar phrasing: the Resource Conservation and Recovery Act of 1976, 42 U.S.C. § 6972(e) ("costs of litigation (including reasonable attorney and expert witness fees)"), and the Natural Gas Pipeline Safety Act Amendments of 1976, 49 U.S.C. App. § 1686(e) ("costs of suit, including reasonable attorney's fees and reasonable expert witnesses fees").

Congress enacted similarly phrased fee-shifting provisions in numerous statutes both before 1976, see, *e.g.*, Endangered Species Act of 1973, 16 U.S.C. § 1540(g)(4) ("costs of litigation (including reasonable attorney and expert witness fees)"), and afterwards, see, *e.g.*, Public Utility Regulatory Policies Act of 1978, 16 U.S.C.

§ 2632(a)(1) ("reasonable attorneys' fees, expert witness fees, and other reasonable costs incurred in preparation and advocacy of [the litigant's] position"). These statutes encompass diverse categories of legislation, including tax, administrative procedure, environmental protection, consumer protection, admiralty and navigation, utilities regulation, and, significantly, civil rights: The Equal Access to Justice Act (EAJA), the counterpart to § 1988 for violation of federal rights by federal employees, states that " 'fees and other expenses' [as shifted by § 2412(d)(1)(A)] includes the reasonable expenses of expert witnesses . . . and reasonable attorney fees." 28 U.S.C. § 2412(d)(2)(A). At least 34 statutes in 10 different titles of the United States Code explicitly shift attorney's fees *and* expert witness fees. * * * We think this statutory usage shows beyond question that attorney's fees and expert fees are distinct items of expense. If, as WVUH argues, the one includes the other, dozens of statutes referring to the two separately become an inexplicable exercise in redundancy.

WVUH suggests that a distinctive meaning of "attorney's fees" should be adopted with respect to § 1988 because this statute was meant to overrule our decision in *Alyeska Pipeline Service Co. v. Wilderness Society*, 421 U.S. 240 (1975). [P]rior to 1975 many courts awarded expert fees and attorney's fees in certain circumstances pursuant to their equitable discretion. In *Alyeska,* we held that this discretion did not extend beyond a few exceptional circumstances long recognized by common law. Specifically, we rejected the so-called "private attorney general" doctrine recently created by some lower federal courts, see, *e.g., La Raza Unida v. Volpe*, 57 F.R.D. 94, 98–102 (N.D. Cal. 1972), which allowed equitable fee shifting to plaintiffs in certain types of civil rights litigation. WVUH argues that § 1988 was intended to restore the pre-*Alyeska* regime—and that, since expert fees were shifted then, they should be shifted now.

Both chronology and the remarks of sponsors of the bill that became § 1988 suggest that at least some members of Congress viewed it as a response to *Alyeska.* See, *e.g.,* S. Rep. No. 94–1011, pp. 4, 6 (1976). It is a considerable step, however, from this proposition to the conclusion the hospital would have us draw, namely, that § 1988 should be read as a reversal of *Alyeska* in all respects.

By its plain language and as unanimously construed in the courts, § 1988 is both broader and narrower than the pre-*Alyeska* regime. Before *Alyeska,* civil rights plaintiffs could recover fees pursuant to the private attorney general doctrine only if private enforcement was necessary to defend important rights benefiting large numbers of people, and cost barriers might otherwise preclude private suits. Section 1988 contains no similar limitation—so that in the present suit there is no question as to the propriety of shifting WVUH's *attorney's* fees, even though it is highly doubtful they could have been awarded under pre-*Alyeska* equitable theories. In other respects, however, § 1988 is not as broad as the former regime. It is limited, for example, to violations of specified civil rights statutes—which means that it would not have reversed the outcome of *Alyeska* itself, which involved not a civil rights statute but the National Environmental Policy Act of 1969, 42 U.S.C. § 4321 *et seq.* Since it is clear that, in many respects, § 1988 was not meant to return us precisely to the pre-*Alyeska* regime, the objective of achieving such a return is no reason to depart from the normal import of the text.

WVUH further argues that the congressional purpose in enacting § 1988 must prevail over the ordinary meaning of the statutory terms. It quotes, for example, the House Committee Report to the effect that "the judicial remedy [must be] full and complete," H.R. Rep. No. 94–1558, p. 1 (1976), and the Senate Committee Report to the effect that "[c]itizens must have the opportunity to recover what it costs them to vindicate [civil] rights in court," S. Rep. No. 94–1011, at 2. As we have observed before, however, the purpose of a statute includes not only what it sets out to change, but also what it resolves to leave alone. See *Rodriguez v. United States*, 480 U.S. 522, 525–526 (1987).

**Food for Thought**

What does Justice Scalia mean when he says that "the purpose of a statute includes not only what it sets out to change, but also what it resolves to leave alone"?

The best evidence of that purpose is the statutory text adopted by both Houses of Congress and submitted to the President. Where that contains a phrase that is unambiguous—that has a clearly accepted meaning in both legislative and judicial practice—we do not permit it to be expanded or contracted by the statements of individual legislators or committees during the course of the enactment process. See *United States v. Ron Pair Enterprises, Inc.*, 489 U.S. 235, 241 (1989) ("[W]here, as here, the statute's language is plain, 'the sole function of the court is to enforce it according to its terms' "), quoting *Caminetti v. United States*, 242 U.S. 470, 485 (1917). Congress could easily have shifted "attorney's fees and expert witness fees," or "reasonable litigation expenses," as it did in contemporaneous statutes; it chose instead to enact more restrictive language, and we are bound by that restriction.

WVUH's last contention is that, even if Congress plainly did not include expert fees in the fee-shifting provisions of § 1988, it would have done so had it thought about it. Most of the pre-§ 1988 statutes that explicitly shifted expert fees dealt with environmental litigation, where the necessity of expert advice was readily apparent; and when Congress later enacted the EAJA, the federal counterpart of § 1988, it explicitly included expert fees. Thus, the argument runs, the 94th Congress simply forgot; it is our duty to ask how they would have decided had they actually considered the question.

This argument profoundly mistakes our role. Where a statutory term presented to us for the first time is ambiguous, we construe it to contain that permissible meaning which fits most logically and comfortably into the body of both previously and subsequently enacted law. See 2 J. Sutherland, Statutory Construction § 5201 (3d F. Horack ed.1943). We do so not because that precise accommodative meaning is what the lawmakers must have had in mind (how could an earlier Congress know what a later Congress would enact?), but because it is our role to make sense rather than nonsense out of the *corpus juris.* But where, as here, the meaning of the term prevents such accommodation, it is not our function to eliminate clearly expressed inconsistency of policy and to treat alike subjects that different Congresses have chosen to treat differently. The facile attribution of congressional "forgetfulness" cannot justify such a usurpation. Where what is at issue is not a contradictory disposition within the same enactment, but merely a difference between the more parsimonious policy of an earlier enactment and the more generous policy of a later one, there is no more basis for saying that the earlier Congress forgot than for saying that the earlier Congress felt differently. In such circumstances, the attribution of forgetfulness rests in reality upon the judge's assessment that the later statute contains the *better* disposition. But that is not for judges to prescribe. We thus reject this last argument for the same reason that Justice Brandeis, writing for the Court, once rejected a similar (though less explicit) argument by the United States:

> "[The statute's] language is plain and unambiguous. What the Government asks is not a construction of a statute, but, in effect, an enlargement of it by the court, so that what was omitted, presumably by inadvertence, may be included within its scope. To supply omissions transcends the judicial function." *Iselin v. United States,* 270 U.S. 245, 250–251 (1926).[7]

For the foregoing reasons, we conclude that § 1988 conveys no authority to shift expert fees. When experts appear at trial, they are of course eligible for the fee provided by § 1920 and § 1821—which was allowed in the present case by the Court of Appeals. [Affirmed.]

JUSTICE MARSHALL, dissenting.

As Justice STEVENS demonstrates, the Court uses the implements of literalism to wound, rather than to minister to, congressional intent in this case. That is a dangerous usurpation of congressional power when any statute is involved. It is troubling for special reasons, however, when the statute at issue is clearly designed to give access to the federal courts to persons and groups attempting to vindicate vital civil rights. * * *

---

7 WVUH at least asks us to guess the preferences of the *enacting* Congress. Justice STEVENS apparently believes our role is to guess the desires of the *present* Congress, or of Congresses yet to be. "Only time will tell," he says, "whether the Court, with its literal reading of § 1988, has correctly interpreted the will of Congress." The implication is that today's holding will be proved wrong if Congress amends the law to conform with his dissent. We think not. The "will of Congress" we look to is not a will evolving from Session to Session, but a will expressed and fixed in a particular enactment. Otherwise, we would speak not of "interpreting" the law but of "intuiting" or "predicting" it. Our role is to say what the law, as hitherto enacted, *is*; not to forecast what the law, as amended, *will be.*

JUSTICE STEVENS, with whom JUSTICE MARSHALL and JUSTICE BLACKMUN join, dissenting.

Since the enactment of the Statute of Wills in 1540, careful draftsmen have authorized executors to pay the just debts of the decedent, including the fees and expenses of the attorney for the estate. Although the omission of such an express authorization in a will might indicate that the testator had thought it unnecessary, or that he had overlooked the point, the omission would surely not indicate a deliberate decision by the testator to forbid any compensation to his attorney.

In the early 1970's, Congress began to focus on the importance of public interest litigation, and since that time, it has enacted numerous fee-shifting statutes. In many of these statutes, which the majority cites at length, Congress has expressly authorized the recovery of expert witness fees as part of the costs of litigation. The question in this case is whether, notwithstanding the omission of such an express authorization in 42 U.S.C. § 1988, Congress intended to authorize such recovery when it provided for "a reasonable attorney's fee as part of the costs." In my view, just as the omission of express authorization in a will does not preclude compensation to an estate's attorney, the omission of express authorization for expert witness fees in a fee-shifting provision should not preclude the award of expert witness fees. We should look at the way in which the Court has interpreted the text of *this statute* in the past, as well as *this statute's* legislative history, to resolve the question before us, rather than looking at the text of the many other statutes that the majority cites in which Congress expressly recognized the need for compensating expert witnesses.

[In *Missouri v. Jenkins*, 491 U.S. 274, 285 (1989), the Court reasoned that a "reasonable attorney's fee" in § 1988 referred to "a reasonable fee for the work product of an attorney." The Court concluded that, under this test, a paralegal's work is compensable under the section 1988's fee-shifting provision.] We explained: "[T]he fee must take into account the work not only of attorneys, but also of secretaries, messengers, librarians, janitors, and others whose labor contributes to the work product for which an attorney bills her client; and it must also take account of other expenses and profit. * * *"

This reasoning applies equally to other forms of specialized litigation support that a trial lawyer needs and that the client customarily pays for, either directly or indirectly. Although reliance on paralegals is a more recent development than the use of traditional expert witnesses, both paralegals and expert witnesses perform important tasks that save lawyers' time and enhance the quality of their work product. * * * To allow reimbursement of these other categories of expenses, and yet not to include expert witness fees, is both arbitrary and contrary to the broad remedial purpose that inspired the fee-shifting provision of § 1988.

The Senate Report on the Civil Rights Attorney's Fees Awards Act of 1976 explained that the purpose of the proposed amendment to 42 U.S.C. § 1988 was "to remedy anomalous gaps in our civil rights laws created by the United States Supreme Court's recent decision in *Alyeska Pipeline Service Co. v. Wilderness Society,* 421 U.S. 240 (1975), and to achieve consistency in our civil rights laws."[7] S. Rep. No. 94–1011, p. 1 (1976). The Senate Committee on the Judiciary wanted to level the playing field so that private citizens, who might have little or no money, could still serve as "private attorneys general" and afford to bring actions, even against state or local bodies, to enforce the civil rights laws. The Committee acknowledged that "[i]f private citizens are to be able to assert their civil rights, and if those who violate the Nation's fundamental laws are not to proceed with impunity, then citizens must have the opportunity to recover *what it costs them* to vindicate these rights in court." *Id.,* at 2 (emphasis added). According to the Committee, the bill would create "no startling new remedy," but would simply provide "the technical requirements" requested by the Supreme Court in *Alyeska,* so that courts could "continue the practice of awarding attorneys' fees which had been going on for years prior to the Court's May decision." *Id.,* at 6.

To underscore its intention to return the courts to their pre-*Alyeska* practice of shifting fees in civil rights cases, the Senate Committee's Report cited with approval not only several cases in which fees had been shifted, but also all of the cases contained in Legal Fees, Hearings before the Subcommittee on Representation of Citizen Interests of the Senate Committee on the Judiciary, 93d Cong., 1st Sess., pt. 3, pp. 888–1024, 1060–1062 (1973) (hereinafter Senate Hearings). See S. Rep. No. 94–1011, at 4, n. 3. The cases collected in the 1973 Senate Hearings included many in which courts had permitted the shifting of costs, including expert witness fees. At the time when the Committee referred to these cases, though several were later reversed, it used them to make the point that prior to *Alyeska,* courts awarded attorney's fees and costs, including expert witness fees, in civil rights cases, and that they did so in order to encourage private citizens to bring such suits. It was to this pre-*Alyeska* regime, in which courts could award expert witness fees along with attorney's fees, that the Senate Committee intended to return through the passage of the fee-shifting amendment to § 1988.

The House Report expressed concerns similar to those raised by the Senate Report. * * * It is fair to say that throughout the course of the hearings, a recurring theme was the desire to return to the pre-*Alyeska* practice in which courts could shift fees, including expert witness fees, and make those who acted as private attorneys general whole again, thus encouraging the enforcement of the civil rights laws.

---

7 In *Alyeska,* the Court held that courts were not free to fashion new exceptions to the American Rule, according to which each side assumed the cost of its own attorney's fees. The Court reasoned that it was not the Judiciary's role "to invade the legislature's province by redistributing litigation costs . . . ," *id.,* at 271, and that it would be "inappropriate for the Judiciary, without legislative guidance, to reallocate the burdens of litigation. . . ." *Id.,* at 247.

The case before us today is precisely the type of public interest litigation that Congress intended to encourage by amending § 1988 to provide for fee shifting of a "reasonable attorney's fee as part of the costs." * * * In January 1986, when the Pennsylvania Department of Public Welfare notified petitioner of its new Medicaid payment rates for Pennsylvania Medicaid recipients, petitioner believed them to be below the minimum standards for reimbursement specified by the Social Security Act. Petitioner successfully challenged the adequacy of the State's payment system under 42 U.S.C. § 1983. * * * This Court's determination today that petitioner must assume the cost of $104,133 in expert witness fees is at war with the congressional purpose of making the prevailing party whole. * * *

In recent years the Court has vacillated between a purely literal approach to the task of statutory interpretation and an approach that seeks guidance from historical context, legislative history, and prior cases identifying the purpose that motivated the legislation. Thus, for example, in *Christiansburg Garment Co. v. EEOC,* 434 U.S. 412 (1978), we rejected a "mechanical construction" of the fee-shifting provision in § 706(k) of Title VII of the Civil Rights Act of 1964 that the prevailing defendant had urged upon us. Although the text of the statute drew no distinction between different kinds of "prevailing parties," we held that awards to prevailing plaintiffs are governed by a more liberal standard than awards to prevailing defendants. That holding rested entirely on our evaluation of the relevant congressional policy and found no support within the four corners of the statutory text. Nevertheless, the holding was unanimous and, to the best of my knowledge, evoked no adverse criticism or response in Congress.

On those occasions, however, when the Court has put on its thick grammarian's spectacles and ignored the available evidence of congressional purpose and the teaching of prior cases construing a statute, the congressional response has been dramatically different. It is no coincidence that the Court's literal reading of Title VII, which led to the conclusion that disparate treatment of pregnant and nonpregnant persons was not discrimination on the basis of sex, see *General Electric Co. v. Gilbert,* 429 U.S. 125 (1976), was repudiated by the 95th Congress; that its literal reading of the "continuous physical presence" requirement in § 244(a)(1) of the Immigration and Nationality Act, which led to the view that the statute did not permit even temporary or inadvertent absences from this country, see *INS v. Phinpathya*, 464 U.S. 183 (1984), was rebuffed by the 99th Congress; [or] that its literal reading of the word "program" in Title IX of the Education Amendments of 1972, which led to the Court's gratuitous limit on the scope of the antidiscrimination provisions of Title IX, see *Grove City College v. Bell*, 465 U.S. 555 (1984), was rejected by the 100th Congress * * *.

In the domain of statutory interpretation, Congress is the master. It obviously has the power to correct our mistakes, but we do the country a disservice when we needlessly ignore persuasive evidence of Congress' actual purpose and require it "to take the time to revisit the matter" and to restate its purpose in more precise English whenever its work product suffers from an omission or inadvertent error. As Judge Learned Hand explained, statutes are likely to be imprecise.

> "All [legislators] have done is to write down certain words which they mean to apply generally to situations of that kind. To apply these literally may either pervert what was plainly their general meaning, or leave undisposed of what there is every reason to suppose they meant to provide for. Thus it is not enough for the judge just to use a dictionary. If he should do no more, he might come out with a result which every sensible man would recognize to be quite the opposite of what was really intended; which would contradict or leave unfulfilled its plain purpose." L. Hand, How Far Is a Judge Free in Rendering a Decision?, in The Spirit of Liberty 103, 106 (I. Dilliard ed.1952).

The Court concludes its opinion with the suggestion that disagreement with its textual analysis could only be based on the dissenters' preference for a "better" statute. It overlooks the possibility that a different view may be more faithful to Congress' command. The fact that Congress has consistently provided for the inclusion of expert witness fees in fee-shifting statutes when it considered the matter is a weak reed on which to rest the conclusion that the omission of such a provision represents a deliberate decision to forbid such awards. Only time will tell whether the Court, with its literal reading of § 1988, has correctly interpreted the will of Congress with respect to the issue it has resolved today. I respectfully dissent.

---

## Points for Discussion

### *a. Touchstones of Interpretation*

Justice Scalia focused on the plain meaning of the statutory text. In determining the meaning of the statute at issue, Justice Scalia considered other fee-shifting statutes that Congress had enacted. What role did those other statutes play in his analysis? Did they demonstrate Congress's intention in omitting specific language about expert fees? Or did they provide context for understanding the meaning of the text of section 1988? If the latter, what does it suggest about just how "plain" the meaning of the statutory text was?

Justice Stevens referred both to congressional purpose and congressional intent. Under his approach, is there a difference between those two things? What evidence did he cite for his conclusion about Congress's purpose or intention? Was he right to be confident about what that evidence revealed?

### *b. Judicial Role*

Justice Scalia rejected Justice Stevens's suggestion that Congress's omission of specific authorization for the recovery of expert fees was simply an oversight, asserting that "there is no more basis for saying that [Congress] forgot than for saying that

[Congress] felt differently." In his view, "the attribution of forgetfulness rests in reality upon the judge's assessment that the [such a reading of the] statute contains the *better* disposition." Do you agree that Justice Stevens's approach essentially involved judicial policy-making? If so, do you agree that such matters are "not for judges to prescribe"?

### c. *Subsequent Events*

Less than a year after the Court's decision in *West Virginia University Hospitals*, Congress enacted the Civil Rights Act of 1991, Pub. L. 102–166 (November 21, 1991). In section 3 of the Act, Congress stated that one of its purposes was "to respond to recent decisions of the Supreme Court by expanding the scope of relevant civil rights statutes in order to provide adequate protection to victims of discrimination." Section 113 of the Act explicitly permitted the recovery of expert fees as part of an attorney's fee award to the prevailing party. The revised 42 U.S.C. § 1988 provides: "In awarding an attorney's fee * * *, the court, in its discretion, may include expert fees as part of the attorney's fee."

Do these subsequent events suggest that Justice Stevens correctly divined Congress's intent? Or do they strengthen Justice Scalia's argument about the meaning of the prior version of the statute and about the proper judicial role in statutory interpretation?

---

## Perspective and Analysis

[The] system of making law by judicial opinion, and making law by distinguishing earlier cases, is what every American law student, every newborn American lawyer, first sees when he opens his eyes. * * * His image of the great judge * * * is the man (or woman) who has the intelligence to discern the best rule of law for the case at hand and then the skill to perform the broken-field running through earlier cases that leaves him free to impose that rule * * *.

All of this would be an unqualified good, were it not for a trend in government that has developed in recent centuries, called democracy. * * * [O]nce we have taken this realistic view of what common-law courts do, the uncomfortable relationship of common-law lawmaking to democracy (if not to the technical doctrine of the separation of powers) becomes apparent. * * *

My point in all of this is not that the common law should be scraped away as a barnacle on the hull of democracy. * * * But [I] do question whether the attitude of the common-law judge—the mind-set that asks, "What is the most desirable resolution of this case, and how can any impediments to the achievement of that result be evaded?"—is appropriate for most of the work that I do * * *. We live in an age of legislation, and most new law is statutory law. * * * It will not do to treat the enterprise [of statutory interpretation] as simply an inconvenient modern add-on to the judge's primary role of common-law lawmaker. Indeed, attacking the enterprise with the Mr. Fix-it mentality of the common-law judge is a sure recipe for incompetence and usurpation.

You will find it frequently said in judicial opinions of my court and others that the judge's objective in interpreting a statute is to give effect to "the intent of the legislature." * * * [But it] is simply incompatible with democratic government, or indeed, even with fair government, to have the meaning of a law determined by what the lawgiver meant, rather than by what the lawgiver promulgated. That seems to me one step worse than the trick the emperor Nero was said to engage in: posting edicts high up on the pillars, so that they could not easily be read. Government by unexpressed intent is similarly tyrannical. It is the law that governs, not the intent of the lawgiver. * * *

In reality, however, if one accepts the principle that the object of judicial interpretation is to determine the intent of the legislature, being bound by genuine but unexpressed legislative intent rather than the law is only the theoretical threat. The practical threat is that, under the guise or even the self-delusion of pursuing unexpressed legislative intents, common-law judges will in fact pursue their own objectives and desires, extending their lawmaking proclivities from the common law to the statutory field. When you are told to decide, not on the basis of what the legislature said, but on the basis of what it meant, and are assured that there is necessary connection between the two, your best shot at figuring out what the legislature meant is to ask yourself what a wise and intelligent person *should* have meant; and that will surely bring you to the conclusion that the law means what you think it ought to mean—which is precisely how judges decide things under the common law. * * *

It is simply not compatible with democratic theory that laws mean whatever they ought to mean, and that unelected judges decide what that is. * * * The text is the law, and it is the text that must be observed.

**Antonin Scalia, *Common-Law Courts in a Civil-Law System: The Role of United States Federal Courts in Interpreting the Constitution and Laws*, in A MATTER OF INTERPRETATION 9–23 (Amy Gutmann ed., 1998).**

---

Justice Scalia's approach to statutory interpretation is called "textualism," because it focuses on the ordinary meaning of the text of the statute rather than on the legislature's purpose or intent. Justice Scalia said that to "be a textualist in good standing, one need not be too dull to perceive the broader social purposes that a statute is designed, or could be designed, to serve; or too hidebound to realize that new times require new laws. One need only hold the belief that judges have no authority to pursue those broader purposes or write those new laws." Are you persuaded that a focus on statutory text limits the ability of judges to substitute their personal views for those of the elected legislature, or that it is more faithful to democracy?

Justice Scalia's textualism has been very influential. But it is not universally accepted, and the debate over the proper touchstone of interpretation continues. Consider the case that follows.

---

## *General Dynamics Land Systems, Inc. v. Cline*

540 U.S. 581 (2004)

JUSTICE SOUTER delivered the opinion of the Court.

The Age Discrimination in Employment Act of 1967 (ADEA or Act), 81 Stat. 602, 29 U.S.C. § 621 *et seq.,* forbids discriminatory preference for the young over the old. The question in this case is whether it also prohibits favoring the old over the young. We hold it does not.

In 1997, a collective-bargaining agreement between petitioner General Dynamics and the United Auto Workers eliminated the company's obligation to provide health benefits to subsequently retired employees, except as to then-current workers at least 50 years old. Respondents (collectively, Cline) were then at least 40 and thus protected by the Act, see 29 U.S.C. § 631(a), but under 50 and so without promise of the benefits. All of them objected to the new terms, although some had retired before the change in order to get the prior advantage, some retired afterwards with no benefit, and some worked on, knowing the new contract would give them no health coverage when they were through.

**Take Note**

The question in this case is whether the statute's prohibition on discrimination "because of * * * age" forbids treating older workers better than younger workers. Before you proceed any further, can you anticipate the respondents' textual argument? Does the employer have a response based on the text? If not, how might a focus on a different touchstone produce a different result? Does it help to think about why Congress likely prohibited discrimination because of age?

[Respondents] claimed that the agreement violated the ADEA, because it "discriminate[d against them] . . . with respect to . . . compensation, terms, conditions, or privileges of employment, because of [their] age," § 623(a)(1). The District Court called the federal claim one of "reverse age discrimination," upon which, it observed, no court had ever granted relief under the ADEA. It dismissed, [reasoning that] "the ADEA does not protect . . . the younger *against* the older." * * * A divided panel of the Sixth Circuit reversed * * *.

The common ground in this case is the generalization that the ADEA's prohibition covers "discriminat[ion] . . . because of [an] individual's age," 29 U.S.C. § 623(a)(1), that helps the younger by hurting the older. In the abstract, the phrase is open to an argument for a broader construction, since reference to "age" carries no express modifier and the word could be read to look two ways. This more expansive possible understanding does not, however, square with the natural reading of the whole provision prohibiting discrimination, and in fact Congress's interpretive clues speak almost unanimously to an understanding of discrimination as directed against workers who are older than the ones getting treated better.

Congress chose not to include age within discrimination forbidden by Title VII of the Civil Rights Act of 1964, § 715, being aware that there were legitimate reasons as well as invidious ones for making employment decisions on age. Instead it called for a study of the issue by the Secretary of Labor, who concluded that age discrimination was a serious problem, but one different in kind from discrimination on account of race. The Secretary spoke of disadvantage to older individuals from arbitrary and stereotypical employment distinctions (including then-common policies of age ceilings on hiring), but he examined the problem in light of rational considerations of increased pension cost and, in some cases, legitimate concerns about an older person's ability to do the job. [United States Dept. of Labor, The Older American Worker: Age Discrimination in Employment (June 1965) (Wirtz Report), at 2.] When the Secretary ultimately took the position that arbitrary discrimination against older workers was widespread and persistent enough to call for a federal legislative remedy, he placed his recommendation against the background of common experience that the potential cost of employing someone rises with age, so that the older an employee is, the greater the inducement to prefer a younger substitute. The report contains no suggestion that reactions to age level off at some point, and it was devoid of any indication that the Secretary had noticed unfair advantages accruing to older employees at the expense of their juniors.

Congress then asked for a specific proposal, Fair Labor Standards Amendments of 1966, § 606, 80 Stat. 845, which the Secretary provided in January 1967. 113 Cong. Rec. 1377 (1967); see also Public Papers of the Presidents, Lyndon B. Johnson, Vol. 1, Jan. 23, 1967, p. 37 (1968) (message to Congress urging that "[o]pportunity . . . be opened to the many Americans over 45 who are qualified and willing to work"). Extensive House and Senate hearings ensued. * * *

The testimony at both hearings dwelled on unjustified assumptions about the effect of age on ability to work. See, *e.g.*, House Hearings 151 (statement of Rep. Joshua Eilberg) ("At age 40, a worker may find that age restrictions become common . . . . By age 45, his employment opportunities are likely to contract sharply; they shrink more severely at age 55 and virtually vanish by age 65"); *id.*, at 422 (statement of Rep.

Claude Pepper) ("We must provide meaningful opportunities for employment to the thousands of workers 45 and over who are well qualified but nevertheless denied jobs which they may desperately need because someone has arbitrarily decided that they are too old"); Senate Hearings 34 (statement of Sen. George Murphy) ("[A]n older worker often faces an attitude on the part of some employers that prevents him from receiving serious consideration or even an interview in his search for employment"). The hearings specifically addressed higher pension and benefit costs as heavier drags on hiring workers the older they got. See, *e.g.*, House Hearings 45 (statement of Norman Sprague) (Apart from stereotypes, "labor market conditions, seniority and promotion-from-within policies, job training costs, pension and insurance costs, and mandatory retirement policies often make employers reluctant to hire older workers"). The record thus reflects the common facts that an individual's chances to find and keep a job get worse over time; as between any two people, the younger is in the stronger position, the older more apt to be tagged with demeaning stereotype. Not surprisingly, from the voluminous records of the hearings, we have found (and Cline has cited) nothing suggesting that any workers were registering complaints about discrimination in favor of their seniors.

Nor is there any such suggestion in the introductory provisions of the ADEA, 81 Stat. 602, which begins with statements of purpose and findings that mirror the Wirtz Report and the committee transcripts. *Id.*, § 2. The findings stress the impediments suffered by "older workers . . . in their efforts to retain . . . and especially to regain employment," *id.*, § 2(a)(1); "the [burdens] of arbitrary age limits regardless of potential for job performance," *id.*, § 2(a)(2); the costs of "otherwise desirable practices [that] may work to the disadvantage of older persons," *ibid.*; and "the incidence of unemployment, especially long-term unemployment[, which] is, relative to the younger ages, high among older workers," *id.*, § 2(a)(3). The statutory objects were "to promote employment of older persons based on their ability rather than age; to prohibit arbitrary age discrimination in employment; [and] to help employers and workers find ways of meeting problems arising from the impact of age on employment." *Id.*, § 2(b).

Such is the setting of the ADEA's core substantive provision, § 4 (as amended, 29 U.S.C. § 623), prohibiting employers and certain others from "discriminat[ion] . . . because of [an] individual's age," whenever (as originally enacted) the individual is "at least forty years of age but less than sixty-five years of age," § 12, 81 Stat. 607. The prefatory provisions and their legislative history make a case that we think is beyond reasonable doubt, that the ADEA was concerned to protect a relatively old worker from discrimination that works to the advantage of the relatively young.

Nor is it remarkable that the record is devoid of any evidence that younger workers were suffering at the expense of their elders, let alone that a social problem required a federal statute to place a younger worker in parity with an older one. Common experience is to the contrary, and the testimony, reports, and congressional findings simply confirm that Congress used the phrase "discriminat[ion] . . . because of [an] individual's age" the same way that ordinary people in common usage might speak of age discrimination any day of the week. One commonplace conception of American society in recent decades is its character as a "youth culture," and in a world where younger is better, talk about discrimination because of age is naturally understood to refer to discrimination against the older.

This same, idiomatic sense of the statutory phrase is confirmed by the statute's restriction of the protected class to those 40 and above. If Congress had been worrying about protecting the younger against the older, it would not likely have ignored everyone under 40. The youthful deficiencies of inexperience and unsteadiness invite stereotypical and discriminatory thinking about those a lot younger than 40, and prejudice suffered by a 40-year-old is not typically owing to youth, as 40-year-olds sadly tend to find out. The enemy of 40 is 30, not 50. See H.R. Rep. No. 805, 90th Cong., 1st Sess., 6 (1967) ("[T]estimony indicated [40] to be the age at which age discrimination in employment becomes evident"). Even so, the 40-year threshold was adopted over the objection that some discrimination against older people begins at an even younger age; female flight attendants were not fired at 32 because they were too young, *ibid.* See also Senate Hearings 47 (statement of Sec'y Wirtz) (lowering the minimum age limit "would change the nature of the proposal from an over-age employment discrimination measure"). Thus, the 40-year threshold makes sense as identifying a class requiring protection against preference for their juniors, not as defining a class that might be threatened by favoritism toward seniors.

The Courts of Appeals and the District Courts have read the law the same way, and prior to this case have enjoyed virtually unanimous accord in understanding the ADEA to forbid only discrimination preferring young to old. * * * The very strength of this consensus is enough to rule out any serious claim of ambiguity, and congressional silence after years of judicial interpretation supports adherence to the traditional view.

Cline and *amicus* EEOC proffer three rejoinders in favor of their competing view that the prohibition works both ways. First, they say (as does Justice THOMAS) that the statute's meaning is plain when the word "age" receives its natural and ordinary meaning and the statute is read as a whole giving "age" the same meaning throughout. And even if the text does not plainly mean what they say it means, they argue that the soundness of their version is shown by a colloquy on the floor of the Senate involving Senator Yarborough, a sponsor of the bill that became the ADEA. Finally, they fall back to the position (fortified by Justice SCALIA's dissent) that we should defer to the EEOC's reading of the statute. On each point, however, we think the argument falls short of unsettling our view of the natural meaning of the phrase speaking of discrimination, read in light of the statute's manifest purpose.

The first response to our reading is the dictionary argument that "age" means the length of a person's life, with the phrase "because of such individual's age" stating a simple test of causation: "discriminat[ion] . . . because of [an] individual's age" is treatment that would not have occurred if the individual's span of years had been longer or shorter. The case for this reading calls attention to the other instances of "age" in the ADEA that are not limited to old age, such as 29 U.S.C. § 623(f), which gives an employer a defense to charges of age discrimination when "age is a bona fide occupational qualification." Cline and the EEOC argue that if "age" meant old age, § 623(f) would then provide a defense (old age is a bona fide qualification) only for an employer's action that on our reading would never clash with the statute (because preferring the older is not forbidden).

**FYI**

The ADEA does not prohibit discrimination because of age when age is a "bona fide qualification" for the job—that is, a legitimate basis for preferring a person of a particular age to another person of a different age, such as when an airline requires pilots to retire at a certain age to ensure that active pilots have the reflexes necessary for safe operation of a plane.

The argument rests on two mistakes. First, it assumes that the word "age" has the same meaning wherever the ADEA uses it. But this is not so, and Cline simply misemploys the "presumption that identical words used in different parts of the same act are intended to have the same meaning." *Atlantic Cleaners & Dyers, Inc. v. United States*, 286 U.S. 427, 433 (1932). Cline forgets that "the presumption is not rigid and readily yields whenever there is such variation in the connection in which the words are used as reasonably to warrant the conclusion that they were employed in different parts of the act with different intent." *Ibid.* * * *. The presumption of uniform usage thus relents when a word used has several commonly understood meanings among which a speaker can alternate in the course of an ordinary conversation, without being confused or getting confusing.

"Age" is that kind of word. As Justice THOMAS agrees, the word "age" standing alone can be readily understood either as pointing to any number of years lived, or as common shorthand for the longer span and concurrent aches that make youth look good. Which alternative was probably intended is a matter of context; we understand the different choices of meaning that lie behind a sentence like "Age can be shown by a driver's license," and the statement, "Age has left him a shut-in." So it is easy to understand that Congress chose different meanings at different places in the ADEA, as the different settings readily show. Hence the second flaw in Cline's argument for uniform usage: it ignores the cardinal rule that "[s]tatutory language must be read in context [since] a phrase 'gathers meaning from the words around it.' " *Jones v. United States*, 527 U.S. 373, 389 (1999) (quoting *Jarecki v. G.D. Searle & Co.*, 367 U.S. 303, 307 (1961)). The point here is that we are not asking an abstract question about the meaning of "age"; we are seeking the meaning of the whole phrase "discriminate . . . because of such individual's age," where it occurs in the ADEA, 29 U.S.C. § 623(a)(1). As we have said, social history emphatically reveals an understanding of age discrimination as aimed against the old, and the statutory reference to age discrimination in this idiomatic sense is confirmed by legislative history. For the very reason that reference to context shows that "age" means "old age" when teamed with "discrimination," the provision of an affirmative defense when age is a bona fide occupational qualification readily shows that "age" as a qualification means comparative youth. As context tells us that "age" means one thing in § 623(a)(1) and another in § 623(f), so it also tells us that the presumption of uniformity cannot sensibly operate here.

The comparisons Justice THOMAS urges to *McDonald v. Santa Fe Trail Transp. Co.*,427 U.S. 273 (1976), and *Oncale v. Sundowner Offshore Services, Inc.*, 523 U.S. 75 (1998), serve to clarify our position. Both cases involved Title VII of the Civil Rights Act of 1964, 42 U.S.C. § 2000e *et seq.*, and its prohibition on employment discrimination "because of [an] individual's *race* . . .[or] *sex*," § 2000e–2(a)(1) (emphasis added).

**FYI**

In *McDonald*, the Court held that Title VII's ban on discrimination because of race protected white employees. In *Oncale*, the Court held that Title VII's ban on discrimination because of sex protected male employees from harassment by male co-workers.

The term "age" employed by the ADEA is not, however, comparable to the terms "race" or "sex" employed by Title VII. "Race" and "sex" are general terms that in every day usage require modifiers to indicate any relatively narrow application. We do not commonly understand "race" to refer only to the black race, or "sex" to refer only to the female. But the prohibition of age discrimination is readily read more narrowly than analogous provisions dealing with race and sex. That narrower reading is the more natural one in the textual setting, and it makes perfect sense because of Congress's demonstrated concern with distinctions that hurt older people.

The second objection has more substance than the first, but still not enough. The record of congressional action reports a colloquy on the Senate floor between two of the legislators most active in pushing for the ADEA, Senators Javits and Yarborough. Senator Javits began the exchange by raising a concern mentioned by Senator Dominick, that "the bill might not forbid discrimination between two persons each of whom would be between the ages of 40 and 65." 113 Cong. Rec. 31255 (1967). Senator Javits then gave his own view that, "if two individuals ages 52 and 42 apply for the same job, and the employer selected the man aged 42 solely . . . because he is younger than the man 52, then he will have violated the act," and asked Senator Yarborough for his opinion. *Ibid.* Senator Yarborough answered that "[t]he law prohibits age being a factor in the decision to hire, as to one age over the other, whichever way [the] decision went." *Ibid.*

Although in the past we have given weight to Senator Yarborough's views on the construction of the ADEA because he was a sponsor, see, *e.g., Public Employees*

*Retirement System of Ohio v. Betts*, 492 U.S. 158, 179 (1989), his side of this exchange is not enough to unsettle our reading of the statute. * * * What matters is that the Senator's remark, "whichever way [the] decision went," is the only item in all the 1967 hearings, reports, and debates going against the grain of the common understanding of age discrimination. Even from a sponsor, a single outlying statement cannot stand against a tide of context and history, not to mention 30 years of judicial interpretation producing no apparent legislative qualms. * * *

The third objection relies on a reading consistent with the Yarborough comment, adopted by the agency now charged with enforcing the statute * * *. When the EEOC adopted [its view] in 1981, shortly after assuming administrative responsibility for the ADEA, it gave no reasons for the view expressed * * *.

[D]eference to [an agency's] statutory interpretation is called for only when the devices of judicial construction have been tried and found to yield no clear sense of congressional intent. Here, regular interpretive method leaves no serious question, not even about purely textual ambiguity in the ADEA. The word "age" takes on a definite meaning from being in the phrase "discriminat[ion] . . . because of such individual's age," occurring as that phrase does in a statute structured and manifestly intended to protect the older from arbitrary favor for the younger.

**Make the Connection**

We will consider the relationship between agency interpretation and judicial interpretation, and the "*Chevron* doctrine," in Chapter 8.

We see the text, structure, purpose, and history of the ADEA, along with its relationship to other federal statutes, as showing that the statute does not mean to stop an employer from favoring an older employee over a younger one. The judgment of the Court of Appeals is reversed.

[Justice Scalia's dissent, asserting that the Court should have deferred to the EEOC's interpretation of the ADEA, has been omitted.]

Justice Thomas, with whom Justice Kennedy joins, dissenting.

This should have been an easy case. The plain language of 29 U.S.C. § 623(a)(1) mandates a particular outcome: that the respondents are able to sue for discrimination against them in favor of older workers. * * * And the only portion of legislative history relevant to the question before us is consistent with this outcome. Despite the fact that these traditional tools of statutory interpretation lead inexorably to the conclusion that respondents can state a claim for discrimination against the relatively young, the Court, apparently disappointed by this result, today adopts a different interpretation. In doing so, the Court, of necessity, creates a new tool of statutory interpretation, and then proceeds to give this newly created "social history" analysis dispositive weight.

Because I cannot agree with the Court's new approach to interpreting antidiscrimination statutes, I respectfully dissent.

The plain language of the ADEA clearly allows for suits brought by the relatively young when discriminated against in favor of the relatively old. The phrase "discriminate . . . because of such individual's age," 29 U.S.C. § 623(a)(1), is not restricted to discrimination because of relatively *older* age. If an employer fired a worker for the sole reason that the worker was under 45, it would be entirely natural to say that the worker had been discriminated against because of his age. I struggle to think of what other phrase I would use to describe such behavior. I wonder how the Court would describe such incidents, because the Court apparently considers such usage to be unusual, atypical, or aberrant.

The parties do identify a possible ambiguity, centering on the multiple meanings of the word "age." As the parties note, "age" does have an alternative meaning, namely, "[t]he state of being old; old age." American Heritage Dictionary 33 (3d ed.1992); see also Oxford American Dictionary 18 (1999); Webster's Third New International Dictionary 40 (1993). First, this secondary meaning is, of course, less commonly used than the primary meaning, and appears restricted to those few instances where it is clear in the immediate context of the phrase that it could have no other meaning. The phrases "hair white with age," American Heritage Dictionary, *supra,* at 33, or "*eyes . . . dim with age,*" Random House Dictionary of the English Language 37 (2d ed.1987), cannot possibly be using "age" to include "young age," unlike a phrase such as "he fired her because of her age." Second, the use of the word "age" in other portions of the statute effectively destroys any doubt. The ADEA's * * * bona fide occupational qualification defense, § 623(f)(1), would [be] rendered incoherent if the term "age" in [the provision] were read to mean only "older age." Although it is true that the "presumption that identical words used in different parts of the same act are intended to have the same meaning" is not "rigid" and can be overcome when the context is clear, *ante,* the presumption is not rebutted here, [because] the plain and common reading of the phrase "such individual's age" refers to the individual's chronological age.

The one structural argument raised by the Court in defense of its interpretation of "discriminates . . . because of such individual's age" is the provision limiting the ADEA's protections to those over 40 years of age. See 29 U.S.C. § 631(a). At first glance, this might look odd when paired with the conclusion that § 623(a)(1) bars discrimination against the relatively young as well as the relatively old, but there is a perfectly rational explanation. Congress could easily conclude that age discrimination directed against those under 40 is not as damaging, since a young worker unjustly fired is likely to find a new job or otherwise recover from the discrimination. A person over 40 fired due to irrational age discrimination (whether because the worker is too young or too old) might have a more difficult time recovering from the discharge and finding new employment. Such an interpretation also comports with the many findings of the Wirtz report [and] the parallel findings in the ADEA itself. See, *e.g.*, 29 U.S.C. § 621(a)(1) (finding that "older workers find themselves disadvantaged in their efforts to retain employment, and especially to regain employment when displaced from jobs") * * *.

This plain reading of the ADEA is bolstered by the interpretation of the agency charged with administering the statute. * * * Even if the Court disagrees with my interpretation of the language of the statute, it strains credulity to argue that such a reading is so unreasonable that an agency could not adopt it. * * *

Finally, the only relevant piece of legislative history addressing the question before the Court—whether it would be possible for a younger individual to sue based on discrimination against him in favor of an older individual—comports with the plain reading of the text. Senator Yarborough, in the only exchange that the parties identified from the legislative history discussing this particular question, confirmed that the text really meant what it said. See 113 Cong. Rec. 31255 (1967). Although the statute is clear, and hence there is no need to delve into the legislative history, this history merely confirms that the plain reading of the text is correct.

Strangely, the Court does not explain why it departs from accepted methods of interpreting statutes. It does, however, clearly set forth its principal reason for adopting its particular reading of the phrase "discriminate . . . based on [an] individual's age" in [its] opinion. "The point here," the Court states, "is that we are not asking an abstract question about the meaning of 'age'; we are seeking the meaning of the whole phrase 'discriminate . . . because of such individual's age.' . . . As we have said, *social history* emphatically reveals an understanding of age discrimination as aimed against the old, and the statutory reference to age discrimination in this idiomatic sense is confirmed by legislative history." (emphasis added). The Court does not define "social history," although it is apparently something different from legislative history, because the Court refers to legislative history as a separate interpretive tool in the very same sentence. * * *

It appears that the Court considers the "social history" of the phrase "discriminate . . . because of [an] individual's age" to be the principal evil that Congress targeted when it passed the ADEA. In each section of its analysis, the Court pointedly notes that there was no evidence of widespread problems of anti-youth discrimination, and that the primary concerns of Executive Branch officials and Members of Congress pertained to problems that workers generally faced as they increased in age. The Court reaches its final, legal conclusion as to the meaning of the phrase (that "ordinary" people employing the common usage of language would "talk about discrimination because of age [as] naturally [referring to] discrimination against the older") only after concluding both that "the ADEA was concerned to protect a relatively old worker from discrimination that works to the advantage of the relatively young" and that "the record is devoid of any evidence that younger workers were suffering at the expense of their elders, let alone that a social problem required a federal statute to place a younger worker in parity with an older one." Hence, the Court apparently concludes that if Congress has in mind a particular, principal, or primary form of discrimination when it passes an antidiscrimination provision prohibiting persons from "discriminating because of [some personal quality]," then the phrase "discriminate because of [some personal quality]" only covers the principal or most common form of discrimination relating to this personal quality.

The Court, however, has not typically interpreted nondiscrimination statutes in this odd manner. "[S]tatutory prohibitions often go beyond the principal evil to cover reasonably comparable evils, and it is ultimately the provisions of our laws rather than the principal concerns of our legislators by which we are governed." *Oncale v. Sundowner Offshore Services, Inc.*, 523 U.S. 75, 79 (1998). The oddity of the Court's new technique of statutory interpretation is highlighted by this Court's contrary approach to the racial-discrimination prohibition of Title VII of the Civil Rights Act of 1964, 78 Stat. 253, as amended, 42 U.S.C. § 2000e *et seq.*

There is little doubt that the motivation behind the enactment of the Civil Rights Act of 1964 was to prevent invidious discrimination against racial minorities, especially blacks. * * * The congressional debates and hearings, although filled with statements decrying discrimination against racial minorities and setting forth the disadvantages those minorities suffered, contain no references that I could find to any problem of discrimination against whites. * * * In light of the Court's opinion today, it appears that this Court has been treading down the wrong path with respect to Title VII since at least 1976. See *McDonald v. Santa Fe Trail Transp. Co.*, 427 U.S. 273 (1976) (holding that Title VII protected whites discriminated against in favor of racial minorities).

[T]he Court's new approach to antidiscrimination statutes would lead us far astray from well-settled principles of statutory interpretation. The Court's examination of "social history" is in serious tension (if not outright conflict) with our prior cases in such matters. Under the Court's current approach, for instance, *McDonald* and *Oncale*[6] are wrongly decided. One can only hope that this new technique of statutory interpretation does not catch on, and that its errors are limited to only this case. * * *

---

6 "[M]ale-on-male sexual harassment in the workplace was assuredly not the principal evil Congress was concerned with when it enacted Title VII." *Oncale*, 523 U.S., at 79. I wonder if there is even a single reference in all the committee reports and congressional debates on Title VII's prohibition of sex discrimination to any "social problem requir[ing] a federal statute [to correct]" arising out of excessive male-on-male sexual harassment.

## Points for Discussion

***a. Statutory Purpose***

Justice Souter's opinion began by explaining the impetus for the enactment of the ADEA and by identifying Congress's purpose, which was to "protect a relatively old worker from discrimination that works to the advantage of the relatively young." The opinion then sought to determine the meaning of the statutory language in light of that background. Would you say that the Court's touchstone was legislative purpose or textual meaning? Or was it both? If the latter, is it a satisfying way to reconcile the competing claims about how to engage in statutory interpretation?

***b. Statutory Text***

Justice Thomas focused on the ordinary meaning of the statutory text. Do you agree with him that the phrase "discriminate * * * because of * * * age" plainly applies to workplace policies that disadvantage younger workers for the benefit of older workers? Does it depend which meaning of "age" we choose? When text is susceptible to more than one meaning, how should a judge committed to enforcing the ordinary meaning of text choose among them?

**Test Your Knowledge**

To assess your understanding of the material in this Chapter, click here to take a quiz.

## Chapter Three

# *Interpreting Text*

In Chapter 2, we considered the debate over how central text should be in the inquiry about statutory meaning. As we saw, some interpreters focus on legislative intent or purpose, while others confine their inquiry to the text. This debate is a profound one, but it is also easy to overstate its importance. After all, there is wide agreement that the statutory text is at least *relevant* in determining statutory meaning. The conflicts over the meaning of the statutes that we examined in Chapter 2 typically arose at the margins, in unusual cases. But even interpreters committed to determining a statute's purpose or the spirit of the law recognize that the text alone can often resolve a case. As Professors Hart and Sacks, who were committed to the Legal Process approach and a focus on statutory purpose, explained, "When the words fit with all the relevant elements of their context to convey a single meaning, as applied to the matter at hand, the mind of the interpreter moves to a confident conclusion almost instantaneously. * * * Interpretation requires a conscious effort when the words do not fit with their context to convey any single meaning." Henry M. Hart, Jr., & Albert M. Sacks, The Legal Process: Basic Problems in the Making and Application of Law 1374 (William N. Eskridge Jr. & Philip P. Frickey eds. 1994).

In this Chapter, we put aside the debate over the correct touchstone for statutory interpretation and consider the rules that apply when we focus on the meaning of statutory text. As we will see, some of those principles are simply rules about how we ordinarily understand language; others are designed to advance particular policies thought to be important; and still others attempt to govern decision-making by injecting a dose of common sense into the act of interpretation. At bottom, because language can be indeterminate and text can be susceptible to multiple meanings, we need a set of default rules about how to break ties among multiple plausible meanings of the text. We consider those rules in this Chapter.

## A. Absurdity and Scrivener's Errors

### *United States v. Kirby*

74 U.S. 482 (1868)

The defendants were indicted for knowingly and wilfully obstructing and retarding the passage of the mail and of a mail carrier, in the District Court for the District of Kentucky. The case was certified to the Circuit Court for that district.

The indictment was founded upon the ninth section of the act of Congress, of March 3, 1825, * * * which provides "that, if any person shall knowingly and wilfully obstruct or retard the passage of the mail, or of any driver or carrier, or of any horse or carriage carrying the same, he shall, upon conviction, for every such offence, pay a fine not exceeding one hundred dollars * * *."

The indictment contained four counts, and charged the defendants with knowingly and wilfully obstructing the passage of the mail of the United States, in the district of Kentucky, on the first of February, 1867, contrary to the act of Congress; and with knowingly and wilfully obstructing and retarding at the same time in that district, the passage of one Farris, a carrier of the mail, while engaged in the performance of this duty; and with knowingly and wilfully retarding at the same time in that district, the passage of the steamboat General Buell, which was then carrying the mail of the United States from the city of Louisville, in Kentucky, to the city of Cincinnati, in Ohio.

To this indictment the defendants, among other things, pleaded specially to the effect, that at the September Term, 1866, of the Circuit Court of Gallation County, in the State of Kentucky, which was a court of competent jurisdiction, two indictments were found by the grand jury of the county against the said Farris for murder; that by order of the court bench warrants were issued upon these indictments, and placed in the hands of Kirby, one of the defendants, who was then sheriff of the county, commanding him to arrest the said Farris and bring him before the court to answer the indictments; that in obedience to these warrants he arrested Farris, and was accompanied by the other defendants as a posse, who were lawfully summoned to assist him in effecting the arrest; that they entered the steamboat Buell to make the arrest, and only used such force as was necessary to accomplish this end; and that they acted without any intent or purpose to obstruct or retard the mail, or the passage of the steamer. To this plea the district attorney of the United States demurred, and upon the argument of the demurrer two questions arose:

First. Whether the arrest of the mail-carrier upon the bench warrants from the Circuit Court of Kentucky was, under the circumstances, an obstruction of the mail within the meaning of the act of Congress.

Second. Whether the arrest was obstructing or retarding the passage of a carrier of the mail within the meaning of that act.

Mr. Justice Field, after stating the case, delivered the opinion of the court, as follows:

There can be but one answer, in our judgment, to the questions certified to us. The statute of Congress by its terms applies only to persons who "knowing and willfully" obstruct or retard the passage of the mail, or of its carrier; that is, to those who know that the acts performed will have that effect, and perform them with the intention that such shall be their operation. When the acts which create the obstruction are in themselves unlawful, the intention to obstruct will be imputed to their author, although the attainment of other ends may have been his primary object. The statute has no reference to acts lawful in themselves, from the execution of which a temporary delay to the mails unavoidably follows. All persons in the public service are exempt, as a matter of public policy, from arrest upon civil process while thus engaged. Process of that kind can, therefore, furnish no justification for the arrest of a carrier of the mail. * * * The rule is different when the process is issued upon a charge of felony. No officer or employee of the United States is placed by his position, or the services he is called to perform, above responsibility to the legal tribunals of the country, and to the ordinary processes for his arrest and detention, when accused of felony, in the forms prescribed by the Constitution and laws. The public inconvenience which may occasionally follow from the temporary delay in the transmission of the mail caused by the arrest of its carriers upon such charges, is far less than that which would arise from extending to them the immunity for which the counsel of the government contends. Indeed, it may be doubted whether it is competent for Congress to exempt the employees of the United States from arrest on criminal process from the State courts, when the crimes charged against them are not merely *mala prohibita*, but are *mala in se*.

**Definition**

*Mala prohibita* is Latin for "wrongs prohibited" and refers to acts that are against the law even though they are not inherently evil. *Mala in se* is the plural of the Latin phrase meaning "wrong in itself" and refers to acts that are inherently wrongful or evil.

But whether legislation of that character be constitutional or not, no intention to extend such exemption should be attributed to Congress unless clearly manifested by its language. All laws should receive a sensible construction. General terms should be so limited in their application as not to lead to injustice, oppression, or an absurd consequence. It will always, therefore, be presumed that the legislature intended exceptions to its language, which would avoid results of this character. The reason of the law in such cases should prevail over its letter.

The common sense of man approves the judgment mentioned by Puffendorf, that the Bolognian law which enacted, "that whoever drew blood in the streets should be punished with the utmost severity," did not extend to the surgeon who opened the vein of a person that fell down in the street in a fit. The same common sense accepts the ruling, cited by Plowden, that the statute of 1st Edward II, which enacts that a prisoner who breaks prison shall be guilty of felony, does not extend to a prisoner who breaks out when the prison is on fire—"for he is not to be hanged because he would not stay to be burnt." And we think that a like common sense will sanction the ruling we make, that the act of Congress which punishes the obstruction or retarding of the passage of the mail, or of its carrier, does not apply to a case of temporary detention of the mail caused by the arrest of the carrier upon an indictment for murder.

The questions certified to us must be answered IN THE NEGATIVE; and it is so ORDERED.

---

## Points for Discussion

### *a. Textual Meaning*

The Court appeared to begin its analysis of the statute by conceding that the plain meaning of the text reached the defendant in the case. After all, there would be no reason to "limit[ ]" the "[g]eneral terms" of the statute to avoid an "absurd consequence," or to depart from the statute's "letter," if the ordinary meaning of the statutory text did not reach the defendant in the first place. Is it obvious to you that, in light of the Court's recital of the facts of the case, the defendant "knowingly and wilfully obstruct[ed] or retard[ed] the passage of the mail, or of any driver or carrier, or of any horse or carriage carrying the same"? On which words of the statute could the defendant have relied in making an argument based on the plain meaning of the statute?

### *b. The Absurdity Doctrine*

The Court construed the statute narrowly to avoid what it called an "absurd consequence," based on the assumption that "the legislature intended exceptions to its language, which would avoid results of this character." In so doing, the Court relied on the so-called "absurdity doctrine." The absurdity doctrine holds that judges may depart from the plain meaning of statutory text to avoid absurd consequences. Accordingly, the doctrine functions like a caveat to, or safety valve from, the plain meaning rule.

In one sense, the absurdity doctrine seems indistinguishable from an approach that focuses on the spirit, rather than the letter, of the law. (Recall, for example, the Court's approach in *Riggs v. Palmer*, which we considered in Chapter 2, in seeking to imagine what the legislature would have decided had it anticipated the question at issue.) Indeed, the Court in *Kirby* explained its conclusion by declaring that the "reason of the law in such cases should prevail over its letter."

But unlike an approach that generally seeks to determine statutory purpose or the spirit of the law, the absurdity doctrine is not particularly controversial. In fact, even textualists—judges and scholars who assert that the act of interpretation should focus on the ordinary meaning of the statutory text rather than the legislature's unenacted intentions—generally accept, and in unusual cases are willing to apply, the absurdity doctrine. For those judges and scholars, the absurdity doctrine functions as a limited exception to the plain meaning approach.

Is the absurdity doctrine—under which judges can depart from the plain meaning of statutory text when it would produce "absurd results"—consistent with an approach that treats the plain meaning of statutory text as the only legitimate touchstone of interpretation? Is there a meaningful difference between the absurdity doctrine, on the one hand, and an approach that more generally considers legislative purpose or statutory spirit, on the other? See John F. Manning, *The Absurdity Doctrine*, 116 HARV. L. REV. 2387 (2003). Even assuming there is a difference, how does a judge applying the absurdity doctrine know when a particular outcome is "absurd"? Is it obvious to you that the outcome in *Kirby* was absurd?

---

## *Green v. Bock Laundry Machine Co.*

490 U.S. 504 (1989)

JUSTICE STEVENS delivered the opinion of the Court.

This case presents the question whether Rule 609(a)(1) of the Federal Rules of Evidence requires a judge to let a civil litigant impeach an adversary's credibility with evidence of the adversary's prior felony convictions. * * *

While in custody at a county prison, petitioner Paul Green obtained work-release employment at a car wash. On his sixth day at work, Green reached inside a large dryer to try to stop it. A heavy rotating drum caught and tore off his right arm. Green brought this product liability action against respondent Bock Laundry Co. (Bock), manufacturer of the machine. At trial Green testified that he had been instructed inadequately concerning the machine's operation and dangerous character. Bock impeached Green's testimony by eliciting admissions that he had been convicted of conspiracy to commit burglary and burglary, both felonies. The jury returned a verdict for Bock. On appeal Green argued that the District Court had erred by denying his pretrial motion to exclude the impeaching evidence. The Court of Appeals summarily affirmed the District Court's ruling.

* * * We begin by considering the extent to which the text of Rule 609 answers the question before us. Concluding that the text is ambiguous with respect to civil cases, we then seek guidance from legislative history and from the Rules' overall structure.

Federal Rule of Evidence 609(a) provides:

> "General Rule. For the purpose of attacking the credibility of a witness, evidence that the witness has been convicted of a crime shall be admitted if elicited from the witness or established by public record during cross-examination but only if the crime (1) was punishable by death or imprisonment in excess of one year under the law under which the witness was convicted, and the court determines that the probative value of admitting this evidence outweighs its prejudicial effect to the defendant, or (2) involved dishonesty or false statement, regardless of the punishment."

**FYI**

During a trial, when a party's adversary calls a witness to testify, the party's attorney has an opportunity to cross-examine the witness. During cross-examination, the attorney usually tries to impeach the credibility of the witness by attempting to solicit testimony that will lead the fact-finder to doubt the witness's veracity. Fairly or not, evidence that the witness has previously been convicted of a crime often leads jurors to view the witness's testimony more skeptically.

By its terms the Rule requires a judge to allow impeachment of any witness with prior convictions for felonies not involving dishonesty "only if" the probativeness of the evidence is greater than its prejudice "to the defendant." It follows that impeaching evidence detrimental to the prosecution in a criminal case "shall be admitted" without any such balancing.

The Rule's plain language commands weighing of prejudice to a defendant in a civil trial as well as in a criminal trial. But that literal reading would compel an odd result in a case like this. Assuming that all impeaching evidence has at least minimal probative value, and given that the evidence of plaintiff Green's convictions had some prejudicial effect on his case—but surely none on defendant Bock's—balancing according to the strict language of Rule 609(a)(1) inevitably leads to the conclusion that the evidence was admissible. In fact, under this construction of the Rule, impeachment detrimental to a civil plaintiff always would have to be admitted.

No matter how plain the text of the Rule may be, we cannot accept an interpretation that would deny a civil plaintiff the same right to impeach an adversary's testimony that it grants to a civil defendant. The Sixth Amendment to the Constitution guarantees a criminal defendant certain fair trial rights not enjoyed by the prosecution, while the Fifth Amendment lets the accused choose not to testify at trial. In contrast, civil litigants in federal court share equally the protections of the

Fifth Amendment's Due Process Clause. Given liberal federal discovery rules, the inapplicability of the Fifth Amendment's protection against self-incrimination, and the need to prove their case, civil litigants almost always must testify in depositions or at trial. Denomination as a civil defendant or plaintiff, moreover, is often happenstance based on which party filed first or on the nature of the suit. Evidence that a litigant or his witness is a convicted felon tends to shift a jury's focus from the worthiness of the litigant's position to the moral worth of the litigant himself. It is unfathomable why a civil plaintiff—but not a civil defendant—should be subjected to this risk. Thus we agree with the Seventh Circuit that as far as civil trials are concerned, Rule 609(a)(1) "can't mean what it says." *Campbell v. Greer*, 831 F.2d 700, 703 (7th Cir. 1987).

Out of this agreement flow divergent courses, each turning on the meaning of "defendant." The word might be interpreted to encompass all witnesses, civil and criminal, parties or not. See *Green v. Shearson Lehman/American Express, Inc.*, 625 F. Supp. 382, 383 (E.D. Pa. 1985). It might be read to connote any party offering a witness, in which event Rule 609(a)(1)'s balance would apply to civil, as well as criminal, cases. *E.g., Howard v. Gonzales*, 658 F.2d 352 (5th Cir. 1981). Finally, "defendant" may refer only to the defendant in a criminal case. See, *e.g., Campbell*, 831 F.2d, at 703. These choices spawn a corollary question: must a judge allow prior felony impeachment of all civil witnesses as well as all criminal prosecution witnesses, or is Rule 609(a)(1) inapplicable to civil cases, in which event Rule 403 would authorize a judge to balance in such cases? Because the plain text does not resolve these issues, we must examine the history leading to enactment of Rule 609 as law.

**FYI**

Rule 403 of the Federal Rules of Evidence provides a general rule that evidence should not be admitted if "its probative value is substantially outweighed by the danger of unfair prejudice, confusion of the issues, or misleading the jury, or by consideration of undue delay, waste of time, or needless presentation of cumulative evidence."

At common law a person who had been convicted of a felony was not competent to testify as a witness. "[T]he disqualification arose as part of the punishment for the crime, only later being rationalized on the basis that such a person was unworthy of belief." 3 J. Weinstein & M. Berger, Weinstein's Evidence ¶ 609[02], p. 609–58 (1988). As the law evolved, this absolute bar gradually was replaced by a rule that allowed such witnesses to testify in both civil and criminal cases, but also to be impeached by evidence of a prior felony conviction or a *crimen falsi* misdemeanor conviction. In the face of scholarly criticism of automatic admission of such impeaching evidence, some courts moved toward a more flexible approach.

**Definition**

*Crimen falsi* is Latin for "crime of falsehood."

[Starting in the 1940s, the American Law Institute and the ABA proposed rules to deal with evidence of prior convictions offered to impeach a witness. In *Luck v. United States*, 348 F.2d 763, 768 (D.C. Cir. 1965), the Court of Appeals interpreted the District of Columbia Code to give judges discretion to exclude evidence of prior convictions of any witness if its probative value was outweighed by the risk of undue prejudice. Congress responded in 1970 by amending the District of Columbia Code to provide that both prior felony and *crimen falsi* impeaching evidence "shall be admitted."]

Amid controversy over *Luck,* a distinguished Advisory Committee appointed at the recommendation of the Judicial Conference of the United States submitted in March 1969 the first draft of evidence rules to be used in all federal civil and criminal proceedings. Rule 6–09, forerunner of Federal Rule of Evidence 609, allowed all *crimen falsi* and felony convictions evidence without mention of judicial discretion. * * * [But] the Advisory Committee embraced the *Luck* doctrine in its second draft. Issued in March 1971, this version of Rule 609(a) authorized the judge to exclude either felony or *crimen falsi* evidence upon determination that its probative value was "substantially outweighed by the danger of unfair prejudice." Revised Draft of Proposed Rules of Evidence, 51 F.R.D. 315, 391 (1971). The Committee specified that its primary concern was prejudice to the witness-accused * * *. Yet the text of the proposal was broad enough to allow a judge to protect not only criminal defendants, but also civil litigants and nonparty witnesses, from unfair prejudice.

As had *Luck*'s interpretation of the District of Columbia Code, the Advisory Committee's revision of Rule 609(a) met resistance. The Department of Justice [and] Senator McClellan objected to the adoption of the *Luck* doctrine and urged reinstatement of the earlier draft. The Advisory Committee backed off. As Senator McClellan had requested, it submitted as its third and final draft the same strict version it had proposed in March 1969. Rules of Evidence, 56 F.R.D. 183, 269–270 (1973). The Committee's Note explained: "Whatever may be the merits of [other] views, this rule is drafted to accord with the Congressional policy manifested in the 1970 legislation." *Id.*, at 270. This Court forwarded the Advisory Committee's final draft to Congress on November 20, 1972.

The House of Representatives did not accept the Advisory Committee's final proposal. A Subcommittee of the Judiciary Committee recommended an amended version similar to the text of the present Rule 609(a), except that it avoided the current Rule's ambiguous reference to prejudice to "the defendant." Rather, in prescribing weighing of admissibility of prior felony convictions, it used the same open-ended reference to "unfair prejudice" found in the Advisory Committee's second draft.

The House Judiciary Committee departed even further from the Advisory Committee's final recommendation, preparing a draft that did not allow impeachment by evidence of prior conviction unless the crime involved dishonesty or false statement.[21] Motivating the change were concerns about the deterrent effect upon an accused who might wish to testify and the danger of unfair prejudice, "even upon a witness who was not the accused," from allowing impeachment by prior felony convictions regardless of their relation to the witness' veracity. H.R. Rep. No. 93–650, p. 11 (1973). Although the Committee Report focused on criminal defendants and did not mention civil litigants, its express concerns encompassed all nonaccused witnesses.

Representatives who advocated the automatic admissibility approach of the Advisory Committee's draft and those who favored the intermediate approach proposed by the Subcommittee both opposed the Committee's bill on the House floor. Four Members pointed out that the Rule applied in civil, as well as criminal, cases. [120 Cong. Rec. 2376–2381 (1974).] The House voted to adopt the Rule as proposed by its Judiciary Committee.

The Senate Judiciary Committee proposed an intermediate path. For criminal defendants, it would have allowed impeachment only by *crimen falsi* evidence; for other witnesses, it also would have permitted prior felony evidence only if the trial judge found that probative value outweighed "prejudicial effect against the party offering that witness." This language thus required the exercise of discretion before prior felony convictions could be admitted in civil litigation. But the full Senate, prodded by Senator McClellan, reverted to the version that the Advisory Committee had submitted. See 120 Cong. Rec. 37076, 37083 (1974).*

Conflict between the House bill, allowing impeachment only by *crimen falsi* evidence, and the Senate bill, embodying the Advisory Committee's automatic admissibility approach, was resolved by a Conference Committee. The conferees' compromise—enacted as Federal Rule of Evidence 609(a)(1)—authorizes impeachment by felony convictions, "but only if" the court determines that probative value outweighs "prejudicial effect to the defendant." The Conference Committee's Report makes it perfectly clear that the balance set forth in this draft, unlike the second Advisory Committee and the Senate Judiciary Committee versions, does not protect all nonparty witnesses:

> "The danger of prejudice to a witness other than the defendant (such as injury to the witness' reputation in his community) was considered and rejected by the Conference as an element to be weighed in determining admissibility. It was the judgment of the

---

21 The version sent to the full House by the Judiciary Committee simply provided: "(a) General Rule—For the purpose of attacking the credibility of a witness, evidence that he has been convicted of a crime is admissible only if the crime involved dishonesty or false statement." 120 Cong. Rec. 2374 (1974).

* The version approved by the full Senate provided: "(a) General rule. For the purpose of attacking the credibility of a witness, evidence that he has been convicted of a crime is admissible but only if the crime (1) was punishable by death or imprisonment in excess of one year under the law under which he was convicted or (2) involved dishonesty or false statement regardless of the punishment." —*Ed.*

> Conference that the danger of prejudice to a nondefendant witness is outweighed by the need for the trier of fact to have as much relevant evidence on the issue of credibility as possible." H.R. Conf. Rep. No. 93–1597, pp. 9–10 (1974).

Equally clear is the conferees' intention that the rule shield the accused, but not the prosecution,[25] in a criminal case. Impeachment by convictions, the Committee Report stated, "should only be excluded where it presents a danger of improperly influencing the outcome of the trial by persuading the trier of fact to convict the defendant on the basis of his prior criminal record." H.R. Conf. Rep. No. 93–1597, *supra,* at 10.

But this emphasis on the criminal context, in the Report's use of terms such as "defendant" and "to convict" and in individual conferees' explanations of the compromise,[26] raises some doubt over the Rule's pertinence to civil litigants. The discussions suggest that only two kinds of witnesses risk prejudice—the defendant who elects to testify in a criminal case and witnesses other than the defendant in the same kind of case. Nowhere is it acknowledged that undue prejudice to a civil litigant also may improperly influence a trial's outcome. Although this omission lends support to [the view] that "legislative oversight" caused exclusion of civil parties from Rule 609(a)(1)'s balance, a number of considerations persuade us that the Rule was meant to authorize a judge to weigh prejudice against no one other than a criminal defendant.

To the extent various drafts of Rule 609 distinguished civil and criminal cases, * * * they did so only to mitigate prejudice to criminal defendants. Any prejudice that convictions impeachment might cause witnesses other than the accused was deemed "so minimal as scarcely to be a subject of comment." Advisory Committee's Note, 51 F.R.D., at 392. Far from voicing concern lest such impeachment unjustly diminish a civil witness in the eyes of the jury, Representative Hogan declared that this evidence ought to be used to measure a witness' moral value. [120 Cong. Rec. 2376 (1974).] Furthermore, Representative Dennis—who in advocating a Rule

---

25 As one Conference Committee Member explained: "[N]ow a defendant can cross examine a government witness about any of his previous felony convictions; he can always do it, because that will not prejudice him in any way. . . . Only the government is going to be limited. . . ." 120 Cong. Rec. 40894 (1974) (remarks of Rep. Dennis).

26 Representative Dennis, who had stressed in earlier debates that the Rule would apply to both civil and criminal cases, see 120 Cong. Rec. 2377 (1974), explained the benefits of the Rule for criminal defendants and made no reference to benefits for civil litigants when he said: "[Y]ou can ask about all . . . felonies on cross examination, only if you can convince the court, and the burden is on the *government,* which is an important change in the law, that the probative value of the question is greater than the damage to the *defendant*; and that is damage or prejudice *to the defendant alone.*" *Id.,* at 40894 (emphases supplied). In the same debate Representative Hogan manifested awareness of the Rule's broad application. While supporting the compromise, he reiterated his preference for a rule "that, for the purpose of attacking the credibility of a witness, *even if the witness happens to be the defendant in a criminal case,* evidence that he has been convicted of a crime is admissible and may be used to challenge that witness' credibility if the crime is a felony or is a misdemeanor involving dishonesty of [*sic*] false statement." *Id.,* at 40895 (emphasis added).

limiting impeachment to *crimen falsi* convictions had recognized the impeachment Rule's applicability to civil trials—not only debated the issue on the House floor, but also took part in the conference out of which Rule 609 emerged. See 120 Cong. Rec. 2377–2380, 39942, 40894–40895 (1974). These factors indicate that Rule 609(a)(1)'s textual limitation of the prejudice balance to criminal defendants resulted from deliberation, not oversight.

Had the conferees desired to protect other parties or witnesses, they could have done so easily. Presumably they had access to all of Rule 609's precursors, particularly the drafts prepared by the House Subcommittee and the Senate Judiciary Committee, both of which protected the civil litigant as well as the criminal defendant. Alternatively, the conferees could have amended their own draft to include other parties. They did not for the simple reason that they intended that only the accused in a criminal case should be protected from unfair prejudice by the balance set out in Rule 609(a)(1).

That conclusion does not end our inquiry. We next must decide whether Rule 609(a)(1) governs all prior felonies impeachment, so that no discretion may be exercised to benefit civil parties, or whether Rule 609(a)(1)'s specific reference to the criminal defendant leaves Rule 403 balancing available in the civil context.

A general statutory rule usually does not govern unless there is no more specific rule. See *D. Ginsberg & Sons, Inc. v. Popkin*, 285 U.S. 204, 208 (1932). * * * Rule 609(a) states that impeaching convictions evidence "shall be admitted." With regard to subpart (2), which governs impeachment by *crimen falsi* convictions, it is widely agreed that this imperative, coupled with the absence of any balancing language, bars exercise of judicial discretion pursuant to Rule 403. Subpart (1), concerning felonies, is subject to the same mandatory language; accordingly, Rule 403 balancing should not pertain to this subsection either.

In summary, we hold that Federal Rule of Evidence 609(a)(1) requires a judge to permit impeachment of a civil witness with evidence of prior felony convictions regardless of ensuant unfair prejudice to the witness or the party offering the testimony. Thus no error occurred when the jury in this product liability suit learned through impeaching cross-examination that plaintiff Green was a convicted felon. [*Affirmed.*]

JUSTICE SCALIA, concurring in the judgment.

We are confronted here with a statute which, if interpreted literally, produces an absurd, and perhaps unconstitutional, result. Our task is to give some alternative meaning to the word "defendant" in Federal Rule of Evidence 609(a)(1) that avoids this consequence; and then to determine whether Rule 609(a)(1) excludes the operation of Federal Rule of Evidence 403.

I think it entirely appropriate to consult all public materials, including the background of Rule 609(a)(1) and the legislative history of its adoption, to verify that what seems to us an unthinkable disposition (civil defendants but not civil plaintiffs receive the benefit of weighing prejudice) was indeed unthought of, and thus to justify a departure from the ordinary meaning of the word "defendant" in the Rule. For that purpose, however, it would suffice to observe that counsel have not provided, nor have we discovered, a shred of evidence that anyone has ever proposed or assumed such a bizarre disposition. The Court's opinion, however, goes well beyond this. Approximately four-fifths of its substantive analysis is devoted to examining the evolution of Federal Rule of Evidence 609 [through the legislative process]—all with the evident purpose, not merely of confirming that the word "defendant" cannot have been meant literally, but of determining what, precisely, the Rule does mean.

I find no reason to believe that any more than a handful of the Members of Congress who enacted Rule 609 were aware of its interesting evolution * * *; or that any more than a handful of them (if any) voted, with respect to their understanding of the word "defendant" and the relationship between Rule 609 and Rule 403, on the basis of the referenced statements in the Subcommittee, Committee, or Conference Committee Reports, or floor debates—statements so marginally relevant, to such minute details, in such relatively inconsequential legislation. The meaning of terms on the statute books ought to be determined, not on the basis of which meaning can be shown to have been understood by a larger handful of the Members of Congress; but rather on the basis of which meaning is (1) most in accord with context and ordinary usage, and thus most likely to have been understood by the *whole* Congress which voted on the words of the statute (not to mention the citizens subject to it), and (2) most compatible with the surrounding body of law into which the provision must be integrated—a compatibility which, by a benign fiction, we assume Congress always has in mind. I would not permit any of the historical and legislative material discussed by the Court, or all of it combined, to lead me to a result different from the one that these factors suggest.

I would analyze this case, in brief, as follows:

(1) The word "defendant" in Rule 609(a)(1) cannot rationally (or perhaps even constitutionally) mean to provide the benefit of prejudice-weighing to civil defendants and not civil plaintiffs. Since petitioner has not produced, and we have not ourselves discovered, even a snippet of support for this absurd result, we may confidently assume that the word was not used (as it normally would be) to refer to all defendants and only all defendants.

(2) The available alternatives are to interpret "defendant" to mean (a) "civil plaintiff, civil defendant, prosecutor, and criminal defendant," (b) "civil plaintiff and defendant and criminal defendant," or (c) "criminal defendant." Quite obviously, the last does least violence to the text. It adds a qualification that the word "defendant" does not contain but, unlike the others, does not give the word a meaning ("plaintiff" or "prosecutor") it simply will not bear. The qualification it adds, moreover, is one that could understandably have been omitted by inadvertence—and sometimes is omitted in normal conversation ("I believe strongly in defendants' rights"). Finally,

this last interpretation is consistent with the policy of the law in general and the Rules of Evidence in particular of providing special protection to defendants in criminal cases.*

**Take Note**

Justice Scalia agreed with the Court's ultimate conclusion about the meaning of Rules 609 and 403. Why didn't he join the Court's opinion?

(3) As well described by the Court, the "structure of the Rules" makes it clear that Rule 403 is not to be applied in addition to Rule 609(a)(1).

I am frankly not sure that, despite its lengthy discussion of ideological evolution and legislative history, the Court's reasons for both aspects of its decision are much different from mine. I respectfully decline to join that discussion, however, because it is natural for the bar to believe that the juridical importance of such material matches its prominence in our opinions—thus producing a legal culture in which, when counsel arguing before us assert that "Congress has said" something, they now frequently mean, by "Congress," a committee report; and in which it was not beyond the pale for a recent brief to say the following: "Unfortunately, the legislative debates are not helpful. Thus, we turn to the other guidepost in this difficult area, statutory language." Brief for Petitioner in *Jett v. Dallas Independent School District,* O.T.1988, No. 87–2084, p. 21.

JUSTICE BLACKMUN, with whom JUSTICE BRENNAN and JUSTICE MARSHALL join, dissenting.

* * * The majority concludes that Rule 609(a)(1) cannot mean what it says on its face. I fully agree. I fail to see, however, why we are required to solve this riddle of statutory interpretation by reading the inadvertent word "defendant" to mean "criminal defendant." I am persuaded that a better interpretation of the Rule would allow the trial court to consider the risk of prejudice faced by any party, not just a criminal defendant. * * *

The majority's lengthy recounting of the legislative history of Rule 609 demonstrates why almost all that history is entitled to very little weight. Because the proposed rule changed so often—and finally was enacted as a compromise between the House and the Senate—much of the commentary cited by the majority concerns versions different from the Rule Congress finally enacted.

* Acknowledging the statutory ambiguity, the dissent would read "defendant" to mean "any party" because, it says, this interpretation "extend[s] the protection of judicial supervision to a larger class of litigants" than the interpretation the majority and I favor, which "takes protection *away* from litigants." But neither side in this dispute can lay claim to generosity without begging the policy question whether judicial supervision is better than the automatic power to impeach. We could as well say—and with much more support in both prior law and this Court's own recommendation—that our reading "extend[s] the protection of [the right to impeach with prior felony convictions] to a larger class of litigants" than the dissent's interpretation, which "takes protection *away* from litigants."

The only item of legislative history that focuses on the Rule as enacted is the Report of the Conference Committee, H.R. Conf. Rep. No. 93–1597 (1974). Admittedly, language in the Report supports the majority's position: the Report mirrors the Rule in emphasizing the prejudicial effect on the defendant, and also uses the word "convict" to describe the potential outcome. But [because] the slipshod drafting of Rule 609(a)(1) demonstrates that clarity of language was not the Conference's forte, I prefer to rely on the underlying reasoning of the Report, rather than on its unfortunate choice of words, in ascertaining the Rule's proper scope. The Report's treatment of the Rule's discretionary standard consists of a single paragraph. After noting that the Conference was concerned with prejudice to a defendant, the Report states:

> "The danger of prejudice to a witness other than the defendant (such as injury to the witness' reputation in his community) was considered and rejected by the Conference as an element to be weighed in determining admissibility. It was the judgment of the Conference that the danger of prejudice to a nondefendant witness is outweighed by the need for the trier of fact to have as much relevant evidence on the issue of credibility as possible. Such evidence should only be excluded where it presents a danger of improperly influencing the outcome of the trial by persuading the trier of fact to convict the defendant on the basis of his prior criminal record."

The Report indicates that the Conference determined that any felony conviction has sufficient relevance to a witness' credibility to be admitted, even if the felony had nothing directly to do with truthfulness or honesty. In dealing with the question of undue prejudice, however, the Conference drew a line: it distinguished between two types of prejudice, only one of which it permitted the trial court to consider.

As the Conference observed, admitting a prior conviction will always "prejudice" a witness, who, of course, would prefer that the conviction not be revealed to the public. The Report makes clear, however, that this kind of prejudice to the witness' life outside the courtroom is not to be considered in the judicial balancing required by Rule 609(a)(1). Rather, the kind of prejudice the court is instructed to be concerned with is prejudice which "presents a danger of improperly influencing the outcome of the trial." Congress' solution to that kind of prejudice was to require judicial supervision: the conviction may be admitted only if "the court determines that the probative value of admitting this evidence outweighs its prejudicial effect to the defendant." Rule 609(a)(1).

Although the Conference expressed its concern in terms of the effect on a criminal defendant, the potential for prejudice to the outcome at trial exists in any type of litigation, whether criminal or civil, and threatens all parties to the litigation. The Report and the Rule are best read as expressing Congress' preference for judicial balancing whenever there is a chance that justice shall be denied a party because of the unduly prejudicial nature of a witness' past conviction for a crime that has no direct bearing on the witness' truthfulness. In short, the reasoning of the Report suggests that by "prejudice to the defendant," Congress meant "prejudice to a party," as opposed to the prejudicial effect of the revelation of a prior conviction to the witness' own reputation.

It may be correct, as Justice SCALIA notes in his opinion concurring in the judgment, that interpreting "prejudicial effect to the defendant" to include only "prejudicial effect to [a] *criminal* defendant," and not prejudicial effect to other categories of litigants as well, does the "least violence to the text," if what we mean by "violence" is the interpolation of excess words or the deletion of existing words. But the reading endorsed by Justice SCALIA and the majority does violence to the logic of the only rationale Members of Congress offered for the Rule they adopted.

**Take Note**

Justice Blackmun agreed with the Court and Justice Scalia that the Rule's plain language would produce absurd results. Why didn't he agree with the Court's conclusion about what the Rule should be read to mean? On which touchstone of interpretation did he rely in reaching that conclusion?

Certainly the possibility that admission of a witness' past conviction will improperly determine the outcome at trial is troubling when the witness' testimony is in support of a criminal defendant. The potential, however, is no less real for other litigants. Unlike Justice SCALIA, I do not approach the Rules of Evidence, which by their terms govern both civil and criminal proceedings, with the presumption that their general provisions should be read to "provid[e] special protection to defendants in criminal cases." Rather, the Rules themselves specify that they "shall be construed to secure fairness in administration . . . to the end that the truth may be ascertained and proceedings justly determined" in *all* cases. [Federal] Rule [of Evidence] 102. The majority's result does not achieve that end.

As I see it, therefore, our choice is between two interpretations of Rule 609(a)(1), neither of which is completely consistent with the Rule's plain language. The majority's interpretation takes protection *away* from litigants—*i.e.,* civil defendants—who would have every reason to believe themselves entitled to the judicial balancing offered by the Rule. The alternative interpretation—which I favor—also departs somewhat from the plain language, but does so by *extending* the protection of judicial supervision to a larger class of litigants—*i.e.,* to all parties. Neither result is compelled by the statutory language or the legislative history, but for me the choice between them is an easy one. I find it proper, as a general matter and under the dictates of Rule 102, to construe the Rule so as to avoid "unnecessary hardship," see *Burnet v. Guggenheim,* 288 U.S. 280, 285 (1933), and to produce a sensible result.

This case should have been decided on the basis of whether the Bock Laundry Machine Company designed and sold a dangerously defective machine without providing adequate warnings. The fact that Paul Green was a convicted felon, in a work-release program at a county prison, has little, if anything, to do with these issues. We cannot know precisely why the jury refused to compensate him for the sad and excruciating loss of his arm, but there is a very real possibility that it was influenced improperly by his criminal record. I believe that this is not a result Congress conceivably could have intended, and it is not a result this Court should endorse.

---

## Points for Discussion

***a. The Absurdity Doctrine***

Justice Stevens, Justice Scalia, and Justice Blackmun all agreed that the result that would follow from strict adherence to the plain language of Rule 609 would be absurd. Why was it so obvious to all of them that the result—that impeachment evidence of past convictions detrimental to a civil plaintiff would always be admissible—was absurd? Does the notion of absurdity have any objective content, or does it simply require reference to the judge's intuition about what is fair and appropriate?

***b. Touchstones of Interpretation***

Even when we can achieve broad consensus about what results count as absurd, we still need a method to determine what the law should mean in spite of its text. In what way was Justice Blackmun's proposed reading of the Rule different from Justice Stevens's? Once a judge is willing to depart from the plain text, how does she know which rule of law to substitute? Can you explain why Justice Scalia chose a different reading of the Rule from the one that Justice Blackmun proposed? Does it turn on their different views about the appropriate touchstone of interpretation?

---

Courts are willing to depart from statutory text not only when the results produced by the plain meaning of the text would be absurd, but also when the statute contains a so-called "scrivener's error." A "scrivener" is a clerk or a scribe—for our purposes, the person who transcribes the legislature's action into statutory text. It seems uncontroversial to suggest that, if the scrivener made an error in writing down the statutory language, or (more likely today) if a legislative aide made a typo and no one in the legislature noticed, courts should not be bound by the mistake. Under the scrivener's error doctrine, courts will depart from the plain meaning of the statutory text when it is very clear that the "meaning genuinely intended" was "inadequately expressed." *United States v. X-Citement Video, Inc.*, 513 U.S. 64, 82 (1994) (Scalia, J., dissenting).

For example, 28 U.S.C. § 1453(c)(1), which governs appeals from a district court's decision granting or denying a motion to remand a removed class action to state court, provides (with emphasis added):

> "Section 1447 shall apply to any removal of a case under this section, except that notwithstanding section 1447(d), a court of appeals may accept an appeal from an

> order of a district court granting or denying a motion to remand a class action to the State court from which it was removed if application is made to the court of appeals *not less than 7 days after entry of the order.*"

Read literally, this provision seems to say that a party must wait a week before appealing such a decision, but that once a week passes, there is no simply deadline for when such an appeal can be filed. When confronted with this provision, the Ninth Circuit concluded that Congress had clearly made a mistake by using the word "less," and that Congress must have intended to use the word "more"—that is, to impose a seven-day limit on filing such appeals. See *Amalgamated Transit Union Local 1309, AFL-CIO v. Laidlaw Transit Serv., Inc.*, 435 F.3d 1140, 1145–46 (9th Cir. 2006).

But it is easier to state the scrivener's error doctrine than it is to apply it. Just how clear must it be that Congress made a drafting error before courts can invoke the doctrine? In this sense, the doctrine functions in a manner similar to the absurdity doctrine. There is an intuitive appeal to a rule that permits courts to depart from the statutory text when the legislature couldn't possibly have meant what it said. But how exactly do we identify those cases?

Consider the statute at issue in *United States v. Locke*, 471 U.S. 84 (1985), which we considered in Chapter 2. The relevant provision stated:

> "The owner of an unpatented lode or placer mining claim located prior to October 21, 1976, shall, within the three-year period following October 21, 1976 and prior to December 31 of each year thereafter, file the instruments required by paragraphs (1) and (2) of this subsection. The owner of an unpatented lode or placer mining claim located after October 21, 1976 shall, prior to December 31 of each year following the calendar year in which the said claim was located, file the instruments required by paragraphs (1) and (2) of this subsection * * *." 43 U.S.C. § 1744(a).

In *Locke*, the plaintiffs had sought to preserve their mining rights and filed their claim with the Bureau of Land Management on December 31. The Court, relying on the plain meaning of the statutory text, concluded that the plaintiffs had filed their claim too late; the statutory deadline—"*prior* to December 31"—meant that the plaintiffs were required to file their claim no later than December 30.

To many people, however, it seems strange that Congress would intentionally have chosen to make the second-to-last day of the year the deadline, especially given that Congress expressly mentioned the last day of the year—a more typical deadline for annual claims—in the statute. Should the Court have concluded that the statute contained a scrivener's error and that Congress actually meant to say "on or before December 31" instead? How can we tell when the legislature made a mistake, as opposed to making a contestable policy choice?

---

## B. Ordinary, Colloquial, or Technical Meaning

For the sake of discussion, let's put aside the absurdity and scrivener's error doctrines—and the approaches that consider touchstones other than the text—and assume that the correct way to interpret a statute is simply to give effect to the ordinary meaning of its text. What do we do about the fact that words often carry multiple meanings?

Part of the difficulty is simply a semantic one. For example, the word "sanction" can mean either a *penalty* for disobeying the law or official *permission* to take a particular action—that is, the word has two meanings that are diametrically opposed. If a statute uses the word "sanction," how do we know which meaning is the correct one?

This problem is compounded by the fact that the meaning of many words and phrases varies depending on usage and context. For example, if your friend tells you to meet her at "midnight on Thursday," you probably understand her to propose a meeting the minute after 11:59 pm on Thursday night. But if NASA announces that a launch will take place at "midnight on Thursday," it means that the launch will take place the minute after 11:59 pm on *Wednesday*. (NASA uses military time, which relies on a 24-hour clock. In military time, midnight is expressed as "0:00," which makes clear that it is the beginning, and not the end, of the day.)

When courts interpret statutory text, they generally seek the "ordinary" or "plain" meaning of the words. But as the midnight example suggests, text sometimes has a colloquial meaning and/or a technical meaning, either of which might constitute (or be different from) the "ordinary" meaning. How do courts know when a statute uses one of those meanings instead of the others? Consider the cases that follow.

---

## *Nix v. Hedden*

149 U.S. 304 (1893)

This was an action brought February 4, 1887, against the collector of the port of New York to recover back duties paid under protest on tomatoes imported by the plaintiff from the West Indies in the spring of 1886, which the collector assessed under "Schedule G.—Provisions' " of the tariff act of March 3, 1883, (chapter 121), imposing a duty on "vegetables in their natural state, or in salt or brine, not specially enumerated or provided for in this act, ten per centum ad valorem;" and which the plaintiffs contended came within the clause in the free list of the same act, "Fruits, green, ripe, or dried, not specially enumerated or provided for in this act." 22 Stat. 504, 519.

At the trial the plaintiff's counsel, after reading in evidence definitions of the words "fruit" and "vegetables" from Webster's Dictionary, Worcester's Dictionary, and the Imperial Dictionary, called two witnesses, who had been for 30 years in the business of selling fruit and vegetables, and asked them, after hearing these definitions, to say whether these words had "any special meaning in trade or commerce, different from those read."

One of the witnesses answered as follows: "Well, it does not classify all things there, but they are correct as far as they go. It does not take all kinds of fruit or vegetables; it takes a portion of them. I think the words 'fruit' and 'vegetable' have the same meaning in trade to-day that they had on March 1, 1883. I understand that the term 'fruit' is applied in trade only to such plants or parts of plants as contain the seeds. There are more vegetables than those in the enumeration given in Webster's Dictionary under the term 'vegetable,' as 'cabbage, cauliflower, turnips, potatoes, peas, beans, and the like,' probably covered by the words 'and the like.' "

The other witness testified: "I don't think the term 'fruit' or the term 'vegetables' had, in March, 1883, and prior thereto, any special meaning in trade and commerce in this country different from that which I have read here from the dictionaries."

The plaintiff's counsel then read in evidence from the same dictionaries the definitions of the word "tomato."

The defendant's counsel then read in evidence from Webster's Dictionary the definitions of the words "pea," "egg plant," "cucumber," "squash," and "pepper."

The plaintiff then read in evidence from Webster's and Worcester's dictionaries the definitions of "potato," "turnip," "parsnip," "cauliflower," "cabbage," "carrot," and "bean."

No other evidence was offered by either party. The court, upon the defendant's motion, directed a verdict for him, which was returned, and judgment rendered thereon. The plaintiffs duly excepted to the instruction, and sued out this writ of error.

MR. JUSTICE GRAY, after stating the facts in the foregoing language, delivered the opinion of the court.

The single question in this case is whether tomatoes * * * are to be classed as "vegetables" or as "fruit," within the meaning of the tariff act of 1883.

The only witnesses called at the trial testified that neither "vegetables" nor "fruit" had any special meaning in trade or commerce different from that given in the dictionaries, and that they had the same meaning in trade to-day that they had in March, 1883.

The passages cited from the dictionaries define the word "fruit" as the seed of plants, or that part of plants which contains the seed, and especially the juicy, pulpy products of certain plants, covering and containing the seed. These definitions have no tendency to show that tomatoes are "fruit," as distinguished from "vegetables," in common speech, or within the meaning of the tariff act.

There being no evidence that the words "fruit" and "vegetables" have acquired any special meaning in trade or commerce, they must receive their ordinary meaning. Of that meaning the court is bound to take judicial notice, as it does in regard to all words in our own tongue; and upon such a question dictionaries are admitted, not as evidence, but only as aids to the memory and understanding of the court.

Botanically speaking, tomatoes are the fruit of a vine, just as are cucumbers, squashes, beans, and peas. But in the common language of the people, whether sellers or consumers of provisions, all these are vegetables which are grown in kitchen gardens, and which, whether eaten cooked or raw, are, like potatoes, carrots, parsnips, turnips, beets, cauliflower, cabbage, celery, and lettuce, usually served at dinner in, with, or after the soup, fish, or meats which constitute the principal part of the repast, and not, like fruits generally, as dessert.

The attempt to class tomatoes as fruit is not unlike a recent attempt to class beans as seeds, of which Mr. Justice Bradley, speaking for this court, said: "We do not see why they should be classified as seeds, any more than walnuts should be so classified. Both are seeds, in the language of botany or natural history, but not in commerce nor in common parlance. On the other hand in speaking generally of provisions, beans may well be included under the term 'vegetables.' As an article of food on our tables, whether baked or boiled, or forming the basis of soup, they are used as a vegetable, as well when ripe as when green. This is the principal use to which they are put. Beyond the common knowledge which we have on this subject, very little evidence is necessary, or can be produced." *Robertson v. Salomon*, 130 U. S. 412, 414 (1889). [Affirmed.]

---

## Points for Discussion

### *a. Textual Meaning*

The Court acknowledged that "botanically speaking" a tomato is a fruit, because fruits, which are the reproductive bodies of plants, contain seeds. But the Court declined to read the statute to classify tomatoes as fruits because in "the common language of the people" tomatoes are vegetables. In other words, the Court chose the colloquial meaning of the words in the statute rather than the technical meaning. What was the Court's standard for when to choose statutory text's colloquial meaning rather than its technical meaning? Should we expect that one of those will more typically provide the "ordinary" meaning?

#### *b. Text and Dictionaries*

Most dictionaries define "fruit" as (something like) "the usually edible reproductive body of a seed plant," whereas they define "vegetable" as "a usually herbaceous plant grown for an edible part that is usually eaten as part of a meal." According to these definitions, is a tomato a fruit or a vegetable? If the former, then how often should we expect dictionaries to be helpful in interpreting statutory text? Would it make sense to say that the "dictionary meaning" of statutory text is presumptively the "ordinary meaning" of that text, and that courts should depart only upon a strong showing that the legislature intended the words to carry a different meaning? If so, how would we know when the legislature intended a different meaning? And what should we do about the fact that most dictionaries have multiple definitions for each word?

---

## *Smith v. United States*

508 U.S. 223 (1993)

JUSTICE O'CONNOR delivered the opinion of the Court.

We decide today whether the exchange of a gun for narcotics constitutes "use" of a firearm "during and in relation to . . . [a] drug trafficking crime" within the meaning of 18 U.S.C. § 924(c)(1). We hold that it does.

Petitioner John Angus Smith and his companion went from Tennessee to Florida to buy cocaine; they hoped to resell it at a profit. While in Florida, they met petitioner's acquaintance, Deborah Hoag. Hoag agreed to, and in fact did, purchase cocaine for petitioner. She then accompanied petitioner and his friend to her motel room, where they were joined by a drug dealer. While Hoag listened, petitioner and the dealer discussed petitioner's MAC–10 firearm, which had been modified to operate as an automatic. The MAC–10 apparently is a favorite among criminals. It is small and compact, lightweight, and can be equipped with a silencer. Most important of all, it can be devastating: A fully automatic MAC–10 can fire more than 1,000 rounds per minute. The dealer expressed his interest in becoming the owner of a MAC–10, and petitioner promised that he would discuss selling the gun if his arrangement with another potential buyer fell through.

Unfortunately for petitioner, Hoag * * * was a confidential informant. Consistent with her post, she informed the Broward County Sheriff's Office of petitioner's activities. The Sheriff's Office responded quickly, sending an undercover officer to Hoag's motel room. * * * Upon arriving at Hoag's motel room, the undercover officer presented himself to petitioner as a pawnshop dealer. Petitioner, in turn, presented the officer with a proposition: He had an automatic MAC–10 and silencer with which he might be willing to part. Petitioner then pulled the MAC–10 out of a black canvas bag and showed it to the officer. The officer examined the gun and asked petitioner what he wanted for it. Rather than asking for money, however, petitioner asked for drugs. He was willing to trade his MAC–10, he said, for two ounces of cocaine. * * *

A grand jury sitting in the District Court for the Southern District of Florida returned an indictment charging petitioner with, among other offenses, two drug trafficking crimes * * *. Most important here, the indictment alleged that petitioner knowingly used the MAC–10 and its silencer during and in relation to a drug trafficking crime. Under 18 U.S.C. § 924(c)(1), a defendant who so uses a firearm must be sentenced to five years' incarceration. And where, as here, the firearm is a "machinegun" or is fitted with a silencer, the sentence is 30 years. The jury convicted petitioner on all counts.

On appeal, petitioner argued that § 924(c)(1)'s penalty for using a firearm during and in relation to a drug trafficking offense covers only situations in which the firearm is used as a weapon. According to petitioner, the provision does not extend to defendants who use a firearm solely as a medium of exchange or for barter. * * *

**Take Note**

The question in this case is whether Smith "use[d]" a firearm "during and in relation to" a drug crime. Before reading further, can you articulate the argument that Smith likely made about the meaning of the statute? What do you suppose the government argued in response?

Section 924(c)(1) requires the imposition of specified penalties if the defendant, "during and in relation to any crime of violence or drug trafficking crime[,] uses or carries a firearm." By its terms, the statute requires the prosecution to make two showings. First, the prosecution must demonstrate that the defendant "use[d] or carrie[d] a firearm." Second, it must prove that the use or carrying was "during and in relation to" a "crime of violence or drug trafficking crime."

Petitioner argues that exchanging a firearm for drugs does not constitute "use" of the firearm within the meaning of the statute. He points out that nothing in the record indicates that he fired the MAC–10, threatened anyone with it, or employed it for self-protection. In essence, petitioner argues that he cannot be said to have "use[d]" a firearm unless he used it as a weapon, since that is how firearms most often are used. Of course, § 924(c)(1) is not limited to those cases in which a gun is used; it applies with equal force whenever a gun is "carrie[d]." In this case, however, the indictment alleged only that petitioner "use[d]" the MAC–10. Accordingly, we do not consider whether the evidence might support the conclusion that petitioner carried the MAC–10 within the meaning of § 924(c)(1). Instead we confine our discussion to what the parties view as the dispositive issue in this case: whether trading a firearm for drugs can constitute "use" of the firearm within the meaning of § 924(c)(1).

When a word is not defined by statute, we normally construe it in accord with its ordinary or natural meaning. Surely petitioner's treatment of his MAC–10 can be described as "use" within the everyday meaning of that term. Petitioner "used" his MAC–10 in an attempt to obtain drugs by offering to trade it for cocaine. Webster's defines "to use" as "[t]o convert to one's service" or "to employ." Webster's New International Dictionary 2806 (2d ed. 1939). Black's Law Dictionary contains a similar definition: "[t]o make use of; to convert to one's service; to employ; to avail oneself of; to utilize; to carry out a purpose or action by means of." Black's Law Dictionary 1541 (6th ed. 1990). Indeed, over 100 years ago we gave the word "use" the same gloss, indicating that it means " 'to employ' " or " 'to derive service from.' " *Astor v. Merritt*, 111 U.S. 202, 213 (1884). Petitioner's handling of the MAC–10 in this case falls squarely within those definitions. By attempting to trade his MAC–10 for the drugs, he "used" or "employed" it as an item of barter to obtain cocaine; he "derived service" from it because it was going to bring him the very drugs he sought.

**Take Note**

The Court starts its inquiry into statutory meaning by citing dictionaries. In so doing, is the Court seeking the ordinary meaning of the phrase in question? The colloquial meaning? Something else?

In petitioner's view, § 924(c)(1) should require proof not only that the defendant used the firearm, but also that he used it *as a weapon*. But the words "as a weapon" appear nowhere in the statute. Rather, § 924(c)(1)'s language sweeps broadly, punishing any "us[e]" of a firearm, so long as the use is "during and in relation to" a drug trafficking offense. Had Congress intended the narrow construction petitioner urges, it could have so indicated. It did not, and we decline to introduce that additional requirement on our own.

Language, of course, cannot be interpreted apart from context. The meaning of a word that appears ambiguous if viewed in isolation may become clear when the word is analyzed in light of the terms that surround it. Recognizing this, petitioner and the dissent argue that the word "uses" has a somewhat reduced scope in § 924(c)(1) because it appears alongside the word "firearm." Specifically, they contend that the average person on the street would not think immediately of a guns-for-drugs trade as an example of "us[ing] a firearm." Rather, that phrase normally evokes an image of the most familiar use to which a firearm is put—use as a weapon. Petitioner and the dissent therefore argue that the statute excludes uses where the weapon is not fired or otherwise employed for its destructive capacity. Indeed, relying on that argument—and without citation to authority—the dissent announces its own, restrictive definition of "use." "To use an instrumentality," the dissent argues, "ordinarily means to use it for its intended purpose."

There is a significant flaw to this argument. It is one thing to say that the ordinary meaning of "uses a firearm" *includes* using a firearm as a weapon, since that is the intended purpose of a firearm and the example of "use" that most immediately comes to mind. But it is quite another to conclude that, as a result, the phrase also *excludes* any other use. Certainly that conclusion does not follow from the phrase "uses . . . a firearm" itself. As the dictionary definitions and experience make clear, one can use a firearm in a number of ways. That one example of "use" is the first to come to mind when the phrase "uses . . . a firearm" is uttered does not preclude us from recognizing that there are other "uses" that qualify as well. In this case, it is both reasonable and normal to say that petitioner "used" his MAC–10 in his drug trafficking offense by trading it for cocaine; the dissent does not contend otherwise.

The dissent's example of how one might "use" a cane suffers from a similar flaw. To be sure, "use" as an adornment in a hallway is not the first "use" of a cane that comes to mind. But certainly it does not follow that the *only* "use" to which a cane might be put is assisting one's grandfather in walking. Quite the opposite: The most infamous use of a cane in American history had nothing to do with walking at all, see J. McPherson, Battle Cry of Freedom 150 (1988) (describing the caning of Senator Sumner in the United States Senate in 1856); and the use of a cane as an instrument of punishment was once so common that "to cane" has become a verb meaning "[t]o beat with a cane." Webster's New International Dictionary, *supra,* at 390. In any event, the only question in this case is whether the phrase "uses . . . a firearm" in § 924(c)(1) is most reasonably read as *excluding* the use of a firearm in a gun-for-drugs trade. The fact that the phrase clearly *includes* using a firearm to shoot someone, as the dissent contends, does not answer it.

We are not persuaded that our construction of the phrase "uses . . . a firearm" will produce anomalous applications. * * * § 924(c)(1) requires not only that the defendant "use" the firearm, but also that he use it "during and in relation to" the drug trafficking crime. As a result, the defendant who "uses" a firearm to scratch his head, or for some other innocuous purpose, would avoid punishment for that conduct altogether: Although scratching one's head with a gun might constitute "use," that action cannot support punishment under § 924(c)(1) unless it facilitates or furthers the drug crime; that the firearm served to relieve an itch is not enough.

In any event, the "intended purpose" of a firearm is not that it be used in any offensive manner whatever, but rather that it be used in a particular fashion—by firing it. The dissent's contention therefore cannot be that the defendant must use the firearm "as a weapon," but rather that he must fire it or threaten to fire it, "as a gun." Under the dissent's approach, then, even the criminal who pistol-whips his victim has not used a firearm within the meaning of § 924(c)(1), for firearms are intended to be fired or brandished, not used as bludgeons. * * * The universal view of the courts of appeals, however, is directly to the contrary. * * *

To the extent there is uncertainty about the scope of the phrase "uses . . . a firearm" in § 924(c)(1), we believe the remainder of § 924 appropriately sets it to rest. Just as a single word cannot be read in isolation, nor can a single provision of a statute. * * * Here, Congress employed the words "use" and "firearm" together not only in § 924(c)(1), but also in § 924(d)(1), which deals with forfeiture of firearms. Under § 924(d)(1), any "firearm or ammunition intended to be used" in the various offenses listed in § 924(d)(3) is subject to seizure and forfeiture. Consistent with petitioner's interpretation, § 924(d)(3) lists offenses in which guns might be used as offensive weapons. But it also lists offenses in which the firearm is ***not*** used as a weapon but instead as an item of barter or commerce. For example, any gun int ed to be "used" in an interstate "transfer, s[ale], trade, gi[ft], transport, or d of a firearm prohibited under § 922(a)(5) where there is a pattern of such a § 924(d)(3)(C), or in a federal offense involving "the exportation of firear (3)(F), is subject to forfeiture. In fact, none of the offenses listed in f subsections of § 924(d)(3) involves the bellicose use of a firearm; each off use as an item in commerce. Thus, it is clear from § 924(d)(3) that one w exports, sells, or trades a firearm "uses" it within the meaning of § 924 though those actions do not involve using the firearm as a weapon. Unle hold that using a firearm has a different meaning in § 924(c)(1) than § 924(d)—and clearly we should not—we must reject petitioner's narrow inte tation.

The dissent suggests that our interpretation produces a "strange dichotomy" between "using" a firearm and "carrying" one. We do not see why that is so. Just as a defendant may "use" a firearm within the meaning of § 924(c)(1) by trading it for drugs *or* using it to shoot someone, so too would a defendant "carry" the firearm by keeping it on his person whether he intends to exchange it for cocaine or fire it in self-defense. The dichotomy arises, if at all, only when one tries to extend the phrase "uses . . . a firearm" to any use "for any purpose whatever." For our purposes, it is sufficient to recognize that, because § 924(d)(1) includes both using a firearm for ***trade*** and using a firearm as a ***weapon*** as "us[ing] a firearm," it is most reasonable to construe § 924(c)(1) as encompassing both of those "uses" as well.

**Make the Connection**

In a case called *Muscarello v. United States*, which follows immediately after this case, the Court addressed the meaning of the statute's prohibition on "carr[ying]" a firearm "during and in relation" to a drug crime.

[The dissent notes] that § 924(c)(1) originally dealt with use of a firearm during crimes of violence; the provision concerning use of a firearm during and in relation to drug trafficking offenses was added later. From this, the dissent infers that "use" *originally* was limited to use of a gun "as a weapon." That the statute in its current form employs the term "use" more broadly is unimportant, the dissent contends, because the addition of the words " 'drug trafficking crime' would have been a peculiar way to *expand* its meaning." Even if we assume that Congress had intended the term "use" to have a more limited scope when it passed the original version of § 924(c) in 1968, we believe it clear from the face of the statute that the Congress that amended § 924(c) in 1986 did not. Rather, the 1986 Congress employed the term "use" expansively, covering both use as a weapon, as the dissent admits, and use as an item of trade or barter, as an examination of § 924(d) demonstrates. Because the phrase "uses . . . a firearm" is broad enough in ordinary usage to cover use of a firearm as an item of barter or commerce, Congress was free in 1986 so to employ it. The language and structure of § 924 indicates that Congress did just that. Accordingly, we conclude that using a firearm in a guns-for-drugs trade may constitute "us[ing] a firearm" within the meaning of § 924(c)(1).

Finally, the dissent and petitioner invoke the rule of lenity, [a canon of construction that provides that an ambiguous criminal statute should be construed in favor of the defendant]. The mere possibility of articulating a narrower construction, however, does not by itself make the rule of lenity applicable. Instead, that venerable rule is reserved for cases where, "[a]fter 'seiz[ing] every thing from which aid can be derived,' " the Court is "left with an ambiguous statute." *United States v. Bass*, 404 U.S. 336, 347 (1971) (quoting *United States v. Fisher*, 2 Cranch 358, 386 (1805)). This is not such a case. Not only does petitioner's use of his MAC–10 fall squarely within the common usage and dictionary definitions of the terms "uses . . . a firearm," but Congress affirmatively demonstrated that it meant to include transactions like petitioner's as "us[ing] a firearm" by so employing those terms in § 924(d).

Imposing a more restrictive reading of the phrase "uses . . . a firearm" does violence not only to the structure and language of the statute, but to its purpose as well. When Congress enacted the current version of § 924(c)(1), it was no doubt aware that drugs and guns are a dangerous combination. * * * The fact that a gun is treated momentarily as an item of commerce does not render it inert or deprive it of destructive capacity. Rather, as experience demonstrates, it can be converted instantaneously from currency to cannon. We therefore see no reason why Congress would have intended courts and juries applying § 924(c)(1) to draw a fine metaphysical distinction between a gun's role in a drug offense as a weapon and its role as an item of barter; it creates a grave possibility of violence and death in either capacity.

We have observed that the rule of lenity "cannot dictate an implausible interpretation of a statute, nor one at odds with the generally accepted contemporary meaning of a term." *Taylor v. United States*, 495 U.S. 575, 596 (1990). That observation controls this case. Both a firearm's use as a weapon and its use as an item of barter fall within the plain language of § 924(c)(1), so long as the use occurs during and in relation to a drug trafficking offense; both must constitute "uses" of a firearm for § 924(d)(1) to make any sense at all; and both create the very dangers and risks that Congress meant § 924(c)(1) to address. We therefore hold that a criminal who trades his firearm for drugs "uses" it during and in relation to a drug trafficking offense within the meaning of § 924(c)(1). * * * The judgment of the Court of Appeals, accordingly, is affirmed.

[JUSTICE BLACKMUN's concurring opinion has been omitted.]

JUSTICE SCALIA, with whom JUSTICE STEVENS and JUSTICE SOUTER join, dissenting.

Section 924(c)(1) mandates a sentence enhancement for any defendant who "during and in relation to any crime of violence or drug trafficking crime . . . uses . . . a firearm." The Court begins its analysis by focusing upon the word "use" in this passage, and explaining that the dictionary definitions of that word are very broad. It is, however, a "fundamental principle of statutory construction (and, indeed, of language itself) that the meaning of a word cannot be determined in isolation, but must be drawn from the context in which it is used." *Deal v. United States*, 508 U.S. 129, 132 (1993). That is particularly true of a word as elastic as "use," whose meanings range all the way from "to partake of" (as in "he uses tobacco") to "to be wont or accustomed" (as in "he used to smoke tobacco"). See Webster's New International Dictionary 2806 (2d ed. 1939).

> **Take Note**
>
> Justice Scalia said that he was seeking the ordinary, and not the technical, meaning of the phrase in the statute. How did he know that the phrase "uses a firearm" didn't have a technical meaning?

In the search for statutory meaning, we give nontechnical words and phrases their ordinary meaning. To use an instrumentality ordinarily means to use it for its intended purpose. When someone asks, "Do you use a cane?," he is not inquiring whether you have your grandfather's silver-handled walking stick on display in the hall; he wants to know whether you *walk* with a cane. Similarly, to speak of "using a firearm" is to speak of using it for its distinctive purpose, *i.e.*, as a weapon. To be sure, "one can use a firearm in a number of ways," including as an article of exchange, just as one can "use" a cane as a hall decoration—but that is not the ordinary meaning of "using" the one or the other.[1] The Court does not appear to grasp the distinction between how a word *can be* used and how it *ordinarily is* used. It would, indeed, be "both reasonable and normal to say that petitioner 'used' his MAC–10 in his drug trafficking offense by trading it for cocaine." It would also be reasonable and normal to say that he "used" it to scratch his head. When one wishes

---

1 The Court asserts that the "significant flaw" in this argument is that "to say that the ordinary meaning of 'uses a firearm' *includes* using a firearm as a weapon" is quite different from saying that the ordinary meaning "also *excludes* any other use" (emphases in original). The two are indeed different—but it is precisely the latter that I assert to be true: The ordinary meaning of "uses a firearm" does *not* include using it as an article of commerce. I think it perfectly obvious, for example, that the objective falsity requirement for a perjury conviction would not be satisfied if a witness answered "no" to a prosecutor's inquiry whether he had ever "used a firearm," even though he had once sold his grandfather's Enfield rifle to a collector.

to describe the action of employing the instrument of a firearm for such unusual purposes, "use" is assuredly a verb one could select. But that says nothing about whether the *ordinary* meaning of the phrase "uses a firearm" embraces such extraordinary employments. It is unquestionably *not* reasonable and normal, I think, to say simply "do not use firearms" when one means to prohibit selling or scratching with them.

Given our rule that ordinary meaning governs, and given the ordinary meaning of "uses a firearm," it seems to me inconsequential that "the words 'as a weapon' appear nowhere in the statute"; they are reasonably implicit. Petitioner is not, I think, seeking to introduce an "additional requirement" into the text, but is simply construing the text according to its normal import.

The Court seeks to avoid this conclusion by referring to the next subsection of the statute, § 924(d), which does not employ the phrase "uses a firearm," but provides for the confiscation of firearms that are "used in" referenced offenses which include the crimes of transferring, selling, or transporting firearms in interstate commerce. The Court concludes from this that *whenever* the term appears in this statute, "use" of a firearm must include nonweapon use. I do not agree. We are dealing here not with a technical word or an "artfully defined" legal term, but with common words that are, as I have suggested, inordinately sensitive to context. Just as adding the direct object "a firearm" to the verb "use" *narrows* the meaning of that verb (it can no longer mean "partake of"), so also adding the modifier "in the offense of transferring, selling, or transporting firearms" to the phrase "use a firearm" *expands* the meaning of that phrase (it then includes, as it previously would not, nonweapon use). But neither the narrowing nor the expansion should logically be thought to apply to *all* appearances of the affected word or phrase. Just as every appearance of the word "use" in the statute need not be given the narrow meaning that word acquires in the phrase "use a firearm," so also every appearance of the phrase "use a firearm" need not be given the expansive connotation that phrase acquires in the broader context "use a firearm in crimes such as unlawful sale of firearms." When, for example, the statute provides that its prohibition on certain transactions in firearms "shall not apply to the loan or rental of a firearm to any person for temporary use for lawful sporting purposes," 18 U.S.C. §§ 922(a)(5)(B), (b)(3)(B), I have no doubt that the "use" referred to is *only* use as a sporting *weapon,* and not the use of pawning the firearm to pay for a ski trip. Likewise when, in § 924(c)(1), the phrase "uses . . . a firearm" is not employed in a context that necessarily envisions the unusual "use" of a firearm as a commodity, the normally understood meaning of the phrase should prevail.

Another consideration leads to the same conclusion: § 924(c)(1) provides increased penalties not only for one who "uses" a firearm during and in relation to any crime of violence or drug trafficking crime, but also for one who "carries" a firearm in those circumstances. The interpretation I would give the language produces an eminently reasonable dichotomy between "using a firearm" (as a weapon) and "carrying a firearm" (which in the context "uses or carries a firearm" means carrying it in such manner as to be ready for use as a weapon). The Court's interpretation, by contrast, produces a strange dichotomy between "using a firearm for any purpose whatever, including barter," and "carrying a firearm."[3]

Finally, although the present prosecution was brought under the portion of § 924(c)(1) pertaining to use of a firearm "during and in relation to any . . . drug trafficking crime," I think it significant that that portion is affiliated with the pre-existing provision pertaining to use of a firearm "during and in relation to any crime of violence," rather than with the firearm trafficking offenses defined in § 922 and referenced in § 924(d). The word "use" in the "crime of violence" context has the unmistakable import of use as a weapon, and that import carries over, in my view, to the subsequently added phrase "or drug trafficking crime." Surely the word "use" means the same thing as to both, and surely the 1986 addition of "drug trafficking crime" would have been a peculiar way to *expand* its meaning (beyond "use as a weapon") for crimes of violence.

Even if the reader does not consider the issue to be as clear as I do, he must at least acknowledge, I think, that it is eminently debatable—and that is enough, under the rule of lenity, to require finding for the petitioner here. "At the very least, it may be said that the issue is subject to some doubt. Under these circumstances, we adhere to the familiar rule that, 'where there is ambiguity in a criminal statute, doubts are resolved in favor of the defendant.' " *Adamo Wrecking Co. v. United States*, 434 U.S. 275, 284–285 (1978), quoting *United States v. Bass*, 404 U.S. 336, 348 (1971).[4]

**Make the Connection**

Justice Scalia invoked the rule of lenity, a canon of construction that teaches that courts should construe ambiguous criminal statutes in favor of the defendant. Do you agree that this statute is ambiguous? We will consider the rule of lenity, and the canons of construction more generally, later in this Chapter.

For the foregoing reasons, I respectfully dissent.

---

3 The Court responds to this argument by abandoning all pretense of giving the phrase "uses a firearm" even a *permissible* meaning, much less its ordinary one. There is no problem, the Court says, because it is not contending that "uses a firearm" means "uses for *any* purpose," only that it means "uses as a weapon or for trade." Unfortunately, that is not one of the options that our mother tongue makes available. "Uses a firearm" can be given a broad meaning ("uses for any purpose") or its more ordinary narrow meaning ("uses as a weapon"); but it cannot possibly mean "uses as a weapon or for trade."

4 The Court contends that giving the language its ordinary meaning would frustrate the purpose of the statute, since a gun "can be converted instantaneously from currency to cannon." Stretching language in order to write a more effective statute than Congress devised is not an exercise we should indulge in. But in any case, the ready ability to use a gun that is at hand as a weapon is perhaps one of the reasons the statute sanctions not only *using* a firearm, but *carrying* one. Here, however, the Government chose not to indict under that provision.

## *Muscarello v. United States*

524 U.S. 125 (1998)

JUSTICE BREYER delivered the opinion of the Court.

A provision in the firearms chapter of the federal criminal code imposes a 5-year mandatory prison term upon a person who "uses or carries a firearm" "during and in relation to" a "drug trafficking crime." 18 U.S.C. § 924(c)(1). The question before us is whether the phrase "carries a firearm" is limited to the carrying of firearms on the person. We hold that it is not so limited. Rather, it also applies to a person who knowingly possesses and conveys firearms in a vehicle, including in the locked glove compartment or trunk of a car, which the person accompanies.

* * * Petitioner in the first case, Frank J. Muscarello, unlawfully sold marijuana, which he carried in his truck to the place of sale. Police officers found a handgun locked in the truck's glove compartment. * * * Petitioners in the second case, Donald Cleveland and Enrique Gray-Santana, placed several guns in a bag, put the bag in the trunk of a car, and then traveled by car to a proposed drug-sale point, where they intended to steal drugs from the sellers. Federal agents at the scene stopped them, searched the cars, found the guns and drugs, and arrested them.

We begin with the statute's language. The parties vigorously contest the ordinary English meaning of the phrase "carries a firearm." Because they essentially agree that Congress intended the phrase to convey its ordinary, and not some special legal, meaning, and because they argue the linguistic point at length, we too have looked into the matter in more than usual depth. Although the word "carry" has many different meanings, only two are relevant here. When one uses the word in the first, or primary, meaning, one can, as a matter of ordinary English, "carry firearms" in a wagon, car, truck, or other vehicle that one accompanies. When one uses the word in a different, rather special, way, to mean, for example, "bearing" or (in slang) "packing" (as in "packing a gun"), the matter is less clear. But, for reasons we shall set out below, we believe Congress intended to use the word in its primary sense and not in this latter, special way.

**Take Note**

The parties agreed that the Court should interpret the phrase "carries a firearm" according to its ordinary meaning. Aside from a dictionary—which might contain multiple, differing definitions of the terms in question—what other sources would you consult to determine the ordinary meaning of the phrase?

Consider first the word's primary meaning. The Oxford English Dictionary gives as its *first* definition "convey, originally by cart or wagon, hence in any vehicle, by ship, on horseback, etc." 2 Oxford English Dictionary 919 (2d ed. 1989); see also Webster's Third New International Dictionary 343 (1986) (*first* definition: "move while supporting (*as in a vehicle* or in one's hands or arms)"); Random House Dictionary of the English Language Unabridged 319 (2d ed. 1987) (*first* definition: "to take or support from one place to another; convey; transport").

The origin of the word "carries" explains why the first, or basic, meaning of the word "carry" includes conveyance in a vehicle. See Barnhart Dictionary of Etymology 146 (1988) (tracing the word from Latin "carum," which means "car" or "cart"); 2 Oxford English Dictionary 919 (tracing the word from Old French "carier" and the late Latin "carricare," which meant to "convey in a car"); Oxford Dictionary of English Etymology 148 (C. Onions ed. 1966) (same); Barnhart Dictionary of Etymology 143 (explaining that the term "car" has been used to refer to the automobile since 1896).

The greatest of writers have used the word with this meaning. See, *e.g.,* The King James Bible, 2 Kings 9:28 ("[H]is servants carried him in a chariot to Jerusalem"); *id.,* Isaiah 30:6 ("[T]hey will carry their riches upon the shoulders of young asses"). Robinson Crusoe says, "[w]ith my boat, I carry'd away every Thing." D. Defoe, Robinson Crusoe 174 (J. Crowley ed. 1972). And the owners of Queequeg's ship, Melville writes, "had lent him a [wheelbarrow], in which to carry his heavy chest to his boarding-house." H. Melville, Moby Dick 43 (U. Chicago 1952). This Court, too, has spoken of the "carrying" of drugs in a car or in its "trunk." *California v. Acevedo,* 500 U.S. 565, 572–573 (1991); *Florida v. Jimeno,* 500 U.S. 248, 249 (1991).

These examples do not speak directly about carrying guns. But there is nothing linguistically special about the fact that weapons, rather than drugs, are being carried. Robinson Crusoe might have carried a gun in his boat; Queequeg might have borrowed a wheelbarrow in which to carry not a chest, but a harpoon. And, to make certain that there is no special ordinary English restriction (unmentioned in dictionaries) upon the use of "carry" in respect to guns, we have surveyed modern press usage, albeit crudely, by searching computerized newspaper databases—both the New York Times data base in Lexis/Nexis, and the "US News" data base in Westlaw. We looked for sentences in which the words "carry," "vehicle," and "weapon" (or variations thereof) all appear. We found thousands of such sentences, and random sampling suggests that many, perhaps more than one-third, are sentences used to convey the meaning at issue here, *i.e.,* the carrying of guns in a car.

The New York Times, for example, writes about "an ex-con" who "arrives home driving a stolen car and carrying a load of handguns," Mar. 21, 1992, section 1, p. 18, col. 1, and an "official peace officer who carries a shotgun in his boat," June 19, 1988, section 12WC, p. 2, col. 1. The Boston Globe refers to the arrest of a professional baseball player "for carrying a semiloaded automatic weapon in his car." Dec. 10, 1994, p. 75, col. 5. The Colorado Springs Gazette Telegraph speaks of one "Russell" who "carries a gun hidden in his car." May 2, 1993, p. B1, col. 2. The Arkansas Gazette refers to a "house" that was "searched" in an effort to find "items that could be carried in a car, such as . . . guns." Mar. 10, 1991, p. A1, col. 2. The San Diego Union-Tribune asks, "What, do they carry guns aboard these boats now?" Feb. 18, 1992, p. D2, col. 5.

Now consider a different, somewhat special meaning of the word "carry"—a meaning upon which the linguistic arguments of petitioners and the dissent must rest. The Oxford English Dictionary's *twenty-sixth* definition of "carry" is "bear, wear, hold up, or sustain, as one moves about; habitually to bear about with one." 2 Oxford English Dictionary, at 921. Webster's defines "carry" as "to move while supporting," not just in a vehicle, but also "in one's hands or arms." Webster's Third New International Dictionary, at 343. And Black's Law Dictionary defines the entire phrase "carry arms or weapons" as "To wear, bear or carry them upon the person or in the clothing or in a pocket, for the purpose of use, or for the purpose of being armed and ready for offensive or defensive action in case of a conflict with another person." Black's Law Dictionary 214 (6th ed. 1990).

These special definitions, however, do not purport to *limit* the "carrying of arms" to the circumstances they describe. No one doubts that one who bears arms on his person "carries a weapon." But to say that is not to deny that one may *also* "carry a weapon" tied to the saddle of a horse or placed in a bag in a car.

Nor is there any linguistic reason to think that Congress intended to limit the word "carries" in the statute to any of these special definitions. To the contrary, all these special definitions embody a form of an important, but secondary, meaning of "carry," a meaning that suggests support rather than movement or transportation, as when, for example, a column "carries" the weight of an arch. 2 Oxford English Dictionary, at 919, 921. In this sense a gangster might "carry" a gun (in colloquial language, he might "pack a gun") even though he does not move from his chair. It is difficult to believe, however, that Congress intended to limit the statutory word to this definition—imposing special punishment upon the comatose gangster while ignoring drug lords who drive to a sale carrying an arsenal of weapons in their van.

**Take Note**

The Court here considers whether Congress "intended" to use the word "carry" in its ordinary sense or instead in a more narrow sense. Does this mean that the Court was seeking a touchstone of interpretation other than the text's ordinary meaning? Or must a court seeking to determine the meaning of the text inevitably ask this question in order to determine which of multiple plausible textual meanings is the correct one?

We recognize, as the dissent emphasizes, that the word "carry" has other meanings as well. But those other meanings (*e.g.*, "carry all he knew," "carries no colours") are not relevant here. And the fact that speakers often do *not* add to the phrase "carry a gun" the words "in a car" is of no greater relevance here than the fact that millions of Americans did *not* see Muscarello carry a gun in his truck. The relevant linguistic facts are that the word "carry" in its ordinary sense includes carrying in a car and that the word, used in its ordinary sense, keeps the same meaning whether one carries a gun, a suitcase, or a banana.

We now explore more deeply the purely legal question of whether Congress intended to use the word "carry" in its ordinary sense, or whether it intended to limit the scope of the phrase to instances in which a gun is carried "on the person." We conclude that neither the statute's basic purpose nor its legislative history support circumscribing the scope of the word "carry" by applying an "on the person" limitation.

This Court has described the statute's basic purpose broadly, as an effort to combat the "dangerous combination" of "drugs and guns." *Smith v. United States*, 508 U.S. 223, 240 (1993). And the provision's chief legislative sponsor has said that the provision seeks "to persuade the man who is tempted to commit a Federal felony to leave his gun at home." 114 Cong. Rec. 22231 (1968) (Rep. Poff). * * *

From the perspective of any such purpose (persuading a criminal "to leave his gun at home"), what sense would it make for this statute to penalize one who walks with a gun in a bag to the site of a drug sale, but to ignore a similar individual who, like defendant Gray-Santana, travels to a similar site with a similar gun in a similar bag, but instead of walking, drives there with the gun in his car? How persuasive is a punishment that is without effect until a drug dealer who has brought his gun to a sale (indeed has it available for use) actually takes it from the trunk (or unlocks the glove compartment) of his car? It is difficult to say that, considered as a class, those who prepare, say, to sell drugs by placing guns in their cars are less dangerous, or less deserving of punishment, than those who carry handguns on their person.

We have found no significant indication elsewhere in the legislative history of any more narrowly focused relevant purpose. We have found an instance in which a legislator referred to the statute as applicable when an individual "has a firearm on his person," *ibid.* (Rep. Meskill); an instance in which a legislator speaks of "a criminal who takes a gun in his hand," *id.*, at 22239 (Rep. Pucinski); and a reference in the Senate Report to a "gun carried in a pocket," S. Rep. No. 98–225, p. 314, n. 10 (1983); see also 114 Cong. Rec. 21788, 21789 (1968) (references to gun "carrying" without more). But in these instances no one purports to define the scope of the term "carries"; and the examples of guns carried on the person are not used to illustrate the reach of the term "carries" but to illustrate, or to criticize, a different aspect of the statute.

Regardless, in other instances, legislators suggest that the word "carries" has a broader scope. One legislator indicates that the statute responds in part to the concerns of law enforcement personnel, who had urged that "carrying short firearms in motor vehicles be classified as carrying such weapons concealed." *Id.*, at 22242

(Rep. May). Another criticizes a version of the proposed statute by suggesting it might apply to drunken driving, and gives as an example a drunken driver who has a "gun in his car." *Id.,* at 21792 (Rep. Yates). Others describe the statute as criminalizing gun "possession"—a term that could stretch beyond both the "use" of a gun and the carrying of a gun on the person. See *id.,* at 21793 (Rep. Casey); *id.,* at 22236 (Rep. Meskill); *id.,* at 30584 (Rep. Collier); *id.,* at 30585 (Rep. Skubitz). * * *

[P]etitioners and the dissent invoke the "rule of lenity." The simple existence of some statutory ambiguity, however, is not sufficient to warrant application of that rule, for most statutes are ambiguous to some degree. "The rule of lenity applies only if, after seizing everything from which aid can be derived, we can make no more than a guess as to what Congress intended." *United States v. Wells,* 519 U.S. 482, 499 (1997). To invoke the rule, we must conclude that there is a "grievous ambiguity or uncertainty in the statute." *Staples v. United States,* 511 U.S. 600, 619, n. 17 (1994). Certainly, our decision today is based on much more than a "guess as to what Congress intended," and there is no "grievous ambiguity" here. The problem of statutory interpretation in these cases is indeed no different from that in many of the criminal cases that confront us. Yet, this Court has never held that the rule of lenity automatically permits a defendant to win.

In sum, the "generally accepted contemporary meaning" of the word "carry" includes the carrying of a firearm in a vehicle. The purpose of this statute warrants its application in such circumstances. The limiting phrase "during and in relation to" should prevent misuse of the statute to penalize those whose conduct does not create the risks of harm at which the statute aims. For these reasons, we conclude that petitioners' conduct falls within the scope of the phrase "carries a firearm." [Affirmed.]

JUSTICE GINSBURG, with whom THE CHIEF JUSTICE, JUSTICE SCALIA, and JUSTICE SOUTER join, dissenting.

Without doubt, "carries" is a word of many meanings, definable to mean or include carting about in a vehicle. But that encompassing definition is not a ubiquitously necessary one. Nor, in my judgment, is it a proper construction of "carries" as the term appears in § 924(c)(1). In line with [the] principle of lenity the Court has long followed, I would confine "carries a firearm," for § 924(c)(1) purposes, to the undoubted meaning of that expression in the relevant context. I would read the words to indicate not merely keeping arms on one's premises or in one's vehicle, but bearing them in such manner as to be ready for use as a weapon.

Unlike the Court, I do not think dictionaries,[2] surveys of press reports,[3] or the Bible[4] tell us, dispositively, what "carries" means embedded in § 924(c)(1). On definitions, "carry" in legal formulations could mean, *inter alia,* transport, possess, have in stock, prolong (carry over), be infectious, or wear or bear on one's person. At issue here is not "carries" at large but "carries a firearm." The Court's computer search of newspapers is revealing in this light. Carrying guns in a car showed up as the meaning "perhaps more than one-third" of the time. One is left to wonder what meaning showed up some two-thirds of the time. Surely a most familiar meaning is, as the Constitution's Second Amendment ("keep and *bear* Arms") (emphasis added) and Black's Law Dictionary, at 214, indicate: "wear, bear, or carry . . . upon the person or in the clothing or in a pocket, for the purpose . . . of being armed and ready for offensive or defensive action in a case of conflict with another person."

On lessons from literature, a scan of Bartlett's and other quotation collections shows how highly selective the Court's choices are. If "[t]he greatest of writers" have used "carry" to mean convey or transport in a vehicle, so have they used the hydra-headed word to mean, *inter alia,* carry in one's hand, arms, head, heart, or soul, sans vehicle. Consider, among countless examples:

> "[H]e shall gather the lambs with his arm, and carry them in his bosom." The King James Bible, Isaiah 40:11.

---

2 I note, however, that the only legal dictionary the Court cites, Black's Law Dictionary, defines "carry arms or weapons" restrictively.

3 Many newspapers, the New York Times among them, have published stories using "transport," rather than "carry," to describe gun placements resembling petitioners'. See, *e.g.,* Atlanta Constitution, Feb. 27, 1998, p. 9D, col. 2 ("House members last week expanded gun laws by allowing weapons to be *carried into restaurants or transported anywhere in cars.*"); Chicago Tribune, June 12, 1997, sports section, p. 13 ("Disabled hunters with permission to hunt from a standing vehicle would be able to *transport a shotgun in an all-terrain vehicle* as long as the gun is unloaded and the breech is open."); Colorado Springs Gazette Telegraph, Aug. 4, 1996, p. C10 (British gun laws require "locked steel cases bolted onto a car for *transporting guns from home to shooting range.*"); Detroit News, Oct. 26, 1997, p. D14 ("It is unlawful to *carry afield or transport a rifle* . . . or shotgun if you have buckshot, slug, ball loads, or cut shells in possession except while traveling directly to deer camp or target range with firearm not readily available to vehicle occupants."); N.Y. Times, July 4, 1993, p. A21, col. 2 ("[T]he gun is supposed to be *transported unloaded,* in a locked box in the trunk."); Santa Rosa Press Democrat, Sept. 28, 1996, p. B1 ("Police and volunteers ask that participants . . . *transport [their guns] to the fairgrounds* in the trunks of their cars."); Worcester Telegram & Gazette, July 16, 1996, p. B3 ("Only one gun can be turned in per person. *Guns transported in a vehicle* should be locked in the trunk.") (emphasis added in all quotations).

4 The translator of the Good Book, it appears, bore responsibility for determining whether the servants of Ahaziah "carried" his corpse to Jerusalem. Compare *ante* with, *e.g.,* The New English Bible, 2 Kings 9:28 ("His servants *conveyed* his body to Jerusalem."); Saint Joseph Edition of the New American Bible ("His servants *brought* him in a chariot to Jerusalem."); Tanakh: The Holy Scriptures ("His servants *conveyed* him in a chariot to Jerusalem."); see also *id.,* Isaiah 30:6 ("They *convey* their wealth on the backs of asses."); The New Jerusalem Bible ("[T]hey *bear* their riches on donkeys' backs.") (emphasis added in all quotations).

> "And still they gaz'd, and still the wonder grew // That one small head could carry all he knew." O. Goldsmith, The Deserted Village, ll. 215–216, in The Poetical Works of Oliver Goldsmith 30 (A. Dobson ed. 1949).
>
> "There's a Legion that never was 'listed // That carries no colours or crest." R. Kipling, The Lost Legion, st. 1, in Rudyard Kipling's Verse, 1885–1918, p. 222 (1920).
>
> "There is a homely adage which runs, 'Speak softly and carry a big stick; you will go far.' " T. Roosevelt, Speech at Minnesota State Fair, Sept. 2, 1901, in J. Bartlett, Familiar Quotations 575:16 (J. Kaplan ed. 1992).[6]

These and the Court's lexicological sources demonstrate vividly that "carry" is a word commonly used to convey various messages. Such references, given their variety, are not reliable indicators of what Congress meant, in § 924(c)(1), by "carries a firearm."

Section 924(c)(1), as the foregoing discussion details, is not decisively clear one way or another. The sharp division in the Court on the proper reading of the measure confirms, "[a]t the very least, . . . that the issue is subject to some doubt. Under these circumstances, we adhere to the familiar rule that, 'where there is ambiguity in a criminal statute, doubts are resolved in favor of the defendant.' " *Adamo Wrecking Co. v. United States*, 434 U.S. 275, 284–285 (1978). "Carry" bears many meanings, as the Court and the "Firearms" statutes demonstrate. The narrower "on or about [one's] person" interpretation is hardly implausible nor at odds with an accepted meaning of "carries a firearm."

Overlooking that there will be an enhanced sentence for the gun-possessing drug dealer in any event, the Court asks rhetorically: "How persuasive is a punishment that is without effect until a drug dealer who has brought his gun to a sale (indeed has it available for use) actually takes it from the trunk (or unlocks the glove compartment) of his car?" * * * Congress, however, hardly lacks competence to select the words "possesses" or "conveys" when that is what the Legislature means. Notably in view of the Legislature's capacity to speak plainly, and of overriding concern, the Court's inquiry pays scant attention to a core reason for the rule of lenity: "[B]ecause of the seriousness of criminal penalties, and because criminal punishment usually represents the moral condemnation of the community, legislatures and not courts should define criminal activity. This policy embodies 'the instinctive distaste against men languishing in prison unless the lawmaker has clearly said they should.' " *United*

---

6 Popular films and television productions provide corroborative illustrations. In "The Magnificent Seven," for example, O'Reilly (played by Charles Bronson) says: "You think I am brave because I carry a gun; well, your fathers are much braver because they carry responsibility, for you, your brothers, your sisters, and your mothers." And in the television series "M*A*S*H," Hawkeye Pierce (played by Alan Alda) presciently proclaims: "I will not carry a gun. . . . I'll carry your books, I'll carry a torch, I'll carry a tune, I'll carry on, carry over, carry forward, Cary Grant, cash and carry, carry me back to Old Virginia, I'll even 'hari-kari' if you show me how, but I will not carry a gun!"

*States v. Bass*, 404 U.S. 336, 348 (1971) (quoting H. Friendly, Mr. Justice Frankfurter and the Reading of Statutes, in Benchmarks 196, 209 (1967)).

The narrower "on or about [one's] person" construction of "carries a firearm" * * * adheres to the principle that, given two readings of a penal provision, both consistent with the statutory text, we do not choose the harsher construction. The Court, in my view, should leave it to Congress to speak "in language that is clear and definite" if the Legislature wishes to impose the sterner penalty. *Bass*, 404 U.S., at 347.

---

## Points for Discussion

### *a. Ordinary Meaning*

What accounts for the different conclusions in the majority and dissenting opinions in *Smith* and *Muscarello*? All of the Justices who wrote opinions announced that they were seeking the ordinary meaning of the statutory text. Is part of the problem that it is not always obvious what a particular word or phrase means? Does the disagreement among the Justices suggest that an approach focused on statutory text is likely to be unsatisfying? Or is it simply inevitable that there will be outlier cases for which the statutory text is ambiguous?

### *b. Words and Phrases*

Should the Court's task in *Smith* and *Muscarello* have been to determine the ordinary meaning of the words "use" and "carry"? Or was the task to determine the meaning of the phrases "use[ ] a firearm" and "carr[y] a firearm"? Is there a difference between these two inquiries? Sometimes a word has a particular meaning in one context and a different meaning when used in conjunction with other words. For example, the word "drop" means something different in the phrase "drop me a line" than it does in the phrase "drop the groceries"; and the word "kick" means something different in the phrase "kick the bucket" than it does in the phrase "kick your sister." How can a judge know when a statute uses words in their ordinary sense rather than in a particular, idiomatic way?

---

## C. Canons of Construction

### 1. Introduction

## *McBoyle v. United States*

283 U.S. 25 (1931)

MR. JUSTICE HOLMES delivered the opinion of the Court.

The petitioner was convicted of transporting from Ottawa, Illinois, to Guymon, Oklahoma, an airplane that he knew to have been stolen, and was sentenced to serve three years' imprisonment and to pay a fine of $2,000. The judgment was affirmed by the Circuit Court of Appeals for the Tenth Circuit. A writ of certiorari was granted by this Court on the question whether the National Motor Vehicle Theft Act applies to aircraft. Act of October 29, 1919, c. 89, 41 Stat. 324, 18 U.S.C. § 408. That Act provides: "Sec. 2. That when used in this Act: (a) The term 'motor vehicle' shall include an automobile, automobile truck, automobile wagon, motor cycle, or any other self-propelled vehicle not designed for running on rails. . . . Sec. 3. That whoever shall transport or cause to be transported in interstate or foreign commerce a motor vehicle, knowing the same to have been stolen, shall be punished by a fine of not more than $5,000, or by imprisonment of not more than five years, or both."

Section 2 defines the motor vehicles of which the transportation in interstate commerce is punished in Section 3. The question is the meaning of the word "vehicle" in the phrase "any other self-propelled vehicle not designed for running on rails." No doubt etymologically it is possible to use the word to signify a conveyance working on land, water or air, and sometimes legislation extends the use in that direction, e. g., land and air, water being separately provided for, in the Tariff Act, September 21, 1922, c. 356, § 401(b), 42 Stat. 858, 948, 19 U.S.C. § 231(b). But in everyday speech "vehicle" calls up the picture of a thing moving on land.

**Take Note**

Which meaning—ordinary, technical, or colloquial—of the word "vehicle" did the Court seek?

Thus in Rev. St. § 4 (1 U.S.C. § 4) intended, the Government suggests, rather to enlarge than to restrict the definition, vehicle includes every contrivance capable of being used "as a means of transportation on land." And this is repeated, expressly excluding aircraft, in the Tariff Act, June 17, 1930, c. 497, § 401(b), 46 Stat. 590, 708 (19 U.S.C. § 1401). So here, the phrase under discussion calls up the popular picture. For after including automobile truck, automobile wagon and motor cycle, the words "any other self-propelled vehicle not designed for running on rails" still indicate that a vehicle in the popular sense, that is a vehicle running on land is the theme. It is a vehicle that runs, not something, not commonly called a vehicle, that flies. Airplanes were well known in 1919 when this statute was passed, but it is admitted that they were not mentioned in the reports or in the debates in Congress. It is impossible to read words that so carefully enumerate the different forms of motor vehicles and have no reference of any kind to aircraft, as including airplanes under a term that usage more and more precisely confines to a different class. The counsel for the petitioner have shown that the phraseology of the statute as to motor vehicles follows that of earlier statutes of Connecticut, Delaware, Ohio, Michigan and Missouri, not to mention the late Regulations of Traffic for the District of Columbia, title 6, c. 9, § 242, none of which can be supposed to leave the earth.

Although it is not likely that a criminal will carefully consider the text of the law before he murders or steals, it is reasonable that a fair warning should be given to the world in language that the common world will understand, of what the law intends to do if a certain line is passed. To make the warning fair, so far as possible the line should be clear. When a rule of conduct is laid down in words that evoke in the common mind only the picture of vehicles moving on land, the statute should not be extended to aircraft simply because it may seem to us that a similar policy applies, or upon the speculation that if the legislature had thought of it, very likely broader words would have been used. *United States v. Bhagat Singh Thind*, 261 U. S. 204, 209 (1923). [Reversed.]

---

## Points for Discussion

### *a. Semantic Canons of Construction*

Justice Holmes did not end his argument about the meaning of the word "vehicle" after seeking the meaning of the word in "everyday speech." In interpreting the phrase "any other self-propelled vehicle not designed for running on rails," Justice Holmes looked at the other specific vehicles mentioned in the statute—automobiles, trucks, and motorcycles—and concluded that "a vehicle running on land is the theme." This is a common way of interpreting lists. For example, if you receive an invitation to a pot-luck dinner that asks you to bring "a salad, an appetizer, or a small plate," you wouldn't bring a tea saucer, even though a tea saucer is, quite literally, a "small plate." Instead, you would understand the phrase "small plate" in light of the terms—salads and appetizers—that precede it, and thus that the phrase means side dish or something similar.

In the field of statutory interpretation, we refer to these rules as "semantic canons of construction." A **canon of construction** is a default rule or background principle for interpreting statutory text; a **semantic canon** is a generalization about how language is conventionally used and understood. As we'll see soon, the semantic canon on which Justice Holmes relied is called *ejusdem generis*, which means "of the same kind." According to that canon of construction, a general term at the end of a list should be read to embrace items similar in nature to the more specific items on the list that precede it. Is that how you would have read the phrase "any other self-propelled vehicle not designed for running on rails"? If so, then why isn't the logical "theme" of the terms on the list vehicles that are motorized, a category that would include airplanes?

#### *b. Substantive Canons of Construction*

Justice Holmes also asserted that "a fair warning should be given to the world in language that the common world will understand, of what the law intends to do if a certain line is passed." Here, Justice Holmes appeared to suggest that, to the extent that the phrase "self-propelled vehicle not designed for running on rails" is ambiguous, it would be inappropriate to send someone to jail for engaging in conduct that is not clearly prohibited under the statute. In so doing, Justice Holmes was relying on the "rule of lenity," which is a different kind of canon of construction. Unlike the semantic canons of construction, which are simply reflections of how we ordinarily understand written English, the rule of lenity is designed to avoid a particular outcome—the conviction and incarceration of a defendant without giving fair notice that his conduct ran afoul of the law.

As such, the rule of a lenity is one of the **substantive canons of construction**. As a semantic matter, an airplane might well be a self-propelled vehicle not designed for running on rails. But because we want to avoid the unfairness of sending someone to jail when the law isn't clear about what exactly is prohibited, we read the statute narrowly to avoid such a result. Substantive canons, in other words, are not based on how people ordinarily use or understand language; instead, they are designed to advance certain policies or avoid certain disfavored outcomes.

As we saw earlier in this Chapter in the *Smith* and *Muscarello* cases, the rule of lenity applies only when the statute is genuinely ambiguous about whether certain conduct is prohibited. Do you agree that the statute at issue in *McBoyle* was sufficiently ambiguous to trigger the application of the rule of lenity?

---

## 2. The Whole Act Rule, the Whole Code Rule, and Related Maxims

As noted above, semantic canons are simply default rules about how we use and understand language. As such, they generally apply outside of the context of statutory interpretation—indeed, outside of the legal context altogether. Substantive canons, on the other hand, are specific to the act of statutory interpretation; they are designed to ensure that courts do not lightly reach disfavored outcomes. As such, they are not a set of rules that we follow when seeking to understand our friend's instructions. We will turn shortly to the semantic canons and the substantive canons.

Before we turn to these two types of canons, however, we begin with a set of maxims that resemble both semantic and substantive canons but that are actually distinct from both types of canons. The **Whole Act Rule** and **Whole Code Rule**, and a set of related corollaries, are similar to substantive canons in that they are specifically designed for the task of statutory interpretation. But like semantic canons—and unlike the substantive canons—they are designed to reflect how a conscientious legislature likely uses language when it enacts a statute.

The Whole Act Rule is based on a straightforward and common-sense intuition: when we try to determine the meaning of one provision in a statute, we should read it in the context of the entire statute of which the provision is a part. As the Supreme Court has explained, in "reading a statute we must not look merely to a particular clause, but consider in connection with it the whole statute." *Dada v. Mukasey*, 554 U.S. 1, 16 (2008) (internal quotations omitted). In other words, in seeking to determine the meaning of the text in the provision in question, the court should consider whether the other provisions of the statute shed any light on the meaning of those words.

Consulting other provisions of the same statute can assist in statutory interpretation in two related ways. First, the structure of the statute—the way that it is organized, and the topics that it addresses—might reveal something about the meaning of the words in the provision at issue. See, e.g., *United States v. Hartwell*, 73 U.S. (6 Wall.) 385, 396 (1867) ("The proper course in all cases is to adopt that sense of the words which best harmonizes with the context, and promotes in the fullest manner the policy and objects of the legislature."). For example, 38 U.S.C. § 2024(d) (which has since been amended) provided that any person who took a leave of absence from civilian employment "to perform active duty for training or inactive duty training in the Armed Forces of the United States" shall, upon release from such duty, "be permitted to return to such employee's position with such seniority, status, pay, and vacation as such employee would have had if such employee had not been absent for such purposes." A man who worked at a hospital was called up for a three-year tour of duty in the Army, and he asked his employer for a leave of absence under the statute. The hospital refused to grant the request, asserting that a three-year leave was unreasonable and that section 2024 did not guarantee reemployment after such a long leave. The Court rejected the hospital's argument, noting that in other sections of the statute Congress had specified limits on the length of time that other categories of personnel could take leaves from civilian employment, and thus that Congress knew how to impose such limits when it wished to do so. *King v. St. Vincent's Hosp.*, 502 U.S. 215 (1991). Courts also sometimes refer to the title of a statute to provide context for understanding the particular words in one provision of the statute, even though the title usually does not have any explicit operative effect. See, e.g., *Church of the Holy Trinity v. United States*, 143 U.S. 457 (1892), which we considered in Chapter 2.

Second, the words used in the provision at issue might be identical to—or different from—words used in other provisions of the same statute. Reference to these other provisions, particularly when their meaning is clear, can shed light on the meaning of the words in the disputed provision of the statute. Courts and commentators sometimes implement this idea by invoking a set of presumptions: the **presumption of consistent meaning**, see *Atlantic Cleaners & Dyers, Inc. v. United States*, 286 U.S. 427, 433 (1932) (describing the "presumption that identical words used in different parts of the same act are intended to have the same meaning"), and, when the argument about the provision's meaning rests on the fact that the words in the provision *differ* in important ways from the words in other provisions of the statute, the **presumption of meaningful variation**, see *Lawrence v. Florida*, 549 U.S. 327 (2007) (rejecting the argument that the provision at issue had the same meaning as another provision in the statute because the other provision "use[d] much different language"). These presumptions serve as commonly cited corollaries of the Whole Act Rule.

We have seen examples of both of these maxims. For example, in *Smith v. United States*, 508 U.S. 223 (1993), which we considered earlier in this Chapter, the Court concluded that the phrase "use[ ] a firearm" embraced the use of a gun as something other than a weapon in part because in another provision of the statute, Congress had utilized the word "use" to mean "use for exchange." And in *West Virginia University Hospitals, Inc. v. Casey*, 499 U.S. 83 (1991), which we considered in Chapter 2, the Court sought to determine the meaning of the phrase "reasonable attorney's fee"—and whether the phrase authorized the recovery of fees for services provided by non-lawyer experts—by comparing the language of the provision at issue to other fee-shifting statutes that used different language.

Although there is a common-sense intuition behind these corollaries to the Whole Act Rule, these maxims function only as presumptions. Like any other presumption, these presumptions can be overcome by a convincing showing that Congress intended a different meaning. For example, in *General Dynamics Land Systems, Inc. v. Cline*, 540 U.S. 581 (2004), which we considered in Chapter 2, the Court refused to read the word "age" to mean simply the "length of a person's life," even though the statute used the word "age" with that connotation in a different provision of the statute. The Court explained that the presumption of consistent usage "is not rigid and readily yields whenever there is such variation in the connection in which the words are used as reasonably to warrant the conclusion that they were employed in different parts of the act with different intent." And although courts sometimes look to the title of a statute to shed light on the meaning of the words in one its provisions, other times they decline to do so. See, e.g., *Caminetti v. United States*, 242 U.S. 470 (1917), which we considered in Chapter 2.

Another commonly invoked corollary of the Whole Act Rule is the **rule against redundancy**, also sometimes called the **rule against surplusage**. Under this maxim, courts "will avoid a reading which renders some words altogether redundant." *Gustafson v. Alloyd Co., Inc.*, 513 U.S. 561, 574 (1995). For example, in *King v. Burwell*, 576 U.S. 473 (2015), the Court considered whether a health care exchange established and operated by the federal government, when a state had declined to create one, counted under a provision of the statute that provided tax credits for taxpayers who enrolled in insurance plans through an "Exchange established by the State." Trying to make sense of a complicated statutory scheme, the Court held that it did. Justice Scalia dissented, asserting (among other things) that the Court's reading left the phrase "by the State" with "no operative effect at all." This, he reasoned, was inconsistent with "elementary principle that requires an interpreter 'to give effect, if possible, to every clause and word of a statute.' " *Id.* at 502 (quoting *Montclair v. Ramsdell*, 107 U.S. 147, 152 (1883)).

**Make the Connection**

We will consider the Court's decision in *King v. Burwell* in Chapter 8.

The Whole Code Rule is similar to the Whole Act Rule. It instructs interpreters to consider the meaning of a provision in light of the entire statutory code (and not just the statute of which the provision was a part). Many of the maxims described above can operate code-wide. Indeed, the example above of the presumption of meaningful variation in fact functioned as a corollary of the whole code rule; after all, in his opinion in *West Virginia University Hospitals v. Casey*, Justice Scalia looked at other statutes, enacted at different times, that provided for the recovery of attorney's fees.

The most commonly cited corollary of the Whole Code Rule is the maxim ***in pari materia***, which is Latin for "on the same subject." Under that maxim, "statutes addressing the same subject matter should generally be read as if they were one law." *Wachovia Bank v. Schmidt*, 546 U.S. 303, 315–16 (2006) (internal quotation omitted). The maxim is based on the assumption that "a legislative body generally uses a particular word with a consistent meaning in a given context" and on the premise that "whenever Congress passes a new statute, it acts aware of all previous statutes on the same subject." *Erlenbaugh v. United States*, 409 U.S. 239, 243–44 (1972).

The Whole Code Rule and its corollaries are based on an assumption that when Congress legislates, it acts with knowledge of already-existing statutes and seeks to create a coherent body of statutory law. Does this assumption reflect the state of affairs in the real world? A comprehensive study of congressional practice found that many of the legislative aides who draft statutory language were unaware of many of the maxims described here and often are unaware of the statutory language used in prior statutes. See Abbe R. Gluck & Lisa Schultz Bressman, *Statutory Interpretation from the Inside—An Empirical Study of Congressional Drafting, Delegation, and the Canons: Part I*, 65 STAN. L. REV. 901 (2013). This is perhaps not surprising, given that there is not usually any coordination between the various congressional committees that might end up drafting statutory language on a topic. See Abbe R. Gluck & Lisa Schultz Bressman, *Statutory Interpretation from the Inside—An Empirical Study of Congressional Drafting, Delegation, and the Canons: Part II*, 66 STAN. L. REV. 725 (2014). Does this suggest that it is misguided for courts to rely on the Whole Act Rule, the Whole Code Rule, and the various corollaries of those rules? Or can you think of reasons why courts might nevertheless choose to follow them, even if they do not reflect the empirical reality of congressional lawmaking?

---

### 3. Grammar Canons

As noted above, the semantic canons of construction are background rules designed to reflect how we ordinarily use and understand language. For example, as we'll see, there are canons that instruct how the interpreter should construe a word that appears on a list with other words. But our intended meaning when we use written commands depends not only on the words that we choose, but also on the structure of our sentences. As a consequence, the ordinary rules of grammar often help us to determine the meaning of written English. What role should the rules of grammar play when we interpret statutes? Consider the two cases that follow.

---

## *Lockhart v. United States*

577 U.S. 347 (2016)

JUSTICE SOTOMAYOR delivered the opinion of the Court.

Defendants convicted of possessing child pornography in violation of 18 U.S.C. § 2252(a)(4) are subject to a 10-year mandatory minimum sentence and an increased maximum sentence if they have "a prior conviction . . . under the laws of any State relating to aggravated sexual abuse, sexual abuse, or abusive sexual conduct involving a minor or ward." § 2252(b)(2).

The question before us is whether the phrase "involving a minor or ward" modifies all items in the list of predicate crimes ("aggravated sexual abuse," "sexual abuse," and "abusive sexual conduct") or only the one item that immediately precedes it ("abusive sexual conduct"). * * *

In April 2000, Avondale Lockhart was convicted of sexual abuse in the first degree under N.Y. Penal Law Ann. § 130.65(1). The crime involved his then–53–year–old girlfriend. Eleven years later, Lockhart was indicted in the Eastern District of New York for attempting to receive child pornography in violation of 18 U.S.C.

§ 2252(a)(2) and for possessing child pornography in violation of § 2252(a)(4)(b). Lockhart pleaded guilty to the possession offense and the Government dismissed the receipt offense.

Lockhart's presentence report calculated a guidelines range of 78 to 97 months for the possession offense. But the report also concluded that Lockhart was subject to § 2252(b)(2)'s mandatory minimum because his prior New York abuse conviction related "to aggravated sexual abuse, sexual abuse, or abusive sexual conduct involving a minor or ward." * * * Lockhart objected, arguing that the statutory phrase "involving a minor or ward" applies to all three listed crimes: "aggravated sexual abuse," "sexual abuse," *and* "abusive sexual conduct." He therefore contended that his prior conviction for sexual abuse involving an *adult* fell outside the enhancement's ambit. The District Court rejected Lockhart's argument and applied the mandatory minimum. The Second Circuit affirmed his sentence.

**Take Note**

Before reading further, ask yourself whether, according to the ordinary rules of grammar or other linguistic conventions, you understand the phrase "involving a minor or ward" to modify all three crimes on the list or instead only the last one. Is there a grammatical rule that influences your interpretation?

The issue before us is whether the limiting phrase that appears at the end of that list—"involving a minor or ward"—applies to all three predicate crimes preceding it in the list or only the final predicate crime. We hold that "involving a minor or ward" modifies only "abusive sexual conduct," the antecedent immediately preceding it. Although § 2252(b)(2)'s list of state predicates is awkwardly phrased (to put it charitably), the provision's text and context together reveal a straightforward reading. A timeworn textual canon is confirmed by the structure and internal logic of the statutory scheme.

Consider the text. When this Court has interpreted statutes that include a list of terms or phrases followed by a limiting clause, we have typically applied an interpretive strategy called the "rule of the last antecedent." See *Barnhart v. Thomas*, 540 U.S. 20, 26 (2003). The rule provides that "a limiting clause or phrase . . . should ordinarily be read as modifying only the noun or phrase that it immediately follows." *Ibid.*

This Court has applied the rule from our earliest decisions to our more recent. The rule reflects the basic intuition that when a modifier appears at the end of a list, it is easier to apply that modifier only to the item directly before it. That is particularly true where it takes more than a little mental energy to process the individual entries in the list, making it a heavy lift to carry the modifier across them all. For example, imagine you are the general manager of the Yankees and you are rounding out your 2016 roster. You tell your scouts to find a defensive catcher, a quick-footed shortstop, or a pitcher from last year's World Champion Kansas City Royals. It would be natural for your scouts to confine their search for a pitcher to last year's championship team, but to look more broadly for catchers and shortstops.

**Take Note**

In Justice Sotomayor's example, do you naturally assume that the phrase "from last year's World Champion Kansas City Royals" modifies only the last item on the list because of a general rule about modifiers that follow lists? Or because each of the other two items on the list is preceded by its own modifying adjective or adjectival phrase?

Applied here, the last antecedent principle suggests that the phrase "involving a minor or ward" modifies only the phrase that it immediately follows: "abusive sexual conduct." As a corollary, it also suggests that the phrases "aggravated sexual abuse" and "sexual abuse" are not so constrained.

Of course, as with any canon of statutory interpretation, the rule of the last antecedent "is not an absolute and can assuredly be overcome by other indicia of meaning." *Barnhart*, 540 U.S., at 26. For instance, take "the laws, the treaties, and the constitution of the United States." A reader intuitively applies "of the United States" to "the laws," "the treaties" and "the constitution" because (among other things) laws, treaties, and the constitution are often cited together, because readers are used to seeing "of the United States" modify each of them, and because the listed items are simple and parallel without unexpected internal modifiers or structure. Section 2252(b)(2), by contrast, does not contain items that readers are used to seeing listed together or a concluding modifier that readers are accustomed to applying to each of them. And the varied syntax of each item in the list makes it hard for the reader to carry the final modifying clause across all three.

More importantly, here the interpretation urged by the rule of the last antecedent is not overcome by other indicia of meaning. To the contrary, § 2252(b)(2)'s context fortifies the meaning that principle commands.

Among the chapters of the Federal Criminal Code that can trigger § 2252(b)(2)'s recidivist enhancement are crimes "under . . . chapter 109A." Chapter 109A criminalizes a range of sexual-abuse offenses involving adults *or* minors and wards. And it places those federal sexual-abuse crimes under headings that use language nearly identical to the language § 2252(b)(2) uses to enumerate the three categories of state sexual-abuse predicates. The first section in Chapter 109A is titled "Aggravated sexual abuse." 18 U.S.C. § 2241. The second is titled "Sexual abuse." § 2242. And the third is titled "Sexual abuse of a minor or ward." § 2243. Applying the rule of the last antecedent, those sections mirror precisely the order, precisely the divisions, and nearly precisely the words used to describe the three state sexual-abuse predicate crimes in § 2252(b)(2): "aggravated sexual abuse," "sexual abuse," and "abusive sexual conduct involving a minor or ward."

This similarity appears to be more than a coincidence. We cannot state with certainty that Congress used Chapter 109A as a template for the list of state predicates set out in § 2252(b)(2), but we cannot ignore the parallel, particularly because the headings in Chapter 109A were in place when Congress amended the statute to add § 2252(b)(2)'s state sexual-abuse predicates. If Congress had intended to limit each of the state predicates to conduct "involving a minor or ward," we doubt it would have followed, or thought it needed to follow, so closely the structure and language of Chapter 109A.

Lockhart argues, to the contrary, that the phrase "involving a minor or ward" should be interpreted to modify all three state sexual-abuse predicates. He first contends, as does our dissenting colleague, that the so-called series-qualifier principle supports his reading. This principle, Lockhart says, requires a modifier to apply to all items in a series when such an application would represent a natural construction.

This Court has long acknowledged that structural or contextual evidence may "rebut the last antecedent inference." *Jama v. Immigration and Customs Enforcement*, 543 U.S. 335, 344, n. 4 (2005). But in none of [the] cases did the Court describe, much less apply, a countervailing grammatical mandate that could bear the weight that either Lockhart or the dissent places on the series qualifier principle. Instead, the Court simply observed that sometimes context weighs against the application of the rule of the last antecedent. Whether a modifier is "applicable as much to the first . . . as to the last" words in a list, whether a set of items form a "single, integrated list," and whether the application of the rule would require acceptance of an "unlikely premise" are fundamentally contextual questions.

> **Food for Thought**
>
> If the applicability of the rule of the last antecedent (or some other gra[…] matical rule) simply depe[…] context, as the Court su[…] then is it really a car[…] simply state one p[…] items on a list can b[…]

Lockhart * * * points out that the final two state predicate[…] "abusive sexual conduct," are "nearly synonymous as a matter […] And, of course, anyone who commits "aggravated sexual abuse" […] committed "sexual abuse." So, he posits, the items in the list are su[…] that a limiting phrase could apply equally to all three of them.

But Lockhart's effort to demonstrate some similarity among the items in the list of state predicates reveals far too much similarity. The three state predicate crimes are not just related on Lockhart's reading; they are hopelessly redundant. Any conduct that would qualify as "aggravated sexual abuse . . . involving a minor or ward" or "sexual abuse . . . involving a minor or ward" would also qualify as "abusive sexual conduct involving a minor or ward." We take no position today on the meaning of the terms "aggravated sexual abuse," "sexual abuse," and "abusive sexual conduct," including their similarities and differences. But it is clear that applying the limiting phrase to all three items would risk running headlong into the rule against superfluity by transforming a list of separate predicates into a set of synonyms describing the same predicate. See *Bailey v. United States*, 516 U.S. 137, 146 (1995) ("We assume that Congress used two terms because it intended each term to have a particular, nonsuperfluous meaning").

The dissent offers a suggestion rooted in its impressions about how people ordinarily speak and write. The problem is that, as even the dissent acknowledges, § 2252(b)(2)'s list of state predicates is hardly intuitive. No one would mistake its odd repetition and inelegant phrasing for a reflection of the accumulated wisdom of everyday speech patterns. It would be as if a friend asked you to get her tart lemons, sour lemons, or sour fruit from Mexico. If you brought back lemons from California, but your friend insisted that she was using customary speech and obviously asked for Mexican fruit only, you would be forgiven for disagreeing on both counts.

Faced with § 2252(b)(2)'s inartful drafting, then, do we interpret the provision by viewing it as a clear, commonsense list best construed as if conversational English? Or do we look around to see if there might be some provenance to its peculiarity? With Chapter 109A so readily at hand, we are unpersuaded by our dissenting colleague's invocation of basic examples from day-to-day life. Whatever the validity of the dissent's broader point, this simply is not a case in which colloquial practice is of much use. Section 2252(b)(2)'s list is hardly the way an average person, or even an average lawyer, would set about to describe the relevant conduct if they had started from scratch.

Finally, Lockhart asks us to apply the rule of lenity. We have used the lenity principle to resolve ambiguity in favor of the defendant only "at the end of the process of construing what Congress has expressed" when the ordinary canons of statutory construction have revealed no satisfactory construction. *Callanan v. United States*, 364 U.S. 587, 596 (1961). That is not the case here. To be sure, Lockhart contends that if we applied a different principle of statutory construction—namely, his "series-qualifier principle"—we would arrive at an alternative construction of § 2252(b)(2). But the arguable availability of multiple, divergent principles of statutory construction cannot automatically trigger the rule of lenity. Cf. Llewellyn, Remarks on the Theory of Appellate Decision and the Rules or Canons About How Statutes Are To Be Construed, 3 Vand. L. Rev. 395, 401 (1950) ("[T]here are two opposing canons on almost every point"). Here, the rule of the last antecedent is well supported by context and Lockhart's alternative is not. We will not apply the rule of lenity to override a sensible grammatical principle buttressed by the statute's text and structure. [Affirmed.]

**Make the Connection**

We will consider the rule of lenity, and some other substantive canons of construction, later in this Chapter.

JUSTICE KAGAN, with whom JUSTICE BREYER joins, dissenting.

Imagine a friend told you that she hoped to meet "an actor, director, or producer involved with the new Star Wars movie." You would know immediately that she wanted to meet an actor from the Star Wars cast—not an actor in, for example, the latest Zoolander. Suppose a real estate agent promised to find a client "a house, condo, or apartment in New York." Wouldn't the potential buyer be annoyed if the agent sent him information about condos in Maryland or California? And consider a law imposing a penalty for the "violation of any statute, rule, or regulation relating to insider trading." Surely a person would have cause to protest if punished under that provision for violating a traffic statute. The reason in all three cases is the same: Everyone understands that the modifying phrase—"involved with the new Star Wars movie," "in New York," "relating to insider trading"—applies to each term in the preceding list, not just the last.

That ordinary understanding of how English works, in speech and writing alike, should decide this case. * * * And if any doubt remained, the rule of lenity would command the same result: Lockhart's prior conviction for sexual abuse *of an adult* does not trigger § 2252(b)(2)'s mandatory minimum penalty. * * *

[T]his Court has made clear that the last-antecedent rule does not generally apply to the grammatical construction present here: when "[t]he modifying clause appear[s] . . . at the end of a single, integrated list." *Jama*, 543 U.S., at 344, n. 4. Then, the exact opposite is usually true: As in the examples beginning this opinion, the modifying phrase refers alike to each of the list's terms. A leading treatise puts the point as follows: "When there is a straightforward, parallel construction that involves all nouns or verbs in a series," a modifier at the end of the list "normally applies to the entire series." A. Scalia & B. Garner, Reading Law: The Interpretation of Legal Texts 147 (2012); compare *id.*, at 152 ("When the syntax involves something other than [such] a parallel series of nouns or verbs," the modifier "normally applies only to the nearest reasonable referent"). That interpretive practice of applying the modifier to the whole list boasts a fancy name—the "series-qualifier canon," see Black's Law Dictionary 1574 (10th ed. 2014)—but, as my opening examples show, it reflects the completely ordinary way that people speak and listen, write and read.

Even the exception to the series-qualifier principle is intuitive, emphasizing both its common-sensical basis and its customary usage. When the nouns in a list are so disparate that the modifying clause does not make sense when applied to them all, then the last-antecedent rule takes over. Suppose your friend told you not that she wants to meet "an actor, director, or producer involved with Star Wars," but instead that she hopes someday to meet "a President, Supreme Court Justice, or actor involved with Star Wars." Presumably, you would know that she wants to meet a President or Justice even if that person has no connection to the famed film franchise. But so long as the modifying clause "is applicable as much to the first and other words as to the last," this Court has stated, "the natural construction of the language demands that the clause be read as applicable to all." *Paroline v. United States*, 572 U.S. 434, 447 (2014). In other words, the modifier then qualifies not just the last antecedent but the whole series.

The majority responds to all this by claiming that the "inelegant phrasing" of § 2252(b)(2) renders it somehow exempt from a grammatical rule reflecting "how people ordinarily" use the English language. But to begin with, the majority is wrong to suggest that the series-qualifier canon is only about "colloquial" or "conversational" English. In fact, it applies to both speech and writing, in both their informal and their formal varieties. Here is a way to test my point: Pick up a journal, or a book, or for that matter a Supreme Court opinion—most of which keep "everyday" colloquialisms at a far distance. You'll come across many sentences having the structure of the statutory provision at issue here: a few nouns followed by a modifying clause. And you'll discover, again and yet again, that the clause modifies every noun in the series, not just the last—in other words, that even (especially?) in formal writing, the series-qualifier principle works. And the majority is wrong too in suggesting that the "odd repetition" in § 2252(b)(2)'s list of state predicates causes the series-qualifier principle to lose its force. *Ibid.* The majority's own made-up sentence proves that much. If a friend asked you "to get her tart lemons, sour lemons, or sour fruit from Mexico," you might well think her list of terms perplexing: You might puzzle over the difference between tart and sour lemons, and wonder why she had specifically mentioned lemons when she apparently would be happy with sour fruit of any kind. But of one thing, you would have no doubt: Your friend wants some produce *from Mexico*; it would not do to get her, say, sour lemons from Vietnam. However weird the way she listed fruits—or the way § 2252(b)(2) lists offenses—the modifying clause still refers to them all.

The majority as well seeks refuge in the idea that applying the series-qualifier canon to § 2252(b)(2) would violate the rule against superfluity. [But] the majority's approach (as it admits) produces superfluity too—and in equal measure. Now (to rearrange the majority's sentence) any conduct that would qualify as "abusive sexual conduct involving a minor or ward" or "aggravated sexual abuse" would also qualify as "sexual abuse." In other words, on the majority's reading as well, two listed crimes become subsets of a third, so that the three could have been written as one. And indeed, the majority's superfluity has an especially odd quality, because it relates to the modifying clause itself: The majority, that is, makes the term "involving a minor or ward" wholly unnecessary. Remember the old adage about the pot and the kettle? That is why the rule against superfluity cannot excuse

**Make the Connection**

We discussed the rule against superfluity—also called the rule against redundancy or the rule against surplusage—earlier in this Chapter when we considered the Whole Act Rule and its corollaries.

the majority from reading § 2252(b)(2)'s modifier, as ordinary usage demands, to pertain to all the terms in the preceding series.

As against the most natural construction of § 2252(b)(2)'s language, * * * the majority relies on a structural argument. The federal sexual-abuse predicates in § 2252(b)(2), the majority begins, are described as crimes "under . . . Chapter 109A," and that chapter "criminalizes a range of sexual-abuse offenses involving adults *or* minors." [And the] headings of the sections in Chapter 109A, it contends, "mirror precisely the order . . . and nearly precisely the words used to describe" the state predicate crimes at issue.

But § 2252(b)(2)'s state predicates are not nearly as similar to the federal crimes in Chapter 109A as the majority claims. That Chapter includes the following offenses: "Aggravated sexual abuse," § 2241, "Sexual abuse," § 2242, "Sexual abuse of a minor or ward," § 2243, and "Abusive sexual contact," § 2244. The Chapter thus contains *four* crimes—one more than found in § 2252(b)(2)'s list of state offenses. If the drafters of § 2252(b)(2) meant merely to copy Chapter 109A, why would they have left out one of its crimes? The majority has no explanation. * * *

Suppose, for a moment, that this case is not as clear as I've suggested. Assume there is no way to know whether to apply the last-antecedent or the series-qualifier rule. Imagine, too, that the * * * majority's "template" argument [is] not quite so strained. Who, then, should prevail?

This Court has a rule for how to resolve genuine ambiguity in criminal statutes: in favor of the criminal defendant. As the majority puts the point, the rule of lenity insists that courts side with the defendant "when the ordinary canons of statutory construction have revealed no satisfactory construction." At the very least, that principle should tip the scales in Lockhart's favor, because nothing the majority has said shows that the modifying clause in § 2252(b)(2) *unambiguously* applies to only the last term in the preceding series.

But in fact, Lockhart's case is stronger. Consider the following sentence, summarizing various points made above: "The series-qualifier principle, [the Code's structure], and the rule of lenity discussed in this opinion all point in the same direction." Now answer the following question: Has only the rule of lenity been discussed in this opinion, or have the series-qualifier principle and the legislative history been discussed as well? Even had you not read the preceding [3] pages, you would know the right answer—because of the ordinary way all of us use language. That, in the end, is why Lockhart should win.

---

## Points for Discussion

### *a. The Rule of the Last Antecedent and the Series-Qualifier Principle*

Justice Sotomayor and Justice Kagan offered dueling grammar canons to resolve the question about the statute's meaning. Does one of the two canons—the rule of the last antecedent or the series-qualifier principle—better reflect how people ordinarily use language? Consider some examples. If you work in a restaurant and a customer tells you that she "would like to order a hamburger, French fries, and broccoli with cheese," would you tell the chef to put cheese on the burger and the fries? (If not, then you are following the rule of the last antecedent.) If your professor tells you that "in honor of St. Patrick's Day, you should wear pants, shirts, and sweaters with lots of green," would you wear green pants and a green shirt? (If so, then you are following the series-qualifier principle.) If you would sometimes follow one of these grammatical rules and other times follow the other, then can either be said to be a genuine default canon of construction?

### *b. Grammar Canons and Certainty*

Even assuming that neither of the grammar canons discussed in *Lockhart* perfectly reflects how we ordinarily use language, is there a reason for courts simply to choose one and follow it? Does it matter whether the legislature is aware of the courts' practice of following a particular canon of construction?

---

## *O'Connor v. Oakhurst Dairy*

851 F.3d 69 (1st Cir. 2017)

BARRON, CIRCUIT JUDGE.

For want of a comma, we have this case. It arises from a dispute between a Maine dairy company and its delivery drivers, and it concerns the scope of an exemption from Maine's overtime law. 26 M.R.S.A. § 664(3). Specifically, if that exemption used a serial comma to mark off the last of the activities that it lists, then the exemption would clearly encompass an activity that the drivers perform. And, in that event, the drivers would plainly fall within the exemption and thus outside the overtime law's protection. But, as it happens, there is no serial comma to be found in the exemption's list of activities, thus leading to this dispute over whether the drivers fall within the exemption from the overtime law or not.

Maine's wage and hour law is set forth in Chapter 7 of Title 26 of the Maine Revised Statutes. The Maine overtime law is part of the state's wage and hour law.

The overtime law provides that "[a]n employer may not require an employee to work more than 40 hours in any one week unless 1 1/2 times the regular hourly rate is paid for all hours actually worked in excess of 40 hours in that week." 26 M.R.S.A. § 664(3). * * *

The delivery drivers * * * are plainly "employees" [under the statutory definition]. But some workers who fall within the statutory definition of "employee" nonetheless fall outside the protection of the overtime law due to a series of express exemptions from that law. The exemption to the overtime law that is in dispute here is Exemption F.

Exemption F covers employees whose work involves the handling—in one way or another—of certain, expressly enumerated food products. Specifically, Exemption F states that the protection of the overtime law does not apply to:

> The canning, processing, preserving, freezing, drying, marketing, storing, packing for shipment or distribution of: (1) Agricultural produce; (2) Meat and fish products; and (3) Perishable foods.

26 M.R.S.A. § 664(3)(F). The parties' dispute concerns the meaning of the words "packing for shipment or distribution."

The delivery drivers contend that, in combination, these words refer to the single activity of "packing," whether the "packing" is for "shipment" or for "distribution." The drivers further contend that, although they do handle perishable foo[...] they do not engage in "packing" them. As a result, the drivers argue that, as e[...]ees who fall outside Exemption F, the Maine overtime law protects them.

Oakhurst responds that the disputed words actually refer to two distinct exempt activities, with the first being "packing for shipment" and the second being "distribution." And because the delivery drivers do—quite obviously—engage in the "distribution" of dairy products, which are "perishable foods," Oakhurst contends that the drivers fall within Exemption F and thus outside the overtime law's protection.

> **Ta[...]**
>
> Can you articulate the competin[...]sitions in the dispute over the mea[...]ing of the statute? Can you see ho[...] the addition of a comma after the word "shipment" would clarify the meaning of the provision?

The delivery drivers lost this interpretive dispute below. They had filed suit against Oakhurst on May 5, 2014 in the United States District Court for the District of Maine. The suit sought unpaid overtime wages under the federal Fair Labor Standards Act, 29 U.S.C. §§ 201 et seq., and the Maine overtime law, 26 M.R.S.A. § 664(3). * * * The District Court * * * granted summary judgment for Oakhurst on the ground that "distribution" was a stand-alone exempt activity.

The delivery drivers now appeal that ruling. They raise a single legal question: what does the contested phrase in Exemption F mean? * * *

Each party recognizes that, by its bare terms, Exemption F raises questions as to its scope, largely due to the fact that no comma precedes the words "or distribution." But each side also contends that the exemption's text has a latent clarity, at least after one applies various interpretive aids. Each side then goes on to argue that the overtime law's evident purpose and legislative history confirms its preferred reading.

We conclude, however, that Exemption F is ambiguous, even after we take account of the relevant interpretive aids and the law's purpose and legislative history. For that reason, we conclude that, under Maine law, we must construe the exemption in the narrow manner that the drivers favor, as doing so furthers the overtime law's remedial purposes. See *Dir. of Bureau of Labor Standards v. Cormier*, 527 A.2d 1297 (Me. 1987). Before explaining our reasons for reaching this conclusion, though, we first need to work our way through the parties' arguments as to why, despite the absent comma, Exemption F is clearer than it looks.

First, the text. See *Harrington v. State*, 96 A.3d 696, 697–98 (Me. 2014) ("Only if the statute is reasonably susceptible to different interpretations will we look beyond the statutory language. . . ."). In considering it, we do not simply look at the particular word "distribution" in isolation from the exemption as a whole. We instead must take account of certain linguistic conventions—canons, as they are often called—that can help us make sense of a word in the context in which it appears. Oakhurst argues that, when we account for these canons here, it is clear that the exemption identifies "distribution" as a stand-alone, exempt activity rather than as an activity that merely modifies the stand-alone, exempt activity of "packing."

Oakhurst relies for its reading in significant part on the rule against surplusage, which instructs that we must give independent meaning to each word in a statute and treat none as unnecessary. See *Stromberg-Carlson Corp. v. State Tax Assessor*, 765 A.2d 566, 569 (Me. 2001). To make this case, Oakhurst explains that "shipment" and "distribution" are synonyms. For that reason, Oakhurst contends, "distribution" cannot describe a type of "packing," as the word "distribution" would then redundantly perform the role that "shipment"—as its synonym—already performs, which is to describe the type of "packing" that is exempt. By contrast, Oakhurst explains, under its reading, the words "shipment" and "distribution" are not redundant. The first word, "shipment," describes the exempt activity of "packing," while the second, "distribution," describes an exempt activity in its own right.

**Food for Thought**

In its opinion, the court invokes several corollaries of the Whole Act Rule, which we considered earlier in this Chapter. Can you identify them and explain how they applied in this case?

Oakhurst also relies on another established linguistic convention in pressing its case—the convention of using a conjunction to mark off the last item on a list. See The Chicago Manual of Style § 6.123 (16th ed. 2010) (providing examples of lists with such conjunctions). Oakhurst notes, rightly, that there is no conjunction before "packing," but that there is one after "shipment" and thus before "distribution." Oakhurst also observes that Maine overtime law contains two other lists in addition to the one at issue here and that each places a conjunction before the last item. See 26 M.R.S.A. § 664(3) ("The regular hourly rate includes all earnings, bonuses, commissions *and* other compensation . . ." (emphasis added)); *id.* at § 664(3)(A) (exempting from overtime law "automobile mechanics, automobile parts clerks, automobile service writers *and* automobile salespersons as defined in section 663" (emphasis added)).

Oakhurst acknowledges that its reading would be beyond dispute if a comma preceded the word "distribution" and that no comma is there. But, Oakhurst contends, that comma is missing for good reason. Oakhurst points out that the Maine Legislative Drafting Manual expressly instructs that: "when drafting Maine law or rules, don't use a comma between the penultimate and the last item of a series." Maine Legislative Drafting Manual 113 (Legislative Council, Maine State Legislature 2009), http://maine.gov/legis/ros/manual/Draftman2009.pdf ("Drafting Manual"); *see also Jacob v. Kippax*, 10 A.3d 1159, 1166 (Me. 2011) (invoking the Drafting Manual to help resolve a statutory ambiguity). In fact, Oakhurst notes, Maine statutes invariably omit the serial comma from lists. And this practice reflects a drafting convention that is at least as old as the Maine wage and hour law, even if the drafting manual itself is of more recent vintage. See, e.g., Me. Stat. tit. 26, § 663(3)(G) (1965) ("processing, canning or packing"); Me. Stat. tit. 26, § 665(1) (1965) ("hours, total earnings and itemized deductions").

If no more could be gleaned from the text, we might be inclined to read Exemption F as Oakhurst does. But, the delivery drivers point out, there is more to consider. And while these other features of the text do not compel the drivers' reading, they do make the exemption's scope unclear, at least as a matter of text alone.

The drivers contend, first, that the inclusion of both "shipment" and "distribution" to describe "packing" results in no redundancy. Those activities, the drivers argue, are each distinct. They contend that "shipment" refers to the outsourcing of the delivery of goods to a third-party carrier for transportation, while "distribution" refers to a seller's in-house transportation of products directly to recipients. And the drivers note that this distinction is, in one form or another, adhered to in dictionary definitions. See New Oxford English American Dictionary 497, 1573–74 (2001); Webster's Third New International Dictionary 666, 2096 (2002).

Consistent with the drivers' contention, Exemption F does use two different words ("shipment" and "distribution") when it is hard to see why, on Oakhurst's reading, the legislature did not simply use just one of them twice. After all, if "distribution" and "shipment" really do mean the same thing, as Oakhurst contends, then it is odd that the legislature chose to use one of them ("shipment") to describe the activity for which "packing" is done but the other ("distribution") to describe the activity itself.

The drivers' argument that the legislature did not view the words to be interchangeable draws additional support from another Maine statute. That statute clearly lists both "distribution" and "shipment" as if each represents a separate activity in its own right. See 10 M.R.S.A. § 1476 (referring to "manufacture, distribution or shipment"). And because Maine law elsewhere treats "shipment" and "distribution" as if they are separate activities in a list, we do not see why we must assume that the Maine legislature did not treat them that way here as well. After all, the use of these two words to describe "packing" need not be understood to be wasteful. Such usage could simply reflect the legislature's intention to make clear that "packing" is exempt whether done for "shipment" or for "distribution" and not simply when done for just one of those activities.[3]

Next, the drivers point to the exemption's grammar. The drivers note that each of the terms in Exemption F that indisputably names an exempt activity—"canning, processing, preserving," and so forth on through "packing"—is a gerund. By, contrast, "distribution" is not. And neither is "shipment." In fact, those are the only non-gerund nouns in the exemption, other than the ones that name various foods.

**Definition**

A "gerund" is a word ending in "-ing" that derives from a verb but that is used as a noun, such as "packing" or "interpreting."

Thus, the drivers argue, in accord with what is known as the parallel usage convention, that "distribution" and "shipment" must be playing the same grammatical role—and one distinct from the role that the gerunds play. See The Chicago Manual of Style § 5.212 (16th ed. 2010) ("Every element of a parallel series must be a functional match of the others (word, phrase, clause, sentence) and serve the same grammatical function in the sentence (e.g., noun, verb, adjective, adverb)."). In accord with that convention, the drivers read "shipment" and "distribution" each to be objects of the preposition "for" that describes the exempt activity of "packing." And the drivers read the gerunds each to be referring to stand-alone, exempt activities—"canning, preserving. . . ."

By contrast, in violation of the convention, Oakhurst's reading treats one of the two non-gerunds ("distribution") as if it is performing a distinct grammatical function from the other ("shipment"), as the latter functions as an object of a preposition while the former does not. And Oakhurst's reading also contravenes the parallel usage convention in another way: it treats a non-gerund (again, "distribution") as if

---

3 We also note that there is some reason to think that the distinction between "shipment" and "distribution" is not merely one that only a lawyer could love. Oakhurst's own internal organization chart seems to treat the two as if they are separate activities.

it is performing a role in the list—naming an exempt activity in its own right—that gerunds otherwise exclusively perform.

Finally, the delivery drivers circle back to that missing comma. They acknowledge that the drafting manual advises drafters not to use serial commas to set off the final item in a list—despite the clarity that the inclusion of serial commas would often seem to bring. But the drivers point out that the drafting manual is not dogmatic on that point. The manual also contains a proviso—"Be careful if an item in the series is modified"—and then sets out several examples of how lists with modified or otherwise complex terms should be written to avoid the ambiguity that a missing serial comma would otherwise create. See Drafting Manual at 114.

Thus, the drafting manual's seeming—and, from a judge's point of view, entirely welcome—distaste for ambiguous lists does suggest a reason to doubt Oakhurst's insistence that the missing comma casts no doubt on its preferred reading. For, as the drivers explain, the drafting manual cannot be read to instruct that the comma should have been omitted here if "distribution" was intended to be the last item in the list. In that event, the serial comma's omission would give rise to just the sort of ambiguity that the manual warns drafters not to create.[5]

Still, the drivers' textual points do not account for what seems to us to be Oakhurst's strongest textual rejoinder: no conjunction precedes "packing." Rather, the only conjunction in the exemption—"or"—appears before "distribution." And so, on the drivers' reading, the list is strangely stingy when it comes to conjunctions, as it fails to use one to mark off the last listed activity.

To address this anomaly, the drivers cite to Antonin Scalia & Bryan Garner, Reading Law: The Interpretation of Legal Texts (2012), in which the authors observe that "[s]ometimes drafters will omit conjunctions altogether between the enumerated items [in a list]," in a technique called "asyndeton," *id.* at 119. But those same authors point out that most legislative drafters avoid asyndeton. *Id.* And, the delivery drivers

---

5 * * * Before leaving our discussion of serial commas, we would be remiss not to note the clarifying virtues of serial commas that other jurisdictions recognize. In fact, guidance on legislative drafting in most other states and in the Congress appears to differ from Maine's when it comes to serial commas. Some state legislative drafting manuals expressly warn that the absence of serial commas can create ambiguity concerning the last item in a list. One analysis notes that only seven states—including Maine—either do not require or expressly prohibit the use of the serial comma. See Amy Langenfeld, Capitol Drafting: Legislative Drafting Manuals in the Law School Classroom, 22 Perspectives: Teaching Legal Res. & Writing 141, 143–144 (2014). Also, drafting conventions of both chambers of the federal Congress warn against omitting the serial comma for the same reason. See U.S. House of Representatives Office of the Legislative Counsel, House Legislative Counsel's Manual on Drafting Style, No. HLC 104-1, § 351 at 58 (1995) (requiring a serial comma to "prevent[ ] any misreading that the last item is part of the preceding one"); U.S. Senate Office of the Legislative Counsel, Legislative Drafting Manual § 321(c) at 79 (1997) (same language as House Manual).

do not provide any examples of Maine statutes that use this unusual grammatical device. Thus, the drivers' reading of the text is hardly fully satisfying.[6]

The text has, to be candid, not gotten us very far. We are reluctant to conclude from the text alone that the legislature clearly chose to deploy the nonstandard grammatical device of asyndeton. But we are also reluctant to overlook the seemingly anomalous violation of the parallel usage canon that Oakhurst's reading of the text produces. And so—there being no comma in place to break the tie—the text turns out to be no clearer on close inspection than it first appeared. As a result, we turn to the parties' arguments about the exemption's purpose and the legislative history. See *Berube v. Rust Eng'g*, 668 A.2d 875, 877 (Me. 1995) ("Our purpose in construing a statute is to give effect to the legislative intent as indicated by the statute's plain language, and we examine other indicia of legislative intent, such as its legislative history, only when the plain language is ambiguous.").

Oakhurst contends that the evident purpose of the exemption strongly favors its reading. The whole point of the exemption, Oakhurst asserts (albeit without reference to any directly supportive text or legislative history), is to protect against the distorting effects that the overtime law otherwise might have on employer decisions about how best to ensure perishable foods will not spoil. And, Oakhurst argues, the risk of spoilage posed by the distribution of perishable food is no less serious than is the risk of spoilage posed by the other activities regarding the handling of such foods to which the exemption clearly does apply.

We are not so sure. Any analysis of Exemption F that depends upon an assertion about its clear purpose is necessarily somewhat speculative. Nothing in the overtime law's text or legislative history purports to define a clear purpose for the exemption.

Moreover, even if we were to share in Oakhurst's speculation that the legislature included the exemption solely to protect against the possible spoilage of perishable foods rather than for some distinct reason related, perhaps, to the particular dynamics of certain labor markets, we still could not say that it would be arbitrary for the legislature to exempt "packing" but not "distributing" perishable goods. The reason to include "packing" in the exemption is easy enough to conjure. If perishable goods

---

6 The drivers do also contend that their reading draws support from the *noscitur a sociis* canon, which "dictates that words grouped in a list should be given related meaning." *Dole v. United Steelworkers of Am.*, 494 U.S. 26, 36 (1990) (citation omitted). In particular, the drivers contend that distribution is a different sort of activity than the others, nearly all of which entail transforming perishable products to less perishable forms—"canning," "processing," "preserving," "freezing," "drying," and "storing." However, the list of activities also includes "marketing," which Oakhurst argues undercuts the drivers' *noscitur a sociis* argument. And even if "marketing" does not mean promoting goods or services, as in the case of advertising, and means only "to deal in a market," see Webster's Third New International Dictionary of the English Language 1383 (2002); see also id. (providing additional definitions, including "to go to market to buy or sell" and "to expose for sale in a market"), it is a word that would have at least some potential commonalities with the disputed word, "distribution." For that reason, this canon adds little insight beyond that offered by the parallel usage convention.

are not packed in a timely fashion, it stands to reason that they may well spoil. Thus, one can imagine the reason to ensure that the overtime law creates no incentives for employers to delay the packing of such goods. The same logic, however, does not so easily apply to explain the need to exempt the activity of distributing those same goods. Drivers delivering perishable food must often inevitably spend long periods of time on the road to get the goods to their destination. It is thus not at all clear that a legal requirement for employers to pay overtime would affect whether drivers would get the goods to their destination before they spoiled. No matter what delivery drivers are paid for the journey, the trip cannot be made to be shorter than it is.

To be clear, none of this evidence is decisive either way. It does highlight, however, the hazards of simply assuming—on the basis of no more than supposition about what would make sense—that the legislature could not have intended to craft Exemption F as the drivers contend that the legislature crafted it. Thus, we do not find either the purpose or the legislative history fully clarifying. And so we are back to where we began.

We are not, however, without a means of moving forward. The default rule of construction under Maine law for ambiguous provisions in the state's wage and hour laws is that they "should be liberally construed to further the beneficent purposes for which they are enacted." *Dir. of Bureau of Labor Standards v. Cormier*, 527 A.2d 1297, 1300 (Me. 1987). The opening of the subchapter of Maine law containing the overtime statute and exemption at issue here declares a clear legislative purpose: "It is the declared public policy of the State of Maine that workers employed in any occupation should receive wages sufficient to provide adequate maintenance and to protect their health, and to be fairly commensurate with the value of the services rendered." 26 M.R.S.A. § 661. Thus, [we] must interpret the ambiguity in Exemption F in light of the remedial purpose of Maine's overtime statute. And, when we do, the ambiguity clearly favors the drivers' narrower reading of the exemption.

Given that the delivery drivers contend that they engage in neither packing for shipment nor packing for distribution, the District Court erred in granting Oakhurst summary judgment as to the meaning of Exemption F. If the drivers engage only in distribution and not in any of the standalone activities that Exemption F covers—a contention about which the Magistrate Judge recognized possible ambiguity—the drivers fall outside of Exemption F's scope and thus within the protection of the Maine overtime law.

Accordingly, the District Court's grant of partial summary judgment to Oakhurst is reversed.

---

## Points for Discussion

### *a. Commas and Punctuation*

The court in *Oakhurst Dairy* referred to many canons of construction, including semantic canons, substantive canons, and grammar canons. At the heart of the ambiguity in the statute was the omission of a comma. Notice how the provision at issue would have been different—or at least clearer—if the legislature had included one more piece of punctuation:

> "The overtime provision of this section does not apply to * * * [t]he canning, processing, preserving, freezing, drying, marketing, storing, packing for shipment, or distribution of * * * [p]erishable foods."

If the statute were written this way, then it would seem clear that distribution of perishable foods—the precise thing that the drivers did in their jobs—would be exempt from the overtime provisions. Conversely, notice how the provision's meaning would be clearer if the legislature had used parentheses at the end of the list:

> "The overtime provision of this section does not apply to * * * [t]he canning, processing, preserving, freezing, drying, marketing, storing, packing (for shipment or distribution) of * * * [p]erishable foods."

Unfortunately, the Maine legislature didn't use either of these devices to clarify the meaning of the provision.

Purely as a grammatical matter, does it make more sense to read the actual provision to have a meaning similar to the first example above or the second? Which grammatical rule leads you to that conclusion?

### *b. Aftermath of the Decision*

Not long after the court's decision in *Oakhurst Dairy*, the Maine legislature amended Exemption F. It now provides:

> "The overtime provision of this section does not apply to: * * * [t]he canning; processing; preserving; freezing; drying; marketing; storing; packing for shipment; or distributing of * * * [p]erishable foods."

Whose view of the statute did the legislature ultimately adopt? How did the legislature use punctuation to make its view clear? What, if anything, does this choice suggest about the correctness of the court's interpretation in *Oakhurst Dairy*?

---

## 4. Semantic Canons

## *Yates v. United States*

574 U.S. 528 (2015)

JUSTICE GINSBURG announced the judgment of the Court and delivered an opinion, in which THE CHIEF JUSTICE, JUSTICE BREYER, and JUSTICE SOTOMAYOR join.

On August 23, 2007, the *Miss Katie,* a commercial fishing boat, was six days into an expedition in the Gulf of Mexico. Her crew numbered three, including Yates, the captain. Engaged in a routine offshore patrol to inspect both recreational and commercial vessels, Officer John Jones of the Florida Fish and Wildlife Conservation Commission decided to board the *Miss Katie* to check on the vessel's compliance with fishing rules. Although the *Miss Katie* was far enough from the Florida coast to be in exclusively federal waters, she was nevertheless within Officer Jones's jurisdiction. Because he had been deputized as a federal agent by the National Marine Fisheries Service, Officer Jones had authority to enforce federal, as well as state, fishing laws.

Upon boarding the *Miss Katie,* Officer Jones noticed three red grouper that appeared to be undersized hanging from a hook on the deck. At the time, federal conservation regulations required immediate release of red grouper less than 20 inches long. 50 C.F.R. § 622.37(d)(2)(ii) (effective April 2, 2007). Violation of those regulations is a civil offense punishable by a fine or fishing license suspension. See 16 U.S.C. §§ 1857(1)(A), (G), 1858(a), (g).

Suspecting that other undersized fish might be on board, Officer Jones proceeded to inspect the ship's catch, setting aside and measuring only fish that appeared to him to be shorter than 20 inches. Officer Jones ultimately determined that 72 fish fell short of the 20-inch mark. A fellow officer recorded the length of each of the undersized fish on a catch measurement verification form. With few exceptions, the measured fish were between 19 and 20 inches; three were less than 19 inches; none were less than 18.75 inches. After separating the fish measuring below 20 inches from the rest of the catch by placing them in wooden crates, Officer Jones directed Yates to leave the fish, thus segregated, in the crates until the *Miss Katie* returned to port. Before departing, Officer Jones issued Yates a citation for possession of undersized fish.

Four days later, after the *Miss Katie* had docked in Cortez, Florida, Officer Jones measured the fish contained in the wooden crates. This time, however, the measured fish, although still less than 20 inches, slightly exceeded the lengths recorded on board. Jones surmised that the fish brought to port were not the same as those he had detected during his initial inspection. Under questioning, one of the crew members admitted that, at Yates's direction, he had thrown overboard the fish Officer Jones had measured at sea, and that he and Yates had replaced the tossed grouper with fish from the rest of the catch.

* * * On May 5, 2010, [Yates] was indicted for destroying property to prevent a federal seizure, in violation of [18 U.S.C.] § 2232(a),* and for destroying, concealing, and covering up undersized fish to impede a federal investigation, in violation of [18 U.S.C.] § 1519.** [Yates was convicted for violating both statutes and sentenced to 30 days in prison followed by three years of supervised release. He challenged his [illegible]ction under § 1519, asserting that fish are not "tangible object[s]" within the [illegible]g of the provision.]

[illegible]ion 1519 was enacted as part of the Sarbanes-Oxley Act of 2002, 116 Stat. [illegible]arbanes-Oxley Act, all agree, was prompted by the exposure of Enron's [illegible]ounting fraud and revelations that the company's outside auditor, Arthur [illegible]LP, had systematically destroyed potentially incriminating documents. [illegible]rnment acknowledges that § 1519 was intended to prohibit, in particular, [illegible] document-shredding to hide evidence of financial wrongdoing. Prior law [illegible] an offense to "intimidat[e], threate[n], or corruptly persuad[e] *another person*" [illegible]red documents. § 1512(b) (emphasis added). Section 1519 cured a conspicuous omission by imposing liability on a person who destroys records himself. * * *

In the Government's view, § 1519 extends beyond the principal evil motivating its passage. The words of § 1519, the Government argues, support reading the provision as a general ban on the spoliation of evidence, covering all physical items that might be relevant to any matter under federal investigation.

We * * * reject the Government's unrestrained reading. "Tangible object" in § 1519, we conclude, is better read to cover only objects one can use to record or preserve information, not all objects in the physical world.

The ordinary meaning of an "object" that is "tangible," as stated in dictionary definitions, is "a discrete . . . thing," Webster's Third New International Dictionary

---

* "DESTRUCTION OR REMOVAL OF PROPERTY TO PREVENT SEIZURE.—Whoever, before, during, or after any search for or seizure of property by any person authorized to make such search or seizure, knowingly destroys, damages, wastes, disposes of, transfers, or otherwise takes any action, or knowingly attempts to destroy, damage, waste, dispose of, transfer, or otherwise take any action, for the purpose of preventing or impairing the Government's lawful authority to take such property into its custody or control or to continue holding such property under its lawful custody and control, shall be fined under this title or imprisoned not more than 5 years, or both." 18 U.S.C. § 2232(a). —*Ed.*

** "DESTRUCTION, ALTERATION, OR FALSIFICATION OF RECORDS IN FEDERAL INVESTIGATIONS AND BANKRUPTCY.—Whoever knowingly alters, destroys, mutilates, conceals, covers up, falsifies, or makes a false entry in any record, document, or tangible object with the intent to impede, obstruct, or influence the investigation or proper administration of any matter within the jurisdiction of any department or agency of the United States or any case filed under title 11, or in relation to or contemplation of any such matter or case, shall be fined under this title, imprisoned not more than 20 years, or both." 18 U.S.C. § 1519. —*Ed.*

1555 (2002), that "possess[es] physical form," Black's Law Dictionary 1683 (10th ed. 2014). From this premise, the Government concludes that "tangible object," as that term appears in § 1519, covers the waterfront, including fish from the sea.

Whether a statutory term is unambiguous, however, does not turn solely on dictionary definitions of its component words. Rather, "[t]he plainness or ambiguity of statutory language is determined [not only] by reference to the language itself, [but as well by] the specific context in which that language is used, and the broader context of the statute as a whole." *Robinson v. Shell Oil Co.*, 519 U.S. 337, 341 (1997). Ordinarily, a word's usage accords with its dictionary definition. In law as in life, however, the same words, placed in different contexts, sometimes mean different things.

**Food for Thought**

The Court declines to interpret the phrase "tangible object" solely according to its dictionary definition. How does the Court know that the phrase, as used in this statute, means something more narrow?

Familiar interpretive guides aid our construction of the words "tangible object" as they appear in § 1519. * * * We note first § 1519's caption: "Destruction, alteration, or falsification of records in Federal investigations and bankruptcy." That heading conveys no suggestion that the section prohibits spoliation of any and all physical evidence, however remote from records. Neither does the title of the section of the Sarbanes-Oxley Act in which § 1519 was placed, § 802: "Criminal penalties for altering documents." 116 Stat. 800. Furthermore, § 1520, the only other provision passed as part of § 802, is titled "Destruction of corporate audit records" and addresses only that specific subset of records and documents. While these headings are not commanding, they supply cues that Congress did not intend "tangible object" in § 1519 to sweep within its reach physical objects of every kind, including things no one would describe as records, documents, or devices closely associated with them. * * *

**Take Note**

The Court here implicitly invokes the Whole Act Rule and one of its corollaries. Can you explain how the Court uses those maxims to give meaning to the statutory provision at issue?

Section 1519's position within Chapter 73 of Title 18 further signals that § 1519 was not intended to serve as a cross-the-board ban on the destruction of physical evidence of every kind. Congress placed § 1519 (and its companion provision § 1520) at the end of the chapter, following immediately after the pre-existing § 1516, § 1517, and § 1518, each of them prohibiting obstructive acts in specific contexts. See § 1516 (audits of recipients of federal funds); § 1517 (federal examinations of financial institutions); § 1518 (criminal investigations of federal health care offenses). See also S. Rep. No. 107–146, at 7 (observing that § 1517 and § 1518 "apply to obstruction in certain limited types of cases, such as bankruptcy fraud, examinations of financial institutions, and healthcare fraud").

The words immediately surrounding "tangible object" in § 1519—"falsifies, or makes a false entry in any record [or] document"—also cabin the contextual meaning of that term. As explained in *Gustafson v. Alloyd Co.*, 513 U.S. 561, 575 (1995), we rely on the principle of *noscitur a sociis*—a word is known by the company it keeps—to "avoid ascribing to one word a meaning so broad that it is inconsistent its accompanying words, thus giving unintended breadth to the Acts of Con- *Gustafson*, we interpreted the word "communication" in § 2(10) of the Securities Act of 1933 to refer to a public communication, rather than any communication, because the word appeared in a list with other words, notably "notice, circular, [and] advertisement," making it "apparent that the list refer[red] to documents of wide dissemination." 513 U.S., at 575–576. And we did so even though the list began with the word "any."

agraphs, the Court relies ntic canons: *noscitur a* *sdem generis.* From the scription, can you articu- fference between the two

The *noscitur a sociis* canon operates in a similar manner here. "Tangible object" is the last in a list of terms that begins "any record [or] document." The term is therefore appropriately read to refer, not to any tangible object, but specifically to the subset of tangible objects involving records and documents, *i.e.*, objects used to record or preserve information. * * * This moderate interpretation of "tangible object" accords with the list of actions § 1519 proscribes. The section applies to anyone who "alters, destroys, mutilates, conceals, covers up, *falsifies*, or *makes a false entry in* any record, document, or tangible object" with the requisite obstructive intent. (Emphasis added.) The last two verbs, "falsif[y]" and "mak[e] a false entry in," typically take as grammatical objects records, documents, or things used to record or preserve information, such as logbooks or hard drives. See, *e.g.*, Black's Law Dictionary 720 (10th ed. 2014) (defining "falsify" as "[t]o make deceptive; to counterfeit, forge, or misrepresent; esp., to tamper with (a document, record, etc.)"). It would be unnatural, for example, to describe a killer's act of wiping his fingerprints from a gun as "falsifying" the murder weapon. But it would not be strange to refer to "falsifying" data stored on a hard drive as simply "falsifying" a hard drive. * * *

A canon related to *noscitur a sociis*, *ejusdem generis*, counsels: "Where general words follow specific words in a statutory enumeration, the general words are [usually] construed to embrace only objects similar in nature to those objects enumerated by the preceding specific words." *Washington State Dept. of Social and Health Servs. v. Guardianship Estate of Keffeler*, 537 U.S. 371, 384 (2003). * * * Had Congress intended "tangible object" in § 1519 to be interpreted so generically as to capture physical objects as dissimilar as documents and fish, Congress would have had no reason to refer specifically to "record" or "document." The Government's unbounded reading of "tangible object" would render those words misleading surplusage.

Finally, if our recourse to traditional tools of statutory construction leaves any doubt about the meaning of "tangible object," as that term is used in § 1519, we would invoke the rule that "ambiguity concerning the ambit of criminal statutes should be resolved in favor of lenity." *Cleveland v. United States*, 531 U.S. 12, 25 (2000). That interpretative principle is relevant here, where the Government urges a reading of § 1519 that exposes individuals to 20-year prison sentences for tampering with *any* physical object that *might* have evidentiary value in *any* federal investigation into *any* offense, no matter whether the investigation is pending or merely contemplated, or whether the offense subject to investigation is criminal or civil. In determining the meaning of "tangible object" in § 1519, "it is appropriate, before we choose the harsher alternative, to require that Congress should have spoken in language that is clear and definite." See *Cleveland*, 531 U.S., at 25.

For the reasons stated, we resist reading § 1519 expansively to create a coverall spoliation of evidence statute, advisable as such a measure might be. Leaving that important decision to Congress, we hold that a "tangible object" within § 1519's compass is one used to record or preserve information. [Reversed.]

JUSTICE ALITO, concurring in the judgment.

[T]hough the question is close, traditional tools of statutory construction confirm that John Yates has the better of the argument. Three features of 18 U.S.C. § 1519 stand out to me: the statute's list of nouns, its list of verbs, and its title. * * *

Start with the nouns. Section 1519 refers to "any record, document, or tangible object." The *noscitur a sociis* canon instructs that when a statute contains a list, each word in that list presumptively has a "similar" meaning. See, *e.g., Gustafson v. Alloyd Co.*, 513 U.S. 561, 576 (1995). A related canon, *ejusdem generis* teaches that general words following a list of specific words should usually be read in light of those specific words to mean something "similar." See, *e.g., Christopher v. SmithKline Beecham Corp.*, 567 U.S. 142, 163 (2012). Applying these canons to § 1519's list of nouns, the term "tangible object" should refer to something similar to records or documents. A fish does not spring to mind—nor does an antelope, a colonial farmhouse, a hydrofoil, or an oil derrick. All are "objects" that are "tangible." But who wouldn't raise an eyebrow if a neighbor, when asked to identify something similar to a "record" or "document," said "crocodile"?

This reading, of course, has its shortcomings. For instance, this is an imperfect *ejusdem generis* case because "record" and "document" are themselves quite general. And there is a risk that "tangible object" may be made superfluous—what is similar to a "record" or "document" but yet is not one? An e-mail, however, could be such a thing. * * * A hard drive [is] tangible and can contain files * * *. Both "record" and "document" can be read [expansively], but adding "tangible object" to § 1519 would ensure beyond question that electronic files are included. To be sure, "tangible object" presumably can capture more than just e-mails; Congress enacts "catchall[s]" for "known unknowns." *Republic of Iraq v. Beaty*, 556 U.S. 848, 860 (2009). But where *noscitur a sociis* and *ejusdem generis* apply, "known unknowns" should be similar to known knowns, *i.e.*, here, records and documents. This is especially true because reading "tangible object" too broadly could render "record" and "document" superfluous.

Next, consider § 1519's list of verbs: "alters, destroys, mutilates, conceals, covers up, falsifies, or makes a false entry in." Although many of those verbs could apply to nouns as far-flung as salamanders, satellites, or sand dunes, the last phrase in the list—"makes a false entry in"—makes no sense outside of filekeeping. How does one make a false entry in a fish? "Alters" and especially "falsifies" are also closely associated with filekeeping. Not one of the verbs, moreover, *cannot* be applied to filekeeping—certainly not in the way that "makes a false entry in" is always inconsistent with the aquatic.

Finally, my analysis is influenced by § 1519's title: "Destruction, alteration, or falsification of *records* in Federal investigations and bankruptcy." (Emphasis added.) This too points toward filekeeping, not fish. Titles can be useful devices to resolve "doubt about the meaning of a statute." *Porter v. Nussle*, 534 U.S. 516, 527–528 (2002). The title is especially valuable here because it reinforces what the text's nouns and verbs independently suggest—that no matter how other statutes might be read, this particular one does not cover every noun in the universe with tangible form.

JUSTICE KAGAN, with whom JUSTICE SCALIA, JUSTICE KENNEDY, and JUSTICE THOMAS join, dissenting.

The plurality [interprets] "tangible object" to cover "only objects one can use to record or preserve information." The concurring opinion similarly, if more vaguely, contends that "tangible object" should refer to "something similar to records or documents"—and shouldn't include colonial farmhouses, crocodiles, or fish. In my view, conventional tools of statutory construction all lead to a more conventional result: A "tangible object" is an object that's tangible. I would apply the statute that Congress enacted and affirm the judgment below.

**Food for Thought**

Does Justice Kagan focus on a different touchstone than does Justice Ginsburg? Or are they both focused on the same touchstone but in disagreement about what that touchstone reveals?

While the plurality starts its analysis with § 1519's heading, * * * I would begin with § 1519's text. When Congress has not supplied a definition, we generally give a statutory term its ordinary meaning. See, *e.g.*, *Schindler Elevator Corp. v. United States ex rel. Kirk*, 563 U.S. 401, 407 (2011). As the plurality must acknowledge, the ordinary meaning of "tangible object" is "a discrete thing that possesses physical form." A fish is, of course, a discrete thing that possesses physical form. See generally Dr. Seuss, One Fish Two Fish Red Fish Blue Fish (1960). So the ordinary meaning of the term "tangible object" in § 1519, as no one here disputes, covers fish (including too-small red grouper).

That interpretation accords with endless uses of the term in statute and rule books as construed by courts. Dozens of federal laws and rules of procedure (and hundreds of state enactments) include the term "tangible object" or its first cousin "tangible thing"—some in association with documents, others not. See, *e.g.,* 18 U.S.C. § 668(a)(1)(D) (defining "museum" as entity that owns "tangible objects that are exhibited to the public"). To my knowledge, no court has ever read any such provision to exclude things that don't record or preserve data; rather, all courts have adhered to the statutory language's ordinary (*i.e.,* expansive) meaning. For example, courts have understood the phrases "tangible objects" and "tangible things" in the Federal Rules of Criminal and Civil Procedure to cover everything from guns to drugs to machinery to . . . animals. No surprise, then, that—until today—courts have uniformly applied the term "tangible object" in § 1519 in the same way. See, *e.g., United States v. McRae,* 702 F.3d 806, 834–838 (5th Cir. 2012) (corpse); *United States v. Maury,* 695 F.3d 227, 243–244 (3d Cir. 2012) (cement mixer).

That is not necessarily the end of the matter; I agree with the plurality (really, who does not?) that context matters in interpreting statutes. [But] here the text and its context point the same way. Stepping back from the words "tangible object" provides only further evidence that Congress said what it meant and meant what it said.

Begin with the way the surrounding words in § 1519 reinforce the breadth of the term at issue. Section 1519 refers to "any" tangible object, thus indicating (in line with *that* word's plain meaning) a tangible object "of whatever kind." Webster's Third New International Dictionary 97 (2002). This Court has time and again recognized that "any" has "an expansive meaning," bringing within a statute's reach *all* types of the item (here, "tangible object") to which the law refers. *Department of Housing and Urban Development v. Rucker,* 535 U.S. 125, 131 (2002). And the adjacent laundry list of verbs in § 1519 ("alters, destroys, mutilates, conceals, covers up, falsifies, or makes a false entry") further shows that Congress wrote a statute with a wide scope. Those words are supposed to ensure—just as "tangible object" is meant to—that § 1519 covers the whole world of evidence-tampering, in all its prodigious variety.

Still more, "tangible object" appears as part of a three-noun phrase (including also "records" and "documents") common to evidence-tampering laws and always understood to embrace things of all kinds. The Model Penal Code's evidence-tampering section, drafted more than 50 years ago, similarly prohibits a person from "alter[ing], destroy[ing], conceal[ing] or remov[ing] any *record, document or thing*" in an effort to thwart an official investigation or proceeding. ALI, Model Penal Code § 241.7(1), p. 175 (1962) (emphasis added). [C]ourts in the more than 15 States that have laws based on the Model Code's tampering provision apply them to all tangible objects, including drugs, guns, vehicles and . . . yes, animals. See, *e.g., State v. Majors*, 318 S.W.3d 850, 859–861 (Tenn. 2010) (cocaine); *Puckett v. State*, 944 S.W.2d 111, 113–114 (Ark. 1997) (gun); *State v. Bruno*, 673 A.2d 1117, 1122–1123 (Conn. 1996) (bicycle, skeleton, blood stains); *State v. Crites*, 2007 Mont. Dist. LEXIS 615, *5–*7 (Dec. 21, 2007) (deer antlers). Not a one has limited the phrase's scope to objects that record or preserve information.

The words "record, document, or tangible object" in § 1519 also track language in 18 U.S.C. § 1512, the federal witness-tampering law covering * * * physical evidence in all its forms. Section 1512, both in its original version (preceding § 1519) and today, repeatedly uses the phrase "record, document, or other object"—most notably, in a provision prohibiting the use of force or threat to induce another person to withhold any of those materials from an official proceeding. § 4(a) of the Victim and Witness Protection Act of 1982, 96 Stat. 1249, as amended, 18 U.S.C. § 1512(b)(2). That language, which itself likely derived from the Model Penal Code, encompasses no less the bloody knife than the incriminating letter, as all courts have for decades agreed. And typically "only the most compelling evidence" will persuade this Court that Congress intended "nearly identical language" in provisions dealing with related subjects to bear different meanings. *Communications Workers v. Beck*, 487 U.S. 735, 754 (1988); see A. Scalia & B. Garner, Reading Law: The Interpretation of Legal Texts 252 (2012). Context thus again confirms what text indicates.

And legislative history, for those who care about it, puts extra icing on a cake already frosted. Section 1519, as the plurality notes, was enacted after the Enron Corporation's collapse, as part of the Sarbanes-Oxley Act of 2002, 116 Stat. 745. But the provision began its life in a separate bill, and the drafters emphasized that Enron was "only a case study exposing the shortcomings in our current laws" relating to both "corporate and criminal" fraud. S. Rep. No. 107–146, pp. 2, 11 (2002). The primary "loophole[ ]" Congress identified, see *id.*, at 14, arose from limits in the part of § 1512 just described: That provision, as uniformly construed, prohibited a person from inducing another to destroy "record[s], document[s], or other object[s]"—of every type—but not from doing so himself. § 1512(b)(2). Congress (as even the plurality agrees) enacted § 1519 to close that yawning gap. But § 1519 could fully achieve that goal only if it covered all the records, documents, and objects § 1512 did, as well as all the means of tampering with them. And so § 1519 was written to do exactly that—"to apply broadly to any acts to destroy or fabricate physical evidence," as long as performed with the requisite intent. S. Rep. No. 107–146, at 14. "When a person destroys evidence," the drafters explained, "overly technical legal distinctions should neither hinder nor prevent prosecution." *Id.*, at 7. Ah well: Congress, meet today's Court, which here invents just such a distinction with just such an effect.

As Congress recognized in using a broad term, giving immunity to those who destroy non-documentary evidence has no sensible basis in penal policy. A person who hides a murder victim's body is no less culpable than one who burns the victim's diary. A fisherman, like John Yates, who dumps undersized fish to avoid a fine is no less blameworthy than one who shreds his vessel's catch log for the same reason. Congress thus treated both offenders in the same way. It understood, in enacting § 1519, that destroying evidence is destroying evidence, whether or not that evidence takes documentary form.

The plurality searches far and wide for anything—*anything*—to support its interpretation of § 1519. But its fishing expedition comes up empty.

The plurality's analysis starts with § 1519's title * * *. That's already a sign something is amiss. I know of no other case in which we have *begun* our interpretation of a statute with the title, or relied on a title to override the law's clear terms. Instead, we have followed "the wise rule that the title of a statute and the heading of a section cannot limit the plain meaning of the text." *Trainmen v. Baltimore & Ohio R. Co.*, 331 U.S. 519, 528–529 (1947).

The plurality next tries to divine meaning from § 1519's "position within Chapter 73 of Title 18." * * * The plurality claims that if § 1519 applied to objects generally, Congress would not have placed it "after the pre-existing § 1516, § 1517, and § 1518" because those are "specialized provisions." But search me if I can find a better place for a broad ban on evidence-tampering. The plurality seems to agree that the law properly goes in Chapter 73—the criminal code's chapter on "obstruction of justice." But the provision does not logically fit into any of that chapter's pre-existing sections. And with the first 18 numbers of the chapter already taken (starting with § 1501 and continuing through § 1518), the law naturally took the 19th place. That is standard operating procedure. * * *

[The plurality also relies on *noscitur a sociis* and *ejusdem generis*.] The first of those related canons advises that words grouped in a list be given similar meanings. The second counsels that a general term following specific words embraces only things of a similar kind. * * * As an initial matter, this Court uses *noscitur a sociis* and *ejusdem generis* to resolve ambiguity, not create it. * * * But when words have a clear definition, and all other contextual clues support that meaning, the canons cannot properly defeat Congress's decision to draft broad legislation.

Anyway, assigning "tangible object" its ordinary meaning comports with *noscitur a sociis* and *ejusdem generis* when applied, as they should be, with attention to § 1519's subject and purpose. Those canons require identifying a common trait that links all the words in a statutory phrase. In responding to that demand, the plurality characterizes records and documents as things that preserve information—and so they are. But just as much, they are things that provide information, and thus potentially serve as evidence relevant to matters under review. And in a statute pertaining to obstruction of federal investigations, that evidentiary function comes to the fore. The destruction of records and documents prevents law enforcement agents from gathering facts relevant to official inquiries. And so too does the destruction of tangible objects—of whatever kind. Whether the item is a fisherman's ledger or an undersized fish, throwing it overboard has the identical effect on the administration of justice. For purposes of § 1519, records, documents, and (all) tangible objects are therefore alike.

And the plurality's invocation of § 1519's verbs does nothing to buttress its canon-based argument. The plurality observes that § 1519 prohibits "falsif[ying]" or "mak[ing] a false entry in" a tangible object, and no one can do those things to, say, a murder weapon (or a fish). But of course someone can alter, destroy, mutilate, conceal, or cover up such a tangible object, and § 1519 prohibits those actions too. The Court has never before suggested that all the verbs in a statute need to match up with all the nouns. And for good reason. It is exactly when Congress sets out to draft a statute broadly—to include every imaginable variation on a theme—that such mismatches will arise. To respond by narrowing the law, as the plurality does, is thus to flout both what Congress wrote and what Congress wanted.

Finally, when all else fails, the plurality invokes the rule of lenity. But even in its most robust form, that rule only kicks in when, "after all legitimate tools of interpretation have been exhausted, 'a reasonable doubt persists' regarding whether Congress has made the defendant's conduct a federal crime." *Abramski v. United States*, 573 U.S. 169, 264 (2014) (SCALIA, J., dissenting) (quoting *Moskal v. United States*, 498 U.S. 103, 108 (1990)). No such doubt lingers here. The plurality points to the breadth of § 1519, as though breadth were equivalent to ambiguity. It is not. Section 1519 *is* very broad. It is also very clear. Every traditional tool of statutory interpretation points in the same direction, toward "object" meaning object. Lenity offers no proper refuge from that straightforward (even though capacious) construction.

[T]he concurrence suggests applying the term "tangible object" in keeping with what "a neighbor, when asked to identify something similar to record or document," might answer. * * * But § 1519's meaning should not hinge on the odd game of Mad Libs the concurrence proposes. No one reading § 1519 needs to fill in a blank after the words "records" and "documents." That is because Congress, quite helpfully, already did so—adding the term "tangible object." The issue in this case is what that term means. So if the concurrence wishes to ask its neighbor a question, I'd recommend a more pertinent one: Do you think a fish (or, if the concurrence prefers, a crocodile) is a "tangible object"? As to that query, "who wouldn't raise an eyebrow" if the neighbor said "no"?

If none of the traditional tools of statutory interpretation can produce today's result, then what accounts for it? The plurality offers a clue when it emphasizes the disproportionate penalties § 1519 imposes if the law is read broadly. * * * That brings to the surface the real issue: overcriminalization and excessive punishment in the U.S. Code. * * * I tend to think, for the reasons the plurality gives, that § 1519 is a bad law—too broad and undifferentiated, with too-high maximum penalties, which give prosecutors too much leverage and sentencers too much discretion. And I'd go further: In those ways, § 1519 is unfortunately not an outlier, but an emblem of a deeper pathology in the federal criminal code.

But whatever the wisdom or folly of § 1519, this Court does not get to rew the law. * * * If judges disagree with Congress's choice, we are perfectly entitl say so—in lectures, in law review articles, and even in dicta. But we are nc to replace the statute Congress enacted with an alternative of our own des

---

## Points of Discussion

### *a.* Noscitur a Sociis

Both the majority and the dissent relied on ***noscitur a sociis***, a semantic canon that means "it is known from its associates." The canon instructs courts to interpret words in statutory lists in light of the other items on the list. There is a common-sense appeal to this canon. For example, if a sign at airport security says that "poison, knives, and arms are prohibited past this point," we would understand the word "arms" to mean weapons that one can carry, rather than limbs. We know this at least in part because the other items on the list—poison and knives—are also lethal types of weapons.

In *Yates*, the statutory phrase in question—"tangible object"—followed the terms "record" and "document." What do those terms tell us about the meaning of the phrase "tangible object"? Is the common theme among the items on the list that they are all methods of storing information? Or that they are all things that might reveal evidence of a defendant's wrongdoing?

### *b.* Ejusdem Generis

The dueling opinions also relied on ***ejusdem generis***, a semantic canon that means "of the same kind." The canon instructs courts to construe catch-all, general terms at the end of a list in light of the items on the list that precede it. For example, a federal statute governing arbitration excluded from its coverage disputes arising from contracts of employment with "seamen, railroad employees, or any other class of workers engaged in foreign or interstate commerce." 9 U.S.C. § 1. An employee at a large electronics chain sued his employer for discrimination, and the company argued that he was subject to the requirements of the federal statute. The employee argued that he was excluded from its reach because he was a worker "engaged in foreign or interstate commerce." The Court, noting that the other items on the list were employees who worked on boats and on railroads, invoked *ejusdem generis*, concluding that the catch-all phrase applied only to workers in the transportation industry. *Circuit City Stores, Inc. v. Adams*, 532 U.S. 105 (2001).

Is the phrase "any tangible object," which was at issue in *Yates*, a general, catch-all term? If so, then does *ejusdem generis* clarify the meaning of the term? As Justice Kagan noted, both *ejusdem generis* and *noscitur a sociis* require the judge to identify "a common trait that links all the words in a statutory phrase." But how does the judge know the right level of generality at which to discern the common trait?

#### c. *Distinguishing Between* Noscitur a Sociis *and* Ejusdem Generis

The Court in *Yates* treated *noscitur a sociis* and *ejusdem generis* as largely interchangeable. Now that you know what these two canons provide, did one seem more clearly applicable in *Yates* than the other?

---

Recall that semantic canons of construction are guides for determining textual meaning. They are supposed to reflect the ways in which we ordinarily use and understand language. Do *noscitur a sociis* and *ejusdem generis* reflect how you understand items on a list? For example, if your friend, who has invited you over to her house for dinner, asks you to bring "beer, wine, or something else," would you bring a football? In this sense, the two semantic canons at issue in *Yates* do seem to reflect our basic intuition that we should understand ambiguous items on a list to derive meaning from the other items on the list. But there are limits to the canons' ability to clarify textual meaning. It might seem clear in our example that you shouldn't bring a football, but what about bottled water or soda? After all, those are beverages, just like beer and wine. But they are not *alcoholic* beverages, and from the text alone we can't tell whether your friend is asking you to bring booze or just something to drink.

There is at least one other semantic canon that applies when courts construe items on a list. The canon of ***expressio unius est exclusio alterius*** (often referred to simply as "*expressio unius*"), which means "the expression of one thing excludes others," provides that the express identification of certain items in a statute means that other items that are not mentioned are not included. For example, if a road sign says that "No trucks or buses may use this road," it is fair to assume that cars and bicycles are permitted to use the road.

But if the semantic canons are designed to reflect the way that we ordinarily use and understand language, is it obvious to you that we should always read lists according to the *expressio unius* canon? For example, if you and your roommate share the cost of groceries and she leaves you a note asking you to go to the store to get "milk, peanut butter, and eggs," would you interpret the request to mean that you should not get ice cream? Sometimes, in other words, lists are not meant to be exhaustive. How can we tell when the express mention of some items is intended to exclude other items not mentioned?

The following problems give you an opportunity to apply the three semantic canons that we've just considered.

---

## Problems

1. 42 U.S.C. § 1983 provides, "Every person who, under c[…] law], subjects, or causes to be subjected, any citizen of the Unit[…] other person within the jurisdiction thereof to the deprivation c[…] privileges, or immunities secured by the Constitution and law[…] liable to the party injured in an action at law, suit in equity, or othe[…] proceeding for redress * * *." State officers sued under section 1983 are imm[…] from liability, however, if the plaintiff cannot demonstrate that their actions were inconsistent with "clearly established law." In addition, in *Monell v. New York City Dept. of Social Services*, 436 U.S. 658 (1978), the Supreme Court held that municipalities can be liable under section 1983, but that they enjoy immunity from suits seeking to recover on a theory of *respondeat superior*.

Police officers in Northern Texas forcibly entered Charlene Leatherman's home after they detected odors associated with the manufacture of narcotics. The officers did not find any drugs, but during the course of the search they shot and killed two of Leatherman's dogs. Leatherman sued the officers, the county narcotics coordination unit, and the county, alleging that the defendants' actions violated the Fourth Amendment and asserting claims under section 1983. She alleged that the narcotics unit and the county were liable for failure adequately to train the police officers involved.

The defendants moved to dismiss, asserting that they were immune from suit. They relied on a Fifth Circuit decision that held: "In cases against governmental officials [and municipal corporations under section 1983] involving the likely defense of immunity, we require of trial judges that they demand that the plaintiff's complaint state with factual detail and particularity the basis for the claim, which necessarily includes why the defendant cannot successfully maintain the defense of immunity." Leatherman's complaint did not specifically allege facts to explain why the defendants were not entitled to immunity.

Federal Rule of Civil Procedure 8(a)(2) provides that a complaint must include "a short and plain statement of the claim showing that the pleader is entitled to relief." Federal Rule of Civil Procedure Rule 9(b) states that "[i]n all averments of fraud or mistake, the circumstances constituting fraud or mistake shall be stated with particularity." How should the court rule on the defendants' motion to dismiss? Which semantic canon of construction is most relevant to the interpretation of the provisions of the Federal Rules of Civil Procedure?

2. The Supreme Court has made clear that the United States has "sovereign immunity" from suits for damages unless Congress has expressly waived the government's immunity. The Federal Tort Claims Act (FTCA) contains an express waiver of sovereign immunity in cases involving negligence com-

mitted by federal employees in the course of their employment, 28 U.S.C. § 1346(b)(1), making the United States liable "in the same manner and to the same extent as a private individual under like circumstances," *id.* § 2674. The Postal Reorganization Act further provides that the FTCA applies to "tort claims arising out of [Postal Service] activities." 39 U.S.C. § 409(c). The FTCA, however, contains several exceptions to the waiver of sovereign immunity, including specific exceptions for cases involving the Postal Service. In particular, Congress has declined to waive sovereign immunity for "[a]ny claim arising out of the loss, miscarriage, or negligent transmission of letters or postal matter." 28 U.S.C. § 2680(b).

Barbara Dolan filed an FTCA suit against the Postal Service for injuries she suffered when she tripped and fell over mail that a postal employee had left on her porch. The government moved to dismiss the suit, arguing that it was barred by sovereign immunity. The government relied on 26 U.S.C. § 2680(b). Dolan argued that her suit did not fall within the scope of the exception in that provision. How should the court rule? Which semantic canon of construction is most relevant to the interpretation of section 2680?

3. Michigan law provides:

> "*Carrying firearm or dangerous weapon with unlawful intent*—Any person who, with intent to use the same unlawfully against the person of another, goes armed with a pistol or other firearm or dagger, dirk, razor, stiletto, or knife having a blade over 3 inches in length, or any other dangerous or deadly weapon or instrument, shall be guilty of a felony, punishable by imprisonment [for] not more than 5 years or by a fine of not more than $2,500." M.C.L.A. § 750.226.
>
> "*Carrying concealed weapons*—Any person who shall carry a dagger, dirk, stiletto, or other dangerous weapon except hunting knives adapted and carried as such, concealed on or about his person, or whether concealed or otherwise in any vehicle operated or occupied by him, except in his dwelling house or place of business or on other land possessed by him; and any person who shall carry a pistol concealed on or about his person, or, whether concealed or otherwise, in any vehicle operated or occupied by him, except in his dwelling house or place of business or on other land possessed by him, without a license to so carry said pistol as provided by law, shall be guilty of a felony, punishable by imprisonment [for] not more than 5 years, or by a fine of not more than $2,500." M.C.L.A. § 750.227.

A police officer in Detroit observed a van make several erratic U-turns. The officer stopped the van and, while approaching the vehicle, observed through the right window what he believed to be the stock of a rifle. He opened the door and found an M1 rifle underneath the seat. The officer also found a cartridge belt and clips containing ammunition on the seat.

Robert Smith, a passenger in the van, was charged with carrying a concealed weapon in violation of M.C.L.A. § 750.227. He has filed a motion to quash the charges. How should the court rule? Which semantic canon of construction is most relevant to the interpretation of the provisions of the Michigan code?

---

## 5. Substantive Canons

Unlike semantic canons of construction, which are supposed to reflect how people ordinarily use or understand language, substantive canons of construction are default rules designed to advance certain policies or avoid certain disfavored outcomes. In this section, we will consider three substantive canons: (1) the rule of lenity; (2) the avoidance canon; and (3) the federalism clear-statement rule. For each substantive canon, pay attention to the substantive policy goal that the canon advances and the role that the canon plays in statutory interpretation.

---

### a. The Rule of Lenity

## *United States v. Bass*

404 U.S. 336 (1971)

MR. JUSTICE MARSHALL delivered the opinion of the Court.

Respondent was convicted in the Southern District of New York of possessing firearms in violation of Title VII of the Omnibus Crime Control and Safe Streets Act of 1968, 18 U.S.C. App. § 1202(a). In pertinent part, that statute reads:

> "Any person who * * * has been convicted by a court of the United States or of a State or any political subdivision thereof of a felony . . . and who receives, possesses, or transports in commerce or affecting commerce . . . any firearm shall be fined not more than $10,000 or imprisoned for not more than two years, or both."

The evidence showed that respondent, who had previously been convicted of a felony in New York State, possessed on separate occasions a pistol and then a shotgun. There was no allegation in the indictment and no attempt by the prosecution to show that either firearm had been possessed "in commerce or affecting commerce." The Government proceeded on the assumption that § 1202(a)(1) banned all possessions and receipts of firearms by convicted felons, and that no connection with interstate commerce had to be demonstrated in individual cases.

[illegible]e conclude that § 1202 is ambiguous in the critical respect. Because its [illegible]e criminal and because, under the Government's broader reading, the [illegible]uld mark a major inroad into a domain traditionally left to the States, we [illegible]adopt the broad reading in the absence of a clearer direction from Congress.

[W]e begin by looking to the text itself. The critical textual question is whether the statutory phrase "in commerce or affecting commerce" applies to "possesses" and "receives" as well as to "transports." If it does, then the Government must prove as an essential element of the offense that a possession, receipt, or transportation was "in commerce or affecting commerce"—a burden not undertaken in this prosecution for possession.

While the statute does not read well under either view, "the natural construction of the language" suggests that the clause "in commerce or affecting commerce" qualifies all three antecedents in the list. *Porto Rico Railway Light & Power Co. v. Mor*, 253 U.S. 345, 348 (1920). Since "in commerce or affecting commerce" undeniably applies to at least one antecedent, and since it makes sense with all three, the more plausible construction here is that it in fact applies to all three. But although this is a beginning, the argument is certainly neither overwhelming nor decisive.[6]

**Food for Thought**

Is the Court's analysis of the provision's grammar consistent with the Supreme Court's approach in *Lockhart*, which we considered earlier in this Chapter? If not, which approach do you find the most persuasive?

In a more significant respect, however, the language of the statute does provide support for respondent's reading. Undeniably, the phrase "in commerce or affecting commerce" is part of the "transports" offense. But if that phrase applies only to "transports," the statute would have a curious reach. While permitting transportation of a firearm unless it is transported "in commerce or affecting commerce," the statute would prohibit all possessions of firearms, and both interstate and intrastate receipts. Since virtually all transportations, whether interstate or intrastate, involve an accompanying possession or receipt, it is odd indeed to argue that on the one hand the statute reaches all possessions and receipts, and on the other hand outlaws only interstate transportations. Even assuming that a person can "transport" a firearm

6 *** The Government, noting that there is no comma after "transports," argues that the punctuation indicates a congressional intent to limit the qualifying phrase to the last antecedent. But many leading grammarians, while sometimes noting that commas at the end of series can avoid ambiguity, concede that use of such commas is discretionary. See, e.g., B. Evans & C. Evans, A Dictionary of Contemporary American Usage 103 (1957); M. Nicholson, A Dictionary of American-English Usage 94 (1957); R. Copperud, A Dictionary of Usage and Style 94–95 (1964); cf. W. Strunk & E. White, The Elements of Style 1–2 (1959). When grammarians are divided, and surely where they are cheerfully tolerant, we will not attach significance to an omitted comma. It is enough to say that the statute's punctuation is fully consistent with the respondent's interpretation, and that in this case grammatical expertise will not help to clarify the statute's meaning.

under the statute without possessing or receiving it, there is no reason consistent with any discernible purpose of the statute to apply an interstate commerce requirement to the "transports" offense alone. * * *

[A]spects of the meager legislative history, however, do provide some [illegible] support for the Government's interpretation. On the Senate floor, Sen[illegible] introduced § 1202, described various evils that prompted his stat[illegible] included assassinations of public figures and threats to the operat[illegible] significant enough in the aggregate to affect commerce. Such evils, [illegible] most thoroughly mitigated by forbidding every possession of any fire[illegible] classes of especially risky people, regardless of whether the gun was p[illegible] or transported "in commerce or affecting commerce." In addition, sp[illegible] the Senator can be read to state that the amendment reaches the mere [illegible] guns without any showing of an interstate commerce nexus.[13] But Senator [illegible] specifically says that no connection with commerce need be shown in the indiv[illegible] case. And nothing in his statements explains why, if an interstate commerce nexus is irrelevant in individual cases, the phrase "in commerce or affecting commerce" is in the statute at all. But even if Senator Long's remarks were crystal clear to us, they were apparently not crystal clear to his congressional colleagues. Meager as the discussion of [the provision] was, one of the few Congressmen who discussed the amendment summarized [it] as "mak(ing) it a Federal crime to take, possess, or receive a firearm across State lines . . . ." 114 Cong. Rec. 16298 (statement of Rep. Pollock).

In short, "the legislative history of (the) Act hardly speaks with that clarity of purpose which Congress supposedly furnishes courts in order to enable them to enforce its true will." *Universal Camera Corp. v. NLRB*, 340 U.S. 474, 483 (1951). * * * Taken together, the statutory materials are inconclusive on the central issue of whether or not the statutory phrase "in commerce or affecting commerce" applies to "possesses" and "receives" as well as "transports." While standing alone, the legislative history might tip in the Government's favor, the respondent explains far better the presence of critical language in the statute. The Government concedes that "the statute is not a model of logic or clarity." After "seiz(ing) every thing from which aid can be derived," *United States v. Fisher*, 2 Cranch 358, 386 (1805) (Marshall, C.J.), we are left with an ambiguous statute.

Given this ambiguity, we adopt the narrower reading: the phrase "in commerce or affecting commerce" is part of all three offenses, and the present conviction must be set aside because the Government has failed to show the requisite nexus with interstate commerce. This result is dictated by two wise principles this Court has long followed.

---

13 For example, Senator Long began his floor statement by announcing: "I have prepared an amendment which I will offer at an appropriate time, simply setting forth the fact that anybody who has been convicted of a felony (or comes within certain other categories) . . . is not permitted to possess a firearm . . . ." 114 Cong. Rec. 13868.

First, as we have recently reaffirmed, "ambiguity concerning the ambit of criminal statutes should be resolved in favor of lenity." *Rewis v. United States*, 401 U.S. 808, 812 (1971). In various ways over the years, we have stated that "when choice has to be made between two readings of what conduct Congress has made a crime, it is appropriate, before we choose the harsher alternative, to require that Congress should have spoken in language that is clear and definite." *United States v. Universal C.I.T. Credit Corp.*, 344 U.S. 218, 221–222 (1952). This principle is founded on two policies that have long been part of our tradition. First, "a fair warning should be given to the world in language that the common world will understand, of what the law intends to do if a certain line is passed. To make the warning fair, so fair as possible the line should be clear." *McBoyle v. United States*, 283 U.S. 25, 27 (1931) (Holmes, J.).[15] Second, because of the seriousness of criminal penalties, and because criminal punishment usually represents the moral condemnation of the community, legislatures and not courts should define criminal activity. This policy embodies "the instinctive distastes against men languishing in prison unless the lawmaker has clearly said they should." H. Friendly Mr. Justice Frankfurter and the Reading of Statutes, in Benchmarks 196, 209 (1967). Thus, where there is ambiguity in a criminal statute, doubts are resolved in favor of the defendant. Here, we conclude that Congress has not "plainly and unmistakably," *United States v. Gradwell*, 243 U.S. 476, 485 (1917), made it a federal crime for a convicted felon simply to possess a gun absent some demonstrated nexus with interstate commerce.

There is a second principle supporting today's result: unless Congress conveys its purpose clearly, it will not be deemed to have significantly changed the federal-state balance. Congress has traditionally been reluctant to define as a federal crime conduct readily denounced as criminal by the States. [W]e will not be quick to assume that Congress has meant to effect a significant change in the sensitive relation between federal and state criminal jurisdiction. In traditionally sensitive areas, such as legislation affecting the federal balance, the requirement of clear statement assures that the legislature has in fact faced, and intended to bring into issue, the critical matters involved in the judicial decision. * * * In the instant case, the broad construction urged by the Government renders traditionally local criminal conduct a matter for federal enforcement and would also involve a substantial extension of federal police

**Make the Connection**

The Court invokes a second substantive canon here, one designed to limit disruption of the federal-state balance. We will consider the extent to which courts should consider federalism when interpreting federal statutes, and the Court's decision in *Gregory v. Ashcroft*, later in this Chapter.

15 Holmes prefaced his much-quoted statement with the observation that "it is not likely that a criminal will carefully consider the text of the law before he murders or steals . . . ." But in the case of gun acquisition and possession it is not unreasonable to imagine a citizen attempting to "(steer) a careful course between violation of the statute (and lawful conduct)," *United States v. Hood*, 343 U.S. 148, 151 (1952).

resources. Absent proof of some interstate commerce nexus in each case, § 1202(a) dramatically intrudes upon traditional state criminal jurisdiction. * * * Absent a clearer statement of intention from Congress than is present here, we do not interpret § 1202(a) to reach the "mere possession" of firearms. * * *

[JUSTICE BRENNAN's opinion concurring in part and concurring in the judgment has been omitted.]

MR. JUSTICE BLACKMUN, with whom THE CHIEF JUSTICE, joins, dissenting.

1. The statute, 18 U.S.C. App. § 1202 (a), when it speaks of one "who receives, possesses, or transports in commerce or affecting commerce," although arguably ambiguous and, as the Government concedes, "not a model of logic or clarity," is clear enough. The structure of the vital language and its punctuation make it refer to one who receives, to one who possesses, and to one who transports in commerce. If one wished to say that he would welcome a cat, would welcome a dog, or would welcome a cow that jumps over the moon, he would likely say "I would like to have a cat, a dog, or a cow that jumps over the moon." So it is here.

2. The meaning the Court implants on the statute is justified only by the addition and interposition of a comma after the word "transports." I perceive no warrant for this judicial transfiguration.

3. In the very same statute the phrase "after the date of enactment of this Act" is separated by commas and undeniably modifies each of the preceding words, "receives," "possesses," and "transports."* Obviously, then, the draftsman—and the Congress—knew the use of commas for phrase modification. We should give effect to the only meaning attendant upon that use.

**Make the Connection**

Do you agree with Justice Blackmun that the punctuation of the provision at issue clarifies its meaning? We considered grammar canons, and specifically the role of commas, earlier in this Chapter.

4. The specific finding in 18 U.S.C. App. § 1201[3] clearly demonstrates that Congress was attempting to reach and prohibit every possession of a firearm by a felon; that Congress found that such possession, whether interstate or intrastate,

* Although the majority omitted this language in the excerpt above, the statute provides, in relevant part: "Any person who * * * has been convicted by a court of the United States or of a State or any political subdivision thereof of a felony [and] who receives, possesses, or transports in commerce or affecting commerce, after the date of enactment of this Act, any firearm shall be fined not more than $10,000 or imprisoned for not more than two years, or both." —*Ed.*

3 "§ 1201. Congressional findings and declaration. The Congress hereby finds and declares that the receipt, possession, or transportation of a firearm by felons . . . constitutes—(1) a burden on commerce or threat affecting the free flow of commerce . . . ."

affected interstate commerce; and that Congress did not conclude that intrastate possession was a matter of less concern to it than interstate possession. That finding was unnecessary if Congress also required proof that each receipt or possession of a firearm was in or affected interstate or foreign commerce.

5. Senator Long's explanatory comments reveal clearly the purpose, the intent, and the extent of the legislation:

> "I have prepared an amendment which I will offer at an appropriate time, simply setting forth the fact that anybody who has been convicted of a felony . . . is not permitted to *possess* a firearm . . . .
>
> "It might be well to analyze, for a moment, the logic involved. When a man has been convicted of a felony, unless—as this bill sets forth—he has been expressly pardoned by the President and the pardon states that the person is to be permitted to *possess* firearms in the future, that man would have no right to *possess* firearms. He would be punished criminally if he is found in *possession* of them." 114 Cong. Rec. 13868 (emphasis supplied).
>
> "So Congress simply finds that the *possession* of these weapons by the wrong kind of people is either a burden on commerce or a threat that affects the free flow of commerce. You cannot do business in an area, and you certainly cannot do as much of it and do it as well as you would like, if in order to do business you have to go through a street where there are burglars, murderers, and arsonists armed to the teeth against innocent citizens. So the threat certainly affects the free flow of commerce." 114 Cong. Rec. 13869 (emphasis supplied).

* * * One cannot detect in these remarks any purpose to restrict or limit the type of possession that was being considered for proscription.

6. The Court's construction of § 1202(a), limiting its application to interstate possession and receipt, shrinks the statute into something little more than a duplication of 18 U.S.C. §§ 922(g) and (h).[**] I cannot ascribe to Congress such a gesture of nonaccomplishment.

I thus conclude that § 1202(a) was intended to and does reach all possessions and receipts of firearms by convicted felons * * *.

---

[**] 28 U.S.C. § 922(g) provided, in relevant part: "It shall be unlawful for any person—who has been convicted in any court of a crime punishable by imprisonment for a term exceeding one year * * * to ship or transport in interstate or foreign commerce, or possess in or affecting commerce, any firearm or ammunition; or to receive any firearm or ammunition which has been shipped or transported in interstate or foreign commerce." 28 U.S.C. § 922(h) provided, in relevant part: "It shall be unlawful for any individual, who to that individual's knowledge and while being employed for any person described [in] subsection (g) of this section, in the course of such employment—(1) to receive, possess, or transport any firearm or ammunition in or affecting interstate or foreign commerce; or (2) to receive any firearm or ammunition which has been shipped or transported in interstate or foreign commerce." —*Ed.*

## Points for Discussion

### *a. The Rule of Lenity*

When it applies, the **rule of lenity** instructs courts to choose a construction of a criminal statute that favors the defendant, even though the statute could plausibly be read to favor the government. In *Bass*, for example, the Court applied the rule of lenity after concluding that the statute was ambiguous; because the statute was susceptible to more than one plausible reading, the Court chose the one that favored the defendant.

What is the justification for the rule of lenity? The Court suggested two rationales for the rule. First, the rule is designed to ensure that the public has fair notice about what conduct can lead to criminal penalties. If a criminal statute is ambiguous, then the public cannot have confidence about what conduct is permissible and what conduct is prohibited. Second, the rule promotes the separation of powers by ensuring that elected members of the legislature, rather than unelected judges, make the moral judgments that are the basis of criminal law. Do you agree that these rationales were implicated by the statute at issue in *Bass*?

### *b. The Role of Substantive Canons*

We have now seen several cases in which at least one Justice has urged application of the rule of lenity. But the Justices who have invoked it have not always agreed on when the rule is triggered and, when it is, what role it should play in the Court's interpretation of the statute in question.

In *Bass*, the Court reasoned that the rule of lenity applied because the statute was ambiguous. But what exactly was the Court's test for when a statute is ambiguous? As we have seen, most statutes are ambiguous at least to some degree or as applied to certain circumstances. After all, it is impossible for the legislature to anticipate every circumstance that might arise, and language always carries some degree of indeterminacy. Just how unclear must a statute be to trigger application of the rule of lenity? In thinking about this question, recall the Court's opinions in *Smith* and *Muscarello*, which we considered earlier in this Chapter; in both of those cases, the Court asserted that ordinary tools for determining statutory meaning rendered an otherwise ambiguous statute sufficiently clear.

Relatedly, how does the rule of lenity function in those cases in which it is invoked? In *Lockhart v. United States*, which we considered earlier in this Chapter, Justice Kagan's dissenting opinion reasoned that, to the extent that the provision at issue was genuinely ambiguous, the rule of lenity should "tip the scales" in the defendant's favor. On this view, the rule of lenity is a tie-breaker when ordinary rules of statutory interpretation leave the interpreter in equipoise. But in *Bass*, the Court asserted that because Congress had not "plainly and unmistakably * * * made it a federal crime for a convicted felon simply to possess a gun absent some demonstrated nexus with interstate commerce," the Court would not read the statute to criminalize such conduct. On this view, even if the best reading of a statute is that it criminalizes the conduct at issue, the court will not construe it to do so if Congress did not speak with unmistakable clarity. This is a considerably stronger version of the rule of lenity.

Which version of the rule of lenity do you think is most sensible?

---

### b. The Avoidance Canon

## *Skilling v. United States*

561 U.S. 358 (2010)

JUSTICE GINSBURG delivered the opinion of the Court.

Founded in 1985, Enron Corporation grew from its headquarters in Houston, Texas, into one of the world's leading energy companies. [Jeffrey] Skilling launched his career there in 1990 when Kenneth Lay, the company's founder, hired him to head an Enron subsidiary. Skilling steadily rose through the corporation's ranks, serving as president and chief operating officer, and then, beginning in February 2001, as chief executive officer. Six months later, on August 14, 2001, Skilling resigned from Enron.

Less than four months after Skilling's departure, Enron spiraled into bankruptcy. The company's stock, which had traded at $90 per share in August 2000, plummeted to pennies per share in late 2001. Attempting to comprehend what caused the corporation's collapse, the U.S. Department of Justice formed an Enron Task Force, comprising prosecutors and Federal Bureau of Investigation agents from around the Nation. The Government's investigation uncovered an elaborate conspiracy to prop up Enron's short-run stock prices by overstating the company's financial well-being. In the years following Enron's bankruptcy, the Government prosecuted dozens of Enron employees who participated in the scheme. In time, the Government worked its way up the corporation's chain of command: On July 7, 2004, a grand jury indicted Skilling, Lay, and Richard Causey, Enron's former chief accounting officer.

These three defendants, the indictment alleged, "engaged in a wide-ranging scheme to deceive the investing public, including Enron's shareholders, . . . about the true performance of Enron's businesses by: (a) manipulating Enron's publicly reported financial results; and (b) making public statements and representations about Enron's financial performance and results that were false and misleading." Skilling and his co-conspirators, the indictment continued, "enriched themselves as a result of the scheme through salary, bonuses, grants of stock and stock options, other profits, and prestige."

Count 1 of the indictment charged Skilling with conspiracy to commit securities and wire fraud; in particular, it alleged that Skilling had sought to "depriv[e] Enron and its shareholders of the intangible right of [his] honest services."[1] The indictment further charged Skilling with more than 25 substantive counts of securities fraud, wire fraud, making false representations to Enron's auditors, and insider trading. * * * Following a four-month trial and nearly five days of deliberation, the jury found Skilling guilty of 19 counts, including the honest-services-fraud conspiracy charge, and not guilty of 9 insider-trading counts. The District Court sentenced Skilling to 292 months' imprisonment, 3 years' supervised release, and $45 million in restitution. The Court of Appeals [rejected] Skilling's challenge to his conviction for conspiracy to commit honest-services fraud. * * *

We [consider] whether Skilling's conspiracy conviction was premised on an improper theory of honest-services wire fraud. The honest-services statute, § 1346, Skilling maintains, is unconstitutionally vague. Alternatively, he contends that his conduct does not fall within the statute's compass.

To place Skilling's constitutional challenge in context, we first review the origin and subsequent application of the honest-services doctrine. Enacted in 1872, the original mail-fraud provision, the predecessor of the modern-day mail- and wire-fraud laws, proscribed, without further elaboration, use of the mails to advance "any scheme or artifice to defraud." In 1909, Congress amended the statute to prohibit, as it does today, "any scheme or artifice to defraud, *or for obtaining money or property by means of false or fraudulent pretenses, representations, or promises*." § 1341 (emphasis added). Emphasizing Congress' disjunctive phrasing, the Courts of Appeals, one after the other, interpreted the term "scheme or artifice to defraud" to include deprivations not only of money or property, but also of intangible rights. [For example, in *Shushan v. United States*, 117 F.2d 110 (5th Cir. 1941),] the Fifth Circuit reviewed the mail-fraud prosecution of a public official who allegedly accepted bribes from entrepreneurs in exchange for urging city action beneficial to the bribe payers. * * * "A scheme to get a public contract on more favorable terms than would likely be got otherwise by bribing a public official," the court observed, "would not only be a plan to commit the crime of bribery, but would also be a scheme to defraud the public." *Id.*, at 115.

The Fifth Circuit's opinion in *Shushan* stimulated the development of an "honest-services" doctrine. Unlike fraud in which the victim's loss of money or

---

1 The mail- and wire-fraud statutes criminalize the use of the mails or wires in furtherance of "any scheme or artifice to defraud, or for obtaining money or property by means of false or fraudulent pretenses, representations, or promises." 18 U.S.C. § 1341 (mail fraud); § 1343 (wire fraud). The honest-services statute, § 1346, defines "the term 'scheme or artifice to defraud' " in these provisions to include "a scheme or artifice to deprive another of the intangible right of honest services."

property supplied the defendant's gain, with one the mirror image of the other, the honest-services theory targeted corruption that lacked similar symmetry. While the offender profited, the betrayed party suffered no deprivation of money or property; instead, a third party, who had not been deceived, provided the enrichment. For example, if a city mayor (the offender) accepted a bribe from a third party in exchange for awarding that party a city contract, yet the contract terms were the same as any that could have been negotiated at arm's length, the city (the betrayed party) would suffer no tangible loss. Even if the scheme occasioned a money or property *gain* for the betrayed party, courts reasoned, actionable harm lay in the denial of that party's right to the offender's "honest services."

"Most often these cases . . . involved bribery of public officials," *United States v. Bohonus*, 628 F.2d 1167, 1171 (9th Cir. 1980), but courts also recognized private-sector honest-services fraud. * * * Over time, "[a]n increasing number of courts" recognized that "a recreant employee"—public or private—"c[ould] be prosecuted under [the mail-fraud statute] if he breache[d] his allegiance to his employer by accepting bribes or kickbacks in the course of his employment," *United States v. McNeive*, 536 F.2d 1245, 1249 (8th Cir. 1976); by 1982, all Courts of Appeals had embraced the honest-services theory of fraud.

In 1987, this Court, in *McNally v. United States*, 483 U.S. 350 (1987), stopped the development of the intangible-rights doctrine in its tracks. *McNally* involved a state officer who, in selecting Kentucky's insurance agent, arranged to procure a share of the agent's commissions via kickbacks paid to companies the official partially controlled. The prosecutor did not charge that, "in the absence of the alleged scheme[,] the Commonwealth would have paid a lower premium or secured better insurance." Instead, the prosecutor maintained that the kickback scheme "defraud[ed] the citizens and government of Kentucky of their right to have the Commonwealth's affairs conducted honestly." *Id.*, at 35. We held that the scheme did not qualify as mail fraud. "Rather than constru[ing] the statute in a manner that leaves its outer boundaries ambiguous and involves the Federal Government in setting standards of disclosure and good government for local and state officials," we read the statute "as limited in scope to the protection of property rights." *Id.*, at 360. "If Congress desires to go further," we stated, "it must speak more clearly." *Ibid.*

Congress responded swiftly. The following year, it enacted a new statute "specifically to cover one of the 'intangible rights' that lower courts had protected . . . prior to *McNally:* 'the intangible right of honest services.' " *Cleveland v. United States*, 531 U.S. 12, 19–20 (2000). In full, the honest-services statute stated:

> "For the purposes of th[e] chapter [of the United States Code that prohibits, *inter alia,* mail fraud, § 1341, and wire fraud, § 1343], the term 'scheme or artifice to defraud' includes a scheme or artifice to deprive another of the intangible right of honest services." § 1346.

Congress, Skilling charges, reacted quickly but not clearly: He asserts that § 1346 is unconstitutionally vague. To satisfy due process, "a penal statute [must] define the criminal offense [1] with sufficient definiteness that ordinary people can understand what conduct is prohibited and [2] in a manner that does not encourage arbitrary and discriminatory enforcement." *Kolender v. Lawson*, 461 U.S. 352, 357 (1983). The void-for-vagueness doctrine embraces these requirements.

According to Skilling, § 1346 meets neither of the two due process essentials. First, the phrase "the intangible right of honest services," he contends, does not adequately define what behavior it bars. Second, he alleges, § 1346's "standardless sweep . . . allows policemen, prosecutors, and juries to pursue their personal predilections," thereby "facilitat[ing] opportunistic and arbitrary prosecutions."

**Food for Thought**

In light of the Court's account of the statute's background, do you agree with Skilling that the statute was so vague that an ordinary person would not be able to determine that the conduct of which he was accused was unlawful?

In urging invalidation of § 1346, Skilling swims against our case law's current, which requires us, if we can, to construe, not condemn, Congress' enactments. See, *e.g., Civil Service Comm'n v. Letter Carriers*, 413 U.S. 548, 571 (1973). * * * We [conclude] that § 1346 should be construed rather than invalidated. First, we look to the doctrine developed in pre-*McNally* cases in an endeavor to ascertain the meaning of the phrase "the intangible right of honest services." Second, to preserve what Congress certainly intended the statute to cover, we pare that body of precedent down to its core: In the main, the pre-*McNally* cases involved fraudulent schem
deprive another of honest services through bribes or kickbacks supplied
party who had not been deceived. Confined to these paramount applicati
presents no vagueness problem.

There is no doubt that Congress intended § 1346 to refer to and i
honest-services doctrine recognized in Courts of Appeals' decisions b
derailed the intangible-rights theory of fraud. Congress enacted § 13
of *McNally* and drafted the statute using that decision's terminology. A
Circuit observed in its leading analysis of § 1346:

> "The definite article 'the' suggests that 'intangible right of honest services' ha
> specific meaning to Congress when it enacted the statute—Congress was recriminalizing mail- and wire-fraud schemes to deprive others of *that* 'intangible right of honest services,' which had been protected before *McNally*, not *all* intangible rights of honest services whatever they might be thought to be." *United States v. Rybicki*, 354 F.3d 124, 137–138 (2d Cir. 2003) (en banc).

Satisfied that Congress, by enacting § 1346, "meant to reinstate the body of pre-*McNally* honest-services law," we have surveyed that case law. In parsing the Courts of Appeals decisions, we acknowledge that Skilling's vagueness challenge has force, for honest-services decisions preceding *McNally* were not models of clarity or consistency. While the honest-services cases preceding *McNally* dominantly and consistently applied the fraud statute to bribery and kickback schemes—schemes that were the basis of most honest-services prosecutions—there was considerable disarray over the statute's application to conduct outside that core category. In light of this disarray, Skilling urges us, as he urged the Fifth Circuit, to invalidate the statute *in toto*.

It has long been our practice, however, before striking a federal statute as impermissibly vague, to consider whether the prescription is amenable to a limiting construction. See, *e.g., Hooper v. California*, 155 U.S. 648, 657 (1895) ("The elementary rule is that *every reasonable construction* must be resorted to, in order to save a statute from unconstitutionality." (emphasis added)). We have accordingly instructed "the federal courts . . . to avoid constitutional difficulties by [adopting a limiting interpretation] if such a construction is fairly possible." *Boos v. Barry*, 485 U.S. 312, 331 (1988); see *United States v. Harriss*, 347 U.S. 612, 618 (1954) ("[I]f the general class of offenses to which the statute is directed is plainly within its terms, the statute will not be struck down as vague . . . . And if this general class of offenses can be made constitutionally definite by a reasonable construction of the statute, this Court is under a duty to give the statute that construction.").

**Take Note**

Did the Court conclude that the statute was unconstitutionally vague? Or did it decline to resolve the question?

Arguing against any limiting construction, Skilling contends that it is impossible to identify a salvageable honest-services core; "the pre-*McNally* caselaw," he asserts, "is a hodgepodge of oft-conflicting holdings" that are "hopelessly unclear." Although some applications of the pre-*McNally* honest-services doctrine occasioned disagreement among the Courts of Appeals, these cases do not cloud the doctrine's solid core: The "vast majority" of the honest-services cases involved offenders who, in violation of a fiduciary duty, participated in bribery or kickback schemes. Indeed, the *McNally* case itself, which spurred Congress to enact § 1346, presented a paradigmatic kickback fact pattern. Congress' reversal of *McNally* and reinstatement of the honest-services doctrine, we conclude, can and should be salvaged by confining its scope to the core pre-*McNally* applications.

As already noted, the honest-services doctrine had its genesis in prosecutions involving bribery allegations. In view of this history, there is no doubt that Congress intended § 1346 to reach *at least* bribes and kickbacks. Reading the statute to proscribe a wider range of offensive conduct, we acknowledge, would raise the due process concerns underlying the vagueness doctrine. To preserve the statute without transgressing constitutional limitations, we now hold that § 1346 criminalizes *only* the bribe-and-kickback core of the pre-*McNally* case law. Interpreted to encompass only bribery and kickback schemes, § 1346 is not unconstitutionally vague. * * *

The Government did not, at any time, allege that Skilling solicited or accepted side payments from a third party in exchange for making these misrepresentations. It is therefore clear that, as we read § 1346, Skilling did not commit honest-services fraud. Because the indictment alleged three objects of the conspiracy—honest-services wire fraud, money-or-property wire fraud, and securities fraud—Skilling's conviction is flawed. See *Yates v. United States*, 354 U.S. 298 (1957) (constitutional error occurs when a jury is instructed on alternative theories of guilt and returns a general verdict that may rest on a legally invalid theory). This determination, however, does not necessarily require reversal of the conspiracy conviction; * * * [such] errors [are] subject to harmless-error analysis. The parties vigorously dispute whether the error was harmless. We leave this dispute for resolution on remand.

Justice Scalia, with whom Justice Thomas joins, and with whom Justice Kennedy joins [in relevant part], concurring in part and concurring in the judgment.

* * * I [agree] that the decision upholding Skilling's conviction for so-called "honest-services fraud" must be reversed, but for a different reason. In my view, the specification in 18 U.S.C. § 1346 (2006 ed.) that "scheme or artifice to defraud" in the mail-fraud and wire-fraud statutes, §§ 1341 and 1343 (2006 ed., Supp. II), includes "a scheme or artifice to deprive another of the intangible right of honest services" is vague, and therefore violates the Due Process Clause of the Fifth Amendment. The Court strikes a pose of judicial humility in proclaiming that our task is "not to destroy the Act . . . but to construe it." But in transforming the prohibition of "honest-services fraud" into a prohibition of "bribery and kickbacks" it is wielding a power we long ago abjured: the power to define new federal crimes. See *United States v. Hudson*, 7 Cranch 32, 34 (1812).

A criminal statute must clearly define the conduct it proscribes, see *Grayned v. City of Rockford*, 408 U.S. 104, 108 (1972). A statute that is unconstitutionally vague cannot be saved by a more precise indictment, see *Lanzetta v. New Jersey*, 306 U.S. 451, 453 (1939), nor by judicial construction that writes in specific criteria that its text does not contain, see *United States v. Reese*, 92 U.S. 214, 219–221 (1876). * * *

The Court maintains that "the intangible right of honest services" means the right not to have one's fiduciaries accept "bribes or kickbacks." Its first step in reaching that conclusion is the assertion that the phrase refers to "the doctrine developed" in cases decided by lower federal courts prior to our decision in *McNally v. United States*, 483 U.S. 350 (1987). I do not contest that. I agree that Congress used the novel phrase to adopt the lower-court case law that had been disapproved by *McNally*—what the Court calls "the pre-*McNally* honest-services doctrine." * * * But the pre-*McNally* Court of Appeals opinions were not limited to fraud by public officials. * * * None of the "honest services" cases, neither those pertaining to public officials nor those pertaining to private employees, defined the nature and content of the fiduciary duty central to the "fraud" offense.

In short, the first step in the Court's analysis—holding that "the intangible right of honest services" refers to "the honest-services doctrine recognized in Courts of Appeals' decisions before *McNally*"—is a step out of the frying pan into the fire. The pre-*McNally* cases provide no clear indication of what constitutes a denial of the right of honest services. * * *

* * * To say that bribery and kickbacks represented "the core" of the doctrine, or that most cases applying the doctrine involved those offenses, is not to say that they *are* the doctrine. All it proves is that the multifarious versions of the doctrine *overlap* with regard to those offenses. But the doctrine itself is much more. Among all the pre-*McNally* smorgasbord offerings of varieties of honest-services fraud, *not one* is limited to bribery and kickbacks. That is a dish the Court has cooked up all on its own. * * * Perhaps it is true that "Congress intended § 1346 to reach *at least* bribes and kickbacks." That simply does not mean, as the Court now holds, that "§ 1346 criminalizes *only*" bribery and kickbacks.

Arriving at that conclusion requires not interpretation but invention. The Court replaces a vague criminal standard that Congress adopted with a more narrow one (included within the vague one) that can pass constitutional muster. I know of no precedent for such "paring down," and it seems to me clearly beyond judicial power. * * *

The canon of constitutional avoidance, on which the Court so heavily relies, states that "when the constitutionality of a statute is assailed, if the statute be reasonably susceptible of two interpretations, by one of which it would be unconstitutional and by the other valid, it is our plain duty to adopt that construction which will save the statute from constitutional infirmity." *United States ex rel. Attorney General v. Delaware & Hudson Co.*, 213 U.S. 366, 407 (1909); see also *United States v. Rumely*, 345 U.S. 41, 45 (1953) (describing the canon as decisive "in the choice of fair alternatives"). Here there is no choice to be made between two "fair alternatives." Until today, no one has thought (and there is no basis for thinking) that the honest-services statute prohibited only bribery and kickbacks.

I certainly agree with the Court that we must, "if we can," uphold, rather than "condemn," Congress's enactments. But I do not believe we have the power, in order to uphold an enactment, to rewrite it. Congress enacted the entirety of the pre-*McNally* honest-services law, the content of which is (to put it mildly) unclear. In prior vagueness cases, we have resisted the temptation to make all things right with the stroke of our pen. See, *e.g.*, *Smith v. Goguen*, 415 U.S. 566, 575 (1974). I would show the same restraint today, and reverse Skilling's conviction on the basis that § 1346 provides no "ascertainable standard" for the conduct it condemns. Instead, the Court today adds to our functions the prescription of criminal law.

[JUSTICE ALITO's opinion concurring in part and concurring in the judgment, and JUSTICE SOTOMAYOR's opinion concurring in part and dissenting in part, have been omitted.]

---

## Points for Discussion

### *a. The Avoidance Canon*

The Court suggested that the provision at issue might be unconstitutionally vague, but it read the statute more narrowly to "avoid constitutional difficulties." In so doing, the Court invoked the **avoidance canon**, also known as the canon of constitutional avoidance. The avoidance canon is another substantive canon; it does not rely simply on understandings about how we ordinarily use the English language, but instead is designed to avoid the disfavored result of a court invalidating a statute. Under the avoidance canon, a court will choose a construction of a statute that avoids constitutional difficulties. Under the Court's interpretation of the statute, Skilling's conduct was not unlawful, and the Court accordingly reversed his conviction for honest-services fraud.

Justice Scalia agreed that Skilling's conviction on that count had to be reversed, but he reached this conclusion because he thought that the statute was unconstitutionally vague. Why did Justice Scalia believe that the avoidance canon was inapplicable in this case? On his view, when should a court invoke the canon? Which view—the Court's or Justice Scalia's—do you find more persuasive?

### *b. Forms of Avoidance*

The Court in *Skilling* did not hold that the statute was unconstitutionally vague. Instead, the Court appears to have held that, because the statute *might* be unconstitutionally vague, the Court should construe the statute to avoid the constitutional difficulty. Does it make sense to read a statute narrowly—and perhaps in some tension with its plain terms or history—in order to avoid a possible constitutional problem? Although the avoidance canon has deep historical roots, courts in the nineteenth century tended to apply the canon differently. Under the older approach, sometimes called "classic avoidance," a reviewing court would decide whether the statute as written violates the Constitution; if so, the court would then choose an alternative (but still plausible) interpretation that avoids the constitutional problem.

The more modern version of the doctrine looks more like what the Court in *Skilling* did: the court considers the range of plausible interpretations of a statute and, if one would raise constitutional problems or doubts, chooses one that avoids the possible constitutional problem. See, e.g., *Ashwander v. Tennessee Valle Authority*, 297 U.S. 288, 348 (1936) (Brandeis, J., concurring) ("When the validity of an act of the

Congress is drawn in question, and even if a serious doubt of constitutionality is raised, it is a cardinal principle that this Court will first ascertain whether a construction of the statute is fairly possible by which the question may be avoided." (quoting *Crowell v. Benson*, 285 U.S. 22, 62 (1932)). What are the virtues of "modern avoidance"? What are its drawbacks? Is it a problem that courts applying this approach resolve fewer constitutional questions, or is it instead a virtue?

#### *c. Aftermath of the Decision*

The Court remanded Skilling's case for consideration in light of the Court's understanding of the statute. On remand, the Court of Appeals affirmed Skilling's conviction, reasoning that there was sufficient evidence to justify a verdict on other theories. The Supreme Court denied certiorari. Skilling then entered a deal with the Department of Justice that reduced his sentence to 14 years. Skilling was released from custody after serving 12 years in prison.

---

### c. The Federalism Clear-Statement Rule

## *Gregory v. Ashcroft*

501 U.S. 452 (1991)

JUSTICE O'CONNOR delivered the opinion of the Court.

Article V, § 26, of the Missouri Constitution provides that "[a]ll judges other than municipal judges shall retire at the age of seventy years." We consider whether this mandatory retirement provision violates the federal Age Discrimination in Employment Act of 1967 (ADEA or Act), 81 Stat. 602, as amended, 29 U.S.C. §§ 621–634 * * *.

Petitioners are Missouri state judges * * * subject to the § 26 mandatory retirement provision. Petitioners were appointed to office by the Governor of Missouri, pursuant to the Missouri Non-Partisan Court Plan, Mo. Const., Art. V, §§ 25(a)–25(g). Each has, since his appointment, been retained in office by means of a retention election in which the judge ran unopposed, subject only to a "yes or no" vote. See Mo. Const., Art. V, § 25(c)(1). [They and two others filed suit challenging the mandatory retirement provision.]

The ADEA makes it unlawful for an "employer" "to discharge any individual" who is at least 40 years old "because of such individual's age." 29 U.S.C. §§ 623(a), 631(a). The term "employer" is defined to include "a State or political subdivision of a State." § 630(b)(2). Petitioners work for the State of Missouri. They contend that the Missouri mandatory retirement requirement for judges violates the ADEA. [The

District Court granted the Governor's motion to dismiss, concluding that the judges are exempted from the protection of the ADEA because of 29 U.S.C. § 630(f), which provides:

> "The term 'employee' means an individual employed by any employer except that the term 'employee' shall not include any person elected to public office in any State or political subdivision of any State by the qualified voters thereof, or any person chosen by such officer to be on such officer's personal staff, or an appointee on the policy-making level or an immediate adviser with respect to the exercise of the constitutional or legal powers of the office."

The Court of Appeals affirmed.]

**Take Note**

Before you read any further, can you guess which clause in section 630(f) the Governor relied on? Just reading the text of the provision, do you think that the Governor's argument that section 630(f) exempts judges from the protections in the ADEA was a strong one?

As every schoolchild learns, our Constitution establishes a system of dual sovereignty between the States and the Federal Government. This Court also has recognized this fundamental principle. In *Tafflin v. Levitt*, 493 U.S. 455, 458 (1990), "[w]e beg[a]n with the axiom that, under our federal system, the States possess sovereignty concurrent with that of the Federal Government, subject only to limitations imposed by the Supremacy Clause." * * *

The Constitution created a Federal Government of limited powers. "The powers not delegated to the United States by the Constitution, nor prohibited by it to the States, are reserved to the States respectively, or to the people." U.S. Const., Amdt. 10. The States thus retain substantial sovereign authority under our constitutional system. * * *

This federalist structure of joint sovereigns preserves to the people numerous advantages. It assures a decentralized government that will be more sensitive to the diverse needs of a heterogeneous society; it increases opportunity for citizen involvement in democratic processes; it allows for more innovation and experimentation in government; and it makes government more responsive by putting the States in competition for a mobile citizenry.

Perhaps the principal benefit of the federalist system is a check on abuses of government power. "The 'constitutionally mandated balance of power' between the States and the Federal Government was adopted by the Framers to ensure the protection of 'our fundamental liberties.' " *Atascadero State Hospital v. Scanlon*, 473 U.S. 234, 242 (1985), quoting *Garcia v. San Antonio Metropolitan Transit Authority*, 469 U.S. 528, 572 (1985) (POWELL, J., dissenting). Just as the separation and independence of the coordinate branches of the Federal Government serve to prevent the accumulation of excessive power in any one branch, a healthy balance of power between the States and the Federal Government will reduce the risk of tyranny and abuse from either front. [As James Madison explained:]

> "In a single republic, all the power surrendered by the people is submitted to the administration of a single government; and the usurpations are guarded against by a division of the government into distinct and separate departments. In the compound republic of America, the power surrendered by the people is first divided between two distinct governments, and then the portion allotted to each subdivided among distinct and separate departments. Hence a double security arises to the rights of the people. The different governments will control each other, at the same time that each will be controlled by itself." [The Federalist No. 51, p. 323 (C. Rossiter ed. 1961).]

One fairly can dispute whether our federalist system has been quite as successful in checking government abuse as Hamilton promised, but there is no doubt about the design. If this "double security" is to be effective, there must be a proper balance between the States and the Federal Government. These twin powers will act as mutual restraints only if both are credible. In the tension between federal and state power lies the promise of liberty.

The Federal Government holds a decided advantage in this delicate balance: the Supremacy Clause. U.S. Const., Art. VI, cl. 2. As long as it is acting within the powers granted it under the Constitution, Congress may impose its will on the States. Congress may legislate in areas traditionally regulated by the States. This is an extraordinary power in a federalist system. It is a power that we must assume Congress does not exercise lightly.

The present case concerns a state constitutional provision through which the people of Missouri establish a qualification for those who sit as their judges. This provision goes beyond an area traditionally regulated by the States; it is a decision of the most fundamental sort for a sovereign entity. Through the structure of its government, and the character of those who exercise government authority, a State defines itself as a sovereign. * * *

Congressional interference with this decision of the people of Missouri, defining their constitutional officers, would upset the usual constitutional balance of federal and state powers. For this reason, "it is incumbent upon the federal courts to be certain of Congress' intent before finding that federal law overrides" this balance. *Atascadero*, 473 U.S., at 243. We explained recently:

> "[I]f Congress intends to alter the 'usual constitutional balance between the States and the Federal Government,' it must make its intention to do so 'unmistakably clear in the language of the statute.' " *Atascadero*, 473 U.S. at 242. *Atascadero* was an Eleventh Amendment case, but a similar approach is applied in other contexts. Congress should make its intention 'clear and manifest' if it intends to pre-empt the historic powers of the States, *Rice v. Santa Fe Elevator Corp.*, 331 U.S. 218, 230

> (1947). . . . 'In traditionally sensitive areas, such as legislation affecting the federal balance, the requirement of clear statement assures that the legislature has in fact faced, and intended to bring into issue, the critical matters involved in the judicial decision.' *United States v. Bass*, 404 U.S. 336, 349 (1971)." *Will v. Michigan Dept. of State Police*, 491 U.S. 58, 65 (1989).

This plain statement rule is nothing more than an acknowledgment that the States retain substantial sovereign powers under our constitutional scheme, powers with which Congress does not readily interfere.

[Our] cases stand in recognition of the authority of the people of the States to determine the qualifications of their most important government officials.* It is an authority that lies at "the heart of representative government." [*Bernal v. Fainter*, 467 U.S. 216, 221 (1984).] It is a power reserved to the States under the Tenth Amendment and guaranteed them by that provision of the Constitution under which the United States "guarantee[s] to every State in this Union a Republican Form of Government." U.S. Const., Art. IV, § 4.

The authority of the people of the States to determine the qualifications of their government officials is, of course, not without limit. Other constitutional provisions, most notably the Fourteenth Amendment, proscribe certain qualifications * * *. Here, we must decide what Congress did in extending the ADEA to the States, pursuant to its powers under the Commerce Clause. See *EEOC v. Wyoming*, 460 U.S. 226 (1983) (the extension of the ADEA to employment by state and local governments was a valid exercise of Congress' powers under the Commerce Clause). * * *

We are constrained in our ability to consider the limits that the state-federal balance places on Congress' powers under the Commerce Clause. See *Garcia v. San Antonio Metropolitan Transit Authority*, 469 U.S. 528 (1985) (declining to review limitations placed on Congress' Commerce Clause powers by our federal system). But there is no need to do so if we hold that the ADEA does not apply to state judges. Application of the plain statement rule thus may avoid a potential constitutional problem.

**Food for Thought**

The Court held in *Garcia* that the Tenth Amendment does not prohibit Congress, when it legislates pursuant to the Commerce Clause, from regulating states in the same way that it regulates private parties. If Congress has power to apply the protections of the ADEA to state employers, and there's no dispute that it has done so, then what "constitutional problem" would arise from concluding that the plaintiffs are protected by the Act?

Indeed, inasmuch as this Court in *Garcia* has left primarily to the political process the protection of the States against intrusive exercises of Congress' Commerce

* The Court cited cases under the Equal Protection Clause of the Fourteenth Amendment involving the states' exclusion of non-citizens from certain government positions. —*Ed.*

Clause powers, we must be absolutely certain that Congress intended such an exercise. "[T]o give the state-displacing weight of federal law to mere congressional *ambiguity* would evade the very procedure for lawmaking on which *Garcia* relied to protect states' interests." L. Tribe, American Constitutional Law § 6–25, p. 480 (2d ed. 1988).

In 1974, Congress extended the substantive provisions of the ADEA to include the States as employers. 29 U.S.C. § 630(b)(2). At the same time, Congress amended the definition of "employee" to exclude all elected and most high-ranking government officials. * * * 29 U.S.C. § 630(f).

Governor Ashcroft contends that the § 630(f) exclusion of certain public officials also excludes judges, like petitioners, who are appointed to office by the Governor and are then subject to retention election. The Governor points to two passages in § 630(f). First, he argues, these judges are selected by an elected official and, because they make policy, are "appointee[s] on the policymaking level."

Petitioners counter that judges merely resolve factual disputes and decide questions of law; they do not make policy. Moreover, petitioners point out that the policymaking-level exception is part of a trilogy, tied closely to the elected-official exception. Thus, the Act excepts elected officials and: (1) "any person chosen by such officer to be on such officer's personal staff"; (2) "an appointee on the policymaking level"; and (3) "an immediate advisor with respect to the exercise of the constitutional or legal powers of the office." Applying the maxim of statutory construction *noscitur a sociis*—that a word is known by the company it keeps—petitioners argue that since (1) and (3) refer only to those in close working relationships with elected officials, so too must (2). Even if it can be said that judges may make policy, petitioners contend, they do not do so at the behest of an elected official.

**Make the Connection**

We considered *noscitur a sociis*, and semantic canons of construction more generally, earlier in this Chapter. Do you find the plaintiffs' argument based on the canon persuasive?

Governor Ashcroft relies on the plain language of the statute: It exempts persons appointed "at the policymaking level." The Governor argues that state judges, in fashioning and applying the common law, make policy. Missouri is a common law state. See Mo. Rev. Stat. § 1.010 (1986) (adopting "[t]he common law of England" consistent with federal and state law). The common law, unlike a constitution or statute, provides no definitive text; it is to be derived from the interstices of prior opinions and a well-considered judgment of what is best for the community. As Justice Holmes put it:

> "The very considerations which judges most rarely mention, and always with an apology, are the secret root from which the law draws all the juices of life. I mean, of course, considerations of what is expedient for the community concerned. Every important principle which is developed by litigation is in fact and at bottom the result

of more or less definitely understood views of public policy; most generally, to be sure, under our practice and traditions, the unconscious result of instinctive preferences and inarticulate convictions, but nonetheless traceable to views of public policy in the last analysis." O. Holmes, The Common Law 35–36 (1881).

The Governor stresses judges' policymaking responsibilities, but it is far from plain that the statutory exception requires that judges actually make policy. The statute refers to appointees "on the policymaking level," not to appointees "who make policy." It may be sufficient that the appointee is in a position requiring the exercise of discretion concerning issues of public importance. This certainly describes the bench, regardless of whether judges might be considered policymakers in the same sense as the executive or legislature.

Nonetheless, "appointee at the policymaking level," particularly in the context of the other exceptions that surround it, is an odd way for Congress to exclude judges; a plain statement that judges are not "employees" would seem the most efficient phrasing. But in this case we are not looking for a plain statement that judges are excluded. We will not read the ADEA to cover state judges unless Congress has made it clear that judges are *included*. This does not mean that the Act must mention judges explicitly, though it does not. Rather, it must be plain to anyone reading the Act that it covers judges. In the context of a statute that plainly excludes most important state public officials, "appointee on the policymaking level" is sufficiently broad that we cannot conclude that the statute plainly covers appointed state judges. Therefore, it does not.

**Food for Thought**

The Court says that "it must be plain to anyone reading the Act" that judges are covered. Would the Court's clear statement rule be satisfied if the text did not clearly cover judges, but there was strong evidence in the legislative history of Congress's intent to protect judges from age discrimination?

The ADEA plainly covers all state employees except those excluded by one of the exceptions. Where it is unambiguous that an employee does not fall within one of the exceptions, the Act states plainly and unequivocally that the employee is included. It is at least ambiguous whether a state judge is an "appointee on the policymaking level."

Governor Ashcroft points also to the "person elected to public office" exception. He contends that because petitioners—although appointed to office initially—are subject to retention election, they are "elected to public office" under the ADEA. Because we conclude that petitioners fall presumptively under the policymaking-level exception, we need not answer this question.

[The Court also concluded that the Missouri Constitution's mandatory retirement provision for judges does not violate the Equal Protection Clause of the Fourteenth Amendment to the United States Constitution.] Affirmed.

JUSTICE WHITE, with whom JUSTICE STEVENS joins, concurring in part, dissenting in part, and concurring in the judgment.

I agree with the majority that neither the Age Discrimination in Employment Act (ADEA) nor the Equal Protection Clause prohibits Missouri's mandatory retirement provision as applied to petitioners, and I therefore concur in the judgment * * *. I cannot agree, however, with the majority's [application of a plain statement rule], which ignores several areas of well-established precedent and announces a rule that is likely to prove both unwise and infeasible. * * *

The dispute in this case [is] not whether Congress has outlawed age discrimination by the States. It clearly has. The only question is whether petitioners fall within the definition of "employee" in the Act, § 630(f), which contains exceptions for elected officials and certain appointed officials. If petitioners *are* "employee[s]," Missouri's mandatory retirement provision clearly conflicts with the antidiscrimination provisions of the ADEA. Indeed, we have noted that the "policies and substantive provisions of the [ADEA] apply with especial force in the case of mandatory retirement provisions." *Western Air Lines, Inc. v. Criswell*, 472 U.S. 400, 410 (1985). Pre-emption therefore is automatic, since "state law is pre-empted to the extent that it actually conflicts with federal law." *Pacific Gas & Elec. Co. v. State Energy Resources Conservation and Development Comm'n*, 461 U.S. 190, 204 (1983).

**FYI**

"Preemption" is a doctrine of constitutional law under which validly enacted federal laws preempt, or displace, state laws that conflict with the federal laws or otherwise stand as an obstacle to the federal regulatory scheme.

The majority's federalism concerns are irrelevant to such "actual conflict" pre-emption. "The relative importance to the State of its own law is not material when there is a conflict with a valid federal law, for the Framers of our Constitution provided that the federal law must prevail.' " *Fidelity Federal Sav. & Loan Assn. v. De la Cuesta*, 458 U.S. 141, 153 (1982).

While acknowledging this principle of federal legislative supremacy, the majority nevertheless imposes upon Congress a "plain statement" requirement. The majority claims to derive this requirement from the plain statement approach developed in our Eleventh Amendment cases, see, *e.g., Atascadero State Hospital v. Scanlon*, 473 U.S. 234, 243 (1985), and applied two Terms ago in *Will v. Michigan Dept. of State Police*, 491 U.S. 58, 65 (1989). The issue in those cases, however, was whether Congress intended a particular statute to extend to the States *at all.* * * * In the present case, by contrast, Congress has expressly extended the coverage of the ADEA to the States and their employees. Its intention to regulate age discrimination by States is thus "unmistakably clear in the language of the statute." *Atascadero*, 473 U.S., at 242. The only dispute is over the precise details of the statute's application. We have never extended the plain statement approach that far, and the majority offers no compelling reason for doing so.

The majority's plain statement rule is not only unprecedented, it directly contravenes our decisions in *Garcia v. San Antonio Metropolitan Transit Authority*, 469 U.S. 528 (1985), and *South Carolina v. Baker*, 485 U.S. 505 (1988). In those cases we made it clear "that States must find their protection from congressional regulation through the national political process, not through judicially defined spheres of unregulable state activity." *Id.,* at 512. We also rejected as "unsound in principle and unworkable in practice" any test for state immunity that requires a judicial determination of which state activities are "traditional," "integral," or "necessary." *Garcia,* 469 U.S., at 546. The majority disregards those decisions in its attempt to carve out areas of state activity that will receive special protection from federal legislation.

The majority's approach is also unsound because it will serve only to confuse the law. First, the majority fails to explain the scope of its rule. Is the rule limited to federal regulation of the qualifications of state officials? Or does it apply more broadly to the regulation of any "state governmental functions"? Second, the majority does not explain its requirement that Congress' intent to regulate a particular state activity be "plain to anyone reading [the federal statute]." Does that mean that it is now improper to look to the purpose or history of a federal statute in determining the scope of the statute's limitations on state activities? If so, the majority's rule is completely inconsistent with our pre-emption jurisprudence. See, *e.g., Hillsborough County v. Automated Medical Laboratories, Inc.*, 471 U.S. 707, 715 (1985) (pre-emption will be found where there is a "clear and manifest *purpose*" to displace state law) (emphasis added). The vagueness of the majority's rule undoubtedly will lead States to assert that various federal statutes no longer apply to a wide variety of state activities if Congress has not expressly referred to those activities in the statute. Congress, in turn, will be forced to draft long and detailed lists of which particular state functions it meant to regulate.

The imposition of such a burden on Congress is particularly out of place in the context of the ADEA. Congress already has stated that all "individual[s] employed by any employer" are protected by the ADEA unless they are expressly excluded by one of the exceptions in the definition of "employee." See 29 U.S.C. § 630(f). The majority, however, turns the statute on its head, holding that state judges are not protected by the ADEA because "Congress has [not] made it clear that judges are *included.*"

The majority asserts that its plain statement rule is helpful in avoiding a "potential constitutional problem." It is far from clear, however, why there would be a constitutional problem if the ADEA applied to state judges, in light of our decisions in *Garcia* and *Baker,* discussed above. * * * In any event, as discussed below, a straightforward analysis of the ADEA's definition of "employee" reveals that the ADEA does not apply here. Thus, even if there were potential constitutional problems in extending the ADEA to state judges, the majority's proposed plain statement rule would not be necessary to avoid them in this case. Indeed, because this case can be decided purely on the basis of statutory interpretation, the majority's announcement of its plain statement rule, which purportedly is derived from constitutional principles, *violates* our general practice of avoiding the unnecessary resolution of constitutional issues.

**Food for Thought**

Is it obvious to you, given the grammatical structure of section 630(f), that there are four, rather than three, categories of exempt state and local employees? We considered the grammar canons, and in particular the role of punctuation in statutory interpretation, earlier in this Chapter.

A parsing of [the ADEA's definition of "employee"] reveals that it excludes from the definition of "employee" (and thus the coverage of the ADEA) four types of (noncivil service) state and local employees: (1) persons elected to public office; (2) the personal staff of elected officials; (3) persons appointed by elected officials to be on the policymaking level; and (4) the immediate advisers of elected officials with respect to the constitutional or legal powers of the officials' offices.

The question before us is whether petitioners fall within the third exception. * * * I assume that petitioners, who were initially appointed to their positions by the Governor of Missouri, are "appointed" rather than "elected" within the meaning of the ADEA. For the reasons below, I also conclude that petitioners are "on the policymaking level."

"Policy" is defined as "a definite course or method of action selected (as by a government, institution, group, or individual) from among alternatives and in the light of given conditions to guide and usu[ally] determine present and future decisions." Webster's Third New International Dictionary 1754 (1976). Applying that definition, it is clear that the decisionmaking engaged in by common-law judges, such as petitioners, places them "on the policymaking level." In resolving disputes, although judges do not operate with unconstrained discretion, they do choose "from among alternatives" and elaborate their choices in order "to guide and . . . determine present and future decisions." * * *

Moreover, it should be remembered that the statutory exception refers to appointees "on the policymaking level," not "policymaking employees." Thus, whether or not judges actually *make* policy, they certainly are on the same *level* as policymaking officials in other branches of government and therefore are covered by the exception. * * *

Petitioners argue that the "appointee[s] on the policymaking level" exception should be construed to apply "only to persons who advise or work closely with the elected official that chose the appointee." In support of that claim, petitioners point out that the exception is "sandwiched" between the "personal staff" and "immediate adviser" exceptions in § 630(f), and thus should be read as covering only similar employees.

Petitioners' premise, however, does not prove their conclusion. It is true that the placement of the "appointee" exception between the "personal staff" and "immediate adviser" exceptions suggests a similarity among the three. But the most obvious similarity is simply that each of the three sets of employees are connected in some way with elected officials: The first and third sets have a certain working relationship with elected officials, while the second is *appointed* by elected officials. There is no textual support for concluding that the second set must *also* have a close working relationship with elected officials. Indeed, such a reading would tend to make the "appointee" exception superfluous since the "personal staff" and "immediate adviser" exceptions would seem to cover most appointees who are in a close working relationship with elected officials.

* * * I would hold that petitioners are excluded from the coverage of the ADEA because they are "appointee[s] on the policymaking level" under 29 U.S.C. § 630(f).

[JUSTICE BLACKMUN, joined by JUSTICE MARSHALL, dissented. They agreed with JUSTICE WHITE that the Court's clear statement rule was unwarranted, but would have concluded that state judges did not fall within the exclusion in section 630(f) for "appointee[s] on the policymaking level."]

---

## Points for Discussion

### *a. The Federalism Clear-Statement Rule*

The Court in *Gregory* declined to read the ADEA to protect the plaintiffs because the statute did not "plainly cover" appointed state judges. The Court thus invoked a substantive canon of construction called the **federalism clear-statement rule**. The rule operates as a substantive canon because it is not based on how we ordinarily understand language. (Indeed, we don't usually insist on such a high standard of clarity before we are willing to assign a particular meaning to text.) The canon is designed to advance federalism goals, and specifically to protect state prerogatives, by limiting the occasions when courts will find that Congress has regulated the states or state functions.

When does the Court's clear-statement rule apply? Does it apply whenever Congress seeks to regulate state employees in the same fashion that it regulates private employees? Only in cases that involve "the authority of the people of the States to determine the qualifications of their government officials"? Or anytime that a federal statute, if read expansively, would "upset the usual constitutional balance of federal and state powers" by regulating the manner in which the state chooses to organize itself? If it applies anytime a federal statute would upset the usual balance of powers, how can we recognize when such a federal statute has such an effect?

### b. *Other Federalism Canons*

The clear-statement rule in *Gregory* is one of several substantive canons of construction that seek to advance federalism goals. First, in *Bass v. United States*, 404 U.S. 336 (1971), which we considered earlier in this Chapter, the Court relied on a canon that holds that, "unless Congress conveys its purpose clearly, it will not be deemed to have significantly changed the federal-state balance." Under this canon, courts will narrowly construe a federal statute that does not regulate the states, but instead regulates conduct historically regulated by state law.

Second, courts often declare that they will not lightly find that a federal statute preempts state regulatory schemes in areas of traditional state responsibility. In *Cippilone v. Liggett Group, Inc.*, 505 U.S. 504 (1992), for example, the Court invoked a "presumption against the pre-emption of state police power regulations." See also *Rice v. Santa Fe Elevator Corp.*, 331 U.S. 218, 237 (1947) (stating that in "ambiguous situations * * * we have refused to hold that state regulation was superseded by a federal law.").

Third, the Court has applied a clear-statement rule in cases involving congressional attempts to abrogate the states' immunity from suit. Courts have interpreted the Eleventh Amendment of the Constitution and background principles implicit in the constitutional scheme to confer on states an immunity from suit in state and federal court. See, e.g., *Alden v. Maine*, 527 U.S. 706 (1999). But the Supreme Court has also recognized that, under limited circumstances, Congress has power to abrogate, or override, that immunity in certain suits seeking relief from the states. See, e.g., *Fitzpatrick v. Bitzer*, 427 U.S. 445 (1976) (holding that Congress has power pursuant to Section 5 of the Fourteenth Amendment to abrogate state sovereign immunity). The Court has held, however, that it will not conclude that Congress exercised that power unless Congress "mak[es] its intention unmistakably clear in the language of the statute." *Kimel v. Florida Bd. of Regents*, 528 U.S. 62, 73 (2000). This standard requires even greater clarity than the other clear-statement rules described above; the Court has stated that Congress must "unequivocally express its intention" to abrogate the states' immunity in the text of the statute. *Atascadero State Hosp. v. Scanlon*, 473 U.S. 234, 242 (1985).

### c. *Semantic Canons and Substantive Canons*

In his concurring opinion in *Gregory*, Justice White asserted that the Court could have reached the same conclusion by applying ordinary rules of statutory interpretation, including semantic canons, without the need to invoke a new substantive canon of construction. Should courts rely on substantive canons to avoid disfavored results when straightforward textual approaches would also avoid those results?

Why do you think the Court felt the need to announce a new substantive canon of construction in *Gregory*?

---

## 6. Review and Assessing the Canons

### Problem

In the early 1970s, the Maryland legislature authorized a public works project with two components. The first part of the project entailed the dredging of material from the bottom of Baltimore Harbor in order to increase the depth of the harbor. The second part of the project involved depositing the dredged material between Hart Island and Miller Island in the Chesapeake Bay. The net effect of the second part of the project would be to link the two islands, thereby creating one larger island at the site.

Section 9 of the Rivers and Harbors Act of 1899, codified at 33 U.S.C. § 401, states that "[i]t shall not be lawful to construct or commence the construction of any bridge, dam, dike, or causeway over or in [any] navigable water of the United States until the consent of Congress to the building of such structures shall have been obtained * * *." Section 10 of the Act, codified at 33 U.S.C. § 403, states that "it shall not be lawful to build or commence the building of any wharf, pier, dolphin, boom, weir, breakwater, bulkhead, jetty, or other structures in [any] navigable [water] of the United States, * * * except on plans recommended by the Chief of [the United States Army Corps of] Engineers * * *."

In 1972, the Maryland Department of Public Works applied to the U.S. Army Corps of Engineers ("the Corps") for a permit pursuant to Section 10 of the Act to construct a "diked dredge spoil disposal area" on and adjacent to Hart and Miller Islands. After holding a hearing about the environmental impact of the project, the Corps granted the permit. Environmentalists sued, seeking an injunction to prevent work on the second part of the project. The plaintiffs contended that only Congress could authorize the second part of the project, and that, because the State had not obtained Congress's consent, the project could not proceed.

How should the court rule? In thinking about the question, pay particular attention to the canons of construction on which the parties would be likely to rely.*

---

* This problem is based on a classroom exercise that my colleague Joshua Schwartz created and graciously gave me permission to use here. —*Ed.*

---

There is a long-running debate over the utility of the canons of construction. Karl Llewelyn mocked the canons as " 'correct,' unchallengeable rules of 'how to read' which lead in happily variant directions." He noted that "the accepted convention still unhappily requires discussion as if only one single correct meaning [of a statute] could exist. Hence there are two opposing canons on almost every point. * * * Every lawyer must be familiar with them all: they are still needed tools of argument. * * * Plainly, to make any canon take hold in a particular instance, the construction contended for must be sold, essentially, by means other than the use of the canon." Karl Llewellyn, *Remarks on the Theory of Appellate Decision and the Rules or Canons About How Statutes are to Construed*, 3 VAND. L. REV. 395, 399, 401 (1950).

Llewelyn then famously provided a series of "thrust[s]"—familiar canons or maxims of statutory interpretation—and corresponding "parr[ies]"—different or competing canons or maxims of interpretation that point in the opposite direction. Below are some of his examples of competing canons that advocates on opposite sides of a dispute could invoke to advance their preferred reading of the statute in question.** Can you recall cases in which judges relied on the thrusts and parries that Llewellyn identified?

| THRUST | BUT | PARRY |
|---|---|---|
| Titles do not control meaning; preambles do not expand scope; section headings do not change language. | | The title may be consulted as a guide when there is doubt or obscurity in the body; preambles may be consulted to determine rationale, and thus the true construction of terms; section headings may be looked upon as part of the statute itself. |
| If language is plain and unambiguous it must be given effect. | | Not when literal interpretation would lead to absurd or mischievous consequences or thwart manifest purpose. |
| Words are to be taken in their ordinary meaning unless they are technical terms or words of art. | | Popular words may bear a technical meaning and technical words may have a popular signification and they should be so construed as to agree with evident intention or to make the statute operative. |
| The same language used repeatedly in the same connection is presumed to bear the same meaning throughout the statute. | | This presumption will be disregarded where it is necessary to assign different meanings to make the statute consistent. |

---

** This excerpt is re-printed with the permission of the Vanderbilt Law Review.

| THRUST | BUT | PARRY |
|---|---|---|
| Expression of one thing excludes another. | | The language may fairly comprehend many different cases where some only are expressly mentioned by way of example. |
| Qualifying or limiting words or clauses are to be referred to the next preceding antecedent. | | Not when evident sense and meaning require a different construction. |

Years later, Justice Scalia and his co-author Bryan Garner responded to Llewellyn's criticism of the canons. They argued that reliance on canons of construction "will curb—even reverse—the tendency of judges to imbue authoritative texts with their own policy preferences" and "provide greater certainty in the law, and hence greater predictability and greater respect for the rule of law." ANTONIN SCALIA AND BRYAN GARNER, READING LAW: THE INTERPRETATION OF LEGAL TEXTS xxvii–xxix (2012).

Now that you have seen a variety of canons of construction and maxims of statutory interpretation, do you think that they are likely to be useful tools in interpreting statutes? Or do you think instead that they are simply manipulable tools for judges to use to justify results that they otherwise want to reach?

**Test Your Knowledge**

To assess your understanding of the material in this Chapter, click here to take a quiz.

## CHAPTER FOUR

# *Legislative History*

As we've seen, there remains considerable debate over the appropriate touchstone for statutory interpretation. A related question, which we have touched on only obliquely, is what evidence is appropriate for courts to consider when seeking to determine the meaning of a statute.

For example, some judges rely on dictionaries to ascertain the ordinary meaning of statutory text. In other cases, judges have looked at background norms to understand the scope of a statute—such as when the court in *Riggs v. Palmer* considered the common-law rule prohibiting a person from profiting from his wrongs, or when the Court in *Church of the Holy Trinity v. United States* considered the nation's commitment to religious liberty. In still other cases, judges have looked at the context for the legislature's enactment of the statute, such as when the court in *People ex rel. Fyfe v. Barnett* considered the population qualified to vote when the legislature enacted a statute governing eligibility for jury service.

**Make the Connection**

We considered *Riggs*, *Church of the Holy Trinity*, *Fyfe*, *Hill*, and *General Dynamics Land Systems* in Chapter 2.

In this Chapter, we consider another source of evidence of statutory meaning: legislative history. We have already seen several cases in which judges have considered legislative history. For example, in *Church of the Holy Trinity*, the Court considered a Senate committee report in concluding that Congress did not intend to prohibit labor contracts with ministers. Similarly, in *Tennessee Valley Authority v. Hill*, the Court looked at the legislative history of the Endangered Species Act to confirm its view of the statute's plain meaning. And in *General Dynamics Land Systems v. Cline*, the Court considered testimony presented at hearings before the congressional committees that drafted the ADEA to determine the meaning of the word "age" in the statute.

In this Chapter, we will consider two principal sets of questions about legislative history. First, is it ever appropriate for courts to consider legislative history when interpreting a statute? Second, if so, which kinds of legislative history are likely to provide the best evidence of statutory meaning?

Before we proceed any further, it helps to clarify our terminology. When courts speak of "legislative history," they are referring to the record of a bill's progress through the legislative process. For example, the sponsor of a bill might make a statement on the floor when introducing the bill; the committee that marks up the bill and sends it to the full body for consideration might issue a report; the members might make statements for or against the bill during the floor debate; and a conference committee might issue a report when the House and Senate have to reconcile competing versions of the bill.

Legislative history is different from statutory history, though the two are related. When we speak of "statutory history," we are usually referring to the evolution of statutory law over time. For example, imagine that Congress enacts a law in 1965. Over time, it becomes clear that the statute has failed to cover an important facet of the problem that Congress had set out to address. In response, Congress in 1982 enacts a new law that amends the 1965 law. A court seeking to ascertain the meaning of the 1982 enactment might consider this statutory evolution. This is, more or less, what happened in *Chishom v. Roemer*, which we considered in Chapter 2. In that case, the Court sought to determine the meaning of an amendment to the Voting Rights Act. In conducting its inquiry, the Court considered the meaning of the amendment in light of the problems with the original provision and the Court's interpretations of that provision.

It is not difficult to see why there is little controversy over reliance on statutory history as evidence of statutory meaning. Even judges who focus exclusively on textual meaning consider the context in which the legislature adopted the statutory language, in order to understand the sense in which the legislature used the terms. For example, in *West Virginia University Hospitals v. Casey*, which we considered in Chapter 2, both Justices Scalia and Stevens relied on statutory history, even though they disagreed about the ultimate meaning of the statutory language.

But there is considerable debate over whether judges should consult legislative history when they interpret statutes. We will consider that debate and then turn to how, assuming it is appropriate, judges consult legislative history in practice.

---

## A. Should Judges Consult Legislative History?

In Chapter 2, we considered the various touchstones of interpretation. Recall that some judges interpret statutes by focusing on legislative intent. In *Tennessee Valley Authority v. Hill*, 437 U.S. 153 (1978), for example, Justice Powell asserted in dissent that Congress had not intended to bar construction of the Tellico Dam project. In making that argument, he pointed to evidence that members of Congress had specifically considered and rejected the claim that the Endangered Species Act prohibited continued progress on the project. When judges focus on legislative intent, they generally seek evidence of the legislature's actual, specific intentions.

Other judges focus on statutory purpose. As we saw in Chapter 2, a focus on statutory purpose considers whether the view of the statute urged by a party comports with the general objectives that motivated the legislature to enact the statute in the first place. In *Bob Jones University v. United States*, 461 U.S. 574 (1983), for example, the Court went "beyond the literal language" of the statute because it thought that "reliance on that language would defeat the plain purpose of the statute," which was that only genuinely charitable organizations—those that were operated consistent with the public interest—were entitled to a tax exemption.

It is not difficult to see why a judge who seeks to interpret a statute by discerning the legislators' specific intentions or general animating purposes would consult the statute's legislative history. After all, the legislative history might contain a discussion of the legislature's views about the precise issue before the court, or an explanation of the reasons why the legislature enacted the statute in the first place. Judges who focus on legislative intent or purpose accordingly often are willing to consult legislative history to inform their understanding of a statute's meaning.

But we also saw that some judges believe that the ordinary or plain meaning of the text should be the focus, and perhaps even the only legitimate touchstone, of interpretation. For example, in *Caminetti v. United States*, 242 U.S. 470 (1917), the Court declared that "the meaning of a statute must, in the first instance, be sought in the language in which the act is framed, and if that is plain, and if the law is within the constitutional authority of the lawmaking body which passed it, the sole function of the courts is to enforce it according to its terms." At a minimum, we can expect a judge who takes this view to be considerably less inclined to consider legislative history in seeking to determine statutory meaning. After all, if the legislature's specific intent or broad, animating purposes are irrelevant in statutory interpretation, or at least presumptively irrelevant, then there is less reason to consult material that might reveal such intentions or purposes.

To be sure, it's possible for legislative history to reveal that members of Congress used a particular term in a specific or technical way, rather than according to its ordinary meaning. See, e.g., *Green v. Bock Laundry Machine Co.*, 490 U.S. 504, 527 (1989) (Scalia, J., concurring in the judgment) ("I think it entirely appropriate to consult all public materials, including the background of Rule 609(a)(1) and the legislative history of its adoption, to verify that what seems to us an unthinkable disposition * * * was indeed unthought of, and thus to justify a departure from the ordinary meaning of the [text of] the Rule."). But for the most part, if one believes that the plain meaning of statutory text should be the sole guide to the meaning of a statute, then it naturally follows that one should generally avoid consulting legislative history to determine the meaning of the statute. Justice Scalia advanced this view in *West Virginia University Hospitals v. Casey*, 499 U.S. 83 (1991). He declared: "Where [a statute] contains a phrase that is unambiguous—that has a clearly accepted meaning in both legislative and judicial practice—we do not permit it to be expanded or contracted by the statements of individual legislators or committees during the course of the enactment process."

In other words, one's choice of interpretive touchstone is highly predictive of one's willingness to consult legislative history. A person who focuses on intent or purpose—and thus starts from the premise that statutory meaning might not be perfectly reflected in the text—is, not surprisingly, substantially more likely to consider legislative history to inform her understanding of the statute's meaning than is a person who focuses on the ordinary meaning of the text.

As we saw in Chapter 2, those who believe that the ordinary meaning of the text should be the touchstone for statutory meaning are usually called "textualists." Although the term is relatively new, Justice Holmes summed up the approach when he wrote: "We do not inquire what the legislature meant; we ask only what the statute means." OLIVER WENDELL HOLMES, COLLECTED LEGAL PAPERS 207 (1920). As Justice Scalia explained, his textualism led him to "object to the use of legislative history in principle, since [he] reject[ed] the intent of the legislature as the proper criterion of the law." Antonin Scalia, *Common-Law Courts in a Civil-Law System: The Role of United States Federal Courts in Interpreting the Constitution and Laws*, in A MATTER OF INTERPRETATION 31 (Amy Gutmann ed., 1998).

But people who focus on the ordinary meaning of text have gone further than simply arguing that legislative history is irrelevant in a proper inquiry about statutory meaning; they have argued that it is usually *illegitimate* for judges to rely on legislative history in determining statutory meaning. For example, Justice Scalia argued that reliance on legislative history "does not even make sense for those who *accept* legislative intent as the criterion." *Id.* at 31–32. First, even assuming that there is such a thing as an identifiable legislative intent—something that Justice Scalia would not concede—he argued that it is unrealistic to imagine that most members of Congress would be aware of a statement made on the floor or in a committee report, let alone that such statements are representative of the views of a majority of the members. *Id.* at 32. Justice Scalia also contended that "the more courts have relied on legislative history, the less worthy of reliance it has become," because "[o]ne of the routine tasks of the Washington lawyer-lobbyist is to draft language that sympathetic legislators can recite in a prewritten 'floor debate'—or, even better, insert into a committee report." *Id.* at 34.

Second, he argued that reliance on legislative history has "facilitated rather than deterred decisions that are based upon the courts' policy preferences, rather than neutral principles of law." *Id.* at 35. He noted that "[i]n any major piece of legislation, the legislative history is extensive, and there is something for everybody. As Judge Harold Leventhal used to say, the trick is to look over the heads of the crowd and pick out your friends. The variety and specificity of result that legislative history can achieve is unparalleled." *Id.* at 36; see also Patricia M. Wald, *Some Observations on the Use of Legislative History in the 1981 Supreme Court Term*, 68 IOWA L. REV. 195, 214 (1983).

But Justice Scalia went beyond simply arguing that reliance on legislative history is misguided; he suggested that it is unconstitutional. He explained:

> " 'All legislative Powers herein granted,' the Constitution says, 'shall be vested in a Congress of the United States, which shall consist of a Senate and House of Representatives.' The legislative power is the power to make laws, not the power to make legislators. It is nondelegable. Congress can no more authorize one committee to 'fill in the details' of a particular law in a binding fashion than it can authorize a committee to enact minor laws. Whatever Congress has not *itself* prescribed is left to be resolved by the executive or (ultimately) the judicial branch. That is the very essence of the separation of powers."

*Common-Law Courts* at 35.

Other textualist scholars have elaborated on this challenge to the use of legislative history in statutory interpretation. Consider the views that follow.

---

## Perspective and Analysis

The prevailing approach to the use of legislative history—which permits the use of almost any available legislative history to discern the legislative intent—has been criticized as circumventing the constitutional enactment process, making it difficult for private citizens to plan their conduct in accordance with positive law, and admitting unreliable evidence of actual legislative intent. These criticisms do more than simply attack certain uses of legislative history. They illustrate the shortcomings of the intent theory of statutory interpretation, or, at least, one of the most widely held versions of that theory. If one recognizes that the proper goal of statutory interpretation is to ascertain the actual meaning of textual language, rather than the meaning that Congress or a part of Congress intended that language to have, the prevailing approach to the use of legislative history must be re-evaluated.

**Office of Legal Policy, United States Department of Justice, *Using and Misusing Legislative History: A Re-Evaluation of the Status of Legislative History in Statutory Interpretation* iii (January 5, 1989).**

---

## Perspective and Analysis

[T]extualists have predicated their resistance to [the] use of legislative history on two important premises, one resting on a hypothesis about legislative behavior and a second rooted in constitutional structure. First, textualist judges argue that a 535-member legislature has no "genuine" collective intent with respect to matters left ambiguous by the statute itself. Even if Congress did have a collective intent, they add, courts act improperly when they equate the views of a committee or sponsor with the intent of the entire Congress and the President. Second, textualists contend that giving decisive weight to legislative history assigns dispositive effect to texts that never cleared the constitutionally mandated process of bicameralism and presentment. Rather than consulting legislative history, textualists maintain that courts should listen for "the ring the words [of a statute] would have had to a skilled user of words at the time, thinking about the same problem." * * *

[But] textualist concerns relating to "genuine" legislative intent and bicameralism and presentment do not alone suffice to explain why textualists reject the interpretive authority of legislative history. Rather, because textualist judges routinely rely on other extrinsic sources of meaning that do not reflect "genuine" legislative intent and have not been enacted by Congress, textualism must rest on a special constitutional injunction against the legislative creation of unenacted interpretive authority. * * * [T]extualism should be understood as a means of implementing a central and increasingly well-settled element of the separation of powers—the prohibition against legislative self-delegation. Viewed in that light, textualism functions to preserve the integrity of the legislative process by stripping congressional agents of the authority to resolve vague and ambiguous texts of Congress's own making.

**John F. Manning, *Textualism as a Non-Delegation Doctrine*, 97 COLUM. L. REV. 673, 674–675 (1997).**

---

Notwithstanding the textualist critique, many judges and scholars defend the use of legislative history in statutory interpretation. First and foremost, as noted above, if one is persuaded that courts should seek to enforce the legislature's intent or broad purposes—and that those intentions and purposes are not always captured by the language that the legislature used—then the use of legislative history is considerably less problematic.

The defense of the use of legislative history is also in part historical. As William Eskridge has observed, "Nothing in the Constitution itself directly indicates the method the Court must follow when it interprets federal statutes, and the practice in the eighteenth century was not to limit a court's consideration to the plain meaning of the statutory text (even as supplemented by the whole statute or other statutes)." William N. Eskridge, Jr., *The New Textualism*, 37 UCLA L. REV. 621, 670 (1990).

Critics of the textualist approach have also questioned Justice Scalia's assertion that a prohibition on consideration of legislative history is likely to constrain judges. Professor Eskridge notes:

> "[I]t is mildly counterintuitive that an approach asking a court to consider materials generated by the legislative process, in addition to statutory text (also generated by the legislative process), canons of construction (generated by the judicial process), and statutory precedents (also generated by the judicial process), leaves the court with *more* discretion than an approach that just considers the latter three sources. Frankly, a result-oriented jurist will refuse to be constrained under any approach, and a modest and diligent jurist will be constrained under either the new textualism or the traditional approach. * * * Justice Scalia considers a great deal of context, and the context he emphasizes is just as manipulable as the context emphasized by the traditional approach. That is, Justice Scalia's approach requires choices among competing evidence just as much as the traditional approach does. Furthermore, he potentially expands upon the judge's range of discretion by his revival of the notoriously numerous and manipulable canons of construction. * * *"

*Id.* at 674–75.

Defenders of reliance on legislative history have also rejected textualists' claim that collective legislative intent is an unknowable fiction. Consider then-Judge Breyer's view.

---

## Perspective and Analysis

Critics sometimes argue that the use of legislative history depends upon a mistaken belief that behind every statute lies a congressional "intent." Congressional intent, they say, is a myth; some say that the concept itself lacks intellectual coherence. * * *

Conceptually, however, one can ascribe an "intent" to Congress in enacting the words of a statute if one means "intent" in its, here relevant, sense of "purpose," rather than its sense of "motive." One often ascribes "group" purposes to group actions. A law school raises tuition to obtain money for a new library. A basketball team stalls to run out the clock. A tank corps feints to draw the enemy's troops away from the main front. Obviously, one of the best ways to find out the purpose of an action taken by a group is to ask some of the group's members about it. But, this does not necessarily mean that the group's purposes and the members' motives or purposes must be identical. The members of the group participating in the group activity—indeed, whose actions are necessary conditions for its action—may have different, private

> *motives* for their own actions; but that fact does not necessarily change the proper characterization of the group's purpose. Perhaps several key members of the faculty voted for the tuition increase, not because they cared about the library, but simply in order to please the Dean. Is a better library any the less the object of the *law school's* action? * * *
>
> All this is to say that ascribing purposes to groups and institutions is a complex business, and one that is often difficult to describe abstractly. But that fact does not make such ascriptions improper. In practice, we ascribe purposes to group activities all the time without many practical difficulties. * * * A legislator, for example, may vote for language that the legislator believes will extend a statute of limitations solely to obtain campaign contributions, to gain political support, or to defeat the bill on the floor. Those personal motives, however, do not change the purpose of the bill's language, namely, to extend the limitations period. * * * To refuse to ascribe a "purpose" to Congress in enacting statutory language simply because one cannot find three or four hundred legislators who have claimed it as a personal purpose, is rather like * * * refusing to believe in the existence of Oxford University because one can find only colleges.

**Stephen Breyer, *On the Uses of Legislative History in Interpreting Statutes*, 65 S. CAL. L. REV. 845, 864–66 (1992).**

---

Finally, defenders of the use of legislative history have responded to textualists' claim that a single-minded judicial focus on statutory text will lead Congress to be more conscientious in drafting statutes. (For an example of such a claim, see *Finley v. United States*, 490 U.S. 545, 556 (1989) (Scalia, J.) ("What is of paramount importance is that Congress be able to legislate against a background of clear interpretive rules, so that it may know the effect of the language it adopts.")) Professor Eskridge argues that "[t]he vast majority of the Court's difficult statutory interpretation cases involve statutes whose ambiguity is either the result of deliberate legislative choice to leave conflictual decisions to agencies or the courts, or the result of social or legal developments the most clairvoyant legislators could not have foreseen." As a consequence, "[e]ven if Congress drafted statutes with a sophisticated appreciation of the Court's ground rules, it is doubtful whether clearer rules would improve the drafting process." William N. Eskridge, Jr., *The New Textualism*, 37 UCLA L. REV. 621, 677 (1990).

In addition,

> "for most of [the twentieth] century the Court [told] Congress, 'We shall attend to committee reports, at least.' That has encouraged Congress to develop conventions by which much of the elaboration of statutes—references to judicial decisions ratified or overruled, purposes to be fulfilled, specific issues thought to be resolved—has been put in committee reports rather than in the statutes themselves, where most of it would be

> cumbersome and out-of-place anyway. If the new textualism displaces the traditional approach entirely, it will undermine the expectations of decades of statutory drafting."

*Id.* at 683. Nor have congressional practices meaningfully changed since the textualist revolution reached the federal courts. A recent study of congressional practices concluded that many of the assumptions on which textualists rely in criticizing consideration of legislative history are unfounded:

> "Perhaps most importantly, legislative history was emphatically viewed by almost all of our respondents—Republicans and Democrats, majority and minority—as the most important drafting and interpretive tool apart from text. Our respondents also made clear that the staff- and committee-focused concerns about delegation cannot be limited to legislative history alone, but rather also apply to statutory text: committees are responsible for text and legislative history alike. Nor is it the case that members of Congress—or even their staffs—are more engaged with textual drafting than with legislative history drafting. In fact, many of our respondents said precisely the opposite: members and their staffs focus more on legislative history, while the nonpartisan professional drafters in the Offices of Legislative Counsel focus on text."

Abbe R. Gluck & Lisa Schultz Bressman, *Statutory Interpretation from the Inside—An Empirical Study of Congressional Drafting, Delegation, and the Canons: Part I*, 65 STAN. L. REV. 901, 965–66 (2013).

The debate over the use of legislative history continues in the academy and in the courts. Sometimes the Supreme Court will declare that the statutory text is the only permissible source of statutory meaning, as the Court seemed to do in *Bostock v. Clayton County*, 140 S.Ct. 1731 (2020) ("This Court normally interprets a statute in accord with the ordinary public meaning of its terms at the time of its enactment. After all, only the words on the page constitute the law adopted by Congress and approved by the President. If judges could add to, remodel, update, or detract from old statutory terms inspired only by extratextual sources and our own imaginations, we would risk amending statutes outside the legislative process reserved for the people's representatives."). Other times the Court considers a range of indicators of statutory meaning, including Congress's objectives and the legislative history. See, e.g., *General Dynamics Land Systems v. Cline*, 540 U.S. 581 (2004) (relying on the "setting" of the statutory provision at issue, and concluding that the "prefatory provisions and their legislative history make a case that we think is beyond reasonable doubt" about the meaning of the statute).

In your view, should judges consult legislative history when they interpret statutes? If so, should they always do so, or only sometimes? If the latter, when?

**Make the Connection**

We considered *General Dynamics Land Systems* in Chapter 2. We will consider *Bostock* in Chapter 5.

---

Debates over the use of legislative history are not unique to the United States' legal system. Consider the case that follows and the judges' views on the appropriateness of considering legislative history in the course of statutory interpretation.

---

## *Pepper v. Hart*

1993 AC 593 (House of Lords)

[Malvern College, a private school in Great Britain, operated a "concessionary fees scheme" that entitled employees at the school to send their sons to the school for one-fifth of the tuition charged to parents of other pupils. It was in the school's discretion whether to offer admission to the children of its employees. The school did so in some years when the school had "surplus pupil capacity," which means that the school had not filled all of its seats with full-paying students.

Appellants were teachers and staff at the school. During some of the years when the school had not filled all of its seats, the school offered admission to appellants' sons, and the appellants had paid one-fifth of the normal tuition rate.

Pepper, the Inspector of Taxes, assessed income tax for the employees under the Finance Act of 1976. The Act provided that benefits (including tuition benefits) for employees were subject to tax as income based on the "cash equivalent of the benefit." Section 63 of the Act provided:

> "(1) The cash equivalent of any benefit chargeable to tax * * * is an amount equal to the cost of the benefit, less so much (if any) of it as is made good by the employee to those providing the benefit.
>
> (2) * * * [T]he cost of a benefit is the amount of any expense incurred in or in connection with its provision, and * * * includes a proper proportion of any expense relating partly to the benefit and partly to other matters."

In calculating the tax owed, the government maintained that the "cash equivalent" of the benefit that the employees received was the ordinary price of tuition, minus the 20% that the employees had paid. In the government's view, the "expense incurred in or in connection with" the provision of education for the appellants' children was exactly the same as the expense incurred in or in connection with the education of all other pupils at the school, and that the expense of educating any one child is a proportionate part of the cost of running the whole school.

The employees argued that the cash equivalent of the benefit was simply the *marginal* cost incurred by the employer for educating their children, minus the fees that the employees had paid. Because most of the school's costs—including tuition and maintenance—were fixed, it was undisputed that the concessionary fees that the appellants paid more than covered the additional cost to the school of educating their children. In other words, because the school had not been able to fill all of its seats with students who were not children of employees, the appellants argued that the marginal cost of educating their children was less than the amount that they had paid in tuition. Accordingly, they argued that they had not received a taxable benefit.

An appellate panel of the House of Lords concluded that, under the plain text of the statute, the "cost of the benefit" was the amount that the school could have charged a non-staff child for tuition. A larger panel of the Lords then reheard the case, in part to address whether it was appropriate to consider the legislative history of the statute in resolving the question presented. To do so would require modification of the long-standing "exclusionary rule." Under that rule, courts were prohibited from considering "Hansard," the official report of parliamentary debates, when construing statutes enacted by Parliament. In their decision, the Lords issued their opinions *seriatim*.]

**Definition**

*Seriatim* means "one after another." For the first decade or so after the ratification of the United States Constitution, United States Supreme Court Justices issued opinions *seriatim*. During the tenure of Chief Justice John Marshall, the Court adopted the practice of having one Justice issue an opinion for the Court. The practice of issuing *seriatim* opinions has lasted much longer in Great Britain.

LORD MACKAY OF CLASHFERN [Lord Chancellor].

* * * The benefit which the taxpayers in this case received was the placing of their children in surplus places at the college, if as a matter of discretion the college agreed to do so. * * * They were in a similar position to the person coming along on a standby basis for an airline seat as against the passenger paying a full fare, and without the full rights of a standby passenger, in the sense that the decision whether or not to accommodate them in the college was entirely discretionary. If one regards the benefit in this light I cannot see that the cost incurred in, or in connection with, the provision of the benefit, can properly be held to include the cost incurred, in any event, in providing education to fee paying pupils at the school who were there as a right in return for the fees paid in respect of them. The expenses incurred by the college were all incurred necessarily in order properly to provide for these pupils. No further expense over and above that was incurred in, or in connection with, the provision of surplus places to the taxpayers' children. * * * I conclude that looking at the matter from the point of view of expense incurred and not from the point of view of loss to the employer no expense could be regarded as having been incurred as a result of the decision of the authorities of the college to provide this particular benefit to the taxpayer. * * * At the very least it appears to me that the manner in which I have construed the relevant provisions in their application to the facts in this appeal is a possible construction and that any ambiguity there should be resolved in favour of the taxpayer.

* * * But much wider issues than the construction of the Finance Act 1976 have been raised in these appeals and for the first time this House has been asked to consider a detailed argument upon the extent to which reference can properly be made before a court of law in the United Kingdom to proceedings in Parliament recorded in Hansard.

The principal difficulty I have on this aspect of the case is that [in appellants' view] reference to Parliamentary material as an aid to interpretation of a statutory provision should be allowed only with leave of the court and where the court is satisfied that such a reference is justifiable: (a) to confirm the meaning of a provision as conveyed by the text, its object and purpose; (b) to determine a meaning where the provision is ambiguous or obscure; or (c) to determine the meaning where the ordinary meaning is manifestly absurd or unreasonable.

[The] exception [to the exclusionary rule] presently proposed is so extensive that I do not feel able to support it in the present state of our knowledge of its practical results in this jurisdiction. For these reasons, I agree that these appeals should be allowed, although I cannot agree on the main issue, for the discussion of which this further hearing was arranged.

Lord Keith of Kinkel.

My Lords, for the reasons set out in the speech to be delivered by my noble and learned friend, Lord Browne-Wilkinson, which I have had the opportunity of considering in draft and with which I agree, I would allow this appeal.

Lord Bridge of Harwich.

My Lords, I was one of those who were in the majority at the conclusion of the first hearing of this appeal in holding the opinion that section 63 of the Finance Act 1976, construed by conventional criteria, supported the assessments to income tax made by the revenue on the appellants * * *. If it were not permissible to take account of the Parliamentary history of the relevant legislation and of ministerial statements of its intended effect, I should remain of that opinion. But once the Parliamentary material was brought to our attention, it seemed to me, as, I believe, to others of your Lordships who had heard the appeal first argued, to raise an acute question as to whether it could possibly be right to give effect to taxing legislation in such a way as to impose a tax which the Financial Secretary to the Treasury, during the passage of the Bill containing the relevant provision, had, in effect, assured the House of Commons it was not intended to impose. It was this which led to the appeal being re-argued before the Appellate Committee of seven which now reports to the House.

Following the further arguments of which we have had the benefit, I should find it very difficult, in conscience, to reach a conclusion adverse to the appellants on the basis of a technical rule of construction requiring me to ignore the very material which in this case indicates unequivocally which of the two possible interpretations of section 63(2) of the Act of 1976 was intended by Parliament. But, for all the reasons given by my noble and learned friend, Lord Browne-Wilkinson, with whose speech I entirely agree, I am not placed in that invidious situation.

LORD GRIFFITHS.

My Lords, I have long thought that the time had come to change the self-imposed judicial rule that forbade any reference to the legislative history of an enactment as an aid to its interpretation. The ever increasing volume of legislation must inevitably result in ambiguities of statutory language which are not perceived at the time the legislation is enacted. The object of the court in interpreting legislation is to give effect so far as the language permits to the intention of the legislature. If the language proves to be ambiguous I can see no sound reason not to consult Hansard to see if there is a clear statement of the meaning that the words were intended to carry. The days have long passed when the courts adopted a strict constructionist view of interpretation which required them to adopt the literal meaning of the language. The courts now adopt a purposive approach which seeks to give effect to the true purpose of legislation and are prepared to look at much extraneous material that bears upon the background against which the legislation was enacted. Why then cut ourselves off from the one source in which may be found an authoritative statement of the intention with which the legislation is placed before Parliament? I have had the advantage of reading the speech of Lord Browne-Wilkinson * * *. [I] agree that the courts should have recourse to Hansard in the circumstances and to the extent he proposes.

As to the question of statutory construction I should myself have construed the section in favour of the taxpayer without recourse to Hansard. * * * In my view this case provides a dramatic vindication of the decision to consult Hansard; had your Lordships not agreed to do so the result would have been to place a very heavy burden of taxation upon a large number of persons which Parliament never intended to impose.

LORD ACKNER.

My Lords, I entirely agree that for the reasons set out in the speech of my noble and learned friend, Lord Browne-Wilkinson, which I have had the advantage of reading in draft, this appeal should be allowed.

LORD OLIVER OF AYLMERTON.

My Lords, I have had the advantage of reading in draft the speech prepared by my noble and learned friend, Lord Browne-Wilkinson. I agree with it in its entirety and would, in the ordinary way, be content to do no more than express my concurrence both in the reasoning and in the result. I venture to add a few observations of my own only because I have to confess to having been a somewhat reluctant convert to the notion that the words which Parliament has chosen to use in a statute for the expression of its will may fall to be construed or modified by reference to what individual members of Parliament may have said in the course of debate or discussion preceding the passage of the Bill into law. A statute is, after all, the formal and complete intimation to the citizen of a particular rule of the law which he is enjoined, sometimes under penalty, to obey and by which he is both expected and entitled to regulate his conduct. We must, therefore, I believe, be very cautious in opening the door to the reception of material not readily or ordinarily accessible to the citizen whose rights and duties are to be affected by the words in which the legislature has elected to express its will.

But experience shows that language—and, particularly, language adopted or concurred in under the pressure of a tight Parliamentary timetable—is not always a reliable vehicle for the complete or accurate translation of legislative intention; and I have been persuaded, for the reasons so cogently deployed in the speech of my noble and learned friend, that the circumstances of this case demonstrate that there is both the room and the necessity for a limited relaxation of the previously well-settled rule which excludes reference to Parliamentary history as an aid to statutory construction.

So far as the merits of the instant appeal are concerned, I, like my noble and learned friends, Lord Bridge of Harwich and Lord Browne-Wilkinson, was in favour of dismissing the appeal at the conclusion of the first hearing. Were it not for the material in the reports of Hansard to which your Lordships have been referred, I, too, would still be of that view * * *.

**Food for Thought**

Did the judges agree on the proper touchstone for interpretation? Did it matter, in persuading many of the judges that it is sometimes appropriate to consider legislative history, that judges focusing on the same touchstone of interpretation had come to conflicting conclusions about the meaning of the statute?

LORD BROWNE-WILKINSON.

The case was originally argued before your Lordships without reference to any Parliamentary proceedings. After the conclusion of the first hearing, it came to your Lordships' attention that an examination of the proceedings in Parliament in 1976 which lead to the enactment of [section 63] might give a clear indication which of the two rival contentions represented the intention of Parliament in using the statutory words. * * *

For reasons which will appear it is necessary first to refer to the legislation affecting the taxation of benefits in kind before 1975. Under the Finance Act 1948, section 39(1), directors and employees of bodies corporate earning more than £2,000 per annum were taxed under Schedule E on certain benefits in kind. The amount charged was the expense incurred by the body corporate "in or in connection with the provision" of the benefit in kind. By section 39(6) it was provided that references to expenses "incurred in or in connection with any matter includes a reference to a proper proportion of any expense incurred partly in or in connection with that matter." Employment by a school or charitable organisation was expressly excluded from the charge: sections 41(5) and 44. These provisions were re-enacted in the Income and Corporation Taxes Act 1970.

[A]fter 1948 the [taxing authority] sought to tax at least two categories of employees in receipt of in-house benefits. Higher paid employees of the railways enjoy free or concessionary travel on the railways. The revenue [service] reached an agreement that such employees should be taxed on 20 per cent (later 25 per cent) of the full fare. Airline employees also enjoy concessionary travel. [I]n the 1960s the revenue [service] sought to tax such employees on that benefit on the basis of the average cost to the airline of providing a seat, not merely on the marginal cost. The tax commissioners rejected such claim: the revenue [service] did not appeal. Therefore in practice from 1948 to 1975 the revenue did not seek to extract tax on the basis of the average cost to the employer of providing in-house benefits.

In 1975 the Government proposed a new tax on vouchers provided by an employer to his employees which could be exchanged for goods or services. Clause 33(1) of the Finance (No. 2) Bill 1975 provided that the employee was to be treated, on receipt of a voucher, as having received an emolument from his employment of an amount "equal to the expense incurred by the person providing the voucher in or in connection with the provision of the voucher and the money, goods or services for which it is capable of being exchanged." The statutory wording of the Bill was therefore similar to that in the Act of 1948 and in section 63(2) of the Finance Act 1976. On 1 July 1975 in the Standing Committee on the Bill (Standing Committee H), the Financial Secretary was asked about the impact of the clause on railwaymen. He gave the following answer (Hansard, column 666):

> "Similarly, the railwayman travelling on his normal voucher will not be taxable either. The clause deals with the situation where a number of firms produce incentives of various kinds. In one or two instances, there is likely to be some liability concerning rail vouchers of a special kind, but in general, the position is as I have said and they will not be taxable."

He was then asked to explain why they would not be taxable and replied:

> "Perhaps I can make clear why there is no taxable benefit in kind, because the provision of the service that he provides falls upon the employer. Clearly, the railways will run in precisely the same way whether the railwaymen use this facility or not, so there is no extra charge to the Railways Board itself, therefore there would be no taxable benefits."

Later he explained that by the words "no extra charge" he meant "no extra cost." Clause 33(1) of the Bill was enacted as section 36(1) of the Finance (No. 2) Act 1975.

The Finance Bill 1976 sought to make a general revision of the taxation of benefits in kind. The existing legislation on fringe benefits was to be repealed. Clause 52 of the Bill as introduced eventually became section 61 of the Act of 1976 and imposed a charge to tax on benefits in kind for higher paid employees, i.e., those paid more than £5,000 per annum. Clause 54 of the Bill eventually became section 63 of the Act of 1976. As introduced, clause 54(1) provided that the cash equivalent of any benefit was to be an amount equal to "the cost of the benefit." Clause 54(2) provided that, except as provided in later subsections "the cost of a benefit is the amount of any expense incurred in or in connection with its provision." Crucially, clause 54(4) of the Bill sought to tax in-house benefits on a different basis from that applicable to external benefits. It provided that the cost of a benefit consisting of the provision of any service or facility which was also provided to the public (i.e., in-house benefits) should be the price which the public paid for such facility or service. Employees of schools were not excluded from the new charge.

**Take Note**

By "external benefits," Lord Browne-Wilkinson was referring to benefits purchased from outside the employer's business, such as a car or medical insurance. By "in-house benefits," he was referring to the enjoyment by the employee of services or facilities that it is part of the employer's business to sell to the public, such as when a railroad employee travels for free on the railroad or a teacher sends his child for free to the school at which he works.

Thus if the 1976 Bill had gone through as introduced, railway and airline employees would have been treated as receiving benefits in kind from concessionary travel equal to the open market cost of tickets and schoolmasters would have been taxed for concessionary education on the amount of the normal school fees.

After second reading, clause 52 of the Bill was committed to a committee of the whole House and clause 54 to Standing Committee E. On 17 May 1976, the House considered clause 52 and strong representations were made about the impact of clause 52 on airline and railway employees. At the start of the meeting of Standing Committee E on 17 June 1976 (before clause 54 was being discussed) the Financial Secretary to the Treasury, Mr. Robert Sheldon, made an announcement (Hansard, columns 893–895) in the following terms:

> "The next point I wish to make concerns services and deals with the position of employees of organisations, bodies, or firms which provide services, where the employee is in receipt of those services free or at a reduced rate. Under clause 54(4) the taxable benefit is to be based on the arm's length price of the benefit received. At present the benefit is valued on the cost to the employer. Representations have been made concerning airline travel and railway employees . . . . It was never intended that the benefit received by the airline employee would be the fare paid by the ordinary passenger. The benefit to him would never be as high as that, because of certain disadvantages that the employee has. Similar considerations, although of a different kind,

apply to railway employees. I have had many interviews, discussions and meetings on this matter and I have decided to withdraw clause 54(4). I thought I would mention this at the outset because so many details, which would normally be left until we reach that particular stage, will be discussed with earlier parts of the legislation. I shall give some reasons which weigh heavily in favour of the withdrawal of this provision. The first is the large difference between the cost of providing some services and the amount of benefit which under the Bill would be held to be received. There are a number of cases of this kind, and I would point out that air and rail journeys are only two of a number of service benefits which have a number of problems attached to them. But there is a large difference between the cost of the benefit to the employer and the value of that benefit as assessed. It could lead to unjustifiable situations resulting in a great number of injustices and I do not think we should continue with it . . . .

The second reason for withdrawing clause 54(4) is that these services would tend to be much less used. The problem would then arise for those who had advocated the continuation of this legislation that neither the employer nor the employee nor the Revenue would benefit from the lesser use of these services. This factor also weighed with me. The third reason is the difficulty of enforcement and administration, which both give rise to certain problems. Finally, it was possible to withdraw this part of the legislation as the services cover not only a more difficult area, but a quite distinct area of these provisions, without having repercussions on some of the other areas . . . .

*A member*: I, too, have talked to many airline employees about this matter, and I am not completely clear as to the purport of my Hon. Friend's remarks. Is he saying that these benefits will remain taxable but that the equivalent cost of the benefit will be calculated on some different basis? Or is he saying that these benefits will not be taxable at all?

*Financial Secretary*: The existing law which applies to the taxation of some of these benefits will be retained. The position will subsequently be unchanged from what it is now before the introduction of this legislation."

The Financial Secretary was then asked to elucidate the impact of this on airline employees. At column 930, he is reported as saying:

* * * "What we are withdrawing is the arm's-length valuation of benefit under clause 54(4) where an employer is providing services to the employee at a cost which may be very little. The employee earning more than £5,000 or the director will be assessed on the benefit received by him on the basis of the cost to the employer rather than the price that would generally be charged to the public. That is the position that we have now brought in, as opposed to the original one in the Bill where it would be assessed on the cost to a member of the public. That position now is the same as it stands before this legislation is passed."

After being further pressed, the Financial Secretary said, at column 931:

* * * "Some companies provide services of a kind where the cost to them is very little. For example, an airline ticket, allowing occupation of an empty seat, costs an airline nothing—in fact, in such a case there could be a negative cost, as it might be an advantage to the airline to have an experienced crew member on the flight. The cost

to the company, then, would be nothing, but the benefit assessable under clause 54(4) could be considerable. We are reverting to the existing practice."

Simultaneously with the announcement to the Standing Committee, a press release was issued announcing the withdrawal of clause 54(4). It referred to the same matters as the Financial Secretary had stated to the Committee and concluded:

"The effect of deleting this subclause will be to continue the present basis of taxation of services, namely the cost to the employer of providing the service."

The point was further debated in committee on 22 June 1976. A member is reported as saying, at column 1013, that

"Like many others, I welcome the concession that has been made to leave out the airline staff and the railway employees and all the others that are left out by the dropping of clause 54(4)."

Another member, after referring to the particular reference in the Financial Secretary's statement to airline and railway employees, asked whether the same distinction applied to services provided by hotel companies to their employees—that is, to rooms which are freely available for the general public in hotels being offered at a concessionary rate to employees of the hotel group. In response, the Financial Secretary said of the position of such employees:

"The position is, as he probably expected, the same as that which, following my announcement last week about the withdrawal of clause 54(4), applies to other employees in service industries; the benefit is the cost to the employer. It is a good illustration of one of the reasons why I withdrew this subsection, in that the cost to the employer in this instance could be much less than the arm's-length cost to the outside person taking advantage of such a service." (Column 1024.)

**Take Note**

The legislative history reveals that members of Parliament discussed the very issue raised by the appellants' case. It appears to show, moreover, that the members of Parliament and witnesses who addressed the matter had a clear understanding of how the provision would apply to the issue in the appellants' case. Is there nevertheless an argument that the court should ignore the legislative history? What would a textualist say about how to resolve this case? Do you find that approach satisfying in this case?

The very question which is the subject matter of the present appeal was also raised. A member said, at columns 1091–1092:

"I should be grateful for the Financial Secretary's guidance on [how his view applies] to private sector, fee-paying schools where, as the Financial Secretary knows, there is often an arrangement for the children of staff in these schools to be taught at less than the commercial fee in other schools. I take it that because of the deletion of clause 54(4) that is not now caught. Perhaps these examples will help to clarify the extent to which the Government amendment goes."

The Financial Secretary responded to this question as follows:

> "He mentioned the children of teachers. The removal of clause 54(4) will affect the position of a child of one of the teachers at the child's school, because now the benefit will be assessed on the cost to the employer, which would be very small indeed in this case." (Column 1098.)

Thereafter, clause 54 was not the subject of further debate and passed into law as it now stands as section 63 of the Act. * * *

Under present law, there is a general rule that references to Parliamentary material as an aid to statutory construction is not permissible ("the exclusionary rule"). This rule did not always apply but was judge made. Thus, in *Ash v. Abdy* (1678) 3 Swans. 664, Lord Nottingham took judicial notice of his own experience when introducing the Bill in the House of Lords. The exclusionary rule was probably first stated by Willes J. in *Millar v. Taylor* (1769) 4 Burr. 2303, 2332. However, the case of *In re Mew and Thorne* (1862) 31 L.J.Bank. 87 shows that even in the middle of the last century the rule was not absolute: in that case Lord Westbury L.C. in construing an Act had regard to its Parliamentary history and drew an inference as to Parliament's intention in passing the legislation from the making of an amendment striking out certain words. The exclusionary rule was later extended so as to prohibit the court from looking even at reports made by commissioners on which legislation was based * * *.

[T]he reasons put forward for the present rule are first, that it preserves the constitutional proprieties leaving Parliament to legislate in words and the courts (not Parliamentary speakers), to construe the meaning of the words finally enacted; second, the practical difficulty of the expense of researching Parliamentary material which would arise if the material could be looked at; third, the need for the citizen to have access to a known defined text which regulates his legal rights; fourth, the improbability of finding helpful guidance from Hansard. * * *

My Lords, I have come to the conclusion that, as a matter of law, there are sound reasons for making a limited modification to the existing rule (subject to strict safeguards) * * *. In my judgment, * * * reference to Parliamentary material should be permitted as an aid to the construction of legislation which is ambiguous or obscure or the literal meaning of which leads to an absurdity. Even in such cases references in court to Parliamentary material should only be permitted where such material clearly discloses the mischief aimed at or the legislative intention lying behind the ambiguous or obscure words. In the case of statements made in Parliament, as at present advised I cannot foresee that any statement other than the statement of the Minister or other promoter of the Bill is likely to meet these criteria.

[M]y main reason for reaching this conclusion is based on principle. Statute law consists of the words that Parliament has enacted. It is for the courts to construe those words and it is the court's duty in so doing to give effect to the intention of Parliament in using those words. It is an inescapable fact that, despite all the care taken in passing legislation, some statutory provisions when applied to the circumstances under consideration in any specific case are found to be ambiguous. One of the reasons for such ambiguity is that the members of the legislature in enacting the statutory provision may have been told what result those words are intended to achieve. Faced with a given set of words which are capable of conveying that meaning it is not surprising if the words are accepted as having that meaning. Parliament never intends to enact an ambiguity. Contrast with that the position of the courts. The courts are faced simply with a set of words which are in fact capable of bearing two meanings. The courts are ignorant of the underlying Parliamentary purpose. Unless something in other parts of the legislation discloses such purpose, the courts are forced to adopt one of the two possible meanings using highly technical rules of construction. In many, I suspect most, cases references to Parliamentary materials will not throw any light on the matter. But in a few cases it may emerge that the very question was considered by Parliament in passing the legislation. Why in such a case should the courts blind themselves to a clear indication of what Parliament intended in using those words? The court cannot attach a meaning to words which they cannot bear, but if the words are capable of bearing more than one meaning why should not Parliament's true intention be enforced rather than thwarted?

It is said that Parliamentary materials are not readily available to, and understandable by, the citizen and his lawyers who should be entitled to rely on the words of Parliament alone to discover his position. It is undoubtedly true that Hansard and particularly records of Committee debates are not widely held by libraries outside London and that the lack of satisfactory indexing of Committee stages makes it difficult to trace the passage of a clause after it is redrafted or renumbered. But such practical difficulties can easily be overstated. It is possible to obtain Parliamentary materials and it is possible to trace the history. The problem is one of expense and effort in doing so, not the availability of the material. In considering the right of the individual to know the law by simply looking at legislation, it is a fallacy to start from the position that all legislation is available in a readily understandable form in any event: the very large number of statutory instruments made every year are not available in an indexed form for well over a year after they have been passed. Yet, the practitioner manages to deal with the problem albeit at considerable expense. Moreover, experience in New Zealand and Australia (where the strict rule has been relaxed for some years) has not shown that the non-availability of materials has raised these practical problems.

Next, it is said that lawyers and judges are not familiar with Parliamentary procedures and will therefore have difficulty in giving proper weight to the Parliamentary materials. Although, of course, lawyers do not have the same experience of these matters as members of the legislature, they are not wholly ignorant of them. If, as I think, significance should only be attached to the clear statements made by a Minister or other promoter of the Bill, the difficulty of knowing what weight to attach to such statements is not overwhelming. In the present case, there were numerous statements of view by members in the course of the debate which plainly do not throw any light on the true construction of section 63. What is persuasive in this case is a consistent series of answers given by the Minister, after opportunities for taking advice from his officials, all of which point the same way and which were not withdrawn or varied prior to the enactment of the Bill.

Then it is said that court time will be taken up by considering a mass of Parliamentary material and long arguments about its significance, thereby increasing the expense of litigation. In my judgment, though the introduction of further admissible material will inevitably involve some increase in the use of time, this will not be significant as long as courts insist that Parliamentary material should only be introduced in the limited cases I have mentioned and where such material contains a clear indication from the Minister of the mischief aimed at, or the nature of the cure intended, by the legislation. Attempts to introduce material which does not satisfy those tests should be met by orders for costs made against those who have improperly introduced the material. Experience in the United States of America, where legislative history has for many years been much more generally admissible than I am now suggesting, shows how important it is to maintain strict control over the use of such material. That position is to be contrasted with what has happened in New Zealand and Australia (which have relaxed the rule to approximately the extent that I favour): there is no evidence of any complaints of this nature coming from those countries.

In sum, I do not think that the practical difficulties arising from a limited relaxation of the rule are sufficient to outweigh the basic need for the courts to give effect to the words enacted by Parliament in the sense that they were intended by Parliament to bear. Courts are frequently criticised for their failure to do that. This failure is due not to cussedness but to ignorance of what Parliament intended by the obscure words of the legislation. The courts should not deny themselves the light which Parliamentary materials may shed on the meaning of the words Parliament has used and thereby risk subjecting the individual to a law which Parliament never intended to enact.

The Attorney-General [argues] that for the court to use Parliamentary material in construing legislation would be to confuse the respective roles of Parliament as the maker of law and the courts as the interpreter. I am not impressed by this argument. The law, as I have said, is to be found in the words in which Parliament has enacted. It is for the courts to interpret those words so as to give effect to that purpose. The question is whether, in addition to other aids to the construction of statutory words, the courts should have regard to a further source. * * * I can see no constitutional impropriety in this.

I therefore reach the conclusion, subject to any question of Parliamentary privilege, that the exclusionary rule should be relaxed so as to permit reference to Parliamentary materials where (a) legislation is ambiguous or obscure, or leads to an absurdity; (b) the material relied upon consists of one or more statements by a

Minister or other promoter of the Bill together if necessary with such other Parliamentary material as is necessary to understand such statements and their effect; (c) the statements relied upon are clear.

I have no hesitation in holding that [section 63 is ambiguous]. The "expense incurred in or in connection with" the provision of in-house benefits may be either the marginal cost caused by the provision of the benefit in question or a proportion of the total cost incurred in providing the service both for the public and for the employee ("the average cost").

The 1976 Finance Bill as introduced proposed to charge in-house benefits on a different basis from that applicable to external benefits, i.e., on the open market price charged to the public * * *. Once the Government announced its intention to withdraw clause 54(4) a number of Members were anxious to elucidate what effect this would have on classes of taxpayers who enjoyed in-house benefits * * *. In answer to these inquiries the Financial Secretary [stated] that in all the cases (except that of the teachers' concessionary education) that the benefits would be taxed on the same basis as under the existing law and (2) that in all cases the amount of the charge would be nil, small or, in the case of the schoolteachers, "very small indeed." In my view these repeated assurances are quite inconsistent with the Minister having had, or communicated, any intention other than that the words "the expense incurred in or in connection with" the provision of the benefit would produce a charge to tax on the additional or marginal cost only, not a charge on the average cost of the benefit.

The question then arises whether it is right to attribute to Parliament as a whole the same intention as that repeatedly voiced by the Financial Secretary. In my judgment it is. It is clear from reading Hansard that the Committee was repeatedly asking for guidance as to the effect of the legislation once subclause (4) of clause 54 was abandoned. That Parliament relied on the ministerial statements is shown by the fact that the matter was never raised again after the discussions in Committee, that amendments were consequentially withdrawn and that no relevant amendment was made which could affect the correctness of the Minister's statement.

Accordingly, in my judgment we have in this case a clear statement by the responsible Minister stating the effect of the ambiguous words used in what became section 63 of the Act of 1976 which the Parliamentary history shows to have been the basis on which that section was enacted.

[T]he Parliamentary history shows that Parliament passed the legislation on the basis that the effect of sections 61 and 63 of the Act was to assess in-house benefits, and particularly concessionary education for teachers' children, on the marginal cost to the employer and not on the average cost. Since the words of section 63 are perfectly capable of bearing that meaning, in my judgment that is the meaning they should be given.

---

## Points for Discussion

### *a. Touchstones of Interpretation in the United Kingdom*

The approach from which the Court in *Pepper* departed—called the "exclusionary rule"—prohibited judges from consulting legislative history in seeking to determine the meaning of statutes enacted by Parliament. As some of the judges explained, the rule was based in part on the assumption that a court's task in construing legislation is to determine the plain meaning of the statutory text. According to the various opinions, what were the justifications for focusing on that touchstone in the United Kingdom? Are they the same justifications that textualists in the United States advance to defend a focus on statutory text?

There are also multiple references in the various opinions to the Parliament's intent and purpose. What were the judges' understandings of the relationship between statutory text and legislative intent or purpose?

Why did the Court in *Pepper* depart from the long-standing prohibition on consideration of legislative history? Was it because the Court no longer treated the ordinary meaning of statutory text as the appropriate touchstone? Or was it because of changing views about the utility of legislative history? Notice that the courts in the United Kingdom have followed more or less the opposite trajectory as those in the United States, where a traditional focus on legislative intent and purpose has increasingly been challenged by those urging a focus on textual meaning.

### *b. Limits on the Use of Legislative History*

According to the court in *Pepper*, when is it appropriate for a British court to consult legislative history? Would it make sense to impose those limits on the use of legislative history in the United States, as well? If legislative history can clarify legislative intent, as several of the judges concluded, then why wouldn't they be willing to consult it in all cases involving questions about the meaning of a statute?

---

## B. Using Legislative History as a Source of Statutory Meaning

For better or worse, the Supreme Court has never accepted the view that courts should categorically disregard legislative history when construing statutes. As a consequence, we must address a second set of questions: when and how should courts use legislative history?

In thinking about these questions, it is useful to recall the federal legislative process, which we considered in Chapter 1. To be enacted into law, a bill must successfully pass both the House and the Senate. In the House, a member introduces a bill; the bill is usually referred to one or more committees, and often a sub-committee, as well; the bill is subject to hearings and revision before those committees; the bill that emerges from the committee process is subject to a "rule" governing debate; and the Members then debate the bill on the floor before a vote. The process is similar in the Senate, where a Member introduces the bill, which is then usually referred to a committee for hearings and mark-up; the bill is subject to debate and sometimes cloture; and then ultimately the bill is the subject of a floor debate and a vote. If the two houses pass bills that are not identical, then they often use a conference to produce a compromise bill, which both houses then consider without amendment.

Legislative history can be produced at each one of these stages in the legislative process, and judges who are open to reliance on legislative history as evidence of statutory meaning are generally willing to cite legislative history from any of these stages. Consider the opinions in *Tennessee Valley Authority v. Hill*, 437 U.S. 153 (1978), which we considered in Chapter 2. In his opinion for the Court, Chief Justice Burger relied on many different sources of legislative history.

As noted above, it is common for a committee in each chamber to hold hearings on a bill, to inform the members about the subject and to explain the justification for the bill's approach. In recent years, committees in both chambers have made video and audio from hearings available on their websites. In addition, the Government Publishing Office publishes transcripts of committee hearings.

**IMPLEMENTATION OF THE NO CHILD LEFT BEHIND ACT**

# HEARING

BEFORE THE

COMMITTEE ON EDUCATION AND THE WORKFORCE

HOUSE OF REPRESENTATIVES

ONE HUNDRED SEVENTH CONGRESS

SECOND SESSION

HEARING HELD IN WASHINGTON, DC, JULY 24, 2002

**Serial No. 107-75**

Printed for the use of the Committee on Education and the Workforce

86-210 pdf

For sale by the Superintendent of Documents, U.S. Government Printing Office
Internet: bookstore.gpo.gov Phone: toll free (866) 512-1800; DC area (202) 512-1800
FAX: (202) 512-2250 Mail: Stop SSOP, Washington, DC 20402-0001

In his opinion for the Court in *Hill*, Chief Justice Burger cited testimony by witnesses before a House committee to support an argument about the reasons why Congress enacted the Endangered Species Act:

> "By 1973, when Congress held hearings on what would later become the Endangered Species Act of 1973, it was informed that species were still being lost at the rate of about one per year, 1973 House Hearings 306 (statement of Stephen R. Seater, for Defenders of Wildlife) * * *. Moreover, Congress was also told that the primary cause of this trend was something other than the normal process of natural selection: '[M]an and his technology [have] continued at any ever-increasing rate to disrupt the natural ecosystem. * * *' 1973 House Hearings 202 (statement of Assistant Secretary of the Interior)."

Chief Justice Burger also cited witness testimony to demonstrate that Congress intended to expand protections for endangered species by ensuring that agency priorities would not prevail over such protections. He wrote:

> "A representative of the Sierra Club, for example, attacked the use of the phrase 'consistent with the primary purpose' in proposed H.R. 4758, cautioning that the qualification 'could be construed to be a declaration of congressional policy that other agency purposes are necessarily more important than protection of endangered species and would always prevail if conflict were to occur.' 1973 House Hearings 335 (statement of the chairman of the Sierra Club's National Wildlife Committee); see *id.*, at 251 (statement for the National Audubon Society)."

Chief Justice Burger also cited testimony from a hearing before a subcommittee of the Senate Committee on Commerce to demonstrate Congress's intent to bar federal agency action that threatens endangered species. His opinion stated:

> "Virtually every bill introduced in Congress during the 1973 session responded to this concern by incorporating language similar, if not identical, to that found in the present § 7 of the Act. These provisions were designed, in the words of an administration witness, 'for the first time [to] *prohibit* [a] federal agency from taking action which does jeopardize the status of endangered species,' Hearings on S. 1592 and S. 1983 before the Subcommittee on Environment of the Senate Committee on Commerce, 93d Cong., 1st Sess., 68 (1973) (statement of Deputy Assistant Secretary of the Interior) (emphasis added) * * *.

House and Senate committees usually publish a report to accompany their decision to send a bill to the full chamber for consideration. The report describes the bill, its provisions, the ways that the original proposal changed during the course of committee consideration, and the committee's reasoning in advancing the bill. Committee reports also often include a description of the committee's understanding about how the bill would apply in a range of circumstances.

| 116TH CONGRESS<br>*2d Session* | HOUSE OF REPRESENTATIVES | REPORT<br>116–669 |
|---|---|---|

# DATA PRESERVATION ACT OF 2020

DECEMBER 18, 2020.—Committed to the Committee of the Whole House on the State of the Union and ordered to be printed

Mr. GRIJALVA, from the Committee on Natural Resources, submitted the following

# REPORT

[To accompany H.R. 4299]

[Including cost estimate of the Congressional Budget Office]

The Committee on Natural Resources, to whom was referred the bill (H.R. 4299) to reauthorize through 2024 the National Geological and Geophysical Data Preservation Program Act of 2005, having considered the same, reports favorably thereon with an amendment and recommends that the bill as amended do pass.

The amendment is as follows:

Strike all after the enacting clause and insert the following:

**SECTION 1. SHORT TITLE.**

This Act may be cited as the "Data Preservation Act of 2020".

**SEC. 2. REAUTHORIZATION OF NATIONAL GEOLOGICAL AND GEOPHYSICAL DATA PRESERVATION PROGRAM ACT OF 2005.**

Subsection (k) of the National Geological and Geophysical Data Preservation Program Act of 2005 (42 U.S.C. 15908(k)) is amended by striking "2006 through 2010" and inserting "2020 through 2024".

## PURPOSE OF THE BILL

The purpose of H.R. 4299 is to reauthorize through 2024 the National Geological and Geophysical Data Preservation Program Act of 2005.

## BACKGROUND AND NEED FOR LEGISLATION

The Data Preservation Act reauthorizes the National Geological and Geophysical Data Preservation Program (NGGDPP) through 2024. The NGGDPP was first authorized by the Energy Policy Act of 2005 but expired in 2016.

Administered by the U.S. Geological Survey, the NGGDPP promotes the preservation and accessibility of geoscientific data, infor-

19–006

In his opinion in *Hill*, Chief Justice Burger relied on committee reports in interpreting the Endangered Species Act. For example, he noted that, "[i]n shaping legislation to deal with the problem * * * presented, Congress started from the finding that '[t]he two major causes of extinction are hunting and destruction of natural habitat.' S. Rep. No. 93–307, p. 2 (1973)." (In support of that view, he also cited testimony at a hearing before a House committee to clarify that, "[o]f these twin threats, Congress was informed that the greatest was destruction of natural habitats; see 1973 House Hearings 236 (statement of Associate Deputy Chief for National Forest System, Dept. of Agriculture).")

In addition, to support the assertion that the Act did not permit accommodation of agency programs and priorities, Chief Justice Burger noted that the version of the bill that the Senate initially approved was more limited. But, he asserted,

> the bill that originally passed the House, H.R. 37, contained a provision which was essentially a mirror image of the subsequently passed [Act]—indeed all phrases which might have qualified an agency's responsibilities had been omitted from the bill. In explaining the expected impact of this provision in H.R. 37 on federal agencies, the House Committee's Report states: "This subsection *requires* the Secretary and the heads of all other Federal departments and agencies to use their authorities in order to carry out programs for the protection of endangered species, and it further *requires* that those agencies take *the necessary action* that will *not jeopardize* the continuing existence of endangered species or result in the destruction of critical habitat of those species." H.R. Rep. No. 93–412, p. 14 (1973).

Chief Justice Burger also referred to an example in the House Committee report of the ways that the Park Service, another federal agency, would have to conform its practices to the need to protect endangered species, " 'by curtailing the destruction of habitat by clearcutting National Forests surrounding the Park, and by preventing hunting until their numbers have recovered sufficiently to withstand these pressures.' H.R. Rep. No. 93–412, p. 14 (1973)."

As noted above, when the two houses pass different bills, they often constitute a conference committee to draft language that will be acceptable to majorities in both houses.

105TH CONGRESS *2d Session* } HOUSE OF REPRESENTATIVES { REPORT 105–780

INTELLIGENCE AUTHORIZATION ACT FOR FISCAL YEAR 1999

OCTOBER 5, 1998.—Ordered to be printed

Mr. GOSS, from the committee of conference, submitted the following

CONFERENCE REPORT

[To accompany H.R. 3694]

The committee of conference on the disagreeing votes of the two Houses on the amendment of the Senate to the bill (H.R. 3694), to authorize appropriations for fiscal year 1999 for intelligence and intelligence-related activities of the United States Government, the Community Management Account, and the Central Intelligence Agency Retirement and Disability System, and for other purposes, having met, after full and free conference, have agreed to recommend and do recommend to their respective Houses as follows:

That the House recede from its disagreement to the amendment of the Senate and agree to the same with an amendment as follows:

In lieu of the matter proposed to be inserted by the Senate amendment, insert the following:

***SECTION 1. SHORT TITLE; TABLE OF CONTENTS.***

*(a) SHORT TITLE.—This Act may be cited as the "Intelligence Authorization Act for Fiscal Year 1999".*

*(b) TABLE OF CONTENTS.—The table of contents for this Act is as follow:*



In his opinion in *Hill,* Chief Justice Burger noted that, after the two houses passed different versions of a bill to protect endangered species, the conference committee "rejected the Senate version [and] adopted the stringent, mandatory language" in the House version.

Both houses of Congress keep a record of debates on the floor, and we can access them by consulting the Congressional Record. (The Congressional Record also includes the texts of bills, resolutions, and motions proposed in the two houses, as well as the results of roll-call votes.)

**H12338** CONGRESSIONAL RECORD — HOUSE *November 4, 2009*

Despite the fact that tort reform would help reduce health care costs, the administration refuses to propose this commonsense solution. Why is that?

According to former Democratic National Committee Chairman Howard Dean, "Tort reform is not in the (health care) bill because the people who wrote it don't want to take on the trial lawyers."

In the handful of States that have enacted tort reform, health care costs have fallen, and the availability of medical care has expanded.

Tort reform and reducing the number of frivolous lawsuits against hospitals and doctors would help all Americans.

NO PUBLIC FUNDING FOR ABORTIONS

(Mr. INGLIS asked and was given permission to address the House for 1 minute and to revise and extend his remarks.)

Mr. INGLIS. Madam Speaker, there are many things wrong with the Pelosi health care bill. Some of them rise to moral issues, and certainly the moral issue that I am focused on right now is the abortion issue.

There are a lot of people who want to say, Well, there won't be public funds used for abortion, but really, please, when we debate this bill, let's not insult the intelligence of other Members of Congress or of the American people. There is a clear commingling of resources. If you set up a public option and then there is money flowing into that from taxpayers, that money will ultimately find its way to abortion services.

So what we need in order to avoid that problem that many of us have of funding abortions with taxpayer money is an expressed prohibition on abortion services. There needs to be a bright line in this bill saying there will be no support for abortion services anywhere in the bill, similar to the Hyde amendment in HHS appropriations.

So, Madam Speaker, this is something that needs to be done in order to make it clear and to avoid this moral challenge.

SPECIAL ORDERS

The SPEAKER pro tempore (Ms. TITUS). Under the Speaker's announced policy of January 6, 2009, and under a previous order of the House, the following Members will be recognized for 5 minutes each.

AFFORDABLE HEALTH CARE FOR AMERICA ACT

The SPEAKER pro tempore. Under a previous order of the House, the gentleman from Maryland (Mr. CUMMINGS) is recognized for 5 minutes.

Mr. CUMMINGS. Madam Speaker, I am compelled to address this body tonight after having listened to my colleagues over the last few days fabricate falsely about the Affordable Health Care for America Act.

Every 12 minutes, an American dies in the greatest country on Earth simply because he cannot afford to live. Americans lie right now, as I speak, in their homes while in pain, suffering because they cannot afford the care that would bring them relief.

I meet people in my district who choose between medication and food, parents who go without medical treatment to pay for heat and clothing for their children, and family members who believe with all their hearts that loved ones have died because they lacked adequate health care.

Like the misrepresentations about this bill, these injustices must stop. The time to act is now. In the words of President Obama, we must have the urgency of now.

H.R. 3962 helps uninsured Americans immediately. It immediately creates an insurance program with financial assistance for those who are uninsured or for those who have been denied policies because of preexisting conditions. It also allows those who are unemployed to keep their COBRA coverage until the exchange is operational.

Health insurance reform will mean greater stability and lower costs for all Americans. That means affordability for the middle class, security for our seniors, and responsibility to our children. It also will mean coverage for 96 percent of Americans. According to the CBO, the bill reduces the deficit by $30 billion over the first 10 years.

In their speeches, Republicans have described this bill as the Speaker's bill. They call it the "Pelosi bill." This bill does not belong to the Speaker, although she has done a phenomenal job in helping us to craft it.

This bill belongs to the hardworking Americans who have insurance but who want a more transparent and stable health care marketplace that focuses on quality, affordable choices for all Americans, and that keeps insurers honest.

It belongs to 47 million Americans who are suffering and who have no help on the horizon.

This bill belongs to the seniors living in rural areas all over our country who will receive better Medicare coverage because of this bill.

It belongs to the children throughout our Nation who are so poor that their parents cannot even afford checkups. These are the children whose lives will be crippled by diabetes simply because doctors have not diagnosed them as being at risk.

Our children are our living messages we send to a future we will never see. The question is: What type of message are we sending? They will suffer simply because they do not know how to reverse the symptoms leading them down a troubled road.

This bill belongs to 44,000 Americans who die every year because they lack insurance. They have been guaranteed life, liberty, and the pursuit of happiness by founding documents to which my colleagues on the other side of the aisle constantly refer. Americans are denied those things by the thousands. They cannot afford care and so they die.

That's right, Madam Speaker. For every page that Republicans have printed out and have used as props, for every page, 22 Americans will die this year because they cannot pay for the care that will save their lives.

It is telling that, using valuable tax dollars, they printed those pages to make copies of a bill that is available, searchable, and downloadable online. It is a perfect metaphor for the millions of dollars this bill will save Americans.

Our health care system will save more than $150 billion every year, a call that President Obama made in the beginning of his campaign. The bill moves America to a health care system with an electronic recordkeeping system, cutting fraud, excessive administrative costs and medical mistakes.

Republicans do not care about those savings or about that progress. Like the pages of the taxpayer-provided paper used here today on this floor, they are props—only interested in being weights to drag down, to slow down, and to eventually stop true health care reform.

It pains me to say these words, but this is how I feel.

The SPEAKER pro tempore. Under a previous order of the House, the gentleman from Texas (Mr. POE) is recognized for 5 minutes.

(Mr. POE of Texas addressed the House. His remarks will appear hereafter in the Extensions of Remarks.)

ABRAHAM LINCOLN ON PRESERVING OUR FREEDOM

The SPEAKER pro tempore. Under a previous order of the House, the gentlewoman from North Carolina (Ms. FOXX) is recognized for 5 minutes.

Ms. FOXX. Madam Speaker, in the ongoing debate over health care reform, the topic of freedom is often overlooked, but it ought not be. The Democrats' health care bill is a massive expansion of government that will alter the lives and livelihoods of every person in America. For many, that means higher taxes; and for even more, it will mean an unprecedented intrusion of Federal Government bureaucrats into the way we receive health care. This is a fundamental erosion of our freedom.

The great freedom fighter, Abraham Lincoln, gave a speech in Springfield, Illinois, in 1838 where he touched on the idea of the loss of freedom. He was very explicit. He explained that our country could one day suffer a loss of freedom, not by an outside attack but from within. I will quote what Lincoln said and then give it in its larger context:

Although Chief Justice Burger did not quote from the Conference Report, he did refer to statements that "the House manager of the bill, Representative Dingell, [made to provide] an interpretation of what the Conference bill would require, making it clear that the mandatory provisions of [the Act] were not casually or inadvertently included." Chief Justice Burger then quoted Representative Dingell's comments:

> "[Section 7] substantially amplifie[s] the obligation of [federal agencies] to take steps within their power to carry out the purposes of this act. A recent article . . . illustrates the problem which might occur absent this new language in the bill. It appears that the whooping cranes of this country, perhaps the best known of our endangered species, are being threatened by Air Force bombing activities along the gulf coast of Texas. Under existing law, the Secretary of Defense has some discretion as to whether or not he will take the necessary action to see that this threat disappears . . . . [O]nce the bill is enacted, [the Secretary of Defense] *would be required to take the proper steps.* * * * The purposes of the bill included the conservation of the species and of the ecosystems upon which they depend, and *every agency of government is committed* to see that those purposes are carried out. . . . [T]he agencies of Government can no longer plead that they can do nothing about it. *They can, and they must. The law is clear.*" 119 Cong. Rec. 42913 (1973).

In other words, in his opinion for the Court in *Hill*, Chief Justice Burger cited all of the main source of legislative history: witness statements provided in hearings before congressional committees; committee reports; conference committee reports; and statements by individual legislators during floor debates. (If you review the opinions in *Hill*, you'll see that Justice Powell's dissent also referred to several sources of legislative history, including House and Senate committee reports about bills appropriating money for the Tellico Project.)

There are other possible sources of legislative history, as well. For example, legislation might be inspired by a proposal from the President or the head of an administrative agency; a committee conducting a hearing might receive written statements from regulated parties or from state or local governments; or lawyers who work for one of the houses might prepare an analysis of a bill.

Assuming that it is appropriate to consult legislative history, are some of these sources more authoritative than others? Are some likely to do a better job of reflecting statutory meaning than others?

Judges who consult legislative history usually consider committee reports to be the best evidence of statutory meaning. Committee reports usually explain, in relatively accessible language, both what the provisions in the bill were designed to mean and why the committee adopted them. For this reason, many members of Congress are more likely to read a committee report in deciding whether to support a bill than to read the bill itself.

Remember, however, that committee reports describe the bill that emerged from committee, which might change in meaningful ways once it is subject to debate on the floor. *Conference* committee reports, on the other hand, essentially never suffer from this problem; both houses' rules prevent amendments to conference reports on the floor. This might make conference committee reports even more reliable statements of legislative intent. On the other hand, conference committee reports (in addition to including the text of the agreed-upon bill) tend to address only those provisions that were sources of disagreement between the houses, rather than those that were included in the bills that both houses originally passed, which can make conference committee reports less helpful as evidence of statutory meaning.

Most judges who are willing to consult legislative history believe that committee reports rank higher in the hierarchy of legislative history than do statements by individual members of the legislature. After all, committee reports are (by definition) collective statements of understanding, even if not statements formally subject to a vote by the full chambers; a statement by an individual member generally represents the views only of that one member. But not all member statements are treated alike; judges often give significant weight to statements by the sponsors or authors of a bill. It is fair to presume that the person who wrote the bill or introduced it has a deep understanding of the bill's provisions and its objectives. At the same time, the sponsor or author of the bill might be inclined to paper over potential problems with the bill and to present the bill in the most flattering possible light. Should this make judges wary about crediting statements by authors or sponsors?

Although judges do not put as much weight on statements by other members of Congress, they do not ignore those statements. A member who takes the time to speak about a bill might point to possible ambiguities in the statutory language and offer a view about how to resolve those ambiguities. Or a member might raise a concern about the bill, which other members then address by stating their understanding of its meaning. Should it matter, in assigning significance to a member statement, whether the member ultimately supported the bill? What role might statements from opponents of a bill play in seeking to determine the statute's meaning?

As we saw in the excerpts above from the Court's opinion in *Hill*, judges also sometimes cite other pieces of legislative history—such as witness testimony before a committee hearing, a colloquy between a member or a legislative aide and a witness, or statements submitted to a committee by interested groups—in seeking to determine the meaning of a statute. But whereas members of Congress often consult committee reports in deciding whether to vote for a bill, few members (other than those on the relevant committee, and even then not necessarily all of them) regularly read the testimony or statements collected during the hearing process. What role, if any, should these other materials play in the process of statutory interpretation? Are they useful for informing the court about what sorts of problems Congress sought to address? For providing context for Congress's decision to enact the law? Or are these sources simply a smorgasbord from which a results-oriented judge can choose in order to "find" evidence of her preferred statutory meaning?

## Perspective and Analysis

[I offer] five rule-based decision theory Principles, akin to canons, for judges and lawyers to make readings of legislative history more objective. The First Principle is a caution against congressional illiteracy: one should never read legislative history without knowing Congress's [rules, such as] the rules of conference committees * * *.

The Second Principle is a rule of reverse sequential consideration: legislative history should focus on the last relevant legislative decision. * * *

The Third Principle is one of proximity and specificity: proximity to text and specificity to the interpretive issue are central to the most reliable history. This rule of relevance can make manageable even some of the largest decisionmaking records * * *.

The Fourth Principle is that one should never cite losers' history as an authoritative source of textual meaning. No judge would ever confuse a dissenting opinion with a majority opinion, yet this is precisely what happens when a judge uses losers' history as Congress's meaning. One of the greatest difficulties with the "intent" metaphor is that it obscures the differences between majorities' decisions and filibustering minorities' opposition. * * *

The Fifth Principle follows from the First: courts and Congress regularly misunderstand each other precisely because courts fail to understand that Congress plays by its own rules, not judicial ones. For example, behavior that follows Congress's own rules may appear to courts as if it produces ambiguity and no resolution where a conscientious legislator would find no ambiguity and a clear decision (based on bills already passed). Similarly, cases that appear as if they could be solved by a simple textual fix may involve significant and difficult structural conflicts within the legislature.

**Victoria F. Nourse, *A Decision Theory of Statutory Interpretation: Legislative History by the Rules*, 122 YALE L.J. 70 (2012).**

---

## Points for Discussion

### *a. Legislative History as Evidence of Statutory Meaning*

One frequent criticism of judicial reliance on legislative history is that there's something for everyone; judges (or their clerks) can comb through a voluminous record to find a few statements here and there that support their preferred outcome, even though those statements might not be representative. This is a serious criticism, but it is worth considering whether this problem is unique to the quest for legislative intent or purpose. After all, judges regularly preside over trials—and sometimes serve as fact-finders at trials—in which a range of contradictory evidence is offered. When self-interested parties introduce competing evidence at trial, we don't ordinarily throw up our hands and declare that it's not possible to determine what really happened. Why is the same not true for judicial efforts to determine statutory meaning from legislative history? Is there a meaningful difference between consulting legislative history to determine what Congress meant, on the one hand, and consulting a body of conflicting evidence to resolve a factual dispute between two parties, on the other?

***b. A Hierarchy of Sources of Legislative History***

As noted above, most judges who consult legislative history have a rough hierarchy of legislative history based on its reliability and authoritativeness. As a consequence, judges are more likely to treat a committee report as authoritative evidence of statutory meaning than they would a statement of a random member during a floor debate. Professor Nourse, on the other hand, suggests that we give more weight to legislative history produced later in time—such as conference committee reports and possibly even floor debates—and to legislative history that speaks most directly to the question at issue, even if it would fall lower on the traditional hierarchy. Which view is more sensible?

**Test Your Knowledge**

To assess your understanding of the material in this Chapter, click here to take a quiz.

# Chapter Five

# *Putting Together (Some of) the Pieces*

We have seen that courts use a range of techniques when they interpret statutes. Sometimes they seek the plain or ordinary meaning of the statutory text; sometimes they consider the legislature's intent; and other times they consider the broad purposes that animate the statutory scheme. Although there is sharp disagreement among judges about which of these touchstones of interpretation should be the object of interpretation, most judges agree that the ultimate goal in statutory interpretation is faithfully to implement the instructions of the legislature. The disagreement, for the most part, is simply about how to determine what the legislature's instructions actually are.

But is that the only plausible understanding of the judge's role in statutory interpretation? Or should judges acknowledge that statutes often do not clearly resolve some questions, and that they instead should exercise policy judgment rather than pretending to determine statutory meaning? Regardless of your answer to that question, do you think that in practice judges—whatever they say about their approach to statutory interpretation—make policy determinations when they apply statutes?

In this Chapter, we will consider these questions. Doing so will also give us an opportunity to review what we have seen so far. We begin with a case that frames these questions in stark terms.

---

Under the Controlled Substances Act, 21 U.S.C. §§ 801–971, it is "unlawful for any person knowingly or intentionally * * * to manufacture, distribute, or dispense, or possess with intent to manufacture, distribute, or dispense, a controlled substance." 21 U.S.C. § 841(a). The case that follows involved an amendment to the Act that identified the penalties for trafficking in controlled substances. See Controlled Substances Penalties Amendments Act of 1984, Pub. L. 98–473. The relevant sections provided:

> **Section 841(b). Penalties.**
>
> Except as otherwise provided in section 849, 859, 860, or 861 of this title, any person who violates subsection (a) of this section shall be sentenced as follows:
>
> (1)(A) In the case of a violation of subsection (a) of this section involving—

(i) 1 kilogram or more of a mixture or substance containing a detectable amount of heroin; * * *

(iii) 280 grams or more of a mixture or substance * * * which contains cocaine base;

(iv) 100 grams or more of phencyclidine (PCP) or 1 kilogram or more of a mixture or substance containing a detectable amount of phencyclidine (PCP);

(v) 10 grams or more of a mixture or substance containing a detectable amount of lysergic acid diethylamide (LSD); * * *

(vii) 1000 kilograms or more of a mixture or substance containing a detectable amount of marihuana, or 1,000 or more marihuana plants regardless of weight; or

(viii) 50 grams or more of methamphetamine, its salts, isomers, and salts of its isomers or 500 grams or more of a mixture or substance containing a detectable amount of methamphetamine, its salts, isomers, or salts of its isomers;

such person shall be sentenced to a term of imprisonment which may not be less than 10 years or more than life and if death or serious bodily injury results from the use of such substance shall be not less than 20 years or more than life, a fine not to exceed the greater of that authorized in accordance with the provisions of Title 18 or $10,000,000 if the defendant is an individual or $50,000,000 if the defendant is other than an individual, or both. * * *

(B) In the case of a violation of subsection (a) of this section involving—

(i) 100 grams or more of a mixture or substance containing a detectable amount of heroin; * * *

(iii) 28 grams or more of a mixture or substance * * * which contains cocaine base;

(iv) 10 grams or more of phencyclidine (PCP) or 100 grams or more of a mixture or substance containing a detectable amount of phencyclidine (PCP);

(v) 1 gram or more of a mixture or substance containing a detectable amount of lysergic acid diethylamide (LSD); * * *

(vii) 100 kilograms or more of a mixture or substance containing a detectable amount of marihuana, or 100 or more marihuana plants regardless of weight; or

(viii) 5 grams or more of methamphetamine, its salts, isomers, and salts of its isomers or 50 grams or more of a mixture or substance containing a detectable amount of methamphetamine, its salts, isomers, or salts of its isomers;

such person shall be sentenced to a term of imprisonment which may not be less than 5 years and not more than 40 years and if death or serious bodily injury results from the use of such substance shall be not less than 20 years or more than life, a fine not to exceed the greater of that authorized in accordance with the provisions of Title 18 or $5,000,000 if the defendant is an individual or $25,000,000 if the defendant is other than an individual, or both. * * *

---

## *United States v. Marshall*

908 F.2d 1312 (7th Cir. 1990) (*en banc*)

EASTERBROOK, CIRCUIT JUDGE.

Two cases consolidated for decision [present] three questions concerning the application and constitutionality of the statute and sentencing guidelines that govern sales of lysergic acid diethylamide (LSD). Stanley J. Marshall was convicted after a bench trial and sentenced to 20 years' imprisonment for conspiring to distribute, and distributing, more than ten grams of LSD, enough for 11,751 doses. Patrick Brumm, Richard L. Chapman, and John M. Schoenecker were convicted by a jury of selling ten sheets (1,000 doses) of paper containing LSD. Because the total weight of the paper and LSD was 5.7 grams, a five-year mandatory minimum applied. The district court sentenced Brumm to 60 months (the minimum), Schoenecker to 63 months, and Chapman to 96 months' imprisonment. All four defendants confine their arguments on appeal to questions concerning their sentences.

> **Definition**
>
> *En banc* is French for "on the bench." In the United States judicial system, the term is used to refer to a decision by the full court. Although the United States Courts of Appeals resolve most appeals with panels of three judges, a decision *en banc* is a decision rendered by the entire membership of the Court of Appeals in question. The judges on a Court of Appeals can vote to rehear *en banc* a case previously decided by a panel of three judges.

The three questions we must resolve are these: (1) Whether 21 U.S.C. § 841(b)(1)(A)(v) and (B)(v), which set mandatory minimum terms of imprisonment—five years for selling more than one gram of a "mixture or substance containing a detectable amount" of LSD, ten years for more than ten grams—exclude the weight of a carrier medium. (2) Whether the weight tables in the sentencing guidelines likewise exclude the weight of any carrier. (3) Whether the statute and the guidelines are unconstitutional to the extent their computations are based on anything other than the weight of the pure drug. * * *

According to the Sentencing Commission, the LSD in an average dose weighs 0.05 milligrams. Twenty thousand pure doses are a gram. But 0.05 mg is almost invisible, so LSD is distributed to retail customers in a carrier. Pure LSD is dissolved in a solvent such as alcohol and sprayed on paper or gelatin; alternatively the paper may be dipped in the solution. After the solvent evaporates, the paper or gel is cut into one-dose squares and sold by the square. Users swallow the squares or may drop them into a beverage, releasing the drug. Although the gelatin and paper are light, they weigh much more than the drug. Marshall's 11,751 doses weighed 113.32 grams; the LSD accounted for only 670.72 mg of this, not enough to activate the five-year mandatory minimum sentence, let alone the ten-year minimum. The ten sheets of blotter paper carrying the 1,000 doses Chapman and confederates sold weighed 5.7

grams; the LSD in the paper did not approach the one-gram threshold for a mandatory minimum sentence. This disparity between the weight of the pure LSD and the weight of LSD-plus-carrier underlies the defendants' arguments.

If the carrier counts in the weight of the "mixture or substance containing a detectable amount" of LSD, some odd things may happen. Weight in the hands of distributors may exceed that of manufacturers and wholesalers. Big fish then could receive paltry sentences or small fish draconian ones. Someone who sold 19,999 doses of pure LSD (at 0.05 mg per dose) would escape the five-year mandatory minimum of § 841(b)(1)(B)(v) and be covered by § 841(b)(1)(C), which lacks a minimum term and has a maximum of "only" 20 years. Someone who sold a single hit of LSD dissolved in a tumbler of orange juice could be exposed to a ten-year mandatory minimum. Retailers could fall in or out of the mandatory terms depending not on the number of doses but on the medium: sugar cubes weigh more than paper, which weighs more than gelatin. One way to eliminate the possibility of such consequences is to say that the carrier is not a "mixture or substance containing a detectable amount" of the drug. Defendants ask us to do this.

**Food for Thought**

Pause here and think about what arguments you would make about the statute's meaning if you represented the defendant. Would you rely on the plain meaning of the statutory text? If so, are there are canons or maxims of statutory interpretation that are relevant? Or would you instead make an argument focused on a different touchstone?

Defendants' submission starts from the premise that the interaction of the statutory phrase "mixture or substance" with the distribution of LSD by the dose in a carrier creates a unique probability of surprise results. The premise may be unwarranted. The paper used to distribute LSD is light stuff, not the kind used to absorb ink. Chapman's 1,000 doses weighed about 0.16 ounces. More than 6,000 doses, even in blotter paper, weigh less than an ounce. Because the LSD in one dose weighs about 0.05 milligrams, the combination of LSD-plus-paper is about 110 times the weight of the LSD. The impregnated paper could be described as "0.9% LSD". Gelatin carrying LSD could be described as "2.5% LSD" * * *.

This is by no means an unusual dilution rate for illegal drugs. Heroin sold on the street is 2% to 3% opiate and the rest filler. Jerome J. Platt, *Heroin Addiction: Theory, Research, and Treatment* 48–50 (1986). * * * Heroin and crack cocaine, like LSD, are sold on the streets by the dose, although they are sold by weight higher in the distributional chain. All of the "designer drugs" and many of the opiates are sold by the dose, often conveniently packaged in pills. * * *

So there may be nothing extraordinary about LSD, no reason to think that the statute operates differently for LSD than for heroin. Heroin comes into this country pure; it is sold diluted on the street, creating the possibility that § 841 will require higher sentences for retailers than for smugglers or refiners. The dilution factor for retail heroin is not significantly different from the factor for LSD on blotter paper. * * * So although § 841 creates the possibility of erratic application in LSD cases, it is important to recognize that the normal case involves neither extreme weight (LSD in orange juice) nor extreme purity (19,999 doses weighing less than a gram). With this understanding, we turn to the statute.

**Take Note**

On which touchstone of interpretation did Justice Easterbrook focus? Do you find his analysis convincing?

It is not possible to construe the words of § 841 to make the penalty turn on the net weight of the drug rather than the gross weight of carrier and drug. The statute speaks of "mixture or substance containing a detectable amount" of a drug. "Detectable amount" is the opposite of "pure"; the point of the statute is that the "mixture" is not to be converted to an equivalent amount of pure drug.

The structure of the statute reinforces this conclusion. The 10-year minimum applies to any person who possesses, with intent to distribute, "100 grams or more of phencyclidine (PCP) or 1 kilogram or more of a mixture or substance containing a detectable amount of phencyclidine (PCP)," § 841(b)(1)(A)(iv). Congress distinguished the pure drug from a "mixture or substance containing a detectable amount of" it. All drugs other than PCP are governed exclusively by the "mixture or substance" language. Even brute force cannot turn that language into a reference to pure LSD. Congress used the same "mixture or substance" language to describe heroin, cocaine, amphetamines, and many other drugs that are sold after being cut—sometimes as much as LSD. There is no sound basis on which to treat the words "substance or mixture containing a detectable amount of," repeated verbatim for every drug mentioned in § 841 except PCP, as *different* things for LSD and cocaine although the language is identical, while treating the "mixture or substance" language as meaning the *same* as the reference to pure PCP in 21 U.S.C. § 841(b)(1)(A)(iv) and (B)(iv).

Although the "mixture or substance" language shows that the statute cannot be limited to pure LSD, it does not necessarily follow that blotter paper *is* a "mixture or substance containing" LSD. That phrase cannot include all "carriers." One gram of crystalline LSD in a heavy glass bottle is still only one gram of "statutory LSD." So is a gram of LSD being "carried" in a Boeing 747. How much mingling of the drug with something else is essential to form a "mixture or substance"? The legislative history is silent, but ordinary usage is indicative.

"Substance" may well refer to a chemical compound, or perhaps to a drug in a solvent. LSD does not react chemically with sugar, blotter paper, or gelatin, and none of these is a solvent. "Mixture" is more inclusive. Cocaine often is mixed with mannitol, quinine, or lactose. These white powders do not react, but it is common ground that a cocaine-mannitol mixture is a statutory "mixture."

LSD and blotter paper are not commingled in the same way as cocaine and lactose. What is the nature of their association? The possibility most favorable to defendants is that LSD sits on blotter paper as oil floats on water. Immiscible substances may fall outside the statutory definition of "mixture." The possibility does not assist defendants—not on this record, anyway. LSD is applied to paper in a solvent; after the solvent evaporates, a tiny quantity of LSD remains. Because the fibers absorb the alcohol, the LSD solidifies inside the paper rather than on it. You cannot pick a grain of LSD off the surface of the paper. Ordinary parlance calls the paper containing tiny crystals of LSD a mixture.

*United States v. Rose*, 881 F.2d 386 (7th Cir.1989), like every other appellate decision that has addressed the question, concludes that the carrier medium for LSD, like the "cut" for heroin and cocaine, is a "mixture or substance containing a detectable amount" of the drug. Although a chemist might be able to offer evidence bearing on the question whether LSD and blotter paper "mix" any more fully than do oil and water, the record contains no such evidence. Without knowing more of the chemistry than this record reveals, we adhere to the unanimous conclusion of the other courts of appeals that blotter paper treated with LSD is a "mixture or substance containing a detectable quantity of" LSD.

Two reasons have been advanced to support a contrary conclusion: that statutes should be construed to avoid constitutional problems, and that some members of the sitting Congress are dissatisfied with basing penalties on the combined weight of LSD and carrier. Neither is persuasive.

A preference for giving statutes a constitutional meaning is a reason to construe, not to rewrite or "improve." Canons are doubt-resolvers, useful when the language is ambiguous and "a construction of the statute is *fairly possible* by which the question may be avoided," *Crowell v. Benson*, 285 U.S. 22, 62 (1932) (emphasis added). "[S]ubstance or mixture containing a detectable quantity" is not ambiguous, avoidance not "fairly possible." Neither the rule of lenity nor the preference for avoiding constitutional adjudication justifies disregarding unambiguous language.

The canon about avoiding constitutional decisions, in particular, must be used with care, for it is a closer cousin to invalidation than to interpretation. It is a way to enforce the constitutional penumbra, and therefore an aspect of constitutional law proper. Constitutional decisions breed penumbras, which multiply questions. Treating each as justification to construe laws out of existence too greatly enlarges the judicial power. And heroic

**Take Note**

The court here considers two substantive canons. Why does the court decline to rely on those canons to read the statute more narrowly?

"construction" is unnecessary, given our conclusion [that] Congress possesses the constitutional power to set penalties on the basis of gross weight.

As for the pending legislation: subsequent debates are not a ground for avoiding the import of enactments. E.g., *Pierce v. Underwood*, 487 U.S. 552, 566–68 (1988). Although the views of a subsequent Congress are entitled to respect, ongoing debates do not represent the views of Congress. [Proposals by two Senators to amend the statute] are more naturally understood as suggestions for change than as evidence of today's meaning. At all events, the Senators [who made such proposals] were speaking for themselves, not for Congress as an institution.

Statements supporting proposals that have not been adopted do not inform our reading of the text an earlier Congress passed and the President signed, see *Firestone Tire & Rubber Co. v. Bruch*, 489 U.S. 101 (1989). We may not, in the name of faithful interpretation of what the political branches *enacted,* treat as authoritative the statements of legislators supporting change. Opinion polls of Senators are not law.

[The court rejected the defendants' argument that the sentencing scheme violated the Eighth Amendment's prohibition on cruel and unusual punishment and the equal protection component of the Due Process Clause of the Fifth Amendment. The court reasoned that the hypothetical difference between the weight of the "pure" drug and the drug on a carrier is immaterial if] in 99% of all cases, LSD is sold in blotter paper. Why reduce the amount to a pure measure if that almost never spells a difference? No one has been prosecuted for distributing LSD in sugar cubes in the last 20 years. Similarly, no one has been prosecuted for possessing significant quantities of pure LSD in the last decade. Why worry about how to treat manufacturers caught red-handed with pure dry LSD if they are never nabbed? Statutes rationally may be addressed to the main cases rather than the exceptions. Congress may count on prosecutorial discretion to take care of the absurd cases (one dose in a quart of lemonade), and it has created the [Continuing Criminal Enterprise statute, 21 U.S.C. § 848,] to take care of Mr. Big. It need not build into each *section* of the United States Code an apparatus sufficient in itself to produce graduated penalties.

**Take Note**

What is Judge Easterbrook's understanding of the judge's role in statutory interpretation? Do you agree with him that reading the statute to avoid unfair (and likely unanticipated) consequences would amount to impermissible judicial policy-making?

Political decisions may be harsh yet within the bounds of power. The Constitution does not compel Congress to adopt a criminal code with all possibility for unjust variation extirpated. Experience with the guidelines suggests the reverse: Every attempt to make the system of sentences "more rational" carries costs and concealed irrationalities, both loopholes and unanticipated severity. Criminals have neither a moral nor a constitutional claim to equal or entirely proportional treatment. Constitutional law is not a device allowing judges to set the "just price" of crime, to prescribe the ratio of retailers' to manufacturers' sentences. That Congress could have written better laws does not mean that it had to. *United States v. Powell*, 423 U.S. 87 (1975). Amendments to the criminal code may be in order, but they are not ours to make under the banner of constitutional adjudication. [Affirmed.]

CUMMINGS, CIRCUIT JUDGE, with whom BAUER, CHIEF JUDGE, and WOOD, JR., CUDAHY, and POSNER, CIRCUIT JUDGES, join, dissenting:

Six courts, including the district court in *Marshall*, have explicitly considered whether the carrier in an LSD case is a mixture or substance within the meaning of 21 U.S.C. § 841. Five of these courts have concluded that the blotter paper is a "mixture or substance" within the meaning of the statute. * * * The sixth court, the United States District Court for the District of Columbia, held that blotter paper was not a mixture or substance within the meaning of the statute. *United States v. Healy*, 729 F. Supp. 140 (D.D.C.1990). The court relied not only on ordinary dictionary definitions of the words mixture and substance but also on a November 30, 1988, Sentencing Commission publication, entitled "Questions Most Frequently Asked About the Sentencing Guidelines," which states that the Commission has not taken a position on whether the blotter paper should be weighed. * * *

The court in *Healy* did not refer to the legislative history of the statute to support the proposition that Congress did not intend the weight of the carrier to be included in LSD cases. This is not surprising since the only reference to LSD in the debates preceding the passage of the 1986 amendments to Section 841 was a passing reference that does not address quantities or weights of drugs. 132 Cong. Rec. S14030 (daily ed. Sept. 27, 1986) (statement of Sen. Harkin).

Two subsequent pieces of legislative history, however, do shed some light on this question. In a letter to Senator Joseph R. Biden, Jr., dated April 26, 1989 (Marshall Appendix at 165), the Chairman of the Sentencing Commission, William W. Wilkens, Jr., noted the ambiguity in the statute as it is currently written:

> "With respect to LSD, it is unclear whether Congress intended the carrier to be considered as a packaging material, or, since it is commonly consumed along with the illicit drug, as a dilutant ingredient in the drug mixture . . . . The Commission suggests that Congress may wish to further consider the LSD carrier issue in order to clarify legislative intent as to whether the weight of the carrier should or should not be considered in determining the quantity of LSD mixture for punishment purposes."

Presumably acting in response to this query, Senator Biden added to the Congressional Record for October 5, 1989, an analysis of one of a series of technical corrections to 21 U.S.C. § 841 that were under consideration by the Senate that day. This analysis states that the purpose of the particular correction at issue was to remove an unintended "inequity" from Section 841 caused by the decisions of some courts to include the weight of the blotter paper for sentencing purposes in LSD cases. According to Senator Biden, the correction "remedie[d] this inequity by removing the weight of the carrier from the calculation of the weight of the mixture or substance." This correction was adopted as part of Amendment No. 976 to S. 1711. 135 Cong. Rec. S12749 (daily ed. Oct. 5, 1989). The amended bill was passed by a unanimous vote of the Senate (*id.* at S12765) and is currently pending before the House.

Comments in more recent issues of the Congressional Record indicate that S. 1711 is not expected to pass the House of Representatives. See 136 Cong. Rec. S943 (daily ed. Feb. 7, 1990). In the meantime, however, a second attempt to clarify Congress' intent in amending 21 U.S.C. § 841 to include the words mixture or substance has now been introduced in the Senate. On April 18, 1990, Senator Kennedy introduced an amendment to S. 1970 (a bill establishing constitutional procedures for the imposition of the death penalty) seeking to clarify the language of 21 U.S.C. § 841. That amendment, Amendment No. 1716, states:

> "Section 841(b)(1) of title 21, United States Code, is amended by inserting the following new subsection at the end thereof:
>
> '(E) In determining the weight of a 'mixture or substance' under this section, the court shall not include the weight of the carrier upon which the controlled substance is placed, or by which it is transported.' "

136 Cong. Rec. S7069 (daily ed. May 24, 1990).

To be sure there are difficulties inherent in relying heavily on this subsequent legislative history. The first is that these initiatives to clarify the manner in which 21 U.S.C. § 841 and the sentencing guidelines treat LSD offenders may never be enacted. The second is that a given amendment may be viewed not as a clarification of Congress' original intent, but as the expression of an entirely new intent. At the very least, however, this subsequent legislative history, coupled with the fact that the Sentencing Commission has yet to resolve its position on the matter, refutes the proposition that the language of the statute and the Guidelines "couldn't be clearer." * * * The words "mixture or substance" are ambiguous, and a construction of those words that can avoid invalidation on constitutional grounds is therefore appropriate.

**Take Note**

On which touchstone of interpretation did Judge Cummings focus?

[Judge Cummings would have concluded that the sentencing scheme, as interpreted by the court, violated the Due Process Clause because it irrationally distinguished between "two defendants convicted of selling the same number of doses of LSD for the same amount of money * * * if they have chosen different inert carrier media to distribute the LSD."]

POSNER, CIRCUIT JUDGE, joined by BAUER, CHIEF JUDGE, and CUMMINGS, WOOD, JR., and CUDAHY, CIRCUIT JUDGES, dissenting.

In each of these cases consolidated for decision *en banc*, the district court sentenced sellers of LSD in accordance with an interpretation of 21 U.S.C. § 841 that is plausible but that makes the punishment scheme for LSD irrational. It has been assumed that an irrational federal sentencing scheme denies the equal protection of the laws and therefore (*Bolling v. Sharpe*, 347 U.S. 497 (1954)) violates the due process clause of the Fifth Amendment. The assumption is proper, and in order to avoid having to strike down the statute we are entitled to adopt a reasonable interpretation that cures the constitutional infirmity, even if that interpretation might not be our first choice were there no such infirmity.

**FYI**

The Sentencing Guidelines are recommendations issued by the United States Sentencing Commission for the sentencing of persons convicted of federal crimes.

The statute fixes the minimum and maximum punishments with respect to each illegal drug on the basis of the weight of the "mixture or substance containing a detectable amount of" the drug. * * * The quoted words are critical. Drugs are usually consumed, and therefore often sold, in a diluted form, and the adoption by Congress of the "mixture or substance" method of grading punishment reflected a conscious decision to mete out heavy punishment to large retail dealers, who are likely to possess "substantial street quantities," which is to say quantities of the diluted drug ready for sale. H.R. Rep. No. 845, 99th Cong., 2d Sess. 11–12 (1986). That decision is well within Congress's constitutional authority even though it may sometimes result in less severe punishment for possessing a purer, and therefore a lighter, form of the illegal drug than a heavier but much less potent form.

The statute fixes only the minimum and maximum punishments and for the actual punishment in a particular case we must go to the Sentencing Guidelines.

They proportion punishment to the weight of the mixture or substance, defined as in the statute. They permit an adjustment upward for sales of unusual purity, but this takes care of the problem identified in the previous paragraph only in part; the statutory mandatory minimum sentences (which, like the Guidelines sentences themselves, are not subject to parole) truncate the effort of the Guidelines' framers to tie the severity of punishment in the particular case to the gravity of the defendant's misconduct.

Based as it is on weight, the system I have described works well for drugs that are sold by weight; and ordinarily the weight quoted to the buyer is the weight of the dilute form, although of course price will vary with purity. The dilute form is the product, and it is as natural to punish its purveyors according to the weight of the product as it is to punish moonshiners by the weight or volume of the moonshine they sell rather than by the weight of the alcohol contained in it. So, for example, under Florida law it is a felony to possess one or more gallons of moonshine, and a misdemeanor to possess less than one gallon, regardless of the alcoholic content. Fla. Stat. §§ 561.01, 562.451.

LSD, however, is sold to the consumer by the dose; it is not cut, diluted, or mixed with something else. Moreover, it is incredibly light. An average dose of LSD weighs .05 milligrams, which is less than two millionths of an ounce. To ingest something that small requires swallowing something much larger. Pure LSD in granular form is first diluted by being dissolved, usually in alcohol, and then a quantity of the solution containing one dose of LSD is sprayed or eyedropped on a sugar cube, or on a cube of gelatin, or, as in the cases before us, on an inch-square section of "blotter" paper. (LSD blotter paper, which is sold typically in sheets ten inches square containing a hundred sections each with one dose of LSD on it, is considerably thinner than the paper used to blot ink but much heavier than the LSD itself.) After the solution is applied to the carrier medium, the alcohol or other solvent evaporates, leaving an invisible (and undiluted) spot of pure LSD on the cube or blotter paper. The consumer drops the cube or the piece of paper into a glass of water, or orange juice, or some other beverage, causing the LSD to dissolve in the beverage, which is then drunk. This is not dilution. It is still one dose that is being imbibed. Two quarts of a 50-proof alcoholic beverage are more than one quart of a 100-proof beverage, though the total alcoholic content is the same. But a quart of orange juice containing one dose of LSD is not more, in any relevant sense, than a pint of juice containing the same one dose, and it would be loony to punish the purveyor of the quart more heavily than the purveyor of the pint. It would be like basing the punishment for selling cocaine on the combined weight of the cocaine and of the vehicle (plane, boat, automobile, or whatever) used to transport it or the syringe used to inject it or the pipe used to smoke it. The blotter paper, sugar cubes, etc. are the vehicles for conveying LSD to the consumer.

The weight of the carrier is vastly greater than that of the LSD, as well as irrelevant to its potency. There is no comparable disparity between the pure and the mixed form * * * with respect to the other drugs in section 841, with the illuminating exception of PCP. There Congress specified alternative weights, for the drug itself and for the substance or mixture containing the drug. For example, the five-year minimum sentence for a seller of PCP requires the sale of either ten grams of the drug itself or one hundred grams of a substance or mixture containing the drug. 21 U.S.C. § 841(b)(1)(B)(iv).

**Food for Thought**

Judge Posner cites here the statutory provision for sentencing persons convicted of trafficking in PCP. Does this provision strengthen Judge Posner's argument about the proper interpretation of the provision addressing LSD, or does it undermine it?

Ten sheets of blotter paper, containing a thousand doses of LSD, weigh almost six grams. The LSD itself weighs less than a hundredth as much. If the thousand doses are on gelatin cubes instead of sheets of blotter paper, the total weight is less, but it is still more than two grams, which is forty times the weight of the LSD. In both cases, if the carrier plus the LSD constitutes the relevant "substance or mixture" (the crucial "if" in this case), the dealer is subject to the minimum mandatory sentence of five years. One of the defendants before us (Marshall) sold almost 12,000 doses of LSD on blotter paper. This subjected him to the ten-year minimum, and the Guidelines then took over and pushed him up to twenty years. Since it takes 20,000 doses of LSD to equal a gram, Marshall would not have been subject to even the five-year mandatory minimum had he sold the LSD in its pure form. And a dealer who sold fifteen times the number of doses as Marshall—180,000—would not be subject to the ten-year mandatory minimum sentence if he sold the drug in its pure form, because 180,000 doses is only nine grams.

At the other extreme, if Marshall were not a dealer at all but dropped a square of blotter paper containing a single dose of LSD into a glass of orange juice and sold it to a friend at cost (perhaps 35 cents), he would be subject to the ten-year minimum. The juice with LSD dissolved in it would be the statutory mixture or substance containing a detectable amount of the illegal drug and it would weigh more than ten grams (one ounce is about 35 grams, and the orange juice in a glass of orange juice weighs several ounces). So a person who sold one dose of LSD might be subject to the ten-year mandatory minimum sentence while a dealer who sold 199,999 doses in pure form would be subject only to the five-year minimum. * * *

All this seems crazy but we must consider whether Congress might have had a reason for wanting to key the severity of punishment for selling LSD to the weight of the carrier rather than to the number of doses or to some reasonable proxy for dosage (as weight is, for many drugs). The only one suggested is that it might be costly to determine the weight of the LSD in the blotter paper, sugar cube, etc., because it is so light! That merely underscores the irrationality of basing the punishment for selling this drug on weight rather than on dosage. But in fact the weight is reported in every case I have seen, so apparently it can be determined readily enough; it *has* to be determined in any event, to permit a purity adjustment under the Guidelines. If the weight of the LSD is difficult to determine, the difficulty is easily overcome by basing punishment on the number of doses, which makes much more sense in any event. To base punishment on the weight of the carrier medium makes about as much sense as basing punishment on the weight of the defendant.

A person who sells LSD on blotter paper is not a worse criminal than one who sells the same number of doses on gelatin cubes, but he is subject to a heavier punishment. A person who sells five doses of LSD on sugar cubes is not a worse person than a manufacturer of LSD who is caught with 19,999 doses in pure form, but the former is subject to a ten-year mandatory minimum no-parole sentence while the latter is not even subject to the five-year minimum. If defendant Chapman, who received five years for selling a thousand doses of LSD on blotter paper, had sold the same number of doses in pure form, his Guidelines sentence would have been fourteen months. And defendant Marshall's sentence for selling almost 12,000 doses would have been four years rather than twenty. The defendant in *United States v. Rose*, 881 F.2d 386, 387 (7th Cir.1989), must have bought an unusually heavy blotter paper, for he sold only 472 doses, yet his blotter paper weighed 7.3 grams—more than Chapman's, although Chapman sold more than twice as many doses. Depending on the weight of the carrier medium (zero when the stuff is sold in pure form), and excluding the orange juice case, the Guidelines range for selling 198 doses (the amount in *Dean*) or 472 doses (the amount in *Rose*) stretches from ten months to 365 months; for selling a thousand doses (*Chapman*), from fifteen to 365 months; and for selling 11,751 doses (*Marshall*), from 33 months to life. In none of these computations, by the way, does the weight of the LSD itself make a difference—so slight is its weight relative to that of the carrier—except of course when it is sold in pure form. Congress might as well have said: if there is a carrier, weigh the carrier and forget the LSD.

This is a quilt the pattern whereof no one has been able to discern. The legislative history is silent, and since even the Justice Department cannot explain the why of the punishment scheme that it is defending, the most plausible inference is that Congress simply did not realize how LSD is sold. The inference is reinforced by the statutory treatment of PCP.

That irrationality is magnified when we compare the sentences for people who sell other drugs prohibited by 21 U.S.C. § 841. Marshall, remember, sold fewer than 12,000 doses and was sentenced to twenty years. Twelve thousand doses sounds like a lot, but to receive a comparable sentence for selling heroin Marshall would have had to sell ten kilograms, which would yield between one and two million doses. To receive a comparable sentence for selling cocaine he would have had to sell fifty kilograms, which would yield anywhere from 325,000 to five million doses. While the corresponding weight is lower for crack—half a kilogram—this still translates into 50,000 doses.

* * * No one believes that LSD is a more dangerous drug than heroin or cocaine (particularly crack cocaine). The general view is that it is *much* less dangerous. Cox, *et al.*, Drugs and Drug Abuse: A Reference Text 313–15 (1983). There is no indication that Congress believes it to be more dangerous, or more difficult to control. The heavy sentences that the law commands for minor traffickers in LSD are the inadvertent result of the interaction among a statutory procedure for measuring weight, adopted without understanding how LSD is sold; a decision to specify harsh mandatory minimum sentences for drug traffickers, based on the weight of the drug sold; and a decision (gratuitous and unreflective, as far as I can see) by the framers of the Guidelines to key punishment to the statutory measure of weight, thereby amplifying Congress's initial error and ensuring that the big dealer who makes or ships the pure

drug will indeed receive a shorter sentence than the small dealer who handles the stuff in its street form. * * *

Well, what if anything can we judges do about this mess? The answer lies in the shadow of a jurisprudential disagreement that is not less important by virtue of being unavowed by most judges. It is the disagreement between the severely positivistic view that the content of law is exhausted in clear, explicit, and definite enactments by or under express delegation from legislatures, and the natural lawyer's or legal pragmatist's view that the practice of interpretation and the general terms of the Constitution (such as "equal protection of the laws") authorize judges to enrich positive law with the moral values and practical concerns of civilized society. * * *

**Definition**

"Positive law" means law that has been created by the institution responsible for making law. The term is generally used in contrast to "natural law," which is an idea that holds that law derives from nature, reason, or God and applies even if the institution responsible for making the law has been silent.

Neither approach is entirely satisfactory. The first buys political neutrality and a type of objectivity at the price of substantive injustice, while the second buys justice in the individual case at the price of considerable uncertainty and, not infrequently, judicial willfulness. It is no wonder that our legal system oscillates between the approaches. The positivist view, applied unflinchingly to this case, commands the affirmance of prison sentences that are exceptionally harsh by the standards of the modern Western world, dictated by an accidental, unintended scheme of punishment nevertheless implied by the words (taken one by one) of the relevant enactments. The natural law or pragmatist view leads to a freer interpretation, one influenced by norms of equal treatment; and let us explore the interpretive possibilities here. One is to interpret "mixture or substance containing a detectable amount of [LSD]" to exclude the carrier medium—the blotter paper, sugar or gelatin cubes, and orange juice or other beverage. That is the course we rejected in *United States v. Rose*, as have the other circuits. I wrote *Rose*, but I am no longer confident that its literal interpretation of the statute, under which the blotter paper, cubes, etc. are "substances" that "contain" LSD, is inevitable. The blotter paper, etc. are better viewed, I now think, as carriers, like the package in which a kilo of cocaine comes wrapped or the bottle in which a fifth of liquor is sold.

Interpreted to exclude the carrier, the punishment schedule for LSD would make perfectly good sense; it would not warp the statutory design. The comparison with heroin and cocaine is again illuminating. The statute imposes the five-year mandatory minimum sentence on anyone who sells a substance or mixture containing a hundred grams of heroin, equal to 10,000 to 20,000 doses. One gram of pure LSD, which also would trigger the five-year minimum, yields 20,000 doses. The comparable figures for cocaine are 3250 to 50,000 doses, placing LSD in about the middle. So Congress may have wanted to base punishment for the sale of LSD on the weight of the pure drug after all, using one and ten grams of the pure drug to trigger the five-year and ten-year minima (and corresponding maxima—twenty years and forty years). This interpretation leaves "substance or mixture containing" without a referent, so far as LSD is concerned. But we must remember that Congress used the identical term in each subsection that specifies the quantity of a drug that subjects the seller to the designated minimum and maximum punishments. In thus automatically including the same term in each subsection, Congress did not necessarily affirm that, for each and every drug covered by the statute, a substance or mixture containing the drug *must* be found.

The flexible interpretation that I am proposing is decisively strengthened by the constitutional objection to basing punishment of LSD offenders on the weight of the carrier medium rather than on the weight of the LSD. Courts often do interpretive handsprings to avoid having even to *decide* a constitutional question. *Gomez v. United States*, 490 U.S. 858 (1989). In doing so they expand, very questionably in my view, the effective scope of the Constitution, creating a constitutional penumbra in which statutes wither, shrink, are deformed. A better case for flexible interpretation is presented when the alternative is to nullify Congress's action: when in other words there is not merely a constitutional question about, but a constitutional barrier to, the statute when interpreted literally. This is such a case.

The sentences stand condemned under [a] principle [implicit in the Due Process Clause of the Fifth Amendment that] forbids the unequal treatment of people identically situated. That this principle exists and is potentially applicable to criminal punishment can scarcely be doubted * * *.

The point is not that the judicial imagination can conjure up anomalous applications of the statute. A statute is not irrational because its draftsmen lacked omniscience. The point is that graduating punishment to the weight of the carrier medium produces, in the case of LSD, a systematically, unavoidably bizarre schedule of punishments that no one is able to justify. * * *

Our choice is between ruling that the provisions of section 841 regarding LSD are irrational, hence unconstitutional, and therefore there is no punishment for dealing in LSD—Congress must go back to the drawing boards, and all LSD cases in the pipeline must be dismissed—and ruling that, to preserve so much of the statute as can constitutionally be preserved, the statutory expression "substance or mixture containing a detectable amount of [LSD]" excludes the carrier medium. Given *this* choice, we can be reasonably certain that Congress would have

**Food for Thought**

Could Judge Posner have reached his conclusion simply by invoking the rule against absurdity, which we considered in Chapter 3? How can a judge know when a particular statute produces "absurd" results?

preferred the second course; and this consideration carries the argument for a flexible interpretation over the top.

The literal interpretation adopted by the majority is not inevitable. All interpretation is contextual. The words of the statute—interpreted against a background that includes a constitutional norm of equal treatment, a (closely related) constitutional commitment to rationality, an evident failure by both Congress and the Sentencing Commission to consider how LSD is actually produced, distributed, and sold, and an equally evident failure by the same two bodies to consider the interaction between heavy mandatory minimum sentences and the Sentencing Guidelines—will bear an interpretation that distinguishes between the carrier vehicle of the illegal drug and the substance or mixture containing a detectable amount of the drug. The punishment of the crack dealer is not determined by the weight of the glass tube in which he sells the crack; we should not lightly attribute to Congress a purpose of punishing the dealer in LSD according to the weight of the LSD carrier. We should not make Congress's handiwork an embarrassment to the members of Congress and to us.

---

## Points for Discussion

### *a. Touchstones of Interpretation*

Judge Easterbrook's opinion for the court focused primarily on the ordinary meaning of the statutory text. He asserted that it "is not possible to construe the words of § 841 to make the penalty turn on the net weight of the drug rather than the gross weight of carrier and drug," because " '[d]etectable amount' is the opposite of 'pure.' " He also concluded that "[o]rdinary parlance calls the paper containing tiny crystals of LSD a mixture." Taking Judge Easterbrook on his own terms, do you agree with his assertions about the plain meaning of the statutory text?

Judge Cummings relied principally on Congress's intent in concluding that a court should not consider the weight of the carrier medium in calculating the sentence for trafficking in LSD. On what evidence did he rely in identifying Congress's intent? Why did Judge Easterbrook disregard that evidence? Do you agree with Judge Cummings's view of Congress's intent with respect to the question presented in the case?

### *b. The Judicial Role in Statutory Interpretation*

As we saw in Chapter 2, the approach that Judge Easterbrook urged is called textualism. On Judge Easterbrook's view, what is a judge's role in interpreting statutes? How does a focus on the plain or ordinary meaning of statutory text advance that role? Judge Easterbrook also declined to invoke the rule of lenity or the avoidance canon, which we considered in Chapter 3. Did he think that those canons are inconsistent with the proper judicial role in statutory interpretation, or did he just think that they were not implicated in this case?

Judge Posner urged a very different approach to statutory interpretation. He described Judge Easterbrook's approach as a form of "positivism," an approach that holds that the law is simply what the body authorized to make law—in this case, Congress—has declared it to be. On that view, judges should not depart from the text of the law because such departures impermissibly substitute the judge as law-maker. In Judge Posner's view, what is the virtue of that approach? What are the drawbacks?

Judge Posner ultimately urged the court to engage in what he described as "pragmatic" interpretation. What does that approach involve? In Judge Posner's view, what is the virtue of that approach? What are the drawbacks? What is Judge Posner's conception of the appropriate judicial role in statutory interpretation?

### *c. Subsequent Developments*

The Supreme Court granted certiorari to review the court's conclusion in *Marshall.* The Court affirmed the Seventh Circuit's conclusion, reasoning that a reading of the statute "that makes the penalty turn on the net weight of the drug rather than the gross weight of the carrier and drug together" is "not a plausible one." *Chapman v. United States,* 500 U.S. 453 (1991). Noting that the "statute refers to a 'mixture or substance containing a detectable amount,' " the Court concluded that "[s]o long as it contains a detectable amount, the entire mixture or substance is to be weighed when calculating the sentence." Justice Stevens, joined by Justice Marshall, dissented, reasoning that the "consequences of the majority's construction of 21 U.S.C. § 841 are so bizarre that I cannot believe they were intended by Congress."

---

In Chapter 2, we considered *Commonwealth v. Maxwell* and *People ex rel. Fyfe v. Barnett,* which involved women's eligibility to serve as jurors, and *In the Matter of Angel Lace M.*, which involved an unmarried gay woman's petition to adopt her partner's biological child. Those cases raised the question of how to apply an old statute whose terms are broad but whose language has not changed to accommodate circumstances that the enacting legislature did not contemplate or anticipate. Should a judge in such a case simply apply the ordinary meaning of the statutory terms? Or should she seek to implement the enacting legislature's intent? If the latter, at what level of generality should the court determine that intent? Does Judge Posner's approach in *United States v. Marshall* suggest another way to approach such questions? Consider the Problem and the case that follows.

---

## Problem

The Supreme Court granted certiorari in three cases. In each of the cases, an employer allegedly fired a long-time employee simply for being gay or transgender. Clayton County, Georgia, fired Gerald Bostock for conduct "unbecoming" a county employee shortly after he began participating in a gay recreational softball league. Altitude Express fired Donald Zarda days after he mentioned being gay. And R. G. & G. R. Harris Funeral Homes fired Aimee Stephens, who presented as a male when she was hired but subsequently informed her employer that she planned to "live and work full-time as a woman." Each employee sued, alleging sex discrimination under Title VII of the Civil Rights Act of 1964.

The relevant provisions of Title VII provide:

> **42 U.S.C. § 2000d–2. Unlawful Employment Practices.**
>
> **(a) Employer practices.** It shall be an unlawful employment practice for an employer—
>
> > **(1)** to fail or refuse to hire or to discharge any individual, or otherwise to discriminate against any individual with respect to his compensation, terms, conditions, or privileges of employment, because of such individual's race, color, religion, sex, or national origin; or
> >
> > **(2)** to limit, segregate, or classify his employees or applicants for employment in any way which would deprive or tend to deprive any individual of employment opportunities or otherwise adversely affect his status as an employee, because of such individual's race, color, religion, sex, or national origin. * * *
>
> **(e) Businesses or enterprises with personnel qualified on basis of religion, sex, or national origin; educational institutions with personnel of particular religion.**
>
> Notwithstanding any other provision of this subchapter, * * * it shall not be an unlawful employment practice for an employer to hire and employ employees, for an employment agency to classify, or refer for employment any individual, for a labor organization to classify its membership or to classify or refer for employment any individual, or for an employer, labor organization, or joint labor-management committee controlling apprenticeship or other training or retraining programs to admit or employ any individual in any such program, on the basis of his religion, sex, or national origin in those certain instances where religion, sex, or national origin is a bona fide occupational qualification reasonably necessary to the normal operation of that particular business or enterprise * * *.
>
> **(m) Impermissible consideration of race, color, religion, sex, or national origin in employment practices.**
>
> Except as otherwise provided in this subchapter, an unlawful employment practice is established when the complaining party demonstrates that race, color, religion,

> sex, or national origin was a motivating factor for any employment practice, even though other factors also motivated the practice.

Before 2017, the federal courts of appeals had uniformly held that the Act does not prohibit discrimination on the basis of sexual orientation.

Several Supreme Court cases were relevant to the issue presented in the three suits. First, in *Price Waterhouse v. Hopkins*, 490 U.S. 228 (1989), the Court confronted a claim that an employer had discriminated against women who behaved in a way that the employer viewed as too "masculine"—by declining to wear makeup and jewelry, or by dressing in a way that the employer viewed as unfeminine. The Court concluded that the practice of gender stereotyping falls within Title VII's prohibition against sex discrimination. The Court held that a plaintiff could prevail on such a claim by demonstrating that sex played a part in the employer's decision, if the employer could not show that it would have made the same decision absent any discriminatory motive.

Second, in *Oncale v. Sundowner Offshore Servs., Inc.*, 523 U.S. 75 (1998), the Court held that a plaintiff can prevail on a claim of sexual harassment even if the harasser is the same sex as the victim. The Court explained:

> "[M]ale-on-male sexual harassment in the workplace was assuredly not the principal evil Congress was concerned with when it enacted Title VII. But statutory prohibitions often go beyond the principal evil to cover reasonably comparable evils, and it is ultimately the provisions of our laws rather than the principal concerns of our legislators by which we are governed. Title VII prohibits 'discriminat[ion] . . . because of . . . sex' in the 'terms' or 'conditions' of employment. Our holding that this includes sexual harassment must extend to sexual harassment of any kind that meets the statutory requirements."

Third, in *Phillips v. Martin Marietta Corp.*, 400 U.S. 542 (1971), the Court concluded that a company violated Title VII by refusing to hire women with young children, despite the fact that the discrimination also depended on being a parent of young children and the fact that the company otherwise favored hiring women over men. In addition, in *Los Angeles Dept. of Water and Power v. Manhart*, 435 U.S. 702 (1978), the Court held that an employer's policy of requiring women to make larger pension fund contributions than men violated Title VII, notwithstanding the policy's basis in statistically accurate assumptions about life expectancy (that is, that women tend to live longer than men).

Fourth, in *Loving v. Virginia*, 388 U.S. 1 (1967), the Court invalidated a Virginia law that prohibited inter-racial marriages. Under *Loving*, accordingly, discrimination on the basis of the race of a person with whom another person associates constitutes impermissible racial discrimination under the Equal Protection Clause of the Fourteenth Amendment. Similarly, the Supreme

Court held in *Obergefell v. Hodges*, 576 U.S. 644 (2015), that the Due Process and Equal Protection Clauses of the Constitution protect the right of same-sex couples to marry.

A few other federal statutes address discrimination on the basis of sexual orientation. For example, 34 U.S.C. § 12291(b)(13)(A), which applies to federal grants distributed pursuant to the Violence Against Women Act, provides: "No person in the United States shall, on the basis of actual or perceived race, color, religion, national origin, sex, gender identity . . ., sexual orientation, or disability, be excluded from participation in, be denied the benefits of, or be subjected to discrimination under any program or activity funded in whole or in part with funds made available under the Violence Against Women Act of 1994." And the Hate Crimes Act, which Congress enacted in 2009, provides enhanced punishment for causing bodily injury to "any person, because of the actual or perceived religion, national origin, gender, sexual orientation, gender identity, or disability of any person." 18 U.S.C. § 249(a)(2)(A).

Finally, the Equal Employment Opportunity Commission, the agency charged with vindicating the interests protected by Title VII, for the first time in 2011 asserted that "discrimination against a transgender individual because that person is transgender" violates Title VII. See *Macy v. Holder*, 2012 WL 1435995, *11, n. 16 (Apr. 20, 2012). In addition, in 2015, the agency first announced its view that the law's prohibition against sex discrimination encompasses discrimination on the basis of sexual orientation. *Baldwin v. Foxx*, EEOC Appeal No. 0120133080, 2015 WL 4397641 (July 15, 2015).

What are the plaintiffs' strongest arguments that the Court should interpret the statute to prohibit discrimination on the basis of sexual orientation or gender identity? What are the employers' strongest arguments that the statute does not prohibit such discrimination? Sketch out the arguments before reading the case that follows.

---

## *Bostock v. Clayton County*

140 S.Ct. 1731 (2020)

JUSTICE GORSUCH delivered the opinion of the Court.

Few facts are needed to appreciate the legal question we face. Each of the three cases before us started the same way: An employer fired a long-time employee shortly after the employee revealed that he or she is homosexual or transgender—and allegedly for no reason other than the employee's homosexuality or transgender status. Gerald

Bostock worked for Clayton County, Georgia, as a child welfare advocate. Under his leadership, the county won national awards for its work. After a decade with the county, Mr. Bostock began participating in a gay recreational softball league. Not long after that, influential members of the community allegedly made disparaging comments about Mr. Bostock's sexual orientation and participation in the league. Soon, he was fired for conduct "unbecoming" a county employee. Donald Zarda worked as a skydiving instructor at Altitude Express in New York. After several seasons with the company, Mr. Zarda mentioned that he was gay and, days later, was fired. Aimee Stephens worked at R. G. & G. R. Harris Funeral Homes in Garden City, Michigan. When she got the job, Ms. Stephens presented as a male. But two years into her service with the company, she began treatment for despair and loneliness. Ultimately, clinicians diagnosed her with gender dysphoria and recommended that she begin living as a woman. In her sixth year with the company, Ms. Stephens wrote a letter to her employer explaining that she planned to "live and work full-time as a woman" after she returned from an upcoming vacation. The funeral home fired her before she left, telling her "this is not going to work out."

* * * Each employee brought suit under Title VII alleging unlawful discrimination on the basis of sex. 78 Stat. 255, 42 U.S.C. § 2000e–2(a)(1). [The Eleventh Circuit held that the law does not prohibit employers from firing employees for being gay, but the Second Circuit concluded that sexual orientation discrimination violates Title VII, and the Sixth Circuit held that Title VII bars employers from firing employees because they are transgender.]

This Court normally interprets a statute in accord with the ordinary public meaning of its terms at the time of its enactment. After all, only the words on the page constitute the law adopted by Congress and approved by the President. If judges could add to, remodel, update, or detract from old statutory terms inspired only by extratextual sources and our own imaginations, we would risk amending statutes outside the legislative process reserved for the people's representatives. And we would deny the people the right to continue relying on the original meaning of the law they have counted on to settle their rights and obligations.

With this in mind, our task is clear. We must determine the ordinary public meaning of Title VII's command that it is "unlawful . . . for an employer to fail or refuse to hire or to discharge any individual, or otherwise to discriminate against any individual with respect to his compensation, terms, conditions, or privileges of employment, because of such individual's race, color, religion, sex, or national origin." § 2000e–2(a)(1). To

**Take Note**

The Court states that, in assessing the meaning of the statutory text, it should "orient" itself "to the time of the statute's adoption." What should the Court do if the ordinary meaning of the statutory terms was different in 1964 than it is today?

do so, we orient ourselves to the time of the statute's adoption, here 1964, and begin by examining the key statutory terms in turn before assessing their impact on the cases at hand and then confirming our work against this Court's precedents.

The only statutorily protected characteristic at issue in today's cases is "sex"—and that is also the primary term in Title VII whose meaning the parties dispute. Appealing to roughly contemporaneous dictionaries, the employers say that, as used here, the term "sex" in 1964 referred to "status as either male or female [as] determined by reproductive biology." The employees counter by submitting that, even in 1964, the term bore a broader scope, capturing more than anatomy and reaching at least some norms concerning gender identity and sexual orientation. But because nothing in our approach to these cases turns on the outcome of the parties' debate, and because the employees concede the point for argument's sake, we proceed on the assumption that "sex" signified what the employers suggest, referring only to biological distinctions between male and female.

Still, that's just a starting point. The question isn't just what "sex" meant, but what Title VII says about it. Most notably, the statute prohibits employers from taking certain actions "because of" sex. And, as this Court has previously explained, "the ordinary meaning of 'because of' is 'by reason of' or 'on account of.' " *University of Tex. Southwestern Medical Center v. Nassar*, 570 U.S. 338, 350 (2013). In the language of law, this means that Title VII's "because of" test incorporates the "simple" and "traditional" standard of but-for causation. *Nassar*, 570 U.S. at 346, 360. That form of causation is established whenever a particular outcome would not have happened "but for" the purported cause. In other words, a but-for test directs us to change one thing at a time and see if the outcome changes. If it does, we have found a but-for cause.

* * * Often, events have multiple but-for causes. * * * When it comes to Title VII, the adoption of the traditional but-for causation standard means a defendant cannot avoid liability just by citing some *other* factor that contributed to its challenged employment decision. So long as the plaintiff's sex was one but-for cause of that decision, that is enough to trigger the law.

As sweeping as [the] but-for causation standard can be, Title VII does not concern itself with everything that happens "because of" sex. The statute imposes liability on employers only when they "fail or refuse to hire," "discharge," "or otherwise . . . discriminate against" someone because of a statutorily protected characteristic like sex. The employers acknowledge that they discharged the plaintiffs in today's cases, but assert that the statute's list of verbs is qualified by the last item on it: "otherwise . . . discriminate against." By virtue of the word *otherwise*, the employers suggest, Title VII concerns itself not with every discharge, only with those discharges that involve discrimination.

Accepting this point, too, for argument's sake, the question becomes: What did "discriminate" mean in 1964? As it turns out, it meant then roughly what it means today: "To make a difference in treatment or favor (of one as compared with others)." Webster's New International Dictionary 745 (2d ed. 1954). To "discriminate against" a person, then, would seem to mean treating that individual worse than others who are similarly situated. See *Burlington N. & S.F.R. Co. v. White*, 548 U.S. 53, 59 (2006). In so-called "disparate treatment" cases like today's, this Court has also held that the difference in treatment based on sex must be intentional. See, *e.g., Watson v. Fort Worth Bank & Trust*, 487 U.S. 977, 986 (1988). So, taken together, an employer who intentionally treats a person worse because of sex—such as by firing the person for actions or attributes it would tolerate in an individual of another sex—discriminates against that person in violation of Title VII.

**FYI**

Title VII prohibits both intentional discrimination on the prohibited bases—known as "disparate treatment"—and some actions that are not motivated by a discriminatory intent but that have discriminatory effects. Cases involving the latter sort of claim are called "disparate impact" cases.

At first glance, another interpretation might seem possible. Discrimination sometimes involves "the act, practice, or an instance of discriminating categorically rather than individually." Webster's New Collegiate Dictionary 326 (1975). * * * Maybe the law concerns itself simply with ensuring that employers don't treat women generally less favorably than they do men. * * * [But the statute] tells us three times—including immediately after the words "discriminate against"—that our focus should be on individuals, not groups: Employers may not "fail or refuse to hire or . . . discharge any *individual*, or otherwise . . . discriminate against any *individual* with respect to his compensation, terms, conditions, or privileges of employment, because of such *individual's* . . . sex." § 2000e–2(a)(1) (emphasis added). And the meaning of "individual" was as uncontroversial in 1964 as it is today: "A particular being as distinguished from a class, species, or collection." Webster's New International Dictionary, at 1267. * * *

From the ordinary public meaning of the statute's language at the time of the law's adoption, a straightforward rule emerges: An employer violates Title VII when it intentionally fires an individual employee based in part on sex. It doesn't matter if other factors besides the plaintiff's sex contributed to the decision. And it doesn't matter if the employer treated women as a group the same when compared to men as a group. If the employer intentionally relies in part on an individual employee's sex when deciding to discharge the employee—put differently, if changing the employee's sex would have yielded a different choice by the employer—a statutory violation has occurred. * * *

[I]t is impossible to discriminate against a person for being homosexual or transgender without discriminating against that individual based on sex. Consider, for example, an employer with two employees, both of whom are attracted to men. The two individuals are, to the employer's mind, materially identical in all respects, except that one is a man and the other a woman. If the employer fires the male employee for no reason other than the fact he is attracted to men, the employer discriminates against him for traits or actions it tolerates in his female colleague. Put differently, the employer intentionally singles out an employee to fire based in part on the employee's sex, and the affected employee's sex is a but-for cause of his discharge. Or take an employer who fires a transgender person who was identified as a male at birth but who now identifies as a female. If the employer retains an otherwise identical employee who was identified as female at birth, the employer intentionally penalizes a person identified as male at birth for traits or actions that it tolerates in an employee identified as female at birth. Again, the individual employee's sex plays an unmistakable and impermissible role in the discharge decision. * * * [H]omosexuality and transgender status are inextricably bound up with sex. Not because homosexuality or transgender status are related to sex in some vague sense or because discrimination on these bases has some disparate impact on one sex or another, but because to discriminate on these grounds requires an employer to intentionally treat individual employees differently because of their sex.

Nor does it matter that, when an employer treats one employee worse because of that individual's sex, other factors may contribute to the decision. Consider an employer with a policy of firing any woman he discovers to be a Yankees fan. Carrying out that rule because an employee is a woman *and* a fan of the Yankees is a firing "because of sex" if the employer would have tolerated the same allegiance in a male employee. Likewise here. When an employer fires an employee because she is homosexual or transgender, two causal factors may be in play—*both* the individual's sex *and* something else (the sex to which the individual is attracted or with which the individual identifies). But Title VII doesn't care. If an employer would not have discharged an employee but for that individual's sex, the statute's causation standard is met, and liability may attach.

Reframing the additional causes in today's cases as additional intentions can do no more to insulate the employers from liability. [I]ntentional discrimination based on sex violates Title VII, even if it is intended only as a means to achieving the employer's ultimate goal of discriminating against homosexual or transgender employees. * * * Imagine an employer who has a policy of firing any employee known to be homosexual. The employer hosts an office holiday party and invites employees to bring their spouses. A model employee arrives and introduces a manager to Susan, the employee's wife. Will that employee be fired? If the policy works as the employer intends, the answer depends entirely on whether the model employee is a man or a woman. To be sure, that employer's ultimate goal might be to discriminate on the basis of sexual orientation. But to achieve that purpose the employer must, along the way, intentionally treat an employee worse based in part on that individual's sex.

An employer musters no better a defense by responding that it is equally happy to fire male *and* female employees who are homosexual or transgender. Title VII liability is not limited to employers who, through the sum of all of their employment actions, treat the class of men differently than the class of women. Instead, the law makes each instance of discriminating against an individual employee because of that individual's sex an independent violation of Title VII. So just as an employer who fires both Hannah and Bob for failing to fulfill traditional sex stereotypes doubles rather than eliminates Title VII liability, an employer who fires both Hannah and Bob for being gay or transgender does the same.

At bottom, these cases involve no more than the straightforward application of legal terms with plain and settled meanings. For an employer to discriminate against employees for being homosexual or transgender, the employer must intentionally discriminate against individual men and women in part because of sex. That has always been prohibited by Title VII's plain terms—and that "should be the end of the analysis." 883 F.3d at 135 (Cabranes, J., concurring in judgment).

If more support for our conclusion were required, there's no need to look far. All that the statute's plain terms suggest, this Court's cases have already confirmed. Consider three of our leading precedents.

In *Phillips v. Martin Marietta Corp.*, 400 U.S. 542 (1971) (*per curiam*), a company allegedly refused to hire women with young children, but did hire men with children the same age. Because its discrimination depended not only on the employee's sex as a female but also on the presence of another criterion—namely, being a parent of young children—the company contended it hadn't engaged in discrimination "because of" sex. The company maintained, too, that it hadn't violated the law because, as a whole, it tended to favor hiring women over men. Unsurprisingly by now, these submissions did not sway the Court. * * *

In *Los Angeles Dept. of Water and Power v. Manhart*, 435 U.S. 702 (1978), an employer required women to make larger pension fund contributions than men. The employer sought to justify its disparate treatment on the ground that women tend to live longer than men, and thus are likely to receive more from the pension fund over time. [But the Court recognized that] a rule that appears evenhanded at the group level can prove discriminatory at the level of individuals. [The Court concluded that the employer] could not "pass the simple test" asking whether an individual female employee would have been treated the same regardless of her sex. *Id.*, at 711.

In *Oncale v. Sundowner Offshore Services, Inc.*, 523 U.S. 75 (1998), a male plaintiff alleged that he was singled out by his male co-workers for sexual harassment. The Court held it was immaterial that members of the same sex as the victim committed the alleged discrimination. * * * "[A]ssuredly," the case didn't involve "the principal evil Congress was concerned with when it enacted Title VII." *Id.*, at 79. But, the Court unanimously explained, it is "the provisions of our laws rather than the principal concerns of our legislators by which we are governed." Because the plaintiff alleged that the harassment would not have taken place but for his sex—that is, the plaintiff would not have suffered similar treatment if he were female—a triable Title VII claim existed.

The lessons these cases hold for ours are by now familiar. First, it's irrelevant what an employer might call its discriminatory practice, how others might label it, or what else might motivate it. * * * [T]oday's employers might describe their actions as motivated by their employees' homosexuality or transgender status. But just as labels and additional intentions or motivations didn't make a difference in *Manhart* or *Phillips*, they cannot make a difference here. * * * Second, the plaintiff's sex need not be the sole or primary cause of the employer's adverse action. * * * Finally, an employer cannot escape liability by demonstrating that it treats males and females comparably as groups. [A]n employer who intentionally fires an individual homosexual or transgender employee in part because of that individual's sex violates the law even if the employer is willing to subject all male and female homosexual or transgender employees to the same rule.

* * * For present purposes, [the employers] do not dispute that they fired the plaintiffs for being homosexual or transgender. * * * Rather, the employers submit that even intentional discrimination against employees based on their homosexuality or transgender status supplies no basis for liability under Title VII. Maybe most intuitively, the employers assert that discrimination on the basis of homosexuality and transgender status aren't referred to as sex discrimination in ordinary conversation. If asked by a friend (rather than a judge) why they were fired, even today's plaintiffs would likely respond that it was because they were gay or transgender, not because of sex. According to the employers, that conversational answer, not the statute's strict terms, should guide our thinking and suffice to defeat any suggestion that the employees now before us were fired because of sex. But this submission rests on a mistaken understanding of what kind of cause the law is looking for in a Title VII case. In conversation, a speaker is likely to focus on what seems most relevant or informative to the listener. So an employee who has just been fired is likely to identify the primary or most direct cause * * *. But these conversational conventions do not control Title VII's legal analysis, which asks simply whether sex was a but-for cause. * * * You can call the statute's but-for causation test what you will—expansive, legalistic, the dissents even dismiss it as wooden or literal. But it is the law.

**Take Note**

On which canon of construction did the employers rely here? Do you find that argument convincing?

Next, the employers turn to Title VII's list of protected characteristics—race, color, religion, sex, and national origin. Because homosexuality and transgender status can't be found on that list and because they are conceptually distinct from sex, the employers reason, they are implicitly excluded from Title VII's reach. Put another way, if Congress had wanted to address these matters in Title VII, it would have referenced them specifically.

* * * We agree that homosexuality and transgender status are distinct concepts from sex. But, as we've seen, discrimination based on homosexuality or transgender status necessarily entails discrimination based on sex * * *. Nor is there any such thing as a "canon of donut holes," in which Congress's failure to speak directly to a specific case that falls within a more general statutory rule creates a tacit exception. Instead, when Congress chooses not to include any exceptions to a broad rule, courts apply the broad rule. * * * As enacted, Title VII prohibits all forms of discrimination because of sex, however they may manifest themselves or whatever other labels might attach to them.

The employers try the same point another way. Since 1964, they observe, Congress has considered several proposals to add sexual orientation to Title VII's list of protected characteristics, but no such amendment has become law. Meanwhile, Congress has enacted other statutes addressing other topics that do discuss sexual orientation. This postenactment legislative history, they urge, should tell us something. But what? There's no authoritative evidence explaining why later Congresses adopted other laws referencing sexual orientation but didn't amend this one. Maybe some in the later legislatures understood the impact Title VII's broad language already promised for cases like ours and didn't think a revision needed. Maybe others knew about its impact but hoped no one else would notice. Maybe still others, occupied by other concerns, didn't consider the issue at all. All we can know for certain is that speculation about why a later Congress declined to adopt new legislation offers a "particularly dangerous" basis on which to rest an interpretation of an existing law a different and earlier Congress did adopt. *Pension Benefit Guaranty Corporation v. LTV Corp.*, 496 U.S. 633, 650 (1990).

Ultimately, the employers are forced to abandon the statutory text and precedent altogether and appeal to assumptions and policy. Most pointedly, they contend that few in 1964 would have expected Title VII to apply to discrimination against homosexual and transgender persons. [But this] Court has explained many times over many years that, when the meaning of the statute's terms is plain, our job is at an end. The people are entitled to rely on the law as written, without fearing that courts might disregard its plain terms based on some extratextual consideration. Of course, some Members of this Court have consulted legislative history when interpreting *ambiguous* statutory language. But that has no bearing here. "Legislative history, for those who take it into account, is meant to clear up ambiguity, not create it." *Milner v. Department of Navy*, 562 U.S. 562, 574 (2011). And as we have seen, no ambiguity exists about how Title VII's terms apply to the facts before us. To be sure, the statute's application in these cases reaches "beyond the principal evil" legislators may have intended or expected to address. *Oncale*, 523 U.S. at 79. But "the fact that [a statute] has been applied in situations not expressly anticipated by Congress" does not demonstrate ambiguity; instead, it simply "demonstrates [the] breadth" of a legislative command. *Sedima, S.P.R.L.* v. *Imrex Co.*, 473 U.S. 479, 499 (1985). And "it is ultimately the provisions of" those legislative commands "rather than the principal concerns of our legislators by which we are governed." *Oncale*, 523 U.S. at 79; see also A. Scalia & B. Garner, Reading Law: The Interpretation of Legal Texts 101 (2012) (noting that unexpected applications of broad language reflect only Congress's "presumed point [to] produce general coverage—not to leave room for courts to recognize ad hoc exceptions").

Still, while legislative history can never defeat unambiguous statutory text, historical sources can be useful for a different purpose: Because the law's ordinary meaning at the time of enactment usually governs, we must be sensitive to the possibility a statutory term that means one thing today or in one context might have meant something else at the time of its adoption or might mean something different in another context. And we must be attuned to the possibility that a statutory phrase ordinarily bears a different meaning than the terms do when viewed individually or literally. To ferret out such shifts in linguistic usage or subtle distinctions between literal and ordinary meaning, this Court has sometimes consulted the understandings of the law's drafters as some (not always conclusive) evidence. For example, in the context of the National Motor Vehicle Theft Act, this Court admitted that the term "vehicle" in 1931 could literally mean "a conveyance working on land, water or air." *McBoyle v. United States*, 283 U.S. 25, 26 (1931). But given contextual clues and "everyday speech" at the time of the Act's adoption in 1919, this Court concluded that "vehicles" in that statute included only things "moving on land," not airplanes too. * * *

The employers, however, advocate nothing like that here. They do not seek to use historical sources to illustrate that the meaning of any of Title VII's language has changed since 1964 or that the statute's terms, whether viewed individually or as a whole, ordinarily carried some message we have missed. * * * Rather than suggesting that the statutory language bears some other *meaning*, the employers and dissents merely suggest that, because few in 1964 expected today's *result*, we should not dare to admit that it follows ineluctably from the statutory text. When a new application emerges that is both unexpected and important, they would seemingly have us merely point out the question, refer the subject back to Congress, and decline to enforce the plain terms of the law in the meantime.

That is exactly the sort of reasoning this Court has long rejected. Admittedly, the employers take pains to couch their argument in terms of seeking to honor the statute's "expected applications" rather than vindicate its "legislative intent." But the concepts are closely related. One could easily contend that legislators only intended expected applications or that a statute's purpose is limited to achieving applications foreseen at the time of enactment. However framed, the employer's logic impermissibly seeks to displace the plain meaning of the law in favor of something lying beyond it.

If anything, the employers' new framing may only add new problems. * * * How many people have to foresee the application for it to qualify as "expected"? Do we look only at the moment the statute was enacted, or do we allow some time for the implications of a new statute to be worked out? Should we consider the expectations of those who had no reason to give a particular application any thought or only those with reason to think about the question? How do we account for those who change their minds over time, after learning new facts or hearing a new argument? How specifically or generally should we frame the "application" at issue? None of these questions have obvious answers, and the employers don't propose any.

One could also reasonably fear that objections about unexpected applications will not be deployed neutrally. Often lurking just behind such objections resides a cynicism that Congress could not *possibly* have meant to protect a disfavored group. * * * But to refuse enforcement just because of that, because the parties before us happened to be unpopular at the time of the law's passage, would not only require us to abandon our role as interpreters of statutes; it would tilt the scales of justice in favor of the strong or popular and neglect the promise that all persons are entitled to the benefit of the law's terms.

The employer's position also proves too much. If we applied Title VII's plain text only to applications some (yet-to-be-determined) group expected in 1964, we'd have more than a little law to overturn. Start with *Oncale*. How many people in 1964 could have expected that the law would turn out to protect male employees? Let alone to protect them from harassment by other male employees? * * * [Indeed,] thanks to the [Act's] broad language, many, maybe most, applications of Title VII's sex provision were "unanticipated" at the time of the law's adoption. * * *

The weighty implications of the employers' argument from expectations also reveal why they cannot hide behind the no-elephants-in-mouseholes canon. That canon recognizes that Congress "does not alter the fundamental details of a regulatory scheme in vague terms or ancillary provisions." *Whitman v. American Trucking Assns., Inc.*, 531 U.S. 457, 468 (2001). But it has no relevance here. We can't deny that today's holding * * * is an elephant. But where's the mousehole? Title VII's prohibition of sex discrimination in employment is a major piece of federal civil rights legislation [written] in starkly broad terms. It has repeatedly produced unexpected applications, at least in the view of those on the receiving end of them. Congress's key drafting choices—to focus on discrimination against individuals and not merely between groups and to hold employers liable whenever sex is a but-for cause of the plaintiff's injuries—virtually guaranteed that unexpected applications would emerge over time. This elephant has never hidden in a mousehole; it has been standing before us all along.

With that, the employers are left to abandon their concern for expected applications and fall back to the last line of defense for all failing statutory interpretation arguments: naked policy appeals. If we were to apply the statute's plain language, they complain, any number of undesirable policy consequences would follow. Gone here is any pretense of statutory interpretation; all that's left is a suggestion we should proceed without the law's guidance to do as we think best. But that's an invitation no court should ever take up. * * * When it comes to statutory interpretation, our role is limited to applying the law's demands as faithfully as we can in the cases that come before us. [T]he same judicial humility that requires us to refrain from adding to statutes requires us to refrain from diminishing them. * * * Whether other policies and practices might or might not qualify as unlawful discrimination or find justifications under other provisions of Title VII are questions for future cases, not these.

* * * Ours is a society of written laws. Judges are not free to overlook plain statutory commands on the strength of nothing more than suppositions about intentions or guesswork about expectations. In Title VII, Congress adopted broad language making it illegal for an employer to rely on an employee's sex when deciding to fire that employee. We do not hesitate to recognize today a necessary consequence of that legislative choice: An employer who fires an individual merely for being gay or transgender defies the law.

JUSTICE ALITO, with whom JUSTICE THOMAS joins, dissenting.

There is only one word for what the Court has done today: legislation. The document that the Court releases is in the form of a judicial opinion interpreting a statute, but that is deceptive. Title VII of the Civil Rights Act of 1964 prohibits employment discrimination on any of five specified grounds: "race, color, religion, sex, [and] national origin." 42 U.S.C. § 2000e–2(a)(1). Neither "sexual orientation" nor "gender identity" appears on that list. For the past 45 years, bills have been introduced in Congress to add "sexual orientation" to the list, and in recent years, bills have included "gender identity" as well. But to date, none has passed both Houses.

Because no such amendment of Title VII has been enacted in accordance with the requirements in the Constitution (passage in both Houses and presentment to the President, Art. I, § 7, cl. 2), Title VII's prohibition of discrimination because of "sex" still means what it has always meant. But the Court is not deterred by these constitutional niceties. Usurping the constitutional authority of the other branches, the Court has essentially taken [an unenacted proposal] and issued it under the guise of statutory interpretation. A more brazen abuse of our authority to interpret statutes is hard to recall.

The Court tries to convince readers that it is merely enforcing the terms of the statute, but that is preposterous. Even as understood today, the concept of discrimination because of "sex" is different from discrimination because of "sexual orientation" or "gender identity." And in any event, our duty is to interpret statutory terms to "mean what they conveyed to reasonable people *at the time they were written*." A. Scalia & B. Garner, Reading Law: The Interpretation of Legal Texts 16 (2012) (emphasis added). If every single living American had been surveyed in 1964, it would have been hard to find any who thought that discrimination because of sex meant discrimination because of sexual orientation—not to mention gender identity, a concept that was essentially unknown at the time.

The Court attempts to pass off its decision as the inevitable product of the textualist school of statutory interpretation championed by our late colleague Justice Scalia, but no one should be fooled. The Court's opinion is like a pirate ship. It sails under a textualist flag, but what it actually represents is a theory of statutory interpretation that Justice Scalia excoriated—the theory that courts should "update" old statutes so that they better reflect the current values of society. See A. Scalia, A Matter of Interpretation 22 (1997). If the Court finds it appropriate to adopt this theory, it should own up to what it is doing.

Many will applaud today's decision because they agree on policy grounds with the Court's updating of Title VII. But the question in these cases is not whether discrimination because of sexual orientation or gender identity *should be* outlawed. The question is *whether Congress did that in 1964*. It indisputably did not.

Title VII, as noted, prohibits discrimination "because of . . . sex," § 2000e–2(a)(1), and in 1964, it was as clear as clear could be that this meant discrimination because of the genetic and anatomical characteristics that men and women have at the time of birth. Determined searching has not found a single dictionary from that time that defined "sex" to mean sexual orientation, gender identity, or "transgender status." * * * The Court * * * "proceed[s] on the assumption that 'sex' . . . refer[s] only to biological distinctions between male and female." * * * If "sex" in Title VII means biologically male or female, then discrimination because of sex means discrimination because the person in question is biologically male or biologically female, not because that person is sexually attracted to members of the same sex or identifies as a member of a particular gender. * * * "Sex," "sexual orientation," and "gender identity" are different concepts, as the Court concedes. And neither "sexual orientation" nor "gender identity" is tied to either of the two biological sexes. Both men and women may be attracted to members of the opposite sex, members of the same sex, or members of both sexes. And individuals who are born with the genes and organs of either biological sex may identify with a different gender.

* * * Contrary to the Court's contention, discrimination because of sexual orientation or gender identity does not in and of itself entail discrimination because of sex. We can see this because it is quite possible for an employer to discriminate on those grounds without taking the sex of an individual applicant or employee into account. An employer can have a policy that says: "We do not hire gays, lesbians, or transgender individuals." And an employer can implement this policy without paying any attention to or even knowing the biological sex of gay, lesbian, and transgender

applicants. * * * [I]f an employer discriminates against individual applicants or employees without even knowing whether they are male or female, it is impossible to argue that the employer intentionally discriminated because of sex. * * *

The Court's remaining argument is based on a hypothetical that the Court finds instructive. In this hypothetical, an employer has two employees who are "attracted to men," and "*to the employer's mind*" the two employees are "materially identical" except that one is a man and the other is a woman. The Court reasons that if the employer fires the man but not the woman, the employer is necessarily motivated by the man's biological sex * * * In an effort to prove its point, the Court carefully includes in its example just two employees, a homosexual man and a heterosexual woman, but suppose we add two more individuals, a woman who is attracted to women and a man who is attracted to women. * * * [Imagine that the employer discharges the woman attracted to women and the man attracted to men.] The discharged employees have one thing in common. It is not biological sex, attraction to men, or attraction to women. It is attraction to members of their own sex—in a word, sexual orientation. And that, we can infer, is the employer's real motive. * * *

Although the Court relies solely on the arguments discussed above, several other arguments figure prominently in the decisions of the lower courts and in briefs submitted by or in support of the employees. * * * One argument, which relies on our decision in *Price Waterhouse v. Hopkins*, 490 U.S. 228 (1989) (plurality opinion), is that discrimination because of sexual orientation or gender identity violates Title VII because it constitutes prohibited discrimination on the basis of sex stereotypes. [But Title VII does not forbid] discrimination based on sex stereotypes. * * * It prohibits discrimination because of "sex," and the two concepts are not the same. * * *

A second prominent argument made in support of the result that the Court now reaches analogizes discrimination against gays and lesbians to discrimination against a person who is married to or has an intimate relationship with a person of a different [race, which several lower courts have held violates Title VII]. * * * This argument totally ignores the historically rooted reason why discrimination on the basis of an interracial relationship constitutes race discrimination. * * * Discrimination because of sexual orientation * * * cannot be regarded as a form of sex discrimination on the ground that applies in race cases since discrimination because of sexual orientation is not historically tied to a project that aims to subjugate either men or women. An employer who discriminates on this ground might be called "homophobic" or "transphobic," but not sexist.

[W]hat matters in the end is the answer to the question[:] How would the terms of a statute have been understood by ordinary people at the time of enactment? Justice Scalia was perfectly clear on this point. The words of a law, he insisted, "mean *what they conveyed to reasonable people at the time.*" Reading Law, at 16 (emphasis added). * * * Thus, when textualism is properly understood, it calls for an examination of the social context in which a statute was enacted because this may have an important bearing on what its words were understood to mean at the time of enactment. Textualists do not read statutes as if they were messages picked up by a powerful radio telescope from a distant and utterly unknown civilization. Statutes consist of communications between members of a particular linguistic community, one that existed in a particular place and at a particular time, and these communications must therefore be interpreted as they were understood by that community at that time.

For this reason, it is imperative to consider how Americans in 1964 would have understood Title VII's prohibition of discrimination because of sex. * * * In 1964, ordinary Americans reading the text of Title VII would not have dreamed that discrimination because of sex meant discrimination because of sexual orientation, much less gender identity. * * * In 1964, the concept of prohibiting discrimination "because of sex" was no novelty. It was a familiar and well-understood concept, and what it meant was equal treatment for men and women. Long before Title VII was adopted, many pioneering state and federal laws had used language substantively indistinguishable from Title VII's critical phrase, "discrimination because of sex." [See, e.g., Cal. Const., art. XX, § 18 (1879) (stipulating that no one, "*on account of sex*, [could] be disqualified from entering upon or pursuing any lawful business, vocation, or profession"); U.S. Const., amend. XIX (banning the denial or abridgment of the right to vote "on account of sex").] * * * In 1961, President Kennedy * * * established a "Commission on the Status of Women" and directed it to recommend policies "for overcoming discriminations in government and private employment *on the basis of sex*." Exec. Order No. 10980, 3 CFR 138 (1961 Supp.) (emphasis added). In short, the concept of discrimination "because of," "on account of," or "on the basis of" sex was well understood. It was part of the campaign for equality that had been waged by women's rights advocates for more than a century, and what it meant was equal treatment for men and women.

Discrimination "because of sex" was not understood as having anything to do with discrimination because of sexual orientation or transgender status. Any such notion would have clashed in spectacular fashion with the societal norms of the day. For most 21st-century Americans, it is painful to be reminded of the way our society once treated gays and lesbians, but any honest effort to understand what the terms of Title VII were understood to mean when enacted must take into account the societal norms of that time. And the plain truth is that in 1964 homosexuality was thought to be a mental disorder, and homosexual conduct was regarded as morally culpable and worthy of punishment. In its then-most recent Diagnostic and Statistical Manual of Mental Disorders (1952), the American Psychiatric Association classified same-sex attraction as a "sexual deviation," a particular type of "sociopathic personality disturbance," *id.*, at 38–39 * * *. Sodomy was a crime in every State but Illinois, see W. Eskridge, Dishonorable Passions 387–407 (2008) * * *. In 1964 and for many years thereafter, homosexuals were barred from the military. * * * That was how our society [saw] things a half century ago.

To its credit, our society has now come to recognize the injustice of past practices, and this recognition provides the impetus to "update" Title VII. But that is not our job. Our duty is to understand what the terms of Title VII were understood to mean when enacted, and in doing so, we must take into account the societal norms of that time. * * * Without strong evidence to the contrary (and there is none here), our job is to ascertain and apply the "*ordinary* meaning" of the statute. And in 1964, ordinary Americans most certainly would not have understood Title VII to ban discrimination because of sexual orientation * * *. [And] they would have been bewildered to hear that this law also forbids discrimination on the basis of "transgender status" or "gender identity," terms that would have left people at the time scratching their heads. * * * While it is likely true that there have always been individuals who experience what is now termed "gender dysphoria," * * * the current understanding of the concept postdates the enactment of Title VII. * * * It defies belief to suggest that the public meaning of discrimination because of sex in 1964 encompassed discrimination on the basis of a concept that was essentially unknown to the public at that time.

[T]he Court relies on Justice Scalia's opinion for the Court in *Oncale v. Sundowner Offshore Services, Inc.*, 523 U.S. 75 (1998). But * * * it would be a wild understatement to say that discrimination because of sexual orientation and transgender status was not the "principal evil" on Congress's mind in 1964. Whether we like to admit it now or not, in the thinking of Congress and the public at that time, such discrimination would not have been evil at all. But the more important difference between these cases and *Oncale* is that here the interpretation that the Court adopts does not fall within the ordinary meaning of the statutory text as it would have been understood in 1964. To decide for the defendants in *Oncale*, it would have been necessary to carve out an exception to the statutory text. Here, no such surgery is at issue. * * *

Because the opinion of the Court flies a textualist flag, I have taken pains to show that it cannot be defended on textualist grounds. But * * * when there is ambiguity in the terms of a statute, [many Justices] have found it appropriate to look to other evidence of "congressional intent," including legislative history. * * * Any assessment of congressional intent or legislative history seriously undermines the Court's interpretation.

[T]he legislative history of Title VII's prohibition of sex discrimination is brief, but it is nevertheless revealing. The prohibition of sex discrimination was "added to Title VII at the last minute on the floor of the House of Representatives," *Meritor Savings Bank, FSB v. Vinson*, 477 U.S. 57, 63 (1986), by Representative Howard Smith, the Chairman of the Rules Committee. See 110 Cong. Rec. 2577 (1964). Representative Smith had been an ardent opponent of the civil rights bill, and it has been suggested that he added the prohibition against discrimination on the basis of "sex" as a poison pill [to make the bill] unacceptable to Members who might have otherwise voted in favor of the bill. But if Representative Smith had been looking for a poison pill, prohibiting discrimination on the basis of sexual orientation or gender identity would have been far more potent. However, neither Representative Smith nor any other Member said one word about the possibility that the prohibition of sex discrimination might have that meaning. Instead, all the debate concerned discrimination on the basis of biological sex. See 110 Cong. Rec. 2577–2584.

Representative Smith's motivations are contested, 883 F.3d at 139–140 (Lynch, J., dissenting), but whatever they were, the meaning of *the adoption of the prohibition* of sex discrimination is clear. * * * It grew out of "a long history of women's rights advocacy that had increasingly been gaining mainstream recognition and acceptance," and it marked a landmark achievement in the path toward fully equal rights for women. *Id.*, at 140. "Discrimination against gay women and men, by contrast, was not on the table for public debate . . . [i]n those dark, pre-Stonewall days." *Ibid.* For those who regard congressional intent as the touchstone of statutory interpretation, the message of Title VII's legislative history cannot be missed.

Post-enactment events only clarify what was apparent when Title VII was enacted. [B]ills to add "sexual orientation" to Title VII's list of prohibited grounds were introduced in every Congress beginning in 1975 * * *. [Although] two such bills were before Congress in 1991 when it made major changes in Title VII, [Congress did not abrogate lower court decisions concluding that] Title VII does not prohibit discrimination because of sexual orientation * * *. After 1991, six other Courts of Appeals reached the issue of sexual orientation discrimination, and until 2017, every single Court of Appeals decision understood Title VII's prohibition of "discrimination because of sex" to mean discrimination because of biological sex. * * * The Court observes that "[t]he people are entitled to rely on the law as written, without fearing that courts might disregard its plain terms," but it has no qualms about disregarding over 50 years of uniform judicial interpretation of Title VII's plain text. * * *

The updating desire to which the Court succumbs no doubt arises from humane and generous impulses. Today, many Americans know individuals who are gay, lesbian, or transgender and want them to be treated with the dignity, consideration, and fairness that everyone deserves. But the authority of this Court is limited to saying what the law *is*. The Court itself recognizes this: "The place to make new legislation . . . lies in Congress. When it comes to statutory interpretation, our role is limited to applying the law's demands as faithfully as we can in the cases that come before us." It is easy to utter such words. If only the Court would live by them.

Justice Kavanaugh, dissenting.

For the sake of argument, I will assume that firing someone because of their sexual orientation may, as a very literal matter, entail making a distinction based on sex. But to prevail in this case with their literalist approach, the plaintiffs must *also* establish one of two other points. The plaintiffs must establish that courts, when interpreting a statute, adhere to literal meaning rather than ordinary meaning. Or alternatively, the plaintiffs must establish that the ordinary meaning of "discriminate because of sex"—not just the literal meaning—encompasses sexual orientation discrimination. The plaintiffs fall short on both counts.

[*First*,] there is no serious debate about the foundational interpretive principle that courts adhere to ordinary meaning, not literal meaning, when interpreting statutes. As Justice Scalia explained, "the good textualist is not a literalist." A. Scalia, A Matter of Interpretation 24 (1997). * * * The ordinary meaning that counts is the ordinary public meaning at the time of enactment—although in this case, that temporal principle matters little because the ordinary meaning of "discriminate because of sex" was the same in 1964 as it is now.

Judges adhere to ordinary meaning for two main reasons: rule of law and democratic accountability. A society governed by the rule of law must have laws that are known and understandable to the citizenry. And judicial adherence to ordinary meaning facilitates the democratic accountability of America's elected representatives for the laws they enact. Citizens and legislators must be able to ascertain the law by reading the words of the statute. Both the rule of law and democratic accountability badly suffer when a court adopts a hidden or obscure interpretation of the law, and not its ordinary meaning.

Consider a simple example of how ordinary meaning differs from literal meaning. A statutory ban on "vehicles in the park" would literally encompass a baby stroller. But no good judge would interpret the statute that way because the word "vehicle," in its ordinary meaning, does not encompass baby strollers. * * * Time and again, this Court has rejected literalism in favor of ordinary meaning. [See, e .g., *Nix v. Hedden*, 149 U.S. 304, 307 (1893); *McBoyle v. United States*, 283 U.S. 25, 26 (1931).] * * *

* * * The difference between literal and ordinary meaning becomes especially important when—as in this case—judges consider *phrases* in statutes. (Recall that the shorthand version of the phrase at issue here is "discriminate because of sex.") Courts must heed the ordinary meaning of the *phrase as a whole*, not just the meaning of the words in the phrase. * * * A "cold war" could literally mean any wintertime war, but in common parlance it signifies a conflict short of open warfare. * * * If the usual evidence indicates that a statutory phrase bears an ordinary meaning different from the literal strung-together definitions of the individual words in the phrase, we may not ignore or gloss over that discrepancy. [T]his Court's precedents and longstanding principles of statutory interpretation teach a clear lesson: Do not simply split statutory phrases into their component words, look up each in a dictionary, and then mechanically put them together again, as the majority opinion today mistakenly does. To reiterate Justice Scalia's caution, that approach misses the forest for the trees. * * *

*Second*, in light of the bedrock principle that we must adhere to the ordinary meaning of a phrase, the question in this case boils down to the ordinary meaning of the phrase "discriminate because of sex." Does the ordinary meaning of that phrase encompass discrimination because of sexual orientation? The answer is plainly no. * * * Both common parlance and common legal usage treat sex discrimination and sexual orientation discrimination as two distinct categories of discrimination—back in 1964 and still today.

* * * In common parlance, Bostock and Zarda were fired because they were gay, not because they were men. [To treat animosity based on sexual orientation as animosity based on sex] rewrites history. Seneca Falls was not Stonewall. The women's rights movement was not (and is not) the gay rights movement, although many people obviously support or participate in both. So to think that sexual orientation discrimination is just a form of sex discrimination is not just a mistake of language and psychology, but also a mistake of history and sociology.

Importantly, [since] enacting Title VII in 1964, * * * Congress has consistently treated sex discrimination and sexual orientation discrimination as legally distinct categories of discrimination. * * * [W]hen Congress wants to prohibit sexual orientation discrimination in addition to sex discrimination, Congress explicitly refers to sexual orientation discrimination. [See, e.g., 18 U.S.C. § 249(a)(2)(A).] * * * As Justice Scalia explained for the Court, "it is not our function" to "treat alike subjects that different Congresses have chosen to treat differently." *West Virginia Univ. Hospitals, Inc. v. Casey*, 499 U.S. 83, 101 (1991). * * * Congress knows how to prohibit sexual orientation discrimination. So courts should not read that specific concept into the general words "discriminate because of sex." * * *

The majority opinion insists that it is not rewriting or updating Title VII, but instead is just humbly reading the text of the statute as written. But that assertion is tough to accept. Most everyone familiar with the use of the English language in America understands that the ordinary meaning of sexual orientation discrimination is distinct from the ordinary meaning of sex discrimination. Federal law distinguishes the two. State law distinguishes the two. This Court's cases distinguish the two. Statistics on discrimination distinguish the two. History distinguishes the two. Psychology distinguishes the two. Sociology distinguishes the two. Human resources departments all over America distinguish the two. Sports leagues distinguish the two. Political groups distinguish the two. Advocacy groups distinguish the two. Common parlance distinguishes the two. Common sense distinguishes the two.

I have the greatest, and unyielding, respect for my colleagues and for their good faith. But when this Court usurps the role of Congress, as it does today, the public understandably becomes confused about who the policymakers really are in our system of separated powers, and inevitably becomes cynical about the oft-repeated aspiration that judges base their decisions on law rather than on personal preference. The best way for judges to demonstrate that we are deciding cases based on the ordinary meaning of the law is to walk the walk, even in the hard cases when we might prefer a different policy outcome. * * *

---

## Points for Discussion

### *a. Touchstones of Interpretation*

Justice Gorsuch declared that the Court's task was to "determine the ordinary public meaning" of Title VII's prohibition on discrimination because of sex. Did the dissenting Justices disagree with this description of the appropriate object of statutory interpretation? If not, then why did the majority and the dissents disagree about the meaning of the statute? If so, is it obvious to you that an approach based on legislative intent or statutory purpose would have produced a different result? Did the various opinions in *Bostock* lead you to rethink your views about the appropriate touchstone of interpretation?

### *b. An Alternative Approach*

Three years before the Court's decision in *Bostock*, the Seventh Circuit, sitting *en banc*, reached a similar conclusion in a suit filed by a lesbian who claimed that she had been denied a full-time position because of her sexual orientation. *Hively v. Ivy Tech Community College of Ind.*, 853 F.3d 339 (7th Cir. 2017) (en banc). Judge Wood's opinion announcing the judgment relied on *Price Waterhouse v. Hopkins*, 490 U.S. 228 (1989), for the proposition that Title VII prohibits adverse employment actions based on failures to conform to gender stereotypes. The opinion also relied on in *Loving v. Virginia*, 388 U.S. 1 (1967), which Judge Wood read to stand for the proposition that "a person who is discriminated against because of the protected characteristic of one with whom she associates is actually being disadvantaged because of her own traits." Judge Flaum's concurring opinion advanced the view that Justice Gorsuch ultimately approved in *Bostock*, that discrimination against a person because he is gay necessarily entails discrimination based on sex.

In a separate concurring opinion, Judge Posner offered "an alternative approach." He began by noting that

> "the interpretation of statutes comes in three flavors. The first and most conventional is the extraction of the original meaning of the statute—the meaning intended by the legislators—and corresponds to interpretation in ordinary discourse. Knowing English I can usually determine swiftly and straightforwardly the meaning of a statement, oral or written, made to me in English * * *. The second form of interpretation, illustrated by the commonplace local ordinance which commands 'no vehicles in the park,' is interpretation by unexpressed intent, whereby we understand that although an ambulance is a vehicle, the ordinance was not intended to include ambulances among the 'vehicles' forbidden to enter the park. * * * Finally and most controversially, interpretation can mean giving a fresh meaning to a statement (which can be a statement found in a constitutional or statutory text)—a meaning that infuses the statement with vitality and significance today. * * * And a common

> form of interpretation it is, despite its flouting "original meaning." Statutes and constitutional provisions frequently are interpreted on the basis of present need and present understanding rather than original meaning—constitutional provisions even more frequently, because most of them are older than most statutes."

Judge Posner acknowledged that "the term 'sex' in the statute, when enacted in 1964, undoubtedly meant 'man or woman,' and so at the time people would have thought that a woman who was fired for being a lesbian was not being fired for being a woman unless her employer would not have fired on grounds of homosexuality a man he knew to be homosexual * * *." Because "Title VII does not mention discrimination on the basis of sexual orientation," he thought that "an explanation is needed for how 53 years later the meaning of the statute has changed and the word 'sex' in it now connotes both gender *and* sexual orientation."

Judge Posner reasoned:

> "Title VII of the Civil Rights Act of 1964, now more than half a century old, invites an interpretation that will update it to the present, a present that differs markedly from the era in which the Act was enacted. But I need to emphasize that [the] third form of interpretation—call it judicial interpretive updating—presupposes a lengthy interval between enactment and (re)interpretation. A statute when passed has an understood meaning; it takes years, often many years, for a shift in the political and cultural environment to change the understanding of the statute."

Judge Posner then asserted that a "broader understanding of the word 'sex' in Title VII than the original understanding" is "essential," because "[f]ailure to adopt it would make the statute anachronistic." He continued:

> "We now understand that homosexual men and women (and also bisexuals, defined as having both homosexual and heterosexual orientations) are normal in the ways that count, and beyond that have made many outstanding intellectual and cultural contributions to society (think for example of Tchaikovsky, Oscar Wilde, Jane Addams, André Gide, Thomas Mann, Marlene Dietrich, Bayard Rustin, Alan Turing, Alec Guinness, Leonard Bernstein, Van Cliburn, and James Baldwin—a very partial list). We now understand that homosexuals, male and female, play an essential role, in this country at any rate, as adopters of children from foster homes * * *. The compelling social interest in protecting homosexuals (male and female) from discrimination justifies an admittedly loose "interpretation" of the word "sex" in Title VII to embrace homosexuality: an interpretation that cannot be imputed to the framers of the statute but that we are entitled to adopt in light of (to quote Holmes) "*what this country has become*," or, in Blackstonian terminology, to embrace as a sensible deviation from the literal or original meaning of the statutory language."

In reaching his conclusion, Judge Posner was "reluctant" to base his interpretation of Title VII on cases such as *Oncale* and *Loving*, or on the assertion that Congress in 1964 "may not have realized or understood the full scope of the words it chose." Judge Posner explained that "[w]hat the framers and ratifiers understandably didn't understand was how attitudes toward homosexuals would change in the following half century. They shouldn't be blamed for that failure of foresight. *We* understand the words of Title VII differently not because we're smarter than the statute's framers and ratifiers but because we live in a different era, a different culture." Judge Posner than declared:

> "I would prefer to see us acknowledge openly that today we, who are judges rather than members of Congress, are imposing on a half-century-old statute a meaning of 'sex discrimination' that the Congress that enacted it would not have accepted. This is something courts do fairly frequently to avoid statutory obsolescence and concomitantly to avoid placing the entire burden of updating old statutes on the legislative branch. We should not leave the impression that we are merely the obedient servants of the 88th Congress (1963–1965), carrying out their wishes. We are not. We are taking advantage of what the last half century has taught."

Do you agree with Judge Posner's assertion that courts should openly and candidly "update" statutes through the process of "interpretation"? What are the virtues of this approach? What are the drawbacks? Is Judge Posner's reasoning a more defensible basis than Justice Gorsuch's reasoning in Bostock for the conclusion that Title VII prohibits discrimination on the basis of sexual orientation or gender identity? A more candid basis?

---

## Problem

The Endangered Species Act of 1973 contains a variety of measures designed to save from extinction species that the Secretary of the Interior designates, pursuant to authority in 16 U.S.C. § 1533, as endangered or threatened. The Act is codified at 16 U.S.C. § 1531 *et seq.* and begins with a statement of congressional purposes. 16 U.S.C. § 1531 states in relevant part:

> "Findings, Purposes, and Policy
>
> * * * (b) Purposes. The purposes of this chapter are to provide a means whereby the ecosystems upon which endangered species and threatened species depend may be conserved, to provide a program for the conservation of such endangered species and threatened species, and to take such steps as may be appropriate to achieve the purposes of treaties and conventions * * *.
>
> (c) Policy. [I]t is further declared to be the policy of Congress that all Federal departments and agencies shall seek to conserve endangered species and threatened species and shall utilize their authorities in furtherance of the purposes of this chapter * * *." 16 U.S.C. § 1531.

The Act provides several means for achieving its goals. First, as we saw when we considered *TVA v. Hill*, 437 U.S. 153 (1978), the Act provides that "[e]ach Federal agency shall, in consultation with and with the assistance of the

Secretary [of the Interior], insure that any action authorized, funded, or carried out by such agency * * * is not likely to jeopardize the continued existence of any endangered species or threatened species or result in the destruction or adverse modification of habitat of such species which is determined by the Secretary * * * to be critical, unless such agency has been granted an exemption for such action by [an interagency committee]." 16 U.S.C. § 1536.

Second, the Act gives the Secretary of the Interior authority to acquire land in order to protect endangered species. 16 U.S.C. § 1534 provides:

> "Land Acquisition
>
> (a) [T]he Secretary * * * shall establish and implement a program to conserve fish, wildlife, and plants, including those which are listed as endangered species or threatened species pursuant to section 1533 of this title. To carry out such a program, the [Secretary]—
>
> > (1) shall utilize the land acquisition and other authority under [other federal statutes], as appropriate; and
> >
> > (2) is authorized to acquire by purchase, donation, or otherwise, lands, waters, or interest therein, and such authority shall be in addition to any other land acquisition authority vested in him. * * *" 16 U.S.C. § 1534.

Third, the Act contains a list of prohibited acts. 16 U.S.C. § 1538 provides in relevant part:

> "Prohibited Acts
>
> (a)(1) Except as provided in [section 1539], with respect to any endangered species of fish or wildlife listed pursuant to section 1533 * * * it is unlawful for any person subject to the jurisdiction of the United States to—
>
> > (A) import any such species into, or export any such species from the United States;
> >
> > (B) take any such species within the United States or the territorial sea of the United States; * * *
> >
> > (D) possess, sell, deliver, carry, transport or ship, by any means whatsoever, any such species * * *;
> >
> > (E) deliver, receive, carry, transport, or ship in interstate or foreign commerce, by any means whatsoever and in the course of a commercial activity, any such species;
> >
> > (F) sell or offer for sale in interstate or foreign commerce any such species; or
> >
> > (G) violate any regulation pertaining to such species or to any threatened species of fish or wildlife listed pursuant to section 1533 of this title and promulgated by the Secretary pursuant to authority provided by this chapter. * * *" 16 U.S.C. § 1538.

The Act contains a list of definitions of words used in the statute. It states that the term "take," which is used in 16 U.S.C. § 1538(a)(1)(B), "means to harass, harm, pursue, hunt, shoot, wound, kill, trap, capture, or collect, or to attempt to engage in any such conduct." 16 U.S.C. § 1532(19).

Finally, 16 U.S.C. § 1540 authorizes civil penalties for "knowing" violations of the Act and criminal penalties for its "willful" violation.

In 1975, the Secretary of the Interior promulgated regulations to implement the Act's prohibition on "tak[ing]" an endangered species. Among other things, the regulation provided further clarification of the meaning of the term "take." The regulation noted that the statutory definition of the term "take" includes "harm." The regulation then defined the term "harm" as follows:

> "*Harm* in the definition of 'take' in the Act means an act which actually kills or injures wildlife. Such act may include significant habitat modification or degradation where it actually kills or injures wildlife by significantly impairing essential behavioral patterns, including breeding, feeding, or sheltering." 50 CFR § 17.3 (1994).

Congress amended the Act in 1982 by adding the provisions in 16 U.S.C. § 1539. That section authorizes the Secretary to grant exceptions to the prohibition on "taking" an endangered species. Specifically, the provision states that the "Secretary may permit, under such terms and conditions as he shall prescribe * * * any taking otherwise prohibited by section 1538(a)(1)(B) * * * if such taking is incidental to, and not the purpose of, the carrying out of an otherwise lawful activity." 16 U.S.C. § 1539(a)(1)(B). The provision further states that no such "permit may be issued by the Secretary * * * unless the applicant therefor submits to the Secretary a conservation plan that specifies * * * the impact which will likely result from such taking" and the "steps the applicant will take to minimize and mitigate such impacts." *Id.* § 1539(a)(2). The provision also requires the Secretary to give an opportunity for public comment before granting a permit, and to determine, among other things, that the "taking will be incidental" and that "the taking will not appreciably reduce the likelihood of the survival and recovery of the species in the wild." *Id.* § 1539(a)(2)(B). Finally, the provision states that the "Secretary may grant exceptions under [this section] only if he finds * * * that (1) such exceptions were applied for in good faith, (2) if granted and exercised will not operate to the disadvantage of such endangered species, and (3) will be consistent with the purposes and policy set forth in section 1531 of this title." 16 U.S.C. § 1539(d).

In the 1970s, the Secretary of the Interior designated the red-cockaded woodpecker as an endangered species and the northern spotted owl as a threatened species. The former lived exclusively in mature pine forests in the American Southeast; the latter lived only in old-growth forests in the Northwest. Several small landowners, logging companies, on the forest-products industries in the Pacific Nort and organizations that represent their interests, fil action against the Secretary of the Interior to ch Secretary's regulation defining "harm." They co was inconsistent with the statute because it defi degradation as a prohibited taking. In their vi prohibited only takings that result from a di force against an endangered or threatened ar

There is legislative history that ar bly is relevan definition of the ter original version of th includ e list of words in the definition o ed in the bill as ultimately enacted. *See* the Subcommittee on Environment of 93d Cong., 1st Sess., pp. 7, 27 (1973). lso defined the term "take" to include nent of [the] habitat or range" of fish he Commerce Committee removed efore sending the bill to the floor. ke' is defined * * * in the broadest way in which a person can 'take' p. No. 93–307, p. 7 (1973).

l in the Senate, subsequently n" to the definition of "take," would "help to achieve the 683 (1973). In describing the bill on also said the following:

> ough [the] land acquisition provisions, we will be able to conserve habitats necessary to protect fish and wildlife from further destruction. Although most endangered species are threatened primarily by the destruction of their natural habitats, a significant portion of these animals are subject to predation by man for commercial, sport, consumption, or other purposes. The provisions of [the bill] would prohibit the commerce in or the importation, exportation, or taking of endangered species." 119 Cong. Rec. 25669 (1973).

The House Committee Report (from the Merchant Marine and Fisheries Committee) on the version of the bill originally approved in the House stated that the term "take" included "harassment, whether intentional or not." H.R. Rep. No. 93–412, p. 11 (1973). The Report also stated that the "broadest possible terms" were used to define the restriction on takings. *Id.* at 15. The Report explained that the definition "would allow, for example, the Secretary to regulate or prohibit the activities of birdwatchers where the effect of those

Regulation as inconsistent
* deliberately struck harm to habitat from original language in statute
↳ arguing that Congresspeople expressed that protection of habitat through land acquisition
↓ taking is meant to prohibit hunting/picking/etc. → direct harm to species
* plain meaning construction
↳ also legislative history

Regulation as consistent
* "take" should be defined as broadly as possible to include every way in which someone can take/attempt to take
* purpose of statute to protect endangered species → regulations should be implemented to do so

activities might disturb the birds and make it difficult for them to hatch or raise their young." *Id.* at 11.

During the floor debate in the House, Representative Sullivan, the House floor manager, stated:

> "[T]he principal threat to animals stems from destruction of their habitat. * * * [The bill] will meet this problem by providing funds for acquisition of critical habitat. * * * It will also enable the Department of Agriculture to cooperate with willing landowners who desire to assist in the protection of endangered species, but who are understandably unwilling to do so at excessive cost to themselves."
>
> "Another hazard to endangered species arises from those who would capture or kill them for pleasure or profit. There is no way that the Congress can make it less pleasurable for a person to take an animal, but we can certainly make it less profitable for them to do so." 119 Cong. Rec. 30162 (1973).

Although the House and Senate bills differed in some respects, the bills that they approved contained the same definition of the word "take." Accordingly, the Conference Committee Report did not discuss the definition of the term included in the bill ultimately approved by both houses. *See* H.R. Conf. Rep. 93–740 (1973).

There is also legislative history from the 1982 amendments to the Act. The House Committee Report (also from the Merchant Marine and Fisheries Committee) stated that "[b]y use of the word 'incidental' [in 16 U.S.C. § 1539] the Committee intends to cover situations in which it is known that a taking will occur if the other activity is engaged in but such taking is incidental to, and not the purpose of, the activity." H.R. Rep. No. 97-567, p. 31 (1982). In addition, both the Senate Report and the Conference Report on the bill pointed, as an example of the types of projects eligible for exemptions, to a cooperative federal-state response to a case in California in which a development project threatened incidental harm to a species of endangered butterfly by modification of its habitat. *See* S. Rep. No. 9-418, p. 10 (1982); H.R. Conf. Rep. No. 97-835, pp. 30–32 (1982). The Conference's joint explanation stated:

> "This provision is modeled after a habitat conservation plan that has been developed by three Northern California cities in the County of San Mateo, and private landowners and developers to provide the conservation of the habitat of three endangered species and other unlisted species of concern within the San Bruno Mountain area of San Mateo County.
>
> "This provision will measurably reduce conflicts under the Act and will provide the institutional framework to permit cooperation between the public and private sectors in the interest of endangered species and habitat conservation. * * * The Secretary, in determining whether to issue a long-term permit to carry out a conservation plan should consider the extent to which the [plan] is likely to enhance

the habitat of the listed species or increase the long-term survivability of the species or its ecosystem.

"Because the San Bruno Mountain Plan is the model for this long-term permit and because the adequacy of similar conservation plans should be measured against the San Bruno Plan, the Committee believes that the elements of this plan should be clearly understood. Large portions of the habitat on San Bruno Mountain are privately owned. * * * The Conservation Plan addressed the habitat throughout the area and preserves sufficient habitat to allow for enhancement of the survival of the species. The plan protects in perpetuity at least 87 percent of the habitat of the listed butterflies." H.R. Conf. Rep. No. 97-835, pp. 30–31 (1982).

What arguments should the parties make to support their respective views of the meaning of the statute?

**Test Your Knowledge**

To assess your understanding of the material in this Chapter, click here to take a quiz.

## Chapter Six

# *Agency Decision-Making*

So far, we have been thinking about statutory interpretation as a drama featuring two main characters: the legislature, which enacts the law, and the court, which interprets it. But we've also seen hints along the way that the plot is often more complex than it is in the more straightforward, two-character production. Congress often gives enforcement power over a particular statute to an *administrative agency*. As a consequence, when courts interpret statutes, they often are not writing on a clean slate; the agency charged with implementing the statute might have already interpreted the statute in its effort to carry out the statute's objectives.

For example, recall *General Dynamics Land Systems, Inc. v. Cline*, 540 U.S. 581 (2004), which we considered in Chapter 2. In that case, the Court had to decide whether the Age Discrimination in Employment Act's prohibition on discrimination "because of * * * age" prohibited a workplace policy that gave preference to older workers over younger workers. The respondents relied in part on guidance that the Equal Employment Opportunity Commission, the agency charged with enforcing the statute, had issued in 1981. The agency's guidance stated:

> "It is unlawful in situations where this Act applies, for an employer to discriminate in hiring or in any other way by giving preference because of age between individuals 40 and over. Thus, if two people apply for the same position, and one is 42 and the other 52, the employer may not lawfully turn down either one on the basis of age, but must make such decision on the basis of some other factor." 29 C.F.R. § 1625.2(a) (2003).

What role should the agency's interpretation of the ADEA have played, if any, in the Court's understanding of the statute's meaning? (Justice Scalia, in dissent, urged the Court to defer to the EEOC's view of the statute; the Court declined to defer because it thought that the EEOC's interpretation was "clearly wrong.")

This question is surprisingly complicated. But before we can tackle it—that is, before we can try to determine how *agency* interpretations of statutes should affect *judicial* interpretation—we need to understand the role of agencies and their status in our constitutional system. Our consideration will be necessarily brief; there is an entire course in law school, called Administrative Law, designed to explore these questions. (You might also explore some of these questions in your course in Constitutional Law.) But we need to develop at least a basic understanding of the administrative state so that we can more confidently explore the debate over the role that agency interpretations should play in judicial interpretation of statutes.

In this Chapter, we will consider two principal questions: (1) How much decision-making power can Congress give to agencies? (2) What is the range of actions that an agency can take in exercising that authority? In Chapter 7, we will consider where and how agencies "fit" in our constitutional system. In addressing those questions, we will consider the forms of oversight that the President, Congress, and the courts exercise over agency decision-making. Finally, in Chapter 8, we will return to the interpretive question and consider what role agency interpretations of statutes should play in judicial efforts to determine statutory meaning.

---

## A. Delegation of Policy-Making Power to Administrative Agencies

### *Whitman v. American Trucking Associations*

531 U.S. 457 (2001)

JUSTICE SCALIA delivered the opinion of the Court.

Section 109(a) of the [Clean Air Act (CAA)] requires the Administrator of the EPA to promulgate [national ambient air quality standards (NAAQS)] for each air pollutant for which "air quality criteria" have been issued under § 108. [Section 109(b)(1) of the CAA instructs the EPA to set "ambient air quality standards the attainment and maintenance of which in the judgment of the Administrator, based on [the] criteria [documents of § 108] and allowing an adequate margin of safety, are requisite to protect the public health."] Once a NAAQS has been promulgated, the Administrator must review the standard (and the criteria on which it is based) "at five-year intervals" and make "such revisions . . . as may be appropriate." CAA § 109(d)(1). These cases arose when, on July 18, 1997, the Administrator revised the NAAQS for particulate matter and ozone. American Trucking Associations, Inc., and its co-respondents—which include, in addition to other private companies, the States of Michigan, Ohio, and West Virginia—challenged the new standards in the Court of Appeals for the District of Columbia Circuit * * *. [The respondents argued that the statute delegated too much decision-making power to the EPA. They also argued that the court should construe the statute to require the EPA to consider the costs imposed on industry when determining the permissible level of emissions of particulate matter and ozone.]

The District of Columbia Circuit accepted some of the challenges and rejected others. It agreed * * * that § 109(b)(1) delegated legislative power to the Administrator in contravention of the United States Constitution, Art. I, § 1, because it found that the EPA had interpreted the statute to provide no "intelligible principle" to guide the agency's exercise of authority. * * *

[S]ince the first step in assessing whether a statute delegates legislative power is to determine what authority the statute confers, we address that issue of interpretation first and reach respondents' constitutional arguments [afterward]. Section 109(b)(1) instructs the EPA to set primary ambient air quality standards "the attainment and maintenance of which . . . are requisite to protect the public health" with "an adequate margin of safety." Were it not for the hundreds of pages of briefing respondents have submitted on the issue, one would have thought it fairly clear that this text does not permit the EPA to consider costs in setting the standards. The language, as one scholar has noted, "is absolute." D. Currie, Air Pollution: Federal Law and Analysis 4–15 (1981). The EPA, "based on" the information about health effects contained in the technical "criteria" documents compiled under § 108(a)(2), is to identify the maximum airborne concentration of a pollutant that the public health can tolerate, decrease the concentration to provide an "adequate" margin of safety, and [illegible] standard at that level. Nowhere are the costs of achieving such a standard ma[illegible] of that initial calculation.

* * * The Court of Appeals held that [section 109(b)(1)] as interpreted by the Administrator did not provide an "intelligible principle" to guide the EPA's exercise of authority in setting NAAQS. "[The] EPA," it said, "lack[ed] any determinate criteria for drawing lines. It has failed to state intelligibly how much is too much." The court hence found that the EPA's interpretation (but not the statute itself) violated the nondelegation doctrine. We disagree.

In a delegation challenge, the constitutional question is whether the statute has delegated legislative power to the agency. Article I, § 1, of the Constitution vests "[a]ll legislative Powers herein granted . . . in a Congress of the United States." This text permits no delegation of those powers, *Loving v. United States*, 517 U.S. 748, 771 (1996), and so we repeatedly have said that when Congress confers decisionmaking authority upon agencies *Congress* must "lay down by legislative act an intelligible principle to which the person or body authorized to

**Take Note**

The Court makes two important points in this paragraph. First, Congress may not delegate "legislative power" to an agency. Second, as a consequence, when Congress gives an agency power to make decisions, it must provide an "intelligible principle" to guide the agency's decision-making. Why does the policy-making power that Congress delegates cease to be the "legislative power" if Congress provides an "intelligible principle" to guide the agency?

[act] is directed to conform." *J.W. Hampton, Jr., & Co. v. United States*, 276 U.S. 394, 409 (1928). * * *

We agree with the Solicitor General that the text of § 109(b)(1) of the CAA at a minimum requires that "[f]or a discrete set of pollutants and based on published air quality criteria that reflect the latest scientific knowledge, [the] EPA must establish uniform national standards at a level that is requisite to protect public health from the adverse effects of the pollutant in the ambient air." Tr. of Oral Arg., p. 5. Requisite, in turn, "mean[s] sufficient, but not more than necessary." *Id.*, at 7. These limits on the EPA's discretion are strikingly similar to the ones we approved in *Touby v. United States*, 500 U.S. 160 (1991), which permitted the Attorney General to designate a drug as a controlled substance for purposes of criminal drug enforcement if doing so was "necessary to avoid an imminent hazard to the public safety." They also resemble the Occupational Safety and Health Act of 1970 provision requiring the agency to "set the standard which most adequately assures, to the extent feasible, on the basis of the best available evidence, that no employee will suffer any impairment of health"—which the Court upheld in *Industrial Union Dept., AFL-CIO v. American Petroleum Institute*, 448 U.S. 607, 646 (1980), and which even then-Justice Rehnquist, who alone in that case thought the statute violated the nondelegation doctrine, see *id.* (opinion concurring in judgment), would have upheld if, like the statute here, it did not permit economic costs to be considered. See *American Textile Mfrs. Institute, Inc. v. Donovan*, 452 U.S. 490, 545 (1981) (Rehnquist, J., dissenting).

**Note**

In this paragraph, the Court describes the "intelligible principle" that constrains the agency's exercise of decision-making power in this case. What is the principle? In your view, does it meaningfully constrain the agency's ability to make policy?

The scope of discretion § 109(b)(1) allows is in fact well within the outer limits of our nondelegation precedents. In the history of the Court we have found the requisite "intelligible principle" lacking in only two statutes, one of which provided literally no guidance for the exercise of discretion, and the other of which conferred authority to regulate the entire economy on the basis of no more precise a standard than stimulating the economy by assuring "fair competition." See *Panama Refining Co. v. Ryan*, 293 U.S. 388 (1935); *A.L.A. Schechter Poultry Corp. v. United States*, 295 U.S. 495 (1935). We have, on the other hand, upheld the validity of § 11(b)(2) of the Public Utility Holding Company Act of 1935, 49 Stat. 821, which gave the Securities and Exchange Commission authority to modify the structure of holding company systems so as to ensure that they are not "unduly or unnecessarily complicate[d]" and do not "unfairly or inequitably distribute voting power among security holders." *American Power & Light Co. v. SEC*, 329 U.S. 90, 104 (1946). We have approved the wartime conferral of agency power to fix the prices of commodities at a level that "will be generally fair and equitable and will effectuate the [in some respects conflicting] purposes of th[e] Act." *Yakus v. United States*, 321 [illegible] have found an "intelligible principle" in various sta[illegible] the "public interest." See, *e.g., National Broadcastin*[illegible] 190, 225–226 (1943) (Federal Communications C[illegible] power to regulate airwaves); *New York Central Securities Corp. v. United States*, 287 U.S. 12, 24–25 (1932) (Interstate Commerce Commission's power to approve railroad consolidations). In short, we have "almost never felt qualified to second-guess Congress regarding the permissible degree of policy judgment that can be left to those executing or applying the law." *Mistretta v. United States*, 488 U.S. 361, 416 (1989) (SCALIA, J., dissenting); see *id.*, at 373 (majority opinion).

It is true enough that the degree of agency discretion that is acceptable varies according to the scope of the power congressionally conferred. While Congress need not provide any direction to the EPA regarding the manner in which it is to define "country elevators," which are to be exempt from new-stationary-source regulations governing grain elevators, it must provide substantial guidance on setting air standards that affect the entire national economy. But even in sweeping regulatory schemes we have never demanded, as the Court of Appeals did here, that statutes provide a "determinate criterion" for saying "how much [of the regulated harm] is too much." In *Touby* for example, we did not require the statute to decree how "imminent" was too imminent, or how "necessary" was necessary enough, or even—most relevant here—how "hazardous" was too hazardous. 500 U.S., at 165–167. Similarly, the statute at issue in *Lichter v. United States*, 334 U.S. 742, 783 (1948), authorized agencies to recoup "excess profits" paid under wartime Government contracts, yet we did not insist that Congress specify how much profit was too much. It is therefore not conclusive for delegation purposes that, as respondents argue, ozone and particulate matter are "nonthreshold" pollutants that inflict a continuum of adverse health effects at any airborne concentration greater than zero, and hence require the EPA to make judgments of degree. "[A] certain degree of discretion, and thus of lawmaking, inheres in most executive or judicial action." *Mistretta v. United States, supra*, at 417 (SCALIA, J., dissenting) (emphasis deleted). Section 109(b)(1) of the CAA, which to repeat we interpret as requiring the EPA to set air quality standards at the level that is "requisite"—that is, not lower or higher than is necessary—to protect the public health with an adequate margin of safety, fits comfortably within the scope of discretion permitted by our precedent.

**Food for Thought**

Is it possible to imagine a statute that leaves no discretion at all for the official administering the statute? Suppose that the statute required the EPA to set a standard for particulate matter at the level that, "regardless of cost, ensures that no person will suffer any material health impairment." Would that statute leave any policy-making discretion to the agency?

JUSTICE THOMAS, concurring.

The parties to these cases who briefed the constitutional issue wrangled over constitutional doctrine with barely a nod to the text of the Constitution. Although this Court since 1928 has treated the "intelligible principle" requirement as the only constitutional limit on congressional grants of power to administrative agencies, see *J.W. Hampton, Jr., & Co. v. United States,* 276 U.S. 394, 409 (1928), the Constitution does not speak of "intelligible principles." Rather, it speaks in much simpler terms: "*All* legislative Powers herein granted shall be vested in a Congress." U.S. Const., Art. 1, § 1 (emphasis added). I am not convinced that the intelligible principle doctrine serves to prevent all cessions of legislative power. I believe that there are cases in which the principle is intelligible and yet the significance of the delegated decision is simply too great for the decision to be called anything other than "legislative."

**Food for Thought**

Justice Thomas laments that the parties did not explain how the text of the Constitution addresses the question at issue in this case. What, if anything, does the text of the Constitution require? Does that text answer the question in this case?

As it is, none of the parties to these cases has examined the text of the Constitution or asked us to reconsider our precedents on cessions of legislative power. On a future day, however, I would be willing to address the question whether our delegation jurisprudence has strayed too far from our Founders' understanding of separation of powers.

JUSTICE STEVENS, with whom JUSTICE SOUTER joins, concurring in part and concurring in the judgment.

The Court has two choices. We could choose to articulate our ultimate disposition of this issue by frankly acknowledging that the power delegated to the EPA is "legislative" but nevertheless conclude that the delegation is constitutional because adequately limited by the terms of the authorizing statute. Alternatively, we could pretend, as the Court does, that the authority delegated to the EPA is somehow not "legislative power." * * * I am persuaded that it would be both wiser and more faithful to what we have actually done in delegation cases to admit that agency rulemaking authority is "legislative power."

The proper characterization of governmental power should generally depend on the nature of the power, not on the identity of the person exercising it. If the NAAQS that the EPA promulgated had been prescribed by Congress, everyone would agree that those rules would be the product of an exercise of "legislative power." The same characterization is appropriate when an agency exercises rulemaking authority pursuant to a permissible delegation from Congress.

My view is not only more faithful to normal English usage, but is also fully consistent with the text of the Constitution. In Article I, the Framers vested "All legislative Powers" in the Congress, Art. I, § 1, just as in Article II they vested the "executive Power" in the President, Art. II, § 1. Those provisions do not purport to limit the authority of either recipient of power to delegate authority to others. * * *

It seems clear that an executive agency's exercise of rulemaking authority pursuant to a valid delegation from Congress is "legislative." As long as the delegation provides a sufficiently intelligible principle, there is nothing inherently unconstitutional about it.

[JUSTICE BREYER's opinion concurring in part and concurring in the judgment is omitted.]

---

## Points for Discussion

### *a. Congressional Power and Agency Discretion*

The dispute in *American Trucking Associations* was over how much policy-making power Congress is permitted to delegate to an administrative agency. Why did Congress see the need to delegate some policy-making power to the EPA to set the permissible levels of exposure for pollutants? Could Congress have set those limits itself? If so, why did it choose not to do so?

### *b. Constitutional Limits*

Article I, § 1 of the Constitution declares that "[a]ll legislative Powers herein granted shall be vested in a Congress of the United States * * *." The Court declared that "[t]his text permits no delegation of those powers." Is it obvious to you that Article I's language prohibits Congress from delegating the legislative power to some other decision-maker? After all, Article II, § 1 provides that the "executive Power shall be vested in the President of the United States of America," yet no one doubts that the President can delegate executive power to other actors. For example, the President can let the Attorney General decide whether to seek an indictment of a person suspected of committing a crime. Is legislative power different from executive power in some crucial way that might lead us to adopt different rules about its delegability?

### *c. The Non-Delegation Doctrine and the Intelligible-Principle Test*

According to the Court, Congress does not impermissibly delegate the legislative power if it provides an "intelligible principle" to guide the agency's exercise of policy-making discretion. Together, these principles are known as the "non-delegation doctrine."

What constitutes an intelligible principle? As the Court noted, it has upheld a statute that gave an agency power to grant licenses to broadcasters when doing so would be consistent with the "public interest," and it has upheld another statute that gave an agency power to set prices at a level that "will be generally fair and equitable and will effectuate" the purposes of the statute. If these statutes satisfied the intelligible-principle test, then what would a statute have to say to fail the test?

***d. Institutional Roles***

Because the Court has permitted Congress to delegate broad decision-making authority to agencies, agencies often have power to make important decisions about policy. What are the virtues of letting agencies make such decisions? What are the costs? Would the alternative—which would require judges to decide which policy questions are so important that only Congress should be permitted to make them—be preferrable?

***e. Discontent with the Non-Delegation Doctrine***

In his dissent in *Gundy v. United States*, 139 S. Ct. 2116 (2019), Justice Gorsuch, joined by Chief Justice Roberts and Justice Thomas, urged the Court to reinvigorate the non-delegation doctrine. He asserted that the modern intelligible-principle test "has no basis in the original meaning of the Constitution, in history, or even in the decision from which it was plucked." Because the Court at the time had only 8 members, Justice Alito declined to join Justice Gorsuch's dissent (to avoid the problem of an evenly divided Court), but he indicated his support for an effort to "reconsider the approach we have taken for the past 84 years"—an approach that, in his view, had "rejected nondelegation arguments * * * pursuant to extraordinarily capacious standards." Since the Court's decision in *Gundy*, Justice Kavanaugh has joined the Court and indicated his interest in revisiting the intelligible-principle test. See *Paul v. United States*, 140 S. Ct. 342 (Mem.) (Nov. 25, 2019) (statement of Kavanaugh, J., respecting the denial of certiorari) ("Justice Gorsuch's scholarly analysis of the Constitution's nondelegation doctrine in his *Gundy* dissent may warrant further consideration in future cases.").

Some scholars have disputed the claim that the modern non-delegation standard is inconsistent with the original meaning of the Constitution. Early practice—under which Congress gave administrators broad statutory authority to regulate—suggests that modern cases are perhaps much closer to the original understanding of Congress's power to delegate authority than critics have suggested. See, e.g., Jerry L. Mashaw, *Recovering American Administrative Law: Federalist Foundations, 1787–1801*, 115 YALE L.J. 1256 (2006); Julian Davis Mortenson & Nicholas Bagley, *Delegation at the Founding*, 121 COLUM. L. REV. 277 (2021). We will revisit this debate in Chapter 8, when we consider the so-called "Major Questions Doctrine."

---

## Problem

Two statutes (19 U.S.C. § 1351 and 19 U.S.C. § 1821) give the President power to enter into trade agreements and to raise or lower tariffs to carry out such agreements. Another statute, the Trade Expansion Act of 1962, gives the President authority to "adjust the imports" of an article if the Secretary of Commerce, after a process of consultation and information-seeking, "finds that [the] article is being imported into the United States in such quantities or under such circumstances as to threaten to impair the national security." 19 U.S.C. § 1862(c)(1)(A).

The Trade Expansion Act lists several "relevant factors" to which the Secretary and the President shall "give consideration" in making their determinations regarding national security. *Id.*, § 1862(d). These factors include the "domestic production needed for projected national defense requirements," the "capacity of domestic industries to meet such requirements," and the "requirements of growth of such domestic industries." *Id.* They also include "the impact of foreign competition on the economic welfare of individual domestic industries" and whether the "weakening of our internal economy may impair the national security." *Id.* The statute enumerates other considerations as well, but the enumeration is set forth "without excluding other relevant factors."

On April 19, 2017, pursuant to section 1862, the Secretary of Commerce opened an investigation into the impact of steel imports on national security. After soliciting comments from the public and holding a public hearing, the Secretary found that many domestic steel mills had been driven out of business due to declining steel prices, global overcapacity, and unfairly traded steel, and that remaining steel mills were financially distressed. The Secretary also found that steel is important to national security because a variety of steel products are needed to support the country's defense and to supply industries that are critical to the economy and basic government operations. The Secretary concluded that the then-current importation of steel threatened the national security by jeopardizing domestic steel production. To alleviate this threat, the Secretary recommended immediately implementing tariffs or quotas in an amount sufficient to enable domestic steel plants to supply steel to meet domestic demand.

On March 8, 2018, the President issued Proclamation 9705, in which he concurred with the Secretary's findings and imposed a 25-percent tariff, effective March 23, 2018, on all steel articles from most countries.

The American Institute for International Steel, a trade group representing foreign steel manufacturers, filed suit challenging the President's order imposing a tariff. The group argued that the order was invalid because the Trade

Expansion Act impermissibly delegates legislative power to the President. How should the court rule?

---

## B. Forms of Agency Decision-Making

Let's assume that Congress has delegated authority to an administrative agency. What happens next? What can the agency do with the power that Congress has given it? We are not particularly concerned right now with the specific substantive policy choices that agencies might make when they exercise delegated authority, although obviously those choices matter a great deal to many people and companies. Those choices are the focus of other law school courses, such as Environmental Law, Securities Law, and so forth. We are going to focus instead on the forms of administrative action that agencies might use.

As an example, recall the rainmaking problem that we considered in Chapter 1. Imagine that Congress decides to regulate the problem of rainmaking and enacts a statute creating the Rainmaking Bureau. The statute instructs the agency to permit rainmaking "except in cases in which rainmaking would threaten fragile ecosystems, impose unreasonable costs on local businesses, or substantially disrupt water supplies."

Let's assume that the statute would survive a challenge under the non-delegation doctrine. (Can you make an argument for why the statute would survive such a challenge?) How might the agency go about implementing Congress's directive?

Ordinarily, when Congress creates an agency, or gives new responsibilities to an existing agency, it also confers specific powers on the agency. Congress can choose from a surprisingly large menu of options. For example, Congress might authorize an agency to conduct studies and issue reports on a matter within its area of expertise. The agency might use the results of such studies to propose legislative reforms to Congress. Or the agency might give guidance and advice to private parties subject to its authority.

Congress might also choose to give an agency the power to regulate the rights and duties of private parties. In our example, Congress might give an agency power to issue rules setting standards for the use of rainmaking technology. Or Congress might give the agency power to grant licenses to businesses that wish to use the technology. Alternatively (or in addition), Congress might choose to give the agency power to adjudicate controversies over the use of rainmaking technology.

Deciding which types of power agencies should be authorized to exercise is in large part a question of regulatory and institutional design, and therefore a bit beyond the scope of this course. Most controversies over agency decision-making are less arcane; they tend to involve the question whether an agency has exceeded limits on its authority. The non-delegation doctrine concerns the scope of Congress's power to give policy-making authority to agencies. But what limits apply to the agencies' exercise of those powers?

We noted above that the first step in creating an agency is the enactment of a statute establishing the agency. This statute is generally known as the agency's **organic statute**. An organic statute does several things: it names the agency; it creates the offices of the people who will be responsible for running the agency; and it confers powers on the agency. An organic statute usually both identifies the subjects that the agency can regulate—for example, it might say that the agency has power to decide when rainmaking is appropriate—and confers specific types of decision-making authority—for example, by giving the agency power to issue rules, grant licenses, or bring enforcement actions against rainmakers who violate the statute.

In conferring these powers—and in withholding others—the organic statute often also includes limits on the power of the agency to act. For example, the organic statute might say that the agency must obtain the permission of the Solicitor General, an official at the Department of Justice, before it can file a lawsuit seeking to enforce the statute. Or it might state that the agency can rescind a license only after giving the license-holder the right to appear in person to offer evidence about why he should be permitted to retain the license.

As an example, here are some of the provisions of the Federal Trade Commission Act of 1914, 15 U.S.C. § 41 *et seq.*, the Federal Trade Commission's organic statute:

> **Section 41. Federal Trade Commission established; membership; vacancies * * *.** A commission is created and established, to be known as the Federal Trade Commission * * *, which shall be composed of five Commissioners, who shall be appointed by the President, by and with the advice and consent of the Senate. Not more than three of the Commissioners shall be members of the same political party. The [Commissioners] shall be appointed for terms of seven years, except that any person chosen to fill a vacancy shall be appointed only for the unexpired term of the Commissioner whom he shall succeed: *Provided, however,* That upon the expiration of his term of office a Commissioner shall continue to serve until his successor shall have been appointed and shall have qualified. The President shall choose a chairman from the Commission's membership. * * * Any Commissioner may be removed by the President for inefficiency, neglect of duty, or malfeasance in office. A vacancy in the Commission shall not impair the right of the remaining Commissioners to exercise all the powers of the Commission. * * *
>
> **Section 42. Employees; expenses.** Each Commissioner shall receive a salary, payable in the same manner as the salaries of the judges of the courts of the United States. The Commission shall appoint a secretary, who shall receive a salary, and it shall have authority to employ and fix the compensation of such attorneys, special experts, examiners, clerks, and other

employees as it may from time to time find necessary for the proper performance of its duties and as may be from time to time appropriated for by Congress.

With the exception of the secretary, a clerk to each Commissioner, the attorneys, and such special experts and examiners as the Commission may from time to time find necessary for the conduct of its work, all employees of the Commission shall be a part of the classified civil service * * *.

Until otherwise provided by law, the Commission may rent suitable offices for its use. * * *

**Section 45. Unfair methods of competition unlawful; prevention by Commission.**

**(a) Declaration of unlawfulness; power to prohibit unfair practices; inapplicability to foreign trade.**

(1) Unfair methods of competition in or affecting commerce, and unfair or deceptive acts or practices in or affecting commerce, are hereby declared unlawful.

(2) The Commission is hereby empowered and directed to prevent persons, partnerships, or corporations [subject to certain exceptions] from using unfair methods of competition in or affecting commerce and unfair or deceptive acts or practices in or affecting commerce. * * *

**(b) Proceeding by Commission; modifying and setting aside orders.**

Whenever the Commission shall have reason to believe that any such person, partnership, or corporation has been or is using any unfair method of competition or unfair or deceptive act or practice in or affecting commerce, and if it shall appear to the Commission that a proceeding by it in respect thereof would be to the interest of the public, it shall issue and serve upon such person, partnership, or corporation a complaint stating its charges in that respect and containing a notice of a hearing upon a day and at a place therein fixed at least thirty days after the service of said complaint. The person, partnership, or corporation so complained of shall have the right to appear at the place and time so fixed and show cause why an order should not be entered by the Commission requiring such person, partnership, or corporation to cease and desist from the violation of the law so charged in said complaint. * * * If upon such hearing the Commission shall be of the opinion that the method of competition or the act or practice in question is prohibited by this subchapter, it shall make a report in writing in which it shall state its findings as to the facts and shall issue and cause to be served on such person, partnership, or corporation an order requiring such person, partnership, or corporation to cease and desist from using such method of competition or such act or practice. * * *

An agency's organic statute is not the only source of limits on an agency's powers. Congress has enacted other statutes that apply broadly to all (or most) federal agencies, such as the National Environmental Policy Act ("NEPA"), which requires most agencies to produce environmental impact statements before taking certain actions.

Although agency organic statutes and other statutes such as NEPA are quite important in the practice of administrative law, there are too many such statutes for us to tackle in a general, introductory course. Instead, we will focus on two sources of limits on agency power that apply generally: the Constitution's Due Process Clauses and the Administrative Procedure Act. As their names suggest, these provisions impose *procedural* requirements on agency action. As a consequence, they are trans-substantive, which means that they apply regardless of the subject matter that the agency is responsible for regulating. We will consider them in turn.

---

## 1. The Due Process Clauses

As we noted above, agencies exercise a wide range of powers. The most important powers—and the ones most likely to provoke controversy—are rulemaking and adjudication. You are almost certainly generally familiar with these concepts. If the legislature enacts a statute that prohibits rainmaking, for example, we recognize that act as one designed to produce a generally applicable rule to govern private conduct. If the government accuses a person of violating the rule, it might bring an enforcement action to enjoin the person from engaging in the unlawful conduct. If the person contests the government's allegations, a court will adjudicate the parties' competing claims.

In other words, we tend to think of rulemaking as something that legislatures do and adjudication as something that courts do. Our intuition, moreover, is that a person whose rights are affected by government action is entitled to much greater participation rights when a court adjudicates her interests than when the legislature enacts a law that affects her interests.

If our intuition is correct, then an agency should provide greater participation rights—at a minimum, notice and an opportunity to be heard—when it adjudicates a particular person's rights than it must provide when it issues a generally applicable rule. But whereas it is not difficult to tell when a legislature or instead a court has acted, it is not uncommon for one agency to have both the power to issue rules and to adjudicate claims arising under the agency's organic statute. How do we know when an agency has acted by generally applicable rules and when it has effectively adjudicated private rights? What consequences flow from that determination? Consider the two cases that follow.

---

## *Londoner v. City and County of Denver*

210 U.S. 373 (1908)

MR. JUSTICE MOODY delivered the opinion of the court.

The plaintiffs in error began this proceeding in a state court of Colorado to relieve lands owned by them from an assessment of a tax for the cost of paving a street upon which the lands abutted. The relief sought was granted by the trial court, but its action was reversed by the supreme court of the state * * *. The supreme court held that the tax was assessed in conformity with the Constitution and laws of the state, and its decision of that question is conclusive.

The tax complained of was assessed under the provisions of the charter of the city of Denver, which confers upon the city the power to make local improvements and to assess the cost upon property specially benefited. * * *

It appears from the charter that, in the execution of the power to make local improvements and assess the cost upon the property specially benefited, the main steps to be taken by the city authorities are plainly marked and separated: 1. The board of public works must transmit to the city council a resolution ordering the work to be done and the form of an ordinance authorizing it and creating an assessment district. This it can do only upon certain conditions, one of which is that there shall first be filed a petition asking the improvement, signed by the owners of the majority of the frontage to be assessed. 2. The passage of that ordinance by the city council, which is given authority to determine conclusively whether the action of the board was duly taken. 3. The assessment of the cost upon the landowners after due notice and opportunity for hearing.

**Take Note**

The Court concluded that the Board did not violate the rights of the objecting homeowners in deciding that improvements should be made on the street where they lived, even though they did not have the opportunity to appear in person prior to the Board's decision and even though there was some question whether in fact a petition seeking the improvements had been signed by the owners of the majority of the frontage to be assessed. Why were the homeowners not entitled to appear at a hearing before the Board made that decision?

In the case before us the board took the first step by transmitting to the council the resolution to do the work and the form of an ordinance authorizing it. It is contended, however, that there was wanting an essential condition of the jurisdiction of the board; namely, such a petition from the owners as the law requires. The trial court found this contention to be true. But, as has been seen, the charter gave the city council the authority to determine conclusively that the improvements were duly ordered by the board after due notice and a proper petition. In the exercise of this authority the city council, in the ordinance directing the improvement to be made, adjudged, in effect, that a proper petition had been filed. * * * The state supreme court held that the determination of the city council was conclusive that a proper petition was filed, and that decision must be accepted by us as the law of the state. The only question for this court is whether the charter provision authorizing such a finding, without notice to the landowners, denies to them due process of law. We think it does not. The proceedings, from the beginning up to and including the passage of the ordinance authorizing the work, did not include any assessment or necessitate any assessment, although they laid the foundation for an assessment, which might or might not subsequently be made. Clearly all this might validly be done without hearing to the landowners, provided a hearing upon the assessment itself is afforded. The legislature might have authorized the making of improvements by the city council without any petition. If it chose to exact a petition as a security for wise and just action, it could, so far as the Federal Constitution is concerned, accompany that condition with a provision that the council, with or without notice, should determine finally whether it had been performed. This disposes of the first assignment of error, which is overruled. * * *

The fifth assignment [of error], though general, vague, and obscure, fairly raises, we think, the question whether the assessment was made without notice and opportunity for hearing to those affected by it, thereby denying to them due process of law. The trial court found as a fact that no opportunity for hearing was afforded, and the supreme court did not disturb this finding. The record discloses what was actually done, and there seems to be no dispute about it. After the improvement was completed, the board of public works, in compliance with § 29 of the charter, certified to the city clerk a statement of the cost, and an apportionment of it to the lots of land to be assessed. Thereupon the city clerk, in compliance with § 30, published a notice, stating, *inter alia*, that the written complaints or objections of the owners, if filed within thirty days, would be "heard and determined by the city council before the passage of any ordinance assessing the cost." Those interested, therefore, were informed that if they reduced their complaints and objections to writing, and filed them within thirty days, those complaints and objections would be heard, and would be heard before any assessment was made. * * * Resting upon the assurance that they would be heard, the plaintiffs in error filed within the thirty days the following paper:

"Denver, Colorado, January 13, 1900.

"To the Honorable Board of Public Works and the Honorable Mayor and City Council of the City of Denver:

"The undersigned, by Joshua Grozier, their attorney, do hereby most earnestly and strenuously protest and object to the passage of the contemplated or any assessing ordinance against the property in Eighth avenue paving district No. 1, so called, for each of the following reasons, to wit:

> "1st. That said assessment and all and each of the proceedings leading up to the same were and are illegal, voidable, and void; and the attempted assessment, if made, will be void and uncollectible.
>
> "2d. That said assessment and the cost of said pretended improvement should be collected, if at all, as a general tax against the city at large, and not as a special assessment.
>
> "3d. That property in said city not assessed is benefited by the said pretended improvement, and certain property assessed is not benefited by said pretended improvement, and other property assessed is not benefited by said pretended improvement to the extent of the assessment; that the individual pieces of property in said district are not benefited to the extent assessed against them and each of them respectively; that the assessment is arbitrary, and property assessed in an equal amount is not benefited equally; that the boundaries of said pretended district were arbitrarily created without regard to the benefits or any other method of assessment known to law; that said assessment is outrageously large. * * *
>
> "8th. Because the city had no jurisdiction in the premises. No petition subscribed by the owners of a majority of the frontage in the district to be assessed for said improvements was ever obtained or presented. * * *
>
> "Wherefore, because of the foregoing and numerous other good and sufficient reasons, the undersigned object and protest against the passage of the said proposed assessing ordinance."

This certainly was a complaint against an objection to the proposed assessment. Instead of affording the plaintiffs in error an opportunity to be heard upon its allegations, the city council, without notice to them, met as a board of equalization, not in a stated, but in a specially called, session, and, without any hearing, adopted the following resolution:

> "Whereas, complaints have been filed by the various persons and firms as the owners of real estate included within the Eighth avenue paving district No. 1, of the city of Denver, against the proposed assessments on said property for the cost of said paving, * * * and Whereas, no complaint or objection has been filed or made against the apportionment of said assessment made by the board of public works of the city of Denver, but the complaints and objections filed deny wholly the right of the city to assess any district or portion of the assessable property of the city of Denver; therefore, be it
>
> "Resolved, by the city council of the city of Denver, sitting as a board of equalization, that the apportionments of said assessment made by said board of public works be, and the same are hereby, confirmed and approved."

Subsequently, without further notice or hearing, the city council enacted the ordinance of assessment whose validity is to be determined in this case. The facts out of which the question on this assignment arises may be compressed into small compass. The first step in the assessment proceedings was by the certificate of the board of public works of the cost of the improvement and a preliminary apportionment of it. The last step was the enactment of the assessment ordinance. From beginning to end of the proceedings the landowners, although allowed to formulate and file complaints and objections, were not afforded an opportunity to be heard upon them. Upon these facts, was there a denial by the state of the due process of law guaranteed by the 14th Amendment to the Constitution of the United States?

In the assessment, apportionment, and collection of taxes upon property within their jurisdiction, the Constitution of the United States imposes few restrictions upon the states. In the enforcement of such restrictions as the Constitution does impose, this court has regarded substance, and not form. But where the legislature of a state, instead of fixing the tax itself, commits to some subordinate body the duty of determining whether, in what amount, and upon whom it shall be levied, and of making its assessment and apportionment, due process of law requires that, at some stage of the proceedings, before the tax becomes irrevocably fixed, the taxpayer shall have an opportunity to be heard, of which he must have notice, either personal, by publication, or by a law fixing the time and place of the hearing. It must be remembered that the law of Colorado denies the landowner the right to object in the courts to the assessment, upon the ground that the objections are cognizable only by the board of equalization.

**Take Note**

The Court here addressed the landowners' claim that the assessment of taxes violated the Due Process Clause. Why did the Court conclude that the assessment violated the Clause? What could the Board have done to cure the problem?

If it is enough that, under such circumstances, an opportunity is given to submit in writing all objections to and complaints of the tax to the board, then there was a hearing afforded in the case at bar. But we think that something more than that, even in proceedings for taxation, is required by due process of law. Many requirements essential in strictly judicial proceedings may be dispensed with in proceedings of this nature. But even here a hearing, in its very essence, demands that he who is entitled to it shall have the right to support his allegations by argument, however brief: and, if need be, by proof, however informal. *Pittsburgh, C. C. & St. L. R. Co. v. Backus*, 154 U. S. 421, 426 (1894); *Fallbrook Irrig. Dist. v. Bradley*, 164 U. S. 112, 171 (1896).

It is apparent that such a hearing was denied to the plaintiffs in error. The denial was by the city council, which, while acting as a board of equalization, represents the state. The assessment was therefore void, and the plaintiffs in error were entitled to a decree discharging their lands from a lien on account of it. [Reversed]

The Chief Justice and Mr. Justice Holmes dissent.

## *Bi-Metallic Investment Co. v. State Board of Equalization of Colorado*

239 U.S. 441 (1915)

MR. JUSTICE HOLMES delivered the opinion of the court.

This is a suit to enjoin the State Board of Equalization and the Colorado Tax Commission from putting in force and the defendant Pitcher, as assessor of Denver, from obeying, an order of the boards, increasing the valuation of all taxable property in Denver 40 per cent. The order was sustained and the suit directed to be dismissed by the supreme court of the state. The plaintiff is the owner of real estate in Denver, and brings the case here on the ground that it was given no opportunity to be heard, and that therefore its property will be taken without due process of law, contrary to the 14th Amendment of the Constitution of the United States. That is the only question with which we have to deal. * * *

For the purposes of decision we assume that the constitutional question is presented in the baldest way—that neither the plaintiff nor the assessor of Denver, who presents a brief on the plaintiff's side, nor any representative of the city and county, was given an opportunity to be heard, other than such as they may have had by reason of the fact that the time of meeting of the boards is fixed by law. On this assumption it is obvious that injustice may be suffered if some property in the county already has been valued at its full worth. But if certain property has been valued at a rate different from that generally prevailing in the county, the owner has had his opportunity to protest and appeal as usual in our system of taxation (*Hagar v. Reclamation Dist.*, 111 U.S. 701, 709, 710 (1884)), so that it must be assumed that the property owners in the county all stand alike. The question, then, is whether all individuals have a constitutional right to be heard before a matter can be decided in which all are equally concerned—here, for instance, before a superior board decides that the local taxing officers have adopted a system of undervaluation throughout a county, as notoriously often has been the case. The answer of this court in the *State R. Tax Cases*, 92 U.S. 575 (1875), at least, as to any further notice, was that it was hard to believe that the proposition was seriously made.

**FYI**

In *Hagar*, the Court held that "where a tax is levied on property not specifically, but according to its value, to be ascertained by assessors appointed for that purpose, upon such evidence as they may obtain," a state satisfies the requirements of due process when the law creates "boards of revision or equalization, sitting at designated periods provided by law, to hear complaints respecting the justice of the assessments" or allows judicial review of board decisions.

Where a rule of conduct applies to more than a few people, it is impracticable that everyone should have a direct voice in its adoption. The Constitution does not require all public acts to be done in town meeting or an assembly of the whole. General statutes within the state power are passed that affect the person or property of individuals, sometimes to the point of ruin, without giving them a chance to be heard. Their rights are protected in the only way that they can be in a complex society, by their power, immediate or remote, over those who make the rule. If the result in this case had been reached, as it might have been by the state's doubling the rate of taxation, no one would suggest that the 14th Amendment was violated unless every person affected had been allowed an opportunity to raise his voice against it before the body intrusted by the state Constitution with the power. In considering this case in this court we must assume that the proper state machinery has been used, and the question is whether, if the state Constitution had declared that Denver had been undervalued as compared with the rest of the state, and had decreed that for the current year the valuation should be 40 per cent higher, the objection now urged could prevail. It appears to us that to put the question is to answer it. There must be a limit to individual argument in such matters if government is to go on. In *Londoner v. Denver*, 210 U.S. 373, 385 (1908), a local board had to determine 'whether, in what amount, and upon whom' a tax for paving a street should be levied for special benefits. A relatively small number of persons was concerned, who were exceptionally affected, in each case upon individual grounds, and it was held that they had a right to a hearing. But that decision is far from reaching a general determination dealing only with the principle upon which all the assessments in a county had been laid. [Affirmed.]

---

## Points for Discussion

### *a. Participation Rights and Government Action*

*Londoner* and *Bi-Metallic* both involved the question whether a person affected by agency action is entitled to some kind of hearing before the agency can act. Why does it matter whether a landowner can appear in person before the Board acts? Are broad participation rights likely to improve the quality or accuracy of administrative decision-making? If not, is there any other reason to permit it? What are the costs of permitting such participation rights?

### *b.* **Londoner** *and Judicial Action*

In *Londoner*, the Court concluded that the Due Process Clause required the Board to give the landowners an opportunity to participate (perhaps in person) before the Board could assess taxes on them. (The Court said that the landowners had "the right to support [their] allegations by argument, however brief: and, if need be, by proof, however informal.") In what way was the Board's action similar to judicial action?

#### *c.* **Bi-Metallic** ***and Legislative Action***

In *Bi-Metallic*, the Court concluded that the Due Process Clause did not require the Board to give the landowner an opportunity to object (perhaps in person) before the Board could apply to the landowner an order increasing the value, for purposes of calculating property taxes, of all taxable property. In what way was the Board's action similar to legislative action? How did the Court distinguish between those types of agency decisions that trigger the requirement of notice and opportunity to be heard, on the one hand, and those that do not, on the other?

Does it make sense to think about the question in terms of the matters that the agency would have to resolve in order to make its decision? Kenneth Culp Davis famously distinguished between "adjudicative facts" and "legislative facts." As Professor Davis explained, "[a]djudicative facts usually answer the question of who did what, where, when, how, why, and with what motive or intent; adjudicative facts are roughly the kind of facts that go to a jury in a jury case." In contrast, "legislative facts do not usually concern the immediate parties but are the general facts that help the tribunal decide questions of law and policy and discretion." 2 KENNETH CULP DAVIS & RICHARD J. PIERCE, JR., ADMINISTRATIVE LAW TREATISE § 10.5, at 140–141 (3d ed. 1994). Professor Davis reasoned that adjudicative facts are likely to be within the particular (and perhaps unique) knowledge of those who would be most affected by the government's decision. Can you see why trial-type proceedings make sense for determining such facts? Legislative facts, in contrast, are more likely to turn on the sorts of information—such as a peer-reviewed study—for which cross-examination seems unnecessary. If this is the right way to think about the distinction between government action that triggers the requirement of a hearing and government action that does not, then is it obvious that the Court correctly drew the line in *Londoner* and *Bi-Metallic*?

#### ***d. The Due Process Clauses***

There are two Due Process Clauses in the Constitution. The Fifth Amendment provides that "[n]o person shall * * * be deprived of life, liberty, or property, without due process of law." In *Barron v. City of Baltimore*, 32 U.S. 243 (1833), the Supreme Court held that the provisions of the Fifth Amendment, like the other provisions in the first eight Amendments, are "intended solely as a limitation on the exercise of power by the government of the United States, and [are] not applicable to the legislation of the states." After the Civil War, Congress adopted, and the states ratified, the Fourteenth Amendment, which provides that "No State shall * * * deprive any person of life, liberty, or property, without due process of law." Accordingly, *Londoner* and *Bi-Metallic*, which involved action by a Colorado state agency, concerned the Due Process Clause of the Fourteenth Amendment. Challenges to federal agency action, on the other hand, are property asserted under the Due Process Clause of the Fifth Amendment.

---

Together, *Londoner* and *Bi-Metallic* suggest that an agency must provide notice and an opportunity to be heard when it takes action that amounts to an adjudication of private rights—that is, makes decisions that concern a "relatively small number of persons" who are "exceptionally affected" on "individual grounds." Can you apply this test to determine when the Due Process Clause requires a hearing for those affected by the government's decision? Consider the Problem that follows.

---

## Problem

[1] In order to avoid rampant inflation in housing costs in areas heavily affected by World War II defense activities, Congress passed a statute that attempted to stabilize rents in those areas. Congress created the Office of Price Administration and gave its Administrator the power: (a) to establish "defense-rental areas" and recommend rents for housing in those areas; and (b) if such recommendations fail to produce lower rents, to set maximum rents that will be "generally fair and equitable," giving "due consideration" to rents prevailing on April 1, 1941, and to other factors, such as property taxes and other costs.

[2] The Administrator established a "defense-rental area" near a major army base and recommended that maximum rents should be those prevailing in the area on April 1, 1941.

[3] Finding that his recommendation did not suffice to bring down rents, the Administrator established rent control in the area, fixing rents at those prevailing on April 1, 1941. For units first rented after that date, the Administrator established as a maximum rent the first rent charged, subject to being later reduced if that first rent was higher than rents generally prevailing on April 1, 1941.

[4] The Administrator ordered a reduction in the maximum rents allowable in two apartments (both first rented after April 1, 1941) owned by Larry Lawson, on the ground that the first rent charged exceeded the rent generally prevailing on April 1, 1941.

[5] The Administrator denied Lawson's protest to the validity of the ordered reduction.

[6] A court reviewed the denial of the protest.

In light of the Court's decisions in *Londoner* and *Bi-Metallic*, at what point (from [1] to [6] above) was the Administrator obligated to give Larry Lawson notice and an opportunity to be heard? (For present purposes, assume that, as Justice Moody suggested in *Londoner*, an "opportunity to be heard" means, at a minimum, "the right to support * * * allegations by argument however brief, and, if need be, by proof, however informal.")

---

At bottom, the Due Process Clauses provide a constitutional baseline for fair procedure. When an agency seeks to adjudicate the rights of one person (or a small number of persons), the applicable Due Process Clause requires the agency to provide some kind of hearing with some opportunity for the persons affected to appear. Successful challenges based on the Due Process Clause to federal agency action are relatively rare, however, because Congress has generally insisted that agencies provide more procedural protections for those affected by agency action than the Due Process Clause of the Fifth Amendment requires. We explore those protections in the sections that follow and in Chapter 7.

**Make the Connection**

We will return to the Due Process Clauses in Chapter 7, when we consider judicial oversight of informal agency adjudication.

---

## 2. The Administrative Procedure Act

# *Wong Yang Sung v. McGrath*

339 U.S. 33 (1950)

Mr. Justice Jackson delivered the opinion of the Court.

This habeas corpus proceeding involves a single ultimate question—whether administrative hearings in deportation cases must conform to requirements of the Administrative Procedure Act of June 11, 1946, 60 Stat. 237.

Wong Yang Sung, native and citizen of China, was arrested by immigration officials on a charge of being unlawfully in the United States through having overstayed shore leave as one of a shipping crew. A hearing was held before an immigrant inspector who recommended deportation. The Acting Commissioner approved; and the Board of Immigration Appeals affirmed.

Wong Yang Sung then sought release from custody by habeas corpus proceedings in District Court for the District of Columbia, upon the sole ground that the administrative hearing was not conducted in conformity with §§ 5 and 11 of the Administrative Procedure Act.[1] The Government admitted noncompliance, but asserted that the Act did not apply. The court, after hearing, discharged the writ and remanded the prisoner to custody, holding the Administrative Procedure Act inapplicable to deportation hearings. The Court of Appeals affirmed.

The Administrative Procedure Act of June 11, 1946, is a new, basic and comprehensive regulation of procedures in many agencies, more than a few of which can advance arguments that its generalities should not or do not include them. Determination of questions of its coverage may well be approached through consideration of its purposes as disclosed by its background.

Multiplication of federal administrative agencies and expansion of their functions to include adjudications which have serious impact on private rights has been one of the dramatic legal developments of the past half-century. Partly from restriction by statute, partly from judicial self-restraint, and partly by necessity—from the nature of their multitudinous and semi-legislative or executive tasks—the decisions of administrative tribunals were accorded considerable finality, and especially with respect to fact finding. The conviction developed, particularly within the legal profession, that this power was not sufficiently safeguarded and sometimes was put to arbitrary and biased use.

Concern over administrative impartiality and response to growing discontent was reflected in Congress as early as 1929, when Senator Norris introduced a bill to create a separate administrative court. Fears and dissatisfactions increased as tribunals

---

1 Particularly invoked are § 5(c), [5 U.S.C. § 554(d)], which provides in part: "The same officers who preside at the reception of evidence pursuant to section 7 shall make the recommended decision or initial decision required by section 8 except where such officers become unavailable to the agency. Save to the extent required for the disposition of *ex parte* matters as authorized by law, no such officer shall consult any person or party on any fact in issue unless upon notice and opportunity for all parties to participate; nor shall such officer be responsible to or subject to the supervision or direction of any officer, employee, or agent engaged in the performance of investigative or prosecuting functions for any agency. No officer, employee, or agent engaged in the performance of investigative or prosecuting functions for any agency in any case shall, in that or a factually related case, participate or advise in the decision, recommended decision, or agency review pursuant to section 8 except as witness or counsel in public proceedings. . . ."; and § 11, which provides in part: "Subject to the civil-service and other laws to the extent not inconsistent with this Act, there shall be appointed by and for each agency as many qualified and competent examiners as may be necessary for proceedings pursuant to sections 7 and 8, who shall be assigned to cases in rotation so far as practicable and shall perform no duties inconsistent with their duties and responsibilities as examiners. Examiners shall be removable by the agency in which they are employed only for good cause established and determined by the Civil Service Commission (hereinafter called the Commission) after opportunity for hearing and upon the record thereof. Examiners shall receive compensation prescribed by the Commission independently of agency recommendations or ratings and in accordance with the Classification Act of 1923, as amended * * *." [Section 11 of the original Act has been amended and is now codified in various sections in Title 5 of the U.S. Code.]

grew in number and jurisdiction, and a succession of bills offering various remedies appeared in Congress. Inquiries into the practices of state agencies, which tended to parallel or follow the federal pattern, were instituted in several states, and some studies noteworthy for thoroughness, impartiality and vision resulted.

The Executive Branch of the Federal Government also became concerned as to whether the structure and procedure of these bodies was conducive to fairness in the administrative process. President Roosevelt's Committee on Administrative Management in 1937 recommended complete separation of adjudicating functions and personnel from those having to do with investigation or prosecution. The President early in 1939 also directed the Attorney General to name "a committee of eminent lawyers, jurists, scholars, and administrators to review the entire administrative process in the various departments of the executive Government and to recommend improvements, including the suggestion of any needed legislation."

So strong was the demand for reform, however, that Congress did not await the Committee's report but passed what was known as the Walter-Logan bill, a comprehensive and rigid prescription of standardized procedures for administrative agencies. This bill was vetoed by President Roosevelt December 18, 1940, and the veto was sustained by the House. But the President's veto message made no denial of the need for reform. Rather it pointed out that the task of the Committee, whose objective was "to suggest improvements to make the process more workable and more just," had proved "unexpectedly complex." The President said, "I should desire to await their report and recommendations before approving any measure in this complicated field."

The committee divided in its views and both the majority and the minority submitted bills which were introduced in 1941. A subcommittee of the Senate Judiciary Committee held exhaustive hearings on three proposed measures, but, before the gathering storm of national emergency and war, consideration of the problem was put aside. Though bills on the subject reappeared in 1944, they did not attract much attention.

The McCarran-Sumners bill, which evolved into the present Act, was introduced in 1945. Its consideration and hearing, especially of agency interests, was painstaking. All administrative agencies were invited to submit their views in writing. A tentative revised bill was then prepared and interested parties again were invited to submit criticisms. The Attorney General named representatives of the Department of Justice to canvass the agencies and report their criticisms, and submitted a favorable report on the bill as finally revised. It passed both Houses without opposition and was signed by President Truman June 11, 1946.

The Act thus represents a long period of study and strife; it settles long-continued and hard-fought contentions, and enacts a formula upon which opposing social and political forces have come to rest. It contains many compromises and generalities and, no doubt, some ambiguities. Experience may reveal defects. But it would be a disservice to our form of government and to the administrative process itself if the courts should fail, so far as the terms of the Act warrant, to give effect to its remedial purposes where the evils it was aimed at appear.

Of the several administrative evils sought to be cured or minimized, only two are particularly relevant to issues before us today. One purpose was to introduce greater uniformity of procedure and standardization of administrative practice among the diverse agencies whose customs had departed widely from each other. We pursue this no further than to note that any exception we may find to its applicability would tend to defeat this purpose.

More fundamental, however, was the purpose to curtail and change the practice of embodying in one person or agency the duties of prosecutor and judge. The President's Committee on Administrative Management voiced in 1937 the theme which, with variations in language, was reiterated throughout the legislative history of the Act. The Committee's report, which President Roosevelt transmitted to Congress with his approval as "a great document of permanent importance," said:

> ". . . the independent commission is obliged to carry on judicial functions under conditions which threaten the impartial performance of that judicial work. The discretionary work of the administrator is merged with that of the judge. Pressures and influences properly enough directed toward officers responsible for formulating and administering policy constitute an unwholesome atmosphere in which to adjudicate private rights. But the mixed duties of the commissions render escape from these subversive influences impossible.
>
> "Furthermore, the same men are obliged to serve both as prosecutors and as judges. This not only undermines judicial fairness; it weakens public confidence in that fairness. Commission decisions affecting private rights and conduct lie under the suspicion of being rationalizations of the preliminary findings which the commission, in the role of prosecutor, presented to itself." Administrative Management in the Government of the United States, Report of the President's Committee on Administrative Management, 36–37 (1937).

The Committee therefore recommended a redistribution of functions within the regulatory agencies. "(I)t would be divided into an administrative section and a judicial section" and the administrative section "would formulate rules, initiate action, investigate complaints . . ." and the judicial section "would sit as an impartial, independent body to make decisions affecting the public interest and private rights upon the basis of the records and findings presented to it by the administrative section." *Id.* at 37.

Another study was made by a distinguished committee named by the Secretary of Labor, whose jurisdiction at the time included the Immigration and Naturalization Service. Some of the committee's observations have relevancy to the procedure under examination here. It said: "The inspector who presides over the formal hearing is in many respects comparable to a trial judge. He has, at a minimum, the function of determining—subject to objection on the alien's behalf—what goes into the written record upon which decision ultimately is to be based. Under the existing practice he has also the function of counsel representing the moving party—he does not merely admit evidence against the alien; he has the responsibility of seeing that such evidence is put into the record. The precise scope of his appropriate functions is the first question to be considered." The Secretary of Labor's Committee on Administrative Procedure, The Immigration and Naturalization Service, 77 (Mimeo. 1940).

Further:

> "Merely to provide that in particular cases different inspectors shall investigate and hear is an insufficient guarantee of insulation and independence of the presiding official. The present organization of the field staff not only gives work of both kinds commonly to the same inspector but tends toward an identity of viewpoint as between inspectors who are chiefly doing only one or the other kind of work. . . .
>
> ". . . We recommend that the presiding inspectors be relieved of their present duties of presenting the case against aliens and be confirmed (sic) entirely to the duties customary for a judge. This, of course, would require the assignment of another officer to perform the task of a prosecuting attorney. The appropriate officer for this purpose would seem to be the investigating inspector who, having prepared the case against the alien, is already thoroughly familiar with it. . . .
>
> "A genuinely impartial hearing, conducted with critical detachment, is psychologically improbable if not impossible, when the presiding officer has at once the responsibility of appraising the strength of the case and of seeking to make it as strong as possible. Nor is complete divorce between investigation and hearing possible so long as the presiding inspector has the duty himself of assembling and presenting the results of the investigation. . . ." *Id.* at 81–82.

And the Attorney General's Committee on Administrative Procedure, which divided as to the appropriate remedy, was unanimous that this evil existed. Its Final Report said: "These types of commingling of functions of investigation or advocacy with the function of deciding are thus plainly undesirable. But they are also avoidable and should be avoided by appropriate internal division of labor. For the disqualifications produced by investigation or advocacy are personal psychological ones which result from engaging in those types of activity; and the problem is simply one of isolating those who engage in the activity. Creation of independent hearing commissioners insulated from all phases of a case other than hearing and deciding will, the Committee believes, go far toward solving this problem at the level of the initial hearing provided the proper safeguards are established to assure the insulation. . . ." Rep. Atty. Gen. Comm. Ad. Proc. 56 (1941), S. Doc. No. 8, 77th Cong., 1st Sess. 56 (1941).

The Act before us adopts in general this recommended form of remedial action. A minority of the Committee had, furthermore, urged an even more thoroughgoing separation and supported it with a cogent report. *Id.*, at 203 et seq.

Such were the evils found by disinterested and competent students. Such were the facts before Congress which gave impetus to the demand for the reform which this Act was intended to accomplish. It is the plain duty of the courts, regardless of their views of the wisdom or policy of the Act, to construe this remedial legislation to eliminate, so far as its text permits, the practices it condemns.

**Food for Thought**

On which touchstone of interpretation did the Court rely in interpreting the APA's requirements?

Turning now to the case before us, we find the administrative hearing a perfect exemplification of the practices so unanimously condemned.

This hearing, which followed the uniform practice of the Immigration Service, was before an immigrant inspector, who, for purposes of the hearing, is called the "presiding inspector." Except with consent of the alien, the presiding inspector may not be the one who investigated the case. 8 C.F.R. 150.6(b). But the inspector's duties include investigation of like cases; and while he is today hearing cases investigated by a colleague, tomorrow his investigation of a case may be heard before the inspector whose case he passes on today. An "examining inspector" may be designated to conduct the prosecution, 8 C.F.R. 150.6(n), but none was in this case; and, in any event, the examining inspector also has the same mixed prosecutive and hearing functions. The presiding inspector, when no examining inspector is present, is required to "conduct the interrogation of the alien and the witnesses [on] behalf of the Government and shall cross-examine the alien's witnesses and present such evidence as is necessary to support the charges in the warrant of arrest." 8 C.F.R. 150.6(b). It may even become his duty to lodge an additional charge against the alien and proceed to hear his own accusation in like manner. 8 C.F.R. 150.6(1). Then, as soon as practicable, he is to prepare a summary of the evidence, proposed findings of fact, conclusions of law, and a proposed order. A copy is furnished the alien or his counsel, who may file exceptions and brief, 8 C.F.R. 150.7, whereupon the whole is forwarded to the Commissioner. 8 C.F.R. 150.9.

The Administrative Procedure Act did not go so far as to require a complete separation of investigating and prosecuting functions from adjudicating functions. But that the safeguards it did set up were intended to ameliorate the evils from the commingling of functions as exemplified here is beyond doubt. And this commingling, if objectionable anywhere, would seem to be particularly so in the deportation proceedings, where we frequently meet with a voteless class of litigants who not only lack the influence of citizens, but who are strangers to the laws and customs in which they find themselves involved and who often do not even understand the tongue in which they are accused. Nothing in the nature of the parties or proceedings suggests that we should strain to exempt deportation proceedings from reforms in administrative procedure applicable generally to federal agencies.

Nor can we accord any weight to the argument that to apply the Act to such hearings will cause inconvenience and added expense to the Immigration Service. Of course it will, as it will to nearly every agency to which it is applied. But the power of the purse belongs to Congress, and Congress has determined that the price for greater fairness is not too high. The agencies, unlike the aliens, have ready and persuasive access to the legislative ear and if error is made by including them, relief from Congress is a simple matter.

This brings us to contentions both parties have advanced based on the pendency in Congress of bills to exempt this agency from the Act. Following an adverse decision, the Department asked Congress for exempting legislation, which appropriate committees of both Houses reported favorably but in different form and substance. Congress adjourned without further action. The Government argues that Congress knows that the Immigration Service has construed the Act as not applying to deportation proceedings, and that it "has taken no action indicating disagreement with that interpretation"; that therefore it "is at least arguable that Congress was prepared to specifically confirm the administrative construction by clarifying legislation." We do not think we can draw that inference from incompleted steps in the legislative process.

On the other hand, we will not draw the inference, urged by petitioner, that an agency admits that it is acting upon a wrong construction by seeking ratification from Congress. Public policy requires that agencies feel free to ask legislation which will terminate or avoid adverse contentions and litigations. We do not feel justified in holding that a request for and failure to get in a single session of Congress clarifying legislation on a genuinely debatable point of agency procedure admits weakness in the agency's contentions. We draw, therefore, no inference in favor of either construction of the Act—from the Department's request for legislative clarification, from the congressional committees' willingness to consider it, or from Congress' failure to enact it.

We come, then, to examination of the text of the Act to determine whether the Government is right in its [contention that] the general scope of § 5 of the Act does not cover deportation proceedings * * *.

The Administrative Procedure Act, § 5, establishes a number of formal requirements to be applicable "[i]n every case of adjudication required by statute to be determined on the record after opportunity for an agency hearing." * * * The Government contends that there is no express requirement for any hearing or adjudication in the statute authorizing deportation, and that this omission shields these proceedings from the impact of § 5. * * *

But the difficulty with any argument premised on the proposition that the deportation statute does not require a hearing is that, without such hearing, there would be no constitutional authority for deportation. The constitutional requirement of procedural due process of law derives from the same source as Congress' power to legislate and, where applicable, permeates every valid enactment of that body. * * * We think that the limitation to hearings "required by statute" in § 5 of the Administrative Procedure Act exempts from that section's application only those hearings which administrative agencies may hold by regulation, rule, custom, or special dispensation; not those held by compulsion. We do not think the limiting words render the Administrative Procedure Act inapplicable to hearings, the requirement for which has been read into a statute by the Court in order to save the statute from invalidity. * * * We would hardly attribute to Congress a purpose to be less scrupulous about the fairness of a hearing necessitated by the Constitution than one granted by it as a matter of expediency.

Indeed, to so construe the Immigration Act might again bring it into constitutional jeopardy. When the Constitution requires a hearing, it requires a fair one, one before a tribunal which meets at least currently prevailing standards of impartiality. A deportation hearing involves issues basic to human liberty and happiness and, in the present upheavals in lands to which aliens may be returned, perhaps to life itself. It might be difficult to justify as measuring up to constitutional standards of impartiality a hearing tribunal for deportation proceedings the like of which has been condemned by Congress as unfair even where less vital matters of property rights are at stake.

We hold that deportation proceedings must conform to the requirements of the Administrative Procedure Act if resulting orders are to have validity. Since the proceeding in the case before us did not comply with these requirements, we sustain the writ of habeas corpus and direct release of the prisoner.

Mr. Justice Douglas and Mr. Justice Clark took no part in the consideration or decision of this case.

[Mr. Justice Reed's dissenting has been omitted.]

---

## Points for Discussion

### *a. The APA's Broad Purposes*

The Court's opinion in *Wong Yang Sung* provides a good overview of the impetus for, and history of, the Administrative Procedure Act and Congress's general objectives in enacting the law. Notice that the bill passed unanimously in both houses, which suggests that there was broad consensus about the need to standardize the procedural rules that govern federal agency action. Why did Congress see the need to enact such a law?

### *b. The APA and Immigration Hearings*

The Court acknowledged that Congress had considered bills to exempt immigration hearings from the requirements from the APA, but at the time of the Court's decision, Congress had not yet acted on those proposals. The following year, Congress legislatively overruled the Court's specific holding in *Wong Yang Sung* by providing that immigration hearings are exempt from the requirements of the APA. Supplemental Appropriation Act, 1951. 64 Stat. 1044, 1048; see also *Ardestani v. INS*, 502 U.S. 129 (1991). Accordingly, although *Wong Yang Sung* identifies Congress's broad goals in enacting the APA, its holding about immigration hearings is no longer good law.

---

The administrative state grew substantially during President Franklin D. Roosevelt's administration. Congress created dozens of agencies to administer statutory programs designed to protect the public health and safety and to prevent market abuses. Courts reviewing agency decisions in this era applied a mix of constitutional principles—such as those embodied in *Londoner* and *Bi-Metallic*—as well as limits included in agency organic statutes and a judicially created common law of administrative action. But this early version of administrative law was not always totally consistent or coherent, and critics charged that it did not do enough to constrain the discretion of administrative agencies.

As the Court explained in *Wong Yang Sung*, Congress eventually responded by enacting the Administrative Procedure Act. The APA provides a statutory framework to govern virtually all actions of federal administrative agencies. The APA's provisions are codified in two parts of the United States Code. The rules governing administrative procedures, which we will begin to consider in this Chapter, are codified at 5 U.S.C. §§ 551–559; the rules governing judicial review of agency action, which we will consider in Chapter 7, are codified at 5 U.S.C. §§ 701–706.

**FYI**

The full text of the APA is reprinted in the appendix of this book. You can also access it on the website of the National Archives.

The statute begins with a set of definitions of terms used in the Act's various provisions. Section 551(1) defines "agency"—and therefore the government entities to which the Act applies—as "each authority of the Government of the United States, whether or not it is within or subject to review by another agency," but specifically excludes Congress, the courts, territorial governments, the District of Columbia government, and (for most purposes) military tribunals. 5 U.S.C. § 551(1). In other words, pretty much every federal agency is subject to the APA's requirements, even if Congress did not so specify when it created the agency. (Indeed, Section 559 states that a "[s]ubsequent statute may not be held to supersede or modify this subchapter

* * * except to the extent that it does so expressly," which means that the APA applies unless Congress specifically exempts an agency. 5 U.S.C. § 559.)

Unlike the Due Process Clause of the Fifth Amendment, which (as interpreted by the Court in *Londoner* and *Bi-Metallic*) essentially divides all administrative action into *two* categories (judicial-type action and legislative-type action), the APA contemplates *four* distinct categories of administrative action: formal adjudication, informal adjudication, formal rulemaking, and informal rulemaking.

Section 553 contains provisions that apply to "rule making," and Section 554 governs agency "adjudications." As these terms suggest, they loosely track the *Londoner* and *Bi-Metallic* distinction between legislative-type action and judicial-type action. As we noted above, for constitutional purposes the line between these categories—which governs the rights of participation to which an interested person is entitled—is hazy at best. The APA defines the terms "rule making" and "adjudication," but unfortunately the definitions raise as many questions as they answer.

Section 551 defines "rule making" as "agency process for formulating, amending, or repealing a rule." 5 U.S.C. § 551(5). It defines "rule," in turn, as "the whole or a part of an agency statement of general or particular applicability and future effect designed to implement, interpret, or prescribe law or policy * * *." *Id.* § 551(4). "Adjudication," in contrast, is the "agency process for the formulation of an order," *id.* § 551(7), and an "order," in turn, is "the whole or a part of a final disposition, whether affirmative, negative, injunctive, or declaratory in form, of an agency in a matter other than rule making but including licensing," *id.* § 551(6).

In other words, according to the APA, an adjudication is essentially anything that is not considered rulemaking, and rulemaking is an agency action designed to produce an "agency statement of general or particular applicability and future effect designed to implement, interpret, or prescribe law or policy." Taken literally, these definitions appear to suggest that any prospective action—even action of "particularly applicability" designed to "implement * * * law or policy"—counts as rulemaking. But courts have read these provisions according to common sense and in light of the Court's distinction in *Londoner* and *Bi-Metallic* between judicial-like and legislative-like actions. Accordingly, courts usually treat decisions to adopt generally applicable, prospective policies as exercises of the power to make rules. Adjudications, in contrast, are determinations concerning one or a small number of persons, based on historical facts unique to that person or persons, and are designed to determine the rights or obligations of those persons in light of the substantive law.

Section 553 governs rulemaking. We will consider its provisions in detail in Chapter 7, but for now notice two important things about it. First, section 553 states that rulemaking ordinarily begins with "general notice of [the] proposed rulemaking * * * in the Federal Register," and that the notice must include "either the terms or substance of the proposed rule or a description of the subjects and issues involved."

5 U.S.C. § 553(b). Section 553 also provides that the agency must "give interested persons an opportunity to participate in the rule making through submission of written data, views, or arguments with or without opportunity for oral presentation." *Id.* § 553(c). In addition, "[a]fter consideration of the relevant matter presented, the agency shall incorporate in the rules adopted a concise general statement of their basis and purpose." *Id.* Because of these provisions, agency rule-making pursuant to section 553 is often called "notice-and-comment rule-making."

In other words, when agencies issue rules, the APA usually requires the agency to provide some opportunity for participation for interested persons. (There are a few exceptions to the notice and comment requirements, but we won't concern ourselves with them right now.) Stated another way, the APA requires greater rights of participation for rulemaking than does the Due Process Clause (as construed in *Bi-Metallic*), but fewer rights of participation than the Due Process Clause (as construed in *Londoner*) requires for adjudication. The APA, for example, does not require personalized notice to interested persons before a rulemaking, and there is no guaranteed right to appear in person at a hearing before the agency.

Second, section 553 states that "[w]hen rules are required by statute to be made on the record after opportunity for an agency hearing, sections 556 and 557 of this title apply instead of this subsection." 5 U.S.C. § 553(c). Sections 556 and 557, in turn, require formal proceedings that include many of the procedural requirements that we associate with judicial decision-making, such as the opportunity for cross-examination and a decision based only on evidence submitted on the record during the proceeding. 5 U.S.C. § 556(d), (e).

In other words, when some other statute—usually, the agency's organic statute—states that rules must be made "on the record after opportunity for an agency hearing," the agency will not follow the relatively lax procedures specified in section 553; instead, it will follow the more formal requirements listed in sections 556 and 557. When an agency makes a rule pursuant to these procedures, it engages in what we call **formal rulemaking**. As we'll see soon, formal rulemaking is quite uncommon today. Because the much more common type—notice-and-comment rule-making—uses comparatively less formal procedures, it is often referred to as **informal rulemaking**.

The APA creates a similar distinction in its provisions that govern agency adjudications. Section 554 states that its provisions apply "in every case of adjudication required by statute to be determined on the record after opportunity for an agency hearing." 5 U.S.C. § 554(a). Its provisions, along with sections 556 and 557, to which it refers, describe something like what one would expect to see in a formal trial in an ordinary court. As a consequence, this form of administrative decision-making is known as **formal adjudication**. Whereas statutes rarely require rulemaking to be done on the record—that is, in a formal proceeding—it is quite common for statutes to require formal adjudications.

In formal proceedings, the APA ordinarily requires a presiding officer (usually called an Administrative Law Judge) who enjoys a good deal of independence from the political appointees at the agency. (These were the provisions at issue in Wong Yang Sung.)The person whose rights are being adjudicated gets all kinds of procedural rights, including the right to introduce oral evidence and the right to a decision that is based only on the evidence introduced during the proceeding.

Whereas the APA specifies the procedures required when an agency engages in formal adjudication, see 5 U.S.C. §§ 554, 556, 557, it says very little about adjudications that are not required by statute to be made on the record after opportunity for an agency hearing—that is, about **informal adjudication**. Part of the reason why the APA says little about informal adjudications is that, as we'll see shortly, a large and varied group of agency decisions count as informal adjudications. It would be difficult in a general statute designed to regulate all agency decision-making to provide requirements for such a diverse group of decisions, each of which raises different concerns and is taken for different reasons. As a consequence, when agencies operate in this category, the Due Process Clause identifies the minimum procedure that the agency must provide. Section 555 also provides some basic procedural requirements, including the right to be represented by a lawyer and the right to prompt notice of the denial of requested action. 5 U.S.C. § 555.

Although we will explore some of the details below and in Chapter 7, we have now identified the four basic categories of administrative action contemplated by the APA: informal rulemaking, formal rulemaking, informal adjudication, and formal adjudication. The procedural requirements with which the agency must comply vary depending on which type of action the agency takes.

| | RULEMAKING | ADJUDICATION |
|---|---|---|
| INFORMAL | Section 553(b) & (c) | Due Process Clause; Section 555 |
| FORMAL | Sections 556 & 557 | Sections 554, 556, & 557 |

It can be difficult to appreciate the nature of the agency actions in these various categories simply from a set of abstract definitions. Accordingly, the cases that follow are included to illustrate the various forms of agency action. By definition, each case involves the response of a court called upon to scrutinize agency action. For now, however, the cases are included simply to help you to identify the various forms of agency action. We'll turn squarely to judicial control of agency action, and the APA's provisions that govern judicial review, in Chapter 7.

---

### a. Formal Adjudication

## *Seacoast Anti-Pollution League v. Costle*

572 F.2d 872 (1st Cir. 1978)

COFFIN, CHIEF JUDGE.

This case is before us on a petition by the Seacoast Anti-Pollution League and the Audubon Society of New Hampshire (petitioners) to review a decision by the Administrator of the Environmental Protection Agency (EPA). * * * The petition presents several important issues relating to the applicability and effect of the Administrative Procedure Act (APA), 5 U.S.C. § 501 et seq., and the interpretation of the Federal Water Pollution Control Act of 1972 (FWPCA), 33 U.S.C. § 1251 et seq. * * *

The Public Service Company of New Hampshire (PSCO) filed an application with the EPA for permission to discharge heated water into the Hampton-Seabrook Estuary which runs into the Gulf of Maine. The water would be taken from the Gulf of Maine, be run through the condensor of PSCO's proposed nuclear steam electric generating station at Seabrook, and then be directly discharged back into the Gulf at a temperature 39° F higher than at intake. The water is needed to remove waste heat, some 16 billion BTU per hour, generated by the nuclear reactor but not converted into electrical energy by the turbine. Occasionally, in a process called backflushing, the water will be recirculated through the condensor, and discharged through the intake tunnel at a temperature of 120° F in order to kill whatever organisms may be living in the intake system.

Section 301(a) of the FWPCA, 33 U.S.C. § 1311(a), prohibits the discharge of any pollutant unless the discharger, the point source operator, has obtained an EPA permit. Heat is a pollutant. 33 U.S.C. § 1362(6). Section 301(b) directs the EPA to promulgate effluent limitations. The parties agree that the cooling system PSCO has proposed does not meet the EPA standards because PSCO would utilize a once-through open cycle system—the water would not undergo any cooling process before being returned to the sea. Therefore, in August, 1974, PSCO applied not only for a discharge permit under § 402 of the FWPCA, 33 U.S.C. § 1342, but also an exemption from the EPA standards pursuant to § 316 of the FWPCA, 33 U.S.C. § 1326. Under § 316(a) a point source operator who "after opportunity for public hearing, can demonstrate to the satisfaction of the Administrator" that the EPA's standards are "more stringent than necessary to assure the projection (sic) and propagation of a balanced, indigenous population of shellfish, fish, and wildlife in and on the body of water" may be allowed to meet a lower standard. Moreover, under § 316(b) the cooling water intake structure must "reflect the best technology available for minimizing adverse environmental impact."

**Make the Connection**

The statute at issue appears to contain a typo, using the word "projection" instead of "protection." Should the court simply read it to mean "protection"? We considered the scrivener's error doctrine in Chapter 3.

In January, 1975, the Regional Administrator of the EPA held a non-adjudicatory hearing at Seabrook. He then authorized the once-through system in June, 1975. Later, in October, 1975, he specified the location of the intake structure. The Regional Administrator granted a request by petitioners that public adjudicative hearings on PSCO's application be held. These hearings were held in March and April, 1976, pursuant to the EPA's regulations establishing procedures for deciding applications for permits under § 402 of the FWPCA, 40 C.F.R. § 125.36. The hearings were before an administrative law judge who certified a record to the Regional Administrator for decision. The Regional Administrator decided in November, 1976, to reverse his original determinations and deny PSCO's application.

**FYI**

"C.F.R." is the Code of Federal Regulations. It is published in the Federal Register and includes regulations issued by federal agencies, organized by agency and subject matter.

PSCO, pursuant to 40 C.F.R. § 125.36(n), appealed the decision to the Administrator who agreed to review it. Thereafter, a new Administrator was appointed, and he assembled a panel of six in-house advisors to assist in his technical review. This panel met between February 28 and March 3, 1977, and submitted a report finding that with one exception PSCO had met its burden of proof. With respect to that exception, the effect of backflushing, the Administrator asked PSCO to submit further information, offered other parties the opportunity to comment upon PSCO's submission, and stated that he would hold a hearing on the new information if any party so requested and could satisfy certain threshold conditions * * *. Petitioners did request a hearing, but the Administrator denied the request.

The Administrator's final decision followed the technical panel's recommendations and, with the additional information submitted, reversed the Regional Administrator's decision, finding that PSCO had met its burden under § 316. It is this decision that petitioners have brought before us for review.

**Take Note**

Pause for a moment and think about the nature of the agency decision at issue in this case. The Administrator reviewed evidence and argument submitted by a regulated party in the course of deciding whether that party was entitled to an exemption from a statutory requirement. Is that decision best characterized as an adjudication or a rulemaking? Why?

*Applicability of the Administrative Procedure Act*

Petitioners assert that the proceedings by which the EPA decided this case contravened certain provisions of the APA governing adjudicatory hearings, 5 U.S.C. §§ 554, 556, and 557. Respondents answer that the APA does not apply to proceedings held pursuant to § 316 or § 402 of the FWPCA, 33 U.S.C. §§ 1326, 1342.

The dispute centers on the meaning of the introductory phrases of § 554(a) of the APA:[4] "This section applies . . . in every case of adjudication required by statute to be determined on the record after opportunity for an agency hearing . . . ." Both § 316(a) and § 402(a)(1) of the FWPCA provide for public hearings, but neither states that the hearing must be "on the record." * * * The Ninth Circuit and the Seventh Circuit have each found that the APA does apply to proceedings pursuant to § 402. *Marathon Oil Co. v. EPA*, 564 F.2d 1253 (9th Cir. 1977); *United States Steel Corp. v. Train*, 556 F.2d 822 (7th Cir. 1977). We agree.

At the outset we reject the position of intervenor PSCO that the precise words "on the record" must be used to trigger the APA. The Supreme Court has clearly rejected such an extreme reading even in the context of rule making under § 553 of the APA. See *United States v. Florida East Coast Ry. Co.*, 410 U.S. 224, 245 (1973). Rather, we think that the resolution of this issue turns on the substantive nature of the hearing Congress intended to provide.

**Make the Connection**

We will consider formal rulemaking, and the Court's decision in *Florida East Coast Railway*, later in this Chapter.

---

4 The determination that the EPA must make under § 316 of the FWPCA is not a rule because it is not "designed to implement, interpret, or prescribe law or policy." 5 U.S.C. § 551(4). Rather the EPA must decide a specific factual question already prescribed by statute. Since the determination is not a rule, it is an order. 5 U.S.C. § 551(6). The agency process for formulating an order is an adjudication. 5 U.S.C. § 551(7). Therefore, § 554 rather than § 553 of the APA is the relevant section. The same result is dictated because § 316(a) of the FWPCA is a licensing, 5 U.S.C. § 551(9), since it results in the granting or denial of a form of permission. See 5 U.S.C. § 551(8). A license is an order. 5 U.S.C. § 551(6).

We begin with the nature of the decision at issue. The EPA Administrator must make specific factual findings about the effects of discharges from a specific point source. On the basis of these findings the Administrator must determine whether to grant a discharge permit to a specific applicant. Though general policy considerations may influence the decision, the decision will not make general policy. Only the rights of the specific applicant will be affected. "As the instant proceeding well demonstrates, the factual questions involved in the issuance of section 402 permits will frequently be sharply disputed. Adversarial hearings will be helpful, therefore, in guaranteeing both reasoned decisionmaking and meaningful judicial review. In summary, the proceedings below were conducted in order 'to adjudicate disputed facts in particular cases,' not 'for the purposes of promulgating policy-type rules or standards.' " *Marathon Oil Co., supra* at 1262.

This is exactly the kind of quasi-judicial proceeding for which the adjudicatory procedures of the APA were intended. * * * One of the developments that prompted the APA was the "(m)ultiplication of federal administrative agencies and expansion of their functions to include adjudications which have serious impact on private rights." *Wong Yang Sung v. McGrath*, 339 U.S. 33, 36–37 (1950). This is just such an adjudication. The panoply of procedural protections provided by the APA is necessary not only to protect the rights of an applicant for less stringent pollutant discharge limits, but is also needed to protect the public for whose benefit the very strict limitations have been enacted. If determinations such as the one at issue here are not made on the record, then the fate of the Hampton-Seabrook Estuary could be decided on the basis of evidence that a court would never see or, what is worse, that a court could not be sure existed. We cannot believe that Congress would intend such a result.

Our holding does not render the opening phrases of § 554 of the APA meaningless. We are persuaded that their purpose was to exclude "governmental functions, such as the administration of loan programs, which traditionally have never been regarded as adjudicative in nature and as a rule have never been exercised through other than business procedures." Attorney General's Manual on the Administrative Procedure Act 40 (1947). Without some kind of limiting language, the broad sweep of the definition of "adjudication," defined principally as that which is not rule making, 5 U.S.C. § 551(6), (7), would include such ordinary procedures that do not require any kind of hearing at all. In short, we view the crucial part of the limiting language to be the requirement of a statutorily imposed hearing. We are willing to presume that, unless a statute otherwise specifies, an adjudicatory hearing subject to judicial review must be on the record. * * * Therefore, we will judge the proceedings below according to the standards set forth in §§ 554, 556, and 557 of the APA.

*Compliance with the Administrative Procedure Act*

Petitioners contend that two steps in the EPA's proceedings in this case violated the APA. We will look at each in turn.

1. The Post-hearing Submissions; The Request for Information

The Regional Administrator, in his initial decision, had determined that the record was insufficient to properly evaluate the environmental effects of backflushing. The Administrator's technical panel agreed. The Administrator asked PSCO to submit supplemental information on that subject. Other parties were given permission to comment on PSCO's submission. In addition, the Administrator provided that a hearing with respect to the submission would be held if four conditions designed to guarantee that the hearing could resolve a substantial issue of fact were met. PSCO submitted the requested information. Other parties, including petitioners, submitted comments, and petitioners requested a hearing. The Administrator denied the hearing because petitioners had failed to meet the threshold conditions.

Petitioners argue, first, that the Administrator could not rely on this information because it was not part of the exclusive record for decision. 5 U.S.C. § 556(e). Second, petitioners argue that even if the information was legitimately part of the record, the Administrator was obligated to provide an opportunity for cross-examination pursuant to 5 U.S.C. § 556(d).

Section 556(e) provides that "(t)he transcript of testimony and exhibits, together with all papers and requests filed in the proceeding, constitutes the exclusive record for decision . . . ." [This section] does not limit the time frame during which any papers must be received. Certainly the submissions at issue were "filed in the proceeding." Moreover, 5 U.S.C. § 557(b) provides that "(o)n appeal from or review of the initial decision, the agency has all the powers which it would have in making the initial decision . . . ." One of those powers is the power to preside at the taking of evidence. 5 U.S.C. § 556(b)(1). For these reasons we can find no fault with the Administrator's decision to seek further evidence. Indeed we think this procedure was a most appropriate way to gather the necessary information without the undue delay that would result from a remand.

The question remains, however, whether the procedures by which the Administrator gathered the information conformed to the governing law. The first point is whether the Administrator was empowered to require that the new evidence be submitted in written form. * * * In this case § 316(a) of the FWPCA requires the EPA to afford an opportunity for a public hearing. We do not believe that an opportunity to submit documents constitutes a public hearing. * * * The public hearing can be especially important in cases such as this one which turn not so much upon the actual baseline data (which presumably all parties will be happy to have submitted in written form) as upon experts' interpretation of the data. The experts' credibility is, therefore, very much at issue here.

While we believe that it was error for the Administrator not to hold a hearing to receive the responses to his request for information, and that therefore the submission was not properly part of the record, we cannot be sure that any purpose would be served by ordering a hearing on this issue at this stage in these proceedings. Petitioners' principal complaints are that either the Administrator could not take any evidence or that he was required to afford an opportunity for cross-examination. The latter complaint has no more basis than the former. A party to an administrative adjudicatory hearing does not have an absolute right to cross-examine witnesses. The plain language of 5 U.S.C. § 556(d) limits that right to instances where cross-examination is "required for a full and true disclosure of the facts."

We will order a remand for the limited purpose of allowing the Administrator to determine whether cross-examination would be useful. * * * If the Administrator finds that cross-examination would help disclose the facts a hearing must be provided at which cross-examination would be available. If, however, the Administrator concludes that cross-examination would not serve any useful purpose then we will not require him to hold a hearing merely to have the already submitted statements read into the record.

2. Participation of the Technical Review Panel

Petitioners object to the Administrator's use of a panel of EPA scientists to assist him in reviewing the Regional Administrator's initial decision. The objection is two-fold: first, that the Administrator should not have sought such help at all; and, second, that the panel's report (the Report) to the Administrator included information not in the administrative record.

* * * [A]dministrative agencies [exist], in part, to enable government to focus broad ranges of talent on particular multi-dimensional problems. The Administrator is charged with making highly technical decisions in fields far beyond his individual expertise. "The strength (of the administrative process) lies in staff work organized in such a way that the appropriate specialization is brought to bear upon each aspect of a single decision, the synthesis being provided by the men at the top." 2 K. Davis, Administrative Law Treatise 84 (1958). Therefore, "(e)vidence . . . may be sifted and analyzed by competent subordinates." *Morgan v. United States*, 298 U.S. 468, 481 (1936). The decision ultimately reached is no less the [Administrator's] simply because agency experts helped him to reach it.

A different question is presented, however, if the agency experts do not merely sift and analyze but also add to the evidence properly before the Administrator. 5 U.S.C. § 556(e) [provides,] "The transcript of testimony and exhibits, together with all papers and requests filed in the proceeding, constitutes the exclusive record for decision . . . ." To the extent the technical review panel's Report included information not in the record on which the Administrator relied, § 556(e) was violated. In effect the agency's staff would have made up for PSCO's failure to carry its burden of proof.

Our review of the Report indicates that such violations did occur. The most serious instance is on page 19 of the Report where the technical panel rebuts the Regional Administrator's finding that PSCO had failed to supply enough data on species' thermal tolerances by saying: "There is little information in the record on the thermal tolerances of marine organisms exposed to the specific temperature fluctuation associated with the Seabrook operation. However, the scientific literature does contain many references to the thermal sensitivity of members of the local biota." * * * [T]the record did not support the conclusion until supplemented by the panel. The panel's work found its way directly into the Administrator's decision at page 27 where he discusses the Regional Administrator's concerns about insufficient data but then precipitously concludes, "On the recommendation of the panel, however, I find that . . . local indigenous populations will not be significantly affected." This conclusion depends entirely on what the panel stated about the scientific literature. * * * The panel did not say that the information missing was unavailable or irrelevant; instead they supplied the information. They are free to do that as witnesses, but not as deciders.

The appropriate remedy under these circumstances is to remand the decision to the Administrator because he based his decision on material not part of the record. We are compelled to treat the use of the Report more severely than the use of the PSCO post-hearing submission because no party was given any opportunity to comment on the panel's Report. By contrast, all parties were given the opportunity to comment on PSCO's submission, and these comments were considered equally part of the record by the Administrator. * * *

The Administrator will have the options of trying to reach a new decision not dependent on the panel's supplementation of the record; of holding a hearing at which all parties will have the opportunity to cross-examine the panel members and at which the panel will have an opportunity to amplify its position; or of taking any other action within his power and consistent with this opinion.

---

## Points for Discussion

### *a. Identifying Adjudications*

The agency decision at issue involved a request by a regulated party for an exemption from a statutory requirement. Why does such a decision count, for purposes of the APA, as an adjudication? The court, quoting the APA, noted that the decision was a not a rule "because it [was] not 'designed to implement, interpret, or prescribe law or policy.' " Is it obvious to you that a decision whether to grant an exemption from a statutory policy is not designed to "implement" that policy? Even if not, a common-sense understanding of the difference between rulemaking and adjudication suggests that what was issue in this case was an adjudication. Can you articulate what about the decision made it seem like an adjudication?

### *b. "On the Record After Opportunity for an Agency Hearing"*

The court held that a statutory requirement that an agency adjudication be made after a hearing, even if there is no specific requirement that the decision be made "on the record," is sufficient to trigger the APA's requirements governing formal adjudications. Why did the court reach this conclusion? Is the requirement of an on-the-record decision such an essential characteristic of an adjudication—a process for determining the rights or obligations of a particular party in light of historical facts and the governing law—that such a requirement can be implied from the fact that the statute also requires a hearing?

### *c. Formal Adjudication*

Because the court concluded that the FWPCA triggered the requirements of section 554 of the APA, the agency decision at issue was a "formal adjudication." With which procedural requirements must an agency comply when conducting a formal adjudication? In what ways are such proceedings comparable to judicial proceedings in Article III courts? In what ways are they different? For example, are the requirements about cross-examination of witnesses the same or different? Should we be troubled that the "judge" in the case was the agency's Administrator, who is also responsible for formulating policy for the agency?

**Make the Connection**

We will return to the APA's procedural requirements for formal adjudications in Chapter 7, when we consider judicial oversight of agency decision-making.

---

Of the four categories of administrative action, formal adjudication is probably the one with which you are most familiar as a conceptual matter. Even if your other classes have not yet fully explored the elements of a civil trial in federal court, you likely have a good sense of what a typical judicial proceeding looks like. Formal adjudications before an agency have much in common with judicial proceedings in a federal court. For example, the APA provides that a "party is entitled to present his case or defense by oral or documentary evidence, to submit rebuttal evidence, and to conduct such cross-examination as may be required for a full and true disclosure of the facts." 5 U.S.C. § 556(d). In addition, the APA prohibits interested parties from *ex parte* contacts—that is, contacts about the merits of the adjudication outside of the proceedings themselves without the presence of all of the interested parties—with the agency decision-makers; such contacts, which by definition are not subject to cross-examination, are similarly prohibited with the judge during the course of a judicial proceeding.

But there are also important differences between formal adjudication by an agency and a judicial proceeding in an Article III court. In *Seacoast Anti-Pollution*

*League*, for example, the decision about entitlement to an exemption from statutory requirements was made by the Administrator of the agency, who presumably had some policy agenda with respect to nuclear power that he sought to advance, rather than a totally impartial decision-maker comparable to an Article III judge. In addition, many agency adjudications are conducted in inquisitorial rather than adversarial proceedings. For example, in the immigration proceeding at issue in *Wong Yang Sung*, which we considered earlier in this Chapter, the government did not have an attorney playing the role of prosecutor; instead, the hearing examiner was responsible for questioning witnesses and compiling a record before reaching a decision. Similarly, Social Security Disability proceedings—of which there are more than two million each year—do not involve a lawyer from the Social Security Administration, but instead involve the claimant and an administrative law judge who is responsible for establishing the facts and rendering a decision.

Formal adjudications can concern a wide range of substantive matters—from claims for disability benefits, to requests for statutory exemptions, to applications for licenses. Does it make sense to have one set of procedural requirements to govern all of these disparate proceedings? If not, would it be efficient and administrable to have a system in which the procedural requirements varied widely depending on the nature of the underlying substantive matter to be decided?

---

### b. Informal Adjudication

As we just saw, an agency decision properly characterized as an adjudication must comply with a set of strict procedural requirements when some other statute requires the decision to be made "on the record after opportunity for an agency hearing." But what about agency decisions that count as adjudications within the meaning of the APA and that are not required to be made on the record after an opportunity for an agency hearing? Not surprisingly, such decisions are called "informal adjudications." They are adjudications because they do not count as rules, and they are informal because they do not have to comply with the formal trial-type requirements identified in sections 554, 556, and 557 of the APA.

It might surprise you to learn that the vast majority of agency decisions count as informal adjudications under the APA. Here are some examples of agency actions that count as informal adjudications: the grant of a permit to a manufacturer that alters its equipment to comply with environmental standards; an inspection of a truck for compliance with safety standards; the seizure of adulterated food that imposes an immediate health risk; and the denial of an application for relief from a student loan. To be sure, these actions don't sound to us like "adjudications." But they nevertheless count as informal adjudications under the APA. Remember, an agency action is an informal adjudication under the APA as long as it is not a rule—that is, not "an agency statement of general or particular applicability and future effect designed to implement, interpret, or prescribe law or policy"—and is not required by some other statute to be made on the record after opportunity for an agency hearing.

The following case provides an example of an informal adjudication, how to recognize that an agency decision counts as an informal adjudication, and what requirements apply when an agency engages in informal adjudication.

---

## *Pension Benefit Guaranty Corporation v. LTV Corp.*

496 U.S. 633 (1990)

Justice Blackmun delivered the opinion of the Court.

In this case we must determine whether the decision of the Pension Benefit Guaranty Corporation (PBGC) to restore certain pension plans under § 4047 of the Employee Retirement Income Security Act of 1974 (ERISA), 88 Stat. 1028, as amended, 100 Stat. 237, 29 U.S.C. § 1347, was, as the Court of Appeals concluded, arbitrary and capricious or contrary to law, within the meaning of the Administrative Procedure Act (APA), 5 U.S.C. § 706.

Petitioner PBGC is a wholly owned United States Government corporation, see 29 U.S.C. § 1302, modeled after the Federal Deposit Insurance Corporation. The Board of Directors of the PBGC consists of the Secretaries of the Treasury, Labor, and Commerce. 29 U.S.C. § 1302(d). The PBGC administers and enforces Title IV of ERISA. Title IV includes a mandatory Government insurance program that protects the pension benefits of over 30 million private-sector American workers who participate in plans covered by the Title. In enacting Title IV, Congress sought to ensure that employees and their beneficiaries would not be completely "deprived of anticipated retirement benefits by the termination of pension plans before sufficient funds have been accumulated in the plans." *Pension Benefit Guaranty Corporation v. R.A. Gray & Co.*, 467 U.S. 717, 720 (1984).

When a plan covered under Title IV terminates with insufficient assets to satisfy its pension obligations to the employees, the PBGC becomes trustee of the plan, taking over the plan's assets and liabilities. The PBGC then uses the plan's assets to cover what it can of the benefit obligations. See 29 U.S.C. § 1344 (1982 ed. and Supp. IV). The PBGC then must add its own funds to ensure payment of most of the remaining "nonforfeitable" benefits, i.e., those benefits to which participants have earned entitlement under the plan terms as of the date of termination. §§ 1301(a)(8), 1322(a) and (b). * * * The cost of the PBGC insurance is borne primarily by employers that maintain ongoing pension plans. * * * The insurance program is also financed by statutory liability imposed on employers who terminate under-funded pension plans. * * *

The PBGC [may] terminate a plan "involuntarily" [whenever the PBGC] determines that "[the] plan has not met the minimum funding standard required [by the statute], [the] plan will be unable to pay benefits when due, [or] "the possible long-run loss of the [PBGC] with respect to the plan may reasonably be expected to increase unreasonably if the plan is not terminated." 29 U.S.C. § 1342(a). [PBGC can also undo a termination—that is, "restore" a plan—if it determines such action to be appropriate and necessary.] When a plan is restored, full benefits are reinstated, and the employer, rather than the PBGC, again is responsible for the plan's unfunded liabilities.

This case arose after respondent The LTV Corporation (LTV Corp.) and many of its subsidiaries, including LTV Steel Company Inc. (LTV Steel), (collectively LTV), in July 1986 filed petitions for reorganization under Chapter 11 of the Bankruptcy Code. At that time, LTV Steel was the sponsor of three defined benefit pension plans (Plans) covered by Title IV of ERISA. Two of the Plans were the products of collective-bargaining negotiations with the United Steelworkers of America (Steelworkers). The third was for nonunion salaried employees. Chronically underfunded, the Plans, by late 1986, had unfunded liabilities for promised benefits of almost $2.3 billion. Approximately $2.1 billion of this amount was covered by PBGC insurance.

It is undisputed that one of LTV Corp.'s principal goals in filing the Chapter 11 petitions was the restructuring of LTV Steel's pension obligations, a goal which could be accomplished if the Plans were terminated and responsibility for the unfunded liabilities was placed on the PBGC. LTV Steel then could negotiate with its employees for new pension arrangements. LTV, however, could not voluntarily terminate the Plans because two of them had been negotiated in collective bargaining. LTV therefore sought to have the PBGC terminate the Plans. [Because the under-funding of the plans was likely only to increase,] the PBGC, invoking * * * 29 U.S.C. § 1342(a)(4), determined that the Plans should be terminated in order to protect the insurance program from the unreasonable risk of large losses * * *. With LTV's consent, the Plans were terminated effective January 13, 1987. [Because the PBGC terminated the plans, the PBGC effectively agreed to cover the existing obligations of the plans.]

[During the bankruptcy reorganization, LTV and the steelworkers union negotiated an agreement that included new pension arrangements intended to make up benefits that plan participants lost as a result of the termination. * * * The PBGC objected to these new pension agreements, characterizing them as "follow-on" plans. It defines a follow-on plan as a new benefit arrangement designed to wrap around the insurance benefits provided by the PBGC in such a way as to provide both retirees and active participants substantially the same benefits as they would have received had no termination occurred. The PBGC's policy against follow-on plans stems from the agency's belief that such plans are "abusive" of the insurance program and result in the PBGC's subsidizing an employer's ongoing pension program in a way not contemplated by Title IV. * * *

In early August 1987, the PBGC determined that the financial factors on which it had relied in terminating the Plans had changed significantly. Of particular significance to the PBGC was its belief that the steel industry, including LTV Steel, was experiencing a dramatic turnaround. As a result, the PBGC concluded it no longer faced the imminent risk, central to its original termination decision, of large unfunded liabilities stemming from plant shutdowns. [The PBGC then] decided to restore the Plans.

The Director issued a notice of restoration on September 22, 1987, indicating the PBGC's intent to restore the terminated Plans. The PBGC notice explained that the restoration decision was based on (1) LTV's establishment of "a retirement program that results in an abuse of the pension plan termination insurance system established by Title IV of ERISA," and (2) LTV's "improved financial circumstances." Restoration meant that the Plans were ongoing, and that LTV again would be responsible for administering and funding them.

**Take Note**

The agency decision at issue in this case is the "restoration" of a pension plan. In what way is such a decision an "adjudication"? What would have to be true in order for the trial-type procedures identified in sections 554, 556, and 557 of the APA to apply to the decision?

LTV refused to comply with the restoration decision. This prompted the PBGC to initiate an enforcement action in the District Court. [The court vacated the PBGC's restoration decision, and the court of appeals affirmed, holding that the PBGC's restoration decision was "arbitrary and capricious" or contrary to law under the APA, 5 U.S.C. § 706. In reaching that conclusion, the court of appeals concluded that the agency's procedures in deciding to restore the plans were inadequate.]

[The court of appeals] held that the PBGC's decision was arbitrary and capricious because the "PBGC neither apprised LTV of the material on which it was to base its decision, gave LTV an adequate opportunity to offer contrary evidence, proceeded in accordance with ascertainable standards . . ., nor provided [LTV] a statement showing its reasoning in applying those standards." 875 F.2d 1008, 1021 (2d Cir. 1989). The court suggested that on remand the agency was required to do each of these things.

The PBGC argues that this holding conflicts with *Vermont Yankee Nuclear Power Corp. v. Natural Resources Defense Council, Inc.*, 435 U.S. 519 (1978), where, the PBGC contends, this Court made clear that when the Due Process Clause is not implicated and an agency's governing statute contains no specific procedural mandates, the APA establishes the maximum procedural requirements a reviewing court

**Make the Connection**

We will consider a court's role in reviewing agency action for compliance with procedural requirements, and the Court's decision in *Vermont Yankee,* in Chapter 7. We will also consider substantive review of agency decision-making, and the Court's decision in *Overton Park,* in Chapter 7.

may impose on agencies. Although *Vermont Yankee* concerned additional procedures imposed by the Court of Appeals for the District of Columbia Circuit on the Atomic Energy Commission when the agency was engaging in informal rulemaking, the PBGC argues that the informal adjudication process by which the restoration decision was made should be governed by the same principles.

Respondents counter by arguing that courts, under some circumstances, do require agencies to undertake additional procedures. As support for this proposition, they rely on *Citizens to Preserve Overton Park, Inc. v. Volpe,* 401 U.S. 402 (1971). In *Overton Park,* the Court concluded that the Secretary of Transportation's "*post hoc* rationalizations" regarding a decision to authorize the construction of a highway did not provide "an [a]dequate basis for [judicial] review" for purposes of the APA. Accordingly, the Court directed the District Court on remand to consider evidence that shed light on the Secretary's reasoning at the time he made the decision. Of particular relevance for present purposes, the Court in *Overton Park* intimated that one recourse for the District Court might be a remand to the agency for a fuller explanation of the agency's reasoning at the time of the agency action. See *id.,* at 420–421. Subsequent cases have made clear that remanding to the agency in fact is the preferred course. See *Florida Power & Light Co. v. Lorion,* 470 U.S. 729, 744 (1985) ("[I]f the reviewing court simply cannot evaluate the challenged agency action on the basis of the record before it, the proper course, except in rare circumstances, is to remand to the agency for additional investigation or explanation"). Respondents contend that the instant case is controlled by *Overton Park* rather than *Vermont Yankee,* and that the Court of Appeals' ruling was thus correct.

We believe that respondents' argument is wide of the mark. We begin by noting that although one initially might feel that there is some tension between *Vermont Yankee* and *Overton Park,* the two cases are not necessarily inconsistent. *Vermont Yankee* stands for the general proposition that courts are not free to impose upon agencies specific procedural requirements that have no basis in the APA. At most, *Overton Park* suggests that § 706(2)(A), which directs a court to ensure that an agency action is not arbitrary and capricious or otherwise contrary to law, imposes a general "procedural" requirement of sorts by mandating that an agency take whatever steps it needs to provide an explanation that will enable the court to evaluate the agency's rationale at the time of decision.

Here, unlike in *Overton Park,* the Court of Appeals did not suggest that the administrative record was inadequate to enable the court to fulfill its duties under § 706. Rather, to support its ruling, the court focused on "fundamental fairness" to

LTV. 875 F.2d, at 1020–1021. With the possible exception of the absence of "ascertainable standards"—by which we are not exactly sure what the Court of Appeals meant—the procedural inadequacies cited by the court all relate to LTV's role in the PBGC's decisionmaking process. But the court did not point to any provision in ERISA or the APA which gives LTV the procedural rights the court identified. Thus, the court's holding runs afoul of *Vermont Yankee* and finds no support in Overton Park.

Nor is *Bowman Transportation, Inc. v. Arkansas-Best Freight System, Inc.*, 419 U.S. 281 (1974), the case on which the Court of Appeals relied, to the contrary. The statement relied upon (which was dictum) said: "A party is entitled, of course, to know the issues on which decision will turn and to be apprised of the factual material on which the agency relies for decision so that he may rebut it." *Id.* at 288, n. 4. That statement was entirely correct in the context of *Arkansas–Best,* which involved a formal adjudication by the Interstate Commerce Commission pursuant to the trial-type procedures set forth in §§ 5, 7 and 8 of the APA, 5 U.S.C. §§ 554, 556–557, which include requirements that parties be given notice of "the matters of fact and law asserted," § 554(b)(3), an opportunity for "the submission and consideration of facts [and] arguments," § 554(c)(1), and an opportunity to submit "proposed findings and conclusions" or "exceptions," § 557(c)(1), (2). The determination in this case, however, was lawfully made by informal adjudication, the minimal requirements for which are set forth in the APA, 5 U.S.C. § 555, and do not include such elements. A failure to provide them where the Due Process Clause itself does not require them (which has not been asserted here) is therefore not unlawful. [Reversed.]

[The separate opinions of Justice White (joined by Justice O'Connor) and Justice Stevens, which addressed parts of the majority opinion that are not included here, have been omitted.]

---

## Points for Discussion

### *a. Identifying Informal Adjudications*

The Court stated that the agency decision to restore the plan "was lawfully made by informal adjudication," rather than by formal adjudication. Although the Court did not explain how it knew that the decision was an informal adjudication, we have now seen enough to characterize the decision. The agency decision involved the determination of the rights or obligations of a particular party in light of historical facts and a statutory standard, and no statute required the determination to be made on the record after opportunity for an agency hearing. Accordingly, even though the decision did not look like an "adjudication" in the conventional sense, it counted as an informal adjudication for purposes of the APA.

### *b. What Makes Informal Adjudications Informal?*

We saw above that adjudicatory decisions required to be made on the record after opportunity for an agency hearing must comply with a set of procedural requirements that look very much like the trial-type requirements that courts follow. Informal adjudications, in contrast, do not have to comply with those requirements, which apply only when some other statute requires the decision to be made on the record after opportunity for an agency hearing. Accordingly, such decisions are called "informal" adjudications because they are not required to use the trial-type procedural requirements that apply in more formal proceedings.

### *c. Procedural Requirements for Informal Adjudications*

If the requirements in sections 554, 556, and 557 of the APA do not apply to informal adjudications, then what procedural requirements do apply to such decisions? The Court cited two sources: section 555 of the APA and the Due Process Clause of the Fifth Amendment. Section 555 provides some very basic rights to all persons affected by agency action, such as the right to be represented by counsel, the right to a reasonably timely determination of the matter in question, and, except "when the denial is self-explanatory," a "brief statement of the grounds for denial" of a petition of requested relief. As we saw earlier in this Chapter, the Due Process Clause presumptively entitles an affected party to "the right to support his allegations by argument, however brief: and, if need be, by proof, however informal." *Londoner v. City and County of Denver*, 210 U.S. 373 (1908).

**Make the Connection**

We will explore the requirements imposed on agency adjudication by the Due Process Clause, and the Court's decisions in *Withrow v. Larkin* and *Mathews v. Eldridge*, in Chapter 7.

---

## c. Formal Rulemaking

# *United States v. Florida East Coast Railway*

410 U.S. 224 (1973)

MR. JUSTICE REHNQUIST delivered the opinion of the Court.

Appellees, two railroad companies, brought this action in the District Court for the Middle District of Florida to set aside the incentive per diem rates established by appellant Interstate Commerce Commission in a rule-making proceeding. Incentive Per Diem Charges—1968, Ex parte No. 252 (Sub.-No. 1), 337 I.C.C. 217 (1970). * * *

The District Court sustained appellees' position that the Commission had failed to comply with the applicable provisions of the Administrative Procedure Act, 5 U.S.C. § 551 et seq. * * *. The District Court held that the language of § 1(14)(a)[1] of the Interstate Commerce Act, 24 Stat. 379, as amended, 49 U.S.C. § 1(14)(a), required the Commission in a proceeding such as this to act in accordance with * * * 5 U.S.C. § 556(d), and that the Commission's determination to receive submissions from the appellees only in written form was a violation of that section * * *.

We here decide that the Commission's proceeding was governed only by § 553 of [the Administrative Procedure] Act, and that appellees received the "hearing" required by § 1(14)(a) of the Interstate Commerce Act.

This case arises from the factual background of a chronic freight-car shortage on the Nation's railroads * * *. Congressional concern for the problem was manifested in the enactment in 1966 of an amendment to § 1(14)(a) of the Interstate Commerce Act, enlarging the Commission's authority to prescribe per diem charges for the use by one railroad of freight cars owned by another. Pub. L. 89–430, 80 Stat. 168. * * *

The Commission in 1966 commenced an investigation "to determine whether information presently available warranted the establishment of an incentive element increase, on an interim basis, to apply pending further study and investigation." 332 I.C.C. 11, 12 (1967). * * * In December 1967, the Commission initiated the rulemaking procedure giving rise to the order that appellees here challenge. It directed * * * railroads to compile and report detailed information with respect to freight-car demand and supply at numerous sample stations for selected days of the week during 12 four-week periods, beginning January 29, 1968.

**FYI**

The Interstate Commerce Commission has power to set rates for railroad services, a power thought necessary due to the oligopolistic nature of the railroad industry. An "incentive element increase" means an increase in the amount that one railroad is permitted to charge another railroad for the use of its rail cars, in order to encourage the prompt return of existing cars and to make the acquisition of new cars financially attractive.

Some of the affected railroads voiced questions about the proposed study or requested modification in the study procedures outlined by the Commission in its notice of proposed rulemaking. In response to petitions setting forth these carriers' views, the Commission staff held an informal conference in April 1968, at which the objections and proposed modifications were discussed. Twenty railroads, including appellee Seaboard, were represented at this conference, at which the Commission's staff sought to answer

1 Section 1(14)(a) provides: "The Commission may, after hearing, on a complaint or upon its own initiative without complaint, establish reasonable rules, regulations, and practices with respect to car service by common carriers by railroad subject to this chapter * * *."

questions about reporting methods to accommodate individual circumstances of particular railroads. The conference adjourned on a note that undoubtedly left the impression that hearings would be held at some future date. * * *

[After a congressional committee urged quicker action, the] Commission, now apparently imbued with a new sense of mission, issued in December 1969 an interim report announcing its tentative decision to adopt incentive per diem charges on standard boxcars based on the information compiled by the railroads. * * * Embodied in the report was a proposed rule adopting the Commission's tentative conclusions and a notice to the railroads to file statements of position within 60 days * * *. Both appellee railroads filed statements objecting to the Commission's proposal and requesting an oral hearing, as did numerous other railroads. In April 1970, the Commission, without having held further "hearings," issued a supplemental report making some modifications in the tentative conclusions earlier reached, but overruling *in toto* the requests of appellees.

In *United States v. Allegheny-Ludlum Steel Corp.*, 406 U.S. 742 (1972), we held that the language of § 1(14)(a) of the Interstate Commerce Act authorizing the Commission to act "after hearing" was not the equivalent of a requirement that a rule be made "on the record after opportunity for an agency hearing" as the latter term is used in § 553(c) of the Administrative Procedure Act. * * *

Both of the district courts that reviewed this order of the Commission concluded that its proceedings were governed by the stricter requirements of §§ 556 and 557 of the Administrative Procedure Act, rather than by the provisions of §§ 553 alone. The conclusion of the District Court for the Middle District of Florida, which we here review, was based on the assumption that the language in § 1(14)(a) of the Interstate Commerce Act requiring rulemaking under that section to be done "after hearing" was the equivalent of a statutory requirement that the rule "be made on the record after opportunity for an agency hearing." Such an assumption is inconsistent with our decision in *Allegheny-Ludlum.*

The District Court for the Eastern District of New York reached the same conclusion by a somewhat different line of reasoning. That court felt that because § 1(14)(a) of the Interstate Commerce Act had required a "hearing," and because that section was originally enacted in 1917, Congress was probably thinking in terms of a "hearing" such as that described in the opinion of this Court in the roughly contemporaneous case of *ICC v. Louisville & Nashville R. Co.*, 227 U.S. 88, 93 (1913). The ingredients of the "hearing" were there said to be that "(a)ll parties must be fully apprised of the evidence submitted or to be considered, and must be given opportunity to cross-examine witnesses, to inspect documents and to offer evidence in explanation or rebuttal." * * * [The district court] concluded that Congress had, in effect, required that these proceedings be "on the record after opportunity for an agency hearing" within the meaning of § 553(c)of the Administrative Procedure Act.

Insofar as this conclusion is grounded on the belief that the language "after hearing" of § 1(14)(a), without more, would trigger the applicability of §§ 556 and 557, it, too, is contrary to our decision in *Allegheny-Ludlum*. The District Court observed that it was "rather hard to believe that the last sentence of § 553(c) was directed only to the few legislative spots where the words 'on the record' or their equivalent had found their way into the statute book." This is, however, the language which Congress used, and since there are statutes on the books that do use these very words, see e.g., the Fulbright Amendment to the Walsh-Healey Act, 41 U.S.C. § 43a, and 21 U.S.C. § 371(e)(3), the regulations provision of the Food and Drug Act, adherence to that language cannot be said to render the provision nugatory or ineffectual. We recognized in *Allegheny-Ludlum* that the actual words "on the record" and "after . . . hearing" used in § 553 were not words of art, and that other statutory language having the same meaning could trigger the provisions of §§ 556 and 557 in rulemaking proceedings. But we adhere to our conclusion, expressed in that case, that the phrase "after hearing" in § 1(14)(a) of the Interstate Commerce Act does not have such an effect.

Inextricably intertwined with the hearing requirement of the Administrative Procedure Act in this case is the meaning to be given to the language "after hearing" in § 1(14)(a) of the Interstate Commerce Act. Appellees, both here and in the court below, contend that the Commission procedure here fell short of that mandated by the "hearing" requirement of § 1(14)(a), even though it may have satisfied § 553 of the Administrative Procedure Act. The Administrative Procedure Act states that none of its provisions "limit or repeal additional requirements imposed by statute or otherwise recognized by law." 5 U.S.C. § 559. Thus, even though the Commission was not required to comply with §§ 556 and 557 of that Act, it was required to accord the "hearing" specified in § 1(14)(a) of the Interstate Commerce Act. * * *

The term "hearing" in its legal context undoubtedly has a host of meanings. Its meaning undoubtedly will vary, depending on whether it is used in the context of a rulemaking-type proceeding or in the context of a proceeding devoted to the adjudication of particular disputed facts. It is by no means apparent what the drafters of the Esch Car Service Act of 1917, 40 Stat. 101, which became the first part of § 1(14)(a) of the Interstate Commerce Act, meant by the term. * * * What is apparent, though, is that the term was used in granting authority to the Commission to make rules and regulations of a prospective nature.

Appellees refer us to testimony of the Chairman of the Commission to the effect that if the added authority ultimately contained in the 1966 amendment were enacted, the Commission would proceed with "great caution" in imposing incentive per diem rates, and to statements of both Commission personnel and Members of Congress as to the necessity for a "hearing" before Commission action. Certainly, the lapse of time of more than three years between the enactment of the 1966 amendment and the Commission's issuance of its tentative conclusions cannot be said to evidence any lack of caution on the part of that body. Nor do generalized references to the necessity for a hearing advance our inquiry, since the statute by its terms requires a "hearing"; the more precise inquiry of whether the hearing requirements necessarily include submission of oral testimony, cross-examination, or oral arguments is not resolved by such comments as these.

Under these circumstances, confronted with a grant of substantive authority made after the Administrative Procedure Act was enacted,[8] we think that reference to that Act, in which Congress devoted itself exclusively to questions such as the nature and scope of hearings, is a satisfactory basis for determining what is meant by the term "hearing" used in another statute. Turning to that Act, we are convinced that the term "hearing" as used therein does not necessarily embrace either the right to present evidence orally and to cross-examine opposing witnesses, or the right to present oral argument to the agency's decisionmaker.

Section 553 excepts from its requirements rulemaking devoted to "interpretative rules, general statements of policy, or rules of agency organization, procedure, or practice," and rulemaking "when the agency for good cause finds . . . that notice and public procedure thereon are impracticable, unnecessary, or contrary to the public interest." This exception does not apply, however, "when notice or hearing is required by statute"; in those cases, even though interpretative rulemaking be involved, the requirements of § 553 apply. But since these requirements themselves do not mandate any oral presentation, it cannot be doubted that a statute that requires a "hearing" prior to rulemaking may in some circumstances be satisfied by procedures that meet only the standards of § 553. * * *

Similarly, even where the statute requires that the rulemaking procedure take place "on the record after opportunity for an agency hearing," thus triggering the applicability of § 556, subsection (d) provides that the agency may proceed by the submission of all or part of the evidence in written form if a party will not be "prejudiced thereby." Again, the Act makes it plain that a specific statutory mandate that the proceedings take place on the record after hearing may be satisfied in some circumstances by evidentiary submission in written form only.

We think this treatment of the term "hearing" in the Administrative Procedure Act affords sufficient basis for concluding that the requirement of a "hearing" contained in § 1(14)(a), in a situation where the Commission was acting under the 1966 statutory rulemaking authority that Congress had conferred upon it, did not by its own force require the Commission either to hear oral testimony, to permit cross-examination of Commission witnesses, or to hear oral argument. Here, the Commission promulgated a tentative draft of an order, and accorded all interested parties 60 days in which to file statements of position, submissions of evidence, and other relevant

---

8 The Interstate Commerce Act was amended in May 1966; [the Administrative Procedure Act was enacted in 1946].

observations. The parties had fair notice of exactly what the Commission proposed to do, and were given an opportunity to comment, to object, or to make some other form of written submission. The final order of the Commission indicates that it gave consideration to the statements of the two appellees here. Given the "open-ended" nature of the proceedings, and the Commission's announced willingness to consider proposals for modification after operating experience had been acquired, we think the hearing requirement of § 1(14)(a) of the Act was met.

*ICC v. Louisville & Nashville R. Co.*, 227 U.S. 88 (1913), involved what the Court there described as a "quasi-judicial" proceeding of a quite different nature from the one we review here. The provisions of the Interstate Commerce Act, 24 Stat. 379, as amended, and of the Hepburn Act, 34 Stat. 584, in effect at the time that case was decided, left to the railroad carriers the "primary right to make rates," 227 U.S., at 92, but granted to the Commission the authority to set them aside, if after hearing, they were shown to be unreasonable. The proceeding before the Commission in that case had been instituted by the New Orleans Board of Trade complaint that certain class and commodity rates charged by the Louisville & Nashville Railroad from New Orleans to other points were unfair, unreasonable, and discriminatory. The type of proceeding there, in which the Commission adjudicated a complaint by a shipper that specified rates set by a carrier were unreasonable, was sufficiently different from the nationwide incentive payments ordered to be made by all railroads in this proceeding so as to make the *Louisville & Nashville* opinion inapplicable in the case presently before us.

The basic distinction between rulemaking and adjudication is illustrated by this Court's treatment of two related cases under the Due Process Clause of the Fourteenth Amendment. In *Londoner v. Denver*, 210 U.S. 373 (1908), [the] Court held that due process had not been accorded a landowner who objected to the amount assessed against his land as its share of the benefit resulting from the paving of a street. Local procedure had accorded him the right to file a written complaint and objection, but not to be heard orally. This Court held that due process of law required that he "have the right to support his allegations by argument, however brief; and, if need be, by proof, however informal." Id., at 386. But in the later case of *Bi-Metallic Investment Co. v. State Board of Equalization*, 239 U.S. 441 (1915), the Court held that no hearing at all was constitutionally required prior to a decision by state tax officers in Colorado to increase the valuation of all taxable property in Denver by a substantial percentage. The Court distinguished *Londoner* by stating that there a small number of persons "were exceptionally affected, in each case upon individual grounds." Id., at 446.

**Make the Connection**

We considered the *Londoner* and *Bi-Metallic* cases, and the distinction between adjudication and rulemaking, earlier in this Chapter.

* * * While the line dividing them may not always be a bright one, these decisions represent a recognized distinction in administrative law between proceedings for the purpose of promulgating policy-type rules or standards, on the one hand, and proceedings designed to adjudicate disputed facts in particular cases on the other. Here, the incentive payments proposed by the Commission in its tentative order, and later adopted in its final order, were applicable across the board to all of the common carriers by railroad subject to the Interstate Commerce Act. No effort was made to single out any particular railroad for special consideration based on its own peculiar circumstances. Indeed, one of the objections of appellee Florida East Coast was that it and other terminating carriers should have been treated differently from the generality of the railroads. But the fact that the order may in its effects have been thought more disadvantageous by some railroads than by others does not change its generalized nature. * * *

The Commission's procedure satisfied both the provisions of § 1(14)(a) of the Interstate Commerce Act and of the Administrative Procedure Act, and were not inconsistent with prior decisions of this Court. We, therefore, reverse the judgment of the District Court, and remand the case so that it may consider those contentions of the parties that are not disposed of by this opinion.

MR. JUSTICE POWELL took no part in the consideration or decision of this case.

MR. JUSTICE DOUGLAS, with whom MR. JUSTICE STEWART concurs, dissenting.

The present decision makes a sharp break with traditional concepts of procedural due process. The Commission order under attack is tantamount to a rate order. Charges are fixed that nonowning railroads must pay owning railroads for boxcars of the latter that are on the tracks of the former. * * * This is the imposition on carriers by administrative fiat of a new financial liability. I do not believe it is within our traditional concepts of due process to allow an administrative agency to saddle anyone with a new rate, charge, or fee without a full hearing that includes the right to present oral testimony, cross-examine witnesses, and present oral argument. That is required by the Administrative Procedure Act, 5 U.S.C. § 556(d); § 556(a) states that § 556 applies to hearings required by § 553. Section 553(c) provides that § 556 applies "(w)hen rules are required by statute to be made on the record after opportunity for an agency hearing." A hearing under § 1(14)(a) of the Interstate Commerce Act fixing rates, charges, or fees is certainly adjudicatory, not legislative in the customary sense. * * * I would hold that appellees were not afforded the hearing guaranteed by § 1(14)(a) of the Interstate Commerce Act and 5 U.S.C. §§ 553, 556, and 557, and would affirm the decision of the District Court.

---

## Points for Discussion

### *a. Ratemaking and Rulemaking*

The Court concluded that the agency decision, which raised the rates that railroads could charge other railroads for borrowing their railcars, was an exercise of the agency's rulemaking power. Yet as Justice Douglas noted in dissent, the decision effectively set the rates that a small number of railroad companies would have to pay. Why did the decision at issue count as a rulemaking rather than an adjudication? The short answer is that the APA's definition of a "rule" includes "the approval or prescription for the future of rates * * *." Accordingly, ratemaking proceedings count as rulemaking under the APA. See 5 U.S.C. § 551(5) (" '[R]ule making' means agency process for formulating, amending, or repealing a rule.").

### *b. Formal Decision-Making and Rulemaking*

Section 553 of the APA, the provision that governs rulemaking, provides a relatively modest set of requirements (including notice of a rulemaking and the opportunity for interested persons to comment on the agency's proposed rule). But it then states: "When rules are required by statute to be made on the record after opportunity for an agency hearing, sections 556 and 557 of this title apply instead of this subsection." 5 U.S.C. § 553(c). In other words, as with adjudications, the more formal set of trial-type requirements specified in sections 556 and 557 apply when some other statute requires the rulemaking to be made on the record after opportunity for an agency hearing.

We saw above, in *Seacoast Anti-Pollution League*, that courts are willing to conclude that the formal requirements in sections 556 and 557 apply to agency adjudications even when a statute requires only a decision after a hearing, with no mention of the requirement that the decision be on the record. Why didn't the Court in *Florida East Coast Railway* apply a similarly generous test for when formal rulemaking is required? The Court based its conclusion in part on the differences between rulemaking and adjudication. Consider the view expressed in the Attorney General's Manual on the Administrative Procedure Act 42–43 (1947), an important early document describing how the government understood the requirements of the Act:

> "It is believed that with respect to adjudication the specific statutory requirement of a hearing, without anything more, carries with it the further requirement of decision on the basis of the evidence adduced at the hearing. With respect to rule making, it was concluded [that] a statutory provision that rules be issued after a hearing, without more, should not be construed as requiring agency action 'on the record,' but rather as merely requiring an opportunity for the expression of views. That conclusion was based on the legislative nature of rule making, from which it was inferred, unless a statute requires otherwise, that an agency hearing on proposed rules would be similar to a hearing before a legislative committee, with neither the legislature nor the agency

> being limited to the material adduced at the hearing. No such rationale applies to administrative adjudication. In fact, it is assumed that where a statute specifically provides for administrative adjudication (such as the suspension or revocation of a license) after opportunity for an agency hearing, such specific requirement for a hearing ordinarily implies the further requirement of decision in accordance with evidence adduced at the hearing. Of course, the foregoing discussion is inapplicable to any situation in which the legislative history or the context of the pertinent statute indicates a contrary congressional intent."

The court in *Seacoast Anti-Pollution League* drew a similar distinction, noting that adjudications decide the rights of specific applicants, often involve disputed questions of fact, and typically aren't designed to resolve general questions of policy. As such, it makes sense to presume that an adjudication that must include a "hearing" is required to follow the trial-type procedures specified for formal adjudications in the APA. But a "hearing serves a very different function in the rule making context. Witnesses may bring in new information or different points of view, but the agency's final decision need not reflect the public input. The witnesses are not the only source of the evidence on which the Administrator may base his factual findings. For these reasons, we place less importance on the absence of the words 'on the record' in the adjudicatory context." Id.

Are you persuaded that agency decisions setting the rates that a small number of railroad companies can charge are sufficiently different from agency adjudications such that the APA's formal requirements should not apply, notwithstanding a statutory requirement that the decision be made after a hearing? If so, would it ever make sense to conduct formal rulemaking?

#### c. *Formal Rulemaking After* **Florida East Coast Railway**

In the early twentieth century and in the years shortly after the enactment of the APA, formal rulemaking was relatively common, particularly in cases involving rate- and price-setting. By the time of *Florida East Coast Railway*, formal rulemaking was considerably less common. Because of the Court's high standard in that case for triggering formal rulemaking, formal rulemaking is quite rare today.

---

### d. Informal Rulemaking

## *Sugar Cane Growers Cooperative of Florida v. Veneman*

289 F.3d 89 (D.C. Cir. 2002)

SILBERMAN, SENIOR CIRCUIT JUDGE:

In the United States, sugar production, which the government supports through a variety of programs, is about evenly divided between sugar cane and sugar beet production. This suit involves the [Department of Agriculture's] choice of a particular method of support. Appellants are self-described small-, medium- and large-sized sugar cane growers, processors, refiners and marketers, who together make up a "significant" portion of the total domestic sugar cane production, which mostly occurs in the Gulf Belt and Hawaii. Sugar beets grow primarily in the North and West, and sugar beet farmers tend to harvest significantly fewer acres per producer than sugar cane farmers. The Department supports sugar production through a program of non-recourse loans; if the market price of sugar drops below the forfeiture price, producers may forfeit their crops to the Department in satisfaction of these loans rather than try to repay in cash, which effectively guarantees a minimum price for harvested and processed sugar. With the low sugar prices over the past several years, the Department has accumulated more than 700,000 tons of sugar, for which it pays approximately $1.35 million per month in storage fees. The presence of that potential supply (or "overhang") may depress somewhat sugar prices and it exacerbates the problem of limited sugar storage, which is particularly troublesome for sugar beet farmers.

> **FYI**
>
> A non-recourse loan is a loan secured by collateral. If the borrower defaults on the loan, the lender accepts the collateral as payment in full, even if the collateral is worth less than the outstanding debt.

The Food Security Act gives the Department authority to implement a payment-in-kind (PIK) program for sugar, which it did for sugar beet farmers in August 2000. For the 2000 PIK program, sugar beet farmers submitted bids to the Department offering to destroy (or "divert") a certain amount of their crops in return for sugar from USDA storage. A farmer's bid is his asking price for that amount of destruction; the price is expressed in terms of a percentage of the three-year average value of the crop yield for the acreage diverted. Thus, a farmer bidding 80 percent would receive eight dollars for every acre destroyed if an average acre of their farm produced ten dollars worth of sugar. In fact, the average bid was approximately 84 percent and resulted in the distribution of about 277,000 tons of government sugar and the diversion of approximately 102,000 acres. Participants were prohibited from participating in future

PIK programs if they increased their acreage planted with sugar beets over 2000 levels. The Agency did not proceed by notice and comment, but no party challenged that decision or the program itself.

Appellants claim the 2000 PIK program unfairly provided participants with below-harvest-cost government sugar which gave them a competitive advantage over appellants. And they claim that the program depressed sugar prices. Actually, the price of sugar rose, but it is not clear what caused the increase. According to appellants, although initial forecasts predicted that the diverted acreage would lead to lower sugar crop volume in 2000, subsequent forecasts increased substantially in the months following implementation of the PIK program—to 23.6 tons per acre in December 2000 from 22.8 tons per acre before August 2000. Appellants contend that the yield increase (or "yield slippage") resulted in part from farmers taking their lowest-yielding crops out of production for the PIK program. With the yield slippage, additional beet sugar supplies ended up on the market, and PIK farmers received more sugar through the program than they would have if they had produced sugar on the diverted acres. And the greater supplies of sugar, it is argued, necessarily depressed sugar prices below that which would otherwise have obtained. The government insists that the program had a positive effect on the price of sugar, at least in part because it reduced the government's sugar supply and storage fees, ameliorating the overhang effect and storage scarcity problem.

In January 2001, the Department met with interested persons (including representatives of appellants) and indicated that while it was considering a PIK program for the 2001 sugar crop, it would not do so without notice and comment. The Agency also asked those present about the effectiveness of the 2000 PIK program and their thoughts on the desirability and structure of a potential 2001 program. Appellants claim that they were unable to comment satisfactorily because the data on the 2000 program was not yet available. Before August 2001, Department employees had approximately a dozen contacts with sugar industry representatives regarding the possibility of a 2001 program.

The Department announced by an August 31, 2001 press release, however, that it was implementing a PIK program for the 2001 sugar crop without using APA rulemaking. The Agency followed that announcement a week later with a "Notice of Program Implementation" in the September 7, 2001 Federal Register. For the 2001 PIK program, the Department set a 200,000 ton limit in order to encourage more competitive bidding and

**Take Note**

The program at issue essentially paid farmers not to grow crops, but for various reasons the appellants could not fully take advantage of the program. As a consequence, in their view the program gave other sugar farmers an unfair competitive advantage. But their challenge had nothing to do with the wisdom of this program; instead, they argued that the agency had failed to comply with the proper procedures under the APA.

made both beet and cane sugar producers eligible. But a statutory restriction limiting payments to $20,000 per producer effectively eliminated appellants' opportunity to participate because of their size. Particularly troubling appellants, the government waived its 2000 PIK program restriction on future eligibility by participants who had increased their crop acreage; it merely included a similar restriction on 2001 participants. * * * After announcing the program, the Department received more than 6,000 bids and accepted 4,655 bids, some as high as 87.9931 percent. * * *

Appellants filed suit shortly after the press release appeared, seeking injunctive and declaratory relief. They argued that the Department did not comply with the APA because it promulgated a rule without notice-and-comment rulemaking * * *. [The district court concluded that appellants failed to establish standing, but the court of appeals disagreed and reached the merits.]

* * * The APA sets forth several steps an agency must take when engaged in rulemaking: it must publish a general notice of proposed rulemaking in the Federal Register; give an opportunity for interested persons to participate in the rulemaking through submission of written data, views, or arguments; and issue publication of a concise general statement of the rule's basis and purpose. 5 U.S.C. § 553(b), (c). The government defends the Department's failure to engage in notice-and-comment rulemaking by asserting the PIK announcement was not really a rule and, even if it were, the failure to engage in rulemaking was a harmless error.[5]

The APA defines a rule very broadly as

> "the whole or a part of an agency statement of general or particular applicability and future effect designed to implement, interpret, or prescribe law or policy or describing the organization, procedure, or practice requirements of an agency and includes the approval or prescription for the future of rates, wages, corporate or financial structures or reorganizations thereof, prices, facilities, appliances, services or allowances therefor or of valuations, costs, or accounting, or practices bearing on any of the foregoing."

5 U.S.C. § 551(4). We have recognized that notwithstanding the breadth of the APA's definition an agency pronouncement that lacks the firmness of a [prescribed] standard—particularly certain policy statements—is not a rule. *See Syncor Int'l Corp. v. Shalala*, 127 F.3d 90, 94 (D.C. Cir. 1997). (Of course, general statements of policy are exempt from notice-and-comment procedures anyway. 5 U.S.C. § 553(b)(A)). But the government does not claim that its package of announcements is a policy statement. Instead, the government argues that because the announcement of the 2001 PIK program was an "isolated agency act" that did not propose to affect sub-

---

5 Although the government also implies that it had good cause not to follow notice-and-comment rulemaking, it does not rely on that position, presumably because the Department did not assert it. Nor do we address amicus' argument that the 2001 PIK program was exempt from APA rulemaking requirements under 5 U.S.C. § 553(a)(2) because it constitutes agency action relating to "public property, loans, grants, benefits, or contracts." As the Department acknowledged, it has essentially waived that APA exemption.

sequent Department acts and had "no future effect on any other party before the agency" it was not a rule. The government would have us see its announcement of the PIK program as analogous to an agency's award of a contract pursuant to an invitation of bids or an agency's decision to approve an application or a proposal—in administrative law terms an informal adjudication (which is the technical term for an executive action).

**Take Note**

The agency action at issue created a payment-in-kind program and announced the requirements and conditions of that program. Can you see why such an action constitutes a rulemaking within the meaning of the APA?

We have little difficulty * * * in rejecting this argument. The August 31 press release, the September Questions and Answers and most notably the September 7 Notice of Program Implementation set forth the bid submission procedures which all applicants must follow, the payment limitations of the program, and the sanctions that will be imposed on participants if they plant more in *future* years than in 2001. It is simply absurd to call this anything but a rule "by any other name."

[T]he government alternatively claims harmless error. We are told that appellants cannot identify any additional arguments they would have made in a notice-and-comment procedure that they did not make to the Department in the several informal sessions. And we are reminded that the Department did make certain changes to the 2001 PIK program in response to appellants' concerns. It is true that we have recognized certain technical APA errors as harmless. For example, in *Sheppard v. Sullivan*, 906 F.2d 756, 761–62 (D.C. Cir. 1990), a challenge to an agency adjudication in a benefits case, we held that a failure to undertake formal notice and comment with respect to a program manual was harmless. But, in so doing, we applied the standard set out in *McLouth Steel Prods. Corp. v. Thomas*, 838 F.2d 1317, 1324 (D.C. Cir. 1988), under which an utter failure to comply with notice and comment cannot be considered harmless if there is any uncertainty at all as to the effect of that failure. And in *Sheppard,* we initially observed that the agency did not even rely on that program manual in its challenged order; furthermore, we expressly concluded that the agency's substantive approach was "the only reasonable one." *Sheppard*, 906 F.2d at 762.

**Make the Connection**

We will consider procedural and substantive judicial review of informal rulemaking in Chapter 7.

Here the government would have us virtually repeal section 553's requirements: if the government could skip those procedures, engage in informal consultation, and then be protected from judicial review unless a petitioner could show a new argument—not presented informally—section 553 obviously would be eviscerated. The government could avoid the necessity of publishing a notice of a proposed rule and perhaps, most important, would not be obliged to set forth a statement of the basis and purpose of the rule, which needs to take account of the major comments—and often is a major focus of judicial review.

In any event, although they need not have, appellants have indicated additional considerations they would have raised in a comment procedure. For example, they would have argued that the Agency should have bound itself to a gradual disbursement of the sugar, rather than merely allowing itself that option. And, they would have challenged the Department's decision to waive the 2000 PIK program restriction on participants who had increased their acreage.

There remains the question of remedy. Normally when an agency so clearly violates the APA we would vacate its action—in this case its "non-rule rule"—and simply remand for the agency to start again. Unfortunately, because we denied preliminary relief in this case, the 2001 program was launched and crops were plowed under. The egg has been scrambled and there is no apparent way to restore the status quo ante. Appellants suggested that if we were to vacate, the Federal Court of Claims would have the responsibility of allocating damages. But that seems an invitation to chaos. Moreover, although the government did not—and could not have for the first time on appeal—assert a good cause for omitting notice and comment, it is at least possible that the Department could establish good cause because of timing exigencies.

Appellants insist that we have no discretion in the matter; if the Department violated the APA—which it did—its actions must be vacated. But that is simply not the law. Instead, "[t]he decision whether to vacate depends on 'the seriousness of the order's deficiencies (and thus the extent of doubt whether the agency chose correctly) and the disruptive consequences of an interim change that may itself be changed.' " *Allied-Signal, Inc. v. United States Nuclear Regulatory Commission*, 988 F.2d 146, 150–51 (D.C. Cir. 1993). We have previously remanded without vacating when the agency failed to follow notice-and-comment procedures. *See, e.g., Fertilizer Institute v. EPA*, 935 F.2d 1303, 1312 (D.C. Cir. 1991).

Accordingly, we reverse the district court's grant of summary judgment and remand to that court to in turn remand to the Department.

---

## Points for Discussion

### *a. Rulemaking*

According to the court, why was the agency action at issue a rulemaking rather than an adjudication? In thinking about that question, consider whether the appellants were challenging the grant of government funds (actually, the grant of sugar) to specific farmers, or instead were challenging the creation of the program pursuant to which the government would grant sugar to farmers. Properly understood, was the agency action a "statement of general or particular applicability and future effect designed to implement, interpret, or prescribe law or policy," 5 U.S.C. § 551(4), or was it a decision that exceptionally affected a small number of interested persons on individual grounds, cf. *Londoner v. City and County of Denver*, 210 U.S. 373 (1908)?

### b. *Informal Rulemaking*

To determine the procedural requirements with which the agency had to comply, the court not only had to decide that the agency action at issue constituted rulemaking, but also had to determine whether the rulemaking was required to be formal or informal. Because no statute required the agency's program to be created by a proceeding "on the record after opportunity for an agency hearing," the action constituted informal rulemaking under the APA.

Not surprisingly, the APA's procedural requirements for informal rulemaking are less strict and rigorous than its requirements for formal rulemaking. Under section 553, an agency that engages in informal rulemaking must give notice of its intention to engage in rulemaking, an opportunity for interested persons to submit comments, and (when it issues the rule) a concise and general statement of basis and purpose for the rule. 5 U.S.C. § 553(b) and (c). Because of these requirements, many people refer to informal rulemaking as "notice-and-comment rulemaking."

The APA exempts certain rulemakings from these requirements; it states that they do not apply to "interpretative rules, general statements of policy, or rules of agency organization, procedure, or practice" or when "the agency for good cause finds * * * that notice and public procedure thereon are impracticable, unnecessary, or contrary to the public interest." *Id.* § 553(b). The notice-and-comment requirements also do not apply to rules "relating to agency management or personnel or to public property, loans, grants, benefits, or contracts." *Id.* § 553(a). The agency likely could have relied on this last provision, but it failed to raise the argument before the trial court. Should the court of appeals have permitted the agency to raise this argument, rather than ordering a remand to the agency?

### c. *Informal Rulemaking and Agency Policy-Making*

Informal rulemaking is a very common way for agencies to implement their policy agendas. In practice, however, significant agency rules take years to issue because of the volume of comments that the agency receives and the need for the agency to craft a statement explaining why it chose to issue the rule in light of (or notwithstanding) the comments that it received. (In Chapter 7, we will consider the ways in which the practice of judicial review of agency rules is partially responsible for the slow pace of agency rulemaking.) Does it make sense to require agencies that hope to issue rules governing private conduct to solicit feedback from any "interested person[ ]"?

---

## C. Choosing a Mode for Policy-Making

We began this Chapter by noting that many agencies enjoy considerable policy-making discretion. Although as a formal matter only Congress may exercise the legislative power—and thus in theory only Congress should be responsible for making important decisions of policy—in practice agencies enjoy significant authority to resolve contested questions of policy. As we noted, even the most conscientious Congress will inevitably leave some gaps in a given statute, which the agency charged with administering the statute will have to fill. Indeed, Congress often expressly delegates substantial policy-making authority to agencies, which it is permitted to do as long as it provides an intelligible principle to guide the agency's exercise of its discretion.

We then noted that Congress might choose to give a particular agency both the power to issue rules and the authority to conduct adjudications. If an agency enjoys both rulemaking and adjudicative power, must it always use the former when it seeks to make policy?

At first blush, rulemaking seems to be the most natural mode for agency policy-making. As we noted in our discussion of the difference between rulemaking and adjudication, the essence of rulemaking is the formulation of generally applicable policy. (Recall that the Court in *Bi-Metallic* treated adjudication as a method of decision for a small number of persons who are exceptionally affected on individual grounds, which doesn't sound like a promising vehicle for the announcement of broadly applicable norms.)

But you have also seen in your classes that focus on common-law subjects such as Torts and Contracts that courts often make policy through their decisions, as well. To take just one prominent example, when the New York Court of Appeals decided in *MacPherson v. Buick Motor Co.*, 111 N.E. 1050 (N.Y. 1916), that the manufacturer of a product enjoys a duty of care even to persons with whom it is not in privity of contract, the court made a policy judgment about who should bear the costs of accidents. And although the court announced its judgment in the course of an adjudication of a claim against just one company, as a matter of *stare decisis* the court's policy judgment became binding on all other manufacturers of dangerous products sold in New York, as well. The same can be true for agency adjudications.

**Make the Connection**

We considered the relative virtues and drawbacks of legislation and common-law decision-making as means of regulation in Chapter 1.

In other words, it is possible for an agency to make policy either by issuing a rule or by conducting an adjudication. If an agency has power to do both, does it matter which means the agency chooses to make policy? Consider the case that follows.

---

## *Securities and Exchange Comm'n v. Chenery Corp.*

332 U.S. 194 (1947)

MR. JUSTICE MURPHY delivered the opinion of the Court.

This case is here for the second time. In *S.E.C. v. Chenery Corporation*, 318 U.S. 80 (1943), we held that an order of the Securities and Exchange Commission could not be sustained on the grounds upon which that agency acted. We therefore directed that the case be remanded to the Commission for such further proceedings as might be appropriate. On remand, the Commission reexamined the problem, recast its rationale and reached the same result. The issue now is whether the Commission's action is proper in light of the principles established in our prior decision.

When the case was first here, we emphasized a simple but fundamental rule of administrative law. That rule is to the effect that a reviewing court, in dealing with a determination or judgment which an administrative agency alone is authorized to make, must judge the propriety of such action solely by the grounds invoked by the agency. If those grounds are inadequate or improper, the court is powerless to affirm the administrative action by substituting what it considers to be a more adequate or proper basis. To do so would propel the court into the domain which Congress has set aside exclusively for the administrative agency.

We also emphasized in our prior decision an important corollary of the foregoing rule. If the administrative action is to be tested by the basis upon which it purports to rest, that basis must be set forth with such clarity as to be understandable. It will not do for a court to be compelled to guess at the theory underlying the agency's action; nor can a court be expected to chisel that which must be precise from what the agency has left vague and indecisive. * * *

**FYI**

Congress enacted the Public Utility Holding Company Act after many public utility companies collapsed in the stock market crash of 1929. A holding company is a company created and organized solely to buy and possess the shares of other companies, which it then controls. Many of the utility companies that collapsed during the Great Depression were controlled by holding companies, which had borrowed considerable sums of money to purchase them. Because the firms were highly leveraged—that is, they carried a significant amount of debt—the collapse of a company that they owned would likely lead to collapse of the entire firm (and possibly other companies that they controlled). The Act directed the SEC to require certain holding companies to reorganize in a manner that would be more financially stable. The Act permitted regulated holding companies to propose voluntary reorganization plans, which the SEC could then approve or disapprove after a hearing, by determining whether the plan was "fair and equitable to persons affected by such plan." The Chenerys, who were the officers, directors, and controlling shareholders of Federal Water Service Corporation, proposed a voluntary reorganization plan under which they would retain substantial control of the new firm.

Applying this rule and its corollary, the Court was unable to sustain the Commission's original action. The Commission had been dealing with the reorganization of the Federal Water Service Corporation (Federal), a holding company registered under the Public Utility Holding Company Act of 1935, 49 Stat. 803, 15 U.S.C. § 79 et seq. During the period when successive reorganization plans proposed by the management were before the Commission, the officers, directors and controlling stockholders of Federal purchased a substantial amount of Federal's preferred stock on the over-the-counter market. Under the fourth reorganization plan, this preferred stock was to be converted into common stock of a new corporation; on the basis of the purchases of preferred stock, the management would have received more than 10% of this new common stock. It was frankly admitted that the management's purpose in buying the preferred stock was to protect its interest in the new company. It was also plain that there was no fraud or lack of disclosure in making these purchases.

But the Commission would not approve the fourth plan so long as the preferred stock purchased by the management was to be treated on a parity with the other preferred stock. It felt that the officers and directors of a holding company in process of reorganization under the Act were fiduciaries and were under a duty not to trade in the securities of that company during the reorganization period. And so the plan was amended to provide that the preferred stock acquired by the management, unlike that held by others, was not to be converted into the new common stock; instead, it was to be surrendered at cost plus dividends accumulated since the purchase dates. As amended, the plan was approved by the Commission over the management's objections.

The Court interpreted the Commission's order approving this amended plan as grounded solely upon judicial authority. The Commission appeared to have treat-

**Definition**

"Preferred stock" is a form of stock that usually entitles the holder to a dividend, the payment of which takes priority over the payment of dividends to holders of "common stock." A "fiduciary duty" is an obligation to act in the best interests of another party.

ed the preferred stock acquired by the management in accordance with what it thought were standards theretofore recognized by courts. If it intended to create new standards growing out of its experience in effectuating the legislative policy, it failed to express itself with sufficient clarity and precision to be so understood. Hence the order was judged by the only standards clearly invoked by the Commission. On that basis, the order could not stand. The opinion pointed out that courts do not impose upon officers and directors of a corporation any fiduciary duty to its stockholders which precludes them, merely because they are officers and directors, from buying and selling the corporation's stock. Nor was it felt that the cases upon which the Commission relied established any principles of law or equity which in themselves would be sufficient to justify this order.

The opinion further noted that neither Congress nor the Commission had promulgated any general rule proscribing such action as the purchase of preferred stock by Federal's management. And the only judge-made rule of equity which might have justified the Commission's order related to fraud or mismanagement of the reorganization by the officers and directors, matters which were admittedly absent in this situation.

After the case was remanded to the Commission, Federal Water and Gas Corp. (Federal Water), the surviving corporation under the reorganization plan, made an application for approval of an amendment to the plan to provide for the issuance of now common stock of the reorganized company. This stock was to be distributed to the members of Federal's management on the basis of the shares of the old preferred stock which they had acquired during the period of reorganization, thereby placing them in the same position as the public holders of the old preferred stock. The intervening members of Federal's management joined in this request. The Commission denied the application in an order issued on February 7, 1945. That order was reversed by the Court of Appeals, which felt that our prior decision precluded such action by the Commission.

**Take Note**

In resolving the respondents' case on remand, the SEC announced a new policy to implement the Act's requirements. The respondents argued that, if the SEC wanted to announce a new, generally applicable policy, it had to do so through rulemaking, not in the course of the agency's adjudication of the lawfulness of the respondents' plan.

The latest order of the Commission definitely avoids the fatal error of relying on judicial precedents which do not sustain it. This time, after a thorough reexamination of the problem in light of the purposes and standards of the Holding Company Act, the Commission has concluded that the proposed transaction is inconsistent with the standards of §§ 7 and 11 of the Act. It has drawn heavily upon its accumulated experience in dealing with utility reorganizations. And it has expressed its reasons with a clarity and thoroughness that admit of no doubt as to the underlying basis of its order.

The argument is pressed upon us, however, that the Commission was foreclosed from taking such a step following our prior decision. It is said that, in the absence of findings of conscious wrongdoing on the part of Federal's management, the Commission could not determine by an order in this particular case that it was inconsistent with the statutory standards to permit Federal's management to realize a profit through the reorganization purchases. All that it could do was to enter an order allowing an amendment to the plan so that the proposed transaction could be consummated. Under this view, the Commission would be free only to promulgate a general rule outlawing such profits in future utility reorganizations; but such a rule would have to be prospective in nature and have no retroactive effect upon the instant situation.

We reject this contention, for it grows out of a misapprehension of our prior decision and of the Commission's statutory duties. We held no more and no less than that the Commission's first order was unsupportable for the reasons supplied by that agency. But when the case left this Court, the problem whether Federal's management should be treated equally with other preferred stockholders still lacked a final and complete answer. It was clear that the Commission could not give a negative answer by resort to prior judicial declarations. And it was also clear that the Commission was not bound by settled judicial precedents in a situation of this nature. Still unsettled, however, was the answer the Commission might give were it to bring to bear on the facts the proper administrative and statutory considerations, a function which belongs exclusively to the Commission in the first instance. The administrative process had taken an erroneous rather than a final turn. Hence we carefully refrained from expressing any views as to the propriety of an order rooted in the proper and relevant considerations.

When the case was directed to be remanded to the Commission for such further proceedings as might be appropriate, it was with the thought that the Commission would give full effect to its duties in harmony with the views we had expressed. * * * The fact that the Commission had committed a legal error in its first disposition of the case certainly gave Federal's management no vested right to receive the benefits of such an order. After the remand was made, therefore, the Commission was bound to deal with the problem afresh, performing the function delegated to it by Congress. It was again charged with the duty of measuring the proposed treatment of the management's preferred stock holdings by relevant and proper standards. Only in that way could the legislative policies embodied in the Act be effectuated.

The absence of a general rule or regulation governing management trading during reorganization did not affect the Commission's duties in relation to the particular proposal before it. The Commission was asked to grant or deny effectiveness to a proposed amendment to Federal's reorganization plan whereby the management would be accorded parity treatment on its holdings. It could do that only in the form of an order, entered after a due consideration of the particular facts in light of the relevant and proper standards. That was true regardless of whether those standards previously had been spelled out in a general rule or regulation. Indeed, if the Commission rightly felt that the proposed amendment was inconsistent with those standards, an order giving effect to the amendment merely because there was no general rule or regulation covering the matter would be unjustified.

It is true that our prior decision explicitly recognized the possibility that the Commission might have promulgated a general rule dealing with this problem under its statutory rule-making powers, in which case the issue for our consideration would have been entirely different from that which did confront us. But we did not mean to imply thereby that the failure of the Commission to anticipate this problem and to promulgate a general rule withdrew all power from that agency to perform its statutory duty in this case. To hold that the Commission had no alternative in this proceeding but to approve the proposed transaction, while formulating any general rules it might desire for use in future cases of this nature, would be to stultify the administrative process. That we refuse to do.

Since the Commission, unlike a court, does have the ability to make new law prospectively through the exercise of its rule-making powers, it has less reason to rely upon ad hoc adjudication to formulate new standards of conduct within the framework of the Holding Company Act. The function of filling in the interstices of the Act should be performed, as much as possible, through this quasi-legislative promulgation of rules to be applied in the future. But any rigid requirement to that effect would make the administrative process inflexible and incapable of dealing with many of the specialized problems which arise. Not every principle essential to the effective administration of a statute can or should be cast immediately into the mold of a general rule. Some principles must await their own development, while others must be adjusted to meet particular, unforeseeable situations. In performing its important functions in these respects, therefore, an administrative agency must be equipped to act either by general rule or by individual order. To insist upon one form of action to the exclusion of the other is to exalt form over necessity.

In other words, problems may arise in a case which the administrative agency could not reasonably foresee, problems which must be solved despite the absence of a relevant general rule. Or the agency may not have had sufficient experience with a particular problem to warrant rigidifying its tentative judgment into a hard and fast rule. Or the problem may be so specialized and varying in nature as to be impossible of capture within the boundaries of a general rule. In those situations, the agency must retain power to deal with the problems on a case-to-case basis if the administrative process is to be effective. There is thus a very definite place for the case-by-case evolution of statutory standards. And the choice made between proceeding by general rule or by individual, ad hoc litigation is one that lies primarily in the informed discretion of the administrative agency.

Hence we refuse to say that the Commission, which had not previously been confronted with the problem of management trading during reorganization, was forbidden from utilizing this particular proceeding for announcing and applying a new standard of conduct. That such action might have a retroactive effect was not necessarily fatal to its validity. Every case of first impression has a retroactive effect, whether the new principle is announced by a court or by an administrative agency. But such retroactivity must be balanced against the mischief of producing a result which is contrary to a statutory design or to legal and equitable principles. If that mischief is greater than the ill effect of the retroactive application of a new standard, it is not the type of retroactivity which is condemned by law.

The problem in this case thus resolves itself into a determination of whether the Commission's action in denying effectiveness to the proposed amendment to the Federal reorganization plan can be justified on the basis upon which it clearly rests. * * * The Commission concluded that it could not find that the reorganization plan, if amended as proposed, would be "fair and equitable to the persons affected (thereby)" within the meaning of § 1 (e) of the Act, under which the reorganization was taking place. Its view was that the amended plan would involve the issuance of securities on terms "detrimental to the public interest or the interest of investors" * * * and would result in an "unfair or inequitable distribution of voting power" among the Federal security holders * * *. It was led to this result "not by proof that [the Chenerys] committed acts of conscious wrongdoing but by the character of the conflicting interests created by [their] program of stock purchases carried out while plans for reorganization were under consideration."

The Commission noted that Federal's management controlled a large multi-state utility system and that its influence permeated down to the lowest tier of operating companies. * * * Drawing upon its experience, the Commission indicated that all [the] powers of the holding company management during the course of a § 11(e) reorganization placed in the management's command "a formidable battery of devices that would enable it, if it should choose to use them selfishly, to affect in material degree the ultimate allocation of new securities among the various existing classes, to influence the market for its own gain and to manipulate or obstruct the reorganization required by the mandate of the statute." In that setting, the Commission felt that a management program of stock purchase would give rise to the temptation and the opportunity to shape the reorganization proceeding so as to encourage public selling on the market at low prices. * * *

The Commission further felt that its answer should be the same even where proof of intentional wrongdoing on the management's part is lacking. Assuming a conflict of interests, the Commission thought that the absence of actual misconduct is immaterial; injury to the public investors and to the corporation may result just as readily. "Questionable transactions may be explained away, and an abuse of investors and the administrative process may be perpetrated without evil intent, yet the injury will remain." Moreover, the Commission was of the view that the delays and the difficulties involved in probing the mental processes and personal integrity of corporate officials do not warrant any distinction on the basis of evil intent, the plain fact being "that an absence of unfairness or detriment in cases of this sort would be practically impossible to establish by proof."

The scope of our review of an administrative order wherein a new principle is announced and applied is no different from that which pertains to ordinary administrative action. The wisdom of the principle adopted is none of our concern. Our duty is at an end when it becomes evident that the Commission's action is based upon substantial evidence and is consistent with the authority granted by Congress.

The Commission's conclusion here rests squarely in that area where administrative judgments are entitled to the greatest amount of weight by appellate courts. It is the product of administrative experience, appreciation of the complexities of the problem, realization of the statutory policies, and responsible treatment of the uncontested facts. It is the type of judgment which administrative agencies are best equipped to make and which justifies the use of the administrative process. Whether we agree or disagree with the result reached, it is an allowable judgment which we cannot disturb. Reversed.

MR. JUSTICE BURTON concurs in the result.

THE CHIEF JUSTICE and MR. JUSTICE DOUGLAS took no part in the consideration or decision of this case.

MR. JUSTICE JACKSON, [joined by JUSTICE FRANKFURTER,] dissenting.

The Court by this present decision sustains the identical administrative order which only recently it held invalid. As the Court correctly notes, the Commission has only "recast its rationale and reached the same result." There being no change in the order, no additional evidence in the record and no amendment of relevant legislation, it is clear that there has been a shift in attitude between that of the controlling membership of the Court when the case was first here and that of those who have the power of decision on this second review.

**FYI**

When the Supreme Court first considered the *Chenery* case, Justice Douglas did not participate, and there was a vacancy on the Court. The Court divided 4–3, and Justice Frankfurter wrote the opinion. When the Court considered the case for a second time, there were three new Justices. Only Justices Frankfurter and Jackson remained on the Court from the four-Justice majority in the first case.

I feel constrained to disagree with the reasoning offered to rationalize this shift. It makes judicial review of administrative orders a hopeless formality for the litigant, even where granted to him by Congress. It reduces the judicial process in such cases to a mere feint. [If the Court's] pronouncements should become governing principles they would, in practice, put most administrative orders over and above the law.

The reversal of the position of this Court is due to a fundamental change in prevailing philosophy. The basic assumption of the earlier opinion as therein stated was, "But before transactions otherwise legal can be outlawed or denied their usual business consequences, they must fall under the ban of some standards of conduct prescribed by an agency of government authorized to prescribe such standards." *Securities and Exchange Commission v. Chenery Corp.*, 318 U.S. 80, 92, 93 (1943). The basic assumption of the present opinion is stated thus: "The absence of a general rule or regulation governing management trading during reorganization did not affect the Commission's duties in relation to the particular proposal before it." This puts in juxtaposition the two conflicting philosophies which produce opposite results in the same case and on the same facts. The difference between the first and the latest decision of the Court is thus simply the difference between holding that administrative orders must have a basis in law and a holding that absence of a legal basis is no ground on which courts may annul them.

As there admittedly is no law or regulation to support this order we peruse the Court's opinion diligently to find on what grounds it is now held that the Court of Appeals, on pain of being reversed for error, was required to stamp this order with its approval. We find but one. That is the principle of judicial deference to administrative experience. That argument is five times stressed in as many different contexts * * *.

What are we to make of this reiterated deference to "administrative experience" when in another context the Court says, "Hence we refuse to say that the Commission, *which had not previously been confronted with the problem of management trading during reorganization*, was forbidden from utilizing this particular proceeding for announcing and applying a new standard of conduct"? (Emphasis supplied.)

The Court's reasoning adds up to this: The Commission must be sustained because of its accumulated experience in solving a problem with which it had never before been confronted!

Of course, thus to uphold the Commission by professing to find that it has enunciated a "new standard of conduct" brings the Court squarely against the invalidity of retroactive law-making. But the Court does not falter. "That such action might have a retroactive effect was not necessarily fatal to its validity." * * * Of course, if what these parties did really was condemned by "statutory design" or "legal and equitable principles," it could be stopped without resort to a new rule and there would be no retroactivity to condone. But if it had been the Court's view that some law already prohibited the purchases, it would hardly have been necessary three sentences earlier to hold that the Commission was not prohibited "from utilizing this particular proceeding for announcing and applying a *new standard of conduct*." (Emphasis supplied.)

I give up. Now I realize fully what Mark Twain meant when he said, "The more you explain it, the more I don't understand it."

* * * [A]dministrative experience is of weight in judicial review only to this point—it is a persuasive reason for deference to the Commission in the exercise of its discretionary powers under and within the law. It cannot be invoked to support action outside of the law. And what action is, and what is not within the law must be determined by courts, when authorized to review, no matter how much deference is due to the agency's fact finding. * * *

The truth is that in this decision the Court approves the Commission's assertion of power to govern the matter without law, power to force surrender of stock so purchased whenever it will, and power also to overlook such acquisitions if it so chooses. The reasons which will lead it to take one course as against the other remain locked in its own breast, and it has not and apparently does not intend to commit them to any rule or regulation. This administrative authoritarianism, this power to decide without law, is what the Court seems to approve in so many words: "The absence of a general rule or regulation governing management trading during reorganization did not affect the Commission's duties . . . ." This seems to me to undervalue and to belittle the place of law, even in the system of administrative justice. It calls to mind Mr. Justice Cardozo's statement that "Law as a guide to conduct is reduced to the level of mere futility if it is unknown and unknowable."

I have long urged, and still believe, that the administrative process deserves fostering in our system as an expeditious and nontechnical method of applying law in specialized fields. I can not agree that it be used, and I think its continued effectiveness is endangered when it is used, as a method of dispensing with law in those fields.

---

## Points for Discussion

### *a. The* Chenery *Cases*

The Chenerys' conflict with the SEC produced two seminal Supreme Court decisions, each announcing an important principle of administrative law. In the first decision, sometimes known as "*Chenery I*," the Court held that a reviewing court should "judge the propriety [of an agency's action] solely on the grounds invoked by the agency" and that, as a result, the agency must set forth the basis of its decision with clarity. In the second decision, sometimes known as "*Chenery II*," the Court held that, in formulating policy, "the choice between proceeding by rule or by individual, ad hoc litigation is one that lies primarily in the informed discretion of the administrative agency."

It is ironic that the Chenerys' conflict with the SEC lasted as long as it did. Accounts of the litigation reveal that the Chenerys were content to accept the SEC's settlement proposal, because all they really wanted was to keep control of the company. But their lawyer thought that the SEC could not constitutionally require them to give up their profits, and he recommended that they fight the SEC every step of the way. This turned out to be a huge blunder. The SEC conducted what today we think of as a formal adjudication—it took place before the enactment of the APA—and concluded (twice) that management had a fiduciary duty not to trade the company's shares during reorganization. Whereas the proposed settlement would have forced the Chenerys to give up $60,000 in profit, the order that the SEC issued after the adjudication cost the Chenerys about $4.5 million dollars and control of the new enterprise.

#### *b. Choice of Policy-Making Mode*

The Court in *Chenery II* permitted the SEC effectively to announce a new policy in the course of a formal adjudication, rather than through informal rulemaking. Did the Court reason that adjudication and rulemaking are equally sensible vehicles for policy-making? If not, why did the Court leave it to the agency's discretion to decide which decision-making mode to use for policy-making? Can you make an argument for why sometimes policy-making through adjudication is likely to produce better or fairer policy?

Regardless of its virtues, some agencies have regularly made policy in the course of formal adjudications. Most prominently, the National Labor Relations Board, which adjudicates disputes between management and labor, almost never engages in informal rulemaking to clarify the rules of labor-management relations. Instead, it announces new rules in the course of formal adjudications, acting essentially as would a common-law court. Notwithstanding frequent criticisms that labor law is unnecessarily unpredictable as a result, the Supreme Court has reaffirmed *Chenery II* specifically as applied to the NLRB. See *National Labor Relations Board v. Bell Aerospace Co.*, 416 U.S. 267 (1974).

Should the Court be more insistent that agencies make new policy through informal rulemaking rather than through adjudication? Consider the following view.

---

### Perspective and Analysis

Judges and academics long ago reached rare consensus on the desirability of agency policymaking through the process of informal rulemaking. [To be sure, the] Supreme Court wisely [recognized] that it is impossible for agencies to make *all* policy decisions generically in advance, and that agencies are best positioned to determine the circumstances in which the many advantages of rulemaking must be sacrificed for the flexibility of ad hoc policymaking through adjudication.

Still, courts consistently recognize the advantages of rulemaking and frequently strive to encourage agencies to make policy primarily through the rulemaking process. Many of the landmark decisions in administrative law are explicable in part by reference to the nearly unanimous judicial preference for policymaking through rulemaking. Judges and scholars have identified eight significant advantages inherent in the rulemaking process as a means of making policy decisions.

Rulemaking yields higher-quality policy decisions than adjudication because it invites broad participation in the policymaking process by all affected entities and groups, and because it encourages the agency to focus on the broad effects of its policy rather than the often idiosyncratic adjudicative facts of a specific dispute. Rulemaking enhances efficiency in three ways. It avoids the needless cost and delay of finding legislative facts through trial-type procedures; it eliminates the need to relitigate policy issues in the context of disputes with no material differences in adjudicative facts; and, it yields much clearer "rules" than can be extracted from a decision resolving a specific dispute. Rulemaking also provides greater fairness in three ways. It provides affected parties with clearer notice of what conduct is permissible and impermissible; it avoids the widely disparate temporal impact of agency policy decisions made and implemented through ad hoc adjudication; and, it allows all potentially affected segments of the public to participate in the process of determining the rules that will govern their conduct and affect their lives.

**Richard J. Pierce, Jr., *Two Problems in Administrative Law: Political Polarity on the District of Columbia Circuit and Judicial Deterrence of Agency Rulemaking*, 1988 DUKE L.J. 300, 308–09.**

---

Now that we have a sense of the types of things that agencies do, we can turn to two principal remaining questions. The first arises because Congress has given agencies such broad power to make policy: should we be concerned about electorally unaccountable actors resolving important questions of policy, or do other actors—the President, Congress, and the courts—exercise sufficient control over agency decision-making to alleviate any such concerns? Once we have answered that question in Chapter 7, we can turn in Chapter 8 to the second question: what role should agency interpretations of the statutes that they are charged with administering play in statutory interpretation by courts? With a more complete understanding of the role and powers of agencies, we will be well positioned to answer this thorny question.

**Test Your Knowledge**

To assess your understanding of the material in this Chapter, click here to take a quiz.

## Chapter Seven

# *Oversight of Agency Decision-Making*

We saw in Chapter 6 that federal agencies often have broad power to make policy that affects the lives of millions of people. The EPA, for example, decides how much pollution manufacturers can emit, which helps to determine both the safety of the air that we breathe and the cost of products that we buy; the Federal Reserve Board decides the nation's monetary policy, which affects interest rates (and thus whether we can afford a mortgage to buy a new home); the Department of Education sets policy about student loans and loan forgiveness, which has long-term financial consequences for millions of graduates of institutions of higher learning. Congress has delegated substantial decision-making authority to these and scores of other agencies, and it has given them power to make rules and to resolve individualized grievances in order to implement that authority.

On the one hand, it makes sense to give agencies authority to resolve important but difficult questions of policy. Many questions of policy are complicated and require a sophisticated understanding of science (in the case of the EPA), economics (in the case of the Federal Reserve and the Department of Education), or other specialized disciplines. Whereas Congress (most charitably viewed) is composed of generalists, agencies maintain staffs of experts in the fields relevant to the agencies' mandates. Many people take comfort in knowing that important questions that affect their lives—such as whether to approve a vaccine or whether to ban a workplace toxin—are in the hands of experts.

On the other hand, as we noted in Chapter 1, many of the policy questions that agencies have authority to resolve are contested and require value judgments. For example, if we know that banning the use of coal as a source of energy will reduce the incidence of asthma and other respiratory illnesses by ten percent, slow the pace of climate change by ten percent, and result in a ten percent increase in energy costs—and thus an increase in the cost of many products—then should the EPA ban the use of coal as a source of energy? Answering this question requires more than simply the ability to determine causes and effects, and more than simply the ability to do the math; it requires a judgment about the value of human and planetary well-being.

To be sure, perhaps there is no reason to expect members of Congress to be better at making such judgments than the dedicated public servants who work at agencies. But because the stakes are so high—and because there is not likely to be broad consensus on what the answers should be—this might be the type of policy decision that "we the people" want to determine. Of course, we won't determine it directly; we don't have a system of direct democracy in the United States, at least not at the federal level. But we do get to vote for our representatives, which means that we still have a meaningful form of control over their resolution of important questions. The decision-makers at federal agencies, on the other hand, are not subject to election, and we do not have a direct form of control over their decision-making.

This conflict—between the virtue of expertise and the desire for accountable decision-making—is at the heart of any law school course in Administrative Law. (Indeed, it played a significant role, even if only implicitly, in our consideration of the non-delegation doctrine in Chapter 6.) But notice that the conflict becomes less acute—even if it doesn't disappear entirely—if there are mechanisms for electorally accountable decision-makers to influence or control agency policy-making. We don't vote for the Administrator of the EPA, but we do vote for the President and for members of Congress; if they can effectively control decision-making at the EPA, then our concerns about unaccountable decision-making diminish substantially. In addition, even if the President and the Congress cannot meaningfully dictate every decision that a federal agency makes, judicial review of agency decisions can ensure that those decisions are within the scope of the substantive authority that Congress has delegated and consistent with procedural requirements that are designed to ensure reasoned decision-making.

In this Chapter, we will consider the forms of control that the political branches and the courts exercise over agency decision-making. We begin with the ways in which the President can control agency decision-making—and whether Congress can impose any limits on the President's ability to do so. We will then turn to the forms of control that Congress can exercise over agency decision-making. Finally, we will consider judicial oversight of agency decision-making.

---

## A. Presidential Control of Agency Decision-Making

### 1. Appointment

The most obvious way that the President can control agency decision-making is by deciding who will get to make decisions at the agencies. The Constitution provides:

> "[The President] shall nominate, and by and with the Advice and Consent of the Senate, shall appoint Ambassadors, other public Ministers and Consuls, Judges of

> the supreme Court, and all other Officers of the United States, whose Appointments are not herein otherwise provided for, and which shall be established by Law: but the Congress may by Law vest the Appointment of such inferior Officers, as they think proper, in the President alone, in the Courts of Law, or in the Heads of Departments." U.S. Const., Art. II, § 2, cl. 2.

In other words, the President has considerable authority (subject only to the Senate's power of advice and consent) to choose who will serve as "officers"—often called "principal officers"—and perhaps less power to decide who will serve as "inferior officers." But the Constitution does not explain how to tell the difference between these two categories of officials.

In *Morrison v. Olson*, 487 U.S. 654 (1988), the Court held that an independent counsel appointed to investigate alleged wrongdoing by an official at the Department of Justice was an inferior officer and thus could be appointed by someone other than the President. The Court acknowledged that the "line between 'inferior' and 'principal' officers is one that is far from clear, and the Framers provided little guidance into where it should be drawn." But without deciding "exactly where the line falls between the two types of officers," the Court concluded that the independent counsel fell "on the 'inferior officer' side of that line." The Court relied on "[s]everal factors" in reaching that conclusion:

> "First, [the independent counsel was] subject to removal by a higher Executive Branch official. [The Attorney General had the power to remove the independent counsel, but only for good cause.] Although [the independent counsel] may not be 'subordinate' to the Attorney General (and the President) insofar as she possesses a degree of independent discretion to exercise the powers delegated to her under the Act, the fact that she can be removed by the Attorney General indicates that she is to some degree 'inferior' in rank and authority. Second, [the independent counsel] is empowered by the Act to perform only certain, limited duties. An independent counsel's role is restricted primarily to investigation and, if appropriate, prosecution for certain federal crimes. * * *
>
> Third, [the independent counsel's] office is limited in jurisdiction. Not only is the [statute authorizing appointment of the independent counsel] itself restricted in applicability to certain federal officials suspected of certain serious federal crimes, but an independent counsel can only act within the scope of the jurisdiction that has been granted by [a Special Division of the United States Court of Appeals for the D.C. Circuit, which appointed the counsel,] pursuant to a request by the Attorney General. Finally, [the independent counsel's] office is limited in tenure. There is concededly no time limit on the appointment of a particular counsel. Nonetheless, the office of independent counsel is 'temporary' in the sense that an independent counsel is appointed essentially to accomplish a single task, and when that task is over the office is terminated, either by the counsel herself or by action of the Special Division. * * * In our view, these factors relating to the 'ideas of tenure, duration . . . and duties' of the independent counsel [are] sufficient to establish that appellant is an 'inferior' officer in the constitutional sense.

Does it make sense to conclude that an official who could not easily be removed by any other official is an "inferior officer" within the meaning of the Appointments Clause?

Even assuming that we can readily tell the difference between principal officers and inferior officers, do those two categories together include every person who works for the federal government? Consider the case that follows.

---

## *Lucia v. Securities and Exchange Commission*

138 S.Ct. 2044 (2018)

JUSTICE KAGAN delivered the opinion of the Court.

The Appointments Clause of the Constitution lays out the permissible methods of appointing "Officers of the United States," a class of government officials distinct from mere employees. Art. II, § 2, cl. 2. This case requires us to decide whether administrative law judges (ALJs) of the Securities and Exchange Commission (SEC or Commission) qualify as such "Officers."

**Make the Connection**

The SEC often adjudicates claims that a person has violated the securities laws. We considered adjudication as a means for implementing policy in Chapter 6.

The SEC has statutory authority to enforce the nation's securities laws. One way it can do so is by instituting an administrative proceeding against an alleged wrongdoer. By law, the Commission may itself preside over such a proceeding. See 17 CFR § 201.110 (2017). But the Commission also may, and typically does, delegate that task to an ALJ. The SEC currently has five ALJs. Other staff members, rather than the Commission proper, selected them all.

**Food for Thought**

ALJs preside over adjudicatory proceedings at administrative agencies. Their decisions are usually subject to review by the head(s) of the agency, whose decisions are in turn usually subject to review in Article III courts. Is this process consistent with your understanding of Article III and the Due Process Clause?

An ALJ assigned to hear an SEC enforcement action has extensive powers—the "authority to do all things necessary and appropriate to discharge his or her duties" and ensure a "fair and orderly" adversarial proceeding. §§ 201.111, 200.14(a). Those powers "include, but are not limited to," supervising discovery; issuing, revoking, or modifying subpoenas; deciding motions; ruling on the admissibility of evidence; administering

oaths; hearing and examining witnesses; generally "[r]egulating the course of" the proceeding and the "conduct of the parties and their counsel"; and imposing sanctions for "[c]ontemptuous conduct" or violations of procedural requirements. §§ 201.111, 201.180; see §§ 200.14(a), 201.230. As that list suggests, an SEC ALJ exercises authority "comparable to" that of a federal district judge conducti
*Butz v. Economou*, 438 U.S. 478, 513 (1978).

After a hearing ends, the ALJ issues an "initial decision." § 20
decision must set out "findings and conclusions" about all "material issues of fact [and] law"; it also must include the "appropriate order, sanction, relief, or denial thereof." § 201.360(b). The Commission can then review the ALJ's decision, either upon request or *sua sponte*. See § 201.360(d)(1). But if it opts against review, the Commission "issue[s] an order that the [ALJ's] decision has become final." § 201.360(d)(2). At that point, the initial decision is "deemed the action of the Commission." § 78d–1(c).

This case began when the SEC instituted an administrative proceeding against petitioner Raymond Lucia and his investment company. Lucia marketed a retirement savings strategy called "Buckets of Money." In the SEC's view, Lucia used misleading slideshow presentations to deceive prospective clients. The SEC charged Lucia under the Investment Advisers Act, § 80b–1 *et seq.*, and assigned ALJ Cameron Elliot to adjudicate the case. After nine days of testimony and argument, Judge Elliot issued an initial decision concluding that Lucia had violated the Act and imposing sanctions, including civil penalties of $300,000 and a lifetime bar from the investment industry. [After a remand from the Commission for more factfinding, Judge Elliot] made additional findings of deception and issued a revised initial decision, with the same sanctions.

On appeal to the SEC, Lucia argued that the administrative proceeding was invalid because Judge Elliot had not been constitutionally appointed [because] the Commission had left the task of appointing ALJs, including Judge Elliot, to SEC staff members. As a result, Lucia contended, Judge Elliot lacked constitutional authority to do his job.

The Commission rejected Lucia's argument. [A panel of the Court of Appeals for the D.C. Circuit concluded that SEC ALJs are employees rather than officers, and so are not subject to the Appointments Clause. The Court of Appeals heard argument *en banc* but divided evenly, resulting in a *per curiam* order denying Lucia's claim. See 868 F.3d 1021 (2017).]

In the court of appeals, the federal government defended the Commission's position that SEC ALJs are not officers. After the presidential election, the government switched sides, arguing that the ALJs are officers and that their appointment was unconstitutional. The Court appointed an *amicus curiae* to defend the judgment below.

The sole question here is whether the Commission's ALJs are "Officers of the United States" or simply employees of the Federal Government. The Appointments Clause prescribes the exclusive means of appointing "Officers." Only the President, a court of law, or a head of department can do so. See Art. II, § 2, cl. 2.[3] And as all parties agree, none of those actors appointed Judge Elliot before he heard Lucia's case; instead, SEC staff members gave him an ALJ slot. So if the Commission's ALJs are constitutional officers, Lucia raises a valid Appointments Clause claim. The only way to defeat his position is to show that those ALJs are not officers at all, but instead non-officer employees—part of the broad swath of "lesser functionaries" in the Government's workforce. *Buckley v. Valeo*, 424 U.S. 1, 126, n. 162 (1976) (*per curiam*). For if that is true, the Appointments Clause cares not a whit about who [illegible] them. See *United States v. Germaine*, 99 U.S. 508, 510 (1879).

[illegible] decisions set out this Court's basic framework for distinguishing between [illegible] and employees. *Germaine* held that "civil surgeons" (doctors hired to perform various physical exams) were mere employees because their duties were "occasional or temporary" rather than "continuing and permanent." *Id.*, at 511–512. Stressing "ideas of tenure [and] duration," the Court there made clear that an individual must occupy a "continuing" position established by law to qualify as an officer. *Id.*, at 511. *Buckley* then set out another requirement, central to this case. It determined that members of a federal commission were officers only after finding that they "exercis[ed] significant authority pursuant to the laws of the United States." 424 U.S., at 126. The inquiry thus focused on the extent of power an individual wields in carrying out his assigned functions.

The standard is no doubt framed in general terms, tempting advocates to add whatever glosses best suit their arguments. And maybe one day we will see a need to refine or enhance the test *Buckley* set out so concisely. But that day is not this one, because in *Freytag v. Commissioner*, 501 U.S. 868 (1991), we applied the unadorned "significant authority" test to adjudicative officials who are near-carbon copies of the Commission's ALJs. As we now explain, our analysis there * * * necessarily decides this case.

The officials at issue in *Freytag* were the "special trial judges" (STJs) of the United States Tax Court. * * * This Court held that the Tax Court's STJs are officers, not mere employees. Citing *Germaine*, the Court first found that STJs hold a continuing office established by law. See 501 U.S., at 881. They serve on an ongoing, rather than a "temporary [or] episodic[,] basis"; and their "duties, salary, and means of appointment" are all specified in the Tax Code. *Ibid.* The Court then considered, as *Buckley* demands, the "significance" of the "authority" STJs wield. 501 U.S., at 881.

---

3 That statement elides a distinction, not at issue here, between "principal" and "inferior" officers. See *Edmond v. United States*, 520 U.S. 651, 659–660 (1997). * * * Both the Government and Lucia view the SEC's ALJs as inferior officers and acknowledge that the Commission, as a head of department, can constitutionally appoint them.

* * * Describing the responsibilities involved in presiding over adversarial hearings, the Court said: STJs "take testimony, conduct trials, rule on the admissibility of evidence, and have the power to enforce compliance with discovery orders." *Id.,* at 881–882. And the Court observed that "[i]n the course of carrying out these important functions, the [STJs] exercise significant discretion." *Id.,* at 882. That fact meant they were officers, even when their decisions were not final.

*Freytag* says everything necessary to decide this case. To begin, the Commission's ALJs, like the Tax Court's STJs, hold a continuing office established by law. Far from serving temporarily or episodically, SEC ALJs "receive[ ] a career appointment." 5 CFR § 930.204(a) (2018). And that appointment is to a position created by statute, down to its "duties, salary, and means of appointment." *Freytag,* 501 U.S., at 881; see 5 U.S.C. §§ 556–557, 5372, 3105.

Still more, the Commission's ALJs exercise the same "significant discretion" when carrying out the same "important functions" as STJs do. *Freytag,* 501 U.S., at 882. Both sets of officials have all the authority needed to ensure fair and orderly adversarial hearings—indeed, nearly all the tools of federal trial judges. See *Butz,* 438 U.S., at 513. * * * And at the close of those proceedings, ALJs issue decisions much like that in *Freytag*—except with potentially more independent effect. * * * In a major case like *Freytag,* a regular Tax Court judge must always review an STJ's opinion. And that opinion counts for nothing unless the regular judge adopts it as his own. See 501 U.S., at 873. By contrast, the SEC can decide against reviewing an ALJ decision at all. And when the SEC declines review (and issues an order saying so), the ALJ's decision itself "becomes final" and is "deemed the action of the Commission." § 201.360(d)(2); 15 U.S.C. § 78d–1(c). That last-word capacity makes this an *a fortiori* case: If the Tax Court's STJs are officers, as *Freytag* held, then the Commission's ALJs must be too.

The only issue left is remedial. * * * Judge Elliot heard and decided Lucia's case without the kind of appointment the [Appointments] Clause requires. * * * This Court has also held that the "appropriate" remedy for an adjudication tainted with an appointments violation is a new "hearing before a properly appointed" official. *Ryder v. United States,* 515 U.S. 177, 183, 188 (1995). And we add today one thing more. That official cannot be Judge Elliot, even if he has by now received (or receives sometime in the future) a constitutional appointment. Judge Elliot has already both heard Lucia's case and issued an initial decision on the merits. He cannot be expected to consider the matter as though he had not adjudicated it before.[5] To cure

---

5 Justice BREYER disagrees with our decision to wrest further proceedings from Judge Elliot, arguing that "[f]or him to preside once again would not violate the structural purposes [of] the Appointments Clause." But our Appointments Clause remedies are designed not only to advance those purposes directly, but also to create "[ ]incentive[s] to raise Appointments Clause challenges." *Ryder v. United States,* 515 U.S. 177, 183 (1995). We best accomplish that goal by providing a successful litigant with a hearing before a new judge. That is especially so because (as Justice BREYER points out) the old judge would have no reason to think he did anything wrong on the merits—and so could be expected to reach all the same judgments. * * *

the constitutional error, another ALJ (or the Commission itself) must hold the new hearing to which Lucia is entitled.[6]

We accordingly reverse the judgment of the Court of Appeals and remand the case for further proceedings consistent with this opinion.

JUSTICE THOMAS, with whom JUSTICE GORSUCH joins, concurring.

I agree with the Court that this case is indistinguishable from *Freytag v. Commissioner*, 501 U.S. 868 (1991). * * * Moving forward, however, this Court will not be able to decide every Appointments Clause case by comparing it to *Freytag*. And, as the Court acknowledges, our precedents in this area do not provide much guidance. While precedents like *Freytag* discuss what is *sufficient* to make someone an officer of the United States, our precedents have never clearly defined what is *necessary*. I would resolve that question based on the original public meaning of "Officers of the United States." * * *

The Founders likely understood the term "Officers of the United States" to encompass all federal civil officials who perform an ongoing, statutory duty—no matter how important or significant the duty. Mascott, *Who Are "Officers of the United States"?* 70 Stan. L. Rev. 443, 454 (2018). "Officers of the United States" was probably not a term of art that the Constitution used to signify some special type of official. Based on how the Founders used it and similar terms, the phrase "of the United States" was merely a synonym for "federal," and the word "Office[r]" carried its ordinary meaning. See *id.*, at 471–479. The ordinary meaning of "officer" was anyone who performed a continuous public duty. See *id.* at 484–507; *e.g., United States v. Maurice*, 26 F. Cas. 1211, 1214 (No. 15,747) (CC Va. 1823) (defining officer as someone in "a public charge or employment" who performed a "continuing" duty); 8 Annals of Cong. 2304–2305 (1799) (statement of Rep. Harper) (explaining that the word officer "is derived from the Latin word *officium*" and "includes all persons holding posts which require the performance of some public duty"). For federal officers, that duty is "established by Law"—that is, by statute. Art. II, § 2, cl. 2. The Founders considered individuals to be officers even if they performed only ministerial statutory duties—including recordkeepers, clerks, and tidewaiters (individuals who watched goods land at a customhouse). See Mascott 484–507. Early congressional practice reflected this understanding. With exceptions not relevant here, Congress required

---

6 While this case was on judicial review, the SEC issued an order "ratif[ying]" the prior appointments of its ALJs. Order (Nov. 30, 2017), online at https://www.sec.gov/litigation/opinions/2017/33-10440.pdf (as last visited June 18, 2018). Lucia argues that the order is invalid. We see no reason to address that issue. The Commission has not suggested that it intends to assign Lucia's case on remand to an ALJ whose claim to authority rests on the ratification order. The SEC may decide to conduct Lucia's rehearing itself. Or it may assign the hearing to an ALJ who has received a constitutional appointment independent of the ratification.

all federal officials with ongoing statutory duties to be appointed in compliance with the Appointments Clause. See *id.,* at 507–545.

Applying the original meaning here, the administrative law judges of the Securities and Exchange Commission easily qualify as "Officers of the United States." These judges exercise many of the agency's statutory duties, including issuing initial decisions in adversarial proceedings. See 15 U.S.C. § 78d–1(a); 17 CFR §§ 200.14, 200.30–9 (2017). As explained, the importance or significance of these statutory duties is irrelevant. All that matters is that the judges are continuously responsible for performing them. * * * Because the Court reaches the same conclusion by correctly applying *Freytag,* I join its opinion.

JUSTICE BREYER, with whom JUSTICE GINSBURG and JUSTICE SOTOMAYOR join as to Part III, concurring in the judgment in part and dissenting in part.

[I] [The Administrative Procedure Act] governs the appointment of administrative law judges. It provides [that] "[e]ach agency shall appoint as many administrative law judges as are necessary for" hearings governed by the Administrative Procedure Act. 5 U.S.C. § 3105. In the case of the Securities and Exchange Commission, the relevant "agency" is the Commission itself. But the Commission did not appoint the Administrative Law Judge who presided over Lucia's hearing. Rather, the Commission's staff appointed that Administrative Law Judge, without the approval of the Commissioners themselves.

I do not believe that the Administrative Procedure Act permits the Commission to delegate its power to appoint its administrative law judges to its staff. We have held that, for purposes of the Constitution's Appointments Clause, the Commission itself is a "Hea[d]" of a "Departmen[t]." *Free Enterprise Fund v. Public Company Accounting Oversight Board,* 561 U.S. 477, 512–513 (2010). Thus, reading the statute as referring to the Commission itself, and not to its staff, avoids a difficult constitutional question, namely, the very question that the Court answers today: whether the Commission's administrative law judges are constitutional "inferior Officers" whose appointment Congress may vest only in the President, the "Courts of Law," or the "Heads of Departments." * * * The upshot, in my view, is that for statutory, not constitutional, reasons, the Commission did not lawfully appoint the Administrative Law Judge here at issue. And this Court should decide no more than that.

[II] [I]n my view, [the] Appointments Clause is properly understood [illegible] Congress a degree of leeway as to whether particular Government workers are [illegible] or instead mere employees not subject to the Appointments Clause. * * * The use of the words "by Law" [in the Appointments Clause] to describe the establishment and means of appointment of "Officers of the United States," together with the fact that Article I of the Constitution vests the legislative power in Congress, suggests that (other than the officers the Constitution specifically lists) Congress, not the Judicial Branch alone, must play a major role in determining who is an "Office[r] of the United States." And Congress' intent in this specific respect is often highly relevant. Congress' leeway is not, of course, absolute—it may not, for example, say that positions the Constitution itself describes as "Officers" are not "Officers." But [illegible] constitutional language, the Court, when deciding whether other positions [illegible] ers of the United States" under the Appointments Clause, should give [illegible] weight to Congress' decision.

I would not answer the question whether the Securities and Exchange Commission's administrative law judges are constitutional "Officers" without first deciding * * * what effect that holding would have on the statutory "for cause" removal protections that Congress provided for administrative law judges. If [saying] administrative law judges are "inferior Officers" will cause them to lose their "for cause" removal protections, then I would likely hold that the administrative law judges are not "Officers," for to say otherwise would be to contradict Congress' enactment of those protections in the Administrative Procedure Act. * * *

[III] Separately, I also disagree with the majority's conclusion that the proper remedy in this case requires a hearing before a *different* administrative law judge. The Securities and Exchange Commission has now itself appointed the Administrative Law Judge in question, and I see no reason why he could not rehear the case. After all, when a judge is reversed on appeal and a new trial ordered, typically the judge who rehears the case is the same judge who heard it the first time. The reversal here is based on a technical constitutional question, and the reversal implies no criticism at all of the original judge or his ability to conduct the new proceedings. For him to preside once again would not violate the structural purposes that we have said the Appointments Clause serves, nor would it, in any obvious way, violate the Due Process Clause.

JUSTICE SOTOMAYOR, with whom JUSTICE GINSBURG joins, dissenting.

The Court today and scholars acknowledge that this Court's Appointments Clause jurisprudence offers little guidance on who qualifies as an "Officer of the United States." * * * This confusion can undermine the reliability and finality of proceedings and result in wasted resources.

As the majority notes, this Court's decisions currently set forth at least two prerequisites to officer status: (1) an individual must hold a "continuing" office established by law, *United States v. Germaine*, 99 U.S. 508, 511–512 (1879), and (2) an individual must wield "significant authority," *Buckley v. Valeo*, 424 U.S. 1, 126 (1976) (*per curiam*). The first requirement is relatively easy to grasp; the second, less so. To be sure, to exercise "significant authority," the person must wield considerable powers in comparison to the average person who works for the Federal Government. As this Court has noted, the vast majority of those who work for the Federal Government are not "Officers of the United States." See *Free Enterprise Fund v. Public Company Accounting Oversight Bd.*, 561 U.S. 477, 506, n. 9 (2010) (indicating that well over

90% of those who render services to the Federal Government and are paid by it are not constitutional officers). But this Court's decisions have yet to articulate the types of powers that will be deemed significant enough to constitute "significant authority."

To provide guidance to Congress and the Executive Branch, I would hold that one requisite component of "significant authority" is the ability to make final, binding decisions on behalf of the Government. Accordingly, a person who merely advises and provides recommendations to an officer would not herself qualify as an officer. * * *

Turning to the question presented here, it is true that the administrative law judges (ALJs) of the Securities and Exchange Commission wield "extensive powers." * * * Nevertheless, I would hold that Commission ALJs are not officers because they lack final decisionmaking authority. * * * Commission ALJs can issue only "initial" decisions. 5 U.S.C. § 557(b). The Commission can review any initial decision upon petition or on its own initiative. 15 U.S.C. § 78d–1(b). The Commission's review of an ALJ's initial decision is *de novo.* 5 U.S.C. § 557(c). It can "make any findings or conclusions that in its judgment are proper and on the basis of the record." 17 CFR § 201.411(a) (2017). * * * Even where the Commission does not review an ALJ's initial decision, as in cases in which no party petitions for review and the Commission does not act *sua sponte*, the initial decision still only becomes final when the Commission enters a finality order. 17 CFR § 201.360(d)(2). And by operation of law, every action taken by an ALJ "shall, for all purposes, . . . be deemed the action of the *Commission.*" 15 U.S.C. § 78d–1(c) (emphasis added). In other words, Commission ALJs do not exercise significant authority because they do not, and cannot, enter final, binding decisions against the Government or third parties. * * * I would conclude that Commission ALJs are not officers for purposes of the Appointments Clause * * *.

---

## Points for Discussion

### *a. Principal Officers, Inferior Officers, and Employees*

As noted above, the Court has struggled to distinguish between principal officers, who must be appointed by the President subject to Senate advice and consent, and inferior officers, who can, if Congress so provides, be appointed by Heads of Departments or the Courts of Law. Does the Constitution also contemplate "employees" who work for the federal government but who can be hired by other means? Does it affect your answer to learn that several million people work for the federal government (but are not currently hired pursuant to the process identified in the Appointments Clause)?

What is the Court's test for distinguishing between inferior officers and employees? Under the Court's test, is an Assistant United States Attorney—one of the thousands of federal prosecutors who staff regional offices around the country—an inferior officer or an employee? How would Justice Thomas have approached these questions? What would be the consequences for the administrative state if the Court adopted Justice Thomas's view?

***b. Inferior Officers, Employees, and Multiple Layers of Protection from Removal***

In *Free Enterprise Fund v. Public Company Accounting Oversight Board*, 561 U.S. 477 (2010), which we will briefly consider later in this Chapter, the Court held that Congress cannot create two layers of "for-cause" protection from removal—that is, Congress cannot restrict the President's power to remove a principal officer who in turn is restricted in his ability to remove an inferior officer who determines the policy and enforces the laws of the United States. Because the President can terminate Commissioners of the SEC only for cause, the Solicitor General of the United States argued in *Lucia* that Congress could not also impose strict good-cause limits on the Commissioners' power to remove ALJs. Would there be any problem with such a conclusion?

ALJs adjudicate claims between the government and private citizens. Although they do not enjoy the protections for independence that Article III confers on federal judges, they have long enjoyed statutory protection from interference by the political appointees at the agency, to ensure a fair and unbiased hearing. If Commissioners at the SEC could terminate them at will, then they would lose much of that independence. But is it problematic to create a class of government officials who exercise power beyond the meaningful control of the President?

Would it make more sense to conclude that agencies lack constitutional power to adjudicate matters involving private parties? Or would that approach substantially undermine the functioning of the administrative state?

---

## 2. Removal

As the discussion above reveals, there is considerable ambiguity in who counts as a "principal officer," who counts as an "inferior officer," and who counts as a mere employee. Let's put those problems aside for present purposes and assume that the person in question is a principal officer who was appointed by the President. Even officials whom the President has appointed might sometimes seek to make decisions with which the President disagrees. Suppose, for example, that the President disagrees with the Secretary of the Treasury on a matter of policy or the President views the Secretary of Treasury's performance as unsatisfactory. What can the President do? Traditionally, the President has exercised control in these kinds of situations by firing, or threatening to fire, subordinates who do not conform to the President's agenda. Indeed, the President might be able to control the decision-making even of officers whom he has *not* appointed if he has the power to remove them from office.

The only thing that the Constitution says about removal of officers, however, is that the "President, the Vice President, and all civil Officers of the United States, shall be removed from Office on Impeachment for, and Conviction of, Treason, Bribery, or other high Crimes and Misdemeanors." U.S. CONST., art. II, § 4. Few people think that a person appointed to office is constitutionally entitled to serve until impeached by the House and convicted by the Senate. But if the impeachment clause does not settle who enjoys constitutional power to remove an officer, then what is the rule?

This question has been controversial since the founding. In 1789, shortly after the ratification of the Constitution, the first Congress set out to create the first federal agencies. During the debate over the creation of the Department of Foreign Affairs, members of Congress disagreed about who should, and who constitutionally could, enjoy the power to remove an officer. A small number of Representatives believed that impeachment was the only way to remove an officer, but the rest of the Members divided more or less evenly among three positions. Some Members thought that the power to remove an officer was within the President's exclusive power; some thought that the power of removal tracked the power of appointment, meaning that the power to remove an officer was jointly vested in the President and the Senate, which would have the power to consent to (or withhold consent for) the termination of an official; and some thought that, because the Constitution is silent on the ordinary mechanism for removal, Congress can settle the question for each office pursuant to its power under the Necessary and Proper Clause. James Madison supported the first position, arguing that the power to remove an official charged with executing the law is in its nature an executive power. (He subsequently acknowledged, however, that Congress could protect from removal officials with duties that "partake of a judiciary quality.") Proponents of the first and third views joined together to support giving the President the power to remove the Secretary of Foreign Affairs.

The political branches had another opportunity to consider this question in the 1860s, during a heated political battle over post-Civil-War efforts to remedy some of the consequences of slavery. Andrew Johnson, who became President after Lincoln's assassination, was widely viewed as unenthusiastic about the project of Reconstruction. To prevent Johnson from undermining Reconstruction by firing administration officials, Congress enacted the Tenure in Office Act, 14 Stat. 430, over Johnson's veto. The law prohibited the President from removing officers without the advice and consent of the Senate.

President Johnson viewed the law as an impermissible interference with his power as President. He responded by seeking to fire Edwin Stanton, whom Lincoln had appointed as the Secretary War. Stanton, relying on the Tenure in Office Act, refused to resign, and the Senate refused to consent to his termination. Johnson, arguing that the Senate lacked power to interfere with his removal of an Executive Branch official, ignored Congress and nominated someone else to serve as Secretary of War. The House responded by impeaching Johnson for violating the Act (among other things), but the Senate failed by one vote to convict and remove Johnson.

The Supreme Court did not address the question of the President's power to remove an officer until 1926, when it decided *Myers v. United States*, 272 U.S. 52 (1926). In 1917, President Wilson appointed Frank Myers as Postmaster of the First Class at Portland, Oregon. The statute governing the office provided that Postmasters of the First Class would serve for terms of four years. In January 1920, however, Wilson demanded Myers's resignation. When Myers refused, Wilson removed him from office. Myers relinquished his position, but he sued, seeking the salary that he would have received had he been permitted to serve the full four-year term. He relied on the Act of Congress of July 12, 1876, 19 Stat. 80, which provided: "Postmasters of the first, second, and third classes shall be appointed and may be removed by the President by and with the advice and consent of the Senate, and shall hold their offices for four years unless sooner removed or suspended according to law." He argued that, because the Senate had not consented to his removal before the expiration of the four-year term, the President had improperly terminated him.

**FYI**

William Howard Taft was the President of the United States from 1909–1913. In his tremendous legal and political career, he also served as Chief Justice of the United States, a federal circuit judge, the solicitor general of the United S[illegible]l governor of [illegible]fessor at Yale [illegible]

The Supreme Court, in an opinion by Chief Justice William Howard Taft, rejected Myers's claim for unpaid salary. Chief Justice Taft canvassed the history, including the congressional debate in 1789 and the controversy over the Tenure in Office Act. In his view, the 1789 debate suggested an early consensus in favor of an exclusive presidential removal power; he thought that the Tenure in Office Act was an aberration. He then reasoned:

> [illegible] executive power in the President was essentially a grant of the [illegible]. But the President alone and unaided could not execute the laws. He must execute them by the assistance of subordinates. * * * As he is charged specifically to take care that they be faithfully executed, the reasonable implication, even in the absence of express words, was that as part of his executive power he should select those who were to act for him under his direction in the execution of the laws. The further implication must be, in the absence of any express limitation respecting removals, that as his selection of administrative officers is essential to the execution of the laws by him, so must be his power of removing those for whom he cannot continue to be responsible.
>
> The power to prevent the removal of an officer who has served under the President is different from the authority to consent to or reject his appointment. When a nomination is made, it may be presumed that the Senate is, or may become, as well advised as to the fitness of the nominee as the President, but in the nature

> of things the defects in ability or intelligence or loyalty in the administration of the laws of one who has served as an officer under the President are facts as to which the President, or his trusted subordinates, must be better informed than the Senate, and the power to remove him may therefore be regarded as confined for very sound and practical reasons, to the governmental authority which has administrative control. The power of removal is incident to the power of appointment, not to the power of advising and consenting to appointment, and when the grant of the executive power is enforced by the express mandate to take care that the laws be faithfully executed, it emphasizes the necessity for including within the executive power as conferred the exclusive power of removal.

Myers's case, however, was a bit more complicated, because a regional postmaster arguably was an inferior officer within the meaning of the Appointments Clause. The Court acknowledged that the "authority of Congress * * * to vest the appointment of such inferior officers in the heads of departments carries with it authority incidentally to invest the heads of departments with power to remove. It has been the practice of Congress to do so and this court has recognized that power." In other words, the Court acknowledged that Congress can effectively limit the President's power directly to remove an inferior officer simply by giving the power to remove to a principal officer, rather than to the President. But, Chief Justice Taft continued,

> the court never has held, nor reasonably could hold, although it is argued to the contrary on behalf of the appellant, that the excepting clause enables Congress to draw to itself, or to either branch of it, the power to remove or the right to participate in the exercise of that power. To do this would be to go beyond the words and implications of that clause, and to infringe the constitutional principle of the separation of governmental powers.

The Court then declared that, "[f]or the reasons given, we must therefore hold that the provision of the law of 1876 by which the unrestricted power of removal of first-class postmasters is denied to the President is in violation of the Constitution and invalid."

Less than a decade later, however, the Court upheld a limitation on the President's power to remove in *Humphrey's Executor v. United States*, 295 U.S. 602 (1935). President Hoover had appointed (and the Senate had confirmed) William E. Humphrey to serve a seven-year term as a member of the Federal Trade Commission. Shortly after taking office in 1933, however, President Roosevelt asked Humphrey to resign, stating that "the aims and purposes of the Administration with respect to the work of the Commission can be carried out most effectively with personnel of my own selection." When Humphrey declined to resign, President Roosevelt removed him. Humphrey subsequently sued to recover salary for the remaining years in his term. He relied on section 1 of the Federal Trade Commission Act, which provided that "any commissioner may be removed by the President for inefficiency, neglect of duty, or malfeasance in office."

The government relied on *Myers*, but the Court held that Congress had constitutionally limited the President's power to remove to cases of good cause. The Court distinguished *Myers* by stating:

> A postmaster is an executive officer restricted to the performance of executive functions. He is charged with no duty at all related to either the legislative or judicial power. The actual decision in the *Myers* Case finds support in the theory that such an officer is merely one of the units in the executive department and, hence, inherently subject to the exclusive and illimitable power of removal by the Chief Executive, whose subordinate and aid he is. [T]he necessary reach of the decision goes far enough to include all purely executive officers. It goes no farther; much less does it include an officer who occupies no place in the executive department and who exercises no part of the executive power vested by the Constitution in the President.

The Court then reasoned:

> [T]he Federal Trade Commission is an administrative body created by Congress to carry into effect legislative policies embodied in the statute in accordance with the legislative standard therein prescribed, and to perform other specified duties as a legislative or as a judicial aid. Such a body cannot in any proper sense be characterized as an arm or an eye of the executive. Its duties are performed without executive leave and, in the contemplation of the statute, must be free from executive control. In administering the provisions of the statute in respect of "unfair methods of competition," that is to say, in filling in and administering the details embodied by that general standard, the commission acts in part quasi legislatively and in part quasi judicially. In making investigations and reports thereon for the information of Congress under section 6, in aid of the legislative power, it acts as a legislative agency. Under section 7, which authorizes the commission to act as a master in chancery under rules prescribed by the court, it acts as an agency of the judiciary. To the extent that it exercises any executive function, as distinguished from executive power in the constitutional sense, it does so in the discharge and effectuation of its quasi legislative or quasi judicial powers, or as an agency of the legislative or judicial departments of the government.
>
> We think it plain under the Constitution that illimitable power of removal is not possessed by the President in respect of officers of the character of those just named. The authority of Congress, in creating quasi legislative or quasi judicial agencies, to require them to act in discharge of their duties independently of executive control cannot well be doubted; and that authority includes, as an appropriate incident, power to fix the period during which they shall continue, and to forbid their removal except for cause in the meantime. For it is quite evident that one who holds his office only during the pleasure of another cannot be depended upon to maintain an attitude of independence against the latter's will.

In the Court's view, the "coercive influence" of the "power of removal here claimed for the President" "threatens the independence of a commission" that Congress created "as a means of carrying into operation legislative and judicial powers, and as an agency of the legislative and judicial departments." The Court concluded by stating:

> Whether the power of the President to remove an officer shall prevail over the authority of Congress to condition the power by fixing a definite term and precluding a removal except for cause will depend upon the character of the office; the *Myers* decision, affirming the power of the President alone to make the removal, is confined to purely executive officers; and as to officers of the kind here under consideration, we hold that no removal can be made during the prescribed term for which the officer is appointed, except for one or more of the causes named in the applicable statute.

The decisions in *Humphrey's Executor* and *Myers* reflected competing impulses. On the one hand, there might be good reason to immunize certain agency decisions from political interference by the President. It would be problematic, for example, for the President to order the Commissioner of the Internal Revenue Service to audit the President's political enemies. But such an order would be considerably less effective if the Commissioner knew that she could not be fired for refusing to comply. The Court in *Humphrey's Executor* defended this view in referring to the "coercive influence" on agency "independence" of an unfettered presidential removal power.

On the other hand, our commitment to representative government might argue in favor of complete presidential control over officials charged with executing the law. We don't get to vote for the Commissioner of the IRS (or the Attorney General or the Secretary of Health and Human Services), even though those officials have authority to make decisions that can affect our lives. But we do get to vote for the President; and if the President can exercise meaningful control over those officers' decision-making, then we can blame the President when we disagree with their decisions (or reward her with re-election when we agree). The Court in *Myers* defended this view when it declared that the President's "selection of administrative officers is essential to the execution of the laws by him," as is "his power of removing those for whom he cannot continue to be responsible."

The Court in *Myers* advanced what is known as the theory of the unitary executive. The theory holds that, because the Constitution vests the executive power in the President, the President must have control over anyone charged with executing the law. On this view, Congress cannot limit presidential control over anyone charged with executing the law, and therefore can't impose any limits on the President's power to fire such officers.

The Court in *Humphrey's Executor* advanced a different understanding of the President's power to oversee administrative decision-making. The Court defended the idea of the independent agency—that is, an administrative agency that is independent, at least to some degree, of presidential control. In the years before and after the Court's decision, Congress created many agencies whose heads are protected from at-will removal by the President. For example, the President's removal power over the heads of the Central Intelligence Agency, the Federal Communications Commission, and the Securities and Exchange Commission, just to name a few, is limited by statute to cases of good cause (such as corruption or dereliction of duty).

Whatever we can say about the virtues of these competing visions of presidential and congressional power, the law after *Humphrey's Executor* was muddled at best. The Court did not overrule *Myers*; instead, it distinguished it on the ground that postmasters exercised executive power, whereas the Commissioners of the Federal Trade Commission exercised quasi-legislative and quasi-judicial power. According to the Court, whether Congress could restrict the President's power to remove an officer depended on the "character of the office," and the *Myers* rule applied only to officers exercising executive power. But is it obvious to you that postmasters, who oversee the delivery of the mail, exercise executive power, and that the Commissioners of the FTC, which is charged with enforcing laws banning unfair trade practices, exercises some other kind of power? (In any event, can Congress constitutionally give legislative or judicial power to a federal agency?)

**FYI**

President Nixon had permitted his Attorney General to appoint a special prosecutor to investigate wrongdoing by the President and close campaign associates in connection with the Watergate scandal. When it appeared that the prosecutor might uncover serious crimes, Nixon ordered the Attorney General to fire him. In the infamous "Saturday Night Massacre," the top two officials at the Department of Justice resigned rather than fire the special prosecutor. Nixon then prevailed upon Robert Bork, who at time was the Solicitor General, to fire him.

The Court again addressed the appropriate scope of the President's removal power in *Morrison v. Olson*, 487 U.S. 654 (1988). The case involved a challenge to the independent counsel provisions of the Ethics in Government Act of 1978, which Congress enacted in the wake of the Watergate scandal and President Nixon's decision to order the removal of a special prosecutor investigating wrongdoing by the President and his close associates.

The statute required the Attorney General to conduct a preliminary investigation after learning of possible misconduct by certain executive branch officials. If the investigation produced reasonable grounds to believe that a high-ranking official might have violated the law, the statute required the Attorney General to ask a special division of the United States Court of Appeals for the D.C. Circuit to appoint an independent counsel to investigate and perhaps prosecute the official. In *Morrison*, an independent counsel was investigating whether Ted Olson, an Assistant Attorney General, had testified truthfully to Congress in a dispute over the invocation of executive privilege. Olson challenged the authority of the independent counsel on the ground that the provisions of the Act that governed her appointment and removal were unconstitutional.

Under the statute, a panel of three judges, rather than the Attorney General or the President, appointed the independent counsel. The Attorney General had authority to fire the independent counsel, but only "for good cause, physical disability, mental incapacity, or other condition that substantially impairs the performance of such independent counsel's duties." The Court held that the removal provisions did not violate the Constitution.

The Court began by noting that, unlike *Myers*, "this case does not involve an attempt by Congress itself to gain a role in the removal of executive officials other than its established powers of impeachment and conviction." Accordingly, the Court stated that "the removal provisions of the Act make this case more analogous to *Humphrey's Executor* than to *Myers*." The Court then responded to Olson's argument that the "decision in *Humphrey's Executor* rests on a distinction between 'purely executive' officials and officials who exercise 'quasi-legislative' and 'quasi-judicial' powers." (Olson argued that "when a 'purely executive' official is involved, the governing precedent is *Myers*, not *Humphrey's Executor*," and that "under *Myers*, the President must have absolute discretion to discharge 'purely' executive officials at will.") The Court stated:

> We undoubtedly did rely on the terms "quasi-legislative" and "quasi-judicial" to distinguish the officials involved in *Humphrey's Executor* [from] those in *Myers*, but our present considered view is that the determination of whether the Constitution allows Congress to impose a "good cause"-type restriction on the President's power to remove an official cannot be made to turn on whether or not that official is classified as "purely executive." The analysis contained in our removal cases is designed not to define rigid categories of those officials who may or may not be removed at will by the President, but to ensure that Congress does not interfere with the President's exercise of the "executive power" and his constitutionally appointed duty to "take care that the laws be faithfully executed" under Article II. *Myers* was undoubtedly correct in its holding, and in its broader suggestion that there are some "purely executive" officials who must be removable by the President at will if he is to be able to accomplish his constitutional role. * * * At the other end of the spectrum[,] the characterization of the [agency] in *Humphrey's Executor* [as] "quasi-legislative" or "quasi-judicial" in large part reflected our judgment that it was not essential to the President's proper execution of his Article II powers that these agencies be headed up by individuals who were removable at will. We do not mean to suggest that an analysis of the functions served by the officials at issue is irrelevant. But the real question is whether the removal restrictions are of such a nature that they impede the President's ability to perform his constitutional duty, and the functions of the officials in question must be analyzed in that light.

The Court acknowledged that "the functions performed by the independent counsel are 'executive' in the sense that they are law enforcement functions that typically have been undertaken by officials within the Executive Branch." But the Court concluded that the "imposition of a 'good cause' standard for removal [did not] unduly trammel[ ] on executive authority." The Court explained:

> [T]he independent counsel is an inferior officer under the Appointments Clause, with limited jurisdiction and tenure and lacking policymaking or significant administrative

> authority. Although the counsel exercises no small amount of discretion and judgment in deciding how to carry out his or her duties under the Act, we simply do not see how the President's need to control the exercise of that discretion is so central to the functioning of the Executive Branch as to require as a matter of constitutional law that the counsel be terminable at will by the President.

Justice Scalia was alone in dissent. He asserted:

> * * * Article II, § 1, cl. 1, of the Constitution provides: "The executive Power shall be vested in a President of the United States." This does not mean *some of* the executive power, but *all of* the executive power. It seems to me, therefore, that the decision of the Court of Appeals invalidating the present statute must be upheld on fundamental separation-of-powers principles if the following two questions are answered affirmatively: (1) Is the conduct of a criminal prosecution (and of an investigation to decide whether to prosecute) the exercise of purely executive power? (2) Does the statute deprive the President of the United States of exclusive control over the exercise of that power? Surprising to say, the Court appears to concede an affirmative answer to both questions, but seeks to avoid the inevitable conclusion that since the statute vests some purely executive power in a person who is not the President of the United States it is void.
>
> Governmental investigation and prosecution of crimes is a quintessentially executive function. As for the second question, whether the statute before us deprives the President of exclusive control over that quintessentially executive activity: * * * That is indeed the whole object of the statute. * * * [I]t is ultimately irrelevant *how much* the statute reduces Presidential control. * * * It is not for us to determine, and we have never presumed to determine, how much of the purely executive powers of government must be within the full control of the President. The Constitution prescribes that they *all* are.

Justice Scalia criticized the Court for replacing "the clear constitutional prescription that the executive power belongs to the President with a 'balancing test.' " He asked:

> What are the standards to determine how the balance is to be struck, that is, how much removal of Presidential power is too much? * * * Once we depart from the text of the Constitution, just where short of that do we stop? The most amazing feature of the Court's opinion is that it does not even purport to give an answer. It simply announces, with no analysis, that the ability to control the decision whether to investigate and prosecute the President's closest advisers, and indeed the President himself, is not "so central to the functioning of the Executive Branch" as to be constitutionally required to be within the President's control. * * * Evidently, the governing standard is to be what might be called the unfettered wisdom of a majority of this Court, revealed to an obedient people on a case-by-case basis. This is not only not the government of laws that the Constitution established; it is not a government of laws at all.

After *Morrison*, the rule seemed to be that Congress could not assign to itself the power to remove an officer (other than by impeachment), see, e.g., *Bowsher v. Synar*, 478 U.S. 714 (1986) (invalidating statute that vested executive power in an officer subject to removal by Congress), but that Congress could limit the President's power to remove an officer as long as the removal limitation did not "impede the President's ability to perform his constitutional duty." Under this test, there likely were some officials—such as the Secretary of State—whose responsibilities were so important to the President's ability to do his job that Congress could not restrict the President's power to remove the official. But by upholding the removal limitations at issue, the Court reaffirmed the constitutional validity of independent agencies.

But what exactly do we mean by an "independent agency"? We noted above that some agencies, by virtue of a limit on the President's power to fire the agencies' heads, are independent of presidential control. But are removal limitations the only thing that might make an agency "independent"? And are all other agencies properly thought of as "executive" agencies, in the sense that the President, as the head of the executive branch, has unfettered control over them? Consider the view that follows.

---

## Perspective and Analysis

Underlying * * * almost all discussions [of] independent agencies are three fundamental assumptions. First, agencies can be divided into two identifiable, distinct sets: independent and executive. Second, the presence of certain characteristics defines the members of each set. And third, those characteristics justify the accompanying legal rules governing the President's ability to interact with each type of agency. These assumptions are incorrect.

Agencies cannot be neatly divided into two categories. Independent agencies are almost always defined as agencies with a for-cause removal provision limiting the President's power to remove the agencies' heads to cases of "inefficiency, neglect of duty, or malfeasance in office." But [the] so-called independent agencies do not share a single form. This Article * * * systematically survey[s] the enabling statutes of both independent and executive agencies for a broad set of indicia of independence: removal protection, specified tenure, multimember structure, partisan balance requirements, litigation authority, budget and congressional communication authority, and adjudication authority. It finds that there is no single feature—not even a for-cause removal provision—that every agency commonly thought of as independent shares. Moreover, many agencies generally considered to be executive agencies exhibit at least some structural attributes of independence. * * *

Instead of falling into two categories, agencies fall along a continuum. * * * The continuum ranges from most insulated to least insulated from presidential control. * * * The continuum view provides a simple answer to questions of whether the President can take a certain action with respect to an agency: straightforward statutory interpretation. The President can take any action toward an agency that is within the scope of his Article II powers unless an agency's enabling statute prohibits such action. The President's ability to gain compliance by the agency will vary based on what features the agency's enabling statute contains. For example, it will be easier for the President to secure compliance if he can threaten to fire the agency head, credibly threaten to reduce the agency's budget request during the next budget cycle, or have his Justice Department refuse to represent the agency in litigation before the federal courts. The outer bounds of presidential power (or powerlessness) are set by the Constitution. Congress cannot insulate an agency to the point where the President cannot perform his Article II duties. Similarly, the President cannot go beyond his Article II powers when interacting with an agency. But beyond those Article II issues, other questions can and should be resolved through basic statutory interpretation.

**Kirti Datla & Richard L. Revesz, *Deconstructing Independent Agencies (and Executive Agencies)*, 98 CORNELL L. REV. 769 (2013).**

---

The Court's decision in *Morrison* was not the last word on the validity of limitations on the President's power to remove an officer. In *Free Enterprise Fund v. Public Company Accounting Oversight Board*, 561 U.S. 477 (2010), the Court considered a challenge to the structure of the Public Company Accounting Oversight Board, which Congress created in 2002 to supervise the accounting industry. As originally structured, the Board had five members, appointed to 5-year terms by the Securities and Exchange Commission (SEC). The SEC had supervisory authority over the Board's functions, but it could remove Board members only "for good cause shown," including willful violation of the Act, willful abuse of authority, or failing to enforce compliance with applicable rule and standards. The Commissioners of the SEC had similar protection for their positions.

The question for the Court was "whether these separate layers of protection may be combined." Stated another way, "May the President be restricted in his ability to remove a principal officer, who is in turn restricted in his ability to remove an inferior officer, even though that inferior officer determines the policy and enforces the laws of the United States?" The Court held, in a 5–4 decision, that "such multilevel protection from removal is contrary to Article II's vesting of the executive power in the President." The Court explained:

> The President cannot "take Care that the Laws be faithfully executed" if he cannot oversee the faithfulness of the officers who execute them. Here the President cannot remove an officer who enjoys more than one level of good-cause protection, even if the President determines that the officer is neglecting his duties or discharging them improperly. That judgment is instead committed to another officer, who may or may not agree with the President's determination, and whom the President cannot remove simply because that officer disagrees with him. This contravenes the President's

"constitutional obligation to ensure the faithful execution of the laws." *Morrison*, 487 U.S. at 693.

The Court acknowledged that it had "previously upheld limited restrictions on the President's removal power [in *Humphrey's Executor* and *Morrison*]. In those cases, however, only one level of protected tenure separated the President from an officer exercising executive power. It was the President—or a subordinate he could remove at will—who decided whether the officer's conduct merited removal under the good-cause standard." The statute in question, however, did "something quite different":

> It not only protects Board members from removal except for good cause, but withdraws from the President any decision on whether that good cause exists. That decision is vested instead in other tenured officers—the Commissioners—none of whom is subject to the President's direct control. The result is a Board that is not accountable to the President, and a President who is not responsible for the Board.
>
> The added layer of tenure protection makes a difference. Without a layer of insulation between the Commission and the Board, the Commission could remove a Board member at any time, and therefore would be fully responsible for what the Board does. The President could then hold the Commission to account for its supervision of the Board, to the same extent that he may hold the Commission to account for everything else it does. * * *
>
> This novel structure does not merely add to the Board's independence, but transforms it. Neither the President, nor anyone directly responsible to him, nor even an officer whose conduct he may review only for good cause, has full control over the Board. The President is stripped of the power our precedents have preserved, and his ability to execute the laws—by holding his subordinates accountable for their conduct—is impaired. That arrangement is contrary to Article II's vesting of the executive power in the President.

The Court's explanation for why the Constitution prohibits multi-level layers of protection from removal could easily have applied as well to one layer of removal limitations:

> The diffusion of power carries with it a diffusion of accountability. The people do not vote for the "Officers of the United States." Art. II, § 2, cl. 2. They instead look to the President to guide the "assistants or deputies . . . subject to his superintendence." The Federalist No. 72, p. 487 (J. Cooke ed. 1961) (A. Hamilton). Without a clear and effective chain of command, the public cannot "determine on whom the blame or the punishment of a pernicious measure, or series of pernicious measures ought really to fall." *Id.*, No. 70, at 476 (same). That is why the Framers sought to ensure that "those who are employed in the execution of the law will be in their proper situation, and the chain of dependence be preserved; the lowest officers, the middle grade, and the highest, will depend, as they ought, on the President, and the President on the community." 1 Annals of Cong., at 499 (J. Madison).

To cure the constitutional problem, the Court invalidated the tenure protections for members of the Board, leaving only one layer of good-cause protection.

Justice Breyer, joined by Justices Stevens, Ginsburg, and Sotomayor, dissented. He noted that the constitutional text does not speak to the question presented, that the question never came up at the Constitutional Convention, and that the Court's precedents did not "fully answer" it. Accordingly, he focused on how multi-level tenure protections were "likely to function" in practice. He concluded that the removal restriction "will not restrict presidential power significantly." He reasoned:

> [T]he restriction directly limits, not the President's power, but the power of an already independent agency. The Court seems to have forgotten that fact when it identifies its central constitutional problem: According to the Court, the President "is powerless to intervene" if he has determined that the Board members' "conduct merit[s] removal" because "[t]hat decision is vested instead in other tenured officers—the Commissioners—none of whom is subject to the President's direct control." But so long as the President is *legitimately* foreclosed from removing the [SEC] *Commissioners* except for cause (as the majority assumes), nullifying the Commission's power to remove Board members only for cause will not resolve the problem the Court has identified: The President will *still* be "powerless to intervene" by removing the Board members if the Commission reasonably decides not to do so.
>
> In other words, the Court fails to show why *two* layers of "for cause" protection—Layer One insulating the Commissioners from the President, and Layer Two insulating the Board from the Commissioners—impose any more serious limitation upon the *President's* powers than *one* layer.

The Court addressed that underlying question in the case that follows.

---

## *Seila Law LLC v. Consumer Financial Protection Bureau*

140 S.Ct. 2183 (2020)

CHIEF JUSTICE ROBERTS delivered the opinion of the Court with respect to Parts I, II, and III.

### I

[In the wake of the 2008 financial crisis, Congress established the Consumer Financial Protection Bureau (CFPB).] Congress tasked the CFPB with "implement[ing]" and "enforc[ing]" a large body of financial consumer protection laws to "ensur[e] that all consumers have access to markets for consumer financial products and services and that markets for consumer financial products and services are fair, transparent, and competitive." 12 U.S.C. § 5511(a). Congress transferred the administration of 18 existing federal statutes to the CFPB, including the Fair Credit

Reporting Act, the Fair Debt Collection Practices Act, and the Truth in Lending Act. See §§ 5512(a), 5481(12), (14). In addition, Congress enacted a new prohibition on "any unfair, deceptive, or abusive act or practice" by certain participants in the consumer-finance sector. § 5536(a)(1)(B). Congress authorized the CFPB to implement that broad standard (and the 18 pre-existing statutes placed under the agency's purview) through binding regulations. §§ 5531(a)–(b), 5581(a)(1)(A), (b).

Congress also vested the CFPB with potent enforcement powers. The agency has the authority to conduct investigations, issue subpoenas and civil investigative demands, initiate administrative adjudications, and prosecute civil actions in federal court. §§ 5562, 5564(a), (f). To remedy violations of federal consumer financial law, the CFPB may seek restitution, disgorgement, and injunctive relief, as well as civil penalties of up to $1,000,000 (inflation adjusted) for each day that a violation occurs. §§ 5565(a), (c)(2); 12 CFR § 1083.1(a), Table (2019). Since its inception, the CFPB has obtained over $11 billion in relief for over 25 million consumers, including a $1 billion penalty against a single bank in 2018.

The CFPB's rulemaking and enforcement powers are coupled with extensive adjudicatory authority. The agency may conduct administrative proceedings to "ensure or enforce compliance with" the statutes and regulations it administers. 12 U. S. C. § 5563(a). When the CFPB acts as an adjudicator, it has "jurisdiction to grant any appropriate legal or equitable relief." § 5565(a)(1). * * *

* * * Rather than create a traditional independent agency headed by a multimember board or commission, Congress elected to place the CFPB under the leadership of a single Director. 12 U.S.C. § 5491(b)(1). The CFPB Director is appointed by the President with the advice and consent of the Senate. § 5491(b)(2). The Director serves for a term of five years, during which the President may remove the Director from office only for "inefficiency, neglect of duty, or malfeasance in office." §§ 5491(c)(1), (3).

Seila Law LLC is a California-based law firm that provides debt-related legal services to clients. In 2017, the CFPB issued a civil investigative demand to Seila Law to determine whether the firm had "engag[ed] in unlawful acts or practices in the advertising, marketing, or sale of debt relief services." The demand (essentially a subpoena) directed Seila Law to produce information and documents related to its business practices. Seila Law

**Take Note**

In arguing this case at the U.S. Court of Appeals for the Ninth Circuit, government lawyers successfully contended that the CFPB's structure was constitutional. But when Seila Law sought certiorari at the Supreme Court, the Solicitor General (from a new Presidential Administration) chose to side with Seila Law and filed a response supporting the grant of certiorari and arguing that the CFPB's structure was unconstitutional. In response, the Supreme Court invited Paul Clement, a former Solicitor General who had previously argued 95 cases before the Supreme Court, to file an *amicus curiae* brief to defend the constitutionality of the agency.

asked the CFPB to set aside the demand, objecting that the agency's leadership by a single Director removable only for cause violated the separation of powers. The CFPB declined to address that claim and directed Seila Law to comply with the demand. [When the CFPB sued Seila Law to enforce the demand, the District Court and Court of Appeals rejected Seila's constitutional challenges.]

## II

[The Court held in Part II that Seila Law had standing to challenge the structure of the CFPB.]

## III

We hold that the CFPB's leadership by a single individual removable only for inefficiency, neglect, or malfeasance violates the separation of powers.

Article II provides that "[t]he executive Power shall be vested in a President," who must "take Care that the Laws be faithfully executed." Art. II, § 1, cl. 1; *id.*, § 3. The entire "executive Power" belongs to the President alone. But because it would be "impossib[le]" for "one man" to "perform all the great business of the State," the Constitution assumes that lesser executive officers will "assist the supreme Magistrate in discharging the duties of his trust." 30 Writings of George Washington 334 (J. Fitzpatrick ed. 1939).

These lesser officers must remain accountable to the President, whose authority they wield. As Madison explained, "[I]f any power whatsoever is in its nature Executive, it is the power of appointing, overseeing, and controlling those who execute the laws." 1 Annals of Cong. 463 (1789). That power, in turn, generally includes the ability to remove executive officials, for it is "only the authority that can remove" such officials that they "must fear and, in the performance of [their] functions, obey." *Bowsher v. Synar*, 478 U.S. 714, 726 (1986).

The President's removal power has long been confirmed by history and precedent. It "was discussed extensively in Congress when the first executive departments were created" in 1789. *Free Enterprise Fund v. Public Company Accounting Oversight Bd.*, 561 U.S. 477, 492 (2010). "The view that 'prevailed, as most consonant to the text of the Constitution' and 'to the requisite responsibility and harmony in the Executive Department,' was that the executive power included a power to oversee executive officers through removal." *Ibid.* (quoting Letter from James Madison to Thomas Jefferson (June 30, 1789), 16 Documentary History of the First Federal Congress 893 (2004)). The First Congress's recognition of the President's removal power in 1789 "provides contemporaneous and weighty evidence of the Constitution's meaning," *Bowsher*, 478 U.S., at 723, and has long been the "settled and well understood construction of the Constitution," *Ex parte Hennen*, 13 Pet. 230, 259 (1839).

The Court recognized the President's prerogative to remove executive officials in *Myers v. United States*, 272 U.S. 52 (1926). Chief Justice Taft, writing for the Court, conducted an exhaustive examination of the First Congress's determination in 1789, the views of the Framers and their contemporaries, historical practice, and our precedents up until that point. He concluded that Article II "grants to the President" the "general administrative control of those executing the laws, including the power of appointment *and removal* of executive officers." Just as the President's "selection of administrative officers is essential to the execution of the laws by him, so must be his power of removing those for whom he cannot continue to be responsible." *Id.*, at 117. "[T]o hold otherwise," the Court reasoned, "would make it impossible for the President . . . to take care that the laws be faithfully executed." *Id.*, at 164.

We recently reiterated the President's general removal power in *Free Enterprise Fund*. "Since 1789," we recapped, "the Constitution has been understood to empower the President to keep these officers accountable—by removing them from office, if necessary." 561 U.S., at 483. Although we had previously sustained congressional limits on that power in certain circumstances, we declined to extend those limits to "a new situation not yet encountered by the Court"—an official insulated by *two* layers of for-cause removal protection. *Id.*, at 483.

*Free Enterprise Fund* left in place two exceptions to the President's unrestricted removal power. First, in *Humphrey's Executor*, decided less than a decade after *Myers*, the Court upheld a statute that protected the Commissioners of the FTC from removal except for "inefficiency, neglect of duty, or malfeasance in office." 295 U.S. 602, 620 (1935). In reaching that conclusion, the Court stressed that Congress's ability to impose such removal restrictions "will depend upon the character of the office." 295 U.S. at 631.

Because the Court limited its holding "to officers of the kind here under consideration," *id.*, at 632, the contours of the *Humphrey's Executor* exception depend upon the characteristics of the agency before the Court. Rightly or wrongly, the Court viewed the FTC (as it existed in 1935) as exercising "no part of the executive power." *Id.*, at 628. Instead, it was "an administrative body" that performed "specified duties as a legislative or as a judicial aid." *Ibid.* It acted "as a legislative agency" in "making investigations and reports" to Congress and "as an agency of the judiciary" in making recommendations to courts as a master in chancery. *Ibid.* "To the extent that [the FTC] exercise[d] any executive *function*[,] as distinguished from executive *power* in the constitutional sense," it did so only in the discharge of its "quasi-legislative or quasi-judicial powers." *Ibid.* (emphasis added).

The Court identified several organizational features that helped explain its characterization of the FTC as non-executive. Composed of five members—no more than three from the same political party—the Board was designed to be "non-partisan" and to "act with entire impartiality." *Id.*, at 624, 619–620. The FTC's duties were "neither political nor executive," but instead called for "the trained judgment of a body of experts" "informed by experience." *Id.*, at 624. And the Commissioners' staggered, seven-year terms enabled the agency to accumulate technical expertise and avoid a "complete change" in leadership "at any one time." *Ibid.*

In short, *Humphrey's Executor* permitted Congress to give for-cause removal protections to a multimember body of experts, balanced along partisan lines, that performed legislative and judicial functions and was said not to exercise any executive power. Consistent with that understanding, the Court later applied "[t]he philosophy of *Humphrey's Executor*" to uphold for-cause removal protections for the members of the War Claims Commission—a three-member "adjudicatory body" tasked with resolving claims for compensation arising from World War II. *Wiener v. United States*, 357 U.S. 349, 356 (1958).

While recognizing an exception for multimember bodies with "quasi-judicial" or "quasi-legislative" functions, *Humphrey's Executor* reaffirmed the core holding of *Myers* that the President has "unrestrictable power . . . to remove purely executive officers." 295 U.S. at 632. The Court acknowledged that between purely executive officers on the one hand, and officers that closely resembled the FTC Commissioners on the other, there existed "a field of doubt" that the Court left "for future consideration." *Ibid.*

We have recognized a second exception for *inferior* officers in two cases, *United States v. Perkins*, 116 U.S. 483 (1886), and *Morrison v. Olson*, 487 U.S. 654 (1988). In *Perkins*, we upheld tenure protections for a naval cadet-engineer. And, in *Morrison*, we upheld a provision granting good-cause tenure protection to an independent counsel appointed to investigate and prosecute particular alleged crimes by high-ranking Government officials. Backing away from the reliance in *Humphrey's Executor* on the concepts of "quasi-legislative" and "quasi-judicial" power, we viewed the ultimate question as whether a removal restriction is of "such a nature that [it] impede[s] the President's ability to perform his constitutional duty." 487 U.S. at 691. Although the independent counsel was a single person and performed "law enforcement functions that typically have been undertaken by officials within the Executive Branch," we concluded that the removal protections did not unduly interfere with the functioning of the Executive Branch because "the independent counsel [was] an inferior officer under the Appointments Clause, with limited jurisdiction and tenure and lacking policymaking or significant administrative authority." *Ibid.*

**Food for Thought**

Does the Court's description of the Court's holding and reasoning in *Morrison* reflect your understanding of the case? Or did the Court in *Morrison* have a more flexible understanding of congressional power to restrict the President's power to remove officials?

These two exceptions—one for multimember expert agencies that do not wield substantial executive power, and one for inferior officers with limited duties and no policymaking or administrative authority—"represent what up to now have been the outermost constitutional limits of permissible congressional restrictions on the President's removal power." *PHH Corp. v. CFPB*, 881 F.3d 75, 196 (D.C. Cir. 2018) (Kavanaugh, J., dissenting).

Neither *Humphrey's Executor* nor *Morrison* resolves whether the CFPB Director's insulation from removal is constitutional. Start with *Humphrey's Executor*. Unlike the New Deal-era FTC upheld there, the CFPB is led by a single Director who cannot be described as a "body of experts" and cannot be considered "non-partisan" in the same sense as a group of officials drawn from both sides of the aisle. 295 U.S. at 624. Moreover, while the staggered terms of the FTC Commissioners prevented complete turnovers in agency leadership and guaranteed that there would always be some Commissioners who had accrued significant expertise, the CFPB's single-Director structure and five-year term guarantee abrupt shifts in agency leadership and with it the loss of accumulated expertise.

In addition, the CFPB Director is hardly a mere legislative or judicial aid. Instead of making reports and recommendations to Congress, as the 1935 FTC did, the Director possesses the authority to promulgate binding rules fleshing out 19 federal statutes, including a broad prohibition on unfair and deceptive practices in a major segment of the U.S. economy. And instead of submitting recommended dispositions to an Article III court, the Director may unilaterally issue final decisions awarding legal and equitable relief in administrative adjudications. Finally, the Director's enforcement authority includes the power to seek daunting monetary penalties against private parties on behalf of the United States in federal court—a quintessentially executive power not considered in *Humphrey's Executor*.

**Make the Connection**

Decision-makers at agencies do not enjoy the same protections as federal judges and might be influenced by political or partisan concerns. Should we be troubled by an agency's exercising the power to "issue final decisions awarding legal and equitable relief in administrative adjudications"? We will consider that question later in this Chapter.

The logic of *Morrison* also does not apply. Everyone agrees the CFPB Director is not an inferior officer, and her duties are far from limited. Unlike the independent counsel, who lacked policymaking or administrative authority, the Director has the sole responsibility to administer 19 separate consumer-protection statutes that cover everything from credit cards and car payments to mortgages and student loans. It is true that the independent counsel in *Morrison* was empowered to initiate criminal investigations and prosecutions, and in that respect wielded core executive power. But that power, while significant, was trained inward to high-ranking Governmental actors identified by others, and was confined to a specified matter in which the

Department of Justice had a potential conflict of interest. By contrast, the CFPB Director has the authority to bring the coercive power of the state to bear on millions of private citizens and businesses, imposing even billion-dollar penalties through administrative adjudications and civil actions.

In light of these differences, the constitutionality of the CFPB Director's insulation from removal cannot be settled by *Humphrey's Executor* or *Morrison* alone.

The question instead is whether to extend those precedents to the "new situation" before us, namely an independent agency led by a single Director and vested with significant executive power. *Free Enterprise Fund*, 561 U.S., at 483. We decline to do so. Such an agency has no basis in history and no place in our constitutional structure.

After years of litigating the agency's constitutionality, the Courts of Appeals, parties, and *amici* have identified "only a handful of isolated" incidents in which Congress has provided good-cause tenure to principal officers who wield power alone rather than as members of a board or commission. *Ibid.* "[T]hese few scattered examples"—four to be exact—shed little light. *NLRB v. Noel Canning*, 573 U.S. 513, 538 (2014).

First, the CFPB's defenders point to the Comptroller of the Currency, who enjoyed removal protection for *one year* during the Civil War. That example has rightly been dismissed as an aberration. It was "adopted without discussion" during the heat of the Civil War and abandoned before it could be "tested by executive or judicial inquiry." *Myers*, 272 U.S., at 165.

Second, the supporters of the CFPB point to the Office of the Special Counsel (OSC), which has been headed by a single officer since 1978. But this first enduring single-leader office, created nearly 200 years after the Constitution was ratified, drew a contemporaneous constitutional objection from the Office of Legal Counsel under President Carter and a subsequent veto on constitutional grounds by President Reagan. In any event, the OSC exercises only limited jurisdiction to enforce certain rules governing Federal Government employers and employees. It does not bind private parties at all or wield regulatory authority comparable to the CFPB.

Third, the CFPB's defenders note that the Social Security Administration (SSA) has been run by a single Administrator since 1994. That example, too, is comparatively recent and controversial. President Clinton questioned the constitutionality of the SSA's new single-Director structure upon signing it into law. In addition, unlike the CFPB, the SSA lacks the authority to bring enforcement actions against private parties. Its role is largely limited to adjudicating claims for Social Security benefits.

The only remaining example is the Federal Housing Finance Agency (FHFA), created in 2008 to assume responsibility for Fannie Mae and Freddie Mac. It regulates primarily Government-sponsored enterprises, not purely private actors. And its single-Director structure is a source of ongoing controversy. Indeed, it was recently held unconstitutional by the Fifth Circuit, sitting en banc. *See Collins v. Mnuchin*, 938 F.3d 553, 587–588 (2019).

The Framers deemed an energetic executive essential to "the protection of the community against foreign attacks," "the steady administration of the laws," "the protection of property," and "the security of liberty." [The Federalist No. 70, at 475 (A. Hamilton)] No. 70, at 471. Accordingly, they chose not to bog the Executive down with the "habitual feebleness and dilatoriness" that comes with a "diversity of views and opinions." *Id.*, at 476. Instead, they gave the Executive the "[d]ecision, activity, secrecy, and dispatch" that "characterise the proceedings of one man." *Id.*, at 472.

To justify and check *that* authority—unique in our constitutional structure—the Framers made the President the most democratic and politically accountable official in Government. Only the President (along with the Vice President) is elected by the entire Nation. And the President's political accountability is enhanced by the solitary nature of the Executive Branch, which provides "a single object for the jealousy and watchfulness of the people." *Id.*, at 479. The President "cannot delegate ultimate responsibility or the active obligation to supervise that goes with it," because Article II "makes a single President responsible for the actions of the Executive Branch." *Free Enterprise Fund*, 561 U.S., at 496–497 (quoting *Clinton v. Jones*, 520 U.S. 681, 712–713 (1997) (Breyer, J., concurring in judgment)).

**Food for Thought**

Under the Court's reasoning, should restrictions on the President's power to remove Commissioners of a multi-member body such as the Federal Trade Commission be unconstitutional, as well?

The CFPB's single-Director structure contravenes this carefully calibrated system by vesting significant governmental power in the hands of a single individual accountable to no one. The Director is neither elected by the people nor meaningfully controlled (through the threat of removal) by someone who is. * * * Yet the Director may *unilaterally*, without meaningful supervision, issue final regulations, oversee adjudications, set enforcement priorities, initiate prosecutions, and determine what penalties to impose on private parties. With no colleagues to persuade, and no boss or electorate looking over her shoulder, the Director may dictate and enforce policy for a vital segment of the economy affecting millions of Americans.

Because the CFPB is headed by a single Director with a five-year term, some Presidents may not have any opportunity to shape its leadership and thereby influence its activities. A President elected in 2020 would likely not appoint a CFPB Director until 2023, and a President elected in 2028 may *never* appoint one. That means an unlucky President might get elected on a consumer-protection platform and enter office only to find herself saddled with a holdover Director from a competing political party who is dead set *against* that agenda. To make matters worse, the agency's single-Director structure means the President will not have the opportunity to appoint any other leaders—such as a chair or fellow members of a Commission or Board—who can serve as a check on the Director's authority and help bring the agency in line with the President's preferred policies.

### IV

* * * The provisions of the Dodd-Frank Act bearing on the CFPB's structure and duties remain fully operative without the offending tenure restriction. Those provisions are capable of functioning independently, and there is nothing in the text or history of the Dodd-Frank Act that demonstrates Congress would have preferred *no* CFPB to a CFPB supervised by the President. Quite the opposite. [T]he Dodd-Frank Act contains an express severability clause. There is no need to wonder what Congress would have wanted if "any provision of this Act" is "held to be unconstitutional" because it has told us: "the remainder of this Act" should "not be affected." 12 U.S.C. § 5302.

Because we find the Director's removal protection severable from the other provisions of Dodd-Frank that establish the CFPB, we remand for the Court of Appeals to consider whether the civil investigative demand was validly ratified.

JUSTICE THOMAS, with whom JUSTICE GORSUCH joins, concurring in part and dissenting in part.

Continued reliance on *Humphrey's Executor* to justify the existence of independent agencies creates a serious, ongoing threat to our Government's design. Leaving these unconstitutional agencies in place does not enhance this Court's legitimacy; it subverts political accountability and threatens individual liberty. We have a "responsibility to 'examin[e] without fear, and revis[e] without reluctance,' any 'hasty and crude decisions' rather than leaving 'the character of [the] law impaired, and the beauty and harmony of the [American constitutional] system destroyed by the perpetuity of error.' " *Gamble v. United States*, 139 S.Ct. 1960, 1984 (2019) (THOMAS, J., concurring) (quoting 1 J. Kent, Commentaries on American Law 444 (1826)). We simply cannot compromise when it comes to our Government's structure. Today, the Court does enough to resolve this case, but in the future, we should reconsider *Humphrey's Executor in toto.* And I hope that we will have the will to do so.

While I think that the Court correctly resolves the merits of the constitutional question, I do not agree with its decision to sever the removal restriction in 12 U.S.C. § 5491(c)(3). To resolve this case, I would simply deny the Consumer Financial Protection Bureau (CFPB) petition to enforce the civil investigative demand.

Because the power of judicial review does not allow courts to revise statutes, the Court's severability doctrine must be rooted in statutory interpretation. But, even viewing severability as an interpretive question, I remain skeptical of our doctrine. As I have previously explained, "the severability doctrine often requires courts to weigh in on statutory provisions that no party has standing to challenge, bringing courts dangerously close to issuing advisory opinions." *Murphy v. NCAA*, 138 S.Ct. 1461, 1487 (2018) (concurring opinion). And the application of the doctrine "does not follow basic principles of statutory interpretation." *Id.*, at 1486. Instead of determining the meaning of a statute's text, severability involves "nebulous inquir[ies] into hypothetical congressional intent." *United States v. Booker*, 543 U.S. 220, 320, n. 7 (THOMAS, J., dissenting in part).

JUSTICE KAGAN, with whom JUSTICE GINSBURG, JUSTICE BREYER, and JUSTICE SOTOMAYOR join, concurring in the judgment with respect to severability and dissenting in part.

The text of the Constitution, the history of the country, the precedents of this Court, and the need for sound and adaptable governance—all stand against the majority's opinion. They point not to the majority's "general rule" of "unrestricted removal power" with two grudgingly applied "exceptions." Rather, they bestow discretion on the legislature to structure administrative institutions as the times demand, so long as the President retains the ability to carry out his constitutional duties. And most relevant here, they give Congress wide leeway to limit the President's removal power in the interest of enhancing independence from politics in regulatory bodies like the CFPB.

What does the Constitution say about the separation of powers—and particularly about the President's removal authority? (Spoiler alert: about the latter, nothing at all.) * * * It is of course true that the Framers lodged three different kinds of power in three different entities. And that they did so for a crucial purpose—because, as James Madison wrote, "there can be no liberty where the legislative and executive powers are united in the same person[ ] or body" or where "the power of judging [is] not separated from the legislative and executive powers." The Federalist No. 47, p. 325 (J. Cooke ed. 1961) (quoting Baron de Montesquieu).

The problem lies * * * in failing to recognize that the separation of powers is, by design, neither rigid nor complete. Blackstone, whose work influenced the Framers on this subject as on others, observed that "every branch" of government "supports and is supported, regulates and is regulated, by the rest." 1 W. Blackstone, Commentaries on the Laws of England 151 (1765). So as James Madison stated, the creation of distinct branches "did not mean that these departments ought to have no partial agency in, or no controul over the acts of each other." The Federalist No. 47, at 325 (emphasis deleted). To the contrary, Madison explained, the drafters of the Constitution—like those of then-existing state constitutions—opted against keeping the branches of government "absolutely separate and distinct." *Id.*, at 327. Or as Justice Story reiterated a half-century later: "[W]hen we speak of a separation of the three great departments of government," it is "not meant to affirm, that they must be kept wholly and entirely separate." 2 J. Story, Commentaries on the Constitution of the United States § 524,

p. 8 (1833). Instead, the branches have—as they must for the whole arrangement to work—"common link[s] of connexion [and] dependence." *Ibid.*

One way the Constitution reflects that vision is by giving Congress broad authority to establish and organize the Executive Branch. Article II presumes the existence of "Officer[s]" in "executive Departments." § 2, cl. 1. But it does not, as you might think from reading the majority opinion, give the President authority to decide what kinds of officers—in what departments, with what responsibilities—the Executive Branch requires. Instead, Article I's Necessary and Proper Clause puts those decisions in the legislature's hands. Congress has the power "[t]o make all Laws which shall be necessary and proper for carrying into Execution" not just its own enumerated powers but also "all other Powers vested by this Constitution in the Government of the United States, or in any Department or Officer thereof." § 8, cl. 18. Similarly, the Appointments Clause reflects Congress's central role in structuring the Executive Branch. Yes, the President can appoint principal officers, but only as the legislature "shall . . . establish[ ] by Law" (and of course subject to the Senate's advice and consent). Art. II, § 2, cl. 2. And Congress has plenary power to decide not only what inferior officers will exist but also who (the President or a head of department) will appoint them. So as Madison told the first Congress, the legislature gets to "create[ ] the office, define[ ] the powers, [and] limit[ ] its duration." 1 Annals of Cong. 582 (1789). The President, as to the construction of his own branch of government, can only try to work his will through the legislative process.

The majority relies for its contrary vision on Article II's Vesting Clause, but the provision can't carry all that weight. Or as Chief Justice Rehnquist wrote of a similar claim in *Morrison v. Olson*, 487 U.S. 654, (1988), "extrapolat[ing]" an unrestricted removal power from such "general constitutional language"—which says only that "[t]he executive Power shall be vested in a President"—is "more than the text will bear." *Id.*, at 690, n. 29. Dean John Manning has well explained why, even were it not obvious from the Clause's "open-ended language." Separation of Powers as Ordinary Interpretation, 124 Harv. L. Rev. 1939, 1971 (2011). The Necessary and Proper Clause, he writes, makes it impossible to "establish a constitutional violation simply by showing that Congress has constrained the way '[t]he executive Power' is implemented"; that is exactly what the Clause gives Congress the power to do. *Id.*, at 1967. Only "a *specific* historical understanding" can bar Congress from enacting a given constraint. *Id.*, at 2024. And nothing of that sort broadly prevents Congress from limiting the President's removal power. * * *

Nor can the Take Care Clause come to the majority's rescue. * * * [T]he text of the Take Care Clause requires only enough authority to make sure "the laws [are] faithfully executed"—meaning with fidelity to the law itself, not to every presidential policy preference. As this Court has held, a President can ensure " 'faithful execution' of the laws"—thereby satisfying his "take care" obligation—with a removal provision like the one here. *Morrison*, 487 U.S., at 692. A for-cause standard gives him "ample authority to assure that [an official] is competently performing [his] statutory responsibilities in a manner that comports with the [relevant legislation's] provisions." *Ibid.*

Finally, recall the Constitution's telltale silence: Nowhere does the text say anything about the President's power to remove subordinate officials at will. * * * That's because removal is a *tool*—one means among many, even if sometimes an important one, for a President to control executive officials. To find that authority hidden in the Constitution as a "general rule" is to discover what is nowhere there.

History no better serves the majority's cause. * * * Begin with evidence from the Constitution's ratification. And note that this moment is indeed the beginning: Delegates to the Constitutional Convention never discussed whether or to what extent the President would have power to remove executive officials. As a result, the Framers advocating ratification had no single view of the matter. In Federalist No. 77, Hamilton presumed that under the new Constitution "[t]he consent of [the Senate] would be necessary to displace as well as to appoint" officers of the United States. *Id.*, at 515. He thought that scheme would promote "steady administration": "Where a man in any station had given satisfactory evidence of his fitness for it, a new president would be restrained" from substituting "a person more agreeable to him." *Ibid.* By contrast, Madison thought the Constitution allowed Congress to decide how any executive official could be removed. He explained in Federalist No. 39: "The tenure of the ministerial offices generally will be a subject of legal regulation, conformably to the reason of the case, and the example of the State Constitutions." *Id.*, at 253. Neither view, of course, at all supports the majority's story.

What is more, the Court's precedents before today have accepted the role of independent agencies in our governmental system. * * * *Humphrey's* found constitutional a statute identical to the one here, providing that the President could remove FTC Commissioners for "inefficiency, neglect of duty, or malfeasance in office." 295 U.S., at 619. The *Humphrey's* Court, as the majority notes, relied in substantial part on what kind of work the Commissioners performed. (By contrast, nothing in the decision turned—as the majority suggests, on any of the agency's organizational features.) According to *Humphrey's*, the Commissioners' primary work was to "carry into effect legislative policies"—"filling in and administering the details embodied by [a statute's] general standard." 295 U.S., at 627–628. In addition, the Court noted, the Commissioners recommended dispositions in court cases, much as a special master does. Given those "quasi-legislative" and "quasi-judicial"—as opposed to "purely executive"—functions, Congress could limit the President's removal authority. *Id.*, at 628. Or said another way, Congress could give the FTC some "independen[ce from] executive control." *Id.*, at 629.

* * * *Morrison* both extended *Humphrey's* domain and clarified the standard for addressing removal issues. The *Morrison* Court, over a one-Justice dissent, upheld for-cause protections afforded to an independent counsel with power to investigate and prosecute crimes committed by high-ranking officials. The Court well understood

that those law enforcement functions differed from the rulemaking and adjudicatory duties highlighted in *Humphrey's* * * *. But that difference did not resolve the issue. An official's functions, *Morrison* held, were relevant to but not dispositive of a removal limit's constitutionality. The key question in all the cases, *Morrison* saw, was whether such a restriction would "impede the President's ability to perform his constitutional duty." 487 U.S., at 691. Only if it did so would it fall outside Congress's power. And the protection for the independent counsel, the Court found, did not. Even though the counsel's functions were "purely executive," the President's "need to control the exercise of [her] discretion" was not "so central to the functioning of the Executive Branch as to require" unrestricted removal authority. *Id.*, at 690–691. True enough, the Court acknowledged, that the for-cause standard prevented the President from firing the counsel for discretionary decisions or judgment calls. But it preserved "ample authority" in the President "to assure that the counsel is competently performing" her "responsibilities in a manner that comports with" all legal requirements. *Id.*, at 692. That meant the President could meet his own constitutional obligation "to ensure 'the faithful execution' of the laws." *Ibid.*

The majority's description of *Morrison* is not true to the decision. (Mostly, it seems, the majority just wishes the case would go away.) First, *Morrison* is no "exception" to a broader rule from *Myers*. *Morrison* echoed all of *Humphrey's* criticism of the by-then infamous *Myers* "dicta." 487 U.S., at 687. It again rejected the notion of an "all-inclusive" removal power. *Ibid.* It yet further confined *Myers*' reach, making clear that Congress could restrict the President's removal of officials carrying out even the most traditional executive functions. And the decision, with care, set out the governing rule—again, that removal restrictions are permissible so long as they do not impede the President's performance of his own constitutionally assigned duties. Second, as all that suggests, *Morrison* is not limited to inferior officers. In the eight pages addressing the removal issue, the Court constantly spoke of "officers" and "officials" in general. 487 U.S., at 685–693. By contrast, the Court there used the word "inferior" in just one sentence (which of course the majority quotes), when applying its general standard to the case's facts. *Id.*, at 691. Indeed, Justice Scalia's dissent emphasized that the counsel's inferior-office status played no role in the Court's decision. See *id.*, at 724 ("The Court could have resolved the removal power issue in this case by simply relying" on that status, but did not). As Justice Scalia noted, the Court in *United States v. Perkins*, 116 U.S. 483, 484–485 (1886), had a century earlier allowed Congress to restrict the President's removal power over inferior officers. See *Morrison*, 487 U.S., at 723–724. Were that *Morrison*'s basis, a simple citation would have sufficed.

The question here, which by now you're well equipped to answer, is whether including that for-cause standard in the statute creating the CFPB violates the Constitution. Applying our longstanding precedent, the answer is clear: It does not. This Court, as the majority acknowledges, has sustained the constitutionality of the FTC and similar independent agencies. The for-cause protections for the heads of those agencies, the Court has found, do not impede the President's ability to perform his own constitutional duties, and so do not breach the separation of powers. There is nothing different here. The CFPB wields the same kind of power as the FTC and similar agencies. And all of their heads receive the same kind of removal protection. No less than those other entities—by now part of the fabric of government—the CFPB is thus a permissible exercise of Congress's power under the Necessary and Proper Clause to structure administration.

And Congress's choice to put a single director, rather than a multimember commission, at the CFPB's head violates no principle of separation of powers. The purported constitutional problem here is that an official has "slip[ped] from the Executive's control" and "supervision"—that he has become unaccountable to the President. So to make sense on the majority's own terms, the distinction between singular and plural agency heads must rest on a theory about why the former more easily "slip" from the President's grasp. But the majority has nothing to offer. In fact, the opposite is more likely to be true: To the extent that such matters are measurable, individuals are easier than groups to supervise.

To begin with, trying to generalize about these matters is something of a fool's errand. Presidential control * * * can operate through many means—removal to be sure, but also appointments, oversight devices (*e.g.*, centralized review of rulemaking or litigating positions), budgetary processes, personal outreach, and more. The effectiveness of each of those control mechanisms, when present, can then depend on a multitude of agency-specific practices, norms, rules, and organizational features. In that complex stew, the difference between a singular and plural agency head will often make not a whit of difference. * * *

But if the demand is for generalization, then the majority's distinction cuts the opposite way: More powerful control mechanisms are needed (if anything) for commissions. Holding everything else equal, those are the agencies more likely to "slip from the Executive's control." Just consider your everyday experience: It's easier to get one person to do what you want than a gaggle. So too, you know exactly whom to blame when an individual—but not when a group—does a job badly. The same is true in bureaucracies. A multimember structure reduces accountability to the President because it's harder for him to oversee, to influence—or to remove, if necessary—a group of five or more commissioners than a single director. Indeed, that is *why* Congress so often resorts to hydra-headed agencies. * * *

Recall again how this dispute got started. In the midst of the Great Recession, Congress and the President came together to create an agency [to] protect consumers from the reckless financial practices that had caused the then-ongoing economic collapse. Not only Congress but also the President thought that the new agency, to fulfill its mandate, needed a measure of independence. So the two political branches, acting together, gave the CFPB Director the same job protection that innumerable other agency heads possess. * * * And now consider how the dispute ends—with five unelected judges rejecting the result of that democratic process. * * * The majority does so even though the Constitution grants to Congress, acting with the President's approval, the authority to create and shape administrative bodies. And even though those branches, as compared to courts, have far greater understanding of political control mechanisms and agency design. * * * Because this Court ignores that sensible—indeed, that obvious—division of tasks, I respectfully dissent.

---

## Points for Discussion

#### *a. Single-Director and Multi-Member Agencies*

The Court in *Seila Law* suggested that the general constitutional rule is that the President must have unfettered removal power over officers of the United States. The Court acknowledged that it had recognized congressional authority to restrict the President's power over members of multi-member, bipartisan commissions under limited circumstances, but it concluded that this exception to the general rule did not extend to single-director agencies. Why can Congress limit the President's power to fire the leaders of a multi-member commission but not the director of a single-member agency? If we were creating a Constitution from scratch, would we craft different rules for the President's removal power depending on the leadership structure of the agency at issue? If not, is it possible to defend the Court's distinction between the agency at issue in *Seila Law* and the agency at issue in *Humphrey's Executor*? What would be the consequences for the administrative state of overruling the Court's holding in *Humphrey's Executor*?

#### *b. The President's Power to Remove After* Seila Law

In *Seila Law*, the Court held that Congress can limit the President's power to remove an agency official only if the official is an inferior officer (and the limitation would not unduly trammel the President's power faithfully to execute the law) or if the official is part of a multimember, bipartisan commission that does not meaningfully exercise executive authority. Did the Court's approach in *Seila Law* follow its prior decisions, clarify its prior decisions, or depart from its prior decisions? If the Court's approach departed from prior decisions, are you persuaded that the departure is warranted?

---

## Perspective and Analysis

[T]he Constitution recognizes the existence of only three kinds of federal governmental power and creates only three institutions of government. * * * [Because the Constitution specifically enumerates the powers granted to the President, Congress, and the judiciary, the] text of the Constitution simply cannot be construed to recognize more than the three traditional powers of government.

[Just as] the constitutional text does not permit historical arguments for the existence of a fourth inherent, unenumerated administrative power of [government, it] also contemplates only three types of institutions of government staffed by three types of personnel. [For example,] the Oaths or Affirmations Clause of Article VI * * * explicitly refers to, and clearly contemplates, only three types of federal officers or personnel.

[As a consequence, any "administrative power"] must somehow be made to fit subordinately into the Constitution's trinitarian framework. * * * Any administrative power or personnel that exists cannot be derivative of or subordinate to the legislative power or the judicial power. Those powers cannot be delegated, even to administrative officers, and administration requires the delegation of power to numerous officials. Moreover, administration cannot be conducted through the procedural hoops that the Constitution imposes on all exercises of legislative and judicial power. It would be impractical to "administer" anything subject to procedural constraints of bicameralism, presentment, or the existence of a case or controversy. If the mechanisms for the use of the legislative and judicial powers are simply unsuitable for employment of the administrative power, only one other constitutional actor remains. The administrative power, if it exists, must be a subset of the President's "executive Power" and not of one of the other two traditional powers of government. * * *

The plain dictionary meaning of the Executive Power Clause [in Article II] suggests that the power the Clause grants the President includes at least the power to execute all federal laws. * * * The Executive Power Clause grants "the executive Power" solely and exclusively to the President; it gives Congress no power whatsoever to create subordinate entities that may exercise "the executive Power" until and unless the President delegates that power in some fashion. * * *

Because the President alone has the constitutional power to execute federal law, it would seem to follow that, notwithstanding the text of any given statute, the President must be able to execute that statute, interpreting it and applying it in concrete circumstances. * * * If the President may make a decision that a statute purports to reserve for an inferior executive officer, by the same logic, the President must be able to nullify an action taken by an inferior executive officer. * * * The President's power over nominations and his exclusively held executive power strongly suggest that he must be able to remove federal officers who he feels are not executing federal law in a manner consistent with his administrative agenda.

**Steven G. Calabresi & Saikrishna B. Prakash, *The President's Power to Execute the Laws*, 104 YALE L.J. 541 (1994).**

---

## Perspective and Analysis

The [theory of the unitary executive] has no substantial basis in either our nation's administrative history or constitutional jurisprudence and subverts our delicately balanced scheme of separated but shared powers. It is Congress that was meant to be the dominant policymaking body in our constitutional scheme and its principal tool to ensure that its will would be carried out is its virtually plenary power to create the administrative bureaucracy and to shape the powers, duties, and tenure of the offices and officers of that infrastructure in a manner best suited to accomplish legislative ends. * * *

Recognition of Congress's substantial authority with respect to the bureaucratic infrastructure is, of course, far from denigrating or denying the powerful role the President plays in the policymaking and policy effectuation processes. The ability to recommend and veto legislation, to appoint and discharge his appointees, to influence (through his powers in the budget and resource allocation process) even those officials not subject to at-will removal, and to bring to bear the force of the office on the bureaucracy and the legislature, ensures the executive's co-equal role in the constitutional scheme. But it does underline the limits of the President's role and subjects the claim of a unitary executive to still further constitutional doubt.

Both literal and structural analysis of the constitutional text fails to suggest a hierarchical executive. * * * Among the powers explicitly granted to the President is the power to "require the Opinion, in writing, of the principal Officer in each of the executive Departments, upon any subject relating to the Duties of their respective Offices." * * * If the President was meant to have full control over the executive, including the power to discharge at will, why was the power to request written opinions put in the Constitution? * * * [The Clause] exists because it was not assumed, or at the very least not obvious, that the President has absolute power over heads of departments. And the Take Care Clause says only that the President "shall take Care that the Laws be faithfully executed," regardless of who executes them—arguably a duty quite different from the claim that the President has an encompassing responsibility for executing all the laws. A literal reading of the Take Care Clause confirms that it is the President's duty to ensure that officials obey

Congress's instructions; the Clause does not create a presidential power so great that it can be used to frustrate statutory congressional intention. * * *

This understanding that the President is legally responsible for seeing that congressional enactments are carried out also diminishes the [related] argument that since he is the only official elected by all the people, he must be accountable to the people for actions of all executive agencies. The contention confuses political accountability with legal responsibility. The former reflects the notion of popular support as a basis of presidential political power. It is a political concept and has been variously cited to imply a free-floating executive responsibility unfettered by legal standards, legal review, or legal consequences. * * *

**Morton Rosenberg, *Congress's Prerogative Over Agencies and Agency Decisionmakers: The Rise and Demise of the Reagan Administration's Theory of the Unitary Executive*, 57 GEO. WASH. L. REV. 627, 634, 688–90 (1989).**

---

After *Seila Law*, there are strict limits on Congress's authority to restrict the President's power to remove officers. But even if the Court had accepted Justice Kagan's view, the President would still have other means of exercising control over agency officials. First, as we noted above, to the extent that the President gets to appoint officials—or oversee those who appoint inferior officers—the President can ensure that the Administration is staffed by those sympathetic to his agenda. Second, although Congress has the power to fund the federal government, the enactment of the budget, like any other law, requires the President's assent. The President can use that power to cajole agency compliance. Indeed, the White House's Office of Management and Budget (OMB) prepares a budget to submit as a proposal to Congress, and the proposal can both reflect the President's priorities and punish those agencies that refuse to comply with the President's wishes.

Third, Presidents since Richard Nixon have required White House review of certain agency actions before they take effect. For the last four decades, this process has been centralized in the OMB's Office of Information and Regulatory Affairs (OIRA), which reviews new rules and legislative proposals to ensure that they are justified. Presidents Reagan and Bush required that new rules be subjected to a rigorous cost-benefit analysis, a requirement designed to advance their Administrations' deregulatory objectives. President Clinton continued the approach of requiring centralized review, though he applied a more expansive understanding of costs and benefits and used the review as a means to promote a pro-regulatory agenda.

---

## Perspective and Analysis

The Clinton OMB continued to manage a regulatory review process, but with certain variations from the Reagan and Bush model: although the process provoked fewer confrontations with agencies, it in fact articulated a broader understanding of the President's appropriate authority to direct administrative actions. More important, the Clinton White House sandwiched regulatory review between two other methods for guiding and asserting ownership over administrative activity, used episodically by prior Presidents but elevated by Clinton to something near a governing philosophy. At the front end of the regulatory process, Clinton regularly issued formal directives to the heads of executive agencies to set the terms of administrative action and prevent deviation from his proposed course. And at the back end of the process (which could not but affect prior stages as well), Clinton personally appropriated significant regulatory action through communicative strategies that presented regulations and other agency work product, to both the public and other governmental actors, as his own, in a way new to the annals of administrative process.

By the close of the Clinton Presidency, a distinctive form of administration and administrative control—call it "presidential administration"—had emerged, at the least augmenting, and in significant respects subordinating, other modes of bureaucratic governance. * * * [I]n comparison with other forms of control, the new presidentialization of administration renders the bureaucratic sphere more transparent and responsive to the public, while also better promoting important kinds of regulatory competence and dynamism. * * *

If presidential administration * * * represents a salutary development in administrative process, then courts should attempt, through their articulation of administrative law, to recognize and promote this kind of control over agency policymaking. * * * The current rules, however, largely disregard the potential of presidential control [to] perform this function. * * * [R]ecognition of this potential would support a body of doctrine granting preferred status to administrative action infused in the appropriate way with presidential authority, and thereby promoting this kind of presidential involvement. * * *

[T]he nondelegation doctrine should tolerate most easily * * * presidentially directed actions taken pursuant to a delegation to an agency official. * * * [A]ll else equal, administrative action taken pursuant to a delegation to an agency official, but clothed with the imprimatur and authority of the President, should receive maximum protection against a nondelegation challenge. The President's involvement, at least if publicly disclosed, vests the action with an increased dose of accountability, which although not (by definition) peculiarly legislative in nature, renders the action less troublesome than solely bureaucratic measures from the standpoint of democratic values. And this kind of presidential participation gives rise to none of the rule of law issues that might loom large in the context of direct delegations. [G]iven the often urgent need for, and resulting omnipresence of, broad delegations, courts should understand and, by so doing, encourage this mechanism of control as mitigating the potential threat that administrative discretion poses.

**Elena Kagan, *Presidential Administration*, 114 HARV. L. REV. 2245, 2250–2252 (2001).**

---

## *EXECUTIVE ORDER 12866*

58 Fed. Reg. 51735 (September 30, 1993)

[B]y the authority vested in me as President by the Constitution and the laws of the United States of America, it is hereby ordered as follows:

**Section 1.** *Statement of Regulatory Philosophy and Principles.*

(a) *The Regulatory Philosophy.* Federal agencies should promulgate only such regulations as are required by law, are necessary to interpret the law, or are made necessary by compelling public need, such as material failures of private markets to protect or improve the health and safety of the public, the environment, or the well-being of the American people. In deciding whether and how to regulate, agencies should assess all costs and benefits of available regulatory alternatives, including the alternative of not regulating. Costs and benefits shall be understood to include both quantifiable measures (to the fullest extent that these can be usefully estimated) and qualitative measures of costs and benefits that are difficult to quantify, but nevertheless essential to consider. Further, in choosing among alternative regulatory approaches, agencies should select those approaches that maximize net benefits (including potential economic, environmental, public health and safety, and other advantages; distributive impacts; and equity), unless a statute requires another regulatory approach.

(b) *The Principles of Regulation.* To ensure that the agencies' regulatory programs are consistent with the philosophy set forth above, agencies should adhere to the following principles, to the extent permitted by law and where applicable:

(1) Each agency shall identify the problem that it intends to address (including, where applicable, the failures of private markets or public institutions that warrant new agency action) as well as assess the significance of that problem.

(2) Each agency shall examine whether existing regulations (or other law) have created, or contributed to, the problem that a new regulation is intended to correct and whether those regulations (or other law) should be modified to achieve the intended goal of regulation more effectively.

(3) Each agency shall identify and assess available alternatives to direct regulation, including providing economic incentives to encourage the desired behavior, such as user fees or marketable permits, or providing information upon which choices can be made by the public.

(4) In setting regulatory priorities, each agency shall consider, to the extent reasonable, the degree and nature of the risks posed by various substances or activities within its jurisdiction.

(5) When an agency determines that a regulation is the best available method of achieving the regulatory objective, it shall design its regulations in the most cost-effective manner to achieve the regulatory objective. In doing so, each agency shall consider incentives for innovation, consistency, predictability, the costs of enforcement and compliance (to the government, regulated entities, and the public), flexibility, distributive impacts, and equity.

(6) Each agency shall assess both the costs and the benefits of the intended regulation and, recognizing that some costs and benefits are difficult to quantify, propose or adopt a regulation only upon a reasoned determination that the benefits of the intended regulation justify its costs.

(7) Each agency shall base its decisions on the best reasonably obtainable scientific, technical, economic, and other information concerning the need for, and consequences of, the intended regulation.

(8) Each agency shall identify and assess alternative forms of regulation and shall, to the extent feasible, specify performance objectives, rather than specifying the behavior or manner of compliance that regulated entities must adopt.

(9) Wherever feasible, agencies shall seek views of appropriate State, local, and tribal officials before imposing regulatory requirements that might significantly or uniquely affect those governmental entities. Each agency shall assess the effects of Federal regulations on State, local, and tribal governments, including specifically the availability of resources to carry out those mandates, and seek to minimize those burdens that uniquely or significantly affect such governmental entities, consistent with achieving regulatory objectives. In addition, as appropriate, agencies shall seek to harmonize Federal regulatory actions with related State, local, and tribal regulatory and other governmental functions.

(10) Each agency shall avoid regulations that are inconsistent, incompatible, or duplicative with its other regulations or those of other Federal agencies.

(11) Each agency shall tailor its regulations to impose the least burden on society, including individuals, businesses of differing sizes, and other entities (including small communities and governmental entities), consistent with obtaining the regulatory objectives, taking into account, among other things, and to the extent practicable, the costs of cumulative regulations.

(12) Each agency shall draft its regulations to be simple and easy to understand, with the goal of minimizing the potential for uncertainty and litigation arising from such uncertainty.

**Sec. 2.** *Organization.* An efficient regulatory planning and review process is vital to ensure that the Federal Government's regulatory system best serves the American people.

(a) *The Agencies.* Because Federal agencies are the repositories of significant substantive expertise and experience, they are responsible for developing regulations and assuring that the regulations are consistent with applicable law, the President's priorities, and the principles set forth in this Executive order.

(b) *The Office of Management and Budget.* Coordinated review of agency rulemaking is necessary to ensure that regulations are consistent with applicable law, the President's priorities, and the principles set forth in this Executive order, and that decisions made by one agency do not conflict with the policies or actions taken or planned by another agency. The Office of Management and Budget (OMB) shall carry out that review function. Within OMB, the Office of Information and Regulatory Affairs (OIRA) is the repository of expertise concerning regulatory issues, including methodologies and procedures that affect more than one agency, this Executive order, and the President's regulatory policies. To the extent permitted by law, OMB shall provide guidance to agencies and assist the President, the Vice President, and other regulatory policy advisors to the President in regulatory planning and shall be the entity that reviews individual regulations, as provided by this Executive order. * * *

**Sec. 4.** *Planning Mechanism.* In order to have an effective regulatory program, to provide for coordination of regulations, to maximize consultation and the resolution of potential conflicts at an early stage, to involve the public and its State, local, and tribal officials in regulatory planning, and to ensure that new or revised regulations promote the President's priorities and the principles set forth in this Executive order, these procedures shall be followed, to the extent permitted by law:

(a) *Agencies' Policy Meeting.* Early in each year's planning cycle, the Vice President shall convene a meeting of the Advisors and the heads of agencies to seek a common understanding of priorities and to coordinate regulatory efforts to be accomplished in the upcoming year.

(b) *Unified Regulatory Agenda.* For purposes of this subsection, the term "agency" or "agencies" shall also include those considered to be independent regulatory agencies, as defined in 44 U.S.C. § 3502(10). Each agency shall prepare an agenda of all regulations under development or review, at a time and in a manner specified by the Administrator of OIRA. * * *

(c) *The Regulatory Plan.* For purposes of this subsection, the term "agency" or "agencies" shall also include those considered to be independent regulatory agencies, as defined in 44 U.S.C. § 3502(10).

(1) As part of the Unified Regulatory Agenda, beginning in 1994, each agency shall prepare a Regulatory Plan (Plan) of the most important significant regulatory actions that the agency reasonably expects to issue in proposed or final form in that fiscal year or thereafter. The Plan shall be approved personally by the agency head * * *.

(2) Each agency shall forward its Plan to OIRA by June 1st of each year. * * *

(5) If the Administrator of OIRA believes that a planned regulatory action of an agency may be inconsistent with the President's priorities or the principles set forth in this Executive order or may be in conflict with any policy or action taken or planned by another agency, the Administrator of OIRA shall promptly notify, in writing, the affected agencies, the Advisors, and the Vice President. * * *

**Sec. 6.** *Centralized Review of Regulations.* The guidelines set forth below shall apply to all regulatory actions, for both new and existing regulations, by agencies other than those agencies specifically exempted by the Administrator of OIRA:

(a) *Agency Responsibilities.*

(1) Each agency shall (consistent with its own rules, regulations, or procedures) provide the public with meaningful participation in the regulatory process. * * *

(3) [E]ach agency shall develop its regulatory actions in a timely fashion and adhere to the following procedures with respect to a regulatory action:

(A) Each agency shall provide OIRA, at such times and in the manner specified by the Administrator of OIRA, with a list of its planned regulatory actions, indicating those which the agency believes are significant regulatory actions within the meaning of this Executive order. * * *

(B) For each matter identified as, or determined by the Administrator of OIRA to be, a significant regulatory action, the issuing agency shall provide to OIRA:

(i) The text of the draft regulatory action, together with a reasonably detailed description of the need for the regulatory action and an explanation of how the regulatory action will meet that need; and

(ii) An assessment of the potential costs and benefits of the regulatory action, including an explanation of the manner in which the regulatory action is consistent with a statutory mandate and, to the extent permitted by law, promotes the President's priorities and avoids undue interference with State, local, and tribal governments in the exercise of their governmental functions.

(C) For those matters identified as, or determined by the Administrator of OIRA to be, a significant regulatory action * * *, the agency shall also provide to OIRA the following additional information developed as part of the agency's decision-making process (unless prohibited by law):

(i) An assessment, including the underlying analysis, of benefits anticipated from the regulatory action (such as, but not limited to, the promotion of the efficient functioning of the economy and private markets, the enhancement of health and safety, the protection of the natural environment, and the elimination or reduction of discrimination or bias) together with, to the extent feasible, a quantification of those benefits;

(ii) An assessment, including the underlying analysis, of costs anticipated from the regulatory action (such as, but not limited to, the direct cost both to the government in administering the regulation and to businesses and others in complying with the regulation, and any adverse effects on the efficient functioning of the economy, private markets (including productivity, employment, and competitiveness), health, safety, and the natural environment), together with, to the extent feasible, a quantification of those costs; and

(iii) An assessment, including the underlying analysis, of costs and benefits of potentially effective and reasonably feasible alternatives to the planned regulation, identified by the agencies or the public (including improving the current regulation and reasonably viable nonregulatory actions), and an explanation why the planned regulatory action is preferable to the identified potential alternatives. * * *

(E) After the regulatory action has been published in the Federal Register or otherwise issued to the public, the agency shall:

(i) Make available to the public the information set forth in subsections (a)(3)(B) and (C);

(ii) Identify for the public, in a complete, clear, and simple manner, the substantive changes between the draft submitted to OIRA for review and the action subsequently announced; and

(iii) Identify for the public those changes in the regulatory action that were made at the suggestion or recommendation of OIRA.

(F) All information provided to the public by the agency shall be in plain, understandable language. * * *

**Sec. 7.** *Resolution of Conflicts.* To the extent permitted by law, disagreements or conflicts between or among agency heads or between OMB and any agency that cannot be resolved by the Administrator of OIRA shall be resolved by the President, or by the Vice President acting at the request of the President, with the relevant agency head (and, as appropriate, other interested government officials). Vice Presidential and Presidential consideration of such disagreements may be initiated only by the Director, by the head of the issuing agency, or by the head of an agency that has a significant interest in the regulatory action at issue. * * * At the end of this review process, the President, or the Vice President acting at the request of the President, shall notify the affected agency and the Administrator of OIRA of the President's decision with respect to the matter. * * *

—William Jefferson Clinton, The White House (September 30, 1993)

---

## Points for Discussion

### *a. White House Review*

President Clinton (and the Presidents who succeeded him) built upon President Reagan's efforts to assert White House control over agency rulemaking. Does presidential control address concerns that some have raised about the broad delegations of power that Congress has given to administrative agencies? Is the addition of another layer of bureaucratic review before agencies can fulfill their regulatory missions likely to promote good policy, or is it likely to frustrate it?

### *b. Accountability and Independence*

Presidential control of agency decision-making promotes a form of accountability for agency action. We cannot vote for agency heads, but we can vote for (or against) the President. If the public disagrees with agency action—such as a burdensome rule issued by the EPA or a lax rule issued by the Federal Communications Commission—then it can hold the President (or his or her party) responsible in the next election. Such accountability seems appropriate as long as the President exercises a meaningful form of control over agency-decision, such as the form of control contemplated by President Clinton's Executive Order.

But this form of presidential oversight also diminishes agency independence, and at least sometimes this might be concerning. We can all imagine agency decisions that we think should not be distorted by crass political concerns, and the ability to vote against the President in the next election might not be much comfort in the meantime. Is it possible to reconcile our competing impulses towards accountability and independence? If not, do you agree with the way that President Clinton, his predecessors, and his successors have struck the balance?

---

## B. Congressional Control of Agency Decision-Making

In considering the President's power to control agency decision-making, we saw some examples of congressional attempts to do the same. For example, in *Myers v. United States*, Congress tried to reserve for the Senate the power to ratify—and thus, by withholding consent, the power to reject—the President's attempt to fire a postmaster. Although the Court held that Congress lacked power to do so, Congress presumably tried to reserve a role for itself in the removal process for the same reason that the President wishes to retain that power for himself: to influence the official's decision-making while in office.

What other means of control over agency decision-making does Congress enjoy? Consider the case that follows.

---

## *Immigration and Naturalization Service v. Chadha*

462 U.S. 919 (1983)

CHIEF JUSTICE BURGER delivered the opinion of the Court.

> **FYI**
>
> At the time of the decision in this case, the Immigration and Naturalization Service was a component of the Department of Justice. Chadha's deportation hearing was held before an administrative law judge, an agency official with a good deal of independence from political decision-makers. But under the statute, the Attorney General was the final decision-maker for the agency. Does this structure itself raise concerns about the separation of powers?

Chadha is an East Indian who was born in Kenya and holds a British passport. He was lawfully admitted to the United States in 1966 on a nonimmigrant student visa. His visa expired on June 30, 1972. On October 11, 1973, the District Director of the Immigration and Naturalization Service ordered Chadha to show cause why he should not be deported for having "remained in the United States for a longer time than permitted." Pursuant to § 242(b) of the Immigration and Nationality Act, a deportation hearing was held before an immigration judge on January 11, 1974. Chadha conceded that he was deportable for overstaying his visa and the hearing was adjourned to enable him to file an application for suspension of deportation under § 244(a)(1) of the Act. Section 244(a)(1) provides [for suspension of deportation for persons of "good moral character" in certain cases of "extreme hardship."]

The immigration judge found that Chadha met the requirements of § 244(a)(1): he had resided continuously in the United States for over seven years, was of good moral character, and would suffer "extreme hardship" if deported. Pursuant to § 244(c)(1) of the Act, the immigration judge suspended Chadha's deportation * * *. [The Attorney General agreed.] Once the Attorney General's recommendation for suspension of Chadha's deportation was conveyed to Congress, Congress had the power under § 244(c)(2) of the Act to veto[2] the Attorney General's determination that Chadha should not be deported. Section 244(c)(2) provides:

> "In the case of an alien specified in paragraph (1) of subsection (a) of this subsection—if during the session of the Congress at which a case is reported, or prior to the close of the session of the Congress next following the session at which a case is reported, either the Senate or the House of Representatives passes a resolution stating in substance that it does not favor the suspension of such deportation, the Attorney General shall thereupon deport such alien or authorize the alien's voluntary departure at his own expense under the order of deportation in the manner provided by law. If, within the time above specified, neither the Senate nor the House of Representatives shall pass such a resolution, the Attorney General shall cancel deportation proceedings."

On December 12, 1975, Representative Eilberg, Chairman of the Judiciary Subcommittee on Immigration, Citizenship, and International Law, introduced a resolution opposing "the granting of permanent residence in the United States to [six] aliens," including Chadha. The resolution was referred to the House Committee on the Judiciary. On December 16, 1975, the resolution was discharged from further consideration by the House Committee on the Judiciary and submitted to the House of Representatives for a vote. The resolution had not been printed and was not made available to other Members of the House prior to or at the time it was voted on. So far as the record before us shows, the House consideration of the resolution was based on Representative Eilberg's statement from the floor that "[i]t was the feeling of the committee, after reviewing 340 cases, that the aliens contained in the resolution [Chadha and five others] did not meet these statutory requirements, particularly as

**FYI**

It is a mystery why the House exercised its legislative veto with respect to Chadha. One controversial theory, often discussed but never proved, was that members of Congress or their staff used the veto power to seek bribes. Chadha's attorney, Alan Morrison (who later became a colleague of this book's author), believed that the "committee was just showing who was the boss, that they had the power and they wanted to be sure that the Immigration Service understood it." *See* Oral History of Alan Morrison: Interviews conducted by Daniel Marcus (2008).

---

2 In constitutional terms, "veto" is used to describe the President's power under Art. I, § 7 of the Constitution. It appears, however, that Congressional devices of the type authorized by § 244(c)(2) have come to be commonly referred to as a "veto." We refer to the Congressional "resolution" authorized by § 244(c)(2) as a "one-House veto" of the Attorney General's decision to allow a particular deportable alien to remain in the United States.

it relates to hardship; and it is the opinion of the committee that their deportation should not be suspended." *Ibid.* The resolution was passed without debate or recorded vote. Since the House action was pursuant to § 244(c)(2), the resolution was not treated as an Article I legislative act; it was not submitted to the Senate or presented to the President for his action.

After the House veto of the Attorney General's decision to allow Chadha to remain in the United States, the immigration judge reopened the deportation proceedings to implement the House order deporting Chadha. Chadha moved to terminate the proceedings on the ground that § 244(c)(2) is unconstitutional.

*The Presentment Clauses*

The records of the Constitutional Convention reveal that the requirement that all legislation be presented to the President before becoming law was uniformly accepted by the Framers. Presentment to the President and the Presidential veto were considered so imperative that the draftsmen took special pains to assure that these requirements could not be circumvented. During the final debate on Art. I, § 7, cl. 2, James Madison expressed concern that it might easily be evaded by the simple expedient of calling a proposed law a "resolution" or "vote" rather than a "bill." 2 M. Farrand, The Records of the Federal Convention of 1787 301–302. As a consequence, Art. I, § 7, cl. 3, was added. *Id.*, at 304–305.

The decision to provide the President with a limited and qualified power to nullify proposed legislation by veto was based on the profound conviction of the Framers that the powers conferred on Congress were the powers to be most carefully circumscribed. It is beyond doubt that lawmaking was a power to be shared by both Houses and the President. In The Federalist No. 73, Hamilton focused on the President's role in making laws:

> "If even no propensity had ever discovered itself in the legislative body to invade the rights of the Executive, the rules of just reasoning and theoretic propriety would of themselves teach us that the one ought not to be left to the mercy of the other, but ought to possess a constitutional and effectual power of self-defense."

The President's role in the lawmaking process also reflects the Framers' careful efforts to check whatever propensity a particular Congress might have to enact oppressive, improvident, or ill-considered measures. [See The Federalist No. 73.] * * * The Court also has observed that the Presentment Clauses serve the important purpose of assuring that a "national" perspective is grafted on the legislative process * * *. *Myers v. United States*, 272 U.S. 52, 123 (1926).

*Bicameralism*

The bicameral requirement of Art. I, §§ 1, 7 was of scarcely less concern to the Framers than was the Presidential veto and indeed the two concepts are interdependent. By providing that no law could take effect without the concurrence of the prescribed majority of the Members of both Houses, the Framers reemphasized their belief, already remarked upon in connection with the Presentment Clauses, that legislation should not be enacted unless it has been carefully and fully considered by the Nation's elected officials. In the Constitutional Convention debates on the need for a bicameral legislature, James Wilson, later to become a Justice of this Court, commented:

> "Despotism comes on mankind in different shapes. Sometimes in an Executive, sometimes in a military, one. Is there danger of a Legislative despotism? Theory & practice both proclaim it. If the Legislative authority be not restrained, there can be neither liberty nor stability; and it can only be restrained by dividing it within itself, into distinct and independent branches. In a single house there is no check, but the inadequate one, of the virtue & good sense of those who compose it." 1 M. Farrand, Records of the Federal Convention of 1787, p. 254 (1911).

Hamilton argued that [were] the Nation to adopt a Constitution providing for only one legislative organ, "we shall finally accumulate, in a single body, all the most important prerogatives of sovereignty, and thus * * * create in reality that very tyranny which the adversaries of the new Constitution either are, or affect to be, solicitous to avert." The Federalist No. 22. These observations are consistent with what many of the Framers expressed, none more cogently than Hamilton* in pointing up the need to divide and disperse power in order to protect liberty: "In republican government, the legislative authority necessarily predominates. The remedy for this inconveniency is to divide the legislature into different branches; and to render them, by different modes of election and different principles of action, as little connected with each other as the nature of their common functions and their common dependence on the society will admit." The Federalist No. 51.

We see therefore that the Framers were acutely conscious that the bicameral requirement and the Presentment Clauses would serve essential constitutional functions. The President's participation in the legislative process was to protect the Executive Branch from Congress and to protect the whole people from improvident laws. The division of the Congress into two distinctive bodies assures that the legislative power would be exercised only after opportunity for full study and debate in separate settings. The President's unilateral veto power, in turn, was limited by the power of two thirds of both Houses of Congress to overrule a veto thereby precluding final arbitrary action of one person. It emerges clearly that the prescription for legislative action in Art. I, §§ 1, 7 represents the Framers' decision that the legislative power of the Federal government be exercised in accord with a single, finely wrought and exhaustively considered, procedure.

---

* The Court mistakenly attributed The Federalist No. 51 to Hamilton. The consensus of scholars is that James Madison wrote The Federalist No. 51, one of the most-cited Federalist Papers of all time. See Ira C. Lupu, *The Most-Cited Federalist Papers*, 15 CONST. COMMENT. 403 (1997). —*Ed.*

Not every action taken by either House is subject to the bicameralism and presentment requirements of Art. I. Whether actions taken by either House are, in law and fact, an exercise of legislative power depends not on their form but upon "whether they contain matter which is properly to be regarded as legislative in its character and effect." S. Rep. No. 1335, 54th Cong., 2d Sess., 8 (1897).

Examination of the action taken here by one House pursuant to § 244(c)(2) reveals that it was essentially legislative in purpose and effect. In purporting to exercise power defined in Art. I, § 8, cl. 4 to "establish an uniform Rule of Naturalization," the House took action that had the purpose and effect of altering the legal rights, duties and relations of persons, including the Attorney General, Executive Branch officials and Chadha, all outside the legislative branch. Section 244(c)(2) purports to authorize one House of Congress to require the Attorney General to deport an individual alien whose deportation otherwise would be cancelled under § 244. The one-House veto operated in this case to overrule the Attorney General and mandate Chadha's deportation; absent the House action, Chadha would remain in the United States. Congress has *acted* and its action has altered Chadha's status.

The legislative character of the one-House veto in this case is confirmed by the character of the Congressional action it supplants. Neither the House of Representatives nor the Senate contends that, absent the veto provision in § 244(c)(2), either of them, or both of them acting together, could effectively require the Attorney General to deport an alien once the Attorney General, in the exercise of legislatively delegated authority,[16] had determined the alien should remain in the United States. Without the challenged provision in § 244(c)(2), this could have been achieved, if at all, only by legislation requiring deportation. Similarly, a veto by one House of Congress under § 244(c)(2) cannot be justified as an attempt at amending the standards set out in § 244(a)(1), or as a repeal of § 244 as applied to Chadha. Amendment and repeal of statutes, no less than enactment, must conform with Art. I.

---

16 Congress protests that affirming the Court of Appeals in this case will sanction "lawmaking by the Attorney General." To be sure, some administrative agency action—rule making, for example—may resemble "lawmaking." [But when] the Attorney General performs his duties pursuant to § 244, he does not exercise "legislative" power. The bicameral process is not necessary as a check on the Executive's administration of the laws because his administrative activity cannot reach beyond the limits of the statute that created it—a statute duly enacted pursuant to Art. I, §§ 1, 7. The constitutionality of the Attorney General's execution of the authority delegated to him by § 244 involves only a question of delegation doctrine. * * * Executive action under legislatively delegated authority that might resemble "legislative" action in some respects is not subject to the approval of both Houses of Congress and the President for the reason that the Constitution does not so require. That kind of Executive action is always subject to check by the terms of the legislation that authorized it; and if that authority is exceeded it is open to judicial review as well as the power of Congress to modify or revoke the authority entirely. A one-House veto is clearly legislative in both character and effect and is not so checked; the need for the check provided by Art. I, §§ 1, 7 is therefore clear. Congress' authority to delegate portions of its power to administrative agencies provides no support for the argument that Congress can constitutionally control administration of the laws by way of a Congressional veto.

Finally, we see that when the Framers intended to authorize either House of Congress to act alone and outside of its prescribed bicameral legislative role, they narrowly and precisely defined the procedure for such action. There are but four provisions in the Constitution, explicit and unambiguous, by which one House may act alone with the unreviewable force of law, not subject to the President's veto: (a) The House of Representatives alone was given the power to initiate impeachments. Art. I, § 2, cl. 6; (b) The Senate alone was given the power to conduct trials following impeachment on charges initiated by the House and to convict following trial. Art. I, § 3, cl. 5; (c) The Senate alone was given final unreviewable power to approve or to disapprove presidential appointments. Art. II, § 2, cl. 2; (d) The Senate alone was given unreviewable power to ratify treaties negotiated by the President. Art. II, § 2, cl. 2. * * * Clearly, when the Draftsmen sought to confer special powers on one House, independent of the other House, or of the President, they did so in explicit, unambiguous terms.

Since it is clear that the action by the House under § 244(c)(2) was not within any of the express constitutional exceptions authorizing one House to act alone, and equally clear that it was an exercise of legislative power, that action was subject to the standards prescribed in Article I.

The veto authorized by § 244(c)(2) doubtless has been in many respects a convenient shortcut; the "sharing" with the Executive by Congress of its authority over aliens in this manner is, on its face, an appealing compromise. In purely practical terms, it is obviously easier for action to be taken by one House without submission to the President; but it is crystal clear from the records of the Convention, contemporaneous writings and debates, that the Framers ranked other values higher than efficiency. The records of the Convention and debates in the States preceding ratification underscore the common desire to define and limit the exercise of the newly created federal powers affecting the states and the people. There is unmistakable expression of a determination that legislation by the national Congress be a step-by-step, deliberate and deliberative process. We hold that the Congressional veto provision in § 244(c)(2) is severable from the Act and that it is unconstitutional.

**Definition**

When a provision of a statute is "severable," it means that the statute "remains operative in its remaining provisions even if a portion of the law is declared unconstitutional." Black's Law Dictionary (2014 ed.)

JUSTICE POWELL, concurring in the judgment.

The Court's decision, based on the Presentment Clauses, apparently will invalidate every use of the legislative veto. * * * One reasonably may disagree with Congress' assessment of the veto's utility, but the respect due its judgment as a coordinate branch of Government cautions that our holding should be no more extensive than necessary to decide this case. In my view, the case may be decided on a narrower ground. When Congress finds that a particular person does not satisfy the statutory criteria for permanent residence in this country it has assumed a judicial function in violation of the principle of separation of powers.

[The Framers were concerned] that trial by a legislature lacks the safeguards necessary to prevent the abuse of power. * * * On its face, the House's action appears clearly adjudicatory. The House did not enact a general rule; rather it made its own determination that six specific persons did not comply with certain statutory criteria. It thus undertook the type of decision that traditionally has been left to other branches.

The impropriety of the House's assumption of this function is confirmed by the fact that its action raises the very danger the Framers sought to avoid—the exercise of unchecked power. In deciding whether Chadha deserves to be deported, Congress is not subject to any internal constraints that prevent it from arbitrarily depriving him of the right to remain in this country. Unlike the judiciary or an administrative agency, Congress is not bound by established substantive rules. Nor is it subject to the procedural safeguards, such as the right to counsel and a hearing before an impartial tribunal, that are present when a court or an agency adjudicates individual rights. The only effective constraint on Congress' power is political, but Congress is most accountable politically when it prescribes rules of general applicability. When it decides rights of specific persons, those rights are subject to "the tyranny of a shifting majority."

Justice White, dissenting.

Today the Court not only invalidates § 244(c)(2) of the Immigration and Nationality Act, but also sounds the death knell for nearly 200 other statutory provisions in which Congress has reserved a "legislative veto." For this reason, the Court's decision is of surpassing importance. And it is for this reason that the Court would have been well-advised to decide the case, if possible, on the narrower grounds of separation of powers, leaving for full consideration the constitutionality of other congressional review statutes operating on such varied matters as war powers and agency rulemaking, some of which concern the independent regulatory agencies.

The prominence of the legislative veto mechanism in our contemporary political system and its importance to Congress can hardly be overstated. It has become a central means by which Congress secures the accountability of executive and independent agencies. Without the legislative veto, Congress is faced with a Hobson's choice: either to refrain from delegating the necessary authority, leaving itself with a hopeless task of writing laws with the requisite specificity to cover endless

**Take Note**

Why did Justice White think that Congress needs the legislative veto? What role did such practical realities play in his analysis?

special circumstances across the entire policy landscape, or in the alternative, to abdicate its law-making function to the executive branch and independent agencies. To choose the former leaves major national problems unresolved; to opt for the latter risks unaccountable policymaking by those not elected to fill that role. Accordingly, over the past five decades, the legislative veto has been placed in nearly 200 statutes. The device is known in every field of governmental concern: reorganization, budgets, foreign affairs, war powers, and regulation of trade, safety, energy, the environment and the economy.

The history of the legislative veto also makes clear that it has not been a sword with which Congress has struck out to aggrandize itself at the expense of the other branches—the concerns of Madison and Hamilton. Rather, the veto has been a means of defense, a reservation of ultimate authority necessary if Congress is to fulfill its designated role under Article I as the nation's lawmaker. While the President has often objected to particular legislative vetoes, generally those left in the hands of congressional committees, the Executive has more often agreed to legislative review as the price for a broad delegation of authority. To be sure, the President may have preferred unrestricted power, but that could be precisely why Congress thought it essential to retain a check on the exercise of delegated authority.

If the legislative veto were as plainly unconstitutional as the Court strives to suggest, its broad ruling today would be more comprehensible. But, the constitutionality of the legislative veto is anything but clearcut. * * * The reality of the situation is that the constitutional question posed today is one of immense difficulty over which the executive and legislative branches—as well as scholars and judges—have understandably disagreed. That disagreement stems from the silence of the Constitution on the precise question: The Constitution does not directly authorize or prohibit the legislative veto. Thus, our task should be to determine whether the legislative veto is consistent with the purposes of Art. I and the principles of Separation of Powers which are reflected in that Article and throughout the Constitution. We should not find the lack of a specific constitutional authorization for the legislative veto surprising, and I would not infer disapproval of the mechanism from its absence. * * * [O]ur Federal Government was intentionally chartered with the flexibility to respond to contemporary needs without losing sight of fundamental democratic principles.

The power to exercise a legislative veto is not the power to write new law without bicameral approval or presidential consideration. The veto must be authorized by statute and may only negative what an Executive department or independent agency has proposed. On its face, the legislative veto no more allows one House of Congress to make law than does the presidential veto confer such power upon the President.

If Congress may delegate lawmaking power to independent and executive agencies, it is most difficult to understand Article I as forbidding Congress from also reserving a check on legislative power for itself. Absent the veto, the agencies receiving delegations of legislative or quasi-legislative power may issue regulations having the force of law without bicameral approval and without the President's signature. It is thus not apparent why the reservation of a veto over the exercise of that legislative power must be subject to a more exacting test. In both cases, it is enough that the initial statutory authorizations comply with the Article I requirements. * * * Under the Court's analysis, the Executive Branch and the independent agencies may make rules with the effect of law while Congress, in whom the Framers confided the legislative power, may not exercise a veto which precludes such rules from having operative force.

The central concern of the presentation and bicameralism requirements of Article I is that when a departure from the legal status quo is undertaken, it is done with the approval of the President and both Houses of Congress—or, in the event of a presidential veto, a two-thirds majority in both Houses. This interest is fully satisfied by the operation of § 244(c)(2). The President's approval is found in the Attorney General's action in recommending to Congress that the deportation order for a given alien be suspended. The House and the Senate indicate their approval of the Executive's action by not passing a resolution of disapproval within the statutory period. Thus, a change in the legal status quo—the deportability of the alien—is consummated only with the approval of each of the three relevant actors. The disagreement of any one of the three maintains the alien's pre-existing status: the Executive may choose not to recommend suspension; the House and Senate may each veto the recommendation. The effect on the rights and obligations of the affected individuals and upon the legislative system is precisely the same as if a private bill were introduced but failed to receive the necessary approval.

[T]he history of the separation of powers doctrine is [a] history of accommodation and practicality. Apprehensions of an overly powerful branch have not led to undue prophylactic measures that handicap the effective working of the national government as a whole. The Constitution does not contemplate total separation of the three branches of Government.

The legislative veto provision does not "prevent the Executive Branch from accomplishing its constitutionally assigned functions." * * * § 244 grants the executive only a qualified suspension authority and it is only that authority which the President is constitutionally authorized to execute. Moreover, the Court believes that the legislative veto we consider today is best characterized as an exercise of legislative or quasi-legislative authority. Under this characterization, the practice does not, even on the surface, constitute an infringement of executive or judicial prerogative. * * * Nor does § 244 infringe on the judicial power, as Justice POWELL would hold. * * * Congressional action does not substitute for judicial review of the Attorney General's decisions.

[The Court's holding] reflects a profoundly different conception of the Constitution than that held by the Courts which sanctioned the modern administrative state. Today's decision strikes down in one fell swoop provisions in more laws enacted by Congress than the Court has cumulatively invalidated in its history. * * * I must dissent.

---

## Points for Discussion

### *a. The Reach of* Chadha

Justice White observed that nearly 200 federal statutes contained legislative veto provisions. After the Court's decision, all of these federal statutes were (at least in part) unconstitutional. For this reason, *INS v. Chadha* could be said to have invalidated more federal statutes than any other decision in the history of the United States. Was the number of statutes containing legislative veto provisions a reason for pause, or was it instead a reason for the Court to act as it did?

### *b. The Legislative Veto as a Form of Control*

Congress included the legislative veto in the statute at issue in *Chadha* (and in many other statutes) in order to ensure a degree of congressional control over agency decision-making. But couldn't Congress have achieved the same goal simply by giving the Attorney General less discretion to suspend deportation (or no discretion at all)? If Congress wanted the final say in which deportable aliens were entitled to remain in the United States, then why did Congress give the Attorney General discretion to suspend their deportation in the first place? In thinking about that question, you might be interested to learn that, before Congress enacted section 244, suspension of deportation was done exclusively by "private bills," which are bills passed by both Houses of Congress and presented to the President and that relate only to one or a small number of persons or entities. Why do you suppose Congress changed that system?

### *c. The Consequences of* Chadha *for Congressional and Presidential Power over Agencies*

What are the consequences of the Court's decision in *Chadha* for Congress's and the President's respective ability to control agency decision-making? Imagine that, after *Chadha*, an agency issues a rule with which a majority of both houses of the current Congress disagrees. What can Congress do if it wants to repeal the rule? What will the President's response to Congress's action likely be?

We started our consideration of the administrative state by noting that broad delegations of power to agencies might be problematic, to the extent that they give important policy-making authority to unelected officials. Did the legislative veto address this concern? If so, does its invalidation mean that agency decision-making will be even less accountable?

---

Congress can no longer rely on the legislative veto to control agency decision-making. What other tools does Congress have at its disposal to influence or control agency decision-making? Are those tools likely to be as effective as the legislative veto? Consider the case that follows.

---

## *Sierra Club v. Costle*

657 F.2d 298 (D.C. Cir. 1981)

Wald, Circuit Judge:

This case concerns the extent to which new coal-fired steam generators that produce electricity must control their emissions of sulfur dioxide and particulate matter into the air. In June of 1979 EPA revised the regulations called "new source performance standards" ("NSPS" or "standards") governing emission control by coal burning power plants. On this appeal we consider challenges to the revised NSPS brought by environmental groups which contend that the standards are too lax and by electric utilities which contend that the standards are too rigorous. * * *

The Clean Air Act provides for direct federal regulation of emissions from new stationary sources of air pollution by authorizing EPA to set performance standards for significant sources of air pollution which may be reasonably anticipated to endanger public health or welfare. In June 1979 EPA promulgated the NSPS involved in this case. The new standards increase pollution controls for new coal-fired electric power plants by tightening restrictions on emissions of sulfur dioxide and particulate matter. Sulfur dioxide emissions are limited to a maximum of 1.2 lbs./MBtu (or 520 ng/j) and a 90 percent reduction of potential uncontrolled sulfur dioxide emissions is required except when emissions to the atmosphere are less than 0.60 lbs./MBtu (or 260 ng/j). When sulfur dioxide emissions are less than 0.60 lbs./MBtu potential emissions must be reduced by no less than 70 percent. In addition, emissions of particulate matter are limited to 0.03 lbs./MBtu (or 13 ng/j).

[Some environmental groups challenged this variable standard, arguing that the stricter reduction requirements should apply to all plants. Other environmental groups argued that the maximum allowable emissions were too high. Utility companies challenged both the limits on emissions and the reduction requirements. One of the environmental groups asserted that EPA had initially decided to adopt a lower allowable limit on emissions, but that the agency changed its mind after an "*ex parte* blitz" from the coal industry, the President, and Senator Robert Byrd of West Virginia. After the comment period for the emissions rule had ended, opponents of

**Definition**

*Ex parte* means "by or for one party" and is used to refer to communications that take place without the participation of, or notice to, representatives of all parties in a dispute. During litigation, an example of an *ex parte* contact would be a conversation about the case between the judge and a lawyer for just one of the parties in the suit. Judges are not supposed to base decisions on *ex parte* contacts because their decisions are supposed to be based only on evidence introduced during the formal proceedings (and thus subject to cross-examination and rebuttal).

the EPA's initial view, which would have imposed stricter requirements on coal plants, repeatedly contacted and pressured the decision-makers at the EPA to modify the proposal to reduce the burdens on the coal industry. The group contended that these contacts were inappropriate.]

The [Clean Air Act] does not explicitly treat the issue of post-comment period meetings with individuals outside EPA. Oral face-to-face discussions are not prohibited anywhere, anytime, in the Act. The absence of such prohibition may have arisen from the nature of the informal rulemaking procedures Congress had in mind. Where agency action resembles judicial action, where it involves formal rulemaking, adjudication, or quasi-adjudication among "conflicting private claims to a valuable privilege," the insulation of the decisionmaker from *ex parte* contacts is justified by basic notions of due process to the parties involved. But where agency action involves informal rulemaking of a policymaking sort, the concept of *ex parte* contacts is of more questionable utility.

Under our system of government, the very legitimacy of general policymaking performed by unelected administrators depends in no small part upon the openness, accessibility, and amenability of these officials to the needs and ideas of the public from whom their ultimate authority derives, and upon whom their commands must fall. As judges we are insulated from these pressures because of the nature of the judicial process in which we participate; but we must refrain from the easy temptation to look askance at all face-to-face lobbying efforts, regardless of the forum in which they occur, merely because we see them as inappropriate in the judicial context. Furthermore, the importance to effective regulation of continuing contact with a regulated industry, other affected groups, and the public cannot be underestimated. Informal contacts may enable the agency to win needed support for its program, reduce future enforcement requirements by helping those regulated to anticipate and shape their plans for the future, and spur the provision of information which the agency needs. The possibility of course exists that in permitting *ex parte* communications with rulemakers we create the danger of "one administrative record for the public and this court and another for the Commission." *Home Box Office, Inc. v. FCC*, 567 F.2d 9, 54 (D.C. Cir. 1977). Under the Clean Air Act procedures, however, "(t)he promulgated rule may not be based (in part or whole) on any information or data which has not been placed in the docket. . . ." 42 U.S.C. § 7607(d)(6)(C). Thus EPA must justify its rulemaking solely on the basis of the record it compiles and makes public.

It still can be argued, however, that if oral communications are to be freely permitted after the close of the comment period, then at least some adequate summary of them must be made in order to preserve the integrity of the rulemaking docket, which under the statute must be the sole repository of material upon which EPA intends to rely. The statute does not require the docketing of all post-comment period conversations and meetings, but we believe that a fair inference can be drawn that in some instances such docketing may be needed in order to give practical effect to section 307(d)(4)(B)(i), which provides that all documents "of central relevance to the rulemaking" shall be placed in the docket as soon as possible after their availability. This is so because unless oral communications of central relevance to the rulemaking are also docketed in some fashion or other, information central to the justification of the rule could be obtained without ever appearing on the docket, simply by communicating it by voice rather than by pen, thereby frustrating the command of section 307 [of the Clean Air Act] that the final rule not be "based (in part or whole) on any information or data which has not been placed in the docket. . . ." 42 U.S.C. § 7607(d)(6)(C).

[Petitioner] is understandably wary of a rule which permits the agency to decide for itself when oral communications are of such central relevance that a docket entry for them is required. Yet the statute itself vests EPA with discretion to decide whether "documents" are of central relevance and therefore must be placed in the docket; surely EPA can be given no less discretion in docketing oral communications, concerning which the statute has no explicit requirements whatsoever. * * *

Turning to the particular oral communications in this case, we find that only two of the nine contested meetings were undocketed by EPA.* The agency has maintained that, as to the May 1 meeting where Senate staff people were briefed on EPA's analysis concerning the impact of alternative emissions ceilings upon coal reserves, its failure to place a summary of the briefing in the docket was an oversight. We find no evidence that this oversight was anything but an honest inadvertence; furthermore, a briefing of this sort by EPA which simply provides background information about an upcoming rule is not the type of oral communication which would require a docket entry under the statute.

The other undocketed meeting occurred at the White House and involved the President and his White House staff. * * * We have already held that a blanket prohibition against meetings during the post-comment period with individuals outside EPA is unwarranted, and this perforce applies to meetings with White House officials. We have not yet addressed, however, the issue whether such oral communications with

* The meetings included multiple briefings for White House officials; a meeting with the National Coal Association (NCA); a meeting in Senator Byrd's office with White House and NCA officials; a briefing for the President; and a briefing for Senate Committee staff members. —*Ed.*

White House staff, or the President himself, must be docketed on the rulemaking record, and we now turn to that issue. * * *

The court recognizes the basic need of the President and his White House staff to monitor the consistency of executive agency regulations with Administration policy. He and his White House advisers surely must be briefed fully and frequently about rules in the making, and their contributions to policymaking considered. The executive power under our Constitution, after all, is not shared—it rests exclusively with the President. The idea of a "plural executive," or a President with a council of state, was considered and rejected by the Constitutional Convention. Instead the Founders chose to risk the potential for tyranny inherent in placing power in one person, in order to gain the advantages of accountability fixed on a single source. To ensure the President's control and supervision over the Executive Branch, the Constitution and its judicial gloss vests him with the powers of appointment and removal, the power to demand written opinions from executive officers, and the right to invoke executive privilege to protect consultative privacy. In the particular case of EPA, Presidential authority is clear since it has never been considered an "independent agency," but always part of the Executive Branch.

The authority of the President to control and supervise executive policymaking is derived from the Constitution; the desirability of such control is demonstrable from the practical realities of administrative rulemaking. Regulations such as those involved here demand a careful weighing of cost, environmental, and energy considerations. They also have broad implications for national economic policy. Our form of government simply could not function effectively or rationally if key executive policymakers were isolated from each other and from the Chief Executive. Single mission agencies do not always have the answers to complex regulatory problems. An overworked administrator exposed on a 24-hour basis to a dedicated but zealous staff needs to know the arguments and ideas of policymakers in other agencies as well as in the White House.

We recognize, however, that there may be instances where the docketing of conversations between the President or his staff and other Executive Branch officers or rulemakers may be necessary to ensure due process. This may be true, for example, where such conversations directly concern the outcome of adjudications or quasi-adjudicatory proceedings; there is no inherent executive power to control the rights of individuals in such settings. Docketing may also be necessary in some circumstances where a statute like this one specifically requires that essential "information or data" upon which a rule is based be docketed. But in the absence of any further Congressional requirements, we hold that it was not unlawful in this case for EPA not to docket a face-to-face policy session involving the President and EPA officials during the post-comment period, since EPA makes no effort to base the rule on any "information or data" arising from that meeting. * * *

The purposes of full-record review which underlie the need for disclosing *ex parte* conversations in some settings do not require that courts know the details of every White House contact, including a Presidential one, in this informal rulemaking setting. After all, any rule issued here with or without White House assistance must have the requisite factual support in the rulemaking record, and under this particular statute the Administrator may not base the rule in whole or in part on any "information or data" which is not in the record, no matter what the source. The courts will monitor all this, but they need not be omniscient to perform their role effectively. Of course, it is always possible that undisclosed Presidential prodding may direct an outcome that is factually based on the record, but different from the outcome that would have obtained in the absence of Presidential involvement. In such a case, it would be true that the political process did affect the outcome in a way the courts could not police. But we do not believe that Congress intended that the courts convert informal rulemaking into a rarified technocratic process, unaffected by political considerations or the presence of Presidential power. In sum, we find that the existence of intra-Executive Branch meetings during the post-comment period, and the failure to docket one such meeting involving the President, violated neither the procedures mandated by the Clean Air Act nor due process.

Finally, [petitioner] challenges the rulemaking on the basis of alleged Congressional pressure, citing principally two meetings with Senator Byrd. [Petitioner] asserts that under the controlling case law the political interference demonstrated in this case represents a separate and independent ground for invalidating this rulemaking.

[Our cases require] that two conditions be met before an administrative rulemaking may be overturned simply on the grounds of Congressional pressure. First, the content of the pressure upon the Secretary is designed to force him to decide upon factors not made relevant by Congress in the applicable statute. * * * Second, the Secretary's determination must be affected by those extraneous considerations.

In the case before us, there is no persuasive evidence that either criterion is satisfied. Senator Byrd requested a meeting in order to express "strongly" his already well-known views that the [proposed] standards' impact on coal reserves was a matter of concern to him. EPA initiated a second responsive meeting to report its reaction to the reserve data submitted by the NCA. In neither meeting is there any allegation that EPA made any commitments to Senator Byrd. The meetings did underscore Senator Byrd's deep concerns for EPA, but there is no evidence he attempted actively to use "extraneous" pressures to further his position. Americans rightly expect their elected representatives to voice their grievances and preferences concerning the administration of our laws. We believe it entirely proper for Congressional representatives vigorously to represent the interests of their constituents before administrative agencies engaged in informal, general policy rulemaking, so long as individual Congressmen do not frustrate the intent of Congress as a whole as expressed in statute, nor undermine applicable rules of procedure. Where Congressmen keep their comments focused on the substance of the proposed rule—and we have no substantial evidence to cause us to believe Senator Byrd did not do so here[539]—administrative agencies are expected to balance Congressional pressure with the pressures emanating from all other sources. To hold otherwise would deprive the agencies of legitimate sources of information and call into question the validity of nearly every controversial rulemaking.

In sum, we conclude that EPA's adoption of the 1.2 lbs./MBtu emissions ceiling was free from procedural error. The post-comment period contacts here violated neither the statute nor the integrity of the proceeding. * * *

---

## Points for Discussion

### *a. Congressional Lobbying as a Form of Control*

One way that Congress can exercise control over agency decision-making is for members of Congress to lobby agency officials to take (or refrain from taking) certain actions. Such efforts are very common. How effective are such efforts likely to be? Are agency officials under any obligation to follow the advice of members of Congress about policy? If not, are there nevertheless reasons why agency officials are likely to accommodate requests by members of Congress? Does it matter whether the White House and Congress are controlled by different political parties?

Under the court's approach, is there ever a time when contacts between members of Congress and agency officials will so taint an agency rulemaking proceeding that the court must set the rule aside? The court's test required both that "the content of the pressure upon the [agency] is designed to force [it] to decide upon factors not made relevant by Congress in the applicable statute" and that the agency's "determination [be] affected by those extraneous considerations." Even if there is no congressional pressure, do you think that courts will uphold agency decisions based on factors "not made relevant" in the applicable statute? We will consider this question later in this Chapter, when we turn to "hard-look" review of agency rules.

---

539 The only hint we are provided that extraneous "threats" were made comes from a newspaper article which states, in part,

> "The ceiling decision came after two weeks of what one Senate source called 'hard-ball arm-twisting' by Byrd and other coal state Senators. Byrd summoned Costle and White House adviser Stuart Eizenstat *strongly hinting* that the Administration needs his support on strategic arms limitation treaty (SALT) and the windfall profits tax, according to Senate and Administration sources."

The Washington Post, May 5, 1979, at A-1 (emphasis supplied). We do not believe that a single newspaper account of strong "hint(s)" represents substantial evidence of extraneous pressure significant enough to warrant a finding of unlawful congressional interference.

#### *b. Political Influence in Rulemaking and Adjudication*

How significant was it for the court's conclusion that the agency action at issue was rulemaking rather than adjudication? The court noted that it does not make sense to impose judicial norms of fair procedure on agency rulemaking proceedings, which are more similar to legislative action than they are to judicial action. Should there be a different rule for attempts by the White House or members of Congress to influence the outcome of an agency adjudication? We will consider this question later in this Chapter, when we consider *Portland Audubon Society v. Endangered Species Committee*, 984 F.2d 1534 (9th Cir. 1993).

---

## C. Judicial Oversight of Agency Decision-Making

We began this Chapter by asking whether electorally accountable decision-makers—the President and Congress—exercised meaningful forms of control over agency decision-making. This question was important both for assessing the virtues and drawbacks of a system in which Congress routinely delegates broad policy-making authority to agencies and for starting to think about what role agency interpretations of statutes should play in determining the meaning of those statutes.

We continue our exploration of these questions in this section, which considers the ways in which courts conduct oversight of agency decision-making. To be sure, judicial oversight of agency action is different in an important respect from political control. Presidential or congressional control or influence over agency decision-making can allay concerns about electorally unaccountable actors making government policy, because we get to vote for the President and for members of Congress. Judges, on the other hand, are largely immune from political and electoral control. But judicial review of agency action can ensure that agencies comply with the limits imposed by statute, which electorally accountable actors were responsible for enacting. Accordingly, judicial oversight of agency decision-making indirectly promotes accountability. It also ensures that agency decision-making takes place within a carefully limited legal framework designed to promote rational policy choices.

We have already seen examples of judicial oversight of agency decision-making. In Chapter 6, for example, when we considered examples of the various forms of agency decision-making, we did so through the lens of judicial decisions that evaluated the lawfulness of the agency actions. In addition, some of the cases that we considered in the Chapters about statutory interpretation—including, for example, *Tennessee Valley Authority v. Hill*, which we considered in Chapter 2—involved the question whether agency action was lawful. We now turn directly to how courts review agency decisions for lawfulness and validity.

---

## 1. Review for Compliance with Procedural Requirements

As we saw in Chapter 6, there are several sources of law that constrain agency action. First, an agency's organic statute often contains limits on the agency's powers and procedural requirements for agency action. Second, Congress has enacted some statutes, such as the National Environmental Policy Act, that impose specific limits on virtually all agency authority. Third, the Administrative Procedure Act identifies procedural requirements with which agency action must comply, and it provides standards for judicial review of agency action. Fourth, the Constitution—in the Due Process Clause of the Fifth Amendment (and, as we'll see, Article III)—guarantees some minimal level of procedure for some agency actions that affect private rights.

In this section, we consider judicial review for compliance with procedural requirements. Recall from Chapter 6 that the APA creates four basic procedural categories—formal and informal rulemaking, and formal and informal adjudication—and that the procedural requirements that it imposes vary depending on the category of agency action at issue. We begin with judicial oversight of agency compliance with the procedural requirements for rulemaking, and then we will turn to judicial review for agency compliance with the procedural requirements for adjudication.

---

### a. Rulemaking

## *Chocolate Mfrs. Ass'n v. Block*

755 F.2d 1098 (4th Cir. 1985)

SPROUSE, CIRCUIT JUDGE:

Chocolate Manufacturers Association (CMA) appeals from the decision of the district court denying it relief from a rule promulgated by the Food and Nutrition Service (FNS) of the United States Department of Agriculture (USDA or Department). CMA protests that part of the rule that prohibits the use of chocolate flavored milk in the federally funded Special Supplemental Food Program for Women, Infants and Children (WIC Program). Holding that the Department's proposed rulemaking did not provide adequate notice that the elimination of flavored milk would be considered in the rulemaking procedure, we reverse.

The WIC Program was established by Congress in 1972 to assist pregnant, postpartum, and breastfeeding women, infants and young children from families with inadequate income whose physical and mental health is in danger because of inadequate nutrition or health care. Under the program, the Department designs food packages reflecting the different nutritional needs of women, infants, and children and provides cash grants to state or local agencies, which distribute cash or vouchers to qualifying individuals in accordance with Departmental regulations as to the type and quantity of food.

In 1975 Congress revised and extended the WIC Program through fiscal year 1978 and, for the first time, defined the "supplemental foods" which the program was established to provide. The term

> "shall mean those foods containing nutrients known to be lacking in the diets of populations at nutritional risk and, in particular, those foods and food products containing high-quality protein, iron, calcium, vitamin A, and vitamin C. . . . The contents of the food package shall be made available in such a manner as to provide flexibility, taking into account medical and nutritional objectives and cultural eating patterns."

Pub. L. No. 94–105, § 17(g)(3), 89 Stat. 511, 520 (1975) (codified at 42 U.S.C. § 1786(g)(3) (1976)) (replaced by 42 U.S.C. § 1786(b)(14) (1982)).

Pursuant to this statutory definition, the Department promulgated new regulations specifying the contents of WIC Program food packages. These regulations specified that flavored milk was an acceptable substitute for fluid whole milk in the food packages for women and children, but not infants. This regulation formalized the Department's practice of permitting the substitution of flavored milk, a practice observed in the WIC Program since its inception in 1973 * * *.

In 1978 Congress, in extending the WIC Program through fiscal year 1982, redefined the term "supplemental foods" to mean:

> "those foods containing nutrients determined by nutritional research to be lacking in the diets of pregnant, breastfeeding, and postpartum women, infants, and children, as prescribed by the Secretary. State agencies may, with the approval of the Secretary, substitute different foods providing the nutritional equivalent of foods prescribed by the Secretary, to allow for different cultural eating patterns."

Pub. L. No. 95–627, § 17(b)(14), 92 Stat. 3603, 3613 (1978) (codified at 42 U.S.C. § 1786(b)(14) (1982)). Congress stated further:

> "The Secretary shall prescribe by regulation supplemental foods to be made available in the program under this section. To the degree possible, the Secretary shall assure that the fat, sugar, and salt content of the prescribed foods is appropriate."

*Id.* at § 17(f)(12), 92 Stat. at 3616 (codified at 42 U.S.C. § 1786(f)(12) (1982)). To comply with this statutory redefinition, the Department moved to redraft its regulations specifying the WIC Program food packages. In doing so it relied upon information collected during an extensive investigative effort which had begun in 1977. * * *

**Take Note**

Although the public's opportunity to participate in the rulemaking process began only after the agency published its proposed rule, the agency spent a considerable amount of time studying the issue and collecting information in the two years before it published its proposal. Does the APA impose any limits on these early, informal processes? Should it?

Using this information as well as its own research as a basis, the Department in November 1979 published for comment the proposed rule at issue in this case. Along with the proposed rule, the Department published a preamble discussing the general purpose of the rule and acknowledging the congressional directive that the Department design food packages containing the requisite nutritional value and appropriate levels of fat, sugar, and salt. Discussing the issue of sugar at length, it noted, for example, that continued inclusion of high sugar cereals may be "contrary to nutrition education principles and may lead to unsound eating practices." It also noted that high sugar foods are more expensive than foods with lower sugar content, and that allowing them would be "inconsistent with the goal of teaching participants economical food buying patterns."

The rule proposed a maximum sugar content specifically for authorized cereals. The preamble also contained a discussion of the sugar content in juice, but the Department did not propose to reduce the allowable amount of sugar in juice because of technical problems involved in any reduction. Neither the rule nor the preamble discussed sugar in relation to flavoring in milk. Under the proposed rule, the food packages for women and children without special dietary needs included milk that could be "flavored or unflavored."

The notice allowed sixty days for comment and specifically invited comment on the entire scope of the proposed rules: "The public is invited to submit written comments in favor of or in objection to the proposed regulations or to make recommendations for alternatives not considered in the proposed regulations." Over 1,000 comments were received from state and local agencies, congressional offices, interest groups, and WIC Program participants and others. Seventy-eight commenters, mostly local WIC administrators, recommended that the agency delete flavored milk from the list of approved supplemental foods.

In promulgating the final rule, the Department, responding to these public comments, deleted flavored milk from the list, explaining:

> "In the previous regulations, women and children were allowed to receive flavored or unflavored milk. No change in this provision was proposed by the Department. However, 78 commenters requested the deletion of flavored milk from the food packages since flavored milk has a higher sugar content than unflavored milk. They indicated that providing flavored milk contradicts nutrition education and the Department's proposal to limit sugar in the food packages. Furthermore, flavored milk is more expensive than unflavored milk. The Department agrees with these concerns. * * *

> Therefore, to reinforce nutrition education, for consistency with the Department's philosophy about sugar in the food packages, and to maintain food package costs at economic levels, the Department is deleting flavored milk from the food packages for women and children. Although the deletion of flavored milk was not proposed, the comments and the Department's policy on sugar validate this change.

45 Fed. Reg. 74854, 74865–66 (1980).

After the final rule was issued, CMA petitioned the Department to reopen the rulemaking to allow it to comment, maintaining that it had been misled into believing that the deletion of flavored milk would not be considered. * * * [The Department] declined to reopen the rulemaking procedure.

On this appeal, CMA contends [that] the Department did not provide notice that the disallowance of flavored milk would be considered * * *. The Department responds * * * by arguing that its notice advised the public of its general concern about high sugar content in the proposed food packages and that this should have alerted potentially interested commenters that it would consider eliminating any food with high sugar content. It also argues in effect that the inclusion of flavored milk in the proposed rule carried with it the implication that both inclusion and exclusion would be considered in the rulemaking process. * * *

The requirement of notice and a fair opportunity to be heard is basic to administrative law. * * * We must decide whether inclusion of flavored milk in the allowable food packages under the proposed rule should have alerted interested persons that the Department might reverse its position and exclude flavored milk if adverse comments recommended its deletion from the program.

Section 4 of the Administrative Procedure Act (APA) requires that the notice in the Federal Register of a proposed rulemaking contain "either the terms or substance of the proposed rule or a description of the subjects and issues involved." 5 U.S.C. § 553(b)(3) (1982). The purpose of the notice-and-comment procedure is both "to allow the agency to benefit from the experience and input of the parties who file comments . . . and to see to it that the agency maintains a flexible and open-minded attitude towards its own rules." *National Tour Brokers Ass'n v. United States*, 591 F.2d 896, 902 (D.C. Cir. 1978). The notice-and-comment procedure encourages public participation in the administrative process and educates the agency, thereby helping to ensure informed agency decisionmaking.

The Department's published notice here consisted of the proposed rule and a preamble discussing the negative effect of high sugar content in general and specifically in relation to some foods such as cereals and juices, but it did not mention high sugar content in flavored milk. The proposed rule eliminated certain foods with high sugar content but specifically authorized flavored milk as part of the permissible diet. In a discussion characterized by pointed identification of foods with high sugar content, flavored milk was conspicuous by its exclusion. If after comments the agency had adopted without change the proposed rule as its final rule, there could have been no possible objection to the adequacy of notice. The public was fully notified as to what the Department considered to be a healthy and adequate diet for its target group. The final rule, however, dramatically altered the proposed rule, changing for the first time the milk content of the diet by deleting flavored milk. The agency concedes that the elimination of flavored milk by the final rule is a complete reversal from its treatment in the proposed rule, but it explains that the reversal was caused by the comments received from 78 interested parties—primarily professional administrators of the WIC Program.

This presents then not the simple question of whether the notice of a proposed rule adequately informs the public of its intent, but rather the question of how to judge the adequacy of the notice when the proposal it describes is replaced by a final rule which reaches a conclusion exactly opposite to that proposed, on the basis of comments received from parties representing only a single view of a controversy. In reviewing the propriety of such agency action, we are not constrained by the same degree of deference we afford most agency determinations. * * *

There is no question that an agency may promulgate a final rule that differs in some particulars from its proposal. Otherwise the agency "can learn from the comments on its proposals only at the peril of starting a new procedural round of commentary." *International Harvester Co. v. Ruckelshaus*, 478 F.2d 615, 632 n. 51 (D.C. Cir. 1973). An agency, however, does not have carte blanche to establish a rule contrary to its original proposal simply because it receives suggestions to alter it during the comment period. An interested party must have been alerted by the notice to the possibility of the changes eventually adopted from the comments. Although an agency, in its notice of proposed rulemaking, need not identify precisely every potential regulatory change, the notice must be sufficiently descriptive to provide interested parties with a fair opportunity to comment and to participate in the rulemaking. *United States v. Allegheny-Ludlum Steel Corp.*, 406 U.S. 742, 758 (1972).

[A]ppellate review of changes in a proposed rule after comments is more specifically controlled by the circumstances of each case than most administrative appeals. Nevertheless, a review of decisions of our sister circuits performing similar tasks is helpful. In *BASF Wyandotte Corp. v. Costle*, 598 F.2d 637 (1st Cir. 1979), cert. denied, 444 U.S. 1096 (1980), the court considered an EPA regulation controlling the discharge of pollutants into navigable waters by the pesticide industry. The EPA originally proposed dividing the organic pesticide industry into three subcategories, setting different pollutant standards for each one. The industry, arguing for expansion of the number of subcategories and, therefore, pollutant standards, submitted comments demonstrating that the proposed three subcategories were indistinguishable. The EPA, while agreeing with the comments, chose a different solution: it altered its initial rule by eliminating the subcategories and applying uniform standards throughout the entire organic pesticide industry. The industry complained that the EPA's decision to contract rather than expand the number of subcategories took them entirely by surprise. "The essential inquiry," the court said, "is whether the commentators have had a fair opportunity to present their views on the contents of the final plan." *Id.* at 642. The First Circuit reasoned that even if the initial rule had proposed uniform standards, the content of petitioner's comments would not have been different for they still would have argued, albeit more voluminously and vociferously, for more subcategories. *Id.* at 644. The petitioners, therefore, "had a fair opportunity to present their views." *Id.*

In *South Terminal Corp. v. EPA*, 504 F.2d 646 (1st Cir. 1974), the court considered an air quality transportation control plan for Boston, Massachusetts, which varied substantially from the proposal described in the notice. The petitioners contended that they had no meaningful notice of the substance of the plan. The *South Terminal* court identified two factors of primary importance in determining whether a substantially revised final rule is promulgated in accordance with the APA: the changes in the original rule must be "in character with the original scheme" and "a logical outgrowth" of the notice and comment already given. *Id.* at 658, 659. In rejecting the petitioners' claim, the court stated: "Although the changes were substantial, they were in character with the original scheme and were additionally foreshadowed in proposals and comments advanced during the rulemaking. [In addition, the parties] had been warned that strategies might be modified in light of their suggestions." 504 F.2d at 658. A proposed rule, therefore, must fairly apprise interested parties of the potential scope and substance of a substantially revised final rule and, under this approach, a substantial change must relate in part to the comments received.

**Take Note**

The court here announces the "logical outgrowth" test for notice of a proposed rulemaking. Under the test, notice of a proposed rulemaking is valid as long as the rule that the agency ultimately issues is a "logical outgrowth" of the proposed rule. Under this test, can an agency modify a proposed rule to respond to concerns or problems raised in the comments? If not, then what is the point of notice-and-comment rulemaking?

The test devised by the First Circuit for determining adequacy of notice of a change in a proposed rule occurring after comments appears to us to be sound: notice is adequate if the changes in the original plan "are in character with the original scheme," and the final rule is a "logical outgrowth" of the notice and comments already given. Other circuits also have adopted some form of the "logical outgrowth" test. * * * Stated differently, if the final rule materially alters the issues involved in the rulemaking or, as stated in *Rowell v. Andrus*, 631 F.2d 699, 702 n. 2 (10th Cir. 1980), if the final rule "substantially departs from the terms or substance of the proposed rule," the notice is inadequate.

There can be no doubt that the final rule in the instant case was the "outgrowth" of the original rule proposed by the agency, but the question of whether the change in it was in character with the original scheme and whether it was a "*logical* outgrowth" is not easy to answer. In resolving this difficult issue, we recognize that, although helpful, verbal formulations are not omnipotent talismans, and we agree that in the final analysis each case "must turn on how well the notice that the agency gave serves the policies underlying the notice requirement." *Small Refiner Lead Phase-Down Task Force v. EPA*, 705 F.2d 506, 547 (D.C. Cir. 1983). Under either view, we do not feel that CMA was fairly treated or that the administrative rulemaking process was well served by the drastic alteration of the rule without an opportunity for CMA to be heard.

It is apparent that for many years the Department of Agriculture has permitted the use of chocolate in some form in the food distribution programs that it administers. The only time the Department has proposed to remove chocolate in any form from its programs was in April 1978 when it sought to characterize chocolate as a candy and remove it from the School Lunch Program. That proposal was withdrawn after CMA commented, supporting chocolate as a part of the diet. Chocolate flavored milk has been a permissible part of the WIC Program diet since its inception and there have been no proposals for its removal until the present controversy.

The Department sponsored commendable information-gathering proceedings prior to publishing its proposed rule. Together with its own research, the information gathered in the pre-publication information solicitations formed the basis for the proposed rule. Most of the same information was presented to Congress prior to enactment of the 1978 statute that precipitated the 1979 rulemaking here in controversy. The National Advisory Council on Maternal, Infant, and Fetal Nutrition provided information and advice. Regional council meetings were open to the public and held in diverse areas of the country. Department of Agriculture personnel attended a number of regional, state, and local meetings and gathered opinions concerning possible changes in the food packages. The agency also gathered a food package advisory panel of experts seeking their recommendations. Food packages were designed based on the information and advice gleaned from these sources. In all of these activities setting out and discussing food packages, including the proposed rule and its preamble, the Department never suggested that flavored milk be removed from the WIC Program.

The published preamble to the proposed rule consisted of twelve pages in the Federal Register discussing in detail factors that would be considered in making the final rule. Two pages were devoted to a general discussion of nutrients * * * and the dangers of overconsumption of sugar, fat, and salt. The preamble discussed some foods containing these ingredients and foods posing specific problems. It did not discuss flavored milk.

In the next eight pages of the preamble, the nutrition content of food packages was discussed—under the general headings of "cereal" and "juice" for infants; and "eggs," "milk," "cheese," "peanut butter and mature dried beans and peas," "juice," "additional foods," "cereals," "iron," "sugar," "whole grain cereals," "highly fortified cereals," and "artificial flavors and colors" for women and children. The only reference to milk concerned the correct quantity to be provided to children, *i.e.,* 24 quarts per month instead of 28 quarts. Although there was considerable discussion of the sugar content of juice and cereal, there was none concerning flavored milk. Likewise, there was considerable discussion of artificial flavor and color in cereal but none concerning flavored milk. The only reference to flavored milk was in the two-page discussion of the individual food packages, which noted that the proposed rule would permit the milk to be flavored or unflavored. The proposed rule which followed the preamble expressly noted that flavored or unflavored milk was permitted in the individual food packages for women and children without special dietary needs.

At the time the proposed rulemaking was published, neither CMA nor the public in general could have had any indication from the history of either the WIC Program or any other food distribution programs that flavored milk was not part of the acceptable diet for women and children without special dietary needs. The discussion in the preamble to the proposed rule was very detailed and identified specific foods which the agency was examining for excess sugar. This specificity, together with total silence concerning any suggestion of eliminating flavored milk, strongly indicated that flavored milk was not at issue. The proposed rule positively and unqualifiedly approved the continued use of flavored milk. Under the specific circumstances of this case, it cannot be said that the ultimate changes in the proposed rule were in character with the original scheme or a logical outgrowth of the notice. We can well accept that, in general, an approval of a practice in a proposed rule may properly alert interested parties that the practice may be disapproved in the final rule in the event of adverse comments. The total effect of the history of the use of flavored milk, the preamble discussion, and the proposed rule, however, could have led interested persons only to conclude that a change in flavored milk would not be considered. Although ultimately their comments may well have been futile, CMA and other interested persons at least should have had the opportunity to make them. We believe that there was insufficient notice that the deletion of flavored milk from the WIC Program would be considered if adverse comments were received, and, therefore, that affected parties did not receive a fair opportunity to contribute to the administrative rulemaking process. That process was ill-served by the misleading or inadequate notice concerning the permissibility of chocolate flavored milk in the WIC Program and "does not serve the policy underlying the notice requirement."

[Reversed.]

## Points for Discussion

### *a. Notice and the Opportunity to Comment*

The APA provides that "[g]eneral notice of proposed rule making shall be published in the Federal Register" and "shall include * * * either the terms or substance of the proposed rule or a description of the subjects and issues involved." 5 U.S.C. § 553(b). The APA provides further that "[a]fter notice required by this section, the agency shall give interested persons an opportunity to participate in the rule making through submission of written data, views, or arguments with or without opportunity for oral presentation." *Id.* § 553(c). Not surprisingly, the APA also contemplates that the agency will consider the comments that it receives before issuing a final rule. See *id.* ("After consideration of the relevant matter presented, the agency shall incorporate in the rules adopted a concise general statement of their basis and purpose.").

When an agency engages in informal rulemaking—also called notice-and-comment rulemaking, because of these procedural requirements—it usually starts by publishing its proposed rule in the Federal Register, with an invitation for interested persons to submit comments. After reviewing the comments, the agency then issues a final rule. According to the court, the final rule must be a "logical outgrowth" of the proposed rule. The justification for this requirement is to ensure that interested persons had genuine notice that the agency might issue a rule that would affect their interests. As a consequence, the logical outgrowth test tends to prohibit agency rules that depart substantially from the original proposal. But what if the final rule departs substantially from the proposed rule because the commenters raised convincing objections to some aspect of the original proposal? Does it make sense to have a standard that effectively prohibits the agency from listening to the concerns raised by commenters? If so, then what is the point of giving interested persons an opportunity to comment in the first place?

### *b. Exceptions to the Notice and Comment Requirements*

The notice and comment requirements do not apply when the rule involves "a military or foreign affairs function of the United States" or a "matter relating to agency management or personnel or to public property, loans, grants, benefits, or contracts." 5 U.S.C. § 553(a). They also do not apply to "interpretative rules, general statements of policy, or rules of agency organization, procedure, or practice"—that is, to rules that do not generally carry the binding force of law—or when "the agency for good cause finds * * * that notice and public procedure thereon are impracticable, unnecessary, or contrary to the public interest." *Id.* § 553(b). If the point of the notice and comment requirements is to ensure that the agency considers the views of interested persons before acting, then does it make sense to create these exceptions to the requirements?

## *Independent U.S. Tanker Owners Committee v. Dole*

809 F.2d 847 (D.C. Cir. 1987)

Bork, Circuit Judge:

These consolidated cases are before us on appeal from a decision of the district court, 620 F. Supp. 1289 (1985), which sustained the validity of a rule promulgated by the Secretary of Transportation. Appellants challenge the rule as exceeding the Secretary's statutory authority and as arbitrary and capricious agency action; they also raise a battery of specific procedural objections to the manner in which the rule was promulgated. We find that the Secretary was well within her statutory authority in promulgating the rule, but that she failed to provide an adequate account of how the rule serves the objectives set out in the governing statute, the Merchant Marine Act of 1936, ch. 858, 49 Stat. 1985 (codified as amended at 46 U.S.C. §§ 1101–1295g (1982)).

The rulemaking that gives rise to this case is the latest of numerous attempts by the Congress, the Maritime Administration, and the Department of Transportation to address the recurrent problems of the United States merchant marine fleet. The American fleet has had great difficulty competing in foreign commerce. American ships typically have higher construction and operating costs than their foreign competitors, not only because they typically must meet more stringent environmental and safety standards, but also because foreign ships often are subsidized and otherwise assisted by their own governments. Congress confronted these problems in 1936 and authorized the United States government to pay up to half the construction costs of American ships that will operate in foreign commerce. 46 U.S.C. §§ 1151–1152 (1982). In addition, Congress authorized the government to subsidize the operating costs of these ships where necessary to meet foreign competition. *Id.* §§ 1171–1172. Despite these provisions, American ships have continued to fare poorly against their competitors in foreign commerce.

Merchant ships that operate in the domestic shipping market do not receive these government subsidies. They are protected from the rigors of foreign competition, however, by the Jones Act, which requires all cargo transported between points in the United States to be carried on ships built in the United States, registered in the United States, and owned by American citizens. 46 U.S.C. § 883 (1982). They are also protected from having to compete against any of the ships that have received construction subsidies or operating subsidies from the government, except in a few specific and very limited instances. Since the Trans-Alaska Pipeline opened in 1977, however, the domestic fleet has been unable to satisfy the great new demand for large tankers to carry Alaskan oil to other points in the country. The Maritime Administration has responded to this situation by invoking its statutory authority to allow certain subsidized ships to operate in the domestic market for up to six months in a given year if the ships repay a proportional share of the construction subsidy that they have received. 46 C.F.R. Part 250 (1984). Yet this step has only partly solved the problem.

The rule at issue in this case permitted tanker vessels built with the assistance of a federal construction-differential subsidy, which had been barred from competing in domestic trade on account of that subsidy, to undertake domestic operations if they agreed to repay the unamortized portion of the subsidy plus interest during a period that began on June 6, 1985, and closed one year later. *See* Construction-Differential Subsidy Repayment; Total Payment Policy, 50 Fed. Reg. 19,170 (1985) (codified at 46 C.F.R. § 276.3 (1985)) (hereafter the "payback rule").

**FYI**

Under conventional accounting practices, the value of an asset is often determined by subtracting an amount from the original cost of the asset to represent the asset's depreciation. In many cases, the holder of the asset can treat a certain amount of the cost as depreciation each year. The "unamortized" portion is the amount that has not yet been subtracted for depreciation.

This rule addressed problems in both the foreign and domestic markets by providing an opportunity for ships that are not competitive in foreign commerce to enter the domestic market where the demand for their services has increased, but only by agreeing to relinquish their financial advantage over unsubsidized ships. The Maritime Administration has considered proposals for individual ships to repay their subsidies at least since 1964. In 1977, several owners of unsubsidized ships challenged the Administration's approval of repayment by one vessel in particular. The Supreme Court upheld the government's authority to approve subsidy repayment in exchange for permission to enter the domestic market. *See Seatrain Shipbuilding Corp. v. Shell Oil Co.*, 444 U.S. 572 (1980). Shortly thereafter, the Administration established an interim rule that extended this authorization to undertake domestic shipping, upon repayment of the full subsidy plus interest, to a limited class of large tankers whose owners demonstrated "exceptional circumstances" of dismal prospects in foreign commerce to justify the application of the rule. *See* 45 Fed. Reg. 68,393 (1980). The interim rule was challenged, and this court invalidated it, finding that although the Administration had statutory authority to promulgate the rule, it had acted arbitrarily and capriciously by providing an inadequate discussion of the basis and purpose of the rule. *See Independent U.S. Tanker Owners Comm. v. Lewis*, 690 F.2d 908, 918–20 (D.C. Cir. 1982). At that point, the Secretary of Transportation proposed the payback rule. This rule is similar to the earlier proposed interim rule except that it covers all tankers and does not require tankers to make any showing of "exceptional circumstances" to qualify for the benefits of subsidy repayment.

Appellants contend that [the payback rule] should be invalidated because it is the product of agency action that was "arbitrary, capricious, an abuse of discretion, or not otherwise in accordance with law." 5 U.S.C. § 706(2)(A). In particular, appellants contend that the Secretary failed to provide a sufficiently reasoned discussion of why this rule was adopted and alternatives were rejected in light of the purposes of the Merchant Marine Act * * *.

It is unfortunate that, once more, we must agree with this contention. This court vacated the previous interim rule because the government "failed completely to fulfill its obligations" to set out an adequate statement of basis and purpose for the rule. *Independent U.S. Tanker Owners Comm.*, 690 F.2d at 919. Now, four years later, we must vacate a similar rule on similar grounds.

Under the Administrative Procedure Act, when an agency initiates a rulemaking that the governing statute does not require to be undertaken "on the record," the agency is nonetheless bound to comply with the requirements for "notice and comment" rulemaking set out in 5 U.S.C. § 553. One requirement is that after the agency considers the comments presented by the participating parties, it "shall incorporate in the rules adopted a concise general statement of their basis and purpose." 5 U.S.C. § 553(c). This statement need not be an exhaustive, detailed account of every aspect of the rulemaking proceedings; it is not meant to be the more elaborate document, complete with findings of fact and conclusions of law, that is required in an on-the-record rulemaking. *See id.* § 557(c). On the other hand, this court has cautioned against "an overly literal reading of the statutory terms 'concise' and 'general'. . . . [which] must be accommodated to the realities of judicial scrutiny." *Automotive Parts & Accessories Ass'n v. Boyd*, 407 F.2d 330, 338 (D.C. Cir. 1968). At the least, such a statement should indicate the major issues of policy that were raised in the proceedings and explain why the agency decided to respond to these issues as it did, particularly in light of the statutory objectives that the rule must serve.

In *Seatrain*, the Supreme Court indicated that Congress gave the government broad power to implement the Merchant Marine Act so that the government could take steps that "directly further the general goals of the Act." 444 U.S. at 558. Those objectives are to foster the development and encourage the maintenance of an American merchant marine, in both foreign and domestic commerce, that is:

> (a) sufficient to carry its domestic water-borne commerce and a substantial portion of the water-borne export and import foreign commerce of the United States and to provide shipping service essential for maintaining the flow of such domestic and foreign water-borne commerce at all times, (b) capable of serving as a naval and military auxiliary in time of war or national emergency, (c) owned and operated under the United States flag by citizens of the United States, insofar as may be practicable, (d) composed of the best-equipped, safest, and most suitable types of vessels, constructed in the United States and manned with a trained and efficient citizen personnel, and (e) supplemented by efficient facilities for shipbuilding and ship repair.

46 U.S.C. § 1101 (1982).

The Secretary's statement of basis and purpose fails to give an adequate account of how the payback rule serves these objectives and why alternative measures were rejected in light of them. The Secretary's treatment of these objectives, and of the concerns raised about them in the comment proceedings, is cursory at best. For example, concerns about whether this rule meets the statutory objective of maintaining an American merchant marine "sufficient to carry its domestic water-borne commerce and a substantial portion of the water-borne export and import foreign commerce" are met with the statement: "The Department believes that the [rule] will benefit the U.S. Merchant Marine." 50 Fed. Reg. 19,170, 19,173 (1985). Her discussion continues further, but it hardly improves:

> "Although it is true, as many commenters pointed out, that some tankers will be forced out of service by more efficient operators, the industry should be more competitive and efficient in the future, especially since some of the most efficient tankers in the U.S. flag fleet would be fully utilized. . . . Overall, the industry should be left in a healthier, more viable condition."

*Id.* at 19,173–74. On the more dubious proposition that the fleet will remain able to carry "a substantial portion" of foreign commerce, the Secretary candidly acknowledges that "the final rule merely recognizes the existing condition of the U.S. tanker fleet. There currently exist few foreign trade employment opportunities for those vessels and the prospects for future employment in the foreign trade are far from bright." *Id.* at 19,174. Though this statement strongly suggests the view that this rule will hasten an American retreat from carriage of foreign commerce, the Secretary surprisingly asserts that the fleet will remain "more than adequate to carry an appropriate share of the U.S. foreign oil commerce if such opportunities should arise." *Id.* This remark is hard to fathom. If there is currently little hope for the employment of American vessels in foreign trade, then the payback rule will permit the total size of the American fleet to follow its natural tendency to decrease toward the level required by the domestic market. Under present conditions, therefore, the rule will make it impossible to retain a fleet that can carry all domestic traffic and "a substantial portion" of foreign traffic "at all times," which is explicitly set out as an objective in section (a) of the statute.

The Secretary's response to concerns about the rule's effects on the fleet as a naval auxiliary, to take another example, is similarly unsatisfying. The Navy warned that the projected loss under this rule of "handy-sized" tankers might have adverse implications for national security. The Secretary brushes aside this comment by stating her belief that "the outlook for these old, small product tankers is poor regardless of whether or not this rule is promulgated because of their age and the decline of the U.S. products trade." *Id.* She also claims that other non-fleet ships could fill in the gap, *id.*, even though this observation may not help to satisfy the statutory objective that the fleet itself should constitute "a naval and military auxiliary in time of war or national emergency." 46 U.S.C. § 1101(b) (1982).

Rather than providing a more extensive discussion of the Merchant Marine Act's objectives, the Secretary chooses to rely on other policies in defending the rule. She identifies some of the "most important" reasons for the rule as being "economic efficiency," "use of underemployed resources," "increased competition," and "deregulation." 50 Fed. Reg. at 19,172. As she later elaborates: "It is the Department's position that the competitive forces of the market, rather than government regulation, should be relied upon, whenever feasible, to allocate transportation capacity and resources in the domestic trade. This rule reflects that position." *Id.* at 19,175. The central thrust of her approach, quite obviously, is to subject the merchant marine fleet to the discipline of the free market. Thus she finds it significant that the rule will leave the industry "in a healthier, more viable condition," *id.* at 19,174, and she finds it permissible that the condition of the fleet should depend on what economic opportunities become available in the world market. *See id.* This policy may well be defensible, yet it is not among the objectives specified in the Act, and if the Secretary has decided that it is implicit in or compatible with the statutory objectives, it would be useful for her to explain this decision somewhat more fully. She has failed to do so. The closest she comes is the conclusory statement that "it would not be appropriate to let the various program objectives reflected in the Act stand in the way of achieving the Act's broader policy mandates, including that of promoting a more competitive and efficient merchant fleet." *Id.* It may, however, be entirely appropriate for the Act's objectives to stand in the way of the payback rule, and perhaps to favor other alternatives, unless the Secretary can offer a fuller and more persuasive explanation for her view that the "broader policy mandates" of the Act include the promotion of a "more competitive and efficient merchant fleet."[4]

The Secretary's failure to link the policies served by this rule to the objectives set out in the Merchant Marine Act is particularly problematic because she does not explain in the statement of basis and purpose why she rejects proposed alternatives to the payback rule. One can find this explanation in the Regulatory Impact Analysis, Joint Appendix ("J.A.") at 1049, where the Secretary considers and rejects at least a half-dozen other suggested measures. Once again, however, her account focuses on non-statutory criteria that favor this rule, such as lower transportation costs, collateral fiscal benefits, and more "efficient" use of the fleet. She admits that the rule "has a number of adverse impacts," including "the displacement of about 13 tankers . . . most of which are militarily useful handy-sized tankers, loss of employment opportunities for about 800 seamen, and the possible default on several government loans," problems that impinge on the statutory objectives and that might be avoided under some of the alternative measures.

---

4 It may be, of course, that present conditions in the world shipping market make it impossible for the Secretary to find a way to meet all of the statutory objectives. If this is the problem, she should discuss it frankly and directly when she considers which measures to adopt in light of the objectives explicitly set out in the Act.

In exercising her decisionmaking authority, the Secretary is certainly free to consider factors that are not mentioned explicitly in the governing statute, yet she is not free to substitute new goals in place of the statutory objectives without explaining how these actions are consistent with her authority under the statute. Her failure to link these non-statutory criteria with Congress' stated objectives in the Act thus makes it impossible for us to uphold the Secretary's decision to reject other measures and adopt this rule in response to the current problems of the merchant marine fleet. Her reliance on these non-statutory criteria is consistently a key point in her justifications for adopting this rule. In order to defend this action as "reasoned decisionmaking," the Secretary must spell out in more detail how her decision to adopt this rule and reject alternative measures by relying on policies of competition and deregulation can be squared with the statutory objectives that Congress specified as the primary guidelines for administrative action in this area. We take no position on whether these policies can be squared with the Act. But in the absence of any such discussion, this court can only conclude that her action is "arbitrary, capricious, . . . or not otherwise in accordance with law." 5 U.S.C. § 706(2)(A).

We therefore conclude that the Secretary violated section 553(c) of the Administrative Procedure Act by adopting this rule. In fashioning a remedy for an agency's failure to present an adequate statement of basis and purpose, this court may either remand for specific procedures to cure the deficiency without vacating the rule, or it may vacate the rule, thus requiring the agency to initiate another rulemaking proceeding if it would seek to confront the problem anew. In this case, we vacate the rule because the Secretary's omissions are quite serious and raise considerable doubt about which of the proposed alternatives would best serve the objectives set out in the Merchant Marine Act. Yet we exercise our power to withhold issuance of our mandate until July 16, 1987, to avoid further disruptions in the domestic market and to allow the Secretary to undertake further proceedings to address the problems of the merchant marine trade. *See* Fed. R. App. P. 41(a). As of that date, the present rule will be vacated and conditions returned to the *status quo ante,* before the payback rule took effect, subject of course to any further action that may have been taken in the interim.

---

## Points for Discussion

### *a. Concise General Statement of Basis and Purpose*

The APA states that, after considering the comments submitted by interested persons, "the agency shall incorporate in the rules adopted a concise general statement of their basis and purpose." 5 U.S.C. § 553(c). According to the court, why was the agency's statement of basis and purpose defective? What must an agency do to satisfy its obligation under section 553(c)? If the proposed rule is complicated and many interested persons submitted comments, is it possible for the statement to be "concise" and "general" and still satisfy the court's test?

***b. Review for Compliance with Procedural Requirements and Review for Substance***

We will soon consider judicial review of agency policy judgments, which is variously called "arbitrary and capricious" review, "hard look" review, or "substantive" review. Unlike judicial review of a rule for compliance with the APA's procedural requirements, judicial review of an agency's policy choices to determine that they are not arbitrary and capricious, 5 U.S.C. § 706, inevitably requires the reviewing court to consider whether the agency has properly justified the policy in the rule.

The court in *Independent U.S. Tanker Owners Committee* held that the Secretary's statement of basis and purpose was defective under the APA's procedural requirements for informal rulemaking. In order to cure the defect, the agency would have to provide a more detailed statement that explained the agency's policy choice in light of the evidence before the agency and the statute's objectives. Is judicial review for compliance with the "concise general statement [of] basis and purpose" requirement meaningfully different from judicial review of the agency's' substantive policy choice?

**Make the Connection**

We will address judicial review of agency's policy choices—so-called "arbitrary and capricious" review or "hard look" review—later in this Chapter, when we consider the Court's decision in *Motor Vehicle Mfrs. Assoc. of U.S. v. State Farm Mut. Auto Ins. Co.*

***c. Formal Rulemaking***

*Chocolate Mfrs. Assoc.* and *Independent U.S. Tanker Owners Committee* both involved challenges to informal rulemaking. As we saw in Chapter 6, formal rulemaking proceedings are quite rare today. When an agency is required to engage in formal rulemaking—when, that is, another statute requires the agency decision "to be made on the record after opportunity for an agency hearing," 5 U.S.C. § 553(c)—the trial-type requirements in sections 556 and 557 of the APA, rather than the notice and comment requirements in section 553, apply.

---

## b. Adjudication

As we saw in Chapter 6, the APA provides a different set of procedural requirements when an agency engages in adjudication. When the adjudication is formal—that is, when another statute requires the adjudication "to be determined on the record after opportunity for an agency hearing," 5 U.S.C. § 554(a)—the trial-type requirements in sections 554, 556, and 557 of the APA apply. When no other statute requires the decision to be on the record after opportunity for a hearing, the considerably more modest requirements of section 555 apply, along with the minimum requirements imposed by the Due Process Clause. Below, we consider some examples of judicial review for compliance with procedural requirements imposed by these sources. As with rulemaking, our consideration will be necessarily illustrative; a more comprehensive treatment will have to wait for your upper-level course in Administrative Law.

---

## *Portland Audubon Society v. The Endangered Species Committee*

984 F.2d 1534 (9th Cir. 1993)

REINHARDT, CIRCUIT JUDGE:

The Endangered Species Act requires that "[e]ach Federal agency shall . . . insure that any action authorized, funded or carried out by such agency . . . is not likely to jeopardize the continued existence of any endangered species . . . or result in the destruction or adverse modification of [critical] habitat of such species." 16 U.S.C. § 1536(a)(2) (1988). However, if the Secretary of the Interior ("Secretary") finds that a proposed agency action would violate § 1536(a)(2), an agency may apply to the [Endangered Species Committee] for an exemption from the Endangered Species Act. §§ 1536(a)(2), (g)(1)–(2). The Committee was created by the Endangered Species Act for the sole purpose of making final decisions on applications for exemptions from the Act, § 1536(e), and it is composed of high level officials.[1] Because it is the ultimate arbiter of the fate of an endangered species, the Committee is known as "The God Squad."

The Secretary must initially consider any exemption application, publish a notice and summary of the application in the Federal Register, and determine whether certain threshold requirements have been met. 16 U.S.C. §§ 1536(g)(1)–(3). If so, the Secretary shall, in consultation with the other members of the Committee, hold a hearing on the application (which is conducted by an ALJ), and prepare a written report to the Committee. § 1536(g)(4); 50 C.F.R. § 452.05(a)(2) (Oct. 1, 1991). Within thirty days of receiving the Secretary's report, the Committee shall make

---

1 The seven-member Committee is composed of: the Secretary of Agriculture, the Secretary of the Army, the Chairman of the Council of Economic Advisors, the Administrator of the Environmental Protection Agency, the Secretary of the Interior, the Administrator of the National Oceanic and Atmospheric Administration, and "one individual from each affected State" appointed by the President. 16 U.S.C. § 1536(e)(3). The Committee members from the affected states have one collective vote. 50 C.F.R. § 453.05(d) (Oct. 1, 1991).

a final determination whether or not to grant the exemption from the Endangered Species Act based on the report, the record of the Secretary's hearing, and any additional hearings or written submissions for which the Committee itself may call. § 1536(h)(1)(A); 50 C.F.R. § 453.04. An exemption requires the approval of five of the seven members of the Committee. § 1536(h)(1).

On May 15, 1992, the Committee [in a 5–2 vote] approved an exemption for the Bureau of Land Management for thirteen of forty-four timber sales. It was only the second exemption ever granted by the Committee. The environmental groups filed a timely petition for review in this court on June 10, 1992. The environmental groups have Article III standing if for no other reason than that they allege procedural violations in an agency process in which they participated. *Cf. Lujan v. Defenders of Wildlife*, 504 U.S. 555 (1992).

Both in their petition and in this motion the environmental groups contend that improper ex parte contacts between the White House and members of the Committee tainted the decision-making process. They base their charges on two press reports, one by Associated Press ("AP") and one by Reuters, and on the facts stated in the declaration of Victor Sher, lead counsel for the environmental groups. Published on May 6, 1992, the AP and Reuters accounts reported that, according to two anonymous administration sources, at least three Committee members had been "summoned" to the White House and pressured to vote for the exemption.[5] In his declaration filed

5 The AP report, in pertinent part, reads as follows:

> The Bush administration is pressuring "God Squad" members to exempt 44 Northwest timber sales from the Endangered Species Act's protection of the northern spotted owl, sources said Tuesday. Two administration sources, speaking on condition of anonymity, said that at least three members of the panel have been summoned to White House meetings to discuss coming decisions on the owl. . . . But a spokesman for Interior Secretary Manuel Lujan Jr. said the conversations pertain to general environmental policy and that no political pressure is being placed on the Endangered Species Committee. According to the sources, each of the meetings was attended by Lujan, the chairman of the committee, and Clayton Yeutter, President Bush's domestic policy adviser. William K. Reilly, head of the Environmental Protection Agency and a committee member, joined Lujan and Yeutter in meeting Tuesday, one source said. John Knauss, head of the National Oceanic and Atmospheric Administration and a committee member, attended a similar meeting within the last two weeks, the source said. Frances Hunt, a forestry specialist for the National Wildlife Federation, said other administration sources had told her that Knauss was pressured at the meeting to vote for the exemption to the Endangered Species Act.
>
> "My understanding is that it was all-out arm-twisting," she said Tuesday. "Lujan is portraying this as something the administration needs." . . . Steve Goldstein, Lujan's chief spokesman, confirmed that Lujan and Reilly met Tuesday with Yeutter.
>
> "Clayton Yeutter is the environmental policy coordinator for the administration. We are part of the administration. But no one from the administration will dictate to any committee member how they should vote," Goldstein said.

Scott Fonner, *Bush Prods "God Squad" to OK Timber Sales, Sources Say,* The Oregonian, May 6, 1992. The Reuters report contained similar information. *See* Sue Kirchhoff, *Debate Over Owl Protection Comes to a Head on the Hill,* Seattle Post-Intelligencer, May 6, 1992.

August 25, 1992, Sher stated that his conversations with "several sources within the Administration," who asked for anonymity, revealed that the media reports were accurate, and further that the pressure exerted by the White House may have changed the vote of at least one Committee member. Sher declared that his sources indicated that, in addition to in-person meetings, at least one Committee member had "substantial on-going contacts with White House staff concerning the substance of his decision on the application for exemption by telephone and facsimile, as well as through staff intermediaries." He also declared that he had learned from his sources that White House staff members had made substantial comments and recommendations on draft versions of the "Endangered Species Committee Amendment," a part of the Committee's final decision. For the purposes of the present motion, the Committee neither admits nor denies that these communications occurred.

[The environmental groups sought leave to conduct discovery into allegedly improper ex parte communications between the White House and individual Committee members, in order to supplement the record on review of the Committee's decision.]

This case raises two important and closely related questions of statutory construction: 1) Are Committee proceedings subject to the ex parte communications ban of 5 U.S.C. § 557(d)(1)? and, 2) are communications from the President and his staff covered by that provision? For the reasons that follow, we answer both questions in the affirmative.

Section 557(d)(1) is a broad provision that prohibits any ex parte communications[9] relevant to the merits of an agency proceeding between "any member of the body comprising the agency" or any agency employee who "is or may reasonably be expected to be involved in the decisional process" and any "interested person outside the agency."[10] 5 U.S.C. §§ 557(d)(1)(A)–(B); *see North Carolina, Envtl. Policy Inst. v. Environmental Protection Agency*, 881 F.2d 1250, 1257–58 (4th Cir.1989) (interpreting § 557(d)(1) broadly "to include anyone who was involved in the decisional process but is no longer an agency employee or has recused himself or herself from further involvement"). The purpose of the ex parte communications prohibition is to ensure that "agency decisions required to be made on a public record are not influenced by private, off-the-record communications from those personally interested in the outcome." *Raz Inland Navigation Co. v. Interstate Commerce Comm'n*, 625 F.2d 258, 260 (9th Cir.1980) (quoting legislative history).[11]

---

9 An "*ex parte* communication" is defined as: "an oral or written communication not on the public record with respect to which reasonable prior notice is not given, but it shall not include requests for status reports on any matter or proceeding covered by this subchapter." 5 U.S.C. § 551(14).

10 The government does not dispute that the Committee is an "agency" within the meaning of the APA. *See* 5 U.S.C. § 551(1).

11 The APA provides that when such an ex parte contact has occurred, it shall be placed on the public record of the proceeding, and if in the interests of justice, the agency may require the party involved

* * * By its terms, section 554 of the APA, which pertains to formal adjudications, applies to "every case of adjudication required by statute to be determined on the record after [the] opportunity for an agency hearing." 5 U.S.C. § 554(a). That section also provides that any hearing conducted and any decision made in connection with such an adjudication shall be "in accordance with sections 556 and 557 of this title." 5 U.S.C. § 554(c)(2). * * * Accordingly, the ex parte communications prohibition applies whenever the three requirements set forth in APA § 554(a) are satisfied: The administrative proceeding must be 1) an adjudication; 2) determined on the record; and 3) after the opportunity for an agency hearing. The question is, therefore, are those three conditions met here? We find our answer primarily in the language of section 1536(h)(1)(A) of the Endangered Species Act.

* * * Under the Endangered Species Act the Committee decides whether to grant or deny specific requests for exemptions based upon specific factual showings. Thus, the Committee's determinations are quasi-judicial. Accordingly, they constitute "adjudications" within the meaning of § 554(a).

**Make the Connection**

We considered the difference between rulemaking and adjudication in Chapter 6, when we considered the *Londoner* and *Bi-Metallic* decisions and the APA's definitions.

The language of the Endangered Species Act explicitly meets the second requirement of section 554(a). Section 1536(h)(1)(A) of the Act mandates that the Committee make its final determination of an exemption application "on the record." * * * It is equally clear that the third requirement of APA § 554(a) is satisfied here. Section 1536(h)(1)(A) of the Endangered Species Act also requires that the Committee's final decision be "*based on* the report of the Secretary, *the hearing* held under (g)(4) of this section * * * and on such other testimony or evidence as it may receive." 16 U.S.C. § 1536(h)(1)(A) (emphasis added). * * * Because Committee decisions are adjudicatory in nature, are required to be on the record, and are made after an opportunity for an agency hearing, we conclude that the APA's ex parte communication prohibition is applicable.

The Endangered Species Act as well as the applicable part of its regulations are intended to ensure that all Committee meetings, hearings, and records are open to the public. 16 U.S.C. § 1536(e)(5)(D); 50 C.F.R. §§ 453.04(b)(4), 453.05(e). Notices of all meetings and hearings must be published in the Federal Register. 50 C.F.R. §§ 453.04(b)(3), 453.05(f). If the Committee determines that written submissions are necessary for it to reach a decision, its invitation of such submissions must also be published in the Federal Register. § 453.04(a). The transcribed proceedings of any Committee hearings are to be available for public inspection.§ 453.04(b)(5). The

---

"to show cause why his claim or interest in the proceeding should not be dismissed, denied, disregarded, or otherwise adversely affected on account of such violation." 5 U.S.C. §§ 557(d)(1)(C)–(D).

Committee's final determination of an exemption application must be documented in a written decision, which itself must be published in the Federal Register. § 453.03(b).

The public's right to attend all Committee meetings, participate in all Committee hearings, and have access to all Committee records would be effectively nullified if the Committee were permitted to base its decisions on the private conversations and secret talking points and arguments to which the public and the participating parties have no access. If ex parte communications with Committee members were permissible, it would render futile the efforts contained in the remainder of the regulations to make the Committee's deliberative process open to the public. * * *

[In addition,] the Committee is, in effect, an administrative court. *See* S. Rep. No. 418, 97th Congress, 2d Sess. 17 (1982) ("the Endangered Species Committee is designed to function as an administrative court of last resort"). Ex parte contacts are antithetical to the very concept of an administrative court reaching impartial decisions through formal adjudication. * * * By definition, ex parte contacts cannot be addressed and rebutted through an adversarial discussion among the parties. Basic fairness requires that ex parte communications play no part in Committee adjudications, which involve high stakes for all the competing interests and concern issues of supreme national importance. *See Professional Air Traffic Controllers Org. v. Federal Labor Relations Auth.*, 672 F.2d 109, 113 (D.C. Cir. 1982). Behind-the-scenes contacts have no place in such a process.

The APA prohibits an "interested person outside the agency" from making, or knowingly causing to be made, an ex parte communication relevant to the merits of the proceeding with a member of the body comprising the agency. 5 U.S.C. § 557(d)(1)(A). Likewise, agency members are prohibited from engaging in such ex parte communication. § 557(d)(1)(B). Although the APA's ban on ex parte communications is absolute and includes no special exemption for White House officials, the government advances three arguments in support of its position that section 557(d)(1) does not apply to the President and his staff.

First, the government argues that because the President is the center of the Executive Branch and does not represent or act on behalf of a particular agency, he does not have an interest in Committee proceedings greater than the interest of the public as a whole. Therefore, the government contends, neither the President nor his staff is an "interested person." Next, the government maintains that the President and his staff do not fall within the terms of section 557(d)(1) because the President's interest as the Chief of the Executive Branch is no different from that of his subordinates on the Committee. Specifically, the government claims that by placing the Chairman of the President's Council of Economic Advisors on the Committee, Congress directly and expressly involved the Executive Office of the President in the decision-making process. In other words, it is the government's position that because the Committee members are Executive Branch officials, communications between them and the White House staff cannot be considered to come from "outside the agency." Finally, the government argues that if the APA's ex parte communications ban encompasses the President and his aides, the provision violates the doctrine of separation of powers. We find all three of the government's arguments to be without merit.

There is little decisional law on the meaning of the term "interested person." * * * A person can be "interested" in at least three different senses. First, an interested person can be someone who has a curiosity or a concern about a matter, although he may be neutral with respect to the outcome. Second, an interested person can have a preference or a bias regarding a matter's outcome but no direct stake in the proceedings. Finally, a person can be "interested" in a matter in the sense of having a legal interest that will be determined or affected by the decision.

Ultimately, the ex parte communication provision must be interpreted in a common sense fashion. Its purposes are to insure open decision-making and the appearance thereof, to preserve the opportunity for effective response, and to prevent improper influences upon agency decision-makers. To achieve these ends we must give the provision a broad scope rather than a constricted interpretation. The essential purposes of the APA require that all communications that might improperly influence an agency be encompassed within the ex parte contacts prohibition or else the public and the parties will be denied indirectly their guaranteed right to meaningful participation in agency decisional processes.

In *Professional Air Traffic Controllers Org. v. Federal Labor Relations Auth.*, 685 F.2d 547, 570 (D.C. Cir.1982) (*PATCO v. FLRA II*), the District of Columbia Circuit found that the Secretary of Transportation was an "interested person" within the meaning of APA § 557(d)(1) * * *. The government does not contest the validity of *PATCO v. FLRA II* as it applies to Cabinet level officials and below. However, it argues that the President's broader policy role places him beyond the reach of the "interested person" language. We strongly disagree. In fact, we believe the proper argument is quite the opposite from the one the government advances. We believe the President's position at the center of the Executive Branch renders him, *ex officio,* an "interested person" for the purposes of APA § 557(d)(1). As the head of government and chief executive officer, the President necessarily has an interest in *every* agency proceeding. No ex parte communication is more likely to influence an agency than one from the President or a member of his staff. No communication from any other person is more likely to deprive the parties and the public of their right to effective participation in a key governmental decision at a most crucial time. The essential purposes of the statutory provision compel the conclusion that the President and his staff are "interested persons" within the meaning of 5 U.S.C. § 557(d)(1).

The government's next argument—that because the President and the members of the Committee are all members of the executive branch the President is, for all intents and purposes, a "member" of the Committee and may attempt to influence its decisions—amounts to a contention that the President is not "outside the agency" for the purposes of APA § 557(d)(1). The Supreme Court soundly rejected the basic logic of this argument in *United States ex rel. Accardi v. Shaughnessy*, 347 U.S. 260 (1954). The Court held that where legally binding regulations delegated a particular discretionary decision to the Board of Immigration Appeals, the Attorney General could not dictate a decision of the Board, even though the Board was appointed by the Attorney General, its members served at his pleasure, and its decision was subject to his ultimate review. Here, the Endangered Species Act explicitly vests discretion to make exemption decisions in the Committee and does not contemplate that the President or the White House will become involved in Committee deliberations. The President and his aides are not a part of the Committee decision-making process. They are "outside the agency" for the purposes of the ex parte communications ban.

The government then argues that *Sierra Club v. Costle* determined that contacts with the White House do not constitute ex parte communications that would contaminate the Committee's decision-making process, and that we should follow that precedent. 657 F.2d 298, 400–10 (D.C. Cir.1981). We disagree. * * * The decision in *Costle* that the contacts were not impermissible was based explicitly on the fact that the proceeding involved was *informal* rulemaking to which the APA restrictions on ex parte communications are not applicable. *Id.* at 400–02, 402 n. 507. In fact, while the *Costle* court recognized that political pressure from the President may not be inappropriate in *informal* rulemaking proceedings, it acknowledged that the contrary is true in formal adjudications. *See id.* at 406–07. Because Congress has decided that Committee determinations are formal adjudications, *Costle* supports, rather than contradicts, the conclusion that the President and his staff are subject to the APA's ex parte communication ban.

**Make the Connection**

We considered *Sierra Club v. Costle*, and *ex parte* contacts in informal rulemakings, earlier in this Chapter. We also considered *Myers v. United States*, and presidential control of agency officials, earlier in this Chapter.

The government next contends that any construction of APA § 557(d)(1) that includes presidential communications within the ban on ex parte contacts would constitute a violation of the separation of powers doctrine. It relies on language in *Myers v. United States* that states that the President has the constitutional authority to "supervise and guide" Executive Branch officials in "their construction of the statutes under which they act." 272 U.S. 52 (1926). The government argues that including the President and his staff within the APA's ex parte communication ban would represent Congressional interference with the President's constitutional duty to provide such supervision and guidance to inferior officials. We reject this argument out of hand.

The Supreme Court established the test for evaluating whether an act of Congress improperly interferes with a presidential prerogative in *Nixon v. Administrator of Gen. Services*, 433 U.S. 425 (1977). First, a court must determine whether the act prevents the executive branch from accomplishing its constitutional functions. If the potential for such disruption exists, the next question is whether the impact is justified by an overriding need to promote objectives within the constitutional authority of Congress. We conclude that Congress in no way invaded any legitimate constitutional power of the President in providing that he may not attempt to influence the outcome of administrative adjudications through ex parte communications and that Congress' important objectives reflected in the enactment of the APA would, in any event, outweigh any *de minimis* impact on presidential power.

* * * [C]arried to its logical conclusion the government's position would effectively destroy the integrity of all federal agency adjudications. It is a fundamental precept of administrative law that when an agency performs a quasi-judicial (or a quasi-legislative) function its independence must be protected. There is no presidential prerogative to influence quasi-judicial administrative agency proceedings through behind-the-scenes lobbying. *Myers* itself clearly recognizes that "there may be duties of a quasi-judicial character imposed on executive officers and members of executive tribunals whose decisions after hearing affect interests of individuals, the discharge of which the President can not in a particular case properly influence or control." 272 U.S. at 135. * * * The government's position in this case is antithetical to and destructive of these elementary legal precepts, and we unequivocally reject it.

Congress might well have established a different procedure for granting exemptions from the Endangered Species Act. However, the language of the Act shows that it intended to create the Committee as a quasi-judicial adjudicatory body subject to the statutory restrictions that the APA imposes on such institutions. Congress clearly has the authority to do so, and thereby to ensure the independence of the agency from presidential control. We conclude that the members of the Committee, despite the Cabinet-level status they otherwise enjoy, are, while serving in their Committee capacities, precisely the kinds of "members of executive tribunals" that *Myers* * * * contemplate[s] are to be free from presidential influence. [W]e hold that communications between the Committee and the President or his staff are subject to the APA's prohibition on ex parte contacts.

* * * Section 706 of the APA provides that judicial review of agency action shall be based on "the whole record." "The whole record" includes everything that was before the agency pertaining to the merits of its decision. * * * When it appears the agency has relied on documents or materials not included in the record, supplementation is appropriate. *Public Power Council v. Johnson*, 674 F.2d 791, 794 (9th Cir. 1982). * * * [T]he discovery requested here involves allegedly improper ex parte contacts between decisionmakers and outside parties. If such ex parte communications occurred, then the record must be supplemented to include those contacts so that proper judicial review may be conducted.

We believe that the better course here is to order a remand for a "vigorous and thorough" adversarial, evidentiary hearing * * *. [We direct] the Committee to hold, with the aid of a specially appointed administrative law judge, an evidentiary hearing to determine the nature, content, extent, source, and effect of any ex parte communications that may have transpired between any member of the Committee or its staff and the President or any member of his staff regarding the determination of the exemption application at issue. * * * The parties will then advise the court what further proceedings, if any, should, in their opinion, be held, either before the Committee or this court.

GOODWIN, CIRCUIT JUDGE, concurring:

In deciding the questions actually presented in this case, I agree that all of the executive and cabinet level officials involved here are subject to APA's ban on ex parte communications. * * * [T]here is no evidence in the record that the then-incumbent President made any ex parte contacts with members of the "God Squad." Accordingly, we have no need to reach the issue whether the President is himself subject to the APA's ban on ex parte communications—a question which presents troubling separation of powers problems. * * * I would not address this question until it is squarely presented.

---

## Points for Discussion

### *a. Procedural Requirements in Formal Adjudications*

The APA contemplates that formal adjudications will look very much like judicial proceedings. The parties will have an opportunity to introduce evidence and impeach adverse witnesses, and the decision-maker will confine her decision to evidence introduced on the record in the proceedings. In ordinary judicial proceedings, *ex parte* contacts—contacts with the decision-maker to which not all of the parties are privy—are prohibited because they create the possibility of a decision based on evidence not introduced on the record during the proceedings.

Does it make sense to import wholesale to agency adjudications the rules about *ex parte* contacts in ordinary judicial proceedings? In the adjudication at issue in *Portland Audubon Society*, the decision-maker was a Committee composed of high-ranking political employees, most of whom had policy agendas that flowed from their positions as heads of federal agencies. Is it realistic to assume that such decision-makers would base their resolution of the matter in question solely on evidence introduced in a hearing? Or did the composition of the committee provide even more reason to insist that the decision be based only on evidence introduced on the record during the proceedings?

### *b. Presidential Control of Agency Decision-Making*

Even assuming that it makes sense to limit *ex parte* contacts during formal adjudications, does it make sense to prevent contacts by the President with agency heads? Earlier in this Chapter, we noted that presidential influence over agency officials is an important corrective for the risks of unaccountable agency decision-making. Shouldn't we want the President to seek to influence agency decision-making, to ensure electoral accountability? On the other hand, what would be the point of carefully structuring an on-the-record hearing process if the committee's decision ultimately would be determined by the President's preferences?

In any event, was the court correct to conclude that the APA's ban on *ex parte* contacts during formal adjudications applies to the President? Can the court's decision survive the more recent decision by the Supreme Court in *Seila Law LLC v. Consumer Financial Protection Bureau*, 140 S.Ct. 2183 (2020), which we considered earlier in this Chapter?

---

The Due Process Clause requires agencies to use fair procedures before they can determine a private party's rights. We have seen that the ordinary rule is that government actions that exceptionally affect a small number of people on individual grounds must be preceded by some kind of opportunity to be heard. See *Londoner v. City and County of Denver*, 210 U.S. 373 (1908); *Bi-Metallic Investment Co. v. State Board of Equalization*, 239 U.S. 441 (1915). What other limits does the Due Process Clause impose on the power of an agency to adjudicate private rights?

---

## *Withrow v. Larkin*

421 U.S. 35 (1975)

Mr. Justice White delivered the opinion for a unanimous Court.

The statutes of the State of Wisconsin forbid the practice of medicine without a license from an Examining Board composed of practicing physicians. The statutes also define and forbid various acts of professional misconduct, proscribe fee splitting, and make illegal the practice of medicine under any name other than the name under which a license has issued if the public would be misled, such practice would constitute unfair competition with another physician, or other detriment to the profession would result. To enforce these provisions, the Examining Board is empowered under Wis. Stat. Ann. §§ 448.17 and 448.18 (1974) to warn and reprimand, temporarily to suspend the license, and "to institute criminal action or action to revoke license when it finds probable cause therefor under criminal or revocation statute . . . ." When an investigative proceeding before the Examining Board was commenced against him, appellee brought this suit against appellants, the individual members of the Board, seeking an injunction against the enforcement of the statutes. [A three-judge] District Court issued a preliminary injunction * * *.

Appellee, a resident of Michigan and licensed to practice medicine there, obtained a Wisconsin license in August 1971 under a reciprocity agreement between Michigan and Wisconsin governing medical licensing. His practice in Wisconsin consisted of performing abortions at an office in Milwaukee. On June 20, 1973, the Board sent to appellee a notice that it would hold an investigative hearing on July 12, 1973, * * * to determine whether he had engaged in certain proscribed acts.[2] The hearing would be closed to the public, although appellee and his attorney could attend. They would not, however, be permitted to cross-examine witnesses. Based upon the evidence presented at the hearing, the Board would decide "whether to warn or reprimand if it finds such practice and whether to institute criminal action or action to revoke license if probable cause therefor exists under criminal or revocation statutes."

[Appellee then filed suit in federal court, eventually asserting that Wis. Stat. Ann. §§ 448.17 and 448.18 were unconstitutional and that appellants' acts with respect to him violated his constitutional rights.] The Board proceeded with its investigative hearing on July 12 and 13, 1973; numerous witnesses testified and appellee's counsel was present throughout the proceedings. * * * On September 18, 1973, the Board sent to appellee a notice that a "contested [adversarial] hearing" would be held on October 4, 1973, to determine whether appellee had engaged in certain prohibited acts[4] and that based upon the evidence adduced at the hearing the Board would determine whether his license would be suspended temporarily under Wis. Stat. § 448.18(7). Appellee [sought] a restraining order [from the District Court] against the contested hearing. The District Court granted the [temporary restraining order, concluding that appellee had raised a substantial federal question.]

The Board complied and did not go forward with the contested hearing. Instead, it noticed and held a final investigative session on October 4, 1973, at which appellee's attorney, but not appellee, appeared. The Board thereupon issued "Findings of Fact," "Conclusions of Law," and a "Decision" in which the Board found that appellee had

---

2 The notice indicated that the hearing would be held "to determine whether the [licensee] has engaged in practices that are inimical to the public health, whether he has engaged in conduct unbecoming a person licensed to practice medicine, and whether he has engaged in conduct detrimental to the best interests of the public."

4 The notice stated that the hearing would be held "to determine whether the licensee has practiced medicine in the State of Wisconsin under any other [name] than that under which he was originally licensed or registered to practice medicine in this state, which practicing has operated to unfairly compete with another practitioner, to mislead the public as to identity, or to otherwise result in detriment to the profession or the public, and more particularly, whether the said Duane Larkin, M.D., has practiced medicine in this state since September 1, 1971, under the name of Glen Johnson." It would also "determine whether the * * * said Duane Larkin, M.D., permitted Young Wahn Ahn, M.D., an unlicensed physician, to perform abortions at his abortion clinic during the year 1972." Finally the Board would "determine whether the said Duane Larkin, M.D., split fees with other persons during the years 1971, 1972, and 1973 in violation of sec. 448.23(1)."

engaged in specified conduct proscribed by the statute. [The Board referred the matter to the District Attorney of Milwaukee County for the purpose of initiating an action to revoke Larkin's medical license and for "initiating appropriate actions for violation of the criminal laws relating to the practice of medicine."

The district court subsequently held that "for the board temporarily to suspend Dr. Larkin's license at its own contested hearing on charges evolving from its own investigation would constitute a denial to him of his rights to procedural due process. Insofar as § 448.18(7) authorizes a procedure wherein a physician stands to lose his liberty or property, absent the intervention of an independent, neutral and detached decision maker, we [conclude] that it was unconstitutional and unenforceable." 368 F. Supp. 796, 797 (E.D.Wis.1973).]

Concededly, a "fair trial in a fair tribunal is a basic requirement of due process." *In re Murchison*, 349 U.S. 133, 136 (1955). This applies to administrative agencies which adjudicate as well as to courts. *Gibson v. Berryhill*, 411 U.S. 564, 579 (1973). Not only is a biased decisionmaker constitutionally unacceptable but "our system of law has always endeavored to prevent even the probability of unfairness." *In re Murchison*, 349 U.S., at 136. In pursuit of this end, various situations have been identified in which experience teaches that the probability of actual bias on the part of the judge or decisionmaker is too high to be constitutionally tolerable. Among these cases are those in which the adjudicator has a pecuniary interest in the outcome and in which he has been the target of personal abuse or criticism from the party before him.

The contention that the combination of investigative and adjudicative functions necessarily creates an unconstitutional risk of bias in administrative adjudication has a much more difficult burden of persuasion to carry. It must overcome a presumption of honesty and integrity in those serving as adjudicators; and it must convince that, under a realistic appraisal of psychological tendencies and human weakness, conferring investigative and adjudicative powers on the same individuals poses such a risk of actual bias or prejudgment that the practice must be forbidden if the guarantee of due process is to be adequately implemented.

That is not to say that there is nothing to the argument that those who have investigated should not then adjudicate. The issue is substantial, it is not new, and legislators and others concerned with the operations of administrative agencies have given much attention to whether and to what extent distinctive administrative functions should be performed by the same persons. No single answer has been reached. Indeed, the growth, variety, and complexity of the administrative processes have made any one solution highly unlikely. Within the Federal Government itself, Congress has addressed the issue in several different ways, providing for varying degrees of separation from complete separation of functions to virtually none at all. For the generality of agencies, Congress has been content with § 5 of the Administrative Procedure Act, 5 U.S.C. § 554(d), which provides that no employee engaged in investigating or prosecuting may also participate or advise in the adjudicating

**FYI**

The APA's exemption of "the agency or a member or members of the body comprising the agency" refers to the person or persons who serve as the head of the agency, such as the Administrator, the Secretary, or the Commissioners. Those persons often make the final decision on behalf of the agency, sometimes disagreeing with the decision of the person who presided over the hearing. In other cases, the head of the agency presides over the hearing as the decision-maker in the first instance.

function, but which also expressly exempts from this prohibition "the agency or a member or members of the body comprising the agency."

It is not surprising, therefore, to find that "(t)he case law, both federal and state, generally rejects the idea that the combination (of) judging (and) investigating functions is a denial of due process . . . ." 2 K. Davis, Administrative Law Treatise § 13.02, p. 175 (1958). Similarly, our cases, although they reflect the substance of the problem, offer no support for the bald proposition applied in this case by the District Court that agency members who participate in an investigation are disqualified from adjudicating. The incredible variety of administrative mechanisms in this country will not yield to any single organizing principle.

Appellee relies heavily on *In re Murchison*, in which a state judge, empowered under state law to sit as a "one-man grand jury" and to compel witnesses to testify before him in secret about possible crimes, charged two such witnesses with criminal contempt, one for perjury and the other for refusing to answer certain questions, and then himself tried and convicted them. This Court found the procedure to be a denial of due process of law not only because the judge in effect became part of the prosecution and assumed an adversary position, but also because as a judge, passing on guilt or innocence, he very likely relied on "his own personal knowledge and impression of what had occurred in the grand jury room," an impression that "could not be tested by adequate cross-examination." 349 U.S., at 138.

Plainly enough, *Murchison* has not been understood to stand for the broad rule that the members of an administrative agency may not investigate the facts, institute proceedings, and then make the necessary adjudications. The Court did not * * * lay down any general principle that a judge before whom an alleged contempt is committed may not bring and preside over the ensuing contempt proceedings. The accepted rule is to the contrary. *Ungar v. Sarafite*, 376 U.S. 575, 584–585 (1964).

Nor is there anything in this case that comes within the strictures of Murchison. When the Board instituted its investigative procedures, it stated only that it would investigate whether proscribed conduct had occurred. Later in noticing the adversary hearing, it asserted only that it would determine if violations had been committed which would warrant suspension of appellee's license. Without doubt, the Board then anticipated that the proceeding would eventuate in an adjudication of the issue; but there was no more evidence of bias or the risk of bias or prejudgment than inhered in the very fact that the Board had investigated and would now adjudicate.[21] Of course, we should be alert to the possibilities of bias that may lurk in the way particular procedures actually work in practice. The processes utilized by the Board, however, do not in themselves contain an unacceptable risk of bias. The investigative proceeding had been closed to the public, but appellee and his counsel were permitted to be present throughout; counsel actually attended the hearings and knew the facts presented to the Board. No specific foundation has been presented for suspecting that the Board had been prejudiced by its investigation or would be disabled from hearing and deciding on the basis of the evidence to be presented at the contested hearing. The mere exposure to evidence presented in nonadversary investigative procedures is insufficient in itself to impugn the fairness of the board members at a later adversary hearing. Without a showing to the contrary, state administrators "are assumed to be men of conscience and intellectual discipline, capable of judging a particular controversy fairly on the basis of its own circumstances." *United States v. Morgan*, 313 U.S. 409, 421 (1941).

We are of the view, therefore, that the District Court was in error when it entered the restraining order against the Board's contested hearing and when it granted the preliminary injunction based on the untenable view that it would be unconstitutional for the Board to suspend appellee's license "at its own contested hearing on charges evolving from its own investigation . . . ." The contested hearing should have been permitted to proceed.

Nor do we think the situation substantially different because the Board, when it was prevented from going forward with the contested hearing, proceeded to make and issue formal findings of fact and conclusions of law asserting that there was probable cause to believe that appellee had engaged in various acts prohibited by the Wisconsin statutes. These findings and conclusions were verified and filed with the district attorney for the purpose of initiating revocation and criminal proceedings. Although the District Court did not emphasize this aspect of the case before it, appellee stresses it in attempting to show prejudice and prejudgment. We are not persuaded.

Judges repeatedly issue arrest warrants on the basis that there is probable cause to believe that a crime has been committed and that the person named in the warrant has committed it. Judges also preside at preliminary hearings where they must decide whether the evidence is sufficient to hold a defendant for trial. Neither of these pretrial involvements has been thought to raise any constitutional barrier against the judge's presiding over the criminal trial and, if the trial is without a jury, against making the necessary determination of guilt or innocence. Nor has it been thought that a judge is disqualified from presiding over injunction proceedings because he has initially

---

21 Appellee does claim that state officials harassed him with litigation because he performed abortions. * * * The District Court made no findings with respect to these allegations, and the record does not provide a basis for finding as an initial matter here that there was evidence of actual bias or prejudgment on the part of appellants.

assessed the facts in issuing or denying a temporary restraining order or a preliminary injunction. It is also very typical for the members of administrative agencies to receive the results of investigations, to approve the filing of charges or formal complaints instituting enforcement proceedings, and then to participate in the ensuing hearings. This mode of procedure does not violate the Administrative Procedure Act, and it does not violate due process of law. We should also remember that it is not contrary to due process to allow judges and administrators who have had their initial decisions reversed on appeal to confront and decide the same questions a second time around.

Here, the Board stayed within the accepted bounds of due process. Having investigated, it issued findings and conclusions asserting the commission of certain acts and ultimately concluding that there was probable cause to believe that appellee had violated the statutes.

The risk of bias or prejudgment in this sequence of functions has not been considered to be intolerably high or to raise a sufficiently great possibility that the adjudicators would be so psychologically wedded to their complaints that they would consciously or unconsciously avoid the appearance of having erred or changed position. Indeed, just as there is no logical inconsistency between a finding of probable cause and an acquittal in a criminal proceeding, there is no incompatibility between the agency filing a complaint based on probable cause and a subsequent decision, when all the evidence is in, that there has been no violation of the statute. * * *

That the combination of investigative and adjudicative functions does not, without more, constitute a due process violation, does not, of course, preclude a court from determining from the special facts and circumstances present in the case before it that the risk of unfairness is intolerably high. Findings of that kind made by judges with special insights into local realities are entitled to respect, but injunctions resting on such factors should be accompanied by at least the minimum findings required by [the Federal Rules of Civil Procedure].

The judgment of the District Court is reversed and the case is remanded to that court for further proceedings consistent with this opinion.

---

## Points for Discussion

### *a. The Due Process Clauses as Limits on Agency Adjudications*

Because *Withrow* involved a challenge to an adjudication by a state agency, the Court applied the Due Process Clause of the Fourteenth Amendment. The same principles apply to federal agencies under the Due Process Clause of the Fifth Amendment. Notice that, by their terms, the Due Process Clauses are conclusory at best; they guarantee all of the process that is "due," but they do not specify any specific procedural entitlements. How does a court applying one of the Due Process Clauses know which procedural rights it requires?

***b. Agency Decision-Makers as Unbiased Judges***

As we saw in Chapter 6 when we considered *Wong Yang Sung v. McGrath*, 339 U.S. 33 (1950), part of the impetus for the enactment of the APA was the concern that administrative hearings were often unfair because some agencies let the same person serve as both "prosecutor" and "judge." Did the Court in *Withrow* agree that a mixing of the job of investigator and judge inevitably constitutes a denial of due process? If not, why not?

In thinking about that question, keep in mind that, in many cases, the final decision in an agency adjudication is rendered by the head of the agency. (A common structure has a hearing before an independent administrative law judge, with an appeal for the aggrieved party to the agency head.) Is it possible for the final decision-maker to be impartial when the final decision-maker has a policy agenda that she wants to accomplish?

In *Federal Trade Commission v. Cement Institute*, 333 U.S. 683 (1948), the Court rejected a challenge to a decision by the Commission finding that a cement company had violated the antitrust laws. The respondents noted that the agency had previously issued public reports and given testimony to Congress stating that the pricing system used in the cement industry was anti-competitive. The respondents argued that the agency could not fairly adjudicate the case because it had prejudged the issue. The Court disagreed, noting that the respondents were permitted to participate in the hearing, present evidence, and cross-examine the Commission's evidence. More important, the Court concluded that Congress had assigned the Commission the power to decide such matters precisely because of its expertise, and that "experience acquired from their work as commissioners" should not "be a handicap instead of an advantage." Should courts be worried about this form of bias by agency decision-makers?

---

## *Mathews v. Eldridge*

424 U.S. 319 (1976)

MR. JUSTICE POWELL delivered the opinion of the Court.

The issue in this case is whether the Due Process Clause of the Fifth Amendment requires that prior to the termination of Social Security disability benefit payments the recipient be afforded an opportunity for an evidentiary hearing.

Cash benefits are provided to workers during periods in which they are completely disabled under the disability insurance benefits program created by the 1956 amendments to Title II of the Social Security Act. 70 Stat. 815, 42 U.S.C. § 423.[1] Respondent Eldridge was first awarded benefits in June 1968. In March 1972, he received a questionnaire from the state agency charged with monitoring his medical condition. Eldridge completed the questionnaire, indicating that his condition had not improved and identifying the medical sources, including physicians, from whom he had received treatment recently. The state agency then obtained reports from his physician and a psychiatric consultant. After considering these reports and other information in his file the agency informed Eldridge by letter that it had made a tentative determination that his disability had ceased in May 1972. The letter included a statement of reasons for the proposed termination of benefits, and advised Eldridge that he might request reasonable time in which to obtain and submit additional information pertaining to his condition.

In his written response, Eldridge disputed one characterization of his medical condition and indicated that the agency already had enough evidence to establish his disability.[2] The state agency then made its final determination that he had ceased to be disabled in May 1972. This determination was accepted by the Social Security Administration (SSA), which notified Eldridge in July that his benefits would terminate after that month. The notification also advised him of his right to seek reconsideration by the state agency of this initial determination within six months.

Instead of requesting reconsideration Eldridge commenced this action challenging the constitutional validity of the administrative procedures established by the Secretary of Health, Education, and Welfare for assessing whether there exists a continuing disability. He sought an immediate reinstatement of benefits pending a hearing on the issue of his disability * * *. In support of his contention that due process requires a pretermination hearing, Eldridge relied exclusively upon this Court's decision in *Goldberg v. Kelly*, 397 U.S. 254, (1970), which established a right to an

---

1 The program is financed by revenues derived from employee and employer payroll taxes. 26 U.S.C. §§ 3101(a), 3111(a); 42 U.S.C. § 401(b). It provides monthly benefits to disabled persons who have worked sufficiently long to have an insured status, and who have had substantial work experience in a specified interval directly preceding the onset of disability. 42 U.S.C. §§ 423(c)(1)(A) and (B). Benefits also are provided to the worker's dependents under specified circumstances. §§ 402(b)–(d). When the recipient reaches age 65 his disability benefits are automatically converted to retirement benefits. §§ 416(i)(2)(D), 423(a)(1). In fiscal 1974 approximately 3,700,000 persons received assistance under the program. Social Security Administration, The Year in Review 21 (1974).

2 Eldridge originally was disabled due to chronic anxiety and back strain. He subsequently was found to have diabetes. The tentative determination letter indicated that aid would be terminated because available medical evidence indicated that his diabetes was under control, that there existed no limitations on his back movements which would impose severe functional restrictions, and that he no longer suffered emotional problems that would preclude him from all work for which he was qualified. In his reply letter he claimed to have arthritis of the spine rather than a strained back.

"evidentiary hearing" prior to termination of welfare benefits.[4] * * * [The District Court held that Eldridge was entitled to a hearing before termination of his benefits, and the Court of Appeals affirmed.]

Procedural due process imposes constraints on governmental decisions which deprive individuals of "liberty" or "property" interests within the meaning of the Due Process Clause of the Fifth or Fourteenth Amendment. The Secretary does not contend that procedural due process is inapplicable to terminations of Social Security disability benefits. He recognizes, as has been implicit in our prior decisions, e. g., *Richardson v. Belcher*, 404 U.S. 78, 80–81 (1971), that the interest of an individual in continued receipt of these benefits is a statutorily created "property" interest protected by the Fifth Amendment. Cf. *Arnett v. Kennedy*, 416 U.S. 134, 166 (1974) (POWELL, J., concurring in part); *Board of Regents v. Roth*, 408 U.S. 564, 576–578 (1972). Rather, the Secretary contends that the existing administrative procedures, detailed below, provide all the process that is constitutionally due before a recipient can be deprived of that interest.

**Food for Thought**

The Fifth and Fourteenth Amendments guarantee due process of law only when a person is deprived of "life, liberty, and property." The Court notes here that the government conceded that an interest in continued receipt of disability benefits constitutes "property" within the meaning of the Due Process Clauses. How should the Court define "property" for purposes of deciding the scope of the Clauses' protections?

This Court consistently has held that some form of hearing is required before an individual is finally deprived of a property interest. * * * Eldridge agrees that the review procedures available to a claimant before the initial determination of ineligibility becomes final would be adequate if disability benefits were not terminated until after the evidentiary hearing stage of the administrative process. The dispute centers upon what process is due *prior* to the initial termination of benefits, pending review.

In recent years this Court increasingly has had occasion to consider the extent to which due process requires an evidentiary hearing prior to the deprivation of some type of property interest even if such a hearing is provided thereafter. In only one case, *Goldberg v. Kelly*, has the Court held that a hearing closely approximating a judicial trial is necessary. * * *

---

4 In *Goldberg* the Court held that the pretermination hearing must include the following elements: (1) "timely and adequate notice detailing the reasons for a proposed termination"; (2) "an effective opportunity (for the recipient) to defend by confronting any adverse witnesses and by presenting his own arguments and evidence orally"; (3) retained counsel, if desired; (4) an "impartial" decisionmaker; (5) a decision resting "solely on the legal rules and evidence adduced at the hearing"; (6) a statement of reasons for the decision and the evidence relied on. 397 U.S., at 266–271. In this opinion the term "evidentiary hearing" refers to a hearing generally of the type required in *Goldberg*.

"[D]ue process, unlike some legal rules, is not a technical conception with a fixed content unrelated to time, place and circumstances." *Cafeteria Workers v. McElroy*, 367 U.S. 886, 895 (1961). "(D)ue process is flexible and calls for such procedural protections as the particular situation demands." *Morrissey v. Brewer*, 408 U.S. 471, 481 (1972). Accordingly, resolution of the issue whether the administrative procedures provided here are constitutionally sufficient requires analysis of the governmental and private interests that are affected. More precisely, our prior decisions indicate that identification of the specific dictates of due process generally requires consideration of three distinct factors: First, the private interest that will be affected by the official action; second, the risk of an erroneous deprivation of such interest through the procedures used, and the probable value, if any, of additional or substitute procedural safeguards; and finally, the Government's interest, including the function involved and the fiscal and administrative burdens that the additional or substitute procedural requirement would entail. See, e.g., *Goldberg*, 397 U.S. at 263–271.

We turn first to a description of the procedures for the termination of Social Security disability benefits and thereafter consider the factors bearing upon the constitutional adequacy of these procedures.

The disability insurance program is administered jointly by state and federal agencies. State agencies make the initial determination whether a disability exists, when it began, and when it ceased. 42 U.S.C. § 421(a). The standards applied and the procedures followed are prescribed by the Secretary, see § 421(b), who has delegated his responsibilities and powers under the Act to the SSA. See 40 Fed. Reg. 4473 (1975).

In order to establish initial and continued entitlement to disability benefits a worker must demonstrate that he is unable "to engage in any substantial gainful activity by reason of any medically determinable physical or mental impairment which can be expected to result in death or which has lasted or can be expected to last for a continuous period of not less than 12 months . . . ." 42 U.S.C. § 423(d)(1)(A).

To satisfy this test the worker bears a continuing burden of showing, by means of "medically acceptable clinical and laboratory diagnostic techniques," § 423(d)(3), that he has a physical or mental impairment of such severity that "he is not only unable to do his previous work but cannot, considering his age, education, and work experience, engage in any other kind of substantial gainful work which exists in the national economy * * *." § 423(d)(2)(A).

The principal reasons for benefits terminations are that the worker is no longer disabled or has returned to work. As Eldridge's benefits were terminated because he was determined to be no longer disabled, we consider only the sufficiency of the procedures involved in such cases.

The continuing-eligibility investigation is made by a state agency acting through a "team" consisting of a physician and a nonmedical person trained in disability evaluation. The agency periodically communicates with the disabled worker, usually by mail in which case he is sent a detailed questionnaire or by telephone, and requests information concerning his present condition, including current medical restrictions and sources of treatment, and any additional information that he considers relevant to his continued entitlement to benefits.

Information regarding the recipient's current condition is also obtained from his sources of medical treatment. If there is a conflict between the information provided by the beneficiary and that obtained from medical sources such as his physician, or between two sources of treatment, the agency may arrange for an examination by an independent consulting physician. Whenever the agency's tentative assessment of the beneficiary's condition differs from his own assessment, the beneficiary is informed that benefits may be terminated, provided a summary of the evidence upon which the proposed determination to terminate is based, and afforded an opportunity to review the medical reports and other evidence in his case file. He also may respond in writing and submit additional evidence.

The state agency then makes its final determination, which is reviewed by an examiner in the SSA Bureau of Disability Insurance. 42 U.S.C. § 421(c). If, as is usually the case, the SSA accepts the agency determination it notifies the recipient in writing, informing him of the reasons for the decision, and of his right to seek de novo reconsideration by the state agency. 20 CFR §§ 404.907, 404.909 (1975). Upon acceptance by the SSA, benefits are terminated effective two months after the month in which medical recovery is found to have occurred.

If the recipient seeks reconsideration by the state agency and the determination is adverse, the SSA reviews the reconsideration determination and notifies the recipient of the decision. He then has a right to an evidentiary hearing before an SSA administrative law judge. The hearing is nonadversary, and the SSA is not represented by counsel. As at all prior and subsequent stages of the administrative process, however, the claimant may be represented by counsel or other spokesmen. If this hearing results in an adverse decision, the claimant is entitled to request discretionary review by the SSA Appeals Council, and finally may obtain judicial review. 42 U.S.C. § 405(g); 20 CFR § 404.951 (1975).

Should it be determined at any point after termination of benefits that the claimant's disability extended beyond the date of cessation initially established, the worker is entitled to retroactive payments. If, on the other hand, a beneficiary receives any payments to which he is later

**Take Note**

Under the Act, the claimant was eventually entitled to a full adversarial hearing with all of the procedural protections of an ordinary trial. In addition, if, after the hearing, the agency concluded that the claimant in fact was still disabled, the claimant would receive retroactive payments to make up for the payments that he missed after the agency terminated his benefits. Given this, why did Eldridge challenge the agency's procedures? In what way did he think that the agency should change those procedures?

determined not to be entitled, the statute authorizes the Secretary to attempt to recoup these funds in specified circumstances.

Despite the elaborate character of the administrative procedures provided by the Secretary, the courts below held them to be constitutionally inadequate, concluding that due process requires an evidentiary hearing prior to termination. In light of the private and governmental interests at stake here and the nature of the existing procedures, we think this was error.

Since a recipient whose benefits are terminated is awarded full retroactive relief if he ultimately prevails, his sole interest is in the uninterrupted receipt of this source of income pending final administrative decision on his claim. His potential injury is thus similar in nature to that of the welfare recipient in *Goldberg* * * *. [In *Goldberg*, the Court] Court held that due process requires an evidentiary hearing prior to a temporary deprivation [of welfare benefits]. It was emphasized there that welfare assistance is given to persons on the very margin of subsistence: "The crucial factor in this context a factor not present in the case of . . . virtually anyone else whose governmental entitlements are ended is that termination of aid pending resolution of a controversy over eligibility may deprive an eligible recipient of the very means by which to live while he waits." 397 U.S., at 264.

Eligibility for disability benefits, in contrast, is not based upon financial need.[24] Indeed, it is wholly unrelated to the worker's income or support from many other sources, such as earnings of other family members, workmen's compensation awards, tort claims awards, savings, private insurance, public or private pensions, veterans' benefits, food stamps, public assistance, or the "many other important programs, both public and private, which contain provisions for disability payments affecting a substantial portion of the work force . . . ." *Richardson v. Belcher*, 404 U.S. 78, 85–87 (1971) (DOUGLAS, J., dissenting).

As *Goldberg* illustrates, the degree of potential deprivation that may be created by a particular decision is a factor to be considered in assessing the validity of any administrative decisionmaking process. The potential deprivation here is generally likely to be less than in *Goldberg*, although the degree of difference can be overstated. As the District Court emphasized, to remain eligible for benefits a recipient must be "unable to engage in substantial gainful activity." 42 U.S.C. § 423; 361 F. Supp., at 523. Thus, [there] is little possibility that the terminated recipient will be able to find even temporary employment to ameliorate the interim loss.

As we recognized last Term in *Fusari v. Steinberg*, 419 U.S. 379, 389 (1975), "the possible length of wrongful deprivation of . . . benefits (also) is an important factor in assessing the impact of official action on the private interests." The Secretary

---

24 The level of benefits is determined by the worker's average monthly earnings during the period prior to disability, his age, and other factors not directly related to financial need, specified in 42 U.S.C. § 415 (1970 ed., Supp. III). See § 423(a)(2).

concedes that the delay between a request for a hearing before an administrative law judge and a decision on the claim is currently between 10 and 11 months. Since a terminated recipient must first obtain a reconsideration decision as a prerequisite to invoking his right to an evidentiary hearing, the delay between the actual cutoff of benefits and final decision after a hearing exceeds one year.

In view of the torpidity of this administrative review process, and the typically modest resources of the family unit of the physically disabled worker,[26] the hardship imposed upon the erroneously terminated disability recipient may be significant. Still, the disabled worker's need is likely to be less than that of a welfare recipient. In addition to the possibility of access to private resources, other forms of government assistance will become available where the termination of disability benefits places a worker or his family below the subsistence level. In view of these potential sources of temporary income, there is less reason here than in *Goldberg* to depart from the ordinary principle, established by our decisions, that something less than an evidentiary hearing is sufficient prior to adverse administrative action.

An additional factor to be considered here is the fairness and reliability of the existing pretermination procedures, and the probable value, if any, of additional procedural safeguards. Central to the evaluation of any administrative process is the nature of the relevant inquiry. In order to remain eligible for benefits the disabled worker must demonstrate by means of "medically acceptable clinical and laboratory diagnostic techniques," that he is unable "to engage in any substantial gainful activity by reason of any medically determinable physical or mental impairment. . . ." § 423(d)(1)(A). In short, a medical assessment of the worker's physical or mental condition is required. This is a more sharply focused and easily documented decision than the typical determination of welfare entitlement. In the latter case, a wide variety of information may be deemed relevant, and issues of witness credibility and veracity often are critical to the decisionmaking process. *Goldberg* noted that in such circumstances "written submissions are a wholly unsatisfactory basis for decision." 397 U.S. at 269.

By contrast, the decision whether to discontinue disability benefits will turn, in most cases, upon "routine, standard, and unbiased medical reports by physician specialists," *Richardson v. Perales*, 402 U.S. 389, 404 (1971), concerning a subject whom they have personally examined. In *Richardson* the Court recognized the "reliability and probative worth of written medical reports," emphasizing that while there may be "professional disagreement with the medical conclusions" the "specter of questionable credibility and veracity is not present." *Id.* at 405, 407. To be sure, credibility and veracity may be a factor in the ultimate disability assessment in some

---

26 *Amici* cite statistics compiled by the Secretary which indicate that in 1965 the mean income of the family unit of a disabled worker was $3,803, while the median income for the unit was $2,836. The mean liquid assets i.e., cash, stocks, bonds of these family units was $4,862; the median was $940. These statistics do not take into account the family unit's nonliquid assets *i.e.*, automobile, real estate, and the like.

cases. But procedural due process rules are shaped by the risk of error inherent in the truthfinding process as applied to the generality of cases, not the rare exceptions. The potential value of an evidentiary hearing, or even oral presentation to the decisionmaker, is substantially less in this context than in *Goldberg*.

The decision in *Goldberg* also was based on the Court's conclusion that written submissions were an inadequate substitute for oral presentation because they did not provide an effective means for the recipient to communicate his case to the decisionmaker. Written submissions were viewed as an unrealistic option, for most recipients lacked the "educational attainment necessary to write effectively" and could not afford professional assistance. In addition, such submissions would not provide the "flexibility of oral presentations" or "permit the recipient to mold his argument to the issues the decision maker appears to regard as important." 397 U.S., at 269. In the context of the disability-benefits-entitlement assessment the administrative procedures under review here fully answer these objections.

The detailed questionnaire which the state agency periodically sends the recipient identifies with particularity the information relevant to the entitlement decision, and the recipient is invited to obtain assistance from the local SSA office in completing the questionnaire. More important, the information critical to the entitlement decision usually is derived from medical sources, such as the treating physician. Such sources are likely to be able to communicate more effectively through written documents than are welfare recipients or the lay witnesses supporting their cause. The conclusions of physicians often are supported by X-rays and the results of clinical or laboratory tests, information typically more amenable to written than to oral presentation.

A further safeguard against mistake is the policy of allowing the disability recipient's representative full access to all information relied upon by the state agency. In addition, prior to the cutoff of benefits the agency informs the recipient of its tentative assessment, the reasons therefor, and provides a summary of the evidence that it considers most relevant. Opportunity is then afforded the recipient to submit additional evidence or arguments, enabling him to challenge directly the accuracy of information in his file as well as the correctness of the agency's tentative conclusions. These procedures, again as contrasted with those before the Court in *Goldberg*, enable the recipient to "mold" his argument to respond to the precise issues which the decisionmaker regards as crucial.

Despite these carefully structured procedures, amici point to the significant reversal rate for appealed cases as clear evidence that the current process is inadequate. Depending upon the base selected and the line of analysis followed, the relevant reversal rates urged by the contending parties vary from a high of 58.6% for appealed reconsideration decisions to an overall reversal rate of only 3.3%. Bare statistics rarely provide a satisfactory measure of the fairness of a decisionmaking process. Their adequacy is especially suspect here since the administrative review system is operated on an open-file basis. A recipient may always submit new evidence, and such submissions may result in additional medical examinations. Such fresh examinations were held in approximately 30% to 40% of the appealed cases, in fiscal 1973, either at the reconsideration or evidentiary hearing stage of the administrative process. In this context, the value of reversal rate statistics as one means of evaluating the adequacy of the pretermination process is diminished. Thus, although we view such information as relevant, it is certainly not controlling in this case.

In striking the appropriate due process balance the final factor to be assessed is the public interest. This includes the administrative burden and other societal costs that would be associated with requiring, as a matter of constitutional right, an evidentiary hearing upon demand in all cases prior to the termination of disability benefits. The most visible burden would be the incremental cost resulting from the increased number of hearings and the expense of providing benefits to ineligible recipients pending decision. No one can predict the extent of the increase, but the fact that full benefits would continue until after such hearings would assure the exhaustion in most cases of this attractive option. Nor would the theoretical right of the Secretary to recover undeserved benefits result, as a practical matter, in any substantial offset to the added outlay of public funds. The parties submit widely varying estimates of the probable additional financial cost. We only need say that experience with the constitutionalizing of government procedures suggests that the ultimate additional cost in terms of money and administrative burden would not be insubstantial.

Financial cost alone is not a controlling weight in determining whether due process requires a particular procedural safeguard prior to some administrative decision. But the Government's interest, and hence that of the public, in conserving scarce fiscal and administrative resources is a factor that must be weighed. At some point the benefit of an additional safeguard to the individual affected by the administrative action and to society in terms of increased assurance that the action is just, may be outweighed by the cost. Significantly, the cost of protecting those whom the preliminary administrative process has identified as likely to be found undeserving may in the end come out of the pockets of the deserving since resources available for any particular program of social welfare are not unlimited.

But more is implicated in cases of this type than ad hoc weighing of fiscal and administrative burdens against the interests of a particular category of claimants. The ultimate balance involves a determination as to when, under our constitutional system, judicial-type procedures must be imposed upon administrative action to assure fairness * * *. All that is necessary is that the procedures be tailored, in light of the decision to be made, to "the capacities and circumstances of those who are to be heard," *Goldberg*, 397 U.S. at 268–269, to insure that they are given a meaningful opportunity to present their case. In assessing what process is due in this case, substantial weight must be given to the good-faith judgments of the individuals charged by Congress with the administration of social welfare programs that the procedures they have provided assure fair consideration of the entitlement claims of individuals. This is especially so where, as here, the prescribed procedures not only provide the claimant with an effective process for asserting his claim prior to any administrative action, but also assure a right to an evidentiary hearing, as well as to subsequent judicial review, before the denial of his claim becomes final.

We conclude that an evidentiary hearing is not required prior to the termination of disability benefits and that the present administrative procedures fully comport with due process. [Reversed.]

MR. JUSTICE BRENNAN, with whom MR. JUSTICE MARSHALL concurs, dissenting.

I agree with the District Court and the Court of Appeals that, prior to termination of benefits, Eldridge must be afforded an evidentiary hearing of the type required for welfare beneficiaries * * *. I would add that the Court's consideration that a discontinuance of disability benefits may cause the recipient to suffer only a limited deprivation is no argument. It is speculative. Moreover, the very legislative determination to provide disability benefits, without any prerequisite determination of need in fact, presumes a need by the recipient which is not this Court's function to denigrate. Indeed, in the present case, it is indicated that because disability benefits were terminated there was a foreclosure upon the Eldridge home and the family's furniture was repossessed, forcing Eldridge, his wife, and their children to sleep in one bed. Finally, it is also no argument that a worker, who has been placed in the untenable position of having been denied disability benefits, may still seek other forms of public assistance.

---

## Points for Discussion

### *a. Trial-Type Hearings and Timing*

Under the procedures at issue in *Mathews*, recipients of disability benefits were entitled to a trial-type hearing before an administrative law judge when the agency decided that they were no longer eligible to receive benefits. The hearing would have been more than sufficient if it had preceded the termination of benefits. The potential problem, however, was that the agency granted the beneficiary a hearing only *after* terminating benefits. Does *Mathews* stand for the proposition that the government can take action that deprives a person of life, liberty, or property without first granting a hearing, as long as it grants a hearing at which to contest the decision after the fact?

In at least some cases, immediate government action, without any pre-action hearing, seems clearly justified by some threat to public health or safety. See, e.g., *North American Cold Storage Co. v. Chicago*, 211 U.S. 306 (1908) (holding that government can seize and destroy rancid food without a pre-seizure hearing). But can you think of cases in which the government should have to give a hearing before taking the action that deprives a person of some property interest?

***b. The Standard for Determining the Procedures Required by the Due Process Clauses***

The Court in *Mathews* explained that determining the procedures required by the Due Process Clauses "generally requires consideration of three distinct factors: First, the private interest that will be affected by the official action; second, the risk of an erroneous deprivation of such interest through the procedures used, and the probable value, if any, of additional or substitute procedural safeguards; and finally, the Government's interest, including the function involved and the fiscal and administrative burdens that the additional or substitute procedural requirement would entail." Under this standard, can an agency know with confidence (without having its programs challenged in court) whether it is required to provide a trial-type hearing to a person affected by its decisions? If not, does that suggest a problem with the Court's standard? Or is the question inherently context specific?

---

When an agency adjudicates a private party's rights, it resolves the same sorts of questions that often are addressed in judicial proceedings in federal court: it resolves contested questions of fact and applies a legal standard to those facts. Unlike federal judges, however, agency decision-makers—both administrative law judges, who often preside over a hearing, and the heads of agencies, who often make the final decision—do not enjoy life tenure as a protection against political influence. Are there any limits on Congress's power to give agencies the power to adjudicate private rights in the first place? Consider the case that follows.

---

## *Commodity Futures Trading Commission v. Schor*

478 U.S. 833 (1986)

JUSTICE O'CONNOR delivered the opinion of the Court.

The [Commodity Exchange Act (CEA or Act), 7 U.S.C. § 1 *et seq.*,] broadly prohibits fraudulent and manipulative conduct in connection with commodity futures transactions. In 1974, Congress "overhaul[ed]" the Act in order to institute a more "comprehensive regulatory structure to oversee the volatile and esoteric futures trading complex." H.R. Rep. No. 93–975, p. 1 (1974). See Pub. L. 93–463, 88 Stat. 1389. Congress also determined that the broad regulatory powers of the CEA were most appropriately vested in an agency which would be relatively immune from the "political winds that sweep Washington." H.R. Rep. No. 93–975, at 44,

70. It therefore created an independent agency, [the Commodity Futures Trading Commission (CFTC or Commission),] and entrusted to it sweeping authority to implement the CEA.

Among the duties assigned to the CFTC was the administration of a reparations procedure through which disgruntled customers of professional commodity brokers could seek redress for the brokers' violations of the Act or CFTC regulations. Thus, § 14 of the CEA, 7 U.S.C. § 18 (1976 ed.), provides that any person injured by such violations may apply to the Commission for an order directing the offender to pay reparations to the complainant and may enforce that order in federal district court. Congress intended this administrative procedure to be an "inexpensive and expeditious" alternative to existing fora available to aggrieved customers, namely, the courts and arbitration. S. Rep. No. 95–850, p. 11 (1978). See also 41 Fed. Reg. 3994 (1976) (CFTC regulations promulgated pursuant to § 14).

In conformance with the congressional goal of promoting efficient dispute resolution, the CFTC promulgated a regulation in 1976 which allows it to adjudicate counterclaims "aris[ing] out of the transaction or occurrence or series of transactions or occurrences set forth in the complaint." *Id.*, at 3995, 4002 (codified at 17 CFR § 12.23(b)(2) (1983)). This permissive counterclaim rule leaves the respondent in a reparations proceeding free to seek relief against the reparations complainant in other fora.

The instant dispute arose in February 1980, when respondents Schor and Mortgage Services of America, Inc., invoked the CFTC's reparations jurisdiction by filing complaints against petitioner Conti Commodity Services, Inc. (Conti), a commodity futures broker, and Richard L. Sandor, a Conti employee. Schor had an account with Conti which contained a debit balance because Schor's net futures trading losses and expenses, such as commissions, exceeded the funds deposited in the account. Schor alleged that this debit balance was the result of Conti's numerous violations of the CEA.

Before receiving notice that Schor had commenced the reparations proceeding, Conti had filed a diversity action in Federal District Court to recover the debit balance. *Conti-Commodity Services, Inc. v. Mortgage Services of America, Inc.*, No. 80–C–1089 (ND Ill., filed Mar. 4, 1980). Schor counterclaimed in this action, reiterating his charges that the debit balance was due to Conti's violations of the CEA. Schor also moved on two separate occasions to dismiss or stay the District Court action, arguing that the continuation of the federal action would be a waste of judicial resources and an undue burden on the litigants in view of the fact that "[t]he reparations proceedings . . . will fully . . . resolve and adjudicate all the rights of the parties to this action with respect to the transactions which are the subject matter of this action."

Although the District Court declined to stay or dismiss the suit, Conti voluntarily dismissed the federal court action and presented its debit balance claim by way of a counterclaim in the CFTC reparations proceeding. Conti denied violating the CEA and instead insisted that the debit balance resulted from Schor's trading, and was therefore a simple debt owed by Schor.

After discovery, briefing, and a hearing, the Administrative Law Judge (ALJ) in Schor's reparations proceeding ruled in Conti's favor on both Schor's claims and Conti's counterclaims. After this ruling, Schor for the first time challenged the CFTC's statutory authority to adjudicate Conti's counterclaim. The ALJ rejected Schor's challenge * * *. The Commission declined to review the decision and allowed it to become final, at which point Schor filed a petition for review with the Court of Appeals for the District of Columbia Circuit. Prior to oral argument, the Court of Appeals, *sua sponte,* raised the question whether CFTC could constitutionally adjudicate Conti's counterclaims in light of *Northern Pipeline Construction Co. v. Marathon Pipe Line Co.*, 458 U.S. 50 (1982), in which this Court held that "Congress may not vest in a non-Article III court the power to adjudicate, render final judgment, and issue binding orders in a traditional contract action arising under state law, without consent of the litigants, and subject only to ordinary appellate review." *Thomas v. Union Carbide Agricultural Products Co.*, 473 U.S. 568, 584 (1985).

**Make the Connection**

We considered the "avoidance canon," under which courts sometimes construe statutes narrowly in order to avoid constitutional problems, in Chapter 3.

[The court of appeals concluded that the CFTC's exercise of jurisdiction over Conti's common law counterclaim gave rise to "[s]erious constitutional problems" under *Northern Pipeline* and construed the CEA not to confer power on the CFTC to adjudicate such claims. The Supreme Court found that interpretation of the statute "untenable."] We therefore are squarely faced with the question whether the CFTC's assumption of jurisdiction over common law counterclaims violates Article III of the Constitution.

Article III, § 1, directs that the "judicial Power of the United States shall be vested in one supreme Court and in such inferior Courts as the Congress may from time to time ordain and establish," and provides that these federal courts shall be staffed by judges who hold office during good behavior, and whose compensation shall not be diminished during tenure in office. Schor claims that these provisions prohibit Congress from authorizing the initial adjudication of common law counterclaims by the CFTC, an administrative agency whose adjudicatory officers do not enjoy the tenure and salary protections embodied in Article III.

Although our precedents in this area do not admit of easy synthesis, they do establish that the resolution of claims such as Schor's cannot turn on conclusory reference to the language of Article III. Rather, the constitutionality of a given congressional delegation of adjudicative functions to a non-Article III body must be assessed by reference to the purposes underlying the requirements of Article III. This inquiry, in turn, is guided by the principle that "practical attention to substance rather than doctrinaire reliance on formal categories should inform application of Article III." *Thomas, supra*, at 587. See also *Crowell v. Benson*, 285 U.S. 22, 53 (1932).

In determining the extent to which a given congressional decision to authorize the adjudication of Article III business in a non-Article III tribunal impermissibly threatens the institutional integrity of the Judicial Branch, the Court has declined to adopt formalistic and unbending rules. Although such rules might lend a greater degree of coherence to this area of the law, they might also unduly constrict Congress' ability to take needed and innovative action pursuant to its Article I powers. Thus, in reviewing Article III challenges, we have weighed a number of factors, none of which has been deemed determinative, with an eye to the practical effect that the congressional action will have on the constitutionally assigned role of the federal judiciary. Among the factors upon which we have focused are the extent to which the "essential attributes of judicial power" are reserved to Article III courts, and, conversely, the extent to which the non-Article III forum exercises the range of jurisdiction and powers normally vested only in Article III courts, the origins and importance of the right to be adjudicated, and the concerns that drove Congress to depart from the requirements of Article III.

An examination of the relative allocation of powers between the CFTC and Article III courts in light of the considerations given prominence in our precedents demonstrates that the congressional scheme does not impermissibly intrude on the province of the judiciary. The CFTC's adjudicatory powers depart from the traditional agency model in just one respect: the CFTC's jurisdiction over common law counterclaims. While wholesale importation of concepts of pendent or ancillary jurisdiction into the agency context may create greater constitutional difficulties, we decline to endorse an absolute prohibition on such jurisdiction out of fear of where some hypothetical "slippery slope" may deposit us. Indeed, the CFTC's exercise of this type of jurisdiction is not without precedent. Thus, in * * * *Katchen v. Landy*, 382 U.S. 323 (1966), this Court upheld a bankruptcy referee's power to hear and decide state law counterclaims against a creditor who filed a claim in bankruptcy when those counterclaims arose out of the same transaction. We reasoned that, as a practical matter, requiring the trustee to commence a plenary action to recover on its counterclaim would be a "meaningless gesture." *Id.*, at 334.

In the instant cases, we are likewise persuaded that there is little practical reason to find that this single deviation from the agency model is fatal to the congressional scheme. * * * The CEA scheme in fact hews closely to the agency model approved by the Court in *Crowell v. Benson*, 285 U.S. 22 (1932). * * *

The CFTC, like the agency in *Crowell*, deals only with a "particularized area of law," whereas the jurisdiction of the bankruptcy courts found unconstitutional in

*Northern Pipeline* extended to broadly "all civil proceedings arising under title 11 or arising in or *related to* cases under title 11." 28 U.S.C. § 1471(b). CFTC orders, like those of the agency in *Crowell,* but unlike those of the bankruptcy courts under the 1978 Act, are enforceable only by order of the district court. See 7 U.S.C. § 18(f). CFTC orders are also reviewed under the same "weight of the evidence" standard sustained in *Crowell,* rather than the more deferential standard found lacking in *Northern Pipeline.* See 7 U.S.C. § 9. *Northern Pipeline, supra,* at 85. The legal rulings of the CFTC, like the legal determinations of the agency in *Crowell,* are subject to *de novo* review. Finally, the CFTC, unlike the bankruptcy courts under the 1978 Act, does not exercise "all ordinary powers of district courts," and thus may not, for instance, preside over jury trials or issue writs of habeas corpus.

**FYI**

In *Crowell,* the Court addressed the constitutionality of a provision of the Longshoremen's and Harbor Workers' Act that created an agency scheme for adjudicating tort claims arising from certain maritime employment. Under the Act, federal district courts reviewed agency conclusions of law *de novo,* but had only limited authority to review agency findings of fact. The Court upheld the scheme, reasoning that Congress can permit agencies to adjudicate claims of "public right"—that is, "between the Government and persons subject to its authority"—as opposed to claims of "private right"—that is, claims between two private parties.

Of course, the nature of the claim has significance in our Article III analysis quite apart from the method prescribed for its adjudication. The counterclaim asserted in this litigation is a "private" right for which state law provides the rule of decision. It is therefore a claim of the kind assumed to be at the "core" of matters normally reserved to Article III courts. See, *e.g., Thomas,* 473 U.S., at 587. Yet this conclusion does not end our inquiry; just as this Court has rejected any attempt to make determinative for Article III purposes the distinction between public rights and private rights, there is no reason inherent in separation of powers principles to accord the state law character of a claim talismanic power in Article III inquiries.

We have explained that "the public rights doctrine reflects simply a pragmatic understanding that when Congress selects a quasi-judicial method of resolving matters that 'could be conclusively determined by the Executive and Legislative Branches,' the danger of encroaching on the judicial powers" is less than when private rights, which are normally within the purview of the judiciary, are relegated as an initial matter to administrative adjudication. *Thomas,* 473 U.S., at 589. * * * The risk that Congress may improperly have encroached on the federal judiciary is obviously magnified when Congress "withdraw[s] from judicial cognizance any matter which, from its nature, is the subject of a suit at the common law, or in equity, or admiralty" and which therefore has traditionally been tried in Article III courts, and allocates the decision of those matters to a non-Article III forum of its own creation. *Murray's Lessee v. Hoboken Land & Improvement Co.,* 18 How. 272, 284 (1856). Accordingly, where private, common law rights are at stake, our examination of the congressional attempt to control the manner in which those rights are adjudicated has been searching. In this litigation, however, "[l]ooking beyond form to the substance of what" Congress has done, we are persuaded that the congressional authorization of limited CFTC jurisdiction over a narrow class of common law claims as an incident to the CFTC's primary, and unchallenged, adjudicative function does not create a substantial threat to the separation of powers.

It is clear that Congress has not attempted to "withdraw from judicial cognizance" the determination of Conti's right to the sum represented by the debit balance in Schor's account. Congress gave the CFTC the authority to adjudicate such matters, but the decision to invoke this forum is left entirely to the parties and the power of the federal judiciary to take jurisdiction of these matters is unaffected. In such circumstances, separation of powers concerns are diminished, for it seems self-evident that just as Congress may encourage parties to settle a dispute out of court or resort to arbitration without impermissible incursions on the separation of powers, Congress may make available a quasi-judicial mechanism through which willing parties may, at their option, elect to resolve their differences. This is not to say, of course, that if Congress created a phalanx of non-Article III tribunals equipped to handle the entire business of the Article III courts without any Article III supervision or control and without evidence of valid and specific legislative necessities, the fact that the parties had the election to proceed in their forum of choice would necessarily save the scheme from constitutional attack. But this case obviously bears no resemblance to such a scenario, given the degree of judicial control saved to the federal courts, as well as the congressional purpose behind the jurisdictional delegation, the demonstrated need for the delegation, and the limited nature of the delegation.

When Congress authorized the CFTC to adjudicate counterclaims, its primary focus was on making effective a specific and limited federal regulatory scheme, not on allocating jurisdiction among federal tribunals. Congress intended to create an inexpensive and expeditious alternative forum through which customers could enforce the provisions of the CEA against professional brokers. Its decision to endow the CFTC with jurisdiction over such reparations claims is readily understandable given the perception that the CFTC was relatively immune from political pressures, and the obvious expertise that the Commission possesses in applying the CEA and its own regulations. This reparations scheme itself is of unquestioned constitutional validity. It was only to ensure the effectiveness of this scheme that Congress authorized the CFTC to assert jurisdiction over common law counterclaims. Indeed, * * * absent the CFTC's exercise of that authority, the purposes of the reparations procedure would have been confounded.

It also bears emphasis that the CFTC's assertion of counterclaim jurisdiction * * * is incidental to, and completely dependent upon, adjudication of reparations claims created by federal law, and in actual fact is limited to claims arising out of the same transaction or occurrence as the reparations claim.

In such circumstances, the magnitude of any intrusion on the Judicial Branch can only be termed *de minimis.* Conversely, were we to hold that the Legislative Branch may not permit such limited cognizance of common law counterclaims at the election of the parties, it is clear that we would "defeat the obvious purpose of the legislation to furnish a prompt, continuous, expert and inexpensive method for dealing with a class of questions of fact which are peculiarly suited to examination and determination by an administrative agency specially assigned to that task." *Crowell,* 285 U.S., at 46. We do not think Article III compels this degree of prophylaxis. [Reversed and] remanded for further proceedings consistent with this opinion.

JUSTICE BRENNAN, with whom JUSTICE MARSHALL joins, dissenting.

Article III, § 1, of the Constitution provides that "[t]he judicial Power of the United States, shall be vested in one supreme Court, and in such inferior Courts as the Congress may from time to time ordain and establish." It further specifies that the federal judicial power must be exercised by judges who "shall hold their Offices during good Behaviour, and [who] shall, at stated Times, receive for their Services a Compensation, which shall not be diminished during their Continuance in Office."

On its face, Article III, § 1, seems to prohibit the vesting of *any* judicial functions in either the Legislative or the Executive Branch. The Court has, however, recognized three narrow exceptions to the otherwise absolute mandate of Article III: territorial courts, see, *e.g., American Ins. Co. v. Canter,* 1 Pet. 511 (1828); courts-martial, see, *e.g., Dynes v. Hoover,* 20 How. 65 (1857); and courts that adjudicate certain disputes concerning public rights, see, *e.g., Crowell v. Benson,* 285 U.S. 22 (1932). Unlike the Court, I would limit the judicial authority of non-Article III federal tribunals to these few, long-established exceptions and would countenance no further erosion of Article III's mandate.

* * * The federal judicial power [must] be exercised by judges who are independent of the Executive and the Legislature in order to maintain the checks and balances that are crucial to our constitutional structure. The Framers [understood] that a principal benefit of the separation of the judicial power from the legislative and executive powers would be the protection of individual litigants from decisionmakers susceptible to majoritarian pressures. Article III's salary and tenure provisions promote impartial adjudication by placing the judicial power of the United States "in a body of judges insulated from majoritarian pressures and thus able to enforce [federal law] without fear of reprisal or public rebuke." *United States v. Raddatz,* 447 U.S. 667, 704 (1980) (MARSHALL, J., dissenting). As Alexander Hamilton observed, "[t]hat inflexible and uniform adherence to the rights of the Constitution, and of individuals, which we perceive to be indispensable in the Courts of justice can certainly not be expected

from Judges who hold their offices by a temporary commission." The Federalist No. 78, p. 546 (H. Dawson ed. 1876). * * *

These important functions of Article III are too central to our constitutional scheme to risk their incremental erosion. The exceptions we have recognized for territorial courts, courts-martial, and administrative courts were each based on "certain exceptional powers bestowed upon Congress by the Constitution or by historical consensus." *Northern Pipeline*, 458 U.S., at 70 (opinion of Brennan, J.). * * * By sanctioning the adjudication of state-law counterclaims by a federal administrative agency, the Court far exceeds the analytic framework of our precedents.

More than a century ago, we recognized that Congress may not "withdraw from [Article III] judicial cognizance any matter *which, from its nature, is the subject of a suit at the common law,* or in equity, or admiralty." *Murray's Lessee*, 18 How., at 284 (emphasis added). * * * The Court attempts to support the substantial alteration it works today in our Article III jurisprudence by pointing, *inter alia,* to legislative convenience [and] to the fact that Congress does not altogether eliminate federal-court jurisdiction over ancillary state-law counterclaims * * *. In my view, the Court's effort fails.

* * * Article III's prophylactic protections were intended to prevent * * * abdication to claims of legislative convenience. The Court requires that the legislative interest in convenience and efficiency be weighed against the competing interest in judicial independence. In doing so, the Court pits an interest the benefits of which are immediate, concrete, and easily understood against one, the benefits of which are almost entirely prophylactic, and thus often seem remote and not worth the cost in any single case. Thus, while this balancing creates the illusion of objectivity and ineluctability, in fact the result was foreordained, because the balance is weighted against judicial independence. The danger of the Court's balancing approach is, of course, that as individual cases accumulate in which the Court finds that the short-term benefits of efficiency outweigh the long-term benefits of judicial independence, the protections of Article III will be eviscerated.

* * * The Court dismisses warnings about the dangers of its approach, asserting simply that it does not fear the slippery slope, and that this litigation does not involve the creation by Congress of a "phalanx of non-Article III tribunals equipped to handle the entire business of the Article III courts." [But Congress] can seriously impair Article III's structural and individual protections * * * by *diluting* the judicial power of the federal courts. And * * * dilution of judicial power operates to impair the protections of Article III regardless of whether Congress acted with the "good intention" of providing a more efficient dispute resolution system or with the "bad intention" of strengthening the Legislative Branch at the expense of the Judiciary.

---

## Points for Discussion

### *a. Article III as a Limit on Agency Power to Adjudicate*

Although the Court in *Schor* upheld the agency's power to adjudicate the claims at issue, the Court acknowledged that Article III of the Constitution, which governs the judicial power of the United States, imposes meaningful limits on Congress's power to assign adjudicatory power to agencies. On this view, Article III prohibits Congress from giving broad power to agencies to adjudicate "private rights."

We have also seen that Congress often gives agencies broad power to issue rules that include important policy judgments, yet the Court has not been willing to impose meaningful limits on Congress's power to do so. (We considered the non-delegation doctrine, and Congress's broad authority to delegate policy-making power to agencies, in Chapter 6.) Should the Court conclude that Article I of the Constitution, which governs the legislative power of the United States, imposes meaningful limits on Congress's power to delegate policy-making authority to agencies? Or should the Court instead be as willing to allow Congress to give adjudicatory power to agencies as it is to allow Congress to give policy-making power to agencies?

### *b. Public Rights and Private Rights*

The Court suggested that there is no constitutional barrier to letting agencies adjudicate so-called "public rights"—that is, disputes "between the Government and persons subject to its authority." Instead, the Court reasoned that, if there were any defect in the grant of adjudicatory power to the CFTC, the problem was with Congress's power to let the CFTC adjudicate claims of "private right"—that is, disputes between two private parties.

Why did the Court think that it was so clear that the CFTC's "primary * * * adjudicative function"—that is, to decide whether a person or firm has violated the Commodities Exchange Act—raises no serious problems under the separation of powers? (The Court said that the CFTC's power to do so was "of unquestioned constitutional validity.") Yet federal courts often adjudicate such claims—such as when the Securities and Exchange Commission institutes an action in federal court against a person accused of violating the securities laws—which means that any effort by Congress to vest the power to adjudicate them in an agency detracts to some extent from the scope of the federal courts' power. Why is agency adjudication of "public rights" any less problematic than agency adjudication of "private rights"?

### *c. Constitutional Claims and Waiver*

As the Court explained, Schor moved to dismiss the action that Conti had filed in federal court so that the CFTC could adjudicate the matter. Later, after the CFTC ruled against him, Schor argued that the CFTC lacked power to adjudicate

Conti's counterclaim against him. Why didn't Schor waive the right to challenge the CFTC's authority to adjudicate?

In a part of the opinion that was omitted above, the Court stated that Article III "serves both to protect 'the role of the independent judiciary within the constitutional scheme of tripartite government' and to safeguard litigants' 'right to have claims decided before judges who are free from potential domination by other branches of government.' " The Court reasoned that Schor's actions resulted in a waiver of "any right he may have possessed to the full trial of Conti's counterclaim before an Article III court" but that he had not waived the "structural principle" implicated in the case.

Justice Brennan responded: "In my view, the structural and individual interests served by Article III are inseparable. The potential exists for individual litigants to be deprived of impartial decisionmakers only where federal officials who exercise judicial power are susceptible to congressional and executive pressure. * * * Because the individual and structural interests served by Article III are coextensive, consent is irrelevant to Article III analysis."

Should a party be permitted to challenge an agency's power to adjudicate a matter, on the ground that it impermissibly interferes with the authority of Article III courts, when the party actively declined an opportunity to litigate the matter in federal court?

---

## 2. Review of the Substance of Agency Decisions

The APA provides: "A person suffering legal wrong because of agency action, or adversely affected or aggrieved by agency action within the meaning of a relevant statute, is entitled to judicial review thereof." 5 U.S.C. § 702. It states further that "[a]gency action made reviewable by statute and final agency action for which there is no other adequate remedy in a court are subject to judicial review." *Id.* § 704. Finally, the APA defines the "scope of review" during such a judicial proceeding as follows:

> To the extent necessary to decision and when presented, the reviewing court shall decide all relevant questions of law, interpret constitutional and statutory provisions, and determine the meaning or applicability of the terms of an agency action. The reviewing court shall—
>
> (1) compel agency action unlawfully withheld or unreasonably delayed; and
>
> (2) hold unlawful and set aside agency action, findings, and conclusions found to be—
>
> (A) arbitrary, capricious, an abuse of discretion, or otherwise not in accordance with law;
>
> (B) contrary to constitutional right, power, privilege, or immunity;

(C) in excess of statutory jurisdiction, authority, or limitations, or short of statutory right;

(D) without observance of procedure required by law;

(E) unsupported by substantial evidence in a case subject to sections 556 and 557 of this title or otherwise reviewed on the record of an agency hearing provided by statute; or

(F) unwarranted by the facts to the extent that the facts are subject to trial de novo by the reviewing court.

In making the foregoing determinations, the court shall review the whole record or those parts of it cited by a party, and due account shall be taken of the rule of prejudicial error.

*Id.* § 706.

We have already seen examples of judicial review "without observance of procedure required by law." In the remaining parts of this Chapter, we will consider judicial review of agency fact-finding and judicial review of agency decision-making to determine whether it is "arbitrary, capricious, an abuse of discretion, or otherwise not in accordance with law."

---

### a. Judicial Review of Agency Fact-Finding

## *Universal Camera Corp. v. National Labor Relations Board*

340 US. 474 (1951)

Mr. Justice Frankfurter delivered the opinion of the Court.

The essential issue raised by this case * * * is the effect of the Administrative Procedure Act and the legislation colloquially known as the Taft-Hartley Act, 29 U.S.C. § 141 et seq., on the duty of Courts of Appeals when called upon to review orders of the National Labor Relations Board.

[One of the National Labor Relations Board's responsibilities is to conduct elections among employees to determine if they wish to be represented during collective bargaining with their employer. A union filed a petition with the Board to institute such a representation proceeding for petitioner's employees. One of the petitioner's employees was fired after he testified in support of the union's position. The employee filed a complaint with the Board, contending that he had been fired for the protected activity of participation in a representation proceeding. The petitioner defended on the ground that the employee had not been fired for his testimony, but rather because he had accused the company's personnel manager of drunkenness. A trial examiner at the Board held a hearing on the matter and, crediting the employer's testimony that anti-union animus did not motivate the employee's termi nation, recommended dismissal of the complaint. A divided Board disagreed, holding the discharge to be an unfair labor practice. On review, the court of appeals affirmed the Board's decision but expressed concern about the Board's assessment of the evidence.]

I

**FYI**

The National Labor Relations Act of 1935, also known as the Wagner Act, created the NLRB and authorized private-sector employees to form unions, engage in collective bargaining, and take collective action to ensure better working conditions and compensation.

Want of certainty in judicial review of Labor Board decisions partly reflects the intractability of any formula to furnish definiteness of content for all the impalpable factors involved in judicial review. But in part doubts as to the nature of the reviewing power and uncertainties in its application derive from history, and to that extent an elucidation of this history may clear them away.

The Wagner Act provided: "The findings of the Board as to the facts, if supported by evidence, shall be conclusive." Act of July 5, 1935, § 10(e), 49 Stat. 449, 454, 29 U.S.C. § 160(e). [Before enactment of the APA, this] Court read "evidence" to mean "substantial evidence," *Washington, V. & M. Coach Co. v. Labor Board*, 301 U.S. 142 (1937), and we said that "(s)ubstantial evidence is more than a mere scintilla. It means such relevant evidence as a reasonable mind might accept as adequate to support a conclusion." *Consolidated Edison Co. v. National Labor Relations Board*, 305 U.S. 197, 229 (1938). Accordingly, it "must do more than create a suspicion of the existence of the fact to be established. . . . [I]t must be enough to justify, if the trial were to a jury, a refusal to direct a verdict when the conclusion sought to be drawn from it is one of fact for the jury." *National Labor Relations Board v. Columbian Enameling & Stamping Co.*, 306 U.S. 292, 300 (1939).

**Take Note**

Under the approach that the Court describes here, reviewing courts would uphold the Board's finding of fact as long as there was some meaningful amount of evidence in support of that finding, even if there was also substantial evidence to the contrary.

The very smoothness of the "substantial evidence" formula as the standard for reviewing the evidentiary validity of the Board's findings established its currency. But the inevitably variant applications of the standard to conflicting evidence soon brought contrariety of views and in due course bred criticism. Even though the whole record may have been canvassed in order to determine whether the evidentiary foundation of a determination by the Board was "substantial," the phrasing of this Court's process of review readily lent itself to the notion that it was enough that the evidence supporting the Board's result was "substantial" when considered by itself. It is fair to say that by imperceptible steps regard for the fact-finding function of the Board led to the assumption that the requirements of the Wagner Act were met when the reviewing court could find in the record evidence which, when viewed in isolation, substantiated the Board's findings.

Criticism of so contracted a reviewing power reinforced dissatisfaction felt in various quarters with the Board's administration of the Wagner Act in the years preceding the war. The scheme of the Act was attacked as an inherently unfair fusion of the functions of prosecutor and judge. Accusations of partisan bias were not wanting. The "irresponsible admission and weighing of hearsay, opinion, and emotional speculation in place of factual evidence" was said to be a "serious menace." No doubt some, perhaps even much, of the criticism was baseless and some surely was reckless. What is here relevant, however, is the climate of opinion thereby generated and its effect on Congress. Protests against "shocking injustices" and intimations of judicial "abdication" with which some courts granted enforcement of the Board's order stimulated pressures for legislative relief from alleged administrative excesses.

The strength of these pressures was reflected in the passage in 1940 of the Walter-Logan Bill. It was vetoed by President Roosevelt, partly because it imposed unduly rigid limitations on the administrative process, and partly because of the investigation into the actual operation of the administrative process then being conducted by an experienced committee appointed by the Attorney General. It is worth noting that despite its aim to tighten control over administrative determinations of fact, the Walter-Logan Bill contented itself with the conventional formula that an agency's decision could be set aside if "the findings of fact are not supported by substantial evidence."

The final report of the Attorney General's Committee was submitted in January, 1941. The majority concluded that "(d)issatisfaction with the existing standards as to the scope of judicial review derives largely from dissatisfaction with the fact-finding procedures now employed by the administrative bodies." Departure from the "substantial evidence" test, it thought, would either create unnecessary uncertainty or transfer to courts the responsibility for ascertaining and assaying matters the significance of which lies outside judicial competence. Accordingly, it recommended against Legislation embodying a general scheme of judicial review.

Three members of the Committee registered a dissent. Their view was that the "present system or lack of system of judicial review" led to inconsistency and uncertainty. They reported that under a "prevalent" interpretation of the "substantial evidence" rule "if what is called 'substantial evidence' is found anywhere in the record to support conclusions of fact, the courts are said to be obliged to sustain the decision without reference to how heavily the countervailing evidence may preponderate—unless indeed the stage of arbitrary decision is reached. Under this interpretation, the courts need to read only one side of the case and, if they find any evidence there, the administrative action is to be sustained and the record to the contrary is to be ignored." Their view led them to recommend that Congress enact principles of review applicable to all agencies not excepted by unique characteristics. One of these principles was expressed by the formula that judicial review could extend to "findings, inferences, or conclusions of fact unsupported, upon the whole record, by substantial evidence." So far as the history of this movement for enlarged review reveals, the phrase "upon the whole record" makes its first appearance in this recommendation of the minority of the Attorney General's Committee. This evidence of the close relationship between the phrase and the criticism out of which it arose is important, for the substance of this formula for judicial review found its way into the statute books when Congress with unquestioning—we might even say uncritical—unanimity enacted the Administrative Procedure Act.

One is tempted to say "uncritical" because the legislative history of that Act hardly speaks with that clarity of purpose which Congress supposedly furnishes courts in order to enable them to enforce its true will. On the one hand, the sponsors of the legislation indicated that they were reaffirming the prevailing "substantial evidence" test. But with equal clarity they expressed disapproval of the manner in which the courts were applying their own standard. The committee reports of both houses refer to the practice of agencies to rely upon "suspicion, surmise, implications, or plainly incredible evidence," and indicate that courts are to exact higher standards "in the exercise of their independent judgment" and on consideration of "the whole record."

> **FYI**
>
> The Taft-Hartley Act, 61 Stat. 136, 29 U.S.C. § 141 et seq., amended the National Labor Relations Act. It prohibited certain union practices and required disclosure of various financial and political activities by unions.

Similar dissatisfaction with too restricted application of the "substantial evidence" test is reflected in the legislative history of the Taft-Hartley Act. * * * Early committee prints in the Senate provided for review by "weight of the evidence" or "clearly erroneous" standards. But, as the Senate Committee Report relates, "it was finally decided to conform the statute to the corresponding section of the Administrative Procedure Act where the substantial evidence test prevails. In order to clarify any ambiguity in that statute, however, the committee inserted the words 'questions of fact, if supported by substantial evidence on the record considered as a whole. . . .' " [Congress ultimately enacted this version of the bill.]

It is fair to say that in all this Congress expressed a mood. And it expressed its mood not merely by oratory but by legislation. As legislation that mood must be respected, even though it can only serve as a standard for judgment and not as a body of rigid rules assuring sameness of applications. Enforcement of such broad standards implies subtlety of mind and solidity of judgment. But it is not for us to question that Congress may assume such qualities in the federal judiciary.

From the legislative story we have summarized, two concrete conclusions do emerge. One is the identity of aim of the Administrative Procedure Act and the Taft-Hartley Act regarding the proof with which the Labor Board must support a decision. The other is that now Congress has left no room for doubt as to the kind of scrutiny which a court of appeals must give the record before the Board to satisfy itself that the Board's order rests on adequate proof. * * * [The] standard of proof specifically required of the Labor Board by the Taft-Hartley Act is the same as that to be exacted by courts reviewing every administrative action subject to the Administrative Procedure Act.

Whether or not it was ever permissible for courts to determine the substantiality of evidence supporting a Labor Board decision merely on the basis of evidence which in and of itself justified it, without taking into account contradictory evidence or evidence from which conflicting inferences could be drawn, the new legislation definitively precludes such a theory of review and bars its practice. The substantiality of evidence must take into account whatever in the record fairly detracts from its weight. This is clearly the significance of the requirement in both statutes that courts consider the whole record. Committee reports and the adoption in the Administrative Procedure Act of the minority views of the Attorney General's Committee demonstrate that to enjoin such a duty on the reviewing court was one of the important purposes of the movement which eventuated in that enactment.

To be sure, the requirement for canvassing "the whole record" in order to ascertain substantiality does not furnish a calculus of value by which a reviewing court can assess the evidence. Nor was it intended to negative the function of the Labor Board as one of those agencies presumably equipped or informed by experience to deal with a specialized field of knowledge, whose findings within that field carry the authority of an expertness which courts do not possess and therefore must respect. Nor does it mean that even as to matters not requiring expertise a court may displace the Board's choice between two fairly conflicting views, even though the court would justifiably have made a different choice had the matter been before it *de novo*. Congress has merely made it clear that a reviewing court is not barred from setting aside a Board decision when it cannot conscientiously find that the evidence supporting that decision is substantial, when viewed in the light that the record in its entirety furnishes, including the body of evidence opposed to the Board's view.

There remains, then, the question whether enactment of these two statutes has altered the scope of review other than to require that substantiality be determined in the light of all that the record relevantly presents. A formula for judicial review of

**Take Note**

The Court here and in the next few paragraphs announces the standard for judicial review of agency fact-finding. Can you identify the ways in which the standard differs from the old approach described earlier in the opinion?

administrative action may afford grounds for certitude but cannot assure certainty of application. Some scope for judicial discretion in applying the formula can be avoided only by falsifying the actual process of judging or by using the formula as an instrument of futile casuistry. It cannot be too often repeated that judges are not automata. The ultimate reliance for the fair operation of any standard is a judiciary of high competence and character and the constant play of an informed professional critique upon its work.

Since the precise way in which courts interfere with agency findings cannot be imprisoned within any form of words, new formulas attempting to rephrase the old are not likely to be more helpful than the old. There are no talismanic words that can avoid the process of judgment. The difficulty is that we cannot escape, in relation to this problem, the use of undefined defining terms.

Whatever changes were made by the Administrative Procedure and Taft-Hartley Acts are clearly within this area where precise definition is impossible. Retention of the familiar "substantial evidence" terminology indicates that no drastic reversal of attitude was intended.

But a standard leaving an unavoidable margin for individual judgment does not leave the judicial judgment at large even though the phrasing of the standard does not wholly fence it in. The legislative history of these Acts demonstrates a purpose to impose on courts a responsibility which has not always been recognized. Of course it is a statute and not a committee report which we are interpreting. But the fair interpretation of a statute is often "the art of proliferating a purpose," ***Brooklyn*** *National Corp. v. Commissioner*, 157 F.2d 450, 451 (2d Cir. 1946), revealed more by the demonstrable forces that produced it than by its precise phrasing. The adoption in these statutes of the judicially-constructed "substantial evidence" test was a response to pressures for stricter and more uniform practice, not a reflection of approval of all existing practices. To find the change so elusive that it cannot be precisely defined does not mean it may be ignored. * * *

We conclude, therefore, that the Administrative Procedure Act and the Taft-Hartley Act direct that courts must now assume more responsibility for the reasonableness and fairness of Labor Board decisions than some courts have shown in the past. Reviewing courts must be influenced by a feeling that they are not to abdicate the conventional judicial function. Congress has imposed on them responsibility for assuring that the Board keeps within reasonable grounds. That responsibility is not less real because it is limited to enforcing the requirement that evidence appear substantial when viewed, on the record as a whole, by courts invested with the authority and enjoying the prestige of the Courts of Appeals. The Board's findings are entitled to respect; but they must nonetheless be set aside when the record before a Court of Appeals clearly precludes the Board's decision from being justified by a fair estimate of the worth of the testimony of witnesses or its informed judgment on matters within its special competence or both.

Our power to review the correctness of application of the present standard ought seldom to be called into action. Whether on the record as a whole there is substantial evidence to support agency findings is a question which Congress has placed in the keeping of the Courts of Appeals. This Court will intervene only in what ought to be the rare instance when the standard appears to have been misapprehended or grossly misapplied.

**II**

The decision of the Court of Appeals is assailed on two grounds. It is said (1) that the court erred in holding that it was barred from taking into account the report of the examiner on questions of fact insofar as that report was rejected by the Board, and (2) that the Board's order was not supported by substantial evidence on the record considered as a whole, even apart from the validity of the court's refusal to consider the rejected portions of the examiner's report.

The latter contention is easily met. * * * [I]t is clear from the court's opinion in this case that it in fact did consider the "record as a whole," and did not deem itself merely the judicial echo of the Board's conclusion. The testimony of the company's witnesses was inconsistent, and there was clear evidence that the complaining employee had been discharged by an officer who was at one time influenced against him because of his appearance at the Board hearing. On such a record we could not say that it would be error to grant enforcement.

The first contention, however, raises serious questions to which we now turn.

**III**

The Court of Appeals deemed itself bound by the Board's rejection of the examiner's findings because the court considered these findings not "as unassailable as a master's." They are not. * * * The responsibility for decision [placed] on the Board is wholly inconsistent with the notion that it has power to reverse an examiner's findings only when they are "clearly erroneous." Such a limitation would make so drastic a departure from prior administrative practice that explicitness would be required.

The Court of Appeals concluded from this premise "that, although the Board would be wrong in totally disregarding his findings, it is practically impossible for a court, upon review of those findings which the Board itself substitutes, to consider the Board's reversal as a factor in the court's own decision. This we say, because we cannot find any middle ground between doing that and treating such a reversal as error, whenever it would be such, if done by a judge to a master in equity." Much as we respect the logical acumen of the Chief Judge of the Court of Appeals, we do not find ourselves pinioned between the horns of his dilemma.

We are aware that to give the examiner's findings less finality than a master's and yet entitle them to consideration in striking the account, is to introduce another and an unruly factor into the judgmatical process of review. But we ought not to fashion an exclusionary rule merely to reduce the number of imponderables to be considered by reviewing courts.

The Taft-Hartley Act provides that "The findings of the Board with respect to questions of fact if supported by substantial evidence on the record considered as a whole shall be conclusive." 29 U.S.C. § 160(e). Surely an examiner's report is as much a part of the record as the complaint or the testimony. According to the Administrative Procedure Act, "All decisions (including initial, recommended, or tentative decisions) shall become a part of the record . . . ." We found that this Act's provision for judicial review has the same meaning as that in the Taft-Hartley Act. The similarity of the two statutes in language and purpose also requires that the definition of "record" found in the Administrative Procedure Act be construed to be applicable as well to the term "record" as used in the Taft-Hartley Act.

It is therefore difficult to escape the conclusion that the plain language of the statutes directs a reviewing court to determine the substantiality of evidence on the record including the examiner's report. * * * Nothing in the statutes suggests that the Labor Board should not be influenced by the examiner's opportunity to observe the witnesses he hears and sees and the Board does not. Nothing suggests that reviewing courts should not give to the examiner's report such probative force as it intrinsically commands. * * *

We do not require that the examiner's findings be given more weight than in reason and in the light of judicial experience they deserve. The "substantial evidence" standard is not modified in any way when the Board and its examiner disagree. We intend only to recognize that evidence supporting a conclusion may be less substantial when an impartial, experienced examiner who has observed the witnesses and lived with the case has drawn conclusions different from the Board's than when he has reached the same conclusion. The findings of the examiner are to be considered along with the consistency and inherent probability of testimony. The significance of his report, of course, depends largely on the importance of credibility in the particular case. To give it this significance does not seem to us materially more difficult than to heed the other factors which in sum determine whether evidence is "substantial."

We therefore remand the cause to the Court of Appeals. On reconsideration of the record it should accord the findings of the trial examiner the relevance that they reasonably command in answering the comprehensive question whether the evidence supporting the Board's order is substantial. But the court need not limit its reexamination of the case to the effect of that report on its decision. We leave it free to grant or deny enforcement as it thinks the principles expressed in this opinion dictate.

Judgment vacated that cause remanded.

MR. JUSTICE BLACK and MR. JUSTICE DOUGLAS concur with parts I and II of this opinion but as to part III agree with the opinion of the court below.

---

## Points for Discussion

### *a. Judicial Review of Agency Fact-Finding*

We have seen that agency proceedings take one of four possible forms: formal adjudication, informal adjudication, formal rulemaking, or informal rulemaking. When agencies engage in formal decision-making—that is to say, when they make on-the-record decisions after formal, trial-type proceedings—they often make findings of fact or base their decisions on their view of the facts. For example, if an agency conducts a formal adjudication to determine whether a person is entitled to a permit to discharge pollutants into a river, the agency might have to determine whether the person has in fact complied with several predicates, such as acquiring the best technology available to minimize environmental harm. See, e.g., *Seacoast Anti-Pollution League v. Costle*, 572 F.2d 872 (1st Cir. 1978).

The APA specifically authorizes judicial review of agency "findings" in cases "subject to sections 556 and 557" of the APA, the provisions that govern formal agency proceedings. In such cases, agencies essentially act as if they were trial courts, and federal courts that review the agencies' decisions act in an "appellate" function. Is it troubling to give agencies what is effectively the judicial power to determine in the first instance facts that will affect private rights, such as the entitlement to a permit? Or does it depend on what standard of review courts apply when they review agency fact-finding?

### *b. The "Substantial Evidence" Test*

According to the APA, "[t]he reviewing court shall * * * hold unlawful and set aside agency * * * findings * * * found to be * * * unsupported by substantial evidence in a case subject to sections 556 and 557 of this title or otherwise reviewed on the record of an agency hearing provided by statute." 5 U.S.C. § 706. Is this standard different from the standard that federal courts of appeals apply when they review fact-finding by a federal district court judge? See F.R.C.P. 52 ("Findings of fact, whether based on oral or other evidence, must not be set aside unless clearly erroneous, and the reviewing court must give due regard to the trial court's opportunity to judge the witnesses' credibility.") If so, would it make sense to apply the same standard that courts of appeals apply for reviewing trial court findings?

Notice that the question is complicated in the context of agency fact-finding because of the multi-tiered decision-making process that many agencies employ. In many cases, including the *Universal Camera* case, a largely independent agency official—an administrative law judge or hearing examiner—presides over the formal hearing, and then the agency itself—the Board, the Secretary, or the Commission—"reviews" the decision and makes findings of its own. How did the Court in *Universal Camera* deal with such a decision-making process? According to the Court, what role should the administrative law judge's findings play in reviewing the agency's ultimate findings in the matter in question?

---

### b. Judicial Review of the Substance of Agency Decisions

Imagine that an agency conducts a formal adjudication. At the conclusion of the proceeding, at which it complied with all applicable procedural requirements, it makes defensible findings of fact. But its decision is based on a policy judgment that seems irrational or inconsistent with statutory objectives. Or imagine that an agency engages in informal rulemaking. It properly gives notice and an opportunity for comment, and it provides a concise general statement of basis and purpose when it issues the final rule. But the rule seems arbitrary or difficult to defend in light of the comments submitted or the statute's purposes. What should a court do when it reviews such agency action? The answer is surprisingly complex.

The APA states that the "reviewing court shall * * * hold unlawful and set aside agency action, findings, and conclusions found to be * * * arbitrary, capricious, an abuse of discretion, or otherwise not in accordance with law." Is it clear to you what sorts of judgments this standard requires a court to make when it reviews agency action? Consider the case that follows for an overview of the competing views about the appropriate judicial role in reviewing the substance of agency decisions.

---

## *Ethyl Corp. v. EPA*

541 F.2d 1 (D.C. Cir. 1976) (*en banc*)

J. SKELLY WRIGHT, CIRCUIT JUDGE:

[This case involved a challenge to a rule that the EPA issued that limited lead additives in gasoline. In issuing the rule, the agency resolved several highly contested factual questions about the likely costs and benefits of the rule. A panel of the D.C. Circuit invalidated the rule on the ground that the agency's predictive and scientific judgments were misguided, but the court, sitting *en banc*, reversed the panel's judgment and upheld the rule.]

Man's ability to alter his environment has developed far more rapidly than his ability to foresee with certainty the effects of his alterations. It is only recently that we have begun to appreciate the danger posed by unregulated modification of the world around us, and have created watchdog agencies whose task it is to warn us, and protect us, when technological "advances" present dangers unappreciated or unrevealed by their supporters. Such agencies, unequipped with crystal balls and unable to read the future, are nonetheless charged with evaluating the effects of unprecedented environmental modifications, often made on a massive scale. Necessarily, they must deal with predictions and uncertainty, with developing evidence, with conflicting evidence, and, sometimes, with little or no evidence at all. Today we address the scope of the power delegated one such watchdog, the Environmental Protection Agency (EPA). We must determine the certainty required by the Clean Air Act before EPA may act to protect the health of our populace from the lead particulate emissions of automobiles.

Section 211(c)(1)(A) of the Clean Air Act authorizes the Administrator of EPA to regulate gasoline additives whose emission products "will endanger the public health or welfare . . . ." 42 U.S.C. § 1857f–6c(c)(1)(A). Acting pursuant to that power, the Administrator, after notice and comment, determined that the automotive emissions caused by leaded gasoline present "a significant risk of harm" to the public health. Accordingly, he promulgated regulations that reduce, in step-wise fashion, the lead content of leaded gasoline. We must decide whether the Administrator properly interpreted the meaning of Section 211(c)(1)(A) and the scope of his power thereunder, and, if so, whether the evidence adduced at the rule-making proceeding supports his final determination. Finding in favor of the Administrator on both grounds, and on all other grounds raised by petitioners, we affirm his determination.

In promulgating the low-lead regulations under Section 211, EPA engaged in informal rule-making. As such, since the statute does not indicate otherwise, its procedures are conducted pursuant to Section 4 of the APA, 5 U.S.C. § 553, and must be reviewed under Section 10 of the Act, 5 U.S.C. § 706(2)(A)–(D). Our review of the evidence is governed by Section 10(e)(2)(A), which requires us to strike "agency action, findings, and conclusions" that we find to be "arbitrary, capricious, an abuse of discretion, or otherwise not in accordance with law . . . ." 5 U.S.C. § 706(2)(A). This standard of review is a highly deferential one. It presumes agency action to be valid. *Citizens to Preserve Overton Park v. Volpe*, 401 U.S. 402, 415 (1971). Moreover, it forbids the court's substituting its judgment for that of the agency, *id.* at 416, and requires affirmance if a rational basis exists for the

**Make the Connection**

We will consider *Overton Park* later in this Chapter.

agency's decision. *Bowman Transportation, Inc. v. Arkansas-Best Freight System, Inc.*, 419 U.S. 281, 290 (1974).

This is not to say, however, that we must rubber-stamp the agency decision as correct. To do so would render the appellate process a superfluous (although time-consuming) ritual. Rather, the reviewing court must assure itself that the agency decision was "based on a consideration of the relevant factors. . . ." Moreover, it must engage in a "substantial inquiry" into the facts, one that is "searching and careful." *Citizens to Preserve Overton Park*, 401 U.S. at 415, 416. This is particularly true in highly technical cases such as this one.

A court does not depart from its proper function when it undertakes a study of the record, hopefully perceptive, even as to the evidence on technical and specialized matters, for this enables the court to penetrate to the underlying decisions of the agency, to satisfy itself that the agency has exercised a reasoned discretion, with reasons that do not deviate from or ignore the ascertainable legislative intent.

There is no inconsistency between the deferential standard of review and the requirement that the reviewing court involve itself in even the most complex evidentiary matters; rather, the two indicia of arbitrary and capricious review stand in careful balance. The close scrutiny of the evidence is intended to educate the court. It must understand enough about the problem confronting the agency to comprehend the meaning of the evidence relied upon and the evidence discarded; the questions addressed by the agency and those bypassed; the choices open to the agency and those made. The more technical the case, the more intensive must be the court's effort to understand the evidence, for without an appropriate understanding of the case before it the court cannot properly perform its appellate function. But that function must be performed with conscientious awareness of its limited nature. The enforced education into the intricacies of the problem before the agency is not designed to enable the court to become a superagency that can supplant the agency's expert decision-maker. To the contrary, the court must give due deference to the agency's ability to rely on its own developed expertise. *Market Street Railway v. Railroad Commission*, 324 U.S. 548, 559–561 (1945). The immersion in the evidence is designed solely to enable the court to determine whether the agency decision was rational and based on consideration of the relevant factors. It is settled that we must affirm decisions with which we disagree so long as this test is met. *Bowman Transportation*, 419 U.S. at 290.

Thus, after our careful study of the record, we must take a step back from the agency decision. We must look at the decision not as the chemist, biologist or statistician that we are qualified neither by training nor experience to be, but as a reviewing court exercising our narrowly defined duty of holding agencies to certain minimal standards of rationality. "Although (our) inquiry into the facts is to be searching and careful, the ultimate standard of review is a narrow one." *Citizens to Preserve Overton Park*, 401 U.S. at 416. We must affirm unless the agency decision is arbitrary or capricious.

**Food for Thought**

What does it mean for a court to hold an agency decision to "minimal standards of rationality"? If judges are not experts in environmental law (or securities law or labor law or the many other subjects that federal agencies regulate), then how can they decide whether an agency's decision is "rational"?

[The court conducted a detailed review of the evidence, mostly about the adverse health effects of lead, on which the agency had relied in issuing the rule.] From a vast mass of evidence the Administrator has concluded that the emission products of lead additives will endanger the public health. He has handled an extraordinarily complicated problem with great care and candor. The evidence did not necessarily always point in one direction and frequently, until EPA authorized research, there was no evidence at all. The Administrator reached his conclusion only after hearings spread over several months, consideration of thousands of pages of documents, publication of three health documents, three formal comment periods, and receipt of hundreds of comments. Each study was considered independently; its worth was assessed only after it was measured against any critical comments. From the totality of the evidence the Administrator concluded that regulation under Section 211(c)(1)(A) was warranted.

In tracking his path through the evidence we, in our appellate role, have also considered separately each study and the objections petitioners make thereto. In no case have we found the Administrator's use of the evidence to be arbitrary or capricious. * * * We find the Administrator's analysis of the evidence and assessment of the risks to be well within the flexibility allowed by the "will endanger" standard. Accordingly, we affirm his determination that lead emissions "present a significant risk of harm to the health of urban populations, particularly to the health of city children." 38 Fed .Reg. 33734.

[The court also rejected the petitioner's claim that the agency failed to follow the required procedures in promulgating the rule. The agency had provided notice and three separate comment periods.] The record in this case clearly demonstrates that EPA fully satisfied the requirements of administrative due process. In fact, EPA's efforts to elicit informed comment on its proposed action went far beyond the measures it was required to take. All health-related documents, including internal EPA policy memoranda, were made public upon receipt, and comments on the documents were accepted until the date of final promulgation. These documents included drafts of the Administrator's decision whose contents were very similar to the version finally published and a draft of the Third Health Document which was substantially identical to the final draft. Both the draft of the Administrator's decision and the regulations and the draft of the Third Health Document were circulated for comment, and comments were received and acted upon. On this record, we cannot find that petitioners were deprived of administrative due process by EPA procedures.

[The court upheld the rule. The court's opinion included an extensive appendix with evidence relating to the EPA's conclusion that lead exposure poses serious health risks.]

Bazelon, Chief Judge, with whom McGowan, Circuit Judge, joins (concurring):

I concur in Judge Wright's opinion for the court, and wish only to further elucidate certain matters.

I agree with the court's construction of the statute that the Administrator is called upon to make "essentially legislative policy judgments" in assessing risks to public health. But I cannot agree that this automatically relieves the Administrator's decision from the "procedural . . . rigor proper for questions of fact." Quite the contrary, this case strengthens my view that

> ". . . in cases of great technological complexity, the best way for courts to guard against unreasonable or erroneous administrative decisions is not for the judges themselves to scrutinize the technical merits of each decision. Rather, it is to establish a decision-making process that assures a reasoned decision that can be held up to the scrutiny of the scientific community and the public." [*International Harvester Co. v. Ruckelshaus*, 478 F.2d 615, 652 (1973) (Bazelon, C. J., concurring).]

This record provides vivid demonstration of the dangers implicit in the contrary view, ably espoused by Judge Leventhal, which would have judges "steeping" themselves "in technical matters to determine whether the agency 'has exercised a reasoned discretion.' " It is one thing for judges to scrutinize FCC judgments concerning diversification of media ownership to determine if they are rational. But I doubt judges contribute much to improving the quality of the difficult decisions which must be made in highly technical areas when they take it upon themselves to decide, as did the panel in this case, that "in assessing the scientific and medical data the Administrator made clear errors of judgment." The process making a de novo evaluation of the scientific evidence inevitably invites judges of opposing views to make plausible-sounding, but simplistic, judgments of the relative weight to be afforded various pieces of technical data.

Because substantive review of mathematical and scientific evidence by technically illiterate judges is dangerously unreliable, I continue to believe we will do more to improve administrative decision-making by concentrating our efforts on strengthening administrative procedures: "When administrators provide a framework for principled decision-making, the result will be to diminish the importance of judicial review by enhancing the integrity of the administrative process, and to improve the quality of judicial review in those cases where judicial review is sought." [*Environmental Defense Fund, Inc. v. Ruckelshaus*, 439 F.2d 584, 598 (1971) (Bazelon, C. J.).]

It does not follow that courts may never properly find that an administrative decision in a scientific area is irrational. But I do believe that in highly technical areas, where our understanding of the import of the evidence is attenuated, our readiness to review evidentiary support for decisions must be correspondingly restrained.

As I read the court's opinion, it severely limits judicial weighing of the evidence by construing the Administrator's decision to be a matter of "legislative policy," and consequently not subject to review with the "substantive rigor proper for questions of fact." Since this result would bar the panel's close analysis of the evidence, it satisfies my concerns. * * *

**Food for Thought**

In Judge Bazelon's view, what is the appropriate judicial role in reviewing agency decisions? When he says that courts should concentrate on "strengthening administrative procedures," does he mean that courts should add procedural requirements beyond those explicitly imposed by the APA? If so, what should they be, and how would courts know to impose them?

Statement of Circuit Judge Leventhal:

I concur without reservation in the excellent opinion for the court.

I write an additional word only because of observations in the concurring opinion authored by Chief Judge Bazelon. * * * What does and should a reviewing court do when it considers a challenge to technical administrative decision-making? In my view, the panel opinion in this case overstepped the bounds of proper judicial supervision in its willingness to substitute its own scientific judgments for that of the EPA. * * * [But Judge Bazelon's opinion] if I read it right advocates engaging in no substantive review at all, whenever the substantive issues at stake involve technical matters that the judges involved consider beyond their individual technical competence.

Taking the opinion in its fair implication, as a signal to judges to abstain from any substantive review, it is my view that while giving up is the easier course, it is not legitimately open to us at present. In the case of legislative enactments, the sole responsibility of the courts is constitutional due process review. In the case of agency decision-making the courts have an additional responsibility set by Congress. Congress has been willing to delegate its legislative powers broadly and courts have upheld such delegation because there is court review to assure that the agency exercises the delegated power within statutory limits, and that it fleshes out objectives within those limits by an administration that is not irrational or discriminatory. Nor is that envisioned judicial role ephemeral * * *.

Our present system of review assumes judges will acquire whatever technical knowledge is necessary as background for decision of the legal questions. It may be that some judges are not initially equipped for this role, just as they may not be technically equipped initially to decide issues of obviousness and infringement in patent cases. If technical difficulties loom large, Congress may push to establish specialized courts. Thus far, it has proceeded on the assumption that we can both have the important values secured by generalist judges and rely on them to acquire whatever technical background is necessary.

The aim of the judges is not to exercise expertise or decide technical questions, but simply to gain sufficient background orientation. Our obligation is not to be jettisoned because our initial technical understanding may be meagre when compared to our initial grasp of FCC or freedom of speech questions. When called upon to make de novo decisions, individual judges have had to acquire the learning pertinent to complex technical questions in such fields as economics, science, technology and psychology. Our role is not as demanding when we are engaged in review of agency decisions, where we exercise restraint, and affirm even if we would have decided otherwise so long as the agency's decisionmaking is not irrational or discriminatory.

The substantive review of administrative action is modest, but it cannot be carried out in a vacuum of understanding. Better no judicial review at all than a charade that gives the imprimatur without the substance of judicial confirmation that the agency is not acting unreasonably. Once the presumption of regularity in agency action is challenged with a factual submission, and even to determine whether such a challenge has been made, the agency's record and reasoning has to be looked at. If there is some factual support for the challenge, there must be either evidence or judicial notice available explicating the agency's result, or a remand to supply the gap.

Mistakes may mar the exercise of any judicial function. While in this case the panel made such a mistake, it did not stem from judicial incompetence to deal with technical issues, but from confusion about the proper stance for substantive review of agency action in an area where the state of current knowledge does not generate customary definitiveness and certainty. In other cases the court has dealt ably with these problems, without either abandoning substantive review or ousting the agency's action for lack of factual underpinning.

On issues of substantive review, on conformance to statutory standards and requirements of rationality, the judges must act with restraint. Restraint, yes, abdication, no.

[JUDGE MACKINNON's dissenting opinion and JUDGE WILKEY's dissenting opinion, joined by JUDGES TAMM and ROBB, have been omitted.]

## Points for Discussion

### *a. "Strengthening Administrative Procedures:" Judge Bazelon's Approach*

Judge Bazelon asserted that judges should eschew approaches to judicial review of agency action that require them to make technical judgments about policy. In Judge Bazleon's view, judges are not experts and are ill-equipped to judge the substantive validity of agency decisions. On this view, judges who nevertheless review agency decisions for rationality risk substituting their views about good policy for those of the agency officials to whom Congress delegated decision-making authority.

On Judge Bazelon's view, what should a reviewing court do when confronted with an agency decision—say, a rule issued after proper notice and the opportunity for comment—that is objectively irrational? And on Judge Bazelon's view, what was the point of the provision in section 706 of the APA requiring courts to set aside "arbitrary and capricious" agency action?

### *b. Substantive Review: Judge Leventhal's Approach*

Judge Leventhal asserted that courts have no choice but to review the substance of agency decisions for rationality. He acknowledged that many challenges to agency action will require judges to come up to speed about some technical matter with which they were not previously familiar, but he argued that even generalist judges have the requisite competence to perform this task. In his view, Judge Bazelon's approach amounted to judicial abdication.

On Judge Leventhal's view, what should a reviewing court do if the judges disagree about whether a challenged agency decision is irrational or arbitrary? How can a judge know if an agency decision about an obscure, technical matter is irrational or arbitrary in the first place?

---

The debate between Judge Bazelon and Judge Leventhal was particularly significant because the D.C. Circuit hears a disproportionate number of administrative law cases. (Many agency organic statutes provide for judicial review of agency actions in the D.C. Circuit.) Two years after the D.C. Circuit's decision in *Ethyl Corp.*, the Supreme Court decided the case that follows, which effectively resolved the debate between the two judges.

---

## *Vermont Yankee Nuclear Power Corp. v. Natural Resources Defense Council, Inc.*

435 U.S. 519 (1978)

Mr. Justice Rehnquist delivered the opinion of the Court.

In 1946, Congress enacted the Administrative Procedure Act, which as we have noted elsewhere was not only "a new, basic and comprehensive regulation of procedures in many agencies," *Wong Yang Sung v. McGrath*, 339 U.S. 33 (1950), but was also a legislative enactment which settled "long-continued and hard-fought contentions, and enacts a formula upon which opposing social and political forces have come to rest." *Id.*, at 40. Section 4 of the Act, 5 U.S.C. § 553 (1976 ed.), dealing with rulemaking, requires in subsection (b) that "notice of proposed rule making shall be published in the Federal Register . . .," describes the contents of that notice, and goes on to require in subsection (c) that after the notice the agency "shall give interested persons an opportunity to participate in the rule making through submission of written data, views, or arguments with or without opportunity for oral presentation. After consideration of the relevant matter presented, the agency shall incorporate in the rules adopted a concise general statement of their basis and purpose." Interpreting this provision of the Act in *United States v. Allegheny-Ludlum Steel Corp.*, 406 U.S. 742 (1972), and *United States v. Florida East Coast R. Co.*, 410 U.S. 224 (1973), we held that generally speaking this section of the Act established the maximum procedural requirements which Congress was willing to have the courts impose upon agencies in conducting rulemaking procedures. Agencies are free to grant additional procedural rights in the exercise of their discretion, but reviewing courts are generally not free to impose them if the agencies have not chosen to grant them. This is not to say necessarily that there are no circumstances which would ever justify a court in overturning agency action because of a failure to employ procedures beyond those required by the statute. But such circumstances, if they exist, are extremely rare.

**Make the Connection**

We considered *Florida East Coast Ry.*, and its conclusion that an agency need not engage in formal rulemaking unless Congress specifically requires a decision based on the record, in Chapter 6.

Even apart from the Administrative Procedure Act this Court has for more than four decades emphasized that the formulation of procedures was basically to be left within the discretion of the agencies to which Congress had confided the responsibility for substantive judgments. In *FCC v. Schreiber*, 381 U.S. 279, 290 (1965), the Court explicated this principle, describing it as "an outgrowth of the congressional determination that administrative agencies and administrators will be familiar with the industries which they regulate and will be in a better position than federal courts or Congress itself to design procedural rules adapted to the peculiarities of the industry and the tasks of the agency involved." * * *

It is in the light of this background of statutory and decisional law that we granted certiorari to review two judgments of the Court of Appeals for the District of Columbia Circuit because of our concern that they had seriously misread or misapplied this statutory and decisional law cautioning reviewing courts against engrafting their own notions of proper procedures upon agencies entrusted with substantive functions by Congress. We conclude that the Court of Appeals has done just that in these cases, and we therefore remand them to it for further proceedings. * * *

Under the Atomic Energy Act of 1954, 68 Stat. 919, as amended, 42 U.S.C. § 2011 *et seq.*, the Atomic Energy Commission[2] was given broad regulatory authority over the development of nuclear energy. Under the terms of the Act, a utility seeking to construct and operate a nuclear power plant must obtain a separate permit or license at both the construction and the operation stage of the project. See 42 U.S.C. §§ 2133, 2232, 2235, 2239. In order to obtain the construction permit, the utility must file a preliminary safety analysis report, an environmental report, and certain information regarding the antitrust implications of the proposed project. See 10 CFR §§ 2.101, 50.30(f), 50.33a, 50.34(a) (1977). This application then undergoes exhaustive review by the Commission's staff and by the Advisory Committee on Reactor Safeguards (ACRS), a group of distinguished experts in the field of atomic energy. Both groups submit to the Commission their own evaluations, which then become part of the record of the utility's application. See 42 U.S.C. §§ 2039, 2232(b). The Commission staff also undertakes the review required by the National Environmental Policy Act of 1969 (NEPA), 83 Stat. 852, 42 U.S.C. § 4321 *et seq.*, and prepares a draft environmental impact statement, which, after being circulated for comment, 10 CFR §§ 51.22–51.25 (1977), is revised and becomes a final environmental impact statement. § 51.26. Thereupon a three-member Atomic Safety and Licensing Board conducts a public adjudicatory hearing, 42 U.S.C. § 2241, and reaches a decision[4] which can be appealed to the Atomic Safety and Licensing Appeal Board, and currently, in the Commission's discretion, to the Commission itself. 10 CFR §§ 2.714, 2.721, 2.786, 2.787 (1977). The final agency decision may be appealed to the courts of appeals. 42 U.S.C. § 2239; 28 U.S.C. § 2342. The same sort of process occurs when the utility applies for a license to operate the plant, 10 CFR § 50.34(b) (1977), except that a hearing need only be held in contested cases and may be limited to the

---

2 The licensing and regulatory functions of the Atomic Energy Commission (AEC) were transferred to the Nuclear Regulatory Commission (NRC) by the Energy Reorganization Act of 1974, 42 U.S.C. § 5801 *et seq.* (1970 ed., Supp. V). Hereinafter both the AEC and NRC will be referred to as the Commission.

4 The Licensing Board issues a permit if it concludes that there is reasonable assurance that the proposed plant can be constructed and operated without undue risk, 42 U.S.C. § 2241; 10 CFR § 50.35(a) (1977), and that the environmental cost-benefit balance favors the issuance of a permit.

matters in controversy. See 42 U.S.C. § 2239(a); 10 CFR § 2.105 (1977); 10 CFR pt. 2, App. A, V(f) (1977).[5]

These cases arise from two separate decisions of the Court of Appeals for the District of Columbia Circuit. In the first, the court remanded a decision of the Commission to grant a license to petitioner Vermont Yankee Nuclear Power Corp. to operate a nuclear power plant. *Natural Resources Defense Council v. NRC*, 547 F.2d 633 (D.C. Cir. 1976). In the second, the court remanded a decision of that same agency to grant a permit to petitioner Consumers Power Co. to construct two pressurized water nuclear reactors to generate electricity and steam. *Aeschliman v. NRC*, 547 F.2d 622 (D.C. Cir. 1976).[*]

In December 1967, after the mandatory adjudicatory hearing and necessary review, the Commission granted petitioner Vermont Yankee a permit to build a nuclear power plant in Vernon, Vt. Thereafter, Vermont Yankee applied for an operating license. Respondent Natural Resources Defense Council (NRDC) objected to the granting of a license, however, and therefore a hearing on the application commenced on August 10, 1971. Excluded from consideration at the hearings, over NRDC's objection, was the issue of the environmental effects of operations to reprocess fuel or dispose of wastes resulting from the reprocessing operations.[6] This ruling was affirmed by the Appeal Board in June 1972.

In November 1972, however, the Commission, making specific reference to the Appeal Board's decision with respect to the Vermont Yankee license, instituted rulemaking proceedings "that would specifically deal with the question of consideration of environmental effects associated with the uranium fuel cycle in the individual cost-benefit analyses for light water cooled nuclear power reactors." The notice of proposed rulemaking offered two alternatives, both predicated on a report prepared by the Commission's staff entitled Environmental Survey of the Nuclear Fuel Cycle. The first would have required no quantitative evaluation of the environmental hazards of fuel reprocessing or disposal because the Environmental Survey had found them to be slight. The second would have specified numerical values for the environmental

---

5 When a license application is contested, the Licensing Board must find reasonable assurance that the plant can be operated without undue risk and will not be inimical to the common defense and security or to the health and safety of the public. See 42 U.S.C. § 2232(a); 10 CFR § 50.57(a) (1977). The Licensing Board's decision is subject to review similar to that afforded the Board's decision with respect to a construction permit.

* The Court's discussion of the Consumers Power Co. case has been omitted. —*Ed.*

6 The nuclear fission which takes place in light-water nuclear reactors apparently converts its principal fuel, uranium, into plutonium, which is itself highly radioactive but can be used as reactor fuel if separated from the remaining uranium and radioactive waste products. Fuel reprocessing refers to the process necessary to recapture usable plutonium. Waste disposal, at the present stage of technological development, refers to the storage of the very long lived and highly radioactive waste products until they detoxify sufficiently that they no longer present an environmental hazard. There are presently no physical or chemical steps which render this waste less toxic, other than simply the passage of time.

impact of this part of the fuel cycle, which values would then be incorporated into a table, along with the other relevant factors, to determine the overall cost-benefit balance for each operating license.

Much of the controversy in this case revolves around the procedures used in the rulemaking hearing which commenced in February 1973. In a supplemental notice of hearing the Commission indicated that while discovery or cross-examination would not be utilized, the Environmental Survey would be available to the public before the hearing along with the extensive background documents cited therein. All participants would be given a reasonable opportunity to present their position and could be represented by counsel if they so desired. Written and, time permitting, oral statements would be received and incorporated into the record. All persons giving oral statements would be subject to questioning by the Commission. At the conclusion of the hearing, a transcript would be made available to the public and the record would remain open for 30 days to allow the filing of supplemental written statements. More than 40 individuals and organizations representing a wide variety of interests submitted written comments. On January 17, 1973, the Licensing Board held a planning session to schedule the appearance of witnesses and to discuss methods for compiling a record. The hearing was held on February 1 and 2, with participation by a number of groups, including the Commission's staff, the United States Environmental Protection Agency, a manufacturer of reactor equipment, a trade association from the nuclear industry, a group of electric utility companies, and a group called Consolidated National Intervenors which represented 79 groups and individuals including respondent NRDC.

**Take Note**

What kind of action—rulemaking or adjudication—did the agency take to resolve the question of environmental effects? Did the agency comply with all of the requirements that the APA imposes for that form of action? (Would you need to know anything else to answer this question?)

After the hearing, the Commission's staff filed a supplemental document for the purpose of clarifying and revising the Environmental Survey. Then the Licensing Board forwarded its report to the Commission without rendering any decision. The Licensing Board identified as the principal procedural question the propriety of declining to use full formal adjudicatory procedures. The major substantive issue was the technical adequacy of the Environmental Survey.

In April 1974, the Commission issued a rule which adopted the second of the two proposed alternatives described above. The Commission also approved the procedures used at the hearing,[7] and indicated that the record, including the

7 The Commission stated: "In our view, the procedures adopted provide a more than adequate basis for formulation of the rule we adopted. All parties were fully heard. Nothing offered was excluded.

Environmental Survey, provided an "adequate data base for the regulation adopted." Finally, the Commission ruled that to the extent the rule differed from the Appeal Board decisions in Vermont Yankee "those decisions have no further precedential significance," but that since "the environmental effects of the uranium fuel cycle have been shown to be relatively insignificant, . . . it is unnecessary to apply the amendment to applicant's environmental reports submitted prior to its effective date or to Final Environmental Statements for which Draft Environmental Statements have been circulated for comment prior to the effective date."

Respondents appealed from both the Commission's adoption of the rule and its decision to grant Vermont Yankee's license to the Court of Appeals for the District of Columbia Circuit.

[T]he court first ruled that in the absence of effective rulemaking proceedings,[13] the Commission must deal with the environmental impact of fuel reprocessing and disposal in individual licensing proceedings. The court then examined the rulemaking proceedings and, despite the fact that it appeared that the agency employed all the procedures required by 5 U.S.C. § 553 (1976 ed.) and more, the court determined the proceedings to be inadequate and overturned the rule. Accordingly, the Commission's determination with respect to Vermont Yankee's license was also remanded for further proceedings.[14]

After a thorough examination of the opinion itself, we conclude that while the matter is not entirely free from doubt, the majority of the Court of Appeals struck down the rule because of the perceived inadequacies of the procedures employed in the rulemaking proceedings. The court first determined the intervenors' primary argument to be "that the decision to preclude 'discovery or cross-examination' denied

---

The record does not indicate that any evidentiary material would have been received under different procedures. Nor did the proponent of the strict 'adjudicatory' approach make an offer of proof—or even remotely suggest—what substantive matters it would develop under different procedures. In addition, we note that 11 documents including the Survey were available to the parties several weeks before the hearing, and the Regulatory staff, though not requested to do so, made available various drafts and handwritten notes. Under all of the circumstances, we conclude that adjudicatory type procedures were not warranted here."

13 In the Court of Appeals no one questioned the Commission's authority to deal with fuel cycle issues by informal rulemaking as opposed to adjudication. Neither does anyone seriously question before this Court the Commission's authority in this respect.

14 After the decision of the Court of Appeals the Commission promulgated a new interim rule pending issuance of a final rule. 42 Fed. Reg. 13803 (1977). * * * As we read the opinion of the Court of Appeals, its view that reviewing courts may in the absence of special circumstances justifying such a course of action impose additional procedural requirements on agency action raises questions of such significance in this area of the law as to warrant our granting certiorari and deciding the case. Since the vast majority of challenges to administrative agency action are brought to the Court of Appeals for the District of Columbia Circuit, the decision of that court in this case will serve as precedent for many more proceedings for judicial review of agency actions than would the decision of another Court of Appeals. Finally, this decision will continue to play a major role in the instant litigation regardless of the Commission's decision to press ahead with further rulemaking proceedings. * * *

them a meaningful opportunity to participate in the proceedings as guaranteed by due process." The court then went on to frame the issue for decision thus: "[W]e are called upon to decide whether the procedures provided by the agency were sufficient to ventilate the issues."

[T]here is little doubt in our minds that the ineluctable mandate of the court's decision is that the procedures afforded during the hearings were inadequate. This conclusion is particularly buttressed by the fact that after the court examined the record, particularly the testimony of Dr. Pittman, and declared it insufficient, the court proceeded to discuss at some length the necessity for further procedural devices or a more "sensitive" application of those devices employed during the proceedings. * * * Accordingly, we feel compelled to address the opinion on its own terms, and we conclude that it was wrong.

In prior opinions we have intimated that even in a rulemaking proceeding when an agency is making a "quasi-judicial" determination by which a very small number of persons are "exceptionally affected, in each case upon individual grounds," in some circumstances additional procedures may be required in order to afford the aggrieved individuals due process.[16] *Florida East Coast R. Co.*, 410 U.S., at 242–245 (quoting from *Bi-Metallic Investment Co. v. State Board of Equalization*, 239 U.S. 441 (1915)). It might also be true, although we do not think the issue is presented in this case and accordingly do not decide it, that a totally unjustified departure from well-settled agency procedures of long standing might require judicial correction.

But this much is absolutely clear. Absent constitutional constraints or extremely compelling circumstances the "administrative agencies 'should be free to fashion their own rules of procedure and to pursue methods of inquiry capable of permitting them to discharge their multitudinous duties." *Schreiber*, 381 U.S., at 290. * * *

Respondent NRDC argues that § 4 of the Administrative Procedure Act, 5 U.S.C. § 553 (1976 ed.), merely establishes lower procedural bounds and that a court may routinely require more than the minimum when an agency's proposed rule addresses complex or technical factual issues or "Issues of Great Public Import." [O]ur decisions reject this view. We also think the legislative history, even the part which it cites, does not bear out its contention. The Senate Report explains what eventually became § 4 thus:

> "This subsection states . . . the minimum requirements of public rule making procedure short of statutory hearing. Under it agencies might in addition confer with industry advisory committees, consult organizations, hold informal 'hearings,' and the like. Considerations of practicality, necessity, and public interest . . . will naturally govern the agency's determination of the extent to which public proceedings should go. Matters of great import, or those where the public submission of facts will be either

16 Respondent NRDC does not now argue that additional procedural devices were required under the Constitution. Since this was clearly a rulemaking proceeding in its purest form, we see nothing to support such a view.

> useful to the agency or a protection to the public, should naturally be accorded more elaborate public procedures." S. Rep. No. 752, 79th Cong., 1st Sess., 14–15 (1945).

And the Attorney General's Manual on the Administrative Procedure Act 31, 35 (1947), a contemporaneous interpretation previously given some deference by this Court because of the role played by the Department of Justice in drafting the legislation, further confirms that view. In short, all of this leaves little doubt that Congress intended that the discretion of the *agencies* and not that of the courts be exercised in determining when extra procedural devices should be employed.

There are compelling reasons for construing § 4 in this manner. In the first place, if courts continually review agency proceedings to determine whether the agency employed procedures which were, in the court's opinion, perfectly tailored to reach what the court perceives to be the "best" or "correct" result, judicial review would be totally unpredictable. And the agencies, operating under this vague injunction to employ the "best" procedures and facing the threat of reversal if they did not, would undoubtedly adopt full adjudicatory procedures in every instance. Not only would this totally disrupt the statutory scheme, through which Congress enacted "a formula upon which opposing social and political forces have come to rest," *Wong Yang Sung*, 339 U.S., at 40, but all the inherent advantages of informal rulemaking would be totally lost.

Secondly, it is obvious that the court in these cases reviewed the agency's choice of procedures on the basis of the record actually produced at the hearing, and not on the basis of the information available to the agency when it made the decision to structure the proceedings in a certain way. This sort of Monday morning quarterbacking not only encourages but almost compels the agency to conduct all rulemaking proceedings with the full panoply of procedural devices normally associated only with adjudicatory hearings.

Finally, and perhaps most importantly, this sort of review fundamentally misconceives the nature of the standard for judicial review of an agency rule. The court below uncritically assumed that additional procedures will automatically result in a more adequate record because it will give interested parties more of an opportunity to participate in and contribute to the proceedings. But informal rulemaking need not be based solely on the transcript of a hearing held before an agency. Indeed, the agency need not even hold a formal hearing. See 5 U.S.C. § 553(c) (1976 ed.). Thus, the adequacy of the "record" in this type of proceeding is not correlated directly to the type of procedural devices employed, but rather turns on whether the agency has followed the statutory mandate of the Administrative Procedure Act or other relevant statutes. If the agency is compelled to support the rule which it ultimately adopts with the type of record produced only after a full adjudicatory hearing, it simply will have no choice but to conduct a full adjudicatory hearing prior to promulgating every rule. In sum, this sort of unwarranted judicial examination of perceived procedural shortcomings of a rulemaking proceeding can do nothing but seriously interfere with that process prescribed by Congress.

In short, nothing in the APA, [the] circumstances of this case, the nature of the issues being considered, past agency practice, or the statutory mandate under which the Commission operates permitted the court to review and overturn the rulemaking proceeding on the basis of the procedural devices employed (or not employed) by the Commission so long as the Commission employed at least the statutory *minima*, a matter about which there is no doubt in this case.

There remains, of course, the question of whether the challenged rule finds sufficient justification in the administrative proceedings that it should be upheld by the reviewing court. Judge Tamm, concurring in the result reached by the majority of the Court of Appeals, thought that it did not. There are also intimations in the majority opinion which suggest that the judges who joined it likewise may have thought the administrative proceedings an insufficient basis upon which to predicate the rule in question. We accordingly remand so that the Court of Appeals may review the rule as the Administrative Procedure Act provides. We have made it abundantly clear before that when there is a contemporaneous explanation of the agency decision, the validity of that action must "stand or fall on the propriety of that finding, judged, of course, by the appropriate standard of review. If that finding is not sustainable on the administrative record made, then the Comptroller's decision must be vacated and the matter remanded to him for further consideration." *Camp v. Pitts*, 411 U.S. 138, 143 (1973). The court should engage in this kind of review and not stray beyond the judicial province to explore the procedural format or to impose upon the agency its own notion of which procedures are "best" or most likely to further some vague, undefined public good. * * * *Reversed and remanded.*

Mr. Justice Blackmun and Mr. Justice Powell took no part in the consideration or decision of these cases.

**Make the Connection**

The Court remanded the case to the court of appeals to determine whether the agency properly justified its rule. We turn to such "substantive" review of agency rulemaking in the cases that follow.

---

## Points for Discussion

### *a. Resolving the Debate on the D.C. Circuit*

In its opinion in *Vermont Yankee*, the Court effectively rejected the view that Judge Bazelon had advanced in *Ethyl Corp.* Why did the Court conclude that courts reviewing agency actions should not impose on agencies procedural requirements beyond those identified in the APA? In implicitly rejecting Judge Bazelon's view, did the Court contemplate a form of substantive review of the form proposed by Judge

Leventhal? If not, then how would courts decide whether a challenged rule or other agency action is "arbitrary, capricious, [or] an abuse of discretion"?

### *b. Informal Rulemaking and Agency Policy-Making*

How much of the Court's conclusion was a function of its view of the utility of informal rulemaking? The Court reasoned that if judges reviewing agency actions could impose additional procedures beyond those explicitly required by the APA, then "all the inherent advantages of informal rulemaking would be totally lost." Does the Court's reasoning apply to other forms of agency decision-making? That is, can courts impose additional procedural requirements—other than in those rare cases in which the Due Process Clause requires more process—on agencies that conduct formal adjudications? Informal adjudications? Formal rulemakings? Is there something distinctive about informal rulemaking that makes it uniquely immune from judicial efforts to strengthen administrative procedures?

---

When a Court reviews the actual substance of an agency's decision, what is its task? For an introduction to this question, consider the case that follows.

---

## *Citizens to Preserve Overton Park, Inc. v. Volpe*

401 U.S. 402 (1971)

Opinion of the Court by MR. JUSTICE MARSHALL, announced by MR. JUSTICE STEWART.

The growing public concern about the quality of our natural environment has prompted Congress in recent years to enact legislation designed to curb the accelerating destruction of our country's natural beauty. We are concerned in this case with § 4(f) of the Department of Transportation Act of 1966, as amended, and § 18(a) of the Federal-Aid Highway Act of 1968, 82 Stat. 823, 23 U.S.C. § 138 (1964 ed., Supp. V).[3] These statutes prohibit the Secretary of Transportation from authorizing

---

3 "It is hereby declared to be the national policy that special effort should be made to preserve the natural beauty of the countryside and public park and recreation lands, wildlife and waterfowl refuges, and historic sites. The Secretary of Transportation shall cooperate and consult with the Secretaries of the Interior, Housing and Urban Development, and Agriculture, and with the States in developing transportation plans and programs that include measures to maintain or enhance the natural beauty of the lands traversed. After August 23, 1968, the Secretary shall not approve any program or project which requires the use of any publicly owned land from a public park, recreation area, or wildlife and waterfowl refuge of national, State, or local significance as determined by the Federal, State, or local officials having jurisdiction thereof, or any land from an historic site of national, State, or local significance as so determined by such officials unless (1) there is no feasible and prudent alternative to

the use of federal funds to finance the construction of highways through public parks if a "feasible and prudent" alternative route exists. If no such route is available, the statutes allow him to approve construction through parks only if there has been "all possible planning to minimize harm" to the park.

Petitioners, private citizens as well as local and national conservation organizations, contend that the Secretary has violated these statutes by authorizing the expenditure of federal funds for the construction of a six-lane interstate highway through a public park in Memphis, Tennessee. Their claim was rejected by the District Court, which granted the Secretary's motion for summary judgment, and the Court of Appeals for the Sixth Circuit affirmed. After oral argument, this Court granted a stay that halted construction and, treating the application for the stay as a petition for certiorari, granted review [on an expedited schedule]. We now reverse the judgment below and remand for further proceedings in the District Court.

Overton Park is 342-acre city park located near the center of Memphis. The park contains a zoo, a nine-hole municipal golf course, an outdoor theater, nature trails, a bridle path, an art academy, picnic areas, and 170 acres of forest. The proposed highway, which is to be a six-lane, high-speed, expressway, will sever the zoo from the rest of the park. Although the roadway will be depressed below ground level except where it crosses a small creek, 26 acres of the park will be destroyed. The highway is to be a segment of Interstate Highway I-40, part of the National System of Interstate and Defense Highways. I-40 will provide Memphis with a major east-west expressway which will allow easier access to downtown Memphis from the residential areas on the eastern edge of the city.

Although the route through the park was approved by the Bureau of Public Roads in 1956 and by the Federal Highway Administrator in 1966, the enactment of § 4(f) of the Department of Transportation Act prevented distribution of federal funds for the section of the highway designated to go through Overton Park until the Secretary of Transportation determined whether the requirements of § 4(f) had been met. Federal funding for the rest of the project was, however, available; and the state acquired a right-of-way on both sides of the park. In April 1968, the Secretary announced that he concurred in the judgment of local officials that I-40 should be built through the park. And in September 1969 the State acquired the right-of-way inside Overton Park from the city.[15] Final approval for the project—the route as well as the design—was not announced until November 1969, after Congress had reiterated in § 138 of the Federal-Aid Highway Act that highway construction through public

---

the use of such land, and (2) such program includes all possible planning to minimize harm to such park, recreational area, wildlife and waterfowl refuge, or historic site resulting from such use." 82 Stat. 824, 49 U.S.C. § 1653(f) (1964 ed., Supp. V). [23 U.S.C. § 138 contained virtually identical language.]

**15** The State paid the City $2,000,000 for the 26-acre right-of-way and $206,000 to the Memphis Park Commission to replace park facilities that were to be destroyed by the highway. The city of Memphis has used $1,000,000 of these funds to pay for a new 160-acre park and it is anticipated that additional parkland will be acquired with the remaining money.

parks was to be restricted. Neither announcement approving the route and design of I-40 was accompanied by a statement of the Secretary's factual findings. He did not indicate why he believed there were no feasible and prudent alternative routes or why design changes could not be made to reduce the harm to the park.

Petitioners contend that the Secretary's action is invalid without such formal findings and that the Secretary did not make an independent determination but merely relied on the judgment of the Memphis City Council. They also contend that it would be "feasible and prudent" to route I-40 around Overton Park either to the north or to the south. And they argue that if these alternative routes are not "feasible and prudent," the present plan does not include "all possible" methods for reducing harm to the park. Petitioners claim that I-40 could be built under the park by using either of two possible tunneling methods, and they claim that, at a minimum, by using advanced drainage techniques the expressway could be depressed below ground level along the entire route through the park including the section that crosses the small creek.

Respondents argue that it was unnecessary for the Secretary to make formal findings, and that he did, in fact, exercise his own independent judgment which was supported by the facts. In the District Court, respondents introduced affidavits, prepared specifically for this litigation, which indicated that the Secretary had made the decision and that the decision was supportable. These affidavits were contradicted by affidavits introduced by petitioners, who also sought to take the deposition of a former Federal Highway Administrator who had participated in the decision to route I-40 through Overton Park.

The District Court and the Court of Appeals found that formal findings by the Secretary were not necessary and refused to order the deposition of the former Federal Highway Administrator because those courts believed that probing of the mental processes of an administrative decisionmaker was prohibited. And, believing that the Secretary's authority was wide and reviewing courts' authority narrow in the approval of highway routes, the lower courts held that the affidavits contained no basis for a determination that the Secretary had exceeded his authority.

We agree that formal findings were not required. But we do not believe that in this case judicial review based solely on litigation affidavits was adequate.

A threshold question—whether petitioners are entitled to any judicial review—is easily answered. Section 701 of the Administrative Procedure Act, 5 U.S.C. § 701 (1964 ed., Supp. V), provides that the action of "each authority of the Government of the United States," which includes the Department of Transportation, is subject to judicial review except where there is a statutory prohibition on review or where "agency action is committed to agency discretion by law." In this case, there is no indication that Congress sought to prohibit judicial review and there is most certainly no "showing of 'clear and convincing evidence' of a . . . legislative intent" to restrict access to judicial review. *Abbott Laboratories v. Gardner*, 387 U.S. 136, 141 (1967).

Similarly, the Secretary's decision here does not fall within the exception for action "committed to agency discretion." This is a very narrow exception. The legislative history of the Administrative Procedure Act indicates that it is applicable in those rare instances where "statutes are drawn in such broad terms that in a given case there is no law to apply." S. Rep. No. 752, 79th Cong., 1st Sess., 26 (1945).

**Make the Connection**

We consider the presumption of reviewability, the Court's decision in *Abbot Laboratories*, and the "committed to agency discretion" exception later in this Chapter.

Section 4(f) of the Department of Transportation Act and § 138 of the Federal-Aid Highway Act are clear and specific directives. Both the Department of Transportation Act and the Federal-Aid to Highway Act provide that the Secretary "shall not approve any program or project" that requires the use of any public parkland "unless (1) there is no feasible and prudent alternative to the use of such land, and (2) such program includes all possible planning to minimize harm to such park . . . ." 23 U.S.C. § 138; 49 U.S.C. § 1653(f). This language is a plain and explicit bar to the use of federal funds for construction of highways through parks—only the most unusual situations are exempted.

Despite the clarity of the statutory language, respondents argue that the Secretary has wide discretion. They recognize that the requirement that there be no "feasible" alternative route admits of little administrative discretion. For this exemption to apply the Secretary must find that as a matter of sound engineering it would not be feasible to build the highway along any other route. Respondents argue, however, that the requirement that there be no other "prudent" route requires the Secretary to engage in a wide-ranging balancing of competing interests. They contend that the Secretary should weigh the detriment resulting from the destruction of parkland against the cost of other routes, safety considerations, and other factors, and determine on the basis of the importance that he attaches to these other factors whether, on balance, alternative feasible routes would be "prudent."

But no such wide-ranging endeavor was intended. It is obvious that in most cases considerations of cost, directness of route, and community disruption will indicate that parkland should be used for highway construction whenever possible. Although it may be necessary to transfer funds from one jurisdiction to another, there will always be a smaller outlay required from the public purse when parkland is used since the public already owns the land and there will be no need to pay for right-of-way. And since people do not live or work in parks, if a highway is built on parkland no one will have to leave his home or give up his business. Such factors are common to substantially all highway construction. Thus, if Congress intended these factors to be on an equal footing with preservation of parkland there would have been no need for the statutes.

Congress clearly did not intend that cost and disruption of the community were to be ignored by the Secretary. But the very existence of the statutes indicates that protection of parkland was to be given paramount importance. The few green havens that are public parks were not to be lost unless there were truly unusual factors present in a particular case or the cost or community disruption resulting from alternative routes reached extraordinary magnitudes. If the statutes are to have any meaning, the Secretary cannot approve the destruction of parkland unless he finds that alternative routes present unique problems.

Plainly, there is "law to apply" and thus the exemption for action "committed to agency discretion" is inapplicable. But the existence of judicial review is only the start: the standard for review must also be determined. For that we must look to § 706 of the Administrative Procedure Act, which provides that a "reviewing court shall . . . hold unlawful and set aside agency action, findings, and conclusions found' not to meet six separate standards. In all cases agency action must be set aside if the action was "arbitrary, capricious, an abuse of discretion, or otherwise not in accordance with law" or if the action failed to meet statutory, procedural, or constitutional requirements. 5 U.S.C. §§ 706(2)(A), (B), (C), (D) (1964 ed., Supp. V). In certain narrow, specifically limited situations, the agency action is to be set aside if the action was not supported by "substantial evidence." And in other equally narrow circumstances the reviewing court is to engage in a de novo review of the action and set it aside if it was "unwarranted by the facts." 5 U.S.C. §§ 706(2)(E), (F) (1964 ed., Supp. V).

**Take Note**

The Court here misstated the provisions of the APA. According to 5 U.S.C. § 706(2)(E), a reviewing court shall "hold unlawful and set aside agency action, findings, and conclusions found to be * * * unsupported by substantial evidence in a case subject to sections 556 and 557 * * * or otherwise reviewed on the record of an agency hearing provided by statute * * *." Cases subject to sections 556 and 557, in turn, are those rulemakings *or adjudications* required to be "on the record after opportunity for an agency hearing." §§ 553(c) and 554(a).

Petitioners argue that the Secretary's approval of the construction of I-40 through Overton Park is subject to one or the other of these latter two standards of limited applicability. First, they contend that the "substantial evidence" standard of § 706(2)(E) must be applied. In the alternative, they claim that § 706(2)(F) applies and that there must be a de novo review to determine if the Secretary's action was "unwarranted by the facts." Neither of these standards is, however, applicable.

Review under the substantial-evidence test is authorized only when the agency action is taken pursuant to a rulemaking provision of the Administrative Procedure Act itself, 5 U.S.C. § 553, or when the agency action is based on a public adjudicatory hearing. See 5 U.S.C. §§ 556, 557. The Secretary's decision to allow the expenditure of federal funds to build I-40 through Overton Park was plainly not an exercise of a rulemaking function. And the only hearing that is required by either the Administrative Procedure Act or the statutes regulating the distribution of federal funds for highway construction is a public hearing conducted by local officials for the purpose of informing the community about the proposed project and eliciting community views on the design and route. 23 U.S.C. § 128. The hearing is nonadjudicatory, quasi-legislative in nature. It is not designed to produce a record that is to be the basis of agency action—the basic requirement for substantial-evidence review.

Petitioners' alternative argument also fails. De novo review of whether the Secretary's decision was "unwarranted by the facts" is authorized by § 706(2)(F) in only two circumstances. First, such de novo review is authorized when the action is adjudicatory in nature and the agency factfinding procedures are inadequate. And, there may be independent judicial factfinding when issues that were not before the agency are raised in a proceeding to enforce nonadjudicatory agency action. Neither situation exists here.

Even though there is no de novo review in this case and the Secretary's approval of the route of I-40 does not have ultimately to meet the substantial-evidence test, the generally applicable standards of § 706 require the reviewing court to engage in a substantial inquiry. Certainly, the Secretary's decision is entitled to a presumption of regularity. But that presumption is not to shield his action from a thorough, probing, in-depth review.

The court is first required to decide whether the Secretary acted within the scope of his authority. This determination naturally begins with a delineation of the scope of the Secretary's authority and discretion. As has been shown, Congress has specified only a small range of choices that the Secretary can make. Also involved in this initial inquiry is a determination of whether on the facts the Secretary's decision can reasonably be said to be within that range. The reviewing court must consider whether the Secretary properly construed his authority to approve the use of parkland as limited to situations where there are no feasible alternative routes or where feasible alternative routes involve uniquely difficult problems. And the reviewing court must be able to find that the Secretary could have reasonably believed that in this case there are no feasible alternatives or that alternatives do involve unique problems.

Scrutiny of the facts does not end, however, with the determination that the Secretary has acted within the scope of his statutory authority. [5 U.S.C. §] 706(2)(A) requires a finding that the actual choice made was not "arbitrary, capricious, an abuse of discretion, or otherwise not in accordance with law." To make this finding the court must consider whether the decision was based on a consideration of the relevant factors and whether there has been a clear error of judgment. Although this inquiry into the facts is to be searching and careful, the ultimate standard of review is a narrow one. The court is not empowered to substitute its judgment for that of the agency.

The final inquiry is whether the Secretary's action followed the necessary procedural requirements. Here the only procedural error alleged is the failure of the Secretary to make formal findings and state his reason for allowing the highway to be built through the park.

Undoubtedly, review of the Secretary's action is hampered by his failure to make such findings, but the absence of formal findings does not necessarily require that the case be remanded to the Secretary. Neither the Department of Transportation Act nor the Federal-Aid Highway Act requires such formal findings. Moreover, the Administrative Procedure Act requirements that there be formal findings in certain rulemaking and adjudicatory proceedings do not apply to the Secretary's action here. See 5 U.S.C. §§ 553(a)(2), 554(a). And, although formal findings may be required in some cases in the absence of statutory directives when the nature of the agency action is ambiguous, those situations are rare. Plainly, there is no ambiguity here; the Secretary has approved the construction of I-40 through Overton Park and has approved a specific design for the project.

**Food for Thought**

What was the form of the decision that the Secretary made in this case? Was it rulemaking or adjudication? Formal or informal? The answers to these questions determine whether the APA required the Secretary to make formal findings.

* * * The lower courts based their review on the litigation affidavits that were presented. These affidavits were merely "post hoc" rationalizations, *Burlington Truck Lines v. United States*, 371 U.S. 156, 168–169 (1962), which have traditionally been found to be an inadequate basis for review. And they clearly do not constitute the "whole record" compiled by the agency: the basis for review required by § 706 of the Administrative Procedure Act.

Thus it is necessary to remand this case to the District Court for plenary review of the Secretary's decision. That review is to be based on the full administrative record that was before the Secretary at the time he made his decision. But since the bare record may not disclose the factors that were considered or the Secretary's construction of the evidence it may be necessary for the District Court to require some explanation in order to determine if the Secretary acted within the scope of his authority and if the Secretary's action was justifiable under the applicable standard.

The court may require the administrative officials who participated in the decision to give testimony explaining their action. Of course, such inquiry into the mental processes of administrative decisionmakers is usually to be avoided. *United States v. Morgan*, 313 U.S. 409, 422 (1941). And where there are administrative findings that were made at the same time as the decision, * * * there must be a strong showing of bad faith or improper behavior before such inquiry may be made. But here there are no such formal findings and it may be that the only way there can be effective judicial review is by examining the decisionmakers themselves. See *Shaughnessy v. Accardi*, 349 U.S. 280 (1955).

The District Court is not, however, required to make such an inquiry. It may be that the Secretary can prepare formal findings * * * that will provide an adequate explanation for his action. Such an explanation will, to some extent, be a "post hoc rationalization" and thus must be viewed critically. If the District Court decides that additional explanation is necessary, that court should consider which method will prove the most expeditious so that full review may be had as soon as possible.

Reversed and remanded.

MR. JUSTICE DOUGLAS took no part in the consideration or decision of this case.

[The separate opinion of JUSTICE BLACK, which JUSTICE BRENNAN joined, and JUSTICE BLACKMUN's concurring opinion have been omitted.]

---

## Points for Discussion

### *a. The Availability of Judicial Review*

Before a court can review agency action—either for compliance with procedural requirements or to ensure that it is substantively defensible—judicial review must be available. As the Court noted, the APA states that judicial review of agency action is available "except to the extent that * * * statutes preclude judicial review" or "agency action is committed to agency discretion by law." 5 U.S.C. § 701(a). In this case, no statute specifically precluded judicial review of the Secretary's determination. In addition, because there were sufficient standards in the governing statutes by which to judge the Secretary's decision, the decision was not "committed to agency discretion by law." Can you think of times when it would make sense to prohibit judicial review of an agency action? If so, what types of agency actions would fall in that category? We will consider the availability of judicial review later in this Chapter.

### *b. Judicial Review of Agency Fact-Finding*

We saw earlier in this Chapter that courts sometimes review agency fact-finding. But as we saw, the APA's "substantial evidence" test applies to fact-finding in formal proceedings, not informal decision-making. What should a reviewing court do when an agency conducts an informal adjudication or an informal rulemaking and its decision turns at least in part on the agency's understanding of the underlying facts?

### c. *Judicial Review for Compliance with Procedural Requirements*

As we have seen, the APA also authorizes judicial review to ensure that agency decision-makers followed the appropriate procedures before taking the action in question. In focusing on the fact that the Secretary did not make formal findings when he decided to authorize the construction of the highway, did the Court effectively conclude that the Secretary's decision failed to comply with all applicable procedural requirements? In thinking about that question, ask yourself what kind of action—formal adjudication, informal adjudication, formal rulemaking, or informal rulemaking—was at issue in the case. Do the APA's provisions governing that form of action require formal findings? If not, is it possible to square the Court's decision with the later decision in *Vermont Yankee Nuclear Power Corp. v. Natural Resources Defense Council, Inc.*, 435 U.S. 519 (1978), which we considered earlier in this Chapter?

Here's what the Court had to say about that question in *Pension Benefit Guaranty Corporation v. LTV Corp.*, 496 U.S. 633 (1990), which we considered in Chapter 6:

> [A]lthough one initially might feel that there is some tension between *Vermont Yankee* and *Overton Park,* the two cases are not necessarily inconsistent. *Vermont Yankee* stands for the general proposition that courts are not free to impose upon agencies specific procedural requirements that have no basis in the APA. At most, *Overton Park* suggests that § 706(2)(A), which directs a court to ensure that an agency action is not arbitrary and capricious or otherwise contrary to law, imposes a general "procedural" requirement of sorts by mandating that an agency take whatever steps it needs to provide an explanation that will enable the court to evaluate the agency's rationale at the time of decision.

Does this persuade you that *Overton Park* is consistent with *Vermont Yankee*?

### d. *Judicial Review of the Substance of Agency Decisions*

The APA requires reviewing courts to "hold unlawful and set aside agency action * * * found to be * * * arbitrary, capricious, an abuse of discretion, or otherwise not in accordance with law" or "in excess of statutory jurisdiction, authority, or limitations, or short of statutory right." A court's task in applying the latter standard seems relatively straightforward; if nothing else, a court should inquire whether Congress has given the agency the power to take the action at issue. But what is a court's task in determining whether an agency action is "arbitrary, capricious, an abuse of discretion, or otherwise not in accordance with law"? The Court's disposition in *Overton Park* suggests that the inquiry, at a minimum, should determine whether the agency's decision was justifiable in light of the information available to the agency when it made its decision. What else is entailed in this form of substantive review? Consider the case that follows.

---

## *Motor Vehicle Manufacturers Ass'n v. State Farm Mutual Automobile Ins. Co.*

463 U.S. 29 (1983)

Justice White delivered the opinion of the Court.

The development of the automobile gave Americans unprecedented freedom to travel, but exacted a high price for enhanced mobility. Since 1929, motor vehicles have been the leading cause of accidental deaths and injuries in the United States. In 1982, 46,300 Americans died in motor vehicle accidents and hundreds of thousands more were maimed and injured. While a consensus exists that the current loss of life on our highways is unacceptably high, improving safety does not admit to easy solution. In 1966, Congress decided that at least part of the answer lies in improving the design and safety features of the vehicle itself. But much of the technology for building safer cars was undeveloped or untested. Before changes in automobile design could be mandated, the effectiveness of these changes had to be studied, their costs examined, and public acceptance considered. This task called for considerable expertise and Congress responded by enacting the National Traffic and Motor Vehicle Safety Act of 1966, (Act), 15 U.S.C. §§ 1381 *et seq.* (1976 and Supp. IV 1980). The Act, created for the purpose of "reduc[ing] traffic accidents and deaths and injuries to persons resulting from traffic accidents," 15 U.S.C. § 1381, directs the Secretary of Transportation or his delegate to issue motor vehicle safety standards that "shall be practicable, shall meet the need for motor vehicle safety, and shall be stated in objective terms." 15 U.S.C. § 1392(a). In issuing these standards, the Secretary is directed to consider "relevant available motor vehicle safety data," whether the proposed standard "is reasonable, practicable and appropriate" for the particular type of motor vehicle, and the "extent to which such standards will contribute to carrying out the purposes" of the Act. 15 U.S.C. § 1392(f)(1), (3), (4).

**Make the Connection**

Congress gave the agency broad power to set standards for motor-vehicle safety. Does the grant of power satisfy the non-delegation doctrine? We considered the non-delegation doctrine in Chapter 6.

The Act also authorizes judicial review under the provisions of the Administrative Procedure Act (APA), 5 U.S.C. § 706 (1976), of all "orders establishing, amending, or revoking a Federal motor vehicle safety standard," 15 U.S.C. § 1392(b). Under this authority, we review today whether NHTSA acted arbitrarily and capriciously in revoking the requirement in Motor Vehicle Safety Standard 208 that new motor vehicles produced after September 1982 be equipped with passive restraints to protect the safety of the occupants of the vehicle in the event of a collision. Briefly summarized, we hold that the agency failed to present an adequate basis and explanation for rescinding the passive restraint requirement and that the agency must either consider the matter further or adhere to or amend Standard 208 along lines which its analysis supports.

I

The regulation whose rescission is at issue bears a complex and convoluted history. Over the course of approximately 60 rulemaking notices, the requirement has been imposed, amended, rescinded, reimposed, and now rescinded again.

As originally issued by the Department of Transportation in 1967, Standard 208 simply required the installation of seatbelts in all automobiles. 32 Fed. Reg. 2408, 2415 (Feb. 3, 1967). It soon became apparent that the level of seatbelt use was too low to reduce traffic injuries to an acceptable level. The Department therefore began consideration of "passive occupant restraint systems"—devices that do not depend for their effectiveness upon any action taken by the occupant except that necessary to operate the vehicle. Two types of automatic crash protection emerged: automatic seatbelts and airbags. The automatic seatbelt is a traditional safety belt, which when fastened to the interior of the door remains attached without impeding entry or exit from the vehicle, and deploys automatically without any action on the part of the passenger. The airbag is an inflatable device concealed in the dashboard and steering column. It automatically inflates when a sensor indicates that deceleration forces from an accident have exceeded a preset minimum, then rapidly deflates to dissipate those forces. The life-saving potential of these devices was immediately recognized, and in 1977, after substantial on-the-road experience with both devices, it was estimated by NHTSA that passive restraints could prevent approximately 12,000 deaths and over 100,000 serious injuries annually. 42 Fed. Reg. 34,298.

In 1969, the Department formally proposed a standard requiring the installation of passive restraints, 34 Fed. Reg. 11,148 (July 2, 1969), thereby commencing a lengthy series of proceedings. In 1970, the agency revised Standard 208 to include passive protection requirements, 35 Fed. Reg. 16,927 (Nov. 3, 1970), and in 1972, the agency amended the standard to require full passive protection for all front seat occupants of vehicles manufactured after August 15, 1975. 37 Fed. Reg. 3911 (Feb. 24, 1972). In the interim, vehicles built between August 1973 and August 1975 were to carry either passive restraints or lap and shoulder belts coupled with an "ignition interlock" that would prevent starting the vehicle if the belts were not connected. On review, the agency's decision to require passive restraints was found to be supported by "substantial evidence" and upheld. *Chrysler Corp. v. Dep't of Transportation*, 472 F.2d 659 (6th Cir. 1972).

In preparing for the upcoming model year, most car makers chose the "ignition interlock" option, a decision which was highly unpopular, and led Congress to amend the Act to prohibit a motor vehicle safety standard from requiring or permitting compliance by means of an ignition interlock or a continuous buzzer designed to indicate that safety belts were not in use. Motor Vehicle and Schoolbus Safety Amendments of 1974, Pub. L. 93–492, § 109, 88 Stat. 1482, 15 U.S.C. § 1410b(b). The 1974 Amendments also provided that any safety standard that could be satisfied by a system other than seatbelts would have to be submitted to Congress where it could be vetoed by concurrent resolution of both houses. 15 U.S.C. § 1410b(b)(2).

**Make the Connection**

After the Court's decision in *Chadha*, could Congress constitutionally have asserted the authority to veto certain safety standards issued by the agency? We considered *Chadha* earlier in this Chapter.

The effective date for mandatory passive restraint systems was extended for a year until August 31, 1976. 40 Fed. Reg. 16,217 (April 10, 1975); *id.*, at 33,977 (Aug. 13, 1975). But in June 1976, Secretary of Transportation William Coleman initiated a new rulemaking on the issue, 41 Fed. Reg. 24,070 (June 9, 1976). After hearing testimony and reviewing written comments, Coleman extended the optional alternatives indefinitely and suspended the passive restraint requirement. Although he found passive restraints technologically and economically feasible, the Secretary based his decision on the expectation that there would be widespread public resistance to the new systems. He instead proposed a demonstration project involving up to 500,000 cars installed with passive restraints, in order to smooth the way for public acceptance of mandatory passive restraints at a later date. Department of Transportation, The Secretary's Decision Concerning Motor Vehicle Occupant Crash Protection (December 6, 1976).

Coleman's successor as Secretary of Transportation disagreed. Within months of assuming office, Secretary Brock Adams decided that the demonstration project was unnecessary. He issued a new mandatory passive restraint regulation, known as Modified Standard 208. 42 Fed. Reg. 34,289 (July 5, 1977); 42 CFR § 571.208 (1977). The Modified Standard mandated the phasing in of passive restraints beginning with large cars in model year 1982 and extending to all cars by model year 1984. The two principal systems that would satisfy the Standard were airbags and passive belts; the choice of which system to install was left to the manufacturers. In *Pacific Legal Foundation v. Dep't of Transportation*, 593 F.2d 1338 (DC Cir. 1979), cert. denied, 444 U.S. 830 (1979), the Court of Appeals upheld Modified Standard 208 as a rational, nonarbitrary regulation consistent with the agency's mandate under the Act. The standard also survived scrutiny by Congress, which did not exercise its authority under the legislative veto provision of the 1974 Amendments.

Over the next several years, the automobile industry geared up to comply with Modified Standard 208. As late as July, 1980, NHTSA reported:

> "On the road experience in thousands of vehicles equipped with airbags and automatic safety belts has confirmed agency estimates of the life-saving and injury-preventing

> benefits of such systems. When all cars are equipped with automatic crash protection systems, each year an estimated 9,000 more lives will be saved and tens of thousands of serious injuries will be prevented." NHTSA, Automobile Occupant Crash Protection, Progress Report No. 3, p. 4 (App. 1627).

In February 1981, however, Secretary of Transportation Andrew Lewis reopened the rulemaking due to changed economic circumstances and, in particular, the difficulties of the automobile industry. 46 Fed. Reg. 12,033 (Feb. 12, 1981). Two months later, the agency ordered a one-year delay in the application of the standard to large cars, extending the deadline to September 1982, 46 Fed. Reg. 21,172 (April 9, 1981) and at the same time, proposed the possible rescission of the entire standard. 46 Fed. Reg. 21,205 (April 9, 1981). After receiving written comments and holding public hearings, NHTSA issued a final rule (Notice 25) that rescinded the passive restraint requirement contained in Modified Standard 208.

## II

In a statement explaining the rescission, NHTSA maintained that it was no longer able to find, as it had in 1977, that the automatic restraint requirement would produce significant safety benefits. Notice 25, 46 Fed. Reg. 53,419 (Oct. 29, 1981). This judgment reflected not a change of opinion on the effectiveness of the technology, but a change in plans by the automobile industry. In 1977, the agency had assumed that airbags would be installed in 60% of all new cars and automatic seatbelts in 40%. By 1981 it became apparent that automobile manufacturers planned to install the automatic seatbelts in approximately 99% of the new cars. For this reason, the life-saving potential of airbags would not be realized. Moreover, it now appeared that the overwhelming majority of passive belts planned to be installed by manufacturers could be detached easily and left that way permanently. Passive belts, once detached, then required "the same type of affirmative action that is the stumbling block to obtaining high usage levels of manual belts." 46 Fed. Reg., at 53421. For this reason, the agency concluded that there was no longer a basis for reliably predicting that the standard would lead to any significant increased usage of restraints at all.

In view of the possibly minimal safety benefits, the automatic restraint requirement no longer was reasonable or practicable in the agency's view. The requirement would require approximately $1 billion to implement and the agency did not believe it would be reasonable to impose such substantial costs on manufacturers and consumers without more adequate assurance that sufficient safety benefits would accrue. In addition, NHTSA concluded that automatic restraints might have an adverse effect on the public's attitude toward safety. Given the high expense and limited benefits of detachable belts, NHTSA feared that many consumers would regard the standard as an instance of ineffective regulation, adversely affecting the public's view of safety regulation and, in particular, "poisoning popular sentiment toward efforts to improve occupant restraint systems in the future." 46 Fed. Reg., at 53424.

State Farm Mutual Automobile Insurance Co. and the National Association of Independent Insurers filed petitions for review of NHTSA's rescission of the passive restraint standard. The United States Court of Appeals for the District of Columbia Circuit held that the agency's rescission of the passive restraint requirement was arbitrary and capricious. 680 F.2d 206 (DC Cir. 1982). * * *

## III

* * * Both the Motor Vehicle Safety Act and the 1974 Amendments concerning occupant crash protection standards indicate that motor vehicle safety standards are to be promulgated under the informal rulemaking procedures of § 553 of the Administrative Procedure Act. 5 U.S.C. § 553 (1976). The agency's action in promulgating such standards therefore may be set aside if found to be "arbitrary, capricious, an abuse of discretion, or otherwise not in accordance with law." 5 U.S.C. § 706(2)(A). We believe that the rescission or modification of an occupant protection standard is subject to the same test. [The Court rejected the Motor Vehicle Manufacturers Association's argument that the rescission of an agency rule should be judged by the more deferential standard that courts apply to agency refusals to promulgate a rule in the first place.]

In so holding, we fully recognize that "regulatory agencies do not establish rules of conduct to last forever," *American Trucking Assoc., Inc. v. Atchison, T. & S.F.R. Co.*, 387 U.S. 397, 416 (1967), and that an agency must be given ample latitude to "adapt their rules and policies to the demands of changing circumstances." *Permian Basin Area Rate Cases*, 390 U.S. 747, 784 (1968). But the forces of change do not always or necessarily point in the direction of deregulation. In the abstract, there is no more reason to presume that changing circumstances require the rescission of prior action, instead of a revision in or even the extension of current regulation. If Congress established a presumption from which judicial review should start, that presumption—contrary to petitioners' views—is not *against* safety regulation, but *against* changes in current policy that are not justified by the rulemaking record. * * *

The scope of review under the "arbitrary and capricious" standard is narrow and a court is not to substitute its judgment for that of the agency. Nevertheless, the agency must examine the relevant data and articulate a satisfactory explanation for its action including a "rational connection between the facts found and the choice made." *Burlington Truck Lines v. United States*, 371 U.S. 156, 168 (1962). In reviewing that explanation, we must "consider whether the decision was based on a consideration of the relevant factors and whether there has been a clear error of judgment." *Bowman Transportation,*

**Take Note**

In this paragraph, the Court explains the standard for deciding whether agency action was arbitrary and capricious. Is it possible for a court to apply the standard without "substitut[ing] its judgment for that of the agency"?

*Inc. v. Arkansas-Best Freight System, Inc.*, 419 U.S. 281, 285 (1974). Normally, an agency rule would be arbitrary and capricious if the agency has relied on factors which Congress has not intended it to consider, entirely failed to consider an important aspect of the problem, offered an explanation for its decision that runs counter to the evidence before the agency, or is so implausible that it could not be ascribed to a difference in view or the product of agency expertise. The reviewing court should not attempt itself to make up for such deficiencies: "We may not supply a reasoned basis for the agency's action that the agency itself has not given." *SEC v. Chenery Corp.*, 332 U.S. 194, 196 (1947). * * *

**V**

The ultimate question before us is whether NHTSA's rescission of the passive restraint requirement of Standard 208 was arbitrary and capricious. We conclude, as did the Court of Appeals, that it was. We also conclude, but for somewhat different reasons, that further consideration of the issue by the agency is therefore required. * * *

**A**

The first and most obvious reason for finding the rescission arbitrary and capricious is that NHTSA apparently gave no consideration whatever to modifying the Standard to require that airbag technology be utilized. Standard 208 sought to achieve automatic crash protection by requiring automobile manufacturers to install either of two passive restraint devices: airbags or automatic seatbelts. There was no suggestion in the long rulemaking process that led to Standard 208 that if only one of these options were feasible, no passive restraint standard should be promulgated. Indeed, the agency's original proposed standard contemplated the installation of inflatable restraints in all cars. Automatic belts were added as a means of complying with the standard because they were believed to be as effective as airbags in achieving the goal of occupant crash protection. 36 Fed. Reg. 12,858, 12,859 (July 8, 1971). At that time, the passive belt approved by the agency could not be detached. Only later, at a manufacturer's behest, did the agency approve of the detachability feature—and only after assurances that the feature would not compromise the safety benefits of the restraint. Although it was then foreseen that 60% of the new cars would contain airbags and 40% would have automatic seatbelts, the ratio between the two was not significant as long as the passive belt would also assure greater passenger safety.

The agency has now determined that the detachable automatic belts will not attain anticipated safety benefits because so many individuals will detach the mechanism. Even if this conclusion were acceptable in its entirety, standing alone it would not justify any more than an amendment of Standard 208 to disallow compliance by means of the one technology which will not provide effective passenger protection. It does not cast doubt on the need for a passive restraint standard or upon the efficacy of airbag technology. In its most recent rule-making, the agency again acknowledged the life-saving potential of the airbag: "The agency has no basis at this time for changing its earlier conclusions in 1976 and 1977 that basic airbag technology is sound and has been sufficiently demonstrated to be effective in those vehicles in current use. . . ." NHTSA Final Regulatory Impact Analysis (RIA) at XI-4 (App. 264). Given the effectiveness ascribed to airbag technology by the agency, the mandate of the Safety Act to achieve traffic safety would suggest that the logical response to the faults of detachable seatbelts would be to require the installation of airbags. At the very least this alternative way of achieving the objectives of the Act should have been addressed and adequate reasons given for its abandonment. But the agency not only did not require compliance through airbags, it did not even consider the possibility in its 1981 rulemaking. Not one sentence of its rulemaking statement discusses the airbags-only option. Because, as the Court of Appeals stated, "NHTSA's . . . analysis of airbags was nonexistent," 680 F.2d, at 236, what we said in *Burlington Truck Lines*, 371 U.S., at 167, is apropos here:

> "There are no findings and no analysis here to justify the choice made, no indication of the basis on which the [agency] exercised its expert discretion. We are not prepared to and the Administrative Procedure Act will not permit us to accept such . . . practice. . . . Expert discretion is the lifeblood of the administrative process, but 'unless we make the requirements for administrative action strict and demanding, *expertise,* the strength of modern government, can become a monster which rules with no practical limits on its discretion.' *New York v. United States*, 342 U.S. 882, 884 (1951) (dissenting opinion)." (footnote omitted).

We have frequently reiterated that an agency must cogently explain why it has exercised its discretion in a given manner, *Atchison, T & S.F.R. Co. v. Wichita Bd. of Trade*, 412 U.S. 800, 806 (1973), and we reaffirm this principle again today.

The automobile industry has opted for the passive belt over the airbag, but surely it is not enough that the regulated industry has eschewed a given safety device. For nearly a decade, the automobile industry waged the regulatory equivalent of war against the airbag and lost—the inflatable restraint was proven sufficiently effective. Now the automobile industry has decided to employ a seatbelt system which will not meet the safety objectives of Standard 208. This hardly constitutes cause to revoke the standard itself. Indeed, the Motor Vehicle Safety Act was necessary because the industry was not sufficiently responsive to safety concerns. The Act intended that safety standards not depend on current technology and could be "technology-forcing" in the sense of inducing the development of superior safety design. If, under the statute, the agency should not defer to the industry's failure to develop safer cars, which it surely should not do, *a fortiori* it may not revoke a safety standard which can be satisfied by current technology simply because the industry has opted for an ineffective seatbelt design.

B

**Take Note**

Whereas the preceding parts of the Court's opinion were joined by all members of the Court, this part of the Court's opinion was for only five Justices.

Although the issue is closer, we also find that the agency was too quick to dismiss the safety benefits of automatic seatbelts. NHTSA's critical finding was that, in light of the industry's plans to install readily detachable passive belts, it could not reliably predict "even a 5 percentage point increase as the minimum level of expected usage increase." 46 Fed. Reg., at 53,423. * * * We agree with petitioners that just as an agency reasonably may decline to issue a safety standard if it is uncertain about its efficacy, an agency may also revoke a standard on the basis of serious uncertainties if supported by the record and reasonably explained. Rescission of the passive restraint requirement would not be arbitrary and capricious simply because there was no evidence in direct support of the agency's conclusion. It is not infrequent that the available data does not settle a regulatory issue and the agency must then exercise its judgment in moving from the facts and probabilities on the record to a policy conclusion. Recognizing that policymaking in a complex society must account for uncertainty, however, does not imply that it is sufficient for an agency to merely recite the terms "substantial uncertainty" as a justification for its actions. The agency must explain the evidence which is available, and must offer a "rational connection between the facts found and the choice made." *Burlington Truck Lines, Inc.*, 371 U.S., at 168. Generally, one aspect of that explanation would be a justification for rescinding the regulation before engaging in a search for further evidence.

In this case, the agency's explanation for rescission of the passive restraint requirement is *not* sufficient to enable us to conclude that the rescission was the product of reasoned decisionmaking. * * * We start with the accepted ground that if used, seatbelts unquestionably would save many thousands of lives and would prevent tens of thousands of crippling injuries. * * * The empirical evidence on the record, consisting of surveys of drivers of automobiles equipped with passive belts, reveals more than a doubling of the usage rate experienced with manual belts. * * * The agency maintained that the doubling of seatbelt usage in these studies could not be extrapolated to an across-the-board mandatory standard because the passive seatbelts were guarded by ignition interlocks and purchasers of the tested cars are somewhat atypical. * * * But accepting the agency's view of the field tests on passive restraints indicates only that there is no reliable real-world experience that usage rates will substantially increase. [The agency's view] that passive belts will not yield substantial increases in seatbelt usage apparently [takes] no account of the critical difference between detachable automatic belts and current manual belts. A detached passive belt does require an affirmative act to reconnect it, but—unlike a manual seat belt—the passive belt, once reattached, will continue to function automatically unless again disconnected. Thus, inertia—a factor which the agency's own studies have found significant in explaining the current low usage rates for seatbelts—works in *favor* of, not *against,* use of the protective device. Since 20 to 50% of motorists currently wear seatbelts on some occasions, there would seem to be grounds to believe that seatbelt use by occasional users will be substantially increased by the detachable passive belts. Whether this is in fact the case is a matter for the agency to decide, but it must bring its expertise to bear on the question.

The agency is correct to look at the costs as well as the benefits of Standard 208. The agency's conclusion that the incremental costs of the requirements were no longer reasonable was predicated on its prediction that the safety benefits of the regulation might be minimal. Specifically, the agency's fears that the public may resent paying more for the automatic belt systems is expressly dependent on the assumption that detachable automatic belts will not produce more than "negligible safety benefits." 46 Fed. Reg., at 53,424. When the agency reexamines its findings as to the likely increase in seatbelt usage, it must also reconsider its judgment of the reasonableness of the monetary and other costs associated with the Standard. In reaching its judgment, NHTSA should bear in mind that Congress intended safety to be the preeminent factor under the Motor Vehicle Safety Act * * *.

Justice Rehnquist, with whom The Chief Justice, Justice Powell, and Justice O'Connor join, concurring in part and dissenting in part.

I join parts I, II, III, IV, and V-A of the Court's opinion. In particular, I agree that, since the airbag and continuous spool automatic seatbelt were explicitly approved in the standard the agency was rescinding, the agency should explain why it declined to leave those requirements intact. In this case, the agency gave no explanation at all. Of course, if the agency can provide a rational explanation, it may adhere to its decision to rescind the entire standard.

I do not believe, however, that NHTSA's view of detachable automatic seatbelts was arbitrary and capricious. The agency adequately explained its decision to rescind the standard insofar as it was satisfied by detachable belts.

The statute that requires the Secretary of Transportation to issue motor vehicle safety standards also requires that "[e]ach such . . . standard shall be practicable [and] shall meet the need for motor vehicle safety." 15 U.S.C. § 1392(a). The Court rejects the agency's explanation for its conclusion that there is substantial uncertainty whether requiring installation of detachable automatic belts would substantially increase seatbelt usage. The agency chose not to rely on a study showing a substantial increase in seatbelt usage in cars equipped with automatic seatbelts *and* an ignition interlock to prevent the car from being operated when the belts were not in place *and* which were voluntarily purchased with this equipment by consumers. It is reasonable for the agency to decide that this study does not support any conclusion concerning the effect of automatic seatbelts that are installed in all cars whether the consumer wants them or not and are not linked to an ignition interlock system.

The Court rejects this explanation because "there would seem to be grounds to believe that seatbelt use by occasional users will be substantially increased by the detachable passive belts," and the agency did not adequately explain its rejection of these grounds. It seems to me that the agency's explanation, while by no means a model, is adequate. The agency acknowledged that there would probably be some increase in belt usage, but concluded that the increase would be small and not worth the cost of mandatory detachable automatic belts. 46 F.R. 53421–54323 (1981). The agency's obligation is to articulate a "rational connection between the facts found and the choice made." I believe it has met this standard.

The agency's changed view of the standard seems to be related to the election of a new President of a different political party. It is readily apparent that the responsible members of one administration may consider public resistance and uncertainties to be more important than do their counterparts in a previous administration. A change in administration brought about by the people casting their votes is a perfectly reasonable basis for an executive agency's reappraisal of the costs and benefits of its programs and regulations. As long as the agency remains within the bounds established by Congress,* it is entitled to assess administrative records and evaluate priorities in light of the philosophy of the administration.

---

## Points for Discussion

### *a. "Hard-Look Review"*

The Court in *State Farm* declared that, in reviewing an agency action under the arbitrary and capricious standard, a court should ensure that the agency has "examine[d] the relevant data" and provided a "satisfactory explanation for its action," including a "rational connection between the facts found and the choice made." Applying that standard, the Court set aside the agency's decision to rescind the passive-restraint rule, concluding that the agency hadn't considered whether requiring airbags in all cars would be a more sensible course. The Court also concluded that the agency was "too quick to dismiss the safety benefits of automatic seatbelts."

The Court's approach in the *State Farm* case is known as "hard-look" review, because the Court took a hard look at the agency's reasoning. Unlike judicial review to determine whether an agency has followed the proper procedures in creating a

---

* Of course, a new administration may not choose not to enforce laws of which it does not approve, or to ignore statutory standards in carrying out its regulatory functions. But in this case, as the Court correctly concludes, Congress has not required the agency to require passive restraints.

rule, hard-look review focuses on the substance of agency decision-making. The Court sought to determine whether the agency's decision was reasonable and made sense, in light of the evidence before the agency. Is it possible for a court to conduct this inquiry without making contestable policy judgments? If not, is there reason to think that judges are better suited to make such determinations than agency officials?

#### *b. Informal Rulemaking and Substantive Judicial Review*

In important and controversial questions of policy, informal rulemaking is often a long and drawn-out process. Agency officials might spend months or years formulating a proposed rule; many months more receiving comments from interested persons, revising the proposal to respond to the comments, and seeking comments again on the revision; and then many months more drafting the final rule. Given the amount of information that an agency in such a case has before it when it issues the rule—comments, studies, and so forth—it is not difficult to imagine a reviewing court later concluding that the final rule did not sufficiently explain a decision to choose one path instead of another. And when a court sets aside a rule under *State Farm* hard-look review, the agency has to go back to the drawing board. Does hard-look review create a disincentive for agencies to engage in informal rulemaking in the first place?

Consider the Department of Transportation's approach to automobile safety regulation after the Court's decision in *State Farm*. The Department became hesitant to expend resources to formulate rules to force the adoption of safety-enhancing technologies. Instead, it began to focus on automobile recall campaigns for technologies that had proved in practice to be unsafe. Are there reasons to think that such an approach to promoting automobile safety is likely to be inferior to an approach that relies on prospective rules requiring the use of certain technologies?

#### *c. Regulation, Deregulation, and Political Change*

As the Court explains, government efforts to require airbags waxed and waned in the years prior to the Court's decision. The agency first issued a rule that would eventually require the installation of passive restraints in all cars, but it extended the deadline for compliance. In 1976, the Secretary of Transportation suspended the requirement. Then, in 1977, a new Secretary of Transportation issued a new rule to require the gradual phasing in of a passive-restraint requirement. And then, in 1981, another new Secretary of Transportation repealed the rule, which led to the challenge in *State Farm*. It is, of course, possible that the passage of time provided more data from which the agency could make a judgment about the likely costs and benefits of a passive-restraint requirement. But does the timing of the various decisions suggest that something else accounts for the changing views? (Notice that Justice Rehnquist said that "the agency's changed view seems to be related to the election of a new President of a different political party.")

If we are concerned about giving power to agency officials who are not subject to direct electoral control—a concern we addressed earlier in this Chapter—then isn't it a good thing when agency decision-making closely follows the President's agenda? Should the Court in *State Farm* have given more leeway to the agency to pursue the Administration's deregulatory agenda? Or did the Court's approach enhance agency accountability, by ensuring that the agency's action complied with the instructions that Congress, another electorally accountable branch, had provided in the governing statute?

#### *d. The Long Struggle over Airbags*

The Department of Transportation responded to the Court's decision in *State Farm* by issuing a new rule that required the phasing in of a passive-restraint requirement for all cars, which car manufacturers could satisfy with airbags, enhanced padding in the car's interior, or automatic seatbelts. The rule also provided that the passive-restraint requirement would be rescinded if, within five years, two-thirds of the population of the United States was covered by state compulsory-seatbelt-usage laws that met certain specified conditions, such as a mandatory minimum fine for car occupants who failed to comply.

In the years that followed, many states adopted mandatory-seatbelt-use laws, but many of them drafted their laws in a way that wouldn't trigger the conditions for rescission of the federal rule. As a consequence, seat belt usage increased dramatically, and car makers remained under the obligation to install passive restraints in all cars. A few years later, in response to public pressure, Congress enacted a law that required all new cars to be equipped with airbags.

---

## 3. The Availability of Judicial Review

As we have seen, courts review agency decisions for compliance with procedural requirements; to determine that agency fact-finding in formal proceedings was supported by evidence in the record; and to ensure that the decisions are substantively defensible. (In Chapter 8, we will see examples of judicial review to ensure that agency actions are within the scope of their statutory authority.)

But a court can review an agency decision only if Congress has authorized judicial review and a plaintiff with standing has challenged the decision. In the cases that follow, we will consider these two threshold requirements for judicial review—reviewability and standing—in turn.

---

### a. Reviewability

## *Abbott Laboratories v. Gardner*

387 U.S. 136 (1967)

Mr. Justice Harlan delivered the opinion of the Court.

In 1962 Congress amended the Federal Food, Drug, and Cosmetic Act, (52 Stat. 1040, as amended by the Drug Amendments of 1962, 76 Stat. 780, 21 U.S.C. § 301 et seq.), to require manufacturers of prescription drugs to print the "established name" of the drug "prominently and in type at least half as large as that used thereon for any proprietary name or designation for such drug," on labels and other printed material, § 502(e)(1)(B), 21 U.S.C. § 352(e)(1)(B). The "established name" is one designated by the Secretary of Health, Education, and Welfare pursuant to § 502(e)(2) of the Act, 21 U.S.C. § 352(e)(2); the "proprietary name" is usually a trade name under which a particular drug is marketed. The underlying purpose of the 1962 amendment was to bring to the attention of doctors and patients the fact that many of the drugs sold under familiar trade names are actually identical to drugs sold under their "established" or less familiar trade names at significantly lower prices. The Commissioner of Food and Drugs, exercising authority delegated to him by the Secretary, 22 Fed. Reg. 1051, 25 Fed. Reg. 8625, published proposed regulations designed to implement the statute, 28 Fed. Reg. 1448. After inviting and considering comments submitted by interested parties the Commissioner promulgated the following regulation for the "efficient enforcement" of the Act:

> "If the label or labeling of a prescription drug bears a proprietary name or designation for the drug or any ingredient thereof, the established name, if such there be, corresponding to such proprietary name or designation, shall accompany each appearance of such proprietary name or designation." 21 CFR § 1.104(g)(1).

A similar rule was made applicable to advertisements for prescription drugs, 21 CFR § 1.105(b)(1).

The present action was brought by a group of 37 individual drug manufacturers and by the Pharmaceutical Manufacturers Association, of which all the petitioner companies are members, and which includes manufacturers of more than 90% of the Nation's supply of prescription drugs. They challenged the regulations on the ground that the Commissioner exceeded his authority under the statute by promulgating an order requiring labels, advertisements, and other printed matter relating to prescription drugs to designate the established name of the particular drug involved every time its trade name is used anywhere in such material.

**Make the Connection**

In issuing the rule in question, the FDA decided that it had authority to force drug manufacturers to take the actions required by the rule. Whether Congress had given the agency that authority was in large part a question of statutory interpretation. Should the district court have deferred to the FDA's interpretation of the statute? Or is such a question of statutory interpretation one solely for the court to resolve, without deference? We will consider this question in Chapter 8.

The District Court, on cross motions for summary judgment, granted the declaratory and injunctive relief sought, finding that the statute did not sweep so broadly as to permit the Commissioner's "every time" interpretation. The Court of Appeals for the Third Circuit reversed without reaching the merits of the case. It held first that under the statutory scheme provided by the Federal Food, Drug, and Cosmetic Act pre-enforcement[1] review of these regulations was unauthorized and therefore beyond the jurisdiction of the District Court. Second, the Court of Appeals held that no "actual case or controversy" existed and, for that reason, that no relief under the Administrative Procedure Act or under the Declaratory Judgment Act, 28 U.S.C. § 2201, was in any event available. * * *

The first question we consider is whether Congress by the Federal Food, Drug, and Cosmetic Act intended to forbid pre-enforcement review of this sort of regulation promulgated by the Commissioner. The question is phrased in terms of "prohibition" rather than "authorization" because a survey of our cases shows that judicial review of a final agency action by an aggrieved person will not be cut off unless there is persuasive reason to believe that such was the purpose of Congress. Early cases in which this type of judicial review was entertained, e.g., *Shields v. Utah Idaho Central R. Co.*, 305 U.S. 177 (1938), have been reinforced by the enactment of the Administrative Procedure Act, which embodies the basic presumption of judicial review to one "suffering legal wrong because of agency action, or adversely affected or aggrieved by agency action within the meaning of a relevant statute," 5 U.S.C. § 702, so long as no statute precludes such relief or the action is not one committed by law to agency discretion, 5 U.S.C. § 701(a). The Administrative Procedure Act provides specifically not only for review of "(a)gency action made reviewable by statute" but also for review of "final agency action for which there is no other adequate remedy in a court," 5 U.S.C. § 704. The legislative material elucidating that seminal act manifests a congressional intention that it cover a broad spectrum of administrative actions,[2] and this Court

1 That is, a suit brought by one before any attempted enforcement of the statute or regulation against him.

2 See H.R. Rep. No. 1980, 79th Cong., 2d Sess., 41 (1946): "To preclude judicial review under this bill a statute, if not specific in withholding such review, must upon its face give clear and convincing evidence of an intent to withhold it. The mere failure to provide specially by statute for judicial review is certainly no evidence of intent to withhold review." See also S. Rep. No. 752, 79th Cong., 1st Sess., 26 (1945).

has echoed that theme by noting that the Administrative Procedure Act's "generous review provisions" must be given a "hospitable" interpretation. *Shaughnessy v. Pedreiro*, 349 U.S. 48, 51 (1955). Again in *Rusk v. Cort*, 369 U.S. 367, 379–380 (1962), the Court held that only upon a showing of "clear and convincing evidence" of a contrary legislative intent should the courts restrict access to judicial review.

Given this standard, we are wholly unpersuaded that the statutory scheme in the food and drug area excludes this type of action. The Government relies on no explicit statutory authority for its argument that pre-enforcement review is unavailable, but insists instead that because the statute includes a specific procedure for such review of certain enumerated kinds of regulations, not encompassing those of the kind involved here, other types were necessarily meant to be excluded from any pre-enforcement review. The issue, however, is not so readily resolved; we must go further and inquire whether in the context of the entire legislative scheme the existence of that circumscribed remedy evinces a congressional purpose to bar agency action not within its purview from judicial review. * * *

In this case the Government has not demonstrated such a purpose; indeed, a study of the legislative history shows rather conclusively that the specific review provisions were designed to give an additional remedy and not to cut down more traditional channels of review. At the time the Food, Drug, and Cosmetic Act was under consideration, in the late 1930's, the Administrative Procedure Act had not yet been enacted, the Declaratory Judgment Act was in its infancy, and the scope of judicial review of administrative decisions under the equity power was unclear. It was these factors that led to the form the statute ultimately took. There is no evidence at all that members of Congress meant to preclude traditional avenues of judicial relief. * * * We conclude that nothing in the Food, Drug, and Cosmetic Act itself precludes this action.

A further inquiry must, however, be made. The injunctive and declaratory judgment remedies are discretionary, and courts traditionally have been reluctant to apply them to administrative determinations unless these arise in the context of a controversy "ripe" for judicial resolution. Without undertaking to survey the intricacies of the ripeness doctrine it is fair to say that its basic rationale is to prevent the courts, through avoidance of premature adjudication, from entangling themselves in abstract disagreements over administrative policies, and also to protect the agencies from judicial interference until an administrative decision has been formalized and its effects felt in a concrete way by the challenging parties. The problem is best seen in a twofold aspect, requiring us to evaluate both the fitness of the issues for judicial decision and the hardship to the parties of withholding court consideration.

As to the former factor, we believe the issues presented are appropriate for judicial resolution at this time. First, all parties agree that the issue tendered is a purely legal one: whether the statute was properly construed by the Commissioner to require the established name of the drug to be used every time the proprietary name is employed. Both sides moved for summary judgment in the District Court, and no claim is made here that further administrative proceedings are contemplated. It is suggested that the justification for this rule might vary with different circumstances, and that the expertise of the Commissioner is relevant to passing upon the validity of the regulation. This of course is true, but the suggestion overlooks the fact that both sides have approached this case as one purely of congressional intent, and that the Government made no effort to justify the regulation in factual terms.

Second, the regulations in issue we find to be "final agency action" within the meaning of [the] Administrative Procedure Act, 5 U.S.C. § 704, as construed in judicial decisions. An "agency action" includes any "rule," defined by the Act as "an agency statement of general or particular applicability and future effect designed to implement, interpret, or prescribe law or policy," 5 U.S.C. §§ 551(4), 551(13). The cases dealing with judicial review of administrative actions have interpreted the "finality" element in a pragmatic way. * * *

The regulation challenged here, promulgated in a formal manner after announcement in the Federal Register and consideration of comments by interested parties is quite clearly definitive. There is no hint that this regulation is informal, or only the ruling of a subordinate official, or tentative. It was made effective upon publication, and the Assistant General Counsel for Food and Drugs stated in the District Court that compliance was expected.

The Government argues, however, that the present case can be distinguished from [earlier] cases like on the ground that in those instances the agency involved could implement its policy directly, while here the Attorney General must authorize criminal and seizure actions for violations of the statute. In the context of this case, we do not find this argument persuasive. These regulations are not meant to advise the Attorney General, but purport to be directly authorized by the statute. Thus, if within the Commissioner's authority, they have the status of law and violations of them carry heavy criminal and civil sanctions. Also, there is no representation that the Attorney General and the Commissioner disagree in this area; the Justice Department is defending this very suit. * * *

**FYI**

The FDA did not have independent litigating authority, which means that it had to rely on the Department of Justice to bring enforcement actions on its behalf.

This is also a case in which the impact of the regulations upon the petitioners is sufficiently direct and immediate as to render the issue appropriate for judicial review at this stage. These regulations purport to give an authoritative interpretation of a statutory provision that has a direct effect on the day-to-day business of all prescription drug companies; its promulgation puts petitioners in a dilemma that it was the very purpose of the Declaratory Judgment Act to ameliorate. * * * The regulations are clear-cut, and were made effective immediately upon publication; [the] agency's counsel represented to the District Court that immediate compliance with their terms was expected. If petitioners wish to comply they must change all their labels, advertisements, and promotional materials; they must destroy stocks of printed matter; and they must invest heavily in new printing type and new supplies. The alternative to compliance—continued use of material which they believe in good faith meets the statutory requirements, but which clearly does not meet the regulation of the Commissioner—may be even more costly. That course would risk serious criminal and civil penalties for the unlawful distribution of "misbranded" drugs.

It is relevant at this juncture to recognize that petitioners deal in a sensitive industry, in which public confidence in their drug products is especially important. To require them to challenge these regulations only as a defense to an action brought by the Government might harm them severely and unnecessarily. Where the legal issue presented is fit for judicial resolution, and where a regulation requires an immediate and significant change in the plaintiffs' conduct of their affairs with serious penalties attached to noncompliance, access to the courts under the Administrative Procedure Act and the Declaratory Judgment Act must be permitted, absent a statutory bar or some other unusual circumstance, neither of which appears here.

Finally, the Government urges that to permit resort to the courts in this type of case may delay or impede effective enforcement of the Act. We fully recognize the important public interest served by assuring prompt and unimpeded administration of the Pure Food, Drug, and Cosmetic Act, but we do not find the Government's argument convincing. First, in this particular case, a pre-enforcement challenge by nearly all prescription drug manufacturers is calculated to speed enforcement. If the Government prevails, a large part of the industry is bound by the decree; if the Government loses, it can more quickly revise its regulation.

The Government contends, however, that if the Court allows this consolidated suit, then nothing will prevent a multiplicity of suits in various jurisdictions challenging other regulations. The short answer to this contention is that the courts are well equipped to deal with such eventualities. The venue transfer provision, 28 U.S.C. § 1404(a), may be invoked by the Government to consolidate separate actions. Or, actions in all but one jurisdiction might be stayed pending the conclusion of one proceeding. A court may even in its discretion dismiss a declaratory judgment or injunctive suit if the same issue is pending in litigation elsewhere. * * *

Further, the declaratory judgment and injunctive remedies are equitable in nature, and other equitable defenses may be interposed. If a multiplicity of suits are undertaken in order to harass the Government or to delay enforcement, relief can be denied on this ground alone. * * *

In addition to all these safeguards against what the Government fears, it is important to note that the institution of this type of action does not by itself stay the effectiveness of the challenged regulation. There is nothing in the record to indicate that petitioners have sought to stay enforcement of the "every time" regulation pending judicial review. See 5 U.S.C. § 705. If the agency believes that a suit of this type will significantly impede enforcement or will harm the public interest, it need not postpone enforcement of the regulation and may oppose any motion for a judicial stay on the part of those challenging the regulation. It is scarcely to be doubted that a court would refuse to postpone the effective date of an agency action if the Government could show, as it made no effort to do here, that delay would be detrimental to the public health or safety.

Lastly, although the Government presses us to reach the merits of the challenge to the regulation in the event we find the District Court properly entertained this action, we believe the better practice is to remand the case to the Court of Appeals for the Third Circuit to review the District Court's decision that the regulation was beyond the power of the Commissioner.

Reversed and remanded.

MR. JUSTICE BRENNAN took no part in the consideration or decision of this case.

MR. JUSTICE FORTAS, with whom THE CHIEF JUSTICE and MR. JUSTICE CLARK join, dissenting.

**FYI**

Justice Fortas issued his dissent in a companion case, in which he addressed the Court's approach in *Abbott Laboratories.*

The Court, by today's [decision,] * * * has opened Pandora's box. Federal injunctions will now threaten programs of vast importance to the public welfare. The Court's holding here strikes at programs for the public health. The dangerous precedent goes even further. It is cold comfort—it is little more than delusion—to read in the Court's opinion that "It is scarcely to be doubted that a court would refuse to postpone the effective date of an agency action if the Government could show . . . that delay would be detrimental to the public health or safety." Experience dictates, on the contrary, that it can hardly be hoped that some federal judge somewhere will not be moved as the Court is here, by the cries of anguish and distress of those regulated, to grant a disruptive injunction. * * * I believe [the Court's] approach improperly and unwisely gives individual federal district judges a roving commission to halt the regulatory process, and to do so on the basis of abstractions and generalities instead of concrete fact situations, and that it impermissibly broadens the license of the courts to intervene in administrative action by means of a threshold suit for injunction rather than by the method provided by statute.

The Court's validation of this shotgun attack upon this vital law and its administration is not confined to these suits, these regulations, or these plaintiffs—or even this statute. It is a general hunting license; and I respectfully submit, a license for mischief because it authorizes aggression which is richly rewarded by delay in the subjection of private interests to programs which Congress believes to be required in the public interest. As I read the Court's opinion, it does not seriously contend that Congress authorized or contemplated this type of relief. It does not rest upon the argument that Congress intended that injunctions or threshold relief should be available. The Court seems to announce a doctrine, which is new and startling in administrative law, that the courts, in determining whether to exercise jurisdiction by injunction, will not look to see whether Congress intended that the parties should resort to another avenue of review, but will be governed by whether Congress has "prohibited" injunctive relief. * * *

Where a remedy is provided by statute, I submit that it is and has been fundamental to our law, to judicial administration, to the principle of separation of powers in our Constitution, that the courts will withhold equitable or discretionary remedies unless they conclude that the statutory remedy is inadequate. Even then, as the Court recognizes, the case must be "ripe" or appropriate for threshold judicial review. Any other doctrine than this * * * is bound to be disruptive. * * *

The Court, [moved] by petitioners' claims as to the expense and inconvenience of compliance and the risks of deferring challenge by noncompliance, * * * says that [the inability to challenge the regulation now would present] the manufacturer with a "real dilemma." But the fact of the matter is that the dilemma is no more than citizens face in connection with countless statutes and with the rules of the SEC, FTC, FCC, ICC, and other regulatory agencies. * * * The overriding fact here is—or should be—that the public interest in avoiding the delay in implementing Congress' program far outweighs the private interest; and that the private interest which has so impressed the Court is no more than that which exists in respect of most regulatory statutes or agency rules. Somehow, the Court has concluded that the damage to petitioners if they have to engage in the required redesign and reprint of their labels and printed materials without threshold review outweighs the damage to the public of deferring during the tedious months and years of litigation a cure for the possible danger and asserted deceit of peddling plain medicine under fancy trademarks and for fancy prices which, rightly or wrongly, impelled the Congress to enact this legislation. I submit that a much stronger showing is necessary than the expense and trouble of compliance and the risk of defiance. Actually, if the Court refused to permit this shotgun assault, experience and reasonably sophisticated common sense show that there would be orderly compliance without the disaster so dramatically predicted by the industry, reasonable adjustments by the agency in real hardship cases, and where extreme intransigence involving substantial violations occurred, enforcement actions in which legality of the regulation would be tested in specific, concrete situations. I respectfully submit that this would be the correct and appropriate result. Our refusal to respond to the vastly overdrawn cries of distress would reflect not only healthy skepticism, but our regard for a proper relationship between the courts on the one hand and Congress and the administrative agencies on the other. It would represent a reasonable solicitude for the purposes and programs of the Congress. And it would reflect appropriate modesty as to the competence of the courts. * * *

---

## *Toilet Goods Ass'n, Inc. v. Gardner*

387 U.S. 158 (1967)

Mr. Justice Harlan delivered the opinion of the Court.

Petitioners in this case are the Toilet Goods Association, an organization of cosmetics manufacturers accounting for some 90% of annual American sales in this field, and 39 individual cosmetics manufacturers and distributors. They brought this action in the United States District Court for the Southern District of New York seeking declaratory and injunctive relief against the Secretary of Health, Education, and Welfare and the Commissioner of Food and Drugs, on the ground that certain regulations promulgated by the Commissioner exceeded his statutory authority under the Color Additive Amendments to the Federal Food, Drug and Cosmetic Act, 74 Stat. 397, 21 U.S.C. §§ 321–376. [The question was whether this pre-enforcement suit was justiciable.]

In [*Abbott Laboratories*, decided today,] we hold that nothing in the Food, Drug, and Cosmetic Act, 52 Stat. 1040, as amended, bars a pre-enforcement suit under the Administrative Procedure Act and the Declaratory Judgment Act. We nevertheless agree with the Court of Appeals that judicial review of this particular regulation in this particular context is inappropriate at this stage because, applying the standards set forth in *Abbott Laboratories*, the controversy is not presently ripe for adjudication.

* * * The Commissioner of Food and Drugs, exercising power delegated by the Secretary, * * * issued the [regulation at issue in this case] after due public notice and consideration of comments submitted by interested parties:

> "(a) When it appears to the Commissioner that a person has:
>
> "(4) Refused to permit duly authorized employees of the Food and Drug Administration free access to all manufacturing facilities, processes, and formulae involved in the manufacture of color additives and intermediates from which such color additives are derived; he may immediately suspend certification service to such person and may continue such suspension until adequate corrective action has been taken." 28 Fed. Reg. 6445–6446; 21 CFR § 8.28.

The petitioners maintain that this regulation is an impermissible exercise of authority, that the FDA has long sought congressional authorization for free access to facilities, processes, and formulae, but that Congress has always denied the agency this power except for prescription drugs. Framed in this way, we agree with petitioners that a "legal" issue is raised, but nevertheless we are not persuaded that the present suit is properly maintainable.

In determining whether a challenge to an administrative regulation is ripe for review a twofold inquiry must be made: first to determine whether the issues tendered are appropriate for judicial resolution, and second to assess the hardship to the parties if judicial relief is denied at that stage.

As to the first of these factors, we agree with the Court of Appeals that the legal issue as presently framed is not appropriate for judicial resolution. This is not because the regulation is not the agency's considered and formalized determination, for we are in agreement with petitioners that * * * this regulation—promulgated in a formal manner after notice and evaluation of submitted comments—is a "final agency action" under [the] Administrative Procedure Act. Also, we recognize the force of petitioners' contention that the issue as they have framed it presents a purely legal question: whether the regulation is totally beyond the agency's power under the statute, the type of legal issue that courts have occasionally dealt with without requiring a specific attempt at enforcement or exhaustion of administrative remedies.

These points which support the appropriateness of judicial resolution are, however, outweighed by other considerations. The regulation serves notice only that the Commissioner may under certain circumstances order inspection of certain facilities and data, and that further certification of additives may be refused to those who decline to permit a duly authorized inspection until they have complied in that regard. At this juncture we have no idea whether or when such an inspection will be ordered and what reasons the Commissioner will give to justify his order. The statutory authority asserted for the regulation is the power to promulgate regulations "for the efficient enforcement" of the Act. Whether the regulation is justified thus depends not only, as petitioners appear to suggest, on whether Congress refused to include a specific section of the Act authorizing such inspections, although this factor is to be sure a highly relevant one, but also on whether the statutory scheme as a whole justified promulgation of the regulation. This will depend not merely on an inquiry into statutory purpose, but concurrently on an understanding of what types of enforcement problems are encountered by the FDA, the need for various sorts of supervision in order to effectuate the goals of the Act, and the safeguards devised to protect legitimate trade secrets. We believe that judicial appraisal of these factors is likely to stand on a much surer footing in the context of a specific application of this regulation than could be the case in the framework of the generalized challenge made here.

We are also led to this result by considerations of the effect on the petitioners of the regulation, for the test of ripeness * * * depends not only on how adequately a court can deal with the legal issue presented, but also on the degree and nature of the regulation's present effect on those seeking relief. * * * This is not a situation in which primary conduct is affected—when contracts must be negotiated, ingredients tested or substituted, or special records compiled. This regulation merely states that the Commissioner may authorize inspectors to examine certain processes or formulae; no advance action is required of cosmetics manufacturers * * *. Moreover, no irremediable adverse consequences flow from requiring a later challenge to this regulation by a manufacturer who refuses to allow this type of inspection. Unlike the other regulations challenged in this action, in which seizure of goods, heavy fines, adverse publicity for distributing "adulterated" goods, and possible criminal liability might penalize failure to comply, refusal to admit an inspector here would at most lead only to a suspension of certification services to the particular party, a determination that can then be promptly challenged through an administrative procedure, which in turn is reviewable by a court. Such review will provide an adequate forum for testing the regulation in a concrete situation.

MR. JUSTICE DOUGLAS dissents for the reasons stated by Judge Tyler of the District Court, 235 F. Supp. 648, 651–652.

MR. JUSTICE BRENNAN took no part in the consideration or decision of this case.

---

## Points for Discussion

### *a. The Presumption of Reviewability*

The Court held in *Abbott Laboratories* that agency action is subject to a presumption of reviewability. In other words, unless Congress has clearly prohibited judicial review of some agency action, courts will conclude that the action is subject to judicial review. What sorts of evidence, short of express statutory language stating that judicial review is prohibited, would be sufficient to lead a court to conclude that judicial review is unavailable? Why would Congress seek to preclude judicial review of some agency action in the first place? If courts cannot review a particular agency action, then do the forms of control that we have been exploring to ensure agency accountability really work? Conversely, if the concern is that regulated parties might use litigation as a way to undermine an otherwise-valid regulatory regime, then should the Court have created a less-searching standard for determining when Congress has precluded judicial review? In other words, does a presumption of reviewability help to prevent agencies from over-reaching? Or does it give regulated parties a powerful weapon to obstruct agencies from fulfilling their statutory mandates?

### *b. Pre-Enforcement Review, Timing, and Ripeness*

Another important question in *Abbott Laboratories* and *Toilet Goods Ass'n.* was about the timing of judicial review: even assuming a rule is subject to judicial review, must a court exercise its power to review it before the rule has been enforced against a regulated party? Both cases involved "pre-enforcement review"—that is, judicial review of an agency rule before the agency has sought to apply it to a party subject to the regulation. Notice that a court's decision not to review a final rule before it has been enforced does not mean that a court will never pass on the rule's validity; it simply means that the regulated party will have to wait until the agency decides to enforce the rule against it. According to the Court, what factors are relevant to determining whether a challenge is sufficiently "ripe" to justify pre-enforcement review? Do you agree with the Court that the standard was satisfied in *Abbott Laboratories*, but not in *Toilet Goods Ass'n*?

---

The APA states that its provisions about judicial review apply "except to the extent that * * * statutes preclude judicial review [or] agency action is committed to agency discretion by law." 5 U.S.C. § 701(a). We had an introduction in *Abbott Laboratories* to the first category of cases for which judicial review is unavailable. (The Court there said that Congress can choose to shield an agency action from judicial scrutiny so as long as it is sufficiently clear about it.) The case that follows is about the second category of case for which judicial review is unavailable: actions that are "committed to agency discretion by law." (We had an introduction to such cases in *Overton Park*, which we considered earlier in this Chapter.)

---

## *Heckler v. Chaney*

470 U.S. 821 (1985)

Justice Rehnquist delivered the opinion of the Court.

This case presents the question of the extent to which a decision of an administrative agency to exercise its "discretion" not to undertake certain enforcement actions is subject to judicial review under the Administrative Procedure Act. * * *

Respondents have been sentenced to death by lethal injection of drugs under the laws of the States of Oklahoma and Texas. Those States, and several others, have recently adopted this method for carrying out the capital sentence. Respondents first petitioned the FDA, claiming that the drugs used by the States for this purpose, although approved by the FDA for the medical purposes stated on their labels, were not approved for use in human executions. They alleged that the drugs had not been tested for the purpose for which they were to be used, and that, given that the drugs would likely be administered by untrained personnel, it was also likely that the drugs would not induce the quick and painless death intended. They urged that use of these drugs for human execution was the "unapproved use of an approved drug" and constituted a violation of the [Federal Food, Drug, and Cosmetic Act's (FDCA)] prohibitions against "misbranding."[1] They also suggested that the FDCA's requirements for approval of "new drugs" applied, since these drugs were now being used for a new purpose. Accordingly, respondents claimed that the FDA was required to approve the drugs as "safe and effective" for human execution before they could be distributed in interstate commerce. See 21 U.S.C. § 355. They therefore requested the FDA to take various investigatory and enforcement actions to prevent these perceived violations; they requested the FDA to affix warnings to the labels of all the drugs stating that they were unapproved and unsafe for human execution, to send statements to the drug manufacturers and prison administrators stating that the drugs should not be so used, and to adopt procedures for seizing the drugs from state prisons and to recommend the prosecution of all those in the chain of distribution who knowingly distribute or purchase the drugs with intent to use them for human execution.

The FDA Commissioner responded, refusing to take the requested actions. The Commissioner first detailed his disagreement with respondents' understanding of the scope of FDA jurisdiction over the unapproved use of approved drugs for human execution, concluding that FDA jurisdiction in the area was generally unclear but in any event should not be exercised to interfere with this particular aspect of state criminal justice systems. He went on to state:

> "Were FDA clearly to have jurisdiction in the area, moreover, we believe we would be authorized to decline to exercise it under our inherent discretion to decline to pursue certain enforcement matters. The unapproved use of approved drugs is an area in which the case law is far from uniform. Generally, enforcement proceedings in this area are initiated only when there is a serious danger to the public health or a blatant scheme to defraud. We cannot conclude that those dangers are present under State lethal injection laws, which are duly authorized statutory enactments in furtherance of proper State functions. . . ."

Respondents then filed the instant suit in the United States District Court for the District of Columbia, claiming the same violations of the FDCA and asking that the FDA be required to take the same enforcement actions requested in the prior petition. * * * The District Court granted summary judgment for petitioner. * * * A divided panel of the Court of Appeals for the District of Columbia Circuit reversed. [The court of appeals concluded that the agency's decision not to take action was reviewable and inconsistent with an] FDA policy statement which indicated that the agency was "obligated" to investigate the unapproved use of an approved drug when such use became "widespread" or "endanger[ed] the public health." 718 F.2d 1174, 1186 (1983) (citing 37 Fed. Reg. 16504 (1972)). * * * The court therefore remanded the case to the District Court, to order the FDA "to fulfill its statutory function." * * *

---

1 See 21 U.S.C. § 352(f): "A drug or device shall be deemed to be misbranded . . . [u]nless its labeling bears * * * adequate directions for use. . . ."

The Court of Appeals' decision addressed three questions: (1) whether the FDA had jurisdiction to undertake the enforcement actions requested, (2) whether if it did have jurisdiction its refusal to take those actions was subject to judicial review, and (3) whether if reviewable its refusal was arbitrary, capricious, or an abuse of discretion. In reaching our conclusion that the Court of Appeals was wrong, however, we need not and do not address the thorny question of the FDA's jurisdiction. For us, this case turns on the important question of the extent to which determinations by the FDA *not to exercise* its enforcement authority over the use of drugs in interstate commerce may be judicially reviewed. That decision in turn involves the construction of two separate but necessarily interrelated statutes, the APA and the FDCA.

The APA's comprehensive provisions for judicial review of "agency actions" are contained in 5 U.S.C. §§ 701–706. Any person "adversely affected or aggrieved" by agency action, see § 702, including a "failure to act," is entitled to "judicial review thereof," as long as the action is a "final agency action for which there is no other adequate remedy in a court," see § 704. The standards to be applied on review are governed by the provisions of § 706. But before any review at all may be had, a party must first clear the hurdle of § 701(a). That section provides that the chapter on judicial review "applies, according to the provisions thereof, except to the extent that—(1) statutes preclude judicial review; or (2) agency action is committed to agency discretion by law." Petitioner urges that the decision of the FDA to refuse enforcement is an action "committed to agency discretion by law" under § 701(a)(2).

This Court has not had occasion to interpret this second exception in § 701(a) in any great detail. On its face, the section does not obviously lend itself to any particular construction; indeed, one might wonder what difference exists between § (a)(1) and § (a)(2). The former section seems easy in application; it requires construction of the substantive statute involved to determine whether Congress intended to preclude judicial review of certain decisions. * * * But one could read the language "committed to agency discretion *by law*" in § (a)(2) to require a similar inquiry. In addition, commentators have pointed out that construction of § (a)(2) is further complicated by the tension between a literal reading of § (a)(2), which exempts from judicial review those decisions committed to agency "discretion," and the primary scope of review prescribed by § 706(2)(A)—whether the agency's action was "arbitrary, capricious, or an *abuse of discretion.*" How is it, they ask, that an action committed to agency discretion can be unreviewable and yet courts still can review agency actions for abuse of that discretion? * * * Mindful, however, of the common-sense principle of statutory construction that sections of a statute generally should be read "to give effect, if

**Make the Connection**

The Court here invoked the rule against surplusage, a corollary of the Whole Act Rule that we considered—along with other maxims and canons of construction—in Chapter 3. We considered the Court's decision in *Overton Park* earlier in this Chapter.

possible, to every clause . . .," see *United States v. Menasche*, 348 U.S. 528, 538–539 (1955), we think there is a proper construction of § (a)(2) which satisfies each of these concerns.

This Court first discussed § (a)(2) in *Citizens to Preserve Overton Park v. Volpe*, 401 U.S. 402 (1971). * * * After setting out the language of § 701(a), the Court stated: * * * "This is a very narrow exception. . . . The legislative history of the Administrative Procedure Act indicates that it is applicable in those rare instances where 'statutes are drawn in such broad terms that in a given case there is no law to apply.' S. Rep. No. 752, 79th Cong., 1st Sess., 26 (1945)." *Overton Park*, 401 U.S., at 410.

The above quote answers several of the questions raised by the language of § 701(a), although it raises others. First, it clearly separates the exception provided by § (a)(1) from the § (a)(2) exception. The former applies when Congress has expressed an intent to preclude judicial review. The latter applies in different circumstances; even where Congress has not affirmatively precluded review, review is not to be had if the statute is drawn so that a court would have no meaningful standard against which to judge the agency's exercise of discretion. In such a case, the statute ("law") can be taken to have "committed" the decisionmaking to the agency's judgment absolutely. This construction avoids conflict with the "abuse of discretion" standard of review in § 706—if no judicially manageable standards are available for judging how and when an agency should exercise its discretion, then it is impossible to evaluate agency action for "abuse of discretion." In addition, this construction satisfies the principle of statutory construction mentioned earlier, by identifying a separate class of cases to which § 701(a)(2) applies.

[The court of appeals read *Overton Park* to require application of a presumption of reviewability even to an agency's decision not to undertake certain enforcement actions. But] *Overton Park* did not involve an agency's refusal to take requested enforcement action. It involved an affirmative act of approval under a statute that set clear guidelines for determining when such approval should be given. Refusals to take enforcement steps generally involve precisely the opposite situation, and in that situation we think the presumption is that judicial review is not available. This Court has recognized on several occasions over many years that an agency's decision not to prosecute or enforce, whether through civil or criminal process, is a decision generally committed to an agency's absolute discretion. See *United States v. Batchelder*, 442 U.S. 114, 123–124 (1979). This recognition of the existence of discretion is attributable in no small part to the general unsuitability for judicial review of agency decisions to refuse enforcement.

**Food for Thought**

Is the Court's conclusion here—that agency refusals to take enforcement steps are presumptively unreviewable—consistent with the Court's conclusion in *Abbott Laboratories* that final agency action is presumptively reviewable? If so, why?

The reasons for this general unsuitability are many. First, an agency decision not to enforce often involves a complicated balancing of a number of factors which are peculiarly within its expertise. Thus, the agency must not only assess whether a violation has occurred, but whether agency resources are best spent on this violation or another, whether the agency is likely to succeed if it acts, whether the particular enforcement action requested best fits the agency's overall policies, and, indeed, whether the agency has enough resources to undertake the action at all. An agency generally cannot act against each technical violation of the statute it is charged with enforcing. The agency is far better equipped than the courts to deal with the many variables involved in the proper ordering of its priorities. * * *

In addition to these administrative concerns, we note that when an agency refuses to act it generally does not exercise its *coercive* power over an individual's liberty or property rights, and thus does not infringe upon areas that courts often are called upon to protect. Similarly, when an agency *does* act to enforce, that action itself provides a focus for judicial review, inasmuch as the agency must have exercised its power in some manner. The action at least can be reviewed to determine whether the agency exceeded its statutory powers. Finally, we recognize that an agency's refusal to institute proceedings shares to some extent the characteristics of the decision of a prosecutor in the Executive Branch not to indict—a decision which has long been regarded as the special province of the Executive Branch, inasmuch as it is the Executive who is charged by the Constitution to "take Care that the Laws be faithfully executed." U.S. Const., Art. II, § 3.

We of course only list the above concerns to facilitate understanding of our conclusion that an agency's decision not to take enforcement action should be presumed immune from judicial review under § 701(a)(2). For good reasons, such a decision has traditionally been "committed to agency discretion," and we believe that the Congress enacting the APA did not intend to alter that tradition. In so stating, we emphasize that the decision is only presumptively unreviewable; the presumption may be rebutted where the substantive statute has provided guidelines for the agency to follow in exercising its enforcement powers.[4] Thus, in establishing this presumption in the APA, Congress did not set agencies free to disregard legislative direction in the statutory scheme that the agency administers. Congress may limit an agency's exercise of enforcement power if it wishes, either by setting substantive priorities, or by otherwise circumscribing an agency's power to discriminate among issues or cases it will pursue. * * *

---

4 We do not have in this case a refusal by the agency to institute proceedings based solely on the belief that it lacks jurisdiction. Nor do we have a situation where it could justifiably be found that the agency has "consciously and expressly adopted a general policy" that is so extreme as to amount to an abdication of its statutory responsibilities. See, *e.g., Adams v. Richardson*, 480 F.2d 1159 (1973) (en banc). Although we express no opinion on whether such decisions would be unreviewable under § 701(a)(2), we note that in those situations the statute conferring authority on the agency might indicate that such decisions were not "committed to agency discretion."

* * * The danger that agencies may not carry out their delegated powers with sufficient vigor does not necessarily lead to the conclusion that courts are the most appropriate body to police this aspect of their performance. That decision is in the first instance for Congress, and we therefore turn to the FDCA to determine whether in this case Congress has provided us with "law to apply." If it has indicated an intent to circumscribe agency enforcement discretion, and has provided meaningful standards for defining the limits of that discretion, there is "law to apply" under § 701(a)(2), and courts may require that the agency follow that law; if it has not, then an agency refusal to institute proceedings is a decision "committed to agency discretion by law" within the meaning of that section.

To enforce the various substantive prohibitions contained in the FDCA, the Act provides for injunctions, 21 U.S.C. § 332, criminal sanctions, §§ 333 and 335, and seizure of any offending food, drug, or cosmetic article, § 334. The Act's general provision for enforcement, § 372, provides only that "[t]he Secretary is *authorized* to conduct examinations and investigations . . ." (emphasis added). * * * § 332 gives no indication of when an injunction should be sought, and § 334, providing for seizures, is framed in the permissive—the offending food, drug, or cosmetic "shall be liable to be proceeded against." The section on criminal sanctions states baldly that any person who violates the Act's substantive prohibitions "shall be imprisoned . . . or fined." Respondents argue that this statement mandates criminal prosecution of every violator of the Act but they adduce no indication in case law or legislative history that such was Congress' intention in using this language, which is commonly found in the criminal provisions of Title 18 of the United States Code. We are unwilling to attribute such a sweeping meaning to this language, particularly since the Act charges the Secretary only with recommending prosecution; any criminal prosecutions must be instituted by the Attorney General. The Act's enforcement provisions thus commit complete discretion to the Secretary to decide how and when they should be exercised.

Respondents nevertheless present three separate authorities that they claim provide the courts with sufficient indicia of an intent to circumscribe enforcement discretion. Two of these may be dealt with summarily. First, we reject respondents' argument that the Act's substantive prohibitions of "misbranding" and the introduction of "new drugs" absent agency approval, see 21 U.S.C. §§ 352(f)(1), 355, supply us with "law to apply." These provisions are simply irrelevant to the agency's discretion to refuse to initiate proceedings.

We also find singularly unhelpful the agency "policy statement" on which the Court of Appeals placed great reliance. We would have difficulty with this statement's vague language even if it were a properly adopted agency rule. Although the statement indicates that the agency considered itself "obligated" to take certain investigative actions, that language did not arise in the course of discussing the agency's discretion to exercise its enforcement power, but rather in the context of describing agency policy with respect to unapproved uses of approved drugs by physicians. In addition, if read to circumscribe agency enforcement discretion, the statement conflicts with the agency rule on judicial review, 21 CFR § 10.45(d)(2) (1984), which states that "[t]he Commissioner shall object to judicial review . . . if [t]he matter is committed by law to the discretion of the Commissioner, e.g., a decision to recommend or not to recommend civil or criminal enforcement action. . . ." But in any event the policy statement was attached to a rule that was never adopted. Whatever force such a statement might have, and leaving to one side the problem of whether an agency's rules might under certain circumstances provide courts with adequate guidelines for informed judicial review of decisions not to enforce, we do not think the language of the agency's "policy statement" can plausibly be read to override the agency's express assertion of unreviewable discretion contained in the above rule.

We therefore conclude that the presumption that agency decisions not to institute proceedings are unreviewable under 5 U.S.C. § 701(a)(2) is not overcome by the enforcement provisions of the FDCA. The FDA's decision not to take the enforcement actions requested by respondents is therefore not subject to judicial review under the APA. The general exception to reviewability provided by § 701(a)(2) for action "committed to agency discretion" remains a narrow one, see *Overton Park,* but within that exception are included agency refusals to institute investigative or enforcement proceedings, unless Congress has indicated otherwise. In so holding, we essentially leave to Congress, and not to the courts, the decision as to whether an agency's refusal to institute proceedings should be judicially reviewable. No colorable claim is made in this case that the agency's refusal to institute proceedings violated any constitutional rights of respondents, and we do not address the issue that would be raised in such a case. The fact that the drugs involved in this case are ultimately to be used in imposing the death penalty must not lead this Court or other courts to import profound differences of opinion over the meaning of the Eighth Amendment to the United States Constitution into the domain of administrative law. [*Reversed.*]

JUSTICE BRENNAN, concurring.

* * * [T]he Court properly does not decide today that nonenforcement decisions are unreviewable in cases where (1) an agency flatly claims that it has no statutory jurisdiction to reach certain conduct; (2) an agency engages in a pattern of nonenforcement of clear statutory language, as in *Adams v. Richardson*, 480 F.2d 1159 (1973) (en banc); (3) an agency has refused to enforce a regulation lawfully promulgated and still in effect; or (4) a nonenforcement decision violates constitutional rights. It is possible to imagine other nonenforcement decisions made for entirely illegitimate reasons, for example, nonenforcement in return for a bribe, judicial review of which would not be foreclosed by the nonreviewability presumption. It may be presumed that Congress does not intend administrative agencies, agents of Congress' own creation, to ignore clear jurisdictional, regulatory, statutory, or constitutional commands, and in some circumstances including those listed above the statutes or regulations at

issue may well provide "law to apply" under 5 U.S.C. § 701(a)(2). Individual, isolated nonenforcement decisions, however, must be made by hundreds of agencies each day. It is entirely permissible to presume that Congress has not intended courts to review such mundane matters, absent either some indication of congressional intent to the contrary or proof of circumstances such as those set out above.

Justice Marshall, concurring in the judgment.

Easy cases at times produce bad law, for in the rush to reach a clearly ordained result, courts may offer up principles, doctrines, and statements that calmer reflection, and a fuller understanding of their implications in concrete settings, would eschew. In my view, the "presumption of unreviewability" announced today is a product of that lack of discipline that easy cases make all too easy. The majority, eager to reverse what it goes out of its way to label as an "implausible result," not only does reverse, as I agree it should, but along the way creates out of whole cloth the notion that agency decisions not to take "enforcement action" are unreviewable unless Congress has rather specifically indicated otherwise. Because this "presumption of unreviewability" is fundamentally at odds with rule-of-law principles firmly embedded in our jurisprudence, because it seeks to truncate an emerging line of judicial authority subjecting enforcement discretion to rational and principled constraint, and because, in the end, the presumption may well be indecipherable, one can only hope that it will come to be understood as a relic of a particular factual setting in which the full implications of such a presumption were neither confronted nor understood.

I write separately to argue for a different basis of decision: that refusals to enforce, like other agency actions, are reviewable in the absence of a "clear and convincing" congressional intent to the contrary, but that such refusals warrant deference when, as in this case, there is nothing to suggest that an agency with enforcement discretion has abused that discretion. * * * First, respondents on summary judgment neither offered nor attempted to offer any evidence that the reasons for the FDA's refusal to act were other than the reasons stated by the agency. Second, as the Court correctly concludes, the FDCA is not a mandatory statute that requires the FDA to prosecute all violations of the Act. Thus, the FDA clearly has significant discretion to choose which alleged violations of the Act to prosecute. Third, the basis on which the agency chose to exercise this discretion—that other problems were viewed as more pressing—generally will be enough to pass muster. Certainly it is enough to do so here, where the number of people currently affected by the alleged misbranding is around 200, and where the drugs are integral elements in a regulatory scheme over which the States exercise pervasive and direct control.

---

## Points for Discussion

### *a. Agency Decisions Not to Initiate Enforcement Actions*

The Court in *Chaney* held that agency decisions not to undertake enforcement actions are presumptively unreviewable. This is an exception to the general rule that the Court announced in *Abbott Laboratories*. The Court anchored this exception in 5 U.S.C. § 701(a)(2), which precludes review when "agency action is committed to agency discretion by law." The Court stated that, under that provision, "review is not to be had if the statute is drawn so that a court would have no meaningful standard against which to judge the agency's exercise of discretion." The Court explained that the presumption will be overcome if Congress "has indicated an intent to circumscribe agency enforcement discretion, and has provided meaningful standards for defining the limits of that discretion," such that "there is 'law to apply' under § 701(a)(2)." Absent such a congressional indication, "an agency refusal to institute proceedings is a decision 'committed to agency discretion by law' within the meaning of that section."

Why are such decisions presumptively unreviewable? If Congress has directed an agency to fulfill some mission—such as ensuring that dangerous drugs are used only for their intended purposes—then is the agency's failure to take action to advance that mission any different, from the perspective of a reviewing court, than an agency action that is inconsistent with that mission? Does it matter that agencies have limited resources and can't reasonably be expected to bring actions in every conceivable case of non-compliance? Note that the Court analogized agency decisions not to begin enforcement proceedings to decisions by prosecutors not to initiate criminal proceedings, which have historically been immune from judicial inquiry. Is there reason to treat agency decisions not to enforce a statute differently?

### *b. Action, Inaction, and the Effects of Agency Choices*

In concluding that agency decisions not to take enforcement actions are presumptively unreviewable, the Court reasoned that such decisions generally do not entail the exercise of the agency's "*coercive* power over an individual's liberty or property rights, and thus [do] not infringe upon areas that courts often are called upon to protect." Is it obvious to you that agency inaction is less likely to burden or affect private parties than agency action? To be sure, the impact of agency enforcement on, say, a drug manufacturer is likely to be considerably greater than an agency decision not to act. But what about the impact on the many people who rely on agency action to protect their interests—such as the many people who might get sick from using drugs that were prescribed for purposes different than those for which they were approved? If you are a beneficiary of a regulatory scheme, rather than the subject of the regulation, then agency inaction can be considerably more problematic than agency action.

In announcing the rule that agency decisions not to take enforcement actions are presumptively unreviewable, did the Court make certain assumptions about the appropriate role of government? If so, what were the Court's assumptions?

---

**Problem**

Section 102(c) of the National Security Act of 1947, 61 Stat. 498, as amended, provides that "[T]he Director of Central Intelligence may, in his discretion, terminate the employment of any officer or employee of the Agency whenever he shall deem such termination necessary or advisable in the interests of the United States * * *." 50 U.S.C. § 403(c). In 1982, a covert electronics technician who worked at the Central Intelligence Agency voluntarily informed the agency that he was gay. He was immediately placed on paid administrative leave and then, after an investigation, discharged by the Director, who invoked his authority under section 102(c). (A CIA security agent informed the technician that the Agency's Office of Security had determined that his sexual orientation posed a threat to security, but he declined to explain the nature of the danger.) The technician then filed suit against the Director of the CIA alleging that his termination was arbitrary and capricious, an abuse of discretion, and reached without observing procedures required by the APA and the CIA's regulations. The Director moved to dismiss, arguing that the termination decision was unreviewable under 5 U.S.C. § 701(a)(2). How should the court rule? (These facts are based on *Webster v. Doe*, 486 U.S. 592 (1988).)

---

### b. Standing

## *Allen v. Wright*

468 U.S. 737 (1984)

JUSTICE O'CONNOR delivered the opinion of the Court.

Parents of black public school children allege in this nation-wide class action that the Internal Revenue Service (IRS) has not adopted sufficient standards and procedures to fulfill its obligation to deny tax-exempt status to racially discriminatory private schools. * * * The issue before us is whether plaintiffs have standing to bring this suit. We hold that they do not.

The IRS denies tax-exempt [status] to racially discriminatory private schools. * * * To carry out this policy, the IRS has established guidelines and procedures for determining whether a particular school is in fact racially nondiscriminatory. * * * In 1976 respondents challenged these guidelines and procedures in a suit [in federal court]. The plaintiffs named in the complaint are parents of black children who, at the time the complaint was filed, were attending public schools in seven States in school districts undergoing desegregation.

**Make the Connection**

We saw the IRS's policy about tax-exempt status, as applied to institutions that discriminate on the basis of race, in Chapter 2, when we considered *Bob Jones University v. United States.*

Respondents allege in their complaint that many racially segregated private schools * * * receive tax exemptions, [and that] some of the tax-exempt racially segregated private schools created or expanded in desegregating districts in fact have racially discriminatory policies. Respondents allege that the IRS grant of tax exemptions to such racially discriminatory schools is unlawful.

**FYI**

There are two related benefits to tax-exempt status under the tax code. First, the tax-exempt institution does not have to pay taxes on income. Second, contributions to the tax-exempt institution are deductible by the people making the contribution—which means that people are more likely to make such contributions (because they are relatively cheaper) and thus that the tax-exempt organization is more likely to receive charitable contributions.

Respondents do not allege that their children have been the victims of discriminatory exclusion from the schools whose tax exemptions they challenge as unlawful. Indeed, they have not alleged at any stage of this litigation that their children have ever applied or would ever apply to any private school. Rather, respondents claim a direct injury from the mere fact of the challenged Government conduct and * * * injury to their children's opportunity to receive a desegregated education. * * * Respondents * * * ask for a declaratory judgment that the challenged IRS tax-exemption practices are unlawful [and] an injunction requiring the IRS to deny tax exemptions to a considerably broader class of private schools than the class of racially discriminatory private schools. * * * In May 1977 the District Court permitted intervention as a defendant by petitioner Allen, the head of one of the private school systems identified in the complaint. [The District Court granted the defendants' motion to dismiss.]

Article III of the Constitution confines the federal courts to adjudicating actual "cases" and "controversies." * * * The several doctrines that have grown up to elaborate that requirement are "founded in concern about the proper—and properly limited—role of the courts in a democratic society." *Warth v. Seldin*, 422 U.S. 490, 498 (1975). The Article III doctrine that requires a litigant to have "standing" to invoke the power of a federal court is perhaps the most important of these doctrines. "In essence the question of standing is whether the litigant is entitled to have the court decide the merits of the dispute or of particular issues." *Warth.* Standing doctrine embraces several judicially self-imposed limits on the exercise of federal jurisdiction, such as the general prohibition on a litigant's raising another person's legal rights, the rule barring adjudication of generalized grievances more appropriately addressed in the representative branches, and the requirement that a plaintiff's complaint fall within the zone of interests protected by the law invoked. The requirement of standing, however, has a core component derived directly from the Constitution. A plaintiff must allege personal injury fairly traceable to the defendant's allegedly unlawful conduct and likely to be redressed by the requested relief.

Like the prudential component, the constitutional component of standing doctrine incorporates concepts concededly not susceptible of precise definition. The injury alleged must be, for example, "distinct and palpable" and not "abstract" or "conjectural" or "hypothetical." The injury must be "fairly" traceable to the challenged action, and relief from the injury must be "likely" to follow from a favorable decision. These terms cannot be defined so as to make application of the constitutional standing requirement a mechanical exercise.

Typically, [the] standing inquiry requires careful judicial examination of a complaint's allegations to ascertain whether the particular plaintiff is entitled to an adjudication of the particular claims asserted. [The question of standing] must be answered by reference to the Art. III notion that federal courts may exercise power only "in the last resort, and as a necessity," and only when adjudication is "consistent with a system of separated powers and [the dispute is one] traditionally thought to be capable of resolution through the judicial process." *Flast v. Cohen*, 392 U.S. 83, 97 (1968).

Respondents allege two injuries in their complaint to support their standing to bring this lawsuit. First, they say that they are harmed directly by the mere fact of Government financial aid to discriminatory private schools. Second, they say that the federal tax exemptions to racially discriminatory private schools in their communities impair their ability to have their public schools desegregated. We conclude that neither suffices to support respondents' standing. The first fails under clear precedents of this Court because it does not constitute judicially cognizable injury. The second fails because the alleged injury is not fairly traceable to the assertedly unlawful conduct of the IRS.[19]

---

19 The "fairly traceable" and "redressability" components of the constitutional standing inquiry were initially articulated by this Court as two facets of a single causation requirement. To the extent there is a difference, it is that the former examines the causal connection between the assertedly unlawful conduct and the alleged injury, whereas the latter examines the causal connection between the alleged injury and the judicial relief requested. Cases such as this, in which the relief requested goes well beyond the violation of law alleged, illustrate why it is important to keep the inquiries separate if

Respondents' first claim of injury can be interpreted in two ways. It might be a claim simply to have the Government avoid the violation of law alleged in respondents' complaint. Alternatively, it might be a claim of stigmatic injury, or denigration, suffered by all members of a racial group when the Government discriminates on the basis of race. Under neither interpretation is this claim of injury judicially cognizable.

**Food for Thought**

The Court seemed to suggest that disputes by persons who simply disagree with the government's choices should be resolved in the political, rather than the judicial, arena. But aren't the plaintiffs in this case contending that the very question that they raise—whether the IRS is properly following the law as mandated by Congress—has already been decided by Congress in the political arena?

This Court has repeatedly held that an asserted right to have the Government act in accordance with law is not sufficient, standing alone, to confer jurisdiction on a federal court. * * * "[A]ssertion of a right to a particular kind of Government conduct, which the Government has violated by acting differently, cannot alone satisfy the requirements of Art. III without draining those requirements of meaning." *Valley Forge Christian College v. Americans United for Separation of Church and State, Inc.*, 454 U.S. 464, 483 (1982). Respondents here have no standing to complain simply that their Government is violating the law.

Neither do they have standing to litigate their claims based on the stigmatizing injury often caused by racial discrimination. There can be no doubt that this sort of noneconomic injury is one of the most serious consequences of discriminatory government action and is sufficient in some circumstances to support standing. Our cases make clear, however, that such injury accords a basis for standing only to "those persons who are personally denied equal treatment" by the challenged discriminatory conduct.

The consequences of recognizing respondents' standing on the basis of their first claim of injury illustrate why our cases plainly hold that such injury is not judicially cognizable. If the abstract stigmatic injury were cognizable, standing would extend nationwide to all members of the particular racial groups against which the Government was alleged to be discriminating by its grant of a tax exemption to a racially discriminatory school, regardless of the location of that school. * * * A black person in Hawaii could challenge the grant of a tax exemption to a racially discriminatory school in Maine. Recognition of standing in such circumstances would transform the federal courts into "no more than a vehicle for the vindication of the value

---

the "redressability" component is to focus on the requested relief. Even if the relief respondents request might have a substantial effect on the desegregation of public schools, whatever deficiencies exist in the opportunities for desegregated education for respondents' children might not be traceable to IRS violations of law—grants of tax exemptions to racially discriminatory schools in respondents' communities.

interests of concerned bystanders." *United States v. SCRAP*, 412 U.S. 669, 687 (1973). Constitutional limits on the role of the federal courts preclude such a transformation.

It is in their complaint's second claim of injury that respondents allege harm to a concrete, personal interest that can support standing in some circumstances. The injury they identify—their children's diminished ability to receive an education in a racially integrated school—is, beyond any doubt, not only judicially cognizable but * * * one of the most serious injuries recognized in our legal system. Despite the constitutional importance of curing the injury alleged by respondents, however, [it] cannot support standing because the injury alleged is not fairly traceable to the Government conduct respondents challenge as unlawful.

The illegal conduct challenged by respondents is the IRS's grant of tax exemptions to some racially discriminatory schools. The line of causation between that conduct and desegregation of respondents' schools is attenuated at best. * * * It is, first, uncertain how many racially discriminatory private schools are in fact receiving tax exemptions. Moreover, it is entirely speculative, as respondents themselves conceded in the Court of Appeals, whether withdrawal of a tax exemption from any particular school would lead the school to change its policies. It is just as speculative whether any given parent of a child attending such a private school would decide to transfer the child to public school as a result of any changes in educational or financial policy made by the private school once it was threatened with loss of tax-exempt status. It is also pure speculation whether, in a particular community, a large enough number of the numerous relevant school officials and parents would reach decisions that collectively would have a significant impact on the racial composition of the public schools.

The links in the chain of causation between the challenged Government conduct and the asserted injury are far too weak for the chain as a whole to sustain respondents' standing. * * * "Carried to its logical end, [respondents'] approach would have the federal courts as virtually continuing monitors of the wisdom and soundness of Executive action; such a role is appropriate for the Congress acting through its committees and the 'power of the purse'; it is not the role of the judiciary, absent actual present or immediately threatened injury resulting from unlawful governmental action." *Laird v. Tatum*, 408 U.S. 1, 15 (1972). When transported into the Art. III context, that principle, grounded as it is in the idea of separation of powers, counsels against recognizing standing in a case brought, not to enforce specific legal obligations whose violation works a direct harm, but to seek a restructuring of the apparatus established by the Executive Branch to fulfill its legal duties. The Constitution, after all, assigns to the Executive Branch, and not to the Judicial Branch, the duty to "take Care that the Laws be faithfully executed." U.S. Const., Art. II, § 3. We could not recognize respondents' standing in this case without running afoul of that structural principle.

[JUSTICE BRENNAN's dissenting opinion has been omitted.]

JUSTICE STEVENS, with whom JUSTICE BLACKMUN joins, dissenting.

Respondents, the parents of black school-children, have alleged that their children are unable to attend fully desegregated schools because large numbers of white children in the areas in which respondents reside attend private schools which do not admit minority children. The Court [and I] agree that this is an adequate allegation of "injury in fact." * * * This kind of injury may be actionable whether it is caused by the exclusion of black children from public schools or by an official policy of encouraging white children to attend nonpublic schools. A subsidy for the withdrawal of a white child can have the same effect as a penalty for admitting a black child. * * * The critical question in these cases, therefore, is whether respondents have alleged that the Government has created that kind of subsidy.

"Both tax exemptions and tax deductibility are a form of subsidy * * *. A tax exemption has much the same effect as a cash grant to the organization of the amount of tax it would have to pay on its income. Deductible contributions are similar to cash grants of the amount of a portion of the individual's contributions." *Regan v. Taxation With Representation of Washington*, 461 U.S. 540, 544 (1983). The purpose of this scheme, like the purpose of any subsidy, is to promote the activity subsidized * * *. If the granting of preferential tax treatment would "encourage" private segregated schools to conduct their "charitable" activities, it must follow that the withdrawal of the treatment would "discourage" them * * *.

This causation analysis is nothing more than a restatement of elementary economics: when something becomes more expensive, less of it will be purchased. [The tax-exemption provisions] are premised on that recognition. If racially discriminatory private schools lose the "cash grants" that flow from the operation of the statutes, the education they provide will become more expensive and hence less of their services will be purchased. Conversely, maintenance of these tax benefits makes an education in segregated private schools relatively more attractive, by decreasing its cost. Accordingly, without tax-exempt status, private schools will either not be competitive in terms of cost, or have to change their admissions policies, hence reducing their competitiveness for parents seeking "a racially segregated alternative" to public schools, which is what respondents have alleged many white parents in desegregating school districts seek. In either event the process of desegregation will be advanced * * *. Thus, the laws of economics, not to mention the laws of Congress embodied in [the tax code], compel the conclusion that the injury respondents have alleged—the increased segregation of their children's schools because of the ready availability of private schools that admit whites only—will be redressed if these schools' operations are inhibited through the denial of preferential tax treatment.

The Court could mean one of three things by its invocation of the separation of powers. First, it could simply be expressing the idea that if the plaintiff lacks Art. III standing to bring a lawsuit, then there is no "case or controversy" within the meaning of Art. III and hence the matter is not within the area of responsibility assigned to the Judiciary by the Constitution. * * * While there can be no quarrel with this proposition, in itself it provides no guidance for determining if the injury respondents have alleged is fairly traceable to the conduct they have challenged. Second, the Court could be saying that it will require a more direct causal connection when it is troubled by the separation of powers implications of the case before it. That approach confuses the standing doctrine with the justiciability of the issues that respondents seek to raise. The purpose of the standing inquiry is to measure the plaintiff's stake in the outcome, not whether a court has the authority to provide it with the outcome it seeks. Third, the Court could be saying that it will not treat as legally cognizable injuries that stem from an administrative decision concerning how enforcement resources will be allocated. * * * However, as the Court also recognizes, this principle does not apply when suit is brought "to enforce specific legal obligations whose violation works a direct harm." * * * Here, respondents contend that the IRS is violating a specific constitutional limitation on its enforcement discretion. There is a solid basis for that contention.

Deciding whether the Treasury has violated a specific legal limitation on its enforcement discretion does not intrude upon the prerogatives of the Executive, for in so deciding we are merely saying "what the law is." Surely the question whether the Constitution or the Code limits enforcement discretion is one within the Judiciary's competence * * *.

---

## Points for Discussion

### *a. Standing and the Right to Obtain Judicial Review*

In cases involving challenges to federal agency action, there are two basic sources of standing doctrine. First, the APA states that "[a] person suffering legal wrong because of agency action, or adversely affected or aggrieved by agency action within the meaning of a relevant statute, is entitled to judicial review thereof." 5 U.S.C. § 702. Under this provision, by negative implication, a person who has not suffered legal wrong or been adversely affected by agency action is not entitled to judicial review of some agency action. Second, Article III of the U.S. Constitution states that the judicial power extends to various "[c]ases" and "[c]ontroversies," which suggests (also by negative implication) that federal courts cannot adjudicate anything other than a proper case or controversy. The Court in *Allen* focused on the constitutional standard, which (in the Court's view) provides the minimum requirements for invoking the judicial power.

What is the justification for a standing requirement? Is it to ensure that the plaintiff has a sufficient stake in the outcome so that the issues will be fully developed in the litigation? If so, is there reason to think that the parents who filed the suit in *Allen* didn't have a sufficient stake in the outcome? Or is the justification to enforce separation-of-powers norms by ensuring that courts do not micromanage the decisions of the Executive Branch? If so, is it problematic that a different plaintiff—say, the headmaster of a private school that does not discriminate on the basis of race but that must compete for students with tax-exempt schools that do—would have standing to assert the identical challenge to the federal regulation that the plaintiffs in *Allen* attempted to assert? In reaching the merits in such a suit, wouldn't the Court be acting as the monitor of "the wisdom and soundness of Executive action"?

#### *b. Injury and Causation*

The Article III standing test requires that the plaintiff allege an "injury in fact" and demonstrate that the injury is "fairly traceable" to the challenged conduct and would be likely to be redressed by the requested relief. The latter two requirements are, loosely speaking, a causation requirement: in order to establish standing, the plaintiff must demonstrate that the government's action is in some meaningful way responsible for the injury.

In concluding that the plaintiffs' injury—to their children's ability to get an integrated public-school education—was not fairly traceable to the agency's lax standards about tax-exempt status, what assumptions did the Court make about the ordinary effects of government action on private conduct? Consider the view of a scholar (and later federal judge) closely associated with the law and economics school of legal analysis:

> "[I]t is hard to take seriously the claim that enforcement of legal rules does not affect bystanders. The rule against murder is designed to prevent other people from slaying me, as well as others, and I suffer an injury if the police announce that they will no longer enforce that rule in my neighborhood. I will keep off the streets, hire guards, pay for locks, and still face an increased chance of being killed. Only a judge who secretly believes that the law does not influence behavior would find no injury in fact. Someone who feeds me a poison that increases my chances of dying next year has injured me, even if I am neither dead nor sure to die, and I may recover damages from him. The reduction in my expected life span is a real injury. This is the basis of recovery in many mass tort cases. The same reasoning establishes injury in fact when the government declines to enforce a law that was designed in part for my benefit. The court cannot know that any identified plaintiff will be better off if the law is enforced, but the law is about probabilities, not certainties. A plaintiff need not show a sure gain from winning in order to prove that some probability of gain is better than none, and thus he suffers injury in fact."

Frank H. Easterbrook, *Foreword: The Court and the Economic System*, 98 HARV. L. REV. 4, 40 (1984). Do you agree with Judge Easterbrook's critique?

## *Lujan v. Defenders of Wildlife*

504 U.S. 555 (1992)

Justice Scalia delivered the opinion of the Court with respect to Parts I, II, III-A, and IV, and an opinion with respect to Part III-B, in which The Chief Justice, Justice White, and Justice Thomas join.

### I.

The [Endangered Species Act of 1973 (ESA), 16 U.S.C. § 1536] seeks to protect species of animals against threats to their continuing existence caused by man. The ESA instructs the Secretary of the Interior to promulgate by regulation a list of those species which are either endangered or threatened under enumerated criteria, and to define the critical habitat of these species. Section 7(a)(2) of the Act then provides, in pertinent part: "Each Federal agency shall, in consultation with and with the assistance of the Secretary [of the Interior], insure that any action authorized, funded, or carried out by such agency [is] not likely to jeopardize the continued existence of any endangered species or threatened species or result in the destruction or adverse modification of [critical] habitat[s] of such species * * *."

**Make the Connection**

We saw this provision of the Endangered Species Act in Chapter 2, when we considered the Court's decision in *Tennessee Valley Authority v. Hill.*

[In 1986, the Fish and Wildlife Service and the National Marine Fisheries Service, on behalf of the Secretary of the Interior and the Secretary of Commerce respectively, promulgated a joint regulation] interpreting § 7(a)(2) to require consultation only for actions taken in the United States or on the high seas * * *. Shortly thereafter, respondents, organizations dedicated to wildlife conservation and other environmental causes, filed this action against the Secretary of the Interior, seeking a declaratory judgment that the [regulation] is in error as to the geographic scope of § 7(a)(2) and an injunction requiring the Secretary to promulgate a new regulation restoring the initial interpretation.

### II.

Over the years, our cases have established that the irreducible constitutional minimum of standing contains three elements. First, the plaintiff must have suffered an "injury in fact"—an invasion of a legally protected interest which is (a) concrete and particularized, and (b) "actual or imminent, not 'conjectural' or 'hypothetical.' " Second, there must be a causal connection between the injury and the conduct complained of—the injury has to be "fairly [traceable] to the challenged action of the defendant, and not [the result of] the independent action of some third party not before the court." Third, it must be "likely," as opposed to merely "speculative," that the injury will be "redressed by a favorable decision."

When the suit is one challenging the legality of government action or inaction, the nature and extent of facts that must be averred (at the summary judgment stage) or proved (at the trial stage) in order to establish standing depends considerably upon whether the plaintiff is himself an object of the action (or forgone action) at issue. If he is, there is ordinarily little question that the action or inaction has caused him injury, and that a judgment preventing or requiring the action will redress it. When, however, as in this case, a plaintiff's asserted injury arises from the government's allegedly unlawful regulation (or lack of regulation) of *someone else,* much more is needed. In that circumstance, causation and redressability ordinarily hinge on the response of the regulated (or regulable) third party to the government action or inaction—and perhaps on the response of others as well. * * * Thus, when the plaintiff is not himself the object of the government action or inaction he challenges, standing is not precluded, but it is ordinarily "substantially more difficult" to establish. *Allen v. Wright*, 468 U.S. 737 (1984).

**Take Note**

The Court says here that persons directly regulated by the government are much more likely to be able to establish standing to challenge the regulation than are persons who are beneficiaries of the government's regulation of others. Why might this be so? Does this distinction presuppose some theory about what the government's proper regulatory role is—a theory that we might expect to find embodied in the very statutes on which plaintiffs such as those in *Lujan* rely?

### III.

### A.

Respondents' claim to injury is that the lack of consultation with respect to certain funded activities abroad "increas[es] the rate of extinction of endangered and threatened species." Of course, the desire to use or observe an animal species, even for purely esthetic purposes, is undeniably a cognizable interest for purpose of standing. See, e.g., *Sierra Club v. Morton*, 405 U.S. 727 (1972). "But the 'injury in fact' test requires more than an injury to a cognizable interest. It requires that the party seeking review be himself among the injured." *Id.* To survive the Secretary's summary judgment motion, respondents had to submit affidavits or other evidence showing, through specific facts, not only that listed species were in fact being threatened by funded activities abroad, but also that one or more of respondents' members would thereby be "directly" affected apart from their " 'special interest' in [the] subject."

[The] Court of Appeals focused on the affidavits of two Defenders' members—Joyce Kelly and Amy Skilbred. Ms. Kelly stated that she traveled to Egypt in 1986 and "observed the traditional habitat of the endangered nile crocodile there and intend[s] to do so again, and hope[s] to observe the crocodile directly." * * * Ms. Skilbred averred that she traveled to Sri Lanka in 1981 and "observed [the] habitat" of "endangered species such as the Asian elephant and the leopard" at what is now the site of [a] project funded by the Agency for International Development (AID), although she "was unable to see any of the endangered species." [She alleged that the project threatened endangered species, and that the threat] harmed her because she "intend[s] to return to Sri Lanka in the future and hope[s] to be more fortunate in spotting at least the endangered elephant and leopard." When Ms. Skilbred was asked at a subsequent deposition if and when she had any plans to return to Sri Lanka, she reiterated that "I intend to go back to Sri Lanka," but confessed that she had no current plans: "I don't know [when]. There is a civil war going on right now. * * * Not next year, I will say. In the future."

We shall assume for the sake of argument that these affidavits contain facts showing that certain agency-funded projects threaten listed species—though that is questionable. They plainly contain no facts, however, showing how damage to the species will produce "imminent" injury to Mses. Kelly and Skilbred. That the women "had visited" the areas of the projects before the projects commenced proves nothing. * * * And the affiants' profession of an "inten[t]" to return to the places they had visited before—where they will presumably, this time, be deprived of the opportunity to observe animals of the endangered species—is simply not enough. Such "some day" intentions—without any description of concrete plans, or indeed even any specification of *when* the some day will be—do not support a finding of the "actual or imminent" injury that our cases require.

Besides relying upon the Kelly and Skilbred affidavits, respondents propose a series of novel standing theories. The first, inelegantly styled "ecosystem nexus," proposes that any person who uses *any part* of a "contiguous ecosystem" adversely affected by a funded activity has standing even if the activity is located a great distance away. [But] a plaintiff claiming injury from environmental damage must use the area affected by the challenged activity and not an area roughly "in the vicinity" of it. * * * To say that the Act protects ecosystems is not to say that the Act creates (if it were possible) rights of action in persons who have not been injured in fact, that is, persons who use portions of an ecosystem not perceptibly affected by the unlawful action in question.

Respondents' other theories are called, alas, the "animal nexus" approach, whereby anyone who has an interest in studying or seeing the endangered animals anywhere on the globe has standing; and the "vocational nexus" approach, under which anyone with a professional interest in such animals can sue. Under these theories, anyone who goes to see Asian elephants in the Bronx Zoo, and anyone who is a keeper of Asian elephants in the Bronx Zoo, has standing to sue because the Director of AID did not consult with the Secretary regarding the AID-funded project in Sri Lanka. This is beyond all reason. Standing is not "an ingenious academic exercise in the conceivable," but as we have said requires, at the summary judgment stage, a factual showing of perceptible harm. It is clear that the person who observes or works with a particular animal threatened by a federal decision is facing perceptible harm, since the very subject of his interest will no longer exist. It is even plausible—though it goes to the outermost limit of plausibility—to think that a person who observes or works with animals of a particular species in the very area of the world where that species is threatened by a federal decision is facing such harm, since some animals that might have been the subject of his interest will no longer exist. It goes beyond the limit, however, and into pure speculation and fantasy, to say that anyone who observes or works with an endangered species, anywhere in the world, is appreciably harmed by a single project affecting some portion of that species with which he has no more specific connection.

**B.**

> **Take Note**
>
> This part of the Court's opinion was only for a plurality of the Justices.

Besides failing to show injury, respondents failed to demonstrate redressability. Instead of attacking the separate decisions to fund particular projects allegedly causing them harm, respondents chose to challenge a more generalized level of Government action (rules regarding consultation), the invalidation of which would affect all overseas projects. * * * Since the agencies funding the projects were not parties to the case, the District Court could accord relief only against the Secretary: He could be ordered to revise his regulation to require consultation for foreign projects. But this would not remedy respondents' alleged injury unless the funding agencies were bound by the Secretary's regulation, which is very much an open question. * * * The short of the matter is that redress of the only injury in fact respondents complain of requires action (termination of funding until consultation) by the individual funding agencies; and any relief the District Court could have provided in this suit against the Secretary was not likely to produce that action.

A further impediment to redressability is the fact that the agencies generally supply only a fraction of the funding for a foreign project. AID, for example, has provided less than 10% of the funding for the [Sri Lanka] project. Respondents have produced nothing to indicate that the projects they have named will either be suspended, or do less harm to listed species, if that fraction is eliminated. [I]t is entirely conjectural whether the nonagency activity that affects respondents will be altered or affected by the agency activity they seek to achieve.

## IV.

The Court of Appeals found that respondents had standing for an additional reason: because they had suffered a "procedural injury." The so-called "citizen-suit" provision of the ESA provides, in pertinent part, that "any person may commence a civil suit on his own behalf [to] enjoin any person, including the United States and any other governmental instrumentality or agency [who] is alleged to be in violation of any provision of this chapter." * * * This is not a case where plaintiffs are seeking to enforce a procedural requirement the disregard of which could impair a separate concrete interest of theirs (*e.g.,* the procedural requirement for a hearing prior to denial of their license application, or the procedural requirement for an environmental impact statement before a federal facility is constructed next door to them).[7] Nor is it simply a case where concrete injury has been suffered by many persons, as in mass fraud or mass tort situations. Nor, finally, is it the unusual case in which Congress has created a concrete private interest in the outcome of a suit against a private party for the government's benefit, by providing a cash bounty for the victorious plaintiff. Rather, the court held that the injury-in-fact requirement had been satisfied by congressional conferral upon *all* persons of an abstract, self-contained, noninstrumental "right" to have the Executive observe the procedures required by law. We reject this view.

Whether the courts were to act on their own, or at the invitation of Congress, in ignoring the concrete injury requirement described in our cases, they would be discarding a principle fundamental to the separate and distinct constitutional role of the Third Branch—one of the essential elements that identifies those "Cases" and "Controversies" that are the business of the courts rather than of the political branches. "The province of the court," as Chief Justice Marshall said in *Marbury v. Madison* "is, solely, to decide on the rights of individuals." Vindicating the *public* interest (including the public interest in Government observance of the Constitution and laws) is the function of Congress and the Chief Executive. The question presented here is whether the public interest in proper administration of the laws (specifically, in agencies' observance of a particular, statutorily prescribed procedure) can be converted into an individual right by a statute that denominates it as such, and that permits all citizens (or, for that matter, a subclass of citizens who suffer no distinctive concrete harm)

---

7 There is this much truth to the assertion that "procedural rights" are special: The person who has been accorded a procedural right to protect his concrete interests can assert that right without meeting all the normal standards for redressability and immediacy. Thus, under our case law, one living adjacent to the site for proposed construction of a federally licensed dam has standing to challenge the licensing agency's failure to prepare an environmental impact statement, even though he cannot establish with any certainty that the statement will cause the license to be withheld or altered, and even though the dam will not be completed for many years. (That is why we do not rely, in the present case, upon the Government's argument that, *even if* the other agencies were obliged to consult with the Secretary, they might not have followed his advice.) What respondents' "procedural rights" argument seeks, however, is quite different from this: standing for persons who have no concrete interests affected—persons who live (and propose to live) at the other end of the country from the dam.

to sue. If the concrete injury requirement has the separation-of-powers significance we have always said, the answer must be obvious: To permit Congress to convert the undifferentiated public interest in executive officers' compliance with the law into an "individual right" vindicable in the courts is to permit Congress to transfer from the President to the courts the Chief Executive's most important constitutional duty, to "take Care that the Laws be faithfully executed." It would enable the courts, with the permission of Congress, "to assume a position of authority over the governmental acts of another and co-equal department," and to become "virtually continuing monitors of the wisdom and soundness of Executive action." *Allen*. We have always rejected that vision of our role. We hold that respondents lack standing to bring this action.

JUSTICE KENNEDY, with whom JUSTICE SOUTER joins, concurring in part and concurring in the judgment.

Although I agree with the essential parts of the Court's analysis, I write separately to make several observations. While it may seem trivial to require that Mses. Kelly and Skilbred acquire airline tickets to the project sites or announce a date certain upon which they will return, this is not a case where it is reasonable to assume that the affiants will be using the sites on a regular basis, nor do the affiants claim to have visited the sites since the projects commenced. With respect to the Court's discussion of respondents' "ecosystem nexus," "animal nexus," and "vocational nexus" theories, I agree that on this record respondents' showing is insufficient to establish standing on any of these bases. I am not willing to foreclose the possibility, however, that in different circumstances a nexus theory similar to those proffered here might support a claim to standing. * * * In light of the conclusion that respondents have not demonstrated a concrete injury here sufficient to support standing under our precedents, I would not reach the issue of redressability that is discussed by the plurality in Part III-B.

I also join Part IV of the Court's opinion with the following observations. As Government programs and policies become more complex and farreaching, we must be sensitive to the articulation of new rights of action that do not have clear analogs in our common-law tradition. Modern litigation has progressed far from the paradigm of Marbury suing Madison to get his commission * * *. In my view, Congress has the power to define injuries and articulate chains of causation that will give rise to a case or controversy where none existed before, and I do not read the Court's opinion to suggest a contrary view. In exercising this power, however, Congress must at the very least identify the injury it seeks to vindicate and relate the injury to the class of persons entitled to bring suit. The citizen-suit provision of the Endangered Species Act does not meet these minimal requirements, because while the statute purports to confer a right on "any person [to enjoin] the United States and any other governmental instrumentality or agency [who] is alleged to be in violation of any provision of this chapter," it does not of its own force establish that there is an injury in "any person" by virtue of any "violation."

While it does not matter how many persons have been injured by the challenged action, the party bringing suit must show that the action injures him in a concrete and personal way. This requirement is not just an empty formality. It preserves the vitality of the adversarial process by assuring both that the parties before the court have an actual, as opposed to professed, stake in the outcome, and that "the legal questions presented [will] be resolved, not in the rarified atmosphere of a debating society, but in a concrete factual context conducive to a realistic appreciation of the consequences of judicial action." In addition, the requirement of concrete injury confines the Judicial Branch to its proper, limited role in the constitutional framework of Government.

JUSTICE BLACKMUN, with whom JUSTICE O'CONNOR joins, dissenting.

I think a reasonable finder of fact could conclude from the information in the affidavits and deposition testimony that either Kelly or Skilbred will soon return to the project sites, thereby satisfying the "actual or imminent" injury standard. * * * By requiring a "description of concrete plans" or "specification of *when* the some day [for a return visit] will be," the Court, in my view, demands what is likely an empty formality. No substantial barriers prevent Kelly or Skilbred from simply purchasing plane tickets to return to the Aswan and Mahaweli projects.

The Court [also] expresses concern that allowing judicial enforcement of "agencies' observance of a particular, statutorily prescribed procedure" would "transfer from the President to the courts the Chief Executive's most important constitutional duty, to 'take Care that the Laws be faithfully executed.' " In fact, the principal effect of foreclosing judicial enforcement of such procedures is to transfer power into the hands of the Executive at the expense—not of the courts—but of Congress, from which that power originates and emanates.

Under the Court's anachronistically formal view of the separation of powers, Congress legislates pure, substantive mandates and has no business structuring the procedural manner in which the Executive implements these mandates. * * * In complex regulatory areas, however, Congress often legislates, as it were, in procedural shades of gray. That is, it sets forth substantive policy goals and provides for their attainment by requiring Executive Branch officials to follow certain procedures, for example, in the form of reporting, consultation, and certification requirements.

The consultation requirement of § 7 of the Endangered Species Act is [an] action-forcing statute. Consultation is designed as an integral check on federal agency action, ensuring that such action does not go forward without full consideration of its effects on listed species. * * * Congress legislates in procedural shades of gray not to aggrandize its own power but to allow maximum Executive discretion in the attainment of Congress' legislative goals. * * * The Court never has questioned

Congress' authority to impose such procedural constraints on Executive power. Just as Congress does not violate separation of powers by structuring the procedural manner in which the Executive shall carry out the laws, surely the federal courts do not violate separation of powers when, at the very instruction and command of Congress, they enforce these procedures.

[I] cannot join the Court on what amounts to a slash-and-burn expedition through the law of environmental standing. In my view, "[t]he very essence of civil liberty certainly consists in the right of every individual to claim the protection of the laws, whenever he receives an injury." *Marbury v. Madison*. I dissent.

---

## Points for Discussion

### *a. Injury in Fact*

What criteria should the courts apply in deciding whether an alleged injury is a cognizable injury for purposes of Article III? If the point of standing doctrine is to ensure that the plaintiff has the requisite stake in the outcome such that the suit is truly an adversarial contest between interested parties, then should intangible, moral, or aesthetic injuries be cognizable in the same way that economic injuries are? Regardless of the answer to that question, should Congress be permitted to authorize people who have not suffered a cognizable injury to challenge agency action in federal court?

### *b. Standing Rules and Agency Action*

How does the Court's standing doctrine affect agency decision-making? Imagine that you are an attorney at the Consumer Products Safety Commission, which is considering adopting a rule about crib design. The agency has a limited budget and would prefer to spend as much of it as possible on scientific research (to determine optimal rules) and enforcement efforts. If you know that an aggressive rule will be subject to challenge by crib manufacturers and that a lax rule might not be subject to challenge by anyone, which rule would you be most likely to recommend? Does this suggest a problem with current standing doctrine?

### *c. The APA and the Zone-of-Interests Test*

Recall that, in addition to Article III's limitation on the judicial power, the APA provides that a person "adversely affected or aggrieved by agency action within the meaning of a relevant statute" is entitled to judicial review. 5 U.S.C. § 702. In *Ass'n of Data Processing Serv. Orgs. v. Camp*, 397 U.S. 150 (1970), the Court concluded that, to establish standing, a plaintiff must demonstrate standing under the Article III test and demonstrate that the interest she seeks to vindicate is "arguably within the zone of interests to be protected or regulated by the statute [in] question." Although the zone-of-interests test is usually easier to satisfy than the Article III test, it can be an obstacle to judicial review in some cases.

For example, in *Air Courier Conf. v. American Postal Workers Union*, 498 U.S. 517 (1991), the Court considered a challenge to a Postal Service regulation that allowed private carriers to provide overnight-delivery services for letters to foreign countries. The regulation at issue implemented a federal statute that created a statutory monopoly for the Postal Service on mail service (but that authorized certain exceptions from the monopoly). Two postal workers filed suit to challenge the rule, but the Court held that they lacked standing. The plaintiffs had suffered a cognizable injury, because their jobs would be less secure if their employer faced more competition in the market for letter delivery. But the Court held that the plaintiffs were not within the zone of interests protected by the statute, which was designed "to ensure that postal services will be provided to the citizenry at large, and not to secure employment for postal workers." How does a court know which plaintiffs are "within the zone of interests to be protected or regulated" by the statute in question?

---

## *Massachusetts v. Environmental Protection Agency*

549 U.S. 497 (2007)

JUSTICE STEVENS delivered the opinion of the Court.

Calling global warming "the most pressing environmental challenge of our time," a group of States, local governments, and private organizations alleged in a petition for certiorari that the Environmental Protection Agency (EPA) has abdicated its responsibility under the Clean Air Act to regulate the emissions of four greenhouse gases, including carbon dioxide. Specifically, petitioners asked us to answer two questions concerning the meaning of § 202(a)(1) of the Act: whether EPA has the statutory authority to regulate greenhouse gas emissions from new motor vehicles; and if so, whether its stated reasons for refusing to do so are consistent with the statute.

Section 202(a)(1) of the Clean Air Act, as added by Pub. L. 89–272, § 101(8), 79 Stat. 992, and as amended by, *inter alia,* 84 Stat. 1690 and 91 Stat. 791, 42 U.S.C. § 7521(a)(1), provides:

> "The [EPA] Administrator shall by regulation prescribe (and from time to time revise) in accordance with the provisions of this section, standards applicable to the emission of any air pollutant from any class or classes of new motor vehicles or new motor vehicle engines, which in his judgment cause, or contribute to, air pollution which may reasonably be anticipated to endanger public health or welfare . . . ."

The Act defines "air pollutant" to include "any air pollution agent or combination of such agents, including any physical, chemical, biological, radioactive . . . substance or matter which is emitted into or otherwise enters the ambient air." § 7602(g). "Welfare" is also defined broadly: among other things, it includes "effects on . . . weather . . . and climate." § 7602(h).

When Congress enacted these provisions, the study of climate change was in its infancy. In 1959, shortly after the U.S. Weather Bureau began monitoring atmospheric carbon dioxide levels, an observatory in Mauna Loa, Hawaii, recorded a mean level of 316 parts per million. This was well above the highest carbon dioxide concentration—no more than 300 parts per million—revealed in the 420,000-year-old ice-core record. By the time Congress drafted § 202(a)(1) in 1970, carbon dioxide levels had reached 325 parts per million.[10]

In the late 1970's, the Federal Government began devoting serious attention to the possibility that carbon dioxide emissions associated with human activity could provoke climate change. In 1978, Congress enacted the National Climate Program Act, 92 Stat. 601, which required the President to establish a program to "assist the Nation and the world to understand and respond to natural and man-induced climate processes and their implications," *id.,* § 3. President Carter, in turn, asked the National Research Council, the working arm of the National Academy of Sciences, to investigate the subject. The Council's response was unequivocal: "If carbon dioxide continues to increase, the study group finds no reason to doubt that climate changes will result and no reason to believe that these changes will be negligible . . . . A wait-and-see policy may mean waiting until it is too late."

Congress next addressed the issue in 1987, when it enacted the Global Climate Protection Act, Title XI of Pub. L. 100–204, 101 Stat. 1407, note following 15 U.S.C. § 2901. Finding that "manmade pollution—the release of carbon dioxide, chlorofluorocarbons, methane, and other trace gases into the atmosphere—may be producing a long-term and substantial increase in the average temperature on Earth," § 1102(1), 101 Stat. 1408, Congress directed EPA to propose to Congress a "coordinated national policy on global climate change," § 1103(b), and ordered the Secretary of State to work "through the channels of multilateral diplomacy" and coordinate diplomatic efforts to combat global warming, § 1103(c). Congress emphasized that "ongoing pollution and deforestation may be contributing now to an irreversible process" and that "[n]ecessary actions must be identified and implemented in time to protect the climate." § 1102(4).

---

10 A more dramatic rise was yet to come: In 2006, carbon dioxide levels reached 382 parts per million, a level thought to exceed the concentration of carbon dioxide in the atmosphere at any point over the past 20 million years. See Intergovernmental Panel on Climate Change, Technical Summary of Working Group I Report 39 (2001).

Meanwhile, the scientific understanding of climate change progressed. In 1990, the Intergovernmental Panel on Climate Change (IPCC), a multinational scientific body organized under the auspices of the United Nations, published its first comprehensive report on the topic. Drawing on expert opinions from across the globe, the IPCC concluded that "emissions resulting from human activities are substantially increasing the atmospheric concentrations of . . . greenhouse gases [which] will enhance the greenhouse effect, resulting on average in an additional warming of the Earth's surface."

Responding to the IPCC report, the United Nations convened the "Earth Summit" in 1992 in Rio de Janeiro. The first President Bush attended and signed the United Nations Framework Convention on Climate Change (UNFCCC), a nonbinding agreement among 154 nations to reduce atmospheric concentrations of carbon dioxide and other greenhouse gases for the purpose of "prevent[ing] dangerous anthropogenic [*i.e.*, human-induced] interference with the [Earth's] climate system." S. Treaty Doc. No. 102–38, Art. 2, p. 5, 1771 U.N.T.S. 107 (1992). The Senate unanimously ratified the treaty.

Some five years later—after the IPCC issued a second comprehensive report in 1995 concluding that "[t]he balance of evidence suggests there is a discernible human influence on global climate"—the UNFCCC signatories met in Kyoto, Japan, and adopted a protocol that assigned mandatory targets for industrialized nations to reduce greenhouse gas emissions. Because those targets did not apply to developing and heavily polluting nations such as China and India, the Senate unanimously passed a resolution expressing its sense that the United States should not enter into the Kyoto Protocol. See S. Res. 98, 105th Cong., 1st Sess. (July 25, 1997) (as passed). President Clinton did not submit the protocol to the Senate for ratification.

On October 20, 1999, a group of 19 private organizations filed a rulemaking petition asking EPA to regulate "greenhouse gas emissions from new motor vehicles under § 202 of the Clean Air Act." Petitioners maintained that 1998 was the "warmest year on record"; that carbon dioxide, methane, nitrous oxide, and hydrofluorocarbons are "heat trapping greenhouse gases"; that greenhouse gas emissions have significantly accelerated climate change; and that the IPCC's 1995 report warned that "carbon dioxide remains the most important contributor to [manmade] forcing of climate change." The petition further alleged that climate change will have serious adverse effects on human health and the environment. As to EPA's statutory authority, the petition observed that the Agency itself had already confirmed that it had the power to regulate carbon dioxide. In 1998, Jonathan Z. Cannon, then EPA's general counsel, prepared a legal opinion concluding that "CO2 emissions are within the scope of EPA's authority to regulate," even as he recognized that EPA had so far declined to exercise that authority. Cannon's successor, Gary S. Guzy, reiterated that opinion before a congressional committee just two weeks before the rulemaking petition was filed.

Fifteen months after the petition's submission, EPA requested public comment on "all the issues raised in [the] petition," adding a "particular" request for comments on "any scientific, technical, legal, economic or other aspect of these issues that may be relevant to EPA's consideration of this petition." 66 Fed. Reg. 7486, 7487 (2001). EPA received more than 50,000 comments over the next five months. See 68 Fed. Reg. 52924 (2003).

Before the close of the comment period, the White House sought "assistance in identifying the areas in the science of climate change where there are the greatest certainties and uncertainties" from the National Research Council, asking for a response "as soon as possible." The result was a 2001 report titled Climate Change Science: An Analysis of Some Key Questions (NRC Report), which, drawing heavily on the 1995 IPCC report, concluded that "[g]reenhouse gases are accumulating in Earth's atmosphere as a result of human activities, causing surface air temperatures and subsurface ocean temperatures to rise. Temperatures are, in fact, rising." NRC Report 1.

On September 8, 2003, EPA entered an order denying the rulemaking petition. 68 Fed. Reg. 52922. The Agency gave two reasons for its decision: (1) that contrary to the opinions of its former general counsels, the Clean Air Act does not authorize EPA to issue mandatory regulations to address global climate change, see *id.*, at 52925–52929; and (2) that even if the Agency had the authority to set greenhouse gas emission standards, it would be unwise to do so at this time, *id.*, at 52929–52931.

In concluding that it lacked statutory authority over greenhouse gases, EPA observed that Congress "was well aware of the global climate change issue when it last comprehensively amended the [Clean Air Act] in 1990," yet it declined to adopt a proposed amendment establishing binding emissions limitations. *Id.*, at 52926. Congress instead chose to authorize further investigation into climate change. *Ibid.* (citing §§ 103(g) and 602(e) of the Clean Air Act Amendments of 1990, 104 Stat. 2652, 2703, 42 U.S.C. §§ 7403(g)(1) and 7671a(e)). EPA further reasoned that Congress' "specially tailored solutions to global atmospheric issues," 68 Fed. Reg. 52926—in particular, its 1990 enactment of a comprehensive scheme to regulate pollutants that depleted the ozone layer, see Title VI, 104 Stat. 2649, 42 U.S.C. §§ 7671–7671q—counseled against reading the general authorization of § 202(a)(1) to confer regulatory authority over greenhouse gases.

EPA stated that it was "urged on in this view," 68 Fed. Reg. 529, by this Court's decision in *FDA v. Brown & Williamson Tobacco Corp.*, 529 U.S. 120 (2000). In that case, relying on "tobacco['s] unique political history," *id.*, at 159, we invalidated the Food and Drug Administration's reliance on its general

**Make the Connection**

We will consider the Court's decision in *Brown & Williamson*, and the so-called "major questions doctrine," in Chapter 8.

authority to regulate drugs as a basis for asserting jurisdiction over an "industry constituting a significant portion of the American economy," *ibid.*

EPA reasoned that climate change had its own "political history": Congress designed the original Clean Air Act to address *local* air pollutants rather than a substance that "is fairly consistent in its concentration throughout the *world's* atmosphere," 68 Fed. Reg. 52927; declined in 1990 to enact proposed amendments to force EPA to set carbon dioxide emission standards for motor vehicles, *ibid.* (citing H.R. 5966, 101st Cong., 2d Sess. (1990)); and addressed global climate change in other legislation, 68 Fed. Reg. 52927. Because of this political history, and because imposing emission limitations on greenhouse gases would have even greater economic and political repercussions than regulating tobacco, EPA was persuaded that it lacked the power to do so. In essence, EPA concluded that climate change was so important that unless Congress spoke with exacting specificity, it could not have meant the Agency to address it.

Having reached that conclusion, EPA believed it followed that greenhouse gases cannot be "air pollutants" within the meaning of the Act. The Agency bolstered this conclusion by explaining that if carbon dioxide were an air pollutant, the only feasible method of reducing tailpipe emissions would be to improve fuel economy. But because Congress has already created detailed mandatory fuel economy standards subject to Department of Transportation (DOT) administration, the Agency concluded that EPA regulation would either conflict with those standards or be superfluous. *Id.*, at 52929.

Even assuming that it had authority over greenhouse gases, EPA explained in detail why it would refuse to exercise that authority. The Agency began by recognizing that the concentration of greenhouse gases has dramatically increased as a result of human activities, and acknowledged the attendant increase in global surface air temperatures. *Id.*, at 52930. EPA nevertheless gave controlling importance to the NRC Report's statement that a causal link between the two "cannot be unequivocally established." *Ibid.* (quoting NRC Report 17). Given that residual uncertainty, EPA concluded that regulating greenhouse gas emissions would be unwise. 68 Fed. Reg. 52930.

The Agency furthermore characterized any EPA regulation of motor-vehicle emissions as a "piecemeal approach" to climate change, *id.*, at 52931, and stated that such regulation would conflict with the President's "comprehensive approach" to the problem. That approach involves additional support for technological innovation, the creation of nonregulatory programs to encourage voluntary private-sector reductions in greenhouse gas emissions, and further research on climate change—not actual regulation. According to EPA, unilateral EPA regulation of motor-vehicle greenhouse gas emissions might also hamper the President's ability to persuade key developing countries to reduce greenhouse gas emissions. *Id.*, at 52931.

Petitioners, now joined by intervenor States and local governments, sought review of EPA's order in the United States Court of Appeals for the District of Columbia Circuit. [The court, with one judge dissenting, denied the petition for review.]

EPA maintains that because greenhouse gas emissions inflict widespread harm, the doctrine of standing presents an insuperable jurisdictional obstacle. We do not agree. At bottom, "the gist of the question of standing" is whether petitioners have "such a personal stake in the outcome of the controversy as to assure that concrete adverseness which sharpens the presentation of issues upon which the court so largely depends for illumination." *Baker v. Carr*, 369 U.S. 186, 204 (1962). * * *

To ensure the proper adversarial presentation, *Lujan v. Defenders of Wildlife*, 504 U.S. 555, 560–561 (1992), holds that a litigant must demonstrate that it has suffered a concrete and particularized injury that is either actual or imminent, that the injury is fairly traceable to the defendant, and that it is likely that a favorable decision will redress that injury. However, a litigant to whom Congress has "accorded a procedural right to protect his concrete interests," *id.*, at 572, n. 7—here, the right to challenge agency action unlawfully withheld, § 7607(b)(1)—"can assert that right without meeting all the normal standards for redressability and immediacy," *ibid.* When a litigant is vested with a procedural right, that litigant has standing if there is some possibility that the requested relief will prompt the injury-causing party to reconsider the decision that allegedly harmed the litigant.

* * * We stress here [the] special position and interest of Massachusetts. It is of considerable relevance that the party seeking review here is a sovereign State and not, as it was in *Lujan,* a private individual. Well before the creation of the modern administrative state, we recognized that States are not normal litigants for the purposes of invoking federal jurisdiction. As Justice Holmes explained in *Georgia v. Tennessee Copper Co.*, 206 U.S. 230, 237 (1907), a case in which Georgia sought to protect its citizens from air pollution originating outside its borders:

> "The case has been argued largely as if it were one between two private parties; but it is not. The very elements that would be relied upon in a suit between fellow-citizens as a ground for equitable relief are wanting here. The State owns very little of the territory alleged to be affected, and the damage to it capable of estimate in money, possibly, at least, is small. This is a suit by a State for an injury to it in its capacity of *quasi*-sovereign. In that capacity the State has an interest independent of and behind the titles of its citizens, in all the earth and air within its domain. It has the last word as to whether its mountains shall be stripped of their forests and its inhabitants shall breathe pure air."

Just as Georgia's independent interest "in all the earth and air within its domain" supported federal jurisdiction a century ago, so too does Massachusetts' well-founded desire to preserve its sovereign territory today. That Massachusetts does in fact own a great deal of the "territory alleged to be affected" only reinforces the conclusion that its stake in the outcome of this case is sufficiently concrete to warrant the exercise of federal judicial power.

When a State enters the Union, it surrenders certain sovereign prerogatives. Massachusetts cannot invade Rhode Island to force reductions in greenhouse gas emissions, it cannot negotiate an emissions treaty with China or India, and in some circumstances the exercise of its police powers to reduce in-state motor-vehicle emissions might well be pre-empted. These sovereign prerogatives are now lodged in the Federal Government, and Congress has ordered EPA to protect Massachusetts (among others) by prescribing standards applicable to the "emission of any air pollutant from any class or classes of new motor vehicle engines, which in [the Administrator's] judgment cause, or contribute to, air pollution which may reasonably be anticipated to endanger public health or welfare." 42 U.S.C. § 7521(a)(1). Congress has moreover recognized a concomitant procedural right to challenge the rejection of its rulemaking petition as arbitrary and capricious. § 7607(b)(1). Given that procedural right and Massachusetts' stake in protecting its quasi-sovereign interests, the Commonwealth is entitled to special solicitude in our standing analysis.

With that in mind, it is clear that petitioners' submissions as they pertain to Massachusetts have satisfied the most demanding standards of the adversarial process. EPA's steadfast refusal to regulate greenhouse gas emissions presents a risk of harm to Massachusetts that is both "actual" and "imminent." There is, moreover, a "substantial likelihood that the judicial relief requested" will prompt EPA to take steps to reduce that risk. *Duke Power Co. v. Carolina Environmental Study Group, Inc.*, 438 U.S. 59, 79 (1978).

* * * According to petitioners' unchallenged affidavits, global sea levels rose somewhere between 10 and 20 centimeters over the 20th century as a result of global warming. These rising seas have already begun to swallow Massachusetts' coastal land. Because the Commonwealth "owns a substantial portion of the state's coastal property," it has alleged a particularized injury in its capacity as a landowner. The severity of that injury will only increase over the course of the next century * * *. EPA does not dispute the existence of a causal connection between manmade greenhouse gas emissions and global warming. At a minimum, therefore, EPA's refusal to regulate such emissions "contributes" to Massachusetts' injuries.

EPA nevertheless maintains that its decision not to regulate greenhouse gas emissions from new motor vehicles contributes so insignificantly to petitioners' injuries that the Agency cannot be haled into federal court to answer for them. For the same reason, EPA does not believe that any realistic possibility exists that the relief petitioners seek would mitigate global climate change and remedy their injuries, * * * because predicted increases in greenhouse gas emissions from developing nations, particularly China and India, are likely to offset any marginal domestic decrease.

But EPA overstates its case. Its argument rests on the erroneous assumption that a small incremental step, because it is incremental, can never be attacked in a federal judicial forum. Yet accepting that premise would doom most challenges to regulatory action. Agencies, like legislatures, do not generally resolve massive problems in one fell regulatory swoop. They instead whittle away at them over time, refining their preferred approach as circumstances change and as they develop a more nuanced understanding of how best to proceed. That a first step might be tentative does not by itself support the notion that federal courts lack jurisdiction to determine whether that step conforms to law.

**Food for Thought**

What was the injury that Massachusetts sought to redress in this suit? Was that injury "particularized"? If so, was it fairly traceable to EPA's failure to regulate? Should it matter that the agency has no authority to restrict carbon dioxide emissions in other countries? If so, then would anyone have standing to challenge the agency's failure to regulate?

And reducing domestic automobile emissions is hardly a tentative step. [T]he United States transportation sector emits an enormous quantity of carbon dioxide into the atmosphere—according to [an expert's] affidavit, more than 1.7 billion metric tons in 1999 alone. That accounts for more than 6% of worldwide carbon dioxide emissions. * * * Judged by any standard, U.S. motor-vehicle emissions make a meaningful contribution to greenhouse gas concentrations and hence, according to petitioners, to global warming.

While it may be true that regulating motor-vehicle emissions will not by itself *reverse* global warming, it by no means follows that we lack jurisdiction to decide whether EPA has a duty to take steps to *slow* or *reduce* it. See also *Larson v. Valente*, 456 U.S. 228, 244, n. 15 (1982) ("[A] plaintiff satisfies the redressability requirement when he shows that a favorable decision will relieve a discrete injury to himself. He need not show that a favorable decision will relieve his *every* injury"). Because of the enormity of the potential consequences associated with manmade climate change, the fact that the effectiveness of a remedy might be delayed during the (relatively short) time it takes for a new motor-vehicle fleet to replace an older one is essentially irrelevant. Nor is it dispositive that developing countries such as China and India are poised to increase greenhouse gas emissions substantially over the next century: A reduction in domestic emissions would slow the pace of global emissions increases, no matter what happens elsewhere. * * * We therefore hold that petitioners have standing to challenge EPA's denial of their rulemaking petition.

The scope of our review of the merits of the statutory issues is narrow. As we have repeated time and again, an agency has broad discretion to choose how best to marshal its limited resources and personnel to carry out its delegated responsibilities.

That discretion is at its height when the agency decides not to bring an enforcement action. Therefore, in *Heckler v. Chaney*, 470 U.S. 821 (1985), we held that an agency's refusal to initiate enforcement proceedings is not ordinarily subject to judicial review. Some debate remains, however, as to the rigor with which we review an agency's denial of a petition for rulemaking.

There are key differences between a denial of a petition for rulemaking and an agency's decision not to initiate an enforcement action. In contrast to nonenforcement decisions, agency refusals to initiate rulemaking "are less frequent, more apt to involve legal as opposed to factual analysis, and subject to special formalities, including a public explanation." [See 5 U.S.C. § 555(e).] They moreover arise out of denials of petitions for rulemaking which (at least in the circumstances here) the affected party had an undoubted procedural right to file in the first instance. Refusals to promulgate rules are thus susceptible to judicial review, though such review is "extremely limited" and "highly deferential." *National Customs Brokers & Forwarders Assn. of America, Inc. v. United States*, 883 F.2d 93, 96 (D.C. Cir. 1989).

EPA concluded in its denial of the petition for rulemaking that it lacked authority [to] regulate new vehicle emissions because carbon dioxide is not an "air pollutant" as that term is defined in § 7602. In the alternative, it concluded that even if it possessed authority, it would decline to do so because regulation would conflict with other administration priorities. As discussed earlier, the Clean Air Act expressly permits review of such an action. § 7607(b)(1). We therefore "may reverse any such action found to be . . . arbitrary, capricious, an abuse of discretion, or otherwise not in accordance with law." § 7607(d)(9).

[The Court concluded that carbon dioxide was an air pollutant within the meaning of the Clean Air Act and that EPA's refusal to regulate its emission was "arbitrary, capricious, . . . or otherwise not in accordance with law."] We hold [that] EPA must ground its reasons for action or inaction in the statute. [Reversed.]

CHIEF JUSTICE ROBERTS, with whom JUSTICE SCALIA, JUSTICE THOMAS, and JUSTICE ALITO join, dissenting.

It is not at all clear how the Court's "special solicitude" for Massachusetts plays out in the standing analysis, except as an implicit concession that petitioners cannot establish standing on traditional terms. But the status of Massachusetts as a State cannot compensate for petitioners' failure to demonstrate injury in fact, causation, and redressability.

When the Court actually applies the three-part [standing] test, it focuses [on] the Commonwealth's asserted loss of coastal land as the injury in fact. If petitioners rely on loss of land as the Article III injury, however, they must ground the rest of the standing analysis in that specific injury. That alleged injury must be "concrete and particularized" and "distinct and palpable." Central to this concept of "particularized" injury is the requirement that a plaintiff be affected in a "personal and individual way," *Defenders of Wildlife*, 504 U.S., at 560, n. 1, and seek relief that "directly and tangibly benefits him" in a manner distinct from its impact on "the public at large," *id.*, at 573–574. Without "particularized injury, there can be no confidence of 'a real need to exercise the power of judicial review' or that relief can be framed 'no broader than required by the precise facts to which the court's ruling would be applied.' " *Warth v. Seldin*, 422 U.S. 490, 508 (1975).

The very concept of global warming seems inconsistent with this particularization requirement. Global warming is a phenomenon "harmful to humanity at large," and the redress petitioners seek is focused no more on them than on the public generally—it is literally to change the atmosphere around the world.

If petitioners' particularized injury is loss of coastal land, it is also that injury that must be "actual or imminent, not conjectural or hypothetical," *Defenders of Wildlife, supra*, at 560, "real and immediate," *Los Angeles v. Lyons*, 461 U.S. 95, 102 (1983), and "certainly impending," *Whitmore v. Arkansas*, 495 U.S. 149, 158 (1990). [A]side from a single conclusory statement, there is nothing in petitioners' 43 standing declarations and accompanying exhibits to support an inference of actual loss of Massachusetts coastal land from 20th-century global sea level increases. It is pure conjecture. The Court's attempts to identify "imminent" or "certainly impending" loss of Massachusetts coastal land fares no better. [A]ccepting a century-long time horizon and a series of compounded estimates renders requirements of imminence and immediacy utterly toothless. * * *

Petitioners' reliance on Massachusetts's loss of coastal land as their injury in fact for standing purposes creates insurmountable problems for them with respect to causation and redressability. To establish standing, petitioners must show a causal connection between that specific injury and the lack of new motor vehicle greenhouse gas emission standards, and that the promulgation of such standards would likely redress that injury. [In concluding that this test is satisfied, the] Court ignores the complexities of global warming, and does so by now disregarding the "particularized" injury it relied on in step one, and using the dire nature of global warming itself as a bootstrap for finding causation and redressability. * * *

Petitioners' difficulty in demonstrating causation and redressability is not surprising given the evident mismatch between the source of their alleged injury—catastrophic global warming—and the narrow subject matter of the Clean Air Act provision at issue in this suit. The mismatch suggests that petitioners' true goal for this litigation may be more symbolic than anything else. The constitutional role of the courts, however, is to decide concrete cases—not to serve as a convenient forum for policy debates. * * *

[Justice Scalia also issued a dissenting opinion, joined by The Chief Justice, Justice Thomas, and Justice Alito. His dissent focused on the merits of the petitioners' claims. He concluded: "The Court's alarm over global warming may or may not be justified, but it ought not distort the outcome of this litigation. This is a straightforward administrative-law case, in which Congress has passed a malleable statute giving broad discretion, not to us but to an executive agency. No matter how important the underlying policy issues at stake, this Court has no business substituting its own desired outcome for the reasoned judgment of the responsible agency."]

---

## Points for Discussion

### *a. State Plaintiffs and Article III Standing*

The Court "stress[ed]" the "special position and interest of Massachusetts" and declared that it "is of considerable relevance that the party seeking review here is a sovereign State." Why did it matter that one of the parties seeking judicial review of the agency's failure to act was a state? Are there cognizable injuries that states suffer that private parties cannot? After all, a private party who owned beach-front land in Massachusetts would also face a threat from rising ocean levels. Or are the traceability and redressability requirements relaxed when a state is the plaintiff? If the Court was suggesting that states can more readily establish Article III standing than can private parties, what was the basis for that suggestion?

### *b. The Availability of Judicial Review for Agency Inaction*

Earlier in this Chapter, we considered *Heckler v. Chaney*, 470 U.S. 821 (1985), which held that agency decisions not to initiate enforcement actions are presumptively unreviewable under the APA. In reaching that conclusion, the Court reasoned that such decisions are inevitably based on discretionary judgments about how to allocate scarce agency resources. The Court also stated that agency decisions not to act do not bring the coercive power of the government to bear on private rights. Why did the Court in *Massachusetts v. EPA* conclude that agency decisions not to issue rules are not subject a similar presumption of unreviewability? Does it matter that the specific agency action subject to review in the case was the agency's denial of a rulemaking petition, which the agency accompanied with a statement of reasons for its decision?

### *c. Subsequent Developments*

After the Court's decision, the EPA's Administrator issued an "Advance Notice of Proposed Rulemaking" but then dragged his feet on taking action. Later that year, Barack Obama was elected President. He appointed a new Administrator, who issued a rule that set emissions standards for cars and light trucks and a rule requiring major "stationary sources" of greenhouse gases to obtain permits. In *Utility Air Regulatory Group v. EPA*, 573 U.S. 302 (2014), the Court upheld most of the stationary source rule.

**Test Your Knowledge**

To assess your understanding of the material in this Chapter, click here to take a quiz.

# Chapter Eight

# *Statutory Interpretation in the Administrative State*

The materials on administrative law in Chapters 6 and 7 provided a general overview of the subject. Our coverage of the topic was abbreviated for two main reasons. First, the upper-level course in Administrative Law is a comprehensive look at the administrative state and the rules that govern agency action, and the nuances of the doctrine are best left for that course. Second, our focus in this course is primarily on statutory interpretation. As we've already noted, a complete account of statutory interpretation in the American legal system requires an understanding of the powers and role of federal agencies, which are often called upon to interpret the statutes that they administer. Our consideration of administrative law was largely designed to help you to understand the debate over (and doctrine about) the role that agency interpretations play in judicial inquiries into statutory meaning. You have now seen enough administrative law to develop a richer understanding of statutory interpretation in the administrative state.

At the outset, it is worth thinking about the circumstances in which agencies offer interpretations of the statutes that they are charged with administering. Imagine that a statute prohibits the use of "toxins" in the workplace if "consistent exposure" to the toxin would be likely to result in "material health impairments" to a "critical mass" of those exposed. Imagine further that the statute directs the Occupational Safety and Health Administration (OSHA) to enforce the statute in proceedings conducted on the record after an opportunity for an agency hearing, and that the statute gives OSHA the power to issue rules.

If nothing else, to decide how to enforce the statute—that is, to decide whether to institute a proceeding against an employer who uses a dangerous toxin, or whether a rule is warranted—the agency has to figure out what exactly the statute requires. Suppose that a factory uses a naturally occurring substance in its manufacturing process. The substance causes three percent of the people exposed to it once weekly for at least six months to develop a nagging cough. To decide whether to bring an action against the factory or to issue a rule banning the use of the substance, the agency will have to resolve several important questions of statutory interpretation: Can a naturally occurring substance (such as arsenic or bromine) count as a "toxin," or does the term describe only chemical combinations that do not occur in nature without human intervention? How frequent must a worker's exposure to a toxin be to count as "consistent exposure"? Does an ailment that can be treated with over-the-counter drugs, such as a chronic cough, count as a material health impairment? And if so, how many workers must suffer the ailment in order to count as a "critical mass"? In other words, merely in the course of deciding its enforcement priorities, an agency can be expected routinely to interpret the statute that it is charged with administering. This form of interpretation is largely informal and happens behind the scenes, but it is obviously of great consequence both for the agency's agenda and for the private parties that are subject to (or benefit from) the agency's mandate.

Agencies also frequently offer official interpretations of the statutes that they are responsible for administering. Imagine that OSHA institutes an agency proceeding against a company that uses bromine in its manufacturing process. The agency seeks to impose fines on the company. In addition to making findings of fact at the conclusion of the hearing about the danger of bromine, the agency will have to decide (among other things) whether bromine, which is a naturally occurring substance, is a toxin within the meaning of the statute; whether a nagging cough counts as a "material health impairment"; and whether an ailment that only three percent of workers develop counts as a "critical mass." To make those determinations, the agency will announce its view about the meaning of the terms in the statute.

Or imagine that the agency, persuaded by studies by its staff scientists, concludes that bromine is sufficiently dangerous that it should be banned in all workplace settings. The agency issues notice of a proposed rule, solicits comments from interested persons, and then issues a final rule that prohibits use of the substance in the workplace. Imagine that the preliminary sections of the rule specifically define "toxin" as any "substance, whether naturally occurring or anthropogenic, that causes material health impairments to a critical mass of humans subject to consistent exposure." The rule further defines "material health impairment" to mean "any affliction that would lead an ordinary person to seek medical treatment or intervention, including over-the-counter remedies." And the rule defines "critical mass" as "at least one percent of persons in the relevant population."

Now imagine that the company subject to the enforcement action seeks judicial review of the agency's decision after the adjudication, or a company that wishes to use bromine in its industrial processes files suit and asks the court to set aside the agency's final rule. The company argues that the agency's action is inconsistent with the statute because the term "toxin," as used in the statute, applies only to substances that are not naturally occurring—or because the term "material health impairment" means something more serious than a cough, or because the term "critical mass" means something more than merely one percent of the persons exposed. When the Court addresses these arguments, what attention, if any, should it give to the agency's interpretation of the contested terms?

One way to think about this question is to analogize judicial review of agency decisions to appellate review of decisions by trial courts. Imagine that the plaintiff sues the defendant after he slips on ice on the sidewalk in front of the eighty-seven-year-old defendant's house. The trial court conducts a bench trial (i.e., there is no jury, and the judge serves as the fact-finder). At the conclusion of the trial, the judge finds that the sidewalk was covered with ice; that the plaintiff slipped at 7:00 a.m., three hours after the end of an ice storm; and that the defendant had not yet cleared the ice on the sidewalk. The judge holds that the appropriate standard of care was "what a reasonable eighty-seven-year-old person would have done." Applying that standard, the judge concludes that the defendant did not breach a duty of care.

An appellate court following conventional rules of appellate review would disturb the trial court's finding of facts only if they are "clearly erroneous"—a highly deferential standard of review—but would review the trial court's determination of the applicable legal standard *de novo*. The standard for reviewing the application of the law to the facts—so-called "mixed questions of law and fact"—is notoriously indeterminate, but courts usually characterize the decision either as one of fact or law and then apply the appropriate standard of review.

In other words, appellate courts review trial court findings of fact with deference and trial court conclusions of law without any deference. Would it make sense to adopt this framework for judicial review of agency decisions about the meaning of statutes? In Chapter 7, we saw that agency fact-finding in formal proceedings is usually subject to the deferential "substantial evidence" test. *See* 5 U.S.C. § 706(2)(E). Should courts review agency determinations about statutory meaning *de novo*, without any deference? Does it matter if the determination turns at least in part on factual assumptions?

**FYI**

The Court has described mixed questions of law and fact as follows: "[T]he historical facts are admitted or established, the rule of law is undisputed, and the issue is whether the facts satisfy the [relevant] statutory [or constitutional] standard, or to put it another way, whether the rule of law as applied to the established facts is or is not violated." *Pullman–Standard v. Swint*, 456 U.S. 273, 289, n. 19 (1982).

---

## A. The Old Approach

In thinking about that question, consider the two cases that follow. The Supreme Court decided both before the enactment of the APA, but the Court continued to follow them for years after Congress passed the APA. As we will see, the Court's approach to agency interpretations of the statutes that they are responsible for administering has evolved in the decades since the Court decided these two cases. We consider these two cases for their historical significance and as context for the doctrinal changes that followed.

---

## *National Labor Relations Board v. Hearst*

322 U.S. 111 (1944)

Mr. Justice Rutledge delivered the opinion of the Court.

These cases arise from the refusal of respondents, publishers of four Los Angeles daily newspapers, to bargain collectively with a union representing newsboys who distribute their papers on the streets of that city. Respondents' contention that they were not required to bargain because the newsboys are not their "employees" within the meaning of that term in the National Labor Relations Act, 29 U.S.C. § 152,[1] presents the important question which we granted certiorari to resolve.

The proceedings before the National Labor Relations Board were begun with the filing of four petitions for investigation and certification by Los Angeles Newsboys Local Industrial Union No. 75. Hearings were held in a consolidated proceeding after which the Board made findings of fact and concluded that the regular full-time newsboys selling each paper were employees within the Act and that questions affecting commerce concerning the representation of employees had arisen. It designated appropriate units and ordered elections. At these the union was selected as their representative by majorities of the eligible newsboys. After the union was appropriately certified, the respondents refused to bargain with it. [The Board then held a hearing and determined that respondents' refusal was an unfair labor practice within the meaning of the statute. The Board ordered respondents to bargain collectively with the union upon request. The court of appeals then set aside the Board's order. The court] independently examined the question whether the newsboys are employees within the Act, decided that the statute imports common-law standards to determine that question, and held the newsboys are not employees.

The [four newspapers at issue] are distributed to the ultimate consumer through a variety of channels, including independent dealers and newsstands often attached to drug, grocery or confectionery stores, carriers who make home deliveries, and newsboys who sell on the streets of the city and its suburbs. Only the last of these are involved in this case.

---

1 Section 2(3) of the Act provides that "The term 'employee' shall include any employee, and shall not be limited to the employees of a particular employer, unless the Act explicitly states otherwise * * *."

The newsboys work under varying terms and conditions. They may be "bootjackers," selling to the general public at places other than established corners, or they may sell at fixed "spots." They may sell only casually or part-time, or full-time; and they may be employed regularly and continuously or only temporarily. The units which the Board determined to be appropriate are composed of those who sell full-time at established spots. Those vendors, misnamed boys, are generally mature men, dependent upon the proceeds of their sales for their sustenance, and frequently supporters of families. Working thus as news vendors on a regular basis often for a number of years, they form a stable group with relatively little turnover, in contrast to schoolboys and others who sell as bootjackers, temporary and casual distributors.

Over-all circulation and distribution of the papers are under the general supervision of circulation managers. But for purposes of street distribution each paper has divided metropolitan Los Angeles into geographic districts. Each district is under the direct and close supervision of a district manager. His function in the mechanics of distribution is to supply the newsboys in his district with papers which he obtains from the publisher and to turn over to the publisher the receipts which he collects from their sales * * *. The newsboys' compensation consists in the difference between the prices at which they sell the papers and the prices they pay for them. The former are fixed by the publishers and the latter are fixed either by the publishers or, in the case of the News, by the district manager. In practice the newsboys receive their papers on credit. They pay for those sold either sometime during or after the close of their selling day, returning for credit all unsold papers. * * * Not only is the "profit" per paper thus effectively fixed by the publisher, but substantial control of the newsboys' total "take home" can be effected through the ability to designate their sales areas and the power to determine the number of papers allocated to each. While as a practical matter this power is not exercised fully, the newsboys' "right" to decide how many papers they will take is also not absolute. In practice, the Board found, they cannot determine the size of their established order without the cooperation of the district manager. And often the number of papers they must take is determined unilaterally by the district managers.

In addition to effectively fixing the compensation, respondents in a variety of ways prescribe, if not the minutiae of daily activities, at least the broad terms and conditions of work. * * * The district managers assign "spots" or corners to which the newsboys are expected to confine their selling activities. * * * Transportation to the spots from the newspaper building is offered by each of respondents. Hours of work on the spots are determined not simply by the impersonal pressures of the market, but to a real extent by explicit instructions from the district managers. Adherence to the prescribed hours is observed closely by the district managers or other supervisory agents of the publishers. Sanctions, varying in severity from reprimand to dismissal, are visited on the tardy and the delinquent. By similar supervisory controls minimum standards of diligence and good conduct while at work are sought to be enforced. * * * In this pattern of employment the Board found that the newsboys are an integral part of the publishers' distribution system and circulation organization. And the record discloses that the newsboys * * * feel they are employees of the papers and respondents' supervisory employees, if not respondents themselves, regard them as such.

The principal question is whether the newsboys are "employees." Because Congress did not explicitly define the term, respondents say its meaning must be determined by reference to common-law standards. In their view "common-law standards" are those the courts have applied in distinguishing between "employees" and "independent contractors" when working out various problems unrelated to the Wagner Act's purposes and provisions.

**FYI**

The Wagner Act, also known as the National Labor Relations Act of 1935, created the NLRB and authorized private-sector employees to form unions, engage in collective bargaining, and take collective action to ensure better working conditions and compensation.

The argument assumes that there is some simple, uniform and easily applicable test which the courts have used, in dealing with such problems, to determine whether persons doing work for others fall in one class or the other. Unfortunately this is not true. Only by a long and tortuous history was the simple formulation worked out which has been stated most frequently as "the test" for deciding whether one who hires another is responsible in tort for his wrongdoing. But this formula has been by no means exclusively controlling in the solution of other problems. And its simplicity has been illusory because it is more largely simplicity of formulation than of application. Few problems in the law have given greater variety of application and conflict in results than the cases arising in the borderland between what is clearly an employer-employee relationship and what is clearly one of independent entrepreneurial dealing. * * *

Two possible consequences could follow. One would be to refer the decision of who are employees to local state law. The alternative would be to make it turn on a sort of pervading general essence distilled from state law. Congress obviously did not intend the former result. It would introduce variations into the statute's operation as wide as the differences the forty-eight states and other local jurisdictions make in applying the distinction for wholly different purposes. Persons who might be "employees" in one state would be "independent contractors" in another. They would be within or without the statute's protection depending not on whether their situation falls factually within the ambit Congress had in mind, but upon the accidents of the location of their work and the attitude of the particular local jurisdiction in casting doubtful cases one way or the other. Persons working across state lines might fall in one class or the other, possibly both, depending on whether the Board and the courts would be required to give effect to the law of one state or of the adjoining one, or to that of each in relation to the portion of the work done within its borders.

Both the terms and the purposes of the statute, as well as the legislative history, show that Congress had in mind no such patchwork plan for securing freedom of employees' organization and of collective bargaining. The Wagner Act is federal legislation, administered by a national agency, intended to solve a national problem on a national scale. * * *

Whether, given the intended national uniformity, the term "employee" includes such workers as these newsboys must be answered primarily from the history, terms and purposes of the legislation. The word "is not treated by Congress as a word of art having a definite meaning . . . ." Rather "it takes color from its surroundings . . . (in) the statute where it appears," *United States v. American Trucking Associations, Inc.*, 310 U.S. 534, 545 (1940), and derives meaning from the context of that statute, which "must be read in the light of the mischief to be corrected and the end to be attained." *South Chicago Coal & Dock Co. v. Bassett*, 309 U.S. 251, 259 (1940).

**Take Note**

On which touchstone of interpretation did the Court focus in interpreting the Wagner Act? If the Court focused on the ordinary meaning of the term "employee," would its inquiry have looked any different?

Congress, on the one hand, was not thinking solely of the immediate technical relation of employer and employee. It had in mind at least some other persons than those standing in the proximate legal relation of employee to the particular employer involved in the labor dispute. It cannot be taken, however, that the purpose was to include all other persons who may perform service for another or was to ignore entirely legal classifications made for other purposes. Congress had in mind a wider field than the narrow technical legal relation of "master and servant," as the common law had worked this out in all its variations, and at the same time a narrower one than the entire area of rendering service to others. The question comes down therefore to how much was included of the intermediate region between what is clearly and unequivocally "employment," by any appropriate test, and what is as clearly entrepreneurial enterprise and not employment.

Congress was not seeking to solve the nationally harassing problems with which the statute deals by solutions only partially effective. It rather sought to find a broad solution, one that would bring industrial peace by substituting, so far as its power could reach, the rights of workers to self-organization and collective bargaining for the industrial strife which prevails where these rights are not effectively established. Yet only partial solutions would be provided if large segments of workers about whose technical legal position such local differences exist should be wholly excluded from coverage by reason of such differences. Yet that result could not be avoided, if choice must be made among them and controlled by them in deciding who are "employees" within the Act's meaning. Enmeshed in such distinctions, the administration of the statute soon might become encumbered by the same sort of technical legal refinement as has characterized the long evolution of the employee-independent contractor dichotomy in the courts for other purposes. The consequences would be ultimately to defeat, in part at least, the achievement of the statute's objectives. Congress no more intended to import this mass of technicality as a controlling "standard" for uniform national application than to refer decision of the question outright to the local law.

The Act, as its first section states, was designed to avert the "substantial obstructions to the free flow of commerce" which result from "strikes and other forms of industrial strife or unrest" by eliminating the causes of that unrest. It is premised on explicit findings that strikes and industrial strife themselves result in large measure from the refusal of employers to bargain collectively and the inability of individual workers to bargain successfully for improvements in their "wages, hours, or other working conditions" with employers who are "organized in the corporate or other forms of ownership association." Hence the avowed and interrelated purposes of the Act are to encourage collective bargaining and to remedy the individual worker's inequality of bargaining power by "protecting the exercise . . . of full freedom of association, self-organization, and designation of representatives of their own choosing, for the purpose of negotiating the terms and conditions of their employment or other mutual aid or protection." 29 U.S.C. § 151.

The mischief at which the Act is aimed and the remedies it offers are not confined exclusively to "employees" within the traditional legal distinctions separating them from "independent contractors." Myriad forms of service relationship, with infinite and subtle variations in the terms of employment, blanket the nation's economy. Some are within this Act, others beyond its coverage. Large numbers will fall clearly on one side or on the other, by whatever test may be applied. But intermediate there will be many, the incidents of whose employment partake in part of the one group, in part of the other, in varying proportions of weight. And consequently the legal pendulum, for purposes of applying the statute, may swing one way or the other, depending upon the weight of this balance and its relation to the special purpose at hand.

[It] cannot be irrelevant that the particular workers in these cases are subject, as a matter of economic fact, to the evils the statute was designed to eradicate and that the remedies it affords are appropriate for preventing them or curing their harmful effects in the special situation. Interruption of commerce through strikes and unrest may stem as well from labor disputes between some who, for other purposes, are technically "independent contractors" and their employers as from disputes between persons who, for those purposes, are "employees" and their employers. Inequality of bargaining power in controversies over wages, hours and working conditions may as well characterize the status of the one group as of the other. The former, when acting alone, may be as "helpless in dealing with an employer," as "dependent . . . on his daily wage" and as "unable to leave the employ and to resist arbitrary and unfair treatment" as the latter. For each, "union . . . (may be) essential to give . . . opportunity to deal on equality with their employer." And for each, collective bargaining may be appropriate and effective for the "friendly adjustment of industrial disputes arising out of differences as to wages, hours, or other working conditions." 29 U.S.C. § 151. In short, when the particular situation of employment combines these characteristics, so that the economic facts of the relation make it more nearly one of employment than of independent business enterprise with respect to the ends sought to be accomplished by the legislation, those characteristics may outweigh technical legal classification for purposes unrelated to the statute's objectives and bring the relation within its protections.

It is not necessary in this case to make a completely definitive limitation around the term "employee." That task has been assigned primarily to the agency created by Congress to administer the Act. Determination of "where all the conditions of the relation require protection" involves inquiries for the Board charged with this duty. Everyday experience in the administration of the statute gives it familiarity with the circumstances and backgrounds of employment relationships in various industries, with the abilities and needs of the workers for self organization and collective action, and with the adaptability of collective bargaining for the peaceful settlement of their disputes with their employers. The experience thus acquired must be brought frequently to bear on the question who is an employee under the Act. Resolving that question, like determining whether unfair labor practices have been committed, "belongs to the usual administrative routine" of the Board. *Gray v. Powell*, 314 U.S. 402, 411 (1941).

In making that body's determinations as to the facts in these matters conclusive, if supported by evidence, Congress entrusted to it primarily the decision whether the evidence establishes the material facts. Hence in reviewing the Board's ultimate conclusions, it is not the court's function to substitute its own inferences of fact for the Board's, when the latter have support in the record. Undoubtedly questions of statutory interpretation, especially when arising in the first instance in judicial proceedings, are for the courts to resolve, giving appropriate weight to the judgment of those whose special duty is to administer the questioned statute. But where the question is one of specific application of a broad statutory term in a proceeding in which the agency administering the statute must determine it initially, the reviewing court's function is limited. Like the commissioner's determination under the Longshoremen's & Harbor Workers' Act, that a man is not a "member of a crew" (*South Chicago Coal & Dock Co.*, 309 U.S. 251 (1940)) or that he was injured "in the course of his employment" (*Parker v. Motor Boat Sales, Inc.*,

**Food for Thought**

In the Court's view, was the matter to be decided in this case a question of law, a question of fact, or a mixed question of law or fact? Did the Court's answer to that question lead inevitably to the Court's conclusion about the appropriate role of the agency's resolution of the matter in determining the meaning of the statute?

314 U.S. 244 (1941)) and the Federal Communications Commission's determination that one company is under the "control" of another (*Rochester Telephone Corp. v. United States*, 307 U.S. 125 (1939)), the Board's determination that specified persons are "employees" under this Act is to be accepted if it has "warrant in the record" and a reasonable basis in law.

In this case the Board found that the designated newsboys work continuously and regularly, rely upon their earnings for the support of themselves and their families, and have their total wages influenced in large measure by the publishers who dictate their buying and selling prices, fix their markets and control their supply of papers. Their hours of work and their efforts on the job are supervised and to some extent prescribed by the publishers or their agents. Much of their sales equipment and advertising materials is furnished by the publishers with the intention that it be used for the publisher's benefit. Stating that "the primary consideration in the determination of the applicability of the statutory definition is whether effectuation of the declared policy and purposes of the Act comprehend securing to the individual the rights guaranteed and protection afforded by the Act," the Board concluded that the newsboys are employees. The record sustains the Board's findings and there is ample basis in the law for its conclusion.

The judgments are reversed and the causes are remanded for further proceedings not inconsistent with this opinion.

MR. JUSTICE REED concurs in the result. * * *

MR. JUSTICE ROBERTS [dissenting].

I think it plain that newsboys are not "employees" of the respondents within the meaning and intent of the National Labor Relations Act. When Congress, in 29 U.S.C. § 152(3), said: "The term 'employee' shall include any employee," it stated as clearly as language could do it that the provisions of the Act were to extend to those who, as a result of decades of tradition which had become part of the common understanding of our people, bear the named relationship. Clearly also Congress did not delegate to the National Labor Relations Board the function of defining the relationship of employment so as to promote what the Board understood to be the underlying purpose of the statute. The question who is an employee, so as to make the statute applicable to him, is a question of the meaning of the Act and, therefore, is a judicial and not an administrative question. [The] common, general, and prevailing understanding [of the term "employee," and the facts stated in this court,] demonstrate that the newsboys were not employees of the newspapers.

---

## Points for Discussion

### *a. Warrant in the Record and a Reasonable Basis in Law*

The question in *Hearst* was whether newsboys were "employees" within the meaning of the Act. The resolution of that issue turned at least in part on the answers to several questions of fact, such as how the newsboys were paid, what forms of control the publishers exercised over the newsboys' hours and selling locations, whether the publishers could discipline the newsboys if they didn't sell enough papers, and so on. But the issue also turned on the answer to an important *legal* question: which workers were included in the statutory category of "employees" (or, stated another way, whom did Congress intend to protect when it provided unionization rights to "employees")?

In the Supreme Court's view, the case raised three discrete questions: (1) Does the term "employee" in the statute incorporate the common-law definition of the term? (2) If not, what factors are relevant in construing the term "employee"? (3) In light of those factors, are newsboys "employees"? The Court answered the first two questions without any apparent deference to the agency's conclusion, although its answer was consistent with the agency's conclusion. That is, the Court's explanation for why it concluded that the statute did not incorporate the common-law definition, and the Court's identification of the factors that are relevant in determining who counts as an employee, did not focus on the fact that the agency, which has considerable expertise in labor relations, had reached a similar conclusion.

But the Court stated that the task of answering the third question—whether newsboys are employees within the meaning of the statute—"has been assigned primarily to the agency," whose "[e]veryday experience in the administration of the statute gives it familiarity with the circumstances and backgrounds of employment relationships," experience that "must be brought frequently to bear on the question who is an employee under the Act." In other words, the Court deferred to the agency's application of the statutory standard to the particular facts in the case. According to the Court, "the Board's determination that specified persons are 'employees' under this Act is to be accepted if it has 'warrant in the record' and a reasonable basis in law."

Why might it make sense for courts to answer questions of statutory interpretation *de novo*—that is, without any deference to the agency's view—but defer to agency conclusions about how a statutory standard applies to a given set of facts? Did it matter that the Board's decision in *Hearst* was made in the course of a formal adjudication, and thus approximated a judicial proceeding? Or was the Court's approach based on the simple intuition that judges are experts in resolving legal questions, whereas agencies are experts in making policy judgments in the fields that they are responsible for regulating?

### *b. Factual Determinations, Legal Determinations, and Mixed Questions*

If the availability of judicial deference to agency decision-making turns on whether the agency is making a factual determination or applying the law to the facts, on the one hand, or resolving a legal question, on the other, then courts need to be able to tell the difference between these two categories of decision. Is it obvious to you that the Board's decision in *Hearst* was a mixed question of law and fact, rather than a pure legal determination? What if the publishers had offered evidence from the legislative history that revealed that Congress had specifically thought about the case of newsboys and concluded that they were independent contractors, rather than employees? Are you confident that you can tell the difference between a mixed question of law and fact, on the one hand, and a pure question of law, on the other?

---

## *Skidmore v. Swift and Co.*

323 U.S. 134 (1944)

Mr. Justice Jackson delivered the opinion of the Court.

Seven employees of the Swift and Company packing plant at Fort Worth, Texas, brought an action under the Fair Labor Standards Act, 29 U.S.C.A. § 201 et seq., to recover overtime, liquidated damages, and attorneys' fees, totalling approximately $77,000. [The relevant section of the Act provided that "no employer shall employ any of his employees * * * for a workweek longer than forty hours unless such employee receives compensation for his employment in excess of the hours above specified at a rate not less than one and one-half times the regular rate at which he is employed." 29 U.S.C. § 207(a)(1).]

It is not denied that the daytime employment of these persons was working time within the Act. Two were engaged in general fire hall duties and maintenance of fire-fighting equipment of the Swift plant. The others operated elevators or acted as relief men in fire duties. They worked from 7:00 a.m. to 3:30 p.m., with a half-hour lunch period, five days a week. They were paid weekly salaries.

Under their oral agreement of employment, however, petitioners undertook to stay in the fire hall on the Company premises, or within hailing distance, three and a half to four nights a week. This involved no task except to answer alarms, either because of fire or because the sprinkler was set off for some other reason. No fires occurred during the period in issue, the alarms were rare, and the time required for their answer rarely exceeded an hour. For each alarm answered the employees were paid in addition to their fixed compensation an agreed amount, fifty cents at first, and later sixty-four cents. The Company provided a brick fire hall equipped with steam heat and air-conditioned rooms. It provided sleeping quarters, a pool table, a domino table, and a radio. The men used their time in sleep or amusement as they saw fit, except that they were required to stay in or close by the fire hall and be ready to respond to alarms. [The trial court concluded] that "the time plaintiffs spent in the fire hall subject to call to answer fire alarms does not constitute hours worked, for which overtime compensation is due them under the Fair Labor Standards Act * * *," and in its opinion observed, "of course we know pursuing such pleasurable occupations or performing such personal chores does not constitute work." The Circuit Court of Appeals affirmed.

[W]e hold that no principle of law found either in the statute or in Court decisions precludes waiting time from also being working time. We have not attempted to, and we cannot, lay down a legal formula to resolve cases so varied in their facts as are the many situations in which employment involves waiting time. * * * Facts may show that the employee was engaged to wait, or they may show that he waited to be engaged. His compensation may cover both waiting and task, or only performance of the task itself. Living quarters may in some situations be furnished as a facility of the task and in another as a part of its compensation. The law does not impose an arrangement upon the parties. It imposes upon the courts the task of finding what the arrangement was.

Congress did not utilize the services of an administrative agency to find facts and to determine in the first instance whether particular cases fall within or without the Act. Instead, it put this responsibility on the courts. *Kirschbaum v. Walling*, 316 U.S. 517, 523 (1942). But it did create the office of Administrator [of the Wage and Hour Division of the Department of Labor], impose upon him a variety of duties, endow him with powers to inform himself of conditions in industries and employments subject to the Act, and put on him the duties of bringing injunction actions to restrain violations. Pursuit of his duties has accumulated a considerable experience in the problems of ascertaining working time in employments involving periods of inactivity and a knowledge of the customs prevailing in reference to their solution. From these he is obliged to reach conclusions as to conduct without the law, so that he should seek injunctions to stop it, and that within the law, so that he has no call to interfere. He has set forth his views of the application of the Act under different circumstances in an interpretative bulletin and in informal rulings. They provide a practical guide to employers and employees as to how the office representing the public interest in its enforcement will seek to apply it. Wage and Hour Division, Interpretative Bulletin No. 13. [The Administrator also filed an *amicus* brief with the Supreme Court specifying his views of the issue presented.]

The Administrator thinks the problems presented by inactive duty require a flexible solution, rather than the all-in or all-out rules respectively urged by the parties in this case, and his Bulletin endeavors to suggest standards and examples to guide in particular situations. In some occupations, it says, periods of inactivity are not properly counted as working time even though the employee is subject to call. Examples are an operator of a small telephone exchange where the switchboard is in her home and she ordinarily gets several hours of uninterrupted sleep each night; or a pumper of a stripper well or watchman of a lumber camp during the off season, who may be on duty twenty-four hours a day but ordinarily "has a normal night's sleep, has ample time in which to eat his meals, and has a certain amount of time for relaxation and entirely private pursuits." Exclusion of all such hours the Administrator thinks may be justified. In general, the answer depends "upon the degree to which the employee is free to engage in personal activities during periods of idleness when he is subject to call and the number of consecutive hours that the employee is subject to call without being required to perform active work." "Hours worked are not limited to the time spent in active labor but include time given by the employee to the employer. * * *"

The facts of this case do not fall within any of the specific examples given, but the conclusion of the Administrator, as expressed in the brief *amicus curiae*, is that the general tests which he has suggested point to the exclusion of sleeping and eating time of these employees from the work-week and the inclusion of all other on-call time: although the employees were required to remain on the premises during the entire time, the evidence shows that they were very rarely interrupted in their normal sleeping and eating time, and these are pursuits of a purely private nature which would presumably occupy the employees' time whether they were on duty or not and which apparently could be pursued adequately and comfortably in the required circumstances; the rest of the time is different because there is nothing in the record to suggest that, even though pleasurably spent, it was spent in the ways the men would have chosen had they been free to do so.

There is no statutory provision as to what, if any, deference courts should pay to the Administrator's conclusions. And, while we have given them notice, we have had no occasion to try to prescribe their influence. The rulings of this Administrator are not reached as a result of hearing adversary proceedings in which he finds facts from evidence and reaches conclusions of law from findings of fact. They are not, of course, conclusive, even in the cases with which they directly deal, much less in those to which they apply only by analogy. They do not constitute an interpretation of the Act or a standard for judging factual situations which binds a district court's processes, as an authoritative pronouncement of a higher court might do. But the Administrator's policies are made in pursuance of official duty, based upon more specialized experience and broader investigations and information than is likely to come to a judge in a particular case. They do determine the policy which will guide applications for enforcement by injunction on behalf of the Government. Good administration of the Act and good judicial administration alike require that the standards of public enforcement and those for determining private rights shall be at variance only where justified by very good reasons. The fact that the Administrator's policies and standards are not reached by trial in adversary form does not mean that they are not entitled to respect. * * *

We consider that the rulings, interpretations and opinions of the Administrator under this Act, while not controlling upon the courts by reason of their authority, do constitute a body of experience and informed judgment to which courts and litigants may properly resort for guidance. The weight of such a judgment in a particular case will depend upon the thoroughness evident in its consideration, the validity of its reasoning, its consistency with earlier and later pronouncements, and all those factors which give it power to persuade, if lacking power to control.

[A]lthough the District Court referred to the Administrator's Bulletin, its evaluation and inquiry were apparently restricted by its notion that waiting time may not be work, an understanding of the law which we hold to be erroneous. Accordingly, the judgment is reversed and the cause remanded for further proceedings consistent herewith.

---

## Points for Discussion

### *a.* Skidmore *Deference*

The Court stated that "the rulings, interpretations and opinions of the Administrator under this Act, while not controlling upon the courts by reason of their authority, do constitute a body of experience and informed judgment to which courts and litigants may properly resort for guidance." The Court explained that the "weight of such a judgment in a particular case will depend upon the thoroughness evident in its consideration, the validity of its reasoning, its consistency with earlier and later pronouncements, and all those factors which give it power to persuade, if lacking power to control."

Does this approach constitute a genuine form of judicial deference to the Administrator's view of the meaning of the statute? After all, *any* view—one advanced by a party in a case or by a professor in a law review article—has at least the "power to persuade"; and if it is actually persuasive, a court will be inclined to accept it. But we do not think of a court's conclusion that a particular argument is persuasive as a form of *deference.* In the law, deference refers to a court's decision to yield to a view advanced by someone else, even if the court, if writing on a clean slate, would have reached a *different* conclusion. If a court defers to an agency's interpretation of the statute that it administers only to the extent that the court agrees with the agency's interpretation, then is the court really deferring at all?

### *b. Forms of Agency Decision and Deference*

At a minimum, the Court's description of the status of the Administrator's view of the statute suggested that it was entitled to less deference than the Board's decision in *Hearst.* (In *Hearst,* the Court said that a reviewing court should uphold the Board's determination as long as it had a warrant in the record and a reasonable basis in law.) What accounts for the difference?

The Court in *Skidmore* noted that "Congress did not utilize the services of an administrative agency to find facts and to determine in the first instance whether particular cases fall within or without the Act," as it had with the National Labor Relations Board. The Court also noted that, to the extent that the Administrator of the Wage and Hour Division issued guidance stating his views, the "rulings of [the] Administrator are not reached as a result of hearing adversary proceedings in which he finds facts from evidence and reaches conclusions of law from findings of fact." How much of the Court's conclusion—that the Administrator's view of the meaning of the statute was entitled only to some modest amount of deference—was a function of the fact that the Administrator's views "are not * * * conclusive, even in the cases with which they directly deal, much less in those to which they apply only by analogy"? If this difference accounts for the different levels of deference, do you agree with the distinction?

---

Two years after the Court's decisions in *Hearst* and *Skidmore*, Congress enacted the APA. As we have seen, the APA sought to rationalize and standardize the procedures for agency decision-making and the approach to judicial review of agency action. We have already considered the APA's provisions that instruct a reviewing court to set aside formal agency action that is "unsupported by substantial evidence" and agency action that is "arbitrary, capricious, an abuse of discretion, or otherwise not in accordance with law." 5 U.S.C. § 706(2)(A) & (E). But the APA also states that, "[t]o the extent necessary to decision and when presented, the reviewing court shall decide all relevant questions of law, interpret constitutional and statutory provisions, and determine the meaning or applicability of the terms of an agency action." *Id.* § 706. In addition, the APA states that the reviewing court should set aside agency action "in excess of statutory jurisdiction, authority, or limitations, or short of statutory right." *Id.* § 706(2)(C).

Do these provisions suggest that courts should not give any deference to agency interpretations of the statutes that they are responsible for administering? Does it matter whether the agency decision is a pure question of law—about, say, the meaning of a statutory mandate—or instead entails the application of a statutory standard to a particular set of facts?

In the four decades after the enactment of the APA, the courts' approach to these questions was not entirely consistent. Courts assumed that the APA had, for the most part, incorporated much of the pre-APA common law of administrative action. As a consequence, courts more or less followed the approaches in the *Hearst* and *Skidmore* cases. But it was never entirely clear when *Hearst*'s deferential approach to agency decision-making applied and when *Skidmore*'s less deferential approach applied. And even if courts could tell the difference between cases that warranted one approach or the other, it was far from obvious what counted as a question of fact, a question of law, or a mixed question of law and fact.

To the extent that one can discern trends from this era, courts tended to resolve "purely legal" questions about the meaning of statutes without deference to agency views. In contrast, courts were more likely to defer to agency resolution of those questions that they viewed as "mixed"—that is, applications of a statute to a particular set of facts. Those questions were most likely to arise in agency formal adjudications. But it was less clear what approach applied when, in the course of issuing a rule after notice and comment, an agency made a decision about the meaning of the statute that it is responsible for administering.

## B. The Modern Approach

In the famous case that follows, the Court offered a framework for judicial review of agency interpretations of the statutes that they are charged with implementing.

---

## *Chevron, U.S.A., Inc. v. Natural Resources Defense Council, Inc.*

467 U.S. 837 (1984)

JUSTICE STEVENS delivered the opinion of the Court.

In the Clean Air Act Amendments of 1977, Pub. L. 95–95, 91 Stat. 685, Congress enacted certain requirements applicable to States that had not achieved the national air quality standards established by the Environmental Protection Agency (EPA) pursuant to earlier legislation. The amended Clean Air Act required these "nonattainment" States to establish a permit program regulating "new or modified major stationary sources" of air pollution. Generally, a permit may not be issued for a new or modified major stationary source unless several stringent conditions are met.[1] The EPA regulation promulgated to implement this permit requirement allows a State to adopt a plantwide definition of the term "stationary source."[2] Under this definition,

---

1 Section 172(b)(6), 42 U.S.C. § 7502(b)(6), provides: "The plan provisions required by subsection (a) shall—. . ."(6) require permits for the construction and operation of new or modified major stationary sources in accordance with section 173."

2 "(i) 'Stationary source' means any building, structure, facility, or installation which emits or may emit any air pollutant subject to regulation under the Act.

"(ii) 'Building, structure, facility, or installation' means all of the pollutant-emitting activities which

an existing plant that contains several pollution-emitting devices may install or modify one piece of equipment without meeting the permit conditions if the alteration will not increase the total emissions from the plant. The question presented by these cases is whether EPA's decision to allow States to treat all of the pollution-emitting devices within the same industrial grouping as though they were encased within a single "bubble" is based on a reasonable construction of the statutory term "stationary source."

**Take Note**

The complicated statutory provisions at issue in this case essentially said that, in states that had not yet met air quality targets, a company that wanted to acquire or modify a "stationary source" of pollution would first have to get a permit. The permit would be granted only if the source of pollution used the best available technology for limiting emissions. The dispute in this case was about the meaning of the term "stationary source." On one view, each apparatus that emits pollution—such as a boiler, a kiln, or something similar—counted as a separate stationary source for which a permit would be required. This view would force factories to get a permit, and thus use the cleanest technology, any time they wanted to change or acquire a new piece of equipment that emits pollution. Under the competing view, the term "stationary source" referred to an entire industrial complex; in effect, it imagined that the entire factory or complex was encased in a "bubble." On this view, a factory that added a new polluting apparatus that didn't comply with the newest standards wouldn't have to get a permit for the new apparatus as long as it found offsetting reductions in pollution from elsewhere at the plant.

[The court of appeals invalidated the agency's rule. The court concluded that the text and legislative history of the statute did not clearly reveal Congress's understanding of the meaning of the term "stationary source," but that the bubble concept was inconsistent with the statute's purpose, which was to improve air quality.]

When a court reviews an agency's construction of the statute which it administers, it is confronted with two questions. First, always, is the question whether Congress has directly spoken to the precise question at issue. If the intent of Congress is clear, that is the end of the matter; for the court, as well as the agency, must give effect to the unambiguously expressed intent of Congress.[9] If, however, the court determines Congress has not directly addressed the precise question at issue, the court does not simply impose its own construction on the statute, as would be necessary in the absence of an administrative interpretation. Rather, if the statute is silent or ambiguous with respect to the specific issue, the question

---

belong to the same industrial grouping, are located on one or more contiguous or adjacent properties, and are under the control of the same person (or persons under common control) except the activities of any vessel." 40 CFR §§ 51.18(j)(1)(i) and (ii) (1983).

9 The judiciary is the final authority on issues of statutory construction and must reject administrative constructions which are contrary to clear congressional intent. If a court, employing traditional tools of statutory construction, ascertains that Congress had an intention on the precise question at issue, that intention is the law and must be given effect.

for the court is whether the agency's answer is based on a permissible construction of the statute.[11]

"The power of an administrative agency to administer a congressionally created . . . program necessarily requires the formulation of policy and the making of rules to fill any gap left, implicitly or explicitly, by Congress." *Morton v. Ruiz*, 415 U.S. 199 (1974). If Congress has explicitly left a gap for the agency to fill, there is an express delegation of authority to the agency to elucidate a specific provision of the statute by regulation. Such legislative regulations are given controlling weight unless they are arbitrary, capricious, or manifestly contrary to the statute. Sometimes the legislative delegation to an agency on a particular question is implicit rather than explicit. In such a case, a court may not substitute its own construction of a statutory provision for a reasonable interpretation made by the administrator of an agency.

We have long recognized that considerable weight should be accorded to an executive department's construction of a statutory scheme it is entrusted to administer, and the principle of deference to administrative interpretations "has been consistently followed by this Court whenever decision as to the meaning or reach of a statute has involved reconciling conflicting policies, and a full understanding of the force of the statutory policy in the given situation has depended upon more than ordinary knowledge respecting the matters subjected to agency regulations. . . . If this choice represents a reasonable accommodation of conflicting policies that were committed to the agency's care by the statute, we should not disturb it unless it appears from the statute or its legislative history that the accommodation is not one that Congress would have sanctioned." *United States v. Shimer*, 367 U.S. 374, 382 (1961).

In light of these well-settled principles it is clear that the Court of Appeals misconceived the nature of its role in reviewing the regulations at issue. Once it determined, after its own examination of the legislation, that Congress did not actually have an intent regarding the applicability of the bubble concept to the permit program, the question before it was not whether in its view the concept is "inappropriate" in the general context of a program designed to improve air quality, but whether the Administrator's view that it is appropriate in the context of this particular program is a reasonable one. Based on the examination of the

**Take Note**

The Court here addressed "whether Congress has directly spoken to the precise question at issue." Notice that the Court did not defer to the agency's view, to the extent that it had one, about this question. What was the Court's approach to answering this question of statutory interpretation? On which touchstone of interpretation did the Court focus?

11 The court need not conclude that the agency construction was the only one it permissibly could have adopted to uphold the construction, or even the reading the court would have reached if the question initially had arisen in a judicial proceeding.

legislation and its history which follows, we agree with the Court of Appeals that Congress did not have a specific intention on the applicability of the bubble concept in these cases, and conclude that the EPA's use of that concept here is a reasonable policy choice for the agency to make.

In the 1950's and the 1960's Congress enacted a series of statutes designed to encourage and to assist the States in curtailing air pollution. The Clean Air Amendments of 1970, Pub. L. 91–604, 84 Stat. 1676, "sharply increased federal authority and responsibility in the continuing effort to combat air pollution," *Train v. Natural Resources Defense Council, Inc.*, 421 U.S. 60, 63–64 (1975), but continued to assign "primary responsibility for assuring air quality" to the several States, 84 Stat. 1678. Section 109 of the 1970 Amendments directed the EPA to promulgate National Ambient Air Quality Standards (NAAQS's) and § 110 directed the States to develop plans (SIP's) to implement the standards within specified deadlines. In addition, § 111 provided that major new sources of pollution would be required to conform to technology-based performance standards; the EPA was directed to publish a list of categories of sources of pollution and to establish new source performance standards (NSPS) for each. Section 111(e) prohibited the operation of any new source in violation of a performance standard.

Section 111(a) defined the terms that are to be used in setting and enforcing standards of performance for new stationary sources. It provided: "For purposes of this section: . . . (3) The term 'stationary source' means any building, structure, facility, or installation which emits or may emit any air pollutant." 84 Stat. 1683. In the 1970 Amendments that definition was not only applicable to the NSPS program required by § 111, but also was made applicable to a requirement of § 110 that each state implementation plan contain a procedure for reviewing the location of any proposed new source and preventing its construction if it would preclude the attainment or maintenance of national air quality standards. * * *

The 1970 legislation provided for the attainment of primary NAAQS's by 1975. In many areas of the country, particularly the most industrialized States, the statutory goals were not attained. In 1976, the 94th Congress was confronted with this fundamental problem, as well as many others respecting pollution control. As always in this area, the legislative struggle was basically between interests seeking strict schemes to reduce pollution rapidly to eliminate its social costs and interests advancing the economic concern that strict schemes would retard industrial development with attendant social costs. The 94th Congress, confronting these competing interests, was unable to agree on what response was in the public interest: legislative proposals to deal with nonattainment failed to command the necessary consensus.

In light of this situation, the EPA published an Emissions Offset Interpretative Ruling in December 1976, see 41 Fed. Reg. 55524, to "fill the gap," as respondents put it, until Congress acted. * * * The Ruling gave primary emphasis to the rapid attainment of the statute's environmental goals. Consistent with that emphasis, the construction of every new source in nonattainment areas had to meet the "lowest achievable emission rate" under the current state of the art for that type of facility. The 1976 Ruling did not, however, explicitly adopt or reject the "bubble concept."

[Congress then enacted the Clean Air Act Amendments of 1977.] Most significantly for our purposes, the statute provided that each plan shall "(6) require permits for the construction and operation of new or modified major stationary sources in accordance with section 173. . . ." Before issuing a permit, § 173 requires [the] state agency to determine that there will be sufficient emissions reductions in the region to offset the emissions from the new source and also to allow for reasonable further progress toward attainment, * * * and [that] the proposed source [complies] with the lowest achievable emission rate (LAER).

The 1977 Amendments contain no specific reference to the "bubble concept." Nor do they contain a specific definition of the term "stationary source," though they did not disturb the definition of "stationary source" contained in [the prior Act.] The legislative history of the portion of the 1977 Amendments dealing with nonattainment areas does not contain any specific comment on the "bubble concept" or the question whether a plantwide definition of a stationary source is permissible under the permit program. It does, however, plainly disclose that in the permit program Congress sought to accommodate the conflict between the economic interest in permitting capital improvements to continue and the environmental interest in improving air quality. * * *

[In January 1979, the EPA announced that it would reject a plant-wide definition of the term "stationary source" in states that did not have revised plans to deal with pollution, but would permit it in certain circumstances if authorized by an approved plan.] In August 1980, however, the EPA adopted a regulation that, in essence, applied the basic reasoning of the Court of Appeals in these cases. [The] EPA adopted a dual definition of "source" for nonattainment areas that required a permit whenever a change in either the entire plant, or one of its components, would result in a significant increase in emissions even if the increase was completely offset by reductions elsewhere in the plant. * * *

**Take Note**

The EPA under President Carter ultimately chose a reading of the statute that would require permits in more cases, and thus would force a quicker reduction in pollution. The EPA under President Reagan disagreed and adopted the "bubble" view of the statute. This was the view that the respondents challenged in this case.

In 1981 a new administration took office and initiated a "Government-wide reexamination of regulatory burdens and complexities." 46 Fed. Reg. 16281. In the context of that review, the EPA reevaluated the various arguments that had been advanced in connection with the proper definition of the term "source" and concluded that the term should be given the same definition in both nonattainment areas and PSD areas.

[The EPA] set forth several reasons for concluding that the plantwide definition was more appropriate. It pointed out that the dual definition "can act as a disincentive to new investment and modernization by discouraging modifications to existing facilities" and "can actually retard progress in air pollution control by discouraging replacement of older, dirtier processes or pieces of equipment with new, cleaner ones." Moreover, the new definition "would simplify EPA's rules by using the same definition of 'source' for PSD, nonattainment new source review and the construction moratorium. This reduces confusion and inconsistency." Finally, the agency explained that additional requirements that remained in place would accomplish the fundamental purposes of achieving attainment with NAAQS's as expeditiously as possible. These conclusions were expressed in a proposed rulemaking in August 1981 that was formally promulgated in October.

[Respondents] contend that the text of the Act requires the EPA to use a dual definition—if either a component of a plant, or the plant as a whole, emits over 100 tons of pollutant, it is a major stationary source. [But the text] sheds virtually no light on the meaning of the term "stationary source." [Respondents also] argue that the legislative history and policies of the Act foreclose the plantwide definition, and that the EPA's interpretation is not entitled to deference because it represents a sharp break with prior interpretations of the Act. Based on our examination of the legislative history, we agree with the Court of Appeals that it is unilluminating.

Our review of the EPA's varying interpretations of the word "source"—both before and after the 1977 Amendments—convinces us that the agency primarily responsible for administering this important legislation has consistently interpreted it flexibly—not in a sterile textual vacuum, but in the context of implementing policy decisions in a technical and complex arena. The fact that the agency has from time to time changed its interpretation of the term "source" does not, as respondents argue, lead us to conclude that no deference should be accorded the agency's interpretation of the statute. An initial agency interpretation is not instantly carved in stone. On the contrary, the agency, to engage in informed rulemaking, must consider varying interpretations and the wisdom of its policy on a continuing basis. Moreover, the fact that the agency has adopted different definitions in different contexts adds force to the argument that the definition itself is flexible, particularly since Congress has never indicated any disapproval of a flexible reading of the statute.

[T]he Administrator's interpretation represents a reasonable accommodation of manifestly competing interests and is entitled to deference: the regulatory scheme is technical and complex, the agency considered the matter in a detailed and reasoned fashion, and the decision involves reconciling conflicting policies. Congress intended to accommodate both interests, but did not do so itself on the level of specificity presented by these cases. Perhaps that body consciously desired the Administrator to strike the balance at this level, thinking that those with great expertise and charged with responsibility for administering the provision would be in a better position to do so; perhaps it simply did not consider the question at this level; and perhaps Congress was unable to forge a coalition on either side of the question, and those on each side decided to take their chances with the scheme devised by the agency. For judicial purposes, it matters not which of these things occurred.

Judges are not experts in the field, and are not part of either political branch of the Government. Courts must, in some cases, reconcile competing political interests, but not on the basis of the judges' personal policy preferences. In contrast, an agency to which Congress has delegated policy-making responsibilities may, within the limits of that delegation, properly rely upon the incumbent administration's views of wise policy to inform its judgments. While agencies are not directly accountable to the people, the Chief Executive is, and it is entirely appropriate for this political branch of the Government to make such policy choices—resolving the competing interests which Congress itself either inadvertently did not resolve, or intentionally left to be resolved by the agency charged with the administration of the statute in light of everyday realities.

When a challenge to an agency construction of a statutory provision, fairly conceptualized, really centers on the wisdom of the agency's policy, rather than whether it is a reasonable choice within a gap left open by Congress, the challenge must fail. In such a case, federal judges—who have no constituency—have a duty to respect legitimate policy choices made by those who do. The responsibilities for assessing the wisdom of such policy choices and resolving the struggle between competing views of the public interest are not judicial ones: "Our Constitution vests such responsibilities in the political branches." *TVA v. Hill*, 437 U.S. 153, 195 (1978).

We hold that the EPA's definition of the term "source" is a permissible construction of the statute which seeks to accommodate progress in reducing air pollution with economic growth. [Reversed.]

Justice Marshall and Justice Rehnquist took no part in the consideration or decision of these cases.

Justice O'Connor took no part in the decision of these cases.

---

## Points for Discussion

### *a. The* **Chevron** *Test*

The Court in *Chevron* announced a two-step test for reviewing agency interpretations of the statutes that they are responsible for administering. First, the court determines "whether Congress has directly spoken to the precise question at issue." This step requires the court to consider whether the statute is clear; if so, "that is the end of the matter; for the court, as well as the agency, must give effect to the unambiguously expressed intent of Congress." Second, "if the statute is silent or ambiguous with respect to the specific issue, the question for the court is whether the agency's answer is based on a permissible construction of the statute." In such cases, the court should not determine the "best" reading of the statute, but instead must accept the agency's interpretation as long as it is "reasonable."

In what ways does this test differ from the approach that the Court had previously used to review agency determinations of matters that were not solely factual in nature? In thinking about that question, consider the nature of the agency's decision in *Chevron*. Was it a purely legal question, based solely on the meaning of a statutory term? Or was it a mixed question of law and fact that required the agency to apply some legal typology to a specific set of facts? Did the agency resolve the matter in a way that didn't bind private parties, or did it reach the decision in the course of a proceeding that resulted in an agency rule with the force of law? Was the agency's view longstanding or consistently held? How would a court have reviewed the agency's determination under the old framework?

***b. Deference***

When courts talk about deference, what they mean is that the reviewing body—here, the court—should accept the decision of the body under review—here, the agency—out of respect for that body's decision, even if it was not the decision that the reviewing body would have reached if it had been able to make the decision in the first instance. Common examples of judicial deference are appellate review of trial court fact-finding and trial court discovery rulings. Appellate courts uphold findings of fact unless they are *clearly* erroneous; they will not reverse findings of fact if they are merely arguably or possibly wrong. Similarly, appellate courts do not reverse discovery rulings merely because the appellate judges might have made a different judgment call on a close question; they reverse such decisions only if they constitute an *abuse* of discretion.

At *Chevron* step two, courts apply a genuine form of deference: they should not set aside the agency's view merely because the court would have reached a different conclusion "if the question initially had arisen in a judicial proceeding." In other words, a court reviewing an agency interpretation of an ambiguous statutes should not endeavor to determine the best reading of the statute; instead, the court should set aside an agency's interpretation of the statute it is charged with implementing only if the agency's view is not reasonable. In your view, was the EPA's interpretation of the phrase "stationary source" reasonable? How does a judge know if a particular interpretation of a statute is "reasonable"?

### c. *Statutory Clarity and Statutory Ambiguity*

Under the Court's test, judicial deference is available to a reasonable agency interpretation of the statute that it is responsible for implementing "if the statute is silent or ambiguous with respect to the specific issue" in question. In other words, the trigger for judicial deference is statutory ambiguity. Just how ambiguous does a statute have to be in order to trigger deference under step two of the *Chevron* test?

Consider some of the statutes that we considered in our unit on statutory interpretation. Was the statute at issue in *Yates v. United States*, 574 U.S. 528 (2015), which made it a crime to conceal any "tangible object with the intent to impede, obstruct, or influence the investigation * * * of any matter within the jurisdiction of any department or agency of the United States," ambiguous in the sense that the Court described in *Chevron*? What about the statute in *Smith v. United States*, 508 U.S. 223 (1993), which required an enhanced sentence for anyone who "uses [a] firearm" "during and in relation to [a] drug trafficking crime"? Had Congress "directly spoken to the precise question at issue" in either of those cases?

**Make the Connection**

We considered *Yates*, which involved the prosecution of a man who threw fish back in the ocean to evade the enforcement of wildlife regulations, and *Smith*, which involved a man who traded a gun for drugs, in Chapter 3.

To be sure, the Court in *Chevron* noted that a court applying step one of the test should employ "traditional tools of statutory construction" in seeking to ascertain whether "Congress had an intention on the precise question at issue." (The Court in *Chevron*, for example, considered legislative history in seeking to determine whether Congress intended to require a particular understanding of the phrase "statutory source.") Even assuming that courts regularly consult legislative history and other extra-textual sources of statutory meaning, do you think we can expect there to be many cases in which Congress has spoken to the precise question at issue?

### d. Chevron *and the Non-Delegation Doctrine*

In Chapter 6, we considered the non-delegation doctrine, which states that Congress cannot delegate the "legislative power"—that is, the power to make very important decisions of policy—to an administrative agency. To ensure that Congress does not delegate the legislative power, Congress must provide an "intelligible principle" to guide the agency's exercise of decision-making authority.

In *Chevron*, after concluding that Congress had not resolved the question whether the term "stationary source" referred to each apparatus capable of emitting pollution or instead to an entire industrial complex, the Court noted that there are several reasons why Congress might not have resolved such a question. The Court stated that Congress might have "consciously desired the Administrator to strike the balance at this level" of specificity; or that Congress might not have "consider[ed] the question at this level" of specificity; or that Congress might have been "unable to forge a coalition on either side of the question, and those on each side decided to take their chances with the scheme devised by the agency."

In other words, Congress might have intentionally delegated the power to the agency to decide the policy question, in the same way that Congress gave the Department of Transportation power to announce automobile safety standards (according to principles identified in the statute); or the question might not have occurred to Congress, but it is fair to assume that Congress would have wanted the agency to resolve such questions; or the question *did* occur to Congress, but it couldn't achieve consensus on a disputed question of policy. According to the Court, for "judicial purposes, it matters not which of these things occurred."

Assume that the last possibility is in fact what happened. Shouldn't it matter, under the non-delegation doctrine, that members of Congress couldn't decide whether to prefer environmental or instead economic interests and, as a result, punted the question to the agency to decide? Or is the opinion in *Chevron* a candid acknowledgment that, notwithstanding the non-delegation doctrine, courts should permit Congress to delegate broad policy-making power to agencies?

***e. Institutional Competence, Comparative Expertise, and Accountability***

At bottom, the Court in *Chevron* addressed an institutional question: who should get to decide the meaning of ambiguous regulatory statutes? In our consideration of statutory interpretation in Chapters 2–5, we proceeded on the assumption that courts should be responsible for that task. What is the argument for why courts should have the last word on the meaning of statutes? Conversely, why might it make sense to leave questions about the meaning of ambiguous statutes to agencies? Are you persuaded by the reasons that the Court offered in *Chevron* for the two-step approach to agency interpretations of regulatory statutes?

***f. Judicial Deference and Judicial Skepticism in Reviewing Agency Action***

The Court in *Chevron* held that agency interpretations of ambiguous regulatory statutes are entitled to judicial deference. Is it possible to reconcile this conclusion with the Court's approach in *Motor Vehicle Manufacturers Ass'n v. State Farm Mutual Automobile Ins. Co.*, 463 U.S. 29 (1983), which we considered in Chapter 7? Recall that in *State Farm*, the Court applied "hard-look review" to determine if the agency had properly justified the repeal of a rule that required passive restraints in new vehicles.

In thinking about that question, it helps to think about the particular legal questions at issue in the two cases. *Chevron* involved a claim that an agency had interpreted its mandate in a way that conflicted with the statute. *State Farm*, in contrast, involved a claim that the agency had failed to justify a decision with reference to the appropriate factors. Notice that in *Chevron*, there was no controversy over whether the agency had properly *explained* its rule in light of the relevant statutory considerations—environmental protection and economic development—or the comments of interested persons; the question was simply whether the agency's interpretation of the term "stationary source" was consistent with the statute. And in *State Farm*, there was no contention that the agency had misunderstood the statute in concluding that it had power to decide which safety features should be required in all new cars; instead, the question was whether the agency had properly explained its decision to ease a requirement that it had previously validly imposed.

In *Chevron*, the Court concluded that agency interpretations of ambiguous statutes are entitled to judicial deference; in *State Farm*, in contrast, the Court held that reviewing courts should conduct a careful review of the reasoning that agencies offer to justify their policy determinations. Does this framework for reviewing agency non-factual determinations make sense? Consider view that follows.

---

## Perspective and Analysis

> [T]he present law of judicial review of administrative decisionmaking, the heart of administrative law, contains an important anomaly. The law (1) requires courts to defer to agency judgments about matters of law, but (2) it also suggests that courts conduct independent, "in-depth" reviews of agency judgments about matters of policy. Is this not the exact opposite of a rational system? Would one not expect courts to conduct a stricter review of matters of law, where courts are more expert, but more lenient review of matters of policy, where agencies are more expert?

**Stephen Breyer, *Judicial Review of Questions of Law and Policy*, 38 ADMIN. L. REV. 363, 397 (1986).** Can you articulate a defense of *Chevron* and *State Farm* in response to then-Judge Breyer's critique?

---

*Chevron* was an incredibly influential decision; even though the Court decided it only a few decades ago, it is one of the most cited cases of all time. But *Chevron*'s significance—the likelihood that it will affect judicial decision-making—depends in large part on how often courts reviewing agency action get to *Chevron* step two. At step two, a reviewing court is supposed to defer to a reasonable agency interpretation, even if the court, if presented with the question on a clean slate, would have reached a different conclusion about the statute's meaning. But if courts routinely resolve cases at step one—by concluding that the statute is clear, and thus that the agency interpretation is not entitled to deference—then *Chevon*'s impact will be considerably diminished.

How exactly does a court decide whether Congress has resolved "the precise question at issue"—or, stated another way, that the statute is not ambiguous? Are ordinary tools of statutory interpretation likely to lead courts to conclude that statutes are sufficiently clear to preclude deference to agency interpretations? Consider the case that follows.

---

## *MCI Telecommunications Corp. v. AT&T*

512 U.S. 218 (1994)

JUSTICE SCALIA delivered the opinion of the Court.

Section 203(a) of Title 47 of the United States Code requires communications common carriers to file tariffs with the Federal Communications Commission, and § 203(b) authorizes the Commission to "modify" any requirement of § 203. These cases present the question whether the Commission's decision to make tariff filing optional for all nondominant long-distance carriers is a valid exercise of its modification authority.

*** An understanding of [this case] requires a brief review of the Commission's efforts to regulate and then deregulate the telecommunications industry. When Congress created the Commission in 1934, AT&T, through its vertically integrated Bell system, held a virtual monopoly over the Nation's telephone service. The Communications Act of 1934, 48 Stat. 1064, as amended, authorized the Commission to regulate the rates charged for communication services to ensure that they were reasonable and nondiscriminatory. The requirements of § 203 that common carriers file their rates with the Commission and charge only the filed rate were the centerpiece of the Act's regulatory scheme.

In the 1970's, technological advances reduced the entry costs for competitors of AT&T in the market for long-distance telephone service. The Commission, recognizing the feasibility of greater competition, passed regulations to facilitate competitive entry. By 1979, competition in the provision of long-distance service was well established, and some urged that the continuation of extensive tariff filing requirements served only to impose unnecessary costs on new entrants and to facilitate collusive pricing. The Commission held hearings on the matter, see *Competitive Carrier Notice of Inquiry and Proposed Rulemaking*, 77 F.C.C.2d 308 (1979), following which it issued a series of rules that have produced this litigation. [Those rules, issued in a series of orders, distinguished between dominant carriers in the long-distance market—that is, carriers with market power, a category that included only AT&T—and nondominant carriers, a category that included all other long-distance providers. The rule at issue exempted nondominant carriers, including MCI, from the requirement of filing rates (and charging only the rates filed). AT&T challenged the rule, arguing that the FCC lacked authority to exempt carriers from the rate-filing requirement.]

Section 203 of the Communications Act contains both the filed rate provisions of the Act and the Commission's disputed modification authority. It provides in relevant part:

> "(a) Filing; public display.
>
> "Every common carrier, except connecting carriers, shall, within such reasonable time as the Commission shall designate, file with the Commission and print and keep open for public inspection schedules showing all charges . . ., whether such charges are joint or separate, and showing the classifications, practices, and regulations affecting such charges. . . .
>
> "(b) Changes in schedule; discretion of Commission to modify requirements.
>
> "(1) No change shall be made in the charges, classifications, regulations, or practices which have been so filed and published except after one hundred and twenty days notice to the Commission and to the public, which shall be published in such form and contain such information as the Commission may by regulations prescribe.
>
> "(2) The Commission may, in its discretion and for good cause shown, modify any requirement made by or under the authority of this section either in particular instances or by general order applicable to special circumstances or conditions except that the Commission may not require the notice period specified in paragraph (1) to be more than one hundred and twenty days. * * *" 47 U.S.C. § 203 (1988 ed. and Supp. IV).

The dispute between the parties turns on the meaning of the phrase "modify any requirement" in § 203(b)(2). Petitioners argue that it gives the Commission authority to make even basic and fundamental changes in the scheme created by that section. We disagree. The word "modify"—like a number of other English words employing the root "mod-" (deriving from the Latin word for "measure"), such as "moderate," "modulate," "modest," and "modicum"—has a connotation of increment or limitation. Virtually every dictionary we are aware of says that "to modify" means to change moderately or in minor fashion. See, *e.g.*, Random House Dictionary of the English Language 1236 (2d ed. 1987) ("to change somewhat the form or qualities of; alter partially; amend"); Webster's Third New International Dictionary 1452 (1981) ("to make minor changes in the form or structure of: alter without transforming"); 9 Oxford English Dictionary 952 (2d ed. 1989) ("[t]o make partial changes in; to change (an object) in respect of some of its qualities; to alter or vary without radical transformation"); Black's Law Dictionary 1004 (6th ed. 1990) ("[t]o alter; to change in incidental or subordinate features; enlarge; extend; amend; limit; reduce").

In support of their position, petitioners cite dictionary definitions contained in, or derived from, a single source, Webster's Third New International Dictionary 1452 (1981) (Webster's Third), which includes among the meanings of "modify," "to

**Take Note**

On which touchstone of interpretation did the Court focus in deciding whether the statute was sufficiently ambiguous to trigger deference under *Chevron* step two? Do you agree that the ordinary meaning of the statute was so clear that the Court could conclude that Congress had resolved the precise question at issue?

make a basic or important change in." Petitioners contend that this establishes sufficient ambiguity to entitle the Commission to deference in its acceptance of the broader meaning, which in turn requires approval of its permissive detariffing policy. *See Chevron U.S.A. Inc. v. Natural Resources Defense Council, Inc.*, 467 U.S. 837, 843 (1984). In short, they contend that the courts must defer to the agency's choice among available dictionary definitions * * *.

Most cases of verbal ambiguity in statutes involve * * * a selection between accepted alternative meanings shown as such by many dictionaries. One can envision (though a court case does not immediately come to mind) having to choose between accepted alternative meanings, one of which is so newly accepted that it has only been recorded by a single lexicographer. (Some dictionary must have been the very first to record the widespread use of "projection," for example, to mean "forecast.") But what petitioners demand that we accept as creating an ambiguity here is a rarity even rarer than that: a meaning set forth in a single dictionary (and, as we say, its progeny) which not only *supplements* the meaning contained in all other dictionaries, but *contradicts* one of the meanings contained in virtually all other dictionaries. Indeed, contradicts one of the alternative meanings contained in the out-of-step dictionary itself—for as we have observed, Webster's Third itself defines "modify" to connote *both* (specifically) major change *and* (specifically) minor change. It is hard to see how that can be. When the word "modify" has come to mean *both* "to change in some respects" *and* "to change fundamentally" it will in fact mean *neither* of those things. It will simply mean "to change," and some adverb will have to be called into service to indicate the great or small degree of the change.

If that is what the peculiar Webster's Third definition means to suggest has happened—and what petitioners suggest by appealing to Webster's Third—we simply disagree. "Modify," in our view, connotes moderate change. It might be good English to say that the French Revolution "modified" the status of the French nobility—but only because there is a figure of speech called understatement and a literary device known as sarcasm. And it might be unsurprising to discover a 1972 White House press release saying that "the Administration is modifying its position with regard to prosecution of the war in Vietnam"—but only because press agents tend to impart what is nowadays called "spin." Such intentional distortions, or simply careless or ignorant misuse, must have formed the basis for the usage that Webster's Third, and Webster's Third alone, reported. It is perhaps gilding the lily to add this: In 1934, when the Communications Act became law—the most relevant time for determining a statutory term's meaning, *see Perrin v. United States*, 444 U.S. 37, 42–45

(1979)—Webster's Third was not yet even contemplated. To our knowledge *all* English dictionaries provided the narrow definition of "modify," including those published by G. & C. Merriam Company. See Webster's New International Dictionary 1577 (2d ed. 1934); Webster's Collegiate Dictionary 628 (4th ed. 1934). We have not the slightest doubt that is the meaning the statute intended.

Beyond the word itself, a further indication that the § 203(b)(2) authority to "modify" does not contemplate fundamental changes is the sole exception to that authority which the section provides. One of the requirements of § 203 is that changes to filed tariffs can be made only after 120 days' notice to the Commission and the public. § 203(b)(1). The *only* exception to the Commission's § 203(b)(2) modification authority is as follows: "except that the Commission may not require the notice period specified in paragraph (1) to be more than one hundred and twenty days." Is it conceivable that the statute is indifferent to the Commission's power to eliminate the tariff-filing requirement entirely for all except one firm in the long-distance sector, and yet strains out the gnat of extending the waiting period for tariff revision beyond 120 days? We think not. The exception is not as ridiculous as a Lilliputian in London only because it is to be found in Lilliput: in the small-scale world of "modifications," it is a big deal.

**FYI**

The Lilliputians were fictional miniature people described in Jonathan Swift's novel *Gulliver's Travels*.

Since an agency's interpretation of a statute is not entitled to deference when it goes beyond the meaning that the statute can bear, *see, e.g., Pittston Coal Group v. Sebben*, 488 U.S. 105, 113, (1988); *Chevron*, 467 U.S., at 842–843, the Commission's permissive detariffing policy can be justified only if it makes a less than radical or fundamental change in the Act's tariff-filing requirement. The Commission's attempt to establish that no more than that is involved greatly understates the extent to which its policy deviates from the filing requirement, and greatly undervalues the importance of the filing requirement itself.

To consider the latter point first: * * * The tariff-filing requirement is [the] heart of the common-carrier section of the Communications Act. * * * It is highly unlikely that Congress would leave the determination of whether an industry will be entirely, or even substantially, rate-regulated to agency discretion—and even more unlikely that it would achieve that through such a subtle device as permission to "modify" rate-filing requirements.

Bearing in mind, then, the enormous importance to the statutory scheme of the tariff-filing provision, we turn to whether what has occurred here can be considered a mere "modification." The Commission stresses that its detariffing policy applies only to nondominant carriers, so that the rates charged to over half of all consumers in the long-distance market are on file with the Commission. It is not clear to us that the proportion of customers affected, rather than the proportion of carriers affected, is the proper measure of the extent of the exemption * * *. But even assuming it is, we think an elimination of the crucial provision of the statute for 40% of a major sector of the industry is much too extensive to be considered a "modification." What we have here, in reality, is a fundamental revision of the statute, changing it from a scheme of rate regulation in long-distance common-carrier communications to a scheme of rate regulation only where effective competition does not exist. That may be a good idea, but it was not the idea Congress enacted into law in 1934.

Finally, petitioners earnestly urge that their interpretation of § 203(b) furthers the Communications Act's broad purpose of promoting efficient telephone service. They claim that although the filing requirement prevented price discrimination and unfair practices while AT&T maintained a monopoly over long-distance service, it frustrates those same goals now that there is greater competition in that market. Specifically, they contend that filing costs raise artificial barriers to entry and that the publication of rates facilitates parallel pricing and stifles price competition. We have considerable sympathy with these arguments (though we doubt it makes sense, if one is concerned about the use of filed tariffs to communicate pricing information, to require filing by the dominant carrier, the firm most likely to be a price leader). * * * But our estimations, and the Commission's estimations, of desirable policy cannot alter the meaning of the federal Communications Act of 1934. For better or worse, the Act establishes a rate-regulation, filed-tariff system for common-carrier communications, and the Commission's desire "to 'increase competition' cannot provide [it] authority to alter the well-established statutory filed rate requirements," *Maislin Industries, U.S., Inc. v. Primary Steel, Inc.*, 497 U.S. 116, 135 (1990). * * * As we observed in the context of a dispute over the filed-rate doctrine more than 80 years ago, "such considerations address themselves to Congress, not to the courts," *Armour Packing Co. v. United States*, 209 U.S. 56, 82 (1908).

Justice O'Connor took no part in the consideration or decision of these cases.

Justice Stevens, with whom Justice Blackmun and Justice Souter join, dissenting.

* * * The Communications Act of 1934 (Act) gives the FCC unusually broad discretion to meet new and unanticipated problems in order to fulfill its sweeping mandate "to make available, so far as possible, to all the people of the United States, a rapid, efficient, Nation-wide and world-wide wire and radio communication service with adequate facilities at reasonable charges." 47 U.S.C. § 151. This Court's consistent interpretation of the Act has afforded the Commission ample leeway to interpret and apply its statutory powers and responsibilities. *See, e.g., United States v. Southwestern Cable Co.*, 392 U.S. 157, 172–173 (1968). The Court today abandons that approach in favor of a rigid literalism that deprives the FCC of the flexibility Congress meant it to have in order to implement the core policies of the Act in rapidly changing conditions.

[The majority] does not take issue with the Commission's conclusions that mandatory filing of tariff schedules serves no useful purpose and is actually counterproductive in the case of carriers who lack market power. As the Commission had noted in its prior detariffing orders, if a nondominant carrier sought to charge inflated rates, "customers would simply move to other carriers." 7 FCC Rcd, at 8079. Moreover, an absence of market power will ordinarily preclude firms of any kind from engaging in price discrimination. The Commission plausibly concluded that any slight enforcement benefits a tariff-filing requirement might offer were outweighed by the burdens it would put on new entrants and consumers. Thus, the sole question for us is whether the FCC's policy, however sensible, is nonetheless inconsistent with the Act.

**FYI**

Before Justice Stevens became a judge (on the U.S. Court of Appeals for the Seventh Circuit), he was an antitrust lawyer in Chicago.

In my view, each of the Commission's detariffing orders was squarely within its power to "modify any requirement" of § 203. Section 203(b)(2) plainly confers at least some discretion to modify the general rule that carriers file tariffs, for it speaks of "*any* requirement." * * * The FCC's authority to modify § 203's requirements in "particular instances" or by "general order applicable to special circumstances or conditions" emphasizes the expansive character of the Commission's authority: modifications may be narrow or broad, depending upon the Commission's appraisal of current conditions. From the vantage of a Congress seeking to regulate an almost completely monopolized industry, the advent of competition is surely a "special circumstance or condition" that might legitimately call for different regulatory treatment.

The only statutory exception to the Commission's modification authority provides that it may not extend the 120-day notice period set out in § 203(b)(1). See § 203(b)(2). The Act thus imposes a specific limit on the Commission's authority to *stiffen* that regulatory imposition on carriers, but does not confine the Commission's authority to *relax* it. It was no stretch for the FCC to draw from this single, unidirectional statutory limitation on its modification authority the inference that its authority is otherwise unlimited.

According to the Court, the term "modify," as explicated in all but the most unreliable dictionaries, rules out the Commission's claimed authority to relieve nondominant carriers of the basic obligation to file tariffs. Dictionaries can be useful aids in statutory interpretation, but they are no substitute for close analysis of what words mean as used in a particular statutory context. Even if the sole possible meaning of "modify" were to make "minor" changes, further elaboration is needed to show why the detariffing policy should fail. The Commission came to its present policy through a series of rulings that gradually relaxed the filing requirements for nondominant carriers. Whether the current policy should count as a cataclysmic or merely an incremental departure from the § 203(a) baseline depends on whether one focuses on particular carriers' obligations to file (in which case the Commission's policy arguably works a major shift) or on the statutory policies behind the tariff-filing requirement (which remain satisfied because market constraints on nondominant carriers obviate the need for rate filing). When § 203 is viewed as part of a statute whose aim is to constrain monopoly power, the Commission's decision to exempt nondominant carriers is a rational and "measured" adjustment to novel circumstances—one that remains faithful to the core purpose of the tariff-filing section. See Black's Law Dictionary 1198 (3d ed. 1933) (defining "modification" as "A change; an alteration which introduces new elements into the details, or cancels some of them, but leaves *the general purpose and effect of the subject-matter* intact").

**Take Note**

On which touchstone of interpretation did Justice Stevens focus in interpreting the statute?

A modification pursuant to § 203(b)(1), like any other order issued under the Act, must of course be consistent with the purposes of the statute. * * * But the Commission has repeatedly explained that (1) a carrier that lacks market power is entirely unlikely to charge unreasonable or discriminatory rates, (2) the statutory bans on unreasonable charges and price discrimination apply with full force regardless of whether carriers have to file tariffs, (3) any suspected violations by nondominant carriers can be addressed on the Commission's own motion or on a damages complaint filed pursuant to § 206, and (4) the FCC can reimpose a tariff requirement should violations occur. See, *e.g.*, 7 FCC Rcd, at 8078–8079. The Court does not adequately respond to the FCC's explanations, and gives no reason whatsoever to doubt the Commission's considered judgment that tariff filing is altogether unnecessary in the case of competitive carriers * * *.

The filed tariff provisions of the Communications Act are not ends in themselves, but are merely one of several procedural *means* for the Commission to ensure that carriers do not charge unreasonable or discriminatory rates. See 84 F.C.C.2d, at 483. The Commission has reasonably concluded that this particular means of enforcing the statute's substantive mandates will prove counterproductive in the case of nondominant long-distance carriers. Even if the 1934 Congress did not define the scope of the Commission's modification authority with perfect scholarly precision, this is surely a paradigm case for judicial deference to the agency's interpretation, particularly in a statutory regime so obviously meant to maximize administrative flexibility. Whatever the best reading of § 203(b)(2), the Commission's reading cannot in my view be termed unreasonable. It is informed (as ours is not) by a practical understanding of the role (or lack thereof) that filed tariffs play in the modern regulatory climate and in the telecommunications industry. Since 1979, the FCC has sought to adapt measures originally designed to control monopoly power to new market conditions. It has carefully and consistently explained that mandatory tariff-filing rules frustrate the core statutory interest in rate reasonableness. The Commission's use of the "discretion" expressly conferred by § 203(b)(2) reflects "a reasonable accommodation of manifestly competing interests and is entitled to deference: the regulatory scheme is technical and complex, the agency considered the matter in a detailed and reasoned fashion, and the decision involves reconciling conflicting policies." *Chevron U.S.A. Inc. v. Natural Resources Defense Council, Inc.*, 467 U.S. 837, 865 (1984). The FCC has permissibly interpreted its § 203(b)(2) authority in service of the goals Congress set forth in the Act. We should sustain its eminently sound, experience-tested, and uncommonly well-explained judgment.

**Take Note**

Did Justice Stevens assert that the Court should uphold the agency's order at step one of the *Chevron* test or at step two?

---

## Points for Discussion

### *a. Agency Interpretations of Statutes*

In some cases, it will be obvious that the agency has offered an interpretation of the statute that it is responsible for administering. For example, if the statute states that the agency should establish limits for exposure to workplace toxins at the level necessary to prevent "material health impairments," the agency might issue a rule that defines "material health impairments" to mean any condition that requires medical treatment, including with over-the-counter drugs. In such a case, the agency's rule expressly defines a statutory term and therefore "interprets" the statute. In a challenge to such a rule, a court would have to decide whether the statute is ambiguous with respect to the range of conditions that the agency should endeavor to prevent; if a court reviewing the rule were to decide that the statute is ambiguous, it would defer to the agency's interpretation at step 2 of the *Chevron* test as long as the interpretation is reasonable.

Is this how the question of interpretation arose in the *MCI* case? The FCC issued a series of orders—the type of decision that an agency issues at the conclusion of an adjudication—that announced the ultimate decision to waive the filing requirement for non-dominant carriers. But the agency did not issue a rule that said something like, "The term 'modify,' as used in section 203, means 'change, either modestly or fundamentally.' " Instead, the agency announced a policy and then, when AT&T challenged it, defended the policy by relying on its statutory authority to "modify any requirement made by or under the authority of this section." In other words, the agency relied on a particular reading of the statute in asserting the power to waive the filing requirement for non-dominant carriers. Such implicit interpretations are a common way for a *Chevron* issue to arise. Would it have mattered, for purposes of applying the *Chevron* test, if the agency had issued a rule, after notice and comment, that announced the agency's view of the meaning of various statutory terms, including the word "modify"?

#### *b. Statutory Interpretation in the Age of* **Chevron**

*Chevron* step one directs courts to decide whether Congress has spoken to the precise question at issue in the case. As the Court explained in *Chevron*, "[i]f a court, employing traditional tools of statutory construction, ascertains that Congress had an intention on the precise question at issue, that intention is the law and must be given effect." But the Court in *Chevron* did not purport to resolve what counts as "traditional" (or appropriate) "tools of statutory construction." Accordingly, judges in *Chevron* cases often reprise many of the debates that we considered in Chapters 2–5 over the appropriate way to read statutes.

Should the fact that an agency has offered an interpretation of a statute that it is responsible for implementing affect the way that judges read statutes when applying step one of the *Chevron* test? Or should all of the reasons why courts might be willing to defer to agency interpretations of ambiguous statutory provisions be irrelevant at step one, when the court is trying to determine whether the statute is ambiguous in the first place?

#### *c. Statutory Clarity, Statutory Ambiguity, and Deference*

As we have noted, the trigger for deference to agency interpretations under the *Chevron* test is the existence of statutory ambiguity. If a reviewing court concludes that the statute is clear—that Congress spoke to the precise question at issue—then there is no reason to defer to the agency's view; as the Court explained in *Chevron*, the "judiciary is the final authority on issues of statutory construction and must reject administrative constructions which are contrary to clear congressional intent." As a consequence, the significance of *Chevron* depends on the willingness to judges to find statutory ambiguity—or, conversely, the tendency of judges to conclude that statutes are clear.

Does a judge's choice of interpretive methodology correlate with the likelihood that the judge will find statutory clarity (or instead ambiguity)? For example, is a textualist judge—one who focuses mostly or exclusively on the ordinary meaning of the statutory text—more (or less) likely to conclude that statutes are clear than a judge who focuses on congressional intent or purpose? Does the disagreement between Justices Scalia and Stevens suggest anything about the answer to this question? Compare Thomas W. Merrill, *Textualism and the Future of the* Chevron *Doctrine*, 72 WASH. U. L.Q. 351, 362 (1994) (arguing that textualist judges will be less inclined than will non-textualist judges to apply deference under *Chevron*), with Orin S. Kerr, *Shedding Light on* Chevron*: An Empirical Study of the Chevron Doctrine in the U.S.*

*Courts of Appeals*, 15 YALE J. REG. 1 (1998) (finding no correlation between a judge's interpretive method and his or her approach to *Chevron*).

---

## *FDA v. Brown & Williamson Tobacco Co.*

529 U.S. 120 (2000)

JUSTICE O'CONNOR delivered the opinion of the Court.

This case involves one of the most troubling public health problems facing our Nation today: the thousands of premature deaths that occur each year because of tobacco use. In 1996, the Food and Drug Administration (FDA), after having expressly disavowed any such authority since its inception, asserted jurisdiction to regulate tobacco products. See 61 Fed. Reg. 44619–45318. * * *

The [Food, Drug, and Cosmetic Act (FDCA or Act), 52 Stat. 1040, as amended, 21 U.S.C. § 301 *et seq.*,] grants the FDA, as the designee of the Secretary of Health and Human Services (HHS), the authority to regulate, among other items, "drugs" and "devices." See 21 U.S.C. §§ 321(g)–(h), 393(1994 ed. and Supp. III). The Act defines "drug" to include "articles (other than food) intended to affect the structure or any function of the body." 21 U.S.C. § 321(g)(1)(C). It defines "device," in part, as "an instrument, apparatus, implement, machine, contrivance, . . . or other similar or related article, including any component, part, or accessory, which is . . . intended to affect the structure or any function of the body." § 321(h). The Act also grants the FDA the authority to regulate so-called "combination products," which "constitute a combination of a drug, device, or biological product." § 353(g)(1). The FDA has construed this provision as giving it the discretion to regulate combination products as drugs, as devices, or as both. See 61 Fed. Reg. 44400 (1996).

On August 28, 1996, [after notice and comment,] the FDA issued a final rule entitled "Regulations Restricting the Sale and Distribution of Cigarettes and Smokeless Tobacco to Protect Children and Adolescents." *Id.*, at 44396. The FDA determined that nicotine is a "drug" and that cigarettes and smokeless tobacco are "drug delivery devices," and therefore it had jurisdiction under the FDCA to regulate tobacco products as customarily marketed—that is, without manufacturer claims of therapeutic benefit. *Id.*, at 44397, 44402. First, the FDA found that tobacco products "affect the structure or any function of the body" because nicotine "has significant pharmacological effects." *Id.*, at 44631. Specifically, nicotine "exerts psychoactive, or mood-altering, effects on the brain" that cause and sustain addiction, have both tranquilizing and stimulating effects, and control weight. *Id.*, at 44631–44632. Second, the FDA determined that these effects were "intended" under the FDCA because they "are so widely known and foreseeable that [they] may be deemed to have been intended by the manufacturers," *id.,* at 44687; consumers use tobacco products "predominantly or nearly exclusively" to obtain these effects, *id.,* at 44807; and the statements, research, and actions of manufacturers revealed that they "have 'designed' cigarettes to provide pharmacologically active doses of nicotine to consumers," *id.,* at 44849. Finally, the agency concluded that cigarettes and smokeless tobacco are "combination products" because, in addition to containing nicotine, they include device components that deliver a controlled amount of nicotine to the body, *id.,* at 45208–45216.

[The FDA also] explained the policy justifications for its regulations, detailing the deleterious health effects associated with tobacco use. * * * [The agency] determined that the only way to reduce the amount of tobacco-related illness and mortality was to reduce the level of addiction, a goal that could be accomplished only by preventing children and adolescents from starting to use tobacco. [The regulations imposed limits on tobacco products' promotion, labeling, and accessibility to children and adolescents.]

Respondents, a group of tobacco manufacturers, retailers, and advertisers, filed suit * * * challenging the regulations. [The court of appeals held that Congress had not granted the FDA jurisdiction to regulate tobacco products.]

The FDA's assertion of jurisdiction to regulate tobacco products is founded on its conclusions that nicotine is a "drug" and that cigarettes and smokeless tobacco are "drug delivery devices." * * * A threshold issue is the appropriate framework for analyzing the FDA's assertion of authority to regulate tobacco products. Because this case involves an administrative agency's construction of a statute that it administers, our analysis is governed by *Chevron U.S.A. Inc. v. Natural Resources Defense Council, Inc.*, 467 U.S. 837 (1984). Under *Chevron,* a reviewing court must first ask "whether Congress has directly spoken to the precise question at issue." *Id.,* at 842. If Congress has done so, the inquiry is at an end; the court "must give effect to the unambiguously expressed intent of Congress." *Id.,* at 843. * * *

**Take Note**

After noting that this case is governed by the *Chevron* framework, the Court invoked the Whole Act Rule and the Whole Code Rule. At which step of the *Chevron* test are these maxims of statutory interpretation relevant? We considered these maxims, and other canons of construction, in Chapter 3.

In determining whether Congress has specifically addressed the question at issue, a reviewing court should not confine itself to examining a particular statutory provision in isolation. The meaning—or ambiguity—of certain words or phrases may only become evident when placed in context. See *Brown v. Gardner*, 513 U.S. 115, 118 (1994) ("Ambiguity is a creature not of definitional possibilities but of statutory context"). It is a "fundamental canon of statutory construction that the words of a statute must be read in their context and with a view to their place in the overall statutory scheme." *Davis v. Michigan Dept. of Treasury*, 489 U.S. 803, 809 (1989). A court must therefore interpret the statute "as a symmetrical and coherent regulatory scheme," *Gustafson v. Alloyd Co.*, 513 U.S. 561, 569 (1995), and "fit, if possible, all parts into an harmonious whole," *FTC v. Mandel Brothers, Inc.*, 359 U.S. 385, 389 (1959). Similarly, the meaning of one statute may be affected by other Acts, particularly where Congress has spoken subsequently and more specifically to the topic at hand. See *United States v. Estate of Romani*, 523 U.S. 517, 530–531 (1998); *United States v. Fausto*, 484 U.S. 439, 453 (1988). In addition, we must be guided to a degree by common sense as to the manner in which Congress is likely to delegate a policy decision of such economic and political magnitude to an administrative agency. Cf. *MCI Telecommunications Corp. v. American Telephone & Telegraph Co.*, 512 U.S. 218, 231 (1994).

With these principles in mind, we find that Congress has directly spoken to the issue here and precluded the FDA's jurisdiction to regulate tobacco products.

Viewing the FDCA as a whole, it is evident that one of the Act's core objectives is to ensure that any product regulated by the FDA is "safe" and "effective" for its intended use. This essential purpose pervades the FDCA. For instance, 21 U.S.C. § 393(b)(2) (1994 ed., Supp. III) defines the FDA's "[m]ission" to include "protect[ing] the public health by ensuring that . . . drugs are safe and effective" and that "there is reasonable assurance of the safety and effectiveness of devices intended for human use." The FDCA requires premarket approval of any new drug, with some limited exceptions, and states that the FDA "shall issue an order refusing to approve the application" of a new drug if it is not safe and effective for its intended purpose. §§ 355(d)(1)–(2), (4)–(5). If the FDA discovers after approval that a drug is unsafe or ineffective, it "shall, after due notice and opportunity for hearing to the applicant, withdraw approval" of the drug. 21 U.S.C. §§ 355(e)(1)–(3). The Act also requires the FDA to classify all devices into one of three categories. § 360c(b)(1). Regardless of which category the FDA chooses, there must be a "reasonable assurance of the safety and effectiveness of the device." 21 U.S.C. §§ 360c(a)(1)(A)(i), (B), (C) (1994 ed. and Supp. III); 61 Fed. Reg. 44412 (1996). Even the "restricted device" provision pursuant to which the FDA promulgated the regulations at issue here authorizes the agency to place conditions on the sale or distribution of a device specifically when "there cannot otherwise be reasonable assurance of its safety and effectiveness." 21 U.S.C. § 360j(e). Thus, the Act generally requires the FDA to prevent the marketing of any drug or device where the "potential for inflicting death or physical injury is not offset by the possibility of therapeutic benefit." *United States v. Rutherford*, 442 U.S. 544, 556 (1979).

In its rulemaking proceeding, the FDA quite exhaustively documented that "tobacco products are unsafe," "dangerous," and "cause great pain and suffering from illness." 61 Fed. Reg. 44412 (1996). It found that the consumption of tobacco products presents "extraordinary health risks," and that "tobacco use is the single leading cause of preventable death in the United States." *Id.,* at 44398. It stated that "[m]ore than 400,000 people die each year from tobacco-related illnesses, such as cancer, respiratory illnesses, and heart disease, often suffering long and painful deaths," and that "[t]obacco alone kills more people each year in the United States than acquired immunodeficiency syndrome (AIDS), car accidents, alcohol, homicides, illegal drugs, suicides, and fires, combined." *Ibid.* Indeed, the FDA characterized smoking as "a pediatric disease," *id.,* at 44421, because "one out of every three young people who become regular smokers . . . will die prematurely as a result," *id.,* at 44399.

These findings logically imply that, if tobacco products were "devices" under the FDCA, the FDA would be required to remove them from the market. [The FDCA] prohibits "[t]he introduction or delivery for introduction into interstate commerce of any food, drug, device, or cosmetic that is adulterated or misbranded." 21 U.S.C. § 331(a). * * * [The FDCA also] requires the FDA to place all devices that it regulates into one of three classifications [to determine] the degree of control and regulation necessary to ensure that there is "a reasonable assurance of safety and effectiveness." [Although the] FDA has yet to classify tobacco products, [given] the FDA's findings regarding the health consequences of tobacco use, the agency would have to place cigarettes and smokeless tobacco in Class III because, even after the application of the Act's available controls, they would "presen[t] a potential unreasonable risk of illness or injury." 21 U.S.C. § 360c(a)(1)(C). As Class III devices, tobacco products would be subject to the FDCA's premarket approval process. See 21 U.S.C. § 360c(a)(1)(C)(1994 ed., Supp. III). Under these provisions, the FDA would be prohibited from approving an application for premarket approval without "a showing of reasonable assurance that such device is safe under the conditions of use prescribed, recommended, or suggested in the proposed labeling thereof." 21 U.S.C. § 360e(d)(2)(A). * * *

The FDCA's misbranding and device classification provisions [make] evident that were the FDA to regulate cigarettes and smokeless tobacco, the Act would require the agency to ban them. In fact, based on these provisions, the FDA itself has previously taken the position that if tobacco products were within its jurisdiction, "they would have to be removed from the market because it would be impossible to prove they were safe for their intended us[e]." Public Health Cigarette Amendments of 1971: Hearings before the Commerce Subcommittee on S. 1454, 92d Cong., 2d Sess., 239 (1972) (hereinafter 1972 Hearings) (statement of FDA Comm'r Charles Edwards). * * *

Congress, however, has foreclosed the removal of tobacco products from the market. A provision of the United States Code currently in force states that "[t]he marketing of tobacco constitutes one of the greatest basic industries of the United States with ramifying activities which directly affect interstate and foreign commerce at every point, and stable conditions therein are necessary to the general welfare." 7 U.S.C. § 1311(a). More importantly, Congress has directly addressed the problem of tobacco and health through legislation on six occasions since 1965. See Federal

Cigarette Labeling and Advertising Act (FCLAA), Pub. L. 89–92, 79 Stat. 282; Public Health Cigarette Smoking Act of 1969, Pub. L. 91–222, 84 Stat. 87; Alcohol and Drug Abuse Amendments of 1983, Pub. L. 98–24, 97 Stat. 175; Comprehensive Smoking Education Act, Pub. L. 98–474, 98 Stat. 2200; Comprehensive Smokeless Tobacco Health Education Act of 1986, Pub. L. 99–252, 100 Stat. 30; Alcohol, Drug Abuse, and Mental Health Administration Reorganization Act, Pub. L. 102–321, § 202, 106 Stat. 394. When Congress enacted these statutes, the adverse health consequences of tobacco use were well known, as were nicotine's pharmacological effects. See, *e.g.*, U.S. Dept. of Health, Education, and Welfare, U.S. Surgeon General's Advisory Committee, Smoking and Health 25–40, 69–75 (1964) (hereinafter 1964 Surgeon General's Report). Nonetheless, Congress stopped well short of ordering a ban. Instead, it has generally regulated the labeling and advertisement of tobacco products, [which reveals] its intent that tobacco products remain on the market. Indeed, the collective premise of these statutes is that cigarettes and smokeless tobacco will continue to be sold in the United States. A ban of tobacco products by the FDA would therefore plainly contradict congressional policy.

The FDA apparently recognized this dilemma and concluded, somewhat ironically, that tobacco products are actually "safe" within the meaning of the FDCA. [T]he FDA reasoned that, in determining whether a device is safe under the Act, it must consider "not only the risks presented by a product but also any of the countervailing effects of use of that product, including the consequences of not permitting the product to be marketed." *Id.*, at 44412–44413. Applying this standard, the FDA found that, because of the high level of addiction among tobacco users, a ban would likely be "dangerous." *Id.*, at 44413. * * * [But several] provisions in the Act require the FDA to determine that the *product itself* is safe as used by consumers. That is, the product's probable therapeutic benefits must outweigh its risk of harm. * * * Thus, although the FDA has concluded that a ban would be "dangerous," it has *not* concluded that tobacco products are "safe" as that term is used throughout the Act.

The dissent contends that our conclusion means that "the FDCA requires the FDA to ban outright 'dangerous' drugs or devices," and that this is a "perverse" reading of the statute. This misunderstands our holding. The FDA, consistent with the FDCA, may clearly regulate many "dangerous" products without banning them. Indeed, virtually every drug or device poses dangers under certain conditions. What the FDA may not do is conclude that a drug or device cannot be used safely for any therapeutic purpose and yet, at the same time, allow that product to remain on the market. Such regulation is incompatible with the FDCA's core objective of ensuring that every drug or device is safe and effective.

In determining whether Congress has spoken directly to the FDA's authority to regulate tobacco, we must also consider in greater detail the tobacco-specific legislation that Congress has enacted over the past 35 years. At the time a statute is enacted, it may have a range of plausible meanings. Over time, however, subsequent acts can shape or focus those meanings. The "classic judicial task of reconciling many laws enacted over time, and getting them to 'make sense' in combination, necessarily assumes that the implications of a statute may be altered by the implications of a later statute." *United States v. Fausto*, 484 U.S. 439, 453 (1988). * * *

Congress has enacted six separate pieces of legislation since 1965 addressing the problem of tobacco use and human health. Those statutes, among other things, require that health warnings appear on all packaging and in all print and outdoor advertisements, see 15 U.S.C. §§ 1331, 1333, 4402; prohibit the advertisement of tobacco products through "any medium of electronic communication" subject to regulation by the Federal Communications Commission (FCC), see §§ 1335, 4402(f); require the Secretary of HHS to report every three years to Congress on research findings concerning "the addictive property of tobacco," 42 U.S.C. § 290aa–2(b)(2); and make States' receipt of certain federal block grants contingent on their making it unlawful "for any manufacturer, retailer, or distributor of tobacco products to sell or distribute any such product to any individual under the age of 18," § 300x–26(a)(1).

In adopting each statute, Congress has acted against the backdrop of the FDA's consistent and repeated statements that it lacked authority under the FDCA to regulate tobacco absent claims of therapeutic benefit by the manufacturer. In fact, on several occasions over this period, and after the health consequences of tobacco use and nicotine's pharmacological effects had become well known, Congress considered and rejected bills that would have granted the FDA such jurisdiction. Under these circumstances, it is evident that Congress' tobacco-specific statutes have effectively ratified the FDA's long-held position that it lacks jurisdiction under the FDCA to regulate tobacco products. Congress has created a distinct regulatory scheme to address the problem of tobacco and health, and that scheme, as presently constructed, precludes any role for the FDA.

Moreover, before enacting the FCLAA in 1965, Congress considered and rejected several proposals to give the FDA the authority to regulate tobacco. In April 1963, Representative Udall introduced a bill "[t]o amend the Federal Food, Drug, and Cosmetic Act so as to make that Act applicable to smoking products." H.R. 5973, 88th Cong., 1st Sess., 1. Two months later, Senator Moss introduced an identical bill in the Senate. S. 1682, 88th Cong., 1st Sess. (1963). In discussing his proposal on the Senate floor, Senator Moss explained that "this amendment simply places smoking products under FDA jurisdiction, along with foods, drugs, and cosmetics." 109 Cong. Rec. 10322 (1963). In December 1963, Representative Rhodes introduced another bill that would have amended the FDCA "by

**Food for Thought**

What does Congress's failure to enact a bill tell us about the meaning of existing statutes? Does it depend on whether we seek the original meaning of the statutory text or instead Congress's intent?

striking out 'food, drug, device, or cosmetic,' each place where it appears therein and inserting in lieu thereof 'food, drug, device, cosmetic, or smoking product.' " H.R. 9512, 88th Cong., 1st Sess., § 3 (1963). And in January 1965, five months before passage of the FCLAA, Representative Udall again introduced a bill to amend the FDCA "to make that Act applicable to smoking products." H.R. 2248, 89th Cong., 1st Sess., 1. None of these proposals became law.

Congress ultimately decided in 1965 to subject tobacco products to the less extensive regulatory scheme of the FCLAA, which created a "comprehensive Federal program to deal with cigarette labeling and advertising with respect to any relationship between smoking and health." Pub. L. 89–92, § 2, 79 Stat. 282. The FCLAA rejected any regulation of advertising, but it required the warning, "Caution: Cigarette Smoking May Be Hazardous to Your Health," to appear on all cigarette packages. *Id.,* § 4, 79 Stat. 283. * * * Not only did Congress reject the proposals to grant the FDA jurisdiction, but it explicitly pre-empted any other regulation of cigarette labeling * * *. The regulation of product labeling, however, is an integral aspect of the FDCA, both as it existed in 1965 and today. * * * In this sense, the FCLAA was—and remains—incompatible with FDA regulation of tobacco products. * * * Subsequent tobacco-specific legislation followed a similar pattern.

Taken together, these actions by Congress over the past 35 years preclude an interpretation of the FDCA that grants the FDA jurisdiction to regulate tobacco products. We do not rely on Congress' failure to act—its consideration and rejection of bills that would have given the FDA this authority—in reaching this conclusion. Indeed, this is not a case of simple inaction by Congress that purportedly represents its acquiescence in an agency's position. To the contrary, Congress has enacted several statutes addressing the particular subject of tobacco and health, creating a distinct regulatory scheme for cigarettes and smokeless tobacco. In doing so, Congress has been aware of tobacco's health hazards and its pharmacological effects. It has also enacted this legislation against the background of the FDA repeatedly and consistently asserting that it lacks jurisdiction under the FDCA to regulate tobacco products as customarily marketed. * * * Under these circumstances, it is clear that Congress' tobacco-specific legislation has effectively ratified the FDA's previous position that it lacks jurisdiction to regulate tobacco.

[O]ur conclusion does not rely on the fact that the FDA's assertion of jurisdiction represents a sharp break with its prior interpretation of the FDCA. Certainly, an agency's initial interpretation of a statute that it is charged with administering is not "carved in stone." *Chevron,* 467 U.S., at 863. As we recognized in *Motor Vehicle Mfrs. Assn. of United States, Inc. v. State Farm Mut. Automobile Ins. Co.,* 463 U.S. 29 (1983), agencies "must be given ample latitude to 'adapt their rules and policies to the demands of changing circumstances.' " *Id.,* at 42. The consistency of the FDA's prior position is significant in this case for a different reason: It provides important context to Congress' enactment of its tobacco-specific legislation. * * * Although not crucial, the consistency of the FDA's prior position bolsters the conclusion that when Congress created a distinct regulatory scheme addressing the subject of tobacco and health, it understood that the FDA is without jurisdiction to regulate tobacco products and ratified that position.

Finally, our inquiry into whether Congress has directly spoken to the precise question at issue is shaped, at least in some measure, by the nature of the question presented. Deference under *Chevron* to an agency's construction of a statute that it administers is premised on the theory that a statute's ambiguity constitutes an implicit delegation from Congress to the agency to fill in the statutory gaps. In extraordinary cases, however, there may be reason to hesitate before concluding that Congress has intended such an implicit delegation. Cf. Breyer, Judicial Review of Questions of Law and Policy, 38 Admin. L. Rev. 363, 370 (1986) ("A court may also ask whether the legal question is an important one. Congress is more likely to have focused upon, and answered, major questions, while leaving interstitial matters to answer themselves in the course of the statute's daily administration").

This is hardly an ordinary case. Contrary to its representations to Congress since 1914, the FDA has now asserted jurisdiction to regulate an industry constituting a significant portion of the American economy. In fact, the FDA contends that, were it to determine that tobacco products provide no "reasonable assurance of safety," it would have the authority to ban cigarettes and smokeless tobacco entirely. Owing to its unique place in American history and society, tobacco has its own unique political history. Congress, for better or for worse, has created a distinct regulatory scheme for tobacco products, squarely rejected proposals to give the FDA jurisdiction over tobacco, and repeatedly acted to preclude any agency from exercising significant policymaking authority in the area. Given this history and the breadth of the authority that the FDA has asserted, we are obliged to defer not to the agency's expansive construction of the statute, but to Congress' consistent judgment to deny the FDA this power.

**Take Note**

Is the Court's conclusion here—that courts should not lightly assume that Congress has delegated power to an agency to resolve major questions of policy—relevant to *Chevron* step one or *Chevron* step two?

Our decision in *MCI Telecommunications Corp. v. American Telephone & Telegraph Co.*, 512 U.S. 218 (1994), is instructive. That case involved the proper construction of the term "modify" in § 203(b) of the Communications Act of 1934. The FCC contended that, because the Act gave it the discretion to "modify any requirement" imposed under the statute, it therefore possessed the authority to render voluntary the otherwise mandatory requirement that long distance carriers file their rates. We rejected the FCC's construction, finding "not the slightest doubt" that Congress had directly spoken to the question. In reasoning even more apt here, we concluded that "[i]t is highly unlikely that Congress would leave the determination of whether an industry will be entirely, or even substantially, rate-regulated to agency discretion—and even more unlikely that it would achieve that through such a subtle device as permission to 'modify' rate-filing requirements."

As in *MCI,* we are confident that Congress could not have intended to delegate a decision of such economic and political significance to an agency in so cryptic a fashion. To find that the FDA has the authority to regulate tobacco products, one must not only adopt an extremely strained understanding of "safety" as it is used throughout the Act—a concept central to the FDCA's regulatory scheme—but also ignore the plain implication of Congress' subsequent tobacco-specific legislation. It is therefore clear, based on the FDCA's overall regulatory scheme and the subsequent tobacco legislation, that Congress has directly spoken to the question at issue and precluded the FDA from regulating tobacco products.

Justice Breyer, with whom Justice Stevens, Justice Souter, and Justice Ginsburg join, dissenting.

The Food and Drug Administration (FDA) has the authority to regulate "articles (other than food) intended to affect the structure or any function of the body . . . ." Federal Food, Drug, and Cosmetic Act (FDCA), 21 U.S.C. § 321(g)(1)(C). Unlike the majority, I believe that tobacco products fit within this statutory language.

In its own interpretation, the majority nowhere denies the following two salient points. First, tobacco products (including cigarettes) fall within the scope of this statutory definition, read literally. Cigarettes achieve their mood-stabilizing effects through the interaction of the chemical nicotine and the cells of the central nervous system. Both cigarette manufacturers and smokers alike know of, and desire, that chemically induced result. Hence, cigarettes are "intended to affect" the body's "structure" and "function," in the literal sense of these words. Second, the statute's basic purpose—the protection of public health—supports the inclusion of cigarettes within its scope.

[N]either the companies nor the majority denies that the FDCA's literal language, its general purpose, and its particular legislative history favor the FDA's present jurisdictional view. * * * The majority nonetheless reaches the "inescapable conclusion" that the language and structure of the FDCA as a whole "simply do not fit" the kind of public health problem that tobacco creates. That is because, in the majority's view, the FDCA requires the FDA to ban outright "dangerous" drugs or devices (such as cigarettes); yet, the FDA concedes that an immediate and total cigarette-sale ban is inappropriate.

This argument is curious because it leads with similarly "inescapable" force to precisely the opposite conclusion, namely, that the FDA *does* have jurisdiction but that it must ban cigarettes. More importantly, the argument fails to take into account the fact that a statute interpreted as requiring the FDA to pick a more dangerous over a less dangerous remedy would be a perverse statute, *causing*, rather than preventing, unnecessary harm whenever a total ban is likely the more dangerous response. And one can at least imagine such circumstances.

Suppose, for example, that a commonly used, mildly addictive sleeping pill * * *, plainly within the FDA's jurisdiction, turned out to pose serious health risks for certain consumers. Suppose further that many of those addicted consumers would ignore an immediate total ban, turning to a potentially more dangerous black-market substitute, while a less draconian remedy (say, adequate notice) would wean them gradually away to a safer product. Would the FDCA still *force* the FDA to impose the more dangerous remedy? For the following reasons, I think not.

[T]he statute's language does not restrict the FDA's remedial powers in this way. * * * [T[he FDCA's "device" provisions explicitly grant the FDA wide remedial discretion. For example, where the FDA cannot "otherwise" obtain "reasonable assurance" of a device's "safety and effectiveness," the agency may restrict by regulation a product's "sale, distribution, or use" upon "*such . . . conditions as the Secretary may prescribe.*" § 360j(e)(1) (emphasis added). * * * It is true, as the majority contends, that "the FDCA requires the FDA to place all devices" in "one of three classifications" and that Class III devices require "premarket approval." But it is not the case that the FDA *must* place cigarettes in Class III * * *. In fact, Class III applies *only* where *regulation* cannot otherwise "provide reasonable assurance of . . . safety." §§ 360c(a)(1)(A), (B). Thus, the statute plainly allows the FDA to consider the relative, overall "safety" of a device in light of its regulatory alternatives, and where the FDA has chosen the least dangerous path, *i.e.*, the safest path, then it can—and does—provide a "reasonable assurance" of "safety" within the meaning of the statute. * * *

Noting that the FDCA requires banning a "misbranded" drug, the majority also points to 21 U.S.C. § 352(j), which deems a drug or device "misbranded" if "it is dangerous to health when used" as "prescribed, recommended, or suggested in the labeling." * * * But this "misbranding" language is not determinative, for it permits the FDA to conclude that a drug or device is *not* "dangerous to health" and that it *does* have "adequate" directions *when regulated so as to render it as harmless as possible.* And surely the agency can determine that a substance is comparatively "safe" (*not* "dangerous") whenever it would be *less* dangerous to make the product available (subject to regulatory requirements) than suddenly to withdraw it from the market. * * *

In the majority's view, laws enacted since 1965 require us to deny jurisdiction, whatever the FDCA might mean in their absence. But why? Do those laws contain language barring FDA jurisdiction? The majority must concede that they do not. * * * Perhaps the later laws "shape" and "focus" what the 1938 Congress meant a generation earlier. But this Court has warned against using the views of a later Congress to construe a statute enacted many years before. See *Pension Benefit Guaranty*

*Corporation v. LTV Corp.*, 496 U.S. 633, 650 (1990) (later history is a " 'hazardous basis for inferring the intent of an earlier' Congress"). * * *

Regardless, the later statutes do not support the majority's conclusion. That is because, whatever individual Members of Congress after 1964 may have assumed about the FDA's jurisdiction, the laws they enacted did not embody any such "no jurisdiction" assumption. And one cannot automatically *infer* an antijurisdiction intent, as the majority does, for the later statutes are both (and similarly) consistent with quite a different congressional desire, namely, the intent to proceed without interfering with whatever authority the FDA otherwise may have possessed. * * *

I now turn to the final historical fact that the majority views as a factor in its interpretation of the subsequent legislative history: the FDA's former denials of its tobacco-related authority. Until the early 1990's, the FDA expressly maintained that the 1938 statute did not give it the power that it now seeks to assert. It then changed its mind. The majority agrees with me that the FDA's change of positions does not make a significant legal difference. Nevertheless, it labels those denials "important context" for drawing an inference about Congress' intent. In my view, the FDA's change of policy, like the subsequent statutes themselves, does nothing to advance the majority's position.

When it denied jurisdiction to regulate cigarettes, the FDA consistently stated *why* that was so. In 1963, for example, FDA administrators wrote that cigarettes did not satisfy the relevant FDCA definitions—in particular, the "intent" requirement—because cigarette makers did not sell their product with accompanying "therapeutic claims." And subsequent FDA Commissioners made roughly the same assertion. * * *

What changed? For one thing, the FDA obtained evidence sufficient to prove the necessary "intent" despite the absence of specific "claims." This evidence, which first became available in the early 1990's, permitted the agency to demonstrate that the tobacco companies *knew* nicotine achieved appetite-suppressing, mood-stabilizing, and habituating effects through chemical (not psychological) means, even at a time when the companies were publicly denying such knowledge. Moreover, scientific evidence of adverse health effects mounted, until, in the late 1980's, a consensus on the seriousness of the matter became firm. * * * Finally, administration policy changed. * * * Commissioners of the current administration simply took a different regulatory attitude.

Nothing in the law prevents the FDA from changing its policy for such reasons. By the mid-1990's, the evidence needed to prove objective intent—even without an express claim—had been found. The emerging scientific consensus about tobacco's adverse, chemically induced, health effects may have convinced the agency that it should spend its resources on this important regulatory effort. * * *

One might nonetheless claim * * * that courts, when interpreting statutes, should assume in close cases that a decision with "enormous social consequences" should be made by democratically elected Members of Congress rather than by unelected agency administrators. If there is such a background canon of interpretation, however, I do not believe it controls the outcome here.

Insofar as the decision to regulate tobacco reflects the policy of an administration, it is a decision for which that administration, and those politically elected officials who support it, must (and will) take responsibility. And the very importance of the decision taken here, as well as its attendant publicity, means that the public is likely to be aware of it and to hold those officials politically accountable. Presidents, just like Members of Congress, are elected by the public. Indeed, the President and Vice President are the *only* public officials whom the entire Nation elects. I do not believe that an administrative agency decision of this magnitude—one that is important, conspicuous, and controversial—can escape the kind of public scrutiny that is essential in any democracy. And such a review will take place whether it is the Congress or the Executive Branch that makes the relevant decision.

The upshot is that the Court today holds that a regulatory statute aimed at unsafe drugs and devices does not authorize regulation of a drug (nicotine) and a device (a cigarette) that the Court itself finds unsafe. Far more than most, this particular drug and device risks the life-threatening harms that administrative regulation seeks to rectify. The majority's conclusion is counterintuitive. And, for the reasons set forth, I believe that the law does not require it.

---

## Points for Discussion

### *a. Statutory Interpretation at* Chevron *Step One*

As we have seen, under the *Chevron* framework, a reviewing court has to decide whether Congress has spoken to the precise question at issue. In *Brown & Williamson*, the precise question was whether the FDA had authority to regulate tobacco products. Do you agree that, applying ordinary tools of statutory interpretation, the statute was unambiguous with respect to this question?

### *b. The "Major Questions" Doctrine*

In concluding that the FDA lacked power under the statute to regulate tobacco products, the Court stated: "Deference under *Chevron* to an agency's construction of a statute that it administers is premised on the theory that a statute's ambiguity constitutes an implicit delegation from Congress to the agency to fill in the statutory gaps. In extraordinary cases, however, there may be reason to hesitate before concluding that Congress has intended such an implicit delegation." The Court then expressed confidence that "Congress could not have intended to delegate a decision of such economic and political significance to an agency in so cryptic a fashion."

Was the Court's point that the importance of the policy question at issue was relevant to the question whether the statute was ambiguous? Or that, even if the statute was ambiguous applying traditional tools of statutory interpretation, deference would be inappropriate at *Chevron* step two? Or was the Court's point that the *Chevron* framework doesn't apply at all to questions of considerable economic and political significance, thereby requiring the Court to resolve the question on its own (even if the statute was ambiguous)?

Some scholars have suggested that this "major questions doctrine" effectively adds a step—"step zero"—to the *Chevron* test. On this view, a court reviewing an agency's interpretation of a statue must first decide whether the ordinary two-step *Chevron* framework applies; in cases involving very important questions of policy, a court might decide that the deference framework simply doesn't apply, or at least applies with less force. See Thomas W. Merrill & Kristin Hickman, Chevron's *Domain*, 89 GEO. L.J. 833, 836 (2001). How can judges decide which types of policy questions are sufficiently "major" such that the ordinary *Chevron* framework does not apply?

---

In *Brown & Williamson*, the Court explained that its "inquiry into whether Congress has directly spoken to the precise question at issue is shaped, at least in some measure, by the nature of the question presented." In other words, the fact that it was "hardly an ordinary case" led the Court "not to defer * * * to the agency's expansive construction of the statute * * *."

When a court applies this "major questions" doctrine, it effectively concludes that Congress has not delegated to the agency the power to resolve some important question of policy. In this sense, the doctrine functions as a soft non-delegation principle: because courts will not defer to agency interpretations that assert authority to resolve (some) important questions of policy, it is less likely in practice that courts will conclude that Congress has in fact delegated such authority.

Is the major questions doctrine a general principle of statutory interpretation, or is it simply an element of the *Chevron* doctrine? Consider the two cases that follow.

---

## *National Federation of Independent Business v. Department of Labor, Occupational Safety and Health Administration*

142 S.Ct. 661 (2022)

PER CURIAM.

The Secretary of Labor, acting through the Occupational Safety and Health Administration, recently enacted a vaccine mandate for much of the Nation's work force. The mandate, which employers must enforce, applies to roughly 84 million workers, covering virtually all employers with at least 100 employees. It requires that covered workers receive a COVID-19 vaccine, and it pre-empts contrary state laws. The only exception is for workers who obtain a medical test each week at their own expense and on their own time, and also wear a mask each workday. * * *

Many States, businesses, and nonprofit organizations challenged OSHA's rule in Courts of Appeals across the country. The Fifth Circuit initially entered a stay. But when the cases were consolidated before the Sixth Circuit, that court lifted the stay and allowed OSHA's rule to take effect. Applicants now seek emergency relief from this Court, arguing that OSHA's mandate exceeds its statutory authority and is otherwise unlawful. Agreeing that applicants are likely to prevail, we grant their applications and stay the rule.

Congress enacted the Occupational Safety and Health Act in 1970. 84 Stat. 1590, 29 U.S.C. § 651 *et seq.* The Act created the Occupational Safety and Health Administration (OSHA), which is part of the Department of Labor and under the supervision of its Secretary. As its name suggests, OSHA is tasked with ensuring *occupational* safety—that is, "safe and healthful working conditions." § 651(b). It does so by enforcing occupational safety and health standards promulgated by the Secretary. § 655(b). Such standards must be "reasonably necessary or appropriate to provide safe or healthful *employment*." § 652(8) (emphasis added). They must also be developed using a rigorous process that includes notice, comment, and an opportunity for a public hearing. § 655(b).

The Act contains an exception to those ordinary notice-and-comment procedures for "emergency temporary standards." § 655(c)(1). Such standards may "take immediate effect upon publication in the Federal Register." *Ibid.* They are permissible, however, only in the narrowest of circumstances: the Secretary must show (1) "that employees are exposed to grave danger from exposure to substances or agents determined to be toxic or physically harmful or from new hazards," and (2) that the "emergency standard is necessary to protect employees from such danger." *Ibid.* Prior to the emergence of COVID-19, the Secretary had used this power just nine times before (and never to issue a rule as broad as this one). Of those nine emergency rules, six were challenged in court, and only one of those was upheld in full.

On September 9, 2021, President Biden announced "a new plan to require more Americans to be vaccinated." Remarks on the COVID-19 Response and National Vaccination Efforts, 2021 Daily Comp. of Pres. Doc. 775, p. 2. As part of that plan, the President said that the Department of Labor would issue an emergency rule requiring all employers with at least 100 employees "to ensure their workforces are fully vaccinated or show a negative test at least once a week." *Ibid.* The purpose of the rule was to increase vaccination rates at "businesses all across America." *Ibid.* In tandem with other planned regulations, the administration's goal was to impose "vaccine requirements" on "about 100 million Americans, two-thirds of all workers." *Id.*, at 3.

After a 2-month delay, the Secretary of Labor issued the promised emergency standard. 86 Fed. Reg. 61402 (2021). Consistent with President Biden's announcement, the rule applies to all who work for employers with 100 or more employees. There are narrow exemptions for employees who work remotely "100 percent of the time" or who "work exclusively outdoors," but those exemptions are largely illusory. *Id.*, at 61460. The Secretary has estimated, for example, that only nine percent of landscapers and groundskeepers qualify as working exclusively outside. *Id.*, at 61461. The regulation otherwise operates as a blunt instrument. It draws no distinctions based on industry or risk of exposure to COVID-19. Thus, most lifeguards and linemen face the same regulations as do medics and meatpackers. OSHA estimates that 84.2 million employees are subject to its mandate. *Id.*, at 61467.

Covered employers must "develop, implement, and enforce a mandatory COVID-19 vaccination policy." *Id.*, at 61402. The employer must verify the vaccination status of each employee and maintain proof of it. *Id.*, at 61552. The mandate does contain an "exception" for employers that require unvaccinated workers to "undergo [weekly] COVID-19 testing and wear a face covering at work in lieu of vaccination." *Id.*, at 61402. But employers are not required to offer this option, and the emergency regulation purports to pre-empt state laws to the contrary. *Id.*, at 61437. Unvaccinated employees who do not comply with OSHA's rule must be "removed from the workplace." *Id.*, at 61532. And employers who commit violations face hefty fines: up to $13,653 for a standard violation, and up to $136,532 for a willful one. 29 C.F.R. § 1903.15(d) (2021).

OSHA published its vaccine mandate on November 5, 2021. Scores of parties—including States, businesses, trade groups, and nonprofit organizations—filed petitions for review, with at least one petition arriving in each regional Court of Appeals. The cases were consolidated in the Sixth Circuit, which was selected at random pursuant to 28 U.S.C. § 2112(a). Prior to consolidation, [the] Fifth Circuit stayed OSHA's rule pending further judicial review * * *. [After consolidation, the Sixth Circuit dissolved the Fifth Circuit's stay, concluding that the mandate likely was] consistent with the agency's statutory and constitutional authority. See *In re*

*MCP No. 165*, 21 F. 4th 357 (6th Cir. 2021). [The Supreme Court heard expedited argument on January 7, 2022, and issued its decision on January 13, 2022.]

The Sixth Circuit concluded that a stay of the rule was not justified. We disagree. Applicants are likely to succeed on the merits of their claim that the Secretary lacked authority to impose the mandate. Administrative agencies are creatures of statute. They accordingly possess only the authority that Congress has provided. The Secretary has ordered 84 million Americans to either obtain a COVID-19 vaccine or undergo weekly medical testing at their own expense. This is no "everyday exercise of federal power." *In re MCP No. 165*, 20 F.4th at 272 (Sutton, C. J., dissenting). It is instead a significant encroachment into the lives—and health—of a vast number of employees. "We expect Congress to speak clearly when authorizing an agency to exercise powers of vast economic and political significance." *Alabama Assn. of Realtors v. Department of Health and Human Servs.*, 141 S.Ct. 2485, 2489 (2021). There can be little doubt that OSHA's mandate qualifies as an exercise of such authority.

**Take Note**

This case involved the question whether OSHA had authority to impose the mandate. To determine whether OSHA had such authority, it was necessary to interpret the statute that conferred power on the agency. Had the agency offered an interpretation of that statute, either explicitly or implicitly? If so, was the *Chevron* doctrine the correct framework for analyzing the question? Did the Court apply the *Chevron* framework?

The question, then, is whether the Act plainly authorizes the Secretary's mandate. It does not. The Act empowers the Secretary to set *workplace* safety standards, not broad public health measures. See 29 U.S.C. § 655(b) (directing the Secretary to set "*occupational* safety and health standards" (emphasis added)); § 655(c)(1) (authorizing the Secretary to impose emergency temporary standards necessary to protect "employees" from grave danger in the workplace). Confirming the point, the Act's provisions typically speak to hazards that employees face at work. See, *e.g.*, §§ 651, 653, 657. And no provision of the Act addresses public health more generally, which falls outside of OSHA's sphere of expertise.

The dissent protests that we are imposing "a limit found no place in the governing statute." Not so. It is the text of the agency's Organic Act that repeatedly makes clear that OSHA is charged with regulating "occupational" hazards and the safety and health of "employees." See, *e.g.*, 29 U.S.C. §§ 652(8), 654(a)(2), 655(b)–(c).

The Solicitor General does not dispute that OSHA is limited to regulating "work-related dangers." She instead argues that the risk of contracting COVID-19 qualifies as such a danger. We cannot agree. Although COVID-19 is a risk that occurs in many workplaces, it is not an *occupational* hazard in most. COVID-19 can and does spread at home, in schools, during sporting events, and everywhere else that people gather. That kind of universal risk is no different from the day-to-day dangers that all face from crime, air pollution, or any number of communicable diseases. Permitting

OSHA to regulate the hazards of daily life—simply because most Americans have jobs and face those same risks while on the clock—would significantly expand OSHA's regulatory authority without clear congressional authorization.

The dissent contends that OSHA's mandate is comparable to a fire or sanitation regulation imposed by the agency. But a vaccine mandate is strikingly unlike the workplace regulations that OSHA has typically imposed. A vaccination, after all, "cannot be undone at the end of the workday." *In re MCP No. 165*, 20 F.4th at 274 (Sutton, C. J., dissenting). Contrary to the dissent's contention, imposing a vaccine mandate on 84 million Americans in response to a worldwide pandemic is simply not "part of what the agency was built for."

That is not to say OSHA lacks authority to regulate occupation-specific risks related to COVID-19. Where the virus poses a special danger because of the particular features of an employee's job or workplace, targeted regulations are plainly permissible. We do not doubt, for example, that OSHA could regulate researchers who work with the COVID-19 virus. So too could OSHA regulate risks associated with working in particularly crowded or cramped environments. But the danger present in such workplaces differs in both degree and kind from the everyday risk of contracting COVID-19 that all face. OSHA's indiscriminate approach fails to account for this crucial distinction—between occupational risk and risk more generally—and accordingly the mandate takes on the character of a general public health measure, rather than an "*occupational* safety or health standard." 29 U.S.C. § 655(b) (emphasis added).

In looking for legislative support for the vaccine mandate, the dissent turns to the American Rescue Plan Act of 2021, Pub. L. 117–2, 135 Stat. 4. That legislation, signed into law on March 11, 2021, of course said nothing about OSHA's vaccine mandate, which was not announced until six months later. In fact, the most noteworthy action concerning the vaccine mandate by either House of Congress has been a majority vote of the Senate disapproving the regulation on December 8, 2021. S. J. Res. 29, 117th Cong., 1st Sess. (2021).

It is telling that OSHA, in its half century of existence, has never before adopted a broad public health regulation of this kind—addressing a threat that is untethered, in any causal sense, from the workplace. This "lack of historical precedent," coupled with the breadth of authority that the Secretary now claims, is a "telling indication" that the mandate extends beyond the agency's legitimate reach. *Free Enterprise Fund v. Public Company Accounting Oversight Bd.*, 561 U.S. 477, 505 (2010).

The equities do not justify withholding interim relief. We are told by the States and the employers that OSHA's mandate will force them to incur billions of dollars in unrecoverable compliance costs and will cause hundreds of thousands of employees to leave their jobs. For its part, the Federal Government says that the mandate will save over 6,500 lives and prevent hundreds of thousands of hospitalizations.

It is not our role to weigh such tradeoffs. In our system of government, that is the responsibility of those chosen by the people through democratic processes. Although Congress has indisputably given OSHA the power to regulate occupational dangers, it has not given that agency the power to regulate public health more broadly. Requiring the vaccination of 84 million Americans, selected simply because they work for employers with more than 100 employees, certainly falls in the latter category. * * * [OSHA's Emergency Temporary Standard] is stayed pending disposition of the applicants' petitions for review in the United States Court of Appeals for the Sixth Circuit and disposition of the applicants' petitions for writs of certiorari, if such writs are timely sought. * * *

JUSTICE GORSUCH, with whom JUSTICE THOMAS and JUSTICE ALITO join, concurring.

The central question we face today is: Who decides? No one doubts that the COVID-19 pandemic has posed challenges for every American. Or that our state, local, and national governments all have roles to play in combating the disease. The only question is whether an administrative agency in Washington, one charged with overseeing workplace safety, may mandate the vaccination or regular testing of 84 million people. Or whether, as 27 States before us submit, that work belongs to state and local governments across the country and the people's elected representatives in Congress. This Court is not a public health authority. But it is charged with resolving disputes about which authorities possess the power to make the laws that govern us under the Constitution and the laws of the land.

* * * There is no question that state and local authorities possess considerable power to regulate public health. * * * The federal government's powers, however, are not general but limited and divided. See *McCulloch v. Maryland*, 4 Wheat. 316, 405 (1819). Not only must the federal government properly invoke a constitutionally enumerated source of authority to regulate in this area or any other. It must also act consistently with the Constitution's separation of powers. And when it comes to that obligation, this Court has established at least one firm rule: "We expect Congress to speak clearly" if it wishes to assign to an executive agency decisions "of vast economic and political significance." *Alabama Assn. of Realtors v. Department of Health and Human Servs.*, 141 S.Ct. 2185, 2189 (2021). We sometimes call this the major questions doctrine. *Gundy v. United States*, 139 S.Ct. 2116, 2141 (2019) (GORUSCH, J., dissenting).

OSHA's mandate fails that doctrine's test. The agency claims the power to force 84 million Americans to receive a vaccine or undergo regular testing. By any measure, that is a claim of power to resolve a question of vast national significance. Yet Congress has nowhere clearly assigned so much power to OSHA. * * * Far less consequential agency rules have run afoul of the major questions doctrine. *E.g., MCI Telecommunications Corp. v. American Telephone & Telegraph Co.*, 512 U.S. 218, 231 (1994) (eliminating rate-filing requirement). It is hard to see how this one does not.

Why does the major questions doctrine matter? It ensures that the national government's power to make the laws that govern us remains where Article I of the Constitution says it belongs—with the people's elected representatives. If administrative agencies seek to regulate the daily lives and liberties of millions of Americans, the doctrine says, they must at least be able to trace that power to a clear grant of authority from Congress.

In this respect, the major questions doctrine is closely related to what is sometimes called the nondelegation doctrine. Indeed, for decades courts have cited the nondelegation doctrine as a reason to apply the major questions doctrine. *E.g., Industrial Union Dept., AFL-CIO v. American Petroleum Institute*, 448 U.S. 607, 645 (1980) (plurality opinion). Both are designed to protect the separation of powers and ensure that any new laws governing the lives of Americans are subject to the robust democratic processes the Constitution demands.

**Make the Connection**

We considered the non-delegation doctrine in Chapter 6.

The nondelegation doctrine ensures democratic accountability by preventing Congress from intentionally delegating its legislative powers to unelected officials. * * * The major questions doctrine serves a similar function by guarding against unintentional, oblique, or otherwise unlikely delegations of the legislative power. Sometimes, Congress passes broadly worded statutes seeking to resolve important policy questions in a field while leaving an agency to work out the details of implementation. *E.g., King v. Burwell*, 576 U.S. 473, 485–486 (2015). Later, the agency may seek to exploit some gap, ambiguity, or doubtful expression in Congress's statutes to assume responsibilities far beyond its initial assignment. The major questions doctrine guards against this possibility by recognizing that Congress does not usually "hide elephants in mouseholes." *Whitman v. American Trucking Assns., Inc.*, 531 U.S. 457, 468 (2001). * * *

Whichever the doctrine, the point is the same. * * * On the one hand, OSHA claims the power to issue a nationwide mandate on a major question but cannot trace its authority to do so to any clear congressional mandate. On the other hand, if the statutory subsection the agency cites really did endow OSHA with the power it asserts, that law would likely constitute an unconstitutional delegation of legislative authority. Under OSHA's reading, the law would afford it almost unlimited discretion—and certainly impose no "specific restrictions" that "meaningfully constrai[n]" the agency. *Touby v. United States*, 500 U.S. 160, 166–167 (1991). OSHA would become little more than a "roving commission to inquire into evils and upon discovery correct them." *A.L.A. Schechter Poultry Corp. v. United States*, 295 U.S. 495, 551 (1935) (Cardozo, J., concurring). * * *

JUSTICE BREYER, JUSTICE SOTOMAYOR, and JUSTICE KAGAN, dissenting.

Every day, COVID-19 poses grave dangers to the citizens of this country—and particularly, to its workers. The disease has by now killed almost 1 million Americans and hospitalized almost 4 million. It spreads by person-to-person contact in confined indoor spaces, so causes harm in nearly all workplace environments. And in those environments, more than any others, individuals have little control, and therefore little capacity to mitigate risk. COVID-19, in short, is a menace in work settings. The proof is all around us: Since the disease's onset, most Americans have seen their workplaces transformed.

So the administrative agency charged with ensuring health and safety in workplaces did what Congress commanded it to: It took action to address COVID-19's continuing threat in those spaces. The Occupational Safety and Health Administration (OSHA) issued an emergency temporary standard (Standard), requiring *either* vaccination *or* masking and testing, to protect American workers. The Standard falls within the core of the agency's mission: to "protect employees" from "grave danger" that comes from "new hazards" or exposure to harmful agents. 29 U.S.C. § 655(c)(1). * * *

The legal standard governing a request for relief pending appellate review is settled. To obtain that relief, the applicants must show: (1) that their "claims are likely to prevail," (2) "that denying them relief would lead to irreparable injury," and (3) "that granting relief would not harm the public interest." *Roman Catholic Diocese of Brooklyn v. Cuomo*, 141 S.Ct. 63, 66 (2020). * * * The applicants are not "likely to prevail" under any proper view of the law. OSHA's rule perfectly fits the language of the applicable statutory provision. Once again, that provision commands—not just enables, but commands—OSHA to issue an emergency temporary standard whenever it determines "(A) that employees are exposed to grave danger from exposure to substances or agents determined to be toxic or physically harmful or from new hazards, and (B) that such emergency standard is necessary to protect employees from such danger." 29 U.S.C. § 655(c)(1). Each and every part of that provision demands that, in the circumstances here, OSHA act to prevent workplace harm.

The virus that causes COVID-19 is a "new hazard" as well as a "physically harmful" "agent." Merriam-Webster's Collegiate Dictionary 572 (11th ed. 2005) (defining "hazard" as a "source of danger"); *id.*, at 24 (defining "agent" as a "chemically, physically, or biologically active principle"); *id.*, at 1397 (defining "virus" as "the causative agent of an infectious disease"). The virus also poses a "grave danger" to millions of employees. As of the time OSHA promulgated its rule, more than 725,000 Americans had died of COVID-19 and millions more had been hospitalized. Since then, the disease has continued to work its tragic toll. And because the disease spreads in shared indoor spaces, it presents heightened dangers in most workplaces.

Finally, the Standard is "necessary" to address the danger of COVID-19. OSHA based its rule, requiring either testing and masking or vaccination, on a host of studies and government reports showing why those measures were of unparalleled use in limiting the threat of COVID-19 in most workplaces. The agency showed, in meticulous detail, that close contact between infected and uninfected individuals spreads the disease; that "[t]he science of transmission does not vary by industry or by type of workplace"; that testing, mask wearing, and vaccination are highly effective—indeed, essential—tools for reducing the risk of transmission, hospitalization, and death; and that unvaccinated employees of all ages face a substantially increased risk from COVID-19 as compared to their vaccinated peers. In short, OSHA showed that no lesser policy would prevent as much death and injury from COVID-19 as the Standard would.

OSHA's determinations are "conclusive if supported by substantial evidence." 29 U.S.C. § 655(f). Judicial review under that test is deferential, as it should be. OSHA employs, in both its enforcement and health divisions, numerous scientists, doctors, and other experts in public health, especially as it relates to work environments. Their decisions, we have explained, should stand so long as they are supported by "such relevant evidence as a reasonable mind might accept as adequate to support a conclusion." *American Textile Mfrs. Institute, Inc. v. Donovan*, 452 U.S. 490, 522 (1981) (quoting *Universal Camera Corp. v. NLRB*, 340 U.S. 474, 477 (1951)). Given the extensive evidence in the record supporting OSHA's determinations about the risk of COVID-19 and the efficacy of masking, testing, and vaccination, a court could not conclude that the Standard fails substantial-evidence review.

The Court does not * * * contest that COVID-19 is a "new hazard" and "physically harmful agent"; that it poses a "grave danger" to employees; or that a testing and masking or vaccination policy is "necessary" to prevent those harms. Instead, the majority claims that the Act does not "plainly authorize[ ]" the Standard because it gives OSHA the power to "set *workplace* safety standards" and COVID-19 exists both inside and outside the workplace. In other words, the Court argues that OSHA cannot keep workplaces safe from COVID-19 because the agency (as it readily acknowledges) has no power to address the disease outside the work setting.

But nothing in the Act's text supports the majority's limitation on OSHA's regulatory authority. Of course, the majority is correct that OSHA is not a roving public health regulator: It has power only to protect employees from workplace hazards. But as just explained, that is exactly what the Standard does. And the Act requires nothing more: Contra the majority, it is indifferent to whether a hazard in the workplace is also found elsewhere. The statute generally charges OSHA with "assur[ing] so far as possible . . . safe and healthful working conditions." 29 U.S.C. § 651(b). That provision authorizes regulation to protect employees from all hazards present in the workplace—or, at least, all hazards in part created by conditions there. It does not matter whether those hazards also exist beyond the workplace walls. * * *

And that should settle the matter. When Congress "enact[s] expansive language offering no indication whatever that the statute limits what [an agency] can" do, the Court cannot "impos[e] limits on an agency's discretion that are not supported by the text." *Little Sisters of the Poor Saints Peter and Paul Home v. Pennsylvania*, 140 S.Ct. 2367, 2380–81 (2020). That is what the majority today does—impose a limit found no place in the governing statute.

Consistent with Congress's directives, OSHA has long regulated risks that arise both inside and outside of the workplace. For example, OSHA has issued, and applied to nearly all workplaces, rules combating risks of fire, faulty electrical installations, and inadequate emergency exits—even though the dangers prevented by those rules arise not only in workplaces but in many physical facilities (*e.g.*, stadiums, schools, hotels, even homes). Similarly, OSHA has regulated to reduce risks from excessive noise and unsafe drinking water—again, risks hardly confined to the workplace. A biological hazard—here, the virus causing COVID-19—is no different. Indeed, Congress just last year made this clear. It appropriated $100 million for OSHA "to carry out COVID-19 related worker protection activities" in work environments of all kinds. American Rescue Plan Act of 2021, Pub. L. 117–2, 135 Stat. 30. That legislation refutes the majority's view that workplace exposure to COVID-19 is somehow not a workplace hazard. Congress knew—and Congress said—that OSHA's responsibility to mitigate the harms of COVID-19 in the typical workplace do not diminish just because the disease also endangers people in other settings.

That is especially so because—as OSHA amply established—COVID-19 poses special risks in most workplaces, across the country and across industries. * * * OSHA determined that the virus causing COVID-19 is "readily transmissible in workplaces because they are areas where multiple people come into contact with one another, often for extended periods of time." 86 Fed. Reg. 61411. In other words, COVID-19 spreads more widely in workplaces than in other venues because more people spend more time together there. And critically, employees usually have little or no control in those settings. * * * The agency backed up its conclusions with hundreds of reports of workplace COVID-19 outbreaks—not just in cheek-by-jowl settings like factory assembly lines, but in retail stores, restaurants, medical facilities, construction areas, and standard offices. *Id.*, at 61412–61416. But still, OSHA took care to tailor the Standard. Where it could exempt work settings without exposing employees to grave danger, it did so. See *id.*, at 61419–61420. In sum, the agency did just what the Act told it to: It protected employees from a grave danger posed by a new virus as and where needed, and went no further. The majority, in overturning that action, substitutes judicial diktat for reasoned policymaking.

The result of its ruling is squarely at odds with the statutory scheme. * * * The entire point of the [emergency standard] provision is to enable OSHA to deal with emergencies—to put into effect the new measures needed to cope with new workplace conditions. The enacting Congress of course did not tell the agency to issue this Standard in response to this COVID-19 pandemic—because that Congress could not predict the future. But that Congress did indeed want OSHA to have the tools needed to confront emerging dangers (including contagious diseases) in the workplace. We know that, first and foremost, from the breadth of the authority Congress granted to OSHA. And we know that because of how OSHA has used that authority from the statute's beginnings—in ways not dissimilar to the action here. OSHA has often issued rules applying to all or nearly all workplaces in the Nation, affecting at once many tens of millions of employees. See, *e.g.*, 29 C.F.R. § 1910.141. It has previously regulated infectious disease, including by facilitating vaccinations. See § 1910.1030(f). And it has in other contexts required medical examinations and face coverings for employees. See §§ 1910.120(q)(9)(i), 1910.134. In line with those prior actions, the Standard here requires employers to ensure testing and masking if they do not demand vaccination. Nothing about that measure is so out-of-the-ordinary as to demand a judicially created exception from Congress's command that OSHA protect employees from grave workplace harms.

If OSHA's Standard is far-reaching—applying to many millions of American workers—it no more than reflects the scope of the crisis. The Standard responds to a workplace health emergency unprecedented in the agency's history: an infectious disease that has already killed hundreds of thousands and sickened millions; that is most easily transmitted in the shared indoor spaces that are the hallmark of American working life; and that spreads mostly without regard to differences in occupation or industry. * * *

Even if the merits were a close question—which they are not—the Court would badly err by issuing this stay. That is because a court may not issue a stay unless the balance of harms and the public interest support the action. See *Trump v. International Refugee Assistance Project*, 137 S.Ct. 2080, 2087 (2017). Here, they do not. The lives and health of the Nation's workers are at stake. And the majority deprives the Government of a measure it needs to keep them safe.

Underlying everything else in this dispute is a single, simple question: Who decides how much protection, and of what kind, American workers need from COVID-19? An agency with expertise in workplace health and safety, acting as Congress and the President authorized? Or a court, lacking any knowledge of how to safeguard workplaces, and insulated from responsibility for any damage it causes?

Here, an agency charged by Congress with safeguarding employees from workplace dangers has decided that action is needed. * * * The agency's Standard is informed by a half century of experience

**Food for Thought**

The Court (and Justice Gorsuch, in his concurring opinion) framed the question in this case as whether Congress or instead the agency should have power to decide health policy. The dissent, in contrast, framed the question as whether the agency or instead the Court should have such power. Which framing do you find more convincing?

and expertise in handling workplace health and safety issues. The Standard also has the virtue of political accountability, for OSHA is responsible to the President, and the President is responsible to—and can be held to account by—the American public.

And then, there is this Court. Its Members are elected by, and accountable to, no one. And we "lack[ ] the background, competence, and expertise to assess" workplace health and safety issues. *South Bay United Pentecostal Church v. Newsom*, 140 S.Ct. 1613, 1614 (2020) (opinion of ROBERTS, C. J.). When we are wise, we know enough to defer on matters like this one. When we are wise, we know not to displace the judgments of experts, acting within the sphere Congress marked out and under Presidential control, to deal with emergency conditions. Today, we are not wise. In the face of a still-raging pandemic, this Court tells the agency charged with protecting worker safety that it may not do so in all the workplaces needed. As disease and death continue to mount, this Court tells the agency that it cannot respond in the most effective way possible. Without legal basis, the Court usurps a decision that rightfully belongs to others. It undercuts the capacity of the responsible federal officials, acting well within the scope of their authority, to protect American workers from grave danger.

---

## Points for Discussion

### *a. Major Questions*

What was the Court's reasoning in concluding that OSHA's assertion of authority concerned a major question of policy? Was it based on the number of people affected by the rule? The amount of money at stake? The consequences of the issue's resolution for the country and the world? How did the Court weigh these factors in deciding that this case involved a question that Congress must address directly, rather than one that an agency, acting pursuant to delegated power, can address?

After concluding that the matter at issue was a major question of policy, the Court stated that the question was "whether the Act *plainly authorizes* the Secretary's mandate." Was the Court applying a clear statement rule? If so, is that your understanding of how the major questions doctrine works? Or is the doctrine simply an on-off switch for the application of *Chevron* deference?

### *b. The* Chevron *Doctrine*

Should the Court have approached the question under the *Chevron* doctrine? After all, wasn't the question whether the agency had properly construed its authority under its organic statute? If we view this as a *Chevron* case, then at which step of *Chevron* did the Court resolve the matter?

### *c. Subsequent Events*

After the Supreme Court's decision, OSHA withdrew the emergency standard but announced that it was working on a revised rule. It has not yet issued a new rule to address COVID-19 vaccination in the workplace.

---

## *West Virginia v. Environmental Protection Agency*

142 S.Ct. 2587 (2022)

CHIEF JUSTICE ROBERTS delivered the opinion of the Court.

The Clean Air Act authorizes the Environmental Protection Agency to regulate power plants by setting a "standard of performance" for their emission of certain pollutants into the air. 84 Stat. 1683, 42 U. S. C. § 7411(a)(1). That standard may be different for new and existing plants, but in each case it must reflect the "best system of emission reduction" that the Agency has determined to be "adequately demonstrated" for the particular category. §§ 7411(a)(1), (b)(1), (d). For existing plants, the States then implement that requirement by issuing rules restricting emissions from sources within their borders.

Since passage of the Act 50 years ago, EPA has exercised this authority by setting performance standards based on measures that would reduce pollution by causing plants to operate more cleanly. In 2015, however, EPA issued a new rule concluding that the "best system of emission reduction" for existing coal-fired power plants included a requirement that such facilities reduce their own production of electricity, or subsidize increased generation by natural gas, wind, or solar sources. The question before us is whether this broader conception of EPA's authority is within the power granted to it by the Clean Air Act.

The Clean Air Act establishes three main regulatory programs to control air pollution from stationary sources such as power plants. Clean Air Amendments of 1970, 84 Stat. 1676, 42 U. S. C. § 7401 *et seq.* One program is the New Source Performance Standards program of Section 111, at issue here. The other two are the National Ambient Air Quality Standards (NAAQS) program, set out in Sections 108 through 110 of the Act, 42 U. S. C. §§ 7408–7410, and the Hazardous Air Pollutants (HAP) program, set out in Section 112, § 7412. * * *

The NAAQS program addresses air pollutants that "may reasonably be anticipated to endanger public health or welfare," and "the presence of which in the ambient air results from numerous or diverse mobile or stationary sources." § 7408(a)(1). After identifying such pollutants, EPA establishes a NAAQS for each. The NAAQS represents "the maximum airborne concentration of [the] pollutant that the public health can tolerate." *Whitman v. American Trucking Assns., Inc.*, 531 U.S. 457, 465 (2001); see § 7409(b). [The states then submit plans to maintain those standards within their boundaries. § 7410.]

* * * The HAP program primarily targets pollutants, other than those already covered by a NAAQS, that [threaten human health.] § 7412(b)(2). [Unlike the NAAQS program, under which EPA determines the maximum safe amount of pollutants in the air, the HAP program requires EPA to] promulgate emissions standards for both new and existing major sources [of pollution]. § 7412(d)(1). [Under the HAP program,] EPA must directly require all covered sources to reduce their emissions to a certain level. * * * [I]n the parlance of environmental law, Section 112 directs the Agency to impose "*technology-based* standard[s] for hazardous emissions," *Alaska Dept. of Environmental Conservation v. EPA*, 540 U.S. 461, 485, n. 12 (2004) (emphasis added). * * *

The third air pollution control scheme is the New Source Performance Standards program of Section 111. § 7411. That section directs EPA to list "categories of stationary sources" that it determines "cause[ ], or contribute[ ] significantly to, air pollution which may reasonably be anticipated to endanger public health or welfare." § 7411(b)(1)(A). Under Section 111(b), the Agency must then promulgate for each category "Federal standards of performance for new sources," § 7411(b)(1)(B). A "standard of performance" is one that

> "reflects the degree of emission limitation achievable through the application of the best system of emission reduction [BSER] which (taking into account the cost of achieving such reduction and any nonair quality health and environmental impact and energy requirements) the [EPA] Administrator determines has been adequately demonstrated." § 7411(a)(1).

**Take Note**

The NAAQS program and the HAP program require EPA to set limits for the emission of particular pollutants. The New Source Performance Standards program, in contrast, requires EPA to regulate new plants that produce emissions. Under that program, EPA determines the "best system of emission reduction," or "BSER," for achieving emissions limits at each new power plant (and other sources of pollution). That program also authorizes EPA to impose similar requirements on existing plants, if the particular pollutant at issue is not already regulated under the NAAQS or HAP programs.

* * * EPA undertakes this analysis on a pollutant-by-pollutant basis, establishing different standards of performance with respect to different pollutants emitted from the same source category.

Although the thrust of Section 111 focuses on emissions limits for *new* [sources,] the statute also authorizes regulation of certain pollutants from *existing* sources. Under Section 111(d), once EPA "has set *new* source standards addressing emissions of a particular pollutant under . . . section 111(b)," 80 Fed. Reg. 64711, it must then address emissions of that same pollutant by existing sources—but only if they are not already regulated under the NAAQS or HAP programs. § 7411(d)(1). * * * Section 111(d) thus "operates as a gap-filler," empowering EPA to regulate harmful emissions not already controlled under the Agency's other authorities. *American Lung Assn. v. EPA*, 985 F.3d 914, 932 (D.C. Cir. 2021).

Reflecting the ancillary nature of Section 111(d), EPA has used it only a handful of times since the enactment of the statute in 1970. For instance, the Agency has established emissions limits on acid mist from sulfuric acid production; sulfide gases released by kraft pulp mills; and emissions of various harmful gases from municipal landfills. * * *

Things changed in October 2015, when EPA promulgated two rules addressing carbon dioxide pollution from power plants—one for new plants under Section 111(b), the other for existing plants under Section 111(d). Both were premised on the Agency's earlier finding that carbon dioxide is an "air pollutant" that "may reasonably be anticipated to endanger public health or welfare" by causing climate change. 80 Fed. Reg. 64530. Carbon dioxide is not subject to a NAAQS and has not been listed as a toxic pollutant.

The first rule announced by EPA established federal carbon emissions limits for new power plants of two varieties: fossil-fuel-fired electric steam generating units (mostly coal fired) and natural-gas-fired stationary combustion turbines. *Id.*, at 64512. Following the statutory process set out above, the Agency determined the BSER for the two categories of sources. [The BSER required new plants to use certain technologies that emit less carbon dioxide.]

The second rule was triggered by the first: Because EPA was now regulating carbon dioxide from *new* coal and gas plants, Section 111(d) required EPA to also address carbon emissions from *existing* coal and gas plants. See § 7411(d)(1). It did so through what it called the Clean Power Plan rule.

In that rule, EPA established "final emission guidelines for states to follow in developing plans" to regulate existing power plants within their borders. *Id.*, at 64662. To arrive at the guideline limits, EPA * * * identified the BSER. The BSER that the Agency selected for existing coal-fired power plants, however, was quite different from the BSER it had chosen for new sources. The BSER for existing plants included three types of measures, which the Agency called "building blocks." *Id.*, at 64667. The first building block [required] practices such plants could undertake to burn coal more efficiently. *Id.*, at 64727. But such improvements, EPA stated, would "lead to only small emission reductions," because coal-fired power plants were already operating near optimum efficiency. On the Agency's view, "much larger emission reductions [were] needed from [coal-fired plants] to address climate change." *Ibid.*

So the Agency included two additional building blocks in its BSER, both of which involve what it called "generation shifting from higher-emitting to lower-emitting" producers of electricity. *Id.*, at 64728. Building block two was a shift in electricity production from existing coal-fired power plants to natural-gas-fired plants [, which emit less carbon dioxide than coal-fired plants.] Building block three worked the same way, except that the shift was from both coal- and gas-fired plants to "new low- or zero-carbon generating capacity," mainly wind and solar. *Id.*, at 64729, 64748. * * *

The Agency identified three ways in which a regulated plant operator could implement a shift in generation to cleaner sources. *Id.*, at 64731. First, an operator could simply reduce the regulated plant's own production of electricity. Second, it could build a new natural gas plant, wind farm, or solar installation, or invest in someone else's existing facility and then increase generation there. Finally, operators could purchase emission allowances or credits as part of a cap-and-trade regime. Under such a scheme, sources that achieve a reduction in their emissions can sell a credit representing the value of that reduction to others, who are able to count it toward their own applicable emissions caps. * * * So coal plants, whether by reducing their own production, subsidizing an increase in production by cleaner sources, or both, would cause a shift toward wind, solar, and natural gas.

* * * EPA then set about determining "the degree of emission limitation achievable through the application" of that system. 42 U.S.C. § 7411(a)(1). [I]n translating the BSER into an operational emissions limit, EPA could choose whether to require anything from a little generation shifting to a great deal. The Agency settled on what it regarded as a "reasonable" amount of shift, which it based on modeling of how much more electricity both natural gas and renewable sources could supply without causing undue cost increases or reducing the overall power supply. Based on these changes, EPA projected that by 2030, it would be feasible to have coal provide 27% of national electricity generation, down from 38% in 2014.

[EPA then] developed a series of complex equations to "determine the emission performance rates" that States would be required to implement. 80 Fed. Reg. 64815. The calculations resulted in numerical emissions ceilings so strict that no existing coal plant would have been able to achieve them without engaging in one of the three means of shifting generation described above. * * * EPA's own modeling concluded that the rule would entail billions of dollars in compliance costs (to be paid in the form of higher energy prices), require the retirement of dozens of coal-fired plants, and eliminate tens of thousands of jobs across various sectors. The Energy Information Administration [projected] that the rule would cause retail electricity prices to remain persistently 10% higher in many States, and would reduce GDP by at least a trillion 2009 dollars by 2040.

These projections were never tested, because [the] same day that EPA promulgated the rule, dozens of parties (including 27 States) petitioned for review in the D.C. Circuit. After that court declined to enter a stay of the rule, [we granted one], preventing the rule from taking effect. *West Virginia v. EPA*, 577 U.S. 1126 (2016). The Court of Appeals later heard argument on the merits en banc. But before it could issue a decision, there was a change in Presidential administrations. The new administration requested that the litigation be held in abeyance so that EPA could reconsider the Clean Power Plan. The D.C. Circuit obliged, and later dismissed the petitions for review as moot.

EPA eventually repealed the rule in 2019, concluding that the Clean Power Plan had been "in excess of its statutory authority" under Section 111(d). 84 Fed. Reg. 32523 (2019). * * * In the same rulemaking, the Agency replaced the Clean Power Plan by promulgating a different Section 111(d) regulation, known as the Affordable Clean Energy (ACE) Rule[,] which required] equipment upgrades and operating practices that would improve facilities' heat rates. *Id.*, at 32522, 32537. The ACE Rule * * * would result in only small reductions in carbon dioxide emissions. *Id.*, at 32561.

A number of States and private parties immediately filed petitions for review in the D.C. Circuit, challenging EPA's repeal of the Clean Power Plan and its enactment of the replacement ACE Rule. Other States and private entities—including petitioners here West Virginia [and several coal companies]—intervened to defend both actions.

The Court of Appeals * * * held that EPA's "repeal of the Clean Power Plan rested critically on a mistaken reading of the Clean Air Act" [and that] the statute could reasonably be read to encompass generation shifting * * *. [The court thus] vacated the Agency's repeal of the Clean Power Plan [and the replacement rule. After another change in Presidential administrations, the court of appeals, at EPA's request, partially stayed the issuance of its mandate to ensure that the Clean Power Plan would not immediately go back into effect, in order to give the agency time to consider whether to issue a new Section 111(d) rule.]

[The Supreme Court decided to review the Court of Appeals' decision. The Court first held that the plaintiffs had standing and that the controversy was not moot.]

* * * The issue here is whether restructuring the Nation's overall mix of electricity generation, to transition from 38% coal to 27% coal by 2030, can be the "best system of emission reduction" within the meaning of Section 111.

"It is a fundamental canon of statutory construction that the words of a statute must be read in their context and with a view to their place in the overall statutory scheme." *Davis v. Michigan Dept. of Treasury*, 489 U.S. 803, 809 (1989). Where the statute at issue is one that confers authority upon an administrative agency, that inquiry must be "shaped, at least in some measure, by the nature of the question presented"—whether Congress in fact meant to confer the power the agency has asserted. *FDA v. Brown & Williamson Tobacco Corp.*, 529 U.S. 120,

**Take Note**

Did this case involve an agency interpretation of the statute it is responsible for administering? If so, did the Court address the question under the *Chevron* framework? If so, at which step of the *Chevron* test did the Court resolve the issue? If not, why not?

159 (2000). In the ordinary case, that context has no great effect on the appropriate analysis. Nonetheless, our precedent teaches that there are "extraordinary cases" that call for a different approach—cases in which the "history and the breadth of the authority that [the agency] has asserted," and the "economic and political significance" of that assertion, provide a "reason to hesitate before concluding that Congress" meant to confer such authority. *Id.*, at 159–160.

Such cases have arisen from all corners of the administrative state. In *Brown & Williamson*, for instance, the Food and Drug Administration claimed that its authority over "drugs" and "devices" included the power to regulate, and even ban, tobacco products. We rejected that "expansive construction of the statute," concluding that "Congress could not have intended to delegate" such a sweeping and consequential authority "in so cryptic a fashion." *Id.*, at 160. In *Alabama Assn. of Realtors v. Department of Health and Human Servs.*, 141 S.Ct. 2485, 2487 (2021) (*per curiam*), we concluded that the Centers for Disease Control and Prevention could not, under its authority to adopt measures "necessary to prevent the . . . spread of" disease, institute a nationwide eviction moratorium in response to the COVID-19 pandemic. We found the statute's language a "wafer-thin reed" on which to rest such a measure, given "the sheer scope of the CDC's claimed authority," its "unprecedented" nature, and the fact that Congress had failed to extend the moratorium after previously having done so. *Id.*, at 2488–2490.

Our decision in *Utility Air Regulatory Group v. EPA* addressed * * * whether EPA could construe the term "air pollutant," in a specific provision of the Clean Air Act, to cover greenhouse gases. 573 U.S. 302, 310 (2014). Despite its textual plausibility, we noted that the Agency's interpretation would have given it permitting authority over millions of small sources, such as hotels and office buildings, that had never before been subject to such requirements. *Id.*, at 310, 324. We declined to uphold EPA's claim of "unheralded" regulatory power over "a significant portion of the American economy." *Id.*, at 324. In *Gonzales v. Oregon*, 546 U.S. 243 (2006), we confronted the Attorney General's assertion that he could rescind the license of any physician who prescribed a controlled substance for assisted suicide, even in a State where such action was legal. The Attorney General argued that this came within his statutory power to revoke licenses where he found them "inconsistent with the public interest," 21 U.S.C. § 823(f). We considered the "idea that Congress gave [him] such broad and unusual authority through an implicit delegation . . . not sustainable." 546 U.S. at 267. Similar considerations informed our recent decision invalidating the Occupational Safety and Health Administration's mandate that "84 million Americans . . . either obtain a COVID-19 vaccine or undergo weekly medical testing at their own expense." *National Federation of Independent Business v. Occupational Safety and Health Administration*, 142 S.Ct. 661, 665 (2022) (*per curiam*). We found it "telling that OSHA, in its half century of existence," had never relied on its authority to regulate occupational hazards to impose such a remarkable measure. *Id.*, at 666.

All of these regulatory assertions had a colorable textual basis. And yet, in each case, given the various circumstances, "common sense as to the manner in which Congress [would have been] likely to delegate" such power to the agency at issue, *Brown & Williamson*, 529 U.S. at 133, made it very unlikely that Congress had actually done so. Extraordinary grants of regulatory authority are rarely accomplished through "modest words," "vague terms," or "subtle device[s]." *Whitman*, 531 U.S. at 468. Nor does Congress typically use oblique or elliptical language to empower an agency to make a "radical or fundamental change" to a statutory scheme. *MCI Telecommunications Corp. v. American Telephone & Telegraph Co.*, 512 U.S. 218, 229 (1994). * * * We presume that "Congress intends to make major policy decisions itself, not leave those decisions to agencies." *United States Telecom Assn. v. FCC*, 855 F.3d 381, 419 (DC Cir. 2017) (Kavanaugh, J., dissenting from denial of rehearing en banc).

Thus, in certain extraordinary cases, both separation of powers principles and a practical understanding of legislative intent make us "reluctant to read into ambiguous statutory text" the delegation claimed to be lurking there. *Utility Air*, 573 U.S. at 324. To convince us otherwise, something more than a merely plausible textual basis for the agency action is necessary. The agency instead must point to "clear congressional authorization" for the power it claims. *Ibid.*

The dissent criticizes us for "announc[ing] the arrival" of this major questions doctrine, and argues that each of the decisions just cited simply followed our "ordinary method" of "normal statutory interpretation." But in what the dissent calls the "key case" in this area, *Brown & Williamson*, the Court could not have been clearer: "In extraordinary cases . . . there may be reason to hesitate" before accepting a reading of a statute that would, under more "ordinary" circumstances, be upheld. 529 U.S. at 159. * * * The dissent attempts to fit the analysis in these cases within routine statutory interpretation, but the bottom line—a requirement of "clear congressional authorization"—confirms that the approach under the major questions doctrine is distinct.

As for the major questions doctrine "label[ ]," it took hold because it refers to an identifiable body of law that has developed over a series of significant cases all addressing a particular and recurring problem: agencies asserting highly consequential power beyond what Congress could reasonably be understood to have granted. Scholars and jurists have recognized the common threads between those decisions. So have we.

Under our precedents, this is a major questions case. In arguing that Section 111(d) empowers it to substantially restructure the American energy market, EPA "claim[ed] to discover in a long-extant statute an unheralded power" representing a "transformative expansion in [its] regulatory authority." *Utility Air*, 573 U.S. at 324. It located that newfound power in the vague language of an "ancillary provision[ ]" of the Act, *Whitman*, 531 U.S. at 468, one that was designed to function as a gap filler and had rarely been used in the preceding decades. And the Agency's discovery allowed it to adopt a regulatory program that Congress had conspicuously and repeatedly declined to enact itself. Given these circumstances, there is every reason to "hesitate before concluding that Congress" meant to confer on EPA the authority it claims under Section 111(d).

Prior to 2015, EPA had always set emissions limits under Section 111 based on the application of measures that would reduce pollution by causing the regulated source to operate more cleanly. It had never devised a cap by looking to a "system" that would reduce pollution simply by "shifting" polluting activity "from dirtier to cleaner sources." 80 Fed. Reg. 64726. And as Justice Frankfurter has noted, "just as established practice may shed light on the extent of power conveyed by general statutory language, so the want of assertion of power by those who presumably would be alert to exercise it, is equally significant in determining whether such power was actually conferred." *FTC v. Bunte Brothers, Inc.*, 312 U.S. 349, 352 (1941).

This consistent understanding of "system[s] of emission reduction" tracked the seemingly universal view, as stated by EPA in its inaugural Section 111(d) rulemaking, that "Congress intended a technology-based approach" to regulation in that Section. 40 Fed. Reg. 53343 (1975). * * * Indeed, EPA nodded to this history in the Clean Power Plan itself, describing the sort of "systems of emission reduction" it had always before selected—"efficiency improvements, fuel-switching," and "add-on controls"—as "more traditional air pollution control measures." 80 Fed. Reg. 64784. * * *

But, the Agency explained, in order to "* * * mitigate the dangers presented by climate change," it could not base the emissions limit on "measures that improve efficiency at the power plants." *Id.*, at 64728. * * * Instead, to attain the necessary "critical CO2 reductions," EPA adopted what it called a "broader, forward-thinking approach to the design" of Section 111 regulations. *Id.*, at 64703. Rather than focus on improving the performance of individual sources, it would "improve the *overall power system* by lowering the carbon intensity of power generation." *Ibid.* (emphasis added). And it would do that by forcing a shift throughout the power grid from one type of energy source to another. * * *

This view of EPA's authority was not only unprecedented; it also effected a "fundamental revision of the statute, changing it from [one sort of] scheme of . . . regulation" into an entirely different kind. *MCI*, 512 U.S. at 231. Under the Agency's prior view of Section 111, its role was limited to ensuring the efficient pollution performance of each individual regulated source. Under that paradigm, if a source was already operating at that level, there was nothing more for EPA to do. Under its newly "discover[ed]" authority, *Utility Air*, 573 U.S. at 324, however, EPA can demand much greater reductions in emissions based on a very different kind of policy judgment: that it would be "best" if coal made up a much smaller share of national electricity generation. And on this view of EPA's authority, it could go further, perhaps forcing coal plants to "shift" away virtually all of their generation—*i.e.*, to cease making power altogether.

* * * On EPA's view of Section 111(d), Congress implicitly tasked it, and it alone, with balancing the many vital considerations of national policy implicated in deciding how Americans will get their energy. EPA decides, for instance, how much of a switch from coal to natural gas is practically feasible by 2020, 2025, and 2030 before the grid collapses, and how high energy prices can go as a result before they become unreasonably "exorbitant."

We [find] it "highly unlikely that Congress would leave" to "agency discretion" the decision of how much coal-based generation there should be over the coming decades. *MCI*, 512 U.S. at 231. The basic and consequential tradeoffs involved in such a choice are ones that Congress would likely have intended for itself. Congress certainly has not conferred a like authority upon EPA anywhere else in the Clean Air Act. The last place one would expect to find it is in the previously little-used backwater of Section 111(d).

The dissent contends that there is nothing surprising about EPA dictating the optimal mix of energy sources nationwide, since that sort of mandate will reduce air pollution from power plants, which is EPA's bread and butter. But that does not follow. * * * We would not expect the Department of Homeland Security to make trade or foreign policy even though doing so could decrease illegal immigration. And no one would consider generation shifting a "tool" in OSHA's "toolbox," even though reducing generation at coal plants would reduce workplace illness and injury from coal dust.

* * * At bottom, the Clean Power Plan essentially adopted a cap-and-trade scheme, or set of state cap-and-trade schemes, for carbon. Congress, however, has consistently rejected proposals to amend the Clean Air Act to create such a program. See, *e.g.*, American Clean Energy and Security Act of 2009, H. R. 2454, 111th Cong., 1st Sess.. It has also declined to enact similar measures, such as a carbon tax. See, *e.g.*, Climate Protection Act of 2013, S. 332, 113th Cong., 1st Sess. * * *

Given these circumstances, our precedent counsels skepticism toward EPA's claim that Section 111 empowers it to devise carbon emissions caps based on a generation shifting approach. To overcome that skepticism, the Government must—under the major questions doctrine—point to "clear congressional authorization" to regulate in that manner. *Utility Air*, 573 U.S. at 324.

**Food for Thought**

What would Congress have to say in a statute delegating power to the EPA to satisfy the Court's test? Are there any drawbacks to insisting on such a level of legislative specificity?

All the Government can offer, however, is the Agency's authority to establish emissions caps at a level reflecting "the application of the best system of emission reduction . . . adequately demonstrated." 42 U.S.C. § 7411(a)(1). As a matter of "definitional possibilities," *FCC v. AT&T Inc.*, 562 U.S. 397, 407 (2011), generation shifting can be described as a "system"—"an aggregation or assemblage of objects united by some form of regular interaction," Brief for Federal Respondents 31—capable of reducing emissions. But of course almost anything could constitute such a "system"; shorn of all context, the word is an empty vessel. Such a vague statutory grant is not close to the sort of clear authorization required by our precedents.

Capping carbon dioxide emissions at a level that will force a nationwide transition away from the use of coal to generate electricity may be a sensible "solution to the crisis of the day." *New York v. United States*, 505 U.S. 144 (1992). But it is not plausible that Congress gave EPA the authority to adopt on its own such a regulatory scheme in Section 111(d). A decision of such magnitude and consequence rests with Congress itself, or an agency acting pursuant to a clear delegation from that representative body. [Reversed.]

JUSTICE GORSUCH, with whom JUSTICE ALITO joins, concurring.

One of the Judiciary's most solemn duties is to ensure that acts of Congress are applied in accordance with the Constitution in the cases that come before us. To help fulfill that duty, courts have developed certain "clear-statement" rules. These rules assume that, absent a clear statement otherwise, Congress means for its laws to operate in congruence with the Constitution rather than test its bounds. In this way, these clear-statement rules help courts "act as faithful agents of the Constitution." A. Barrett, Substantive Canons and Faithful Agency, 90 B.U. L. Rev. 109, 169 (2010).

The major questions doctrine works [to] protect the Constitution's separation of powers. In Article I, "the People" vested "[a]ll" federal "legislative powers . . . in Congress." Preamble; Art. I, § 1. As Chief Justice Marshall put it, this means that "important subjects . . . must be entirely regulated by the legislature itself," even if Congress may leave the Executive "to act under such general provisions to fill up the details." *Wayman v. Southard*, 10 Wheat. 1, 42–43 (1825). Doubtless, what qualifies as an important subject and what constitutes a detail may be debated. See, *e.g.*, *Gundy v. United States*, 139 S.Ct. 2116 (2019). But [the] Constitution's rule vesting federal legislative power in Congress is "vital to the integrity and maintenance of the system of government ordained by the Constitution." *Marshall Field & Co. v. Clark*, 143 U.S. 649, 692 (1892).

It is vital because the framers believed that a republic—a thing of the people—would be more likely to enact just laws than a regime administered by a ruling class of largely unaccountable "ministers." The Federalist No. 11, p. 85 (C. Rossiter ed. 1961) (A. Hamilton). [B]y vesting the lawmaking power in the people's elected representatives, the Constitution sought to ensure "not only that all power [w]ould be derived from the people," but also "that those [e]ntrusted with it should be kept in dependence on the people." *Id.*, No. 37, at 227 (J. Madison). * * *

Admittedly, lawmaking under our Constitution can be difficult. But that is nothing particular to our time nor any accident. The framers believed that the power to make new laws regulating private conduct was a grave one that could, if not properly checked, pose a serious threat to individual liberty. See The Federalist No. 48, at 309–312 (J. Madison); see also *id.*, No. 73, at 441–442 (A. Hamilton). As a result, the framers deliberately sought to make lawmaking difficult by insisting that two houses of Congress must agree to any new law and the President must concur or a legislative supermajority must override his veto.

The difficulty of the design sought to serve other ends too. By effectively requiring a broad consensus to pass legislation, the Constitution sought to ensure that any new laws would enjoy wide social acceptance, profit from input by an array of different perspectives during their consideration, and thanks to all this prove stable over time. See *id.*, No. 10, at 82–84 (J. Madison). The need for compromise inherent in this design also sought to protect minorities by ensuring that their votes would often decide the fate of proposed legislation—allowing them to wield real power alongside the majority. See *id.*, No. 51, at 322–324 (J. Madison). The difficulty of legislating at the federal level aimed as well to preserve room for lawmaking "by governments more local and more accountable than a distant federal" authority, *National Federation of Independent Business v. Sebelius*, 567 U.S. 519, 536 (2012) (plurality opinion), and in this way allow States to serve as "laborator[ies]" for "novel social and economic experiments," *New State Ice Co. v. Liebmann*, 285 U.S. 262, 311 (1932) (Brandeis, J., dissenting).

Permitting Congress to divest its legislative power to the Executive Branch would "dash [this] whole scheme." *Department of Transportation v. Association of American Railroads*, 575 U.S. 43, 61 (2015) (ALITO, J., concurring). Legislation would risk becoming nothing more than the will of the current President, or, worse yet, the will of unelected officials barely responsive to him. In a world like that, agencies could churn out new laws more or less at whim. Intrusions on liberty would not be difficult and rare, but easy and profuse. Stability would be lost, with vast numbers of laws changing with every new presidential administration. Rather than embody a wide social consensus and input from minority voices, laws would more often bear the support only of the party currently in power. * * *

* * * Article I's Vesting Clause has [a corollary clear statement rule]: the major questions doctrine. * * * The Court has applied the major questions doctrine for the same reason it has applied other similar clear-statement rules—to ensure that the government does "not inadvertently cross constitutional lines." Barrett at 175. * * * At stake [are] basic questions about self-government, equality, fair notice, federalism, and the separation of powers. * * * In our Republic, "[i]t is the peculiar province of the legislature to prescribe general rules for the government of society." *Fletcher v. Peck*, 6 Cranch 87, 136 (1810). Because today's decision helps safeguard that foundational constitutional promise, I am pleased to concur.

JUSTICE KAGAN, with whom JUSTICE BREYER and JUSTICE SOTOMAYOR join, dissenting.

Today, the Court strips the Environmental Protection Agency (EPA) of the power Congress gave it to respond to "the most pressing environmental challenge of our time." *Massachusetts v. EPA*, 549 U.S. 497, 505 (2007). Climate change's causes and dangers are no longer subject to serious doubt. * * * Congress charged EPA with addressing those potentially catastrophic harms, including through regulation of fossil-fuel-fired power plants. Section 111 of the Clean Air Act directs EPA to regulate stationary sources of any substance that "causes, or contributes significantly to, air pollution" and that "may reasonably be anticipated to endanger public health or welfare." 42 U.S.C. § 7411(b)(1)(A). Carbon dioxide and other greenhouse gases fit that description. See *Massachusetts*, 549 U.S. at 528–532. EPA thus serves as the Nation's "primary regulator of greenhouse gas emissions." *American Elec. Power*, 564 U.S. at 428. And among the most significant of the entities it regulates are fossil-fuel-fired (mainly coal- and natural-gas-fired) power plants. Today, those electricity-producing plants are responsible for about one quarter of the Nation's greenhouse gas emissions. See EPA, Sources of Greenhouse Gas Emissions (Apr. 14, 2022). Curbing that output is a necessary part of any effective approach for addressing climate change.

To carry out its Section 111 responsibility, EPA issued the Clean Power Plan in 2015. * * * This Court has obstructed EPA's effort from the beginning. Right after the Obama administration issued the Clean Power Plan, the Court stayed its implementation. * * * Never before had the Court stayed a regulation then under review in the lower courts. The effect of the Court's order, followed by the Trump administration's repeal of the rule, was that the Clean Power Plan never went into effect. [In the ensuing years, market] forces alone caused the power industry to meet the Plan's nationwide emissions target—through exactly the kinds of generation shifting the Plan contemplated. * * * For that reason, the Biden administration announced that, instead of putting the Plan into effect, it would commence a new rulemaking. Yet this Court determined to pronounce on the legality of the old rule anyway. * * * The Court today issues what is really an advisory opinion on the proper scope of the new rule EPA is considering. [T]his Court could not wait—even to see what the new rule says—to constrain EPA's efforts to address climate change.

The limits the majority now puts on EPA's authority fly in the face of the statute Congress wrote. The majority says it is simply "not plausible" that Congress enabled EPA to regulate power plants' emissions through generation shifting. But that is just what Congress did when it broadly authorized EPA in Section 111 to select the "best system of emission reduction" for power plants. § 7411(a)(1). The "best system" full stop—no ifs, ands, or buts of any kind relevant here. The parties do not dispute that generation shifting is indeed the "best system"—the most effective and efficient way to reduce power plants' carbon dioxide emissions. And no other provision in the Clean Air Act suggests that Congress meant to foreclose EPA from selecting that system;

to the contrary, the Plan's regulatory approach fits hand-in-glove with the rest of the statute. The majority's decision rests on one claim alone: that generation shifting is just too new and too big a deal for Congress to have authorized it in Section 111's general terms. But that is wrong. A key reason Congress makes broad delegations like Section 111 is so an agency can respond, appropriately and commensurately, to new and big problems. Congress knows what it doesn't and can't know when it drafts a statute; and Congress therefore gives an expert agency the power to address issues—even significant ones—as and when they arise. That is what Congress did in enacting Section 111. The majority today overrides that legislative choice. In so doing, it deprives EPA of the power needed—and the power granted—to curb the emission of greenhouse gases.

The majority claims it is just following precedent, but that is not so. The Court has never even used the term "major questions doctrine" before. And in the relevant cases, the Court has done statutory construction of a familiar sort. It has looked to the text of a delegation. It has addressed how an agency's view of that text works—or fails to do so—in the context of a broader statutory scheme. And it has asked, in a common-sensical (or call it purposive) vein, about what Congress would have made of the agency's view—otherwise said, whether Congress would naturally have delegated authority over some important question to the agency, given its expertise and experience. In short, in assessing the scope of a delegation, the Court has considered—without multiple steps, triggers, or special presumptions—the fit between the power claimed, the agency claiming it, and the broader statutory design.

The majority's effort to find support in *Brown & Williamson* for its interpretive approach fails. It may be helpful here to quote the full sentence that the majority quotes half of. "In extraordinary cases," the Court stated, "there may be reason to hesitate before concluding that Congress has intended such an implicit delegation." 529 U.S. at 159. For anyone familiar with this Court's *Chevron* doctrine, that language will ring a bell. The Court was saying only—and it was elsewhere explicit on this point—that there was reason to hesitate before giving FDA's position *Chevron* deference. And what was that reason? The Court went on to explain that it would not defer to FDA because it read the relevant statutory provisions as negating the agency's claimed authority. See *id.*, at 133 (finding at *Chevron*'s first step that "Congress has directly spoken to the issue here and precluded the FDA's" asserted power). In reaching that conclusion, the Court relied * * * not on any special "clear authorization" demand, but on normal principles of statutory interpretation: look at the text, view it in context, and use what the Court called some "common sense" about how Congress delegates. *That* is how courts are to decide, in the majority's language, whether an agency has asserted a "highly consequential power beyond what Congress could reasonably be understood to have granted."

The Court has applied the same kind of analysis in subsequent cases—holding in each that an agency exceeded the scope of a broadly framed delegation when it operated outside the sphere of its expertise, in a way that warped the statutory text or structure. [Justice Kagan discussed the Court's decisions in *Gonzales v. Oregon*, 546 U.S. 243 (2006), *Utility Air Regulatory Group v. EPA*, 573 U.S. 302 (2014), and *Alabama Assn. of Realtors v. Department of Health and Human Servs.*, 141 S.Ct. 2485 (2021).] In each case, the Court thought, the agency had strayed out of its lane, to an area where it had neither expertise nor experience. The Attorney General making healthcare policy, the regulator of pharmaceutical concerns deciding the fate of the tobacco industry, and so on. And in each case, the proof that the agency had roamed too far afield lay in the statutory scheme itself. The agency action collided with other statutory provisions; if the former were allowed, the latter could not mean what they said or could not work as intended. * * *

[N]othing in the Clean Air Act (or, for that matter, any other statute) conflicts with EPA's reading of Section 111. Notably, the majority does not dispute that point. [N]owhere does the majority provide evidence from within the statute itself that the Clean Power Plan conflicts with or undermines Congress's design. That fact alone makes this case different from all the cases described above. * * *

Some years ago, I remarked that "[w]e're all textualists now." Harvard Law School, The Antonin Scalia Lecture Series: A Dialogue with Justice Elena Kagan on the Reading of Statutes (Nov. 25, 2015). It seems I was wrong. The current Court is textualist only when being so suits it. When that method would frustrate broader goals, special canons like the "major questions doctrine" magically appear as get-out-of-text-free cards. Today, one of those broader goals makes itself clear: Prevent agencies from doing important work, even though that is what Congress directed. That anti-administrative-state stance shows up in the majority opinion, and it suffuses the concurrence.

The kind of agency delegations at issue here go all the way back to this Nation's founding. "[T]he founding era," scholars have shown, "wasn't concerned about delegation." E. Posner & A. Vermeule, Interring the Nondelegation Doctrine, 69 U. Chi. L. Rev. 1721, 1734 (2002). The records of the Constitutional Convention, the ratification debates, the Federalist—none of them suggests any significant limit on Congress's capacity to delegate policymaking authority to the Executive Branch. And neither does any early practice. The very first Congress gave sweeping authority to the Executive Branch to resolve some of the day's most pressing problems, including questions of "territorial administration," "Indian affairs," "foreign and domestic debt," "military service," and "the federal courts." J. Mortenson & N. Bagley, Delegation at the Founding, 121 Colum. L. Rev. 277, 349 (2021). * * *

It is not surprising that Congress has always delegated, and continues to do so—including on important policy issues. As this Court has recognized, it is often "unreasonable and impracticable" for Congress to do anything else. *American Power & Light Co. v. SEC*, 329 U.S. 90, 105 (1946). In all times, but ever more in "our increasingly complex society," the Legislature "simply cannot do its job absent an ability to delegate power under broad general directives." *Mistretta v. United States*, 488 U.S. 361, 372 (1989). Consider just two reasons why.

First, Members of Congress often don't know enough—and know they don't know enough—to regulate sensibly on an issue. Of course, Members can and do provide overall direction. But then they rely, as all of us rely in our daily lives, on people with greater expertise and experience. Those people are found in agencies. Congress looks to them to make specific judgments about how to achieve its more general objectives. And it does so especially, though by no means exclusively, when an issue has a scientific or technical dimension. * * *

Second and relatedly, Members of Congress often can't know enough—and again, know they can't—to keep regulatory schemes working across time. Congress usually can't predict the future—can't anticipate changing circumstances and the way they will affect varied regulatory techniques. Nor can Congress (realistically) keep track of and respond to fast-flowing developments as they occur. Once again, that is most obviously true when it comes to scientific and technical matters. The "best system of emission reduction" is not today what it was yesterday, and will surely be something different tomorrow. So for this reason too, a rational Congress delegates. It enables an agency to adapt old regulatory approaches to new times, to ensure that a statutory program remains effective.

Over time, the administrative delegations Congress has made have helped to build a modern Nation. Congress wanted fewer workers killed in industrial accidents. It wanted to prevent plane crashes, and reduce the deadliness of car wrecks. It wanted to ensure that consumer products didn't catch fire. It wanted to stop the routine adulteration of food and improve the safety and efficacy of medications. And it wanted cleaner air and water. If an American could go back in time, she might be astonished by how much progress has occurred in all those areas. It didn't happen through legislation alone. It happened because Congress gave broad-ranging powers to administrative agencies, and those agencies then filled in—rule by rule by rule—Congress's policy outlines.

This Court has historically known enough not to get in the way. Maybe the best explanation of why comes from Justice Scalia. See *Mistretta*, 488 U.S. at 415–416 (dissenting opinion). * * * He started with the inevitability of delegations: "[S]ome judgments involving policy considerations," he stated, "must be left to [administrative] officers." Id., at 415. Then he explained why courts should not try to seriously police those delegations, barring—or, I'll add, narrowing—some on the ground that they went too far. The scope of delegations, he said,

> "must be fixed according to common sense and the inherent necessities of the governmental co-ordination. Since Congress is no less endowed with common sense than we are, and better equipped to inform itself of the necessities of government; and since the factors bearing upon those necessities are both multifarious and (in the nonpartisan sense) highly political . . . it is small wonder that we have almost never felt qualified

to second-guess Congress regarding the permissible degree of policy judgment that can be left to those executing or applying the law." *Id.*, at 416.

In short, when it comes to delegations, there are good reasons for Congress (within extremely broad limits) to get to call the shots. Congress knows about how government works in ways courts don't. More specifically, Congress knows what mix of legislative and administrative action conduces to good policy. Courts should be modest.

Today, the Court is not. Section 111, most naturally read, authorizes EPA to develop the Clean Power Plan—in other words, to decide that generation shifting is the "best system of emission reduction" for power plants churning out carbon dioxide. Evaluating systems of emission reduction is what EPA does. And nothing in the rest of the Clean Air Act, or any other statute, suggests that Congress did not mean for the delegation it wrote to go as far as the text says. In rewriting that text, the Court substitutes its own ideas about delegations for Congress's. And that means the Court substitutes its own ideas about policymaking for Congress's. The Court will not allow the Clean Air Act to work as Congress instructed. The Court, rather than Congress, will decide how much regulation is too much.

The subject matter of the regulation here makes the Court's intervention all the more troubling. Whatever else this Court may know about, it does not have a clue about how to address climate change. And let's say the obvious: The stakes here are high. Yet the Court today prevents congressionally authorized agency action to curb power plants' carbon dioxide emissions. The Court appoints itself—instead of Congress or the expert agency—the decision-maker on climate policy. I cannot think of many things more frightening. Respectfully, I dissent.

---

## Points for Discussion

### *a. Major Questions*

What was the Court's reasoning in concluding that the EPA's assertion of authority concerned a major question of policy? Was it based on the amount of money at stake? The number of people affected by the issue? The consequences of the issue's resolution for the country and the world? How did the Court weigh these factors in deciding that this case involved a question that Congress must directly address, rather than one that an agency, acting pursuant to delegated power, can address?

### *b. The* Chevron *Doctrine*

In *Brown & Williamson* and *MCI*, the Court relied in part on the nature of the questions at issue in applying the *Chevron* doctrine. In *Brown & Williamson*, for example, the question was whether the Court was obligated to defer to the FDA's interpretation of the statute and its application to tobacco products. Is that how the Court applied the major questions doctrine in *West Virginia*? Did the Court treat the case as a *Chevron* case, involving an agency's interpretation of the statute that it is charged with administering? If not, then what was the role of the major questions doctrine?

### *c. Clear Statement Rules*

The Court reasoned that, because the policy question at issue was a major question, the agency should not be deemed to have authority to act unless Congress has spoken clearly and specifically in conferring such authority. Was that your understanding of how the major questions doctrine operates? What exactly must Congress say to satisfy the Court's clear statement test? Is the major questions doctrine simply another substantive canon, like the federalism canon, that requires courts to interpret statutes with a thumb on the scale for certain outcomes? If so, what is the outcome that the Court is trying to produce (or avoid)?

**Make the Connection**

We considered the substantive canons, including the federalism canon, in Chapter 3.

### *d. The Non-Delegation Doctrine*

Although the Court's opinion does not mention the non-delegation doctrine, Justice Gorsuch's concurring opinion asserts that the major questions doctrine, and its corollary clear statement rule, is designed to limit broad delegations of authority from Congress to agencies. If concerns about excessive delegation are the impetus for the Court's approach, would it make more sense for the Court simply to add teeth to the non-delegation doctrine? Or do you agree with Justice Kagan that the Court is wrong to seek to impose such limits (or at least most such limits) in the first place?

---

As we have just seen, when an agency purports to interpret a statute that it is charged with administering—either by expressly construing its terms or by making a judgment about the scope of its authority—courts sometimes decline to defer to the agency because of the significance of the policy question at issue. In other words, the major questions doctrine can function as an on-off switch for the application of the *Chevron* framework. Is the major questions doctrine the only exception to the more general rule of *Chevron*'s two-step test? Consider the case that follows.

---

## *United States v. Mead Corp.*

533 U.S. 218 (2001)

JUSTICE SOUTER delivered the opinion of the Court.

The question is whether a tariff classification ruling by the United States Customs Service deserves judicial deference. The Federal Circuit rejected Customs's invocation of *Chevron U.S.A. Inc. v. Natural Resources Defense Council, Inc.*, 467 U.S. 837 (1984), in support of such a ruling, to which it gave no deference. We agree that a tariff classification has no claim to judicial deference under *Chevron*, there being no indication that Congress intended such a ruling to carry the force of law, but we hold that under *Skidmore v. Swift & Co.*, 323 U.S. 134 (1944), the ruling is eligible to claim respect according to its persuasiveness.

Imports are taxed under the Harmonized Tariff Schedule of the United States (HTSUS), 19 U.S.C. § 1202. 19 U.S.C. § 1500(b) provides that Customs "shall, under rules and regulations prescribed by the Secretary [of the Treasury,] . . . fix the final classification and rate of duty applicable to . . . merchandise" under the HTSUS. Section 1502(a) provides that "[t]he Secretary of the Treasury shall establish and promulgate such rules and regulations not inconsistent with the law (including regulations establishing procedures for the issuance of binding rulings prior to the entry of the merchandise concerned), and may disseminate such information as may be necessary to secure a just, impartial, and uniform appraisement of imported merchandise and the classification and assessment of duties thereon at the various ports of entry."

The Secretary provides for tariff rulings before the entry of goods by regulations authorizing "ruling letters" setting tariff classifications for particular imports. 19 CFR § 177.8 (2000). A ruling letter "represents the official position of the Customs Service with respect to the particular transaction or issue described therein and is binding on all Customs Service personnel in accordance with the provisions of this section until modified or revoked. * * *" § 177.9(a). After the transaction that gives it birth, a ruling letter is to "be applied only with respect to transactions involving articles identical to the sample submitted with the ruling request or to articles whose description is identical to the description set forth in the ruling letter." § 177.9(b)(2). As a general matter, such a letter is "subject to modification or revocation without notice to any person, except the person to whom the letter was addressed," § 177.9(c), and the regulations consequently provide that "no other person should rely on the ruling letter or assume that the principles of that ruling will be applied in connection with any transaction other than the one described in the letter." Since ruling letters respond to transactions of the moment, they are not subject to notice and comment before being issued, may be published but need only be made "available for public inspection,"

19 U.S.C. § 1625(a), and, at the time this action arose, could be modified without notice and comment under most circumstances, 19 CFR § 177.10(c) (2000). * * *

Any of the 46 port-of-entry Customs offices may issue ruling letters, and so may the Customs Headquarters Office, in providing "[a]dvice or guidance as to the interpretation or proper application of the Customs and related laws with respect to a specific Customs transaction * * *." 19 CFR § 177.11(a) (2000). Most ruling letters contain little or no reasoning, but simply describe goods and state the appropriate category and tariff. A few letters, like the Headquarters ruling at issue here, set out a rationale in some detail.

Respondent, the Mead Corporation, imports "day planners," three-ring binders with pages having room for notes of daily schedules and phone numbers and addresses, together with a calendar and suchlike. The tariff schedule on point falls under the HTSUS heading for "[r]egisters, account books, notebooks, order books, receipt books, letter pads, memorandum pads, diaries and similar articles," HTSUS subheading 4820.10, which comprises two subcategories. Items in the first, "[d]iaries, notebooks and address books, bound; memorandum pads, letter pads and similar articles," were subject to a tariff of 4.0% at the time in controversy. Objects in the second, covering "[o]ther" items, were free of duty. HTSUS subheading 4820.10.40.

Between 1989 and 1993, Customs repeatedly treated day planners under the "other" HTSUS subheading. In January 1993, however, Customs changed its position, and issued a Headquarters ruling letter classifying Mead's day planners as "Diaries . . ., bound" subject to tariff under subheading 4820.10.20. That letter was short on explanation, but after Mead's protest, Customs Headquarters issued a new letter, carefully reasoned but never published, reaching the same conclusion. This letter considered two definitions of "diary" from the Oxford English Dictionary [and referred to] commercial usage * * *. Customs concluded that [the term "bound" referred to binding by "reinforcements or fittings of metal, plastics, etc." Mead filed suit to challenge the tariff classification.]

* * * We hold that administrative implementation of a particular statutory provision qualifies for *Chevron* deference when it appears that Congress delegated authority to the agency generally to make rules carrying the force of law, and that the agency interpretation claiming deference was promulgated in the exercise of that authority. Delegation of such authority may be shown in a variety of ways, as by an agency's power to engage in adjudication or notice-and-comment rulemaking, or by some other indication of a comparable congressional intent. The Customs ruling at issue here fails to qualify, although the possibility that it deserves some deference under *Skidmore* leads us to vacate and remand.

When Congress has "explicitly left a gap for an agency to fill, there is an express delegation of authority to the agency to elucidate a specific provision of the statute by regulation," *Chevron*, 467 U.S., at 843–844, and any ensuing regulation is binding in the courts unless procedurally defective, arbitrary or capricious in substance, or manifestly contrary to the statute. See *id.*, at 844; APA, 5 U.S.C. §§ 706(2)(A), (D). But whether or not they enjoy any express delegation of authority on a particular question, agencies charged with applying a statute necessarily make all sorts of interpretive choices, and while not all of those choices bind judges to follow them, they certainly may influence courts facing questions the agencies have already answered. "[T]he well-reasoned views of the agencies implementing a statute 'constitute a body of experience and informed judgment to which courts and litigants may properly resort for guidance,' " *Bragdon v. Abbott*, 524 U.S. 624, 642 (1998) (quoting *Skidmore*, 323 U.S., at 139–140), and "[w]e have long recognized that considerable weight should be accorded to an executive department's construction of a statutory scheme it is entrusted to administer . . . ." *Chevron, supra*, at 844. The fair measure of deference to an agency administering its own statute has been understood to vary with circumstances, and courts have looked to the degree of the agency's care, its consistency, formality, and relative expertness, and to the persuasiveness of the agency's position. The approach has produced a spectrum of judicial responses, from great respect at one end, see, *e.g., Aluminum Co. of America v. Central Lincoln Peoples' Util. Dist.*, 467 U.S. 380, 389–390 (1984) ("substantial deference" to administrative construction), to near indifference at the other, see, *e.g., Bowen v. Georgetown Univ. Hospital*, 488 U.S. 204, 212–213 (1988) (interpretation advanced for the first time in a litigation brief). Justice Jackson summed things up in *Skidmore v. Swift & Co.*: "The weight [accorded to an administrative] judgment in a particular case will depend upon the thoroughness evident in its consideration, the validity of its reasoning, its consistency with earlier and later pronouncements, and all those factors which give it power to persuade, if lacking power to control." 323 U.S., at 140.

Since 1984, we have identified a category of interpretive choices distinguished by an additional reason for judicial deference. This Court in *Chevron* recognized that Congress not only engages in express delegation of specific interpretive authority, but that "[s]ometimes the legislative delegation to an agency on a particular question is implicit." 467 U.S., at 844. Congress, that is, may not have expressly delegated authority or responsibility to implement a particular provision or fill a particular gap. Yet it can still be apparent from the agency's generally conferred authority and other statutory circumstances that Congress would expect the agency to be able to speak with the force of law when it addresses ambiguity in the statute or fills a space in the enacted law, even one about which "Congress did not actually have an intent" as to a particular result. When circumstances implying such an expectation exist, a reviewing court has no business rejecting an agency's exercise of its generally conferred authority to resolve a particular statutory ambiguity simply because the agency's chosen resolution seems unwise, but is obliged to accept the agency's position if Congress has not previously spoken to the point at issue and the agency's interpretation is reasonable, see *id.*, at 842–845; cf. 5 U.S.C. § 706(2) (a reviewing court shall set aside agency action, findings, and conclusions found to be "arbitrary, capricious, an abuse of discretion, or otherwise not in accordance with law").

We have recognized a very good indicator of delegation meriting *Chevron* treatment in express congressional authorizations to engage in the process of rulemaking or adjudication that produces regulations or rulings for which deference is claimed. See, *e.g., EEOC v. Arabian American Oil Co.*, 499 U.S. 244, 257 (1991) (no *Chevron* deference to agency guideline where congressional delegation did not include the power to "promulgate rules or regulations"). It is fair to assume generally that Congress contemplates administrative action with the effect of law when it provides for a relatively formal administrative procedure tending to foster the fairness and deliberation that should underlie a pronouncement of such force. Thus, the overwhelming number of our cases applying *Chevron* deference have reviewed the fruits of notice-and-comment rulemaking or formal adjudication. That said, and as significant as notice-and-comment is in pointing to *Chevron* authority, the want of that procedure here does not decide the case, for we have sometimes found reasons for *Chevron* deference even when no such administrative formality was required and none was afforded, see, *e.g., NationsBank of N.C., N.A. v. Variable Annuity Life Ins. Co.*, 513 U.S. 251, 256–257, 263 (1995). The fact that the tariff classification here was not a product of such formal process does not alone, therefore, bar the application of *Chevron*.

**Take Note**

The Court declared that *Chevron* deference ordinarily is available when an agency uses a "relatively formal administrative procedure tending to foster the fairness and deliberation that should underlie a pronouncement" of agency action with the force of law. The Court specifically noted that formal adjudication and informal rulemaking are usually sufficient to warrant application of *Chevron* deference for ambiguous statutes. Under the Court's approach, is *Chevron* deference available for agency decisions reached through informal adjudication?

There are, nonetheless, ample reasons to deny *Chevron* deference here. The authorization for classification rulings, and Customs's practice in making them, present a case far removed not only from notice-and-comment process, but from any other circumstances reasonably suggesting that Congress ever thought of classification rulings as deserving the deference claimed for them here.

No matter which angle we choose for viewing the Customs ruling letter in this case, it fails to qualify under *Chevron*. On the face of the statute, to begin with, the terms of the congressional delegation give no indication that Congress meant to delegate authority to Customs to issue classification rulings with the force of law. We are not, of course, here making any global statement about Customs's authority, for it is true that the general rulemaking power conferred on Customs, see 19 U.S.C. § 1624, authorizes some regulation with the force of law * * *. It is true as well that Congress had classification rulings in mind when it explicitly authorized, in a parenthetical, the issuance of "regulations establishing procedures for the issuance of binding rulings prior to the entry of the merchandise concerned," 19 U.S.C. § 1502(a).[15] The reference to binding classifications does not, however, bespeak the legislative type of activity that would naturally bind more than the parties to the ruling, once the goods classified are admitted into this country. * * *

It is difficult, in fact, to see in the agency practice itself any indication that Customs ever set out with a lawmaking pretense in mind when it undertook to make classifications like these. Customs does not generally engage in notice-and-comment practice when issuing them, and their treatment by the agency makes it clear that a letter's binding character as a ruling stops short of third parties; Customs has regarded a classification as conclusive only as between itself and the importer to whom it was issued, 19 CFR § 177.9(c) (2000), and even then only until Customs has given advance notice of intended change, §§ 177.9(a), (c). Other importers are in fact warned against assuming any right of detrimental reliance. § 177.9(c).

Indeed, to claim that classifications have legal force is to ignore the reality that 46 different Customs offices issue 10,000 to 15,000 of them each year. Any suggestion that rulings intended to have the force of law are being churned out at a rate of 10,000 a year at an agency's 46 scattered offices is simply self-refuting. Although the circumstances are less startling here, with a Headquarters letter in issue, none of the relevant statutes recognizes this category of rulings as separate or different from others; there is thus no indication that a more potent delegation might have been understood as going to Headquarters even when Headquarters provides developed reasoning, as it did in this instance.

In sum, classification rulings are best treated like "interpretations contained in policy statements, agency manuals, and enforcement guidelines." *Christensen v. Harris County*, 529 U.S. 576, 587 (2000). They are beyond the *Chevron* pale.

To agree with the Court of Appeals that Customs ruling letters do not fall within *Chevron* is not, however, to place them outside the pale of any deference whatever. *Chevron* did nothing to eliminate *Skidmore*'s holding that an agency's interpretation may merit some deference whatever its form, given the "specialized experience and broader investigations and information" available to the agency, 323 U.S., at 139, and given the value of uniformity in its administrative and judicial understandings of what a national law requires, *id.*, at 140.

There is room at least to raise a *Skidmore* claim here, where the regulatory scheme is highly detailed, and Customs can bring the benefit of specialized experience to bear on the subtle questions in this case: whether the daily planner with room for brief daily entries falls under "diaries," when diaries are grouped with "notebooks and address books, bound; memorandum pads, letter pads and similar articles"; and

15 The ruling in question here, however, does not fall within that category.

whether a planner with a ring binding should qualify as "bound," when a binding may be typified by a book, but also may have "reinforcements or fittings of metal, plastics, etc." A classification ruling in this situation may therefore at least seek a respect proportional to its "power to persuade." Such a ruling may surely claim the merit of its writer's thoroughness, logic, and expertness, its fit with prior interpretations, and any other sources of weight.

**Food for Thought**

Is a "*Skidmore* claim," on the Court's own account, really a claim for *deference*? Isn't any argument—including a lawyer's argument on behalf of a party about the meaning of a statute—entitled to respect proportional to its "power to persuade"? If so, what does it really mean to speak of "*Skidmore* deference"?

Underlying the position we take here, like the position expressed by Justice Scalia in dissent, is a choice about the best way to deal with an inescapable feature of the body of congressional legislation authorizing administrative action. That feature is the great variety of ways in which the laws invest the Government's administrative arms with discretion, and with procedures for exercising it, in giving meaning to Acts of Congress. Implementation of a statute may occur in formal adjudication or the choice to defend against judicial challenge; it may occur in a central board or office or in dozens of enforcement agencies dotted across the country; its institutional lawmaking may be confined to the resolution of minute detail or extend to legislative rulemaking on matters intentionally left by Congress to be worked out at the agency level.

Although we all accept the position that the Judiciary should defer to at least some of this multifarious administrative action, we have to decide how to take account of the great range of its variety. If the primary objective is to simplify the judicial process of giving or withholding deference, then the diversity of statutes authorizing discretionary administrative action must be declared irrelevant or minimized. If, on the other hand, it is simply implausible that Congress intended such a broad range of statutory authority to produce only two varieties of administrative action, demanding either *Chevron* deference or none at all, then the breadth of the spectrum of possible agency action must be taken into account. Justice Scalia's first priority over the years has been to limit and simplify. The Court's choice has been to tailor deference to variety. This acceptance of the range of statutory variation has led the Court to recognize more than one variety of judicial deference, just as the Court has recognized a variety of indicators that Congress would expect *Chevron* deference.[18]

---

18 It is, of course, true that the limit of *Chevron* deference is not marked by a hard-edged rule. But *Chevron* itself is a good example showing when *Chevron* deference is warranted, while this is a good case showing when it is not. Judges in other, perhaps harder, cases will make reasoned choices between the two examples, the way courts have always done.

Our respective choices are repeated today. Justice SCALIA would pose the question of deference as an either-or choice. On his view that *Chevron* rendered *Skidmore* anachronistic, when courts owe any deference it is *Chevron* deference that they owe. Whether courts do owe deference in a given case turns, for him, on whether the agency action (if reasonable) is "authoritative." The character of the authoritative derives, in turn, not from breadth of delegation or the agency's procedure in implementing it, but is defined as the "official" position of an agency, and may ultimately be a function of administrative persistence alone.

The Court, on the other hand, said nothing in *Chevron* to eliminate *Skidmore*'s recognition of various justifications for deference depending on statutory circumstances and agency action; *Chevron* was simply a case recognizing that even without express authority to fill a specific statutory gap, circumstances pointing to implicit congressional delegation present a particularly insistent call for deference. * * *

We think, in sum, that Justice SCALIA's efforts to simplify ultimately run afoul of Congress's indications that different statutes present different reasons for considering respect for the exercise of administrative authority or deference to it. Without being at odds with congressional intent much of the time, we believe that judicial responses to administrative action must continue to differentiate between *Chevron* and *Skidmore*, and that continued recognition of *Skidmore* is necessary for just the reasons Justice Jackson gave when that case was decided.

Since the *Skidmore* assessment called for here ought to be made in the first instance by the Court of Appeals for the Federal Circuit or the [Court of International Trade], we go no further than to vacate the judgment and remand the case for further proceedings consistent with this opinion.

JUSTICE SCALIA, dissenting.

Today's opinion makes an avulsive change in judicial review of federal administrative action. Whereas previously a reasonable agency application of an ambiguous statutory provision had to be sustained so long as it represented the agency's authoritative interpretation, henceforth such an application can be set aside unless "it appears that Congress delegated authority to the agency generally to make rules carrying the force of law," as by giving an agency "power to engage in adjudication or notice-and-comment rulemaking, or . . . some other [procedure] indicati[ng] comparable congressional intent," and "the agency interpretation claiming deference was promulgated in the exercise of that authority."[1] What was previously a general presumption of authority in agencies to resolve ambiguity in the statutes they have been authorized to enforce has been changed to a presumption of no such authority, which must be overcome by affirmative legislative intent to the contrary. And whereas

1 It is not entirely clear whether the formulation newly minted by the Court today extends to both formal and informal adjudication, or simply the former.

previously, when agency authority to resolve ambiguity did not exist the court was free to give the statute what it considered the best interpretation, henceforth the court must supposedly give the agency view some indeterminate amount of so-called *Skidmore* deference. We will be sorting out the consequences of the *Mead* doctrine, which has today replaced the *Chevron* doctrine, for years to come. I would adhere to our established jurisprudence, defer to the reasonable interpretation the Customs Service has given to the statute it is charged with enforcing, and reverse the judgment of the Court of Appeals.

Only five years ago, the Court described the *Chevron* doctrine as follows: "We accord deference to agencies under *Chevron* . . . because of a presumption that Congress, when it left ambiguity in a statute meant for implementation by an agency, understood that the ambiguity would be resolved, first and foremost, by the agency, and desired the agency (rather than the courts) to possess whatever degree of discretion the ambiguity allows," *Smiley v. Citibank (South Dakota), N.A.*, 517 U.S. 735, 740–741 (1996). Today the Court collapses this doctrine, announcing instead a presumption that agency discretion does not exist unless the statute, expressly or impliedly, says so. While the Court disclaims any hard-and-fast rule for determining the existence of discretion-conferring intent, it asserts that "a very good indicator [is] express congressional authorizations to engage in the process of rulemaking or adjudication that produces regulations or rulings for which deference is claimed." Only when agencies act through "adjudication[,] notice-and-comment rulemaking, or . . . some other [procedure] indicati[ng] comparable congressional intent [whatever that means]" is *Chevron* deference applicable—because these "relatively formal administrative procedure[s] [designed] to foster . . . fairness and deliberation" bespeak (according to the Court) congressional willingness to have the agency, rather than the courts, resolve statutory ambiguities. Once it is determined that *Chevron* deference is not in order, the uncertainty is not at an end—and indeed is just beginning. Litigants cannot then assume that the statutory question is one for the courts to determine, according to traditional interpretive principles and by their own judicial lights. No, the Court now resurrects, in full force, the pre-*Chevron* doctrine of *Skidmore* deference, whereby "[t]he fair measure of deference to an agency administering its own statute . . . var[ies] with circumstances," including "the degree of the agency's care, its consistency, formality, and relative expertness, and . . . the persuasiveness of the agency's position." The Court has largely replaced *Chevron,* in other words, with that test most beloved by a court unwilling to be held to rules (and most feared by litigants who want to know what to expect): th' ol' "totality of the circumstances" test.

The Court's new doctrine is neither sound in principle nor sustainable in practice. As to principle: The doctrine of *Chevron*—that all *authoritative* agency interpretations of statutes they are charged with administering deserve deference—was rooted in a legal presumption of congressional intent, important to the division of powers between the Second and Third Branches. When, *Chevron* said, Congress leaves an ambiguity in a statute that is to be administered by an executive agency, it is presumed that Congress meant to give the agency discretion, within the limits of reasonable interpretation, as to how the ambiguity is to be resolved. By committing enforcement of the statute to an agency rather than the courts, Congress committed its initial and primary interpretation to that branch as well.

There is some question whether *Chevron* was faithful to the text of the Administrative Procedure Act (APA), which it did not even bother to cite. But it was in accord with the origins of federal-court judicial review. Judicial control of federal executive officers was principally exercised through the prerogative writ of mandamus. See L. Jaffe, Judicial Control of Administrative Action 166, 176–177 (1965). That writ generally would not issue unless the executive officer was acting plainly beyond the scope of his authority. * * * Statutory ambiguities, in other words, were left to reasonable resolution by the Executive.

The basis in principle for today's new doctrine can be described as follows: The background rule is that ambiguity in legislative instructions to agencies is to be resolved not by the agencies but by the judges. Specific congressional intent to depart from this rule must be found—and while there is no single touchstone for such intent it can generally be found when Congress has authorized the agency to act through (what the Court says is) relatively formal procedures such as informal rulemaking and formal (and informal?) adjudication, and when the agency in fact employs such procedures. The Court's background rule is contradicted by the origins of judicial review of administrative action. But in addition, the Court's principal criterion of congressional intent to supplant its background rule seems to me quite implausible. There is no necessary connection between the formality of procedure and the power of the entity administering the procedure to resolve authoritatively questions of law. The most formal of the procedures the Court refers to—formal adjudication—is modeled after the process used in trial courts, which of course are not generally accorded deference on questions of law. The purpose of such a procedure is to produce a closed record for determination and review of the facts—which implies nothing about the power of the agency subjected to the procedure to resolve authoritatively questions of law.

As for informal rulemaking: While formal adjudication procedures are *prescribed* (either by statute or by the Constitution), see 5 U.S.C. §§ 554, 556, informal rulemaking is more typically *authorized* but not required. Agencies with such authority are free to give guidance through rulemaking, but they may proceed to administer their statute case-by-case, "making law" as they implement their program (not necessarily through formal adjudication). See *SEC v. Chenery Corp.*, 332 U.S. 194, 202–203 (1947).

**Make the Connection**

We considered the different forms of agency decision-making, and an agency's discretion to choose a policy-making mode (and the Court's decision *Chenery*), in Chapter 6.

Is it likely—or indeed even plausible—that Congress meant, when such an agency chooses rulemaking, to accord the administrators of that agency, *and their successors*, the flexibility of interpreting the ambiguous statute now one way, and later another; but, when such an agency chooses case-by-case administration, to eliminate all future agency discretion by having that same ambiguity resolved authoritatively (and forever) by the courts? Surely that makes no sense. It is also the case that certain significant categories of rules—those involving grant and benefit programs, for example, are exempt from the requirements of informal rulemaking. See 5 U.S.C. § 553(a)(2). Under the Court's novel theory, when an agency takes advantage of that exemption its rules will be deprived of *Chevron* deference, *i.e.,* authoritative effect. Was this either the plausible intent of the APA rulemaking exemption, or the plausible intent of the Congress that established the grant or benefit program?

As for the practical effects of the new rule: The principal effect will be protracted confusion. As noted above, the one test for *Chevron* deference that the Court enunciates is wonderfully imprecise: whether "Congress delegated authority to the agency generally to make rules carrying the force of law, . . . as by . . . adjudication[,] notice-and-comment rulemaking, or . . . some other [procedure] indicati[ng] comparable congressional intent." But even this description does not do justice to the utter flabbiness of the Court's criterion, since, in order to maintain the fiction that the new test is really just the old one, applied consistently throughout our case law, the Court must make a virtually open-ended exception to its already imprecise guidance: In the present case, it tells us, the absence of notice-and-comment rulemaking (and "[who knows?] [of] some other [procedure] indicati[ng] comparable congressional intent") is not enough to decide the question of *Chevron* deference, "for we have sometimes found reasons for *Chevron* deference even when no such administrative formality was required and none was afforded." The opinion then goes on to consider a grab bag of other factors—including the factor that used to be the sole criterion for *Chevron* deference: whether the interpretation represented the *authoritative* position of the agency. It is hard to know what the lower courts are to make of today's guidance.

Another practical effect of today's opinion will be an artificially induced increase in informal rulemaking. Buy stock in the GPO.

> **FYI**
>
> The "GPO" is the Government Publishing Office, which is responsible for publishing compilations of agency decisions and regulations.

Since informal rulemaking and formal adjudication are the only more-or-less safe harbors from the storm that the Court has unleashed; and since formal adjudication is not an option but must be mandated by statute or constitutional command; informal rulemaking—which the Court was once careful to make voluntary unless required by statute, see *Chenery*—will now become a virtual necessity. As I have described, the Court's safe harbor requires not merely that the agency have been given rulemaking authority, but also that the agency have *employed* rulemaking as the means of resolving the statutory ambiguity. (It is hard to understand why that should be so. Surely the mere *conferral* of rulemaking authority demonstrates—if one accepts the Court's logic—a congressional intent to allow the agency to resolve ambiguities. And given that intent, what difference does it make that the agency chooses instead to use another perfectly permissible means for that purpose?) Moreover, the majority's approach will have a perverse effect on the rules that do emerge, given the principle (which the Court leaves untouched today) that judges must defer to reasonable agency interpretations of their own regulations. See, *e.g., United States v. Cleveland Indians Baseball Co.*, 532 U.S. 200, 2201 (2001). Agencies will now have high incentive to rush out barebones, ambiguous rules construing statutory ambiguities, which they can then in turn further clarify through informal rulings entitled to judicial respect.

Worst of all, the majority's approach will lead to the ossification of large portions of our statutory law. Where *Chevron* applies, statutory ambiguities remain ambiguities subject to the agency's ongoing clarification. They create a space, so to speak, for the exercise of continuing agency discretion. * * * For the indeterminately large number of statutes taken out of *Chevron* by today's decision, however, ambiguity (and hence flexibility) will cease with the first judicial resolution. *Skidmore* deference gives the agency's current position some vague and uncertain amount of respect, but it does not, like *Chevron*, *leave* the matter within the control of the Executive Branch for the future. Once the court has spoken, it becomes *unlawful* for the agency to take a contradictory position; the statute now *says* what the court has prescribed. * * *

**Take Note**

"Ossification" means a tendency toward being molded into a rigid condition. In what way might statutory law become "ossified" under the Court's approach, which makes *Chevron* deference less available for agency decisions than it would have been under Justice Scalia's approach?

One might respond that such ossification would not result if the agency were simply to readopt its interpretation, after a court reviewing it under *Skidmore* had rejected it, by repromulgating it through one of the *Chevron*-eligible procedural formats approved by the Court today. Approving this procedure would be a landmark abdication of judicial power. It is worlds apart from *Chevron* proper, where the court does not *purport* to give the statute a judicial interpretation—except in identifying the scope of the statutory ambiguity, as to which the court's judgment is final and irreversible. (Under *Chevron* proper, when the agency's authoritative interpretation comes within the scope of that ambiguity—and the court therefore approves it—the agency will not be "overruling" the court's decision when it later decides that a different interpretation (still within the scope of the ambiguity) is preferable.) By contrast, under this view, the reviewing court will not be holding the agency's authoritative interpretation within the scope of the ambiguity; but will be holding that the agency has not used the "delegation-conferring" procedures, and that the court must therefore *interpret the statute on its own*—but subject to reversal if and when the agency uses the proper procedures.

I know of no case, in the entire history of the federal courts, in which we have allowed a judicial interpretation of a statute to be set aside by an agency—or have allowed a lower court to render an interpretation of a statute subject to correction by an agency. * * * There is, in short, no way to avoid the ossification of federal law that today's opinion sets in motion. What a court says is the law after according *Skidmore* deference will be the law forever, beyond the power of the agency to change even through rulemaking.

And finally, the majority's approach compounds the confusion it creates by breathing new life into the anachronism of *Skidmore,* which sets forth a sliding scale of deference owed an agency's interpretation of a statute that is dependent "upon the thoroughness evident in [the agency's] consideration, the validity of its reasoning, its consistency with earlier and later pronouncements, and all those factors which give it power to persuade, if lacking power to control" * * *. Justice Jackson's eloquence notwithstanding, the rule of *Skidmore* deference is an empty truism and a trifling statement of the obvious: A judge should take into account the well-considered views of expert observers.

It was possible to live with the indeterminacy of *Skidmore* deference in earlier times. But in an era when federal statutory law administered by federal agencies is pervasive, and when the ambiguities (intended or unintended) that those statutes contain are innumerable, totality-of-the-circumstances *Skidmore* deference is a recipe for uncertainty, unpredictability, and endless litigation. To condemn a vast body of agency action to that regime (all except rulemaking, formal (and informal?) adjudication, and whatever else might now and then be included within today's intentionally vague formulation of affirmative congressional intent to "delegate") is irresponsible.

To decide the present case, I would adhere to the original formulation of *Chevron.* "The power of an administrative agency to administer a congressionally created . . . program necessarily requires the formulation of policy and the making of rules to fill any gap left, implicitly or explicitly, by Congress," 467 U.S., at 843. We accordingly presume—and our precedents have made clear to Congress that we presume—that, absent some clear textual indication to the contrary, "Congress, when it left ambiguity in a statute meant for implementation by an agency, understood that the ambiguity would be resolved, first and foremost, by the agency, and desired the agency (rather than the courts) to possess whatever degree of discretion the ambiguity allows," *Smiley,* 517 U.S., at 740–741. *Chevron* sets forth an across-the-board presumption, which operates as a background rule of law against which Congress legislates: Ambiguity means Congress intended agency discretion. Any resolution of the ambiguity by the administering agency that is authoritative—that represents the official position of the agency—must be accepted by the courts if it is reasonable.

There is no doubt that the Customs Service's interpretation represents the authoritative view of the agency. Although the actual ruling letter was signed by only the Director of the Commercial Rulings Branch of Customs Headquarters' Office of Regulations and Rulings, the Solicitor General of the United States has filed a brief, cosigned by the General Counsel of the Department of the Treasury, that represents the position set forth in the ruling letter to be the official position of the Customs Service. No one contends that it is merely a "*post hoc* rationalizatio[n]" or an "agency litigating positio[n] wholly unsupported by regulations, rulings, or administrative practice," *Bowen v. Georgetown Univ. Hospital*, 488 U.S. 204, 212 (1988).[6]

There is also no doubt that the Customs Service's interpretation is a reasonable one, whether or not judges would consider it the best. I will not belabor this point, since the Court evidently agrees: An interpretation that was unreasonable would not merit the remand that the Court decrees for consideration of *Skidmore* deference.

For the reasons stated, I respectfully dissent from the Court's judgment. * * * I dissent even more vigorously from the reasoning that produces the Court's judgment, and that makes today's decision one of the most significant opinions ever rendered by the Court dealing with the judicial review of administrative action. Its consequences will be enormous, and almost uniformly bad.

---

## Points for Discussion

### *a.* **Chevron** ***and Default Rules for Determining Congressional Intent***

In *Chevron*, the Court stated:

"If Congress has explicitly left a gap for the agency to fill, there is an express delegation of authority to the agency to elucidate a specific provision of the statute by regulation.

---

6 The Court's parting shot, that "there would have to be something wrong with a standard that accorded the status of substantive law to every one of 10,000 'official' customs classifications rulings turned out each year from over 46 offices placed around the country at the Nation's entryways," misses the mark. I do not disagree. The "authoritativeness" of an agency interpretation does not turn upon whether it has been enunciated by someone who is actually employed by the agency. It must represent the judgment of central agency management, approved at the highest levels. I would find that condition to have been satisfied when, a ruling having been attacked in court, the general counsel of the agency has determined that it should be defended. If one thinks that that does not impart sufficient authoritativeness, then surely the line has been crossed when, as here, the General Counsel of the agency and the Solicitor General of the United States have assured this Court that the position represents the agency's authoritative view. * * * The *authoritativeness* of the agency ruling may not be a bright-line standard—but it is infinitely brighter than the line the Court asks us to draw today * * *. And, most important of all, it is a line that focuses attention on the right question: not whether Congress "affirmatively intended" to delegate interpretive authority (if it entrusted administration of the statute to an agency, it did, because that is how our system works); but whether it is truly the agency's considered view, or just the opinions of some underlings, that are at issue.

> Such legislative regulations are given controlling weight unless they are arbitrary, capricious, or manifestly contrary to the statute. Sometimes the legislative delegation to an agency on a particular question is implicit rather than explicit. In such a case, a court may not substitute its own construction of a statutory provision for a reasonable interpretation made by the administrator of an agency."

In other words, the Court in *Chevron* announced a default rule for determining whether Congress wanted agency decision-makers to have authority to resolve statutory ambiguities

Did the Court in *Mead* change the default rule? According to the Court in *Mead*, is the mere existence of statutory ambiguity sufficient to assume that Congress delegated to the agency power to resolve statutory ambiguity and to fill in the gaps in the statutory regime? If not, what must be true for a court to conclude that an agency interpretation of an ambiguous statute is entitled to deference?

### *b.* Mead *and* Chevron *Step Zero*

The Court's approach in *Mead* is another example of what some scholars have called *Chevron* "step zero." See Cass R. Sunstein, Chevron *Step Zero*, 92 VA. L .REV. 187 (2006). According to the Court, whether *Chevron* deference is available for an agency interpretation of a statute is not solely a function of statutory ambiguity; instead, a reviewing court must first conclude that the agency decision is the type for which Congress would have wanted deference to be available. In other words, before a court can apply *Chevron* deference, it must first decide whether "Congress delegated authority to the agency generally to make rules carrying the force of law, and that the agency interpretation claiming deference was promulgated in the exercise of that authority." Are you persuaded that it makes sense for courts to give *Chevron* deference only to a subset of agency interpretations? Or do you agree with Justice Scalia that it would be better to make the availability of *Chevron* deference turn solely on statutory ambiguity and whether the agency's interpretation is authoritative?

### *c. The Continuing Vitality of* Skidmore

According to the Court in *Mead*, agency interpretations that are not entitled to *Chevron* deference—because Congress did not delegate "authority to the agency generally to make rules carrying the force of law" or because the "agency interpretation claiming deference was [not] promulgated in the exercise of that authority"—might still be entitled to *Skidmore* deference. Recall that the Court held in *Skidmore* that an agency interpretation of a statute that is "not controlling upon the courts by reason of their authority" nevertheless "constitute[s] a body of experience and informed judgment to which courts and litigants may properly resort for guidance." According to the Court, the "weight of such a judgment in a particular case will depend upon the thoroughness evident in its consideration, the validity of its reasoning, its consistency with earlier and later pronouncements, and all those factors which give it power to persuade, if lacking power to control."

If nothing else, this form of "deference" is considerably less deferential than *Chevron* deference, which requires a reviewing a court to accept any reasonable agency interpretation of an ambiguous statute that the agency is responsible for administering. How does a court know which agency interpretations are entitled to deference under *Skidmore*? Then again, how does a court know that an agency interpretation is "reasonable" under the *Chevron* test?

#### *d. Deference to Agency Interpretations of Their Regulations*

Justice Scalia noted in his dissent that courts usually defer to agency interpretations of their own regulations. In *Auer v. Robbins*, 519 U.S. 452 (1997), the Court held that a reviewing court should accept an agency's interpretation of its own rules unless the interpretation is "plainly erroneous or inconsistent with the regulation." See also *Bowles v. Seminole Rock & Sand Co.*, 325 U.S. 410 (1945). Agencies often offer interpretations of their rules in informal guidance that has not gone through the notice and comment procedure. In light of the Court's conclusion in *Mead*, does it make sense to defer to an agency's interpretation of its previous rule if the new interpretation is not made using a form of decision-making that carries the force of law?

---

## C. Putting Together (All of) the Pieces

We have now seen how courts approach the task of statutory interpretation, and how an agency's interpretation of the statute that it is responsible for administering can affect the courts' approach. As you read the first part of the case that follows, think about how you would have approached the question with which the Court was presented.

---

## *King v. Burwell*

576 U.S. 473 (2015)

CHIEF JUSTICE ROBERTS delivered the opinion of the Court.

The Patient Protection and Affordable Care Act adopts a series of interlocking reforms designed to expand coverage in the individual health insurance market. First, the Act bars insurers from taking a person's health into account when deciding whether to sell health insurance or how much to charge. Second, the Act generally requires each person to maintain insurance coverage or make a payment to the Internal Revenue Service. And third, the Act gives tax credits to certain people to make insurance more affordable.

In addition to those reforms, the Act requires the creation of an "Exchange" in each State—basically, a marketplace that allows people to compare and purchase insurance plans. The Act gives each State the opportunity to establish its own Exchange, but provides that the Federal Government will establish the Exchange if the State does not.

This case is about whether the Act's interlocking reforms apply equally in each State no matter who establishes the State's Exchange. Specifically, the question presented is whether the Act's tax credits are available in States that have a Federal Exchange.

[The Act's] three reforms are closely intertwined. * * * Congress found that the guaranteed issue and community rating requirements would not work without the coverage requirement.* 42 U.S.C. § 18091(2)(I). And the coverage requirement would not work without the tax credits. The reason is that, without the tax credits, the cost of buying insurance would exceed eight percent of income for a large number of individuals, which would exempt them from the coverage requirement. * * *

In addition to those [reforms], the Act requires the creation of an "Exchange" in each State where people can shop for insurance, usually online. 42 U.S.C. § 18031(b)(1). An Exchange may be created in one of two ways. First, the Act provides that "[e]ach State shall . . . establish an American Health Benefit Exchange . . . for the State." *Ibid.* Second, if a State nonetheless chooses not to establish its own Exchange, the Act provides that the Secretary of Health and Human Services "shall . . . establish and operate such Exchange within the State." § 18041(c)(1).

The issue in this case is whether the Act's tax credits are available in States that have a Federal Exchange rather than a State Exchange. The Act initially provides that tax credits "shall be allowed" for any "applicable taxpayer." 26 U.S.C. § 36B(a). The Act then provides that the amount of the tax credit depends in part on whether the taxpayer has enrolled in an insurance plan through "an Exchange *established by the State* under section 1311 of the Patient Protection and Affordable Care Act [hereinafter 42 U.S.C. § 18031]." 26 U.S.C. §§ 36B(b)–(c) (emphasis added).

The IRS addressed the availability of tax credits by promulgating a rule that made them available on both State and Federal Exchanges. 77 Fed. Reg. 30378 (2012). * * * At this point, 16 States and the District of Columbia have established their own Exchanges; the other 34 States have elected to have HHS do so.

* The guaranteed issue and community rating requirements prohibit insurance companies from discriminating against persons with pre-existing conditions or against persons who have insurance and then get sick. Because these provisions create an incentive for healthy people to wait to get insurance until they get sick, they create the risk that the pool of insured persons will be disproportionately unhealthy, which would lead to higher insurance rates for everyone. To address this problem, Congress required virtually all persons to obtain health insurance. —*Ed.*

Petitioners are four individuals who live in Virginia, which has a Federal Exchange. They do not wish to purchase health insurance. In their view, Virginia's Exchange does not qualify as "an Exchange established by the State under [42 U.S.C. § 18031]," so they should not receive any tax credits. That would make the cost of buying insurance more than eight percent of their income, which would exempt them from the Act's coverage requirement. 26 U.S.C. § 5000A(e)(1).

Under the IRS Rule, however, Virginia's Exchange *would* qualify as "an Exchange established by the State under [42 U.S.C. § 18031]," so petitioners would receive tax credits. That would make the cost of buying insurance *less* than eight percent of petitioners' income, which would subject them to the Act's coverage requirement. The IRS Rule therefore requires petitioners to either buy health insurance they do not want, or make a payment to the IRS.

**Food for Thought**

The plaintiffs in this case sought a declaration that they were not entitled to valuable tax credits under the Affordable Care Act to subsidize the purchase of health insurance. Why would they have taken on the expense of litigating a suit that, if successful, would deprive them of a valuable government benefit?

When analyzing an agency's interpretation of a statute, we often apply the two-step framework announced in *Chevron, USA v. Natural Resources Defense Council, Inc.*, 467 U.S. 837 (1984). Under that framework, we ask whether the statute is ambiguous and, if so, whether the agency's interpretation is reasonable. This approach "is premised on the theory that a statute's ambiguity constitutes an implicit delegation from Congress to the agency to fill in the statutory gaps." *FDA v. Brown & Williamson Tobacco Corp.*, 529 U.S. 120, 159 (2000). "In extraordinary cases, however, there may be reason to hesitate before concluding that Congress has intended such an implicit delegation." *Ibid.*

This is one of those cases. The tax credits are among the Act's key reforms, involving billions of dollars in spending each year and affecting the price of health insurance for millions of people. Whether those credits are available on Federal Exchanges is thus a question of deep "economic and political significance" that is central to this statutory scheme; had Congress wished to assign that question to an agency, it surely would have done so expressly. *Utility Air Regulatory Group v. EPA*, 134 S.Ct. 2427, 2444 (2014). It is especially unlikely that Congress would have delegated this decision to the *IRS*, which has no expertise in crafting health insurance policy of this

**Take Note**

The Court declined to apply the *Chevron* framework to the IRS's rule construing the statute's provisions about eligibility for tax credits. Why didn't the Court apply *Chevron*? If it had, would it likely have resolved the case at step one or step two? If step two, do you think that the agency's view of the statute was reasonable?

sort. See *Gonzales v. Oregon*, 546 U.S. 243, 266–267 (2006). This is not a case for the IRS.

It is instead our task to determine the correct reading of Section 36B. If the statutory language is plain, we must enforce it according to its terms. *Hardt v. Reliance Standard Life Ins. Co.*, 560 U.S. 242, 251 (2010). But oftentimes the "meaning—or ambiguity—of certain words or phrases may only become evident when placed in context." *Brown & Williamson*, 529 U.S., at 132. * * *

We begin with the text of Section 36B. Section 36B allows an individual to receive tax credits only if the individual enrolls in an insurance plan through "an Exchange established by the State under [42 U.S.C. § 18031]." In other words, three things must be true: First, the individual must enroll in an insurance plan through "an Exchange." Second, that Exchange must be "established by the State." And third, that Exchange must be established "under [42 U.S.C. § 18031]." We address each requirement in turn.

[First,] Section 18031 provides that "[e]ach State shall . . . establish an American Health Benefit Exchange . . . for the State." § 18031(b)(1). Although phrased as a requirement, the Act gives the States "flexibility" by allowing them to "elect" whether they want to establish an Exchange. § 18041(b). If the State chooses not to do so, Section 18041 provides that the Secretary "shall . . . establish and operate *such Exchange* within the State." § 18041(c)(1) (emphasis added).

By using the phrase "such Exchange," Section 18041 instructs the Secretary to establish and operate the *same* Exchange that the State was directed to establish under Section 18031. See Black's Law Dictionary 1661 (10th ed. 2014) (defining "such" as "That or those; having just been mentioned"). * * *

Second, we must determine whether a Federal Exchange is "established by the State" for purposes of Section 36B. At the outset, it might seem that a Federal Exchange cannot fulfill this requirement. After all, the Act defines "State" to mean "each of the 50 States and the District of Columbia"—a definition that does not include the Federal Government. 42 U.S.C. § 18024(d). But when read in context, "with a view to [its] place in the overall statutory scheme," the meaning of the phrase "established by the State" is not so clear. *Brown & Williamson*, 529 U.S., at 133.

After telling each State to establish an Exchange, Section 18031 provides that all Exchanges "shall make available qualified health plans to qualified individuals." 42 U.S.C. § 18031(d)(2)(A). Section 18032 then defines the term "qualified individual" in part as an individual who "resides in the State that established the Exchange." § 18032(f)(1)(A). And that's

**Take Note**

As you read the Court's opinion, consider which maxims and canons of construction the Court relied upon. Can you think of others that would have been relevant, as well?

a problem: If we give the phrase "the State that established the Exchange" its most natural meaning, there would be *no* "qualified individuals" on Federal Exchanges. But the Act clearly contemplates that there will be qualified individuals on *every* Exchange. * * * This problem arises repeatedly throughout the Act. See, *e.g.*, § 18031(b)(2) (allowing a State to create "one Exchange . . . for providing . . . services to both qualified individuals and qualified small employers," rather than creating separate Exchanges for those two groups).

These provisions suggest that the Act may not always use the phrase "established by the State" in its most natural sense. Thus, the meaning of that phrase may not be as clear as it appears when read out of context.

Third, [the] Act defines the term "Exchange" to mean "an American Health Benefit Exchange established under section 18031." § 300gg–91(d)(21). If we import that definition into Section 18041, the Act tells the Secretary to "establish and operate such 'American Health Benefit Exchange established under section 18031.' " That suggests that Section 18041 authorizes the Secretary to establish an Exchange under Section 18031, not (or not only) under Section 18041. Otherwise, the Federal Exchange, by definition, would not be an "Exchange" at all.

This interpretation of "under [42 U.S.C. § 18031]" fits best with the statutory context. * * * If Federal Exchanges were not established under Section 18031, * * * literally none of the Act's requirements would apply to them. Finally, the Act repeatedly uses the phrase "established under [42 U.S.C. § 18031]" in situations where it would make no sense to distinguish between State and Federal Exchanges. See, *e.g.*, 26 U.S.C. § 125(f)(3)(A) (2012 ed., Supp. I) ("The term 'qualified benefit' shall not include any qualified health plan . . . offered through an Exchange established under [42 U.S.C. § 18031]"); 26 U.S.C. § 6055(b)(1)(B)(iii)(I) (2012 ed.) (requiring insurers to report whether each insurance plan they provided "is a qualified health plan offered through an Exchange established under [42 U.S.C. § 18031]"). A Federal Exchange may therefore be considered one established "under [42 U.S.C. § 18031]."

The upshot of all this is that the phrase "an Exchange established by the State under [42 U.S.C. § 18031]" is properly viewed as ambiguous. * * * The conclusion that Section 36B is ambiguous is further supported by several provisions that assume tax credits will be available on both State and Federal Exchanges. For example, the Act requires all Exchanges to create outreach programs that must "distribute fair and impartial information concerning . . . the availability of premium tax credits under section 36B." § 18031(i)(3)(B). * * * And the Act requires all Exchanges to report to the Treasury Secretary information about each health plan they sell * * *.

Petitioners and the dissent respond that the words "established by the State" would be unnecessary if Congress meant to extend tax credits to both State and Federal Exchanges. But "our preference for avoiding surplusage constructions is not absolute." *Lamie v. United States Trustee*, 540 U.S. 526, 536 (2004). And specifically with respect to this Act, rigorous application of the canon does not seem a particularly useful guide to a fair construction of the statute.

The Affordable Care Act contains more than a few examples of inartful drafting. (To cite just one, the Act creates three separate Section 1563s. See 124 Stat. 270, 911, 912.) Several features of the Act's passage contributed to that unfortunate reality. Congress wrote key parts of the Act behind closed doors, rather than through "the traditional legislative process." Cannan, A Legislative History of the Affordable Care Act: How Legislative Procedure Shapes Legislative History, 105 L. Lib. J. 131, 163 (2013). And Congress passed much of the Act using a complicated budgetary procedure known as "reconciliation," which limited opportunities for debate and amendment, and bypassed the Senate's normal 60-vote filibuster requirement. *Id.,* at 159–167. As a result, the Act does not reflect the type of care and deliberation that one might expect of such significant legislation. Cf. Frankfurter, Some Reflections on the Reading of Statutes, 47 Colum. L. Rev. 527, 545 (1947) (describing a cartoon "in which a senator tells his colleagues 'I admit this new bill is too complicated to understand. We'll just have to pass it to find out what it means.' ").

Anyway, we "must do our best, bearing in mind the fundamental canon of statutory construction that the words of a statute must be read in their context and with a view to their place in the overall statutory scheme." *Utility Air Regulatory Group,* 134 S.Ct., at 2441. After reading Section 36B along with other related provisions in the Act, we cannot conclude that the phrase "an Exchange established by the State under [Section 18031]" is unambiguous.

**Take Note**

What role did the Court's conclusion that the statutory provision at issue was ambiguous play in its analysis of the statute's meaning? Did the Court mean that, based on its text alone, the provision was ambiguous? If so, what other tools of statutory interpretation were available to the Court to determine the provision's meaning?

Given that the text is ambiguous, we must turn to the broader structure of the Act to determine the meaning of Section 36B. "A provision that may seem ambiguous in isolation is often clarified by the remainder of the statutory scheme . . . because only one of the permissible meanings produces a substantive effect that is compatible with the rest of the law." *United Sav. Assn. of Tex. v. Timbers of Inwood Forest Associates, Ltd.,* 484 U.S. 365, 371 (1988). Here, the statutory scheme compels us to reject petitioners' interpretation because it would destabilize the individual insurance market in any State with a Federal Exchange, and likely create the very "death spirals" that Congress designed the Act to avoid. See *New York State Dept. of Social Servs. v. Dublino,* 413 U.S. 405, 419–420 (1973) ("We cannot interpret federal statutes to negate their own stated purposes.").[3]

3 The dissent notes that several other provisions in the Act use the phrase "established by the

It is implausible that Congress meant the Act to operate in this manner. See *National Federation of Independent Business v. Sebelius*, 567 U.S. 519, 702 (2012) (SCALIA, KENNEDY, THOMAS, and ALITO, JJ., dissenting) ("Without the federal subsidies . . . the exchanges would not operate as Congress intended and may not operate at all."). Congress made the guaranteed issue and community rating requirements applicable in every State in the Nation. But those requirements only work when combined with the coverage requirement and the tax credits. So it stands to reason that Congress meant for those provisions to apply in every State as well.

**Take Note**

On which touchstone of interpretation did the Court focus in these paragraphs?

Section 18041 refutes the argument that Congress believed it was offering the States a deal they would not refuse. That section provides that, if a State elects not to establish an Exchange, the Secretary "shall . . . establish and operate such Exchange within the State." 42 U.S.C. § 18041(c)(1)(A). The whole point of that provision is to create a federal fallback in case a State chooses not to establish its own Exchange. Contrary to petitioners' argument, Congress did not believe it was offering States a deal they would not refuse—it expressly addressed what would happen if a State *did* refuse the deal.

Finally, the structure of Section 36B itself suggests that tax credits are not limited to State Exchanges. Section 36B(a) initially provides that tax credits "shall be allowed" for any "applicable taxpayer." Section 36B(c)(1) then defines an "applicable taxpayer" as someone who (among other things) has a household income between 100 percent and 400 percent of the federal poverty line. Together, these two provisions appear to make anyone in the specified income range eligible to receive a tax credit.

We have held that Congress "does not alter the fundamental details of a regulatory scheme in vague terms or ancillary provisions." *Whitman v. American Trucking Assns., Inc.*, 531 U.S. 457, 468 (2001). But in petitioners' view, Congress made the viability of the entire Affordable Care Act turn on the ultimate ancillary provision: a sub-sub-sub section of the Tax Code. We doubt that is what Congress meant to do. Had Congress meant to limit tax credits to State Exchanges, it likely would have done so in the definition of "applicable taxpayer" or in some other prominent manner. It would not have used such a winding path of connect-the-dots provisions about the amount of the credit.

---

State," and argues that our holding applies to each of those provisions. But "the presumption of consistent usage readily yields to context," and a statutory term may mean different things in different places. *Utility Air Regulatory Group*, 134 at 2441–2442 (2014). That is particularly true when, as here, "the Act is far from a *chef d'oeuvre* of legislative draftsmanship." *Ibid.* Because the other provisions cited by the dissent are not at issue here, we do not address them.

Petitioners' arguments about the plain meaning of Section 36B are strong. But while the meaning of the phrase "an Exchange established by the State under [42 U.S.C. § 18031]" may seem plain "when viewed in isolation," such a reading turns out to be "untenable in light of [the statute] as a whole." *Department of Revenue of Ore. v. ACF Industries, Inc.*, 510 U.S. 332, 343 (1994). In this instance, the context and structure of the Act compel us to depart from what would otherwise be the most natural reading of the pertinent statutory phrase.

In a democracy, the power to make the law rests with those chosen by the people. Our role is more confined—"to say what the law is." *Marbury v. Madison*, 1 Cranch 137, 177 (1803). That is easier in some cases than in others. But in every case we must respect the role of the Legislature, and take care not to undo what it has done. A fair reading of legislation demands a fair understanding of the legislative plan.

Congress passed the Affordable Care Act to improve health insurance markets, not to destroy them. If at all possible, we must interpret the Act in a way that is consistent with the former, and avoids the latter. Section 36B can fairly be read consistent with what we see as Congress's plan, and that is the reading we adopt.

JUSTICE SCALIA, with whom JUSTICE THOMAS and JUSTICE ALITO join, dissenting.

Words no longer have meaning if an Exchange that is *not* established by a State is "established by the State." It is hard to come up with a clearer way to limit tax credits to state Exchanges than to use the words "established by the State." And it is hard to come up with a reason to include the words "by the State" other than the purpose of limiting credits to state Exchanges. "[T]he plain, obvious, and rational meaning of a statute is always to be preferred to any curious, narrow, hidden sense that nothing but the exigency of a hard case and the ingenuity and study of an acute and powerful intellect would discover." *Lynch v. Alworth-Stephens Co.*, 267 U.S. 364, 370 (1925) (internal quotation marks omitted). Under all the usual rules of interpretation, in short, the Government should lose this case. But normal rules of interpretation seem always to yield to the overriding principle of the present Court: The Affordable Care Act must be saved.

I wholeheartedly agree with the Court that sound interpretation requires paying attention to the whole law, not homing in on isolated words or even isolated sections. Context always matters. Let us not forget, however, *why* context matters: It is a tool for understanding the terms of the law, not an excuse for rewriting them.

Reading the rest of the Act also confirms that, as relevant here, there are *only* two ways to set up an Exchange in a State: establishment by a State and establishment by the Secretary. §§ 18031(b), 18041(c). So saying that an Exchange established by the Federal Government is "established by the State" goes beyond giving words bizarre meanings; it leaves the limiting phrase "by the State" with no operative effect at all. That is a stark violation of the elementary principle that requires an interpreter "to

**Take Note**

Justice Scalia suggested here that there is a difference between the rule against redundancy and the rule against surplusage. Do you understand these to be two different Whole Act Rule corollaries, or simply two different ways to express the same idea?

give effect, if possible, to every clause and word of a statute." *Montclair v. Ramsdell*, 107 U.S. 147, 152 (1883). In weighing this argument, it is well to remember the difference between giving a term a meaning that duplicates another part of the law, and giving a term no meaning at all. Lawmakers sometimes repeat themselves—whether out of a desire to add emphasis, a sense of belt-and-suspenders caution, or a lawyerly penchant for doublets (aid and abet, cease and desist, null and void). Lawmakers do not, however, tend to use terms that "have no operation at all." *Marbury v. Madison*, 1 Cranch 137, 174 (1803). So while the rule against treating a term as a redundancy is far from categorical, the rule against treating it as a nullity is as close to absolute as interpretive principles get. The Court's reading does not merely give "by the State" a duplicative effect; it causes the phrase to have no effect whatever.

Making matters worse, the reader of the whole Act will come across a number of provisions beyond § 36B that refer to the establishment of Exchanges by States. Adopting the Court's interpretation means nullifying the term "by the State" not just once, but again and again throughout the Act. * * *

Equating establishment "by the State" with establishment by the Federal Government makes nonsense of other parts of the Act. The Act requires States to ensure (on pain of losing Medicaid funding) that any "Exchange established by the State" uses a "secure electronic interface" to determine an individual's eligibility for various benefits (including tax credits). 42 U.S.C. § 1396w–3(b)(1)(D). How could a State control the type of electronic interface used by a federal Exchange? The Act allows a State to control contracting decisions made by "an Exchange established by the State." § 18031(f)(3). Why would a State get to control the contracting decisions of a federal Exchange? The Act also provides "Assistance to States to establish American Health Benefit Exchanges" and directs the Secretary to renew this funding "if the State . . . is making progress . . . toward . . . establishing an Exchange." § 18031(a). Does a State that refuses to set up an Exchange still receive this funding, on the premise that Exchanges established by the Federal Government are really established by States? It is presumably in order to avoid these questions that the Court concludes that federal Exchanges count as state Exchanges only "for purposes of the tax credits." (Contrivance, thy name is an opinion on the Affordable Care Act!)

It is probably piling on to add that the Congress that wrote the Affordable Care Act knew how to equate two different types of Exchanges when it wanted to do so. The Act includes a clause providing that "[a] *territory* that . . . establishes . . . an Exchange . . . shall be treated as a State" for certain purposes. § 18043(a) (emphasis added). Tellingly, it does not include a comparable clause providing that the *Secretary* shall be treated as a State for purposes of § 36B when *she* establishes an Exchange.

The Court persists that these provisions "would make little sense" if no tax credits were available on federal Exchanges. Even if that observation were true, it would show only oddity, not ambiguity. Laws often include unusual or mismatched provisions. The Affordable Care Act spans 900 pages; it would be amazing if its provisions all lined up perfectly with each other. This Court "does not revise legislation . . . just because the text as written creates an apparent anomaly." *Michigan v. Bay Mills Indian Community*, 134 S.Ct. 2024, 2033 (2014). At any rate, the provisions cited by the Court are not particularly unusual. Each requires an Exchange to perform a standardized series of tasks, some aspects of which relate in some way to tax credits. It is entirely natural for slight mismatches to occur when, as here, lawmakers draft "a single statutory provision" to cover "different kinds" of situations. *Robers v. United States*, 134 S.Ct. 1854, 1858 (2014). * * *

Least convincing of all, however, is the Court's attempt to uncover support for its interpretation in "the structure of Section 36B itself." The Court finds it strange that Congress limited the tax credit to state Exchanges in the formula for calculating the *amount* of the credit, rather than in the provision defining the range of taxpayers *eligible* for the credit. Had the Court bothered to look at the rest of the Tax Code, it would have seen that the structure it finds strange is in fact quite common. Consider, for example, the many provisions that initially make taxpayers of all incomes eligible for a tax credit, only to provide later that the amount of the credit is zero if the taxpayer's income exceeds a specified threshold. See, *e.g.*, 26 U.S.C. § 24 (child tax credit); § 32 (earned-income tax credit); § 36 (first-time-homebuyer tax credit). * * *

For what it is worth, lawmakers usually draft tax-credit provisions the way they do—*i.e.*, the way they drafted § 36B—because the mechanics of the credit require it. Many Americans move to new States in the middle of the year. Mentioning state Exchanges in the definition of "coverage month"—rather than (as the Court proposes) in the provisions concerning taxpayers' eligibility for the credit—accounts for taxpayers who live in a State with a state Exchange for a part of the year, but a State with a federal Exchange for the rest of the year. * * *

For its next defense of the indefensible, the Court turns to the Affordable Care Act's design and purposes. * * * This reasoning suffers from no shortage of flaws. To begin with, "even the most formidable argument concerning the statute's purposes could not overcome the clarity [of] the statute's text." *Kloeckner v. Solis*, 133 S.Ct. 596, 607, n. 4, (2012). Statutory design and purpose matter only to the extent they help clarify an otherwise ambiguous provision. Could anyone maintain with a straight face that § 36B is unclear? To mention just the highlights, the Court's interpretation clashes with a statutory definition, renders words inoperative in at least seven separate provisions of the Act, overlooks the contrast between provisions that say "Exchange" and those that say "Exchange established by the State," gives the same phrase one meaning for purposes of tax credits but an entirely different meaning for other purposes, and (let us not forget) contradicts the ordinary meaning of the words Congress used. On the other side of the ledger, the Court has come up with nothing more than a general provision that turns out to be controlled by a specific one, a handful of clauses that are consistent with either understanding of establishment by the State, and a resemblance between the tax-credit provision and the rest of the Tax Code. If that is all it takes to make something ambiguous, everything is ambiguous.

Perhaps sensing the dismal failure of its efforts to show that "established by the State" means "established by the State or the Federal Government," the Court tries to palm off the pertinent statutory phrase as "inartful drafting." This Court, however, has no free-floating power "to rescue Congress from its drafting errors." *Lamie v. United States Trustee*, 540 U.S. 526, 542 (2004). Only when it is patently obvious to a reasonable reader that a drafting mistake has occurred may a court correct the mistake. The occurrence of a misprint may be apparent from the face of the law, as it is where the Affordable Care Act "creates three separate Section 1563s." But the Court does not pretend that there is any such indication of a drafting error on the face of § 36B. The occurrence of a misprint may also be apparent because a provision decrees an absurd result—a consequence "so monstrous, that all mankind would, without hesitation, unite in rejecting the application." *Sturges v. Crowninshield*, 4 Wheat. 122, 203 (1819). But § 36B does not come remotely close to satisfying that demanding standard. It is entirely plausible that tax credits were restricted to state Exchanges deliberately—for example, in order to encourage States to establish their own Exchanges. We therefore have no authority to dismiss the terms of the law as a drafting fumble.

**Take Note**

Which doctrines for determining textual meaning did Justice Scalia refer to here? Do you agree that those doctrines did not warrant a departure from the "plain" meaning of the text in this case?

Let us not forget that the term "Exchange established by the State" appears twice in § 36B and five more times in other parts of the Act that mention tax credits. What are the odds, do you think, that the same slip of the pen occurred in seven separate places? No provision of the Act—none at all—contradicts the limitation of tax credits to state Exchanges. And as I have already explained, uses of the term "Exchange established by the State" beyond the context of tax credits look anything but accidental. If there was a mistake here, context suggests it was a substantive mistake in designing this part of the law, not a technical mistake in transcribing it.

The Court's decision reflects the philosophy that judges should endure whatever interpretive distortions it takes in order to correct a supposed flaw in the statutory machinery. That philosophy ignores the American people's decision to give *Congress* "[a]ll legislative Powers" enumerated in the Constitution. Art. I, § 1. They made Congress, not this Court, responsible for both making laws and mending them. This Court holds only the judicial power—the power to pronounce the law as Congress has enacted it. We lack the prerogative to repair laws that do not work out in practice, just as the people lack the ability to throw us out of office if they dislike the solutions we concoct. We must always remember, therefore, that "[o]ur task is to apply the text, not to improve upon it." *Pavelic & LeFlore v. Marvel Entertainment Group, Div. of Cadence Industries Corp.*, 493 U.S. 120, 126 (1989).

Trying to make its judge-empowering approach seem respectful of congressional authority, the Court asserts that its decision merely ensures that the Affordable Care Act operates the way Congress "meant [it] to operate." First of all, what makes the Court so sure that Congress "meant" tax credits to be available everywhere? Our only evidence of what Congress meant comes from the terms of the law, and those terms show beyond all question that tax credits are available only on state Exchanges. More importantly, the Court forgets that ours is a government of laws and not of men. That means we are governed by the terms of our laws, not by the unenacted will of our lawmakers. * * *

Even less defensible, if possible, is the Court's claim that its interpretive approach is justified because this Act "does not reflect the type of care and deliberation that one might expect of such significant legislation." It is not our place to judge the quality of the care and deliberation that went into this or any other law. A law enacted by voice vote with no deliberation whatever is fully as binding upon us as one enacted after years of study, months of committee hearings, and weeks of debate. Much less is it our place to make everything come out right when Congress does not do its job properly. It is up to Congress to design its laws with care, and it is up to the people to hold them to account if they fail to carry out that responsibility.

Rather than rewriting the law under the pretense of interpreting it, the Court should have left it to Congress to decide what to do about the Act's limitation of tax credits to state Exchanges. If Congress values above everything else the Act's applicability across the country, it could make tax credits available in every Exchange. * * * And if Congress thinks that the present design of the Act works well enough, it could do nothing. Congress could also do something else altogether, entirely abandoning the structure of the Affordable Care Act. The Court's insistence on making a choice that should be made by Congress both aggrandizes judicial power and encourages congressional lassitude.

Perhaps the Patient Protection and Affordable Care Act will attain the enduring status of the Social Security Act or the Taft-Hartley Act; perhaps not. But this Court's two decisions on the Act will surely be remembered through the years. The somersaults of statutory interpretation they have performed ("penalty" means tax, "further [Medicaid] payments to the State" means only incremental Medicaid payments to

FYI

In *National Federation of Independent Businesses v. Sebelius*, 567 U.S. 519 (2012), the Court upheld most of the ACA against a constitutional challenge. Justice Scalia dissented from the parts of the Court's opinion concluding that Congress had power to enact the statute.

the State, "established by the State" means not established by the State) will be cited by litigants endlessly, to the confusion of honest jurisprudence. And the cases will publish forever the discouraging truth that the Supreme Court of the United States favors some laws over others, and is prepared to do whatever it takes to uphold and assist its favorites.

## Points for Discussion

### a. *Statutory Interpretation*

The dueling opinions in *King* advance many of the arguments about how to determine statutory meaning that we have considered in this course. How many of them can you identify? Notice the progression of arguments about statutory meaning in the Court's opinion: first the Court sought the ordinary meaning of the words used in the provision at issue; then it considered the meaning of the text in light of the statute as a whole, including in light of various Whole Act Rule corollaries; and finally it interpreted the language in light of the structure and purposes of the Act as a whole. (In addition, the Court confronted an agency interpretation of the statute, which turned out to be consistent with the Court's understanding of the best reading of the statute.) In what way did Justice Scalia's approach differ? Having seen the range of arguments about how to determine the meaning of statutes, do you now think that there is one correct way to engage in the task?

### b. *Agency Interpretations of Statutes*

What role did the IRS's interpretation of the contested provision play in the Court's analysis? Notice that the Court concluded that the provision at issue was "ambiguous." In light of that conclusion, should the Court have deferred to the IRS's interpretation? Why did the Court decline to defer to the agency's view? (Notice that the Court ultimately concluded, in effect, that the agency's view was correct.) Is there some predictable test we can use to determine when the *Chevron* framework applies to agency interpretation of statutes and when it does not?

### c. *The Legislative Process*

The Affordable Care Act was an enormous and complicated piece of legislation. (The text of the bill was over 900 pages long.) The Court noted that there were several puzzling inconsistencies in the Act's provisions and that it contained "more than a few examples of inartful drafting." What should a Court do when presented with such a statute? Wouldn't it be logical to assume that Congress, which drafted a hugely complex statute, did not notice or realize the inconsistencies in the text? If so, what should a court's role be in interpreting the statute? Does the answer depend on the court's understanding of how the legislative process operates?

What was the Court's view of the legislative process? The Court noted that Congress used an atypical procedure to pass the ACA and suggested that, as a result, the Act "does not reflect the type of care and deliberation that one might expect of such significant legislation." How did this premise affect the Court's conclusion about the meaning of the statute? What was Justice Scalia's response?

**Test Your Knowledge**

To assess your understanding of the material in this Chapter, click here to take a quiz.

## Appendix A

# *The Constitution of the United States of America*

We the People of the United States, in Order to form a more perfect Union, establish Justice, insure domestic Tranquility, provide for the common defence, promote the general Welfare, and secure the Blessings of Liberty to ourselves and our Posterity, do ordain and establish this Constitution for the United States of America.

### Article I

Section 1. All legislative Powers herein granted shall be vested in a Congress of the United States, which shall consist of a Senate and House of Representatives.

Section 2. [1] The House of Representatives shall be composed of Members chosen every second Year by the People of the several States, and the Electors in each State shall have the Qualifications requisite for Electors of the most numerous Branch of the State Legislature.

[2] No Person shall be a Representative who shall not have attained to the Age of twenty five Years, and been seven Years a Citizen of the United States, and who shall not, when elected, be an Inhabitant of that State in which he shall be chosen.

**Take Note**

The bracketed text has been modified by Section 2 of the Fourteenth Amendment.

[3] [Representatives and direct Taxes shall be apportioned among the several States which may be included within this Union, according to their respective Numbers, which shall be determined by adding to the whole Number of free Persons, including those bound to Service for a Term of Years, and excluding Indians not taxed, three fifths of all other Persons.] The actual Enumeration shall be made within three Years after the first Meeting of the Congress of the United States, and within every subsequent Term of ten Years, in such Manner as they shall by Law direct. The Number of Representatives shall not exceed one for every thirty Thousand, but each State shall have at Least one Representative; and until such enumeration shall be made, the State

of New Hampshire shall be entitled to chuse three, Massachusetts eight, Rhode-Island and Providence Plantations one, Connecticut five, New-York six, New Jersey four, Pennsylvania eight, Delaware one, Maryland six, Virginia ten, North Carolina five, South Carolina five, and Georgia three.

[4] When vacancies happen in the Representation from any State, the Executive Authority thereof shall issue Writs of Election to fill such Vacancies.

[5] The House of Representatives shall chuse their Speaker and other Officers; and shall have the sole Power of Impeachment.

SECTION 3. [1] The Senate of the United States shall be composed of two Senators from each State, [chosen by the Legislature thereof for six Years]; and each Senator shall have one Vote.

[2] Immediately after they shall be assembled in Consequence of the first Election, they shall be divided as equally as may be into three Classes. The Seats of the Senators of the first Class shall be vacated at the Expiration of the second Year, of the second Class at the Expiration of the fourth Year, and of the third Class at the Expiration of the sixth Year, so that one third may be chosen every second Year; [and if Vacancies happen by Resignation, or otherwise, during the Recess of the Legislature of any State, the Executive thereof may make temporary Appointments until the next Meeting of the Legislature, which shall then fill such Vacancies.]

**Take Note**

The bracketed text in the first two clauses of Section 3 has been modified by the Seventeenth Amendment.

[3] No Person shall be a Senator who shall not have attained to the Age of thirty Years, and been nine Years a Citizen of the United States, and who shall not, when elected, be an Inhabitant of that State for which he shall be chosen.

[4] The Vice President of the United States shall be President of the Senate, but shall have no Vote, unless they be equally divided.

[5] The Senate shall chuse their other Officers, and also a President pro tempore, in the Absence of the Vice President, or when he shall exercise the Office of President of the United States.

[6] The Senate shall have the sole Power to try all Impeachments. When sitting for that Purpose, they shall be on Oath or Affirmation. When the President of the United States is tried, the Chief Justice shall preside: And no Person shall be convicted without the Concurrence of two thirds of the Members present.

[7] Judgment in Cases of Impeachment shall not extend further than to removal from Office, and disqualification to hold and enjoy any Office of honor, Trust or Profit

under the United States: but the Party convicted shall nevertheless be liable and subject to Indictment, Trial, Judgment and Punishment, according to Law.

Section 4. [1] The Times, Places and Manner of holding Elections for Senators and Representatives, shall be prescribed in each State by the Legislature thereof; but the Congress may at any time by Law make or alter such Regulations, except as to the Places of chusing Senators.

[2] The Congress shall assemble at least once in every Year, and such Meeting shall be [on the first Monday in December], unless they shall by Law appoint a different Day.

**Take Note**

The bracketed text has been modified by Section 2 of the Twentieth Amendment.

Section 5. [1] Each House shall be the Judge of the Elections, Returns and Qualifications of its own Members, and a Majority of each shall constitute a Quorum to do Business; but a smaller Number may adjourn from day to day, and may be authorized to compel the Attendance of absent Members, in such Manner, and under such Penalties as each House may provide.

[2] Each House may determine the Rules of its Proceedings, punish its Members for disorderly Behaviour, and, with the Concurrence of two thirds, expel a Member.

[3] Each House shall keep a Journal of its Proceedings, and from time to time publish the same, excepting such Parts as may in their Judgment require Secrecy; and the Yeas and Nays of the Members of either House on any question shall, at the Desire of one fifth of those Present, be entered on the Journal.

[4] Neither House, during the Session of Congress, shall, without the Consent of the other, adjourn for more than three days, nor to any other Place than that in which the two Houses shall be sitting.

Section 6. [1] The Senators and Representatives shall receive a Compensation for their Services, to be ascertained by Law, and paid out of the Treasury of the United States. They shall in all Cases, except Treason, Felony and Breach of the Peace, be privileged from Arrest during their Attendance at the Session of their respective Houses, and in going to and returning from the same; and for any Speech or Debate in either House, they shall not be questioned in any other Place.

[2] No Senator or Representative shall, during the Time for which he was elected, be appointed to any civil Office under the Authority of the United States, which shall have been created, or the Emoluments whereof shall have been encreased during such time; and no Person holding any Office under the United States, shall be a Member of either House during his Continuance in Office.

SECTION 7. [1] All Bills for raising Revenue shall originate in the House of Representatives; but the Senate may propose or concur with Amendments as on other Bills.

[2] Every Bill which shall have passed the House of Representatives and the Senate, shall, before it become a Law, be presented to the President of the United States: If he approve he shall sign it, but if not he shall return it, with his Objections to that House in which it shall have originated, who shall enter the Objections at large on their Journal, and proceed to reconsider it. If after such Reconsideration two thirds of that House shall agree to pass the Bill, it shall be sent, together with the Objections, to the other House, by which it shall likewise be reconsidered, and if approved by two thirds of that House, it shall become a Law. But in all such Cases the Votes of both Houses shall be determined by yeas and Nays, and the Names of the Persons voting for and against the Bill shall be entered on the Journal of each House respectively. If any Bill shall not be returned by the President within ten Days (Sundays excepted) after it shall have been presented to him, the Same shall be a Law, in like Manner as if he had signed it, unless the Congress by their Adjournment prevent its Return, in which Case it shall not be a Law.

[3] Every Order, Resolution, or Vote to which the Concurrence of the Senate and House of Representatives may be necessary (except on a question of Adjournment) shall be presented to the President of the United States; and before the Same shall take Effect, shall be approved by him, or being disapproved by him, shall be repassed by two thirds of the Senate and House of Representatives, according to the Rules and Limitations prescribed in the Case of a Bill.

SECTION 8. [1] The Congress shall have Power To lay and collect Taxes, Duties, Imposts and Excises, to pay the Debts and provide for the common Defence and general Welfare of the United States; but all Duties, Imposts and Excises shall be uniform throughout the United States;

[2] To borrow Money on the credit of the United States;

[3] To regulate Commerce with foreign Nations, and among the several States, and with the Indian Tribes;

[4] To establish an uniform Rule of Naturalization, and uniform Laws on the subject of Bankruptcies throughout the United States;

[5] To coin Money, regulate the Value thereof, and of foreign Coin, and fix the Standard of Weights and Measures;

[6] To provide for the Punishment of counterfeiting the Securities and current Coin of the United States;

[7] To establish Post Offices and post Roads;

[8] To promote the Progress of Science and useful Arts, by securing for limited Times to Authors and Inventors the exclusive Right to their respective Writings and Discoveries;

[9] To constitute Tribunals inferior to the supreme Court;

[10] To define and punish Piracies and Felonies committed on the high Seas, and Offences against the Law of Nations;

[11] To declare War, grant Letters of Marque and Reprisal, and make Rules concerning Captures on Land and Water;

[12] To raise and support Armies, but no Appropriation of Money to that Use shall be for a longer Term than two Years;

[13] To provide and maintain a Navy;

[14] To make Rules for the Government and Regulation of the land and naval Forces;

[15] To provide for calling forth the Militia to execute the Laws of the Union, suppress Insurrections and repel Invasions;

[16] To provide for organizing, arming, and disciplining, the Militia, and for governing such Part of them as may be employed in the Service of the United States, reserving to the States respectively, the Appointment of the Officers, and the Authority of training the Militia according to the discipline prescribed by Congress;

[17] To exercise exclusive Legislation in all Cases whatsoever, over such District (not exceeding ten Miles square) as may, by Cession of particular States, and the Acceptance of Congress, become the Seat of the Government of the United States, and to exercise like Authority over all Places purchased by the Consent of the Legislature of the State in which the Same shall be, for the Erection of Forts, Magazines, Arsenals, dock-Yards, and other needful Buildings;—And

[18] To make all Laws which shall be necessary and proper for carrying into Execution the foregoing Powers, and all other Powers vested by this Constitution in the Government of the United States, or in any Department or Officer thereof.

SECTION 9. [1] The Migration or Importation of such Persons as any of the States now existing shall think proper to admit, shall not be prohibited by the Congress prior to the Year one thousand eight hundred and eight, but a Tax or duty may be imposed on such Importation, not exceeding ten dollars for each Person.

[2] The Privilege of the Writ of Habeas Corpus shall not be suspended, unless when in Cases of Rebellion or Invasion the public Safety may require it.

[3] No Bill of Attainder or ex post facto Law shall be passed.

**Take Note**

The bracketed text has been modified by the Sixteenth Amendment.

[4] No Capitation, or other direct, Tax shall be laid, [unless in Proportion to the Census or enumeration herein before directed to be taken.]

[5] No Tax or Duty shall be laid on Articles exported from any State.

[6] No Preference shall be given by any Regulation of Commerce or Revenue to the Ports of one State over those of another; nor shall Vessels bound to, or from, one State, be obliged to enter, clear, or pay Duties in another.

[7] No Money shall be drawn from the Treasury, but in Consequence of Appropriations made by Law; and a regular Statement and Account of the Receipts and Expenditures of all public Money shall be published from time to time.

[8] No Title of Nobility shall be granted by the United States: And no Person holding any Office of Profit or Trust under them, shall, without the Consent of the Congress, accept of any present, Emolument, Office, or Title, of any kind whatever, from any King, Prince, or foreign State.

SECTION 10. [1] No State shall enter into any Treaty, Alliance, or Confederation; grant Letters of Marque and Reprisal; coin Money; emit Bills of Credit; make any Thing but gold and silver Coin a Tender in Payment of Debts; pass any Bill of Attainder, ex post facto Law, or Law impairing the Obligation of Contracts, or grant any Title of Nobility.

[2] No State shall, without the Consent of the Congress, lay any Imposts or Duties on Imports or Exports, except what may be absolutely necessary for executing [its] inspection Laws: and the net Produce of all Duties and Imposts, laid by any State on Imports or Exports, shall be for the Use of the Treasury of the United States; and all such Laws shall be subject to the Revision and Controul of the Congress.

[3] No State shall, without the Consent of Congress, lay any Duty of Tonnage, keep Troops, or Ships of War in time of Peace, enter into any Agreement or Compact with another State, or with a foreign Power, or engage in War, unless actually invaded, or in such imminent Danger as will not admit of delay.

## ARTICLE II

SECTION 1. [1] The executive Power shall be vested in a President of the United States of America. He shall hold his Office during the Term of four Years, and, together with the Vice President, chosen for the same Term, be elected, as follows:

[2] Each State shall appoint, in such Manner as the Legislature thereof may direct, a Number of Electors, equal to the whole Number of Senators and Repre-

sentatives to which the State may be entitled in the Congress: but no Senator or Representative, or Person holding an Office of Trust or Profit under the United States, shall be appointed an Elector.

[3] [The Electors shall meet in their respective States, and vote by Ballot for two Persons, of whom one at least shall not be an Inhabitant of the same State with themselves. And they shall make a List of all the Persons voted for, and of the Number of Votes for each; which List they shall sign and certify, and transmit sealed to the Seat of the Government of the United States, directed to the President of the Senate. The President of the Senate shall, in the Presence of the Senate and House of Representatives, open all the Certificates, and the Votes shall then be counted. The Person having the greatest Number of Votes shall be the President, if such Number be a Majority of the whole Number of Electors appointed; and if there be more than one who have such Majority, and have an equal Number of Votes, then the House of Representatives shall immediately chuse by Ballot one of them for President; and if no Person have a Majority, then from the five highest on the List the said House shall in like Manner chuse the President. But in chusing the President, the Votes shall be taken by States, the Representation from each State having one Vote; A quorum for this purpose shall consist of a Member or Members from two thirds of the States, and a Majority of all the States shall be necessary to a Choice. In every Case, after the Choice of the President, the Person having the greatest Number of Votes of the Electors shall be the Vice President. But if there should remain two or more who have equal Votes, the Senate shall chuse from them by Ballot the Vice President.]

**Take Note**

The bracketed text has been superseded by the Twelfth Amendment, part of which in turn was modified by Section 3 of the Twentieth Amendment.

[4] The Congress may determine the Time of chusing the Electors, and the Day on which they shall give their Votes; which Day shall be the same throughout the United States.

[5] No Person except a natural born Citizen, or a Citizen of the United States, at the time of the Adoption of this Constitution, shall be eligible to the Office of President; neither shall any Person be eligible to that Office who shall not have attained to the Age of thirty five Years, and been fourteen Years a Resident within the United States.

[6] [In Case of the Removal of the President from Office, or of his Death, Resignation, or Inability to discharge the Powers and Duties of the said Office, the Same shall devolve on the Vice President, and the Congress may by Law provide

**Take Note**

The bracketed text has been modified by the Twenty-Fifth Amendment.

for the Case of Removal, Death, Resignation or Inability, both of the President and Vice President, declaring what Officer shall then act as President, and such Officer shall act accordingly, until the Disability be removed, or a President shall be elected.]

[7] The President shall, at stated Times, receive for his Services, a Compensation, which shall neither be increased nor diminished during the Period for which he shall have been elected, and he shall not receive within that Period any other Emolument from the United States, or any of them.

[8] Before he enter on the Execution of his Office, he shall take the following Oath or Affirmation:—"I do solemnly swear (or affirm) that I will faithfully execute the Office of President of the United States, and will to the best of my Ability, preserve, protect and defend the Constitution of the United States."

SECTION 2. [1] The President shall be Commander in Chief of the Army and Navy of the United States, and of the Militia of the several States, when called into the actual Service of the United States; he may require the Opinion, in writing, of the principal Officer in each of the executive Departments, upon any Subject relating to the Duties of their respective Offices, and he shall have Power to grant Reprieves and Pardons for Offences against the United States, except in Cases of Impeachment.

[2] He shall have Power, by and with the Advice and Consent of the Senate, to make Treaties, provided two thirds of the Senators present concur; and he shall nominate, and by and with the Advice and Consent of the Senate, shall appoint Ambassadors, other public Ministers and Consuls, Judges of the supreme Court, and all other Officers of the United States, whose Appointments are not herein otherwise provided for, and which shall be established by Law: but the Congress may by Law vest the Appointment of such inferior Officers, as they think proper, in the President alone, in the Courts of Law, or in the Heads of Departments.

[3] The President shall have Power to fill up all Vacancies that may happen during the Recess of the Senate, by granting Commissions which shall expire at the End of their next Session.

SECTION 3. He shall from time to time give to the Congress Information of the State of the Union, and recommend to their Consideration such Measures as he shall judge necessary and expedient; he may, on extraordinary Occasions, convene both Houses, or either of them, and in Case of Disagreement between them, with Respect to the Time of Adjournment, he may adjourn them to such Time as he shall think proper; he shall receive Ambassadors and other public Ministers; he shall take Care that the Laws be faithfully executed, and shall Commission all the Officers of the United States.

SECTION 4. The President, Vice President and all civil Officers of the United States, shall be removed from Office on Impeachment for, and Conviction of, Treason, Bribery, or other high Crimes and Misdemeanors.

## Article III

Section 1. The judicial Power of the United States shall be vested in one supreme Court, and in such inferior Courts as the Congress may from time to time ordain and establish. The Judges, both of the supreme and inferior Courts, shall hold their Offices during good Behaviour, and shall, at stated Times, receive for their Services a Compensation, which shall not be diminished during their Continuance in Office.

Section 2. [1] The judicial Power shall extend to all Cases, in Law and Equity, arising under this Constitution, the Laws of the United States, and Treaties made, or which shall be made, under their Authority;—to all Cases affecting Ambassadors, other public Ministers and Consuls;—to all Cases of admiralty and maritime Jurisdiction;—to Controversies to which the United States shall be a Party;—to Controversies between two or more States;[—between a State and Citizens of another State;]—between Citizens of different States;—between Citizens of the same State claiming Lands under Grants of different States, [and between a State, or the Citizens thereof, and foreign States, Citizens or Subjects.]

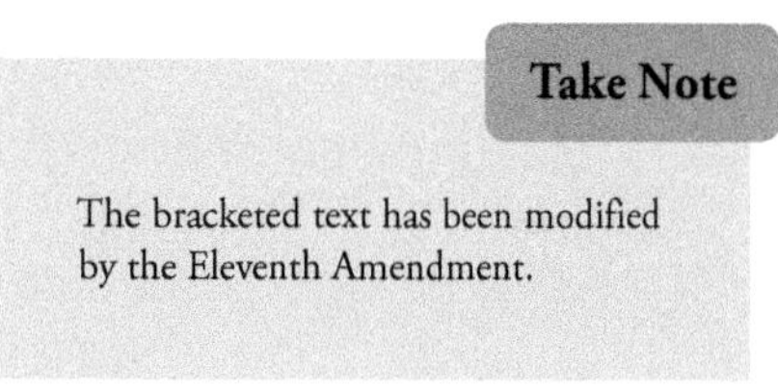


[2] In all Cases affecting Ambassadors, other public Ministers and Consuls, and those in which a State shall be Party, the supreme Court shall have original Jurisdiction. In all the other Cases before mentioned, the supreme Court shall have appellate Jurisdiction, both as to Law and Fact, with such Exceptions, and under such Regulations as the Congress shall make.

[3] The Trial of all Crimes, except in Cases of Impeachment, shall be by Jury; and such Trial shall be held in the State where the said Crimes shall have been committed; but when not committed within any State, the Trial shall be at such Place or Places as the Congress may by Law have directed.

Section 3. [1] Treason against the United States, shall consist only in levying War against them, or in adhering to their Enemies, giving them Aid and Comfort. No Person shall be convicted of Treason unless on the Testimony of two Witnesses to the same overt Act, or on Confession in open Court.

[2] The Congress shall have Power to declare the Punishment of Treason, but no Attainder of Treason shall work Corruption of Blood, or Forfeiture except during the Life of the Person attainted.

## ARTICLE IV

SECTION 1. Full Faith and Credit shall be given in each State to the public Acts, Records, and judicial Proceedings of every other State. And the Congress may by general Laws prescribe the Manner in which such Acts, Records and Proceedings shall be proved, and the Effect thereof.

SECTION 2. [1] The Citizens of each State shall be entitled to all Privileges and Immunities of Citizens in the several States.

[2] A Person charged in any State with Treason, Felony, or other Crime, who shall flee from Justice, and be found in another State, shall on Demand of the executive Authority of the State from which he fled, be delivered up, to be removed to the State having Jurisdiction of the Crime.

[3] [No Person held to Service or Labour in one State, under the Laws thereof, escaping into another, shall, in Consequence of any Law or Regulation therein, be discharged from such Service or Labour, but shall be delivered up on Claim of the Party to whom such Service or Labour may be due.]

**Take Note**

The bracketed text has been superseded by the Thirteenth Amendment.

SECTION 3. [1] New States may be admitted by the Congress into this Union; but no new State shall be formed or erected within the Jurisdiction of any other State; nor any State be formed by the Junction of two or more States, or Parts of States, without the Consent of the Legislatures of the States concerned as well as of the Congress.

[2] The Congress shall have Power to dispose of and make all needful Rules and Regulations respecting the Territory or other Property belonging to the United States; and nothing in this Constitution shall be so construed as to Prejudice any Claims of the United States, or of any particular State.

SECTION 4. The United States shall guarantee to every State in this Union a Republican Form of Government, and shall protect each of them against Invasion; and on Application of the Legislature, or of the Executive (when the Legislature cannot be convened), against domestic Violence.

## ARTICLE V

The Congress, whenever two thirds of both Houses shall deem it necessary, shall propose Amendments to this Constitution, or, on the Application of the Legislatures of two thirds of the several States, shall call a Convention for proposing Amendments, which, in either Case, shall be valid to all Intents and Purposes, as Part of this

Constitution, when ratified by the Legislatures of three fourths of the several States, or by Conventions in three fourths thereof, as the one or the other Mode of Ratification may be proposed by the Congress; Provided that no Amendment which may be made prior to the Year One thousand eight hundred and eight shall in any Manner affect the first and fourth Clauses in the Ninth Section of the first Article; and that no State, without its Consent, shall be deprived of its equal Suffrage in the Senate.

## Article VI

[1] All Debts contracted and Engagements entered into, before the Adoption of this Constitution, shall be as valid against the United States under this Constitution, as under the Confederation.

[2] This Constitution, and the Laws of the United States which shall be made in Pursuance thereof; and all Treaties made, or which shall be made, under the Authority of the United States, shall be the supreme Law of the Land; and the Judges in every State shall be bound thereby, any Thing in the Constitution or Laws of any State to the Contrary notwithstanding.

[3] The Senators and Representatives before mentioned, and the Members of the several State Legislatures, and all executive and judicial Officers, both of the United States and of the several States, shall be bound by Oath or Affirmation, to support this Constitution; but no religious Test shall ever be required as a Qualification to any Office or public Trust under the United States.

## Article VII

The Ratification of the Conventions of nine States, shall be sufficient for the Establishment of this Constitution between the States so ratifying the Same.

**Articles in addition to, and Amendment of the Constitution of the United States of America, proposed by Congress, and ratified by the Legislatures of the several States, pursuant to the fifth Article of the original Constitution:**

## Amendment I [1791]

Congress shall make no law respecting an establishment of religion, or prohibiting the free exercise thereof; or abridging the freedom of speech, or of the press; or the right of the people peaceably to assemble, and to petition the Government for a redress of grievances.

## AMENDMENT II [1791]

A well regulated Militia, being necessary to the security of a free State, the right of the people to keep and bear Arms, shall not be infringed.

## AMENDMENT III [1791]

No Soldier shall, in time of peace be quartered in any house, without the consent of the Owner, nor in time of war, but in a manner to be prescribed by law.

## AMENDMENT IV [1791]

The right of the people to be secure in their persons, houses, papers, and effects, against unreasonable searches and seizures, shall not be violated, and no Warrants shall issue, but upon probable cause, supported by Oath or affirmation, and particularly describing the place to be searched, and the persons or things to be seized.

## AMENDMENT V [1791]

No person shall be held to answer for a capital, or otherwise infamous crime, unless on a presentment or indictment of a Grand Jury, except in cases arising in the land or naval forces, or in the Militia, when in actual service in time of War or public danger; nor shall any person be subject for the same offence to be twice put in jeopardy of life or limb; nor shall be compelled in any criminal case to be a witness against himself, nor be deprived of life, liberty, or property, without due process of law; nor shall private property be taken for public use, without just compensation.

## AMENDMENT VI [1791]

In all criminal prosecutions, the accused shall enjoy the right to a speedy and public trial, by an impartial jury of the State and district wherein the crime shall have been committed, which district shall have been previously ascertained by law, and to be informed of the nature and cause of the accusation; to be confronted with the witnesses against him; to have compulsory process for obtaining witnesses in his favor, and to have the Assistance of Counsel for his defence.

## Amendment VII [1791]

In Suits at common law, where the value in controversy shall exceed twenty dollars, the right of trial by jury shall be preserved, and no fact tried by a jury, shall be otherwise re-examined in any Court of the United States, than according to the rules of the common law.

## Amendment VIII [1791]

Excessive bail shall not be required, nor excessive fines imposed, nor cruel and unusual punishments inflicted.

## Amendment IX [1791]

The enumeration in the Constitution, of certain rights, shall not be construed to deny or disparage others retained by the people.

## Amendment X [1791]

The powers not delegated to the United States by the Constitution, nor prohibited by it to the States, are reserved to the States respectively, or to the people.

## Amendment XI [1798]

The Judicial power of the United States shall not be construed to extend to any suit in law or equity, commenced or prosecuted against one of the United States by Citizens of another State, or by Citizens or Subjects of any Foreign State.

## Amendment XII [1804]

The Electors shall meet in their respective states and vote by ballot for President and Vice-President, one of whom, at least, shall not be an inhabitant of the same state with themselves; they shall name in their ballots the person voted for as President, and in distinct ballots the person voted for as Vice-President, and they shall make distinct lists of all persons voted for as President, and of all persons voted for as Vice-President, and of the number of votes for each, which lists they shall sign and certify, and transmit sealed to the seat of the government of the United States, directed to the President of the Senate;—the President of the Senate shall, in the presence of the Senate and House of Representatives, open all the certificates and the votes shall then be counted;—The person having the greatest number of votes for President, shall be the President, if such number be a majority of the whole number of Electors appointed; and if no person have such majority, then from the persons having the highest numbers not exceeding three on the list of those voted for as President, the House of Representatives shall choose immediately, by ballot, the President. But in choosing the President, the votes shall be taken by states, the representation from each state having one vote; a quorum for this purpose shall consist of a member or members from two-thirds of the states, and a majority of all the states shall be necessary to a choice. [And if the House of Representatives shall not choose a President whenever the right of choice shall devolve upon them, before the fourth day of March next following, then the Vice-President shall act as President, as in case of the death or other constitutional disability of the President.] The person having the greatest number of votes as Vice-President, shall be the Vice-President, if such number be a majority of the whole number of Electors appointed, and if no person have a majority, then from the two highest numbers on the list, the Senate shall choose the Vice-President; a quorum for the purpose shall consist of two-thirds of the whole number of Senators, and a majority of the whole number shall be necessary to a choice. But no person constitutionally ineligible to the office of President shall be eligible to that of Vice-President of the United States.

**Take Note**

The bracketed text has been superseded by the Twentieth Amendment.

## AMENDMENT XIII [1865]

SECTION 1. Neither slavery nor involuntary servitude, except as a punishment for crime whereof the party shall have been duly convicted, shall exist within the United States, or any place subject to their jurisdiction.

SECTION 2. Congress shall have power to enforce this article by appropriate legislation.

## AMENDMENT XIV [1868]

SECTION 1. All persons born or naturalized in the United States, and subject to the jurisdiction thereof, are citizens of the United States and of the State wherein they reside. No State shall make or enforce any law which shall abridge the privileges or immunities of citizens of the United States; nor shall any State deprive any person of life, liberty, or property, without due process of law; nor deny to any person within its jurisdiction the equal protection of the laws.

Section 2. Representatives shall be apportioned among the several States according to their respective numbers, counting the whole number of persons in each State, excluding Indians not taxed. [But when the right to vote at any election for the choice of electors for President and Vice-President of the United States, Representatives in Congress, the Executive and Judicial officers of a State, or the members of the Legislature thereof, is denied to any of the male inhabitants of such State, being twenty-one years of age, and citizens of the United States, or in any way abridged, except for participation in rebellion, or other crime, the basis of representation therein shall be reduced in the proportion which the number of such male citizens shall bear to the whole number of male citizens twenty-one years of age in such State.]

**Take Note**

The bracketed text has been modified by the Nineteenth and Twenty-Sixth Amendments.

Section 3. No person shall be a Senator or Representative in Congress, or elector of President and Vice-President, or hold any office, civil or military, under the United States, or under any State, who, having previously taken an oath, as a member of Congress, or as an officer of the United States, or as a member of any State legislature, or as an executive or judicial officer of any State, to support the Constitution of the United States, shall have engaged in insurrection or rebellion against the same, or given aid or comfort to the enemies thereof. But Congress may by a vote of two-thirds of each House, remove such disability.

Section 4. The validity of the public debt of the United States, authorized by law, including debts incurred for payment of pensions and bounties for services in suppressing insurrection or rebellion, shall not be questioned. But neither the United States nor any State shall assume or pay any debt or obligation incurred in aid of insurrection or rebellion against the United States, or any claim for the loss or emancipation of any slave; but all such debts, obligations and claims shall be held illegal and void.

Section 5. The Congress shall have the power to enforce, by appropriate legislation, the provisions of this article.

## Amendment XV [1870]

Section 1. The right of citizens of the United States to vote shall not be denied or abridged by the United States or by any State on account of race, color, or previous condition of servitude.

SECTION 2. The Congress shall have the power to enforce this article by appropriate legislation.

## AMENDMENT XVI [1913]

The Congress shall have power to lay and collect taxes on incomes, from whatever source derived, without apportionment among the several States, and without regard to any census or enumeration.

## AMENDMENT XVII [1913]

[1] The Senate of the United States shall be composed of two Senators from each State, elected by the people thereof, for six years; and each Senator shall have one vote. The electors in each State shall have the qualifications requisite for electors of the most numerous branch of the State legislatures.

[2] When vacancies happen in the representation of any State in the Senate, the executive authority of such State shall issue writs of election to fill such vacancies: Provided, That the legislature of any State may empower the executive thereof to make temporary appointments until the people fill the vacancies by election as the legislature may direct.

[3] This amendment shall not be so construed as to affect the election or term of any Senator chosen before it becomes valid as part of the Constitution.

## AMENDMENT XVIII [1919]

**Take Note**

The Eighteenth Amendment was repealed by the Twenty-First Amendment.

SECTION 1. After one year from the ratification of this article the manufacture, sale, or transportation of intoxicating liquors within, the importation thereof into, or the exportation thereof from the United States and all territory subject to the jurisdiction thereof for beverage purposes is hereby prohibited.

SECTION 2. The Congress and the several States shall have concurrent power to enforce this article by appropriate legislation.

SECTION 3. This article shall be inoperative unless it shall have been ratified as an amendment to the Constitution by the legislatures of the several States, as provided in the Constitution, within seven years from the date of the submission hereof to the States by the Congress.

## Amendment XIX [1920]

[1] The right of citizens of the United States to vote shall not be denied or abridged by the United States or by any State on account of sex.

[2] Congress shall have power to enforce this article by appropriate legislation.

## Amendment XX [1933]

Section 1. The terms of the President and the Vice President shall end at noon on the 20th day of January, and the terms of Senators and Representatives at noon on the 3d day of January, of the years in which such terms would have ended if this article had not been ratified; and the terms of their successors shall then begin.

Section 2. The Congress shall assemble at least once in every year, and such meeting shall begin at noon on the 3d day of January, unless they shall by law appoint a different day.

Section 3. If, at the time fixed for the beginning of the term of the President, the President elect shall have died, the Vice President elect shall become President. If a President shall not have been chosen before the time fixed for the beginning of his term, or if the President elect shall have failed to qualify, then the Vice President elect shall act as President until a President shall have qualified; and the Congress may by law provide for the case wherein neither a President elect nor a Vice President shall have qualified, declaring who shall then act as President, or the manner in which one who is to act shall be selected, and such person shall act accordingly until a President or Vice President shall have qualified.

Section 4. The Congress may by law provide for the case of the death of any of the persons from whom the House of Representatives may choose a President whenever the right of choice shall have devolved upon them, and for the case of the death of any of the persons from whom the Senate may choose a Vice President whenever the right of choice shall have devolved upon them.

Section 5. Sections 1 and 2 shall take effect on the 15th day of October following the ratification of this article.

Section 6. This article shall be inoperative unless it shall have been ratified as an amendment to the Constitution by the legislatures of three-fourths of the several States within seven years from the date of its submission.

## Amendment XXI [1933]

Section 1. The eighteenth article of amendment to the Constitution of the United States is hereby repealed.

Section 2. The transportation or importation into any State, Territory, or Possession of the United States for delivery or use therein of intoxicating liquors, in violation of the laws thereof, is hereby prohibited.

Section 3. This article shall be inoperative unless it shall have been ratified as an amendment to the Constitution by conventions in the several States, as provided in the Constitution, within seven years from the date of the submission hereof to the States by the Congress.

## Amendment XXII [1951]

Section 1. No person shall be elected to the office of the President more than twice, and no person who has held the office of President, or acted as President, for more than two years of a term to which some other person was elected President shall be elected to the office of President more than once. But this Article shall not apply to any person holding the office of President when this Article was proposed by Congress, and shall not prevent any person who may be holding the office of President, or acting as President, during the term within which this Article becomes operative from holding the office of President or acting as President during the remainder of such term.

Section 2. This article shall be inoperative unless it shall have been ratified as an amendment to the Constitution by the legislatures of three-fourths of the several States within seven years from the date of its submission to the States by the Congress.

## Amendment XXIII [1961]

Section 1. The District constituting the seat of Government of the United States shall appoint in such manner as Congress may direct:

A number of electors of President and Vice President equal to the whole number of Senators and Representatives in Congress to which the District would be entitled if it were a State, but in no event more than the least populous State; they shall be in addition to those appointed by the States, but they shall be considered, for the purposes of the election of President and Vice President, to be electors appointed by a State; and they shall meet in the District and perform such duties as provided by the twelfth article of amendment.

SECTION 2. The Congress shall have power to enforce this article by appropriate legislation.

## AMENDMENT XXIV [1964]

SECTION 1. The right of citizens of the United States to vote in any primary or other election for President or Vice President, for electors for President or Vice President, or for Senator or Representative in Congress, shall not be denied or abridged by the United States or any State by reason of failure to pay poll tax or other tax.

SECTION 2. The Congress shall have power to enforce this article by appropriate legislation.

## AMENDMENT XXV [1967]

SECTION 1. In case of the removal of the President from office or of his death or resignation, the Vice President shall become President.

SECTION 2. Whenever there is a vacancy in the office of the Vice President, the President shall nominate a Vice President who shall take office upon confirmation by a majority vote of both Houses of Congress.

SECTION 3. Whenever the President transmits to the President pro tempore of the Senate and the Speaker of the House of Representatives his written declaration that he is unable to discharge the powers and duties of his office, and until he transmits to them a written declaration to the contrary, such powers and duties shall be discharged by the Vice President as Acting President.

SECTION 4. [1] Whenever the Vice President and a majority of either the principal officers of the executive departments or of such other body as Congress may by law provide, transmit to the President pro tempore of the Senate and the Speaker of the House of Representatives their written declaration that the President is unable to discharge the powers and duties of his office, the Vice President shall immediately assume the powers and duties of the office as Acting President.

[2] Thereafter, when the President transmits to the President pro tempore of the Senate and the Speaker of the House of Representatives his written declaration that no inability exists, he shall resume the powers and duties of his office unless the Vice President and a majority of either the principal officers of the executive department or of such other body as Congress may by law provide, transmit within four days to the President pro tempore of the Senate and the Speaker of the House of Representatives their written declaration that the President is unable to discharge the powers and duties of his office. Thereupon Congress shall decide the issue, assembling within

forty-eight hours for that purpose if not in session. If the Congress, within twenty-one days after receipt of the latter written declaration, or, if Congress is not in session, within twenty-one days after Congress is required to assemble, determines by two-thirds vote of both Houses that the President is unable to discharge the powers and duties of his office, the Vice President shall continue to discharge the same as Acting President; otherwise, the President shall resume the powers and duties of his office.

## AMENDMENT XXVI [1971]

SECTION 1. The right of citizens of the United States, who are eighteen years of age or older, to vote shall not be denied or abridged by the United States or by any State on account of age.

SECTION 2. The Congress shall have power to enforce this article by appropriate legislation.

FYI

The Twenty-Seventh Amendment was proposed on September 25, 1789, along with the Amendments that became the Bill of Rights. The amendment was ratified quickly by six states, but not by the rest of the states. The amendment had no "sunset provision," however, and over time it was ratified by other states until, in 1992, Michigan became the 38th state to ratify it, satisfying the three-fourths requirement.

## AMENDMENT XXVII [1992]

No law, varying the compensation for the services of the Senators and Representatives, shall take effect, until an election of representatives shall have intervened.

# Appendix B

# *Administrative Procedure Act (5 U.S.C.)*

## § 551. Definitions

For the purpose of this subchapter—

(1) "agency" means each authority of the Government of the United States, whether or not it is within or subject to review by another agency, but does not include—

(A) the Congress;

(B) the courts of the United States;

(C) the governments of the territories or possessions of the United States;

(D) the government of the District of Columbia;

or except as to the requirements of section 552 of this title—

(E) agencies composed of representatives of the parties or of representatives of organizations of the parties to the disputes determined by them;

(F) courts martial and military commissions;

(G) military authority exercised in the field in time of war or in occupied territory; or

(H) functions conferred by sections 1738, 1739, 1743, and 1744 of title 12; chapter 2 of title 41; or sections 1622, 1884, 1891–1902, and former section 1641(b)(2), of title 50, appendix;

(2) "person" includes an individual, partnership, corporation, association, or public or private organization other than an agency;

(3) "party" includes a person or agency named or admitted as a party, or properly seeking and entitled as of right to be admitted as a party, in an agency proceeding, and a person or agency admitted by an agency as a party for limited purposes;

(4) "rule" means the whole or a part of an agency statement of general or particular applicability and future effect designed to implement, interpret, or prescribe law or policy or describing the organization, procedure, or practice requirements of an agency and includes the approval or prescription for the future of rates, wages, corporate or financial structures or reorganizations thereof, prices, facilities, appliances, services or allowances therefore or of valuations, costs, or accounting, or practices bearing on any of the foregoing;

(5) "rule making" means agency process for formulating, amending, or repealing a rule;

(6) "order" means the whole or a part of a final disposition, whether affirmative, negative, injunctive, or declaratory in form, of an agency in a matter other than rule making but including licensing;

(7) "adjudication" means agency process for the formulation of an order;

(8) "license" includes the whole or a part of an agency permit, certificate, approval, registration, charter, membership, statutory exemption or other form of permission;

(9) "licensing" includes agency process respecting the grant, renewal, denial, revocation, suspension, annulment, withdrawal, limitation, amendment, modification, or conditioning of a license;

(10) "sanction" includes the whole or a part of an agency—

(A) prohibition, requirement, limitation, or other condition affecting the freedom of a person;

(B) withholding of relief;

(C) imposition of penalty or fine;

(D) destruction, taking, seizure, or withholding of property;

(E) assessment of damages, reimbursement, restitution, compensation, costs, charges, or fees;

(F) requirement, revocation, or suspension of a license; or

(G) taking other compulsory or restrictive action;

(11) "relief" includes the whole or a part of an agency—

(A) grant of money, assistance, license, authority, exemption, exception, privilege, or remedy;

(B) recognition of a claim, right, immunity, privilege, exemption, or exception; or

(C) taking of other action on the application or petition of, and beneficial to, a person;

(12) "agency proceeding" means an agency process as defined by paragraphs (5), (7), and (9) of this section;

(13) "agency action" includes the whole or a part of an agency rule, order, license, sanction, relief, or the equivalent or denial thereof, or failure to act; and

(14) "ex parte communication" means an oral or written communication not on the public record with respect to which reasonable prior notice to all parties is not given, but it shall not include requests for status reports on any matter or proceeding covered by this subchapter.

## § 552. Public information; agency rules, opinions, orders, records, and proceedings

[This provision, adopted as the Freedom of Information Act, has been omitted.]

## § 553. Rule making

(a) This section applies, according to the provisions thereof, except to the extent that there is involved—

(1) a military or foreign affairs function of the United States; or

(2) a matter relating to agency management or personnel or to public property, loans, grants, benefits, or contracts.

(b) General notice of proposed rule making shall be published in the Federal Register, unless persons subject thereto are named and either personally served or otherwise have actual notice thereof in accordance with law. The notice shall include—

(1) a statement of the time, place, and nature of public rule making proceedings;

(2) reference to the legal authority under which the rule is proposed; and

(3) either the terms or substance of the proposed rule or a description of the subjects and issues involved.

Except when notice or hearing is required by statute, this subsection does not apply—

(A) to interpretative rules, general statements of policy, or rules of agency organization, procedure, or practice; or

(B) when the agency for good cause finds (and incorporates the finding and a brief statement of reasons therefore in the rules issued) that notice and public procedure thereon are impracticable, unnecessary, or contrary to the public interest.

(c) After notice required by this section, the agency shall give interested persons an opportunity to participate in the rule making through submission of written data, views, or arguments with or without opportunity for oral presentation. After consideration of the relevant matter presented, the agency shall incorporate in the rules adopted a concise general statement of their basis and purpose. When rules are required by statute to be made on the record after opportunity for an agency hearing, sections 556 and 557 of this title apply instead of this subsection.

(d) The required publication or service of a substantive rule shall be made not less than 30 days before its effective date, except—

(1) a substantive rule which grants or recognizes an exemption or relieves a restriction;

(2) interpretative rules and statements of policy; or

(3) as otherwise provided by the agency for good cause found and published with the rule.

(e) Each agency shall give an interested person the right to petition for the issuance, amendment, or repeal of a rule.

### § 554. Adjudications

(a) This section applies, according to the provisions thereof, in every case of adjudication required by statute to be determined on the record after opportunity for an agency hearing, except to the extent that there is involved—

(1) a matter subject to a subsequent trial of the law and the facts de novo in a court;

(2) the selection or tenure of an employee, except a [sic] administrative law judge appointed under section 3105 of this title;

(3) proceedings in which decisions rest solely on inspections, tests, or elections;

(4) the conduct of military or foreign affairs functions;

(5) cases in which an agency is acting as an agent for a court; or

(6) the certification of worker representatives.

(b) Persons entitled to notice of an agency hearing shall be timely informed of—

(1) the time, place, and nature of the hearing;

(2) the legal authority and jurisdiction under which the hearing is to be held; and

(3) the matters of fact and law asserted.

When private persons are the moving parties, other parties to the proceeding shall give prompt notice of issues controverted in fact or law; and in other instances agencies may by rule require responsive pleading. In fixing the time and place for hearings, due regard shall be had for the convenience and necessity of the parties or their representatives.

(c) The agency shall give all interested parties opportunity for—

(1) the submission and consideration of facts, arguments, offers of settlement, or proposals of adjustment when time, the nature of the proceeding, and the public interest permit; and

(2) to the extent that the parties are unable so to determine a controversy by consent, hearing and decision on notice and in accordance with sections 556 and 557 of this title.

(d) The employee who presides at the reception of evidence pursuant to section 556 of this title shall make the recommended decision or initial decision required by section 557 of this title, unless he becomes unavailable to the agency. Except to the extent required for the disposition of ex parte matters as authorized by law, such an employee may not—

(1) consult a person or party on a fact in issue, unless on notice and opportunity for all parties to participate; or

(2) be responsible to or subject to the supervision or direction of an employee or agent engaged in the performance of investigative or prosecuting functions for an agency.

An employee or agent engaged in the performance of investigative or prosecuting functions for an agency in a case may not, in that or a factually related case, participate or advise in the decision, recommended decision, or agency review pursuant to section 557 of this title, except as witness or counsel in public proceedings. This subsection does not apply—

(A) in determining applications for initial licenses;

(B) to proceedings involving the validity or application of rates, facilities, or practices of public utilities or carriers; or

(C) to the agency or a member or members of the body comprising the agency.

(e) The agency, with like effect as in the case of other orders, and in its sound discretion, may issue a declaratory order to terminate a controversy or remove uncertainty.

## § 555. Ancillary matters

(a) This section applies, according to the provisions thereof, except as otherwise provided by this subchapter.

(b) A person compelled to appear in person before an agency or representative thereof is entitled to be accompanied, represented, and advised by counsel or, if permitted by the agency, by other qualified representative. A party is entitled to appear in person or by or with counsel or other duly qualified representative in an agency proceeding. So far as the orderly conduct of public business permits, an interested person may appear before an agency or its responsible employees for the presentation, adjustment, or determination of an issue, request, or controversy in a proceeding, whether interlocutory, summary, or otherwise, or in connection with an agency function. With due regard for the convenience and necessity of the parties or their representatives and within a reasonable time, each agency shall proceed to conclude a matter presented to it. This subsection does not grant or deny a person who is not a lawyer the right to appear for or represent others before an agency or in an agency proceeding.

(c) Process, requirement of a report, inspection, or other investigative act or demand may not be issued, made, or enforced except as authorized by law. A person compelled to submit data or evidence is entitled to retain or, on payment of lawfully prescribed costs, procure a copy or transcript thereof, except that in a nonpublic investigatory proceeding the witness may for good cause be limited to inspection of the official transcript of his testimony.

(d) Agency subpoenas authorized by law shall be issued to a party on request and, when required by rules of procedure, on a statement or showing of general relevance and reasonable scope of the evidence sought. On contest, the court shall sustain the subpoena or similar process or demand to the extent that it is found to be in accordance with law. In a proceeding for enforcement, the court shall issue an order requiring the appearance of the witness or the production of the evidence or data within a reasonable time under penalty of punishment for contempt in case of contumacious failure to comply.

(e) Prompt notice shall be given of the denial in whole or in part of a written application, petition, or other request of an interested person made in connection with any agency proceeding. Except in affirming a prior denial or when the denial is self-explanatory, the notice shall be accompanied by a brief statement of the grounds for denial.

### § 556. Hearings; presiding employees; powers and duties; burden of proof; evidence; record as basis of decision

(a) This section applies, according to the provisions thereof, to hearings required by section 553 or 554 of this title to be conducted in accordance with this section.

(b) There shall preside at the taking of evidence—

(1) the agency;

(2) one or more members of the body which comprises the agency; or

(3) one or more administrative law judges appointed under section 3105 of this title.

This subchapter does not supersede the conduct of specified classes of proceedings, in whole or in part, by or before boards or other employees specially provided for by or designated under statute. The functions of presiding employees and of employees participating in decisions in accordance with section 557 of this title shall be conducted in an impartial manner. A presiding or participating employee may at any time disqualify himself. On the filing in good faith of a timely and sufficient affidavit of personal bias or other disqualification of a presiding or participating employee, the agency shall determine the matter as a part of the record and decision in the case.

(c) Subject to published rules of the agency and within its powers, employees presiding at hearings may—

(1) administer oaths and affirmations;

(2) issue subpoenas authorized by law;

(3) rule on offers of proof and receive relevant evidence;

(4) take depositions or have depositions taken when the ends of justice would be served;

(5) regulate the course of the hearing;

(6) hold conferences for the settlement or simplification of the issues by consent of the parties or by the use of alternative means of dispute resolution as provided in subchapter IV of this chapter;

(7) inform the parties as to the availability of one or more alternative means of dispute resolution, and encourage use of such methods;

(8) require the attendance at any conference held pursuant to paragraph (6) of at least one representative of each party who has authority to negotiate concerning resolution of issues in controversy;

(9) dispose of procedural requests or similar matters;

(10) make or recommend decisions in accordance with section 557 of this title; and

(11) take other action authorized by agency rule consistent with this subchapter.

(d) Except as otherwise provided by statute, the proponent of a rule or order has the burden of proof. Any oral or documentary evidence may be received, but the agency as a matter of policy shall provide for the exclusion of irrelevant, immaterial, or unduly repetitious evidence. A sanction may not be imposed or rule or order issued except on consideration of the whole record or those parts thereof cited by a party and supported by and in accordance with the reliable, probative, and substantial evidence. The agency may, to the extent consistent with the interests of justice and the policy of the underlying statutes administered by the agency, consider a violation of section 557(d) of this title sufficient grounds for a decision adverse to a party who has knowingly committed such violation or knowingly caused such violation to occur. A party is entitled to present his case or defense by oral or documentary evidence, to submit rebuttal evidence, and to conduct such cross-examination as may be required for a full and true disclosure of the facts. In rule making or determining claims for money or benefits or applications for initial licenses an agency may, when a party will not be prejudiced thereby, adopt procedures for the submission of all or part of the evidence in written form.

(e) The transcript of testimony and exhibits, together with all papers and requests filed in the proceeding, constitutes the exclusive record for decision in accordance with section 557 of this title and, on payment of lawfully prescribed costs, shall be made available to the parties. When an agency decision rests on official notice of a material fact not appearing in the evidence in the record, a party is entitled, on timely request, to an opportunity to show the contrary.

### § 557. Initial decisions; conclusiveness; review by agency; submissions by parties; contents of decisions; record

(a) This section applies, according to the provisions thereof, when a hearing is required to be conducted in accordance with section 556 of this title.

(b) When the agency did not preside at the reception of the evidence, the presiding employee or, in cases not subject to section 554(d) of this title, an employee qualified to preside at hearings pursuant to section 556 of this title, shall initially decide the case unless the agency requires, either in specific cases or by general rule, the entire record to be certified to it for decision. When the presiding employee makes an initial decision, that decision then becomes the decision of the agency without further proceedings unless there is an appeal to, or review on motion of, the agency within time provided by rule. On appeal from or review of the initial decision, the agency has all the powers which it would have in making the initial decision except as it may limit the issues on notice or by rule. When the agency makes the decision without having presided at the reception of the evidence, the presiding employee or an employee qualified to preside at hearings pursuant to section 556 of this title shall first recommend a decision, except that in rule making or determining applications for initial licenses—

(1) instead thereof the agency may issue a tentative decision or one of its responsible employees may recommend a decision; or

(2) this procedure may be omitted in a case in which the agency finds on the record that due and timely execution of its functions imperatively and unavoidably so requires.

(c) Before a recommended, initial, or tentative decision, or a decision on agency review of the decision of subordinate employees, the parties are entitled to a reasonable opportunity to submit for the consideration of the employees participating in the decisions—

(1) proposed findings and conclusions; or

(2) exceptions to the decisions or recommended decisions of subordinate employees or to tentative agency decisions; and

(3) supporting reasons for the exceptions or proposed findings or conclusions.

The record shall show the ruling on each finding, conclusion, or exception presented. All decisions, including initial, recommended, and tentative decisions, are a part of the record and shall include a statement of—

(A) findings and conclusions, and the reasons or basis therefore, on all the material issues of fact, law, or discretion presented on the record; and

(B) the appropriate rule, order, sanction, relief, or denial thereof.

(d)(1) In any agency proceeding which is subject to subsection (a) of this section, except to the extent required for the disposition of ex parte matters as authorized by law—

(A) no interested person outside the agency shall make or knowingly cause to be made to any member of the body comprising the agency, administrative law judge, or other employee who is or may reasonably be expected to be involved in the decisional process of the proceeding, an ex parte communication relevant to the merits of the proceeding;

(B) no member of the body comprising the agency, administrative law judge, or other employee who is or may reasonably be expected to be involved in the decisional process of the proceeding, shall make or knowingly cause to be made to any interested person outside the agency an ex parte communication relevant to the merits of the proceeding;

(C) a member of the body comprising the agency, administrative law judge, or other employee who is or may reasonably be expected to be involved in the decisional process of such proceeding who receives, or who makes or knowingly causes to be made, a communication prohibited by this subsection shall place on the public record of the proceeding:

(i) all such written communications;

(ii) memoranda stating the substance of all such oral communications; and

(iii) all written responses, and memoranda stating the substance of all oral responses, to the materials described in clauses (i) and (ii) of this subparagraph;

(D) upon receipt of a communication knowingly made or knowingly caused to be made by a party in violation of this subsection, the agency, administrative law judge, or other employee presiding at the hearing may, to the extent consistent with the interests of justice and the policy of the underlying statutes, require the party to show cause why his claim or interest in the proceeding should not be dismissed, denied, disregarded, or otherwise adversely affected on account of such violation; and

(E) the prohibitions of this subsection shall apply beginning at such time as the agency may designate, but in no case shall they begin to apply later than the time at which a proceeding is noticed for hearing unless the person responsible for the communication has knowledge that it will be noticed, in which case the prohibitions shall apply beginning at the time of his acquisition of such knowledge.

(2) This subsection does not constitute authority to withhold information from Congress.

### § 558. Imposition of sanctions; determination of applications for licenses; suspension, revocation, and expiration of licenses

(a) This section applies, according to the provisions thereof, to the exercise of a power or authority.

(b) A sanction may not be imposed or a substantive rule or order issued except within jurisdiction delegated to the agency and as authorized by law.

(c) When application is made for a license required by law, the agency, with due regard for the rights and privileges of all the interested parties or adversely affected persons and within a reasonable time, shall set and complete proceedings required to be conducted in accordance with sections 556 and 557 of this title or other proceedings required by law and shall make its decision. Except in cases of willfulness or those in which public health, interest, or safety requires otherwise, the withdrawal, suspension, revocation, or annulment of a license is lawful only if, before the institution of agency proceedings therefore, the licensee has been given—

(1) notice by the agency in writing of the facts or conduct which may warrant the action; and

(2) opportunity to demonstrate or achieve compliance with all lawful requirements.

When the licensee has made timely and sufficient application for a renewal or a new license in accordance with agency rules, a license with reference to an activity of a continuing nature does not expire until the application has been finally determined by the agency.

### § 559. Effect on other laws; effect of subsequent statute

This subchapter, chapter 7, and sections 1305, 3105, 3344, 4301(2)(E), 5372, and 7521 of this title, and the provisions of section 5335(a)(B) of this title that relate to administrative law judges, do not limit or repeal additional requirements imposed by statute or otherwise recognized by law. Except as otherwise required by law, requirements or privileges relating to evidence or procedure apply equally to agencies and persons. Each agency is granted the authority necessary to comply with the requirements of this subchapter through the issuance of rules or otherwise. Subsequent statute may not be held to supersede or modify this subchapter, chapter 7, sections 1305, 3105, 3344, 4301(2)(E), 5372, or 7521 of this title, or the provisions of section 5335(a)(B) of this title that relate to administrative law judges, except to the extent that it does so expressly.

### § 701. Application; definitions

(a) This chapter applies, according to the provisions thereof, except to the extent that—

(1) statutes preclude judicial review; or

(2) agency action is committed to agency discretion by law.

(b) For the purpose of this chapter—

(1) "agency" means each authority of the Government of the United States, whether or not it is within or subject to review by another agency, but does not include—

(A) the Congress;

(B) the courts of the United States;

(C) the governments of the territories or possessions of the United States;

(D) the government of the District of Columbia;

(E) agencies composed of representatives of the parties or of representatives of organizations of the parties to the disputes determined by them;

(F) courts martial and military commissions;

(G) military authority exercised in the field in time of war or in occupied territory; or

(H) functions conferred by sections 1738, 1739, 1743, and 1744 of title 12; subchapter II of chapter 471 of title 49; or sections 1884, 1891–1902, and former section 1641(b)(2), of title 50, appendix; and

(2) "person", "rule", "order", "license", "sanction", "relief", and "agency action" have the meanings given them by section 551 of this title.

### § 702. Right of review

A person suffering legal wrong because of agency action, or adversely affected or aggrieved by agency action within the meaning of a relevant statute, is entitled to judicial review thereof. An action in a court of the United States seeking relief other than money damages and stating a claim that an agency or an officer or employee thereof acted or failed to act in an official capacity or under color of legal authority shall not be dismissed nor relief therein be denied on the ground that it is against the United States or that the United States is an indispensable party. The United States may be named as a defendant in any such action, and a judgment or decree may be entered against the United States: Provided, That any mandatory or injunctive decree shall specify the Federal officer or officers (by name or by title), and their successors in office, personally responsible for compliance. Nothing herein (1) affects other limitations on judicial review or the power or duty of the court to dismiss any action or deny relief on any other appropriate legal or equitable ground; or (2) confers authority to grant relief if any other statute that grants consent to suit expressly or impliedly forbids the relief which is sought.

### § 703. Form and venue of proceeding

The form of proceeding for judicial review is the special statutory review proceeding relevant to the subject matter in a court specified by statute or, in the absence or inadequacy thereof, any applicable form of legal action, including actions for declaratory judgments or writs of prohibitory or mandatory injunction or habeas corpus, in a court of competent jurisdiction. If no special statutory review proceeding is applicable, the action for judicial review may be brought against the United States, the agency by its official title, or the appropriate officer. Except to the extent that prior, adequate, and exclusive opportunity for judicial review is provided by law, agency action is subject to judicial review in civil or criminal proceedings for judicial enforcement.

### § 704. Actions reviewable

Agency action made reviewable by statute and final agency action for which there is no other adequate remedy in a court are subject to judicial review. A preliminary, procedural, or intermediate agency action or ruling not directly reviewable is subject to review on the review of the final agency action. Except as otherwise expressly required by statute, agency action otherwise final is final for the purposes of this section whether or not there has been presented or determined an application for a declaratory order, for any form of reconsideration, or, unless the agency otherwise requires by rule and provides that the action meanwhile is inoperative, for an appeal to superior agency authority.

### § 705. Relief pending review

When an agency finds that justice so requires, it may postpone the effective date of action taken by it, pending judicial review. On such conditions as may be required and to the extent necessary to prevent irreparable injury, the reviewing court, including the court to which a case may be taken on appeal from or on application for certiorari or other writ to a reviewing court, may issue all necessary and appropriate process to postpone the effective date of an agency action or to preserve status or rights pending conclusion of the review proceedings.

## § 706. Scope of review

To the extent necessary to decision and when presented, the reviewing court shall decide all relevant questions of law, interpret constitutional and statutory provisions, and determine the meaning or applicability of the terms of an agency action. The reviewing court shall—

(1) compel agency action unlawfully withheld or unreasonably delayed; and

(2) hold unlawful and set aside agency action, findings, and conclusions found to be—

(A) arbitrary, capricious, an abuse of discretion, or otherwise not in accordance with law;

(B) contrary to constitutional right, power, privilege, or immunity;

(C) in excess of statutory jurisdiction, authority, or limitations, or short of statutory right;

(D) without observance of procedure required by law;

(E) unsupported by substantial evidence in a case subject to sections 556 and 557 of this title or otherwise reviewed on the record of an agency hearing provided by statute; or

(F) unwarranted by the facts to the extent that the facts are subject to trial de novo by the reviewing court.

In making the foregoing determinations, the court shall review the whole record or those parts of it cited by a party, and due account shall be taken of the rule of prejudicial error.

# Index

***References are to Pages***